The Strategic Management of Organisations

ADRIAN HABERBERG AND ALISON RIEPLE

UNIVERSITY OF WESTMINSTER

FT Prentice Hall

FINANCIAL TIMES

An imprint of **Pearson Education**

Harlow, England • London • New York • Boston • San Francisco • Toronto • Sydney • Singapore • Hong Kong
Tokyo • Seoul • Taipei • New Delhi • Cape Town • Madrid • Mexico City • Amsterdam • Munich • Paris • Milan

Pearson Education Limited
Edinburgh Gate
Harlow
Essex CM20 2JE
England

and Associated Companies throughout the world

Visit us on the World Wide Web at:
http://www.pearsoned.co.uk

First published 2001

ISBN 0 130 21971 1

British Library Cataloguing-in-Publication Data
A catalogue record for this book is available from the British Library

Library of Congress Cataloging-in-Publication Data
Haberberg, Adrian.
   The strategic management of organisations / Adrian Haberberg and Alison Rieple.
      p. cm.
   Includes bibliographical references and index.
   ISBN 0–13–021971–1
   1. Strategic planning. I. Rieple, Alison. II. Title.

HD30.28. H27 2001
658.4'012–dc21   00–033990

10   9   8   7   6   5   4
07   06   05   04

Typeset by 3 in Stone Serif 9/12 pt
Printed in China
SWTC/04

To our families:

Gordon, Manuela, Claudia and Julia

Contents

PART 1 Core concepts   1

Preface

Several things motivated us when we decided to write this book. Firstly we believed that few, if any of the textbooks currently available on strategic management, business policy or corporate strategy truly addressed the needs of undergraduate students. Most undergraduates, in our experience, find strategic management a particular challenge. The concepts are difficult and span a number of disciplines, the problems are complex and hardly ever have a clearcut 'right' answer. The textbook author, therefore, has to tackle complexity and ambiguity without being complex or ambiguous. As you can imagine, this is a difficult challenge.

We found that many of the texts that had been written for undergraduates tended to shirk this challenge, by presenting an oversimplified view. The more rigorous texts, on the other hand, are written primarily for the MBA market and assume a sophisticated acquaintance with the way real organisations operate. Not many undergraduates have this type of background, which is important if they are to make sense of how the theoretical models work out in practice. What they often do possess, on the other hand, is knowledge of the theory of economics and organisation studies. Yet hardly any strategy textbooks seek to build on this base, by linking strategic management theory to familiar concepts from these other disciplines, even though strategic management is often taught as a 'capstone' module that is intended to integrate the learning from earlier ones.

We also had reservations about the theory presented in other textbooks. The resource-based view of the firm has been at the centre of strategic management orthodoxy for at least five years, and yet few textbooks cover it in much depth. Related topics such as organisational learning and knowledge management are also neglected, along with such aspects of theory as hybrid organisational forms and the economics of increasing returns.

The international aspects of strategy formed another area that we felt needed better treatment than it received in most existing texts. We live in an era when almost all large firms operate on at least a continental scale, and where neighbourhood shops can serve a worldwide market via the internet while having to compete with firms that can source products from across the globe. We therefore felt strongly that it was time to accept that an international business context was the norm, rather than an oddity to be relegated to a separate chapter. We also felt that it was important to the educational process to expose students to a wide variety of national contexts, not just the USA and the UK (or, in the case of the more enlightened authors, NAFTA and the European Union).

Finally, we found it impossible to find a book that gave a truly balanced and comprehensive view of the subject. Most strategic management textbooks are written by former economists, and tend to present strategic decision-making as a rational exercise, unaffected by considerations of politics, power and human emotion and fallibility. (How they are able to reconcile this with their own experience of work in a university department is quite beyond us!) As well as presenting a rather unrealistic picture of organisational life, these books tend to skimp on their treatment of vital topics like culture, the management of change, and the strategic *management* process, or ignore them altogether. Books written from a more socio-logical or anthropological viewpoint, on the other hand, give an excellent treat-ment of culture and change, but when considering those parts of strategic management theory that are based on industrial and organisational economics, they lack rigour, depth and clarity.

What we have tried to do, therefore, is to give a comprehensive, balanced and up-to-date account of strategic management theory in simple, readable prose. We have attempted to show how considerations of economics, power, politics and individual psychological processes, *taken together*, can help us to understand that most fascinating of puzzles: Why do certain organisations experience success and others failure, and what can a manager do to achieve one and avoid the other? Students who encounter strategic management as a 'capstone' course should, we hope, be able to relate it to their earlier studies, while those who meet these topics for the first time will find sufficient detail here to get them started. We have taken our examples from a wide variety of industries – manufacturing, services and knowledge-based – and from every continent where there is meaningful economic activity.

We have made a considerable effort to emphasise the way in which quantitative analysis complements qualitative analysis in strategy. We hope we have gone beyond the standard treatment of 'Make sure you compute all the standard accounting ratios'. We have, instead, attempted to emphasise the role of *all kinds* of numbers, ratios and recorded events in raising questions about what is really happening inside an organisation, and avoiding the trap of taking management claims at face value.

Lastly, we have tried to tackle one of the main challenges of teaching strategic management – that it cannot easily be taught, as many subjects are, as a series of discrete topics, because all are interrelated. We have provided hypertext-style cross-references between related material within the book, to help our readers under-stand the links and, if necessary, revise or read ahead. We hope that, by using four internationally well-known companies – Sony, McDonald's, Benetton and British Airways – as examples throughout the book, we can help people to see how the dif-ferent aspects of theory knit together.

There are many people to whom our thanks are due. To Harvey Gordon and Ian Beesley for their coaching in how to express complex concepts in clear prose – we hope that they can recognise the results in the chapters that follow. To friends and colleagues who have contributed case studies – Tony Fowler, Jon Gander, Clive Helm, Adam Simmons – or have read and suggested improvements to tracts of this book – Jesper Hornberg, Mick Kemp and our panel of reviewers. To Penelope Woolf and Sacha Taylor of Prentice Hall (as it then was) for getting the project off the ground, and to Sadie McClelland, Geraldine Lyons, Lyn Roberts and Mary Lince of Pearson Education (as it now is) for nursing us through the closing stages. And, of course to our respective families, for their encouragement, love and tolerance of the late hours, long absences and fits of temper and despair that seem to accom-pany any creative enterprise.

ADRIAN HABERBERG
ALISON RIEPLE
London, 2000

Acknowledgements

The publishers are grateful to the following for permission to reproduce copyright material:

Administrative Science Quarterly for an extract from the article 'Fading memories: a process theory of strategic business exit in dynamic environments' by Robert Burgelman in *Administrative Science Quarterly* volume 39#1, March 1994; Amazon.com Inc for 290 words approx. from *Amazon.com 1998 company report*; AMD for an extract from *AMD* website (Advanced Micro Devices); Aviation Week and Space Technology for an extract from *Aviation Week and Space Technology* Sept. 28 1998, vol. 149, Issue 13 p. 32; British Airways for an extract from British Airways website www.british-airways.com; Coca-Cola Company for extracts from Coca-Cola case study and mission statements, information taken from *Coca-Cola* website; The Economist Newspaper Ltd for the articles 'The Kingdom inside a republic' in *The Economist*, 13.4.96, xv pp. 84–5 and 'Small banks in America, the value of good housekeeping' in *The Economist* 03.01.00 Vol. 346, Issue 8049 from *'Finance and Economics' Supplement*; and for an extract from the 'Management Brief' section in *The Economist* 26.11.94; Free Press, New York for an extract adapted from *Managing Acquisitions: Creating Value through corporate renewal* by Haspeslagh/ Jemison (1986); Friends of the Earth 2000 for extracts from *Friends of the Earth* Website; General Electric Co for an extract and statistics from General Electric Reports on *General Electric* website; Greenpeace Ltd for extract and statistics from *Greenpeace* website; Harvard Business School Publishing for extracts from the articles 'Evolution and revolution as organisations grow' by Larry Greiner in *Harvard Business Review* May/June 1968 and 'What holds the modern company together' by R. Goffee and G. Jones in *Harvard Business Review* Nov.–Dec. 1996; Houghton Mifflin Company for an adapted extract from 'Case Study – Merck' in Charles W.L. Hill & Gareth R. Jones in *Strategic Management: An Integrated Approach*. Copyright © 1995 by Houghton Mifflin Company; the author, Gareth R. Jones for an extract from 'The Rise and Fall of IBM' case prepared by Gareth R. Jones and Susan L. Peters in *Strategic Management; an Integrated Approach* (1995), Texas A&M University. Copyright © 1993 by Gareth R. Jones; McDonald's Corporation for extracts and 'Tables of Statistics' from *McDonald's Annual Reports* 1998, 1999 and data taken from various McDonald's annual reports available on website www.mcdonalds.com; Pearson Education Ltd for an extract and Table 'Managerial political actions for change' from Boddy/Buchanan *The Expertise of the Change Event. Public performance and Backstage Activity* (1992), published by Prentice Hall 1992 and an extract from *Managing Change: a strategic approach to organisational dynamics* by Bernard Burnes, published by Pitman, 1996 © Bernard Burnes; Penton Media, Inc. for an extract from 'Driving success at a new blue' from *Industry Week*, December 1999, © Penton Media, Inc., Cleveland, Ohio; Random House UK Ltd for an adapted extract from *Beyond Certainty* by Charles Handy. Published by Hutchinson 1995; La Repubblica Newspaper for an extract translated by the author Adrian Haberberg from an article by Maurizio Crosetti in *La Repubblica* 14.10.96; Sony Europe Finance plc for extracts from 'Founding Prospectus of the Tokyo Engineering Corp.' (Management Policies section), extracts and various tables of statistics from Sony's 1996, 1997 and 1998, 1999 *Annual Reports* (accessed from www.sony.com); Telegraph Group Ltd for extracts from the articles 'Sweet Charity for top bosses' in the *Daily Telegraph* 26.07.98 and 'ROH in crisis' in the *Daily Telegraph* 23.11.99; Time Inc for an adapted extract from article by Nina Munk in *Fortune Magazine* 12.04.99 pp. 33–8, extracts from *Fortune Magazine* 21.12.98 and an article by Jeremy Khan in *Fortune Magazine* 8.11.99; News International on behalf of Times Newspapers Ltd for the article 'Under Fire' by Kirstie Hamilton in *The Sunday Times* 19.11.95 © Sunday Times, London 1995 and an extract from the article 'The Enterprise Network' by David Sumner Smith in *The Sunday Times* 15.02.98 © Sunday Times, London 1998; Louis Vuitton for an adapted extract from LVMH Mission Statement, taken from their website.

Exhibit 1.1 from Burns, McInerney and Swinbank, *The Food Industry Economies and Policies* by permission of Commonwealth Agricultural Bureau, Wallingford; Figure 1.2 based on Mintzberg & Waters, 'Of Strategies, Deliberate and Emergent', (1985) *Strategic Management Journal*, 6/3, pp. 257–72, reproduced by permission of John Wiley & Sons Limited; Exhibits 1.2 and 1.3 by permission of Institute of Grocery Distribution; Exhibit 1.4 by permission of Taylor and Francis on behalf of UCL Press; Exhibit 1.5 by permission of Euromonitor International plc; Exhibit 1.6 from *The Economist*, 23rd February 1991; Exhibit 1.14 by permission of Wm Morrison Supermarkets PLC: Exhibit 1.17 by permission of J. Sainsbury plc; Exhibit 1.19: by permission of Safeway plc; Exhibit 1.20 by permission of Somerfield plc; Exhibits 2.5, 2.7, 2.8, 2.9, and 2.10 by permission of IFPI Secretariat; Exhibit 2.6 by permission of C. Dane, Media Research Publishing Limited, Exhibits 2.16 to 2.19 and Exhibits 3.1 to 3.4 and 3.6 from *Music and Copyright* by permission of Informa Publishing; Figures 3.3, 6.1 and 13.4 adapted from Johnson & Scholes, *Exploring Corporate Strategy* (1999) by permission from Pearson Education Limited; Exhibit 4.2 from *Economic Trends and Financial Statistics* and Exhibit 4.18 from *Overseas Travel and Tourism* by permission of National Statistics © Crown Copyright 2000; Table 4.4(b) from *Airline Business* (September 1996), a Reed Aerospace Publication; Exhibits 4.4, 4.10, 4.15, 4.16 and 4.19 by permission of Civil Aviation Authority; Exhibit 4.8 'Analysis of passenger volume at Dublin Airport 1997–98' by permission of Aer Rianta; Exhibit 4.13 by permission of Steven Jackson; Figure 6.2 adapted from Faulkner & Bowman, *The Essence of Competitive Strategy* (1995) by permission of Pearson Education Limited; Figure 6.3 based on model by Ansoff in Ansoff, I., *Corporate Strategy* (revised edition) 1987, Penguin Books Limited by permission of H. Igor Ansoff; Figure 6.4 by permission of Simon & Schuster on behalf of The Free Press; Figures 8.2 and 8.3 from Stabell & Fjeldstad, 'Configuring Value for Competitive Advantage: on chains, shops and networks' (1998) *Strategic Management Journal*, Vol. 19, pp. 413–37, reproduced by permission of John Wiley & Sons Limited; Figure 8.4 adapted from *Long Range Planning*, Vol. 26 (6), BSM Bossard, quoted in Talway and Rohit, *Business Re-engineering – a Strategy-driven Approach*, pp. 22–40 (1993) with permission from Elsevier Science; Figure 9.1 adapted from Goold & Campbell, *Strategies and Styles: The Role of the Centre in Managing Diversified Corporations* (1987) by permission from Blackwell Publishers; Figure 9.5 reprinted from *Long Range Planning*, Vol. 21, June 1978, Robinson, Hitchens & Wade, *The Directional Policy Matrix – tool for strategic planning*, by permission of Elsevier Science; Figure 10.7 and Table 11.1(a) by permission of Investor Relations, Sony Corporation; Figure 10.11 from Barrie James, The Global Pharmaceutical Industry in the 1990s, *The Challenge of Change*, (1990) reproduced by permission of The Economist Intelligence Unit Limited; Figure 10.12 adapted from Ghoshal, S. & Bartlett, Christopher A. (1998) *The Individualized Corporation* (Heinemann), by permission from Random House Group UK Limited; Figure 12.1 from Poister & Streib, 'Strategic management in the public sector', *Public Productivity and Management Review*, March 1999, Volume 22, Issue 3, pp. 308–25, reprinted by permission of Sage Publications Inc; Figure 13.3 from Carnall, *Managing Change in Organizations 2nd ed.* (1995) by permission from Pearson Education Limited; Figure 15.2 from Faulkner, D., *International Strategic Alliances* (1995) by permission of Dr. David Faulkner; Figure 16.1 'Schools of strategic theorising' from Whittington, R., *What is Strategy and Does it Matter?* (1993) by permission of Routledge; Figure 16.2 'Evolution of the ten schools' from Mintzberg et al, *The Strategy Safari* (1998) by permission of Pearson Education Limited.

A Companion Web Site accompanies *The Strategic Management of Organisations*, by Haberberg and Rieple

Visit the *The Strategic Management of Organisations* Companion Web Site at www.booksites. net/habriep to find valuable teaching and learning material including:

For Students:

- Study material designed to help you improve your results
- Useful web links
- Details of up-to-date readings pertinent to each chapter
- Internet exercises
- A search facility to locate specific information on the site

For Lecturers:

- A secure, password protected site with teaching material
- A downloadable version of the full Instructor's Manual
- OHPs to use in your lectures
- Up-to-date links for extra case material
- A syllabus manager that will build and host a course web page

Introduction

How to use this book

This book is intended to help you to understand the theory of strategic management and competitive advantage and, most importantly, to *apply* it so that you can understand organisations' past strategies, assess their present situation and, as a result, make reasoned, relevant proposals for what they should do in the future. This introduction describes the features we have included in the book, and the way that we have structured it, to help you achieve this understanding.

In-chapter features

Each chapter begins with a set of **Learning Objectives**, lays out the concepts that you will need to meet those objectives and shows how they will be relevant to a strategic analysis. **Definitions** of all the main concepts are given in the margin, for easy future reference, at the point where they are first encountered. There are extended **Concept** boxes to explain some of the more complicated ideas, or to deal with topics that you may already have encountered in courses on marketing, economics or organisation theory, but which have a slightly different usage in strategic management theory. For the most important analytical frameworks we set out **Practical Dos and Don'ts**, designed to help you sharpen your analysis and avoid the most common errors and misunderstandings.

Alongside the main discussion you will find **Advanced Topics**, which may be of interest to students who have the time and the desire to deepen their understanding of the subject, or to pursue ideas that are slightly outside the theoretical mainstream. Most chapters also include **Theoretical Perspectives**, which deal in depth with the ideas of a particularly influential group of theorists, give an extended extract from a key article or book, or summarise an important theoretical debate.

At the end of each chapter you will find a **Summary** on the main learning points. This concludes (except in the first and last chapters) with a review of some **Typical Questions** that you might be asked relating to that chapter, and some suggestions about how you might use the concepts in that chapter to organise your answers. Each chapter finishes with a set of exercises intended for seminar work: some **Questions for Discussion** and a short **Case Study**, along with suggested questions.

Navigational aids

One of the unusual features of strategic management theory, which can pose difficulties for both tutor and student, is that the various topics tend to be intertwined. There is no one obvious logical order in which to tackle the different ideas, and concepts taught in one place frequently reappear in another. We have used three devices to help you make sense of this. You will find numerous **hyperlinks** in the margin, which will point you to the place earlier or later in the book where a particular concept was defined for the first time or will be discussed in greater depth. At the start of each chapter we show the **analytical schema** or **map** around which the book is based, to show you where you are in the overall scheme of things. And we use Part 1 of the book, and Chapter 1 in particular, to introduce you to the essential vocabulary of strategic management. This should enable you to understand what is going on, even if you use the chapters in a different order from that in which they have been set out.

The structure of the book

The schema around which the book is organised is shown in Figure 1. You will see that it is divided into two parts. In the left-hand column a number of overview chapters are listed. The four right-hand columns form a structure (explained in detail at the end of Chapter 3) that you can use for your analysis of case studies and real-life competitive situations.

Figure 1   The schema of this book

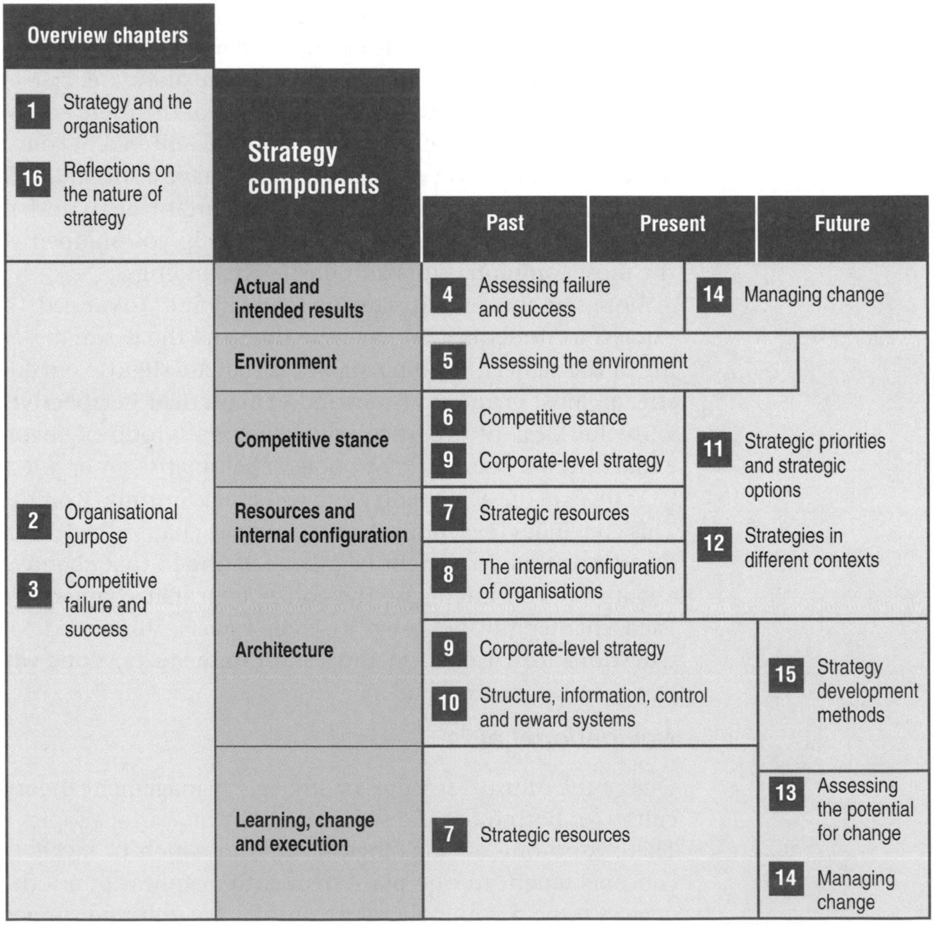

In Part 1, as we have already mentioned, we aim to give you the vocabulary and basic understanding that you need to tackle any of the subsequent topics:

- Chapter 1 sets out the basic vocabulary needed to discuss organisations and their strategies.
- Chapter 2 discusses the purpose of organisations – for whose benefit they exist, the relative importance of economic and non-economic objectives, and the governance mechanisms used to enforce those objectives.
- Chapter 3 covers the essentials of how organisations became and remain successful, and why some organisations fail. It introduces a number of important concepts that are built upon in Part 2.
- Chapter 4 completes the analytical toolkit by laying down some guidelines on how quantitative and qualitative evidence can be combined in a rigorous strategic analysis.

In Part 2 we give a comprehensive review of the theory and practice of how organisations compete, and look at how to assess the source of a firm's past and present competitive advantage.

- Chapter 5 shows how to analyse the impact of an organisation's environment on its strategies and activities.
- Chapter 6 looks at how to assess the decisions an organisation takes about which products to launch into which markets.
- Chapter 7 considers how to assess the quality of an organisation's resources, and its capacity to learn.
- Chapter 8 investigates the internal configuration of organisations – their value chains, culture and architecture.
- Chapter 9 reviews the particular problems faced by large organisations active in more than one area of business, and discusses how they can gain advantage.
- Chapter 10 looks at the organisation's structure, control, reward and information systems and considers how these can influence the strategies they choose and the way in which they are implemented.

In Part 3 the emphasis moves away from what the organisation has achieved in the past to look more at what it might do in the future.

- Chapter 11 sets out a comprehensive framework for (a) identifying the issues confronting an organisation at present and (b) developing proposals for the future.
- Chapter 12 reviews what is known about the strategies that appear to be appropriate in a number of specific competitive contexts. It also looks in some depth at strategies for public sector and not-for-profit organisations.

In Part 4 we study the problems associated with implementing strategies.

- Chapter 13 presents frameworks for viewing the power relationships and culture in an organisation as a prelude to understanding potential constraints on strategy implementation and change.
- Chapter 14 looks at the processes of managing organisational change.

- Chapter 15 reviews the different ways of achieving a chosen strategy, including the management of innovation, acquisitions and alliances.

In Part 5 you are invited to reflect upon the nature of strategy.

- Chapter 16, the only chapter in this part of the book, discusses a number of schools of strategic management theory and invites you to compare and contrast them with those that have been used earlier.

Part 6 contains six case studies designed to give you practice in applying strategic management theory to real-life organisations. They are longer than the Case Studies at the end of the chapters, and require you to combine several different strands of theory in order to arrive at a deep understanding of the issues.

Core concepts

Conceptualisations of strategy and strategic management are discussed in Chapter 1, and in more detail in Chapter 16. ▶

This book is about organisations and the way in which they adapt (or fail to adapt) to the world around them. The things they do to adapt over time are what we call *strategies*, and the process of adaptation is called *strategic management*. Although the word 'management' often calls to mind a deliberate, rational process, organisations' strategies are not always shaped in that way. Sometimes, they come about by accident, or as the result of political activity within the organisation. In this book, the term *strategic management* is used to cover **all** these kinds of strategy making.

In Part 1 we explore the basic concepts that are used in discussing strategy, and examine the links between them. These concepts are drawn from many disciplines: mainly economics and organisation theory, but also sociology, anthropology and psychology.

After reading Part 1, you should know:

● the basic vocabulary of strategic management that you need to understand the rest of the book;

● the different ways in which organisations function and how this affects their ability to survive and compete;

● the meaning of strategy and strategic management;

● the purposes for which organisations exist, and the forces which bear upon them to make them efficient and ethical;

● the types of thought process you need to master in order to understand and analyse organisations and their strategic behaviour.

Strategy and the organisation

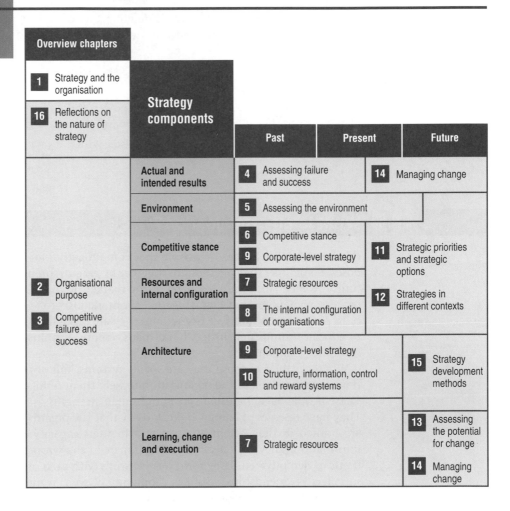

Since a strategy is something that an organisation does, or tries to do, we begin with a discussion of what organisations are, and work towards a definition of strategy. In the process, we cover a number of key concepts about organisations and strategy, and show how they relate to each other. When, in later chapters, you meet these concepts again and explore them in greater depth, you will be able to place them in a broader context.

Learning objectives

After reading this chapter you should have a basic understanding of:

- four different ways of looking at an organisation – as a collection of people, an economic actor, an accumulation of knowledge and learning and a bundle of resources;

- the relationship between these different views of the organisation and the reason why it is important to use them all to understand an organisation's success or failure;

- how organisations develop over time, and why this is relevant to understanding how they compete;

- the concepts of stakeholders, politics, power and culture, and how they are relevant to the development of strategy and strategic objectives;

- what strategy is, and the different levels at which it takes place.

1.1 What is an organisation?

Organisations are **bodies of people** that come together for a particular set of purposes. Sometimes they are brought together by an entrepreneur who sees an opportunity to meet an unfulfilled need in the market place and to become rich in the process. Sometimes they come together spontaneously to fight poverty or injustice, or to play music or football. Sometimes they are brought together by governments to educate, administer justice, build roads, empty dustbins or regulate banks and insurance companies.

Whatever their purpose they are **social systems**, full of people who have ambitions that they look to the organisation to help them fulfil, or at least not to block. These people have the usual spread of human strengths, frailties and peculiarities. They have reserves of energy and creativity that the organisation can tap, but they are limited in their attention span and in their capacity to absorb and process information. They may also, on a bad day or in the wrong environment, be apathetic or demotivated. They form relationships with each other and with users and suppliers – friendships, dislikes, sometimes even romances. These personal relationships have important consequences. They shape the way in which different parts of an organisation work (or fail to work) together, and organisations' decisions about which firms they will buy from and collaborate with.

These social systems **interact with their environment**, buying or leasing space in which to work or perform, purchasing inputs, selling products or services. Thus, they are **economic actors** that, alongside their other purposes, have economic goals. If they are commercial organisations, they must meet the financial expectations of their founders or of financial institutions that may own their shares. If they are clubs, charities or government bodies, they may not be expected to make a profit, but will have to survive within a limited budget.

When we study strategic management, we are really studying what makes these collections of people effective or ineffective economic performers over a period of time. Two other aspects of organisations are important in helping us to understand this. One is the way in which they **process information** from outside and inside the organisation and the extent to which they are able to store it as useful **knowledge** and use it to reach good, informed decisions. The second is how organisations accumulate **resources**, such as technology and brands, and then configure them so as to be able to do things that other organisations cannot.

The following sections explore these ideas in more depth, using a number of examples, many drawn from the organisations that we introduce in Real-Life Application 1.1.

REAL-LIFE APPLICATION 1.1

Four interesting organisations

This box introduces four organisations that we shall be using as illustrations throughout the book. Each of them shows a track record of success along with a number of instructive setbacks.

Sony Corporation is one of the world's leading manufacturers of consumer electronics. It was founded just after World War II by Akio Morita and Masura Ikuba. It came to prominence by being the first company to make a pocket-sized radio, using transistor technology licensed from the USA. This was followed by the world's first transistorised TV, and the Trinitron colour television system. It became one of the world's premier suppliers of high-quality TVs, videos and audio equipment to home and corporate users, with production and R&D facilities in four continents. It cemented a reputation for innovation when in 1979 it introduced the Walkman, a portable cassette player designed to be clipped to a belt and worn while walking or skating. It moved into the business of making the music and film 'software' to be played on its consumer 'hardware' with the 1988 acquisition of CBS Records (now Sony Music) and its 1989 acquisition of the US entertainment combine, Columbia Pictures Entertainment. Its most recent success has been its Playstation videogames console, launched in 1994, which has outsold the products of established players such as Sega and Nintendo. In 1997, it was the world's 30th-largest company (ranked by turnover), with revenues of $53 billion, profits of $1.4 billion and 177,000 employees.

McDonald's Inc. is the world's largest food chain, serving 38 million customers each day in 23,000 restaurants in over 100 countries. It came into being in 1948 when Dick and Sam McDonald worked out how to redesign their kitchen along mass-production lines, producing high volumes of a limited menu for sale at low prices. The firm grew slowly until Ray Kroc, a milkshake machine salesman intrigued by the brothers' high milkshake sales, saw the concept's potential and became the exclusive franchising agent for the USA. Through tireless promotion, he grew the business 16-fold in four years. Its restaurants, with their distinctive golden arch insignia, are now a common sight throughout the world. Apart from its food, the chain is famous for the way that all staff are trained in its distinctive operating procedures, at the company's own 'Hamburger University'. In 1997 it was the world's 16th-largest employer, with 284,000 employees world wide. It made profits of $1.6 billion on a turnover of $12 billion, which made it the world's 361st-largest company measured by revenues.

Benetton SpA is an Italian manufacturer and retailer of clothing. It was founded by Luciano Benetton and his sister Giuliana in 1965, to market her unusual and striking knitwear designs. It pioneered several innovations in its industry, including the use of information systems to monitor worldwide sales on a daily basis and dyeing the finished garments rather than the unprocessed cloth, so that customers' fashion preferences could be responded to with shorter lead times and less risk of unsold stock. It outsources part of its manufacturing to small suppliers and sells only through its own retail outlets, of which it now has several thousand throughout the world. Its contracts with these smaller partners are often informal and shield them from a lot of the risk inherent in the fashion business. It also has major interests in sports goods, where it owns Nordica (skis), Prince (tennis equipment) and Rollerblade (in-line skates). Unlike the other three companies in this Real-Life Application, it is too small to be included among the world's 500-largest companies. Figures for Benetton's turnover, profits and numbers of employees are available from the firm's website, www.benetton.com.

British Airways plc is the world's fourth-largest airline and the largest outside the USA measured by flight miles. Since being sold off into the private sector by the UK government in 1984, it has become one of the world's most profitable airlines. For much of the 1980s and 1990s it moved faster than competitors in control-

ling its cost base, and its customer service gained high ratings from travel magazines. Since 1997, however, it has lost ground to competitors in both of these areas. It also controls a large share of the traffic at Heathrow, the world's busiest international airport and an important air transport hub. In 1997 it was the world's 275th-largest company, with revenues of $15 billion, profits of $340 million and 64,000 employees.

1.2 Organisations as collections of people

In this section we introduce a number of concepts which are important for making sense of the way organisations behave as social systems: stakeholders, culture, politics, power, bounded rationality, and paradigms.

1.2.1 Stakeholders

Stakeholders

People with an interest in an organisation's success, failure or activities, and therefore a desire to influence its behaviour.

Most organisations are subject to a range of stakeholder influences, such as those listed in Table 1.1. Stakeholders shape an organisation's objectives and also the yardsticks that are used to assess its success or failure. Also, different stakeholder groups can be a powerful influence on the extent to which an organisation can change its strategy.

Internal stakeholders

In organisations where the owners or founders still have a management role, they

Methods of identifying stakeholders and assessing their influence are discussed in Section 3.5. ▶

Table 1.1   Examples of stakeholders

Internal stakeholders	Mixed internal and external stakeholders	External stakeholders
Owners/founders	Unions	Users of products and services
Managers	Employees' families	Customers
Staff	Communities where the organisation is based	Distributors
Board of directors	Network partners	Suppliers
	Franchisees	Bankers Shareholders Investment fund managers Pension fund trustees Regulatory bodies Governments

will frequently be dominant stakeholders. This is the case at Benetton, where the founding family retains a great deal of influence on strategy, even though day-to-day control was notionally handed over to professional managers in 1988. Also in most public sector organisations, the owner, in this case the government, has a great deal of control.

In large organisations, it is common for there to be a variety of distinct stakeholder groups, such as different levels of staff, divisions and functions, each with differing views and aspirations. The effective management of this kind of internal tension is an important strategic challenge.

Mixed internal and external stakeholders

Some stakeholders, while not really part of the organisation, may have strong personal links with the organisation's members, which give them an interest in the organisation's affairs. Unions can be influential in some countries and firms, though they have lost power in Anglo-Saxon cultures over the last 20 years. Where a company is a major local employer, it can face strong pressure not to reduce its staffing levels and to contribute time and money to its community. Sometimes the pressure is in the other direction. In 1998, the mayor of New York City, Rudolph Giuliani, offered millions of dollars of public money to the New York Yankees baseball team and the New York Stock Exchange. He was trying to induce them not to move across the Hudson River to New Jersey. Both organisations generated employment in New York, and were prominent symbols of the city and sources of civic pride.

Other examples of mixed stakeholders occur in organisations that have developed as networks. Here, it is difficult to draw a neat boundary to show which stakeholders are 'inside' the organisation and which are 'outside'. For example, while Benetton's suppliers and retailers are separate legal entities, they are mostly dependent on it for their livelihood. Benetton in turn depends upon these firms for its production and sales.

External stakeholders

Users
The people or organisations who actually use an organisation's products or services.

Customers
The people or organisations that pay for an organisation's services or products.

Different attitudes to financial stakeholders, and different forms of corporate ownership and governance, are reviewed in Chapter 2. ▶

Among the most important external stakeholders are an organisation's **users** and **customers**, on whom it depends for survival.

Attitudes to other outside stakeholders vary from country to country. The traditional Western attitude to *suppliers* has been to seek the cheapest source and not to let long-standing relationships stand in the way of getting the cheapest quote. This attitude has softened as Japanese companies, notably automobile manufacturer Toyota, have shown how long-term collaborative relationships can lead to better quality and lower costs. McDonald's has strong links with its suppliers of key inputs like French fried potatoes. British Airways has been involved in helping its main aircraft supplier, Boeing, to design a new generation of airliners.

The relative importance of financial stakeholders, such as banks and shareholders, also differs between countries. In Anglo-Saxon cultures, shareholders are held, as the owners of a firm, to be the most important stakeholders of all. Other models of capitalism start out from the view that companies exist for the benefit of the societies that they belong to, and give unions and employees legal rights to consultation on key decisions or representation on a supervisory board.

| Concept | **Users and customers** |

Users and customers are often the same people or firms. But for many public organisations, and for firms that sell mainly through important distributors such as large supermarket chains, they are not.

Organisation	Users	Customers
Sony	Individual purchasers	Dealers
McDonald's, Benetton	Individual purchasers	Same as users
British Airways	Passengers	Sometimes users, but often their employers
Public university	Students Research sponsors Consultancy clients	Students who pay own fees, sponsors, clients, governments who pay for/subsidise students

If a distributor takes the decision about what to purchase, and the risk if it fails to estimate demand correctly, then it can be regarded as a customer. On this basis Sony's dealers are customers while Benetton's retailers are not, since Benetton takes much of the risk.

Under any model of capitalism, managers sometimes try to divert the firm's resources for their own benefit. Systems of 'corporate governance' have been developed to ensure that firms are run for the benefit of the proper stakeholders, whether they be shareholders alone or some wider group.

1.2.2 Organisations, politics and power

Given the existence of different stakeholder groups in organisations, it is likely that their interests will differ and that there will sometimes be tension between them. Such tension can be destructive, but it can also stimulate creativity and help move organisations forward.

Organisational politics

These tensions within organisations are resolved through **political** processes, which are an important part of strategic decision-making. Decisions may depend upon how much information the decision-makers have at their disposal, how well the different arguments are presented and the decision-makers' desire to further their personal interests. Decision-makers may also be influenced by their past (see Section 1.2.3). They may be more inclined to listen to people from parts of the company where they themselves have spent a substantial part of their career. They may be influenced by sentimental attachments, or because those people know how to put their arguments in language which will appeal to the decision-maker. Some of these considerations are illustrated in Real-Life Application 1.2.

REAL-LIFE APPLICATION 1.2

Stakeholders, politics, power and strategy

British Airways

For many years, British Airways has bought aircraft from Boeing, the US manufacturer that has been the market leader for over a decade. Boeing's aircraft have an excellent reputation, and there are good arguments for sourcing from a single manufacturer, since it saves on the costs of spares and training.

The European Commission has been a strong lobbyist on behalf of Boeing's main rival, Airbus Industrie, a joint venture of four European aerospace firms. During the 1990s, Airbus has steadily gained market share at Boeing's expense. In July 1998, British Airways announced its decision to purchase aircraft from Airbus for the first time.

Undoubtedly, this decision was influenced by the merits of Airbus's products. But it is quite likely that British Airways also wanted to create a good impression with the European Commission, which was due that same month to announce its decision on whether to permit BA to set up a strategic alliance with American Airlines, the largest US carrier, and the terms it would demand for allowing the alliance.

Banque Nationale de Paris

In March 1999, Michel Pébereau, chairman of Banque Nationale de Paris (BNP), surprised observers by launching a takeover bid for two of his bank's main French rivals, Banque Paribas and Société Générale (SG), who had themselves announced plans for an agreed merger earlier that same month.

There had been several large banking mergers in the USA and Europe during the late 1990s. By combining, banks could save money by sharing the 'back office' systems for processing cheques and other transactions, and by closing branches.

However, in France, the banking unions were very powerful, so one of Pébereau's first acts after the takeover bid was to promise that there would be no mass redundancies. The three banks were to retain their separate branch networks and brand identities. Observers were left questioning the rationale behind the proposed takeover.

Meanwhile, the French finance minister and the head of the country's central bank issued a joint statement: 'The public authorities trust that all the actors concerned will favour solutions that are the most respectful of the proper functioning of the market, of social and industrial interests as well as the national interest.'

The role of power in strategic choice

Power
The ability to get other people to do what you want, even if this is not something that they would otherwise have done.

We look at power and power structures again in Chapters 10, 13 and 14. ▶

Real-Life Applications 1.2 (and 1.3, see p. 12) illustrate how the relative power of different stakeholders to make or influence decisions can affect strategic choices. Not everyone has the same ability to bring about strategies. Most of the time, the chief executive is the most powerful person in the organisation. Most of the time, most of the strategic decisions that are taken will come from him or her, or be approved by them at least. This is no doubt why many people have assumed that it is the chief executive who makes the decisions, and who effectively *is* the organisation. But chief executives do not operate in isolation. Why, then, is the chief executive powerful? Or, for that matter, why are some individuals within the organisation more powerful than others?

Power may be based on coercion, such as the use of weapons, or other factors such as the ability to do some things better than other people can. A powerful individual in an army, for example, might be able to induce his or her colleagues to enter into hostile territory, because that person is thought to have the expertise to bring about the desired capture of an enemy position with minimal loss of life. Power is not necessarily the same as authority – the position allocated to someone, which formally entitles them to take certain decisions – although they are very closely associated, and authority is an important source of power. It is also not quite the same as influence, which tends to use persuasion or the force

9

of argument to achieve its effects, although you may very well feel 'persuaded' to do something by the fact that someone is standing over you with an axe in their hand!

Chief executives or other senior managers often become powerful because they are perceived to possess something that the people appointing them think the organisation needs. In the Anglo-Saxon capitalistic world, firms need to have people leading them who have expertise in the management of financial information, able to build good relationships with key sources of finance, such as investment companies, and the ability to manage complex organisations. In Germanic cultures, engineering expertise and training are highly prized. Some more detailed examples of the sources of power are listed below:

- *Expertise* What this is will depend on what is valued by those in the social environment in which it is to be used. In a hospital, expertise may relate to how to carry out heart transplants; in a firm, it may relate to the ability to make appropriate strategic decisions.

- *Control over or access to resources* Once again, the resources which are required by the organisation will vary according to its context. In a commercial firm, resources will include money (and it may be for this reason why finance departments are often extremely powerful), but also may include things such as proprietary technology or knowledge which is critical to a particular aspect of the company's work.

- *Control of or access to information* In a commercial company, important information may relate to customer requirements, future regulatory changes, or to the profitability of certain divisions and activities.

- *Physical strength* It is a simple fact that those who are stronger physically are likely to be able to achieve their objectives over those who are relatively weak. In human society, other factors moderate this, and physical strength is less important than in some areas of the animal world. However, physical fitness is an important source of power; it allows someone to be at work and concentrating, and not languishing at home in bed!

- *Preparedness to fight/confront* A linked source of power to physical strength is someone's preparedness to fight for what they want. Most people like to avoid conflict, and therefore those that show their willingness to stand up for themselves may get their own way over those who do not want a fight.

- *Charisma/referent power* Charisma means a personal quality which inspires devotion. This can even result in people laying down their lives for someone who possesses it. Many of the great warrior or religious leaders had it, such as Napoleon Bonaparte, and yet it is extraordinarily difficult to isolate or define. Many great political or business leaders also have it, Bill Clinton being one recent well-known example. Referent power, another way of describing this, comes from the desire of some people to be associated with the charismatic individual – to be part of their 'gang'.

- *Relationships* Finally, relationships are also a source of power. This is partly because having good relationships gives one access to a wider base of resources, information or expertise on which to call, but is also due to the favours which accrue over time within almost all relationships. If you 'owe' me a good deed, I can call that in at a later time of my choosing.

In a firm, power becomes enshrined in the organisation's structure, so that the departments which have the most critical expertise, or access to important resources, will tend to be larger and have bigger budgets than those which are considered relatively marginal. These are the *power echelons* in an organisation. It is the powerholders, and the power echelons in which they sit, which dictate what strategies are accepted and implemented. The people who appoint new leaders are typically current internal powerholders, who in this way perpetuate their beliefs, values and assumptions. One researcher, Edgar Schein,[1] pointed out that these can often be traced as far back as the founders.

However, even the most powerful individuals within an organisation have to recognise some constraints on their actions. Jeffery Pfeffer, a leading researcher on power, reminds us that even dictators need the 'consent of the governed' to maintain a power position over time.[2] If, for some reason, a leader's expertise declines or is flawed, then their formalised power positions can be overturned through losing the support of subordinates.

Power, politics and rationality

The interplay of power and politics can result in strategic decisions that seem irrational to an outside observer. Such decisions may, however, make perfect sense to people who are conditioned to the way in which the organisation sees the world. It is important to keep this in mind when considering some of the economic models that you will meet later in this book. Economic thinking is largely based on the assumption that organisations and individuals behave rationally. These assumptions are simplifications of reality.

1.2.3 Bounded rationality

Bounded rationality
Bounded rationality is a reasoning process which is not free, but shaped or determined – **bounded** – by factors which make particular ways of thinking about problems much more likely than others. These factors may be preconceptions, or lack of time, information or motivation to take a better decision.

Considerations of power and politics are not the only factors that may affect the 'rationality' of organisational decisions. Even the most gifted managers, as we have already remarked, are fallible human beings. They cannot process all available information and reach a perfectly rational decision, in the way that classical economics assumes that they will. They are too busy, or too tired, to deal with all the stimuli hitting their various senses, and to think deeply about each and every decision. They are predisposed to accept information that reinforces their view of the world and their existing patterns of behaviour. Conversely, they tend to filter out information that challenges their beliefs and behaviour patterns (see Real-Life Application 1.3).

In deciding what they need to notice, people give priority to what has been important in the past, and devise simplifying rules (known as heuristics) based on their previous experience, to help them to decide what to do. Rather than **optimising** – trying to reach the very best decision in the circumstances – people **satisfice**: they settle for the first proposal that appears to give an acceptable outcome. For example, rather than maximising profits, managers simply look for a way of meeting acceptable profit targets. This kind of decision-making is said to be *boundedly rational* and is explored in more detail in the advanced topic that follows.

Banque Nationale de Paris (continued)

In Real-Life Application 1.2 we saw how BNP had bid to take over two French rivals even though powerful stakeholders would make it difficult to obtain the commercial benefits. The deal was also criticised because it involved only French firms. Many observers believed that a successful major bank in the twenty-first century would need to be international in scope.

Why then, did BNP propose the deal? If its two bid targets, Société Générale and Paribas, had pressed ahead with their own merger, then BNP would have lost its position as the largest and most profitable bank in France. BNP's managers are unlikely to have welcomed this prospect. The urge to respond in some way would have been great.

Why not a cross-border merger rather than an all French deal? There is a long history in France of building 'national champions' in certain industries and in limiting foreign participation in key business sectors. Privatisations in France are structured so as to keep strategic shareholdings in French hands, and the government discouraged Germany's Deutsche Bank from bidding for Société Générale. Top French business people and government officials tend to be drawn from a small number of élite universities ('grandes écoles') and seem to share a similar mindset.

Thus it was that BNP might have been predisposed to think of an all-French solution to a European or global competitive problem.

ADVANCED TOPIC
Bounded rationality and enacted environments

The theory of bounded rationality was developed by the Carnegie 'school': Herbert Simon, Richard Cyert and James March. They were pioneers in exploring how managers' human limitations might make them likely to focus their attention on familiar problems and solutions, leading to decisions that are highly determined by history and past experience. They also (March and Simon, 1958) used the term 'satisficing' to indicate some of the constraints of organisational decision-making, which they suggested are rarely optimal or directed at a single goal, but often are a compromise.

According to the Carnegie school, decision-makers are rarely able to process all available information to reach an optimal decision, as the 'rational actor' view assumes. This way of making sense of the complexity of the world around us is called *selective perception*. This means that we tend to focus on stimuli that make us feel comfortable or which are familiar.

There are other reasons why people will focus attention on a relatively narrow range of stimuli, diagnoses and solutions, and simply not consider strategic options that are too far away from what the organisation already does:

- Individuals tend to assume that the future will resemble the past.

- Experience results in routinised responses to familiar situations – we carry round with us packages of behaviours that we are looking to use somewhere. Cyert and March (1963) termed this *problemistic search* – solutions looking for familiar problems.

- People tend to communicate with other people who share the same frames of reference, in language that excludes outsiders.

● Individuals may be more likely to join organisations that appear to share their own values and beliefs.

All this means that people in organisations can never see a full, objective picture of the world. Instead, they work with an imperfect image of reality shaped by their own perceptions and desires, and by those of the people around them. They are said to *enact* their environment (Weick, 1995) – they bring it into existence and then work within it, just as lawmakers do when they enact a piece of legislation.

Strategic drift is covered in Chapter 3. Chapter 14 discusses outsiders and organisational change. ▶

When an organisation becomes misaligned with its environment, this focus on the familiar may be an important cause of strategic slip or drift. It may take an outsider, who does not share the same experiences or possibly even values, to bring about strategic change.

Experience, upbringing and emotions

People's upbringing and past experience are important influences which shape the kinds of decisions that they will prefer.[3] A high level of educational attainment has been shown to be linked with a preference for entrepreneurial, innovative strategies, as is relative youth. Managers with finance backgrounds are likely to pursue unrelated diversification or conglomerate strategies; managers with marketing or production backgrounds are likely to pursue vertical integration or single-business strategies; and managers who have been with their firms a relatively short time are likely to choose diversification strategies. Managers are also likely to incline towards re-using strategies that have worked for them in the past.

More recently, there has been an increasing awareness that other factors play an important part in strategic processes.[4] Real-Life Application 1.4 gives a recent example.

REAL-LIFE APPLICATION 1.4

Economics, emotions and European defence

In December 1998, the merger between DASA, the defence and aerospace division of DaimlerChrysler, and British Aerospace (BAe – since renamed BAE Systems) seemed unstoppable. The two companies had held long negotiations, the economic benefits of the merger were clear, and both firms wanted closer ties to increase their leverage over Aerospatiale, the major French aerospace firm. DASA and BAe agreed that Airbus, the civil aviation consortium in which they and Aerospatiale were all major partners, needed to be incorporated as a 'normal' company if it were to remain competitive. Aerospatiale and its majority shareholder, the French government, were blocking this move.

However, quite suddenly, a decision by its long-standing British rival, the General Electric Company (GEC), to withdraw from the defence industry threw up another possibility for BAe. By purchasing Marconi Electronics, the defence arm of GEC, BAe could propel itself to the number 2 position in the world defence industry, behind only Lockheed-Martin of the USA. The prospect was rendered even more tempting by the possibility of turning the tables on GEC, which under its former chairman, Lord Weinstock, had made repeated noises about acquiring BAe.

BAe decided to go ahead with the £7.7 billion Marconi Electronics deal, which was signed in January ▶

Real-Life Application continued

1999, over the strong objections of the UK prime minister, Tony Blair, who preferred a pan-European merger. Once this was completed, BAe turned its attention back to DASA. The economic and political benefits of a link between the two firms were, to British eyes, as persuasive as ever, and BAe's managers must have been convinced that their German colleagues would eventually 'see sense'.

The sense that Daimler-Chrysler saw, though, was very different. British Aerospace's last-minute change of direction was to it evidence that it was not, after all, a predictable partner. For several months Daimler-Chrysler refused to return calls from BAe's chairman, who when he finally got through, was curtly told: 'We are not interested. You have had your chance.'

DaimlerChrysler instead injected DASA into the newly formed EADS alliance, which included Aerospatiale and CASA, the Spanish aerospace contractor that is the fourth participant in the Airbus consortium. EADS now controls 80% of the Airbus consortium to BAe's 20%. In December 1999, DASA was vying with BAe to see which of them would link up with Italy's Alenia, one of the few remaining independent players in the European defence and aerospace industries.

Sources: David Gow, Mark Milner and Richard Norton-Taylor, 'Analysis: Defence: The politics spoiling a City fairy tale. The mega-merger of British Aerospace and GEC's Marconi division will have serious consequences for Tony Blair's ambitions of tying Britain's defence closer to Europe', *The Guardian*, Manchester, 20 January 1999; 'Britain opts out of Europe', *The Economist*, London, 23 January 1999; Andrew Lorenz and Michael Woodhead, 'BAe weathers Franco-German flak', *Sunday Times*, London, 17 October 1999; 'Flagging out', *The Economist*, London, 27 November 1999; 'Eurofighter rival threatens BAe's Italian link-up', *The Daily Telegraph*, London, 30 December 1999.

1.2.4 Dominant logic and the paradigm

As we have seen in previous sections, people in an organisation tend to reject information that conflicts with their past experience and to recruit and mix with like-minded individuals. Training, the passing on of traditional ways of doing things, the telling of stories about successes and failures, also ensure that over time people in organisations develop similar world views and think about things in a similar way.

Thus, most organisations acquire a set of values and assumptions about the world, their industry and their organisation that become more homogeneous over time. This set of deeply held, often unspoken beliefs is known as the organisation's **dominant logic** or **paradigm**, or sometimes its **theory-in-use** or **organisational code**. It forms a standard against which all new activities are measured, consciously or unconsciously, to determine how credible they are, or indeed whether they are to be considered at all.

1.2.5 Organisational culture

Organisational culture
Culture is 'how things are done around here'. It is what is typical of the organisation, the habits, the prevailing attitudes, the grown-up pattern of accepted and expected behaviour.
(Drennan, 1992)

'Organisations do not have *cultures – they* are *cultures' (Karl Weick)*

The paradigm lies at the centre of the distinctive culture that every organisation develops over time, as the various stakeholders in and around an organisation reach a way of working and living together. It is shaped by a variety of factors (see Real-Life Application 1.5):

● The company's leaders, past and present, may leave a lasting imprint upon an organisation.[5]

We look at ways of analysing how corporate culture contributes to a firm's competitiveness in Chapter 8, and the way it affects an organisation's capacity to change in Chapter 13. ▶

- Events in the history of the organisation will shape its responses to current and future events.
- The industrial environment in which it developed will leave an imprint.
- The national environment in which the organisation developed will also shape the attitudes and behaviours of the people within it.

Corporate culture affects an organisation's activities and strategic effectiveness in three ways. Firstly, it shapes people's behaviour towards outside stakeholders. This in turn influences the purchasing decisions of customers, and the extent to which suppliers, customers and financiers will co-operate with the organisation.

REAL-LIFE APPLICATION 1.5

Four companies, four cultures

	Sony	McDonald's	Benetton	British Airways
Leaders	Both Ibuka and Morita shaped Sony as an innovator. Morita instilled a regard for the importance of good marketing.	Ray Kroc laid down basic values of Quality, Service, Cleanliness, Value which are still central to McDonald's culture and strategy.	Strong design tradition from Giuliana. Luciano Benetton laid down an open culture emphasising personal acquaintance in selecting key staff.	Lord King and Colin Marshall, Chairman and CEO after privatisation, shaped BA's pugnacious attitude to competition and its marketing-driven culture.
History	The loss of control of the standard for video cassettes to arch-rival Matsushita created fear of losing control of future standards. Drove Sony to acquire CBS and Columbia.		Company grew out of poor Veneto region of Italy. Tradition of making do with few resources, led to a culture of self-reliance in development of technology and design.	History as flag carrier for UK shapes attitude to UK government, which it expects to fight its cause with other governments and the European Commission. Recent history – successful turnaround after privatisation – source of corporate pride.
Industry			Rhythms driven by cycles and consistent need for change of a fashion house.	Many airlines drew flight staff from military. Reflected in uniforms and job titles of flight crew.
National culture	Typically Japanese in the long-term commitment it gives and expects from employees (though atypical in other respects).	Very American in the values it portrays to outside world and in aggressive, capitalist stance to competition.	Italian design flair is prominent. Many Italian expatriates involved in building global network.	

Secondly, it shapes the *motivation* of people in the organisation. In order for an organisation to prosper, the people within it need to be motivated to put the organisation's interests alongside (or even ahead of) their own. There are three basic ways of doing this:

1. *Greed* – people can be given incentives with high commission on sales or with share options to behave in certain ways.
2. *Fear* – people can be coaxed through fear of losing their jobs, or of ridicule from their bosses or fellow workers.
3. *Goodwill and commitment* – people share or identify with the aims of the organisation.

There are numerous case studies which suggest that the third way – based on cultural identification – has the greatest impact on organisational effectiveness, although many successful organisations use a combination of all three.

The third important way in which culture influences strategy is by affecting organisations' capacity to react and change. People's patterns of behaviour, and the ways in which they view the world, develop gradually over time, and may alter only slowly. If managers are confronted with a problem, then the solutions they tend to favour are conditioned by experience of what has worked in the past. To use the examples in Real-Life Application 1.5, if confronted with a competitive problem, Sony or Benetton might tend to look for a solution based upon product innovation or design, while McDonald's and British Airways might favour aggressive pricing or marketing. The stronger the organisation's culture, the more difficult it can be for people to force themselves to consider new types of strategy. However, new strategies may be needed if, for example, new technologies are developed or economic conditions change.

1.3 Organisations as economic actors

Our second way of looking at the organisation is as an economic actor. After reading the previous section, and watching the way in which corporate life is depicted in the cinema and on television, you might emerge with the impression that organisations are there only to satisfy the tastes, whims, sexual desires and personal ambition of the powerful people inside them. This can indeed be the case for some organisations, some of the time. However, the key stakeholders also have financial objectives (see Table 1.2) which demand that organisations also function effectively as economic units. The range of things that organisations, and the people within them, can do is constrained by this necessity.

If they fail, the management team may be sacked, or the organisation sold or closed down. If they succeed, on the other hand, people can be rewarded. They may benefit financially from increased salaries, bonuses or stock options, or more indirectly from improvements to the working environment. They may also gain in self-esteem from working for a successful organisation, as well as taking satisfaction from a job well done.

Organisations must do a number of things in order to fulfil their stakeholders' financial objectives: They must generate revenue, by providing **products and services** that satisfy the needs of customers and users, and deliver them at an

Table 1.2 Different types of organisation and their financial objectives

Organisation	Controlling stakeholder	Financial objective
Sony	Japanese banks	Sufficient profits to satisfy expectations of banks (typically lower than those of Western shareholders)
McDonald's	US shareholders	Profit maximisation
Benetton	Benetton family	Cash flow to fund expansion
British Airways	British and US financial institutions	Profit maximisation
A medical research charity	Sponsors and donors	Break-even between income from donations, sponsorship and commercial activities, and expenditure to fund research
A state prison	Government	To use up allocated budget, but not overspend it

acceptable **cost**. In order to do this they develop a **configuration** that enables them to operate effectively and they **interact**, as a buyer, seller or competitor, with individuals and other firms in **industries and markets**. In the following sections we explore each of these concepts in turn.

1.3.1 Products, services and effectiveness

If organisations are to meet these financial objectives, they must serve their users effectively. This is what gives commercial organisations revenues from customers, keeps donations and sponsorship income flowing into a charity's bank account, and persuades governments to keep open, or even expand, a prison or a university.

Organisations serve users by taking inputs and *adding value* to them, i.e. transforming them into outputs that customers are willing to pay for. The inputs may be raw materials, information or human labour. An organisation's outputs may be:

- Tangible products, such as computers or clothing or hamburgers.
- Software, which includes not only programs that run on computers, but also music and films. Although these often take a tangible form, such as a CD or video cassette, the valuable element is the intangible intellectual property, which may be the result of many person-years of creative effort. These types of output are of increasing importance in developed economies. The stock market value of Microsoft, the dominant force in computer software, now exceeds those of most of the oil firms and automobile manufacturers that have been America's largest companies for many decades.
- Services, like a restaurant meal, a retail transaction or an airline flight. Services are intangible and are consumed at the point of production. One of the main trends of the late twentieth century has been the decline in importance of manufacturing industries and the growth of services. Services account for over 80% of the output of the USA and the UK.

The differences between products and services can be exaggerated. Almost all services rely on the efficient manipulation of physical items: a McDonald's restaurant is a small masterpiece of carefully designed mass production, and a British Airways flight depends on aircraft maintenance facilities that are managed and equipped like a factory. Many physical products are sold as a package with a bundle of services, such as design, delivery and after-sales maintenance. It is best to think of organisations as producing a mixture of physical outputs, intellectual property and services, and in this book we shall often use the words 'outputs', 'products' and 'services' interchangeably to cover all parts of this mix.

If the organisation is to succeed, this conversion from inputs into outputs needs to be **effective**: the outputs must do what the users need them to.

1.3.2 Costs and efficiency

Many organisations also strive to be **efficient**, and keep their costs as low as possible. They may try to reduce the variable costs of obtaining the inputs and converting them into outputs. They may also try to minimise their fixed costs: plant, buildings and overheads such as sales and administration. Where high fixed costs are unavoidable, the firm may try to utilise its assets as intensively as possible, to minimise the unit costs of its outputs.

Organisations that at first sight seem very efficient are not always the most successful – keeping costs low can sometimes interfere with innovation or customer service, which may be important to an organisation's effectiveness. However, any organisation must meet a minimum standard of efficiency – it must keep the cost of the inputs plus the costs of the conversion process below what it receives as income. Normally, of course, there needs to be a surplus to allow a firm to renew its assets and show the required level of profit.

Hidden within the organisation's cost base are two particular types of cost that economists have identified and that are important in strategic management:

● *Transaction costs* – the hidden costs of doing business with other organisations.
● *Agency costs* – the hidden costs of keeping the people inside the organisation focused upon that organisation's objectives.

Transaction costs
The cost to an organisation of being exploited by independent suppliers and distributors, or the costs of the administration and control systems needed to avoid such exploitation.

Transaction costs are examined in detail in Section 8.1.2. ▶

Transaction costs

When a firm uses outside firms, such as suppliers, contractors, retailers or distributors, it runs the risk that they will be opportunistic – that they will try to cheat it in some way. For example, a supplier might lie about its costs to try to inflate its prices. A distributor might pretend to have sold more than it really has, to obtain a greater discount or commission than it is entitled to.

There are various ways that organisations can seek to reduce their transaction costs. They can pursue strategies of **vertical integration** – do as much as possible in-house. They can try to do business only with firms that they know and trust, or that have strong reputations for fair dealing. Or they can try to put control systems in place to police the relationship, although the costs of those systems themselves count as part of the organisation's transaction costs.

Concept | **Vertical integration**

An organisation's degree of vertical integration is the extent to which it has extended its activities forwards or downstream (towards the customer or end user) and backwards or upstream (towards the production of its raw materials). Vertical integration decisions relate to whether to produce components or other inputs in-house or to buy them in, and whether to use a firm's own resources or third parties to distribute its outputs.

Agency costs
The costs of controlling the actions of managers and employees, together with any profits lost because of ineffective control.

Agency costs

For quite long periods of time, a firm's managers and employees may use the firm's resources to further their own ambitions rather than to do what their owners, shareholders or controlling stakeholders require. Economists term this a **principal–agent problem** (the owners are the principals, the managers are the agents).

Managers may, for example, use corporate jets for personal holidays or carry out their own businesses using the firm's equipment. They may purchase unnecessarily luxurious offices in order to boost their status and self-esteem at the organisation's expense. Other examples of agency costs include the costs of control and audit systems and of the people that run them, or excessive expense claims by managers who are trying to 'milk' their company for a few extra euros.

We discuss control systems again in Chapter 10. ▶

An organisation can attempt to reduce its agency costs by setting up a supervisory structure and a set of control systems that make it difficult for employees to cheat it. It may also try to develop a culture in which such cheating is socially unacceptable.

1.3.3 Configuration

An organisation has choices to make in how it configures its operations to produce its outputs efficiently and effectively. These choices together constitute its **value chain** and **architecture**.

Value chain
The way an organisation decides to undertake the important activities at each stage in the development, production and delivery of its products and services.

The value chain

An organisation's value chain determines how effectively it serves its users, and at what cost. It includes:

- The way that the organisation chooses to develop new products and services – for example through intensive prior research and test-marketing of a small number of products, or by launching a lot of new products and seeing which ones become popular with customers.

- The way that outputs are produced. Products or services may be highly standardised to keep costs down, like the service in a chain of budget-priced hotels or a mass-produced product like a TV set. Alternatively, they may be highly customised, like a prestige office building or a luxury car. Outputs may be processed along traditional mass-production lines, with inputs being purchased cheaply in bulk and processed in long production runs. Or an organisation may choose more flexible 'lean production' methods, with suppliers delivering the inputs 'just-in-time' to be processed, inventories being kept low and the process structured so as to allow frequent changeovers between one product line and another.

- The way in which products are distributed and marketed. A firm may sell its products through specialist dealers, or general retailers such as supermarkets, or use its own salesforce or sell direct via mail order or the Internet. Each of these may be an effective way of reaching a particular market segment. A firm may choose to invest heavily in advertising to make a lot of people aware of its services, target a narrower group of customers by direct mail, or rely upon word-of-mouth.

- The way in which customers are looked after once they have bought the product, for example through maintenance and repair services, customer help-lines and complaints-handling procedures.

The design of the value chain is one way in which an organisation can make itself different from its competitors (see Real-Life Application 1.6).

We discuss the value chain in a great deal more detail in Chapter 8. ▶

An important set of decisions within the value chain relates to an organisation's degree of vertical integration: what it produces in-house, where it can control delivery times and quality to its own requirements, and what it buys in from outside. In Real-Life Application 1.6, Levi-Strauss is more vertically integrated than Benetton, which keeps direct control of only a few key operations. By using outside suppliers, it may get inputs more cheaply, but may find it has less control over their standards of service or delivery.

REAL-LIFE APPLICATION 1.6

Value chains in the fashion industry

Benetton's value chain is very distinctive. Its use of subcontractors in making its clothes, and franchisees to sell them, helped to keep capital costs low, while linking it to a network of entrepreneurs who are strongly motivated to keep their part of the operation efficient and effective. Historically, it has kept in-house only technically difficult processes that are difficult to carry out and crucial for product quality, like the dyeing of the clothes. This it does as late as possible in the production process, so that if one colour is selling better than another that season, clothes can be produced quickly to meet demand. Recently, it has brought more of its manufacturing in-house, investing heavily in automation to reduce costs.

Other fashion stores configure their value chains differently. For example, Levi-Strauss, the American maker of jeans and casual clothing, designs its own products and manufactures them in plants that it owns and controls. It sells most of them through independ-

ent retailers, though it does have its own stores in major cities as a way of keeping its brand in the public eye.

America's The Gap and the UK's Marks and Spencer have clothing made up to their own design by suppliers around the world, but have a policy of owning, rather than franchising, their stores. (Marks and Spencer does use franchises in some markets, such as South-East Asia.) Other clothing chains act simply as retailers, selling clothes that are designed and manufactured by independent firms.

No one value chain is inherently better than another – effectiveness tends to be context-specific. What makes Benetton effective is the way in which it is able to *manage the relationships and information flows* in its value chain in order to respond effectively and flexibly to customer needs. The management of relationships and information flows comes about through the organisation's *architecture*.

Other important decisions within the value chain relate to:

Economies of scale are
defined in detail in
Chapter 3. ▶

- the scale of operations – large to try and gain lower costs through economies of scale, or small to gain flexibility;
- the scope of operations – whether to focus on a few products or go for a broader range;
- location – e.g. close to customers, to give them fast service, or far away, in a country where labour costs are low.

Architecture[6]

Architecture
The structures, systems and practices that shape the way that information flows into and out of the organisation, and the way that decisions are taken (or avoided) on the basis of that information.

An organisation's architecture is its way of structuring the relationships between its different elements. As an organisation grows more complex, it needs more managers to supervise the different parts of its operations, and systems to help them. Architecture includes an organisation's structure and its control and reward systems, which shape the motivation of people to share information and process and act upon it. This has an important effect upon its agency costs.

One way in which organisations can motivate their people is by giving them a sense of a common destiny and identification with fellow employees. Some do this through their **mission** or **vision**, an important element of many organisations' architecture and also a way in which they signal their 'identity' so as to attract like-minded people.

The concept of
architecture, and the
difference between
culture and architecture,
are discussed in detail in
Chapter 8. ▶

The concept of architecture also embraces the relationships between the organisation and other organisations in its immediate environment, such as its customers, suppliers and distributors. It is an important influence on an organisation's transaction costs. For example, because of the strong personal relationships in its network (Real-Life Application 1.6), Benetton does not encounter opportunistic behaviour from its tied suppliers and retailers.

There are strong links between the concepts of architecture and culture, since both affect the motivation of individuals within an organisation. Architecture also includes mechanisms through which the organisation exchanges information with its environment and distributes it internally. These may be formal information systems, or informal personal contacts. Thus, it is also important to the way in which an organisation accumulates knowledge (Section 1.4).

1.3.4 The organisation's relationship with its environment[7]

A firm's value chain can be viewed as a link in a more extensive chain in which basic raw materials, such as wood, iron ore, silicon, petrochemicals, water and electricity are transformed, through the addition of labour and more raw materials, into products and services. These may then be incorporated into other customers' products, and so on down the chain (Figure 1.1). The end point of the chain is a product like a stereo, or a service like a retail transaction or an education, which is paid for by individual consumers, either as a private transaction or through their taxes.

Figure 1.1 illustrates some important things about the organisation's environment:

Computer memory shortages and the demand for security services

In the early 1990s, a major Asian fabrication plant for Random Access Memory (RAM), the chips that hold data inside a computer while it is being processed, burnt down. This led to a sudden shortage of RAM chips, which trebled in price in the space of a few months.

Because RAM is small, easy to carry and difficult to trace, it became a tempting target for thieves. Large organisations were broken into and the RAM stolen from their PCs.

The result of this was an upsurge in the demand for security services and security devices. If you had been in the security business, would you have started to recruit new staff when you heard about the fire in the RAM factory?

The word 'complex' is used here in its colloquial form, but it can also have a very specific meaning relating to the behaviour of certain types of physical, biological and social systems (see Advanced Topic 3.6). ▶

- It is a *system*; you cannot understand it fully just by looking at one or two elements.
- It is *complex*; anything that happens to any part of the system may affect the demand for an organisation's services, or the prices of its inputs.
- It is *unpredictable* (see Real-Life Application 1.7); not only because of the large number of components, but also because each component is in itself a complex social system full of unpredictable human beings.

Competition and collaboration

If you look again carefully at Figure 1.1, you will see how the total amount of profits that firms in the chain can make is limited. The total amount of revenue that they can extract is limited by the amount that consumers are willing or able

Figure 1.1   The organisation in its environment – a link in a chain

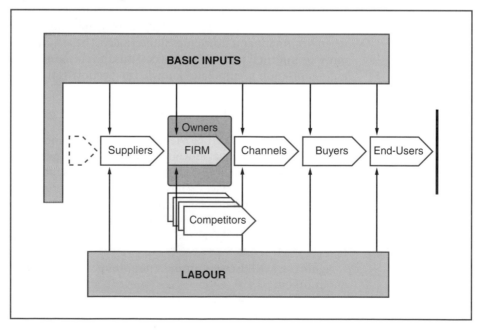

to pay for the services they get. This is governed by macro-economic factors, like consumer spending power, and social factors, like popular tastes, which few firms can influence directly. At the other end of the chain, the costs of labour and raw materials are set by markets of government policies, and most companies cannot influence them either.

So, if a firm within the chain wants to increase its profits, it has a limited number of options on which to base its strategies:

1. It can become more efficient, reducing the quantities of raw materials and labour that it uses, or finding ways of using cheaper ones.

2. It can make its products more attractive so that its customers are willing to pay more for them, or buy more of them. Sometimes this will be because they are more attractive than other items of expenditure or competing products. Sometimes it will be because using the firm's services actually saves the customer money (for example, using an energy consultant can save money spent on fuel). This type of strategy is known as *differentiation*.

3. It can use *power* over the other firms in the chain to drive down the prices it pays for its inputs or to drive up the prices it charges for its outputs.

4. It can *collaborate* with other firms in the chain to drive down the *total cost* of delivering services to the final consumer, so that all can share the benefits.

None of these options is inherently superior to any of the others, so organisations may choose any of them, or a combination. Whichever one is chosen will depend in part on the organisation's culture – some organisations are more competitive by nature than others. But it will also depend upon their perceptions of the **industry** in which they operate, and the likely **reactions** of suppliers, competitors and customers to the moves they make.

Industries and markets

Industry
A group of firms (competitors) that produce a set of similar outputs – products and services that fulfil the same broad function.

The size of an **industry** is measured in terms of the total sales of these outputs. The competing organisations may be single-product companies, or they may be divisions of larger organisations. An organisation may compete in several industries.

An industry's products may be sold in a range of markets. The size of each **market** is represented by the total purchases made by these customers, and may be measured in terms of volume (quantity of outputs sold), value (sales turnover) or sometimes numbers of customers. (Market size is also sometimes used to mean *potential* sales or customers.)

Market
A group of customers.

Markets can be further subdivided into **segments** – buyers who are linked by some common characteristic. It may be that they are located in the same place (a **geographic** segment) or are similar in terms of age or purchasing behaviour. You will sometimes see geographic segments referred to as geographic markets (e.g. 'the UK market for fast food'). You may also see references to **vertical markets**. These are groups of firms or consumers with similar characteristics, such as 'financial services firms' or 'retired people'.

One market may be served by several industries. For example, the market for holidays is served by tour operators, who buy airline seats and hotel rooms in bulk and put them into packages aimed at different types of holidaymaker, and by travel agents who sell their products. But travel agents also sell the services of airlines, rail, coach and ferry operators, cruise lines, hotels and car-hire firms who in turn are quite happy to sell their products directly to any consumers that feel happier making their own arrangements. The holiday market consists of part of the output of all of these industries.

The outputs of different industries serving the same market are said to be **substitutes** for one another. If they perform very much the same task, they can be said to be close substitutes. For example, for travel between major cities in Europe, rail services are close substitutes for air services – they offer the traveller similar journey times and degrees of comfort. On the other hand, for a journey from Europe to the United States, a cruise on a ship is not a close substitute for an airline journey.

We look at industries and substitutes in more detail in Chapter 5. ▶

Concept	Substitutes

The use of the term 'substitute' in strategic management theory may be different from the one you have met if you have studied economics. Some economics textbooks say that nearly identical products from different firms (such as Sony and Philips televisions) are substitutes for one another. We, however, would refer to them as **competing** products. Strategic management theory would class a trip to the cinema, a hi-fi and a personal computer as substitutes for a TV set.

Just as one market may be served by many industries, one industry may serve several markets. The airline, hotel and car-hire industries do not just sell to the holiday market. For most of them, the business travel market is more important. Some of them develop specialised products tailored to the needs of the business traveller, such as business class air travel. However, business class travel cannot usefully be considered a separate industry. Its users will travel on the same planes as holiday travellers and be served by the same crew, while the aircraft may also carry mail and freight – two other services offered by the airline industry.

Not all airline firms serve all these markets. Some carry only packages or freight, some are charter airlines that carry very few business travellers. Such firms form discrete parts of an industry, which some writers confusingly refer to as segments (e.g. the 'charter airline segment'). In this book, we shall refer to a part of an industry as a subsector, and use segment to denote a part of a market.

It can be difficult to determine the boundaries of an industry. Scheduled airlines compete with one another, but also to some extent with charter airlines, railways and cruise liners. Does it make most sense to speak of the scheduled airline industry (containing only firms like British Airways), the passenger airline industry (containing charter airlines as well), the airline industry (containing these plus specialist freight airlines) or the travel industry (containing airlines, rail, bus and boat operators)?

For more detail on how to assess where an industry stops and another begins, see Section 5.7. ▶

There is, unfortunately, no easy answer to this or to the similar problem regarding the dividing line between markets and segments. Where the line should be drawn is a matter of what makes most sense when analysing a particular situation. This judgement really comes down to assessing how close the different substitutes are to one another. If you consider the substitutes to be very close, then it makes most sense to view them as competing products in a single industry.

1.3.5 Interactions between stakeholders – game theory

The different players in the chain depicted in Figure 1.1 are interdependent. Very few organisations can achieve their strategic aims unless other players assist them, or at least fail to obstruct them. A supplier may fail to deliver inputs of the required quality. A failing competitor may cut its prices to suicidal levels in an attempt to win back market share. A potential customer may feel committed to a relationship with a competitor.

This means that no organisation can consider its strategy in isolation. It needs to take account of the likely reactions of these other players. When McDonald's, in its early days, decided to sell hamburgers for 15 cents instead of the prevailing price of 30 cents, it needed to be confident that there was no competitor that would start to undercut it by selling at 12 cents. Otherwise, the result would have been a price war in which no one would have made profits. However, the McDonald brothers could be confident in 1948 that no competitor had the technology to produce burgers as cheaply as they. And most of their local competitors probably made the mistake of assuming that they were mad, and would quickly go bankrupt, so that it was not worthwhile for them to react.

Important insights have been gained from a branch of economics known as **game theory**.[8] The word 'game' in this context has a specialised meaning: it refers to the structure of the interaction between two or more 'players' in a relationship. Two competitors in an industry, a firm and its suppliers or customers, a firm's owners and its managers, can all be seen as involved in games of this kind. In a game theory simulation, each player is assumed to have an objective – normally, though not always, to maximise its profits – and some form of mathematical function is used to model the 'payoffs' to the two players of different combinations of their decisions.

Game theory models are not precise enough to help firms plan actual competitive situations, such as McDonald's contest with Pizza Hut and Burger King. Rather, they give theorists a method of simulating what might happen in particular types of interaction.

One insight from game theory has been to show the allure of strategies that minimise the risk of short-term losses over those that offer the best chance of long-term gain. For example, if you believe that there is a danger that your competitors will cut their prices, it makes sense for you to cut yours first, rather than risk losing market share. This is true even if you can see that profits would be higher all round if everyone kept their prices high. You may be an employee and believe there is a significant chance of your being fired, or of the firm going bankrupt, before you can realise your personal objectives. There is a temptation for you to take what you can from the firm now rather than work for its long-term benefit – this is the basis of the principal–agent problem. Similarly, transaction costs arise because, in the game between supplier and customer, one player may see short-term gains from exploiting the other.

These short-term strategies are more attractive if it is clear that the game will only be played once, or a few times. Researchers have found that, if participants do not know how many times the game will be played, they are more likely to try strategies that increase the long-term benefit to all players – for example, to keep prices high in the hope that their competitors will do likewise.

This difference between *single* and *repeated games* is helpful in a variety of contexts. It helps to explain why some firms might build long-term collaborative relationships with particular suppliers, rather than shopping around for the lowest price each time they order. Similarly, it helps to explain why some firms try to build relationships of trust with their staff, rather than being authoritarian.

Another insight from game theory is the potential importance of *committing* significant resources before competitors do. If, for example, one firm has already built a factory with the capacity to supply 80% of likely demand for a product, game theory shows that a rational profit-maximising competitor is best off building a much smaller plant. On the other hand, if both were making their plans at the same time, each would do best to build a factory able to supply around half the potential market.

This kind of strategy only works, of course, if the competitors are 'rational' in the economic sense of the word. On the other hand, if they are driven by the desire to show how good they are, or by a personal hatred of your organisation because you fired them five years ago, or by national pride, they may still go ahead and build a bigger plant than yours, knowing that the market is not big enough for you both. Later in the book, we shall meet examples of precisely this kind of 'irrational' behaviour.

To anticipate the reactions of competitors, suppliers and customers, one needs information and psychological insights. Some firms have sophisticated competitive intelligence systems to gather data on other firms' resources and cultures, since one clue about how firms will react in the future is their behaviour in the past.

1.3.6 The organisation's picture of its environment

Much of the above discussion has assumed that managers are working with unlimited, good-quality information, and are capable of digesting and responding to it. However, in practice, neither of these things is entirely true.

An organisation's ability to anticipate and react to changes in its environment is constrained by the quality of the information available to it. Market research and competitive intelligence are always likely to have gaps. It is quite unlikely that in real life McDonald's would have been able to predict, with any real precision, the likely outcomes of the pricing decisions in the competitive games we looked at in Section 1.3.5.

Similarly, as we have seen in Section 1.2.3, managers are boundedly rational individuals working with imperfect information. For the organisation to prosper, it is of course necessary for important details within their imperfect picture of the world to be 'correct'. For example, their picture of what customers require must be close to the customers' own picture. Organisations need to be able to learn about their environment in order to keep those key details up-to-date. In the next section, we look at organisations as learning systems.

1.4 The organisation as an accumulation of knowledge and learning

Our third way of looking at an organisation is as a system for processing information and knowledge, and for learning. Organisations come into being to fulfil particular purposes, but they do not always start out with clearly defined methods for achieving them. They often build upon existing practices in their industry and on the personal experience of their members. People will develop solutions to particular operational problems, some after much thought and rehearsal, others on the spur of the moment. They will share these solutions with other people inside the organisation over a cup of coffee or in a formal training session.

In this way, organisations *learn* ways of coping with the situations that they meet most often. These are called *routines* (Nelson and Winter, 1982), a term which covers a wide range of behaviours by both individuals and groups within the organisation (see Real-Life Application 1.8).

REAL-LIFE APPLICATION 1.8

Examples of routines

Factory workers develop routines that enable them to machine difficult components quickly and with minimum waste.

In motor sport, teams develop precisely rehearsed routines to shave vital fractions of a second off the time it takes to change a car's tyres during a race.

Management consultants have routines for managing projects to ensure that they come in on time and within budget, and other routines for putting together a convincing presentation to a client.

Some routines may be written down and widely understood within an organisation. The knowledge that they employ is *explicit knowledge* – it can be packaged and transferred easily. Other routines may have been built up over time from a variety of experiences, have never been written down and may not even be capable of being put into words. This is *tacit knowledge* (see Real-Life Application 1.9 for a discussion of the difference).

REAL-LIFE APPLICATION 1.9

Explicit and tacit knowledge

Explicit knowledge may be carefully documented and widely understood throughout a whole industry, for example:

- accountants' procedures for carrying out the annual audit of a company;
- hospital emergency procedures for treating a broken leg or a heart attack.

Tacit knowledge may be much more personal and more intuitive:

- a chef *knows* when mayonnaise is about to curdle;
- an experienced machine operator *knows*, from long practice, which sequence of machining operations gives the best results for a particular component and can *feel* when it is finished;
- in a group of rock or jazz musicians who play together frequently, everyone *understands* when to start and when to pause.

Learning and knowledge are not just about internal problems and solutions. Organisations also learn about patterns in their environment. McDonald's has learnt what types of food are most in demand in particular seasons of the year and at particular times of day. British Airways has learnt, for each particular destination, when to expect surges of demand and what types of food to serve to cater for the cultural and religious preferences of its customers.

Sometimes, they have learnt about these things by thinking ahead – both firms would have been able to predict surges of demand in their home markets around Christmas. However, to learn how to meet the dietary requirements of Muslim or Hindu customers, they will have needed careful research, or may simply have learnt from making mistakes and then addressing the complaints.

1.4.1 How learning happens

Learning is not automatic. Some organisations learn only how to deal with a particular set of customers at a particular point in time, and then stop. This leaves them very vulnerable when the environment changes – when there is a recession, for example, or when customers suddenly insist upon being able to place their orders through a computer network.

Firstly, people must be able to gather *data* about what is going on in the organisation and its environment. They then need to analyse those data to see what they tell them about the organisation's efficiency, or about customer behaviour. At that point the data have been turned into *information*. Further effort and experience are then required to see patterns in the information. At that stage, the information has become knowledge (see Real-Life Application 1.10).

The learning process thus requires the organisation to have sources, inside and outside the organisation, from which to gather the data, and the technology to process and distribute those data. Benetton's global network linking the Point of Sale tills in each store to the central computer in Italy is an example.

Equally important is that the organisational culture favours learning. People must be motivated to make the effort to gather data and convert them into information and knowledge. And if they are to make the effort, they need to be fairly confident that their colleagues will listen to what they have learnt, and want to share it.

REAL-LIFE APPLICATION 1.10

Data, information and knowledge

Suppose that I have in front of me last month's sales figures for my company in four areas (call them North, South, East and West). These are *data* – they tell me very little, apart from which has the largest and which the smallest sales.

If I then compare the figures with those from earlier months, I may discover that sales in the North are growing at 2% per month and those in the East at 1% per month, while those in the South are stagnant and those in the West are declining sharply. These growth patterns are *information*. I might combine that with other information that I already have about my most dangerous competitor, who is:

● not very active in the North or East;

● competing strongly on price in the West, where my manager has kept prices high;

● also competing strongly on price in the South, where my manager has reduced her prices to just 2% above competitors'.

Now that I see recurring patterns in the information, I have *knowledge*. I know that:

● our products are good enough to stand a 2% price premium, but not much more;

● other competitors are not dangerous to me.

I may also decide that I know that the sales manager in the South is more competent than the one in the West.

1.4.2 Path dependency and stickiness

We have painted a picture of learning as a combination of deliberate thought and haphazard invention. In either case, the results will depend on the specific information that an organisation has available at a given place and time, and on the individual people who look at it and reflect on it. This means that an organisation's routines will depend on the particular path that it has taken through the learning process.

Even though people move from company to company, and take their learning with them, the routines that they set up will never be *quite* the same as those in the organisation they left behind. Different organisations, even within the same industry, have a very different 'feel' to them. This is true even in industries like medicine and accountancy, where important elements of operating procedures are specified at a national level.

This phenomenon is called *'path dependency'*. It is important because it offers a basis for understanding how one organisation can be more successful than another, even when both seem to be pursuing very similar strategies.

Another aspect of routines is that they are *sticky* – they change slowly once they are established, and can sometimes persist even after their original purpose has disappeared (see Real-Life Application 1.11).

REAL-LIFE APPLICATION 1.11

Sticky routines

In the aftermath of the RAM shortage (see Real-Life Application 1.7), many UK organisations, including the university where both authors of this book were working, implemented tighter security procedures to counter thefts of computer memory.

RAM prices have now fallen back below their level before the shortage, and the spate of thefts has diminished. However, the security procedures remain in place.

1.5 Organisations as bundles of resources

Our final way of looking at the organisation is as a set of *resources* that are accumulated over time. Knowledge and routines are also examples of resources. We look now at the different classes of resource: physical, financial, human, intellectual and reputational.

1.5.1 Types of resource

Physical resources

Most organisations acquire physical locations, such as offices, laboratories and factories, together with the furniture, computers and other equipment that go inside them. Many of these resources will simply be the usual things that organisations need to stay in business. More interesting to the strategist are the unusual ones, such as specialised equipment or important locations for retail stores, which can give an organisation the edge over its competitors. British Airways' slots at Heathrow Airport, which give it the right to take off or land at popular times of the day, can be considered as examples of this kind of resource. Of course, a take-off slot is not 'physical', like a building, but, for strategic purposes, a slice of time (the ownership of a time-slot at an airport) can be considered in the same way as a slice of space (the ownership of a piece of land).

Financial resources

One of the rewards of success can be strong cash flow and cash reserves. These give organisations the ability to survive temporary setbacks, such as downturns in demand or strategic mistakes. They also give it the ability to purchase other types of resource if needed.

Human resources

It is a cliché, echoed in many company reports, that an organisation's most important resource is its people. Like most clichés, it contains an element of truth. Machines cannot work without people to design, operate and maintain them. Learning cannot take place unless the people have the intelligence and the skills to use the information. No organisational culture can take hold unless the people are susceptible to the type of motivation that the organisation favours.

Intellectual resources

Knowledge is the source of most intellectual resources. It can be manifested as patents, research programmes and various types of intellectual property. It can also show up more subtly within *capabilities and competences* – things that an organisation knows how to do, which make a difference to its ability to do business. For example, Sony has the capability consistently to produce innovative electronics products.

Many contemporary theorists believe that intellectual resources are the most important source of enduring competitive advantage. British Airways flies the same aircraft as many of its competitors, but the one thing that has historically distinguished it from most of them is its capability to deliver good, consistent in-flight service.

Reputation

As a result of their capabilities, organisations may build a good reputation. This may be a brand built deliberately, using market campaigns such as Benetton's 'United Colours'. Or it may arise from word-of-mouth as a result of good products or excellent service.

Reputation can be important in giving organisations access to sources of finance or to good staff. In a competitive industry, it can be useful to have a reputation as the kind of company that will fight back if provoked.

1.5.2 The durability of resources

Not all resources retain their value over time. Some, like reputation, can be quite durable. Benetton's reputation has endured for over thirty years, though its clothes are arguably less fashionable than they were in the 1980s, and it courted controversy in the 1990s with advertising showing a dying AIDS victim. Although IBM has made some costly mistakes in the computer market, its reputation as a supplier of quality hardware is still unsurpassed.

However, some assets lose value as the environment changes. Benetton's capability in meeting demand flexibly has been imitated by competitors like The Gap, a US chain. British Airways' dominance of Heathrow is under attack from UK competitors such as Virgin and from US competitors who want access to the airport and have powerful supporters in the US government. Competitors are also striving to match its capabilities in in-flight service.

Therefore, a great deal of emphasis is placed upon innovation as a means of anticipating environmental change and ensuring that resources can be adapted.

1.6 How the different views of the organisation fit together

The four views of the organisation – as a collection of people, an economic actor, an accumulation of knowledge and learning, and a bundle of resources – are not alternatives, but complementary. If you want fully to understand an organisation's strategy, and why it succeeds or fails, you need to combine all four aspects, and understand how they interact.

In order for an organisation to be operationally viable at any point in time, it must be a viable economic actor, otherwise its controlling stakeholders will close it down or sell it off. In order to do this, it needs to deploy its resources within its value chain so as to generate value for its users. In this way, it will generate financial resources and a good reputation.

For that same organisation to *continue* to be viable as the environment *changes* over time, it must adapt and innovate. This implies that it must learn effectively, so that it can build new capabilities and adjust its value chain to the changing requirements of its users. Information must be brought into the organisation, processed, absorbed and distributed as knowledge.

Underlying all of this is the way the organisation operates as a social system. If this social system fails, then the organisation will frighten away its customers and its staff, or spend too much time on internal conflict to fulfil its original purpose. If it works well, then the people who encounter the organisation will enjoy the experience and the organisation is likely to prosper.

If people are motivated to further the aims of the organisation, then they are more likely to make the effort to ensure that products and services are delivered on time and at the desired level of quality. Less well-motivated people take fewer pains to achieve top-quality results, and leave urgent jobs unfinished at the end of the working day.

The way the organisation functions as a social system will also affect how well it learns. People who like and believe in their organisation are more likely to make the effort to ensure that information is accurate and reaches the person who can use it most effectively. In a poorly functioning social system, information is used as a political weapon by one department against another.

The final interaction relates to an organisation's ability to change. Most researchers seem to agree that most organisations find it difficult to embrace change. Political manoeuvring to preserve the interests of powerful stakeholders can slow down change processes. Sometimes, it can require the threat of bankruptcy or takeover to overcome these factors. Organisations that are effective learning systems suffer less from this than others, because they become accustomed to a constant rhythm of gradual adaptation.

The need for the effective absorption and use of information by an organisation, to enable it to compete effectively and to learn, highlights the importance of its architecture.

1.7   Strategy: a definition and basic concepts

An organisation, as we have seen, is a social system with an economic purpose. The ways in which it uses its knowledge and other resources to achieve that economic purpose are called *strategies*.

Concept	**Strategy**
This is just one of many different ways of looking at strategy. Some of the alternatives are examined in Chapter 16. ▶	A strategy is the set of actions through which an organisation, by accident or design, develops resources and uses them to deliver services or products in a way which its users find valuable, while meeting the financial and other objectives and constraints imposed by key stakeholders. Most successful strategies give an organisation: ● some property that is unique, or at least rare; ● the means for renewing its competitive advantage as the environment changes.

1.8   Strategic decisions

Not all decisions made within an organisation contribute equally to its strategy. A *strategic decision* can be distinguished from other types of decision in three ways:

● **Magnitude**   Strategic decisions are big decisions. They affect an entire organisation or a large part of it, such as a whole division or a major function. And they entail a **significant degree of interaction** with the world around it – the organisation's suppliers or customers, for example.

● **Time-scale**   Strategic decisions have their impact over the medium- to long-term. They will naturally have a short-term impact as well – the medium term may finish in several years' time, but it starts at the end of this sentence! Different organisations will, of course, have different conceptions about what constitutes medium or long term. In a fast-moving industry, such as computer software or consumer goods, eighteen months may be a long time to think ahead. In capital goods industries like electricity generation or oil production, where new facilities take several years to plan and bring on stream, 10–15 years may be a realistic time horizon. It is helpful to measure timescales in terms of product life-cycles, with the short term being one product life-cycle and the medium term two. For most industries, this gives a time horizon for the strategist of around 3–5 years.

We discuss the important concept of commitment in more detail in Section 3.4.1. ▶

- **Commitment**   Strategic decisions involve making choices, and committing resources in ways that cannot be reversed cheaply or easily. This may mean investing large amounts of money in buildings or high-profile, long-term, marketing campaigns, or large amounts of management time in changing the way an organisation operates.

It is not always simple to tell what is and what is not a strategic decision. When a confectionery company, such as Nestlé, launches a new chocolate bar, that is not necessarily a strategic decision. Companies like this launch new products all the time, and expect most of them to fail. The investment in advertising and new manufacturing skills may be tens of thousands of euros, but this is still affordable for a firm like Nestlé. The failure of that one product is unlikely to seriously affect its profits or future viability. This is a short-term decision requiring little commitment.

However, for a small confectionery company with only one established product, launching a second brand *would* be a strategic decision. In absolute terms, the smaller firm might spend less on a product launch than Nestlé would. However, measured in relation to the size of the firm, the degree of impact of commitment is far higher. Similarly, when an aircraft manufacturer such as Airbus or Boeing decides to launch a new product, that is a strategic decision. The investment needed in design, new manufacturing facilities and marketing will be millions of euros or dollars. The product will be expected to make returns over ten years or more – the Boeing 747 has been in service for over thirty years.

If the product in the last two cases fails in the market place, it will hit the organisations' reputations. Customers, banks and shareholders may start to have doubts about the future of those companies, which will affect the sales of their other products, and also their ability to raise funds. So, these are examples of long-term, high-commitment decisions – what Americans call 'betting the company'.

1.9   Deliberate and emergent strategies

In our definition of strategy, we refer to actions coming about 'by accident or design'. This may seem a little strange – and is, as we shall see, rather controversial. Surely a strategy is something thought out by a chief executive and their top

Concept

Deliberate and emergent strategy

A **deliberate** strategy is one that is conceived by senior managers as a planned response to the challenges confronting an organisation. Often (though not always) it will be the result of a systematic analysis of the organisation's environment and of its resources, and attempt to 'fit' them together.

An **emergent** strategy is one that 'emerges' from lower down the organisation without direct senior management intervention.

management team, and passed down the organisation for carefully planned implementation. One can think of these strategies as being *deliberate* or *intentional*.

The earliest thinkers on strategy took it for granted that strategy was deliberate, the prerogative of the chief executive. He (and it was always he) would make a decision, which was evaluated against alternatives in a rational manner, and its outcomes assessed down to the last little detail. Many influential theorists still believe that strategy is, or ought to be, like this. And yet, you or I might have an idea that would benefit the organisation as a whole over the long term – which is one of the classic attributes of strategy. Such thinking is not simply the preserve of the chief executive.

In fact there is quite a lot of research evidence to say that it is not just the chief executive who shapes strategy. Many senior managers spend very little (less than 10%) of their time conceiving strategy – most of it is devoted to other high-profile tasks, like communicating inside and outside the organisation and solving operational problems (Mintzberg, 1975). On the other hand, managers at other levels can have a substantial role in forming strategy. Lower-level, operational managers feed detailed technological and market knowledge into the strategy process. Middle managers act as a kind of glue that holds the process together. They translate top management's intentions into language that operational staff can understand and act upon. They influence top managers' strategic thinking by making them aware of issues that operational staff think are important, and sometimes using their influence to promote proposals made by junior employees.[9]

Other researchers (e.g. Quinn, 1989) have found that in many organisations the strategies that were implemented were not those that had been developed through

THEORETICAL PERSPECTIVE 1.1

Deliberate, emergent, intended and enforced strategies

Henry Mintzberg and James Waters (1985) wrote one of the earliest papers in the strategy field to suggest that strategies happen at all levels in an organisation, and also that not all the strategies which an 'organisation' wants to happen will actually come to fruition. Individuals make strategy: people have ideas, make sense of the world about them, make decisions about where they think an organisation should go, and take whatever actions they think necessary to get their ideas implemented.

Mintzberg and Waters said that some strategies were decided on in advance by the leadership of the organisation – *intended* strategies. Some were put into operation – *deliberate* strategies. However, they also pointed out that not all intended or deliberate strategies actually happened. Products may not sell because of changing customer tastes; economies may go into recession; and political environments can change suddenly. These strategies then became *unrealised*.

They also said that strategies can come about at all levels in an organisation, in an *emergent* fashion, perhaps to be adopted in a mainstream way when they are shown to work on a smaller scale. Finally, they identified strategies that are *imposed* on an organisation – in other words, about which the members of an organisation have no choice. Many public sector organisations' strategies, for example, are subject to the control of government agencies that dictate what they do and when they do it. However, commercial organisations can also be forced to do things – at least if they wish to stay in business. Legislation on greenhouse gas emissions has forced some companies to restructure their manufacturing processes. Even competitors can sometimes effectively impose strategies. There have been many examples of price wars where companies have had to respond to the short-term price cutting tactics of a competitor, or lose market share to such an extent that they are severely weakened when prices are increased again.

The imposed strategies, *plus* some emergent strategies, *plus* those (few) intended strategies that are, in the end, deliberately adopted, together constitute the realised strategies – i.e. what the organisation as a whole does (Figure 1.2).

Figure 1.2   Deliberate, emergent and realised strategy processes (adapted from Mintzberg and Waters, 1985)

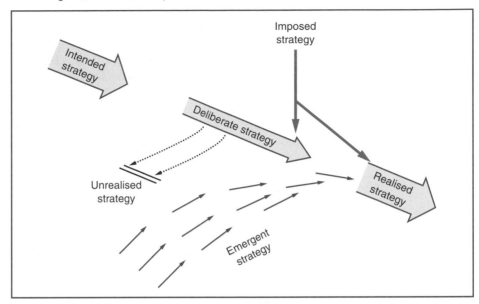

painstaking planning processes. They were *emergent* strategies, routines that people had developed themselves as a response to operational problems and opportunities.

This may be the result of employees sharing ideas and practices among themselves. For example, an enterprising salesperson may discover that a product that is intended to be sold to schools is also attractive to banks or hospitals, and pass this on to some of their colleagues. As a result, the firm ends up entering the financial services or medical markets. Emergent strategies may also come about as the result of control or rewards systems. For example, if middle managers are given profit targets and start to cut corners on quality, then the emergent strategy might be to take the company down market. In this book, we treat both deliberate and emergent decisions as being strategies, provided that they meet the three criteria of size, timescale and commitment.

Can the organisation shape its environment?

A particular type of intended strategy is one where the organisation deliberately sets out to transform its environment. All organisations, in interacting with their environment, will change it to some degree. However, when Henry Ford perfected the production line, Apple launched the Apple II personal computer, and Mosaic (later absorbed into Netscape) gave the world the first functioning Internet browser, they achieved something more. They laid the foundation for a wide-ranging transformation of their industries, and of the lives of the people that bought those industries' outputs. In other spheres, organisations like Greenpeace have managed, from small beginnings, to change the attitudes of people and governments to issues such as pollution, wildlife conservation and the relationships between developed and developing nations.

These examples show that organisations can play a role in changing their environment. There is still, however, a debate among strategy theorists as to whether organisations can realistically expect to set out to *transform* their environment. Two influential writers, Gary Hamel and C.K. Prahalad (1989, 1993, 1994), believe that organisations are capable of 'inventing their own future'. They give examples of organisations which, in their view, have succeeded by developing a 'strategic intent' that involved making a major impact in an industry where they were only a minor force. These firms, according to Hamel and Prahalad, set themselves seemingly impossible 'stretch' goals and then, through an effort of corporate will, achieved them, in the teeth of competition from strong established players. One example they used, and which has since been widely cited by other writers, was Komatsu, a minor Japanese manufacturer of earthmoving equipment, whose objective was 'Maru-C2 – encircle Caterpillar'. Caterpillar was the industry leader with a strong reputation for product quality, but Komatsu grew quickly, aided by aggressive price-cutting, to be number two in the industry, and forced Caterpillar to incur heavy losses fighting them off.

Other scholars, such as John Kay (1993), believe that wishes are not enough – that organisations can achieve them only if the wishes are realistic in the light of environmental conditions. (Komatsu, in the end, could not sustain its aggressive posture. It allowed its prices to drift upwards and its market share to fall, and abandoned the Maru-C objective.)

For details of population ecology, see Advanced Topic 5.3.2. ▶

'Population ecology' theorists take a more extreme view – that organisations are largely at the mercy of forces beyond their control. Whether or not a firm remains in business, according to this view, depends on whether the resources it has picked up in its lifetime happen to be those that are needed to survive in that industry at that time.

1.10 Corporate, business and functional strategies

As organisations grow and sometimes diversify, the levels at which strategic decisions are taken can multiply. When the first airlines started operating in the early days of flying, many would have had a single plane, with a single person who might have been responsible for advertising the firm's services, piloting the aeroplane and possibly servicing it as well. However, as the number of destinations and passengers multiplied, and the technology became more complicated, the need arose for the different specialised *functions* that can be seen in most modern airlines: ticketing, reservations and marketing staff to sell the services, specialist planners to schedule them, aircrew to fly the aircraft, engineers to maintain them, cabin crew and ground crew to serve the passengers, purchasing staff to obtain the food needed in-flight, finance staff to keep control of costs and make sure everything is sold at a profit, human resources specialists to make sure that staff are recruited with the right qualifications and given appropriate training, IT specialists to run the computing services, etc.

Business-level strategy

A modern airline such as British Airways has all these functions, and more. The crucial task of its managers is to knit these disparate groups of specialists together into a coherent value chain that delivers an all-round service to its customers. The planes must be ready to fly at the scheduled time, with motivated, helpful and well-trained staff on board, serving palatable food in planes which are as full as possible of fare-paying passengers. A failure by any one function, however remote from the user, can lead to poor service and customer dissatisfaction, as anyone can testify who has had to wait at an airport check-in when the computer was down.

This linking of different activities together to add value to users is the essence of *business-level strategy*. Business-level strategies relate to:

- choosing which users an organisation should serve and which services it should offer them;
- utilising the organisation's resources within a value chain that delivers those services effectively and reasonably efficiently;
- developing an architecture that enables information to flow into, out of and around the organisation, to allow the value chain to function effectively and the organisation to learn and adapt.

Contemporary theory places a lot of emphasis on business-level strategies, since they determine how well an organisation competes in its chosen markets (they are sometimes referred to as *competitive strategies*). We cover them in some detail throughout the book, particularly in Chapters 5, 6 and 7.

Apart from business-level strategies, it is common to refer to two other levels of strategy (Figure 1.3).

Functional strategies

We review some elements of functional strategy when we look at individual value chain activities, in Appendix 8.1 to Chapter 8. ▶

Each of an organisation's individual functions will have its own *functional strategy*. For example, BA might have a marketing strategy to increase customer recognition of its Club Europe brand with specific targets to be achieved over the next two years, or to increase direct mail activity to certain market segments. A maintenance

Figure 1.3   Levels of strategy

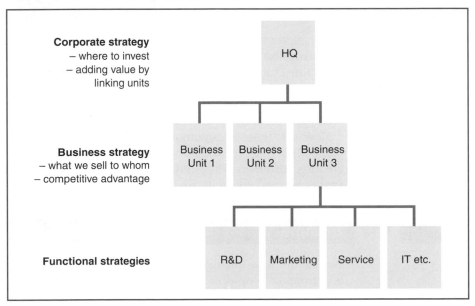

strategy might be to reduce the frequency of unplanned aircraft breakdowns, again with specific targets to be achieved in a given time period. Because functional strategies are not of particularly great magnitude, and are likely to be short-term, we do not discuss them in great detail in this book.

As we shall see in Section 3.1.4, many organisations diversify their activities as they grow. British Airways runs charter flights, which are aimed at a different group of customers (families on holiday) than the scheduled airline, whose core market is the business traveller. The charter flights offer lower levels of comfort and food than would be acceptable to a business class passenger, and aim for higher load factors. The differences in target market and operations are large enough to make the charter airline a different 'business' from the scheduled airline. Other airlines own hotels, or have in-flight catering services that they sell to their competitors. They gather a *portfolio* of more or less related businesses.

Corporate-level strategies

We discuss corporate strategy in more detail in Chapter 9. ▶

An organisation with a diversified portfolio of business is referred to as a corporation, and it has an additional level of strategies that do not relate directly to serving users in individual markets. These *corporate-level strategies*, the uppermost level in Figure 1.3, relate mainly to establishing appropriate structures and control systems, looking at which businesses to enter and exit and managing relationships between them. Each of the businesses may be a significant concern in its own right, pursuing its own business-level strategies. However, resources may be shared across a number of businesses, and there may be common elements in the different businesses' architectures as a result of their common ownership.

However, not all organisations diversify to the extent where they have or need corporate-level strategies. Some very large firms, such as McDonald's, are essentially single businesses.

1.11 Strategies in the public sector

We look at public sector strategies again in Chapter 12. ▶

Public sector managers confront different issues from those in commercial organisations. Most public sector organisations do not have to face the problems of attracting customers, building sales and market share, or of developing new products. Many are in a monopolistic position, with a stable and defined user base, and no competition (although there are arguments that this is changing, and the public sector is becoming more like business).

However, these organisations do face a tricky problem in responding to the demands of a variety of stakeholders. It can be very difficult to define precisely who are their customers. They must respond to the political and democratic procedures that define and constrain what they do.

1.12 Summary

You should have emerged from this chapter with a picture of the organisation. It is a group of people, each of them in differing degrees creative, enthusiastic and ambitious, but sometimes also ignorant, unpredictable and selfish. They are probably prepared to learn and can be persuaded to work towards the organisation's aims. Their ability to take stupid or selfish decisions is constrained by economic necessity – if they get too far out of line with what their users want, for too long, their employing organisation will be shut down or taken over. Equally, economic success can reward organisations and the people inside them for finding ways of serving those users better than their competitors.

The people in this group are feeling their way forward in a complex and uncertain world, sometimes by small steps, sometimes through bold leaps. They gather information to reduce the uncertainty. If they are successful, they can build a body of knowledge about which actions tend to work well in certain circumstances, and which do not. They can also accumulate other resources, such as machinery, cash and a good reputation. These resources can help the organisation prosper for as long as they are valuable.

Changes in the environment can destroy the value of these assets, so organisations need to be able to detect changes and adapt to them – or, better still, to predict or even trigger change. However, many organisations become used to a set of routines and find it difficult to change, or even to recognise the need to do so. Organisations are shaped by their past, and can find it difficult to recognise that things are different in the present and to adapt to the future.

Strategic management is the art (it will probably never be a science) of helping people in organisations to make sense of this complexity and unpredictability and to move forward in a sensible fashion. We shall never prevent you, or the organisations you will eventually work for, from making mistakes. If we tried, we would risk eliminating experimentation and creativity, and that would be a worse mistake than any you could make if left to your own devices. But we do believe that, by using appropriate models and analytical frameworks, and by learning from the success and failure of other organisations, it is possible for you to make better decisions more consistently. In other words, we believe that, even if many strategic decisions are emergent, they will be improved if the people involved can apply deliberate analysis to them. That is why we have written this book, and that is what the rest of this book is about.

Questions for discussion

1. What can organisations do to limit the extent to which managers' rationality is bounded? What would be the possible drawbacks of putting these ideas into practice?

2. Which of the following would count as strategic decisions for a small firm? And for a large one?

- Entering the market in Greece.
- Moving to an expensive office building close to where major customers are located.
- Launching a major advertising campaign for its most important product.
- Changing the supplier of an important component that has a major impact on the quality of the finished product.
- Buying 5% of the shares of the new supplier.

3. In an ideal world, would all strategies be deliberate?

CASE STUDY

Ferrero SpA

Sources: Crosetti, Maurizio, 'Ciocollato e Cultura', *La Repubblica*, 14 October 1996, p. 14; Serrao, Teresa, 'Nutella story – Un pezzo d'Italia', *La Repubblica*, 6 November 1999.

There can be few of us who have not, in our past, absorbed a little piece of Ferrero. Based in Alba, a town of fewer than 30,000 inhabitants in the Piedmont region of Italy's north-west, Ferrero has subsidiaries and strategic partners as far afield as Australia and Argentina. In 1996 it was the world's fourth-largest confectionery group after Switzerland's Nestlé and the US corporations Mars and Philip Morris, with 14,000 employees and a turnover from the Italian operations alone of 2,850 billion Italian lire (roughly £1 billion at 1996 exchange rates).

The company, which celebrated its fiftieth anniversary in 1996, had its origins in a shortage of cocoa in an Italy recovering from the devastation of the Second World War. An Italian cake-maker, Pietro Ferrero, developed a chocolate substitute, a soft paste made from hazelnuts and vegetable oil. His brother Giovanni would load aluminium-wrapped slabs of this 'Pasta Gianduja' into the back of his car and hawk them up and down the Langa (the area around Alba).

Although its taste was less than distinguished, this first product sold tolerably well in post-war Italy. However, Ferrero's major breakthrough came about through two strokes of inspiration on the part of Pietro's son, Michele, who in the 1960s was responsible for the firm's marketing. Firstly, he reformulated the product to be softer and to include milk solids and a little cocoa, by then available again in Italy. Secondly, he developed a new name for it, combining the English word 'nut' and the Italian suffix 'ella'. Nutella, which first saw the light of day in 1964, had tripled its Italian sales by 1967 and then spread through Europe and the USA. The product, whose precise formula remains a closely guarded trade secret, has played a starring role in Italian films and has been rhapsodised by the *New Yorker*, an American literary magazine. English fans have incorporated the product into a body paint designed for the enhancement of erotic pleasures. Today, there are Nutella fanclub websites in Italian, English and German, featuring impassioned cries for help from unfortunate fans stranded in those parts of the world where not one of the 19 million jars produced each month is available for sale.

Nutella is far from being Ferrero's only successful product. The Italian company has given the world Kinder Surprise (inexpensive hollow chocolate eggs with a small toy in the middle), Mon Cheri (chocolates containing a cherry and cherry liqueur), Tic-Tac (tiny fruit- or mint-flavoured sweets dispensed from a coloured plastic box) and Ferrero Rocher. This last product, which features layers of chocolate, wafer and praline around a hazelnut centre, took ten years to develop and is produced on unique, purpose-built machinery.

The firm backs this R&D effort with marketing designed to emphasise their products' uniqueness. Often it tries to give their sweets an upmarket image – it was to this end that 'Mon Cheri' acquired its French name. Ferrero spends 500 billion lire (about £200 million) on advertising each year. The most famous example is the advertising campaign for Ferrero Rocher, which positioned it as the preferred sweet of diplomats and high society. Although widely ridiculed in the UK, it coincided with a substantial increase in sales.

Nowadays it is Michele who is in charge of the company that his father and uncle founded. A private man who does not allow himself to be interviewed or photographed, his home is in Brussels but his influence is everywhere in the company. When he attends meetings at headquarters, managers queue for his attention. He is said to frequent Alba's supermarkets, observing the reactions of children shopping for Kinder Surprises. And every Wednesday morning at 8.30 a.m., he seats himself in the middle of a horseshoe-shaped table to preside over an extraordinary ceremony. 'Taste, please', he murmurs to the employees gathered around the table – and they do. An average of eighty different mouthfuls of Ferrero's and its competitors' products are tasted, compared and then spat out. A purpose-built system of little trucks runs under the table to carry the debris discreetly away.

Alongside its own traditions, Ferrero integrates those of the Langa, retaining a profound feel for the local people and culture. Even in management meetings, Michele converses exclusively in the local dialect. The firm runs buses into the surrounding region each day to pick up and drop off employees at their homes in the countryside. People are able to combine a job at Ferrero with work on their family farms – important, in an area where the agricultural tradition runs deep, and which is renowned for wine and truffles as much as for chocolate. Ferrero has also set up a community centre offering a cinema, theatre, games rooms, sports pitches and free medicine for the retired.

Labour unrest and strikes are almost non-existent at Ferrero, and when Alba was affected by flooding in 1994, 1,000 employees laboured as volunteers to help put right the damage. They were aided by the prompt provision of assistance by the Italian government.

Case study questions

1. Who are the main stakeholders in Ferrero? What are their objectives, and how does the firm strive to meet them?

2. What factors have shaped Ferrero's culture? How does it show through in the way that the firm competes?

3. What distinctive routines has the firm developed?

4. What distinctive resources has the firm developed?

5. What disadvantages is Ferrero likely to risk if it continues with its present style of operations?

NOTES

1. Schein (1983).
2. Pfeffer (1992).
3. Writers who have identified links between particular strategic preferences and the background or experience of the organisation's key decision-makers include Hambrick and Mason (1984), Wiersema and Bantel (1992, 1993), Guthrie and Olian (1991); Guthrie et al. (1991); Gupta (1984, 1986); Child (1974); Smith et al. (1994); Miles and Snow (1978); Chaganti and Sambharya (1987); and Hellgren and Melin (1993).
4. For further reading on emotions in organisations see Fineman (1993); Goleman (1996); Ashforth (1994); Ashforth and Lee (1990); Weick (1993, 1995). There is also a recent edition of the *European Journal of Work and Organizational Psychology*, 8 (3; September), 1999, devoted entirely to this issue.
5. See, for example, Harris and Ogbonna (1999).
6. The concept of architecture we use here is developed from that used by Kay (1993).
7. Some writers use the term 'external environment' to distinguish what goes on outside the organisation, from the 'internal environment' inside it. In this book, environment is used exclusively to refer to what is *outside* the organisation.
8. Kay (1993) contains a readable account of game theory. For a more detailed account of the implications for strategic management see Camerer (1991) and Saloner (1991).
9. The role of operational managers is set out in Chakvravarthy and Lorange (1991). There is a whole raft of research relating to middle management's role in strategy formulation. American researchers Steven Floyd and Bill Wooldridge have specialised in this area and their 1994 article in the *Academy of Management Review*, 8 (4), pp. 47–57, gives a readable summary of their work. The role of middle management is also featured strongly in the writings of Burgelman (1994), Nonaka and Takeuchi (1995) and Ghoshal and Bartlett (1998).

Organisational purpose

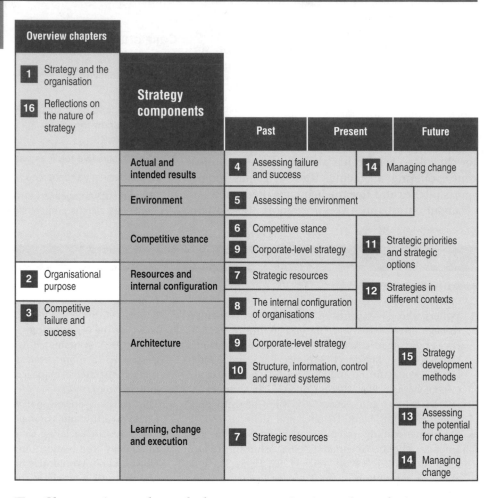

In Chapter 1 we showed that an organisation, through its strategy, attempts to meet 'the financial and other objectives and constraints imposed by key stakeholders'. In this chapter we review a number of ideas, stemming from different conceptions of capitalism, about who the 'key stakeholders' are, or ought to be. We consider the different types of 'financial and other objectives' that these stakeholders may impose, and look at the arguments about the appropriate balance between economic and non-economic considerations in defining an organisation's purpose. Lastly, we look at the mechanisms that have been tried, or advocated, for ensuring that an organisation's managers achieve its stakeholders' objectives rather than – or as well as – their own.

By the end of this chapter you should understand:

● different conceptions of capitalism, including the shareholder value and stakeholder views;

● the strengths and drawbacks of economic profit maximisation as a motivating force;

● the main non-economic factors that influence an organisation's purpose – mission, leadership and ethical considerations;

● the systems of corporate governance which key internal and external stakeholders can use to try and ensure that an organisation's managers comply with their view of the organisation's purpose.

2.1 For whose benefit does the firm exist?

In Anglo-Saxon cultures, great importance is attached to the idea that the shareholders are the owners of the company, so that their interests take precedence over those of other stakeholders. The notion of *shareholder value* currently in vogue among financial theorists is an explicit version of this theory.

Concept | Shareholder value

The theory of shareholder value states that organisations belong to their shareholders, whose interests take priority over those of any other stakeholders, and that it is the duty of the managers to maximise the economic value of the firm. The measure of whether they are performing this duty is the firm's stock market value, which is held to express the net present value of the firm's resources and all profits likely to flow from them.

This gives great influence to the pension funds and insurance companies, who own the vast majority of all traded equities in those economies, and to the fund managers who select the shares for them. Companies like McDonald's and British Airways that are quoted on the UK and US stock markets often invest considerable time and effort in keeping these stakeholders informed and happy.

In most other European countries, such as France and Germany, and also in Japan, the supremacy of the equity shareholder is regarded as less obvious.[1] Long-term bank lending plays a greater role in the firm's capital than is usual in the UK or the USA, and the bank is an influential stakeholder with board representation. France, Germany and Japan were devastated by the war, and their people needed to marshal a huge effort to rebuild their economies. All three countries came to adopt what has been called **stakeholder capitalism**, where firms assumed partial responsibility for the welfare of their workers and local communities.

In countries such as France or Germany, the culture and the legal system give more weight to the interests of employees and communities than to those of shareholders. Workers' representatives are entitled to participate in key decisions, and local and national governments often have considerable influence on decisions like plant openings and closures.

Shareholders in these countries seemed content to live with lower returns on their investment than they might have obtained in, say, the United States. Firms instead spent money on salaries for employees they did not always need, and on government taxes that funded a comprehensive social welfare system. This gave individual some kind of guarantee of personal security – they would not usually lose their jobs, and if they did, they would still not live in poverty. This guarantee helped motivate them for the task of economic reconstruction. Over the four decades following the Second World War, all three economies grew much faster than the UK or the USA, and gave rise to innovative and highly competitive companies such as Toyota, Sony, Daimler and Alcatel. Proponents of this model of capitalism point also to the lower crime rates and higher degree of social cohesion in these countries.

More recently, however, economic growth in these countries has slowed and unemployment has risen sharply. This has led to some of their business leaders and politicians to question whether the firms' social obligations have become too burdensome, raising their costs and slowing their adjustment to change in the competitive environment. There is some evidence (see Section 2.2.1) that these countries are gradually moving towards the Anglo-Saxon shareholder value model.

2.2 Different drivers of organisational purpose

Let us now consider what it is that drives organisations forward, and what it might be that managers are trying to achieve when they create strategies. As we saw in Chapter 1, an important facet of any organisation is that it is an economic actor, and we first look at how economic and financial considerations might shape its purpose. However, Chapter 1 also pointed out that organisations are very much social systems, and we discuss below how social and cultural considerations can also shape its strategic direction.

2.2.1 Economic rationality and wealth creation

We look at Michael Porter's various and hugely influential writings in more detail in Chapters 5 and 6. ▶

Much strategy writing proceeds from the assumption that man is a rational economic actor: that we all do what we can to maximise our wealth and that organisations exist in order to fulfil their owners' wealth-creating objectives. For example, in Michael Porter's writings he assumes that firms aim to make 'super-normal' profits. Igor Ansoff, whom many people see as the father of strategic management theory, similarly assumes that the aim of the strategies he recommends (see Chapter 6) is to increase return on capital.

For true profit-maximising and wealth-maximising behaviour to be possible, managers need good information about their competitors' actions and intentions, about their own cost structures and about the likely reaction of consumers to changes in prices and product quality. They also need the time, technology and mental capacity to process that information, so as to determine the optimal action to take. We have already (Section 1.1.4) encountered an important body of theory that casts doubt on whether true rationality of that kind is possible in management decision-making.

In fact, some 'behavioural economists' have started to question whether people really display the kind of rationality that traditional economic models assume. They have studied taxi drivers in New York and found that they set themselves an income target for the day and stop work when they have reached it. This means that the drivers work longer on a day when few people are about than on a busy one, although 'rationally' they should work longer on the busiest days, when they get the highest return on the time invested. However, failing to make the target feels like a loss, and studies have found that people are 'loss averse'. They will go to far greater lengths to avoid losing €100 than they will to gain a similar sum, even if the probabilities of winning and losing are the same.[2]

The pursuit of wealth creation in practice

There are other grounds for doubting that managers are always economically rational, or even that they should be. Wealth creation may be at least one of the reasons why many companies (though not, of course, public sector organisations) exist in capitalistic societies. However, as we saw in Section 2.1, shareholder value and profit maximisation are not regarded as equally important in all cultures or in all firms in the same country. The concept of wealth being the be-all and end-all of life is likely to be anathema to an Indian Buddhist, for example. Even within capitalist cultures, there are many variations on the Anglo-Saxon model that gives wealth creation a supreme role. Charles Hampden-Turner and Fons Trompenaars (1993) have identified distinctly different variants of managerial priorities for the USA, the UK, Japan, Germany, France, Sweden and the Netherlands, and yet managers seem quite able to function under such varying systems. Organisations exist, and take strategic decisions (often very profitably), in all of these countries.

As we have discussed in Chapter 1, organisations do not all come into being for the purpose of creating wealth. Some may exist to provide social contact, or something to do for the proprietor. Even in publicly owned companies that *are* meant to maximise shareholder wealth, there is evidence that profit-maximising is actually a *rare* activity for managers. Managers may seek to fulfil their own objectives, whatever they may be, rather than maximise the wealth of the firm's shareholders.[3]

The effectiveness of profit-maximising strategies

Paradoxically, it is not always clear that profit-maximising strategies are the best way to maximise profits! There is a tension between short- and long-term profitability. In the USA, the tendency of company managers to focus on short-term financial objectives was widely blamed in the 1980s for eroding the country's innovativeness and long-term wealth. This was because maximising profits in the short-term mitigated against costly investments in innovation and development, which may be beneficial in the long term.[4]

A focus on profit maximisation can sometimes tempt managers into unethical behaviour that can alienate customers, suppliers and employees alike. Real-Life Application 2.1 gives an example of some of these dilemmas. We return to business ethics in Section 2.2.2.

REAL-LIFE APPLICATION 2.1

'Under fire'

Taken from an article by Kirstie Hamilton, Deputy City Editor, *The Sunday Times*, 19 November 1995.

Shell has caused outrage by pressing on with a £2.6 billion gas project in Nigeria, fuelling the debate on big-business ethics. For the second time this year, Shell has become the corporate bad guy in the minds of thousands of customers. Its decision to push ahead with a £2.6 billion investment in a Nigerian gas plant days after the Nigerian government executed Ken Saro-Wiwa, the writer and political activist, caused outrage. Coming close on the heels of Shell's climbdown over the disposal of the Brent Spar oil rig, the furore over Nigeria has raised public consciousness about Shell's activities to the highest level for years.

All this attention is deeply unwelcome to a company not comfortable in the limelight. Most outsiders had only the dimmest perception of how the firm worked, but most would have banked on Shell being a good corporate citizen.

According to many, that description is accurate. But environmental campaigners, politicians and the Ogoni Community Association, the group Saro-Wiwa founded, tell a different story. They maintain that Shell is responsible for the environmental damage inflicted on the Niger Delta over the past 40 years that Shell has been drilling for oil. It is the largest foreign oil company in the country. Much of Nigeria's drilling is on land. This makes the oil cheap and easy to produce, but brings environmental hazard. There are more than 3,000 miles of pipeline in the Niger Delta.

Shell produces nearly 1 million barrels of oil a day and owns 30% of what it drills. Analysts estimate that the after-tax return on each barrel is $2.50 (£1.60), adding £200 million to profits. That may sound a lot – and margins on oil production in developing countries are higher than elsewhere – but it accounts for only 4% of Shell's £4.5 billion of revenues last year.

But Nigeria's future is more important. Oil experts say that, unlike the North Sea, Nigeria has a long-term future.

The battle and the publicity generated have instilled fear in the hearts of other oil producers and other multinational companies. Customer and investors are increasingly demanding higher standards from the companies they deal with. And those that do not match up are being penalised. Sumantra Ghoshal, a London Business School professor, said: 'There is no longer a question that business is just business. It is much more than that. Big institutions have to recognise they are social as well as economic institutions.' Shell has acknowledged the need to consider more than just profits in a fightback campaign it launched on Friday.

So far, the City has remained unmoved by the fuss and Shell shares climbed 50½p to 787½p last week. But brokers report that many small investors were selling Shell, and some bigger investors, such as charities, are reconsidering their holdings. While it remains a smaller-investor issue, Shell can withstand the pressure. But if campaigners whip up a product boycott, as the Germans did over Brent Spar, big investors will start to get nervous.

So it is not clear what 'profit-maximising' behaviour actually means in practice. Managers face a trade-off between profits in the short term, which are relatively predictable, and profits in the long term, which are not. Ethical behaviour and investment in R&D both have very noticeable short-term costs, but the benefits will only be apparent after a few years, and may never arrive at all if things go wrong! The same is true of spending on marketing and equipment maintenance.

To complicate things still further, there is research evidence which questions the link between profit-maximising behaviour and competitive advantage. There have been examples in the steel castings and petrochemicals industries of unprofitable or inefficient firms that have survived, when more profitable and efficient firms have abandoned the industry.[5] What seems to happen is that the 'irrational' behaviour of the unprofitable firms drives down returns in the industry (for example, by keeping prices low). Profit-maximising managers then conclude that the only 'rational' thing to do is to quit the industry, and invest the firm's capital somewhere else.

The sustainability of non-profit-maximising policies

Does this mean that profit-maximising behaviour is a total myth? Non-profit-maximising policies can persist for quite a long time, particularly when they have support from governments and the community. Arguably, the history of the economic success of Japan, Germany and France in the second half of the twentieth century demonstrates this. Another non-profit-maximising behaviour that lasted several decades came from the banks in Japan and other Asian countries that, often under instruction from their governments, offered loans at low interest rates to selected firms. These loans enabled firms like Korea's Samsung to expand rapidly in a variety of industrial sectors, from heavy engineering through consumer goods to retailing.

Nevertheless, despite the long-standing success of stakeholder capitalism, there is a case for believing that 'economic fundamentals' such as the need to make profits eventually reassert themselves. In Germany, top managers in large firms are starting to protest against the high social costs imposed upon German enterprise. In Germany, France and Italy, firms have begun to engage in contested takeover bids to restructure their sectors, a practice previously frowned upon. In South Korea, the artificially low cost of loans is now believed to have led to firms making unproductive investments that have generated poor returns. South Korean firms now have problems in servicing their debts, and many of the country's banks have become technically insolvent. As part of the restructuring process, some of South Korea's major firms (the chaebol) are being forced to reverse some of their investment decisions (see Real-Life Application 2.2).

There are several possible explanations as to why companies in Europe and Asia appear to be adopting traditionally Western, and more specifically American, styles of capitalistic business. The change may be simply a temporary aberration caused by an economic downturn in some Western European countries and South-East Asia. It may be because employees, who benefited from employment guarantees when they were younger, are now reaching pensionable age and are keener that the firms in which their pension funds are invested should make large profits. It may be that these countries' social policies are not sustainable over the long term when there is more ruthless competition elsewhere, and that profit-maximising behav-

---

REAL-LIFE APPLICATION 2.2

Samsung and economic rationality

Samsung began life in 1938 as a manufacturer of noodles and agricultural machinery. In the 1960s, it was selected by the South Korean government as one of the firms that would lead the country's economic development. Korea's government directed low-cost loans to these firms, which became the chaebol, highly diversified groups that dominate the country's economy. Samsung diversified into insurance, credit cards, electronics, telecommunications, hotels, construction and shipbuilding. By 1994 it was the world's 14th-largest firm with sales of $64 billion.

In 1995, Samsung made the controversial decision to enter the automobile industry. This was an industry where there was already one Korean competitor (Hyundai) and which suffered from chronic global overcapacity.

When the banking crisis hit South Korea in 1998, the government forced Samsung to sell its automobile division to Hyundai. Perhaps this was a case of an irrational decision being reversed; but Samsung had already revolutionised the economics of the manufacture of microwave ovens, another established industry that it entered late. Who is to say that could not have done the same for automobiles?

iour and the consequent striving for economic efficiency is the best guarantee of everyone's social welfare – what Adam Smith, the pioneer of economic theory, called 'the hidden hand'.

2.2.2 Non-economic determinants of organisational purpose

If economic rationality is not the only factor that drives managers' strategic decisions, then what are the others? To answer this question, we need to recall that an organisation is a social entity, a group of people who interact and bond with others inside it and in the communities in which it operates. Most organisations tend to develop sets of **values** that drive their strategies. These frequently stem from, and are sustained by, the organisation's **leadership**. At the same time, most are influenced by **ethical** ties to the wider community.

Mission
An organisation's *mission* is the set of goals and purposes that its members and other major stakeholders agree that it exists to achieve.

Vision
An organisation's *vision* is a description of what its leaders aspire to achieve over the medium to long term, and of how it will feel to work in or do business with the organisation once the vision has taken effect.

Values
An organisation's *values* are the philosophical principles that the great majority of its members hold in common.

Mission, vision and values

Although the definitions of **mission**, **vision** and **values** given here will be recognisable to most managers, the three concepts overlap, and different authors use conflicting terminology. Americans James Collins and Jerry Porras, who are two of the most prolific writers in this area, use 'vision' as an overall term that encompasses mission and values. You may also encounter other terms, such as 'strategic intent' (for vision) and 'superordinate goals' (for values).

Mission, vision and values are manifestations of an organisation's distinctive identity, its 'personality', which is visible to employees and customers alike through what it does and says, and how it presents visual elements such as buildings, logos and advertisements. Images of this identity leak into the public domain through a number of channels:

- a firm's products, and their design and performance;
- Such visible things as brand images, staff uniforms or graphics;
- articles and industry reports prepared by journalists or stockbrokers;
- press statements issued by the company itself;
- formalised statements of mission and vision.

REAL-LIFE APPLICATION 2.3

Statements of mission and values

(1) LVMH (French luxury goods and fashion corporation)
Mission statement

The mission of the LVMH group is to represent around the world the most refined qualities of Western 'Art de Vivre'. LVMH must continue to be synonymous with both elegance and creativity. Our products, and the cultural values they embody, blend tradition and innovation, and kindle dream and fantasy.

In view of this mission, five priorities reflect the fundamental values shared by all Group stakeholders.

LVMH values
Be creative and innovate

- Group companies are determined to nurture and grow their creative resources. Their long-term success is rooted in a combination of artistic creativity and technological innovation: they have always been and always will be creators.

- Their ability to attract the best creative talents, to empower them to create leading-edge designs is the lifeblood of our Group.
- The same goes for technological innovation. The success of the companies' new products – particularly in cosmetics – rests squarely with research and development teams.
- This dual value – creativity/innovation – is a priority for all companies. It is the foundation of their continued success.

Aim for product excellence

Group companies pay the closest attention to every detail and ensure the utter perfection of their products. They symbolise the nobility and perfection of traditional craftsmanship. Each and every one of the objects their customers buy and use exemplifies our brands' tradition of impeccable quality. Never should Group companies disappoint, but rather continue to surprise their customers with the quality, endurance, and finish of their products. They never compromise when it comes to product quality.

Their search for excellence goes well beyond the simple quality of their products: it encompasses the layout and location of our stores, the display of the items they offer, their ability to make their customers feel welcome as soon as they enter our stores. All around them, their clients see nothing but quality.

Bolster the image of our brands with passionate determination

Group brands enjoy exceptional reputations. This would not amount to much, and could not be sustained, if it was not backed by the creative superiority and extreme quality of their products. However, without this aura, this extra dimension that somewhat defies logic, this force of expression that transcends reality, the sublime that is the stuff of our dreams, Dior would not be Dior, Louis Vuitton would not be Louis Vuitton, Moët would not be Moët. ... The power of the companies' brands is part of LVMH's heritage. It took years and even decades to build their image. They are an asset that is both priceless and irreplaceable.

Therefore, Group companies exercise stringent control over every minute detail of their brands' image. In each of the elements of their communications with the public (announcements, speeches, messages, etc.), it is the brand that speaks. Each message must do right by the brand. In this area as well, there is absolutely no room for compromise.

Act as entrepreneurs

The Group's organisational structure is decentralised, which fosters efficiency, productivity, and creativity.

This type of organisation is highly motivating and dynamic. It encourages individual initiative and offers real responsibilities – sometimes early on in one's career. It requires highly entrepreneurial executive teams in each company.

This entrepreneurial spirit requires a healthy dose of common sense from managers, as well as hard work, pragmatism, efficiency, and the ability to motivate people in the pursuit of ambitious goals. One needs to share and enjoy this entrepreneurial spirit to – one day – manage a subsidiary or company of the LVMH group.

Strive to be the best in all we do

Last but not least is our ambition to be the best. In each company, executive teams strive to constantly improve, never be complacent, always try to broaden our skills, improve the quality of our work, and come up with new ideas.

The Group encourages this spirit, this thirst for progress, among all of its associates.

Source: LVMH website http://www.LVMH.com/GROUP/12a0000a.htm

(2) General Electric (US diversified engineering and financial services conglomerate)

Statement of values

GE leaders, always with unyielding integrity:

- have a passion for excellence and hate bureaucracy
- are open to ideas from anywhere and committed to work-out
- live quality and drive cost and speed for competitive advantage
- have the self-confidence to involve everyone and behave in a boundaryless fashion
- create a clear, simple, reality-based vision and communicate it to all constituencies
- have enormous energy and the ability to energise others
- stretch, set aggressive goals and reward progress, yet understand accountability and commitment
- see change as opportunity, not threat
- have global brains and build diverse and global teams.

Source: General Electric's 1999 annual report: http://www.GE.com/ANNUAL99/INITIATIVES/INDEX.HTML

Some further examples of mission statements can be found in Chapter 8, where we discuss the importance of mission and vision to an organisation's competitiveness. ▶

If an organisation's mission, vision and values are clear and inspiring, as is clearly the intention in the statements reproduced in Real-Life Application 2.3, they will help drive the organisation forward by giving employees a shared objective to which all can aspire. It also gives them a clear reference point for their decisions, both short term and long term. This helps to avoid unnecessary costs that might arise if objectives were constantly being renegotiated or if its policies on products, service levels, customers and markets were continually being altered.

Many writers suggest that a strong sense of mission and corporate purpose is important for an organisation's success.[6] However, if a firm develops a very strong sense of purpose, it paradoxically may risk blinding itself to opportunities that are outside this remit.

Leadership

An organisation's personality, vision and values are frequently the legacy of a strong leader, past or present. Indeed, several contemporary theorists see the building of a clear and inspiring mission and vision as a key task of an organisation's senior management. However, the personal qualities and ambition of the organisation's leader may in themselves be a force that drives the organisation forward.

The qualities of an effective change agent are described in Chapter 14. ▶

Effective leaders may have a number of attributes. The most famous are those who have shown themselves to be effective agents of change by taking a stagnating or declining company and leading it to a significantly higher level of performance. Examples are managers like Jack Welch of the US corporation General Electric (nominated by *Fortune* magazine as the leading manager of the twentieth century), Percy Barnevik of ABB, a Swedish–Swiss engineering group or Lars Kolind of Oticon (see the case study at the end of Chapter 13).

Some change agents are charismatic individualists, who drive an organisation forward and inspire the people around them, through the sheer force of their personality. This characteristic is also often found in people, such as Walt Disney or Anita Roddick, the founder of cosmetics retailer Body Shop, who have built large firms from scratch.

Some researchers[7] believe, however, that leaders who rely too heavily upon charisma are not always effective in the long term. This is because few individuals, however talented and energetic, are able to handle all types of business problems alone. They require people around them who are able to support them, and who are prepared to tell them when things are going wrong. Charismatic leaders are not always willing to listen to bad news, or to let talented people flourish if they may one day turn into rivals.

A number of attributes have been cited for effective leaders.[8] These include:

- A deep understanding of the business. Sir Colin Marshall, who along with Lord King built British Airways into a major force, and Sam Walton, founder of Wal-Mart, the world's largest retailer, were both renowned for their attention to the detail of everyday operations.

- The ability to choose and motivate people. This includes coaching people so that they grow into their jobs.

- A measure of ruthlessness, or a preparedness to get rid of people when it is clear that they cannot perform.[9]

- The ability to listen, and to understand what is going on in the environment.

There is no one style of leadership that is appropriate for all circumstances. The **transformational leadership** skills required to lead a company through a period of major change may not be appropriate to when a company is in a settled environment. The need then may be for a **transactional leader** who can persuade people to work efficiently and run operations smoothly.[10] Some of the best leaders are those who, as Barnevik did at ABB, recognise in time that their skills are no longer the ones that are needed, and hand over to a more suitable successor.

THEORETICAL PERSPECTIVE 2.1

Leadership approaches

Farkas and Wetlaufer (1996), in a study of 160 chief executives, found that 'in effective companies, CEOs do not simply adopt the leadership style that suits their personalities but instead adopt the approach that will best meet the needs of the organization and the business situation at hand'. They identified five successful approaches to leadership:

- **The strategy approach** was used in firms like Dell Computer. Leaders with this style believe that their position at the top of the organisation makes them uniquely qualified to take strategic decisions. They spend their time gathering competitive, market and technological data to inform those decisions. This approach was used by fewer than 20% of CEOs.

- **The human-assets approach**, used by 22% of the sample, including the CEOs of Gillette and PepsiCo, starts from the notion that if the organisation has the right people, then it will develop an appropriate strategy. The leader spends a lot of time travelling around the organisation, becoming involved in recruitment and career planning for even quite junior staff.

- **The expertise approach** was the least common, used by less than 15% of the CEOs interviewed. It involved leaders devoting their time to championing the adoption of certain vital skills and knowledge within the organisation. At Motorola, the electronics firm, the CEO spent much of his time promoting the firm's exceptionally rigorous quality programme.

- **The box approach** was the most common among the firms researched by Farkas and Wetlaufer. It was employed by British Airways, and by France's AXA, the world's largest insurer. Leaders using this approach see their main task as building a 'box' of control systems that defines the norms that people in the organisation must conform to. These might be financial systems, corporate values, expected behaviours or even a common language to link different units across the world.

- **The change agent approach** was used by approximately 15% of the leaders in the sample. These people see it as their role to reshape their organisation from top to bottom, and to create 'a climate of continual reinvention', even if, in Farkas and Wetlaufer's words 'such an environment produces anxiety and confusion, leads to some strategic mistakes and temporarily hurts financial performance'. Such leaders travel widely through the organisation, holding meetings and giving motivational speeches.

Business ethics and corporate responsibility

The Anglo-Saxon model of shareholder capitalism, at its most extreme, can be summarised in the famous phrase of the Chicago monetarist economist Milton Friedman: 'the business of business is business' – that is, if business concentrates on making profits for its shareholders then everyone will benefit in the long run. This implies that firms should feel themselves under no obligation to behave any more ethically towards employees, suppliers or customers than the law demands.

Managers are certainly sometimes tempted into unethical behaviour. In 1999, there were revelations of dubious relationships between, for example, firms and government ministers or officials, which resulted in the resignations of the whole of the European Commission and several members of the International Olympic Committee. Some of the forces which make people behave unethically are to do with the pressures from external sources to produce constantly increasing returns as seen in the Shell example in Real-Life Application 2.1. Others are to do with the competitive nature of companies and the managers who rise to the top of them. Risk-taking is a well-known component of the entrepreneurial personality, and striving to win is necessary to get to the top in most walks of life.

However, those who go beyond normal bounds of ethical behaviour are relatively rare, and there is some evidence that ethical behaviour can help firms survive longer. Customers and consumers have, for their part suddenly found that they have considerable power to influence the decisions that organisations make. There has been a long-term decline in meat-eating, partly due to consumer abhorrence of factory farming methods and an increasing interest in organic produce. In 1999, a Europe-wide consumer revolt against genetically modified (GM) foodstuffs resulted in many retailers committing themselves to phase out food items containing GM ingredients. This in turn has led to a radical change of policy (and loss of profits) on the part of Monsanto, the market leader in GM technology – and, ironically, a firm that has in the past taken some pride in its ethical standards. Lending institutions and pension fundholders in their turn are reflecting consumers' ethical concerns in their lending and investment policies towards companies.

Consumers do not restrict themselves to issues that effect their own way of life. Sports goods maker Nike was badly hit in 1997 by a boycott of its products after reports that Vietnamese workers employed to manufacture them were exploited and exposed to toxic fumes. Other companies that place a lot of production work in developing countries, such as Disney and Mattel, the world's leading toy manufacturer, have taken the initiative in making sure that their own practices are above criticism. They have set up codes of conduct for their managers and subcontractors and have their plants inspected by independent auditors.[11]

There are increasing numbers of examples of firms that have discovered that they can be not only ethical, but successful businesses as a result. This can come about in a number of ways:

- Selling products, or pursuing policies, designed to appeal to the ethical sensitivities of a particular market segment. The Body Shop, a UK-based international retailer of beauty products made from natural ingredients, became successful partly as a result of tapping into consumers' concerns about animal testing. The Co-operative Bank in the UK has positioned itself entirely as the ethical bank, assuring customers that their bank deposits will never be lent onwards to firms that manufacture arms or pollute the environment.

- Treating employees well, so as to lure the best and keep them motivated. This pays off most obviously when labour markets are tight, as is presently the case in the USA. Firms there offer employees not only stock options, but child care, exercise facilities, take-home meals and even places to sleep when they are overcome by stress. This helps their employees to sustain a reasonable home life at the same time as a very demanding job (60+ hour weeks are common), and results in staff turnover rates well below the industry average. However, this behaviour can also pay off in developing countries. Mining companies Placer Dome and RTZ have helped the World Health Organisation to develop and fund a 'business plan for health' in Papua. One scheme helps to train local villagers to treat malaria and deliver babies. The payoff to the contributors comes partly in increased goodwill, and partly in having a happier, healthier and so more productive workforce.

● Contributing cash and seconding staff to charities and to the local community, as is the practice of firms such as The Body Shop, British Telecom and Marks and Spencer. De Beers, the diamond producer, contributed $2.7 million to a World Health Organisation programme to eliminate polio in Angola. It also insists on having its local employees contribute their marketing skills to raise awareness of the campaign. As well as improving a firm's reputation with its potential customers, this kind of giving can improve employees' image of themselves and of the firm, and help them to develop new skills.

● Pursuing environmentally friendly 'green' policies. BP Amoco, having spent $45 million to purchase Solarex, a solar energy firm, has started to fit solar panels to generate electricity at 200 of its filling stations. It has become the first major oil firm to support the aims, agreed in 1997 at the UN's Kyoto summit, to reduce emissions of greenhouse gases. A number of other firms have found that, by disciplining themselves to cut waste and pollution, they can discover radical ways to reduce costs and improve efficiency.[12]

THEORETICAL PERSPECTIVE 2.2

Business ethics – the theoretical debate

Scholars such as Milton Friedman (quoted above) and Theodore Levitt, a well-known marketing theorist, hold that businesses have no special social responsibility other than to operate within the law. These views tend to proceed from the idea that corporations are created by individuals rather than by society. The argument is that companies should have the same freedoms as individuals do to set their own moral standards and to use their property as they see fit.[13]

Those who disagree with this view tend to argue that businesses are so intertwined with the rest of society that they cannot act without considering its obligations to it. According to these arguments, businesses have obligations to stakeholders or constituents, on whom they depend for their survival and who are affected by their actions. Organisations' social power brings social responsibilities as well, and if they want to focus upon shareholders to the exclusion of all other stakeholders, then they should not attempt to influence political processes or government policy.[14]

2.3 Specific requirements of key stakeholder groups

Aside from the more general drivers reviewed in the previous sections, strategy will be driven by the particular requirements of certain powerful stakeholders. These key stakeholders fall into four main categories: shareholding institutions and stockmarkets; private owners; major funding bodies; government and regulatory bodies. These are normally the only stakeholders that have the power to enforce major changes in management or strategy, or to close an organisation down, although the organisation may also *choose* to meet certain requirements of other stakeholders, such as its staff. We look at their likely requirements in the following sections.

2.3.1 Shareholding institutions and stock markets

Shareholding institutions have particular significance in Anglo-Saxon economies and a growing influence in continental Europe and Japan, as notions of shareholder value take hold there. Most outside shareholders hold shares as financial investments. These are required to generate a return, and this requirement will influence the way shareholders look at firms' performances. They tend to look above all for steadily increasing profits and share prices, and also in some cases for a steady flow of dividends. There are also a number of other, financially based objectives that they may set for the firm.

Earnings per share and financial engineering

Earnings per share (EPS) has been widely adopted as a measure of shareholder value. Entire corporate strategies have been built around EPS, including acquisitions of companies with the sole aim of enhancing the earnings per share of the acquiring company.

Suppose that a company with a high price/earnings (p/e) ratio acquires a firm with a lower p/e ratio. It pays for the acquisition with shares of its own, whose value is the same as the market value of the acquired company's shares. Then, as if by magic, the EPS of the combined company becomes higher than that of the high p/e company before the acquisition. Such acquisitions are technically called 'earnings enhancing'. However, from the strategic point of view, they may be questionable unless the acquiring company has the skills and resources to manage its new subsidiary effectively. Such 'financial engineering' has become discredited, and so, slowly, has EPS as a performance measure.[15]

Economic value added

Economic value added, or EVA[16] is a newer measure of shareholder value that is becoming widely accepted. It is intended to measure the true economic value of the firm. Policies aimed at increasing EVA should, in theory, increase a firm's value to its shareholders.

A number of firms, such as LucasVarity, a UK autoparts manufacturer and Monsanto, a major US chemicals and biotechnology corporation, have incorporated EVA into their management control systems. A 1999 study showed that firms using EVA achieved better stock market returns than their immediately competitors,[17] while there are no indications as yet that EVA has led to the kind of strategically questionable policies observed in firms that targeted their strategies on the basis of EPS.

2.3.2 Private owners

Private owners frequently, like shareholders in public companies, seek financial returns on their investments, but these do not necessarily have to take the form of declared profits. They have the option of taking their returns in the form of benefits, such as accommodation or generous pension schemes paid for by the firm, as salaries for their own work as managers, or as dividends on their shareholdings. They may also have important motivations that are not measurable in financial terms. They may, for example, see the organisation as a means of securing employment for themselves and members of their immediate family, or for people in the locality where they live, as is the case with Benetton. Or, they may view the building of a substantial organisation was a way of demonstrating their worth to themselves and to the world at large. They may seek strategies that promote growth or local employment or that make it more likely that the firm will survive to be handed on to the next generation.

2.3.3 Major funding bodies

Funding bodies' requirements are most often relevant to the public sector or non-profit organisations, which rely on them for sponsorship or revenue. For example, grants by the UK government's Arts Council to theatre groups may be made subject to certain conditions. A group may be required to put on a certain minimum number of productions, to make a certain number of tickets available at prices affordable by people with low incomes or to arrange sessions in local schools to help to give young people an interest in live theatre. UK government funding to universities is partially dependent on those universities achieving a certain level of published research output and achieving certain minimum levels of competence in their teaching and financial management.

2.3.4 Government and regulatory bodies

Governments and regulators are relevant to both public sector organisations, where they may be the controlling stakeholders, and commercial firms. In the UK, they have a particularly strong role in firms that are now privatised but were previously in the public sector. In such cases, it has been UK government policy to set up a regulator to ensure that firms do not abuse local monopoly positions.

Laws and regulations that monitor and control firms are common in most industrialised countries. The types of requirements that they impose will vary from sector to sector, for example:

- Firms may face regulations on the health and safety of employees, laws which prescribe what emissions and effluents may be discharged into the environment, and legislation on the use and abuse of proprietary knowledge.
- Retailers are frequently regulated on their location and their hours of opening.
- Financial services firms must meet international standards on the financial reserves they carry to back up their activities, and local regulations in terms of what they are allowed to sell, and to what types of customer.
- Educational organisations are frequently regulated in terms of what must, as a minimum, be included in their curriculum, the qualification levels of the staff they employ and sometimes the standards of their internal administration.
- Transport firms may have to meet standards in terms of frequency of service, reliability (number of timetabled services that actually run) and punctuality.

All of these constrain the choices that are available to organisations, and the profits they can accrue.

One of the most important external constraints on strategy-making is related to the abuse of monopolistic positions. Monopolies allow firms to make extraordi-

The concept of increasing returns is introduced in Section 5.5.3. ▶

nary profits, at the expense of the customers who have to pay for essential services. Monopolistic firms also tend to be inefficient, or can become so as there is little incentive for managers to strive to minimise costs or achieve high levels of quality. It is the goal of most profit-maximising firms to achieve this position, however. The closer they get to a dominant market position, the more profits they are likely to make, and, unless they are controlled, powerful firms tend to become more powerful, as they can set the basis of competition to favour themselves. Indeed, the recent development of thinking on increasing returns suggests that, in some industries, an initial dominance will never be lost unless deliberately controlled by forces external to the industry. It is this that has led the US authorities to move against the software giant Microsoft, on the grounds that it was acting to limit competition and that competitive forces would not be able to restrain it.

Because most industrialised countries appear to see monopolies as a bad thing, the majority have legal frameworks which act to minimise the power of dominant firms, through blocking their ability to buy up competing firms, or regulating the price they can charge for their products. In the EU, this is carried out under the aegis of the European Commission and through such country agencies as the Office of Fair Trading in the UK, or the Bundeskartellamt in Germany.

2.4 Stakeholder controls on strategic choices

It is quite common for different sets of stakeholders to hold differing views about a firm's direction. External shareholders' desire for growth in both profits and the share price may conflict with the founders' desire for slow, manageable growth and jobs for their children. Managers' bonuses may be threatened by the cost of implementing government legislation. There are several mechanisms that various stakeholders, including external ones, can use to control and influence managers to comply with their objectives.

2.4.1 External controls

The way in which owners and financial stakeholders exert their influence will vary according to the norms in the organisation's home country. In Anglo-Saxon countries, and increasingly elsewhere in Europe, control may be exerted through the **market for corporate control**. Dissatisfied shareholders sell their shares in the market until the price falls to a point where another firm will find it worth while to acquire the firm and reform its strategy. Elsewhere, shareholders and bankers may exert their influence on strategy more directly, through seats on the board or direct lobbying of management. A bank also has the option of withdrawing its funding, or refusing new loans, forcing the firm into bankruptcy.

For public sector and not-for-profit organisations, funding bodies may exert control equivalent to the threat of bankruptcy or the market for corporate control for a commercial firm. Funds may be withdrawn, radical management changes may be imposed or the organisation may be closed down or merged with another.

Infringements of legal and regulatory requirements may lead to organisations' facing fines, having changes imposed in their management systems or being forced to close. (See Real-Life Application 2.4.)

REAL-LIFE APPLICATION 2.4

Regulation in financial services

In 1991, traders at Salomon Brothers, a prestigious New York investment bank, broke regulations designed to stop a single bidder from 'cornering the market' in US Treasury bonds. On two separate occasions, as well as placing a bid in its own name for 35% (the maximum it was allowed to hold) of a particular bond issue, the firm placed further orders in the names of customers who had not authorised the bids. The bank's top management hesitated before reporting this to the Treasury. Top managers in the firm were forced to resign and given personal fines. The firm was fined, banned from participating in bond auctions for several months and forced to strengthen its systems for supervising traders.

Also in 1991, the presidents of Nomura, a Japanese bank that is one of the world's largest, and Nikko, Japan's third-largest brokerage, were forced to resign. Both firms admitted making unjustified payments and loans to people linked to organised crime, and to making good clients' investment losses (against the rules in Japan). The firms in question faced sanctions from the Japanese authorities. The regulatory regime governing financial services in Japan was tightened, and long-standing opposition by the country's finance ministry to allowing foreign firms to compete with its securities firms was reversed.

In 1993, a number of major UK insurers were found to have taken advantage of a change in UK pension regulations to persuade customers to take out a pension with them, when their existing arrangements would actually have guaranteed a better retirement income. The firms in question were fined and forced to pay to have the customers in question reinstated in their former pension schemes. They were also forced to recall their pension salesforces for retraining. Many firms faced further fines when the regulator judged that they were taking too long to identify and compensate the customers affected.

External controls can be more subtle than this. An influential school of thought known as institutional theory holds that organisations adopt new strategic ideas, like total quality and business process re-engineering, mainly as matter of fashion. Ideas pass from one firm to another through intermediaries such as consultants, and are adopted because influential stakeholders, such as major shareholders, are also subject to the same fashions.[18]

2.4.2 Corporate governance

At the firm level there are also external controls, but they are more localised. These include the boards of directors. In the UK and the USA, these boards usually comprise both executive and non-executive directors (directors who are not at the same time managers in the company). In other European countries, for example Germany and Holland, the boards are divided into two tiers: the upper tier supervises the lower tier, is separate from it and often includes representatives of the workforce.

There has been widespread concern over principal–agent problems in public companies, where chief executives and other board members have been seen to be profiting at the expense of shareholders and other stakeholders. In the USA, and to a lesser extent in the UK, there has been controversy because senior executive remuneration has been increasing much faster than general salary levels, and often bears no relationship to profits or share prices. US directors have also been criticised for putting in place 'poison pills' – legal devices to protect their firms from hostile takeover bids – and 'golden parachutes' – provisions to give them large payments if their firms are taken over. Many theorists believe that these provisions work against the interests of shareholders, by protecting managers from the consequences of poor decisions.

In the UK, this led to the Greenbury Report, which investigated the level and structure of remuneration schemes for senior executives of public companies and recommended that directors' pay should be disclosed in annual reports and set by independent committees. It has recently been noted that the same people appear to be being appointed to these committees!

The Cadbury Committee in the UK, the Dey Report in Canada, the Hilmer Report in Australia and the Veinot Report in France looked into the issues of board membership and disclosure of information. The various recommendations included the separation of the roles of chairman and chief executive, the inclusion of more non-executive directors and the setting up of codes of best practice. All are concerned to protect small shareholders and weaker organisational stakeholders whose interests may be too fragmented to be powerful. However, research has found no evidence at all that separating the role of chairman and chief executive makes any difference to firms' performance. It also indicates that US boards dominated by outside directors fail to limit the adoption of golden parachutes and poison pills.[19]

2.5 Summary

In this short chapter we have looked at some of the factors that influence an organisation's strategic direction and at some of the controls and constraints placed upon it:

- The culture in many countries encourages firms to take account of a wide variety of stakeholder groups in formulating their strategies. However, the Anglo-Saxon shareholder value culture, which places the interests of shareholders above those of all other stakeholders, is becoming more widespread.

- Strategies aimed purely at maximising profits are very difficult to formulate and implement, and may not work well in practice because they give too much weight to short-term considerations. However, there is increasing evidence that strategies that neglect economic returns in favour of other objectives, such as growth or employment generation, may not be viable in the long term.

- An organisation's mission, vision and values and leadership are often important in driving its strategy. Charismatic change agents may make good leaders in some circumstances, but effective leaders have a variety of qualities.

- Although some people still hold to the view that ethics are not the concern of businesses, ethical considerations are becoming increasingly important to consumers and financial institutions. Ethical behaviour does not necessarily conflict with profitability.

- Specific stakeholder groups will have particular expectations of the firm. Shareholders will look for rises in profits and share prices, while private owners, funding bodies and governments may have other, non-financial, objectives.

- Stakeholders may use a number of mechanisms to ensure that managers comply with their objectives, including the market for corporate control, legislation and changes to corporate governance.

Typical questions

We conclude this chapter by reviewing some of the questions you may be asked about its contents and how you might go about answering them.

1. *Why did the organisation pursue a given set of strategies?*

You may wish to look at the country in which the organisation was located, and the type of expectations that its culture and legislation imposed upon management (Section 2.1). You might also look how the organisation's historic values and leadership might have influenced the strategy pursued (Section 2.2.2), having regard to what was said in Chapter 1 about bounded rationality. You should then look at the specific requirements of the main stakeholders (Section 2.3), perhaps using the material in Section 1.2.2 to help you to assess which of them had the most power.

2. *How effective are the organisation's procedures for corporate governance?*

You might want to look at the organisation's governance structure, including the constitution of its board, in the light of the material presented in Section 2.4.2. You may also want to look for evidence of principal–agent conflicts (Section 1.3.2), and judge the extent to which stakeholder requirements (Section 2.3) are being fulfilled.

Questions for discussion

1. Can shareholders be said to own a company, in the same way that they own a car or house?

2. '[S]ecurities analysts will never understand . . . business, because they believe that money is real. Securities analysts believe that companies make money. Companies make shoes' (Peter Drucker[20]). Discuss.

3. What are the arguments *in favour* of companies *avoiding* any entanglement in ethical issues?

4. Do managers behave ethically for moral reasons or for practical ones?

The tribulations of a rational man: Doug Ivester and The Coca-Cola Company

Although the entire Coca-Cola Company must have been saddened when Roberto Goizueta, its Chief Executive Officer, died of lung cancer in 1997, the staff and shareholders were comforted to know that there was an obvious successor. Doug Ivester, Giozueta's 50-year-old Chief Operating Officer and protégé, stepped up to the position of CEO and set to work to implement the strategy that he, along with his predecessor, had been instrumental in developing.

The Coca-Cola Company

The Coca-Cola Corporation traced its history back to 1886, when pharmacist John Stith Pemberton first offered his home-made syrup for sale at a local drugstore in Atlanta, Georgia. An Atlanta entrepreneur, Asa G. Candler, bought the business in 1891 and expanded distribution nationwide. The Coca-Cola trademark, how the world's best known, was registered in 1893. The beverage was first bottled for sale in Mississippi in 1894, using syrup shipped from Atlanta. The distinctive bottle was introduced in 1915 to distinguish the product from imitators.

Coca-Cola was first offered for sale outside the USA at the end of the nineteenth century, in Canada and Mexico, and was introduced into Europe in 1920. However, the company's international expansion really took wings during the Second World War when its CEO, Robert Woodruff, famously promised 'Every man in uniform gets a bottle of Coca-Cola for 5 cents, wherever he is and whatever it costs'. With assistance from the US government, the company built 64 bottling plants world wide to enable it to fulfil this promise. In 1997, the company derived two-thirds of its revenues and three-quarters of its operating profits from outside North America.

At the close of the twentieth century, The Coca-Cola Company was the world's largest and most profitable producer of soft drinks, with 30,000 employees and profits in 1998 of $3.5 billion on a turnover of $19 billion. Alongside its flagship soft drink, the company marketed three other leading brands: Diet Coke, Fanta and Sprite, selling more than one billion servings of soft drinks every day.

The company had a formidable reputation as a marketing machine, honed through nearly fifty years of sometimes bitter competition with PepsiCo, its American rival. Its advertising slogans 'It's the real thing' (introduced in 1942) and 'Things go better with Coke' (1963) achieved lasting resonance throughout the English-speaking world. In 1997 it held some 50% of the world's soft-drink market. Coca-Cola's mission statement (see opposite) makes it clear how seriously it took its leadership position and the attendant responsibilities.

Roberto Goizueta

Roberto Goizueta took over from J. Paul Austin as Chairman and Chief Executive Officer in 1981. Cuban by birth and a chemical engineer by training, he was a surprise choice, nominated by Robert Woodruff himself over the head of Austin's own chosen successor. By divesting non-core assets, enhancing efficiency, luring key distributors away from Pepsi and consolidating the distribution network to use fewer, larger bottlers, Goizueta revitalised the organisation, enabling it to increase the volume of drinks it sold at a rate of over 7% per year, and profits by 18% per annum. During his sixteen-year tenure, the company added over $100 billion of shareholder value, and the share price rose 4,000%. In this he was helped by the strength of the US economy, which boosted consumption in the world's largest soft-drinks market, and by the weakness of the US currency, which enhanced the dollar value of profits earned abroad.

For the first thirteen years, Goizueta's right-hand man, President and Chief Operating Officer was Donald Keough, a Nebraskan described by *The Economist* as having 'an intuitive grasp of Coke's brand'. When Keough left in 1994 to become chairman of Allen & Co., a New York investment bank, Douglas Ivester, who had earned a reputation for his brilliant financial brain, took over as number 2. There was little doubt that Ivester, who had first come to Coca-Cola as an outside auditor, was Goizueta's preferred successor. His skills in finance and accounting had been complemented with training in areas like marketing, global affairs and public speaking, to prepare him for the leading role.

Doug Ivester's management style

Alongside his deep-seated belief in Coca-Cola and all it stood for – he described Coke as 'the most noble business on earth' – the hallmark of Ivester's management style was his firm belief in rationality and discipline. In an interview with *Fortune* magazine, he said: 'The most highly disciplined organizations are the most creative. If you can create high discipline, in effect you've created security and safety.'

Ivester exemplified this system through his personal behaviour. He scheduled meetings a year ahead and was meticulous in answering telephone calls and letters – and in pursuing people who did not respond to his own memos. He had also developed a comprehensive set of procedures. According to Jack Stahl, the head of the firm's North American operations and a colleague of Ivester for twenty years, 'Doug probably has 100 models for how to get through things, whether it's a discussion with an employee, a review of a marketing programme, an approach to a crisis, a talk with a government official or remarks to a community group'.

These models, however, were not intended to foster rigid thinking; rather, they were meant to help people to respond quickly in a given situation, and to have contingency plans available if events did not go according to plan. Nor was Ivester short term in his outlook. He had a vision of Coca-Cola as the ultimate Learning Organization, to which end he invested heavily in sophisticated IT and had a thirst for information, including daily updates by voice-mail from his senior executives around the world. When he and his team (unlike Goizueta, he declined to nominate a second-in-command) encountered criticism from outside the firm, he urged them to 'just keep focusing on the long term'.

With those outside his team, Ivester could be insensitive at times. In 1994 he had delivered a speech to a gathering of beverage industry executives, warning them that he was no statesmanlike industry leader, but a fierce competitor who wanted all their shelf space for his brands. When he began seeking more public credit for his part in his prede-

---

The Coca-Cola Company's Mission

We exist to create value for our share owners on a long-term basis by building a business that enhances The Coca-Cola Company's trademarks. This also is our ultimate commitment.

As the world's largest beverage company, we refresh that world. We do this by developing superior soft drinks, both carbonated and non-carbonated, and profitable non-alcoholic beverage systems that create value for our Company, our bottling partners, our customers, our share owners and the communities in which we do business.

In creating value, we succeed or fail based on our ability to perform as worthy stewards of several key assets:

Coca-Cola, the world's most recognised trademark, and other highly valuable trademarks.

The world's most effective and pervasive distribution system.

Satisfied customers, who make a good profit selling our products.

Our people, who are ultimately responsible for building this enterprise.

Our abundant resources, which must be intelligently allocated.

Our strong global leadership in the beverage industry in particular and in the business world in general.

Source: http://www.thecocacolacompany.com/tccc/mission.html, accessed on 3 February 2000.

cessor's successes he upset Donald Keough, who retained strong links to his old employer and felt his own role was being retrospectively downplayed.

Ivester's strategy

Ivester took control of Coca-Cola just as the dollar was strengthening and a financial crisis was devastating many Asian economies, so that profits came under pressure. He and his team responded in several ways. They raised the price of the concentrate – the crucial raw ingredient that Coca-Cola supplied to its bottlers. They continued the Goizueta strategy of eliminating their weaker bottlers and placing more business with the most powerful ones. And they pursued growth through a new strategy – the acquisition of other soft-drinks brands.

The bottlers were less than happy at the price increase of their key raw material, and the structure of Coke's operations meant that their opinion counted. Their role was not just to mix the concentrate with water and carbon dioxide and bottle or can the finished product. Essentially they controlled Coke's distribution through their local network of retailers, restaurants and vending machines. Although nominally independent of The Coca-Cola Company, the eleven major 'anchor' bottlers had strong links to the company, which had minority stakes in several of them and gave them a total of $1.5 billion as marketing support in 1998. $900 million of this, together with a further £300 million for infrastructure investment, went to Coca-Cola Enterprises (CCE), the largest anchor bottler, which handled 70% of the USA bottling plus much of Europe. The Coca-Cola Company owned 42% of CCE's equity, and several CCE directors had more indirect links to the parent. One, Howard Buffet, was the son of Warren Buffett, chairman of Berkshire Hathaway, a Nebraskan firm that was The Coca Cola Company's largest shareholder.

Coke's North American bottlers had little choice but to put up their prices, at the same time that its arch-rival, PepsiCo, launched a new marketing campaign, the 'Joy of Cola', devised by a marketing executive lured from outside the industry. Ivester had appointed Charles Frenette, the son of a bottler

with a background in operations management, as Coca-Cola marketing chief. His predecessor, Sergio Zyman, described by *The Economist* as 'quirky but sometimes brilliant', had been associated with the 'New Coke' episode some years earlier, when Coke had replaced its time-honoured formula with a sweeter version, only to be forced to reinstate the original after consumers rebelled.

Ivester and Frenette made some important gains. Fast-food chain Burger King, attracted by Ivester's long-term perspective as well as by offers of substantial discounts, switched its soft-drinks account to Coca-Cola. They initiated a major marketing partnership with entertainment firm Universal, although this rather upset Universal's competitor Disney, one of Coke's three most important customers. Frenette also increased spend on advertising and sponsorship, but the firm's seven-year-old 'Always Coca-Cola' campaign looked tired besides Pepsi's fresher effort. In 1998 PepsiCo won back market share from Coke for the first time in a decade.

Trouble in Europe

Meanwhile, another part of the strategy – the attempt to acquire new brands – encountered unanticipated problems. Coca-Cola had agreed terms with France's Pernod-Ricard, to buy its Orangina brand for $844 million, and with UK conglomerate Cadbury Schweppes, owner of the brands, to purchase its Schweppes and Dr Pepper soft-drinks brands outside the US for $1.85 billion. The business logic behind the deal was impeccable: Coca Cola would be able to squeeze more value out of the brands by putting them through its unparalleled distribution network, while the vendor firms got much-needed funds to invest in their other businesses.

However, in November 1999 the French authorities blocked the Orangina purchase, claiming that it would have left Coke with 70% of the French market for non-alcoholic carbonated drinks. Regulators in Mexico and Australia, where Coca-Cola also had more than half the carbonated soft-drinks market, objected to the Schweppes acquisition. An Australian official commented that his department, if consulted, could have warned Coke much earlier that the deal with face problems.

The Schweppes deal also faced opposition in Europe from the German authorities and then, in April 1999, from the European Union's competition commissioner, Karel van Miert. Coca-Cola had structured the acquisition so that it would be scrutinised by individual country regulators, rather than by the European Commission. Van Miert was vehement in his criticism of this attempt to circumvent the regulations, and threatened to investigate the deal anyway. In the end, the acquisition had to be restructured to exclude Europe altogether.

Later the same year, Coca-Cola's European bottlers were to confront the European Commission over allegations that they had used a system of bonuses and discounts to tie retailers to them and discourage them from stocking rival products. Commission officials raided the offices of several bottlers in July 1999, looking for evidence of such practices, which under European law were forbidden to a firm with a dominant market position. In August that same year, Italian regulators claimed to have found proof of these illegal tactics.

Accidents

It was perhaps unfortunate that van Miert's home country, Belgium, should be the site of another of Coke's problems. On 8 June 1999, 26 Belgian schoolchildren complained of headaches, stomach cramps and palpitations after drinking bottled Coca-Cola. Within 24 hours, some 170 other people in Belgium and northern France reported the same symptoms. The company investigated and claimed to have found two causes for the problems – a batch of faulty carbon dioxide in its Antwerp plant in Belgium, and some fungicide sticking to cans of Coke on the pallets on which they had been shipped from Dunkirk, France. Independent tests and Belgium's chief food inspector supported the company's views that its products were safe, and Ivester, who was in the firm's Paris office at the time, flew home to Atlanta.

Belgium's health minister, new to his post, did not feel able to dismiss the matter so lightly. His predecessor had been driven from office by failing to take adequate action over a scandal involving contaminated beef and chicken. His ban on all sales of Coca-Cola products was replicated by health authorities in France, Luxembourg and the Netherlands. The company waited eight days before issuing a brief statement and apology. Eventually, after Ivester had flown to Brussels and taken out full-page newspaper advertisements apologising to his Belgian customers, and the local bottler (CCE) had withdrawn 14 million cases of drinks from sale, the ban was lifted.

Many observers criticised the company for being slow to respond, but not everyone would agree. The following month, a letter appeared in the *Lancet*, a reputable British medical journal, from four members of the Belgian Health Council. The cause of the Belgian problems, they wrote, appeared to be neither contaminated carbon dioxide nor fungicide residues, but 'mass sociogenic illness' (more commonly known as mass hysteria).

Decline and fall

Ivester's final brush with controversy came in an interview with a Brazilian magazine in October 1999, when he foresaw the introduction of vending machines that might be intelligent enough to raise the price at which the drinks were sold at the weather grew hotter. A company spokesman later disavowed this idea, which proved unpopular with both consumers and the bottlers who controlled the vending machine network.

On 1 December 1999, Ivester, in Chicago for a meeting with McDonald's, a long-standing Coke client, was called to a private conference with two leading members of his board, Herbert Allen (whose family controlled the bank where Donald Keough was chairman) and Warren Buffett. Buffett had until then been very supportive of Ivester, but the pair now told him quietly that they had lost confidence in his leadership. Four days later, at an emergency board meeting that he had summoned, Douglas Ivester announced his resignation. During the two years in which he had been CEO, net profits had fallen from $4.1 billion to $3.2 billion, return on equity had declined from 57% to 35%

CASE STUDY *continued*

and the company's stock price had risen only 10% while the Standard and Poors 500 stock market index had risen 50%.

Case study questions

1. How appropriate was Ivester's leadership style to the challenges confronting Coca-Cola in 1997?

2. Would Ivester have succeeded better if he had been more, or less, 'rational'?

3. How ethically did The Coca Cola Company behave in its reaction to the Belgian contamination scare in 1999?

4. Comment on the corporate governance of The Coca-Cola Company and of Coca-Cola Enterprises.

NOTES

1. For a discussion of different models of capitalism, see Albert (1993), Hofstede (1991) and Hampden-Turner and Trompenaars (1993).

2. 'Rethinking thinking', *The Economist*, 18 December 1999, pp. 77–79.

3. This is another reference to the principal–agent problem we alluded to in Chapter 1. For summaries of the research evidence, see Eisenhardt (1989) and Jensen and Meckling (1976).

4. See, for example, Hayes and Abernathy (1980).

5. The steel castings example comes from Baden-Fuller (1989); the petrochemicals one from van Witteloostuijn (1998).

6. See, for example, Campbell and Nash (1992); Drucker (1994); Hamel and Prahalad (1992); and Peters and Waterman (1982).

7. For example, Pettigrew and Whipp (1991) and Nadler and Tushman (1988).

8. Pettigrew and Whipp (1991); Charan and Colvin (1999).

9. See Rieple and Vyakarnam (1996).

10. The distinction between transactional and transformational leadership comes from Burns (1978).

11. 'Sweatshop wars', *The Economist*, 27 February 1999, pp. 78–79.

12. See Useem (2000); Levering and Moskowitz (2000); 'How green is Browne?' *The Economist*, 17 April 1999, p. 104; 'Corporate Hospitality', *The Economist*, 27 November 1999, p. 100; Porter and van der Linde (1995); Hutchison (1996). For an interesting case study on environmental strategy in the carpet industry, one of the most polluting of all, see Kinkead (1999). Some success factors for environmental strategies are suggested in Chiesa et al. (1999).

13. Beauchamp and Browe (1983) contains papers by both Friedman (pp. 81–83) and Levitt (pp. 83–86).

14. The case for businesses having a social responsibility ethos is put in papers by Bruno and Nichols and Davis in Hoffman and Moore (1990). The argument that organisations should not intervene politically unless they are prepared to take account of non-shareholder constituencies is made by Reich (1998).

15. For a critique of EPS and an explanation of EVA, see Stern et al. (1998).

16. EVA has been registered as a trademark in the USA by Stern, Stewart and Co. A very similar concept 'added value' is advocated by Kay (1993).

17. See Tulle (1999).

18. DiMaggio and Powell (1983) started this idea. See also Oliver (1997) and O'Neill et al. (1998).

19. Boyd et al. in Thomas et al. (eds) (1997), pp. 237–59.

20. 'Peter Drucker takes the long view', *Fortune*, 28 September 1998, p. 99. A securities analyst is a person working for an American investment firm who forms a view on a company's worth and advises clients whether to buy, sell or hold the shares.

Competitive failure and success

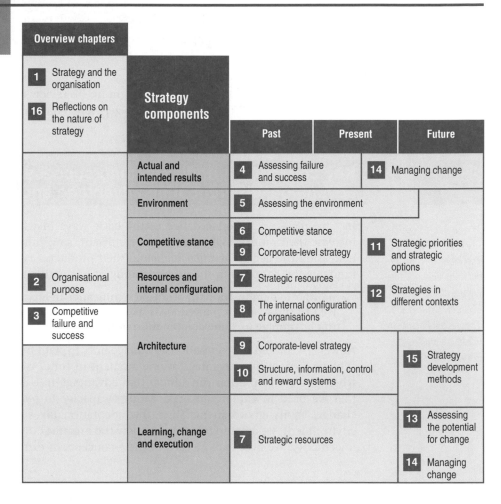

In the previous chapter we have looked at some basic definitions relating to strategy and organisations. We have also examined the theoretical debate about how writers have conceptualised the 'strategy' process within organisations. In this chapter we summarise current theory on competitive effectiveness. We build on the concepts introduced in Chapters 1 and 2 to show how they fit together to help us to understand competitive success or failure.

After reading this chapter, you should understand:

- the essentials of current theory about what makes certain organisations more successful than others;
- how to analyse the basis of an organisation's past competitive success or failure, and assess the likelihood that that success will continue in future;
- how to go about analysing a case study.

Before getting into this chapter, you might like to review the important concepts of cost advantage, differentiation advantage, value chain and architecture, which we defined in Chapter 1.

3.1 Key concepts in understanding success: cost advantage, differentiation advantage and sustainability

In Chapter 1 we introduced two of the basic ways in which organisations can increase their profits: by becoming more efficient, so gaining *cost advantage*, or by increasing the degree of *differentiation* in their products or services. These are two fundamental concepts in the understanding of competitive success and failure.

The ideas of cost and differentiation advantage were first popularised by Michael Porter (1980). Theoretical Perspective 6.1 has a critique of Porter's ideas. ▶

In order to demonstrate the strategic significance of any decision or action, you need to show how it has led, or is likely to lead, to cost advantage, differentiation advantage or some combination of the two.

However, cost and differentiation advantage only explain how an organisation can achieve competitive advantage at one moment in time. We are interested also in whether an organisation can *sustain* that advantage into the future. This means that we need to explore an organisation's capacity to *innovate* and to adapt to changes in its environment. Since this adaptation takes place in an uncertain environment, we are also interested in now the organisation attempts to cope with uncertainty. We now explore each of these concepts in turn.

3.1.1 Cost advantage

There are various ways in which organisations can try gain cost advantage. Two frequently cited ones are through gaining **economies of scale** or **economies of scope**.

Economies of scale and scope can arise at different levels. For example, McDonald's enjoys local economies of scale and cope; larger restaurants with a broader menu are more economic than smaller ones, since the costs of buildings and kitchen equipment and, to a lesser extent, staff can be spread across a greater volume and variety of output. It also enjoys national and global economies of scale through its purchasing power for items which are purchased centrally for all its operations world wide.

Economies of scale are widespread in a whole variety of industries. However, if

Concept	**Economies of scale and scope**

Economies of scale arise when producing a greater quantities makes the average cost per unit significantly smaller. Typically, economies of scale come about because an organisation has a substantial fixed cost base (plant, administration, etc.) and relatively low variable costs per unit of output. If output volumes increase, then the fixed cost per unit will fall rapidly. Economies of scale can also come from purchasing: suppliers will often offer discounts for purchases in bulk.

Economies of scale come from producing greater quantities of a *single* product. *Economies of scope*, on the other hand, arise from producing or selling a greater variety of products, which might, for example, share the same warehousing and distribution network.

In most cases, an organisation has to operate at a certain minimum level of output (called the **minimum economic size** or MES) in order to get any economies of scale. If the MES is large in comparison with the size of the market, then the number of competitors is likely to be small.

you want to claim economies of scale or scope for a firm, you must be able to show *precisely* how they arise. For example, Sony generates economies of scale and scope from its R&D expenditure and marketing. Benetton obtains economies of scale through its bulk purchases of wool.

It is a common error to assume that a firm will automatically generate economies of scale by getting larger. Not all business benefit from them – some service industries, where most of the cost of an item comes from the skilled labour that is needed to provide the service, will have hardly any economies of scale. Sometimes businesses suffer from **diseconomies of scale** – as they grow beyond a certain point, overhead costs will increase, because of the need to employ more supervisors and managers, at a rate which outweighs any economies of scale from other sources.

Economies of scale are not the only sources of cost advantage.[1] It helps if a company uses its production capacity intensively: it may be most cost-effective to use a small plant to its full capacity than a larger one at below full capacity. In some industries, such as the aircraft industry, firms are able to reduce their costs over time through a process of learning. As it produces a particular aircraft in large volumes over a number of years, Boeing is able to make the production process more efficient and cheaper. This is because Boeing's staff learn how to do things faster and more reliably. They also learn what does not need to be done, and so economise by eliminating unnecessary steps in the production process.

However, newer strategic thinking places more emphasis upon an organisation's resources as sources of cost advantage, in particular its knowledge and competences. We look more closely at these in Chapter 7 and Section 3.4 in this chapter.

3.1.2 Differentiation advantage

Differentiation advantage is considered is more detail in Section 6.3. ▶

An organisation obtains differentiation advantage by doing something that customers find valuable, perhaps by saving them time, effort or money, but also by conferring prestige or some other intangible benefit.

Differentiation advantage may come from developing products or services that are better designed to meet customers' needs or are more reliable than competing ones. Sony attempts to differentiate its televisions in this way, by emphasising their product features and design. It may also be obtained from the organisation's value chain, through superior after-sales service for example.

A firm may differentiate on the basis of value for money, by matching a competitors' service levels and product features at a lower price. Part of Benetton's strategy has been to offer well-made, fashionable clothes at an affordable price. Or an organisation may use image as a basis for differentiation, either by associating the product with particular brand values or by using the organisation's reputation (e.g. for reliability) to sell the product.

3.1.3 Innovativeness and sustainability

An organisation's mix of cost and differentiation advantage defines what makes it viable in economic terms. If it has neither type of advantage, then there is nothing to attract customers to it, and no reason why anyone should want to invest in it.

It may be possible for an organisation to survive for a short time with neither kind of advantage. Sometimes, its customers may need more experience or better information before they are able to tell the difference between good and poor suppliers. Sometimes the customers may have no choice, because the organisation has a local monopoly, or because demand for a product is running a long way ahead of supply. However, sooner or later, in any reasonably open market economy, competition will expose such companies.

Understanding what kind of advantage an organisation has achieved, and how it has managed to achieve it, is an important step in the analysis of its strategic situation. That kind of analysis, though, relates to the *past* and the *present*, while a strategist's main concern is with the *future*. The fact that an organisation has cost or differentiation advantage at the moment does not imply that that advantage can be sustained in future:

● *The environment is likely to change.* New technologies will appear, customer tastes and needs will change, and new competitors may enter the fray. These changes may threaten the organisation's existing sources of advantage. Equally, they may signal the arrival of new opportunities for it to profit from its resources.

● *Competitors are not stupid.* They will be looking at ways to copy and improve upon the strategies that a successful organisation has followed. Unless something about a firm's resources makes them rare and difficult to imitate, any advantage that they confer is likely to be short-lived.

So there are two further steps to take after establishing the nature and extent of an organisation's cost or differentiation advantage. Firstly, we need to analyse how the environment is likely to change – a topic we address in detail in Chapter 5. Secondly, we need to evaluate how *sustainable* the advantage is likely to be, in the light of those environmental changes, by answering questions like these:

● How unusual are the sources of the current cost and differentiation advantage, and how difficult are they for other firms to match? Has the firm managed to build any unique competences, strong brands or other resources, or has it just gained a temporary advantage in a particular market segment that competitors are equally able to serve?

● How good is the firm at adapting to changes in the environment? Even if the current sources of advantage can be copied, an organisation's advantage may still be sustainable if it can keep one step ahead of the competition. Does the firm have a good track record of learning and innovation? Has it periodically reinvented itself, changing its structure and systems and adapting its culture to meet the changing needs of its customers or to embrace new technology? Or has it tended to rely upon a few tried and trusted resources?

● Are the organisation's strategies *consistent* with one another? Are its key resources being directed to their most profitable use, or are they being spread thinly over a number of products and markets? Are people being pulled in different directions – for example, by being asked to provide too many different standards of service to too many different customer groups?

For many organisations, it is not clear exactly how the environment is going to change, how drastic those changes are likely to be and what impact they will have on the firm and its competitors. This exposes the organisation to uncertainty and risk, and the need to take decisions with uncertain outcomes. We explore these concepts in the next section.

3.1.4 Risk, commitment and trade-offs

Diversification is discussed in more detail in Chapter 9. ▶

There are two logical, and so superficially attractive, ways for companies to manage risk and uncertainty. One is through **diversification** – on the basis that if a firm spreads its interests over many businesses, it might be less likely to suffer fatal damage from unexpected problems or poor decisions in just one. Another is through **flexibility** – avoiding taking decisions that cannot be reversed or amended as circumstances change.

Both of these policies are sound – up to a point. A firm *usually* has better survival prospects if it has many customers and several product lines than if it is reliant on just one or two key customers and products. But firms that diversify into a wide variety of unrelated products have, on average, lower profitability than those that focus on a relatively narrow area. By trying to do too many things adequately, organisations often find that they are unable to do any of them excellently. They risk being out-competed in each of their businesses by firms which are more focused and therefore more expert.

Similarly, if an organisation tries to keep its options open, it risks being beaten by competitors who are far-sighted enough (or foolish enough) to commit their resources earlier. As falling trade barriers and better telecommunications open up more markets to more firms, the more likely it is that an organisation will be confronted by a focused competitor that has, through luck or good judgement, made a timely, early investment.

Here we have encountered two extremely important, related aspects of strategic decisions. The first is the idea of **commitment** – that, in order to succeed, organisations have to invest their resources in a way that will make it difficult for other firms to compete with them. The second is the notion of **trade-offs** – that by investing in one aspect of strategy, a firm is likely to end up compromising in another area. It is almost impossible for any organisation to excel at everything.

Concept	**Risk and its management**

Risk is a combination of two things: the degree of uncertainty that a particular event will or will not happen, and the impact it will have if it does occur.

Uncertainty is a measure of the extent to which a particular factor may fluctuate. For example, there is relatively little uncertainty in knowing the number of 25-year-old people that there will be in the European Union in five years' time – it can be estimated quite easily from the number of 20-year-olds now. Only very unlikely events, such as a war or a devastating epidemic, would upset the calculations.

On the other hand, the future exchange rate of the euro is subject to considerably uncertainty. Foreign currency markets are inherently volatile, and the euro, as a young currency, has not had time to build up a track record from which to predict its future behaviour.

For a company like Benetton, which exports much of its output and imports much of its raw material such as wool and cotton, the exchange rate of the euro versus other major currencies is a source of risk, because the degree of uncertainty is high and so is the likely impact on the firm's profits. This is a risk the firm may want to manage, for example, through hedging on the currency markets.

The number of 25-year-old people, which form part of Benetton's target market, is important to the firm but, because there is little uncertainty in it, involves little risk. Benetton does not try, as part of its strategy, to influence the number of 25-year-olds – something that would, in any case, be rather difficult to manage!

The fluctuations in taste among people in that age group, on the other hand, are a very real source of risk – one that the firm must manage carefully. The firm can try to influence those tastes, to its own benefit, through its advertising. It can try to get advance warning of changes in tastes, through market research – or by hiring lots of 25-year-olds. Or it can diversify, as it has done with its range of children's clothes, so that it is less reliant upon one age group.

We explore both of these concepts in more depth in Section 3.4. In the next section, we look at how sustainable advantage is built over time, and what to look for when assessing whether or not it exists.

3.2 The building blocks of business-level success: competitive arena, value chain, architecture and strategic resources

In Chapter 1 we saw how an organisation evolved over time, accumulating knowledge and developing routines that, if successful, gave it a set of strategic resources. In this section, we relate these concepts to the way in which an organisation establishes, and then holds on to, competitive advantage over time.

REAL-LIFE APPLICATION 3.1

How Sony built its competitive advantage

The company that is now Sony Corporation was founded in 1946 by Akio Morita and Masura Ibuka, who had worked together researching weapons systems during the Second World War. From the beginning, their aims stressed innovation and the common good, including:

- Establishing an ideal factory, emphasising a spirit of freedom and open-mindedness, where engineers with sincere motivation can exercise their technological skills to the highest level.

- Reconstructing Japan and elevating the nation's culture through dynamic technological and manufacturing activities.

- Promptly applying advanced technologies developed during the war to common households.

Morita's father helped with funds derived from the family saké business, but components were in short supply, so the two engineers had to rely on their own ingenuity. The tape in the firm's first successful product, Japan's first tape recorder, was originally made of paper, because of a shortage of plastic.

Because there was no obvious market for Ibuka's rather expensive tape recorder, it fell to Morita to find one. One of the first markets turned out to be Japan's courts of justice, which were suffering from a shortage of people to take notes of proceedings.

On a trip to research the US tape-recorder industry Morita and Ibuka came across a new concept, the transistor, for which they were able to obtain a licence, though Bell Labs, its inventor, famously believed its only commercial application was in hearing aids.

The firm had originally aimed to produce radio and communications devices and measuring equipment. However, its initial successes with tape recorders and its good fortune in getting access to transistor technology led to further developments in audio-visual products. It introduced Japan's first transistor radio in 1955, its first pocket-sized radio (the world's smallest) in 1957 and the world's first transistor television in 1960. Other innovations in video-cassette recorders and colour television manufacture following during the 1960s and 1970s. In 1979 it launched one of its most famous innovations, the Walkman.

Sony decided early on that it would benefit from an international presence. Sony Corporation of America was founded in 1960 and Sony Overseas SA the following year. During the early 1970s it opened a TV manufacturing facility in the USA and the UK. Overseas subsidiaries were usually run by managers from the countries in question, who were given a lot of autonomy. It was felt that this was the best way to ensure sensitivity to local market and employment practices. This policy seemed to work well, and by the early 1980s, over 75% of Sony's turnover derived from outside Japan. Morita himself lived in the USA for eleven years to enhance his understanding of this key market, and overseas experience became the norm for rising Sony executives.

Source: Nathan (1999) and numerous public sources.

3.2.1 Understanding past success and failure: how organisations build their competitive positions

In Real-Life Application 3.1. we get some insights into the early history of Sony, from its origins with a handful of engineers working in an abandoned shop in war-ravaged Tokyo to its emergence as a leading multinational player in consumer and professional electronics. As with many tales of corporate start-ups, this one has a strong flavour of emergent strategy in the early days – of the founders improvising in response to the opportunities and constraints that they encountered. They moved, for no clear reason, away from the communications sector they had originally targeted, to the tape recorder and thence to transistorised radios and televisions. Morita had to work out how to market the tape recorder as he went along, after the product had been launched.

However, some consistent threads can also be made out. A great deal rested on the founders' technical expertise in electronics. Which they brought into the firm from their wartime experiences. Their initial desire to innovate and to share widely the benefits of technological progress also seems to have shaped the company's growth over its first few decades.

In short, Sony developed into a large company through a process of experience and learning, fuelled by the expertise and values of its founders. This is one example of a typical process of developing competitive advantage mapped out in Figure 3.1. We will now look at the elements of this map in more detail.

Most organisations start with a few people with some skills, some personal contacts, and a business idea – a market that needs to be served, a product or service that 'someone must want'. Some organisations have a clear idea of both product

Figure 3.1   How new organisations develop competitive advantage

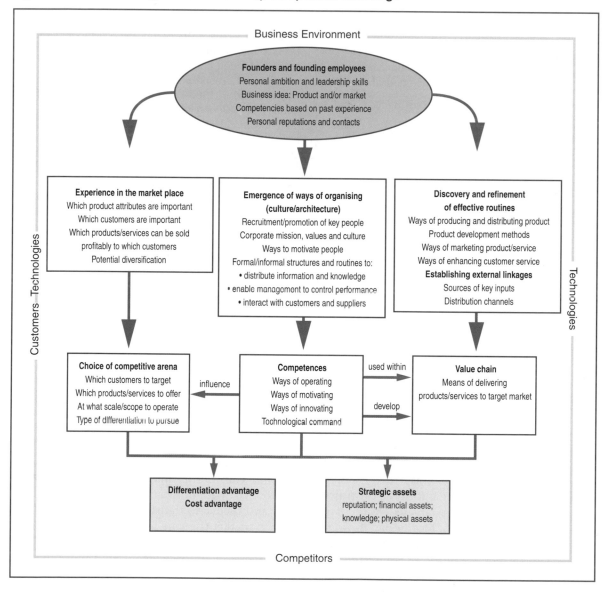

and market, or are brought into being by a government or a larger organisation to provide a particular service. Many, like Sony, only find their place in the world by a process of trial and error. In most cases, what follows is a period of experimentation and learning (the second tier of boxes in Figure 3.1).

- From **experience in the market place**, the organisation learns which customers are really keen on its services, and how much they are prepared to pay. It interacts with customers to learn about the product features they really want, and incorporates new technologies as they become available.

- The organisation begins to develop as a social structure, with the **emergence of ways of organising**. The people learn how to work together with one another and with the new people they recruit as they grow. They may have a vision of the environment in which they would like to work, like Sony's founders' 'ideal factory'. They can try to make that vision a reality, or they may be forced to alter it to please their customers or their investors. Over time the organisation develops a distinctive **culture** and **architecture**.

- The people in the organisation develop **effective routines** to deliver the product or service. The organisation discovers where to obtain reliable supplies of key inputs and establishes routines for dealing with suppliers. It discovers which distribution channels its customers prefer, and how to operate through them. Routines are established for transforming inputs into finished outputs, taking on board new production technologies as they arrive. Other routines are developed for making sure that customers are aware of the products and why they should buy them.

To some extent, this is an idealised picture. Some organisations die before they are able to find a niche in the market place or establish effective architectures or routines. Other organisations survive even though they seem flawed in some important way – their culture may be beset with conflict, or their production systems faulty.

Nonetheless, if an organisation, however flawed initially, survives long enough for you to be asked to study it, it is likely to have emerged from a learning process with five discernible aspects to its strategy:

1. A choice of **competitive arena**. It will have chosen whether it wants to target a broad range of customers all over the world, or to focus on selected countries, or regions, or income groups. It will have chosen whether it wants to offer a broad range of products or limit itself to a few. It will have chosen what form of differentiation it wants to use to position itself in its chosen markets. Sony chose to offer a broad range of audio-visual products to customers across the globe and to attack both professional and consumer markets, differentiating itself on quality and innovation. By contrast, Denmark's Bang and Olufsen offers a more restricted range of far more expensive products. Its target market is narrower, consisting of wealthy people, and it differentiates on price and on the aesthetics of its products.

2. Its **culture**. This is shown in the way that strategic decisions are taken. It includes the organisation's belief and value systems, and the cultural artefacts, such as symbols and stories, which are manifestations of what is regarded as important.

3. Its **architecture**. This comprises the structure, systems and practices that shape the way that information flows into and out of the organisation, and the way that decisions are taken (or avoided) on the basis of that information. Sony's architecture strongly reflected the influence of its founders, especially their fondness for innovation and their belief in internationalisation. It also reflected Morita's links with the Japanese business establishment, which started with financial support from his father and continued to give him access to support from friendly shareholders.

4. Its **value chain**. This represents the routines that have been developed over time in order to serve the organisation's users.

5. Its **capabilities** and **competences**. These are what the organisation knows how to do. They are strongly related to the architecture, since competence comes from having capable, well-informed and well-motivated people who work effectively together. Competences in marketing help an organisation in its choice of competitive arena. Other competences will help it shape and enhance its value chain. A final class of competence relates to aspects of technology of which a firm may have particular command. Sony had competences in miniaturisation, in colour TV and tape technology and in managing product innovation.

Not every organisation is distinctive in all these areas. For example, there is little that is distinctive about Sony's value chain. The ways in which it manufactures and distributes its products, while competent, are not different enough from its competitors' to give it any advantage. However, its choice of a broad competitive arena gave it some economies of scale and scope. These were supported by its architecture, which included well-developed systems for managing its international operations. Its architecture also favoured innovation, which generated technological competences and innovative, highly featured products. These in turn gave Sony a substantial differentiation advantage in many of its markets, reflected in its ability to charge premium prices.

> **A crucial part of a strategic analysis is to understand what is distinctive about an organisation's choice of arena, architecture, culture, competences and value chain, and to show how these five factors have contributed to an organisation's cost and differentiation advantage.**

An initial period of competitive success may generate some enduring *strategic assets*. Successful firms may build up reserves of cash and other financial assets, physical assets such as advanced factories and IT, and knowledge of their customers, markets and technologies.[2] Good products and service, complemented by effective marketing, are likely to give the organisation a good reputation in the market place. Sony's reputation was such that people not only trusted its established products, but were predisposed to give its new products the benefit of the doubt.[3]

These strategic assets may help to explain not only how the organisation builds advantage at the beginning, but also how that advantage may be sustained in the future.

3.2.2 Predicting future success and failure: assessing sustainability in the face of environmental change

In many strategy case studies, and many real life management situations, an organisation with an established track record has to cope with changes in its circumstances. Sometimes these changes may be internally generated – an organisation grows, and finds suddenly that the management practices that worked well with 100 people on a single site are no longer adequate to manage 1,000 people spread across several locations and countries.

REAL-LIFE APPLICATION 3.2

Sony overcomes environmental change

In the early 1980s some fundamental changes affected Sony. A severe recession hit its crucial European and American markets. As a result, customers became more price-sensitive and low cost imitations of Sony's products from new Asian competitors became more attractive to them. Sony's profits fell 30% between 1981 and 1982. It also became clear that consumer markets for audio and video products were becoming saturated and offered limited growth prospects.

The company responded in several ways. It reorganised its international operations to improve co-ordination between the autonomous overseas subsidiaries and reduce wasteful duplication of effort and resources. It imposed exacting cost reduction targets on its new global product units. It moved more of its manufacturing out of high-cost Japan, and developed new products for industrial markets, such as semiconductors and floppy disk drives (the 3½ inch computer floppy was a Sony invention).

The new strategy proved successful for much of the 1980s and 1990s. However, by the mid-1990s, Sony was facing renewed competition from Japanese and Korean firms, which had made inroads into its industrial markets. The company responded by entering new consumer markets. It established a dominant standard in computer games with its Playstation. It became a major force in the very competitive market for laptop computers by launching its Vaio range, which included a number of innovative features, such as photo-editing facilities, unavailable on competitors' machines.

These moves played to Sony's traditional strengths in innovation. However, at the same time, in 1999, it announced moves to improve its cost-competitiveness by shedding 14,000 jobs world wide. This went against the firm's long-standing policy, shared by many Japanese firms, of avoiding major sackings, so as to build staff loyalty and retain a full range of competences. In making this announcement, Sony was widely seen to have signalled a major change in the Japanese business environment.

Often, though, the changes will be triggered by some major movement in the business environment, as happened to Sony in the 1980s in Real-Life Application 3.2. We have already worked out what made the organisation successful in the first place. Our task is now to assess how, or if it can, *sustain* its competitive advantage in the new circumstances. The analysis needed is summarised in Figure 3.2.

The natural starting point is with the factors that made the organisation strong in the first place – its choice of arena, its architecture, its value chain and its strategic resources (capabilities, competences and assets). We then need to look at the extent of the change in the environment, to assess what kinds of strategies are likely to be successful in future. We can then gauge which parts of the existing strategy are likely to continue to work and which will need to change.

For Sony in 1982, the recession, new competitors and the saturation of the consumer market all pointed towards a future need to compete on price. Although a product positioning based on high-quality, innovative products might still be viable, the price premium that could be charged would need to fall. While there was no actual need to change the company's competitive arena, Sony's decision to

Figure 3.2 How existing organisations sustain competitive advantage

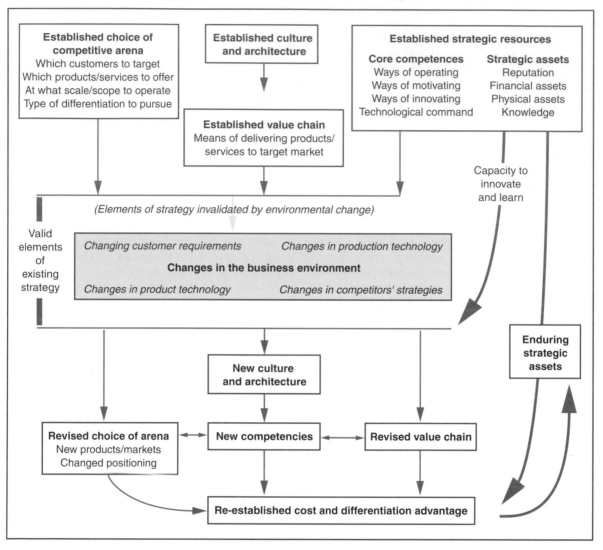

diversify into non-consumer products was logical. It might let the company benefit from access to less price-sensitive markets, and from economies of scope.

However, if the firm was to be competitive in its consumer businesses, then its value chain and architecture needed to change. Tailoring products to local tastes made sense in the 1970s, when the customers were affluent enough to pay for premium products. In the 1980s it made sense to alter the architecture to curtail local autonomy and gain greater economies of global scale. Similarly, the organisation's value chain and management systems needed to be oriented more towards cost advantage, and competences gained on low-cost manufacturing.

Being able to identify the changes needed, however, is only one part of the story. If we had been evaluating Sony's competitive position in 1982, we should have been looking for indications that they could come through these changes successfully. We would have been looking (the right-hand side of Figure 3.2) for strategic assets that could help to carry them through their problems, and for indications that they had the capacity to change in response to the demands of the new situation.

In Sony's case, its formidable reputation for reliable, innovative products was still an asset, as was its wide base of technological and customer knowledge. It had ample cash reserve and the support of rich financial institutions. It had a proven ability to innovate, although its ability to change its structure and culture on the scale that was needed had never been tested. In the event, the company proved equal to that task as well.

To summarise, when assessing the sustainability of a firm's strategic advantage, we need to assess:

- the sources of the organisation's present strategic advantage;
- the extent of the difference between the environment that we see developing and the environment in which the company established its strategies;
- the extent to which the firm's existing strategies and strategic assets will still be valid in the future;
- the ways in which existing strategies will need to change;
- the extent to which the organisation, on the basis of its past performance, has demonstrated the capacity to innovate, learn and change to meet the demands of the future.

3.3 The building blocks of corporate-level success: synergy and parenting advantage

3.3.1 The costs of diversification

Once organisations establish themselves in one business, they quite frequently diversity into others. This can be viewed as a way of spreading risk (as we shall discuss in Section 3.3.2), or as the result of a natural process of managers' seeking out new uses for their firm's resources (Penrose, 1959).

The theory of why organisations diversify and when it is advantageous to do so is discussed in Chapter 9. ▶

However natural the process, it is not always beneficial. It is possible for organisations to diversify too far, into areas where they do not have the knowledge or other resources to compete effectively. Even if the skills are available, they may be spread too thinly if the firm expands too ambitiously.

There are invariably costs involved in having different businesses working together, under a common owner, rather than as separate organisations:

- **People**   The owner (or *parent*) needs, at the very least, some administrative staff to add up the various sets of accounts. Normally, the parent will also have a layer of corporate management 'looking after' the various businesses.
- **Management time**   Business unit managers will spend time reporting their activities to the corporate management that might otherwise be used in improving or expanding their operations.
- **Delay**   Quite frequently, business decisions, particularly if they involve capital investment, will need to be referred up to corporate management for

approval. This may leave the business at a disadvantage if competitors with faster decision processes are able to get to key suppliers or customers more quickly.

3.3.2 Adding value at the corporate level

For a corporation to be viable, it has to add enough value to the businesses it owns to outweigh these costs. Corporations do this in two main ways: through developing synergies between their different businesses, and by adding value themselves through their corporate activities.

Both of these things are quite difficult to achieve in practice, however. Goold and Campbell,[4] who have written widely on these issues, make the point that managers often have a tendency to overestimate the potential for synergy between different parts of their corporations.

Concept | **Synergy**

One of the most common and simplest definitions of synergy is to say that is creates something that is greater than the sum of its parts. There is synergy between two areas of activity if putting the two together leads to their activities being carried out more efficiently than if they were kept separate.

For example, there are synergies between several of Sony's businesses. The expertise that they develop for their audio equipment is also useful for developing TV and video equipment with good sound reproduction. The innovative Trinitron technology that they developed for their consumer TV business also gave them a leading position in computer monitors and other commercial video uses.

There are also some synergies between British Airways' scheduled and charter passenger operations. They can share the same administration, maintenance and training functions, although the style and target of the marketing is likely to be different.

Identifying and realising **synergies** between their businesses is one way in which managers of parent corporations can seek to add value to their businesses. However, Goold et al. (1994) say some parents are able to add value in other ways. They can use their experience in certain types of business to help to improve the performance of the subsidiaries. They can organise corporate centers of excellence and training for particular skills that are important to the entire corporation. They can also identify new businesses that can be acquired to fit well within their existing portfolio. These kinds of skill on the part of the corporate parent are termed **parenting advantage**. When we examine a diversified corporation, two key questions to ask are whether the parent has any such advantages to offer, and whether all the subsidiaries are the right kind of business to benefit from them.

The concept of parenting advantage is examined in far more detail, with examples, in Chapter 9. ▶

Management attention is a scarce resource in most organisations. If it is dissipated between too many different businesses or too many different types of businesses, there is a risk that some of them will be neglected. They may be allowed to get away with decisions that are not in the overall interest of the corporation, or be forced into poor business decisions by corporate managers who do not have the time to gain a full understanding of their products or markets.

Thus, a corporation, in order to be successful, does not just need to consist of sound businesses, each with a competitive advantage in its own sphere of operations. It should also be formed from businesses that have something in common in terms of the knowledge and other resources they deploy. These must be effectively controlled and co-ordinated by the corporate head office,[5] in a way that makes the best use of top management attention. Organisations, like America's General Electric, which have developed routines to do this effectively, are quite rare. However, they are among the most profitable and widely admired corporations in the world.

3.3.3 Overlap between corporate- and business-level strategy

In can be very hard to distinguish between corporate- and business-level strategies (see Real-Life Application 3.3). Broadly speaking, decisions about what businesses belong in the portfolio and how they interact are **corporate-level** decisions, decisions about which customers to serve and how to serve them are **business-level** decisions. Decisions relating to the fine detail of the value chain are **functional** decisions.

REAL-LIFE APPLICATION 3.3

The overlap between corporate- and business-level strategy

General Motors, the American automobile manufacturer, has long had powerful, autonomous divisions, producing cars aimed at a particular income and age group, with separate factories and product development units. It is unclear whether these are different businesses, or different products within a single business.

Many hospitals have specialist units dealing with children and with heart disease. The patients will rarely be the same, the skills of the doctors and nursing staff very different, but they may share the same buildings, maintenance and administration staff. Is this a single business or a corporation?

Most theorists classify the management of alliances as a corporate activity. But Benetton's alliances with the suppliers and independent retailers of its clothing business are absolutely intrinsc to the competitive strategy of that business. Its other businesses, such as sports goods, are run on more traditional lines.

However, that allows quite a lot of scope for ambiguity. LVMH is a French corporation that owns a portfolio of companies making up-market brands of luggage, clothing and drinks. It would be most unlikely to permit any of its subsidiaries to move into mass market products, or take a prominent brand down-market. In LVMH's case, decisions about brand positioning, which for most firms would be business or even functional decisions, become corporate decisions. Some corporations try hard to build a common architecture across all their businesses – for them, the design of control systems and the management of the development of key managers is a corporate activity. Other organisations are happy to delegate such decisions to business level.

New forms of organising, with key activities being outsourced to members of a network of firms, also make it difficult to classify activities and decisions between corporate and business level (see the Benetton example in Real-Life Application 3.3).

Since it is not always clear at which point a growing organisation turns into a corporation, the questions about synergy and parenting advantage can be usefully asked about any organisation that has moved from selling a single product in a single market to a more diversified set of activities.

3.4 The management of uncertainty and paradox

Practising managers face many sources of uncertainty in their strategic decisions. They are trying to make decisions that enable their organisations to cope with an uncertain environment and the unpredictable reactions of human beings inside their organisation. And they have to face the near certainty that they will be wrong, at least some of the time. Successful organisations therefore need some way of addressing risk.

There is an important difference between *managing* risk and *avoiding* it. In the 1960s, several firms developed corporate-level strategies that were aimed at diversifying away their risk. They deliberately bought businesses that they thought would generate high profits in economic circumstances that would reduce returns from their core businesses. This strategy was intended to let the corporation generate stable, high returns from its portfolio.

These risk-avoidance strategies were rarely successful. They were based on earlier strategic theories that tended to overestimate the ability of managers to add value to unrelated businesses, and underestimate the costs of diversification discussed in Section 3.3.1. These strategies also overlooked the economic relationship between risk and reward – by diminishing their exposure to risk, these firms also reduced the probability of their making exceptionally high returns.

Risk management strategies, by contrast, involve acquiring a detailed knowledge of the risks involved in a narrow range of businesses. Managers then try to ensure that the firm has sufficient cash and other resources to remain viable when the environment is unfavourable, and can make exceptional profits in favourable circumstances (see Real-Life Application 3.4).

One factor that distinguishes successful risk management from risk avoidance is making the right strategic commitments.

REAL-LIFE APPLICATION 3.4

Diversification and risk management

RTZ has long been one of the world leaders in the mining and refining of metals such as zinc and copper. The demand for and prices of these commodities are very cyclical, however, and RTZ looked for a way to protect itself against periodic dips in its profits.

During the 1970s, RTZ diversified into a number of areas. Some, like coal-mining, appeared at first to be related to its core business. However, they proved on closer acquaintance to require rather different types of expertise in exploration and extraction, and RTZ's attempts to find synergies proved unsuccessful. Other diversifications were undertaken purely to diminish risk.

The result of this strategy was a fall in RTZ's profitability. During the late 1980s and early 1990s, RTZ sold off all its non-core businesses and focused on becoming a low-cost producer that would be profitable even when metal prices fell. It also built sufficient reserves of cash to enable it to survive a severe economic downturn.

RTZ has diversified its risk to some extent by having a broad product portfolio, since different metals and minerals have different demand cycles. It also spreads the risk of economic and political problems by operating in 35 countries. However, it has managed its risk by keeping to businesses that it understands. Between 1985 and 1994 its market capitalisation increased more than fivefold, even though conditions in many key markets were unfavourable.

Source: 'The Pit and the Pendulum', *Management Today*, October 1994, pp. 45–8.

3.4.1 Commitment, trade-offs and paradox

Pankaj Ghemawat (1991) points out the ways in which strategic decisions involve commitment:

- They 'lock in' resources so that they cannot easily be redeployed. For example, when firms decide to launch a new generation of products or introduce new technologies, they will commit cash, expertise and management time. They may need to build new, specialised research and production facilities. If the original product or technology concept is wrong, then this time and money is likely to have been wasted (although there may occasionally be profitable spin-offs from the research activity) and another firm will take the market. This kind of commitment can be seen in its most extreme form in firms like Intel, the microprocessor manufacturer, or Boeing, the aircraft maker. In both cases, the investment required for a new generation of products is so large that a product failure might bankrupt the firm – yet, if they do not make the investment, rivals will emerge to threaten their position.

- They 'lock out' alternative opportunities. A decision *not* to do something – to pull back from an investment, or to exit from an industry – is as strategic as a decision to go ahead. For example, automobile firms that had not entered the Chinese market by 1997 knew that they would not be able to do so for the foreseeable future. The Chinese government had already announced that no new entrants would be permitted after that time, and the Chinese culture tends to favour people and organisations that are prepared to build relationships over a long period. Although China represents a vast potential market for cars, firms are finding it difficult to operate there at present. It is quite possible that a decision to stay out of the market there is correct – but it is certain that it is irrevocable.

- They commit resources to changing the organisation. This may involve cash spent on training and consultancy, management time spent developing and implementing change programmes and staking the organisation's reputation with customers and employees on getting the change right. If the change fails, the cash and time will have been wasted and the firm's reputation damaged.

Here with see a paradox. On the one hand flexibility – the avoidance of **premature** commitments – can be valuable in reducing risk, and authors such as Hamel and Prahalad (1994) advocate a phased approach to investment in key capabilities and technologies. On the other hand, some form of commitment is essential to a viable strategy. There are three main reasons for this:

1. Without commitment of time, cash or other resources, it is impossible for an organisation to do anything that cannot easily and quickly be copied by a competitor. As we saw in Chapter 1, strategies that are simple to copy afford no prospect of lasting advantage.

2. Commitment sends important messages to stakeholders. It tells customers, employees and host governments that the organisation is committed to a long-term presence. It tells competitors that the firm will not easily be brushed aside, or that it is intent upon taking a major slice of a market. Game theory simulations show that sometimes, by signalling intent in this way, a firm persuades less committed competitors to withdraw from a sector.

3. Many theorists, most notably Michael Porter (1996), believe that in order to arrive at a sustainable competitive position an organisation has to make *trade-offs*. It must decide which users it wishes to focus its efforts upon, and set up all its systems and processes and its structure to deliver the services that those users desire, in the way that they want to receive it. The organisation may have to decide that it cannot serve users whose needs are different from those of its core customers, or that it will only take them on its own terms – at a premium price, or by making them wait longer for service than the primary clients. This tailoring of organisational resources and value chains is a form of commitment (see Real-Life Application 3.5). Sometimes it may be possible for a firm to straddle a number of customer groups, using the same resources to serve them all. But it must be very careful, in trying to satisfy everyone, that it does not end up diluting its service to its core customers and satisfying no one.

REAL-LIFE APPLICATION 3.5

Trade-offs and commitment

(1) Southwest Airways vs Continental Airlines

Southwest Airways is a cut-price air carrier that operates profitably in the United States. It has carefully kept its costs down. It sells only direct, rather than through travel agents. It has developed routines to refuel and reload aircraft very quickly after they land, so that they can make more trips per day than competitors' planes. It does not accept transfers from other airlines' services.

Continental, a full-service airline, decided that it would compete with Southwest in the cut-price segment. It launched a new service, Continental Lite, that used its existing fleet and facilities. But it faced problems reconciling the two services. In order to make money on the lower fares, it could not afford to pay travel agents the commission they were used to on full-priced tickets. So it cut commissions on *all* its tickets, full- and cut-price, alienating the agents. It accepted transfers from its own and other airlines' services – but the baggage from these transfers slowed down the loading of Continental Lite planes, resulting in delays and customer complaints. Continental tried to do two things at once, and in the end did neither of them well. It lost hundreds of millions of dollars as a result, and had to withdraw from the cut-price business.

Source: Porter (1996).

(2) Amazon.com vs Barnes and Noble

Amazon.com is a bookseller that operates through the Internet. It is located near one of the USA's largest wholesalers of books, and so can offer a massive selection of titles, four or five times larger than can be accommodated on the shelves of the largest bookshop. Because it does not need to maintain expensive premises, it can offer lower prices than most booksellers – it sells its books at 30% below list price. However, because it has no physical outlets, it must deliver its books by post or courier. People who shop at Amazon.com must be prepared to wait a few days for delivery, and to pay a delivery charge that on small orders is greater than the price discount. Amazon.com is not interested in small orders of best-selling books – it knows that most people can get them cheaply and reliably from a bookstore or a large supermarket. It serves people who want less common titles and can be more certain of getting what they want from Amazon than from a normal bookstore, or people who are willing to buy several books at once and derive full benefit from the discounted prices. As long as there are enough people who want books on these terms, Amazon should be commercially viable, though at the time of writing it had never made a profit.

Barnes and Noble is one of the largest chains of retail booksellers in the USA. It has led a change in the industry towards larger bookstores where people can browse in comfort over a cup of good coffee. It also has a website through which people can buy books, and is collaborating with the German multimedia group, Bertelsmann, to develop this part of its business. It has yet to be demonstrated whether it can successfully straddle the two types of bookselling. There is a danger that the demands of serving Internet customers will mean that deliveries to the bookstores become less frequent or reliable.

3.4.2 Common paradoxes and trade-offs

A number of tricky questions arise from the preceding sections. At what stage does prudent diversification of products and customers turn into dangerous diversification into unrelated businesses? How can one tell whether a commitment is premature? How does one know when it is right to straddle?

The best answer that strategy theory is able to give is 'it all depends'. For different firms in different industries, the amount of diversification and the degree of commitment that is manageable and appropriate will differ. There are no 'right answers' to strategic questions. This means that there is always scope to be creative and develop new strategies, subtly different from those already tried in an industry. Unfortunately, it also means that manager will sometimes take plausible decisions that turn out badly.

So far we have encountered two sets of trade-offs and their associated paradoxes: between diversification and focus, and between flexibility and commitment. We shall encounter more of these as we examine different types of strategic decision; the most common ones are summarised in Table 3.1.

3.4.3 Is it possible to circumvent paradox and trade-offs?

Not all theorists accept Porter's ideas about trade-offs,[6] and even where they do exist, advances in technology and theory may enable organisations to find ways around them.

Total quality is reviewed in Chapter 14. ▶

For example, for at least fifty years people believed that there was a trade-off between production costs and number of defects. Improvements in product quality were thought to require more elaborate and expensive production and quality control procedures. However, the total quality movement established that it was

Table 3.1   Common trade-offs and paradoxes

Trade-off	*On the one hand . . .*	*. . . but on the other hand*
Flexibility versus commitment	Premature commitment can waste resources. Prolonged commitment can lock resources into unproductive areas. Flexibility helps diminish risk	Failure to commit sufficient resources early enough may lead to markets being lost to more adventurous or committed players
Diversification versus focus	Too much reliance on one set of customers and markets can render an organisation vulnerable to their whims	Too wide a spread can leave each constituent business vulnerable to more focused competitors
Control versus empowerment	Rigid controls can lead to slow, expensive decision-making. Empowerment can improve innovation and customer responsiveness	Lax controls can lead to agency problems or to maverick entrepreneurial behaviour that undermines corporate image
Globalisation versus local responsiveness	Unified global products, brands and management can generate economies of scale and learning	Products designed to be acceptable in every country may end up being second best everywhere. Global managers may overlook the needs of local employees and customers

often possible to have both highly reliable production processes and low production costs. The savings from not having to find and rectify faulty output more than paid for any extra costs associated with the newer manufacturing procedures.

Transnational strategies are discussed in Chapter 6. ▶

Some people now believe that the trade-off described in Table 3.1 between global operations and local cultural sensitivity is similarly a false one – that it is possible for 'transnational' corporations to get the best of both worlds (Ghoshal and Bartlett, 1987).

3.5 How strategies can go wrong

Almost all of the previous discussion in this chapter has considered strategic processes that are intended to be beneficial for the organisation. Unfortunately, they do not always end up that way in practice. In this section we consider how strategies can go wrong. We show how good intentions can lead to competitive *disadvantage*, and how strategies which once were a source of considerable strength to a firm can lead to its decline and even death. In order to look at these issues we will have to return briefly to looking at why and how strategies come about.

Remember the organisation can be considered to be the outcome of previous strategies that have been selected for their success. Future strategies are selected at least in part because of:

- the organisation's culture, which has developed over time and become relatively homogeneous;
- the organisation's considerable investment of time and resources in learning how to do some things very well;
- the organisation's information and gathering systems, which are focused on specific, currently important, environmental features;
- the organisation's existing powerholders, who are unlikely to be willing to cede their decision-making rights to others.

◀ These psychological blocks are discussed in Section 1.2.3.

There are also a number of psychological and sociological influences that are likely to be important. We expect the future to resemble the past; we like to be successful and therefore tend to want to repeat previous successes; and we are often reluctant to change. Organisations are also unwieldy beasts, which cannot change direction fast, even if they want to. The interplay between these various factors means that organisations' strategies sometimes become inappropriate to their environment. We will now look at some of the ways that this can happen.

3.5.1 Strategic drift and punctuated equilibrium

Gerry Johnson (1987) described a process in which a company's strategies become increasingly distanced from the needs of its customers or the environment in which it operates. He called this process **strategic drift** (Figure 3.3).

◀ The concept of paradigm is defined in Section 1.2.5.

Strategic drift happens gradually as the strength of the organisation's sense of what it is about – its paradigm – and the homogeneity of employees' values and beliefs, shuts out 'deviant' strategies, which are rejected as being not what the organisation 'does'. These deviant strategies, however, may be those which would allow the organisation to adjust to its customers' changing needs or seek out new

Figure 3.3 **Strategic drift** (adapted from Johnson and Scholes, 1999: 82)

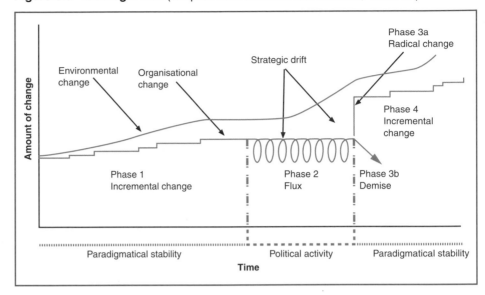

customers. Strategic drift also happens because managers think they are managing change, in line with what they perceive to be changes in their environment. However, what they are actually doing is measuring changes against their own expectations of what change should be – which is not the same thing! Another explanation is that existing powerholders within the organisation are likely to reject strategic suggestions which are outside what they already do – because by its very novelty something different may undermine their own power positions. We return to this issue in Chapter 13.

Some changes may be implemented and improve performance to some extent, thus deluding the company's managers that they are managing change effectively. Over time, however, the firm's financial performance becomes increasingly weak and it becomes apparent that something radical needs to be done. Sometimes the necessary change is achieved through the takeover of the firm, or it may require a new executive to be brought in from outside to 'turn the company around'. Occasionally existing managers can themselves bring about this change, as they realise the seriousness of their position. However, because their beliefs will be strongly shaped by the organisation's paradigm, which is, after all, one of the reasons why the company found itself in its predicament in the first place, this can be quite hard to achieve.

Johnson's theory implies that organisations will experience periods of relative organisational stability interspersed with periods of significant change, a state of affairs known as **punctuated equilibrium**. Research by Romanelli and Tushman[7] suggests that this is quite common in many organisations, perhaps implying that this strategic drift is not only common but almost inevitable, as Johnson (1984) himself claims.

Punctuated equilibrium is a term which comes from chaos theory which we return to in Section 3.6.2. ▶

However, Brown and Eisenhardt (1997) have found a different mode of evolution in certain high technology industries, although their work has yet to be replicated in other settings. They suggest that organisations proceed in what they describe as a process of time-paced evolution, a form of continuous product and organisational development which is nevertheless too radical to be considered incremental.

3.5.2 The Icarus paradox

Another distinguished academic, who has written on the inevitability of strategic decline over time and the increasing inappropriateness of strategic decisions, is Danny Miller. He suggests that the seeds of decline are actually sown in the very success of past strategies. These successes have the potential to lead to a lack of diversity in an organisation's skills base and organisation structures or belief systems, which can lead to failure. Danny Miller calls this decline the Icarus paradox[8] in acknowledgment of the Greek myth which tells of Icarus, the son of Daedalus, who built wings of wax and feathers in order to fly to the sun. Because his wings were so successful he was able to fly *too* close to the sun. As a result, the wax melted and he fell to earth. The parable is clear; organisations which are successful can fall from grace, seduced into excess by their very strengths.

This process happens as an extension of strategic drift. Success appears able to add a layer of complacency or arrogance to the desire to repeat what has worked well in the past. Thus the normal processes of rejection of deviant strategies which come about through selective information-gathering and processing systems or through the dominance of the paradigm, is strengthened and even appears to gather momentum, so even sensible suggestions which point out external threats are rejected. Perhaps the most often-cited example of this problem is IBM. In the early 1970s, IBM was hugely successful; it dominated the world-wide mainframe computer market, and had developed a very strong culture – such that the 'Big Blue' style was famous even outside the company. Many of the most senior managers came from within the mainframe division, and the resources and structure were focused on this division. As a result, the threat from the embryonic personal computer was at best ignored and at worst dismissed as a complete no-hoper. Of course we now know what happened; almost everyone has a PC on their desk, and IBM had to weather two years of heavy losses in the early nineties before discovering an appropriate response.

However, not all strategic mistakes are due to poor decision-making, and in the following Advanced Topic we consider some of the sheer cussedness and unpredictability of organisations and their environment – factors which can also cause huge strategic problems for managers.

3.6 ADVANCED TOPIC
Ambiguity, unpredictability and complexity

The previous sections have highlighted some important limitations that affect strategic decision-making in any organisation. The outcome of a decision will be determined, to some extent at least, by the organisation's environment and the cultural and political processes inside it. The information available to managers about what is going on inside and outside their organisation is usually incomplete, inaccurate or out-of-date. Managers are fallible human beings who will not often have sufficient time or resources to make the best use of the information they have, or to understand its limitations. As you have seen they use **heuristics**; short-cuts based upon their own past experience, or industry 'rules of thumb' to make decisions (see Real-Life Application 3.6). But these heuristics are not always appropriate in a different situation.

REAL-LIFE APPLICATION 3.6

Rules of thumb

Context	Rule of thumb	Basis
Share trading	'Always leave some profit for the next man'	It can be very difficult to calculate precisely when a share price has reached its peak. Traders are often well advised to lock in a good profit on a share whose price has risen. If they hold on in the hope that the price will rise further, it may fall instead
US television	'No one ever went bust by underestimating the intelligence of the audience'	It is more difficult to get large audiences for intellectual programmes than for undemanding quiz shows or thrillers.

Remember that strategies are *path dependent* (see Chapter 1, Section 1.4): their results may vary according to the time and place in which they are executed. It is difficult for people to be *sure* that rules and actions that have worked for them before will work again in the same way. Quite small changes in the environment, or differences between one organisation and another, may mean that rules and policies that have worked well in one context are inappropriate in a different time and place.

The outcomes of strategic decisions are therefore not totally predictable. Sometimes strategies will work as planned, sometimes they will yield results that are quite close to what the strategist hoped for, and sometimes the results will be precisely the opposite (Real-Life Application 3.7).

REAL-LIFE APPLICATION 3.7

Ambiguity and paradox in association football

Tottenham Hotspur (popularly known as 'the Spurs') is a north London Association Football (soccer) club with a proud history. In the 1960s and 1970s it had won numerous trophies and had been the first English club to win a major European competition. It also had a tradition of producing teams that played flowing, attractive attacking football.

However, by 1996 the club and its supporters were hungry for success. In five years it had not won a major trophy and had rarely risen above the middle places in the English championship (the Premiership). This meant that the club had not qualified to compete in European competitions, which were both prestigious and lucrative.

The club was quoted on the London Stock Exchange, but effectively controlled by Alan Sugar, who had invested in the club part of the wealth he had earned from Amstrad, his consumer electronics firm.

Spurs had made an indifferent start to the 1996–97 season, and early in 1997 they recruited Christian Gross to take charge of the team. Gross had enjoyed considerable success in his native Switzerland, and was one of several managers from continental Europe to take charge of English football clubs that year. His arrival was generally welcomed as part of a trend to rejuvenate English football with ideas from their continental rivals.

Gross put in place a number of changes, including new training programmes designed to improve the fitness of his players. However, Tottenham's results

Real-Life Application continued

failed to improve, partly because many of their best players, far from getting fitter, developed serious injuries.

Tottenham narrowly avoided a humiliating (and financially disastrous) relegation from the Premiership by recruiting veteran stars on short-term contracts to fortify the team at the end of the season. The frustration caused by the team's problems was intensified by the success of Arsenal, their near neighbours and historical rivals. Arsenal, managed by a Frenchman, Arsene Wenger, whose policies were superficially quite similar to Gross's, won both the Premiership and the FA Cup that year, a rare and prestigious 'double' that Spurs had last achieved more than thirty years previously.

When Tottenham, with their first-choice players fit once more, began the season with a run of poor results, Gross was replaced at short notice. The appointment of his successor, George Graham, was greeted with surprise by the team's supporters and many observers. Firstly, he had gained his fame, both as player and manager, with hated rivals Arsenal. Secondly, his reputation was for producing teams that played dour defensive football, a world away from the Spurs' swashbuckling traditions. Several commentators doubted whether he could last long at the club.

However, under Graham's leadership, the team's results quickly improved, while the quality of their attacking football seemed, unexpectedly and paradoxically, to be sharpened by his arrival.

It was far from predictable that a Swiss, Gross, would

find it more difficult to prosper in the English system than a Frenchman, Wenger. It was not at all clear that Graham would find success given the apparent conflict between his own and Spurs' preferred style of play. Yet that is what appears to have happened. Spurs' performance has improved significantly. They finished the 1998–99 season half way up the league, a considerable improvement on their position in recent years, and won a coveted place in one of the European club competitions.

It is also difficult to pin down a single, unambiguous set of explanations for the outcomes. Was Gross's failure due to his own personal inability to communicate effectively with his players? Or were the players themselves too egocentric? Did Gross lack the network of contacts that enabled Wenger to identify and recruit promising young French players to Arsenal? All of these have been advanced as possible explanations.

And why did Graham apparently succeed where Gross had failed, and in such an unexpected fashion? Perhaps he was forced to focus on Spurs' assets in attack, because of Sugar's policies and a world-wide shortage of quality players to bolster his defence. Perhaps he, as a straightforward Scot, was better able than Gross to communicate his ideas. But only one-half of his players were British. Would Graham have been so readily accepted by a club whose culture was so different from his own if he had not been preceded by the unpopular Gross?

Chapter 16 is a more detailed review of the positions of different schools of strategic thinking. ▶

There is no consensus among strategic management theorists as to why this should be. Some might argue that this shows the need for better information and more precise planning processes, others see it as evidence that organisations are at the mercy of environmental forces they cannot predict or control. Others still would attribute the unpredictability to the interplay of complex human processes – social, cultural and political.

3.6.1 Systems thinking and systems dynamics

An increasingly influential school of thought, in particular Senge (1990), emphasises the importance of understanding organisations and their environments as parts of a system in which every action by one actor has repercussions right through the system. This view has been shaped in part by the work of *systems dynamics* theorists, notably Jay Forrester of the Massachusetts Institute of Technology. These researchers point out that the many strategic decisions are affected by:

● feedback loops between the different elements;

- lags between taking a decision and its having an effect, and between the effect taking place and the information reaching the decision-maker; for example, most reporting systems collect their data every month or three months, and take 1–2 weeks to process the data into management reports.

Systems dynamics theorists have developed methods of modelling systems with these time lags and feedback loops. These systems tend to be *non-linear*: sometimes a large change in a policy variable such as prices or salary rates may produce very little change in profits or employee behaviour; at other times a small variation in a variable may make a large difference to the outcomes. They may also show unexpected or *paradoxical* behaviour (see Real-Life Application 3.8), where an intervention has the opposite effect to that which the instigator desired and expected.

REAL-LIFE APPLICATION 3.8

Feedback loops and information lags

A bonus scheme is introduced to motivate staff

Possibility 1: The desired 'virtuous circle' (a positive feedback loop)

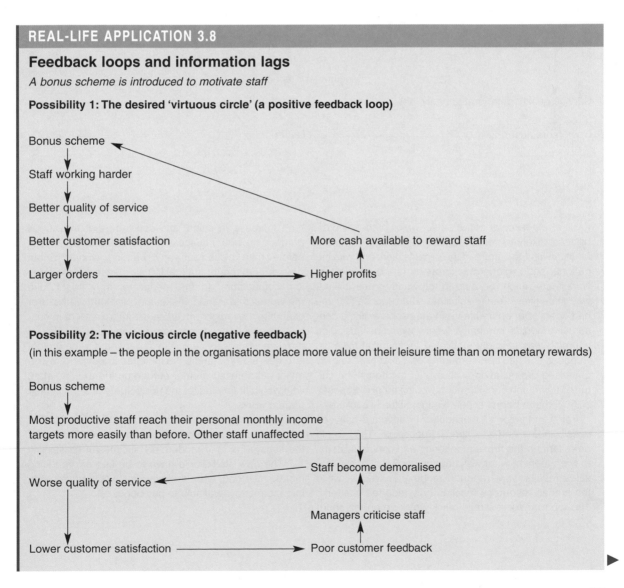

Possibility 2: The vicious circle (negative feedback)
(in this example – the people in the organisations place more value on their leisure time than on monetary rewards)

Real-Life Application continued

Possibility 3: The scheme is too successful

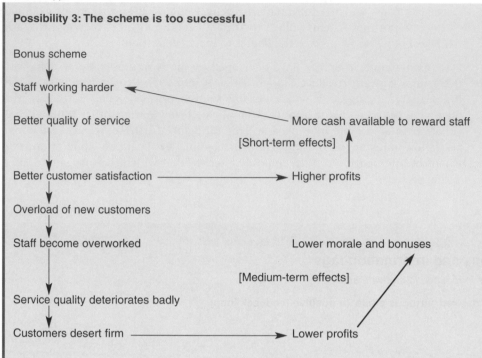

It will rarely be clear at the outset which of these possibilities is likely to occur in practice. Managers who are familiar with the culture of the organisation, and with the national and regional backgrounds of the people that work there, might be able to tell whether possibility 2 was more likely than possibility 1. But suppose that you had spent your entire life in an atmosphere, like a consumer products company, where everyone (including yourself) was strongly motivated by financial rewards. Suppose you had been brought into a charity or a newly privatised organisation, with a brief to change the culture. How much consideration would you give to possibility 2, that a bonus scheme might actually backfire?

For a manager to distinguish in advance between possibilities 1 and 3 is almost impossible. They would be reliant on the firm's monitoring and control systems to warn them of what was happening. But suppose that sales results were reported monthly or weekly, while the human resources function only reported quarterly. The top managers would quickly pick up on the short-

term increase in sales, and conclude that the bonus programme was a success. It would be several weeks before they picked up any warning signals about greater numbers of staff taking sick leave or leaving to join competitors. In the meantime, they might take measures that would make the problem worse. For example, they might advertise the improvement in customer service, exposing more customers to the firm at the time when service quality collapsed. Or they might hire new staff to handle the increase in demand, which might put an even greater burden on the existing staff, who would fit training for the newcomers alongside their normal work.

A manager might think ahead and hire new staff in anticipation of the increase in demand. But what then if the scheme is only moderately successful (possibility 1)? The new staff would have to be laid off, reducing morale all round, while their salaries would have eaten into the money available to pay bonuses!

3.6.2 Chaos and complexity theory

Another explanation of the unpredictability of strategic outcomes is found in **complexity theory**. Complexity theory and its close cousin, **chaos theory**, are both based around the study of systems found in the natural world: weather systems, flocks of birds, biological organisms and chemical reactions. All of these natural systems exhibit the properties of path dependence and non-linearity that some scholars have observed in organisations. Certain theorists have therefore investigated whether organisations themselves behave as *complex systems* – a term here used in the very special sense of systems that behave in the way explained by the mathematics of complexity theory.

An intriguing aspect of complex systems in the physical sciences and mathematics is that, although they behave in complicated and unpredictable ways, they can be modelled by a few, quite simple underlying equations. Depending upon the starting values of the parameters driving these equations, the systems may, over time, end up in one of a variety of states. Sometimes they will converge rapidly to a set of end values and stay there, or oscillate between a few, fixed end states. Sometimes they will exhibit completely unstable behaviour, moving between wildly different states without any pattern or any sign of equilibrium. This type of behaviour is technically known as *chaos*.

Another type of pattern observed in complex systems is *punctuated equilibrium*. Sometimes systems will appear to settle down close to an end value, for a certain period of time. They will then veer off into what looks like chaotic behaviour before settling down again close to another equilibrium. The end values which are the focal points of these phases of equilibrium are called *strange attractors*. Behaviour shown by systems in this state is known as **edge of chaos**, because the system is constantly on the verge of becoming chaotic, but spends most of the time in a more stable state. When moving from a state of chaos to a state of equilibrium, edge of chaos systems seem to be *self-organising*, a property sometimes known as 'autopoesis'.

In experiments with networks of electric circuits, the kind of complex behaviour shown by a system turned out to be related to the number and density of the interconnections within the network. If there were few connections, the system ended up in a state of chaos. If there were very many connections, the system quickly ended up in a static state. With the right number of interconnections, the system would end up on the edge of chaos. The parallels with organisations are quite appealing: the chaotic network corresponds to an organisation without proper controls, which dissolves into anarchy, while the static system has similarities with a stiff bureaucracy whose unbending controls render it incapable of change. The idea of an organisation on the edge of chaos, and so capable of reinventing itself spontaneously at irregular intervals, has proved to be a seductive metaphor for some writers (e.g. Lissack, 1997).

Only a few writers have gone beyond using complexity as a metaphor, to claim that organisations actually *are*, and behave *as*, complex systems. One who does – Ralph Stacey (1992, 1995) – believes that organisations and their environments are essentially chaotic, so that the outcomes of any long-term decision are completely unpredictable. He believes that managers should focus their attention on developing excellent information and control systems to assist their short-term decision-making, and on developing self-organising cultures.

However, there are reasons to be cautious in adopting this approach. Firstly, just because a system shows some of the traits associated with a complex system does not prove that it is one. Authors such as Nelson and Winter (1982) have been able to justify the existence of path dependence without invoking complexity theory. Secondly, organisations are composed of human beings, capable of adapting to their environment, rather than the inanimate particles in a chemical reaction or an electronic circuit. Some interesting simulations at Aston University have gone some way towards demonstrating that, by building into a complex system a human's ability to learn, the extent of any chaotic behaviour is dramatically reduced (Whitby et al., 1998).

3.7 Summary: a framework for strategic analysis

In this chapter we have looked at how to analyse an organisation's present competitive situation – how it was arrived at and how sustainable it might be. The aim of this book is to equip you with the ability to turn your analysis of the past and the present into sensible proposals for an organisation's future. The framework mapped out in Figure 3.4, a modified version of the schema set out in the Introduction to this book, shows one possible approach to this task. Figure 3.4 is set out in the form of a matrix containing a series of questions. If you start at the top left-hand corner of the matrix and work systematically down each column in turn, answering each set of questions as they arise, you should end up with a comprehensive analysis of a strategic situation. The chapter references in that matrix indicate where the theory needed to answer each question can be found.

It is a common mistake by students to overlook the ways in which the passage of time can invalidate an established strategic position. This is why our framework, like the earlier sections in this chapter, clearly distinguishes between the analysis that is needed to understand an organisation's past success or failure, and the analysis that is needed to assess what changes are necessary or desirable for the future.

The starting point for your analysis should always be an organisation's results. You should judge its strategies by the actions it has taken and the outcomes it has obtained, not by its declared intentions. You need to understand how well the organisation has performed in the past, and whether the trend in its current performance is upwards or downwards. However, you should bear in mind that improvement is not the same as strength, and so should seek to make comparisons with other firms in the industry wherever possible. You may want to look out for evidence of strategic drift.

Once you have assessed how well or poorly the organisation is performing, you can then start to establish the reasons for this, using any clues from your analysis of the results. Firstly, you should look at the organisation's environment in the past, and how this helped or inhibited the organisation's development.

Next, you should analyse how the organisation built its advantage in the past. At business level, this means examining its choice of competitive arena and its development of an infrastructure – its architecture and value chain – and a set of strategic resources, competences and strategic assets. For diversified organisations, you are interested in whether there is synergy between the different businesses, and whether the corporation is an appropriate parent for all the businesses

Figure 3.4   A schema for strategic analysis

	Past	Present		Future
Actual and intended results	Against which criteria are results to be judged? How well did the organisation perform in the past? How well is the organisation performing *now*? (Chapter 4)			What level of present and future performance is/will be needed to satisfy key stakeholders? (Chapter 14)
Environment	What were the main features of the environment in the past? How did the environment affect the organisation's early success or failure? (Chapter 5)	How is the present environment different from the past? How will the changes in the environment affect the way that firms compete in the industry? What is the *minimum* that firms will need to achieve to *survive* after these changes? What further things will they need to do in order to be among the *most successful* competitors? (Chapters 5 and 11)	What are the main trends in the environment?	
Competitive stance (business and corporate level)	Which arenas has the firm chosen to compete in, and why? How appropriate were these choices? (Chapters 6 and 9)			Is present competitive advantage *sustainable*? What strategic changes are *needed* for survival? What further changes are *desirable* for success? (Chapter 11) What strategies are available to: • enhance the organisation's existing position? • overhaul existing competitors? • exploit new opportunities? (Chapter 11) What is the most appropriate set of strategies to take the organisation forward? (Chapters 11 and 12) What kinds of systems and structures would be appropriate in the changed strategic circumstances? (Chapters 10 and 12)
Resources and internal configuration	How has the organisation been able to compete successfully in these arenas? What strategic resources has it developed? What value chain has been constructed to deploy these resources? (Chapters 7 and 8)			
Architecture	What are the features of the organisation's culture, structure, information and reward systems that underlie its competences and value chain? (Chapters 8 and 10) How has the organisation been able to organise itself to manage diversity? What parenting skills has the organisation been able to develop? How well has it been able to use them? (Chapters 9 and 10)			
				How can the organisation develop internally or through mergers or alliances? (Chapter 15)
Learning, change and execution	Does the organisation have a track record of learning and change? (Chapter 7)			Are people in the organisation open to change? What obstacles exist? (Chapters 13) How can the needed change be achieved? (Chapter 14)

in its portfolio. You should also see whether the organisation has given any indication in the past of a capacity to learn, innovate and change, or whether, on the other hand, the overconfidence and bounded thinking that characterises the Icarus paradox appears to have taken hold.

Then you should look at how the environment has been changing, and is likely to change in the future. This gives some indications of how strongly the organisation's current strategies will be challenged. You can then assess whether the organisation has the capacity to sustain its competitive advantage, and whether it is likely to be able to adapt its strategies to renew its advantage in the future.

You then move on to considering what strategies the organisation might adopt to meet the challenges of the future, considering the alternatives that it has at its disposal and deciding which best meets its needs. In doing this, you take account of what is necessary in order to survive in the changed environment, of the resources the organisation has, of the demands of its key stakeholders and of the extent to which there is likely to be resistance to change from within the organisation.

Finally, you should consider ways in which particular changes can be implemented, and obstacles to change can be surmounted.

Throughout this process, you need to bear in mind that there are no right answers in strategic analysis. Strategic situations and strategic decisions involve uncertainty, paradox and trade-offs. Resources need to be committed in order to gain competitive advantage, but you will never be *sure* that the organisation could not have derived greater benefit by committing them somewhere else. Nor will anyone else!

3.8 Postscript: SWOT analysis

You are quite likely to have encountered the SWOT framework (Figure 3.5, sometimes known as the TOWS matrix) in your earlier studies, and may be used to using it as a starting point for appraising an organisation's position. It is worth spending a little time on understanding how it fits in with the analysis we are recommending.

SWOT analysis involves identifying:

- the things an organisation does particularly well (strengths) or badly (weaknesses) *at present*;

- the factors that *in future* may give the organisation potential to grow and increase its profits (opportunities) or may make its position weaker (threats). Opportunities and threats normally arise from changes in the environment, but sometimes have their origins inside the organisation – for example, if key machinery or people, functioning very effectively at present, are likely to break down or retire in a few years' time, that is a threat.

SWOT has a long history as a tool of strategic and marketing analysis. Its advocates say that it can be used to gauge the degree of 'fit' between the organisation's strategies and its environment, and to suggest ways in which the organisation can profit from strengths and opportunities and shield itself against weaknesses and threats. However it has come under criticism recently. Because it is so simple, both students and practising managers have a tendency to use it without a great deal of

Figure 3.5   SWOT analysis

Type of Factor	Internal *(usually static)*	External *(usually dynamic)*
Positive	Strength	Opportunity
Negative	Weakness	Threat

thought, so that the results are often useless.[9] Another problem is that SWOT, having been conceived in simpler times, does not cope very well with some of the subtler aspects of modern strategic theory, such as trade-offs (Real-Life Application 3.9).

Because SWOT is such a familiar and comforting tool, many students use it at the start of their analysis. **This is a mistake**. In order to arrive at a proper SWOT appraisal, other analyses need to be carried out first.

- Since opportunities and threats mostly arise from the environment, SWOT analysis needs to take account of the results of a full environmental analysis (Chapter 5).

- It is impossible to gauge what an organisation's real strengths are until you have assessed its strategic resources (Chapter 7) – in fact, strategic resources and strength are the same thing. There is a tendency for students to put down anything vaguely favourable that they can think of about a company as a strength. This temptation needs to be resisted – a strength is not a strength unless it makes a genuine difference to an organisation's competitiveness. The same is true of weaknesses.

We believe that SWOT analysis has been superseded by newer techniques. However, if you want to continue with it, we suggest you read Appendix 3.1 for guidelines on using it properly!

REAL-LIFE APPLICATION 3.9

Trade-offs and SWOT

Look again at Southwest Airlines and Amazon.com, the companies in Real-Life Application 3.5. Both have important groups of potential customers to whom they offer poor service. Southwest ignores business passengers, and will not accept transfers from other airlines. Amazon makes people wait days to receive books that they can obtain instantly from their neighbourhood bookstore, and pay a delivery charge for the privilege. Surely, these are major weaknesses.

But think again. Southwest and Amazon have *chosen* not to give those customers priority. Serving them would divert resources from the firm's core markets, and dilute service to their main customers. Not serving them is certainly not a weakness; in a paradoxical way, it may be a strength!

Appendix 3.1: SWOT analysis

No one knows who first invented SWOT analysis. It has featured in strategy text-books since at least 1972 and can now be found in textbooks on marketing and many other business disciplines.

Even though we believe that SWOT analysis is now outdated (for reasons we discussed in Section 3.8), we are devoting a few pages to it. One reason for this is that many strategy teachers still believe that SWOT is a useful tool. Another is that students who have been taught to use SWOT at school and in the early years of their university education may be familiar with it, and want to continue with it. However, many of the SWOT analyses that we see from students are superficial and internally contradictory. If you are going to carry out a SWOT, you should try to do it properly.

It is important to bear in mind what a SWOT is for. It is intended to summarise a strategic situation, with a view to deciding what the organisation should do next. A SWOT analysis should contain sufficient information for any reader to be able to see **why** a particular issue counts as a strength, weakness, opportunity or threat, and what the **implications** are for the firm that you are analysing.

For the same reason, there is no room for equivocation in a SWOT analysis – a factor can be a strength *or* a weakness, but not both. For example, a firm's IT system may provide good management reports but poor production control information. It is pointless to put his down as *both* a strength *and* a weakness that partially cancel each other out, since managers have only two choices: either they upgrade the system or they do not. This means that you need to come to definite answer to the question: *On balance*, is the IT system a strength or a weakness? Perhaps the lack of good production information is important, in which case the system needs to be upgraded. Perhaps it is vital to maintain the flow of management information, in which case the system should not be touched.

SWOT analyses should only pick out issues that have a substantial effect on a firm's competitive situation. You should avoid the temptation to put down under 'Strengths' almost everything you can think of that is vaguely favourable to the firm, and to classify anything remotely unfavourable as a weakness. It is rare for any firm to have more than half-a-dozen genuine strengths or weaknesses. A real strength should be rare, difficult to copy and make a genuine difference to the

---

REAL-LIFE APPLICATION 3.10

A poorly conceived, superficial SWOT analysis

Strengths
Profitable company
Market leader
Serves youth segment
High level of customer awareness of brand
Décor consistent in all stores
Has recently upgraded computer systems

Opportunities
Overseas expansion
Brand extension

Weaknesses
Factories thirty years old
Ageing top management
Does not address needs of older consumers
High marketing costs
Mature market

Threats
Exchange rate fluctuations

organisation's profitability – a strategic resource. A weakness, similarly, is something that affects the organisation's cost or differentiation advantage. Old-fashioned equipment and authoritarian management styles, for example, are only weaknesses if they lead to increased costs, poor quality or bad customer service.

Lists of strengths and weaknesses should not include factors that are common to every firm in an industry. For example, you could not count 'well-known brand' as a strength for a firm in the jeans or cosmetics industries, since many brands are equally famous.

Some of these points will become clearer when we see what a *bad* SWOT looks like. Real-Life Application 3.10 shows one for a fictitious manufacturer and retailer of consumer goods. You may find it helpful to look at each point in turn, and work out what is wrong with it, before reading on.

The first thing to say about Real-Life Application 3.10 is that it is not really an analysis at all – it is just a list. *All* the points in it are too brief – we cannot see why any of them are of strategic interest, or why they count as strengths, weaknesses, opportunities or threats. Moreover, each of the individual points is flawed in some way, as the following table shows.

Point	What is wrong with it	How it might have read and why this would be an improvement
Strengths		
1. Profitable company	This is a meaningless statement. Profit is just an accountant's way of measuring success, so what this point says, in effect, is 'The company's strength is that it is successful'. This tells us nothing useful! We need to know *why* it is successful and *what* it is doing right	'Strong cashflow enabling investment in marketing and state-of-the-art logistics systems' *Cash is not an accounting convention, like profit. It represents real money that a firm can invest. The revised point shows how this investment leads to competitive advantage.*
2. Market leader	Like profit, market share is a way of measuring success – so we want to know *how* the company *became* market leader. But if market leadership *does* give the organisation an advantage, then it comes from economies of scale and bargaining power. *These* would be the strengths that we are really interested in	'High market share and global scope give strong economies of scale in purchasing raw materials. Resulting cost advantage over nearest competitor equivalent of 1% of sales' *Far more precise and more useful for developing strategic recommendations*
3. Serves youth segment	This may be a source of strength, but only if the youth segment is a desirable market to serve, and if the firm serves it better than its competitors	'Dominant (20%) share of expenditure on similar products by 15–24-year-olds – largest and most fashion-conscious segment'

Point	What is wrong with it	How it might have read and why this would be an improvement
4. High level of customer awareness of brand	This may be a genuine strength – assuming that people are aware of the brand for the right reasons!	'Strong brand within target customer group: 74% could name brand unprompted, and 80% associated it with fashion and "cool"'
		Precision is all!
5. Décor consistent in all stores	This is probably not a strength at all, since it will be equally true of most competing retailers	*No suggestions*
6. Has recently upgraded computer systems	Improvement is not the same as strength! Are the new systems any better than those of competitors? And if so, what precisely do they yield by way of cost or differentiation advantage?	'State-of-the-art ordering and logistics systems have reduced inventory to 5 days' sales, as against 10 days for nearest competitor'
Weaknesses		
7. Factories are thirty years old	Does not indicate why this is a problem. Are competitors' factories any newer? Do they need to be new?	'Proportion of defective output twice the industry average, due to obsolete machinery'
8. Ageing top management	We all get old eventually! Have the managers made any questionable decisions, or overlooked any important industry trends? If not, where is the problem?	*No suggestions. This point may be valid as a threat if there is evidence that the firm will have difficulty in replacing present generation of top managers*
9. Does not address needs of older consumers	Of course it doesn't! The firm focuses on the 15–24 age group. This point directly contradicts point 3 in the list of strengths	*No suggestions. This is an example of a deliberate strategic trade-off (see Sections 3.4.1 and 3.8)*
10. High marketing costs	Of course they are! How else did the firm get its high brand awareness (point 4)? This is another example of an internal contradiction within the SWOT. This would only be a valid weakness if you could demonstrate that other firms were getting similar brand awareness at lower cost	'Total marketing spend as proportion of sales double that of nearest competitors, but brand awareness only two percentage points higher' *And even this would only be valid if you could demonstrate that the extra brand awareness did not generate enough profit to compensate for the extra marketing expenditure*

Point	What is wrong with it	How it might have read and why this would be an improvement
11. Mature market	This is an external factor that applies equally to all firms in the market. So it is not a weakness	*Should probably be reclassified as a threat, although some firms do perfectly well in mature markets*
Opportunities 12. Overseas expansion	This point is too vague to be useful. In which parts of the world do the opportunities lie? And what makes us believe that the firm might be successful there?	'Eastern European markets, with developing spending power and a proven appetite for Western consumer brands, represent opportunity. 25% of existing sales in airport outlets are to customers travelling to these countries'
13. Brand extension	This is the kind of suggestion that could be made about any company, anywhere and at any time. What makes brand extension a particularly relevant thing for this company to consider?	'Competing firms have extended brands to cosmetics, spectacles, jeans and stationery. Likely opportunity for this firm to follow suit'
Threats 14. Exchange rate fluctuation	Any company with international operations needs to manage foreign currency exposures. They are as much a fact of life as Christmas, which nobody would rank as a threat, even though it destabilises sales and inventory levels	'Appreciation of euro versus dollar likely to lead to reduce value of US profits (25% of total)' *This is a specific threat that affects this firm because of its high proportion of US sales*

Practical dos and don'ts   **SWOT analysis**

- Make your points long enough, and include enough detail, to make it plain why a particular factor is important, and why it can be considered as a strength, weakness, opportunity or threat. Include precise evidence, and cite figures, where possible.

- Be as specific as you can about the precise nature of a firm's strength and weakness. Do not be content with general factors like economies of scale.

- Avoid vague, general opportunities and threats that could be put forward for just about any organisation under any circumstances.

- Do not mistake the outcomes of strength (such as profits and market share) for strengths in their own right.

- Improvement is not the same as strength – do not confuse the two.

- Avoid contradicting yourself in the course of the analysis, by having strengths and weaknesses that are essentially different aspects of the same strategy or resource. Come to a reasoned conclusion about whether the good points outweigh the bad ones, or vice versa.

CASE STUDY

The value of good housekeeping

Sources: *The Economist*, 3 January 1998; *Finance and Economics*, Vol. 346, Issue 8049. © *The Economist*, London 1998.

In the age of the megabank, being small can be very profitable

With America's banks showing no sign of curbing their urge to merge, it is tempting to conclude that size and success go hand in hand. Tempting but unwise, especially with people like John Forlines around. Even in Granite Falls, a town of 3,253 in the hills of western North Carolina, Mr Forlines's bank is no colossus. Three of America's biggest financial institutions, NationsBank, First Union and Wachovia, have offices in the area. Yet year after year, Bank of Granite, with only 12 branches and $550m in assets, puts its big-city brethren to shame. Since 1954, when Mr Forlines, who turns 80 next week, joined as chairman, Bank of Granite has raised its dividend payout every year. At 2.7%, its return on assets is a full percentage point over that of the average commercial bank. The shares of most of America's banks have done well in recent years, but the shares of Bank of Granite have left them in the dust (see Figure 3.6).

Figure 3.6   Granite rises

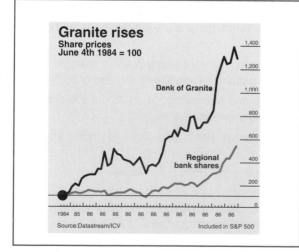

How to explain this edge? It is certainly not the result of heady expansion (the bank has never made an acquisition) or advanced computers (branch technology is basic). As Mr Forlines tells it, success comes from following the basic rules of small-town banking: keep it cheap, motivate employees, and treat customers like humans.

Cost control, it seems, comes naturally to Mr Forlines. The chairman keeps an eye even on the smallest purchases, to the point of telling a branch employee to look into repairing a tattered carpet rather than replacing it. A tight rein on hiring means that Bank of Granite has two-thirds as many employees per dollar of assets as the average small bank, with many wearing several hats. The bank did recently buy advice from consultants, but only to help cut utilities bills. The result of this parsimony is that costs consume only 32% of income, half the figure for many of America's big banks. Mr Forlines inspires loyalty as well as leanness. He likes to promote from within the 170-strong 'Granite family', so there are plenty of stories like that of Pam Harwell, who joined as a teenage book-keeper in 1971 and now runs a large branch. Another motivation is a profit-sharing scheme that pays out on leaving or retirement. Last year a sum equivalent to 15% of salaries went into the pot.

And then there is old-fashioned service. Customers are greeted by name and get an invitation to their local branch's annual Christmas buffet. They also get a say in the bank's running, thanks to regular Customer Satisfaction Days, when clipboard-wielding employees ask how service could be improved. While many banks now push customers to use cash machines or bank by phone rather than visiting the office, Granite has furnished some of its branches with sofas and armchairs for that homely feel.

Know your market

None of this would benefit the bottom line if Bank of Granite had not carved out a narrow but well-defined niche. Its depositors are mostly older folk ('the ones with all the money', says Mr Forlines). Loan customers are mostly medium-sized local businesses, which might be too small to get much attention from a bank with national aspirations. Smaller companies with fewer choices, of course, must pay a bit more for their money: Granite's average loan margin – the difference between the interest it pays depositors and the interest it collects from borrowers – is 5%, a full percentage point over the industry mean.

The bank keeps its risks under control by selling off mortgage and credit-card receivables to bigger institutions. Bad loans stand at a mere 0.3% of the total, because retrieving debts can be easier in a small town than in a big city. 'You'd be surprised what you can recover by tugging at a borrower's conscience', Mr Forlines says by way of explanation. The bank can also thank its connections and its rivals' mistakes for its success. It has set up advisory boards in the towns around Granite Falls, made up of local dignitaries who help it to find worthy borrowers. And Mr Forlines is able to poach customers from banks which have faced difficulties maintaining good service in the wake of repeated mergers.

Small need not mean backward. Earlier this year Granite set up an Internet site and bought a cheque-scanning machine to cut processing costs and help with marketing. The bank has also introduced 24-hour phone banking to lure younger customers, and has started to diversify into leasing, insurance and annuities. Fees from such businesses grew by 50% last year.

Will these initiatives ensure continued success? Banking rivals pose a threat. In the past year, two start-up banks have opened nearby, hoping to replicate Bank of Granite's success. First Union and NationsBank, both based 60 miles away in Charlotte, are also eager to expand their local market shares. These huge institutions offer a palette of products – shares, bonds, mutual funds – that are beyond Bank of Granite's reach. For now, many small-town savers still prefer to park their money in insured accounts with local banks. But as they become more aware of alternatives offering higher returns, small banks will come under pressure to give them a better deal. Still, Bank of Granite's competitors have their work cut out. Mr Forlines shows no sign of cutting back on the 60-odd hours he works each week, much of it spent zipping from branch to branch in a Buick equipped with a radar detector. When, or if, he does eventually retire, the bank will be in safe hands: those of his 62-year-old chief executive, Charles Snipes, who is said to be even more frugal than his boss. Bank of Granite is certainly no threat to America's new breed of superbanks. But it serves as a constant and irritating reminder, in the midst of the banking industry's frenzied consolidation, that mergers are no substitute for good housekeeping.

Case study questions

1. Analyse Bank of Granite's strategy in 1998.

2. To what extent can Bank of Granite be said to have a sustainable competitive advantage?

NOTES

1 This analysis derives from Porter (1985).

2. There is a subtle difference between a knowledge asset and a competence. Knowledge may exist in databases or in people's heads, without the competence to use it to add value.

3 This insight comes from Kay (1993).

4 See, for example, Goold and Campbell (1987, 1998), Goold et al. (1994).

5 For a view on the importance of head office control and co-ordination, see Collis and Montgomery (1998).

6 For a stimulating view on how conflicting strategic imperatives can be analysed and confronted, see Hampden-Turner (1990).

7 See, for example, Romanelli and Tushman (1988, 1994) or Tushman et al. (1986).

8 See Miller (1990, 1992). Other theorists with similar concepts include Peter Drucker (1994) and Ghoshal and Bartlett (1998).

9 See Hill and Westbrook (1997).

CHAPTER 4

Assessing failure and success

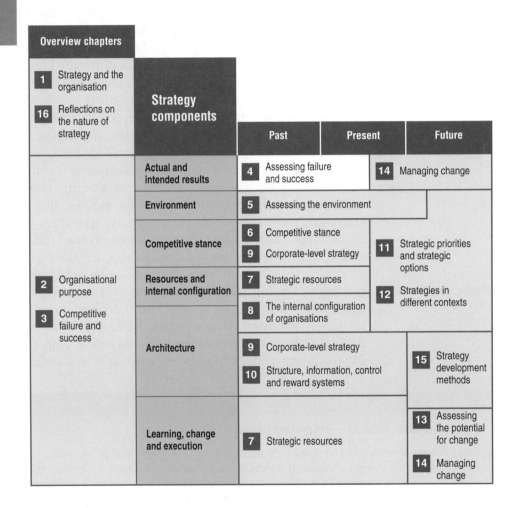

Overview chapters	Strategy components		Past	Present	Future
1 Strategy and the organisation					
16 Reflections on the nature of strategy					
2 Organisational purpose	**Actual and intended results**		**4** Assessing failure and success		**14** Managing change
3 Competitive failure and success	**Environment**		**5** Assessing the environment		
	Competitive stance		**6** Competitive stance		**11** Strategic priorities and strategic options
			9 Corporate-level strategy		
	Resources and internal configuration		**7** Strategic resources		**12** Strategies in different contexts
			8 The internal configuration of organisations		
	Architecture		**9** Corporate-level strategy		**15** Strategy development methods
			10 Structure, information, control and reward systems		
	Learning, change and execution		**7** Strategic resources		**13** Assessing the potential for change
					14 Managing change

In Chapter 2, we saw how an organisation's purpose is shaped by its mission, its leaders and its other powerful stakeholders. Chapter 3 set out the ways in which an organisation moves over time towards achieving that purpose, by choosing one or more competitive arenas, and developing a value chain, culture, architecture and set of strategic resources to compete in them. These deliberate and emergent strategic choices govern the organisation's competitive success or failure. If we are to assess the organisation's competitive position, we need to evaluate how appropriate each of these components is, and how well they fit together.

One part of this assessment will be **qualitative**. Do these strategies 'feel' right? Do they fit in with strategies that have succeeded or failed for other organisations in similar circumstances? Are they the kinds of choices that theory would recommend for this kind of industry?

However, as we have seen, strategic choices have unpredictable outcomes, and what works in one organisation may not work in another. So there is another, equally important question to answer: How well is the strategy working? The answer to this question comes from **quantitative** analysis of an organisation's financial and operational performance.

Quantitative analysis also offers the answer to another question: To what extent is the organisation achieving its purpose? This is important in two ways. Firstly, if an organisation is not achieving the aims it sets itself, then we are entitled to question the quality of its management, and its viability. But there is a subtler angle to this type of analysis. Sometimes, it is only by looking at what a company measures, and seeing what *precisely* it does well, that you can work out what its strategy really is.

Of course, many firms say what their strategy is supposed to be, and you will see these declarations – mission statements, and lists of objectives – reproduced in annual reports and case studies. But even in a successful company, these statements are not always true (Real-Life Application 4.1). Sometimes a firm may deliberately try to mislead its competitors. In other cases, its managers may paint an optimistic picture of its strategic prospects to win time from creditors or shareholders, and stave off the prospect of being sacked. Sometimes a firm chooses to keep its strategy deliberately flexible and vague. And there are times when a firm may be genuinely confused about what its strategy really is, or why people buy (or decline to buy) its services, perhaps because it is in the process of changing from one strategy to another, when it is in a state of flux, for example.

For the debate about whether organisations can exist without a strategy, see Chapter 16. ▶

REAL-LIFE APPLICATION 4.1

Actions and words – two examples

Many computer hardware and software manufacturers are infamous for making misleading announcements about their product strategy. They issue press releases announcing plans to launch products which never materialise. These announcements serve two purposes. Firstly, customers are less likely to buy competitors' equipment if they believe that a superior product is on the way. Secondly, competitors may be fooled into diverting resources into developing products to compete with 'vapourware' (as these products became known). How many of these proposed products are genuine projects that fail, and how many are intended as a smokescreen to hide the developer's real intentions, we shall never know.

In 1986, one of the authors was consulting with a small subsidiary of a medium-sized UK engineering firm. This subsidiary's managers prided themselves on the lengths to which they would go to meet customer requirements on quality and delivery. They believed that customers purchased their products because of this dedication to customer service. Customers indeed had a high opinion of the firm, but in interviews they all said that the main reason why they bought its products was because of its very competitive prices. The firm was highly profitable, and its staff's dedication to customer service was completely sincere, but the emergent low-price strategy turned out to be far more important than the deliberate strategy of differentiation on quality.

To get a full picture of a firm's strategies and how well they are succeeding thus demands a very hard-headed kind of analysis, which looks at actions rather than words and results rather than intentions or opinions. This is equally true for a student preparing a case study for an assessment, or a practising manager trying to come to grips with real-life strategic problems. This chapter shows you how to carry out an analysis of this kind.

Learning objectives

After reading this chapter, you should understand how to:

- analyse an organisation's results, both financial and non-financial;
- assess the extent to which a firm can be said to be successful;
- identify precise areas in which the organisation is performing strongly or weakly;
- use an organisation's actions and achievements to determine what its strategy is in practice.

4.1 Assessing strategic performance

In assessing an organisation's success or failure, there are three stages: working out what to observe and measure, establishing the standards against which to measure performance, and drawing conclusions.

4.1.1 Working out what to observe and measure

Since almost all organisations have an economic purpose, part of their success will be measured in financial and economic terms, using a **financial performance measure** like return on capital employed. Usually we are also interested in how fast the organisation is **growing** relative to competitors. We also need to see how well the organisation is succeeding in meeting **key stakeholder requirements**, particularly in public sector and non-profit organisations. A school, for example, may be measured more by its pupils' examination results than by its success in keeping within the budget.

These will give us general measures of an organisation's overall success or failure. However, if we are to make useful proposals for its future, we need to be able to diagnose the strength or weakness of specific elements of its strategy. We want to know whether it is performing better in some competitive arenas than in others – so we should try, where possible, to compare the performance of different business units. We want to know which particular elements of the value chain, or which specific strategic resources, are important to the organisation's success or failure. This requires the use of ratios that assess particular elements of strategic performance, such as inventory control or quality.

There are a number of **operational performance measures** that are applicable to a wide variety of organisations. As well as helping us assess the efficiency and effectiveness of particular parts of the strategy, these also give us insights into how well the organisation is managed. However, further insights can be gained by assessing how well the organisation is performing by the standards of its own industry, and also by the standards that it has set itself. For example, Sony competes in industries where innovation is important to sustaining competitive advantage, and part of its corporate mission relates to being a leader in product innovation. We shall therefore want to measure how innovative it really is. This kind of analysis requires the use of performance measures that are **tailored** to the organisation and its industry.

4.1.2 Assessing the standards against which to measure performance

Most organisations have internal measures of success. Owners and other major stakeholders will set goals for the organisation, which will typically be expressed in financial terms. The organisation's managers (who are not always its owners) will often set operational targets against which they assess their own progress. In theory, by achieving these targets the organisation should also satisfy the requirements of the major stakeholders.

However, an organisation that is meeting, or even surpassing, its internal goals may still be performing poorly when compared against other measures. Performance needs, if at all possible, to be gauged **externally** – against that of competitors or other comparable firms, against industry norms and even against how the organisation itself has performed in the past.

4.1.3 Drawing conclusions about how strong or weak is the performance

Analysis of the organisation's results gives us a relatively *objective* way of assessing whether the organisation's performance is good, mediocre or poor, and whether or not it is improving relative to competition. The analysis can also give clues about which particular functions or business units give rise to this good or poor performance, and whether the organisation can claim to have any particular competences.

In drawing these conclusions, the quantitative analysis needs to be brought together with qualitative evidence. An organisation may be making losses, but are these because it is poorly managed or because it is a new venture that is investing aggressively? Poor performance may be due to economic conditions that are beyond managers' short-term control. One also has to understand how good and objective the evidence is. Does it all come from the organisation's managers, who might normally be expected to give an optimistic point of view, or from customers or outside experts?

In the following sections, we go into more depth on each of these points, using British Airways (Real-Life Application 4.2) as an example.

4.2 Overall measures of financial performance

Strategy is about using resources to add value to customers and users, and the first stage in any assessment of strategic performance is to try to assess, in broad terms, how well the organisation is doing so – how effective its strategy is.

In Real-Life Application 4.2 British Airways (BA) starts by quoting its **profits** for

A review of common accounting terms and ratios can be found in Appendix 4.1 at the end of this chapter. ▶

1996–97, and for any commercial organisation, the logical starting point for the analyst is to look at profitability.

BA quotes both pre-tax profits and profit attributable to shareholders (net of tax and interest charges). From the strategist's point of view, the most appropriate measure of profit is **before interest and tax**, since the management of tax and interest by the treasury function, while valuable to shareholders, does not normally add value to users of the company's products. (There are some types of business, such as financial services firms, where the treasury function *is* crucial to adding value. In cases like these, which we discuss below, profit is best measured after interest and tax.)

However, the **absolute** level of profit does not help us to assess BA's strategic performance in comparison with that of other airlines, or with its own past results. This is because it does not take account of the quantity or value of the resources that are needed to produce that profit. The starting point for a strategic analysis is therefore a **ratio** that expresses profits as a percentage of the resources invested in the business. This is an illustration of a very basic rule that:

a well-chosen ratio generates more useful information than a raw number such as revenue or profit.

For a commercial organisation, we strongly suggest that you start your analysis by computing one or more of the ratios described in the following paragraphs according to the type of business.

For a firm that has an extensive fixed asset base, such as a manufacturing firm or a retailer, look at the ratio of profit before interest and tax to assets. In the UK, the most commonly employed ratio is **return on capital employed** (ROCE), while US analysts often prefer **return on (total) assets** (ROA). Which you use will depend upon the data available and on personal taste, although it is of course important to use the same ratio for each company and each year of data that you analyse.[1]

For a firm where the management of financial assets is a crucial part of the business, look at the ratio of profits *after* interest and tax to assets. For these companies, the management of debt and taxation *is* crucial to competitiveness, so performance measures need to take account of profits (or losses) from these areas of operations. Typically, you will look at **return on equity** (ROE), but sometimes you will see commentators talk about post-tax returns on total assets. Firms in this category will include banks, insurers and other financial service providers, but also property companies (which typically take on a lot of debt to finance the purchase and development of land). ROE will also be of interest for firms engaged in long-term projects such as power station development, because they get large payments in advance that need to be carefully invested.

For a firm whose main assets are highly trained professionals, such as consultancies and advertising agencies, classic accounting measures of return on assets are deceptive, since they take no account of human capital. This kind of business may have few balance sheet assets beyond some office equipment and a small amount of working capital, so their ROCE may seem absurdly high. There is no perfect overall measure for this kind of business; **profit per employee** is perhaps the best available.

British Airways in fact straddles all these categories. Like many companies it uses a basket of financial measures to assess its performance and does not just rely on one. It has a large investment in buildings and aircraft, but many of the aircraft are leased (putting a premium on financial management). It also has a major invest-

How British Airways assessed its position in 1999

British Airways remains one of the world's successful airlines. In 1996–97, it announced pre-tax profits up 9.4 per cent on the previous year to £640 million. This was achieved on revenues rising by 7.7 per cent to £8,359 million. Profit attributable to shareholders was up 16.9 per cent to £553 million, and represented adjusted earnings of 55.9 pence a share against 49.4 pence in the previous year. Group operating profit, excluding the exceptional operating charge, declined by 7.6 per cent to £673 million – the reduction being more than explained by the rise in the price of aviation fuel, worth £142 million in the year. Excluding this, operating profit would have risen by 12 per cent, reflecting growth in passenger revenue and continued focus on cost efficiencies.

The British Airways Group, including Deutsche BA, and Air Liberté, carried a record 38.2 million passengers during 1996–97. This was up 6 per cent on the previous year. More than 33.4 million people flew on mainline British Airways – a rise of 3.6 per cent. Revenue passenger kilometres on mainline services were up 6.4 per cent, against a capacity increase of 7.3 per cent. This resulted in a mainline passenger load factor of 73.2 per cent, down 0.6 points against the record achieved in 1995–96. A total of 721,000 tonnes of freight and mail were also carried, with cargo tonne kilometres climbing by 9 per cent.

British Airways also remains the world's largest international passenger airline. Its mainline scheduled route network is one of the world's most extensive. In 1996–97 the airline operated an average of over one thousand flights a day, on an unduplicated route network of about 759,000 kilometres. The British Airways Group fleet as at 31 March 1997 comprised 308 aircraft.

The airline's main base is London Heathrow Airport, the largest international airport in the world. It also operates an increasing number of services out of London Gatwick Airport which was a tremendous success for the airline in 1996–97 – British Airways passengers handled through Gatwick rose by 18 per cent, passenger load factors were held steady, yields were up and profits from Gatwick were up. In March 1996, a number of East African routes were transferred from Heathrow to Gatwick; and in March 1997, a number of Latin American routes were also moved from Heathrow to Gatwick.

A total of 58,210 staff were employed by the Group worldwide in 1996–97, 82 per cent of them based in the UK. Unlike many of the world's other airlines, British Airways is owned entirely by private investors – with almost 235,000 shareholders, among them some 87 per cent of the Company's own employees.

The airline's record of success has been built upon quality service provided by a dedicated workforce, combined with marketing and continued cost reduction. The financial year 1996–97 was a landmark year for the company as it set its sights on reshaping itself to meet the challenges which the new millennium will bring. The company introduced a new Mission, 'To be the undisputed leader in world travel' and also changed its corporate Goals and Values. The new Goals are to be the 'Customers' Choice', to have 'Inspired People', 'Strong Profitability' and to be 'Truly Global'. The new Values are to be 'Safe and Secure', 'Honest and Responsible', 'Innovative and Team Spirited', 'Global and Caring', and a 'Good Neighbour'. During the year, the company also began its Business Efficiency Programme which is essential to building continued future success. It will deliver to the business, annual efficiencies of £1 billion by the year 2000. To signal to the world that it was changing, the company launched on June 10, 1997 a new corporate identity featuring new and exciting world images on the tails of aircraft. The new identity does not detract from the company's British heritage in any way, but reflects its position as a global carrier – an airline of the world, born and based in Britain – a community of people passionately committed to serving the communities of the world.

A further element in the airline's future profitability has been the formation of its global alliance. The alliance with Qantas goes from strength to strength – in Singapore and Bangkok, British Airways and Qantas operate as one airline, under a Joint Service Agreement, sharing revenues on services between Europe and Australia over Singapore and Bangkok. Code-sharing with Canadian Airlines International has also been expanded. Presence in Europe was expanded by the acquisition of a majority stake in Air Liberté in the French market. Combined with the existing investment in TAT European Airlines, this represents a significant presence in France, Europe's largest domestic market. Subsequent to the end of the financial year, the airline also announced code-sharing with LOT Polish Airlines and with Finnair in North Europe, and also confirmed that it was in discussions on a co-operation with Iberia of Spain.

A notable development in June 1996 was the announcement of our intended alliance with American

Airlines. At the time of writing, the proposed alliance was in the process of gaining ratification from the British Government, the United States Government, and the Commission of the European Union.

The airline has also franchised smaller carriers to feed passengers onto the wider British Airways network. Taken together with its own extensive route network, these partnerships give British Airways a presence in all major world markets. The British Airways' global alliance, at March 31, 1997 covered some 474 scheduled destinations in 103 countries.

The company reached a significant milestone in February 1997 when we celebrated the tenth anniversary of British Airways' privatisation. The company has made great progress in the time since then, and continues to pursue strategies that will enable it to meet the challenges of an increasingly competitive industry.

Source: http://www.british-airways.com/inside/factfile/overview/overview.shtml accessed on 20 January 1999.

ment in highly trained pilots, engineers and cabin crew. Accordingly, in assessing BA's performance, we would look at all three measures.

For a public sector or not-for-profit organisation, there will be few financial measures of this kind. Instead you might want to review whether the organisation is meeting its budgetary targets. However, unless it is competing in commercial markets with private sector firms, like a publicly owned airline or broadcaster, a public sector unit will not normally be expected to generate commercial-style financial returns. The overall measures of effectiveness in such organisations were reviewed in Chapter 2, Section 2.3.

4.3 Measures of size and growth

Size and growth are important to British Airways. In Real-Life Application 4.2 they write of themselves as 'the world's largest international passenger airline'. They quote the number of flights, the size of their fleet and the length of their route network as evidence of their success. They also refer to the growth over the past year in their profits, in the numbers of passengers carried and in revenue passenger kilometres and cargo tonne kilometres.[2]

It is quite usual in a strategic analysis to look at the size of an organisation and the rate at which it is growing. Typically this analysis will examine sales and profits and, if the data are available, non-financial measures of volume such as numbers of product units produced and sold, numbers of customers, of contracts and of outlets. Such figures need to be put in the context of what is happening in the industry as a whole, so the organisation's market share will also be of interest.

The assumptions underlying this type of analysis are that successful organisations are able to grow, perhaps at the expense of unsuccessful ones, and that large organisations are better able to compete than small ones, partly because they may be able to achieve economies of scale or scope.

4.4 Specific stakeholder requirements

A firm is successful only if its key stakeholders are happy to keep it in existence. The requirements of these stakeholders may not always be expressed in terms of the straightforward accounting measures reviewed In the previous sections. The owners and shareholders of commercial organisations are looking for financial returns on their investments, measured by indicators like share prices and earnings per share. Different kinds of measure are needed for public sector and not-for-profit organisations.

4.4.1 Shareholding institutions and stock markets

As we saw in Section 2.3.1, individuals and institutions hold shares as financial investments that are required to generate a return, through dividends, share price increases or both. They are interested in ROCE, ROE and similar measures of overall performance, together with the firm's profit and growth record, which has a strong influence on its share price. They use measures like **earnings per share** (EPS) and **economic value added** (EVA). However, they also use measures such as dividend per share and net asset value per share, which have no particular strategic significance. The proportion of profits that are distributed as dividends, for example, is not related to the strategies that determine how those profits are earned (unless so much cash is paid out in dividends that it leads to liquidity problems).

Stock market measures, shareholder value and strategic analysis

You will sometimes see stock market indicators quoted as measures of strategic performance. We would caution you against doing this unless no good alternative data are available. Measures like EPS and share prices can tell how likely it is that shareholders will sell a firm's stock, allow a firm to be taken over or try to change its top management. However, they are only indirect measures of strategic performance that supplement, but should not take the place of, your own more detailed analysis.

Earnings per share has frequently been used as a strategic performance measure – in Real-Life Application 4.2, British Airways cites its increasing EPS as evidence of its success. However, it is difficult to see any real link between the ratio of profits to the number of shares in issue, and an organisation's ability to add value to its customers. At best, EPS constitutes a substitute for ROE in cases where detailed accounting data are unavailable.

The newer measure, economic value added (EVA), holds more promise as a valid strategic performance measure. However, a company's EVA (operating profit, less taxes and a charge for the economic cost of the capital tied up in the firm's assets) is difficult to compute from a firm's published accounts. Adjustments are needed to items such as depreciation before EVA can be calculated, and it is not always clear what a firm's cost of capital might be. It is unlikely, therefore, that you will be able to calculate EVA for the firms that you analyse.

The firm's share price may itself be cited as a performance measure. In evaluating what share prices say about a firm's success or failure, it is important to bear in mind the imperfections of stock markets. Share prices are, in essence, an expression of a number of people's estimates of what a firm's profits will be in the future. Some of those people may never have gone near the firm or sampled its products or services, but their bonuses often depend upon their ability to sell its shares at high prices. The more professional analysts will have analysed the firm's financial data, and may have been able to visit the company and assess the quality of its strategy and its managers. However, even they are fallible human beings who may make errors of judgement. They may even have been given misleading or incorrect information.

Share prices may also be influenced by the degree of scarcity of a certain type of stock. Internet firms that have floated themselves on stock markets in Europe and the USA have tended to sell only a limited proportion of their equity – 20%, in the case of Freeserve, the British internet service provider, for example. This means that people who want internet shares in their portfolio tend to bid up the price of the stock.

In summary, share price movements are only indirect evidence of how well a firm is performing. They tell you how likely stock market analysts believe it to be that firms will generate the kind of profits that they expect, as quickly as they would like. In order to evaluate this evidence, you need to know whether the markets are well informed, their judgement is strategically sound and their expectations are realistic. The simplest, and best, way for you to do this is to analyse the company for yourself and draw your own conclusions!

In our view, the strategic situation of the firm is best assessed using measures of strategic performance that we discuss elsewhere in this chapter. Over the long term, if the firm can generate competitive advantage, it will also generate shareholder value so that its share price, EVA and EPS should rise. However, you should beware of companies that focus on improving their share price through short-term and financial manoeuvres. These kinds of policy by themselves give only the appearance of shareholder value. They need to be supported through what we would call 'real' strategies, designed to generate value for customers.

4.4.2 Other stakeholders

◀ *The specific requirements of other stakeholder groups were reviewed in Sections 2.3.2–2.3.4.*

Other stakeholders will measure the organisation's performance in ways that correspond to their particular requirements, and you will need to take account of those requirements in assessing the organisation's success. Private owners may measure the firm on its ability to generate cash for their retirement. Governments want to know whether their investments are achieving their political ends, such as providing housing services cost-effectively. Donors are interested in whether a medical charity is using their money productively to fight disease.

4.4.3 The impact of changing stakeholders

An organisation's stakeholders may change in the future – small firms grow and are floated on the stock exchange, and government bodies are privatised. This means that you need to be alert for changes over time in the way in which an organisation's success will be judged. Its strategy may need to change to satisfy the new criteria – for example, by shedding surplus staff that government or private owners were happy to retain.

4.5	Standard measures of operating performance

There are several measures of different aspects of efficiency and effectiveness that are more or less standard for all types of firm, although the precise definition of the performance measure may vary slightly from industry to industry.

Firstly, there are three types of measure that together give insights into why the company's overall financial returns might be rising or falling. Sales and profits may rise (or fall) because the organisation's assets are generating more (or fewer) orders, because the value of the average order is increasing (or decreasing) or because the profit margin on the average order is changing. Each of these three elements can be assessed by the following:

- *Measures of how productively assets are being utilised.* The classic accounting measures are net asset turnover or fixed asset turnover, but in many cases you will find that particular industries have their own, specific measures. Airlines measure passenger load factors, retailers measure sales per square metre (or square foot) of shopping area and consultants measure staff utilisation (the proportion of staff time spent on fee-earning work).

- *Measures of unit sales value.* BA uses yield (measured as sales per revenue passenger kilometre), while most other organisations measure the value of the average order or transaction.

- *Measures of profitability* – typically gross profit margin or operating profit as a percentage of sales. Improvements in margins might be due to improved effectiveness in product quality (enabling the firm to command higher prices), to improvements in cost efficiency or to better market conditions.

There are two other useful general indicators of the effectiveness of a firm's management, which also measure particular aspects of a firm's strategy:

- *Debtors* (measured in days of sales). When the average number of days it takes an organisation to obtain payment rises, it can indicate one of a number of problems. The firm may be overtrading, and so choosing its customers without fully checking their creditworthiness. It may be selling customers products that they do not really want, and so are reluctant to pay for. Goods may be being delivered broken or in the wrong quantities, the invoicing systems may be faulty, or there may simply be weak management in the finance area, so that outstanding invoices are not properly followed up.

- *Stock turnover.* When inventory (measured in relation to total sales or cost of sales) rises, it can be a sign of emerging problems with sales, of poor production or purchasing controls or of general slackness in management.

Finally, it is important to gauge an organisation's financial strength. The most important strategic indicator of this is the debt/equity ratio (also known as gearing or leverage). If this is persistently growing and reaches abnormal levels (above 50% is a normal 'rule of thumb') then it may indicate that the firm has expanded beyond the limits its cash flow permits. *Interest cover* (the number of times interest payments can be covered from profits) is also a useful check, to see if interest charges are manageable. If the debt/equity ratio is low then the organisation has spare financial resources that might be used for expansion. However, short-term measures of liquidity are not of great interest in strategic analysis, except where they show that a firm is in imminent danger of bankruptcy.

4.6 Tailored measures of performance

One of the most difficult aspects of strategic analysis is to work out *specific* ways of measuring how well an organisation is performing. These specific measures can, however, be very useful. Firstly, they give more precise insights into the nature of an organisation's competitive advantage than the more general indicators we have reviewed earlier in the chapter. Secondly, they can show whether there is a mismatch between what the organisation says it is doing and what it really is doing. Finally, the process of developing these measures can offer insights into the strategies that are being pursued by the organisation and its competitors.

This last sort of insight comes from looking at what the organisation and its competitors measure. If we return to Real-Life Application 4.2, there are clear indications of some of BA's key goals and aspirations. It hopes to become a global airline, and achieve high levels of profits. However, an interesting feature of the Real-Life Application is that several measures are quoted that do not directly relate to any of BA's explicitly declared goals. This is an illustration of an important principle of strategic analysis:

> **you will get better indications of an organisation's true strategy from observing what it measures and does than from its declared goals or what it says it does.**

In the words of an old management saying, 'What gets measured, gets done.' In this particular case, BA quotes figures relating to passenger load factors (broadly, an indicator of how full the average passenger aircraft is when it takes off) and yields (a measure of how much revenue each passenger generates). It also talks about actions to achieve cost efficiencies. It is legitimate to conclude that each of these represents an important element in BA's strategy even though they do not feature in its list of goals.

Other industries also have their standard measures of efficiency and effectiveness. Steel firms measure the number of person-hours required to produce a ton of steel, and automobile manufacturers measure the number of cars per staff-year – both of which are examples of labour-intensive industries measuring labour productivity. Retailers and many other service businesses measure sales per employee for similar reasons. The measures that firms in an industry employ to monitor their own operational performance provide a useful starting point for our analysis.

Sometimes, however, it will be necessary to invent our own measures of the organisation's progress towards its declared goals. For example, if an organisation like Sony has set itself up to be a leader in product innovation, then we shall want to measure its innovativeness. This can be done in a number of quite simple ways – measurement rarely needs sophisticated mathematics. For example we could review Sony's R&D expenditure as a proportion of sales. This is an *input* measure – it shows how seriously Sony is trying to be innovative. We could also count the number of new products that Sony has launched, or the number of patents that it has filed, over the last three years. This is an *outcome* measure – it shows how effective this innovation process really is. **A balanced strategic appraisal looks at both inputs and outcomes.**

The first goal mentioned on BA's web page is to have strong profitability, and the firm's success in achieving it can be assessed using standard accounting measures.

But how might we measure the company's progress towards the second goal: being 'truly global'? The declared intention is not sufficient evidence – we must look for **actions and events**.

In Real-Life Application 4.2 the company writes about the numbers of alliances and code-sharing agreements it has struck up. It also highlights its (rather controversial) decision to replace the British flag on its tail-planes with 'world images'. These are simple input measures – evidence that the company is taking concrete steps in pursuit of its goal.

However, the fact that BA has taken these steps does not mean that it has achieved the goal. In order to understand the extent to which British Airways has become global, we need to have an image of what a global firm would look like. We can then try to measure how close the company is to that image. In fact, strategists attach a precise meaning to the term 'global', which we discuss in detail in Chapters 5 and 6. It involves, among other things, having a single global brand and an international management team. Neither of these aspects of strategy is mentioned in the extract, so we would have to qualify our judgement for lack of evidence.[3] However, we might look at the geographic spread of BA's revenues and profits, on the assumption that a global firm would not be concentrated in a single country or region (a point we return to in Section 4.7.3).

If we wanted to measure the extent to which BA has 'inspired people', we could look for evidence of relevant inputs, such as expenditure on training (total for the firm and expenditure per employee) and whether there was a suggestion scheme. We would also look for outcomes – number and value of employee improvement suggestions, and evidence from employee surveys of the extent to which staff felt motivated, creative or otherwise 'inspired'.

Thinking of appropriate measures like this, and then calculating them from the evidence available, is a key feature of a thorough strategic analysis.

4.7 Assessing the standards for comparison

Quite understandably, the message conveyed by BA's website (Real Life Application 4.2) is upbeat and optimistic. Improvements and growth are highlighted and plausible reasons given for the downturn in profits. It would however be a mistake to accept this message unchallenged. We need to place these results in some kind of context, to evaluate how good (or bad) they really are.

4.7.1 Comparison with past performance

The simplest and most natural starting point is to compare these results with the organisation's own past performance. This means looking at the underlying trends in each of the kinds of measure we have discussed in Sections 4.2–4.6: overall strategic performance indicators and standard and tailored measures of operational performance. The data that will enable you to do this for BA are contained in the case study at the end of this chapter.

The quantitative data can be used to help us question the claims that you will see made about organisations in case studies and their annual reports. An upward trend in BA's results would justify the optimistic tone of its website, while a decline in some of the key indicators would cast doubt upon it – and, by implication, upon the willingness of its managers to face facts. This questioning process is another very important element of strategic analysis.

4.7.2 Comparison with other organisations

However, even if an organisation is performing worse than it did in the past, this does not mean that it is weak, just as improvement in performance is not the same as strength. Confusing the two is a common error.

For example, Singapore Airlines' return on equity fell between 1994 and 1998 – from 10.6% to 9.4% – but *Fortune* magazine still felt this performance good enough to nominate Singapore Airlines' CEO as Asia's Businessman of the Year.[4] They judged that he had made the best of a harsh operating environment.

Strength and weakness both need to be measured relative to an organisation's competitors. An improvement in performance may appear impressive, until one learns that competitors are improving at double the rate. Equally, a seemingly cat-astrophic decline in profits may be the result of a sudden economic collapse in the firm's main markets. The firm may actually have sound strategies that have helped it survive these problems better than its competitors (as *Fortune* judged to be the case with Singapore Airlines).

Competitive comparisons are not always possible, however. Many strategy writers think that directly comparable firms are difficult to find, as few organis-ations operate across *exactly* the same range of products and markets as others. Many case studies only give data for the organisation around which the case was written. However, wherever possible, you should look out for external data against which to gauge the performance of the firm you are analysing.

It is helpful to know whether an organisation is growing faster or slower than the industry as a whole, and how its profitability compares with that of the average firm. Use can be therefore made of industry norms and averages, but unless the industry is unusually homogeneous, this will only give part of the picture.

In most industries, there are a few leading firms that set the standards for the rest. They are more profitable, more innovative, faster growing, can respond faster to orders or produce their outputs more cheaply than their competitors. For example, in the auto industry, Toyota has long been the standard against which other manufacturers assess their efficiency. It is important to assess a firm against such industry leaders. This is true even if factors like trade barriers or different cus-tomer focus stop them competing directly with the organisation you are analysing. The difference in performance between the leader and the rest gives some measure of the opportunities available if performance can be improved.

Organisations that serve similar customer segments and/or act in similar ways are sometimes said to be part of the same 'strategic group' – see Chapter 5. ▶

It is also important to assess an organisation's performance against its closest competitors – those that are serving similar customer segments. For example, it would make little sense to compare British Airways with low-cost carriers like Ireland's Ryanair or America's Southwest Airlines, or with charter airlines like the UK's Britannia. All of these have set up their value chains in a different way, to deliver a low-cost, low-priced service. One would expect their profit margins to be far lower than those of 'full service' carriers like BA. Their passenger load factors, on the other hand, are higher – Britannia's in 1996 was over 90%, well above BA's 'highest ever' 74%. In order to make money, they have to use their assets very intensively.

British Airways' close competitors are full-service airlines that specialise, as BA does, in carrying Business (or Club) class passengers on medium- and long-distance flights. These are companies like American Airlines and United Airlines in the USA, Lufthansa, KLM and SAS in Europe and Singapore Airlines in Asia.

We also need to be alert to any possible inconsistencies between different data sources. For example, the ROE figures for Singapore Airlines may well not be strictly comparable to those for BA, since they are likely to have been prepared under different accounting conventions. Data in different exhibits, or from different sources, may span slightly different time periods.

Most strategy case studies will adjust their data to compensate for differences in accounting practices between firms and countries, although you need to be alert to these differences when doing your own research. However, the data in many cases have holes and inconsistencies – just like the information we give at the end of the chapter for BA! This is not just a way of making sure that the reader is awake; it reflects the incomplete and sometimes contradictory information that managers and consultants have to make do with in real life.

4.7.3 Internal comparisons

Another source of comparison, and one that students often overlook, is between different parts of the same organisation. This can help us to identify whether good or bad performance comes from one part of the organisation, or whether all divisions or functions are performing at more or less the same level. It also helps us to ask questions about the kind of standards against which an organisation's managers might judge its overall performance. The managing director or CEO might ask, for example, why every part of an organisation is not performing at the level of its most profitable division.

Normally, these data require a bit of massaging before they can tell their story, as we can see when we examine the geographical breakdown of BA's turnover and profit (Table 4.1).

These figures tell us very little at the moment. It seems, interestingly, that the European home market is unprofitable and a lot of 1998's profits came from flights to the USA. BA's turnover appears to be spread across the world's markets, giving some substance to the airline's claim to be 'global'.

However, in order to make sense of the data, some calculations are necessary to show the percentage breakdown of turnover and profits by region. And it is almost always helpful, when given two sets of data like profits and sales, or profits and assets, to calculate the ratio, just to see if anything interesting emerges. This kind of calculation represents the difference between analysing data and simply copy-

Table 4.1 British Airways' profit and turnover by destination, 1994–98 (£ million)

By area of destination	Turnover		Operating profit	
	1998	1994	1998	1994
Europe	3,214	2,734	(127)	16
The Americas	3,073	2,029	395	140
Africa, Middle East and Indian subcontinent	1,118	900	125	209
Far East and Australasia	1,237	939	111	103
Total	8,642	6,602	504	468

Source: British Airways Annual Report, 1998.

Table 4.2 Analysis of British Airways' turnover, profit and ROS

	Turnover break-down by region		Operating profit breakdown by region		Operating profit/sales	
	1998	1994	1998	1994	1998	1994
Europe	37%	41%	(25)%	3%	(4.0)%	0.6%
The Americas	36%	31%	78%	30%	12.9%	6.9%
Africa, Middle East and Indian subcontinent	13%	14%	25%	45%	11.2%	23.2%
Far East and Australasia	14%	14%	22%	22%	9.0%	11.0%
Total	100%	100%	100%	100%	5.8%	7.1%

ing it. The results are given in Table 4.2 – we suggest you pause and examine this table to see what it tells you.

Here some interesting features emerge:

- The proportion of turnover coming from outside Europe and America has hardly changed between 1994 and 1998. In the two columns headed 'Turnover breakdown by region', Africa, Middle East and the Indian subcontinent plus Far East and Australia amounted to 27% in 1998, slightly less than the 28% they generated in 1994. To put it another way, the great majority of BA's revenue continues to come from Europe and the USA.

- The share of profit from Africa, Middle East and the Indian subcontinent has fallen as well as the share from Europe (the two columns headed 'Operating profit breakdown by region'). It is on flights to the Americas that BA made most (78%) of its money in 1998.

- Margins on flights to Europe are consistently lower than they are elsewhere (the two columns headed 'Operating profit/sales'). Indeed, BA seems to have lost money on flights to Europe in 1998 (always look out for the odd few negative numbers in a sea of positive ones – or vice versa!).

- Operating profit margins are falling everywhere except on flights to the USA.

4.8 Drawing conclusions

There are two longer, and more detailed 'worked examples' of this kind of analysis in Section 11.2.1. ▶

So, what have we learned about British Airways? We are in a position to draw one or two firm conclusions. On the basis of the analysis in the previous section, It is clear that BA would be threatened by a downturn in demand or by increased competition on its transatlantic routes.

But for the most part, the implications of the data will be ambiguous. Is BA's reliance upon Europe and America evidence that the company is neglecting developing markets or that it is justly sticking to its areas of strength. If some key operating ratios are showing a decline, does this indicate a falling away of performance, or is it because an organisation is expanding, and needs time to train staff and build efficiency in its new operations?

It invariably appears, annoyingly, that the more information we have, the more questions we have to ask in order to make sense of it. And gathering more statistics, which is a comforting thing to do when confronted with uncertainty, may not help. Looking in more detail at an organisation, while answering some questions, is likely to raise more!

The next step, therefore, is to introduce qualitative data. Even this sometimes just leads simply to further questions rather than answers. For example, if we introduce the fact that the European airline market is still in the early stages of deregulation of routes and prices, so that competition is less intense that in the USA, we start to wonder why margins on flights to European destinations are so low.

So what is the 'right' answer? How well is British Airways performing, and how is the company placed in strategic terms? In order to get a better answer to this question, we need to look harder at BA's assumptions about the future. Is the airline industry really becoming global? Is competition going to intensify in the way that they predict, and will it be the low-cost airline that wins the day? And even if all this is true, has BA the resources to become that low-cost producer? The rest of this book aims to equip you with the theory and techniques you need to approach these questions.

However well you use that theory, of course, the fact remains that no one *knows* in advance how the airline industry will look in 2002, or how well BA will be able to adjust to any changes. The best that you will be able to do is to reach a reasoned assessment that seems to fit the limited data in your case study. And that is also the best that we can do.

It is extremely important to understand that there are no 'right answers' to strategic questions. For nervous students looking for safe answers to put in their assignments and examination papers, this may seem frightening news. However, this uncertainty has a positive aspect. If you analyse thoroughly and put forward carefully argued conclusions that are compatible with the evidence, then you cannot be wrong. Your view, in such circumstances, is as good as your professor's, or ours. Just be careful – and rigorous!

4.9   Summary

This chapter has taken you through the process of using quantitative data to broaden your understanding of an organisation's strategy, how well it is succeeding and what specific areas seem to be performing well or badly.

- It is important not to rely upon what organisations say about their strategy, but to examine actions and events, and measure results.

- A complete analysis starts with general measures of strategic effectiveness (like return on capital employed and growth rate).

- It makes use of measures of operational performance (like debtor turnover) and combines them with tailored indicators designed to show how well the organisation is performing by the normal criteria for its industry.

- Tailored indicators are also used to show how well an organisation is meeting its specific strategic objectives. It is desirable to measure both how hard the organisation is trying (inputs) and how effectively it is succeeding (outcomes).

- In most cases, a well-chosen ratio generates the most valuable information, although useful insights can be gained simply by counting things like numbers of alliances and new product launches.

Table 4.3 Measures to be used in assessing an organisation's strategic performance

Type of measure	Examples
Overall measures of financial performance	Return on capital employed Return on total assets Return on equity Profit per employee
Measures of stakeholder satisfaction	(Specific measures for each organisation)
Measures of profit margin	Operating profit/sales
Measures of asset utilisation	Fixed asset turnover Sales/square metre Staff utilisation
Measures of unit sales value	Turnover/units sold
Operational measures	Debtor turnover Stock turnover Sales/employee Output/employee
Measures of financial strength	Debt/equity Interest cover
Tailored measures of strategy achievement	Input measures Outcome measures

The measures that we recommend you look at in assessing a firm's performance are summarised in Table 4.3. In interpreting these measures, it is desirable, where possible, to make comparisons with other organisations in the same industry. Also, please bear in mind that **improvement is not the same as strength** – even if a company is getting better, it may still be being outperformed by its competitors.

Appendix 4.1: Standard accounting terms and ratios, and their significance

The following table summarises the most frequently used accounting terms and ratios, and the way in which they are calculated. It also gives a brief review of the significance of each item in a strategic analysis. Please bear in mind that, although accountancy is supposed to be a precise discipline, not even accountants agree on the definitions of all these terms. There is a possibility that they may differ slightly from those you have read or been taught elsewhere.

For a more detailed account of what these terms and ratios signify, and a description of basic accounting theory, you should consult a specialist textbook.[5]

Term or ratio	Definition	Significance and points to watch
Sales, revenue, turnover	Equivalent ways of speaking of the money brought in from selling goods and services	Some firms include sales tax or value added tax in their turnover figures, others do not
Cost of goods sold	The cost of the inputs needed to produce the goods – raw materials, labour costs and depreciation of equipment	

LEVELS OF PROFIT (All best assessed as ratios to sales or to assets)		
Gross profit	Sales less cost of goods sold	Measures whether production process is profitable
Operating profit Trading profit Operating income Profit before interest and tax (PBIT)	Gross profit less selling, administrative and general expenses	Measures whether customers are served at a profit
Profit before tax	Operating profit plus interest earned less interest charges	
Net profit	Profit before tax less tax	Measures profit accruing to shareholders and effectiveness of entire firm (including treasury function)
Retained profits	Net profits less dividends paid	Measures money left in firm for reinvestment

BALANCE SHEET ITEMS		
Stocks, inventory	Value of raw materials held awaiting processing, materials being processed (work-in-progress – WIP) and finished items awaiting sale or shipment	Aim is normally to keep stocks to the minimum level needed to ensure continuity of supply of goods to customers
Debtors, receivables	Value of goods/services invoiced but unpaid	
Creditors, payables	Value of inputs received but not paid for. Sometimes also includes loans repayable within 12 months	This is money that suppliers effectively lend a firm. If this number rises, a firm gets extra free money, at the risk of antagonising suppliers
Current assets	Stocks plus debtors plus cash	
Current liabilities	Creditors plus short-term loans	
Net current assets Working capital	Current assets less current liabilities	Needs to be financed through debt or equity. The lower the working capital, the more funds are available for investment in fixed assets

Term or ratio	Definition	Significance and points to watch
Fixed assets	Long-term investments made by the firm, include tangible assets (land, buildings, equipment) and intangible assets such as financial investments	
Net assets	Working capital plus fixed assets	Arithmetically equal to capital employed
Shareholders' equity Shareholders' funds	Money received by firm for the purchase of its shares, plus retained profits accumulated over time. Sometimes also includes various reserves against future liabilities	The money invested in the firm by its shareholders
Capital employed	Shareholders' funds plus long-term debt	The total money invested in the firm. Some people believe this should also include short-term bank loans, if the firm is in the habit of rolling them over from year to year

OVERALL PROFITABILITY RATIOS		
Return on capital employed (ROCE, ROK) Return on net assets (RONA)	Operating profit/capital employed	Probably the best overall measure of most firms' financial performance
Return on (total) assets (ROA)	Operating profit/total assets	An alternative to ROCE. Sometimes computed using net profit instead of operating profit, as alternative to ROE
Return on equity (ROE)	Net profit/shareholders' funds	Measures return on equity-holders' investments. Good overall performance measure for financial firms
Profit/employee	Operating profit/no. of employees	Overall measure of profitability in 'people' businesses

PROFIT MARGINS		
Gross margin	Gross profit/sales	Measures extent to which production costs are covered
Operating profit margin Return on sales (ROS)	Operating profit/sales	Measures extent to which overall costs are covered. Indicator of strength of competition in industry
Net profit margin	Net profit/sales	Alternative to ROS for financial and similar firms

Term or ratio	Definition	Significance and points to watch
ASSET UTILISATION		
Net asset turnover	Sales/net assets	Measures intensity with which asset base being used. Higher is better
Fixed asset turnover	Sales/fixed assets	Measures intensity with which fixed assets being used
Sales/employee	Sales/no. of employees	Measures intensity of staff utilisation
Stock turnover	$365 \times$ stocks/cost of sales (to give result measured in days). Cost of sales/stocks (to give result as no. of times stocks 'turned over' in the year)	Measures size of inventory relative to consumption. Fewer days or higher turnover is better. See Section 4.5 for detailed interpretation. Can be calculated as ratio to sales if cost of sales data not available
Debtor turnover	$365 \times$ debtors/sales (gives result measured in days)	Measures time taken to collect payment – lower is better. In most industries there are standard payment terms – 30, 60 and 90 days are typical. An efficient firm will have debtors around this norm
LIQUIDITY		
Current ratio	Current assets/current liabilities	These measures show how easily a company could repay its short-term liabilities if the need arose. Important if you are planning to lend the company money or offer it credit. Of little significance in a strategic analysis
Acid test ratio	Debtors/current liabilities	
INDEBTEDNESS		
Debt/equity ratio, gearing	Long-term debt/shareholders' funds	See Section 4.5. Rule of thumb says that should be no greater than 50%
Interest cover	Operating profit/interest charge	No. of times interest can be paid out of profits. Measures sensitivity of firm to fluctuations in profits or interest rates, and so soundness of its funding strategy
STOCK MARKET RATIOS		
Dividend cover	Net profit/dividend expense	Shows to what extent dividends are justified by current profits. A consistently low figure may mean that the firm is dipping into reserves to maintain its dividend, in order to keep its share price high

Term or ratio	Definition	Significance and points to watch
Earnings per share (EPS)	Net profit/no. of shares in issue	See Section 4.4.1. Imperfect substitute for ROE that has virtue of being easy to calculate
Net assets/share	Net assets/no. of shares in issue	Indicates extent to which the company's share price reflects the value of its 'hard' assets. Sometimes used by analysts to assess how over- or under-valued a share is
Price/earnings (p/e) ratio	Quoted share price $\times$ no. of shares in issue/net profit	Can be calculated using last reported profits ('historic p/e') or forecast profits ('projected p/e'). Shows how many years of profits are built into the share price – a high number shows optimism about future profits growth
Dividend yield	Dividend per share/share price (normally expressed as a percentage)	Indicates annual income that investor gets from investment in the share. Can be compared to the interest rate on a loan or the yield on a bond

Questions for discussion

1. What input and output measures would be appropriate for organisations whose major strategic objectives were:
   (a) to be the lowest-cost producer in its industry?
   (b) to demonstrate to US industry that environmentally-friendly practices were not just feasible, but also profitable?
   (c) to allow its 25-year-old founder and chief executive to retire by the age of 32?
   (d) to bring opera to the people?

2. Companies sometimes use hidden reserves, restructuring charges and other accounting devices to 'massage' their earnings figures, normally to give the appearance of steady, unbroken growth in profits. Why would they do this? What kinds of data would you look for to give you clues about the true situation?

3. Is our focus on quantifiable results a mistaken attempt to bring scientific precision to the inexact art of strategic management?

CASE STUDY

British Airways

Table 4.4(a) shows five years' selected performance data for British Airways and Table 4.4(b) shows selected comparative performance data.

Table 4.4(a)   British Airways' historical data, 1994–98
(Figures relate to £ millions except where otherwise stated)

Measures*	1998	1997	1996	1995	1994
Measures of size					
Passengers carried (000)	34,377	33,440	32,272	30,552	28,656
Unduplicated route (000 km)	769	769	767	743	643
Turnover	8,642	8,359	7,760	7,177	6,602
Measures of raw profitability					
Operating expenditure	(8,138)	(7,813)	(7,032)	(6,559)	(6,134)
Operating profit	504	546	728	618	468
Income from associated undertakings	61	114	61	58	22
Other income and charges	183	162	19	(134)	2
Net interest payable	(168)	(182)	(223)	(215)	(212)
Profit before taxation	580	640	585	327	280
Profit for the year	460	553	473	250	274
Stock market measures					
Dividends	(176)	(154)	(131)	(119)	(106)
Earnings per share (p)	44.7	55.9	49.4	39.3	30.0
Dividends per share (p)	16.60	15.05	13.65	12.40	11.10
Balance sheet information					
Fixed assets	9,055	8,272	7,357	6,634	6,406
Current assets	2,245	2,164	2,684	2,429	2,433
Current liabilities	(2,821)	(3,160)	(2,824)	(2,320)	(2,114)
Total assets less current liabilities	8,479	7,276	7,217	6,743	6,725
Long-term borrowings, leases and provisions	(5,158)	(4,292)	(4,723)	(4,663)	(4,995)
Net assets, shareholders funds	3,321	2,984	2,494	2,090	1,730
Overall profitability measures					
Return on capital employed (%)	6.7	9.1	10.9	10.0	7.3
Return on total assets (%)	5.0	6.3	7.9	7.5	5.5
Return on equity (%)	14	19	19	12	16
Profit/employee	N/A	13,881	16,891	12,062	9,027
Tailored performance measures					
Return on sales (%)	5.8	6.5	9.4	8.6	7.1
Passenger load factor (%)	71.3	73.2	73.8	71.6	70.0
Passenger revenue per RPK* (p)	6.38	6.47	6.39	6.36	6.32
Current assets (days)	95	94	126	124	135
Average fuel price (US cents/US gallon)	64.70	75.90	63.16	59.79	63.64
Punctuality – within 15 minutes (%)	80	82	82	84	85
Regularity (%)	98.0	99.2	99.1	99.5	99.3
Measures of financial strength					
Debt/equity (%)	155	144	189	223	289
Interest cover	4.45	4.52	3.62	2.52	2.32

* RPK = Revenue passenger kilometre.
Source: British Airways 1998 published accounts and authors' calculations. Information on route mileage, load factors, etc., relates to the mainline airline operation and excludes BA's newer subsidiaries. Earnings per share have been adjusted to exclude various exceptional charges and credits in 1995 and 1997.

Table 4.4(b)   British Airways' ranking on selected criteria in 1996

Criterion	Ranking
Numbers of passengers carried world wide	10th
Total traffic (passengers plus freight)	5th
Operating profits	1st
Net profits	2nd
European sales	2nd
Passenger load factor	17th

Source: Airline Business, September 1996.

Case study questions

1.   Use the data in Tables 4.4(a) and 4.4(b), together with the other information given about BA and its competitors in this chapter, to appraise BA's strategic performance. (Look hard. As in many case studies, some relevant information is buried in obscure places.)

2.   BA suffered a lengthy strike by its cabin staff in 1997 that appeared to damage staff morale. Passengers seemed largely sympathetic to the cabin staff. How does this extra qualitative information affect your assessment of BA's performance and position?

NOTES

1.   The difference between ROCE and ROA is rarely important when interpreting trends and comparisons. It hangs on whether you see the resources invested in the business as being the *total* asset base (ROA), or whether you deduct the part of the organisation's working capital that is financed by credit from suppliers (ROCE).

2.   Revenue passenger kilometres (RPK) and cargo tonne kilometres are combined measures of the quantity of passengers or cargo carried and the distances they were conveyed. An airline notches up one RPK for each kilometre it carries a fare-paying passenger, so a 200 kilometre flight with 120 passengers on board would generate 24,000 RPK. Cargo tonne kilometres are calculated similarly.

3.   In point of fact, the evidence is ambiguous: BA's brands are global, but its management team is overwhelmingly British.

4.   See, for example, Kraar (1999). 'Asia's Businessman of the Year', *Fortune*, 139 (2): 45–50.

5.   See, for example, Reid and Myddelton (1996).

PART 2

Understanding the bases of competitive advantage

In Part 1, you were introduced to the basic concepts and vocabulary of strategy and to the nature of strategic thinking. In Part 2, we apply this learning to an understanding of a crucial – perhaps *the* crucial – question in management theory: What is it that makes some organisations more successful than others?

For the first two decades in the history of the theory of strategic management and corporate strategy, most theorists appeared to believe that successful organisations were those that had the best physical and financial resources, and made carefully planned decisions about which markets to deploy them in. Strategy was about making good marketing decisions, and good investment decisions. In the late 1970s, market share was believed to be an important factor. Firms with a high market share enjoyed something called market power, which made them difficult to compete with, and also were able to obtain an important cost advantage because their extra production volume helped them ride down the 'experience curve' more quickly than their competitors.

In the 1980s, with the publication of Michael Porter's book *Competitive Strategy*, the emphasis switched. It was still important to choose to compete in the right arena, but as well as looking at how promising the market was in terms of growth, it was also important to see how competitive the industry was. This development reflected the fact that supply had begun to outstrip demand in many industries, so that firms needed to compete more carefully for customers. Porter also focused attention on the kinds of strategy that firms could use to compete effectively, saying that they needed either to have the lowest costs or to offer some differentiating feature that justified a price premium.

Attention was then turned to the question: what makes some firms cost leaders, or more effective differentiators than their competitors? Porter's own answer to this question came in 1985 with his book *Competitive Advantage*: the most effective competitors were those with the most effective value chains. Essentially, he still holds to that view, with some modifications (Porter, 1996).

However, the theoretical consensus has now swung behind a view that says that choosing the right industry and the most effective value chain does not give lasting advantage, because these decisions are too easy for competitors to copy. According to this, the 'resource-based view' of the firm, it is the resources that they have accumulated over time, and that cannot be copied by other organisations, that make the difference between successful and unsuccessful firms. This view really took hold in the early 1990s, following the publication of Prahalad and Hamel's 1990 article 'The core competence of the corporation', although most of the theoretical spadework had been done several years earlier (see Chapter 7 for details). More recently, scholars' attention has started to focus upon the knowledge that underlies effective competences, and the processes, systems and structures which enable organisations to learn, to distribute knowledge and to acquire competences and other intangible resources.

Because academics are as jealous and quarrelsome as any other group of competitors, there has been a tendency to show each new set of theories as superseding and invalidating those that have gone before. Our view, however, is that these various views of competitive advantage mostly complement each other, with each contributing an understanding of an important facet of strategic decision-making. In Part 2, we explore each of these areas of theory in detail and show how, individually and together, they contribute to an understanding of organisations' competitive advantage. So, after reading Part 2, you should understand how to:

- analyse an organisation's, past, present and future environment, and
  - show how the past environment has shaped its past success or failure
  - evaluate how the environment is changing
  - assess what the implications are for the organisation's present and future strategy;
- analyse how an organisation's choice of product, market and competitive positioning has contributed to its success or failure, within an individual business and also at an overall corporate level;
- identify the different strategic resources that an organisation has accumulated over time, show how they have contributed to its success or failure and assess whether they have given the organisation a competitive advantage;
- identify the role of the organisation's architecture and value chain in its success and failure, and analyse its culture, structure and systems to establish how they have contributed to its competitive position.

Assessing the environment and the nature of competition

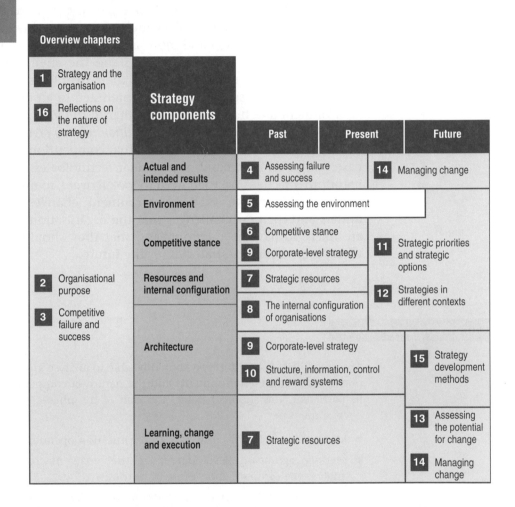

Overview chapters

1 Strategy and the organisation

16 Reflections on the nature of strategy

2 Organisational purpose

3 Competitive failure and success

Strategy components

	Past	Present	Future
Actual and intended results	4 Assessing failure and success	14 Managing change	
Environment	5 Assessing the environment		
Competitive stance	6 Competitive stance 9 Corporate-level strategy	11 Strategic priorities and strategic options	
Resources and internal configuration	7 Strategic resources 8 The internal configuration of organisations	12 Strategies in different contexts	
Architecture	9 Corporate-level strategy 10 Structure, information, control and reward systems	15 Strategy development methods	
Learning, change and execution	7 Strategic resources	13 Assessing the potential for change 14 Managing change	

If an organisation is to be an effective economic unit, its managers must have an understanding of the environment in which it operates. They need to understand the requirements of its customers and users, so as to be able to design its services to please them and market those services effectively. If its customers are businesses, they will have customers of their own, and our organisation may need to appreciate their needs as well. Those needs will not be constant over time, so the organisation needs to be alert to the ways in which they will change. It may even try to influence these developments to its own advantage.

At the same time, changing technology or economic circumstances may alter the economics of production. It may become necessary to improve economies of scale in purchasing, to cut labour costs to meet competition from emerging economies or to increase the organisation's access to new skills and technologies. Sometimes, the first organisation to notice these possibilities can gain an advantage in the market place or can get the pick of the people with rare but necessary skills.

Lastly, organisations need to be alert to the activities of competitors, both existing and potential. They must understand the nature of competition in their industry, and how and whether it is likely to change. Organisations that assess and understand the environment better than their competitors tend to outperform them over time.[1]

As students or researchers, we are interested in an organisation's *present* environment and how it is likely to alter in the *future*. Above all, we need to understand the *nature of the competition that an organisation confronts*.

We need to understand how fierce that competition is, and whether it is based on price, command of particular technologies, marketing superiority or other factors. We then need to look *forward*, to understand how competition may evolve as the environment changes. This helps us to understand the new challenges that the organisation and its competitors are likely to have to confront, and that they should take into account when they formulate strategies for the future.

Learning objectives

After reading this chapter, you should be able to analyse an organisation's past, present and future environments and the nature of competition within them. In particular, you should be able, for each of the phases in an organisation's development to:

- identify the industries in which an organisation operates or has operated;
- identify significant developments in the broad 'macro-environment' and analyse their impact upon those industries;
- analyse the nature of competition in these industries, and in particular whether it was, is or is likely to become
  - global, continental, regional, national or local in scope
  - fierce or benign

  and to identify the factors making it so;
- assess the extent to which the firm's environment and its choice of industry in which to operate have been responsible for its success or failure to date;
- assess the strategic factors determining whether firms survive in a particular industry, and the further factors that might lead to superior performance.

An analysis of the *past* environment can also yield useful information. It tells us whether an organisation has been lucky in growing up in a favourable environment, or has had to fight for survival in tough circumstances. More generally, it shows what kinds of environment the organisation is used to and has developed routines to cope with, and what has shaped the outlook of the principal decision-makers. It tells us how different the present and future are likely to be from the past, and how great a change an organisation will be need to make to its routines, and even its culture, if it is to adjust successfully to the new circumstances.

You may find it useful to review the concepts of industry, market, segments and sub-sectors from Chapter 1, Section 1.3.4.

5.1 Steps in analysing the environment and the nature of competition

We shall define the concept of global competition later in this chapter. ▶

An analysis of the environment and the nature of the competition has four main parts. Looking on the right-hand side of Figure 5.1, you will see that there are three key questions to be answered about the nature of competition in an industry: about its economics (mainly to do with how concentrated or fragmented it is), its intensity (fierce or benign) and its scope (global or local). We can answer these questions by observing the behaviour of the organisations in the industry, and by looking at the economic factors that might influence that behaviour.

One set of economic factors has to do with the stage that the industry has reached in its *life-cycle*. The more mature the industry, the fiercer competition is likely to be.

Figure 5.1 Analysing the nature of competition

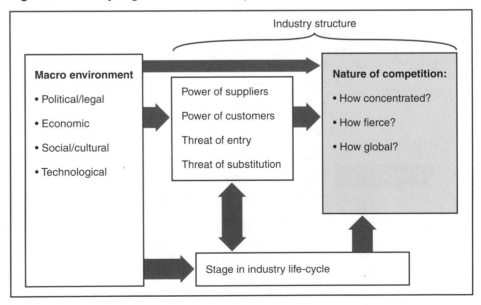

Concept	**The industry life-cycle**

A typical industry goes through four phases:

- an introductory phase when its products and firms are just starting to be noticed by potential customers;
- a growth phase when the industry becomes established and the number of firms and sales of the product grow rapidly;
- a maturity phase when the industry's sales are stagnant or growing only slowly;
- a decline phase when the industry's sales fall.

We return to industry life-cycles in Section 5.3. ▶

These four phases together are known as the industry life-cycle. Not every industry follows this sequence precisely, but the life-cycle model is sufficiently accurate to provide some useful generalisations about competitive behaviour.

There are four other important determinants of competitive behaviour in an industry: the power of its customers and suppliers, the threat of new firms entering the industry and the threat of substitute products. The stronger each of these four forces becomes, the more difficult it is for firms in the industry to make profits, and more fiercely they are likely to compete with one another.

The strength of each of the four forces, and the nature of competition in the industry, are influenced by the industry's structure – how many organisations are involved, and how large they are relative to their customers and suppliers. They are also influenced by the histories and corporate cultures of those organisations, and by the stage of the industry's life-cycle – as an industry matures, customers become more knowledgeable and so more powerful. These industry forces are all in turn heavily influenced by the **macro-environment**.

The macro-environment
The set of factors and influences that are not specific to an organisation or the industry in which it operates, but that nonetheless affect them.

The macro-environment triggers changes in an industry's structure and in the industry life-cycle. For example, it is quite usual for technological advances to bring about the decline of an industry by making substitute products more attractive.

These four environmental features – macro-environment, industry life-cycle, industry structure and nature of competition – are intimately linked and analysis of them needs to be undertaken together. For a complete picture of an industry, this set of analyses needs to be carried out three times: for the past, the present and the future.

Concept	**The macro-environment**

Examples of macro-environmental factors are:

- global and national macro-economic booms, recessions or inflation;
- broad social and cultural developments such as the emergence of a middle class with significant spending power in Asia, and increasing assertiveness on the part of consumers in the developed economies;
- new technologies such as the Internet and fuel cells.

In the interests of logical flow, we shall look at the analytical frameworks in the order in which they appear from left to right in Figure 5.1. However, you will not necessarily want to use them in that same order. Many students also experience problems in working out which industry or industries to incorporate into the analysis and how broadly to cast their review of the macro-environment. We look at these practical questions in Section 5.7; they will make more sense after the detailed review of the theory in Sections 5.2–5.6.

5.2 Analysing the macro-environment – PEST analysis

In analysing the macro-environment, we are trying to identify the factors that might in turn affect a number of vital variables (Table 5.1) that are likely to influence the organisation's supply and demand levels and its costs.

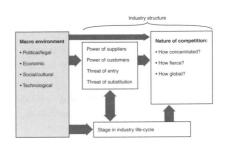

A number of checklists have been developed as ways of cataloguing the vast number of possible issues that might affect an industry. We recommend the simplest of these checklists, the PEST framework,[2] where PEST stands for:

> Political/legal
>
> Economic
>
> Social/cultural
>
> Technological

We explore each of these headings in turn.

5.2.1 Political/legal factors

Political and legal factors encompass actions by local and national administrations and political parties, and by international bodies such as the European Commission, the United Nations and the World Trade Organisation. These affect the stability of an industry's environment, the extent to which firms can take decisions without reference to governments, the costs of operating in a particular area and the facilities and infrastructure available.

Uncertainty makes it more difficult for managers to develop strategies, so that most organisations find life easier within a stable political system. Wars, revolutions and governments that change frequently or are unable to assert their authority can disrupt individual markets or whole industrial sectors. The 1991 war that followed Iraq's invasion of Kuwait caused global demand for hotel and airline services to plummet, as tourists were deterred from flying abroad by the threat of terrorist action. Not all industries suffer from such conflicts. Demand for arms and ammunition rose, for example, and the global oil industry, to which both Iraq and Kuwait are major suppliers, was not greatly affected, since other producers were able to step in and maintain supplies.

Table 5.1   Factors to be captured in an analysis of the macro-environment

Demand for an industry's products
- Changes in the tastes or purchasing power of the industry's customers, or *their* customers, or so on down the supply chain.
- New technologies that make the products or services more attractive.
- New services that might replace the industry's current offerings.
- Economic and political developments that open up markets in new countries.

The way the industry produces and distributes its outputs
- Changes in the technology used within the product or service, making it cheaper or more powerful.
- New production or distribution methods and technologies.

The price and availability of key inputs
- Factors affecting the supply of raw materials, such as political unrest in the countries that produce them, or new technologies that make production cheaper or more reliable.
- Factors affecting the availability of people and skills, such as improving educational standards in developing countries and rises or falls in the number of young people entering labour markets.

The way in which organisations are able to compete with one another
- New regulations liberalising international trade and tariff regimes.
- Changes of government which may lead to the liberalisation or regulation of particular markets.
- New laws governing pollution standards or minimum wages.

There may also be direct political intervention in the operation of industries and markets, for example through:

- *entry standards* – for example, directives that certain medicinal products may only be sold by qualified pharmacists;

- *operational regulations* – for example, regulations (presently being reformulated) exist to say that the ratio of reserves to loans on a bank's balance sheet must not be less than 8%. These standards are set by an international body, the Bank of International Settlements, but national governments choose how strictly to enforce them;

- *controls on merger and acquisition activity* – most national governments, and the European Union, have set up bodies for this purpose;

- *the use of subsidies or nationalisation* – to encourage certain industries or to rescue major firms from bankruptcy;

- *the building of infrastructure* such as ports, roads, railways, telecommunications links, and of training and education systems that give firms a source of skilled labour.

Political and legal actions often impose costs upon organisations. Employers may be called upon to bear part of the cost of their employees' health or unemployment insurance, to pay their staff a minimum wage or to install expensive equipment to control pollution. However, political and legal restraints are not always bad for an industry's competitiveness. In the USA, organic farmers have *asked* the federal government to regulate their industry.[3] They believe that having a clear legal definition of 'organic' produce will help them, by preventing competitors who grow food by cheaper methods from passing their produce off as organic. Most German firms have not objected to their country's expensive system of compulsory training and apprenticeship, because they have obtained benefits, in terms of increased worker productivity, which outweigh the costs.

Paradoxically political and legal action, by imposing heavy costs upon organisations, can sometimes actually enhance their competitiveness. This is because, in order to reduce those costs, firms are forced to develop new routines and technologies that may give them competitive advantage. For example, US firms that have been forced to reconfigure their value chains to meet tough new environmental laws have round that they have made gains in terms of reduced wastage and improved efficiency that far outweigh the costs. In Germany. firms have been forced, by that country's exacting legislation, to develop technologies to reduce their own pollution. In compensation, they have been able to establish global leadership positions in the pollution control industry, beating off international competitors who have not been forced to develop such high standards.

The other side of this paradox is that measures designed to protect firms and encourage new industries may be counter-productive. Governments often try to protect firms in their countries from foreign competition through tariffs and import restrictions, and to encourage their development through cheap loans and large government contracts. These policies can sometimes help domestic producers establish themselves but, in the long term, they risk breeding firms that are made complacent by the easy profits from their home markets. Such organisations are often unable to compete with efficient foreign competitors. Japan's automobile industry was originally protected from competition from cheap carmakers like Fiat in Italy. However, within the Japanese market there was fierce competition among half a dozen domestic firms, the most efficient of which, Toyota and Honda, found great success in export markets in Europe and the USA. By contrast carmakers in France, Italy and the UK, where the governments had encouraged the development of just one or two 'national champions' with large shares of their own markets, were unable to sustain a presence in highly competitive markets such as the USA.

5.2.2 Economic factors

All products and services are either purchased directly by consumers, form inputs into things that are bought by consumers, or are purchased by government departments that are funded by taxes and duties that are eventually paid by consumers. Consumer spending power is thus a major factor in the prosperity of any industry. In most developed and a number of developing countries, personal disposable income has been steadily increasing for the past three decades.

If an economy booms, as happened in many countries during the mid 1980s and 1990s, it will promote the growth of many industries, particularly those producing highly differentiated or luxury goods. Economic downturns or slumps, such as occurred at the beginning of both the 1980s and 1990s, cause difficulties for most industries. However, they may help the growth of subsectors that offer exceptional value for money. For example, low-priced, 'no-frills' airlines first appeared in the USA in the early 1980s. They were made possible by a political factor, the deregulation of the US airline industry, which loosened the hold of established airlines on the route network. However, their development was aided by a severe economic recession, which made both business and leisure travellers more price sensitive, and so more open to the kind of service these airlines offered. It also led established airlines to put unwanted aircraft on the market at affordable prices.

Factors such as rates of economic growth, unemployment and interest rates, which affect the spending power of consumers and businesses, usually have a major impact on the nature of competition in an industry. Increasingly, strategists are more interested in the state of the global economy rather than that of individual countries, and many firms, large and small, operate internationally. The major world economies are increasingly interdependent, with interest rates in Japan, USA and Europe affected by global currency markets.

Within individual countries, governments' macro-economic policies will affect inflation and exchange rates. Very low or negative inflation, such as that experienced in Japan during 1999, can deflate demand for non-essential items, because consumers postpone purchases in the expectation that prices will fall further. High inflation can lead to a demand for products, such as land and jewellery, that consumers regard as a hedge against inflation, and to a reluctance to invest, because interest rates are high and returns unpredictable. It may also lead employees to make high wage demands and to be unwilling to make sacrifices for the long-term good of the organisation, because they too are uncertain what kind of returns they will get on their time and effort.

A low exchange rate may fuel inflation because it makes imported goods dearer, but may assist industries that export a lot of their output. Conversely, a high exchange rate may make it difficult for an organisation to compete in export markets, although there have been instances, such as in Japan in the late 1980s, where high exchange rates stimulated firms to enhance their competitiveness through innovation and improved efficiency.

Other important economic factors relate to the supply of and demand for key inputs, such as oil, metals, minerals and skilled labour. Shortages of these inputs result in prices (or salaries) increasing, which may affect the profitability of industries that need to purchase them.

5.2.3 Social and cultural factors

Just as consumer purchasing power ultimately determines the magnitude of demand for all goods and services, so consumer tastes ultimately determine where that demand is directed. Sometimes these tastes are manifested in what consumers themselves actually buy. In other cases they are expressed through voting, lobbying and other political processes, which influence the decisions of politicians and civil servants.

Certain social trends have a life of only a few years. Sometimes they last long enough and are widespread enough to be noticed by sociologists or journalists, and glorified with a name. Examples are the 'me generation' of the mid-1980s, which was said to favour ostentatious consumption of consumer goods, food and drink, and the more nihilistic 'Generation X' of the early 1990s. Sometimes, these trends are linked to phases of economic boom or bust.

Some trends have a life of several decades and widespread relevance across Europe, the USA and other developed economies. A good environmental analysis would usually take the following factors into account:

- Consumer awareness of 'green' environmental issues, which dates back to the early 1970s and continues to be important.

- Growing consumer assertiveness and intolerance of poor service. This is related to a change in the balance of power between producers and consumers that followed the recovery of industry from the Second World War, so that in most industries supply now exceeds demand rather than vice versa. New sources of consumer information have sprung up in the mass media and, more recently, on the Internet. These are a response to this trend, but at the same time have amplified it.

- Increases in the proportion of households which contain either just one person or two adults, both working. While average household income has risen, the time available to spend it has decreased, and there has been a resulting increase in demand for childcare services and for products such as ready-prepared meals and fast food.

- An increasing awareness of other countries as sources of food and fashion, and as places to visit. This has been fuelled by the decreasing cost of air travel and increases in personal disposable income.

- Growing acceptance of computers and the Internet as tools for education, leisure, information-gathering and purchasing goods and services.

5.2.4 Technological factors

Many major transformations in the ways firms compete can be traced to technological change. Sometimes these changes span the boundaries of many industries, and trigger changes in society itself.

In the field of *product* technology, the clearest trend has been the incorporation of electronics into everyday objects. Starting in the late 1940s with the invention of the transistor, this trend has continued through the introduction of integrated circuits in 1958 and microprocessors in 1978. The story of the last two decades has been the increasing power and memory capacity of microchips which, as well as making possible new industries like personal computers and mobile communications, have been incorporated into established products like washing machines, drinks dispensers and toys.

The increasing power and decreasing size and cost of microprocessors has revolutionised **information and communications technology**. Computers have become more freely available, enabling small firms to afford technologies such as computer-aided design that were once limited to large organisations. Related technologies such as bar-coding and EPOS (electronic point of sale) equipment have enabled firms to gather more data than ever before about their operations and their customers. Developments in telecommunications and computer networking have made it feasible to share that information quickly and cheaply, so that headquarters' decisions in international organisations need no longer be based upon data that are weeks or months old. Organisations that have been able to adapt their systems and cultures to make use of these technologies may have an advantage over those that have not.

These technologies in their turn have assisted developments in production, logistics and marketing technology. Modem production technology dates from post-war Japan, in particular the **lean production** methods pioneered by Toyota, the Japanese automobile manufacturer. Toyota's system is based around minimising inventories, having raw materials and subassemblies delivered 'just-in-time' to the place where they are needed, and reconfiguring manufacturing equipment so that it becomes easier to switch equipment from one type of product to another. It contrasts with the classical mass production system invented by Henry Ford in the early years of the twentieth century, where firms aimed for long production runs and kept enough inventory on hand to minimise the possibility of production being halted by lack of parts. This revolution in production methods has been assisted by the development of CNC (computer numerically controlled) machine tools that can be easily reprogrammed to switch between tasks and manufacture parts to fine tolerances, reducing waste. Integrated CAD/CAM (computer-aided design/computer-aided manufacturing) systems enable designs to be tested on computers before they are manufactured, and then quickly translated into instructions for the production systems. Computerised manufacturing systems have helped firms plan their production schedules and keep track of work in progress. All of these developments started to find their way into factories in the USA and Europe around the mid-1980s.

Information technology has influenced the way in which ideas, as well as physical items, are produced and stored. CAD software helps designers visualise and test their concepts. Newer **groupware** products enable several people in different locations to comment on a drawing or document and suggest alterations. They are also a way for people who have solved a particular professional problem to put those solutions on to a database that can be accessed by colleagues involved in similar projects. These technologies help both people in manufacturing industry and those in pure service firms such as architects and consultancies.

The 'lean' philosophy that has been so influential in manufacturing has also been incorporated into the technology of logistics, the function that deals with the storage and distribution of inputs and finished products. Sophisticated sensors have been developed to monitor the condition of items while they are being stored or delivered, reducing wastage. New networking technologies have enabled producers and retailers to link their ordering systems directly to their suppliers through EDT (electronic data interchange), so that items are ordered automatically and manufacturers/retailers need to carry less stock.

Marketing technology has benefited from an improved understanding of consumer psychology and the availability of more detailed survey data on consumer habits and preferences. This has led firms to move from mass marketing, where a limited range of products was marketed to a broad audience, to closer targeting of particular products at particular market segments. With the availability of more powerful computers to store and analyse customer data, and new **data-mining** software to analyse the data to find underlying patterns in customers' purchases, organisations can potentially track their buyers' requirements more precisely than ever before.

Most recently, with the advent of the world wide web, the world has seen the emergence of **electronic commerce** (e-commerce or e-business). This has given businesses the ability to offer consumers, and other businesses, a broad range of items such as books, toys, electronic components or chemicals – far broader than if they were constrained by the size of their own physical warehouses. They can also make those catalogues easily searchable and add value by offering extra services, such as feedback from other users.

While political, economic and social forces affecting an industry are always external,[4] technological change can be triggered either inside or outside an industry. For example, the invention of the microprocessor, while transforming many industries, had a major impact on competition in the electronic components industry where the innovation took place. It gave power to firms like Intel that mastered the new technology, and removed it from early industry leaders that did not, like Fairchild Semiconductor.

This section may seem like a litany of praise for new technology. However, not all technologies are right for all industries or types of firm, and not everyone finds them beneficial. In small firms, for example, conversations may be more effective than computers for passing information around the organisation and controlling progress. Small firms are sometimes unable to persuade their suppliers to keep to just-in-time delivery schedules, and are forced to hold buffer stocks instead. Firms dealing in items that do not deteriorate with storage can sometimes do better by buying stock in bulk and keeping it until needed, rather than implementing complex just-in-time systems. Just-in-time delivery and EDT systems, while beneficial to producers and retailers, can be very disruptive to the suppliers that have to implement new systems and conform to very demanding production schedules. And e-commerce, while potentially powerful, has yet (at the time of writing) to force many traditional firms out of business or to produce more than a handful of profitable firms, although that is a situation that may well change in the next few years.

Practical dos and don'ts — PEST analysis

1. When carrying out a PEST analysis it is important to show **how** and **how much** the factors that you pick out influence the nature of competition. It is this appraisal of the impact of each factor that distinguishes an analysis from a mere list.

2. Keep your analysis of past developments separate from that of the present situation and future trends. A common error is to try and devise a single analysis to try and cover the entire history of a firm or an industry. Depending upon the question you are trying to answer, you may only be interested in a particular period.

3. When analysing PEST factors in the present, make it plain why the present is different from the past, and how the industry may need to change. Similarly, explain to what extent and why the future may be different from the present.

4. Do not agonise too long over whether a particular item is political, economic, social or technological in nature. Many important factors transcend the simple PEST categories. The advent of the microprocessor is a technological event that has had a broad economic and social impact. The 'green' movement may have started as a socio-cultural phenomenon, but it has been translated into legislation and has stimulated technological change.

5. It is perfectly legitimate when using a checklist like PEST to leave some categories empty. If there are no important political/legal influences on a

▶

Practical dos and don'ts continued

particular industry, do not waste time trying to find factors that do not exist! Limit yourself to the important and relevant factors.

6. PEST is not a set of rigid compartments into which ideas need to be painstakingly sorted. It is better thought of as a set of hooks that can be used to fish for important facts – once the factors have been 'fished out', it does not matter which hook they were attached to. When you come to write up your analysis, you need not mention the PEST labels at all.

5.3 The industry life-cycle

Figure 5.2 shows a typical industry life-cycle, comprising four phases (other models have five; the basic principles remain the same).

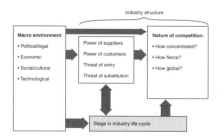

1. In the introductory phase of an industry, new products and their technologies are in their infancy and can be rather unreliable. Customers may be enthusiasts who like and understand the technology well enough to cope with its unreliability, like the people who bought the first personal computers in kit form and then assembled them. Or they may be people or firms, often wealthy, who like progress for its own sake or want to be seen to be progressive. This phase may last a few months or many years – the introductory phase for the electric car industry has lasted over a century!

2. In the growth phase, the product starts to become established, and there may be some improvements in the product and in the process technology used to produce it. Demand may be so high that firms face problems keeping up with it. If they can, however, and their products keep pace with the changing technology, they may be able to survive even if their quality is still indifferent. New firms may enter the industry to take advantage of opportunities there, or because they have some technological innovation that they believe will give them an advantage.

3. In the mature phase, the rate of industry sales growth slows. Typically, this coincides with a settling down in the rate of technological progress, so that product and process development become more stable. Firms can invest in large production facilities with less risk that they will become quickly outdated. Differentiation advantage based on product innovation becomes less important than cost advantage gained through process improvements.

4. During the decline phase, sales in the industry fall, perhaps because everyone who wants the product has already bought one or because substitute products have become more attractive. Because demand is in decline, firms will not want

Figure 5.2 The industry life-cycle

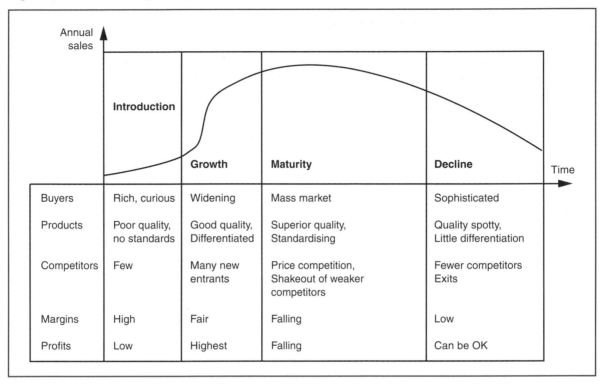

	Introduction	Growth	Maturity	Decline
Buyers	Rich, curious	Widening	Mass market	Sophisticated
Products	Poor quality, no standards	Good quality, Differentiated	Superior quality, Standardising	Quality spotty, Little differentiation
Competitors	Few	Many new entrants	Price competition, Shakeout of weaker competitors	Fewer competitors Exits
Margins	High	Fair	Falling	Low
Profits	Low	Highest	Falling	Can be OK

to invest a great deal in new product or process technologies. It is possible for declining industries to be quite profitable, as long as there are not too many companies competing for a shrinking customer base.

Industries in the introductory or growth phases are sometimes called *emerging industries*. Some authors identify a fifth 'shakeout phase', just before the maturity phase, when a slowing of an industry's growth rate causes a lot of firms to exit. However, recent research (Klepper and Simons, 1996) has shown that shakeouts can occur at any stage in an industry's development and are not necessarily more common when the rate of sales growth is falling.

Like many strategic models, the industry life-cycle is a simplification of reality that glosses over a lot of exceptions. Not all industries go through all these phases. Some, like housing, will naturally stay in the mature phase, although demand may fluctuate greatly from year to year depending on the state of a country's economy. Some may move to maturity or even decline before being rejuvenated by a change in consumer tastes or by a technological development that moves them back to the growth phase (Real-Life Application 5.1).

We return to the different industry life-cycle stages in Chapter 12. ▶ When analysing the nature of competition in an industry, the crucial point to look out for is the changes between the different stages, for example from growth to maturity. At these points the basis of competition may change; firms may move from seeking differentiation advantage (on the basis of innovation and functionality) and give greater weight to cost advantage.

REAL-LIFE APPLICATION 5.1

Mature industries that rediscover their youth

By the early 1980s, demand for bicycles had reached a low point, as alternative, more comfortable, means of transport such as the car became more affordable by more people. However, a renewed interest in healthy lifestyles, particularly in the USA, gave consumers a new reason to buy bicycles. Producers responded with a new product, the mountain bike, which quickly became the new industry standard. Together, these two developments moved the bicycle industry into a new phase of growth.

At the end of the 1980s, the Personal Computer industry appeared to have matured. Technology had stabilised, and new competitors had appeared emphasising cost rather than quality, supported by new suppliers offering good-quality standard components at low prices. Customers had grown accustomed to specifying and using PCs, and were becoming more discriminating in their purchases. Increasingly, they were reluctant to purchase unnecessary upgrades and were price-selective, partly because a slowing economy was putting pressure on their own margins. However, the incorporation of multimedia technology into PCs opened up new markets in the home, and a new growth phase began.

5.3.1 Influence of PEST factors on the industry life-cycle

The two cases in Real-Life Application 5.1 illustrate the kinds of factor that make customers reappraise whether they really want or need the industry's products:

- Socio-cultural changes may trigger changes in customer tastes.
- Political or technological changes may make substitute products more attractive.
- Economic changes may alter people's ideas of what constitutes value for money.

It was changes in these PEST factors that caused the bicycle and PC industries to move from growth to maturity and back again. Industry life-cycle analysis can thus be seen as an extension of PEST analysis, and a way of showing how certain PEST factors influence the development of an industry over time.

More rarely, industries become mature when everyone who needs a product has already bought one, so that sales are largely replacements for broken or worn-out goods. This phenomenon is known as demand (or market) saturation.

5.3.2 ADVANCED TOPIC
Population ecology of organisations

The industry life-cycle was developed as a way of making sense of a pattern that many researchers had observed in a number of industries. It has been widely used in the strategy literature, particularly after Michael Porter employed it as the organising framework for his influential 1980 book, *Competitive Strategy*. However, there has been little rigorous research to validate it, or investigate how well it explains the evolution of particular types of industry.

Some careful research by sociologists, led by Hannan and Freeman,[5] has shown that, for a wide variety of industries, the number of firms in an industry follows an inverted U-shape over time, a pattern that is quite similar to the industry life-cycle. For example, Figure 5.3 shows the shape of the curve charting numbers of auto-

Figure 5.3   Variations in numbers of automobile manufacturers over time in a typical European country.

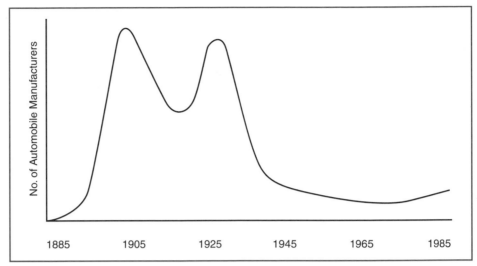

Source: Derived from data presented in Hannan et al. (1995).

mobile manufacturers in a typical European country. If one discounts the sharp dip around 1915 (which corresponds to the First World War) this could easily be an industry life-cycle curve.

Hannan, Freeman and their associates are known as the population ecology school, because they study patterns in the birth and death of organisations in the same way that biologists study patterns in populations of plants and animals. Alongside the inverted U-shape pattern in the number of firms remaining, they have identified a high rate of collapse in the early and late years of an industry so that the number of firms exiting an industry follows a U-shaped curve.

Population ecologists have developed hypotheses to explain the shape of these two curves. During an industry's early years, they believe that the number of firms grows as a result of **legitimation,** as word spreads about the industry and its products and new firms become attracted to it. They attribute the high exit rate during this same period to a phenomenon called the **liability of newness.** New organisations take time to develop the stable routines needed to survive, and during that period there is a high probability that they will collapse. If an organisation survives long enough to develop these routines, it becomes less vulnerable. However, as it grows older and larger, those routines become more and more entrenched and difficult to change. Population ecologists believe that this **inertia** makes it difficult for mature organisations to change as fast as their environment. They claim that inertia explains why the number of organisations fall, and the number of failures rise, later in an industry's life.

Population ecology theory does not allow any role to micro-economic factors like competition and profits in its explanation of why firms enter and leave an industry. It holds that, after making allowance for major events like wars and recessions, the number of firms entering an industry depends solely upon the number of firms already in it. Sophisticated mathematical models have been developed to demonstrate this relationship.

In general, population ecologists take a fatalistic view of individual organisations' prospects. They do not believe that there is much that managers can do about either the liability of newness or inertia. Whether a particular firm survives or not is largely due to how well it is adapted to its environment. Most of strategic management theory on the other hand, is devoted to working out how managers should act to improve their organisations' prospects of survival and success. If the population ecologists are right, most of this book is a waste of time and paper.

There is little doubt that the results of population ecology studies are valid: the inverted U-shaped industry population curve and the U-shaped organisational mortality curve have been demonstrated in many industries. However, the population ecologists' explanations of those results are more open to dispute. While they have shown for some industries that legitimation occurs at the same time as industry growth, they have not found overwhelming evidence that it *causes* industry growth. While the concept of inertia has elements in common with what other theorists have called competency traps, core rigidities and the 'Icarus paradox', no other branch of theory holds it to be as inevitable or irreversible as the population ecologists do. There have been no studies within organisations to test the concept of inertia, to demonstrate that it is related to organisational mortality or to show that it is as inevitable that large organisations will change more slowly than their environment.

We look at competency traps and core rigidities in Chapter 7, and the Icarus paradox can be reviewed in Chapter 3. ▶

Throughout this book, and in particular in Chapters 7 and 14, you will see evidence from case studies and research that managers *can* influence the survival prospects of their firms, and that firms are able to respond to, and sometimes influence, environmental change. In our view, this evidence is more persuasive than the population ecologists' arguments.

5.4 Industry analysis: Porter's five forces

The PEST analysis deals with factors outside an industry that influence the nature of competition within it. Next we look at the forces *inside* the industry that influence the way in which firms compete, and so the industry's likely profitability. Michael Porter (1979, 1980) identified five such forces:

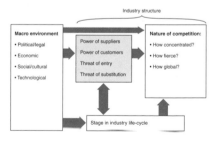

1. *The bargaining power of suppliers* – if this is strong, then the suppliers will be able to charge high prices and take for themselves a lot of the profit that might otherwise have gone to firms in the industry.

2. *The bargaining power of buyers* – if this is strong, then firms in the industry will be limited in how high they can set their prices, and may be forced to incur high costs in order to meet their customers' demands.

3. *The threat of new entrants* – if this is high, then every time industry profits reach an attractive level, new firms will come into the industry, competition will intensify and profits will fall.

4. *The threat of substitution* – if this is high, then customers will switch to a different product if they feel that they are being overcharged, or receiving poor value for money from the industry.

5. *The intensity of rivalry between firms in the industry* – if this is high, then firms will compete away much of the profit that might be extracted from the industry.

In this section, we look at the first four of these five forces in turn and give some practical tips on how to analyse them. The fifth force, the intensity of industry rivalry, is dealt with separately (Section 5.5) as it is the most important of the five and the others are really just contributory factors. (In Porter's own diagram, rivalry among existing firms stands at the centre, with the other four forces influencing it.)

Industry structures change over time as the underlying PEST factors change and the industry moves through its life-cycle. This means that, as with PEST analysis, you should carry out separate five forces analyses for the past, the present and the future.

5.4.1 Supplier power

Supplier power
The degree to which the suppliers to an industry have the power to dictate prices, quality standards, delivery lead times and other terms and conditions to the firms that they are supplying.

In most industries, firms rely upon suppliers to ensure that their goods and services are available on time and at a high enough quality. Fast-food firms like McDonald's need supplies of meat, bread, fuel, premises and cooking equipment. Airlines need supplies of aeroplanes, fuel and airport facilities, together with the time 'slots' during which its aircraft are able to take off and land. Service organisations like banks, advertising agencies or local governments need supplies of office buildings and equipment, as well as skilled people. The balance of power between an industry and its suppliers depends on who needs whom the more.

By and large, if firms in an industry have a **wide variety of suppliers to choose from**, then those suppliers have little power. Fast-food firms have power over suppliers of burger buns, for example. Even if the supplier firms are large, they may still not be very powerful – major airlines have power over the oil companies that supply their aviation fuel, which are among the largest corporations in the world. That is because aviation fuel is largely **undifferentiated** – one supplier is as good as another, and in most locations there are no **switching costs** – all suppliers offer similar facilities. In all these cases, it is the supplier that needs to win the business, while the firms in the industry can shop around.

Switching costs
Costs that a firm incurs when it changes from one supplier or type of product to another.

On the other hand, suppliers can be powerful if they are **relatively few in number** and their **inputs are vital to the quality of the finished product**. It is important to many travellers to be able to arrive at their destination in time for the start of the working day, and airlines that can deliver this are more attractive than those that cannot. For this reason, the airports or governments that control the allocation of take-off and landing slots have power over the airlines.[6] Firms that supply major subsystems like braking and fuel injection to the automobile industry are becoming increasingly powerful, even though their customers are themselves large and powerful firms. For each subsystem, there are only two or three firms with the necessary technological competences. The quality of these subsystems makes a major difference to the performance of the vehicle, so it is in the car manufacturer's interest to spend a little extra to be sure of getting these components exactly right.

One reason why the makers of automobile subsystems are becoming powerful is because the technology in their area is increasingly too complex for a non-specialist firm to master. This means that there is little **threat of backward integration** by the automobile manufacturers. By contrast, many automobile manufacturers have long retained the capability to make more traditional, low-technology components themselves. This increases their power versus the suppliers of this kind of part.

Sometimes, even sophisticated suppliers with few competitors may have little power. There are only two major suppliers of airliners: Boeing and Airbus. Airline companies have no prospect of being able to integrate backwards into aircraft manufacturing and their switching costs are high, since a fleet consisting solely of Boeing or Airbus aircraft is far cheaper for airlines to maintain than a mixed fleet. However, the two firms compete strongly on price for every order, partly for reasons of national pride, and partly because of the economics of airliner production. It is **important for them to get a high volume of orders** if they are to recover the very high costs of developing new aircraft. This gives the airline companies a great deal of power over their suppliers of aircraft.

It will be clear from these examples that industries may have several types of supplier, some powerful and some not. If the powerful suppliers only account for a small proportion of the cost of the industry's outputs, then supplier power overall can be judged to be low. If, on the other hand, a large proportion of the product's value to the customer is in the hands of powerful suppliers, then overall supplier power will be high.

One way of working out where the balance of power lies is to look at profit margins and returns on capital. If the suppliers are more profitable than the firms in the industry, then that is a sign that they are powerful enough to be able to negotiate a share of the industry's profits.

Relationship with PEST and life-cycle analysis

Political decisions may give, or remove, a monopoly from particular classes of supplier, as has happened with electricity supply, for example, in the UK, India and parts of South America. Political or economic instability can also lead to disruption

---

| Practical dos and don'ts | Supplier power |

1. Remember that the aim is to **assess the power** of suppliers. If all that you have done is to list who the suppliers are, then you have not finished the analysis – in fact, you have hardly started it!

2. Remember that you are **not** looking at the power of the firms in the industry *as suppliers* – that is analysed under buyer power. You are looking at the power of those firms *vis-à-vis* the organisations that *supply them*. (It is quite common for students to get confused about this.)

3. Look at the way in which the various players in the industry actually behave, rather than the way you might expect them to behave. In the last example, you might expect Airbus and Boeing to be powerful suppliers, but most of the time they are not.

of supply from one country, and this may increase the power of the remaining suppliers. Technological change may make substitutes available for certain kinds of input. Sometimes this leaves all the suppliers weakened, because firms can play the new producers off against the old. Drinks firms used to be restricted to glass bottles and steel cans, but can now choose PET bottles or aluminium cans. If the new input is clearly superior, on the other hand, its suppliers may start from a position of strength. Entrepreneurs who have switched from bank finance to venture capital find that their new suppliers are very powerful indeed.

Early in an industry's life-cycle, when the technologies are new, firms that can supply key components to it may start from a position of strength, particularly as they are likely to be larger and financially stronger than the companies they are supplying. As an industry matures, the technologies settle down and the firms in the industry become larger and more sophisticated. One would expect this to reduce supplier power but, if key technologies are outsourced, as has happened in the automobile industry it may actually increase it.

5.4.2   Buyer power

Buyer power

The extent to which an industry's customers have the power to dictate prices, quality standards and other terms and conditions to the firms that are supplying them.

Many of the same considerations that we looked at in the previous section apply, in reverse, when considering the bargaining power that an industry's buyers have *vis-à-vis* the firms in the industry. If the industry's customers have a *wide variety of firms to choose from* and if the industry's products are largely **undifferentiated**, then the buyers will have considerable power.

Switching costs are a particularly important consideration in looking at the relationship between the firms in an industry and their customers. It can be irksome for an individual to change bank, because of the sheer tedium of notifying all the utilities and other firms that may regularly put money into the account or take payments from it. This constitutes a switching cost. There are switching costs for firms in changing their accounting systems, because of the time needed to retrain users and to transfer data from one format to another.

It is tempting to think, for example, that because retailers like Benetton and McDonald's are large firms and able to exert a lot of power over their own suppliers, they are also more powerful than their buyers, who are just individuals and families. However, there are very few switching costs for a family when it decides to buy its food or clothing from one retailer rather than another. This means that it is often the customer who has the power. A single customer who switches will make little difference to McDonald's, because the proportion that they contribute to the company's turnover will be small. However, if a firm's prices rise or quality standards fall, it may be only the switching costs that determine whether or not the customers defect en masse.

The relative size of the financial investment is also an important determinant of power. Buyer power may be low if a product accounts for a small proportion of their costs, so that they do not notice much if prices rise. However, this will not be the case where this product also makes a major difference to the performance of their own output. An example is the switch that controls the cooling fan in a car – it costs very little in relation to the whole vehicle, but if it fails the car is unusable.

In theory, buyers' power is diminished if the quality of what they are buying is important to them or to the performance of their own products. However, even in cases like pharmaceuticals (of vital importance to the end user) or automobiles (major items of expenditure where the user cannot normally afford a mistake), the balance of power lies with the buyers because they have so many reliable producers to choose from. In both industries, this is leading to consolidation as firms merge to try and maximise economies of scale.

One factor in the pharmaceuticals industry is that it is not the end-user that specifies the product, but the doctors, who in many countries choose drugs from a list drawn up by a central administration or a health insurer. These intermediaries compensate for the fact that most sick people know far less about the products they are buying than the pharmaceuticals firms do. One factor that does reduce buyer power is *lack of information* on what distinguishes a good product from a bad one, which producers are reliable and which are not. In most established industries, such information is freely available, particularly since the advent of the Internet.

Another factor that is often quoted as reducing buyer power is if firms in an industry have a credible threat of integrating forwards. Here again, it pays to be sceptical. Many clothing manufacturers have integrated forwards into retailing, but this does not seem to make buyer power any less for the clothing industry as a whole. Meanwhile, some vertically integrated groups, like the UK's Laura Ashley, have found it difficult to manage the different sets of competences involved in manufacturing and retailing, and have experienced financial problems as a result.

Practical dos and don'ts   **Buyer power**

1. For most modern industries, it is best to start with the assumption that buyer power is high, and then look for reasons, such as unusually high profits, to believe otherwise.

2. Be careful **not** to do the same piece of analysis twice, analysing the power of firms in the industry versus their suppliers under supplier power, and their own power as buyers under buyer power. Under buyer power, we are looking at firms' power *vis-à-vis* their own customers.

3. Even though one or two firms in an industry may have found ways of making themselves indispensable to their customers, for example by providing excellent service at low prices, this does **not** mean that buyer power *for the whole industry* is low. In this analysis, we are looking at normal practice for the industry. If one firm has managed to do better (or worse) than average, then that is part of its business strategy, and can be analysed using the techniques we outline in Chapters 6, 7 and 8.

4. As with supplier power, the aim of this analysis is to **assess the power** of the buyers, not simply to list them.

Relationship with PEST and life-cycle analysis

As we have seen, buyer power is low when it is difficult to find reliable producers within an industry or reliable information about the product. For this reason, one can expect buyer power to be at its lowest during the introductory and growth phases of an industry and to increase as the industry matures. There can be exceptions to this, where the buyers are technologically sophisticated and there are serviceable substitutes already available. In that case, the customers will have the power throughout the industry's life-cycle.

PEST factors will affect buyer power largely by making an industry's products more or less attractive relative to substitutes, so triggering changes in the industry life-cycle. In addition, economic changes will tend to alter buyer power (or, more precisely, their willingness to use their power) by making them more or less cost-conscious. As a rule, buyer power tends to be more evident in a recession than in a boom.

5.4.3 The threat of substitution

Buyer power is strongly influenced by the availability of substitute products. If customers have a choice, not just between rival producers but between rival products, then this will increase their power. This will make it more difficult for the firms in either of the rival industries to sustain high profits.

The threat of substitution is probably the most difficult of all the five forces to assess. Not all products have realistic substitutes – there are few for some medical items like blood plasma for transfusions for example. When personal computers were introduced, the substitutes – calculators, typewriters, abacuses – were so weak as to be negligible. Indeed, for much of the 1980s it was the PC that was posing a threat of substitution to other products.

Working out what constitutes a substitute can require a degree of insight. There are three types of substitute:

- Things that carry out the same function as the product or service – so audio-cassettes are substitutes for CDs, CD-ROMs for books.

- Dissimilar items that fulfil the same psychological need – for example, chocolates or champagne are substitutes for roses.

- Items that compete for the same spending power. These are the most difficult to spot. For example it appears that mobile telephones are substitutes for CDs, even though they do not (at the time of writing) play music or calm you down after a hard day. But one way in which young people afford their mobile phones is by cutting down on music and so (according to anecdotal evidence we have heard) as mobile phone penetration rates rise, CD sales fall.

The strength of the threat posed by a substitute depends on whether it offers better value for money than an industry's own products – whether it is cheaper, more durable, more convenient to use. Plastic and cardboard cartons have mostly replaced glass bottles for many drinks, because they are cheaper to buy and also to transport and stack in supermarkets. However, some people prefer the appearance of glass, believe it makes the contents taste better than plastic or cardboard and are prepared to pay a premium for a glass container. For some applications, glass remains the preferred medium, but the threat of substitution by plastic grows ever stronger.

Like buyer power, the threat of substitution can be moderated if customers incur switching costs when changing between substitute products.

Practical dos and don'ts **Threat of substitution**

1. Beware of confusing substitutes with competitors. Competition occurs between firms in the same industry, substitution between firms in different industries. However, by deciding which firms count as competitors rather than sources of substitutes, you are essentially defining the boundaries of an industry, which are not always clear. We return to this problem in Section 5.6.

2. Don't just list the substitutes – assess the strength of the threat that they pose!

Relationship with PEST and life-cycle analysis

Technological developments have an obvious and important influence on the threat of substitution. They can lead to the development of new products and services that may make one industry's products uncompetitive, driving it into the maturity or decline phase in its life-cycle.

Sometimes political, legal and social changes are needed to prepare the ground for a technological change. Technological advances in biotechnology have led to the development of foodstuffs that are genetically modified (GM) to repel certain pests. These pose a threat of substitution to firms in the pesticide industry that is likely to grow over time. However, many European consumers (though not as yet their counterparts in the USA) seem concerned about eating foods prepared using genetically modified ingredients. Some UK supermarkets have undertaken to stop selling such products, while there has been agitation for GM products to be specially labelled, or even banned outright.

5.4.4 The threat of new entrants

Barrier to entry
Any advantage that firms already operating in an industry hold over other firms that might potentially decide to start operating in it.

The height of **barriers to entry** determines the strength of the threat that new entrants pose to firms in an industry. Researchers have identified a number of types of potential barriers to entry, and we discuss each of them below. However, it is worth noting that much of the fundamental research on barriers to entry dates from the 1950s. Its conclusions cannot be taken for granted in a modern environment, where venture capital is increasingly freely available and the Internet is altering some of the rules of marketing. Theory in this area also assumes that firms are

Concept **Barriers to entry**

A *high* barrier to entry:

● **either** makes it very likely that new entrants will be forced to close down before they are able to establish themselves – for example, because no one buys their output, preferring to buy from established producers.

● **or** makes it unlikely that they will ever make an acceptable return on their investment – for example, because they are saddled with costs that established producers no longer have to bear, or because their entry disrupts competition in the industry to the extent where no one makes any money.

◀ For a critique of the concept of firms as rational economic actors see Section 2.2.1.

rational economic actors whose main objective is to make a super-normal return on capital. Many barriers to entry do not hold against an organisation that is prepared, for whatever reason, to tolerate low returns over a long period.

The barriers to entry that spring most easily to most people's minds are to do with size. Some industries require a **great deal of capital** to enter – for example, even the smallest manufacturing facility for computer processor or memory chips costs millions of euros or dollars. Even in industries that it is theoretically possible to enter for a modest capital outlay, the production economics may be such that small-scale producers suffer from major cost disadvantages. In industries like this – the automobile industry is one example – where **economies of scale** are important, a new entrant may be forced to risk considerable amounts of capital on large-scale manufacturing and marketing facilities. However, such a high-profile entry may well provoke established firms to cut prices or step up their marketing efforts to prevent the new competitor from getting a foothold in the market. Such **threats of retaliation** are also a potential barrier to entry.

Considerations like these, however, have not prevented new firms from entering both the microchip and automobile industries. The computer memory industry saw large-scale entry by Japanese and later Korean firms, who saw it as strategically important, and later drove out established American competitors like Intel. In the automobile industry, Malaysia's Proton and Korea's Daewoo have both entered during the last decade, even though they operate on a far smaller scale than the industry leaders, and the industry itself suffers from chronic overcapacity.

This illustrated that, if potential entrants have sufficient financial backing and motivation, then capital requirements and economies of scale effectively do not function as barriers to entry. The Korean and Malaysian firms referred to in the previous paragraph benefited from cheap finance from their national governments, which approved of their ventures into industries they saw as prestigious and strategically important. Some firms accumulate massive financial resources of their own which they can use to enter into almost any industry they wish: Microsoft, the computer software giant, and Ford, the US car maker, each has cash reserves of $20 billion. Nor are they likely to be deterred by the threat of retaliation – they have the resources to survive a price or advertising war.

Product differentiation is another factor often cited as a barrier to entry. Here, it is important to understand what kind of differentiation we are dealing with. If it is **easy** for one producer to differentiate itself from its competitors, then this **lowers** barriers to entry. An example is the restaurant business, where it is easy for a new entrant to differentiate on the basis of offering a new dish or a slightly different type of cuisine. Differentiation *can* become a barrier to entry in industries where firms have invested strongly in building reputation, and where reputation is generally important to customers in making their choices.

Here again, though, it is important to analyse carefully. There are many well-known, long-established brands in the hotel industry, such as Hilton and Holiday Inn. However, these did not prevent France's Novotel from building a global hotel chain from scratch during the 1970s. Nor do they inhibit small, family-run hotels from opening in holiday resorts. The world's best-known brand, and one of its strongest corporate reputations, is owned by The Coca-Cola Company. However, this has not prevented food retailers in many countries from introducing their own brands of cola. These soft drinks are often provided by Cotts, a Canadian firm, while the supermarket chains use their own reputations, gained from serving customers over long periods of time, to help offset the price advantages that Coca-Cola and Pepsi-Cola enjoy from their established brands. These own-label colas may not always be very profitable, but they help to improve the supermarkets' own power in negotiating with a strong supplier.

There are factors that genuinely can act as deterrents to entry. **Switching costs**, where they exist, can act to reduce the threat of entry, in the same way as we have already seen that they can reduce buyer power and the threat of substitution. If existing competitors have **strong relationships with their distribution channels**, then it can be difficult for new entrants' products to find a place on the supermarket shelves or in the warehouse. Distributors may not want to take the risk of stocking an untried brand, particularly if it involves antagonising a powerful incumbent firm. Successful entry strategies in such cases often involve the use of untried distribution channels, or vertical integration. Daewoo has penetrated the UK automobile market by selling through its own outlets, rather than using the industry's normal practice of recruiting established dealers. One of the reasons that the Body Shop plc was able to enter the toiletries industry in the 1970s was because it set up its own chain of franchised outlets to bypass the powerful retailers that favoured established brands.

There are other advantages that incumbent firms can enjoy, which make it difficult for new firms to enter. If existing firms have taken up all the reasonably priced sources of raw materials, or all the good locations, then it can be difficult for new firms to compete. It is at present difficult for new firms to enter the UK food retailing industry, because most of the good sites for hypermarkets and large supermarkets have been taken. Existing firms may also have knowledge assets, accumulated through research or from experience of producing and marketing the industry's outputs, which newer entrants can struggle to match. Here again, however, it is possible to overestimate the advantage that incumbents have. It is not easy to protect know-how: key staff can be lured away, products can be 'reverse engineered' (i.e. taken apart to see how they work and how they are put together) and legal protection can be difficult to enforce. Patents, for example, are often easy for competitors to circumvent through minor modifications, and to get one a firm must reveal key technical information. Quite minor advances in product or production technology can sometimes nullify the benefits of years of experience.[7]

| **Practical dos and don'ts** | **Threat of entry** |

1. As with buyer power, it is best to start with the assumption that the threat of entry is high – i.e. that barriers to entry are low – and then look for reasons to believe otherwise.

2. The clearest test of whether barriers to entry are high or low lies in looking at how many firms are actually entering the industry. If there is a steady stream of new entrants then, however imposing the capital and other barriers may look in theory, they are not functioning as a real deterrent.

3. Some firms in the industry may have strong brands or proprietary know-how, but these do not constitute barriers to entry unless just about all the other viable firms in the industry have similar assets. A new entrant may not need to out-compete the best firms in an industry – it may be able to establish itself simply by taking market share away from the weaker ones.

Perhaps the only truly insuperable barriers to entry are political and legal – and even these are not foolproof, as the world's flourishing trade in drugs and pornography shows. Legal restrictions frequently limit entry into industries like medicine, law, banking, airlines and telecommunications. Planning regulations can prevent the building of new airports, hotels or, as in the UK, supermarkets, thus increasing the advantage of incumbent firms that already have the necessary assets.

Relationship with PEST and life-cycle analysis

It should be clear from the earlier discussion that political and legal moves can have a major effect upon barriers to entry. European Union 'open skies' legislation has significantly reduced barriers to entry in the European airlines industry, by giving any European airline the right to carry passengers between any European cities.

Changes in the availability and price of raw materials, and technological advances can all affect ease of entry to an industry. For example, the Internet has dramatically reduced the cost of entry into banking by enabling firms to offer banking services without the need to invest in expensive branch networks.

Most barriers to entry are not affected by an industry's progression through its life-cycle. However, the transition from growth to maturity, and the resulting intensification of competition in an industry, is likely to reduce the threat of entry by making the industry less attractive, and by making it more likely that incumbent firms will take defensive action against a new entrant.

5.5 The nature of competition in an industry

As stated at the start of Section 5.4, the nature of competition in an industry is strongly affected by the other four of Porter's five forces. The stronger the power of buyers and suppliers, and the stronger the threats of entry and substitution, the more intense competition is likely to be within an industry.

However, these four factors are not the only ones that determine how firms in an industry will compete – the structure of the industry itself may play an important role. Indeed, the whole five-forces framework is based on an economic theory known as the 'Structure–Conduct–Performance' (SCP) model: the *structure* of an industry determines organisations' competitive behaviour (*conduct*), which in turn determines their profitability (*performance*). In concentrated industries, according to this model, organisations would be expected to compete less fiercely, and make higher profits, than in fragmented ones. However, as we shall see, the histories and cultures of the firms in the industry also play a very important role in shaping competitive behaviour, and the predictions of the SCP model need to be modified accordingly.

In the following section we look at the types of competitive behaviour that can occur in an industry. We then look at how economic structure is normally expected to influence this kind of behaviour.

5.5.1 Competitive behaviour

It is helpful to start with a review of how we recognise competition when we see it. Firms compete in a number of ways, of which the most common are:

- **Price.** The first think to look for in assessing whether competition in an industry is fierce or benign is for evidence of price wars, fiercely contested competitive tenders, discounting and other forms of price-based competition.

- **Marketing and advertising.** Firms can compete through expensive advertising campaigns, by offering promotional gifts to customers and distributors or by offering inducements to shops and distributors to display and promote their products and services. Sometimes these are inexpensive alternatives to price competition. The free gifts sometimes offered by fast food firms to lure younger customers, for example, are far less expensive than a price cut would be. Sometimes, as in the soft drinks industry, marketing-based competition may involve costly advertising campaigns and expensively bought endorsements from music and sports stars, and be accompanied by price competition.

- **Investment and product development.** In some industries, where differentiation on product features is important, firms will compete to bring the latest products to market. Sometimes, this is just for show. Although there are frequent product innovations in the personal computer and hi-fi industries, for example, the new features tend to appear on every producer's offerings at more or less the same time. These innovations serve to enhance the image of the industry as a whole, and to encourage customers to upgrade – they do not help one firm to gain advantage over another. However, in the airline industry, British Airways and Virgin Atlantic have both publicised their decisions to invest millions of dollars in upgrading their cabins to offer more comfortable sleeping arrangements to long-distance travellers. These decisions represent significant commitments of resources, both financial and reputational. Although they are quite easy to copy, both airlines are hoping that competitors lack the money and motivation to follow them.

  An extreme example of this kind of behaviour is an investment war, when every producer makes massive investment commitments in order to gain maximum economies of scale and frighten competitors into quitting the industry. This occurred in the computer memory industry in the 1980s, where a number of Asian producers simultaneously invested in new plant, leading to overcapacity in the industry and a subsequent price war.

- **Litigation.** Particularly in the USA, but increasingly also elsewhere, organisations may turn to the courts to delay a competitor from launching a new product or to drain its resources. For example, in the microprocessor industry, Intel launched a protracted lawsuit to prevent American Micro Devices (AMD) from marketing its clone of Intel's 80386 chip. Although AMD had a respectable case, it eventually settled out of court, so that it could use its money and management time in developing a range of products that contained no Intel technology.

The intensity of competition

We can say that there is *fierce* or *intense* competition in an industry if we can observe one or more of these forms of competitive behaviour and they are making a significant impact on firms' profitability. *In a fiercely competitive industry, most firms' operating profit margins are likely to decline over time*, although the industry leaders may find individual strategies that help them improve their profitability.

The scope of competition

Alongside the intensity of competition, we are interested in its scope. At one extreme are industries such as antiques retailing, where most firms may serve just one locality in a single country. At the other extreme, industries such as soft drinks or automobiles may be dominated by multinational firms serving markets around the world. In these global industries a local firm may struggle to compete. In between come industries like confectionery and airlines, where competition is to some extent limited to a single country or region, though in many cases it may be becoming more global.

Intensity and **scope of competition** are different things. Some international industries like automobiles are intensely competitive, others less so. The same is true of localised industries. As we shall see in Section 5.5.3, industry structure has an influence on both fierceness and scope of competition, but the habits that firms have evolved over time are also important.

Industry recipes and 'rules of the game'

◀ *These recipes are the equivalent of a firm's paradigm (see Section 1.2.5).*

In most industries, firms settle over time into recognisable patterns of competitive behaviour. For example, most clothing retailers will introduce new lines of merchandise twice a year, and hold periodic sales where out-of-date merchandise is sold at heavily discounted prices to make room for the newer lines. These patterns of behaviour often have a basis in the economics of the industry – clothing firms cannot sell the same merchandise in the summer and winter, and have not enough shelf or warehouse space to carry both types of clothing all the year round. Over time, though, this economic rational may become less important, but the routines persist because they become part of the cultures of many of the organisations in the industry. People learn these routines when they join one organisation, and carry them with them as they move from firm to firm. These ingrained routines are known as **industry recipes** (Spender, 1989).

Industry recipes can cover a wide variety of routines, such as ways of negotiating with suppliers, manufacturing methods and the number of days of credit offered to customers. The competitive aspects of these behaviours are sometimes known as the 'rules of the game'. These are accepted and expected pricing and marketing practices that define the boundaries of what firms can do without inciting their competitors to retaliate. No one will think Benetton is starting a price war if it holds a sale in January or July. Other examples of 'rules of the game' are the tacit[8] acceptance that certain firms within one industry will work closely with particular suppliers and distributors, or will be the leaders in certain markets where they have historically been strong. Competitors do not challenge these practices, because to do so would provoke retaliation and all firms in the industry would lose out.

Acceptance of these kinds of rules of the game rests on the recognition that in most industries competition is a fact of life, and that a manageable degree of competition is actually beneficial in stopping an organisation from becoming complacent and stale.

Strategic groups

It is quite rare for there to be just one type of competitive behaviour in an industry. For example, in clothes retailing, alongside the 'normal' retailers with their twice-yearly collections and sales, there are firms that differentiate on the basis of having very low prices at all times. Others, designer labels such as Armani or Chanel, differentiate on the basis of image, style and high price, and try to avoid discounting – their out-of-fashion merchandise is sold off discreetly through different outlets.

In Section 6.2 we look in more detail at how to identify and analyse strategic groups. ▶

These different types of behaviour define *strategic groups* within an industry. Each group has its own recipe and rules of the game, and there are *mobility barriers* that make it difficult for firms to move from one group to another. For example, Benetton at present occupies a mid-market group along with firms such as The Gap and H&M. If it were to want to move to the 'designer label' group, it would need to reposition its image and learn how to work with different fabrics.

5.5.2 Hypercompetition

Since a moderate amount of competition is beneficial, most firms are content to live with a few competitors that play by the same rules, and only retaliate strongly against those whose behaviour is unpredictable and potentially disruptive.[9] However, some theorists[10] claim to have identified a particularly fierce type of competition known as **hypercompetition**, where firms refuse to accept any competitors at all. Hypercompetition involves using all the forms of competition described above, together and sequentially, to overstretch competitors and force them to quit the industry. Perhaps the closest real-life approximation to this form of intensely competitive behaviour comes in the video-games industry, where different organisations have built commanding market shares through a combination of technological innovation, aggressive pricing and marketing and closed software standards that competitors are forbidden to imitate (Real-Life Application 5.2).

REAL-LIFE APPLICATION 5.2

The video-game industry

The first home video-games consoles came onto the market in 1977 and quickly became popular. By 1982, the Californian firm Atari had carved out a market share of over 60%. However, Atari allowed its main competitors to make compatible machines and did not restrict the right of independent developers to make software for its consoles. As a result, the market was flooded with poor quality games, and console sales collapsed.

The next generation of games, using 8-bit proces-sors, was dominated by Nintendo, a Japanese firm. It started a number of practices that were to become industry standards. It used a character, Mario the plumber, as the lead attraction for its system. It sold the games console relatively cheaply, determined to build volume and make its profits on the sales of games. It made its games' cartridges incompatible with other systems, and restricted the number of software houses that were licensed to produce games, to ensure good quality. Its Famicom and NES systems gained 90% of the market.

However, Nintendo was late into the market with the next generation of consoles, based on 16-bit processors. Although its Super Famicom system sold well initially, it was eventually outsold by Sega's Mega-Drive system (also known as the Genesis). Aggressive pricing and marketing and a popular character, Sonic the Hedgehog, gave Sega 50% of the market by the mid-1990s.

However, both firms were outmanoeuvred by Sony for command of the next generation of technology. Sony's PlayStation was based on a 32-bit processor and used CD-ROMS in place of cartridges for its software. It bought a well-regarded British game developer, Psygnosis, to ensure a supply of high-quality software. It also benefited from exclusive access to film characters from Sony's cinema business. It was able successfully to weather a counter-attack from Nintendo, which launched a 64-bit machine. To keep control of its hardware, it has used legal proceedings to stop the distribution of software that might enable a normal personal computer to run PlayStation games.

Each successive generation of games has brought a massive improvement in the quality of sound and graphics. The main battle for supremacy in 128-bit consoles is between Sega and Sony, although Microsoft

has also announced that it intends to enter the industry. Sega's Dreamcast was launched in Japan in 1998. It offers 3-D graphics, and uses a version of Microsoft Windows as its operating system. This makes it easy for independent houses to develop games for the machine, and also allows the use of some PC peripherals, such as modems.

However, in March 1999, Sony announced its PlayStation 2, which promised graphics and animation of similar quality and realism to those found in a top-quality animated film. Its graphics processor will be over 20 times as fast as the Dreamcast's and 200 times as quick as the original PlayStation. Although no PlayStation 2 consoles have yet been built, many industry observers are prepared to wait for it rather than commit to the proven but less breathtaking Sega machine.

Sony has made a major commitment in developing the PlayStation 2. In order to make a good return on its $500 million investment, it will need to sell 50 million units, approximately as many as Nintendo managed during its five-year period of near-monopoly during the 1980s.

Sources: Champion, D. and Kjellberg, A. (1998), Nintendo Case Study, INSEAD, France; Schofield, Jack, 'Consoles of War', *Guardian Online*, 11 March 1999, pp. 2–3.

5.5.3 Industry structure and competitive behaviour

Typically, strategists classify industries as *concentrated* (containing few producers) or *fragmented* (containing many producers). Concentrated industries fall into two categories:

- **Monopolies** are formally defined in economics textbooks as industries where there is just one producer. In practice, any industry where one producer dominates with, say 40% or more of the market, and where there are no competitors of comparable size, tends to be considered a monopoly.

- **Oligopolies** are industries where a small number of firms (say, six or fewer) account for almost all output.

Fragmented industries tend to be examples of what economists term 'monopolistic competition', where each producer tries to differentiate its products or services from its competitors' and/or to control a small market segment. In theory, there is another structure known as 'perfect competition', where the product is a commodity (so no differentiation is possible) and buyers have perfect information. However, in practice there is almost always some way in which firms can differentiate themselves (see Real-Life Application 5.3).

REAL-LIFE APPLICATION 5.3

A 'commodity' product

Salt is often cited as an example of a product that is a pure commodity – i.e. it is the same everywhere, and no differentiation is possible.

However, in fact over one hundred varieties of salt are sold, with different chemical compositions and crystal sizes. Salt sold for de-icing roads is coarser than table salt, while salt for water softeners is purer. Not all producers offer all these varieties of salt, and they also differ in their ability to serve particular customers. Salt is bulky, and costly to ship over long distances. Producers with access to a waterway have an advantage over those without.

The influence of scale and high up-front costs

An important influence on an industry's degree of concentration is the extent to which a firm's size and scale are significant. An industry where large firms have no particular advantages over small ones is quite likely to remain fragmented. One where there are significant economies of scale and scope is likely to become more concentrated over time. This is even more likely if the minimum economic firm size is a large proportion of the market size, so that there is only room for a few firms.

The extreme case of this is where there is only room for one firm in the market. Such industries are known as 'natural monopolies'. They require such expensive infrastructure that only a monopolist can make sufficient profits to justify the investment involved. Often governments fund the early development of these industries in the public interest. Examples are power, postal services and telecommunications industries, which many governments are now seeking to privatise.

Sometimes governments will set up monopolies on their own account: the Swedish government has a monopoly of the sales of alcoholic drinks, and the Italian government of tobacco sales. However, monopolies are usually held to operate against the public interest, so where they do exist government competition or anti-trust authorities tend to step in to break them up.

In most industries that are not natural monopolies, diminishing returns will make it difficult for a monopolist to serve all customers cheaply and effectively. However, if an industry shows increasing returns to scale it might tend towards a monopolistic structure.

Increasing versus diminishing returns

Most industries show diminishing returns to scale – the profit per unit decreases after a certain production volume is reached, until eventually the firm would make a loss if it tried to produce or sell any more goods or services. This is because it gradually becomes more difficult to find good sources of raw materials and appropriately qualified people to run the operations, and because once the 'easy' customers have bought the product, more effort and cost is required to penetrate more difficult markets.

Recently, theorists (e.g. Arthur, 1996) have identified certain industries – especially high-technology and knowledge-based ones – as having **increasing returns to scale**. The more that firms in these industries can produce, the more they can sell and the higher their profits. The products of these industries typically have **high up-front R&D costs**, which need to be recouped through high sales volumes. Their unit production costs, however, are low compared with the up-front costs and the sales price. Unit production costs do not rise as output increases. There are also **network effects** – the more people that use a particular product, the more desirable it becomes to all its users, and so the more people are likely to want to buy it.

A good example of increasing returns leading to an effective monopoly comes from the PC operating systems industry. It may cost over $50 million to develop a new version of an operating system, like Microsoft's Windows 98. Copies of the system typically sell for over €100/£50/$100, but the CD-ROM and documentation will cost less than 5% of the sales price to produce. There are no real limits on production – there are plenty of subcontractors who can reproduce CD-ROMs and printed matter in large volumes at high quality. Nor are there any real limits on demand: everyone who buys a computer needs an operating system and wants a widely used one that runs lots of common applications. As a result, Microsoft's operating systems, which have become the standard for most users, command 98% of the market.[11]

The effect of concentration on the intensity of competition

Economic theory has two main predictions regarding the effect of industry structure on the intensity of competition: competition in fragmented industries is expected to be fierce, as small firms struggle for a place in the market, while competition in concentrated industries is expected to be relatively benign. For example, profit margins in food retailing in the UK, where the five largest firms have almost 80% of the market, are far higher than in other countries where the industry is less concentrated.

However, not all industries follow this pattern. The restaurant industry is highly fragmented, yet competition is often on non-price factors, such as the quality of the cooking and service, and the variety of dishes on the menu. The soft-drinks industry, on the other hand, is very concentrated. In most countries, it is dominated by The Coca-Cola Company, PepsiCo Inc. and perhaps one or two local competitors. Yet Coke and Pepsi compete fiercely through expensive advertising campaigns, on price and by trying to woo each other's local bottlers. A rational justification for this behaviour is that by broadcasting their reputation as fearsome competitors, the two firms create a barrier to entry to the industry. But the rivalry between the firms has at least as much to do with the firms as social systems as with economic rationality. It dates from the 1950s, when an ex-Coca-Cola executive, Alfred Steele, joined Pepsi as CEO, and instilled into his new colleagues a deep dislike of his former employer.

Increasing returns may give rise to hypercompetitive behaviour. In these industries, once one firm's product is established as a standard, network effects can make it very difficult for even a technologically superior product to dislodge it – users' switching costs will be too high. Thus, it pays firms to try to establish their products as the industry standard and then reap the benefits. Microsoft is alleged to have used a variety of tactics against PC manufacturers to ensure that they installed Explorer, its Internet browser, to help to establish it as a standard. It feared that if users became too familiar with Netscape, a rival piece of software, then Netscape might threaten Microsoft's dominance by developing its browser into an alternative operating system. The video-games industry (Real-Life Application 5.2) is another example of hypercompetitive behaviour in a world of increasing returns.

Co-opetition

Although high up-front costs may move an industry towards increasing returns and hypercompetition, it may also, paradoxically, encourage organisations to collaborate in developing new products of markets. Collaboration may be necessary because the financial risk is too great for one firm to bear alone or because the development needs firms to pool their knowledge assets and capabilities. Firms collaborate to develop new products or services but may compete fiercely to produce and market them. This appears to be becoming increasingly common in today's systemic, mutually-dependent and interlinked global business environment. This hybrid form of competitive behaviour has been given the name 'co-opetition' (Brandenberger and Nalebuff, 1997; Burton, 1995).

Some of the best examples of this type of behaviour can be found in knowledge-intensive industries such as recorded music. In the world-wide music industry co-opetitive behaviour between firms is commonplace. Some of the most common examples are between *independent* record companies and the *majors*, companies such as Sony, Bertelsmann Music Group, or EMI, who in other circumstances could be considered to be in direct competition with each other. Each of these company types has what the other needs to succeed, however, and they have to collaborate. The *majors* bring competence in marketing and financial management, and a global distribution network; the *independents* are able to find and nurture the creative talent – new artistes – which are the foundation for important new musical trends, and which the rather more bureaucratic majors find harder to attract and develop themselves.

The effect of exit barriers on competition

Exit barrier
A factor that makes it difficult or expensive for a firm to leave an industry.

Alongside the degree of concentration in an industry and the industry paradigm, the presence of **exit barriers** may influence the intensity of competition. If there are high exit barriers, organisations are more likely to compete fiercely in order to try to survive, or at least to get the best return they can on their sunk investment costs.

The most frequent type of exit barrier is when firms have invested in equipment that has no alternative use. For example, when a firm builds a steelworks, it invests huge resources in furnaces and casting and rolling machinery that can only be used for processing steel. However, there may also be legislative and psychological barriers to exit. A steelworks is invariably a major employer, whose closure would be very damaging to the community where it is located. Governments may forbid it to close, or provide subsidies to keep it open. They may impose expensive conditions about providing training or alternative employment for staff who are made redundant. The organisations themselves may have strong ties to their communities and be reluctant to wound them. Managers may also have strong sentimental ties to the industry that may make them unwilling or unable to recognise that exit is needed. They may instead decide to hang in and await the next upturn. All of these exit barriers have been present in the steel industry, which, as a result, has suffered overcapacity and periodic price wars for three decades.

5.5.4 Industry structure and the scope of competition

Global product/market strategies are discussed in more detail in Section 6.5.1. ▶

As well as influencing the fierceness of competition in an industry, structural factors also influence whether it is conducted on a local, national, regional or global level. George Yip (1992) has outlined a number of factors that determine the extent to which an industry is likely to be global.

Concept ◼ **Global industry**

A global industry is one where firms compete using uniform products across the entire world. Often (although not always) they will use the same brand in every country. They will also tend to use centralised sourcing for their major inputs, buying raw materials wherever in the world they are cheapest or are available at the highest quality, rather than purchasing them from local suppliers in each country of operation. For example, many banks and airlines use Indian firms to handle their data processing, because that country boasts many highly qualified and reliable people, but has low labour costs.

Some industries, such as soft drinks, computer components, and aircraft, are highly globalised. Others, such as automobiles, operate at a regional level. There may be one product range for North America, a second for Western Europe, a third for Japan and another for sale in developing countries.

Although the industry structure may favour globalisation, firms often differ in the extent to which they choose to follow a global strategy that takes full advantage of this potential.

Cost drivers

Certain elements in an industry's cost structure may predispose it to be global. If firms can gain extra economies of scale from serving more than one national market from a single location, then they are more likely to try to use a single product across different markets. If up-front R&D costs are high and product life-cycles short, then it will make sense to try to recover the up-front costs from sales in as many markets as possible. Both of these factors have contributed to making computer processors a global industry.

Sometimes, however, transport costs may make it difficult to profit from these economies. Packaging products, for example, are sold in similar form across a number of markets, but because the cost of shipping polystyrene foam or empty tin cans is high in comparison with the value of the goods, it is not economic to ship them more than 100 km or so.

Global sourcing will only make sense if there are significant differences between different countries' cost structures. If a firm can find the same inputs, at more or less the same cost and quality, just about anywhere, then it will probably prefer to let each manufacturing unit obtain them locally. One set of theories about why different countries develop different cost structures is discussed in Advanced Topic 5.5.6 below.

Market drivers

Of course, however favourable the cost structure, it makes little sense to globalise an industry if people are unwilling to buy the products. Products like microprocessors or pharmaceuticals are equally effective and acceptable anywhere. Other products, like soft drinks, can be made acceptable to a wide variety of tastes through subtle local adaptations and clever marketing.

In industries like foodstuffs, on the other hand, consumers have strong preferences for local products. This can often be accentuated by the presence of strong local distribution channels that may be reluctant to adopt foreign products, or have strong links with local producers.

It can help an industry to globalise if its customers are aware of what is on offer in different countries. Multinational companies, for example, may look for the same brands of office equipment in Africa as they use in Europe or Japan. In the automobile industry, many companies ask key suppliers to expand with them when they enter a new market. Even in consumer goods, business travellers have been a major influence in helping brands like Canon (in cameras) and Gucci (in clothing) become internationally famous.

Industry paradigms and globalisation

If one firm has been able to make a success of a global strategy, then it may change the industry paradigm so that its competitors have to follow suit. This is in part because globalisation can bring a firm some strategic benefits, such as economies of scale and access to a wider variety of ideas. For example, in chocolate confectionery, Mars, the American industry leader, has followed a global strategy for a number of years, and Nestlé–Rowntree, its main competitor, has gradually followed in making a more uniform selection of products available in different markets. This is despite the strong preferences that consumers in different countries have for chocolate with a particular cocoa, sugar or milk content.

Political/legal influences

Industries can only globalise or regionalise if inputs and outputs can be freely imported and exported. International agreements such as the GATT (General Agreement on Tariffs and Trade) and its successor, the WTO (World Trade Organisation) have been important in underpinning the move to globalisation. So have regional initiatives such as the European Union's Single European Market. However, in certain countries and in certain products and services, tariffs and trade barriers remain as obstacles to globalisation. Some countries also insist that, in order to avoid tariffs or other penalties, firms must use local sources for a certain minimum proportion of raw materials or other inputs. In other cases, there are ownership restrictions for certain types of firm that are seen as strategically important. In the USA, for example, broadcasting firms cannot be controlled by non-US citizens, and airlines may not have foreigners as majority shareholders.

Practical dos and don'ts	**Nature of competition**

1. For your analysis of competition in the past and present, you should remember to look at how organisations *actually* compete, not how economic theory predicts that they should. You should look for *signs* of fierce competition – falling margins, price wars and so on. If you do not find these signs, then competition is not fierce, no matter how fragmented the industry, how low the barriers to entry, and how high the barriers to exit may be.

2. When you come to look at the future of the industry, it is more legitimate to use theory as a guide to what might be expected to happen. You may come across an industry where buyer power is high and growing, there is an increasing threat of substitution and exit barriers are high, and yet competition is not intense. In that case, it is quite reasonable to conclude that competition in that industry will intensify. (Or it may be that the companies in the industry know something that you don't – go back and check your analysis!)

3. We are looking at the overall structure of the industry, not the behaviour of a few firms. One or two firms in an industry may try to differentiate on low prices, but unless this results in consistent price competition that affects most of the competitors, it is not a symptom of fierce competition. In the UK petrol retailing industry, the presence of a small group of discounters has not made competition fierce for other strategic groups.

5.5.5 Relationship with PEST and life-cycle analysis

We have already mentioned in Section 5.5.4 some political and legal factors that can affect the nature of competition in an industry. As well as determining the extent to which monopolies and global competition are tolerated, governments can promote or discourage consolidation in an industry, raise or lower barriers to exit and impose regulations on prices or profits. These interventions are most likely in sectors like energy, telecommunications, water, transport and financial services, where state ownership is common and where there is a threat to people's way of life if competition leads organisations to neglect their infrastructure or take undue risks.

Technological factors may be important in determining the extent to which an industry globalises. In particular, developments in computer networking have made it easier for service industries to globalise, since it has helped firms to monitor performance and service standards across their operations. The Internet has also promoted globalisation by making it easier for firms to locate suppliers in other countries.

We have also already mentioned the main relationship between the industry life-cycle and the nature of competition. In the introductory phase, competition is likely to be quite mild, since there are few competing firms, firms are concentrating on controlling their own internal processes, and they have plenty of potential customers to go for. In the growth phase, as there are still enough customers to go around, competition is unlikely to be fierce and is often based on non-price factors. As the industry matures, competition is likely to intensify and price competition tends to become more frequent.

The industry life-cycle was developed to describe industries with diminishing returns to scale, and it is unclear if it applies to conditions of increasing returns. There are some cases where industries that start off as showing increasing returns have reverted over time to more orthodox forms. For example, the video-cassette recorder (VCR) industry started off as a struggle between two incompatible standards: VHS, backed by Matsushita, and Betamax, promoted by Sony. Matsushita won the battle and reaped the benefits of increasing returns as everyone licensed its technology. Now, however, the technology is mature and competition in the industry is a matter of who can make the most user-friendly machines at the lowest cost.

5.5.6 ADVANCED TOPIC

The competitive advantage of nations: why different countries have different cost structures

One particular theory on the relationship between PEST factors and industry structure comes from Michael Porter's third major book, *The Competitive Advantage of Nations* (Porter, 1990) which extends the notion of corporate competitive advantage to countries. He shows how certain types of organisation are more likely to be founded and be successful in certain geographical settings. His theory identifies the importance of infrastructure and the systemic nature of firms and the markets they operate in. Competitors and customers become partners in the development of knowledge about a particular industry, aiding the development of innovation and new products that are based on a deep understanding of customer needs. Firms that operate in such a supportive environment have a considerable advantage over firms in other countries. Organisations that are not in tune with the contingent factors in their country are likely to have to work harder to succeed. Governments can have a major impact on these environmental factors. They may try to protect their most important assets (e.g. the Japanese government's post-war protection of its manufacturing base), or to destroy the power of economic groups which appear to be becoming too powerful (the UK government's action against powerful mining unions in the 1980s).

Porter draws links between the historical development of industries and the economic and social structures that arise around them over many years. Knowledge and skills about, for example, manufacturing techniques, do not stay simply the property of a single firm, but spread through the network of organisations in the area as employees move between them. Systems of supplier firms develop to provide necessary and often specialist inputs, while roads and transportation systems are built to distribute the finished product. These factors shape the types of products firms sell, and also companies' type, size and structure.

Firms in some lesser developed countries are constrained in their strategic choices by the lack of a distribution network, or availability of finance and venture capital, infrastructure components which those of us in the West take for granted.

Firms in these countries as a result are typically small, family owned, and with narrow distribution and supply networks. However, such 'cottage industries', if given the additional factors which would allow them to compete internationally, may become extremely successful. The Italian woollen clothes industry has become the basis for a world-beating fashion industry, which emerged from the network of small family-owned operations making small-scale items. Benetton, the international clothes manufacturer and retailer still uses such networks in its supply chain – and has turned this structure into a source of considerable competitive advantage.

These factors can be summarised in what has come to be known as Porter's diamond (Figure 5.4). Below is a brief summary of what Porter considers to be the competitive advantage of selected country/industry combinations.

USA

Porter describes the development of the $1 billion American patient-monitoring equipment industry as one where the USA has world-wide advantage. This industry began in Europe, but took off in the 1930s when US firms developed innovative product improvements faster and more in line with developing customer needs. Many new firms emerged in the USA in clusters located close to the major research hospitals, in which the USA also led the way. More recently, patient-monitoring equipment has become increasingly dependent on computerisation, thus the industry has been able to also draw on America's developing world-leading competences in computer systems and software.

Figure 5.4   Porter's diamond – the determinants of national advantage

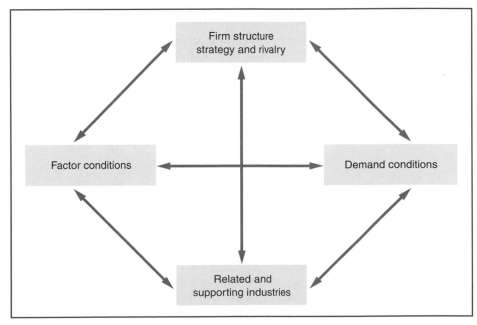

Other American industries which Porter considers to have international competitive advantage include automobiles, defence, aircraft, electronics, computing, oil services, and marketing.

Germany

Porter uses the printing press industry as his example of one where Germany has world-wide advantage. This industry has a very long history, going back to the very earliest days of mechanical printing when Gutenberg printed his bible, although it really began to take off in the early 1800s. Although early presses had been developed in the UK, initial financial incentives and a recession in Britain led to a relocation to Germany. Competitors, many of whose founders had worked for the original firm, entered the market and began to develop innovative processes. In time German firms formed 50% of the world's major competitors. Such innovations were able to draw on Germany's competences in ink and paper technologies, and also its supply of highly trained engineers who emerged from Germany's strong educational system. It also benefited from highly discerning consumers who demanded high-quality paper, and complained if print was smudged.

Other industries in which Germany has international competitive advantage include iron, steel and other metals, chemicals, transportation equipment, and machine engineering of many types. Germany has a particularly broad range of industries in which it has global competitive advantage.

Japan

Porter identifies robotics as his example of a world-beating Japanese industry. This is a relatively young industry. Robots were first conceived in the 1950s in the United States, but it was another country that was to take away its early dominance when Japan began importing robots from the USA in 1967. Japanese inventiveness in improving the early, rather ineffectual, prototypes combined to produce a leading industry. Development was in response to a number of factors. Japan in this period was the world's leading manufacturer across a range of industries such as machinery and micro-electronics. It also had a shortage of skilled workers and a recession which led to heightened cost-consciousness. Thus demand for improved processes in manufacturing was strong.

Other industries in which Japan has competitive advantage include consumer electronics, engines, transportation, office equipment, audio-visual equipment and ceramic packaging.

Italy

Porter cites the $10 billion ceramic tile industry as an example of an Italian industry with international competitive advantage – accounting for 30% of world production and 60% of exports. The industry is located in a small region around one town, near which hundreds of tile firms are located. The industry can trace its origins to the earthenware that was manufactured over centuries from the clay which is found in the region. Tiles themselves, however, took off after the Second World War as a result of the demand for building materials, although the clay used,

Kaolin, was not available locally but was imported from the UK and the kilns were also imported, in this case from Germany. In time Italian firms themselves developed expertise in kiln manufacturing and imports declined. Because of the concentration of firms in the area, supporting firms grew up with expertise in areas like mould formation and glazes, and competitive rivalry was also intense. All acted to improve standards. Finally, Italy's competence in design was used to develop artistically sophisticated and attractive 'designer tiles'.

Italy also has international competences in leather and leather shoes, clothes, household products, domestic appliances, machinery manufacturing, food and wine, and wool.

United Kingdom

The UK has strengths in consumer goods; foods and drinks; cosmetics; diamonds; trading; aircraft engines; wool, petrochemicals; and household products and furnishings. However, Porter chooses Britain as the principal example of a country which had considerable sources of competitive advantage, many of which were lost. As a result, at the time of his analysis (1985) strong industries such as machinery manufacturing, speciality inputs, and transportation had declined substantially. In addition, Porter identified the fact that many of the most successful British firms are broadly distributed across a large number of different industries. They are therefore located in relatively small, specialised and relatively weak pockets within the wider economy. They are less able to draw on competition or factor conditions to build competitive strength than other major economic powers.

5.6   The outcomes of environmental analysis

Once we understand the nature of competition in an industry, we can start to use the results of this analysis to help understand and shape the strategies of organisations. An assessment of the attractiveness of an industry can help us to understand whether the firms inside it should consider quitting, and whether those outside it should contemplate entering. An analysis of success and survival factors helps us to understand how firms have succeeded in the past, and the strategic choices that are available to them in the future.

5.6.1 Industry attractiveness

The Porter five-forces framework was developed as a way of gauging *industry attractiveness*. An industry with low buyer and supplier power, a low threat of substitution and high barriers to entry could be expected to have a mild competitive environment, particularly if the structure of the industry did not promote heavy competition. According to Porter, this would make it an attractive industry – firms already operating in it should consider expanding, and firms not in it should consider entering it. Conversely, if an industry is in decline or is otherwise unattractive, firms should consider exiting.

Although broadly sensible, these recommendations have one drawback – that many firms will be undertaking the same analysis and coming to broadly the same conclusions. Thus, when the PC industry started to expand, many new firms were formed, and many existing electronics and computing firms tried to enter it. This means that it is unlikely that any organisation will be able to gain an advantage by spotting an attractive industry before anyone else. It may also mean that an attractive industry quickly becomes overcrowded and so, paradoxically, loses its attractiveness.

5.6.2 Survival and success factors

An industry's structure, its stage in its life-cycle and the developments in the macro-environment together form a set of parameters within which a firm must work if it is to be viable. Unless a firm believes that is has some specialist competences or innovative ability that will transform the industry, it will need to tailor its strategy to take account of these factors. Not every strategy will make sense.

In all industries, firms' survival depends upon their staying abreast of technological developments, changes in their customer base and modifications to those customers' needs. One aim of a PEST analysis is to identify *precisely* what those needs and technologies are, and how they are changing.

In an industry where competition is relaxed, and based on non-price factors, the list of survival factors may be quite short – an adequate command of the latest technology, for example, a production capability that is adequate to serve existing or emerging markets and a reasonable reputation. The successful competitors are most likely to be those with capabilities that enable them to differentiate in a way that is particularly valuable to the industry's customers. PEST analysis should show whether customers value convenience, or technological leadership, or some other aspect of differentiation.

◄ *Types of differentiation advantage are discussed in Section 3.2.2.*

All these survival factors will apply in an industry where competition is fierce, but there will be other, more exacting ones as well. Where competition is based upon price, firms' cost structures will need to be competitive. This may in turn mean that organisations will need to be of a certain minimum size in order to take advantage of economies of scale or scope. Where competition is based upon marketing or investment, firms will need adequate sources of finance.

Success in a fiercely competitive industry will depend upon taking some aspect of survival and developing it so that it becomes exceptional in some way. If buyer power is high, then close relationships with customers and the capability to meet their needs better than competitors may yield success. If competition is based upon research and development, then the ability to innovate faster than competitors may be a success factor. If cost is all-important, then being the market leader and having maximum economies of scale may be crucial, which may imply having a substantial distribution network.

In a global industry, success may come from globalising faster than competitors and gaining a foothold in all the most important geographic markets. Survival may be a matter of gaining sufficient scale in one or two markets to be competitive on cost, while focusing on the needs of particular groups of customers that do not want or like standardised global products.

In an increasing returns industry, success is likely to come from control of the industry standard. Survival may come from being a collaborator of the industry leader's, or by having a secondary standard – the kind of strategy followed by Apple Computer in competing with Microsoft.

In most cases you should be able to identify more than one way of surviving or succeeding in an industry. In many industries, there is a strategic group that addresses the top of the market with a differentiation strategy and another that addresses the lower part of the market by differentiating on price. There will often be survival and success factors that can be identified with the strategies followed by these two groups, and others for firms wishing to steer a course between these two extremes.

5.7 Defining the industry and the scope of the analysis

Finally in this chapter we return to the problem of defining which industries need to be analysed. For a firm that spans a number of industries, because it is diversified or vertically integrated, a separate environmental analysis is needed for each of the industries involved. An analysis of one of the major mobile telephone manufacturers, such as Nokia or Motorola, would need to take account of their involvement in the manufacture of both handsets and infrastructure. Mobile telephone handsets are small and sold by the million to individual consumers. Mobile telephone infrastructure consists of large items of radio transmission and reception equipment, sold in small quantities to the firms that operate telephony services. Although there are linkages between the two industries, one could certainly not make a single five-forces analysis stretch to both.

This leads to the problem of deciding when two or more related sets of products come from a single industry, or from separate ones. When we defined industries and markets in Chapter 1, we remarked that this is not always simple, but a number of factors can help with the judgement:

- Are the inputs and product technologies similar?
- Are the competitors making each product mostly the same?
- Do the firms in making each of the products look to the same resources as the basis of competitive advantage, and have broadly similar value chains?
- Is there a significant degree of overlap between the different products' customers and end-users?

Real-Life Application 5.4 gives some examples of how these factors can be applied.

REAL-LIFE APPLICATION 5.4

How many industries does Sony's computing business cover?

Sony manufactures laptop computers, computer games consoles and computer components, including floppy drives and CD-ROM drives. Does this constitute one industry or three? And do laptop computers qualify as an industry in their own right, or are they a subsector of the personal computer industry?

	Inputs	Typical competitors	Resources and value chain	Customers and end-users
Games consoles	Specialised processor and graphics chips, displays, joysticks, CD-ROM drives or specialised cartridges	Sony, Nintendo, Sega	Capabilities in graphics technology. Access to innovative games developers. Sell through non-specialist outlets	Customers are electrical stores, bookshops, etc. End-users are consumers, mainly young
PCs: Desktop subsector	Generic components – processors, disc drives, boards, displays, etc.	Compaq, IBM, Dell, Hewlett-Packard (plus many small competitors)	Technical capabilities in combining components. Capabilities in low-cost manufacture	Customers are distributors, firms and individuals. End-users are consumers of all ages
PCs: Laptop subsector	Modified versions of desktop computer components, LCD displays	Sony, Toshiba, Compaq, IBM, Hewlett-Packard	Capabilities in designing lightweight machines with low energy consumption	Same as desktop subsector
Computer components	Silicon chips, wiring, circuit boards, precision optical and mechanical components	Acer, Sharp	Specialist design capabilities, low-cost manufacture	Most customers and end-users are computer manufacturers. Some sales to hobbyists via distributors

On the basis of the above table, it is fairly clear that the desktop and laptop subsectors are close enough to be considered a single industry, but the components and games consoles businesses each reside in a separate industry, despite a superficial overlap in technology.

5.8 Summary

In this chapter you have seen how to assess the nature of competition in an industry, and analyse how it develops over time. Competition is shaped by a complex combination of:

- macro-environmental factors, including:
  - political and legal activity by governments and international organisations
  - economic developments, locally and world-wide, which affect the purchasing power of customers and end-users, and the availability of raw materials and human resources
  - social and cultural changes, which affect the behaviour and desires of customers and end-users

- technological developments, which affect the technologies used in products and services, as well as the way in which they are produced, marketed, distributed and accounted for;
- an industry's progress through its life-cycle, through growth and maturity through eventual decline. Changes from one stage in the life-cycle are often triggered by macro-environmental change;
- forces – relating to the structure of the industry itself, which are shaped by changes in the macro-environment and the industry's stage within its life-cycle – which include:
  - *the power of buyers and suppliers* – if these groups are powerful, they will be able to negotiate deals that reduce the profits of firms in the industry
  - *the threat of substitution* – if this is high, firms will be unable to make high profits, because customers will turn to alternative products or services. Organisations need to be alert to social-cultural or technological changes that may make substitutes more attractive and push an industry into the maturity or decline phase of the life-cycle
  - *the threat of entry* – if this is high, new firms will enter as soon as the industry starts making decent profits, and make competition more intense
  - *the extent to which the industry is concentrated or fragmented* – this is in turn affected by the extent to which economies of scale are important to competitive advantage, and whether the industry shows increasing or decreasing returns to scale
  - *the industry recipe and rules of the game* – the cultures of the firms within the industry, developed over time, have a major influence over how fiercely they will compete.

All these factors combine to determine:

- whether the competition in the industry is mild, fierce or hypercompetitive;
- whether firms in the industry compete at a global, regional, national or local level;
- how attractive the industry is – a fiercely competitive industry might be thought less attractive than a less competitive one;
- the types of strategies that firms can consider to gain competitive advantage, and the factors required for survival and success in the industry.

Typical questions

We conclude this chapter with a review of some of the questions you are likely to be asked about industry structure and the nature of competition, and how you can use the theory in this chapter to answer them.

1. *How much of the organisation's success was due to its being in the right place at the right time?*

   This question related to your analysis of the environment in the *past*. You may want to use PEST analysis (Section 5.2) to isolate the factors that helped (or prevented) the industry's growth and profitability. You may also want to identify where the industry stood in its life-cycle (Section 5.3). You can then show how these factors affected the industry structure (Sections 5.4 and 5.5) and evaluate how intense competition was in the industry as a result.

   Once you have reached a conclusion about the nature of the environment, you need to see how well or badly the firm was able to cope with the circumstances, using the concepts introduced in Chapter 3. Some firms are able to cope well with unfavourable environments and intense competition. Others profit from a favourable environment to build strategic resources that give them an enduring advantage. Others still may make healthy profits while the environment is favourable, then squander the profits on executive perks or poorly judged diversification.

2. *Should a firm exit (or enter) this industry?*

   This is a question about industry attractiveness in the present and future. You should use the tools in this chapter to assess the competitive environment for the present, and see whether competition is likely to be intense or benign, and whether the industry is likely to show high or low profitability. You should then use your PEST analysis for the future to assess whether the nature of competition is likely to change, for better or worse. For example, will technological change lead to the arrival of more powerful substitutes, and so to fiercer competition and falling margins in the industry?

   You then need to compare the industry's success and survival factors, for the present and the future, with your assessment of the firm's capabilities and other strategic resources. Firms with the right resources might do well even if competition is intense and the industry is superficially unattractive. Firms without the technological capabilities needed for survival may struggle in an otherwise attractive industry.

3. *What challenges confront the organisation?*

   Although this question appears to be about the organisation, it has a great deal to do with its environment. Here, you will want to use all three sets of analyses – of the past, the present and the future – for all the major industries in which the firm is active.

   You will need to compare the success and survival factors of each industry for the past, the present and the future, to see how (if at all) they are changing. This gives some measure of the extent to which the firm will need to modify its strategy in order to adapt to changes in the environment. You may also want to look at the firm's performance, to see how it has coped with changes in the environment between the past and the present. Finally, as with the previous question, you may want to look at the firm's strategic resources to see how well adapted they are to the future survival and success factors.

Questions for discussion

1. Is McDonald's in the food industry, the restaurant industry, the fast-food industry or the hamburger industry? Which industries is Benetton in?

2. The Porter five-forces framework is sometimes criticised as being static – that it only gives a snapshot of an industry at a particular moment in time. Do you agree with this criticism? How big a problem do you think it is?

3. What are the weaknesses of PEST analysis?

4. How many industries can you think of, apart from those mentioned in the chapter, that feature increasing returns?

5. 'Unattractive industries are more attractive than attractive ones.' Discuss.

The personal computer industry in 1999

The first Apple I personal computers (PCs), introduced in 1975, were kits, designed for use by hobbyists. The first PC suitable for use by people without skills in electronics was the Apple II, introduced in 1977, quickly followed by a variety of imitators based upon a similar processor. Sales of these machines were fuelled by the invention of VisiCalc, the first spreadsheet. Business customers were attracted to PCs by the availability of this cheap and flexible alternative to the existing financial analysis software that ran on mainframe computers. Some also made use of WordStar, the first word-processing package to find widespread acceptance, although the word-processing market was dominated by equipment built for that specific purpose.

Although PC sales grew steadily in popularity throughout the late 1970s and early 1980s, the industry remained fragmented with conflicting hardware and software standards – software that ran on one make of PC could not be guaranteed to run on another. The hardware itself was unreliable and prone to crash. However, in 1981 IBM, the world's largest computer company, launched its own brand of PCs, using Intel processors and an operating system, PC-DOS, sourced from a new firm, Microsoft.

IBM had intended its PC technology to be proprietary, but ingenious engineers at Compaq and other firms were able to imitate the important elements of IBM's own technology, while buying in Intel processors and Microsoft's operating system. As a result, the IBM PC became the basis of a set of open standards for PC hardware and software, whose existence, together with IBM's presence, reassured both suppliers and customers that their investments were unlikely to be wasted. 'Killer applications' such as Lotus-123 – a far more powerful spreadsheet than VisiCalc – and dBase-II, a powerful database package, gave business customers reasons to buy PCs. With the launch in the mid-1980s of WordPerfect, PCs also became the preferred platform for office word-processing.

The launch of the IBM PC coincided with a global economic recession, but the recovery of the world's major economies from this low point helped demand for PCs to grow strongly throughout the 1980s. The development of successively more powerful generations of Intel processor and of cheaper, faster and higher capacity hard disk storage and memory chips also sustained demand for PCs. Prices of many components fell as low-cost producers based in Taiwan and South Korea entered the industry. New generations of software came onto the market that required more powerful hardware, and this persuaded customers to upgrade their equipment. In particular, Microsoft Windows, which gave IBM PC users an intuitive way of interacting with their computer through a mouse, required computers with more processing power and better graphics than were needed to run DOS applications.

Portable PCs became available in the mid-1980s, and have gradually increased in power and decreased in size. The industry now supplies two distinct types of machine: those designed for lightness and portability, but lacking some of the power and features of a desktop machine, and heavier, more fully featured machines with larger screens designed to take the place of a desktop computer. Even smaller, 'palmtop' computers became popular towards the end of the 1990s. Portable computers have flat LCD screens rather than the bulkier, cheaper CRT screens used in desktops, and they use components designed to consume less energy than those used in desktop computers, so that the portable's batteries will need recharging less often. These differences mean that a portable computer may sell for double the price of a comparably featured desktop machine, although the price differential is narrowing.

Throughout the 1980s and 1990s, the cycle continued of improved hardware technology driving software improvements that persuaded users to buy newer, more powerful hardware. A slowing of the global economy in 1989–90, combined with a pause in the development of new technology, led to an interruption in the industry's growth. Business users became cost-conscious and lacked a strong reason to upgrade their equipment. However, the development of cheaper multimedia technology – CD-ROM, sound and graphics hardware – led to a new market for PCs in the home, for games and educational purposes. In the developed economies, two factors contributed to the attractiveness of this market: economic growth during the 1990s, with the resulting rise in real household incomes, and an increasing trend for professional and office workers to work at least part of the time from home.

The most recent 'killer application' driving PC sales is the web browser. Electronic mail access is becoming commonplace in many countries as a way of communicating with friends and of keeping home-workers in touch with their office. The World Wide Web is used increasingly as a tool in business and education – in the year to August 1998, the number of servers connected to the Internet grew 46% to over 43 million. An increasing variety of financial and retail services are becoming available to consumers through the Internet. There is much speculation about the extent to which electronic commerce will replace traditional banks, stockbrokers and retailers.

The leading PC makers have always been American. IBM was the clear industry leader in the early 1980s, but was slow to introduce computers based upon successive generations of the Intel processor. This allowed Compaq, another US firm that had made the first workable portable PCs to run IBM software, to grab technological leadership of the industry. IBM made a further error when it introduced its PS/2 range, which was intended to replace the original IBM range, but used a different operating system, OS/2, and a range of proprietary components. IBM was betting that its formidable reputation would persuade the industry to adopt its new architecture. However, competitors and customers saw the danger of giving control of the industry standard back to IBM, and preferred to stay with adapted versions of the existing open standards.

Compaq has been able to retain the industry leadership it seized from IBM, which by 1999 ranked only No. 5 in PC market share, but it is under increasing pressure from lower-cost producers. In particular, Dell, which pioneered a system of selling its computers direct by phone and later over the Internet, and building them to order, has overtaken it in the United States, with 16% of the market to Compaq's 15.7%. Compaq is still the leading player in Europe, where its 15% share is double that of third-placed Dell, and worldwide, with 13% of the market. However, Dell's growth rate in both the USA (over 50%) and Europe (36%) was considerably higher than Compaq's (17% and 15% respectively), even though it had stopped trying to undercut the market leader on price.[12] The differential between Compaq's and Dell's prices, $100–$200 for much of the 1990s, had all but disappeared.

Dell is widely praised for the quality of its systems, which minimise its sales and marketing overheads, and enable it to manage with just six days of inventory, far less than any competitor. These systems also enable Dell to tailor its services to its large corporate clients, for whom it can load customised software while the computers are being manufactured, and who can order a range of custom-designed machines through a private website.

The strongest PC manufacturers outside the USA are based in Japan (where Toshiba and Sony both have strong positions in the portable PC segment) and Taiwan. Some European governments tried, in the early days of the industry, to promote national champions like Bull in France, just as they had in the mainframe computer industry. Such firms have mostly proved incapable of withstanding competition from larger, more efficient Taiwanese and US firms. The British champion, ICL, is now part of Japan's Fujitsu which, having also absorbed the PC business of Germany's Siemens, holds second place in the European market. However, in many countries there are small and medium-sized local firms that assemble PCs from the same components as the major global manufacturers. Although they lack the purchasing economies of scale of the largest firms, their overheads are often lower, or they are able to offer service that is tailored to the needs of local buyers.

175

CASE STUDY *continued*

PC prices continued to decline. Some Internet service providers are experimenting with giving PCs away. Compaq, IBM and Hewlett-Packard all make very little money from PC manufacture, and even Dell's margins are said to be under pressure. Many US and Japanese manufacturers of PCs and components have moved their manufacturing to China and South East Asia, to take advantage of the low labour costs there. The economic and political instability in these countries in the late 1990s threatened briefly to disrupt supply in the industry, at least temporarily.

Apart from Compaq, the main beneficiary of IBM's 1980s error of judgement was Microsoft. Originally a partner with IBM in developing the OS/2, it saw its opportunity and launched version 3.0 of its DOS/Windows operating system. This gave it an almost unchallenged grip on the market for operating systems for PCs. The only potential challenger, Apple, preferred to restrict its operating system to use on its proprietary hardware. Although many people believed that Apple's system was superior, its hardware was expensive and used a Motorola processor that was incompatible with the Intel chip used in almost all other PCs. Applications written for one system would not run on the other.

Microsoft also benefited from decisions by WordPerfect and Lotus to focus their development efforts on applications to run under OS/2. Microsoft's own word processor and Excel spreadsheet were clearly the best available applications for Windows and, when OS/2 flopped, they became the industry standards. Today, Microsoft has more than 90% of the market for operating systems and applications software, and is one of the most profitable firms in the world.

Intel has also benefited strongly from its position as standards-setter in the PC processor market, although it does not have as dominant a share as Microsoft. It has faced competition from AMD and Cyrix, which originally marketed clones of Intel's processors, and later developed their own products that some believe are superior to Intel's. Even though the two ranges of processors are not 100% compatible, PC-makers seem happy to design machines for both.

Although the PC market is still growing at 17% per annum in Europe and similar rates in the USA, a leading industry consultancy, Dataquest, predicts that growth will decline by about four percentage points in 2000. Some observers believe that in future many tasks will be carried out on simpler, faster devices than the modern personal computer. The latest computer-game consoles, digital televisions and cellular telephones are all able to access the Internet. However, simple devices such as dedicated word processors never made much impact on the sales of PCs, and an attempt in the mid-1990s to develop 'network computers' failed. These were intended to be simple devices, cheap to buy and to maintain, designed to download software and data from larger central servers whenever needed. However, in the end, their selling price could not be made low enough to justify their lack of features compared to standard PCs.

Case study questions

1. How many industries does the personal computer industry consist of?

2. How well does the industry life-cycle model fit the PC industry?

3. How has the nature of competition in PC manufacture changed over time, and what factors have led to those changes?

4. Why might firms like Compaq find it difficult to make profits in the present-day PC industry? Are their problems likely to increase or diminish in the future?

NOTES

1. Pettigrew and Whipp (1991), being two key academics who have demonstrated this. Others have found similarly.

2. You may also encounter STEP (same factors as PEST in a different order), PEEST (the extra E stands for environmental), PESTEL (E for environmental, L for legal) or other, longer checklists. Properly used, these all lead to the same result.

3. 'Let's keep it clean', *The Economist*, 17 April 1999, pp. 70–1.

4. Of course, influential firms, like influential people, can sometimes help shape political change, by lobbying governments, or affect social trends by introducing new products or even clever advertising campaigns. But new products, lobbying and advertising campaigns only work if they catch the mood of the public. Technological change, on the other hand, can be imposed by one company upon the rest of the world, even if many people hate it, provided that the technology works and its advantages are powerful enough. Look at mobile phones, for example!

5. See, for example, Hannan and Freeman (1989), Hannan and Carroll (1992); Amburgey et al. (1993) and Hannan et al. (1995). You are encouraged to review the population ecologists' arguments for yourselves. However, you are warned that their work contains a lot of complicated mathematics, and can be heavy going even for the hardened professional.

6. There are certain exceptions to this, where legislation or local customs gives airlines control over the slots that they have traditionally held.

7. For an account of an industry where quite small advances in the design of a product's formulation led to the replacement of most of the leading firms in the industry by new entrants, see Henderson and Clark (1990).

8. These types of tacit understanding are different from cartels, *explicit* collaborations between competitors to set prices and carve up markets, which are illegal in most countries.

9. Michael Porter (1985) advocates that firms should choose their competitors: see *Competitive Advantage*, ch. 6.

10. D'Aveni (1994) claims that hypercompetition is becoming more common, and will in future become the norm for competitive behaviour, but few other scholars agree.

11. In the interests of fairness, we must record that Microsoft strenuously denies that it has a monopoly in this industry. The US anti-trust authorities and most commentators disagree with them.

12. US and global market data come from Dataquest and IDC, and were obtained from Ticehurst, Jo, 'Compaq hangs on to worldwide PC market lead' accessed on www.vnunet.com on 25 January 2000. European market data are from Context Computer Information Services and were accessed on www.Itnetwork.com on 21 February 2000.

Competitive stance

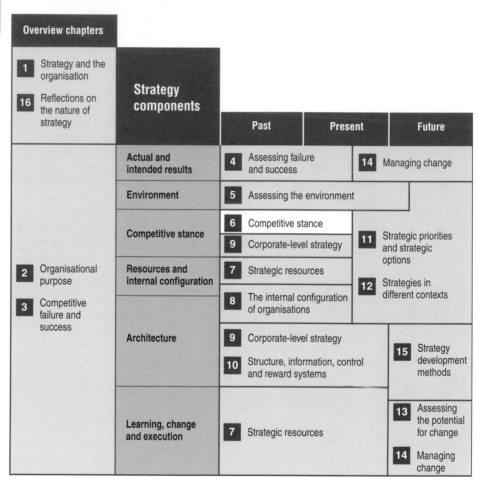

Overview chapters

1 Strategy and the organisation

16 Reflections on the nature of strategy

Strategy components

		Past	Present	Future
	Actual and intended results	4 Assessing failure and success		14 Managing change
	Environment	5 Assessing the environment		
	Competitive stance	6 Competitive stance		11 Strategic priorities and strategic options
		9 Corporate-level strategy		
	Resources and internal configuration	7 Strategic resources		12 Strategies in different contexts
		8 The internal configuration of organisations		
	Architecture	9 Corporate-level strategy		15 Strategy development methods
		10 Structure, information, control and reward systems		
	Learning, change and execution	7 Strategic resources		13 Assessing the potential for change
				14 Managing change

2 Organisational purpose

3 Competitive failure and success

In this chapter we start to consider the effect of some of the basic strategic choices available to firms, and how these relate to some of the most important external influences on a company's activities: its customers and competitors, both current and potential.

We start by looking at how organisations analyse potential customer groupings and decide which they wish to target. We then show how firms can seek to gain advantage by developing products to satisfy the requirements of its target segments, and by positioning those products successfully, in the eyes of those customers, in terms of price and quality. We go on to look at ways in which organisations can position themselves relative

We look at these issues again in Chapters 11 and 12 when we consider strategic options. ▶

to their competitors. We examine the impact of choice of scope and scale on organisations' competitive position, and extend this thinking to looking at some of the international strategies considered by firms in the increasingly global business environment of today.

Our main concern in this chapter is business-level strategy – we are looking at the problems confronting an organisation, or a part of an organisation, operating across a limited range of industries and markets. More highly diversified organisations face a further set of challenges, which we consider in Chapter 9.

Learning objectives

After reading this chapter, you should be able to:

- understand the concept of customer segmentation, analyse the different customer segments in a particular market, and show how a firm's choices of target customer segment and of product have affected its success or failure;
- understand and analyse the effect of different price/quality positions on a firm's strategic viability;
- understand an organisation's basic choices in terms of the scope and scale of its operations and assess their appropriateness;
- understand the difference between locally responsive, global and transnational strategies and be able to assess which is appropriate for a particular firm;
- analyse an organisation's position *vis-à-vis* its principal competitors.

6.1 | Segmentation, positioning, scope and scale

We look at how organisations can select strategies in Chapter 11. ▶

There are a number of ways in which organisations can be classified, and indeed classify themselves. Perhaps the most important of these is the customer groups they choose to serve. We have already seen that companies cannot do everything. They have value chains, cultures, architectures, and resources that are more suited to one type of operation than another. Because of this they have to *position* themselves so that what they can do matches up with the needs of customers – whether these are existing ones or potential future ones. A company which wishes to target extremely high price consumers (the Italian clothes manufacturer Gucci, or Rolls-Royce motor cars for example) cannot afford to compromise quality in its manufacturing processes, and also has to maintain high standards of service. Meeting this target group's needs is not compatible with a 'pile it high and sell it cheap' philosophy, or with systems which ignore quality in order to minimise costs. This is not the same as thinking that Gucci or Rolls-Royce will not want to minimise their costs – of course they will, but this will be far lower down their list of priorities than achieving high quality at all stages of their value chains.

At the same time, organisations need to decide **how large** the segments are that they can serve profitably, and **how many** they can serve at the same time. These decisions about scale and scope also need to be compatible with the firm's value chain. Gucci or Rolls-Royce would have great difficulty in sustaining their standards of production quality and customer service if they tried to serve a mass market. This makes it all the more important for them to **focus** on a smaller, 'niche' market segment, containing customers that are rich enough, and choosy enough, to pay the prices that these firms need to charge in order to make a profit at their very low production volumes.

6.1.1 Generic strategies

◀ *Porter also identified five forces which impact on a firm's performance (see Chapter 5). Differentiation and cost advantage were introduced in Chapter 3.*

Michael Porter in his ground-breaking book *Competitive Strategy* was one of the first people to discuss the bases of organisational competitive advantage in terms of the two dimensions of positioning and scope. He developed the concept of generic business-level strategies. His position was that two factors determine whether firms can achieve high returns – if their costs are lower than those of competitors, or if they can differentiate their products to provide what their customers want, according to their segmented needs. He further drew a distinction between businesses that addressed a broad target (in many geographic markets, and/or across a broad range of customer segments) and those that chose to focus on a narrower one.

Because of its simplicity, Porter's framework is very widely used. However, as we shall see in Theoretical Perspective 6.1, it has not stood the test of time particularly well.

THEORETICAL PERSPECTIVE 6.1

Porter's generic strategy framework

Porter identified three categories of sustainable competitive advantage:

● A **differentiation** strategy involves offering customers something unique, for which they are ready to pay more. The price premium they pay must more than outweigh the extra costs of providing the unique aspects of the product or service.

● A **cost leadership** strategy involves one firm setting out to be '*the* lowest cost producer in the industry' by maximising economies of scale and other sources of cost advantage. Porter holds that there is room for only one cost leader in any industry, and that if several firms compete for that position, the result is cut-throat competition.

● A **focus** strategy involves a firm concentrating on a narrow customer segment. It can be further subdivided into cost focus and differentiation focus strategies, depending on whether the firm tries to achieve cost or differentiation advantage in this particular segment. A focus strategy depends on there being significant differences between the focuser's target segment and the rest of the industry. If these differences are not pronounced enough,

then a broadly based competitor can serve the segment as well, and probably more cheaply.

The implementation of the different generic strategies requires different resources and skills, different organisational processes, different styles of leadership and will mean very different cultures (see Table 6.1).

This framework has been widely adopted by strategy and marketing theorists. However, Porter's views have been criticised since his pioneering writing was published, and recent thinking on strategy is less inclined to put a firm's sources of competitive advantage into such narrow or constrained 'boxes'. Porter's analysis is static – it takes no account of how customer tastes and competitors' strategies may change over time and it appears to see businesses as reacting to what they perceive as customer requirements. Other theorists, such as Hamel and Prahalad (1994) emphasise the scope for firms to be proactive, creating customers by dint of the innovative products or services that emerge from their own capabilities.

Porter's original conceptualisation of a cost-leadership strategy implied that only one firm in an industry could succeed in this – the firm with the *lowest* costs. In fact it is very difficult to find companies that answer to Porter's notion of

Table 6.1   Requisite skills and generic strategies

Generic strategy	Commonly required skills and resources	Common organisational requirements
Low cost	Sustained capital investment and access to capital Process engineering skills Intense supervision of labour Products designed for ease in manufacture Low-cost distribution system	Tight cost control Frequent, detailed control reports Structured organisation and responsibilities Incentives based on meeting strict quantitative targets
Differentiation	Strong marketing abilities Product engineering Creative flair Strong capability in basic research Corporate reputation for quality of technological leadership Long tradition in the industry or unique combination of skills drawn from other businesses Strong co-operation from channels	Strong co-ordination among functions in R&D, product development, and marketing Subjective measurement and incentives instead of quantitative measures Amenities to attract high skilled labour, scientists or creative people
Focus	Combination of the above policies directed at the particular strategic target Strong understanding of market segments and buyer behaviour	Combination of the above policies directed at the particular strategic target

'the' cost leader in their industry. Several other criticisms can be made of this. In the first place it is, as we have seen in Chapters 1 and 5, very difficult to state what an industry is – there are too many 'fuzzy' boundaries between customers of the products they buy.

Another criticism is that Porter did not compare like with like – a differentiation strategy is applied at the **product** level, while cost leadership is typically a property of the **firm**. Cost advantage would be applied across a range of products, not all of which will be in the same industry. However, perhaps one of the biggest problems is the use of the word 'cost'. Low cost is often, in our experience, confused with a low *price* strategy. They are not the same thing, although clearly a company which has high costs and a low price strategy is asking for trouble (see Section 6.4).

Porter's original thinking also implied that his categories were alternatives. Firms could concentrate on *either* minimising costs *or* creating expensive sources of differentiation – if they did not, they were 'stuck in the middle'. This – one of Porter's most famous phrases – has been one of the major sources of criticism subsequently. Although research tends to confirm that the concepts of cost and differentiation advantage explain something meaningful about an organisation's strategy, researchers have consistently failed to establish that there is a trade-off between them. Empirical research shows that the most profitable companies in most industries pursue a mixture of the two.[1] The danger of being 'stuck in the middle' appears to be far less than Porter hypothesised it would be.

Finally, Porter's division of strategies into broad and narrow targets appears to be an oversimplification. The concept of a narrow target brings together firms that supply a broad range of customers in a single geographic market, as many retailers do, with those that supply a carefully defined customer group right across the world, as do Gucci, Rolls-Royce and many medium-sized German engineering firms. Yet the value chains and architectures required for these two strategies are very different. Also, as we shall see shortly, it is rarely obvious where the border lies between broad and narrow target.

We can illustrate these problems by looking at the automobile industry. For many years, the car manufacturer with the lowest production costs has been Toyota, the Japanese manufacturer that ranks Number 3 in world-wide sales. Its cost advantage comes from the very efficient manufacturing techniques that it has pioneered over the last forty years, and which it continues to improve upon. However, these same manufacturing techniques have made Toyota's cars very reliable, with fewer manufacturing faults than most of its rivals. This avoidance of errors, and of the costs of putting them right, contributes to Toyota's cost advantage, but is also a source of differentiation. Toyota's cars are rarely the cheapest – rival manufacturers, with poorer reputations, tend to undercut it on price, even though their costs are higher.[1] ▶

Theoretical Perspective continued

Toyota is not the undisputed cost leader, however. Its Japanese rival, Honda, has pursued similar strategies, and has costs that are nearly as low. On particular models such as the Chrysler Neon, American manufacturers are able to match Honda and Toyota. The second largest US manufacturer, Ford, has reorganised its world-wide operations to try to reap global economies of scale, and become cost leader in its own right.

Toyota, Honda and Ford all obviously conform to Porter's notion of a firm pursuing a broad target. They have a range of models from luxury saloons to small family cars, which they sell in most countries. At the other end of the scale, one can find clear examples of Porter's focus strategies. Germany's Porsche focuses upon fast sports cars, and its customers are rich (or want people to think they are). Russia's Moskvitch focuses upon its home market and upon people who want, or need, to pay for their car in roubles. Its products lack the design features and reliability to appeal to customers outside that market.

But what of Italy's Fiat? It has a wide range of models, though not as broad as Ford's or Volkswagen's. It sells throughout Europe and South America, but lacks a presence in Japan or the USA. Its target is narrower than that of Ford or Toyota, but far broader than those of Porsche or Moskvitch, or even France's Peugeot-Citroën. Can it be called a focuser?

In fact, you might want to question why any of Porter's categories should be *alternatives*. A business which chooses to *focus* on a group of highly price-sensitive customers would also need to control its *costs* (in order to provide the lowest price products) and *differentiate* its offer by, for example providing only a small range of goods with few added service benefits, as the Aldi or Netto supermarket chains do. It would quite naturally combine all three elements of Porter's recommendations.

This is a point which two British researchers, Charles Baden-Fuller and John Stopford (1992) make forcibly. They say that generic strategies are 'a fallacy' as the best firms at all times are trying to reconcile all of these factors – to be low cost *and* high quality. As a result, they suggest that no generic strategies, by themselves, can be enduring sources of competitive advantage. Instead, strategic resources and architecture are more important bases of strategic effectiveness. Miller and Dess (1993) have also demonstrated through statistical analysis of firms' performance that cost and differentiation are best considered as separate dimensions of strategy, rather than as opposite extremes of the same dimension.

6.1.2 Analysing competitive stance

In this book, we make only sparing use of the concepts of 'cost leadership' and 'stuck in the middle'. We expect successful organisations to set themselves up like Toyota, to deliver a judiciously chosen mix of cost and differentiation advantage – to be positioned in the middle, rather than stuck there. For the analysis of this element of competitive positioning, we suggest the use of the 'Strategy Clock' (Section 6.4).

In place of Porter's single distinction between broad and narrow target, we prefer to focus on the organisation's choice of **scope** – how many market segments it chooses to serve, with how great a range of products – and **scale** – how large each segment should be (see Sections 6.5 and 6.6).

First, however, we look in more detail at segmentation – why it is important, how segments can be defined and recognised, and how a segmentation strategy contributes to a firm's competitive advantage.

6.2 Segmentation

Grouping customers together according to common characteristics has been a well-known aspect of marketing theory and practice for many years, but such activities at the functional level apply equally to strategies at the business level. This is called **segmentation**. Such a classification process can be applied to individuals, businesses, countries, or any other type of targeting which might underpin a firm's generic strategies.

6.2.1 Why firms segment their markets

This process of segmentation involves categorising groups of customers who need different products. Ideally, firms would like to produce exactly the right product for their customers' unique needs. However, this process would result in complete customisation of products, something which is generally too expensive for most firms and most buyers. Segmentation is a compromise between customisation and mass marketing. Most of us are different from other people, but we also have some things in common, and segmenting a market according to these common elements allows some degree of a customised product to be offered to buyers.

Segmentation also encourages managers to consider how they can apply a firm's resources to a significant enough number of target customers. A company needs to be able to develop sources of competitive advantage in its chosen segments in order for these to be worth considering. Segmentation allows firms better to match their products to the needs of their customers and end users, and thereby *retain* them.

Segmentation and targeting specific customer needs with different price or quality products can also lead to increased profits. Peter Doyle (1998) uses the example of British Airways (Real-Life Applications 6.1). In its early days the airline business was pretty unaware of the needs of its passengers. Over time it became aware that some people were prepared to pay much more than others; thus first-class and economy class seats were born. Subsequently this classification was divided yet further to add a business class, although only on some routes initially. Business trav-

---

REAL-LIFE APPLICATION 6.1

Segmentation and profitability

Without segmentation

A British Airways plane carries 240 passengers, each of whom pays the same price €250. The airline can achieve 80% load at this price. In this case the profit from this trip is €5,200.

However, the price of €250 is already too much for some budget travellers, whilst business or first-class travellers might be prepared to pay much more to achieve the quality levels they desire, thus . . .

With segmentation

If customers are segmented into three categories, first, business- and economy-class passengers, profits can be increased hugely to €37,840. For example, price-insensitive first-class passengers will be prepared to pay €1,000 for their tickets – four times the undifferentiated price. In addition, the needs of each different customer group are better achieved, increasing their levels of satisfaction and making return purchases more likely. Table 6.1 summarises these calculations.

Table 6.1 Effects of segmentation on profits (adapted from Doyle, 1998, p. 67) (All prices in €)

Class	Passengers	Price	Variable unit cost	Revenue	Variable costs	Fixed costs	Profit
			Undifferentiated strategy				
	240	250	20	60,000	4,800	50,000	5,200
			Differentiated strategy				
Economy	144	250	20	36,000	2,880		
Business	72	500	40	36,000	2,880		
First	24	1,000	100	24,000	2,400		
Total	240			96,000	8,160	50,000	37,840

ellers valued convenience, comfort and space to work; they seldom paid for their own tickets, so the price was of less importance. In contrast, leisure travellers wanted cheap tickets, and because they did not fly often were prepared to suffer the loss of comfort on the relatively rare occasions they travelled. Using differential price/quality mixes allowed British Airways to increase its profit.

6.2.2 Segmentation and competitive advantage

The British Airways example illustrates two things about a successful use of segmentation:

- The segments chosen must be in some way attractive – it must be possible to serve them at a profit.

- It must be possible to **tailor the products and services** offered to the demands of the segment. There would have been no point in BA's identifying the three different segments if the company had not been able to adapt its offer to the demands of the three different types of customer. No-one would pay a first-class fare if the service was little different from that in economy or business class. In fact, several of BA's competitors stopped offering first-class travel because they were not able to differentiate it from business class, or did not think that it was worth while to do so. We look at the concept of differentiation in more detail in Section 6.3.

Thus, when you look at a company and try to assess how its competitive stance has contributed to its success or failure, you need to assess how astutely it has chosen its segments, and how well it has designed the products and services it offers them. There are a number of attributes that might make a segment attractive.

If a segment is **broad**, containing a lot of customers, then it offers a substantial target market. Firms in a number of industries, such as automobiles and pharmaceuticals, have decided to target the Chinese market for this reason, even though the people and firms there have limited spending power at present. A broad segment is even more attractive if it is **homogeneous** – the customers within it all have similar tastes and preferences. This means that they can be satisfied with a limited product range, which means that a company can look forward to potential economies of scale.

If a segment is **easily accessible** this may make it attractive. One way in which new firms can get started, and may be able to defend their position afterwards, is by targeting segments to which they have easier access than their competitors, for example because they are located close by or because their staff have good contacts with potential customers. An established firm, on the other hand, may decide to target a segment because it can be **easily served through the existing value chain** – for example, because the distribution channels are already in place.

If the people or firms in the segment are **affluent**, with a lot of spending power, then this is also likely to make the segment a desirable target, and may compensate for the size of the segment being small. Rolls-Royce and Gucci both have target segments of this kind. The segment becomes still more attractive if, as well as being wealthy, the target customers are **not price sensitive**, so that they are willing to pay the price premiums that a firm must charge if it is to offer a differentiated service and still make a decent return.

Brand loyal customers also make a segment attractive, since it means that, once a company has successfully penetrated the segment, it is likely to be able to establish a sustainable advantage there. A company with established brands may also target existing, brand-loyal customer segments when it enters a new industry. The UK's Virgin Group targets many of its products, such as cosmetics, cola, contraceptives and financial services, at a youngish customer group that it believes is loyal to its brand values.

A segment may be attractive simply because it has been **ignored or overlooked by competitors**. The Body Shop's early success came in part because it located (essentially by accident) a new customer segment, the 'environmentally concerned consumer'. Established toiletries firms did not realise that this segment existed, and Body Shop was able to develop products and a value chain to serve it before they could react.

Real-Life Application 6.2 gives some examples of how segmentation decisions have helped firms to gain competitive advantage.

REAL-LIFE APPLICATION 6.2

Segmentation, products and competitive advantage

Benetton in its early days targeted young Italian people anxious to have their spirits raised after the war. It did so by offering inexpensive woollen garments in bright colours.

The Sony Walkman was originally targeted at young, active people such as roller-skaters. The product provided them, and later many other types of people, with a way of listening to music on the move.

McDonald's targets a number of segments, including teenagers and families with young children. For teenagers, the company provides low prices and a non-threatening environment in which shy young people are not intimidated while ordering. For families, McDonald's offers children's meals including safe toys, and a birthday party service that relieves parents of the duty of having to pretend that they know how to amuse their children.

6.2.3 Ways of segmenting markets

Segmentation is most commonly applied to individuals in consumer markets and business buyers. Some of the most common factors that are used to group buyers together are geographic, demographic, psychographic and behavioural variables.

- *Geographic* variables include: the country of residence; region, north or south, county/district or town; neighbourhood, rural or urban, government housing or privately owned. One of the best-known geographic classifications in the UK is ACORN – A Classification Of Residential Neighbourhoods. It provides a means of identifying broad social categories according to where people live – for example, government housing; multi-occupation rented houses; country houses; owner-occupied housing estates, first-buyer apartments, etc. This allows companies to site their operations better. The British supermarket chain Asda is careful to locate its stores in areas where there are high numbers of its target customers – families who are interested in value for money. Similar schemes have been developed elsewhere, such as Omnidat in the Netherlands and Postaid in Sweden, and used by companies to target particular customer groups in direct mailshots, for example.

- *Psychographic* variables include: social class; life-style; personality, and ethical stance. One of the best-known and oldest psychographic classifications in the

Table 6.2   **Social class groups**

	Social status	Occupation of household head	Approx. percentage of adults
A	Upper middle class	Higher managerial – administrative or professional	3
B	Middle class	Middle managerial – administrative or professional	15
C1	Lower middle class	Supervisory Junior managerial – administrative or professional	23
C2	Skilled working class	Skilled manual	28
D	Working class	Semi and unskilled manual	18
E	Subsistence level	Pensioners Widows Casual workers Lowest paid/ welfare recipients	15

UK is the A, B, C1 and C2, D and E groupings of social class (Table 6.2). This is based on census returns, and is still in common use despite its age and flaws, such as the lack of match between spending power and aspirations in some of the categories.

- *Behavioural* variables include: purchasing pattern, attitude towards novelty (buyers can be classified into, for example, early adopters, laggards, or mainstreamers, according to their willingness to buy innovative new products); taste preferences; brand loyalty; and product benefits required.

- *Demographic* variables include: age; gender; race; religion; nationality; marital status, family size, educational level; employment type, and income. Nike, the US sports shoe manufacturer, is an example of a company that has used demographic variables extremely effectively to target a wide number of different segments. It has over 300 varieties of training shoes, many of which are aimed at very specific age or gender-related subsegments of wider segment groups, such as sports, leisure or 'life-style' wearers of the shoes.

All of these classifications will give an idea of spending power, product preferences, and buying and distribution channel preferences of individual consumers.

Not all firms sell to consumers; some sell to other firms. Business customers can also be classified and targeted according to a number of variables, although these are likely to be somewhat different from those used to categorise individuals.

One of the most common variables here is that of SIC (standard industrial classification) codes – companies' product types, for example engineering; retailers; advertising; building; motors; or fast moving consumer goods. Other segmentation can be on profitability levels or cash strength; the size of the firm, or the place of the purchasing decision – for example whether it is within the marketing department centrally, or locally at, say, depot level. Some of the major segmentation variables for business markets include:

Demographic

- *Industry:* Which industries should be served?
- *Company size and type:* Large, small, family owned, public sector, or publicly quoted?
- *Location:* Which geographic areas should be served? National, international, or local?

Operations

- *Technology:* What customer technologies should be focused on?
- *Customer capabilities:* Do buyers need many or few services? Are they technically knowledgeable or unskilled?

Purchasing approaches

- *Power structure:* Are companies dominated by engineering, finance, or other functions?
- *General purchase policies:* Should companies that prefer leasing be targeted? Services contracts? Systems purchases? Sealed bidding?
- *Purchasing criteria:* Do target companies seek quality? Service? Are they price sensitive?

Situational factors

- *Urgency:* Do target companies need quick and sudden delivery of service, or are they more concerned about low costs, so that time is less of an issue?
- *Size of order:* Large or small orders?

Personal characteristics

- *Identification:* Should companies be targeted whose people and values are similar to ours?
- *Loyalty:* Should we only serve companies that show high loyalty to their suppliers?

Firms can use some of the same fundamental segmentation variables when operating internationally, even though different countries may be at different levels of economic or social development. There is a commonality in the types of product that consumers demand as their income levels increase. Some of the most expensive products, Gucci or Rolex for example, are not modified to cater for country differences. Consumers who regularly purchase these types of branded items have more in common with each other, across national boundaries, than they do with other groups of people in their own countries.

6.3 Differentiation

Once a segment has been identified and targeted, the organisation then faces the problem of how to distinguish itself from other firms that are serving the same group of customers. A customer needs to see a benefit from choosing one product, or one organisation, over another, which implies some form of differentiation.

6.3.1 Forms of differentiation[2]

One way of differentiating an organisation's offer is through the attributes of the product or service itself. This can be done through:

- *Functionality* – a product or service has superior functionality if it offers things that few others do. Sega's Dreamcast games console offers (at the time of writing) far superior quality graphics to any competing machine, although Sony has promised to launch a product with even better graphics.

- *Appearance* – some products, such as clothes and cars, may be bought simply because they look good.

- *Build quality and reliability* – products or services that reach the customer with fewer faults than competitors and/or perform more reliably in use. Volkswagen attempts to differentiate its cars in this fashion, and McDonald's hamburgers are consistent in their taste and hygiene.

- *Price* – products can be differentiated on price in two ways
  - By making their products or services more expensive than competitors', firms hope to signal the superior value of what they offer. This type of differentiation frequently goes together with differentiation on reputation and brand image (see below) and is employed by suppliers of up-market fragrances, designer clothing and top-range management consultancy
  - By selling their products more cheaply than their rivals, firms hope to signal that they offer value for money and expect to make up in higher sales volumes what they lose in low profit margins. Food retailers like Aldi and Netto and clothing chains like the Spanish firm, Zara, pursue this kind of differentiation. Remember that, as we pointed out in Theoretical Perspective 6.1, differentiation on low price is not the same as having a cost advantage. The lowest cost producer does not always have the lowest prices.

  Customers purchasing decisions are not always made on the basis of the product alone. The qualities of the organisation that is providing it may also play a major role. Organisations can mark themselves out from their competitors through their value chain and resources, in particular:

The roles of the sales and after-sales service activities in generating differentiation are examined in Section 8.2.1. ▶

- *Support* – the quality of sales and after-sales service may be a valuable feature. In retailing, Marks and Spencer differentiated itself from its UK competitors by its willingness to refund money to dissatisfied customers with no questions asked. BMW differentiates itself through the quality of its dealer and service agent network.

Reputation and brands are examined in Section 7.2.5. ▶

● *Reputation and brand image* – these factors offer value to customers in two ways. Firstly, by buying a prestigious brand of machinery or clothing, buyers hope acquire some of that prestige for themselves; they hope to be recognised as possessing wealth or good taste. Secondly, by purchasing from a supplier with a good reputation, they hope to save themselves *search costs*: the time and effort needed to evaluate competing products and make an informed choice between them.

Differentiation is not always effective – there are cases, like computers and video machines, where it is more important for a product to be compatible with industry standards. And not all attempts to differentiate work equally well in every market. It will be the specific needs of the target segment and the actions of competitors that will determine whether a particular combination of differentiation features succeeds or not. When Marks and Spencer entered the Canadian market, it found that its 'no questions asked' refund policy, so powerful in the UK, was not a differentiating factor, as most Canadian retailers offered a similar guarantee. Apple Computer (Real-Life Application 6.3) offers another example of failed and successful differentiation.

6.3.2 Identifying customer requirements

In order to achieve an effective differentiation strategy a firm needs to know the needs of its customers. Bowman describes a process of assessing the use needs of customers, which can then be aligned with the internal competences and abilities of the firm. An example is shown in Figure 6.1, in relation to the electrical engineering industry.

A firm wishing to differentiate its products to attract buyers from company A in Figure 6.1 would have to ensure that it provided high levels of product quality, tested for reliability before sales, but should not waste too much money on pro-

---

REAL-LIFE APPLICATION 6.3

Successful and failed differentiation at Apple Computer

The American personal computer manufacturer, Apple, has long emphasised differentiation as a major plank in its strategy. Its Macintosh range of computers was originally differentiated from the IBM-PC and compatible machines through their superior and easy-to-use interface, but also through their price, which was considerably higher than that charged for IBM-compatible machines. Despite this (or perhaps because of it) they attracted a fiercely loyal following, particularly in the design, publishing and education markets that Apple targeted, since the Macintosh's functionality advantages were particularly valuable to those customers.

However, Macintosh's package of differentiation features became less valuable. Successive versions of Microsoft's Windows software gave buyers of other PCs most of the graphics and other features that were previously only available to Apple users. It became increasingly difficult to justify the Macintosh's price premium over Windows PCs, particularly since software houses did not feel it worth the expense of producing special versions of their products to run on the Macintosh.

In 1998, Apple revived its flagging fortunes with the introduction of the iMac, which it targeted at the consumer market. The company has successfully differentiated this new range of computers in this new target segment on the basis of the iMac's colourful appearance and functionality benefits – particularly its networking. It is also easy to set up and use. It is priced at a similar level to a Windows PC of comparable power.

Figure 6.1   Perceived value by customers in the electrical engineering industry (adapted from Johnson and Scholes, 1999; p. 133)

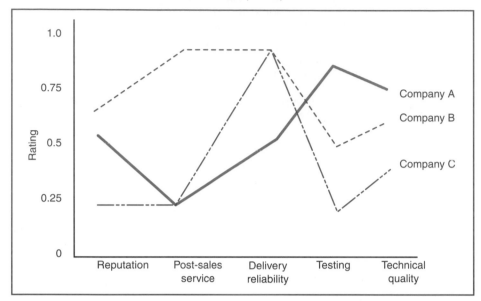

viding high levels of after-sales service. In contrast, if the same firm wanted to service customers from company C, it should invest more in having reliable deliveries and less in providing high quality pre-sales testing. On such bases can products be made different from their competitors. This implies that the same firm is unlikely to want to, or be able to, service the different buyers at the same time.

However, it is sometimes difficult to assess what it is exactly that customers want. There is a famous saying in marketing, that customers are 'irreducibly human' – in other words, unpredictable, unmanageable and inconsistent. They often do not realise what they want until they have it, and then realise that they really wanted something else. Indeed, this underpins one of the major criticisms of this type of model, and provides support for the organisational experimentation and innovation of schools of thought where strategy comes from the internal abilities of the firm. Even if customers are fairly reliable in knowing what they want, the firm has to find out what that is – and this may mean an expensive (and imitable) market research project. In fact, many firms are engaged in a regular discourse with most of their most valuable customers, and do have a pretty good idea of what they need. However, in order to sustain a differentiated position, one needs to know what the competitors' products are, and how they are different. As this is not likely to be a static picture, the basis of differentiated competition may change regularly. Competitors may imitate the firm's products and the firm in its turn may adopt some aspects of their products or service. We return to these issues in Section 6.7.

6.4   Positioning: the strategy clock

We now move on to consider how a firm can profitably position its business-level strategies to meet the segmented needs of customers. Cliff Bowman has neatly brought these two aspects – positioning and segmentation – together in a model

Figure 6.2   The strategy clock (from Faulkner and Bowman, 1995)

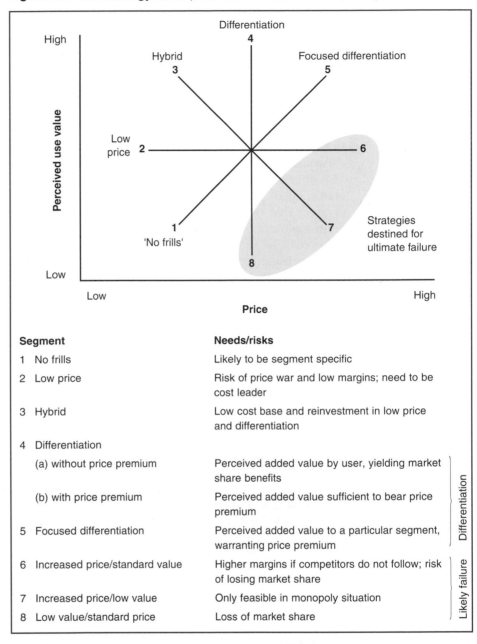

Segment		Needs/risks
1	No frills	Likely to be segment specific
2	Low price	Risk of price war and low margins; need to be cost leader
3	Hybrid	Low cost base and reinvestment in low price and differentiation
4	Differentiation	
	(a) without price premium	Perceived added value by user, yielding market share benefits
	(b) with price premium	Perceived added value sufficient to bear price premium
5	Focused differentiation	Perceived added value to a particular segment, warranting price premium
6	Increased price/standard value	Higher margins if competitors do not follow; risk of losing market share
7	Increased price/low value	Only feasible in monopoly situation
8	Low value/standard price	Loss of market share

that he has called a *strategy 'clock'*. This says that what a firm or business unit does in relation to the *perceived use values* or PUVs of its customers – existing or potential – is what creates competitive advantage. His model (Figure 6.2) develops and adds to Porter's original three categories of generic strategy. Because of this, some aspects of it can be criticised for similar reasons (for example, the focus on static external factors), although it is a more sophisticated model and as such deals with some of the problems in Porter's original.

We will now look at these categories in turn.

1   No frills

A 'no-frills' strategy provides few added features, and targets a price-sensitive segment of a particular market. This is a potentially viable strategy if there are enough consumers who cannot afford to buy higher priced goods or services, and indeed a number of firms appear to have profitably pursued just this type of approach over many years. Ireland's Ryanair and America's SouthWestern airlines offer a cheap, basic point-to-point air travel service, with no meals on their flights and no facilities for people who want to transfer to a connecting flight on arrival at their destination. They have now been imitated by British Airways (with Go!) and KLM Royal Dutch Airlines (with Buzz).

Two other examples in the European food retailing industry are Netto and Aldi, who offer the lowest prices for a limited range of well-known and popular supermarket goods. They typically have around 10,000 lines compared with the 30,000 or more that other supermarkets such as Carrefour or Tesco stock. They sell a limited amount of fresh produce, thus minimising wastage. These stores' branches are housed in warehouse type accommodation, with limited parking facilities. Merchandising is functional as opposed to appealing, reminiscent of a cash and carry operation. No added-value services are on offer, such as free plastic bags, toilets, customer service, or different versions of trolleys.

2   Low price

This strategy aims to charge lower prices for the same levels of quality and service as the firm's competitors offer. As a result, it is a risky strategy which, for success, requires the firm to have lower costs than its competitors, or to be able to block imitation of its prices and survive price wars – both quite difficult to achieve. Price wars can damage an industry in the long term, by blocking the firms' ability to reinvest in long-term development. However, for firms that are able to maintain lower costs than their competitors, and have the financial strength to survive a price war, this route may be sustainable. It seems likely, however, that this strategy will have a short lifespan and will change over time to a stance based either on no frills or on clearer differentiation.

Bowman suggests that some firms that have succeeded in this strategy adopt a highly focused targeting of particular customers, such as the companies that manufacture own-label products for the supermarket groups. Because of their specialised focus they can minimise the costs of seeking new customers, and can tailor their value chains efficiently to the specific requirements of a small group of buyers.

3   Hybrid

A hybrid strategy aims to achieve differentiation from competing products, while charging lower prices. Many organisations appear to be following this strategic path successfully, although Porter condemned it as leading a firm to become 'stuck in the middle'. Charging lower prices for products offering valued benefits is likely to lead to higher levels of turnover than would be achieved simply by differentiation. It may be possible to cut costs (and therefore charge lower prices) in area that are not important to the customer. Firms following this route include Benetton, with its emphasis on fashionable goods at affordable prices, McDonald's, with its offer of reliable quality at low prices, and a number of Japanese and Taiwanese car firms, such as Daewoo and Toyota. Such firms made it their business to cut costs and therefore prices, through reducing their dependence on expensive dealerships in the case of Daewoo, and through manufacturing competences in the case of Toyota. However, their cars fulfilled much the same needs as their competitors' offerings.

4   Differentiation

Differentiation is perhaps the most common of the generic strategies and, as we have explained earlier, can really be said to be present in all the other 'routes'. A differentiation strategy in this model aims to produce products that are *different* from those of competitors in ways which are valued by consumers, who are prepared to pay higher prices, or to remain loyal, as a result. Differentiated products are of higher quality, provide additional benefits, or are accompanied by higher levels of service, either at the time of purchase or subsequently.

Sony, with its emphasis on innovation, reliable but highly featured products and above-average prices, has pursued this kind of strategy for much of its history in televisions, audio equipment, and most recently with its PlayStation games consoles and its Vaio portable computers. The Vaio, which featured striking good looks and facilities for video editing never before seen on a laptop, is an excellent example of a differentiation strategy succeeding in an already crowded industry.

5   Focused differentiation

A focused differentiation strategy seeks to achieve high prices for a highly specialised product, for which there are likely to be few competing firms. In order to achieve this, the firm is likely to have particularly strong competences in areas of particular importance to that narrow range of customers. Perhaps the technology used in production is particularly sophisticated, the product/service specification particularly high, or the relationships with customers particularly strong. This implies that the firm will as a whole be focused on a relatively small range of important issues, where its value chain is specialised, and where it serves relatively few, and therefore powerful, buyers.

This kind of strategy is pursued by high-fashion houses, by top hotels such as the Savoy in London and by Switzerland's private banks, which offer discreet banking services and high-powered financial advice to extremely wealthy individuals.

In this strategy, the relationship and trust between the firm and its buyer is likely to be particularly critical, with considerable mutual interdependency. This is likely to prove problematic if the firm wishes to grow significantly as other customers with similarly specialised needs may be hard to find.

6, 7 and 8   Failure strategies

All three of the following strategies appear likely to result in failure – in the long term at least. Strategy 6 is based on high price and standard value. This, of course, is a wonderful strategy to adopt, if competitors do not offer the same product at lower prices. It is only likely to be sustainable if customers do not have access to

◄ *We looked at natural monopolies in Section 5.5.2.*

the information that would tell them where to obtain better value, or if legal or historical factors give the firm an effective monopoly of a particular segment. Otherwise, it is likely that competitors will take market share. Apple's Macintosh computer (see Real-Life Application 6.3) is an example of how this kind of strategy eventually comes unstuck. Path 7 is even more problematic; prices are increased at the same time as value declines.

Strategy 8, providing low value at a standard price, is likely to result in loss of market share as customers begin to realise that they are being short-changed. However, there are occasions when this strategy can succeed, in the short term at least, as brand loyalty or inability to perceive the relatively low value provided by the firm act to sustain turnover. Some brands of supermarket foods have adopted this strategy recently, reducing the quantity of products in tins or jars. For the most part this reduction in value goes unnoticed, although these tactics may rebound. Throughout the 1970s Cadbury, a British confectioner, gradually reduced the size of its chocolate bars. Its rival, Rowntree, launched a much chunkier bar that immediately took a large share of a market that Cadbury had dominated for decades.

6.5 Choice of scope and scale

Alongside their segmentation and positioning decisions, organisations need to take decisions about the scope and scale at which they operate. Of course these decisions are not independent of one another. Sometimes a decision to attack a particular segment only makes economic sense if that segment is large, or if it is treated as a global segment rather than simply a British or German one. Sony would never have recovered the costs of its development costs on the PlayStation games console if it had focused on Japanese teenagers. It had to sell the product in Europe and, crucially, the USA – and the hardware and software needed to be designed accordingly.

◄ *Global industries were discussed in Section 5.5.3.*

The impact of scale and scope on a firm's value chain is reviewed in Sections 8.1.3 and 8.1.4. ►

Sometimes, the decision relating to appropriate scope and scale will be dictated by industry conditions. Industries may be global, regional, national or local. Different firms may choose to operate at any one of those levels, with a broad or narrow range of products. These decisions will also be very strongly influenced by the firm's value chain, which will determine whether it can operate profitably at a given scale and scope.

6.5.1 Choice of scope

Choosing particular customer groups allows the different elements of a firm's value chain to be set up to cater specifically for the needs of a particular segment. One of the most important issues that a firm needs to consider is how widely to spread itself. Should it concentrate on one product in one market, or spread itself more widely across a number of different products and/or different markets? Some companies have different divisions, with differently configured value chains, providing products tailored for specific segments. In other cases the whole organisation chooses to specialise in one relatively narrow type of business. There are arguments for and against both types of strategy.

Such decisions influence a firm's structure – single or multidivisional; with syn-

◀ *We briefly mentioned the structures and parenting styles of corporations in Chapters 1 and 3 and return to them in Chapter 9.* ▶

We return to these competing choices in Chapter 11. ▶

ergistic links between divisions, or stand-alone divisions with few links between the different sides of the company.

These decisions can be considered against a model of product/market choices (Figure 6.3). Although a bit simplistic, this model is useful if you remember that the word 'new' equals risk. Companies which attempt to move into new markets with existing products are taking some risk; companies which attempt to develop new products for their existing customers are also taking some risk, but innovation or diversification (particularly if unrelated) is the most risky strategy of all.

Thus firms which are moving away from a focus on a single product with a single customer base have to believe that the risks involved are outweighed by the potential benefits of a move away from their home base. If they do this on a number of different businesses or products, then the complexity and risks increase. However, we are *not* saying that firms should not take these risks – simply that their relative downsides and upsides have to be assessed.

There are also risks in *not* moving into new products or markets. Imagine a company whose only product is the manufacture of a single drug sold to a specific market – orthopaedic surgeons. They have a unique product and a captive market. Success! Until, that is, a medical researcher finds that this drug causes cancer. Overnight the sales of this product will stop – either legislated out of business or subject to market forces. So there are reasons why a firm would wish to protect itself against such a thing happening, and the spreading of risk by diversifying into different products or markets, which are perhaps at a different stage of their lifecycle, has been an important traditional method of hedging against such risks.

Another compelling argument for diversifying is to achieve *economies of scope* from sharing resources or capacity across a number of different products or businesses. The firm as a whole may benefit from increased utilisation of its plant, greater buying power, shared advertising campaigns, or cross-selling of a range of products by the same sales team – synergy. It allows costs to be spread across more products, therefore unit costs are lower and prices can be lower. Nevertheless, it is questionable how much synergy is achievable. There have to be considerable similarities between a firm's products or markets for this to work, and as discussed in Chapter 3, diversification at both product and business level can lead to increased transaction costs as the complexity of the business increases.

Complexity is an important issue in considering how much to move away from the core business or product. Senior managers in firms which diversify too much

Figure 6.3 Product/market strategies

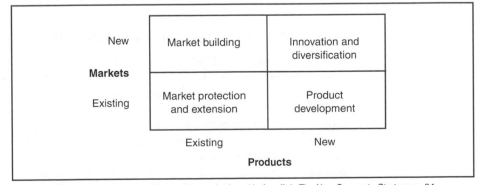

Note: An updated, current version of the model may be found in Ansoff, I. *The New Corporate Strategy*, p. 84

(although how much is too much is difficult to say) appear to lose the ability to oversee the different products or businesses in their portfolio – the co-ordination of all these different activities results in high administrative costs. Their time, resources and expertise are diluted, allowing competitors who are specialists (and therefore more likely to have knowledge which is unique, intangible and inimitable – the basis for core competences) to gain advantage – a process which happens individually in each product or market in which the diversified firm competes.

The fashion for diversified corporations reached its peak in the 1970s and 1980s, after which it was discovered that their performance may actually have been no better, and in many cases was considerably worse, than firms which were specialists – or which, to use Peters and Waterman's (1982) strange but memorable term, 'stuck to the knitting'. Since then many companies have shed peripheral interests and cut back to their core businesses. We look at these issues in more detail in Chapter 9.

6.5.2 Choice of scale

◀ *Economies of scale are defined in Section 3.1.1.*

The firm's value chain and areas of economies of scale or scope are covered in Chapter 8. ▶

Another basic strategic decision for a firm is to decide how many of a particular product it makes – whether it customises every one of its products, reduces costs by making the same product in greater numbers to achieve *economies of scale*, or does something in between these two extremes.

Economies of scale are particularly important in certain industries, such as those with high fixed costs like aircraft manufacturing, high development coses, such as pharmaceuticals, or high advertising costs, such as fast-moving consumer goods. In any industry, however, the firm with the greatest economies of scale for the same type of product will have certain advantages over its competitors. It is one of the reasons why market share appears to lead to greater profits. The search for increasing scale economies is an important factor driving merger decisions, although experience in industries like banking shows how difficult it can be to achieve economies of scale in practice.

The need to push down costs is also an important factor driving the increasing globalisation of business, as we shall see in Section 6.6, although the need for local customisation of products is a counter to this pressure. As with most things in strategy, weighing up the contradictory forces of consumer demand for customisation versus the need to reduce costs is a balancing act without any easy or indeed right answer.

6.5.3 How much advantage does this explain?

One of the criticisms of strategies which are based on achieving economies of either scale or scope is that they can be emulated. Market positions can be overturned, product ranges copied, and economies of scale and scope are open to anyone. Efficiencies of both scale and scope usually have limits beyond which no more benefits can be accrued, so they are not a universal panacea.

So is there any point in attempting to achieve them? The answer has to be yes, because if a firm does not attempt to achieve the lowest possible costs then its competitors surely will. But, over the long term, competitive advantage has to come from other sources. Paradoxically these advantages will automatically result in scale economies because more of the company's products are sold – because they bring new benefits, are of higher quality, distributed through convenient locations, or because the buyer has a strong bond or relationship with the firm.

This line of reasoning points to more complex factors as being the source of enduring competitive advantage. They have to do with the firm's control of rare and valuable resources which no other firm can access, with its competences and capabilities – aspects of performance which are unique, intangible, and not easily copied – and with its relationships with key individuals – its architecture. It is this chain of logic that forms the basis for the resource based view of strategy, to which we return in detail in the next chapter.

6.6 International strategies

One of the most common issues said to be affecting businesses today is the globalisation of their markets. This provides a number of different problems for companies in addition to the 'normal' strategic dilemmas that they have to resolve. In the first place, a company has to decide if it wants to target customers across the globe, simply focus on a local niche, or do something in between. If it decides that it wants to compete internationally, then it has to also decide whether to sell the same product to everyone, or attempt to customise it for local needs. It needs to think about how it sells its products – whether to use local agents, who might understand the local market conditions better, or to employ its own staff to set up fully owned subsidiary divisions, or to use the Internet as a medium through which to search for interested buyers and to submit tenders.

On a small scale, a firm may decide simply to export part of its output to customers that want it. It may leave it to interested buyers to track it down, take payment only in its home currency and bill customers for the cost of shipment. The World Wide Web makes this form of low-key internationalisation far easier and less expensive now than it was, since it gives any business with a website, however new, small and specialised it may be, a global shop window.

However, for any organisation going beyond this simple form of exporting, 'going international' adds a layer of complexity to the normal management problems of a national firm, such as those in the finance function. Different levels of interest and exchange rates across countries, and the need to take these into account when pricing a product in different currencies, make an international firm's treasury function an important one. Large companies can lose millions by getting exchange rates wrong. International firms must also consider where to locate their various value chain activities and how to manage political risks in different countries of operation; should manufacturing take place near where the products will be sold, thereby reducing transportation costs, or where manufacturing costs are lowest, but where there is an unstable political situation? Last but not least, they must attend to the problems of managing people who speak a different language and who may not share, or even be aware of, many of the owners' cultural assumptions.

So going international is an important decision for any company. It has to weigh up the increased management problems against the opportunities a much larger market offers. However, it also needs to consider what happens if it does not expand abroad, because competitors, who are now potentially from all over the world, are quite likely to step in and seize the initiative. The increasing internationalisation of business means that companies may need to compete with firms that are able to achieve economies of scale or low costs by operating internationally. We will look at some of these issues in some detail later, but first we will consider the different international product/market options available to firms.

6.6.1 Locally responsive, global and transnational strategies

There has been quite a debate in the strategy literature over the last ten or fifteen years over whether there is such a thing as a truly global product – one which is sold the world over, and which is exactly the same in each market in which it is found. Underlying this debate, which we summarise at the end of this section, is the question of whether there are fundamental differences between countries in the ways that their residents live and work, the products that they buy and the ways that they buy them. The debate about this can be polarised into, at the one end, the assumption that everyone is the same – the global view, and at the other extreme the assumption that people are very different – the countries' view.

◄ Pressures for globalisation are discussed in Section 5.5.3.

For most products and markets therefore there is a need to reconcile two potentially conflicting pressures: for local responsiveness (through customisation) and global cost minimisation (through manufacturing, development, and sourcing locations and developing economies of scale). These pressures and the strategies they result in are mapped in Figure 6.4.

Firms may deal with these pressures within strategies that are **global** (or *geocentric*) – where the product itself is standardised. Global products tend to be sold under a single brand-name throughout the world and to be supplied to the world-wide market from a small number of key locations where costs are favourable.

George Yip (1992) has described a number of theoretical advantages that a firm obtains from following a global strategy, *if* the industry structure is favourable:

● It can maximise any available economies of scale, and share investments in R&D and marketing across its various markets. British Airways spends over £1 million on its advertisements, featuring hundreds of people and spectacular effects such as islands being swathed in colour. Because BA is a global brand,

Figure 6.4 Costs–responsiveness model

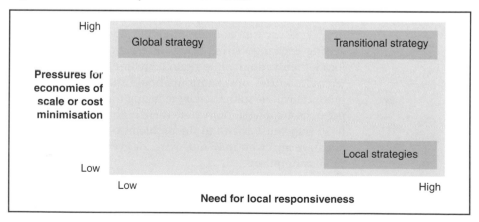

the advertisements, which are almost wordless, can be used throughout the world, allowing each market to achieve a far greater advertising impact than it could afford on its own.

- It can be exposed to developments in all key markets, so it is not taken by surprise by competitors, who will typically test-market a new product in one place before launching it globally. It can also gauge the reaction of the world's most demanding consumers to their products and services. These might, for example, be Japanese people for electronics products, Germans for cars and engineering products and Americans for services. Goods and services that pass the test posed by these buyers are likely to be viable in any market in the world.

- It can fight competitive moves in one country with a counter-move in another. For example, if an American firm starts a price war in your home market, you can counter with a similar move in the USA. Without this ability to play on a global scale, you would be vulnerable to competitors who can keep prices low in your key markets, cutting into your profits. They are able to fund this from the high profits that they can obtain in the markets where you do not have a presence, and so cannot retaliate.

At the other extreme, using a **locally responsive** (sometimes known as a *multi-local*, *multi-domestic* or *polycentric*) strategy, a firm may serve each local market with products that are tailored specifically to it, and produced in that country. Local strategies tend to need a complete range of value-chain activities in each country, and because of duplication are likely therefore to have a higher cost structure. Multinational companies adopting this strategy sometimes have a problem in transferring learning from one market to another and co-ordinating strategies between countries. One example of this was Philips, whose V2000 video format developed in the Netherlands was not taken up by its US subsidiary, who instead chose to adopt the Japanese-developed VHS format. This effectively killed Philips' chances of establishing V2000 as a viable alternative to VHS, and meant that the development cost was wasted.

An intermediate view, which has become very fashionable under the slogan 'think global, act local', or what has now been termed 'glocal', can be described as a **transnational** approach to products and markets. The challenge to global companies is to localise products, while still retaining economies of scale. Industries where this approach might be appropriate include motor cars, many of whose components might be sourced globally but which are customised for local requirements (left- or right-hand drive, for example), and many consumer goods such as soap powders, household items and fashion clothes. Companies that espouse this approach include Unilever, the Anglo-Dutch food, detergent and toiletries firm, and ABB, the Swedish–Swiss engineering combine. It is important to emphasise that a transnational strategy is not an easy compromise between a global and a locally responsive strategy. In order to get the best (rather than the worst) of both worlds, strong management control systems and a particular type of structure and culture are needed.

Prahalad and Doz (1987), however, caution that whichever product/market stance an organisation may choose, its competitive environment is still likely to be global. Even a locally based firm may supply, or be supplied by, global firms. It may also confront the threat of entry into its niche markets from international companies with sufficient financial strength and management competences to see off more purely local competitors.

In fact, most international organisations are likely to be operating a mix of these strategies simultaneously, and even those offering only a single product may not be so easily categorised. Many of the most commonly cited global products (McDonald's or Coca-Cola for example) might be categorised as transnational – because their packaging, advertising, or even content is changed, if only slightly, to adjust to local taste. Coca-Cola is said to have a higher sugar content in some markets, and McDonald's does not put beef in its 'beefburgers' in its Indian branches.

Even in electronic commerce, which some observers thought was likely to lead to further harmonisation of tastes around the world, there has proved to be a need

THEORETICAL PERSPECTIVE 6.2

Global products and global strategies

One of the main proponents of the *global* product argument is a very well known American marketing expert, Theodore Levitt. In an article in the *Harvard Business Review* entitled 'The globalization of markets' (Levitt, 1983), he suggested that the globalisation of industries was inevitable. According to him, 'the world's needs and desires have been irrevocably homogenized'. He suggested that this process was driven by technology, which facilitates communication, transport and travel, and at the same time enables superior products to be produced at low prices. This leads to standardised products sold in standardised ways to customers the world over. Levitt cited, as examples of global products, McDonald's, which is found from the Champs Elysée to the Ginza, Coca-Cola and Pepsi-Cola which can be bought in Bahrain and in Moscow, rock music, Greek salad, Hollywood movies, Revlon cosmetics, Sony televisions, and Levi jeans everywhere. Also placeable in this category are some computer components, some car parts, commodities such as refined sugar or wool, or compact disks. George Yip, C.K. Prahalad and Yves Doz are other prominent proponents of the idea of the global product.

Douglas and Wind (1987) are at the opposite end of the spectrum from Levitt – and advocate a *countries* or *local* approach to competition which aims to customise products for local needs. They suggested that markets are not as homogeneous as Levitt claimed. They offered a range of examples of how customers in different parts of the world have differing needs that cannot be met by a standardised product. They also argued that the emphasis on economies of scale and production and marketing is not the irreversible driving force that Levitt emphasises. Many new technologies actually lower the minimum efficient scale of production and, anyway, for many industries economies of scale are not a

competitive success factor. In the local category are restaurants, local foodstuffs such as cheese, and many services or utilities, such as gas or water supply, car repair shops and hairdressers.

Others have taken a less polarised view of international competition. Kenichi Ohmae, writing in the *Harvard Business Review* in 1989,[3] suggested that customer needs around the world have become similar, whilst the fixed costs of meeting those needs have soared, making global products a necessity. But, in Ohmae's opinion, there are still sufficient differences in the needs of local markets to make totally universal products unrealistic. His may be classified as the transnational view, which is also favoured by Sumantra Ghoshal and Christopher Bartlett.

The debate is complicated by the insistence of some theorists that a global of transnational competitive stance **has** to be associated with a particular value chain and architecture. Ghoshal and Bartlett advocate that transnational firms should have structures that combine strong local managers, who supervise the customisation and marketing of their products, with strong global supervision of the production process. George Yip paints a picture of an idealised 'global company' that has a single point of sourcing for every part of the product, whose managers move easily between operations in different countries and whose senior management team includes representatives from around the world. There are firms who take this to heart – US automaker Ford's present CEO was born in Lebanon and educated in Australia, and his predecessor was a Scot. However, there are plenty of firms, American (e.g. McDonald's), European (Benetton) and Asian (Samsung), that profitably operate internationally even though much of their production and almost all of their top managers come from the company's home country.

to respond to local differences. Internet retailer Amazon.com spends a great deal of time and money in adapting its website and inventory to take account of local customer preferences in each new country it enters.

Perhaps, then, the truly global product is a myth – almost all products have some elements of local customisation, in packaging or their service component for example. The theoretical debate around this issue is explored in Theoretical Perspective 6.2. However, these categorisations – multi-local, global and transnational – serve to point out ways in which firms can think about how much they need to standardise their products in order to benefit from a standardised global customer base. Similarly, they also provide a basis for thinking about which elements of a firm or product's value chain can be located in parts of the world where cost advantages can be obtained.

6.6.2 International cultural differences

One of the reasons why firms might choose a locally responsive strategy is that there are cultural differences between people in different countries. Such differences are also likely to influence how business is carried out in these countries. In fact, assessing and coping with the cultural differences between different countries and the ways in which business is typically conducted in them, provides considerable challenges for international firms. The understanding that not everyone in the world thinks alike has increased substantially over recent years, although there have been some very expensive mistakes made by firms along the way. As globalisation has taken hold, such problems are probably becoming fewer, although international management is a competence in its own right which not all organisations have been able to develop. Even some of the best managed firms have experienced problems. In retailing, Carrefour, the French supermarket chain, withdrew from its attempted entry into the UK because of poor performance. UK food and clothing retailer Marks and Spencer's international expansion, particularly into the USA,

---

THEORETICAL PERSPECTIVE 6.3

International cultural differences

Two Dutch writers, Geert Hofstede and Fons Trompenaars (along with Trompenaars' collaborator, Charles Hampden-Turner, a Briton),[4] have been extremely influential in identifying the cultural differences between countries.

Hofstede's research looked at the differences in management style and other factors which impacted on the ways which companies went about their business in different parts of the world. His work pointed out some of the ways in which managers who worked for international companies could get things very wrong, simply by assuming that others shared their view of the way that things should be done.

Hofstede identified four main dimensions of national cultures: power distance, uncertainty avoidance, individualism–collectivism and masculinity–femininity:

Power distance

This refers to how ready people are to accept the authority of others. Countries with a high power distance tend to be quite hierarchical, with an acceptance that others have the right to exercise power. In low power distance countries superiors tend to consider subordinates to be 'people like them' and vice versa, and there is little expectation that powerholders should have additional privileges.

A boss who has learned about management in a higher power distance culture is likely to assume that she is deemed to speak for her department's views. She may not see the need to attribute specific ideas to her individual staff. She is also likely to assume that it is expected of her that she will make most, if not all, of the important decisions.

Countries with relatively high power distance cultures include Arab countries, Malaysia, India, Brazil and France. Countries with a low power distance include all the Germanic and Scandinavian countries (Netherlands, Germany, Denmark, Sweden, Finland and Norway), South Africa, Italy, and all Anglo-Saxon countries such as Canada, New Zealand, Australia, the USA and the UK.

Individualism–collectivism

Some countries have a much greater sense of society or group-belonging than others. *Individualism* implies a loosely knit social framework in which people have to take care of themselves, while *collectivism* is characterised by a social framework of groups whose members are expected to look after other members. In exchange, absolute loyalty is expected. Organisations are examples of such groups, and in such cultures working for a particular firm is considered rewarding in itself. In collective cultures there is little expectation that everybody has a right to a private life, and decisions which benefit the group are valued over decisions which are individualistic.

Broadly speaking, all the Anglo-Saxon cultures are more individualistic and Asian countries such as Japan, Pakistan, and India show a much greater sense of collectivity. Countries in Latin America ranged from relatively individualistic (Argentina and Brazil) to highly collective (Mexico, Venezuela, Colombia, Chile and Peru). Incidentally, Hofstede also found a strong correlation between national wealth and individualism, although Japan as medially individualistic was an exception to this rule.

Uncertainty avoidance

This indicates the extent to which people in a society feel threatened by uncertain and ambiguous situations. Career stability, the establishing of formal rules of conduct, an intolerance of deviant ideas and behaviours, and a belief in absolute truths and expertise are characteristics of countries with strong uncertainty avoidance. Countries with weak levels of uncertainty avoidance are characterised by risk-taking competition and entrepreneurialness. In such countries people wish for as few rules as possible, which are changed if they do not appear to be working.

Countries with lower levels of uncertainty avoidance include the UK, USA, India and Malaysia. Countries with high levels of uncertainty avoidance include Greece, Japan, France and Spain.

Masculinity/femininity

This dimension describes the extent to which the dominant values in society are considered to be 'masculine' – i.e. assertiveness, the acquisition of money and things, and *not* caring for others, the quality of life, the environment, or

people. Even in 1980, Hofstede was aware of the potential dangers in such stereotypical values and explained his labelling because men scored higher on these factors even though the society of which they were a part as a whole might veer towards the 'feminine' pole. The more an entire society scores to the masculine side, the wider the gap Hofstede found between the values of its men and women. Other masculine traits referred to the perception that women had different roles in life, which were of lower status than men's.

'Masculine' cultures include Japan, the Anglo-Saxon countries, Germany, Italy and Israel. 'Feminine' cultures are mostly the Scandinavian countries.

Other areas of difference

Hofstede's original work has since been extended and other cultural characteristics identified, such as the extent to which a country is religious, believes in the here and now or in deferred rewards, and towards time in general. Different cultures have different perceptions of time, for example, whether they value the past or are more future oriented. The UK and France are past-oriented, whereas the USA is more geared towards the future. Similar differences apply to whether the culture is concerned with the long term or the short term. Most of the Anglo-Saxon cultures are relatively short termist, whereas many Asian and some European countries are more oriented to the long term. Lateness is another area of difference. Behaviour in meetings can be significantly affected by attitudes to time. To join a meeting late in some countries requires an apology, as it is taken to belittle the participants' importance. In Italy or Spain, lateness would not be taken to imply lack of commitment or concern.

Fons Trompenaars was another writer to identify differences between national cultures and organisational behaviour. He identified seven principal areas of difference:

1. Universalism versus particularism – whether rules are rigidly adhered to and accepted to be always applicable and right, or bent according to the needs of a specific relationship without consideration of abstract societal codes.

2. Individualism versus communitarianism – whether the individual or group is considered more important.

3. Emotionality – how acceptable it is to express emotions visibly versus the view that interactions should always be as objective and as detached as possible.

4. Specific versus diffuse – how specifically task-oriented is a particular business relationship, relative to how much the 'whole' person becomes involved.

5. Achievement versus ascription – whether success and

individual accomplishment is valued as opposed to ascribed status according to, for example, age, kinship or gender.

6. Temporality – whether the future is more important than the past.

7. Attitude to the environment – whether it is believed that human action is determined by factors outside the individual's control or whether we are masters of our own fate.

The work of Trompenaars, Hampden-Turner and Hofstede can, however, be criticised because of their assumption that these characteristics are predictive of individual behaviour, and also because, in a multicultural world, such nationalistic characterising is insufficiently sophisticated to cope with the range of cultural mixes found within countries. How would an Indian-born British citizen behave, for example? Or an American with Canadian, Greek and Italian grandparents? These characteristics are also assumed to be stable over time, and there is considerable evidence that exposure to different cultures modifies one's own beliefs and values. Given the increasing levels of international travel, it is quite possible that some of these features will be modified considerably through exposure to alternative cultures. On the other hand, it is also well known that culture is hugely resistant to change. Where you stand on these issues is an individual choice – and, dare we say, is likely to be influenced by your own cultural background!

was much less successful than had been expected, and Aldi and Lidl, the German supermarket chains, have recently experienced less success in their international expansion than hoped.

Identifying the cultural differences between countries is an important task for anyone managing international operations. People who favour a global convergence perspective would argue that differences between countries are becoming less, and that it is differences between industries that are actually more relevant. However, many genuine cultural differences have been identified (see Theoretical Perspective 6.3). Some are quite subtle, and easily overlooked by someone not familiar with the local situation. For this reason too, firms may choose to employ someone local to act as their agent, or set up joint ventures with local firms.

6.7 Competitor analysis

Firms are not totally independent in their choices of which markets to attack, which products to offer and at what scale and scope to operate. Strategies have to take some account of what is 'out there', and in many cases they are based on being different from what competitors do, or in responding to their activities. The competitive environment is a dynamic place, in which a static assessment of the situation is likely to result in a moribund strategic posture, and probable loss of competitive position.

Competitors innovate, they build market positions, and they sell their products in some cases to exactly the same customers, who can be extremely fickle in their choice of suppliers. Food shopping is a good example of this. Although some of the major supermarket chains have made considerable efforts to ensure the loyalty of their customers, it seems that there is very little brand loyalty within the industry. Customers will choose to buy in competing shops at different times, and convenience of location is the most important factor determining this. Firms that do not copy their competitors' innovations, block attempts to usurp their own market share, or develop better responses to the needs of their customers, are not likely to survive long. Therefore understanding what a firm's competitors do, their competences, strategies and market positions are important factors influencing its choice of strategies.

As with customers, competitors can be segmented according to the types of products they offer, what customer groups they service, whether they have cost advantages, superior technological know-how, or innovative capabilities, and their financial positions. However, as with the definition of an industry, defining a competitor is not as easy as it sounds. Are they the firms that sell directly competing products to exactly the same customers? This would be a very narrow interpretation, in which there is no differentiation between the various firms' product offerings. However, when does a differentiated product become a completely different product, and therefore not a competitor? Think of a portable computer. These can be differentiated according to whether they are palmtop, think-pad, or laptop sized, according to the operating system they use, and the features and benefits they provide – an integral CD player, hard disk size, etc. You may think that there are considerable similarities between many of the 'normal' laptops, but are these the same products as palmtops, or a different product altogether? Are Apple laptops competing for the same customers as products based on Microsoft's Windows operating system? We know of very few people who would willingly transfer from one system to the other.

6.7.1 The practice of competitor analysis

Despite these definitional problems, most firms develop over time a very good idea of who their major competitors are, especially if the industry in which they all compete is mature and oligopolistic. Companies will be aware of other firms' activities, and are likely to monitor closely what they are doing. An astute organisation understands its competitors' strategies in as much detail as it does its own – their products, the market segments that each has decided to target and avoid, their resources, value chains, cultures and architectures.

It can be very helpful to understand a competitor's paradigm, so as to be able to predict how it is likely to react to a particular move, such as a new product launch or a price change. Firms may want to **choose** their competitors by not competing in industries or segments where there are competitors that do not abide by the industry rules of the game, or by trying to drive these rogue competitors out of the industry through aggressive pricing.

To have a complete grasp of an organisation's competitive position, you too will need a detailed grasp of its competitors' strategies and mindsets. You will also need to compare the results – profitability, market share, etc. – of different firms' strategies to see which has been most, and least, successful. However, in a fragmented or geographically dispersed industry, it is almost impossible for any organisation to monitor every single competitor in such detail. This is why managers tend to focus their attention on their closest rivals.

◀ See also Section 5.5.1 on industry analysis.

Competitors can be grouped in segments in the same way as customers are. These segments, or strategic groups – consist of companies that compete in similar markets and provide similar products in similar ways. Advanced Topic 6.7.2 describes strategic groups analysis, and contains a brief example.

6.7.2 ADVANCED TOPIC
Strategic groups analysis

Strategic groups are competing firms segmented according to the products they sell and the ways in which they produce these. Strategic groups comprise companies who are in competition with each other, but more than that, compete in similar ways in similar markets with similar products and similar distribution channels. The common features between companies in such groups distinguish them from other companies, who may be serving the same type of customer but do so with different products in different ways.

For example in the pharmaceutical industry, companies such as Glaxo-Wellcome, Merck, AstraZeneca, Glaxo, and Eli Lilley spend a high proportion of their profits on R&D, and focus on innovation. They charge a large premium for their new drugs, in order to recoup their high investment in development, and retain competitive advantage from their patents for many years after the products are launched. Theirs is a high risk/high return approach. Companies in other strategic groups within the same pharmaceutical industry, such as Johnson and Johnson, Hoechst, Ciba-Geigy and Boots focus on, for example, the production of low value drugs, for which the patents have expired and compete principally on brand name, price or own-brand production. Other firms have deliberately outsourced their R&D through the establishment of strategic alliances with small independent biotech firms.

Understanding the nature of a firm's strategic-group is important in a number of ways. Firstly, barriers to entry differ for each strategic group. Secondly, if a company successfully enters one of the groups, the members of that group become its key competitors. If it hopes to succeed, it needs to have some potential advantage in the specific elements of competition that are important in that group. Thirdly, once in a particular strategic group, it may find itself confined there by mobility barriers – factors such as reputation that make it difficult for a firm to move from say, a no frills position to a differentiated one.

Although competition is most intense within a strategic group, there is also likely to be rivalry between different groups. Firms in neighbouring groups may appeal to over-lapping customers. Drug customers may choose to go for generic over the counter (OTC) drugs on one occasion, and be issued with prescription drugs from a doctor on another. These customers may not perceive much different in the benefits they received from one company or another. Companies in different groups might also want to expand the scope of their product range, especially if the firms are fairly equal in size and power and the mobility barriers betwen the groups are low. Merck, under the leadership of a new chief executive Richard Markham, decided to move into the manufacturing of generic drugs. As it happened this was a strategy which was resisted by many of the company's existing managers, and so Merck withdrew from this market – but not because of the mobility barriers between groups.

A proper analysis of strategic groups in an industry is a complex business. It involves taking account of a range of variables relating to firms' products, positioning and resources. A fully rigorous strategic groups analysis necessitates the gathering of several years performance data and the use of a statistical technique known as cluster analysis.[5]

Real-Life Application 6.4 illustrates customer segmentation and strategic groups.

REAL-LIFE APPLICATION 6.4

The European truck industry

The European truck industry in the early 1990s included a van segment, and light, medium and heavy weight truck segments. Most demand was for vans and light weight trucks. The market was served by a rapidly decreasing number of producers. In the medium and heavy truck segments Daimler-Benz was market leader, with a market share of 23%, followed by Fiat/Iveco with 20%. Renault, Volvo, MAN, DAF and Scania had market shares of around 10% each and some smaller specialised producers served the rest of the market. The van and the light truck segment showed a similar division of market shares. The leader was Renault with 20% followed by PSA (Peugeot/Citroën) with 16%. PSA was a car company which was present in the van and light weight truck segments but had no presence in the medium and heavy weight truck segments.

Research and development costs were significant in the truck industry. Expenditures varied from 4 to 8% on sales, depending on the size and the degree of vertical integration of a producer. Technological innovation and increasing sophistication of trucks in terms of fuel efficiency, ergonomy and electronics content had gradually pushed up development costs and favoured competitors with scope for cost-efficient research. Smaller players had been forced to focus their R&D on particular components and enter into strategic alliances aimed at sharing the R&D costs.

The firms

Daimler-Benz

The truck division of Daimler-Benz was part of one of Germany's largest conglomerates with interests in cars, aircraft and electronics. Daimler-Benz was not only the truck market leader in Europe, but also at world level. In Europe it marketed a full line of products and its presence was especially strong in the medium range of trucks. Daimler-Benz produced medium and heavy trucks in West Germany and vans and light trucks in Spain. In 1989 it had acquired DTV, an originally independent supplier of diesel engines, thereby increasing its already high degree of vertical integration.

Figure 6.5 Strategic map of competitors in the European truck industry

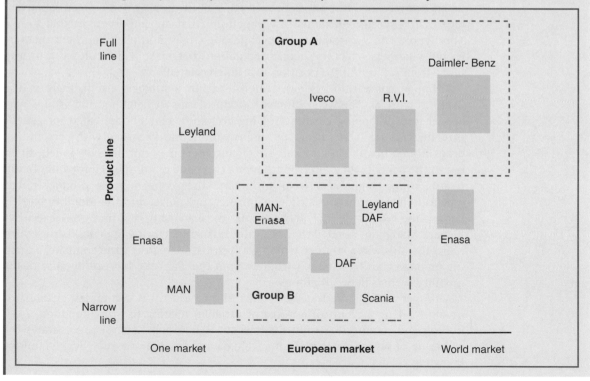

Iveco

Since the early 1980s Iveco had belonged to the Fiat group, which was the main Italian car maker. It marketed a full line of products and almost completely controlled the Italian market. Iveco had a low degree of vertical integration, but had many co-operation agreements with suppliers. Due to acquisitions in Spain (Enasa) and Germany (Magirius Deutz) and a joint venture with Ford (UK) in 1986, Iveco had obtained a relatively strong position in these markets.

Renault

The French group Renault was state-controlled and received large amounts of government support which had had to be discontinued. The group was a major force in the European car industry. Apart from France, Renault also owned plants in Spain and the UK. Renault was also active in the USA and had a strong export presence in the African market. In early 1990, Renault and Volvo had taken considerable cross-holdings in each other's shares and announced the intention to merge the companies completely in the medium term. Within Europe, Renault was the overall market leader in the van and light truck segment. It had an average degree of vertical integration.

Volvo

The Swedish firm Volvo had a world-wide presence in the medium and the heavy truck segment and was also active in the car business. Although Sweden was not an EC member, Volvo profited from European Union advantages because of its plants in Belgium and Scotland. In the USA Volvo had a joint venture, and had some smaller production facilities in Latin America and Australia. Volvo was a producer with a high degree of vertical integration.

MAB/Steyr

In 1989, the German firm MAN acquired the Austrian truck manufacturer Steyr. Its intended acquisition of Enasa in the following year was blocked by the German anti-trust authorities. Besides a strong presence in the medium and heavy truck segments, MAN also had access to the van and the light truck segment through co-operation agreements with Volkswagen. This allowed MAN to offer a full line of trucks. In the industry, MAN was a producer with a relatively low degree of vertical integration. For some parts MAN and Daimler-Benz used the same suppliers.

DAF

In 1987 the Dutch company DAF acquired the formerly state-owned UK company Leyland. This merger gave DAF an improved access to the UK market and provided an extension of its product line, originally focused on the medium and the heavy segment, to a full range. DAF had a relatively low degree of vertical integration.

Scania

Scania was a Swedish producer with many similarities to Volvo both in terms of its product strategy and in its degree of vertical integration. However, its market share was essentially confined to Western Europe.

The players in the industry showed variation in their international presence, in the scope of their product line and in the degree of vertical integration. As a result, various strategic groups could be mapped (Figure 6.5). Strategic Group A comprises Iveco, RVI, and Daimler-Benz, large international companies which provide a large range of products. Group B comprises a group of smaller companies, DAF, Leyland-DAF, Scania, and MAN-Enasa, which compete exclusively in Europe and provide a relatively small number of specialised products.

Source: Haan, F., Thomas, H. and Verdin, P. (1992), 'The European Truck Industry in 1990; Preparing for the post-1992 era', Case Study, IESE, Barcelona.

6.8 Summary

This chapter has discussed some of the basic ways in which firms compete – the fundamental product and market decisions that they make:

● Successful firms strive for a mix of cost and differentiation advantage.

● An important element of strategy is to target appropriate customer segments –

those that are large and homogeneous, easily accessible, affluent and price insensitive or simply overlooked by competitors. There are various methodologies available for segmenting consumer and industrial markets.

- Firms need to develop appropriate products and services to meet the needs of these target markets, and differentiate them from competitors' offerings. Possible ways of obtaining differentiation advantage include product functionality, appearance and price, the support offered by the firm and firm reputation and brand image.

- The strategy clock identifies a number of potentially successful positioning strategies, including no frills, low price, hybrid, differentiation and focused differentiation. Other strategies are unlikely to succeed in the long term.

- The choice of segment and positioning must be complemented by an appropriate choice of scope and scale. The choice of scale must be made in the light of the availability of economies of scale. The choice of appropriate scope comes down to a trade-off between:
  - on the one hand, the costs of administering the complexity that comes with a broad range of products and markets
  - on the other hand, the synergies and economies of scope available from a broad product range, and the benefits of having other product lines and markets to fall back on if there are problems in one of them.

- It is important to consider whether consumers across the globe have to be segmented according to their own national characteristics – local – or multi-local products – or whether there are sufficient similarities between people in different countries to warrant the manufacturing and sales of global products. Strategies which combine customisation and global elements are called transnational. However, whatever strategy it chooses, or even if it limits itself to its home market, a firm is likely to face international competitors.

- Competitors can influence a firm's strategic stance, and how firms within the same industry behave. Firms which operate in the same types of business and behave in similar ways can be considered to be a strategic group. In mature industries firms are very aware of what their competitors are doing, and strategies and strategic ideas often arise in response to actions taken by competitors.

Typical questions

We conclude this chapter by providing some questions you may be asked about an organisation's competitive stance, to do with its generic and international strategics, and how you can use the theory in this chapter to answer them.

1. *How has the firm's choice of consumer segment contributed to its competitive advantage?*

This is a fairly straightforward application of the theory outlined in Section 6.2. Use an appropriate framework based upon those in Section 6.2.3 to analyse the company's customer segments. Then use the material in Section 6.2.2 to guide you in assessing what made the customer segments attractive, and in seeing how the firm designed products and services to target them. You may want to look at the firm's value chain, to see what gave it the ability to serve those segments well, and analyse its competitors (Section 6.7) to show why they did not or could not respond effectively.

It may also be necessary to repeat this analysis at various stages in the firm's development to show how well it kept pace with changes in customer tastes and competitors' strategies. An analysis of the environment (Chapter 5) may help you present these changes in a systematic fashion.

2. *How appropriate was the firm's positioning (or generic strategy) in its different businesses?*

This is an extension of the previous question. After identifying the segments that the firm was targeting and assessing their attractiveness, you might use the strategy clock (Section 6.4) to determine whether the firm was using a viable strategy in the light of its customers' requirements.

3. *What strategy did the firm use for attacking international markets? Was this appropriate?*

This calls for the use of the theory in Section 6.6. Use Section 6.6.1 to help you to identify the firm's strategy as global, locally responsive or transnational. You may then want to use the material in Chapter 5, Section 5.5.4, to help you assess whether the industry's structure was favourable to a global strategy, Theoretical Perspective 6.2 to guide your thinking on whether there was any scope for establishing global products and brands, and Sections 6.6.2 and Theoretical Perspective 6.3 to help you identify any strong cultural differences that might have made it difficult to operate in different markets.

Questions for discussion

1. What are the main arguments in favour of a firm's choosing a locally responsive strategy when competing internationally?

2. How does understanding what a firm's competitors do help to understand what strategies the firm itself may adopt?

3. How might the internet influence international competition in the future?

CASE STUDY

The kingdom inside a republic

Taken from *The Economist*, 13 April 1996: 84–85 © The Economist; London 1996.

He was a Frenchman of sorts. A couple of Walt Disney's forebears are said to have come from Isigny, a Normandy town better known for its cream and butter, and to have taken part in the invasion of England in 1066. Given this ancestry, and the fact that there had already been a successful Disneyland in Japan, what could have seemed more natural back in the 1980s than for Disney to build a theme park in the old world?

Euro Disney looked at first like a sure bet. The brand was known from Prague to Peterborough; spending on leisure in Europe was high; no existing European theme park had been built on the lavish scale that Disney planned; and Europe was enjoying an economic boom.

In the event, the sure bet was wrong. A Europe-wide recession, along with a series of gaffes by the park's management, brought the park to the edge of bankruptcy. In 1994 Euro Disney reported a loss for the year to the end of September of FFr.8 billion ($317 million). Attendance was 10% down on 1993. The firm's share price fell from a peak of FFr68 just before the park opened to only FFr6 in October 1994. Disaster was averted only by means of a FFr6 billion rights issue and a financial restructuring, negotiated with the project's banks and the parent company in America. With a new top management, drastic cost-cutting, changes in pricing and market-ing, and subtle adjustments to the park itself, attendance and spending at Disneyland Paris (as the park has been rechristened) have begun to pick up. Thanks to this – and to 1994's financial rescue – Euro Disney last year announced its first net profits, of FFr14m. Its loss for the low season from October to December was FFr57m, half the level of a year earlier. Such improvements might seem modest. In fact they are a sign that Euro Disney's torments were the result not so much of a flawed idea, but of errors in the way the idea was brought to life.

It is always hard to expand into a foreign market. Consumer tastes differ in a thousand baffling ways.

Although Disney films are as much a part of child-hood as chocolate and fizzy drinks, Euro Disney was Disney's first large commercial venture abroad. (Its Tokyo park is a franchise owned by Japanese investors.) Disney was introducing a theme park aimed at consumers who were more used to the dodgem cars and Ferris wheels of funfairs. Worse, it was trying to launch this new sort of product on several national markets at once.

Plutocrats

More than that, Euro Disney was embarking on a vast property development – including hotels, shops, office and residential housing – over an area a fifth the size of Paris. And it was doing so with a severe handicap: demanding, and potentially unre-alistic, financial obligations to its American parent.

Indeed, some of the management's worst mis-takes were financial. Long before the first giant mouse costume arrived in France, Disney took the one decision that mattered most about its foray into Europe: that the park would be Disney's suc-cess and nobody else's. This was because Disney was fed up with outsiders making money on the back of its brilliance.

Walt Disney opened his first park at Anaheim in California in 1955 on only 100 acres (40 hectares) of land. When it drew crowds bigger than anyone had imagined, many of those lucky enough to own nearby property made fortunes that Disney thought should have belonged to its shareholders.

Even though the company secured 30,000 acres when it built Disney World in Florida in 1971, it again underestimated the demand for accommo-dation, and another opportunity was wasted. But the most irksome misjudgment of all was in Tokyo, where a fantastically successful park was built, financed and owned by a Japanese consortium. Disney, which had been nervous about investing in such a big venture on the other side of the world, collects only 10% of gross earnings on rides and 5% on food and merchandise.

When Disney set up in Europe it was determined

to avoid making the same mistake a fourth time. Euro Disney was to be owned and managed by Disney, and it would be surrounded by land owned by the company. (The zeal knows no limits: virtually every mention of Disney in the firm's literature is accompanied by an intrusive 'R', to warn off intellectual-property thieves.)

The plan was for Disney to finance and build the resort's hotels, and then sell them off at a large profit once their value was proven. Because the French government was providing the land cheaply, it made sense to develop offices and commercial space as well. In this way a determination not to see others profit on the back of Disney turned a theme park into one of Europe's most ambitious property developments with a total budget of roughly FFr30 billion.

Protecting the parent

The same thinking shaped Disney's complicated financial arrangements. In return for all the public help it showered on Disney – not just cheap land but a cheap loan, and extensions to railways, roads and utilities – the French government insisted on the American firm owning no more than 49% of Euro Disney. Disney sold the remaining 51% in a way that turned this condition brilliantly to its advantage.

This sale reduced the American parent's risk and recovered some of its initial investment. But Disney also created a complex series of royalties, management fees and incentive payments to be paid by Euro Disney. This meant that the American firm could in theory make money from Euro Disney even if the park was making a loss. A case study by academics at the Darden Business School at the University of Virginia and Insead, a management school outside Paris, looked at how the initial public offering revalued the original equity contribution of Disney to Euro Disneyland. At a discount rate of 15% (slightly higher than that recommended by Disney's merchant bank at the time the 51% of Euro Disney was sold to the public) the value of the park had increased from FFr12 billion to FFr21 billion.

However, much as this brilliance suited Disney in

America, it left Euro Disney fearfully exposed. When the Gulf war began to affect tourism and the bottom fell out of the French property market, the project was scaled back. Although the firm recently announced that it would continue with further property developments, a second park to be based on the MGM Studios has been delayed (although the firm insists it has not been cancelled).

When the extent of the disappointment began to dawn, Euro Disney's American boss left, as did its finance director, another American. They were replaced by Frenchmen. At first, Michael Eisner, head of Disney in America, pooh-poohed the critics. By 1994 he was calling the park's performance 'dreadful'.

If the park was to survive, the first job of Philippe Bourguignon, the new chief executive who took over in 1993, was to renegotiate Euro Disney's interest payments and fees. A nail-biting marathon between the banks, Euro Disney and its American parent eventually resulted in a deal in the spring of 1994. This provided a holiday on payments of interest and royalties, with some interest payments resuming in 1996. Mr Bourguignon gives the agreement 60% of the credit for the move into profit last year – though analysts think it mattered even more.

However, though it bought the management some time, financial restructuring could never secure the park's prosperity, if only because under the terms of the agreement the interest and royalties must eventually be resumed. From this year, there will be an increase in Euro Disney's financial charges. After 1999 management and incentive fees will again become payable. Revenues will have to grow if the park is not to sink back into loss. The park could survive only if the new management could bring in more customers, and at the same time cut costs.

The princess's mange tout

The first job was to put right some cultural mistakes. From the outset, Euro Disney had been afraid that its American product would offend 'sophisticated' European taste. And, true to form, French intellectuals were infuriated when the park opened for business in the spring of 1992. They accused

CASE STUDY *continued*

Disney of stifling the imagination of young people, of turning children into consumers, even of creating 'a cultural Chernobyl'.

In truth, Disney had all along been too fearful that Europeans would sneer at anything ersatz. As a result, as it now admits, it spent too much money when it built the park. In America 'The Walt' restaurant has wallpaper but in Europe its walls are lined with Moroccan leather. In order to merge with the French surroundings, the turret which the company's 'imagineers' built outside Paris was modelled not on Neuschwanstein, the Bavarian castle reconstructed at Disney's other theme parks, but on a drawing from a 15th-century French manuscript.

In order to improve disappointing sales inside the park, Euro Disney has now redesigned the merchandise. Disney had been convinced that Europeans used to Lacoste and Polo would prefer to have their favourite animals tastefully embroidered on their sweatshirts and rucksacks. Now the firm knows better. Articles are emblazoned with a huge, grinning cartoon mouse, just as in America.

It was the same with food and drink. Although it originally banned alcohol in its restaurants, the menus Euro Disney came up with were in other respects all too European: sitdown, intricate and expensive. The firm now recognises, Mr Bourguignon says, that 'people do not come to the park for a gastronomic experience.' Posh lunches (with alcohol) are still to be had, but so is fast food in self service restaurants.

A better mouse-trap

If Disney proved over-sensitive to European tastes when it was building the park, it was strangely insensitive when it came to marketing it. Initially, this treated Europe as if it were a single country, and tried to market it using the methods that have succeeded well in America. The company was soon to discover that tourists' habits varied a great deal from one European country to the next, that demand was more seasonal than the firm had expected, and that its prices were so high that it put off the French, the park's most numerous visitors.

The guiding principle of Euro Disney's new approach is that people visit the park but for an 'authentic' Disney day-out. They may not be completely sure what that means, except that it entails something American – which is why the park's name has evolved. The 'Euro' in Euro Disney was first shrunk in the logo (and the word 'land' added) and then removed altogether in October 1994. The park is now called simply Disneyland Paris.

The original advertising campaigns were aimed at children and featured Mickey or Pluto introducing the rides and parades on offer inside the park. This had worked in America, where many adults had themselves visited a Disney theme park as children. In Europe, however, the Disney brand was associated with magazines, films and toys, not with a day out. To baffled European parents, a 'theme park' sounded rather like an ordinary funfair – and at FFr250 (up until last April the price of entry) a prohibitively expensive one.

The advertising is now designed to make adults susceptible to their children's pleas. Although it does not show the park in action, it features children impatient to depart for and thrilled to arrive at the Magic Kingdom; or a grandfather delighted by his grand-daughter's excitement at the prospect of seeing Mickey; or grown-ups sitting tensely before riding on the Space Mountain, one attraction that is likely to appeal to fathers left cold by a flying elephant.

At the same time, Euro Disney has begun to treat national markets separately. The firm found that it was spreading its advertising too broadly, and that different nationalities prefer different types of accommodation. Over the past two years, marketing offices have been opened in London, Frankfurt, Milan, Brussels, Amsterdam and Madrid. Each is responsible for tailoring packages to its own market. Perhaps Mr Bourguignon's most daring decision was to cut prices for tickets by more than 20% from FFr250 to FFr195 for an adult in the high season; and by more than a third for the cheapest hotel rooms. Potential customers are bombarded with special offers during the quiet winter months. All this made sense in light of the discovery that those who have come once tend to come again, and because Disney's research showed that each visitor recommends the park to an average of 18 people. In a business where fixed costs are high, attendance is all.

Wonderland

Although Euro Disney is unlikely ever to be the money machine Disney dreamed of, improvements are beginning to come through. Attendance climbed by 20% last year to a record 10.7milion and is expected to grow to over 11.5 million this year. Hotel occupancy has grown from 55% in 1993 to 68% in 1995 – compared with an average of roughly 60% for hotels in the area around Paris.

Operating costs per visitor fell by almost 20% last year, mainly through improved productivity. Mr Bourguignon who breakfasted with some of his 10,000 staff twice a week for two years to pick up tips on how to improve the park, says that some of the best ideas came from his own junior 'cast members', as staff are gushingly called.

In many ways, keeping its 'cast members' sweet has been one of Disney's most impressive achievements. A company that is selling an experience rather than a physical product cannot afford miserable employees. And it cannot have been easy for Euro Disney's employees to keep on grinning at all those children, knowing that bankruptcy was just around the corner. By and large, despite a pay dispute earlier this year, Euro Disney's staff have kept on smiling. But with the financial charges gathering momentum and Europe's economy still shaky even their ability to smile may be severely tested.

Authors' Postscript

In fact, the improvement at Disneyland Paris continued to the point where in September 1999 Euro Disney (the name still used by the company that owns the attraction) announced that it was to open a second theme park, next to the existing one, in 2002. Visitor numbers increased to 12 million, and for the year ending September 2000, the firm was able to announce profits (after royalty payments to The Walt Disney Company) of €38.7 million (FFr 264 million) on revenues of €959 million. This was in spite of freak weather that had closed one of the hotels for four months and forced the whole park to shut for a short period.

Case study questions

1. Who are Disneyland Paris' customers and what are their requirements? (You may want to supplement the data in the case study with your own experience or research).

2. What initial problems did Euro Disney encounter in positioning its product correctly? How did Philippe Bourguignon improve Disneyland Paris' positioning?

3. What suggestions would you make to The Walt Disney Company (Euro Disney's American parent) regarding its future strategy in global markets?

NOTES

1. See Miller and Dess (1993) and Cronshaw, Davis and Kay (1995). Both studies found that firms pursuing clear differentiation strategies tended to be more profitable than those following cost leadership strategies, but that firms that combined cost and differentiation strategies were the most profitable of all.
2. The following analysis has adapted and developed from Mintzberg (1991).
3. Kenichi Ohmae (1989) 'Managing in a borderless world', *Harvard Business Review*.
4. See, for example, Hofstede (1980a, 1980b, 1991) and Trompenaars and Hampden-Turner (1997).
5. For a discussion of the problems associated with strategic groups analysis, and the insights it can offer, see Flavian, Haberberg and Polo (1999).

Strategic resources

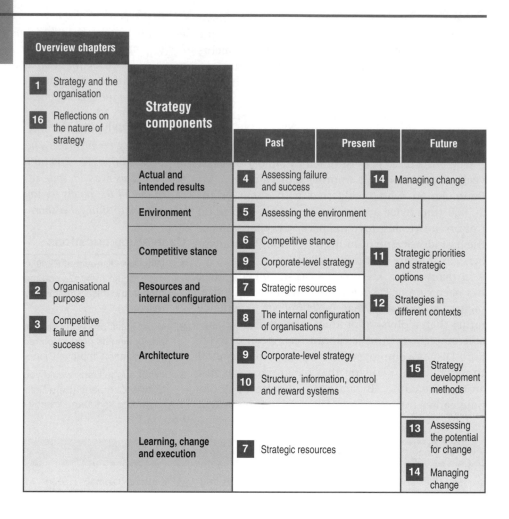

Overview chapters

1	Strategy and the organisation
16	Reflections on the nature of strategy
2	Organisational purpose
3	Competitive failure and success

Strategy components

Strategy components	Past	Present	Future
Actual and intended results	4 Assessing failure and success		14 Managing change
Environment	5 Assessing the environment		
Competitive stance	6 Competitive stance 9 Corporate-level strategy		11 Strategic priorities and strategic options
Resources and internal configuration	7 Strategic resources 8 The internal configuration of organisations		12 Strategies in different contexts
Architecture	9 Corporate-level strategy 10 Structure, information, control and reward systems		15 Strategy development methods
Learning, change and execution	7 Strategic resources		13 Assessing the potential for change 14 Managing change

In the previous chapter we discussed how to evaluate an organisation's choice of target market – which customers or users it will serve. In order to serve them it must have resources at its disposal that it can use to develop and supply products that they value, and to persuade customers to buy its services, rather than competitors'. In this chapter we look in detail at the kinds of resources that organisations may possess, and what it is that makes a resource valuable. In the following chapter we complete the picture by showing how organisations deploy those resources to serve their target market, through their value chain and architecture.

Differences in resources are now widely believed to be the most important factor in explaining why some organisations do better over time than others, and this chapter will summarise the theory that underpins that belief. As we saw in Chapter 1 (Section 1.5) resources with a high knowledge content, such as capabilities and competences, are particularly important, so this chapter also looks at how organisations learn and how they use their knowledge. We also, however, consider the cost and risk for organisations of investing time and effort in building excellent resources. An organisation may develop 'competency traps' and core rigidities.

Our focus in this chapter is on understanding how the strategic use of resources at *business* level, in a single industry, makes the difference between success and mediocrity. Strategic resources are also important in understanding how diversified firms can be successful across a variety of industries, a topic we consider in Chapter 9.

Learning objectives

After reading this chapter you should be able to:

- identify the resources that an organisation possesses;
- evaluate the importance of those resources to the organisation's competitive position, and the extent to which they form the basis of a sustainable advantage;
- understand how the management of knowledge and intellectual resources contributes to the development of capabilities and competences;
- understand how organisations learn, and why these learning processes are important.

7.1 Strategic resources and why they are important

Concept

◄ *Industry success and survival factors were discussed in Section 5.6. Customer segmentation was discussed in Chapter 6.*

Strategic and threshold resources

A **resource** is anything that a firm has or has learned to do that enables it to conceive and implement strategies that improve its efficiency and effectiveness. Resources include assets, competences, capabilities, organisational processes, firm attributes, information and knowledge.[1]

A **strategic resource** is a resource that makes a particular difference to a firm's strategic position – to its cost or differentiation advantage. For a resource to qualify as strategic, it must correspond to one or more of the *success factors* that emerge within the industry and develop over time. It must also be rare and difficult to imitate or substitute. Technological innovation or changing customer tastes may see established resources lose their strategic importance and newer ones gain it.

Resources that are not strategic, but which are still important because they help the firm meet the criteria for *survival* in an industry are called **threshold resources**.

7.1.1 The importance of firm resources

In Chapter 6 (Section 6.5.3), we pointed out that organisations could not achieve sustainable competitive advantage *just* by selecting the right combination of products and services, and positioning them to appeal to attractive target market segments. Although these strategic marketing decisions are a vital part of strategy, and may lead to desirable economies of scale and scope, they are not sufficient in themselves, because they are too easy for competitors to copy.

Strategic management theorists began to wake up to these issues in the late 1980s, and the years 1989–91 saw the publication of a number of important articles that established what went on inside organisations that might be difficult to copy, or to buy on the open market. By 1995, what had become known as the 'resource-based view of the firm' was firmly entrenched in the mainstream of strategic management theory. The evolution of the theory is discussed in greater detail in Theoretical Perspective 7.1.

Resources are also regarded as important for another reason: they help explain the way in which firms grow and diversify, and why some diversifications work better than others. Resource-based theory was actually applied earlier in this area than in the examination of firm competitiveness; we look at it in Chapter 9.

7.1.2 Types of resource

Over the years, a number of different terms have been used for strategic resources. The term 'distinctive capabilities' has a long pedigree, and other authors have used 'strategic assets' and 'core competences'.[2] To complicate matters further, some theorists include all kinds of resource under the heading of 'assets' or 'capabilities', while others give these words specialised meanings. In this book, we use 'resources' as the umbrella term and 'assets', 'capabilities' and 'competences' for particular types of resource.

Concept | **Assets, competences and capabilities**

We can divide resources into three further categories.

Things that a firm **has**, like a reputation, a distribution infrastructure or a customer database, can be termed **assets**, and if they are important and rare enough to qualify as strategic resources, we call them **strategic assets**.

Things that a firm has **learned to do** with its assets are called **competences** or **capabilities**.[3] A **capability** makes a direct difference to an organisation's competitive advantage – for example, by enabling it to cut costs, or serve customers quickly and responsively. A **competence** is deeper-seated, and underlies an organisation's capabilities – for example, a deep understanding of a specialised field of information technology, human psychology, engineering or chemistry. Competences and capabilities usually incorporate routines that have been built up over time. If they meet the criteria for being considered strategic resources, they are termed **core competences** or **distinctive capabilities**.

All competences or capabilities make a difference to an organisation's cost or differentiation position at a given point in time. **Dynamic capabilities** are resources that **also** help an organisation to **develop** that position over time and as the environment changes by, for example, identifying new customer groups or developing new products or more efficient production processes.

THEORETICAL PERSPECTIVE 7.1

The resource-based view of the firm

By common consent, the mother of resource-based theory is a British economics professor, Edith Penrose. She was probably the first economist to look at *how* firms took decisions about what to produce at what price, and *how* and *why* they decided to move from one product and market to another. Her 1959 book, *The Theory of the Growth of the Firm*, pioneered a number of concepts to explain these decisions. She showed how over time firms built up human and physical resources and the capability to use them to provide different kinds of services, some of which could be used in different products and markets from the ones for which they were developed. She explained firms' expansion decisions in terms of managers making best use of those resources. She also explored the importance of knowledge to a firm.

Other important elements of the theory were put in place by two American economists, Richard Nelson and Sidney Winter of Yale University, in their 1982 book *An Evolutionary Theory of Economic Change*. Using insights from organisation theory and philosophy, they showed the importance of routines, tacit knowledge and organisational capabilities in understanding differences between firms. In particular, they showed how two firms might start from a common skill base and end up over time with different sets of routines, in an example of what we now call path dependence. They also discussed how an innovation might enable one firm to grow at the expense of others, if it were difficult to imitate.

Apart from their discussion of innovation, Nelson and Winter did not really look at why one firm might outperform another – their interest was in analysing the behaviour of industries. Penrose, for her part, was concerned with why firms grew and diversified over time, but not with how they competed. The first application of their ideas to the understanding of competition *between* firms, and the first mainstream use of the term 'a resource-based view of the firm' came in a 1984 article of that name by Birger Wernerfelt, which explored how a firm's control of particular resources might give it high financial returns.

During the 1980s, scholars wrestled with the question of how some firms came to control more valuable resources than others. Jay Barney (Barney, 1986a) of Texas A&M University hypothesised that some firms were able to achieve superior returns on their investment in strategic resources, either because they had better information about what the resources would eventually be worth, or through sheer luck. In 1989, Ingemar Dierickx and Karel Cool of INSEAD, in France, used some of Nelson and Winter's ideas to show why resources that a firm had accumulated over time might be difficult to imitate, introducing concepts like time compression diseconomies,

asset mass economies and causal ambiguity, which we explore in Section 7.1.4.

In his 1991 article 'Firm resources and sustained competitive advantage', Jay Barney summed up the criteria that a resource needed to meet in order to be a source of sustainable advantage. They must be valuable, rare, imperfectly imitable and not easily substituted with other resources – concepts that are explored in depth in Section 7.1.3. In 1993, Raphael Amit and Paul Schoemaker expanded on what made a resource valuable, showing that the profit to be derived from a resource depended on the extent to which it overlapped with 'strategic industry factors' (what in Chapter 5 we called industry success factors).

Margaret Peteraf (1993) summarised the kinds of market imperfections that must hold in an industry for any firm to be able to achieve competitive advantage and earn above-normal profits ('economic rents'). For any firm to be able to earn economic rents, it must possess resources that others do not – there must be differences in the resources that firms possess. There must be some forces at work to prevent valuable resources from being imitated or substituted, otherwise those rents cannot be sustained over time. Resources must be imperfectly mobile, otherwise no one firm will be able to hold on to its source of rents. Finally, there must be some factors that limit competition for resources while they are being acquired – for example, some firms must have a better appreciation than others of the potential value of those resources. Otherwise, the costs of those resources would be bid up to the point where no-one could earn rents from them.

The types of advantage described by Barney and others were only valid as long as the environment did not alter so dramatically that the resources lost their value. In 1997 David Teece, a noted US authority on the economics of innovation, Gary Pisano and Amy Shuen described the qualities an organisation needed in order to be able to adjust dynamically to frequent environmental change. Their theory states that an organisation's dynamic capabilities are shaped by its organisational processes (architecture and culture), by its strategic resources and by its history, which to some extent determines the path it is able to follow in the future.

Meanwhile, in 1990, the resource-based view found its way into the mainstream of management thinking through C. K. Prahalad and Gary Hamel's *Harvard Business Review* article, 'The core competence of the corporation'. This reworking of Penrose's, Wernerfelt's and Barney's ideas incorporated some striking case studies of US and Japanese firms. Their term 'core competence' struck a chord with management audiences[4] and is now in common ▶

Theoretical Perspective continued

use in both business and academic circles. Hamel (an American affiliated to London Business School) and Prahalad (originally from India, but now at the University of Michigan) elaborated their ideas in a series of subsequent articles and a 1994 book, *Competing for the Future.*

Theorists then turned their attention to the question of where capability and competence came from. This focused attention on the importance of organisational learning as a means of acquiring competence, and on knowledge as a key resource in sustaining and extending it. This remains one of the main focuses of research in strategic management.

How well-founded is the resource-based view?

The resource-based view of the firm now represents the mainstream of orthodox strategic management theory. Only Michael Porter among prominent strategy thinkers holds out against the idea of resources as being the key to competitive advantage. However, as we said in Chapter 4, the fact that everyone believes something does not mean that it is true.

The resource-based view is based upon a great deal of careful economic reasoning, but there is almost no empirical evidence to support it. A number of writers cited the findings of a 1991 study by Richard Rumelt as supporting the resource-based view.[5] Rumelt used a statistical analysis of American manufacturing companies between 1974 and 1977 to estimate the proportion of the variance in their profits that could be explained by different factors, such as the industry it was in and the corporation that owned it. They interpreted Rumelt's data (summarised in Table 7.1) as showing that a firm's choice of industry (line 2 in Table 7.1) was much less significant than decisions that firms took at business level (line 4). This was seen as contradicting the views of Michael Porter and his followers.

One problem with this interpretation is that the data Rumelt used for his study did not allow him to be very

Table 7.1 Rumelt's findings: proportion of the variation in the profits of US manufacturing firms, 1974–1977, attributable to different causes

Corporate parent effects – differences in ownership	0.8%
Industry in which a firm operates	8.3%
Differences in conditions from year to year	7.8%
Business-unit specific effects	46.4%
Unexplained factors	36.7%

specific about what was included under the different factors. In particular, there is nothing to suggest that the business unit effect is derived from firms' strategic resources. It could in theory be due to anything: their market positions or even the type of buildings they occupy! These doubts are reinforced by some more recent research by Anita McGahan and Michael Porter (1997). They based their findings on data that covered a longer and more recent time period (1982–94) than Rumelt's, and also covered a range of industry sectors, not just manufacturing. They found (Table 7.2) that, overall, firms' choice of industry accounted for a much greater proportion of the variation in profits than Rumelt's study suggested – 19% as against 8%. The difference appeared to be largely due to the inclusion of data from non-manufacturing firms. In service sectors (transport, retailing, lodging and entertainment and other services), industry choice is the largest single influence on profitability, accounting for 40–65% of the variance.

McGahan and Porter still found that, across all industry sectors, business segment factors account for more of the variation in profits than industry ones. However, except in the manufacturing and services sectors, business segment effects were quite small and much less important than choice of industry or corporate parent effects, which

Table 7.2 McGahan and Porter's findings: factors explaining the variation in US company profits, 1982–94

	All sectors	Agriculture and mining	Manufacturing	Transport	Wholesale and retail	Lodging and entertainment	Services
Corporate parent effects	4.3%	22.4%	N/A	28.3%	44.1%	14.7%	N/A
Industry	18.7%	29.4%	10.8%	39.5%	41.8%	64.3%	47.4%
Less overlap between parent and industry*	−5.5%	−9.5%	−2.3%	−16.5%	−20.2%	−29.8%	−23.0%
Year-to-year differences	2.4%	2.3%	2.3%	3.3%	2.6%	N/A	4.2%
Business segment effects	31.7%	5.0%	35.5%	9.7%	2.0%	19.4%	33.5%
Unexplained factors	48.4%	50.5%	53.7%	35.7%	29.7%	31.4%	39.0%

* This item takes account of the fact that certain corporate parents are more likely to have subsidiaries in particular industries.

played a greater role than Rumelt's data suggested. In a separate study, they discovered that industry effects also seemed to be more persistent over time than business-unit effects.

This is, of course, not a refutation of the resource-based view, but it adds up to much less clear-cut support for it than comes from Rumelt's study. There have been a few empirical studies whose results do support the resource-based view. A study by Richard Makadok (1998) of the US money-market fund industry, where products can easily be copied, found that the first firms to introduce a product appeared to be able to develop resources that gave them an advantage over later imitators. Sustained advantage in the US pharmaceutical industry has been linked to firm resources in the marketing and R&D functions (Yeoh and Roth, 1999).

None of these studies offers conclusive proof of the importance of firms' resources. Indeed, it is unlikely that the resource-based view *can* be proved or disproved; in the end, its popularity rests on the strength of the underlying economic logic – and the absence of a more persuasive theory.

7.1.3 What makes a resource 'strategic'

In Chapter 1, Section 1.5, we discussed the types of resource that an organisation might have: physical, financial, human, intellectual and reputational. Most organisations have some resources in each of these categories, but not all of them will qualify as 'strategic' resources. In this section we set out the criteria that a resource must meet in order to be considered strategic. Later in this chapter we shall look at the kinds of resources in each category that are likely to lead to competitive advantage.

According to Barney (1991), a strategic resource must meet four criteria:

1. **It must be rare within the industry.** If every firm in an industry has the same resource, then it is likely to be a threshold resource, rather than a strategic one. Quite often, a certain type of resource will start out being strategic, and then become a threshold resource as competitors over time manage to work out how to copy or use it, or it becomes available on the open market. In the early 1980s, when computer-aided design (CAD) systems cost tens of thousands of euros and were difficult to use, very few architecture practices could afford them. They were a strategic resource for the firms that had invested time and money in acquiring them and training people to use them. Once cheaper, user-friendly systems became available for the PC, they ceased to be rare and to be a strategic resource. They turned into a threshold resource – very few architects could look credible to their customers if they did not have a CAD system.

2. **It must be valuable.** A resource is only strategic if it makes an *appreciable* difference to a firm's cost and/or differentiation advantage, or to its capacity to adapt and innovate. This also implies that it will correspond to one or more of the success factors identified for the industry. The early CAD systems enabled architects to reduce the cost of repetitive design work, and to differentiate by getting work done more quickly and by appearing more up-to-date in the eyes of their clients.

3. **It must be difficult for other firms in the industry to acquire or copy.** A resource will not stay rare for very long if competing organisations can emulate it. As we show in the next section, resources may be difficult to acquire or copy because they are in short supply, prohibitively expensive or difficult to learn how to use effectively.

4. **There should be no freely available substitute resources.** For an architect, the only alternative to a CAD system was employing large numbers of people to make the drawings, with all the consequent dangers of human error. With rigorous training, this danger could be minimised – but the investment to give staff the right skills and motivation would have been huge, and would still not have matched a CAD system for flexibility and speed of presentation.

It is important that all four of these criteria are met:

- A resource that has taken a lot of time and effort to develop, but is not valuable, represents nothing more than wasted effort. There are many stories of organisations adding expensive features to their products or services because enthusiastic product developers felt they were a good idea. These features might well have been very difficult to copy, but if they held no attraction for the customers then they did not constitute a source of differentiation – they were not valuable.

- A valuable resource that is rare, but not difficult to acquire or copy, will not stay rare for long – competitors will buy it or develop their own version.

- Similarly, a valuable resource will not retain its value if substitutes are freely available, since competitors will be able to use the substitute resource to gain the same cost or differentiation advantages.

- Resources that are difficult to copy, but not rare, will not give any one company in the industry an advantage over its competitors. These resources may constitute barriers to entry to the industry for firms that do not have them, and enable *all* the companies in the industry to make reasonable profits. However, they will not make the difference between being an industry leader and one of the also-rans, and they will not protect a small firm in the industry from a larger competitor that wants to invade its markets.

7.1.4 What makes a resource difficult to acquire or copy?

There are two basic reasons why resources may be difficult to acquire copy: because it is simply not possible to replicate them, or because it would be prohibitively expensive to do so.

Resources that cannot be acquired or copied

Sometimes resources cannot be obtained because they are in genuinely short supply, not just within the industry but throughout the world. For example, deposits of metal ores that are close to the surface (and so cheap to mine) with a high metal content and low in bothersome impurities (and so cheap to process) are rare. A firm that finds one will have an enduring cost advantage over its competitors. Similarly, if a firm has managed to attract the world's leading experts in a particular technology, it will have a competitive advantage for as long as they stay with the firm.

Another factor that can prevent resources being copied is because they have a high tacit knowledge content – the people who develop the products or operate the service may not have documented what they do. In extreme cases, perhaps in a very new firm or industry, people may genuinely not understand the difference between success and failure, so there is nothing to imitate. It took the makers of microchips a long time to work out why some batches of silicon wafers would result in usable products, while others would not.

Tacit knowledge content is one example of how inimitable resources result from the way that they are built up over time.[6] Often, organisations are shaped by the particular time and place where they originate. We saw in Chapter 3 how Sony's culture and capabilities were shaped by its origins in post-war Japan, and the vision of its founders. A contemporary firm in Europe or the USA would approach problems with a different attitude and arrive at different solutions. An organisation's capabilities are dependent on the path it has followed.

Time shapes resources in other ways, too. Research and development and advertising are two examples of investments that can take a long time to take effect. It may take several years of experimentation and contemplation before researchers come up with a new technology. According to Dierickx and Cool (1989), investing, say, 2 million euros per year for four years is likely to yield better results than a crash R&D programme of 4 million euros per year over two years. Similarly, it would be difficult for a newcomer to catch up with a brand like McDonald's, which has benefited, not just from years of advertising expenditure, but from countless casual mentions in TV programmes and movies. These are two examples of what have been inelegantly termed 'time compression diseconomies'.

Resources that are expensive to copy

Even where time is not a factor, there are cases where firms' **sunk costs** – their investments in an existing base of resources – may confer an enduring advantage. Consider the case of two competing mobile telephone operators, one an established firm that already serves one-third of the country, the other a new start-up. If they both invest €20 million in new equipment, the first firm will end up with an appreciably larger network than the second, and will be more attractive to both new and existing customers as a result. This is an example of 'asset mass efficiencies', where an investment that adds to a strong base makes a greater improvement to an organisation's position than one that reinforces a weak one. The new competitor may still be able to catch up, by making larger investments or offering a more reliable service, but in principle the entrenched competitor has the advantage. An extreme example is the case of a natural monopoly, such as electricity distribution, where there is simply no point in one firm investing to duplicate an existing network of assets.

Another instance of sunk costs conferring advantage is where other, complementary assets are needed in order to make a resource work to its best advantage. For example, a firm may successfully invest in the knowledge needed to develop an innovative new product, but may still lose out to a firm with an inferior product but a superior sales network.

7.1.5 Resources, success and survival

As we noted at the beginning of the chapter, we are trying to understand how resources make the difference between a successful firm and its competitors in the same industry. Barriers to imitating the leading firms' resources, which we have been discussing in this section, are not the same as barriers to entry to the

---

Practical dos and don'ts   **Analysis of strategic resources**

1. The tests we have described in Section 7.1.3 – that in order to be strategic, a resource must be rare, valuable and difficult to copy and have no substitute – are very exacting. *Not many resources can be expected to pass them, and a firm may have only one or two.* If you come up with a list with more than four or five strategic resources, then it is quite likely that you have not been rigorous enough in applying those tests.

2. Not all firms develop strategic resources. Even apparently successful organisations may flourish for a while, in a favourable environment, and then find that they cannot stand up to a strong competitor. In our experience, it is far more common to find a firm with no strategic resources than one with ten or twelve.

---

industry. It may be perfectly possible for new firms to enter an industry where there are established competitors with strong resources and, if the industry is structurally attractive, they may make decent returns. Around the world, companies are queuing up for licences to run mobile phone networks, and new fast-food brands still appear to challenge McDonald's and Pizza Hut. However, firms that have developed strategic resources are likely to:

- be more profitable than their competitors in the medium term;
- remain profitable as competition intensifies, whereas newer or weaker competitors may struggle;
- be more resilient in the face of changes in the environment.

Strategic resources do not necessarily guarantee advantage forever, however. New technologies or changes in customer tastes may destroy their value. Successful firms may become complacent and neglect their resource base, allowing competitors to overtake them. However, strong resources do make it considerably more likely that a firm will prosper. In the next section, we look at particular types of resource, and how they may contribute to sustainable competitive advantage.

7.2 The strategic importance of different types of resource

In this section, we look in turn at different categories of resource and the extent to which they are likely to qualify as strategic. For the moment, we are focusing on what an organisation *has* – what we are calling its assets – rather than what it can do. Unfortunately there is a considerable confusion over these two terms, so that what we have called physical assets may be termed physical resources by other writers. We have, however, used the standard term human resources rather than the more strictly accurate human assets.

7.2.1 Physical assets

It is actually quite unusual for physical assets to be the basis of sustainable competitive advantage. Exceptionally cheap or pure sources of raw materials, such as the mineral deposits discussed in Section 7.1.4, may count as strategic assets if they are genuinely rare and valuable. The South African minerals corporations, De Beer's, has for decades had control of 90% of the world's sources of diamonds. This undoubtedly qualifies as a strategic asset, since diamonds are valuable and there are few ready substitutes for them.

Most common types of physical assets, such as factories, offices, computer systems and retail outlets, can be bought on the open market. However new and up-to-date they may be, they are also available to competitors, who may even be able to buy cheaper and more powerful facilities. These kinds of assets are normally only strategic if:

- *They incorporate a firm's proprietary technology.* For example, some Japanese firms insist on making their own machine tools rather than purchasing them off the shelf. If they genuinely deliver lower wastage or higher throughputs than commercially available products, they can be considered as strategic assets.

- *They have been bought cheaply, before other firms woke up to their value.* UK retailer Marks & Spencer had for many years a strategic asset in its retail locations, many of which had been purchased cheaply some years ago, while its competitors were paying for expensive leases based upon modern property prices. The value of this asset has diminished, however. Many of the stores are now too small for the range of goods that M&S wants and needs to stock. Also, they are located in traditional town centres, and UK consumers increasingly prefer newer shopping centres with ample car-parking facilities.

7.2.2 Financial assets

Financial assets are rarely strategic, because money is freely available from banks, stock markets and venture capitalists across the globe. There are however, exceptions to this general rule.

Sometimes a company has access to funds in such quantity that it can use them to strike deals from which poorer firms are excluded. In 1999, the US conglomerate General Electric was able to win an exclusive contract to supply jet engines for the long-range version of Boeing's 777 aircraft, by promising to fund one-half of the aircraft's $1 billion development cost. Competitors were only able to offer a contribution of $200 million.[7] A strong balance sheet is most often a source of competitive advantage in banking and insurance, but does figure in other industries too, such as aircraft and defence, where the ability to offer customers attractive finance terms can be an important part of the marketing package.

'Deep pockets' – large cash reserves or borrowing capacity – can offer an advantage in other ways, by giving a company a superior ability to survive a price war or a recession. However, money in itself rarely confers competitive advantage – it usually needs to be converted into some other form of resource in order to make a difference. A rich firm may have better access than its competitors to state-of-the-art physical assets, if these are expensive and important to gaining competitive advantage, or to top lawyers, which can be useful in defending it. Deep-pocketed organisations may also be better able to attract key personnel, particularly in industries like sport, entertainment and banking, where a few 'star' individuals may have a disproportionately large impact on organisational performance (see Real-Life Application 7.1).

REAL-LIFE APPLICATION 7.1

Financial and human resources in football

'Unto he that has, more shall be given.'

Over many years, there has been a clear, self-reinforcing relationship in soccer between financial performance and competitive success (as measured by a team's position in the league table). The richer teams are able to buy, and pay attractive salaries to, the most talented players, and also to build larger squads so that, if a star player is injured, a good-quality substitute is immediately available. This enables them to win trophies, so attracting new supporters and commercial sponsors and boosts sales of replica shirts and other branded merchandise. The televising of

football has emphasised this phenomenon by weakening the traditional link between football fans an their home-town team, and enabling top clubs like Manchester United and Juventus to build support around the world.

As a result, in most European countries, only the members of a small élite of rich clubs are realistic contenders for the top trophies. Some clubs are able to penetrate this élite for a while if they can attract funding from a rich corporation or individual.

Source: Stefan Szymanski and Tim Kuypers, *Winners and Losers: the Business Strategy of Football*, Viking, 1999.

Financial assets usually need to be very substantial – in the billions, or at least the hundreds of millions, of dollars or euros – to count as strategic. Even if a firm has more cash or borrowing capacity than its immediate competitors, it still needs to measure itself against potential competitors like Ford or Microsoft, whose 'war chests' are estimated to be around $20 billion. And even spending on this scale cannot always *guarantee* results. Football teams may spend a fortune on good players, and still be relegated because they do not blend into a coherent team.[8] In the 1980s and 1990s many British, German and Japanese banks spent large sums in recruiting staff to attempt to match American investment banks in the lucrative corporate finance business, but most of them failed to build a sustainable position.

There can even be occasions where having a cash surplus appears to be a positive liability for an organisation. This is when it lulls management into a sense of complacency, or causes them to divert attention from the core business to seek diversification opportunities. The UK's Rank Organisation for many years got an assured income from its 49% share of Rank Xerox, a profitable photocopier firm, which it dissipated on a series of questionable acquisitions in the property and leisure sectors.

This is why firms will occasionally voluntarily take on large amounts of debt, normally to buy back its shares from shareholders. This leveraging strategy (leverage is the American word for gearing) is believed by some theorists to make managers more focused in their drive to cut costs and improve sales, particularly if the managers themselves buy some or all of the remaining shares in what is known as a leveraged buy-out. The effect of the debt is to magnify (or 'leverage') the effect of a small increase in operating profit on the firm's net profit, and hence its share price.[9] The risk, of course, is that if trading conditions suddenly worsen, or interest rates rise sharply, the weight of debt could drive a firm into insolvency.

7.2.3 Human resources

Human resources (we are using the term only because it is in common usage; to be consistent, we should really call them human assets) are more heterogeneous than physical or financial assets – there are considerable differences in the way that

Strategic human resources at Sun Microsystems

Sun Microsystems was founded in 1982 to produce small but powerful desktop computers, known as workstations, for use in running computer networks and for applications such as computer-aided design that needed more computing power than was available on the early PCs. The firm was a runaway success, and quickly seized leadership in the segment. In 1999, it had revenues of over $11 billion and was the largest single supplier of computers to Internet service providers.

The firm made some important marketing decisions that contributed to its early and subsequent success. It priced its systems low, to gain market share. It targeted customers in education, in the belief that students who had learnt their computing on Sun machines would be more likely to ask their employers for them later in their careers. And, it offered 'Open Systems' running the Unix operating system, which attracted customers who did not want to be tied to a single supplier.

Many computers could run the Unix system, but Sun's resource advantage lay in its ability to attract the very best Unix programmers, who knew how to fine-tune the hardware to make best use of the operating system. The most prominent of those programmers was Bill Joy, who as a graduate student at Berkeley University had played a major role in developing Unix. He was attracted by Sun's product idea, and also formed a powerful personal bond with Andreas Bechtolsheim, who had designed Sun's prototype hardware.

Joy went on to play a crucial role in designing the SPARC microprocessors that power Sun's equipment. He is also credited with spotting the potential of the Java language that is used in most World Wide Web applications, and has since designed the Jini language that many people believe will become the standard for allowing computers and electrical appliances to communicate with one another. In many people's eyes, he is the second-most influential person in modern computing (after Microsoft's Bill Gates).

Sources: *Fortune*, 15 February 1999, 10 May 1999; Allen, SA Case study, Sun Microsystems, Inc (A), Babson College, MA, 1994.

human beings behave in different countries and in different organisations. They are therefore much more likely to give rise to advantages that are rare and difficult to copy. This is particularly true in 'people businesses' such as advertising, consultancy and financial services, but may also be true in capital intensive industries, since it is people who are needed to design or operate the machinery.

Some human resources are rare because they require the brain to be 'wired' in a particular and unusual way, so as to make split-second judgements about whether to shoot, pass or run with a football, or to buy or sell a share. Football clubs and merchant banks pay a great deal to attract individuals with these rare skills. Other valuable human skills are less dependent on individual aptitude, but are rare because they are relatively new, and education and training systems have not been developed to produce them in quantity. An organisation that is able to get access to these people will have an advantage over at least some of its competitors. Organisations may offer money or share options, a pleasant working environment or the opportunity for people to be creative, and to mix with stimulating people in an attempt to retain these individuals (see Real-Life Application 7.2). However, they must be on their guard that these people are not lured away to other firms. This is a particular danger during acquisitions, since in that situation the people in the acquired firm may doubt the integrity or competence of their new owners. When Germany's Deutsche Bank acquired the US merchant bank, Banker's Trust, it found that whole teams of valuable people defected to competitors, partly because of clashes of style with the firm's new owners.

Sometimes, organisations derive their strategic human resources from the country in which they are located. Indian information processing firms, for example, have a strategic human resource advantage over their competitors in other countries. Their workforce is well educated and has a good grasp of English, but wage levels are very low by the standards of most other countries. The extent to which *any one firm* will derive an *enduring* advantage will depend on other factors, such as their managers' business skills and ability to maintain quality and staff motivation as the firms grow.

Sometimes a large part of a firm's competitive advantage may seem to rest with a single individual, because of their industry knowledge, technological abilities or their ability to inspire the people around them. Someone like Bill Joy (see Real-Life Application 7.2), who has been a consistent source of ideas over twenty years, is undoubtedly a strategic asset. On the other hand, some entrepreneurs, although they inspire people that work for them, may also so dominate their firms that it is difficult for others to develop their talents. Sometimes it is an outsider that comes in as Chief Executive to give a company new direction after a long-serving leader has left, as was the case with The Walt Disney Company and IBM.

7.2.4 Intellectual assets

◄ *Barriers to entry were reviewed in Section 5.4.4.*

Intellectual assets such as databases, patents and research programmes generally have the capacity to be the source of competitive advantage. If a firm's customer database is larger and more detailed than its competitors' or if it has patents or other forms of technological knowledge, then these may be strategically important. However, they really must be *significantly* better than other firms' assets, and be *genuinely* difficult to copy, in order to be considered strategic. As we saw when looking at barriers to entry, intellectual assets can be quite difficult to defend from imitation.

This is why organisational assets with a **high tacit knowledge content** are often considered to be particularly valuable. Because the knowledge is not written down, it cannot be copied or stolen. It may be possible for a competitor to lure away personnel, but this may not give them access to the relationships or **shared** knowledge those people have acquired over time. Research in cognitive psychology has also shown that people's ability to use knowledge is influenced by the setting in which they are asked to employ it.[10] People may depend upon other resources in the company, such as specially designed workstations or information systems, to make full use of their knowledge. This is an illustration of the difference between an asset (knowledge) and a capability.

Management attention is a particularly important class of intellectual asset.[11] Top managers are often (though not always) the people in an organisation with the greatest ability to find fast solutions to business problems. Either they have seen a similar problem in the past, or they have deep, tacit knowledge of the firm's operations and customers that tells them where to look for a workable solution. However, organisations have only a few of these people, and they can only give proper attention to a limited number of issues at a time. Management attention is therefore scarce and must be allocated carefully. An organisation's information and control systems need to draw attention to important issues quickly, and minimise the amount of top management attention that is wasted on minor matters.

7.2.5 Reputational assets[12]

Reputational assets covers two main types of resource: firms' *brands* – the names they use in the market-place – and their *reputation* – the degree of esteem in which they are held by current or potential customers. The two are not quite the same – brands tend to be associated with products, or families of products, while reputation[13] tends to belong to an organisation. A firm will hope that, by investing in advertising to build one or more brands, it will create a good reputation, but brands have other functions, too.

The functions of brands

When a firm builds a brand, it wants it to symbolise certain things to prospective purchasers.[14] It hopes that, when buyers choose between products, its brand will be strong enough to make its product a more or less automatic choice. The buyer is spared the time, money and mental anguish associated with a long selection process. The seller hopes that its strong brand will lead to repeated purchases of its existing products, easier launches for its new ones, and the ability to charge premium prices. Companies get further benefits if they can associate a brand with a particular market segment. This helps them to focus their marketing effort, so that they can tailor their products and their marketing message to their target customer group, and try and win their loyalty to the brand. Equally, they waste less money trying to sell to customers who are unlikely to be interested in what they offer.

Marketers therefore try to associate brands with an image or 'personality' – fun-loving or serious, enduring or disposable and so on. This is a particular element of differentiation that aims to target particular products at a specific market segment. Ideally, it aims to get customers to buy a particular product because they aspire to the brand values embodied in, say, a BMW car, a Gucci bag or a Budweiser beer. If the market segment is appropriate and the targeting well executed, then a firm can gain at least a temporary advantage. In theory, another producer could then copy the same positioning by using similar messages. However, in practice copycat strategies like these are not all that common, since having several brands with almost exactly the same image creates 'noise' in the market place. This confuses customers and reduces the value of all the brands in that market segment.

The value of brands

The strategic value of brands is coming under debate in both industrial and consumer markets. In industrial markets, brands have traditionally been seen as having limited value, because customers were thought to use price and performance as the main criteria for choosing which product to buy. Industrial advertising has therefore tended to give detailed product information rather than trying to establish brand personalities. However, some theorists such as Ward et al. (1999) now believe that industrial products are becoming so similar that it is increasingly difficult to differentiate on the basis of price and functionality. They say that, increasingly, brands are becoming important for industrial buyers as well. Leading computer manufacturers Hewlett-Packard and IBM are examples of firms that have tried to build brands based on the quality of the support they offer their customers.

REAL-LIFE APPLICATION 7.3

Brands in the jeans industry

The jeans industry contains hundreds of brands. Levi-Strauss, the long-standing industry leader, is 150 years old, while some of its competitors were unknown at the beginning of the 1990s (Tommy Hilfiger, Diesel) or were known for other things (Caterpillar – a market leading brand of earthmoving equipment). Levi-Strauss and its long-standing American competitors Lee and Wrangler specialise in jeans, while for Benetton and The Gap they are just one element in a much broader product portfolio.

In this kind of environment, it is very difficult to say how much enduring advantage a brand confers. People certainly buy Benetton jeans – denim clothing accounts for around one-third of the company's sales – but is this because of the 'United Colours' brand values, or because of the convenience of buying jeans alongside a range of other clothing? The Versace or Dolce e Gabanna brands have more Italian designer chic. Tommy Hilfiger or Diesel are sportier.

Even a brand as venerable as Levi's is not immune to competition. Its share of the US men's jeans market has been eroded from 48% in 1990 to 25% in 1998. Lee and Wrangler have picked up ten percentage points of market share between them, but most of the damage suffered by Levis has been at the hands of retailers' private label brands, many of them new and unprestigious.

Levi-Strauss is still extremely profitable, but faces the problem that many young people do not want to be seen in the same brands of trousers as their parents. One way that it is confronting this issue is through new labels like Red Line, which it launched in 1998. However, to let the new brand appear 'cool', the company is carefully avoiding any public association between Red Line and Levi-Strauss. When marketing to young US males, at least, the Levi's brand appears to be more of a liability than an asset.

Adapted, with additions, from: Nina Munk, 'How Levi's Trashed a Great American Brand', *Fortune*, 12 April 1999, pp. 33–38.

In consumer goods industries, on the other hand, brands have traditionally been regarded as a strategic resource par excellence. The French conglomerate, LVMH, has built its entire corporate-level strategy around the acquisition of prestigious brands such as Moët et Chandon (champagne), Louis Vuitton (luggage), Tag Heuer (watches), Dior and Kenzo (fashion). Firms like Diageo, the British drinks and food corporation, have taken to including brands like Johnny Walker (a best-selling whisky) and Burger King as assets in their balance sheet. In Diageo's case they accounted for over 50% of the company's book value in its 1998 accounts. Brands like McDonald's, Coca-Cola or Rolls-Royce, that have been established long enough to benefit from time compression diseconomies (see Section 7.1.4), are likely to count as a strategic asset.

However, in some industries, like popular music or jeans, brands are relatively easy to create. All the main competitors have them and few firms are credible competitors without them. In cases like these (Real-Life Application 7.3), it is debatable whether a brand is a strategic asset or just a threshold one.

Even long-standing, prestigious brands cannot guarantee advantage, or even survival. Japanese car manufacturers were able to set up their Lexus and Infiniti brands and win share from the German and British luxury car marques, BMW, Mercedes and Jaguar, in the 1980s. Jaguar in particular was badly hit by this, and was eventually taken over by the Ford Motor Company.

The value of reputation

Branding and advertising may establish an organisation's reputation, or it may arise from word-of-mouth – customers or suppliers telling one another about good

---

REAL-LIFE APPLICATION 7.4

Two different types of reputation

In 1992, British Airways (BA) was sued by a UK competitor, Virgin Airways. BA's data processing division had won a contract to maintain Virgin's customer records on BA's computers. It emerged that BA's airline marketing staff had gained unauthorised access to those computer records. They had extracted the names and details of some of Virgin's customers and tried to persuade them to change their bookings to BA flights.

Virgin won the case, and improved its reputation as a small firm that took on established corporations and beat them. British Airways' reputation with its customers was mildly damaged, although surveys found that other issues, such as quality of customer service, were more important to travellers. BA's reputation within the industry as a tough competitor was undoubtedly enhanced.

---

or bad experiences, researchers discussing the company at conferences or trade associations, industry gossip in the trade or financial press. A firm may have a reputation for reliable, well designed or innovative products, for good customer service, for financial soundness, for paying its bills promptly, for being a good employer or for being a tough competitor (Real-Life Application 7.4).

A good reputation can be valuable to the organisation or its customers in a number of ways. It can help reduce customers' search costs. In industries like clothes or fresh fruit, where consumers will typically look at a number of possible suppliers before buying, reputation can help a supplier be one of the places where they will look for good quality or good value. If customers are pressed for time, they may head straight for a retailer which has a reputation for offering reasonable prices, rather than laboriously compare prices in different shops.

For larger items like hi-fi, washing machines or cars, or for services like consultancy or accountancy, reputation can be a key factor in consumers' choice. Buying a product or service like this represents a major commitment for most people, and yet they cannot tell, at the time of purchase, how good it will be. Suppliers with good reputations take some of the risk away, and for this they often charge a premium.

A good reputation can be valuable to an organisation in its relationship with a variety of stakeholders. It can give employees a positive image of themselves, help motivate them to give of their best and help the firm attract talented staff. It can help persuade suppliers to become associated with a firm, to co-operate on delivery schedules and grant favourable credit terms. It can persuade retail outlets to stock an untried product, or engineers to recommend it. It can help the firm persuade bankers to make loans on risky projects, and has been shown to keep its stock price high. A reputation as a tough competitor helps a company deter other firms from entering its markets.[15]

Practising managers attach a great deal of importance to corporate reputation[16] which, unless overstated or badly mismanaged, can be an exceptionally durable asset, one of the most important issues here being *conformity* or *coherence* between reputation and the characteristics of the product (see Real-Life Application 7.5). Very occasionally, it becomes expensive for a firm to live up to its reputation. An American clothing retailer, Nordstrom, built up a fearsome reputation for exceptional customer service. Customers who came in late in the working day, needing an outfit for an important meeting the following morning, would find the garment, altered to their specifications, delivered to their hotel several hundred kilo-

REAL-LIFE APPLICATION 7.5

Enduring and mismanaged reputations

IBM used sometimes to be accused of giving more weight to the desires of its engineers than to the needs of its customers. However, its products have enjoyed a strong reputation for durability and reliability. This was important in sustaining the company's recovery from its record losses of $7.8 billion in the two years 1991–92, which would have threatened the credibility of a lesser firm.

The history of Britain's Jaguar car company goes back to the early years of the twentieth century. It produced cars that, because of their looks and performance, were some of the world's most sought-after luxury models. However, the cars' build quality became so bad that a joke circulated in the USA to the effect that the only way to be sure of having a roadworthy Jaguar was to buy two.[17] Sales declined, but never disappeared. The firm was bought by Ford and, after much effort, the production process was transformed to meet modern

standards of reliability. The firm's product launches, such as that of the recently announced F-type, are still eagerly awaited by car fanatics everywhere.

The French bottled water producer, Perrier, caught on early to the emerging market for bottled water in the UK. Its raindrop-shaped green glass bottle was a design icon, and imaginative advertising helped propel it to market leadership. In 1988 it had 70% of the UK market for bottled water. However, in February 1990, it was discovered that a fault in its bottling process had led to the water being slightly contaminated with a carcinogenic chemical, benzene. The company's first reaction was to downplay the problem; by the time it awoke to the true extent of consumer concern, and recalled all potentially contaminated bottles, it was too late. Although the contamination scare is long forgotten, Perrier has never regained its former market share.

metres away. When in 1997 the firm's profits slumped, some observers wondered whether it could afford to maintain such extravagant service levels, although the firm has stuck with its policy.

In your analysis, you should look carefully at the nature of competition in the industry, before deciding that a firm's reputation counts as a strategic asset. If products in an industry are of uniformly good quality, then firm reputations are not necessarily important to customers. In the 1960s, television sets broke down frequently, and so it made sense to pay extra for a reputable brand. Nowadays, the technology is so reliable that there is far less risk in buying from an unfamiliar producer. For inexpensive goods like beer or newspapers, users run little risk from trying a new product – if they don't like what they buy, they can simply throw it away and try something else. In a fiercely competitive industry with high supplier power, a reputation as a tough competitor that pays promptly for its raw materials may be a threshold resource, rather than a strategic one.

7.2.6 Assets, competences and capabilities

Up to this point, our discussion has focused on a firm's assets – the things that it has accumulated over time. However, an asset – a machine, or a sum of money, or a reputation – is of limited use unless it is intelligently directed towards serving the organisation's target users. It needs to contribute to a capability.

The relationship between assets and competences/capabilities is a close one. Just as an asset is useless without the capability to apply it, so a capability is pointless without the assets to deploy it. A capability in lean manufacturing requires physical assets, in the form of a serviceable factory, although they may not be anything exceptional (see Real-Life Application 7.6). On the other hand, the way in which a firm *acquires* its assets is often by *applying* its capabilities. An oil company's reserves

Assets and capabilities

British Telecommunications

British Telecommunications plc (BT) is the world's sixth-largest telecommunications company with a 1998 turnover of £20 billion. Since its privatisation in 1984 it has worked hard to throw off the bureaucratic culture that it used to have as part of the UK's civil service, to become more responsive to customer requirements and to acquire skills in marketing. Most observers believe that it has succeeded.

One of BT's assets is its subscriber database. For a long time, it tried to keep this proprietary, and to stop other information providers from publishing CD-ROMs containing its full subscriber list. Eventually, market pressures forced it to make this information available on CD-ROM and the World Wide Web. However, it was another, smaller firm, i-CD Publishing, that published a CD-ROM where the telephone directory is cross-referenced to business directories and to the UK's official list of registered voters. i-CD has capabilities in gathering and marketing data that have enabled it to overcome the head start BT had through its superior intellectual and financial assets.

General Motors

In the 1980s, General Motors (GM) committed billions of dollars of investment to fit its brand new Hamtramck factory in Detroit, Michigan with state-of-the-art robots, automated guided vehicles, laser measurement and computing equipment. Its aim was to overcome the cost advantage that Japanese competitors Toyota and Honda had gained through their application of lean manufacturing techniques. By applying sophisticated American information technology, GM hoped to save heavily on labour costs and improve reliability. However, on its opening day in 1985, the plant was a disaster, with the robots destroying each other or the cars they were meant to be building. GM lacked the skills to use the new technology to its best advantage – for example, its workers could not handle the mass of information produced by the laser measurement systems. In the end, some of the automated equipment had to be removed, and it was estimated that 20% of GM's investment had been wasted.

Its Japanese rivals, on the other hand, believed that for car manufacturing, carefully nurtured capabilities were more important than ultra-sophisticated physical assets. They focused upon ways of making their staff more productive, rather than replacing them. While they did invest in robots, these were mainly to assist people and make their working conditions more pleasant.

of cheap, high-grade crude oil are the result of capabilities in exploration. McDonald's brand and reputation are the result of competences in marketing, and in the consistent production of edible hamburgers. Microsoft's $20 billion cash reserves are the result of a raft of competences in areas like software development, marketing and the assessment of the environment.

A really strong strategic asset can have a longer-lasting effect than competences and capabilities. Reputations are durable (Real-Life Application 7.5), low-cost mineral reserves will confer cost advantage as long as the mineral is in demand, and large cash reserves will retain their value for as long as inflation or managerial inertia does not dilute them.

Competences and capabilities, on the other hand, require constant attention to ensure that they do not become outdated, or do not freeze the organisation into a rigid way of behaving. However, it is more common for a capability or competence to be truly distinctive, and therefore strategic, than it is for an asset. This is because capabilities are 'home-grown' within each organisation, whereas competing firms will tend to purchase their physical assets from the same suppliers and recruit their human resources from the same pool of talent.

7.3 Capabilities and competences

We now move on to look at competences and capabilities in more detail – the difference between them, what kinds there are, and what gives rise to them.

The difference between capabilities and competences is a subtle one and, as we noted earlier, many authors do not distinguish between them. However, when trying to get a deep understanding of an organisation's competitive advantage, it is useful to distinguish between *competences*, which are routines that have potential uses in many places in an organisation, and *capabilities*, which are specific, useful, things that organisations do in specific situations.

Capabilities are things that customers and other stakeholders notice when they are dealing with an organisation. They notice whether orders are met within 24 hours, whether unusual requests are dealt with or pushed aside, whether invoices are sent out accurately and on time, whether the firm is willing to take risks with untried customers in new markets. On the basis of these observations, they decide whether they want to do business with a firm, and, if so, whether they are willing to pay any kind of price premium. Capabilities like these have a direct impact on a firm's differentiation advantage; there are others that have a similar impact on its cost advantage.

Customers care whether their orders are met accurately and quickly. They do not necessarily care whether that is because an organisation has a state-of-the-art computer system, or an army of well-trained, well-motivated clerks – that is the firm's problem. However we, as analysts trying to work out whether the firm will be around and profitable in five years' time, will care quite a lot about whether the firm has underlying **competences** in IT or in staff training. We may hold the view that, in future, the IT competence is likely to be more valuable, because of the way the environment is going to change.

From this discussion, it should be clear that capabilities and competences are both important. Without underlying general competences, there can be no capabilities. Unless competences can be translated into useful capabilities, they are of no advantage to the organisation.

We now move on to look at examples of different types of capability and competence, to give some clues about what to look for in your own analysis. It is not a complete list, since human ingenuity consistently comes up with new ones. We shall show how different types of organisational capability lead to cost or differentiation advantage, and what sorts of competence can underlie them.

7.3.1 Types of capability

We look at innovation and its management in more detail in Chapter 15. ▶

Many theorists (e.g. John Kay, 1993, Ch. 7) emphasise the importance of innovation as a capability. By innovation, we do not mean simply an organisation's ability to improve products or processes as they go along, but their ability to produce something genuinely new and different. Classic examples of innovative products are:

- **3M's Post-It note.** When it emerged in the 1970s, no-one had ever thought of producing a note that could stick reliably to one surface, and then be removed, without damaging either the note or the object it was stuck to, and re-struck on another surface. It was a genuine novelty, though competitors have now managed to imitate it.

- **The Sony Walkman.** The idea of a tape player that was actually made to be used while people were in motion (as against small enough to be portable) was completely new at the time.

- **The Dyson cyclonic, bagless vacuum cleaner,** which offers the user more sustained suction power than traditional technologies.

Genuine innovations do not occur very often and some companies, after producing one, never repeat the trick. Although Dyson has invested millions of pounds in nurturing new inventions, it has yet to find a successor to its original breakthrough. Meanwhile, established manufacturers like Hoover and Electrolux, who had earlier rejected Dyson's concept when the inventor tried to interest them in it, have now gone some way towards imitating it.

Only those rare companies like Sony, which over fifty years has produced numerous genuine innovations in audio, TV and computer games equipment, can be said to have a **distinctive** capability in innovation. 3M similarly has innovated in many fields, from sandpaper through stationery to non-woven fabrics.

Most **product** innovations provide differentiation advantage, by giving a firm's products superior functionality, but may also give cost advantage if the innovation is cheaper to produce than competitors' offerings. No less important is **process** innovation, which tends to improve an organisation's cost position. McDonald's process for cooking and serving hamburgers was a considerable innovation in 1940, and enabled the firm to offer cheaper food, at more consistent quality, than its competitors. Similarly, Benetton's invention of a process for dyeing finished garments, rather than dyeing the yarn first and knitting the clothes from coloured wool, gave it a cost advantage. The firm wasted less money on producing garments that would not be sold because they were the wrong colour. They were also able to respond more quickly than competitors if it became clear that there was unexpectedly strong demand for a particular colour – a form of differentiation advantage.

Although both Benetton and McDonald's have produced genuine innovations in the past, neither could really claim a distinctive capability in innovation – they have not followed up their initial breakthrough with others, as Sony has. However, each has managed to build upon their initial innovation to establish distinctive capabilities in other areas.

McDonald's has a distinctive capability in the area of **reliability** – it has learned how to reproduce and control its processes, so that a McDonald's burger tastes similar, and is of equivalent quality, in suburban Los Angeles or London, or central Frankfurt or Moscow.[18] Some international hotel chains have similarly mastered the challenge of making their hospitality and décor of similar standard across the world. People who want a reasonably priced hotel or meal with low risk of disappointment will be drawn to these firms, who thus gain differentiation advantage. The standardisation of inputs can also give economies of scale in areas such as purchasing and staff training, and reduce wastage, so cost advantage can result as well.

For hotels and airlines, reliability needs to go hand in hand with **sensitivity to customer requirements**. These organisations need to be able to detect, often in real time, what their customers need, and respond. Capabilities of this kind are important not only in service businesses, but also in fast-moving industries such as fashion and computing. Cisco Systems, which dominates the market for the routers – computers used to direct messages on the Internet – is renowned for the way in which it stays close to its customers' developing technological needs and satisfies them with the next generation of its hardware. Along with differentiation advantage, this capability may lower costs, by reducing the amount of unsaleable merchandise that is produced, and sometimes by reducing the amount of time and effort needed by the sales function.

Like most profitable fashion businesses, Benetton would boast at least a threshold capability in the area of customer sensitivity. However, its *distinctive* capability lies in its **speed of reaction** to customer requirements; its internal processes enable it to get fashionable items into its stores more quickly than most of its competitors. Similarly, Seven-Eleven Japan, one of the world's largest convenience store chains, pioneered a system whereby orders are placed with its suppliers to replenish stocks automatically as goods are purchased from the stores. This kind of capability also affects both cost and differentiation advantage. On the cost side, it reduces waste and may allow firms to operate with lower inventories because of their faster response times. The differentiation comes from the customer's being sure that the desired goods are always available.

Many people would also say Benetton had a distinctive capability in the area of **communication** – building a brand image and knowledge of the firm and its products – in the eyes of consumers and other stakeholders – through its unusual and sometimes controversial 'United Colours of Benetton' advertising. This kind of capability can be particularly important in fashion, luxury goods and fast-moving consumer goods industries, where differentiation on reputation and brand image is often a success factor.

There are two other types of more subtle capability that can be important. The first is in **negotiation**: the ability to 'manage the expectations' of customers, governments and other stakeholders. For firms involved in minerals extraction and heavy construction projects, such as power stations, being able to negotiate the right terms, timescales and prices with host governments, and to liaise effectively with host communities is as important as the technical skills needed to locate the site and undertake the project. If unhappy local people disrupt a project, or put political pressure on the government to cancel a deal because it is seen as unfair, then the delay can wipe out any profit. These skills are also important for consultants and other professional service firms. If customers feel that the service delivered is different from what was promised, they may refuse to pay or demand costly extra work. They will certainly not employ the firm again, and may attack its reputation. For many other organisations, the ability to negotiate with suppliers to get lower prices or better co-operation than they give competing firms can also be a source of cost advantage.

The final class of business-level capability we would like to highlight is in **risk management**, which is becoming increasingly significant in a number of ways. For banks and insurers, the ability to manage risk in their financial portfolios can be crucial, and the absence of such a capability can lead to huge losses, or even bankruptcy.[19] Superior risk management, knowing when to buy and when to take profits, can be a source of cost advantage. It can also give differentiation advantage for firms like the large US investment banks, who seek to attract investors into funds that they manage, and to help clients to manage their own financial risks. However, risk management can be of value to any firm that is required to take potentially costly leaps into the unknown, such as major investments in new products or new markets (Real-Life Application 7.7).

REAL-LIFE APPLICATION 7.7

Risk management

1. Merck and the pharmaceuticals industry

The process of developing a new drug consists of a number of potentially costly stages. A firm has to identify a promising compound, and then conduct preliminary trials of its effectiveness on animals or on laboratory samples of human tissue. If these are successful, then larger-scale tests on animals are needed to try and predict if there are any unwanted side effects. A drug that passes this stage then needs to be tested on human beings to see if it is effective. If so, then approval must be sought from drug licensing authorities in the major markets, and production and marketing facilities set up. A drug which initially looks promising may fall at any one of these hurdles, causing the drugs company that is developing it to write off millions of dollars of investment.

Merck is the world's largest pharmaceuticals company, with 1998 sales of $27 billion, and has for many years been among the most profitable. One of its distinctive capabilities was the way it used a financial technique, option theory, to evaluate the value of proceeding from one stage to the next in the drug evaluation process. Observers credited this technique with saving the firm many millions of dollars in research investment that was unlikely to result in profitable products.

Source: Nichols, N. (1994) 'Scientific Management at Merck' *Harvard Business Review*, January–February. pp. 88–89.

2. Canon and the US photocopier industries

When Canon, the Japanese electronics corporation, wanted to launch a photocopier in the 1970s, it confronted a number of problems. It did not have a workable process for plain-paper copying, but only for copying on to coated paper. This technology was cheaper than plain-paper copying, but the copies were of inferior quality, had an unpleasant feel and smell and tended to deteriorate with age. Canon needed to preserve the good reputation it had built up for its photographic products, and be wary of the powerful Xerox Corporation, which dominated the market.

Canon entered the US market by supplying its coated-paper copiers to the US firm Nashua, which marketed them under its own brand. As well as limiting the risk to Canon's corporate reputation, this also persuaded Xerox that Canon was not a serious competitor. Only when it had a reliable plain-paper copier that did not infringe Xerox's patents did Canon launch its own brand of machines in the USA, by which time it had learned a great deal about the American market through its association with Nashua. Xerox for many years believed that the main threat to its market dominance came from US firms like IBM and Kodak. It did not react fully to Japanese competitors until the early 1980s, when its market share had fallen from over 70% to under 40%.

◄ *We introduced the concept of parenting skills in Section 3.3.2.*

Alongside the capabilities that we discuss here, there are some capabilities that are more relevant to corporate-level strategy, such as the ability to value a potential acquisition and to integrate it within a firm. These are aspects of a corporation's parenting skills, which we discuss in Chapter 9.

7.3.2 Types of competence

We now move on to look at the types of competence that underlie some of the capabilities we used as examples in the previous section.

Technological competences were the first to be extensively discussed by strategy theorists, and they are important for capabilities in innovation. 3M's invention of the Post-It note resulted from the corporation's competences in coating technology. Hamel and Prahalad in their various writings showed that Canon's development of its plain-paper copier was made possible by its command of precision engineering and optics.[20] However, technology in the sense we are using it here is not limited to fields like science and engineering. Seven-Eleven Japan's capabilities in customer responsiveness are based on competences in information technology. The quality of Benetton's capabilities in communication depends on the strength of its competences in design and in consumer psychology, while Merck's capability in risk management rests on competences in applied financial economics.

Another important class of competences lies in the area of **control**; the ability to appreciate better or faster than competitors what is happening within and to one's organisation. Project management competences can be important for effective innovation and risk management. The reliability of McDonald's or an international hotel chain, is built upon effective control systems. Benetton's ability to update sales and stock information on a daily or even hourly basis is important for its speed of reaction to customer needs.

Research carried out by Andrew Pettigrew and Richard Whipp (1991) has identified the ability to **detect and assess environmental change** as one of the things that distinguishes more successful from less successful firms. Peter Senge, an influential theorist, believes that it is important for managers to be able to understand the firm and its environment as an integrated system.[21] If a firm is to innovate effectively, it needs these kinds of competence, to identify how customer needs are changing and to pick up on new technologies. Similarly, if a firm is to be responsive to customer needs, and to react to them quickly, it needs to be able to detect changes in them, which means it needs the kind of linkages that Cisco Systems has with its environment.

If an organisation is to make use of the information it receives from its environment and from its control systems then it needs to be able to change its behaviour to reflect that information. It needs the ability to **learn** new routines and **unlearn** old ones. Opinions differ as to whether an organisation's ability to learn is a competence like any other, or something more fundamental. Certainly, the theory of organisational learning is now so important to strategic management that it warrants a section of its own (Section 7.4.1 below).

Related to the ability to learn is the **ability to manage transitions**. Shona Brown and Kathleen Eisenhardt[22] have found, in looking at a number of high-technology US firms, that their capability of innovating effectively was related to the way in which they managed the movement of people from one project to another, to sustain the momentum of innovation. They see a similar competence as being important to the new product development process in established firms like Gillette, the US manufacturer of razors and other consumer products. They also identify it as underpinning corporate-level competences such as the ability to manage acquisitions.

7.3.3 Core and distributed competences

It should be becoming clear that many organisations possess a large number of competences. Some of these qualify as *core competences* – they are rare, valuable and difficult to copy and to substitute.[23] If a business' existing capabilities are not underpinned by one or more core competences, there is a risk that any advantage they give the organisation will be gradually eroded.

However, core competences are not the whole story. A study of US patents has shown that organisations undertake research, and develop competences, in many

---

REAL-LIFE APPLICATION 7.8

The distributed competences of large corporations

Core business of firm	Proportion of patents related to			Examples of other fields
	Core business	Machinery	Other fields	
Electrical/Electronic	66%	20%	16%	Telecoms, materials, photography, chemical applications
Chemicals	67%	16%	17%	Plastics, bleaching and dyeing, photography
Automobiles	30%	46%	24%	Metallurgy, computers, textiles, cloth and wood, semiconductors

Source: Granstrand et al. (1997).

The relative benefits of broad and narrow portfolios, and the importance of using management attention carefully, are discussed in Chapter 9. ▶

areas. Some of these, like production machinery, have an obvious link to their core business, and so represent a potential source of advantage there. However, others may be a long way away from the core, in fields where firms might logically be expected to get their specialist knowledge from subcontractors. According to Granstrand et al. (1997), the Ford Motor Company has patents not just in vehicle engineering, but in fields like instrumentation, chemical processes, semiconductors, power plants and textiles (Real-Life Application 7.8).

The same research has shown that, even as organisations have been focusing their activities on fewer *businesses*, the numbers of fields in which they undertake research and development has tended to broaden. Another study (Gambardella and Torrisi, 1998) of European and US electronics firms, has shown that high corporate performance tends to go together with a highly diversified portfolio of technologies, but a small, focused portfolio of products. This implies that, for firms to be innovative, it is important for their staff to be exposed to a wide range of influences. However, to use that innovativeness effectively, they then need to focus their attention on a narrower range of customer segments.

It is reasonable to wonder at this point how this mass of competences, capabilities and assets comes together to form a coherent source of competitive advantage. We shall come back to that point at the end of the chapter. First, however, we look at the equally important question of where competences and capabilities come from, and how organisations acquire them.

7.4 Learning and knowledge

Up to this point, this chapter has followed a very economics-driven approach to the notion of resources. They are things that an organisation has or does, and the ones that are rare, valuable and difficult to copy are important to allowing a firm to generate economic rents. It follows, logically, that an organisation should be able to develop more of these desirable attributes, or to replace the ones that might have outlived their usefulness. Once we probe how it might do this, however, we find that economic theory has little to offer us. We have to remember that organisations are collections of people, and therefore need to introduce insights from sociology and psychology.

In order to understand why this is so, think for a moment about what a competence actually *is*. It is something that *people* do. They may use machines or computers to help them – they may even programme them to carry out some parts of the routine without human intervention. Nonetheless, competences have their roots in human experience and in the regularised practices that people in an organisation develop over time.

A routine comes about because people within an organisation confront a problem. A customer may want a new feature added to a product for a special order, or the department's managers may have problems in staying within their budget. It may even be that people are bored and want a more entertaining way of passing their working hours. Through some combination of chance, inspiration and contemplation, a solution is developed. The customer's requirement is met by finding a way to reprogramme the product's electronics. The budget problem may be solved by developing a system to analyse and then cut the excess costs – or addressed in a less productive way, by developing a routine that diverts certain costs to another budget account. The boredom 'problem' is solved by inventing a computer game to pass the time.

None of these may be the best possible solution, but each of them works for a while. Over time, and as other people become involved, the routine may undergo subtle changes to deal with new circumstances. The reprogramming routine becomes the basis of a capability in new product design. The cost-cutting routine is expanded to other areas and turns into part of a cost leadership strategy. The 'time-wasting' computer game is recognised as a potential new product, and is adopted by other departments. Or the routine may be discarded as inadequate, or banned, so that new routines are introduced in its place.

What we have just described is a **learning** process, in which routines are developed and enhanced over time. If an organisation is to sustain its competitiveness, it needs to learn to serve its customers better or more efficiently. Learning also underpins an organisation's dynamic capabilities, which determine its ability to adapt to change in the environment. In this section we shall look at the theory of how organisations learn and, since the outcome of learning is knowledge, at how organisations use their knowledge assets.

7.4.1 Organisational learning

Organisations are not living things with minds of their own, although the people that write about them sometimes portray them as though they were. 'Organisations have no other brains and senses than those of their members' (Hedberg, 1981: 6). However, the concepts of a *learning organisation* or *organisational learning* are important ones in strategy theory these days, which imply a collectivity of people who *as a group* are able to learn themselves but also learn from each other. In order for this to happen individual experiences need (Nevis et al., 1995) to be translated into new, shared, work practices in a three-stage process:

1. **Knowledge acquisition** – the development or creation of skills, insights and relationships by *individuals*. People learn by making sense of their individual concrete experiences. They observe what happens to them and reflect upon it. This process may be instant and intuitive 'I told you when we launched this product that the packaging is wrong' or may involve a longer period of reflection 'I hate this type of packaging, but all the other products using it are selling fine. However, this is the first time we've tried to sell through department stores rather than pharmacies'. The upshot is some theory or

◀ We introduced the concepts of tacit and explicit knowledge in Section 1.4.

generalisation about what is going on, which can then be tested – we change the packaging, or the distribution strategy – which leads to a new experience, after which the learning process starts all over again, as people refine their knowledge further.[24]

2. **Knowledge sharing** – The fact that certain people in an organisation have learned something does not signify that the organisation has done so, so their learning needs to be shared and utilised on a wider scale. A study of photocopier engineers at work has shown how individual learning passes between members of the same work group, or *community of practice* (a concept first used in this way by Brown and Duguid (1991)). This is very much a social process, with people sharing experiences and tips, and formal documentation and procedures often ignored.

3. **Knowledge utilisation** – the integration of learning so it is broadly available and can be generalised to new situations. The outcome of this process is often a new organisational competence.

The leap from group learning to organisational learning is something that researchers do not yet fully understand.[25] One model of how it might occur comes from two Japanese researchers, Ikujiro Nonaka and Hirotaka Takeuchi (1995). They see it as a repeated four-stage process:

● People share their tacit knowledge through **socialisation**. They watch one another at work or brainstorm problems together. Socialisation can be between members of the same work group, or can come about by staff mingling with customers and watching how they use the products or services.

● People find a way of putting this tacit knowledge into words, often using some kind of striking image to help others understand it. This part of the process, which makes the tacit knowledge more widely available, is called **externalisation**.

● There is a **combination** of explicit knowledge from different sources to make something new. Data analysis may be used to combine a new production technique from one source with some market research data, to come up with a new product. Formal training can be used to make the new idea more widely available, to other people in the organisation and to customers and suppliers.

● Individuals take the new idea back to their work place and experiment with it. This process of learning by doing is called **internalisation**, and at the end of it, the newly created explicit knowledge has been supplemented with additional, tacit knowledge.

The organisation's knowledge is enhanced as these four stages are repeated in '*the spiral of knowledge creation*' (what Nonaka and Takeuchi term 'knowledge creation' is very close to what other researchers call learning). The knowledge also becomes more widely available, as successive bouts of socialisation and combination bring more people into contact with it.

An important source of knowledge and learning is the accumulated experience within organisations. Studies of many products have shown that, as production volumes accumulate over time, the labour element of production cost tends to fall. The more that organisations make of something, the better that they get at doing it. This is the basis of what has been called the 'experience curve', and has led some theorists to conclude, incorrectly, that if a firm can become market leader and stay there, it will have an insurmountable cost advantage.[26]

There are several reasons why this is not the case. Firstly, organisations learn from outside sources – from their suppliers, by copying their competitors, from trade associations and conferences – as well as from their own experience. Secondly, not all organisations learn at the same rate. A firm that is more open to outside influences may learn faster than one that has higher production volumes, but is more introverted. Thirdly, there are different types of learning. Experience is most useful for *exploitation*, or *single-loop learning*, where an organisation focuses upon refining existing competences. However, firms also need *exploration*, or *double-loop learning*, where they 'learn to learn', and to move beyond their existing knowledge, for example through innovation or radical organisational change.[27]

7.4.2 Single- and double-loop learning

◀ *The concept of paradigm was introduced in Section 1.2.5.*

At the basis of most organisations' activities is a paradigm[28] – a set of assumptions about the world, the way the organisation needs to function and what it should be achieving. McDonald's, for example, has long seen the world as full of potential hamburger buyers, believes that it is good at making and selling hamburgers, and has targets for the profits it expects to make.

Most organisations, as a matter of course, use *single-loop learning* (Loop 1 in Figure 7.1) if there is a problem, or if they simply feel that there is scope for improving a routine. For example, if McDonald's profits are out of line with expectations, they will look at their pricing, their advertising, at new products that Pizza Hut or Burger King might have launched, and see if this explains what is going on. They may experiment with lower prices or new products and, if sales recover, they will have learned how to fix that particular problem. If they do not, McDonald's may look at other parts of the way it does business, to see if the quality of its ingredients or of its customer service had somehow been allowed to deteriorate.

Figure 7.1   Single- and double-loop learning

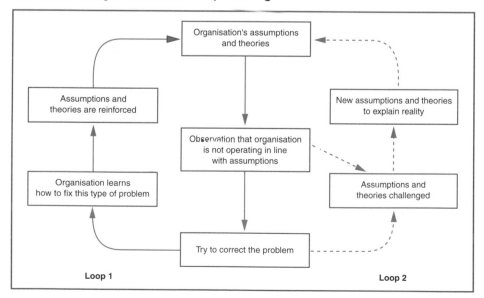

The factors that inhibit
double-loop learning are
similar to those that make
it difficult for organisations
to change (Chapter 13). ▶

All these kinds of enquiry fall within McDonald's basic assumptions that, if the burgers are good enough and served with a smile at an attractive price, then people will want them. Because assumptions like these become so deeply ingrained into organisations and the people that work for them, they can be difficult to challenge. McDonald's would take a lot of convincing that the world had fallen out of love with the hamburger, although in the 1980s it eventually took that possibility seriously enough to introduce McDonald's pizza to counter the threat from Pizza Hut. More recently, it has started to challenge the assumption that it was only good at selling fast-food, and to consider the possibility that its resources might be useful in other businesses. In 1999 it acquired Aroma, a British chain of coffee houses, and was looking for acquisitions outside its core brand.

That is an example of *double-loop learning* (Loop 2 in Figure 7.1) – someone in McDonald's has been able to challenge and change some of its deeply held assumptions and theories. Because of the psychological wrench involved, few organisations seem to be consistently capable of double-loop learning, and even fewer are able to challenge their assumptions unless confronted by an insoluble problem, or even a crisis.

It is important to strike a balance between the two types of learning. Single-loop learning is necessary to build core competences, since routines are rarely perfect the first time they are put into practice. Double-loop learning is important if an organisation is to adapt to major changes in its environment. Evidence that a firm is capable of double-loop learning is thus a useful indicator that it may have a sustainable advantage.

7.4.3 The learning organisation

All organisations appear to be capable of some degree of learning.[29] However, some appear to learn more consistently and easily than others. This has prompted some writers to identify what has been called **the learning organisation**, which is defined as:

> 'an organisation *skilled* at creating, acquiring and transferring knowledge, and at *modifying its behaviour* to reflect new knowledge and insights.'
> (Garvin, 1993: 80; our italics)

The key words highlighted in the above definition are that the organisation is **skilled** at learning – that is, it does so consistently and well – and that it **modifies its behaviour** as a result of what it has learnt. Most theorists would add that a learning organisation would show evidence of double-loop as well as single-loop learning.

Just because a firm has learnt one or two important things over a long period of time does not make it a learning organisation. Similarly, a firm that takes in lots of information, but does not change its behaviour as a result, does not qualify. Learning organisations are those that are open to information from the outside and react quickly to it. They may be innovators in their own right, such as Sony or 3M, or they may make sure that they catch up quickly with other people's innovations. They are able to recognise when they have made a mistake, and take swift action to put it right (Real-Life Application 7.9).

Many researchers (e.g. Senge, 1990; Schein, 1993; Nevis et al., 1995; Argyris and

---

REAL-LIFE APPLICATION 7.9

Microsoft – a learning organisation?

Although Microsoft, the US software giant, is a firm many people like to hate, it has many of the features of a learning organisation. It has a hunger for information from all sources. This sometimes creates controversy, as when it built features into its Windows 98 operating system to help it track how people were using the software. Users reacted strongly against what they saw as an invasion of privacy.

One of the most impressive aspects of Microsoft is its ability to recover from its mistakes. It built a number of features into its Office 97 suite of applications to try to help inexperienced users, but has taken them out of the successor product, Office 2000, because users found them bothersome. In 1994 it underestimated the importance of the World Wide Web, and tried to set up

its own proprietary computer network, MSN. However, once it realised its error, it redirected its resources. It reconfigured MSN to use the World Wide Web, and within a year had launched its own browser software, Explorer, to compete with the market leader Netscape. Although Netscape had a two-year head start, most experts now reckon that Explorer is as good or better.

The need to compete fiercely is deeply embedded in Microsoft's culture. This has led it to be prosecuted by the US anti-trust authorities for abuse of monopoly power, and the initial judgement had, at the time of writing, gone against it. The stiffest test of Microsoft as a learning organisation will be whether it is able to learn from this, and to change its behaviour as a result.

Schön, 1978; Garvin, 1993) have tried to identify what it is that makes an effective learning organisation. Their most important conclusions are that, in learning organisations:

- Top managers are committed to the learning process and set an example by becoming 'star learners'.
- People have a strong understanding of the assumptions they make about their organisation and the world in which it operates.
- The culture encourages openness, so that people own up to not performing as well as they might and experiment to find new solutions.
- There is systematic use of quantitative measurement and logical tools for analysing and solving problems and monitoring the results of actions taken.[30]
- The organisation already has some prior knowledge in fields related to those where it is trying to learn, and people routinely take part in research and learning activities, even though it may be in other areas. Both these factors are important in boosting the organisation's **absorptive capacity** (Cohen and Levinthal, 1990) – its ability to absorb information, recognise when it has found something important, and make practical use of it.

Practical dos and don'ts   **The learning organisation**

1. True learning organisations are very uncommon. Be *extremely* careful before concluding that you have discovered one!

2. Top management commitment, an open culture and so on are helpful if you want to try to create a learning organisation – but they do not guarantee that you will get one. Look for outcomes – evidence of sustained, effective learning – rather than inputs.

7.4.4 So ... what can go wrong? The paradoxes of organisational learning

Organisational learning is currently a very fashionable topic, and from its more passionate advocates it is easy to get the impression that no organisation can learn too much, or too fast. However, there are a number of traps into which organisations can fall (see Levitt and March, 1998; Levinthal and March, 1993).

◀ *This is another form of the Icarus paradox we met in Chapter 3.*

- **Too much single-loop learning.** Some single-loop learning is essential. There is a danger, however, that if an organisation gets too good at it, it will cease to see the need for double-loop learning, which offers less certain returns. This can make the organisation vulnerable to long-term environmental change.

- **Too much double-loop learning.** Sometimes organisations are so intent upon innovation and change that they neglect the basics of running an efficient business. This can be a particular problem where an organisation is locked into a cycle of failure, and tries ever riskier ways of getting out of it.

- **Learning too fast.** This is the organisational equivalent of a person's jumping to conclusions, and can happen if everyone in an organisation has a very similar mindset. According to James March (1991), simulation exercises show that organisations that take their time learning arrive at a better understanding of their environment than those that learn faster. A creative tension between people who want to move forward quickly and those who want to preserve the old values can actually help an organisation to learn more effectively.

- **Misinterpreting success or failure.** Sometimes an organisation can be misled by good results into thinking it has strong capabilities, when it may just have benefited from, say, an economic boom. This leads it to use its assets to develop those capabilities further, when in fact they are not sources of enduring strength (Real-Life Application 7.10). Failure can be equally misleading – sometimes an organisation strives desperately for a solution, when in fact it has just been unlucky, or has set itself unrealistic goals. This kind of misreading of success or failure is called *superstitious learning*.

7.4.5 Knowledge and intellectual capital

The raw material of learning is knowledge, and since 1995, the way in which

---

REAL-LIFE APPLICATION 7.10

Superstitious and genuine learning in the UK water industry

When the UK water companies were privatised in the 1980s, many of them felt that their high profits showed that they had strong management skills. Some tried to capitalise on this 'strength' by diversifying into other businesses, such as plumbing services, and lost a lot of money thereby. Their initial 'success' was in large part due to the regime under which they were privatised. They were given a local monopoly, allowed to charge generous prices and not forced to upgrade their infra-structure as quickly as many observers thought they should.

Many of the companies were eventually taken over by foreign water firms, such as France's Lyonnaise des Eaux and Vivendi, which had long-standing experience in running a commercial operation. Others, such as Thames Water, have built successful new businesses in areas where they had genuine expertise, running water supply operations in developing countries.

organisations create and manage it has become one of the most fashionable management topics. A 1998 article in *Fortune* (Stewart, 1998) hailed it as 'The Next Big Idea', and pointed out that most large companies now have a chief knowledge or learning officer.

This is partly because academics and practising managers came to recognise how knowledge, in particular tacit knowledge, underpinned organisational capabilities. Another stimulus came from researchers, managers and accountants in Sweden, who recognised that the physical assets that feature on firms' balance sheets account for a very low proportion of the true value of firms, as measured by their stockmarket valuations and the prices that acquirers would pay for them. To take an extreme example, corporations that acquired US software firms between 1981 and 1993 typically paid nine times their book value.[31]

Led by Skandia, a major Swedish insurer, firms in Europe have begun to value their 'intellectual capital' and to feature it in supplements to their annual reports. The precise framework that they use varies, but typically **intellectual capital** is defined as the difference between a firm's net assets, according to its accounts, and its market value. It is subdivided into three categories: **human capital** – the skills of individuals and groups; **structural capital** – the value that resides in the company's systems and intellectual property; and **customer capital** – the value of relationships with suppliers, customers and allies.

The method for calculating the value of intellectual capital is beyond the scope of this book.[32] Intellectual capital is a broader concept than intellectual resources or knowledge, since it includes human resources and reputational assets. Nor is it entirely new – it overlaps with the concept of goodwill, which has been included on firms' balance sheets for many years. However, the publicity given to intellectual capital has helped to give knowledge management a prominent place on the business agenda.

Measuring something is only one step towards managing it. Organisations typically have a lot of knowledge scattered around in a variety of databases, in people's heads and in their filing cabinets (Real-Life Application 7.11). The aim of knowledge management is to make it more widely available, so that it can be used in the learning processes discussed in Section 7.4.1. Theorists and practising managers have come up with a number of ideas about how to manage their firms' knowledge, which can be placed in three categories:[33]

- **Create knowledge repositories.** Firms can set up central libraries and databases containing scientific and market research reports, copies of marketing materials and technical and sales manuals. The aim is to prevent people from needlessly having to rediscover or reinvent something that already exists. Some firms, including most major management consultancies, have set up 'discussion databases', often using 'groupware' software. After a major project, staff summarise the lessons they have learned and put it on the database for the benefit of anyone who might need to do a similar job.

- **Improve knowledge access.** One way of giving people better access to knowledge is by having a readily accessible directory that sets out who knows what in the organisation. British Petroleum/Amoco (BP), the world's third largest oil company, and Bain and McKinsey, two of the world's most prestigious and successful management consultancies, have all established 'Yellow Pages'-style directories to help their staff locate employees with the right expertise. No less

Knowledge management at Hewlett Packard and Royal Dutch/Shell

At HP [Hewlett Packard, the world's second-largest computer manufacturer] a large, successful project called 'Electronic Sales Partner' provided technical product information, sales presentations, sales and marketing tactics, customer/account information, and anything else that might have benefitted field personnel in the sales process. The leaders of this project . . . tried to add value to the repository through careful categorisations and pruning. Calling it the 'most successful implementation of software I have seen in twenty years,' the manager of the sales support area reported 'phenomenal feedback from both submitters [of knowledge] and users' . . .

In HP's corporate education division . . . a knowledge project was capturing tips, tricks, insights and experiences into a Lotus Notes database and making them available to some 2,000 trainers and educators scattered throughout the corporation's many sites.'

Source: Davenport et al. (1998: 45)

At Royal Dutch/Shell [an Anglo-Dutch firm, the world's second largest oil corporation] . . . one business problem is that people who need to pick each other's brains – instrumentation engineers, say – may be perched on separate oil rigs worlds apart. To connect them, Shell has funded nearly 150 communities of practice, supported by websites, editorial help and facilitation. Each expertise network – which includes E-mail, chat rooms and a library of best practices produced and warranted by members – costs between $500,000 and $1 million to set up . . . so nothing gets funded unless network sponsors put up a business case; for example, engineers in Shell's polypropylenes business have promised that by sharing tips and best practices globally, they can get rid of $16 million of machine downtime.

Source: Fortune, 21 December 1998, p. 83

important is the communications infrastructure that enables people to communicate. For a large, international organisation, this might include e-mail chat rooms, intranets and video-conferencing facilities. BP has invested heavily in these, and encourages any employee to set up a home page on the intranet.

- **Enhance the knowledge environment.** Busy consultants and sales staff will not always welcome sitting down at the end of a hard day to type their experiences into a database. Organisations can try and give them incentives to share knowledge, and to use knowledge from elsewhere. Quite often, knowledge sharing is underpinned by strong cultural norms. At McKinsey, the norm is that consultants will respond quickly to queries from colleagues. An Australian consultant could leave voice-mail messages for colleagues in the USA or Europe at the end of a working day, and confidently expect to have most of their replies the following morning.

The way in which an organisation manages its knowledge needs to take account of the kind of problems that it faces. A firm that confronts similar problems all the time, like a McDonald's or an information systems consultancy, should consider a 'codification' strategy. This would involve having staff document their knowledge and experience, and investing heavily in IT systems to make the documents available to others. For an organisation that never encounters quite the same problem twice, like McKinsey or Sony's product designers, that kind of investment would probably be wasteful. They might be better off following a 'personalisation' strategy (Hansen et al., 1999) which involves bringing people together as needed to discuss problems and exchange experiences.

7.5 Analysing competitive advantage

A large number of concepts have been thrown at you in the course of this chapter: strategic and threshold resources and assets, distinctive capabilities, core competences, learning, knowledge and intellectual capital. These are the nuts and bolts of competitive advantage. In this section, we show you how you can use these concepts to arrive at an understanding of where an organisation's competitive advantage comes from, and how sustainable it is.

7.5.1 Assets, capabilities, competences and competitive advantage

Let us begin with a company that is just taking its first steps along the road to success. It is a small organisation, consisting of the founder, a few close friends or colleagues and maybe one or two other people. They have a new idea for providing money-saving advice to firms. The company has just found its first customers, people whom the founder and his friends got to know in their previous jobs and who trust them enough to give their new ideas a try. What is the nature of this firm's competitive advantage?

- They have assets: a moderate amount of start-up capital, the human resources in the firm, their personal reputations and their knowledge. Of those, the reputation and the actual product idea are distinctive.

- They have some basic competences in the technology of their product – enough to make their advice service work adequately well. They may experience a few problems from time to time, but the customers will be understanding, as long as the basic product, and its price, are good enough.

- This know-how plus the basic competences give them the capability of delivering the product. They have worked out which questions to ask to which people in an organisation, which costs to focus on and so on. Because they are first in the field, this capability is rare, and therefore distinctive.

Figure 7.2   Initial competitive advantage in a young firm

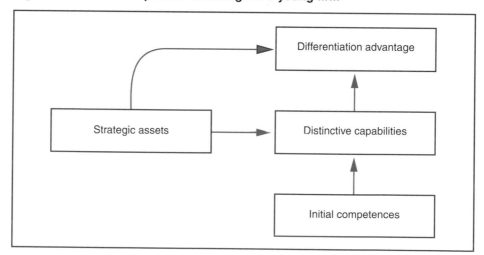

- This distinctive capability, plus the founders' reputations, plus the basic distinctiveness of the product, together add up to a differentiation advantage. This happy picture is shown in Figure 7.2.

Now let's roll the scene forward about two years. More clients have come on board as word has spread about the power of the new company's money-saving methodology. The firm has had to take on more staff, and find ways of training them to run jobs by themselves, since the founders find themselves spending more time preparing proposals and making presentations to new clients, and less in supervising projects. In order to do this, they have had to document their procedures and pool their ideas on how to deliver advice effectively. This has had the welcome side-effect of improving the consistency of the work that they do. There are fewer mistakes, fewer complaints and fewer cost overruns. Some of these new consultants have good computer skills and have come up with small pieces of software to help analyse clients' energy usage and to assist in costing projects.

Of course, this success has not gone unnoticed. Some one-man consultancies have started offering copycat services at lower prices, while the founder's former employers have come out with a directly competing product. Nonetheless, the firm still finds that it is winning an increasing proportion of the jobs that it pitches for, partly because the original partners have developed a shrewd idea of what kind of cost-saving opportunities will appeal to different types of client, and are organising their presentations accordingly.

Naturally, the firm still has problems. Although it has a solid record of winning work from small and medium-sized clients, it invariably loses when it competes with the largest, most prestigious consultancies for work with multinational firms, even though the larger firms' methodology is less innovative and less effective. One of the founding group has left, complaining that the firm has become too big and that the atmosphere 'is not the way it was when we started, and everyone shared everything'.

What is the nature of the firm's competitive advantage at this stage (Figure 7.3)?

- Their earlier success in differentiating themselves has given them a stronger set of assets. They have more money in the bank than their smaller competitors, though less than the largest consultancies. Their reputation is strong enough to count as a strategic asset when competing with small and medium-sized competitors, though it is not as strong as that of the largest, longest-established ones. Experience has given them some proprietary knowledge, part of it in the heads of consultants who have developed a 'feel' for where to look for cost savings, part of it written down for the training manual and in the software.

- There is evidence of continued single-loop learning in all areas of the business. However, there is no real evidence of double-loop learning – their basic strategy and outlook has remained unchanged.

- The learning has generated new competences. Their original technological skill in locating cost savings for customers has been honed to the point where it is genuinely rare, and so counts as a core competence. They have also enhanced their competences in the technology of marketing and customer psychology, and have new ones in information technology. They have also gained a control competence, in the project management area.

Figure 7.3   Competitive advantage in an established firm

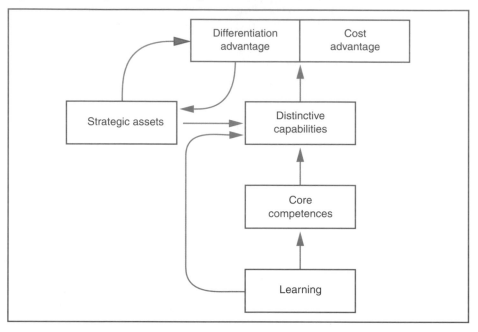

- As a result they have a distinctive capability in reliability – they are getting the work done professionally and on time. This goes together with a distinctive capability in negotiation – specifying and selling the work to client's satisfaction – that gives them both differentiation advantage when compared with smaller rivals, and cost advantage. Their reputation, together with the basic distinctiveness of their product, are other sources of differentiation advantage compared with smaller rivals.

- There are other types of capability that they do **not** possess. Though they have developed enhancements to the basic product, this falls short of a capability in innovation. If they were to develop their software into stand-alone products, or find a way of making their services available over the Internet, then they might seriously be thought of as innovative. They have shown no particular capabilities in communication – their marketing is largely by word of mouth. There is no evidence that they are any more responsive to customer requirements, or quicker to respond to them, than their competitors – they are largely exploiting the same market niche they spotted two years previously. And perhaps they are weak in risk management – they are still spending time and money pitching for work for multinational clients, even though they might be hard-pressed to carry it out if they won a contract, as they lack competences in languages and multi-cultural management.

Apart from showing how the different elements fit together, this little example, fictional but by no means unrealistic, illustrates two important points:

- **Very few firms, however successful they may seem, are good at everything.** The firm in the example had distinctive capabilities in reliability and negotiation. They had threshold capabilities in the other areas, which may well be all that they required to stay competitive.

- **The strength of a resource depends on the market and industry segment where you are using it.** The firm's reputation and negotiation skills would count as strategic resources when being marketed to small and medium-sized clients, since the competitors are small firms that lack those resources. In the multinational market segment, they are not strategic because they are not rare. Most of the competitors will have stronger reputations and negotiating skills that are as good or better. In that same segment, the firm's capability in reliability may still be distinctive, but it is not valuable – clients place more value upon reputation, and on other skills, like those needed to manage multinational projects.

7.5.2 Dynamic capabilities and sustainable competitive advantage

Section 7.5.1 shows how to analyse how organisations have arrived at a position of advantage in the *past*, and how their resources contribute to their cost and differentiation position in the *present*. How does this need to be adapted to judge whether the organisation's advantage is sustainable for the *future*?

This kind of judgement requires a view on how the environment is likely to change. In our example in Section 7.5.1, the firm was confronting increased competition from small competitors and one larger rival, the founder's former employer. To this we would want to add data on PEST factors. As well as evaluating what is likely to happen to demand for the firm's products or services, we would then look to assess how valuable and rare the firm's resources are likely to be.

Some strategic assets, as we have already said, retain their value well even if the environment changes. Factors like a strong reputation, access to low cost inputs and extremely large financial reserves are likely to help to sustain a firm's advantage, no matter what happens to the environment.

There are some tougher judgements to be made about a firm's other resources. We need to judge whether they will become more or less rare, valuable or difficult to copy as the environment changes. Sometimes, a firm's resources can be devalued by environmental change (Real-Life Application 7.12).

The third judgement we need to take relates to the organisation's *dynamic capabilities* – its capacity to learn, adapt and innovate in the face of environmental change. Here we would look for evidence of three things:

- **Learning.** Sustained single-loop learning demonstrates at least that a firm has the capacity to move forward. However, if the environment seems likely to

---

REAL-LIFE APPLICATION 7.12

Environmental change that destroys the value of strategic resources

In the 1980s, one of the authors consulted briefly for a UK engineering firm that produced the turbine blades for large generators. These blades, several metres in diameter, would eventually find their way into power stations. The firm had developed, over several decades, the capability needed to machine these massive pieces of metal reliably to the very fine toler-ances needed for these applications. It was one of a few firms in the world with that capability, and was highly regarded. However, with the invention of computer-numerically-controlled machine tools that capability ceased to be difficult to imitate. Anyone with sufficient money to buy the right equipment could do the job as well, if not better.

change radically, then double-loop learning – the ability to conceive substantial shifts in strategy – would be important, and we would look for evidence of that.

- **Competences in detecting and assessing environmental change**, since this gives the organisation the data from which to learn constructively.
- **Capabilities in innovation**, which demonstrate that the organisation can use its learning to good effect.

7.5.3 Culture and architecture

It is possible to push this analysis deeper still, by asking why certain organisations seem able to learn and to develop their assets into capabilities, while others cannot. In order to answer this question, we have to think again about what capabilities and competences are.

A capability comes down to a group of people using an organisation's resources to do something unusual, and probably difficult. They need the right resources at their disposal, and the right information about what to do with them. And, not least, they need the motivation to do things properly, to develop the capability and then use it to its full potential.

If we look underneath capabilities at competences and learning, we see the same combination of information and motivation at work. All the types of competence we have discussed – technological, control, detecting and assessing environmental change, and managing transitions – require access to good information, and the motivation to make effective use of it. Learning, as we have seen, is a social process. The organisation also needs to provide the motivation and the means – meetings, or information systems – for people to communicate.

◄ *The concepts of corporate culture and architecture were defined in Sections 1.2.6 and 1.3.3.*

Motivation arises from a firm's culture and from its architecture, which also shapes the way that information flows into and around an organisation. This is why theorists have found links between culture and architecture, on the one hand and competitive advantage on the other.[34] This theory is supported by the findings of experience of managers trying to value a firm's intellectual capital. They find that in most established businesses, the structural capital (essentially, culture and architecture) is more valuable than the human capital (Edvinsson, 1997: 370). Most writers on the learning organisation and knowledge management also emphasise the importance of an appropriate culture.

We return to this point when we look at how to analyse culture and architecture in Chapter 8.

7.5.4 Paradoxes and trade-offs in resource creation

Like any other commitment made by a firm, the development of strategic resources has an opportunity cost. The investment of time and assets in developing competences and capabilities, in particular, carries with it the risk that the organisation will be caught in a *competency trap*. Once managers recognise that a particular competence or capability is strategically important, they will be tempted to invest in refining it. The organisation will want to keep its head start over competition, and may see that they will get a better return on investment in existing resources than in newer, riskier ones. This is an example of a strategy that seems rational in the

---

REAL-LIFE APPLICATION 7.13

Core rigidity at Novotel

Novotel, the international hotel chain, was founded by two French entrepreneurs in 1967. Its steady expansion during the 1970s and 1980s owed much to distinctive capabilities in reliability. It developed a standard fomat for hotel room designs, for furnishing and for standards of service that enabled it to offer business travellers, in particular, a uniform standard of comfort throughout Europe and, later, the world. This capability was backed up with competences in control that enabled the firm to make sure standards were maintained.

In 1987, Novotel began to extend the use of this competence in control. It developed a rigid set of rules and procedures, the '95 Bolts' that governed every aspect of the operation of their hotels in minute detail. For example, the words used to greet guests were standardised world wide.

Even though it made the guests' experience even more reliably uniform, this strategy was not a success. The new systems made it difficult for staff to show per-sonal warmth towards their guests and react spontaneously to their requirements, making Novotel seem less hospitable. New competitors appeared, but Novotel's procedures prevented managers from matching their prices or from offering priority to regular guests. The hotels started losing business, and Novotel recorded a sharp decline in profits.

By basing its entire strategy around its competence in control, Novotel transformed that core competence into a core rigidity. In 1992, and after widespread consultation within Novotel, a new management team scrapped the 95 Bolts system and adopted a new strategy, which improved hotel occupancy rates and financial results. Hotel general managers were given greater autonomy to respond to guests' needs and competitors' moves. New systems and structures were put in place to help hotel managers to learn from one another – for example, an interest group was set up where managers of all airport hotels could share their experiences.

---

short term, but may turn out badly in the longer term since, generally speaking, organisations need a spread of competences in order to be successful.

If economic reasons may tempt an organisation to over-invest in their competences, socio-cultural factors may tempt it to over-use them. When a group of people has a routine that has worked well, they will tend to use it again. They may not stop to look at subtle differences between the way it has operated in the past and the way they want to use it now. However, even small differences in the technology that is being used or the target market that is being addressed may call for a different way of working (Real-Life Application 7.13). Dorothy Leonard-Barton (1992) coined the term **core rigidity** for a routine like this that somehow 'takes over' the organisation.

In order to sustain its advantage, an organisation has to balance two conflicting priorities. It must make sure that its core competences and distinctive capabilities are kept up-to-date and efficient. However, it must also make sure that attention is not focused upon them to the extent that they squeeze out innovation and learning in other areas.

7.6   Summary

- Strategic resources are:
  - rare – only a few firms in the industry have them
  - valuable, making a genuine difference to a firm's cost and/or differentiation advantage, and corresponding to success factors within the industry

- difficult to acquire or copy, because they are in genuinely short supply, because they have a high tacit knowledge content or because the way they have developed over time makes them impossible to copy
- difficult to substitute with other resources.

● Threshold resources are needed for a firm to survive in the industry, but do not meet the criteria to be considered strategic resources.

● Physical and financial assets are not usually rare enough or difficult enough to copy to be considered strategic. Human, intellectual and reputational assets are more often difficult to imitate, and so can be the source of advantage.

● A firm's competitiveness depends on different types of resources.
  - *Assets* are things like patents, human resources and reputation that a firm accumulates over time, often through effective use of its capabilities.
  - *Capabilities* are things that a firm is able to do with its assets that make a genuine difference to its cost or differentiation advantage. Examples of types of capability are:
    ● product or process innovation
    ● reliability
    ● sensitivity to customer requirements
    ● speed of reaction
    ● communication
    ● negotiation
    ● risk management.
  - *Competences* are deeper understandings or routines that a firm acquires over time. Firms may have threshold competences in a variety of areas, together with a few core competences that are rare, valuable to the core business and difficult to emulate. Types of competences include
    ● the command of technologies in areas such as science, IT or consumer psychology
    ● the ability to control operations and projects
    ● the ability to detect and assess environmental change
    ● the ability to manage transitions effectively.

● The ability to learn is essential for the development of competences and capabilities. Most organisations learn to some extent, but some learning organisations do so more consistently and effectively than others. They are also capable of double-loop learning, which enables an organisation to challenge its deeply held assumptions, and make radical shifts in strategy. Many organisations are only capable of single-loop learning, which enables them to refine existing competences.

● Some organisations have been able to improve their ability to learn by improving the way in which they manage their knowledge.

● An organisation's culture and architecture are important to the way in which it uses its existing capabilities and creates new ones.

● An organisation's competitive position at any given point in time depends on its having assets and capabilities that generate cost and/or differentiation advantage. Resources that are valuable in one industry or market segment may not be valuable in another.

● Whether or not an organisation has a sustainable advantage depends on whether it has assets and capabilities that will remain valuable as the environment changes, and on its dynamic capabilities – its capacity to learn, to detect and assess environmental change, and to innovate.

Finally we need to re-emphasise that strategic resources are rare. Few organisations have more than two or three. Hardly any organisation has strategic resources in every one of the categories listed in this chapter. If you come up with a long list of strategic resources, it means you have not been rigorous enough in deciding what is rare, valuable and difficult to acquire or copy. Go back and do the analysis again!

Typical questions

We conclude this chapter with a look at some of the questions that you may be asked that relate to strategic resources, and how you can use the theory in this chapter to answer them.

1. *What was the source of the organisation's competitive advantage?*

You would be advised to start with an assessment of the organisation's environment for the relevant point in time, to determine what the success and survival factors were, using the techniques outlined in Chapter 5. You might also want to use the theory in Chapter 6 to analyse the organisation's choice of market segments and the competitors it was facing in them. The analytical techniques described in Chapter 4 will help you to assess the strength of the organisation's advantage, and give you some clues about the areas where its resources are strong or weak.

Then you might look at the organisation's cost and differentiation advantage, seeing in what way it was due to the particular products it was offering, and to what extent it came from particular strategic assets or capabilities. The material in Sections 7.2 and 7.3 may be of help. You may also look further to see if the organisation has demonstrated the ability to learn, and whether there are any features of its culture and architecture that support its capabilities.

(An analysis of a business' value chain (Chapter 8) is a useful way of bringing these factors together, if you feel like reading ahead.)

2. *Does the organisation have a sustainable competitive advantage?*

This is a development of the previous question. Use the processes described above to analyse the source of the organisation's competitive advantage at present. Then use the theory described in Chapter 5 to assess how the environment is likely to change, and in particular whether technology and customer needs are likely to change as a result.

You can then assess the effect that this environmental change is likely to have on the organisation's cost and differentiation advantage, and on the capabilities and assets that support it. You may also want to look at the detail of the organisation's competences, to see if they will be affected by the change in the environment. You would also be advised to assess the organisation's dynamic capabilities (Section 7.5.2) to determine if the organisation has shown the capacity to adapt.

You would want to be on the look-out for signs of internal strains – conflict and staff turnover – within the organisation, and for indications that profitability or customer satisfaction were declining.

Questions for discussion

1. Take an organisation you know well (perhaps the university or business school where you study). What is the basis of its competitive advantage? Is that advantage sustainable?

2. Do McDonald's human resources constitute a strategic asset? Why (or why not)?

3. What might an organisation do to avoid:
   ● Competency traps and core rigidities?
   ● Superstitious learning?

4. In Table 7.2 on page 218, the final line relates to 'unexplained factors' – the part of the variance in firms' profits that is not accounted for by any of the factors in McGahan and Porter's statistical model. What kinds of influence might account for these unexplained factors?

A rescue at sea in South Korea

Management Brief © *The Economist*, London 1994.

Admiral Yi Sun Sin was a fearsome character. When Japan invaded Korea in 1592, he built what were probably the world's first iron-clads. These so-called 'turtle ships' sank more than 500 Japanese vessels in less than six months.

In 1993 South Korea clocked up another ship-building triumph: it overtook Japan to win the largest share of the world's orders. At the heart of this achievement is the once notorious Okpo ship-yard, which the government more or less forced the giant Daewoo group to take over two decades ago. Even six years ago, the yard looked as if it might have to be closed. Daewoo has instead turned it into one of the world's most efficient shipbuilders.

The turnaround says much about the resilience of South Korean businesses, and about their ability to rethink their basic assumptions about management. A decade ago, the shipyard was synonymous with management-by-bullying, characterised by strikes, riots and police brutality. Today, it is a model of management-by-consensus.

Daewoo produced this change partly by borrowing techniques from business-school textbooks. Thus downsizing, empowerment and delayering all featured heavily in the rescue. But it also emphasised Confucian ideals, such as self-discipline, family spirit and social harmony. The blend might be called corporate paternalism with Korean characteristics.

Picking losers

Daewoo is one of a group of vast conglomerates known as chaebols, which include firms such as Hyundai, Samsung and Lucky-Goldstar. They all compete in most areas of business, and dominate more than half the country's economy. Daewoo now has 100,000 employees around the world and group sales last year of $34 billion, making it one of Asia's biggest firms.

Its roots, however, are surprisingly recent. Daewoo was founded in 1967 by Kim Woo Choong with three associates, a typist and $18,000 of capital. It started in the rag trade, but its activities now range from construction to financial services, electronics, domestic goods, heavy machinery and car making.

Mr Kim, now a 57-year-old workaholic, found himself in shipbuilding in 1978, when the government twisted his arm to take over a near-bankrupt project to build a giant shipyard at Okpo, on Koje island near the southern port of Pusan. 'I did not have a chance to say no', says Mr Kim. Indeed, the government simply announced the move when he was out of the country.

At that time the yard – which had been due to open in 1975 – was only 30% complete. It had an ideal location, a natural harbour surrounded by mountains, and it would possess the world's biggest dry dock. But the ambitious project had been planned before the 1973 oil shock set the scene for a global shipping recession.

Liquidating the shipyard – which is what most Western businesses might have done in the circumstances – was not an option open to Daewoo, not least because the company would have lost face amongst its peers. Instead Mr Kim was able to obtain a guarantee that the government would provide some work for the yard, mainly in the shape of big industrial projects, such as parts for power stations (which could be assembled in the dry dock and floated to wherever they were needed).

Then came two setbacks. First, in 1979, Park Chung Hee, the country's president, was assassinated, ushering in a period of turmoil and martial law. Then, in the year following the completion of Okpo's dry dock in 1981, another slump in shipping halved the price of vessels.

After roaming the world in a hopeless search for orders, Mr Kim changed tactics. He clinched a deal with a Norwegian shipping company to build a stainless-steel chemical tanker at no profit. The Norwegians even reserved the right to refuse to take delivery of the ship. This order provided a showcase project, a complex vessel that would demonstrate

CASE STUDY *continued*

Okpo's technical capabilities. The ship won awards and more orders followed.

Daewoo Shipbuilding and Heavy Machinery (DSHM), as the yard was then called, finally had some revenue coming in. Then, flushed by success, Mr Kim made a mistake. Betting on a quick recovery in the shipping market, he allowed DSHM to grow rapidly. The workforce increased from 8,600 in 1981 to 31,480 by 1984. The justification for this optimism was a 1982 order for 12 vast container ships, worth a total of $570 million, from US Lines.

But the shipping recession dragged on. Worse, within months of taking delivery of the last of its ships in 1986, US Lines went bankrupt. DSHM was unable to collect about $150 million in payments, and reimbursement through export insurance was delayed for years. As the shipyard's losses mounted, trade unions came on the scene, thanks to the abolition of old, coercive labour laws as South Korea became more democratic. South Korean businessmen could no longer rely on a cheap, compliant labour force.

By the late 1980s DSHM was at a standstill, close to total collapse. The shipyard workers and their families had been traumatised by a series of brutal strikes and clashes with riot police, in which scores of people had been injured and some killed. The crisis began to threaten other Daewoo companies, which had been subsidising the shipyard.

Even then, Mr Kim now says, he could not have contemplated liquidation. Although he talks about the local social problems such a move would have caused, his biggest fear was clearly that the shipyard had the Daewoo name attached to it. And the last thing a person should lose, says Mr Kim, is his reputation.

In November 1988 he worked out a rescue package with the government. The state-owned Korea Development Bank, which had retained a stake in the shipyard, agreed to extend the repayment time for existing loans of 250 billion won ($359 million) and provide new loans of 150 billion won. For its part, Daewoo agreed to invest 400 billion won.

To do so, Daewoo undertook to sell some shares and property. Mr Kim himself raised 142 billion won by selling his personal shareholdings in a sub-

sidiary, Daewoo Securities. Together, Daewoo and Mr Kim ended up pumping 775 billion won in cash and materials into DSHM between 1989 and 1992.

It was a huge risk. Had it failed, says Mr Kim, he had an escape route planned. With Okpo's mild climate, huge dry dock and workers' quarters, the shipyard could have been converted into a huge water-based theme park. This story is told with a smile, but Mr Kim is probably not joking.

Moving into the office

Mr Kim also decided to introduce a new approach to management, one which rested on co-operation and consensus rather than conflict and coercion. To dramatise his decision, he cleared his desk in Seoul and went to live at the shipyard. He spent 18 months there, accompanied by Kim Tae Gou, a member of his corporate headquarters staff who is now president of Daewoo Motors.

Moving to Okpo sent a strong message to the workforce: that even the most senior members of management were committed to doing everything they could to save the shipyard. This went beyond bosses simply putting on the same uniform as their workers and eating with them in the same cafeteria.

Wave of the future: global tanker replacement demand (m gross tonnes, forecast)

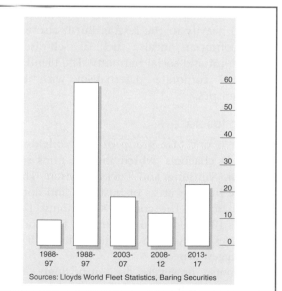

Sources: Lloyds World Fleet Statistics, Baring Securities

Mr Kim mingled with his workers daily to hear their grievances. He visited them at home, usually for breakfast.

There followed a period of intensive training, the aim of which was to teach the workforce not how to build ships (they already knew how to do that) but to get on with one another and to heal the wounds between management and unions. 'Family training' courses were offered to develop a sense of community. Cultural classes were organised for wives. Entire families were sent on trips around the country.

Technical training was introduced only when the workforce had been organised into small groups of about 12. Workers and managers visited other Daewoo companies and travelled abroad to see the most efficient Japanese firms. The object was for the workers themselves to assess how good their skills were, and come up with improvements.

One benefit of the small groups, says David Upton of the Harvard Business School, was that the members (both managers and staff) learnt to know one another well – and began to trust each other. The groups produced a new way of working, based on devolved power instead of centralised command.

Home and dry

As is often the case in such revolutions, these changes were individually small but their cumulative effect was large. In 1989 the semi-automatic welding machines at the shipyard each required one operator. Within three years, six machines were being operated by one man, and now eight are. Instead of gawping at the machines, the operators have found better things to do with their time.

Daewoo also reorganised its production process around what is both its chief advantage and its biggest bottleneck: the giant dry dock, which has to be flooded so that completed ships can be floated out. The dock, which measures 530 metres (580 yards) by 131 metres, allows Daewoo to build five large ships at the same time, but it is unlikely that all the ships will be ready to float simultaneously. To balance the workflow, the firm now concentrates on reducing the time each ship needs to spend in the dock.

This entailed a change in the conventional techniques of shipbuilding. Instead of laying down a keel in the dry dock and building the ship up, Okpo builds sections of ships outside the dry dock, and then lifts them by crane into the dry dock to be welded together – a process rather like building a ship out of Lego. This requires great accuracy as the sections must fit together exactly, but less labour because it is easier to assemble the blocks outside the dock.

As the dry dock at Okpo is spanned by a monster crane that is able to lift 900 tonnes (more than the cranes at rival shipyards can), DSHM is able to pre-assemble larger sections of ships. It also divides the pre-assembly work into specialist areas (one making bow sections, another middle sections, a third sterns). Whereas other shipyards might build, say, a supertanker from about 120 blocks, DSHM can construct the same vessel from about 80 'super-blocks', some the size of an office building.

The reorganisation, dubbed the 'new shipbuilding system', resulted in some 85% of the ship being built in pre-assembly areas, compared with about half before. The effect on lead-times was striking. In 1989 it took 15 months (not counting strikes) to build a supertanker; today it takes only eight months. By 1991, DSHM had begun to turn the corner. In 1993 it won the largest number of new orders of any shipyard in the world: 54 vessels worth a total of $2.8 billion.

Park Dong Kyu, the shipyard's general manager, says that total production has increased 2.4 times since 1989 and quality is far better. Such numbers are difficult to quantify, but one customer says that, although DSHM is not particularly cheap, he is prepared to pay more for its reliability and quality, which he considered well up to Japanese standards.

DSHM has tried to spread its expertise across a range of products. It is a specialist in building supertankers, particularly those with double hulls to prevent spills. It also makes other bulk carriers, oil platforms and even submarines for tourists.

Another sign of DSHM's transformation could be seen in the country's annual wage negotiations. The shipbuilding division of the giant Hyundai group, the biggest shipbuilder in South Korea

CASE STUDY *continued*

Bobbing back: Daewoo Shipbuilding and Heavy Machinery.

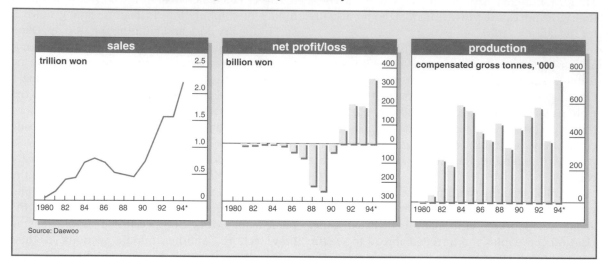

Source: Daewoo

(Daewoo is now second), was crippled by a long strike this year. In June a general strike was called at DSHM too, but it fizzled out within 24 hours when most of the workers, having talked with management, ignored it.

Since its peak, the workforce has shrunk to about 11,000. That was achieved by not replacing people who left and by absorbing workers into other Daewoo group firms, especially the car-making business, which has been revving up for a big expansion, and on which Mr Kim now spends most of his time.

Learning how to learn

Can Okpo keep up the pace? This year, a spurt by Japan's hungry shipbuilders may recapture the international lead temporarily. The Okpo yard will also have to watch the low-price competition from shipyards in China and Eastern Europe. And there is the recurrent problem of the meddlesome South Korean government.

One of the conditions that arose from the government's rescue deal back in 1988 was an undertaking that DSHM would merge with publicly traded Daewoo Heavy Industries. This took place in October this year. Yune Won Seok, president of Daewoo Heavy Industries, says that shipyard products will now account for about 40% of the combined group's sales. The government's idea was

that, come another shipbuilding slump, the Okpo yard could be supported by other divisions.

The managers at the shipyard do not think that will happen. They have a backlog of orders representing three years' work. Vessels built before the shipping recession are also getting older and will soon need replacing. New regulations are demanding safer ships, while technological advances, such as computerised controls, are bringing down costs.

However, Okpo's best defence against the cyclical nature of its industry is its efficiency. DSHM's benchmarking studies suggest that it is improving its performance more rapidly than its rivals. As Harvard's Mr Upton points out, Daewoo has built what many companies are still striving for: a plant that has learned how to learn. Old Admiral Yi would have been most impressed.

Case study questions

1. What strategic resources did the Okpo shipyard possess at the time that Daewoo took it over?

2. What were the crucial decisions and actions that Mr Kim and his colleagues took to turn Okpo around? How did they help build competitive advantage?

3. To what extent could Okpo be said to have a sustainable competitive advantage at the time of the article (1994)? What might go wrong to spoil their competitiveness?

NOTES

1. The definition of resource is taken from Barney (1991: 101). Our definition of strategic resource is based on Amit and Schoemaker's (1993) definition of strategic *assets*. As we mention later in this section, the whole area is a minefield of conflicting terminology.

2. 'Distinctive capability' dates back at least to Kenneth Andrews' 1971 book, *The Concept of Corporate Strategy*. 'Core competence', although relatively new, is probably the most widely used term in the whole of resource-based theory. It was first introduced by Prahalad and Hamel (1990).

3. Many writers use the two words 'competences' and 'capabilities' interchangeably. The distinction we draw between them is similar to that in Stalk et al. (1992: 57–69) and Day (1994: 37–52).

4. This illustrates the importance of a good brand, even if all you are selling is an idea. Somehow, 'time compression diseconomies' does not have the same ring to it as 'core competence'!

5. For example, Kay (1993), Baden-Fuller and Stopford (1992), and Levinthal (1995). Richard Rumelt himself did not link his findings to any particular theory.

6. The analysis in this and the following paragraphs draws heavily on Dierickx and Cool (1989).

7. Lorenz, Andrew, 'Rolls Royce fuels industrial power deals', *Sunday Times*, Business Section, p. 3.3, 1 August 1999.

8. Followers of English football will recognise the plights of Middlesbrough in 1997 and Blackburn in 1999.

9. Try this for yourself. If a firm with no debt increases its profits from €100m to €120m, the operating profits and net profits will both rise 20%, and the share price should do likewise. If the firm has a lot of debt and is paying €50m in interest charges, then net profit will rise from €50m to €70m, a 40% increase. If this looks like magic, then try calculating the impact of a 50% increase in interest rates plus a 20% *decline* in operating profits, as can happen when a central bank raises interest rates to control inflation.

10. Lave, Jean (1988), *Cognition in Practice: Mind, Mathematics and Culture in Everyday Life*. Cambridge University Press. Lave's most-quoted example is of people doing their shopping, who were capable of quite sophisticated calculations and feats of memory while in the supermarket working out which products to buy, but could not reproduce those calculations in another context – for example, seated at a desk. This, of course, also explains why students cannot remember in the exam room what we teach them in the classroom – nothing at all to do with the quality of our lectures!

11. For a full discussion of the concept of attention, and what influences it, see Ocasio, William (1997) 'Towards an attention-based view of the firm', *Strategic Management Journal*, Vol. 18 (Summer Special Issue), pp. 187–206.

12. The theory presented in this section owes a great deal to Kay, (1993: chs 6 and 16).

13. Reputation is the term used by economists, but there are equivalent terms in other disciplines: 'prestige' in sociology, 'image' in marketing and 'goodwill' in law and accounting. Shenkar and Yuchtman-Yaar (1997) offer a useful summary and discussion.

14. Much of the following discussion of brands is based on Berthon et al. (1999), Grunert (1996) and de Chernatony and McDonald (1998).

15. Shenkar and Yuchtman-Yaar (1997) showed that US firms' share-price performance is related to their standing in *Fortune* magazine's annual survey of America's most respected corporations. Vergin and Qoronfleh (1998), showed a relationship between corporate reputation and stock market valuations. Milgrom and Roberts (1982) showed the value of reputation on deterring competition.

16. It is rated by chief executives as their most important intangible resource, according to Hall (1992).

17. Here we see a subtle difference between brand and reputation. You might still in the mid-1990s have decided to be associated with Jaguar's brand values.

18. The point here is not that a Big Mac tastes *precisely* the same in all these cities. It doesn't: the firm sometimes makes some substantial concessions to local tastes. But wherever you go, you will get something that looks and tastes pretty close to what you are used to, and is prepared in hygienic conditions from good quality ingredients.

19. This is particularly the case with the increasingly common use of financial instruments like options and futures, which when employed judiciously help to limit the risk in a portfolio of securities, but when overused can leave investors exposed to the risk of massive losses. For further details, you are referred to any good textbook on corporate finance.

20. See, for example, Prahalad and Hamel (1990) and Hamel and Prahalad (1994).

21. See Senge (1990); he calls this competence 'systems thinking'.

22. See Brown and Eisenhardt (1997) and Eisenhardt and Brown (1998).

23. Hamel and Prahalad's definition stipulates that a core competence should provide the basis for expansion into new businesses. This does not seem relevant when looking at the contribution of core competences to success at business level, but we shall return to it in Chapter 9.

24. This theory is called 'experiential learning', and the learning cycle described in this paragraph was set out by the psychologist, Kurt Lewin. For details see Kolb (1984).

25. For a model of how it *might* happen, see Kim (1993).

26. For a discussion of learning curve issues and effects see Yelle (1979) and Hedley (1976).

27. The distinction between single- and double-loop learning is due to two of the pioneers of organisational learning research, Chris Argyris of Harvard University and Donald Schön of the Massachusetts Institute of Technology. See Argyris and Schön (1978 and 1996). The distinction between exploitation and exploration is due to Jim March; see March (1991) and Levinthal and March (1993), both of which are reprinted in March (1999).

28. Following Argyris and Schön (1978), most organisational learning theory prefers the term 'theory-in-use' which, as we remarked in Chapter 1, means very much the same thing as paradigm.

29. This was the conclusion reached by Nevis, DiBella and Gould after their study of four large US and European organisations.

30. If you have not yet come to grips with Chapter 4, this may prompt you to try again.

31. The US Securities and Exchange Commission, in a 1996 report quoted in Edvinsson (1997).

32. Indeed, it is difficult to find a published example of a clear methodology, probably because it would be too commercially valuable to put into the public domain. Interested students might look at Roos and Roos (1997) or Edvinsson and Malone (1997), or try and get hold of Skandia's annual report and its CD-ROM on intellectual property valuation.

33. This framework comes from Davenport et al. (1998). See also Prokesch (1997) and the *Long Range Planning* Special Issue on 'The Management of Intellectual Capital' Volume 30 (3), June 1997, in particular the articles by Quintas, P., P. Lefrere and G. Jones 'Knowledge Management: a Strategic Agenda', pp. 385–391 and Wiig, K.M. 'Integrating Intellectual Capital and Knowledge Management' pp. 399–405. Ghoshal and Bartlett (1998) have some very interesting examples of knowledge sharing, including the McKinsey example we use in this section.

34. Corporate culture first came to prominence in the early 1980s as a result of two books by alumni of the McKinsey management consultancy: *Corporate Cultures: The Rites and Rituals of Corporate Life*, by Terence Deal and Allen Kennedy (Addison-Wesley, 1982) and *In Search of Excellence*, by Tom Peters and Robert Waterman (Harper and Row, 1982). Strategic management academics started to take the topic seriously about four years later – see Barney (1986b), Leonard-Barton (1992) and Fiol (1991). The importance of architecture is discussed by Kay (1993: ch. 5).

The internal configuration of organisations

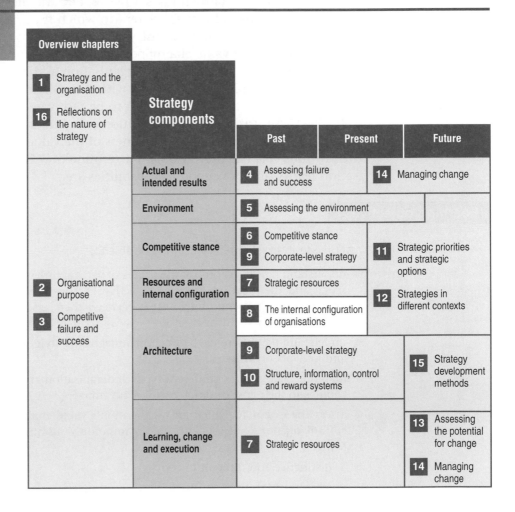

In this chapter, we look at how a business uses its resources (discussed in Chapter 7) to serve its target market segments (Chapter 6). This involves several elements of strategy:

- selecting the right resources for a particular customer group;
- combining them with resources brought in from other organisations – suppliers, distributors and customers;
- deciding what scale and location of operations will allow the organisation to make the most profitable use of its resources;

- finding ways of linking different types of resources to serve the customer better and/or at lower cost.

The way in which an organisation combines these different elements of strategy so as to add value is called its **value chain**.[1] In this chapter, as in Chapter 7, the emphasis is on what gives individual businesses a sustainable position in their chosen market places, and the measure of how well a business is adding value is the extent to which it gains costs and/or differentiation advantage in its industry.

In order to make a value chain operate effectively, information needs to be able to flow into and out of the organisation and between its different parts. Also the people involved, both within the organisation and outside – its suppliers and distributors – need to be motivated to make it operate well. For these reasons, the organisation's **architecture** and **culture** are important influences on the effectiveness of the value chain. As we saw in the previous chapter, they also help determine how effectively the organisation learns, and how good its capabilities are.

Learning objectives

After reading this chapter you should be able to:

- understand how decisions on the degree of vertical integration, the scale, the scope and the location of different activities, together with the resources deployed within them and linkages between them, can affect an organisation's competitive advantage;

- understand the difference between manufacturing-style, professional service and network organisations;

- map the value chain of different types of organisation and show how it contributes to their cost or differentiation advantage;

- assess the extent to which an organisation's value chain, architecture and culture *together* contribute to an organisation's sustainable advantage by being:

  - distinctive and difficult to copy

  - appropriate to the organisation's circumstances.

The value chain is purely a business-level concept, but architecture and culture have implications at corporate level that will be discussed in Chapter 9.

8.1 Value chain analysis

The basic idea of the value chain is quite simple, and is based on the chain of events that every product must go through. First of all, someone has to invent it, and develop the processes that will allow it to be produced. Next, the raw materials and parts need to be brought together to make it. Then, it needs to be manufactured, after which it must be distributed to customers or retail outlets. During and after the production and distribution process, customers must be persuaded to buy the product. Finally, once it is delivered, the firm needs to take care of any problems that arise, and offer spare parts and routine maintenance.

Value chain analysis is a way of seeing where in this *chain* of activities an organisation is successfully adding *value*. It lets us pinpoint the *particular* capabilities and assets that are important to an organisation and show *precisely* where and how they are being applied. A number of frameworks have been developed to help map firms' activities and compare them between different organisations. Most of these frameworks, following the lead given by Michael Porter in his 1985 book, *Competitive Advantage*, set up checklists of the different activities that occur in a firm, under two broad headings: **primary and support activities.**

Concept

Primary activities

Primary activities are those directly involved with delivering products or services to a user.

Support activities

Support activities contributes indirectly to the adding of value, through supporting one or more of the primary activities.

Primary and support activities

The **primary activities** in a value chain include manufacturing operations, sales and marketing and after-sales service for a manufactured product like a car, journalism and advertising sales for a magazine, till service and cheque handling for a bank. Different types of value chain have different types of primary activity.

Support activities include things like the purchasing function, process development, human resource management, planning and financial control.

It is important to bear in mind that the activities in a value chain are not the same as the functions in an organisation structure, even if they may, confusingly, have the same names. The sales and marketing **activity**, for example, includes all marketing that goes on in any **function** in the organisation – whether it be sales people on their rounds, marketing executives developing promotional campaigns, senior managers lunching with prospective clients or the finance department helping to calculate price levels. The planning and financial control activity, similarly, includes all inputs to planning and control from everyone in the organisation, not just those with job titles like 'accountant' or 'planner'.

◄ *An organisation's resources, and what makes them the source of competitive advantage, are discussed in Chapter 7.*

Table 8.1 Strategic decisions in the value chain

Deployment of resources	Which assets and capabilities an organisation chooses to use in connection with specific activities.
Vertical integration	Whether the organisation decides to carry out an activity itself, or to outsource it to a specialist supplier or a franchisee.
Scale of operations	Whether an organisation tries to gain economies of scale, or other types of advantage, from the scale of its operations in a particular activity.
Scope of operations	Whether an organisation tries to share one or more activities across different products and markets.
Location of operations	In which country or region an organisation chooses to locate particular activities.
Linkages	Whether the organisation tries to gain advantage by linking its activities together in a new and different way.

A value chain analysis looks at how each primary and support activity adds value – that is, leads to cost or differentiation advantage. Table 8.1 lists the types of strategic decision that determine how well they will achieve this. We now look at each of these in more detail.

8.1.1 Deployment of resources

If the organisation can utilise some strategic asset or distinctive capability in an activity, then that activity is likely to add value. Strong brands and reputations can be deployed to give differentiation in marketing and sales, or to attract good staff. Capabilities in reliability can be deployed in production or in after-sales service.

Sometimes an organisation may need to be selective about the resources it uses. It may have many assets and capabilities at its disposal, but will not necessarily want to deploy all of them in every market that it serves. (See Real-Life Application 8.1.)

8.1.2 Vertical integration and outsourcing

Vertical integration (sometimes known as 'make or buy') decisions involve important trade-offs between keeping control of important activities and profiting from other firms' specialist resources. Broadly, there are three ways in which a firm can obtain the products or services that it needs in order to produce and sell its own products or services (Williamson, 1975, 1991):

- It can buy them from third-party suppliers on the **open market**. This is sometimes known as *outsourcing*, and can be a short-term or a long-term commitment. Some firms make it clear to their suppliers that they will always purchase at the lowest price, and that a supplier is only as good as its last delivery and its next price quote. Other firms look for longer-term relationships that are close to being a strategic alliance.

- It can produce them within the organisation's **hierarchy**, so that the people

---

REAL-LIFE APPLICATION 8.1

Selective use of resources by Volkswagen

Germany's Volkswagen (VW) is the world's fifth-largest car manufacturer and the market leader in Europe. In 1998 it paid $790 million to acquire Bentley, a prestigious luxury car marque that was formerly part of Rolls-Royce Motors. VW plans to follow its rivals, BMW and Mercedes, in extending its luxury car brand by launching a range of smaller, less expensive Bentleys.

The Bentley brand is undoubtedly an asset, but VW must be careful how it uses it. If the new Bentley is too small and too cheap, then the value of the brand will diminish.

VW has other capabilities that it can use to enhance Bentley's value chain. It plans to transfer some of its manufacturing and design skills, getting Bentley cars to share a 'platform' (the chassis and other basic structures) with its other large cars. However, part of the attraction of Bentley cars is their image of old-fashioned craftsmanship. Although VW's manufacturing capabilities are strong, and its cars get high ratings in the influential JD Power survey of automobile quality, if it uses them all for Bentleys, it risks antagonising their own customers.

Sources: Guyon, Janet, 'Getting the bugs out at Volkswagen', *Fortune*, 29 March 1999, pp. 38–42; authors' own analysis.

providing the service are under direct management control and have (in theory) to do what they are told.

- It can use other, hybrid forms of organisation that are **intermediate** between markets and hierarchies, such as networks, strategic alliances and franchising arrangements. In these cases, although the supplier is not under the direct control of its clients, there is a continuing relationship between them that is likely to make each more sensitive to the needs of the other.

In manufacturing companies, the issue of which components to make in-house and which to buy in from outside suppliers has always been important. Similarly, the question of whether a firm should sell directly to customers – through a direct salesforce, over the telephone or through the Internet – or sell its products through franchisees, distributors or retailers, has long been important in marketing strategy. Some support functions, like cleaning and catering, are outsourced almost as a matter of course.

But companies have been known to use third-party suppliers for almost any activity in the value chain, including advertising, product and packaging design, brand development, manufacturing, distribution, sales and after-sales product maintenance. Crucial support activities may also be carried out by external firms. The outsourcing of the IT function has attracted most attention,[2] but some organisations have experimented with third-party suppliers in areas like human resource management and accounting.

In all these cases, an organisation has to arrive at a trade-off between five factors:

- Production and set-up costs
- Transaction costs
- Flexibility and incentive
- Quality
- Control of key resources.

Production and set-up costs

By using an outside supplier, an organisation can take advantage of that firm's economies of scale and its learning. These economies often outweigh any margin that the supplier charges for its services. This means that sourcing from an experienced third-party supplier is quite likely to be cheaper than in-house production.

Outsourcing may also be the better option if it would be expensive or time-consuming for a firm to set up an activity in its own right. This is particularly true when the potential suppliers have core capabilities that a firm would have difficulty in matching (Barney, 1999).

Transaction costs

◀ *Transaction costs were defined in Section 1.3.2.*

The downside of buying goods and services on the open market is that there is a danger that the supplier may try to exploit the situation for extra profit. There are three main ways in which this may happen:[3]

1. A supplier may increase the amount it charges for its services, because it believes that the client has become dependent upon it, a practice sometimes known as

holdup. It may believe that the client has invested so much in the relationship, for example by changing its information systems or changing its factory layout to make space for the supplier's personnel, that it cannot afford to pull out. Or it may have control of an important resource, such as a firm's information processing.

2. The supplier may promise more than it can deliver – for example, it claims experience in writing particular kinds of software, or selling to customers in the banking sector or in emerging markets, that it does not really have. There are many stories of young firms doing this to win their first contract. Sometimes they are able to learn on the job, but if they cannot, their client will lose time, money and maybe customers as well. Economists call this *adverse selection*, because it leads firms to select the wrong supplier.[4]

3. The supplier might cut corners when it comes to delivering the product or service, a danger known as *moral hazard*. It may use inferior quality components, skimp on quality assurance procedures or use people with lower qualifications than those that it promised. Management consultants, for example, routinely parade a team of highly qualified partners and staff when pitching for a project, but try as far as possible to use less experienced consultants to carry it out. This is because they make higher margins on junior than on senior staff, who in any case are needed to sell the next project.

Economists believe that firms behave in a way that minimises the transaction costs that arise from holdup, adverse selection and moral hazard.[5] If outsourcing involves making major investments that commits it to a single supplier, then an organisation might prefer to perform the activity in-house, to avoid the risk of suppliers exploiting its vulnerability. Firms may also give preference to vertical integration if the industry is complex and reliable information is difficult to come by. In such cases it is difficult to tell a good supplier from a bad one, or to work out if they are doing as they promised. Situations like these may occur when the supplier's industry is at the introductory or growth stages of its life-cycle. For example, during the 1970s and 1980s, when the management consultancy industry was growing strongly, a number of individuals and firms sold themselves as consultants although their experience and qualifications were negligible. The UK industry reacted by forming the Management Consultants Association and the Institute of Management Consultants to help clients to distinguish between genuine professionals and frauds.

In more stable or less complex industries, it can be easier for an organisation to find a reliable supplier, and to write and enforce a contract that will protect it from being exploited. It may also be able, for example, to inspect suppliers' factories and review their quality assurance procedures, something that it can only do properly if it has a good understanding of those suppliers' business. In such cases, a firm may be able to benefit from using outside suppliers.

Some people believe that transaction cost economics places too much emphasis on the negative aspects of human behaviour[6] and argue that it is possible to build relationships of trust between firms and their suppliers. These relationships reduce the likelihood of exploitation, so that organisations can take advantage of savings on production costs with less fear of incurring high transaction costs.

Flexibility and incentive

Not all suppliers are crooks, and the profit motive does not necessarily make them try to exploit their clients in the ways described in the previous section. It also gives them an incentive to do things that the customer probably welcomes, such as keeping down production and delivery costs and keeping inventory levels low. Third-party suppliers may well feel these incentives more keenly than people within the firm's hierarchy. This is one of the reasons why Benetton's system of outsourcing its manufacturing to independent suppliers, and its selling to independent retail partners, is so effective.

That same system illustrates one of the other benefits of outsourcing – flexibility. If demand turns up or down, a firm can increase or decrease the number of suppliers, without having to worry about new investment or redundancy costs. The supplier is in effect taking away some of the client's risk.

Quality

Considerations of quality can influence a firm either away from or towards outsourcing activities. A dedicated supplier may have capabilities superior to those a firm could develop on its own. In the motor industry, firms such as Bosch have better innovative capabilities for specialist products like brakes and fuel injection systems than even the largest carmaker.

However, particularly in a young industry, a firm may be unable to locate a supplier or distributor with the right expertise. It may also decide that an activity is so important to its overall cost or differentiation advantage that it has to control the quality directly, and if necessary learn how to do it well. British Airways during the 1980s believed that the process of getting to and from a plane, quickly and comfortably, was important in shaping passenger's attitudes to an airline. To keep control of the quality of this activity, it ran the bus service that ferried passengers around its Heathrow airport hub, making it, for a time, the UK's second largest bus operator.

Control of key resources

There are other grounds, apart from quality, why a firm may decide that an activity is too strategically important to allow a supplier to take it over. It may fear that the supplier may exploit control of an important resource, or because it wants the knowledge it has of the activity to remain proprietary. For example, Benetton, although it outsources much of the fabrication of its clothes, does the dyeing itself. The dyeing makes an important difference to how the finished garment looks, and Benetton has developed proprietary processes that it does not want to share.

Virtual value chains and value chain deconstruction

There has been a heated debate on whether outsourcing is a good or bad strategy in principle. Many theorists and practitioners have argued that it is a fundamental mistake for firms to outsource key activities, because it may erode their distinctive capabilities.[7] Against this must be set the benefits that firms can derive from tapping into their suppliers' own distinctive capabilities.[8] As well as having greater expertise and assuming some of the risk involved in an activity, an outside contractor may offer better co-ordination of an activity across a large organisation. This is especially true of unglamorous but important activities like tax reporting or energy management, which may not otherwise get a lot of senior management attention.

Consultants such as the Boston Consulting Group (BCG) now advocate the outsourcing of any activity in which the organisation does not have world-class capabilities. They argue that it is no longer possible for a firm to survive, as it once could, with a value chain that is excellent in a few areas but merely adequate in others. Such a firm is in danger of being outmanoeuvred by a rival that focuses on only a few strategically important activities where it can develop distinctive capabilities. If this rival picks the right outside suppliers for its other activities, it will have a value chain that will outperform any other.

The logical outcome of this kind of strategy is a **virtual value chain** (Benjamin and Wigland, 1995; Rayport and Sviokla, 1995), where almost all activities are outsourced. Cisco Systems, the world leader in Internet routers, is an example of a firm that conducts only product development, marketing and some support activities in-house. All manufacturing, distribution and installation are contracted out.

Networks are discussed in Chapter 10 and strategic alliances in Chapter 15. ▶

Value chains that might once have been contained within a single organisation are increasingly being **deconstructed** – split up across networks of specialist suppliers. Firms like Cisco and Benetton, which sit at the centre of these networks, specify the outputs and determine which supplier should do what, are called **orchestrators** or **servers**. Running a network like this requires particular skills and an appropriate architecture (see Section 8.5.5). However, the arrival of electronic commerce has made locating suppliers and managing relationships with them considerably easier (Real-Life Application 8.2). This makes it more difficult for a firm to gain a sustainable competitive advantage as an orchestrator, since its competitors can often gain access to the same excellent suppliers on the same terms (Edeleman, 1998).

REAL-LIFE APPLICATION 8.2

Outsourcing in the electronics industry

Although Sony has many factories of its own, it outsources considerable amounts of its manufacturing to specialist contract manufacturers like Flextronics and Solectron. So do many of its competitors – in fact, sometimes a contract manufacturer may end up making directly competing products on neighbouring production lines.

There are several benefits from using a contract manufacturer. Their production costs are lower, because they get very large discounts from component suppliers. They have greater experience than their clients in operating the complex robots used to surface-mount electronics components on to printed circuit boards. This keeps their costs low and their quality high. They also give firms like Sony extra flexibility – Solectron and Flextronics each have over twenty factories worldwide, and can use spare capacity in one to meet unexpected demand elsewhere.

Transaction costs are kept low in several ways. Firstly, the contract manufacturers frequently operate as strategic partners, helping their clients design their products to be cheap and easy to manufacture. They also are open with their financial information, so the client can see what is being spent and why. This builds trust within the relationship. At the same time, clients' control costs are kept low by making up-to-date production information available via the Internet, so that Sony and its competitors can intervene in the event of any problems.

Source: 'Have factory, will travel', *The Economist*, 12 February 2000, pp. 81–2. © *The Economist*, London 2000.

Vertical integration and corporate-level strategy

Vertical integration decisions may also be taken at corporate level, when firms decide they want to own their suppliers or customers to capture the profits that they make, or to prevent competitors from controlling them. These decisions, which may involve an acquisition or the start-up of a new business unit with its own value chain, are discussed in Chapter 9.

8.1.3 Scale of operations

◀ *Economies of scale and scope are defined in Section 3.1.1. The marketing aspects of choosing the right scale and scope for an organisation's operations are covered in Section 6.5.2.*

In an activity that offers significant economies of scale, an organisation faces important trade-offs. It may try to maximise the scale of its operations in order to try to get a cost advantage. Alternatively, if it believes it has capabilities in responding to user needs, it may opt for a smaller scale of operation. It would hope to gain a differentiation advantage by offering a high level of service to a limited set of users, either external (customers) or internal (other parts of the organisation). Organisations will often decide to operate at different scales at different stages in their value chain, and for different market segments. Ikea, the Swedish furniture retailer, centralises its product design and procurement for the entire globe in its home country. It serves most markets from a few, very large stores, strategically placed so as to be accessible to a large population. Its UK subsidiary, Habitat, serves a slightly different, more affluent market segment. It has a larger network of smaller stores located in city centres.

To get the maximum benefit from a large-scale operation, it must be intensively utilised. Factories try to use expensive equipment for two or three shifts every day, preferably seven days a week, stopping only for retooling and maintenance. Accounting firms try to keep their staff fully occupied on fee-earning client work. Organisations face a trade-off in deciding whether they will be better off with a small operation, where capacity may more easily be fully utilised, or a larger one where there is a risk that it will not be. Lower capacity may offer higher profits and lower risk in the short term, but this must be balanced against the danger that the company will be unable to respond quickly if the market starts to grow strongly.

8.1.4 Scope of operations

An activity may provide a range of outputs for a variety of market segments or internal users. It can be divided into more or less separate businesses, each serving a distinct market with its own products and value chain. Benetton has used different distribution channels for its two main clothing brands, Benetton and Sisley, which target slightly different market segments, and others still for its sports brands such as Rollerblade. British Airways markets its main airline services mostly through travel agents, while tickets for its no-frills subsidiary, Go, are mainly sold direct via telephone or the Internet. These companies hope that, by tailoring the value chain precisely to the needs of the target market, they will satisfy customers better and avoid wasting resources where they are not needed or useful. Benetton did not want to give over valuable shelf space to sports goods in its smaller clothing stores, which were not designed to attract the kinds of people who buy Rollerblade inline skates.

Alternatively, a firm can use parts of the same value chain to serve several market segments. Many car manufacturers use the same dealer and service network for both their mass-market smaller cars and their more luxurious and expensive executive models. They obviously believe that standards of comfort and service at their dealers are high enough to satisfy their more up-market customers. They also hope that mass-market customers will feel comfortable trading up to an executive car as they get older and richer. This kind of strategy hopes to leverage a resource base (such as physical assets and capabilities in customer service) across a number of compatible markets.

8.1.5 Location of resources

By choosing the right country or region to locate a particular part of the value chain, a company can get access to local expertise or to low-cost resources. Any firm with enough cash can copy these location decisions, of course. However, not all firms have the mindset that enables them to adopt a global perspective, and those that do may not have the culture or architecture that enables them to motivate people from other cultures. Decisions about where key elements of the value chain are located need to balance several different elements:

- The characteristics of the product or service
- Knowledge and learning
- Relative attractiveness of different locations
- Operational advantages.

The characteristics of the product or service

◀ *The characteristics of a global product are covered in Theoretical Perspective 6.2.*

Global products like pharmaceuticals or microchips may be manufactured in greater bulk than those that need customisation to local tastes. The firm can use a small number of larger plants in strategic locations, to try to maximise economies of scale.

For products that need to be produced in small batches, there are no economies of scale, so manufacturing locations may be more dispersed. If local preferences are strong, as they are in foodstuffs, for example, the firm may want to locate close to the customer so as to be in tune with local tastes. Some firms have been able to combine some of the benefits of centralised mass production with those of local customisation by using regional distribution centres to add local touches to global products. This is known as a **postponement** strategy – certain value-chain activities are postponed until closer to the point of sale (see Real-Life Application 8.3).

Products that have a short shelf-life, like some foodstuffs, or are difficult to transport because of their fragility, may need to be manufactured close to their final market destinations. Similarly, if a firm needs inputs with a short life, it should put its production plant close to the source of the raw materials. Service organisations like hotels and fast-food restaurants, whose outputs are consumed as they are produced, have to locate their outlets where the customers are.

Products that are expensive to transport, perhaps because of their bulk or special needs (live animals for example) may also need to be manufactured close to their final destination.

REAL-LIFE APPLICATION 8.3

Postponement strategies at Hewlett-Packard

Hewlett-Packard carries out the majority of the manufacturing work on its Deskjet printers at a factory in Singapore that supplies the global market. However, certain components – power supplies, instruction manuals and packaging – need to be tailored to individual markets. These are added at the distribution centres in Europe and Asia, which are also responsible for sourcing the necessary components. Through this combination of global and local sourcing, the total manufacturing, transportation and inventory costs of the Deskjet are 25% lower than when the entire product was produced and packed in Singapore.

Source: van Koek, Remko I., Vos, Bart and Commandeur, Harry R. (1999) 'Restructuring European Supply Chains by Implementing Postponement Strategies', *Long Range Planning*, 32 (5), pp. 505–18.

Knowledge and learning

Even in products that are very international, such as fashion, and could easily be designed and produced at a single location, a firm may decide to have extra locations in influential markets. This helps the organisation to stay in touch with the tastes and requirements of opinion formers, gives them credibility and helps them gather information about what competitors are doing and why. This is why almost every information technology firm of any size has an office in Silicon Valley in California, and Kao, a Japanese cosmetics firm, has set up a centre of excellence for perfume development in Paris.

On the other hand, the sharing of knowledge and learning across borders can present problems. Although the Internet has made it far easier to communicate between different countries and time zones, differences between national cultures and languages may still create problems of understanding.

Relative attractiveness of different locations

◀ *International cultural differences are the subject of Section 6.2.*

◀ *The processes that lead to certain nations developing competitive advantage in particular industries are covered in Section 5.5.*

Different countries and regions will hold different degrees of attractiveness. In an industry like clothing or shoes, where low production costs are important, it makes sense to locate production facilities in markets like Thailand or China where labour costs are very low. The availability of cheap electricity or other inputs may influence location decisions in industries such as aluminium smelting. However, costs are not everything. Firms will take account of broader social and economic factors, such as countries' transport, education, financial and political systems. They will want to be sure that they can find qualified and motivated staff, that they can move goods in and out of the country and that profits are not eroded by high taxes, corrupt officials or organised crime. They will also be interested in whether countries possess specialised knowledge and competencies in areas like engineering or information technology.

Many of these infrastructure factors point strongly to certain locations being more favourable than others. In recent years the Pacific Rim countries have been able to develop suitable infrastructures while at the same time retaining considerable cost advantages over the more highly paid and socially supported labour markets of Western Europe. As a result many European firms have chosen to locate manufacturing plants there, a considerable distance away from some of their markets.

Operational advantages

There can be actual advantages to having a facility located in a different time zone. Western banks that send their cheques to India for processing can have their records updated during the Indian working day, and have the data available when they return to work the following morning. Organisations that run call centres to handle customer enquiries may find it better to refer calls to sister centres in other time zones than to employ a night shift in Europe.

Balancing the different factors

Different firms will arrive at different decisions in balancing these various considerations. A firm whose strategy depends on low prices may be attracted by the cost advantages of locating in the Pacific Rim. A competitor in the same industry that is trying to differentiate on customer service may derive greater value from a more expensive supplier, or an in-house operation, located close to the target market. Other considerations will also come into play – the organisation might need to decide how easily it would adapt to managing a lot of small operations spread across a number of time zones and national cultures. Its organisational culture and architecture might be better suited to managing fewer, larger operations in locations where it understands the people and their business practices. In a single operation in its home country, the organisation might find it relatively easy to exert control and to ensure that information and learning are shared and acted upon.

Firms may also arrive at different decisions for different elements of the value chain. A retail bank may centralise its cheque processing in Asia, to take advantage of economies of scale and low labour costs. However, it may maintain an extensive network of small branches in Europe, so as to be close to its customers, while a competitor chooses to serve its customers through a telephone call centre, or via the Internet.

8.1.6 Linkages

One of the most subtle and difficult parts of value chain analysis is the identification of how *linkages* between different activities can generate value. There are several ways that this can happen (Porter, 1985: 48–53):

- One activity can partially substitute for another. For example, an investment in systems to screen potential clients may improve sales productivity (because it reduces the amount of time salespeople waste with people who are unlikely to buy the service) and reduce debt collection costs – although it may also screen out some marginal leads that a good salesperson might have converted into orders. Increasing the amount of training in quality procedures offered to factory workers can lead to a reduction in the amount of finished goods inspection and after-sales service that is needed.

- One activity can improve the performance of another. For a train or bus operator, more frequent maintenance keeps vehicles in better order and improves the reliability of operations.

- One activity can generate information that can be used by another. A firm with

Table 8.2   Trade-offs in the value chain

Type of decision	Different alternatives and their potential advantages	
Resources deployed	*Proprietary* Potential source of distinctiveness.	*Generic* Cheap, quick and easy to acquire and update.
Vertical integration	*Make (hierarchy)* High degree of control of resources and quality, no risk of exploitation, potential for developing distinctive capabilities.	*Buy (market)* Set-up costs may be lower, flexibility likely to be greater, can profit from suppliers' distinctive capabilities and economies of scale.
Scale and scope	*Large scale, broad scope* Economies of scale and scope, leverage resources across many products and groups of users.	*Small scale, narrow niche* Achieve specialist excellence in narrow field, avoid wasting resources in places where they are not appropriate.
Location	*Everything in one place* Economies of scale, relatively easy to control activities and share information and learning.	*Distributed* Tap into local knowledge and expertise, stay responsive to user requirements, cost advantages.
Linkages	Enable activities to collaborate to meet customer needs in coherent way. Possible source of sustainable advantage.	

its own service operation can keep track of customers' problems and suggestions, and feed them back to the product development activity. A sales system can take details of customer orders that can be used for factory scheduling.

Firms can alter their activities to fit in with the value chains of suppliers, distributors, retailers and end-users. These *vertical linkages* between different organisations' value chains generate benefits on both sides that can be shared.[9] By investing in new vehicles with improved temperature controls, a food distribution firm can reduce the amount of wastage suffered by its customers, for example.

8.1.7 Decisions and trade-offs in the value chain

The previous sections have shown that an organisation faces a variety of trade-offs when configuring each activity in the value chain. These are summarised in Table 8.2.

8.2   Types of value chain

Value chain analysis uses a set of 'generic' value chains which vary slightly across different types of organisation, and which are based on a number of common elements which have been observed in these different settings. These models serve as a kind of checklist to help us know what kinds of activity to look for and analyse in particular organisational settings. In this section, we look at generic value chains that have been developed for three different types of organisation.[10]

- **Manufacturing-style organisations.** These are the kinds of organisation where a set of inputs is translated into a set of outputs using a classic path, from product development through to after-sales service, that we sketched in the introduction to Section 8.1. Along with most manufacturing firms, what we are calling **service-manufacturers** – organisations like retailers, fast-food providers and hotels, which produce a standardised product that happens to have a strong service component to it – also use this kind of value chain. One way to judge whether an organisation falls into this category is to look at the way it measures its outputs and judges its success. Manufacturing-style firms' outputs are measured in volume terms (numbers of computers, hamburgers or hotel room-nights produced and sold) and unit costs are an important measure of efficiency.

- **Professional services.** These organisations exist to solve difficult problems for individual clients, each of which is likely to require a customised service. Examples are consultancies, educational and scientific research institutions, oil exploration firms and government departments. Professional services add value by solving their clients' problems in a creative and effective manner. They measure themselves by the size, prestige and value of the projects they win, rather than the volume of outputs that they produce.

- **Networks.** These are organisations that have the linking of people together as their main function. The bigger they are, the more people they link together and the more attractive they become. Sometimes the linkages are obvious – a telephone operator or on-line auctioneer adds value by being able to link more people together, to talk to or buy things from one another. However, other types of organisation also fit into this category. A retail bank like Lloyds–TSB or Deutsche Bank is a network, not because it exists to bring its customers together, but because, the larger the pool of deposits that it has, the more secure it becomes and the better able to make profitable loans. A newspaper is a network partly because many readers like to feel part of an influential 'club', but mainly because a large readership makes it more attractive to advertisers.[11] These organisations will measure themselves by the size of their customer or asset base.

By this stage in the book, you should not be surprised to read that it is not always clear into which of these categories an organisation falls, and that different parts of an organisation may have different types of value chain. Some professional services may have standardised or 'manufactured' elements such as a training manual or programme, although these are not likely to be the most important part of the overall service. A newspaper is a network, but its printing press has a manufacturing function and will assess its performance like a manufacturer, using measures like 'cost per copy'. A retail bank is a network, but its corporate finance division, which advises commercial clients on how to fund major transactions, is a professional service organisation.

We shall now look at some of the different types of generic value chain and the various activities within them. In Appendix 8.1, which you may prefer to omit on a first reading of this chapter, we explore in detail how each activity may use resources, vertical integration, scope, scale, location and linkages to generate cost and differentiation advantage.

8.2.1 Manufacturing-style organisations

The generic value chain for a manufacturing-style organisation is shown in Figure 8.1.[12] It includes six primary activities:

- **Production design and development** – pure and applied research in areas like materials science and electronics, product development and testing and product design.

- **Supply** – the mechanical and operational procedures that bring inputs into the organisation: ordering and delivery procedures, the inspection of components to make sure that they meet quality requirements, and so on.

- **Operations** – the transformation of inputs into the finished product or service. In a factory it embraces all the functions related to production, including scheduling, production engineering, quality assurance and maintenance. In a restaurant it includes the cooking and serving of food and the washing of dishes, cutlery and linen. A retailer's operations include the stacking of shelves and serving of customers at the counter or checkout.

- **Distribution** – the physical transportation of products from the point of production to the point of sale, and then on to the end-user. It also includes the process of managing relationships with distributors, wholesalers or retailers to ensure that they have adequate stocks of the products they require. For some retailers, the distribution activity covers the process of getting goods from centralised depots to the stores.

- **Marketing and sales** – locating customers, identifying their requirements, making them aware of the organisation through promotional activity and setting the prices at which the product is to be sold, and the discount structure for large purchases. This activity has responsibility for the selection and management of salespeople, distributors and retailers to make sure that they have the knowledge and motivation to 'push' the organisation's products and services.

- **After-sales service** – everything that an organisation provides to customers after the goods or service has been delivered. It includes repair and maintenance services, complaints handling, customer training and telephone help-lines.

Figure 8.1   The value chain for manufacturing style organisations

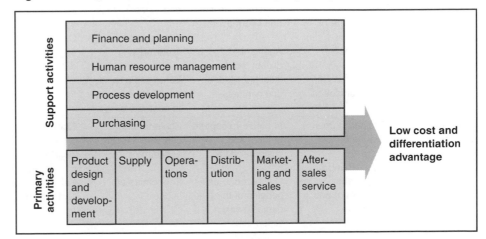

Table 8.3 Possible sources of competitive advantage in the primary activities of a manufacturing-style value chain

	Resources	Vertical integration	Scale and scope	Location	Linkages
Product design and development	Capabilities in: ● innovation ● customer responsiveness ● risk management Laboratories IT facilities Designers	Use alliances and partnerships (May be dangerous to outsource activity fully)	Large scale and broad scope to allow cross-fertilisation of ideas ● between people ● across products and markets	Close to customers and competitors to allow exposure to latest ideas	Operations Distribution Marketing and sales After-sales service
Supply	IT systems (EDI and extranets)	Activity devolved to suppliers		Suppliers located nearby for speedy response	Operations Purchasing *Vertical linkage*: suppliers
Operations	Proprietary equipment Capabilities in innovation, reliability, customer responsiveness, speed of response	Retain *core* activities and develop capabilities. Outsource other activities to world-class suppliers	Economies of scale and scope, plant utilisation	Low-cost locations Close to customer to gain responsiveness	Product design and development Supply Marketing and sales Distribution Human resource management
Distribution	Specialised vehicles, depots and handling equipment Capabilities in reliability, customer responsiveness, speed of response	Keep in-house to ensure customer satisfaction Use top-class wholesalers, retailers	Economies of scale and scope	Many distribution points for speedy customer response Few, strategically located points for economies of scale	Distribution Sales *Vertical linkage*: wholesalers and retailers
Marketing and Sales	Reputational assets. Customer databases. Knowledge of consumer preferences Capabilities in communication	In-house sales to retain control of customer service and information Agents and distributors for local knowledge and contacts	Economies of scope in branding and sales Economies of scale in advertising Large scale to maximise exposure to customers	Close to customer for local sensitivity Clustered near competitors' outlets	All other internal activities. *Vertical linkage*: distributors and retailers
After-sales service	Trained human resources Testing and diagnostic equipment and software	In-house to capture product and customer data Outsource to gain benefits of third parties' scale, scope, local availability	Scale to offer customers local service Economies of scope	Close to customer for local sensitivity Call centre for cost advantage	Product design and development Marketing and sales Human resource management

Table 8.3 summarises the main alternative ways in which organisations might try to gain competitive advantage through these primary activities. These possibilities are discussed in more detail in Sections A–F of Appendix 8.1.

The manufacturing-style value chain also includes four support activities, which also appear in the generic value chains for professional service and network organisations:

- **Purchasing** – the identification of potential suppliers and negotiation of prices and delivery terms.
- **Process development**[13] – all activities to do with enhancing the routines and technologies that the organisation uses.
- **Human resource management** – the recruitment and training of employees and design of appraisal, payment and employee welfare systems.
- **Finance and planning** – invoicing, treasury, accounting, budgeting, planning and related activities.[14]

Table 8.4 summarises the main ways in which these support activities can contribute to competitive advantage. Sections G–J of Appendix 8.1 give further details.

The purchasing activity is sometimes grouped together with the supply and distribution activities and called **supply chain management**. In this book, we shall consider the three as separate activities.

Table 8.4 Possible sources of competitive advantage in the support activities of a value chain

	Resources	Vertical integration	Scale and scope	Location	Linkages
Purchasing	Supplier databases Capabilities in negotiation		Economies of scale and scope: discounts and spreading of overheads	Centralise to maximise scale and scope economies. Devolve to maximise flexibility and responsiveness	All primary activities *Vertical linkage*: suppliers
Process development	Substantial human and financial resources	Keep in-house to give tailored solutions and preserve expertise Outsource to specialist system suppliers and consultants	Larger scale and scope bring exposure to more technologies and markets	Central management to transfer best practices around organisation	Most other activities *Vertical linkage*: suppliers and researchers in other firms
Human resource management	Communications and training systems				Most other activities
Finance and Planning	IT and financial control systems Planning systems (rarely)		Small, low-cost and non-intrusive		Most other activities *Vertical linkage*: financial institutions, governments

8.2.2 Professional services organisations

A professional services value chain is illustrated in Figure 8.2. The support activities are very similar to those in the manufacturing-style value chain, but the primary activities are different. They comprise:

- **Problem acquisition and diagnosis** – persuading clients to bring their problem to the organisation, making and recording an initial assessment of the problem and then choosing an overall approach. For example, a dentist will conduct an initial examination of a patient, determine if there are any problems with their teeth and then map out a plan of treatment. For organisations that are in competitive market places, like consultancies and architecture practices, problem acquisition and diagnosis may involve a number of marketing activities, including advertising and making presentations to clients. In less competitive situations, it will involve liaising with funding and administrative bodies that control the flow of 'problems' and allocate them to one organisation rather than another. For example, schools and hospitals will maintain relationships with local administrations and government departments, to make sure they understand the rules for deciding where to send a particular person for education or treatment.

- **Finding possible solutions** – where the organisation uses its professional knowledge to develop a set of alternative answers to a problem. A doctor may be able to treat a patient through drugs or surgery. An architect may have several possible designs to fit a house or a hospital to the topography of the chosen site.

- **Choice between solutions** – choosing between the various alternatives proposed. It may be quite a brief phase in each project, and involve few resources, but it is crucial to obtaining a workable solution to the problem.

Figure 8.2   Generic value chain for a professional services organisation
(from Stabell and Fjeldstad, 1998: 425)

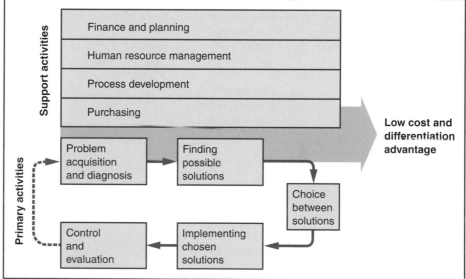

- **Implementing chosen solutions** – communicating the proposed solution to the client and putting it into effect.

- **Control and evaluation** – monitoring the extent to which the implementation process is actually solving the problem. It includes activities like the monitoring of patient progress in a hospital, client feedback meetings for an architect or consultant and safety testing in a new building by a construction firm.

The ways in which the organisation can try to seek competitive advantage from each of these primary activities are summarised in Table 8.5, with details in Sections K–P of Appendix 8.1.

Table 8.5 Possible sources of competitive advantage in the primary activities of a professional services value chain

	Resources	Vertical integration	Scale and scope	Location	Linkages
Problem acquisition and diagnosis	Reputation Capabilities in communication, negotiation and management of expectations				Finding possible solutions Control and monitoring (of previous projects) *Vertical linkage:* Customer networks, professional networks
Finding possible solutions	Knowledge assets Capabilities in innovation	Development of in-house expertise Astute use of out-sourced specialist professionals	Large scale/scope offers customer 'one-stop shop' and access to genuine specialists		Implementing chosen solutions
Choice between solutions	Ability to manage interactions between professions		Small scale/scope for focused expertise and low overheads		Implementing chosen solutions *Vertical linkage:* Professionals in other firms
Implementing chosen solutions	Project management systems Capabilities in customer sensitivity	Involvement of client in implementation			Control and evaluation *Vertical linkage:* Customers
Control and evaluation	Monitoring systems				Problem acquisition Finding and choosing solutions

279

Professional services organisations differ from manufacturing organisations in a number of important ways:

- There is far less division of labour between activities. The people who bring work in to the organisation are frequently the same people that work on the problem-solving and implementation. In fact the most important inputs everywhere in this value chain are specialised human resources.

- The activities are frequently more like a cycle than a chain. Successful solution of one problem may lead to the identification of more problems, leading to more work for the same client. In an accountancy firm, the discovery and resolution of a problem with a client's accounts may throw up other, smaller irregularities. Alternatively, it may lead to a contract to design a system to prevent the problem from recurring. In a research institute, one research programme invariably highlights unanswered questions that form the starting point of the next one.

- The value chain is configured to deal with unique cases. Although organisations will frequently develop standard routines to handle many simple problems such as audit procedures in accountancy, modular programmes in education and methods for open-heart surgery in medicine, the professional normally needs to look out for unusual problems: accounting irregularities, failing students and surgical complications.

- There is no strong correlation between the cost of an activity and its importance. The process of finding possible solutions, for example, may take far fewer resources than their implementation, but be equally as vital to the success of a project.

8.2.3 Networks

Network organisations exist to bring people together and act as intermediaries between them. A newspaper links journalists with readers and advertisers with potential customers. A bank links depositors who have money with people who want to borrow it. An on-line service provider links people who put content on the Internet with people who want to view it.

In network organisations, it can sometimes be difficult to distinguish between a supplier and a customer. The people who advertise in newspapers or run investment advice services on proprietary on-line services like AOL are suppliers in one sense, since they provide part of the content that people pay for. However, they are also charged for the space they consume. It is simpler to think of them as customers.

The generic value chain for this kind of organisation is shown in Figure 8.3. Again, the support activities are similar to those for manufacturing-style organisations, but there are different primary activities. The primary activities are shown overlapping, rather than as a sequence (like the manufacturing value chain) or a cycle (the professional services one). This is because they all have to happen simultaneously if the network is to function. (The difference in size between the three activities in Figure 8.3 is not intended to show their relative importance – it is simply to make them all legible.) They are:

- **Network promotion and contract management** – this involves four basic classes of activity:
  - Marketing the network to potential users. For a newspaper or magazine this would involve finding distributors and arranging subscriptions. For a retail bank, it means finding credit-worthy individuals or companies and persuading them to take out a loan. For an on-line service provider (OSP), it means advertising the service and distributing software by mail or with computer magazines.
  - Marketing the network to potential providers. For a newspaper this involves selling advertising, for a retail bank persuading people to open accounts and deposit money. An on-line service provider has to find providers of information and advice, and persuade them to make some part of their service exclusive to that particular network.
  - Setting up and terminating contracts: opening and closing customer accounts or subscriptions.
  - Screening potential members, for example assessing their credit-worthiness.
- **Service provisioning** – the day-to-day operation of the network: initiating, maintaining and ending contacts through the network, keeping track of customers' use of it, billing them and handling complaints. It includes activities

Concept	**Network organisations and network structures**

It is important to distinguish between network **organisations** (of the type discussed in this section) and network **structures** (discussed in Chapter 10). A network structure is a way of linking different internal stakeholders (often firms in their own right) together to serve customers, and may be used by manufacturing and professional service, as well as by network organisations. A network organisation exists to link different types of external stakeholder together – its internal structure may be along functional or divisional lines.

Network, functional and divisional structures are described in Chapter 10. ▶

Figure 8.3 Generic value chain for a network (from Stabell and Fjeldstad, 1998: 430)

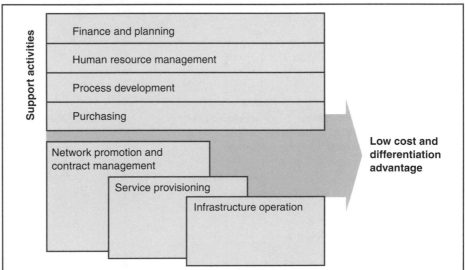

like writing and printing a newspaper, the operation of the servers and modems for an on-line network and the processing of deposits, withdrawals and interest payments in a bank.

- **Infrastructure operation** – keeping the network ready to service customers. It involves the specification and maintenance of physical resources, including buildings, and the IT and telecommunications infrastructure. It has a strong linkage with the procurement activity. For a newspaper, this activity might include the maintenance of delivery vehicles and the operation of telecommunications links between the editorial office and printing plants in other cities or countries. For a bank, it includes the operation of branch offices and ATMs, maintaining relations with the central bank and with correspondent banks in other countries, and the management of the bank's funds to ensure that it has adequate ready cash to service its customers.

The ways in which these primary activities may deliver competitive advantage to a network organisation are summarised in Table 8.6 and detailed in Sections Q–T of Appendix 8.1.

Table 8.6   Possible sources of competitive advantage in the primary activities of a network value chain

	Resources	Vertical integration	Scale and scope	Location	Linkages
Network promotion and contract management	Brand and reputation. Capabilities in communication, negotiation, risk management	Outsource to top-grade supplier		Centralised for economies of scale Close to customer for personal service	Service provisioning Infrastructure operation *Vertical linkage:* Customers
			Economies of scale or increasing returns to scale		
Service provisioning	Computers and other physical resources Capabilities in reliability, customer sensitivity, speed of response	Retention in-house of activities crucial to competitive advantage Choice of world-class supplier		Centralised, possibly in low-cost country with skilled human resources	Other primary activities Purchasing Process development *Vertical linkage:* suppliers
Infrastructure operation	Technological competences: e.g. IT, building maintenance				

8.3   How to analyse a value chain

Value chain analysis is potentially a very powerful tool for understanding an organisation's strategy. It brings together a number of different aspects of the organisation – decisions about scale and scope and vertical integration, strategic resources – and shows how they combine to generate competitive advantage. However, as you will have seen, it can get quite complex and difficult, particularly if you try to incorporate every single detail about every single activity. In this section, we look at how to simplify the analysis to make it less daunting and more useful.

8.3.1   What do you include in a value chain analysis?

There are three possible approaches to value chain analysis: the comprehensive list, the selective approach and financial analysis. Most people use the second of these, and we recommend that you do likewise.

The comprehensive approach

There is a strong temptation, when confronted with a value chain diagram for the first time, to try to fill in every square in meticulous detail using a large number of the categories we have described above. One can certainly learn a lot about an organisation in this way, particularly if you are unfamiliar with its industry.

The problem with this approach is that, although your list would include the important aspects of a firm's strategy, they will be obscured by a lot of mundane and unimportant ones. You may be able to say that a company has up-to-date machine tools in its factory, or employs a top agency to do its advertising. However, the same is quite likely to be equally true of most of its competitors, and indeed of most large firms in any manufacturing industry.

This is why most textbooks (including this one) tend to favour the selective approach.

The selective approach

Under the selective approach, your value chain analysis becomes a tool for picking out the *important* elements of a firm's strategy and operations. The analysis focuses upon the capabilities and decisions that enable a firm to achieve cost and/or differentiation advantage, and ignores the others.

For an innovative firm that has invented a new way of doing business, this may still yield quite a long list of distinctive elements. However, **for an established firm in an established industry the list is likely to be shorter, and some of the cells in the value chain diagram are likely to be empty.** This is because, as we emphasised in Chapter 7, most firms have only a few distinctive capabilities, while decisions relating to things like scale and location are likely to be copied by competitors if they are seen to be effective.

Financial analysis using the value chain

In *Competitive Advantage*, Porter proposes using the value chain as a framework for the financial analysis of a firm. He suggests analysing the cost and assets associated with each activity, to see whether the amount the firm is investing in an activity is in line with its strategic value. As we have seen (Section 8.2.2) in professional service organisations there are activities whose value is out of all proportion to their cost. However, for a manufacturing organisation, there is little doubt that an exercise like this is valuable and revealing.

However, it is very difficult to do this in practice, because the data needed are very detailed, and most firms' information systems are not geared to provide it. Financial information is normally only available by department or function, and the value chain activities usually cut across functional boundaries. For example, to count the cost of sales and marketing activity in a firm, you would want to include the cost of the time that the chief executive and product designers spend with clients, along with the costs of the salesforce and marketing department.

In summary, it is very unlikely that you will ever have the opportunity to carry out the kind of analysis that Porter proposed. Certainly, we have never seen a case study that contains sufficient detail to be analysed in that way.

8.3.2 What about weaknesses?

The value chain approach focuses upon identifying factors that contribute *positively* to competitive advantage. There is a vast range of possible ways in which an organisation may add value, so that no two successful firms are likely to deploy precisely the same mix of factors in the same activities.

This means that, because there are so many ways in which different organisations can achieve success, it can be very difficult to identify the precise elements of the value chain that lead to failure. It will never be clear which element of which firm's strategy an organisation should be copying. Is Company X failing because it lacks Company A's reputation and operations reliability, or Company B's highly trained salesforce and economies of scale? Could it succeed just on the basis of reputation plus economies of scale? Does it need the capability in reliability as well, or would a capability in customer responsiveness do instead?

This limits the extent to which value chain analysis can help identify areas where a firm is subtracting value rather than adding it. However, if all the leading firms are following very similar strategies, or if there is a single leading firm that you can use for the purposes of comparison, then a value chain analysis may reveal areas of weakness alongside distinctive strengths.

8.3.3 How many value chains do you need?

Normally, value chain analysis is used to analyse the strategies of a single business unit in a single firm. It can sometimes be useful to use it in a more general way, to show what distinguishes the firms in an industry from those marketing substitute products and services, or to work out what makes one strategic group different from another. For example, in understanding McDonald's competitive advantage, it might be helpful to do a single value chain for all global fast-food firms, to show how they gain advantage over smaller local competitors. This can then be complemented with another value chain showing how McDonald's gains advantage over Burger King, Pizza Hut and KFC.

A value chain tracks how a firm adds value to a particular set of customers. If it

---

Practical dos and don'ts   **Value chain analysis**

1. Determine whether the organisation you are analysing is a manufacturing-style organisation, a professional services organisation or a network. This involves looking at the nature of its business and the kinds of measures it uses or might use to measure performance, as outlined in Section 8.2.

2. Determine the activities that you are analysing. The relevant generic value chain for a manufacturing-style, professional service or network organisation can serve as a guide. However, it is perfectly in order for you to 'tweak' the generic chain, by adding, subtracting or renaming activities, if you feel that this gives a better picture of the organisation and the way it competes.

3. Go through the activities systematically, picking out how each of them uses resources, vertical integration, scale and scope or location to generate cost and/or differentiation advantage. Look also for linkages between the activities that are unusual.

4. Be discriminating in selecting what to include in your value chain. There is no law that says that, if a box appears on a diagram, you have to write something in it. Be careful that the resources that you include are rare, valuable, difficult to acquire and copy and have no ready substitutes. If you identify scale in an activity as part of an organisation's value chain, be sure in your mind that the scale of that activity is generally exceptional, and identify how it leads to advantage. Similarly scope, vertical integration or location should only feature in your analysis if they are genuinely unusual in the industry in question.

5. Neither a list of value chain factors nor a filled-in value chain diagram constitutes a value chain analysis. You need, in addition, to show in your analysis, using quantitative and qualitative evidence:

   ● **why** you believe that each feature you have highlighted is exceptional
   ● **how** it leads to cost and/or differentiation advantage.

6. You may also want to highlight in your analysis why some elements of an organisation's strategy do **not** feature in its value chain. It may be that the firm's managers obviously believe its scale, or its state-of-the-art computing facilities, or its training programmes, are extremely important. You may conclude that the managers are wrong, and that the company is not significantly better than average in those areas. In such cases, it is helpful to state these conclusions explicitly, and to show why you have reached them.

---

is attacking more than one target market however, then it might be helpful to draw more than one value chain within the business unit or firm as a whole. The way in which Sony adds value to individuals purchasing its consumer electronics will be different from the way in which it adds value to corporate purchasers of its audio-visual equipment. Its innovation capability in the product design activity is important to both sets of customers. However, its reputation is more of an asset in the consumer market than in the corporate market. Corporate buyers will have more expertise and, because they purchase these items more frequently, will have been able to form their own opinions about whose products work best – they do not need reputation as a guide. The sales and after-sales service channels are also different for the two markets.

8.4   ADVANCED TOPIC
Business processes

The value chain is not the only way of mapping activities in an organisation. Another method, in vogue since the early 1990s, is to regard the organisation as a set of *business processes*. Figure 8.4 shows a set of generic business processes developed by Bossard, a French consulting firm. Business processes are sets of activities that run through an organisation, spanning all the traditional functions from marketing and R&D through to service and administration. Each business process typically includes a number of subprocesses, each of which involves one of two functions, as follows:

- Customer service: enquiry handling (which involves the sales and administration functions), sales (the sales function again), order processing (administration), order fulfilment (manufacturing), delivery (distribution), after-sales service (service and administration) and account management (administration).

- New product development: market research, competitor analysis, concept proving, detailed design, product approvals, product trials, process design.

- Supply chain management: physical network design, inbound/outbound logistics, service and cost measurement, contract management, partnership management, resource management.

Figure 8.4   **Generic business processes** (adapted from BSM Bossard, quoted in Talwar (1993))

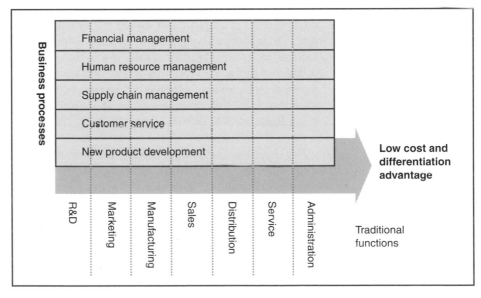

- Human resource management: recruitment, performance appraisal, training and development, counselling and guidance, disciplinary action, promotion and selection.

- Financial management: activity costing, budgeting, cash forecasting, revenue budgeting/forecasting, tax planning, financial reporting.

As can be seen from Figure 8.4, there is a lot of common ground between business process analysis and value chain analysis. There is very little to be gained from doing both – rather, they should be regarded as alternatives.

Business process re-engineering is described in detail in Chapter 14. ▶

By and large, value chain analysis is the more widely used of the two techniques. We mention business processes partly in the interests of completeness, and partly because of their importance in a popular change management technique known as business process engineering (Hammer and Champy, 1993). Some firms have also begun to use business processes as building blocks in an organisation structure, in place of the traditional functions. Some commentators believe that this kind of structure, by cutting across traditional functional boundaries, helps organisations manage their processes more effectively (Garvin, 1995; Hammer and Stanton, 1999).

Not all firms use Bossard's generic process names. Xerox Corporation, the US photocopier and document processing firm, has given its processes more exotic names such as 'time to market' and 'market to collection' (Garvin, 1995).

8.5 | Architecture and culture

The value chain provides a framework for bringing together a great deal of information about how an organisation operates, and relating it to its effectiveness in serving its users. However, it does not give a complete picture of how a firm achieves and sustains competitive advantage. There are a number of threads left hanging loose within the value chain framework, and we need two further, complementary concepts to help us gather those threads together.

8.5.1 The questions that value chain analysis does not answer

The first loose thread is left over from Chapter 7, where we questioned why certain organisations seemed able to learn and to develop their assets into capabilities, while others could not. The answer given there was that capabilities and competences resided in people, and that for those people to function effectively, they needed to have sufficient information, and be motivated to use it for the good of the organisation and its customers.

There is another loose thread hanging from the concept of vertical integration that we deploy within the value chain. There is nothing difficult to emulate about a vertical integration decision. If one firm decides to outsource the management of its IT infrastructure or to bring its after-sales service in-house, any of its competitors can easily follow suit. They can hire the same consultants as advisers, and perhaps even outsource to the same service provider. So why do firms make different decisions in this area? And how are some able to use outsourcing and franchising as the basis of a successful strategy, while others, that are very successful in other ways, try and fail? (See Real-Life Application 8.4.)

REAL-LIFE APPLICATION 8.4

Dell and the direct model

One of the most distinctive value chains is that of the Dell Computing Corporation, an American firm that is second in the world market for personal computers. In 1984 Dell was one of the pioneers of what is known as the 'direct model' of PC marketing. Its marketing and sales activity has always worked by mail, telephone and, nowadays, through the Internet. It does not have a salesforce or distributor network – it pioneered the use of helplines within the after-sales service activity. Its production activity makes each PC to order, so that customers are able to order a PC to their precise specification (a differentiation factor) and Dell is not burdened with stocks of machines that it may not sell (a cost advantage). Dell's inventory levels are well below the industry average and are declining – between the second quarter of 1999 and the second quarter of 2000, they fell from the equivalent of 8 days of sales to 6 days.

Dell's value chain has other advantages. Because its inventories are so lean, it does not have to worry about how to get rid of obsolete computers or components when its suppliers introduce a new generation of products. This gives Dell both cost and differentiation

advantage: it does not have to write off obsolete stock, and it always appears to be marketing the latest technology. It also is able to capture all the information about customer preferences and helpline enquiries, and use it to improve its product development and marketing.

In order to make this value chain work and avoid running out of components, Dell obviously needs very effective procurement and inbound logistics activities. This in turn means that it has to be able to manage vertical linkages with suppliers, since it makes hardly any components in-house.

However good it is at managing a supplier network, Dell is unable to extend that capability to managing networks of distributors or retailers. It experimented with other sales channels in the early 1990s, but found them unprofitable. In the words of Dell's chief financial officer: 'Every time we steer away from the direct model, we get a cold shower.'

Sources: 'Selling PC's like Bananas', *The Economist*, 5 October 1996; www.dell.com

A similar query arises from the concept of linkages in the value chain. It does not take a genius to see the advantages that come from the sales function sharing information with the production and invoicing functions, or from marketing, manufacturing and R&D staff collaborating closely on product development. However, in some organisations these different groups of people are able to forge harmonious linkages, while in others they are constantly at war with one another. Why?

8.5.2 Culture, architecture and relationships

Stories, symbols and other aspects of culture are, however, extremely important when it comes to looking at change in organisations – see Chapter 14. ▶

The answer to these questions comes from two closely related concepts, culture and architecture. As Figure 8.5 shows, there is considerable overlap between them, but some areas of difference. The concept of culture was coined by sociologists and anthropologists, who are interested in how organisations, and other societies, evolve as social structures over time. Research into organisational culture thus covers phenomena like the stories people tell each other, and the symbols they use. These particular aspects of culture are interesting objects of study, but do not directly help us to understand an organisation's competitiveness.

The concept of architecture, by contrast, comes from economics and information technology. It focuses on the aspects of an organisation that are useful in establishing its competitiveness, and extends outside the firm to relationships with suppliers, distributors and franchisees.

At the heart of both concepts are important ideas about relationships between

Figure 8.5 Culture and architecture

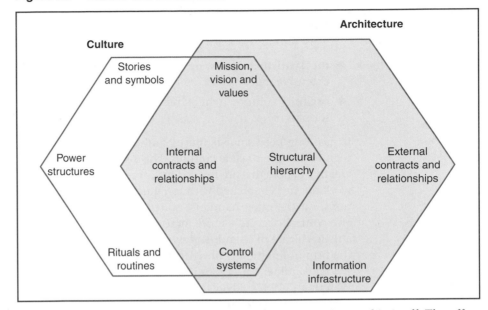

the people in an organisation and between the organisation and its staff. The effectiveness of an organisation has been shown to be affected by the warmth of interpersonal relationships, the extent to which people identify with the firm's aims and values, and the nature of the contractual relationship that people have with the organisation that employs them. The formal manifestations of these relationships, in structures and control systems, also have a significant impact on the way that organisations are able to operate.

Culture and architecture together can thus be viewed as forming the atmosphere within which a value chain must function. If they are either too weak, or too dense and pervasive, then the people in the organisation struggle for breath and for direction. In the following sections, we look at different aspects of culture and architecture, and their effect, indirect but extremely powerful, upon an organisation's competitive position.

8.5.3 Internal relationships and culture

We look at organisational structures and their relationships to culture and strategy in Chapter 10. ▶

As Figure 8.5 shows, culture has a number of aspects. Some of these, such as stories, symbols, power structures and rituals, are mainly of interest when trying to work out how to change an organisation, and are reviewed in Chapter 14. Others, such as control systems, structural hierarchy, mission, vision and values, are considered separately later in this chapter although, as we shall see, the various elements of culture and architecture are quite tightly interwoven. In this section we look at how routines and interpersonal relationships affect an organisation's capacity to compete.

We have already encountered routines as ways of working and operating. These kinds of routine are important parts of organisations' competences and capabilities. However, there are other kinds of routines that people develop for interacting with one another in organisations. They influence, and are influenced by, things like the degree of formality or informality in relationships between people and the extent of their attachment to the organisation and its aims. These factors in turn are reflected in the types of hierarchical structures and control systems that an organisation may develop – or decide not to develop.

A very famous classification of culture along these lines is between:

- **mechanistic** cultures, in which relationships are very formalised and there are extensive, bureaucratic control systems, and
- **organic** cultures, where relationships and control systems are much less formal.

It has long been known (Burns and Stalker, 1961) that innovative organisations tend to develop organic cultures. This seems to be because the highly qualified and creative people that are needed for successful innovation become frustrated if their working life is burdened with too much bureaucracy and control. Mechanistic cultures, on the other hand, are suited to organisations where conditions are stable and control of costs is more important than innovation. If you encounter a mechanistic culture in an industry where innovation is a success or survival factor, then the firm in question is likely to experience problems.

Some influential 1980s writers on corporate culture, notably Peters and Waterman (1982), advocated that firms should adopt a particular type of organic culture. Their research indicated that successful firms tended to have cultures that favoured working in teams and that were shaped by strong sets of corporate values, widely shared by people in the organisation. Rob Goffee and Gareth Jones (1996) later classified these types of culture as 'communal'.

However, Goffee and Jones are sceptical about the idea that the communal culture represents the 'one best way' for any organisation. In Theoretical Perspective 8.1, they identify three other types of culture – networked, mercenary and fragmented – and show how each might be appropriate in certain circumstances. They also point out that communal cultures can be difficult to maintain, a point of view that is supported by the problems that Peters and Waterman's 'excellent' firms had in sustaining their performance.[15]

THEORETICAL PERSPECTIVE 8.1

The impact of culture on competitiveness

Culture, in a word, is community. It is an outcome of how people relate to one another. Communities exist at work just as they do outside the commercial arena. They are built on shared interests and mutual obligations and thrive on co-operation and friendships. It is because of the commonality of all communities that we believe a business's culture can be better understood when viewed through the same lens that has illuminated the study of human organizations for nearly 150 years.

That is the lens of sociology, which divides community into two types of distinct human relations: sociability and solidarity. Briefly, *sociability* is a measure of sincere friendliness among members of a community. *Solidarity* is a measure of a community's ability to pursue shared objectives quickly and effectively, regardless of personal ties. These two categories may at first seem not to capture the whole range of human behaviors, but they have stood the test of close scrutiny, in both academia and the field.

What do sociability and solidarity have to do with culture? The answer comes when you plot the dimensions against each other. The result is four types of community: networked, mercenary, fragmented, and communal. (See Figure 8.6.)

None of these cultures is 'the best'. In fact each is appropriate for different business environments.

The Networked Organization: High Sociability, Low Solidarity

It is perhaps the rituals of what we call networked organizations that are most noticeable to outsiders. People frequently stop to talk in the hallways; lunch is an event in which groups often go out and dine together – and after-hours socializing is not the exception but the rule. Many of these organizations celebrate birthdays and hold parties to honour an employee's long service or retirement. There may be nicknames, in-house jokes, or a common language drawn from shared experiences.

Inside the office, networked cultures are characterized not by a lack of hierarchy but by a profusion of ways to get around it. Friends or cliques of friends make sure that decisions about issues are made before meetings are held to discuss them. People move from one position to another without the "required" training. Employees are hired without going though official channels in the human resources department – they know someone inside the network. This informality can lend flexibility to an organization and be a healthy way of cutting through the bureaucracy. But it also means that the people in these cultures have developed two of the networked organization's key competencies: the ability to collect and selectively disseminate soft information, and the ability to acquire sponsors or allies in the company who will speak on their behalf both formally and informally.

What are the other hallmarks of networked organizations? Their low levels of solidarity mean that managers often have trouble getting functions or operating companies to cooperate. At one large European manufacturer, personal relations among senior executives of business in France, Italy, the United Kingdom, and Germany were extremely friendly. Several executives had known one another for years; some even took vacations together. But when the time came for corporate headquarters to parcel out resources, those same executives fought acrimoniously. At one point, they individually subverted attempts by headquarters to introduce a Europe-wide marketing strategy designed to combat the entry of US competition.

Finally, a networked organization is usually so political that individuals and cliques spend much of their time pursuing personal agendas. It becomes hard for colleagues to agree on priorities and for managers to enforce them. It is not uncommon to hear frequent calls for strong leadership to overcome the divisions of subcultures, cliques, or warring factions in networked organizations.

In addition, because there is little commitment to shared business objectives, employees in networked organizations often contest performance measures, procedures, rules, and systems.

[. . .] despite the political nature of this kind of community, there are many examples of successful networked corporations. These organizations have learned how to overcome the negatives of sociability, such as cliques, gossip, and low productivity, and how to reap its benefits, such as increased creativity and commitment.

We have observed that the networked organization functions well under the following business conditions:

- When corporate strategies have a long time frame. Sociability maintains allegiance to the organization when short-term calculations of interest do not. Consider the case of a company expanding into Vietnam. It might be years before such an effort is profitable, and in the meantime the process of getting operations running may be difficult and frustrating. In a networked culture, employees are often willing to put up with risk and discomfort.
- When knowledge of the peculiarities of local markets is a critical success factor. The reason is that networked

Figure 8.6   Two dimensions, four cultures

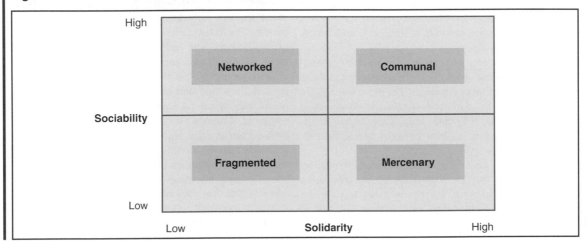

organizations are low on solidarity: members of one unit don't willingly share ideas or information with members of another. This would certainly be a strategic disadvantage if success came from employees having a broad, big-picture perspective. But when success is driven by deep and intense familiarity with a unit's home turf, low solidarity is no hindrance.

● When corporate success is an aggregate of local success. Again, this is a function of low solidarity. If headquarters can do well with low levels of interdivisional communication, then the networked culture is appropriate.

The Mercenary Organization: Low Sociability, High Solidarity

At the other end of the spectrum from the networked organization, the mercenary community is low on hallway hobnobbing and high on data-laden memos. Indeed, almost all communication in a mercenary organization is focused on business matters. The reason: individual interests coincide with corporate objects, and those objectives that are often linked to a crystal clear perception of the "enemy" and the steps required to beat it. As a result, mercenary organizations are characterized by the ability to respond quickly and cohesively to a perceived opportunity or threat in the marketplace. Priorities are decided swiftly – generally by senior management – and enforced throughout the organization with little debate.

Mercenary organizations are also characterized by a clear separation of work and social life. (Interestingly, these cultures often consist of people whose work takes priority over their private life.)

Because of the absence of strong personal ties, mercenary organizations are generally intolerant of poor performance. Those who are not contributing fully are fired or given explicit instructions on how to improve, with a firm deadline. There is a hardheartedness to this aspect of mercenary cultures, and yet the high levels of commitment to a common purpose mean it is accepted, and usually supported, in the ranks.

Employees may very well respect and like their organizations; after all, these institutions are usually fair to those who work hard and meet standards. But those feelings are not sentimental or tied to affectionate relationships between individuals. People stay with high-solidarity companies for as long as their personal needs are met, and then they move on.

[. . .] because of their focused activity, many mercenary organizations are very productive. Moreover, unhindered by friendships, employees are not reluctant to compete, further enhancing performance as standards get pushed even higher.

But mercenary communities have disadvantages as well. Employees who are busy chasing specific targets are often disinclined to cooperate, share information, or exchange new or creative ideas. To do so would be a distraction. Co-operation between units with different goals is even less likely. Consider the example of Warner Brothers, the entertainment conglomerate. The music and film divisions have trouble achieving synergy. Compare this situation with that at Disney, a major competitor, which relentlessly and profitably exploits synergies between its movie characters – from Snow White to Simba – and its merchandising divisions.

The mercenary organization works effectively under the following business conditions:

● When change is fast and rampant. This type of situation calls for a rapid, focused response, which a mercenary organization is able to mount.

● When economies of scale are achieved, or competitive advantage is gained, through creating corporate centers of excellence that can impose processes and procedures on operating companies or divisions. For example, the Zurich-based diversified corporation ABB Asea Brown Boveri builds worldwide centers of excellence for product groups.

● When corporate goals are clear and measurable, and there is therefore little need for input from the ranks or for consensus building.

● When the nature of the competition is clear. Mercenary organizations thrive when the enemy – and the best way to defeat it – are obvious.

The Fragmented Organization: Low Sociability, Low Solidarity

Perhaps most notably, employees of fragmented organizations display a low consciousness of organizational membership. They often believe that they work for themselves or they identify with occupational groups – usually professional. Asked at a party what he does for a living, for instance, a doctor at a major teaching hospital that happens to have this kind of culture might reply, "I'm a surgeon," leaving out the name of the institution where he is employed. Likewise, employees engage in none of the extra-curricular rites and rituals that characterize high-sociability cultures, considering them a waste of time.

People work with their doors shut or, in many cases, at home, going to the office only to collect mail or make long-distance calls. They are often secretive about their projects and progress with co-workers, offering information only when asked point-blank. In extreme cases, members of fragmented organizations attempt to sabotage the work of their "colleagues" through gossip, rumor, or overt criticism delivered to higher-ups in the organization.

This culture also has low levels of solidarity: its members rarely agree about organizational objectives, critical success factors, and performance standards. [...] Leaders often feel isolated and routinely report feeling as if there is no action they can take to effect change. Their calls fall on deaf ears.

But situations do exist that invite, or even benefit from, such a culture, and further, this kind of environment is attractive to individuals who prefer to work alone or to keep their work and personal lives entirely separate.

In our research, we have seen fragmented organizations operate successfully in several forms. First the culture functions well in manufacturing concerns that rely heavily on the outsourcing of piecework. Second, the culture can succeed in professional organizations, such as consulting and law firms, in which highly trained individuals have idiosyncratic work styles. Third, fragmented cultures often accompany organizations that have become virtual: employees work either at home or on the road, reporting in to a central base mainly by electronic means. Of course, fragmented organizations sometimes reflect dysfunctional communities in which ties of sociability or solidarity have been torn asunder by organizational politics, downsizing or other forms of disruption.

The last unhealthy scenario aside however, a fragmented culture is appropriate under the following business conditions:

● When there is little interdependence in the work itself. This might occur, for example, in a company in which pieces of furniture or clothing are subcontracted to individuals who work out of their homes and then assembled at another site. A second example might be a firm composed of tax lawyers, each working for different clients.

● When significant innovation is produced primarily by individuals rather than by teams. This, it should be noted, is becoming increasingly rare in business, as cross-disciplinary teams demonstrate the power of unlike minds working together.

● When standards are achieved by input controls, not process controls. In these organizations, time has proven that management's focus should be on recruiting the right people; once they have been hired and trained, their work requires little supervision.

● When there are few learning opportunities between individuals or when professional pride prevents the transfer of knowledge. In an international oil-trading company we have worked with, for example, employees who traded Nigerian oil never shared market information with employees trading Saudi crude. For one thing, they weren't given any incentive to take the time to do so; for

another, each group of traders took pride in knowing more than the other.

The Communal Organization: High Sociability, High Solidarity

A communal culture can evolve at any stage of a company's life cycle, but when we are asked to illustrate this form, we often cite the characteristics of a typical small, fast-growing, entrepreneurial start-up.

But, as we have said, start-ups don't own this culture. Indeed, communal cultures can be found in mature companies in which employees have worked together for decades to develop both friendships and mutually beneficial objectives.

Regardless of their stage of development, communal organizations share certain traits. First, their employees possess a high, sometimes exaggerated consciousness of organizational identity and membership. [...] Some employees at Nike, it is said, have the company's trademark symbol tattooed above their ankles.

The high solidarity of communal cultures is often demonstrated through an equitable sharing of risks and rewards among employees. Communal organizations, after all, place an extremely high value on fairness and justice, which comes into sharp focus particularly in hard times. For example, during the 1970 recession, rather than lay people off, Hewlett-Packard introduced a 10% cut in pay and hours across every rank. It should be noted that the company's management did not become demonized or despised in the process. In fact, what happened at Hewlett-Packard is another characteristic of communal companies: their leaders command widespread respect, deference, and even affection. Although they invite dissent, and even succeed in receiving it, their authority is rarely challenged.

Solidarity also shows itself clearly when it comes to company goals and values. The mission statement is often given front-and-center display in a communal company's offices, and it evokes enthusiasm rather than cynicism.

Finally, in communal organizations, employees are very clear about the competition. They know which companies threaten theirs – what they do well, how they are weak – and how they can be overcome. And not only is the external competition seen clearly, its defeat is also perceived to be a matter of competing values.

Given all these characteristics, it is perhaps not surprising that many managers see the communal organization as the ideal. [...] where both sociability and solidarity are high, a company gets the best of both worlds – or does it?

The answer is that the communal culture may be an inappropriate and unattainable ideal in many business contexts. Our research suggests that it seems to work best in religious, political, and civic organizations. It is much harder to

▶

293

find commercial enterprises in this quadrant. The reason is that many businesses that achieve the communal form find it difficult to sustain. There are a number of possible explanations. First, high levels of sociability and solidarity are often formed around particular founders or leaders whose departure may weaken either or both forms of social relationship. Second, the high-sociability half of the communal culture is often antithetical to what goes on inside an organization during periods of growth, diversification, or internationalization. These massive and complex change efforts require focus, urgency, and performance – the stuff of solidarity in its undiluted form.

More profoundly, though, there may be a built-in tension between relationships of sociability and solidarity that makes the communal business enterprise an inherently unstable form. The sincere geniality of sociability doesn't usually coexist – it can't – with solidarity's dispassionate, sometimes ruthless focus on achievement of goals.

In what situations, then, does a communal culture function well?

● When innovation requires elaborate and extensive teamwork across functions and perhaps locations. Increasingly, high-impact innovation cannot be achieved by isolated specialists. Rather, as the knowledge base of organizations deepens and diversifies, many talents need to combine (and combust) for truly creative change. For example, at the pharmaceutical company Glaxo

Wellcome, research projects are undertaken by teams from different disciplines – such as genetics, chemistry, and toxicology – and in different locations. Without such teamwork, drug development would be much slower and competitive advantage would be lost.

● When there are real synergies among organizational subunits and real opportunities for learning. We emphasize the word real because synergy and learning are often held up as organizational goals without hard scrutiny. Both are good – in theory. In practice, opportunities for synergy and learning among one company's divisions may not actually exist or be worth the effort.

● When strategies are more long-term than short-term. That is to say, when corporate goals won't be reached in the foreseeable future, managerial mechanisms are needed to keep commitment and focus high. The communal culture provides high sociability to bolster relationships and the commitment that accompanies them and high solidarity to sustain focus.

● When the business environment is dynamic and complex. In these industries, organizations interface with their environment through multiple connections involving technology, customers, the government, competition, and research institutions. A communal culture is appropriate in this kind of environment because its dynamics aid in the synthesis of information from all these sources.

8.5.4 Internal contracts and relationships

In the previous section, we explored how an organisation's culture shapes the way in which relationships are formed between its people, using the language of sociology. In this section, we examine the nature of relationships between people and the organisation. For this, we use the language of law and of game theory.

It can be helpful to think of the relationship between an organisation and its employees as a contract, which specifies what people are expected to do and what they can expect in return. Most people, when they join an organisation, are given a *formal* contract, that sets out the hours that they are expected to work and certain other obligations. For example, most contracts specify that employees should respect the confidentiality of their employer's information, and pass to the firm the rights to anything they invent in the course of their work. The contract also sets out their pay and other rights, such as bonuses, pensions and holidays. It may be supplemented by other documents, such as staff handbooks and job descriptions, which are also part of this formal contract.

In a highly mechanistic culture, such as a government office or a traditional bank, the formal contract may be quite an accurate description of what people actually do. It may be quite common in such cultures for people to arrive promptly at 9.00, spend their day doing precisely the work set out in their job description and depart promptly at 17.30 in the evening. If they are called upon to do work that falls outside their formal job description they may refuse, or accept only in return for extra pay, or after consultation with their union representative. In predictable environments where new challenges are infrequent, this may be a highly efficient way of organising work. People who like to know exactly where they stand and how they will be measured will be attracted to such an organisation, and are quite likely to perform well in it.

However, even in these stable environments, the formal contract often does not cover important aspects of working life. There may be an expectation that everyone will work late and at weekends at certain times of peak workload, such as the end of the financial year. Equally, it may be accepted practice for people to go home early when the workload has subsided, and for an entire department to take a long lunch together on a Friday. These informal, unwritten practices are part of what is known as a **relational contract** (sometimes referred to as a psychological contract) between the firm and its employees.

Relational contracts typically govern a number of important areas, such as promotion and supervision. In some firms, people are promoted automatically after a certain period of time in which they have avoided making mistakes. In others, they are promoted only if they show entrepreneurial flair and are prepared to work long hours. Some people join organisations knowing that their work will be closely supervised, others in the expectation that they will be left alone to develop new products or markets. In some organisations, the relational contract includes a great deal of support for employees – counselling for personal problems, rest-rooms and subsidised meals. The stores of UK retailer Marks & Spencer are periodically visited by a chiropodist – important for staff who spend most of their working day on their feet. In other cases, such as merchant banks or management consultancies, the relational contract is much more brutal: high rewards for those that achieve good results and bring in new business, dismissal for those that do not.

A formal contract may be an adequate framework for a relationship that is not expected to continue for very long. Game theorists call this a finite game – both participants know that it will end after a few periods. In such cases, game theory shows that it is not rational for either player to offer anything more than the minimum required by the contract. So, when McDonald's takes on students to serve in one of its restaurants, it gives them a formal contract that specifies the desired behaviour very tightly, because it knows that most of those people will leave after a few months.

When, however, an organisation and an employee embark on a relationship that both hope will continue indefinitely, the nature of the game changes. In a repeated game, it becomes more rational for the players to experiment with policies that may cost them a certain amount in the short term, but will bring them benefits as long as the other player eventually collaborates. Moreover, if the game has no fixed end, then there is no obvious stage at which it becomes rational for the players to stop collaborating and revert to doing the contractual minimum. So when Sony takes on some new engineers, it makes sense for the firm to offer them an implicit promise of long-term employment and an opportunity to exercise their skills creatively. On the other side of this relational contract, the engineers are expected to devote more time and energy to the job than is required by the formal contract. If the relationship lasts long enough, the company and the engineers will both benefit.

Getting the right relational contracts in place is not simple, since it involves managers right through the organisation behaving consistently over time, and

REAL-LIFE APPLICATION 8.5

Formal and relational contracts at the British Geological Survey

In 1990, the British Geological Survey (BGS) was a government research establishment that had custody of geological records for the United Kingdom, and mapped the geology of the British Isles and the seas and oceans that surrounded it. It undertook research projects for government and commercial clients, in the UK and abroad. Its scientific expertise was (and still is) widely respected.

There was a strong tradition within BGS that once a scientist had been recruited, he or she was there for life. Those who had been given a permanent contract were referred to as having 'tenure' – the same term used for their counterparts in traditional British universities, whose jobs were protected by law. Although in theory, a BGS scientist, unlike a university professor, could be sacked, in practice they rarely left the organisation. Like their university colleagues, they were expected to publish in learned journals.

Many of the survey's scientists worked on projects with a 15-year time span, involving painstaking and arduous work, gathering and analysing rock samples and then writing detailed reports ('memoirs') of their findings. For work of this nature, a relational contract that emphasised long-term commitment on both sides could be said to be appropriate.

However, geological consultancy for commercial and government clients was becoming increasingly important to BGS, as government funding for education and research was under threat. Although some of its scientists were astute commercial operators, others found it difficult to distinguish between the demands of commercial and non-commercial work. They would prolong a project beyond its deadline, and overspend its budget, in order to pursue their scientific interests. The organisation's traditional relational contract was not well-adapted to such work.

UK government policy meant that most of BGS's younger scientists were not permanent employees, but recruited on contracts with a fixed 3–5-year term. The traditional relational contract in BGS did not hold for these limited period appointees (LPAs), who strongly resented what they saw as their second-class status. Although committed scientists, they were conscious of the need to advance their professional standing and find a permanent post elsewhere. This meant that, rationally enough, they would spend much of the final year of their time at BGS looking for their next job. Since a new recruit typically needed one year to become fully effective, LPAs on three year contracts might only spend one-third of their time at BGS working at full capacity. The government's emphasis on formal contracts, although intended to improve BGS's efficiency, probably ended up having the opposite effect.

behaving in a way that makes it clear to employees what the relational contract really is. In the case of Sony, it would ruin the relational contract if engineers were frequently redirected to mundane duties because their manager had overspent on his research budget. Trust is an important element of a relational contract, and if that trust is broken at any stage, the contract is broken too.

Even where a strong relational contract is in place, it may not always benefit the organisation (see Real-Life Application 8.5). It can also be difficult to achieve an appropriate balance between formal and relational contracts – when Sony announced it was to make 17,000 staff redundant in 1999, it was signalling that the term in its relational contract that offered lifetime employment was only valid if the staff could give it commercial success.

Because relational contracts are so difficult to manage, they are a possible source of competitive advantage (Kay, 1993). They are not a direct form of advantage – people do not buy a Sony Discman because they like the way the firm treats its engineers. However, strong and appropriate relational contracts can form the basis of competences and capabilities in areas like customer responsiveness and innovation.

REAL-LIFE APPLICATION 8.6

Internal and external relational contracts at Sony

We shall guide and foster subcontracting factories in ways that will help them become independent, and we shall strive to expand and strengthen mutual cooperation with such factories.

We shall carefully select employees, and our firm shall be comprised of minimal number of employees. We shall avoid to have formal positions for the mere sake of having them, and shall place emphasis on a person's ability, performance and character, so that each individual can fully exercise his or her abilities and skills.

We shall distribute the company's surplus earnings to all employees in an appropriate manner, and we shall assist them in practical manner to secure a stable life. In return, all employees shall exert their utmost effort into their job.

Source: Extracted from the 'Management Policies' section of the 1946 Founding Prospectus of the Tokyo Telecommunications Engineering Corporation – later to become the Sony Corporation.

8.5.5 External contracts and relationships

The balance of formal and relational contracts is not only significant in a firm's relationship with its own staff. It also applies to its relationships with its suppliers, distributors and customers (Real-Life Application 8.6).

Here again, a firm may hope that, by building long-term relationships and bonds of trust, it can persuade its partners to invest extra time, effort and money in developing the business. For a company that has opted for a virtual value chain, or one with a very low degree of vertical integration, the nature of these relational contracts is likely to be vitally important. They may represent the only way that it can obtain advantage over competing firms that are tapping into the same supplier/distributor network.

Benetton is a good example of how relational contracts and a virtual value chain can operate in practice. As we have already pointed out, much of its manufacturing and distribution are outsourced to captive suppliers and to independent retail partners. Suppliers are able to rely upon Benetton for loans to upgrade their equipment, retailers on a prompt response to their demands for stock. Neither of these commitments is written down – they have grown over time as the various participants have grown to understand each other's needs. Luciano Benetton is himself famous for taking on his original retail partners on the basis of a handshake, with no written agreement. Even his company's system for dyeing whole garments, rather than knitting them from coloured wool, was originally developed by a consultant, a friend of the Benetton family. Although he had no formal contract at the time, he has been handsomely rewarded for his discovery.

Although strong relational contracts can be very effective, they are not a panacea. Benetton's relational contracts were originally developed with a network of friends and contacts, mainly from the Benettons' native Veneto region in northern Italy. It may not be possible to get the same benefit out of them when operating in a different country, region or industry. As Real-Life Application 8.7 shows, not all firms are open to this kind of relationship, and it is possible to compete without it.

8.5.6 Mission, vision and values

Part of the relational contract between a firm and its other stakeholders – staff,

REAL-LIFE APPLICATION 8.7

Formal and relational contracts in the automobile industry

In the automobile industry, the traditional carmakers, Ford and General Motors, had highly adversarial relationships with their suppliers in which formal contracts and short-term relationships predominated. Suppliers were selected largely on the basis of price and their performance in fulfilling recent contracts.

The Japanese competitors in the 1960s and 1970s did not have access to Ford's and GM's suppliers, and had to develop their own. They established a form of relational contract: the carmaker would work with the supplier to improve quality and reduce costs. The two parties would commit to a long-term relationship and share the benefits and the learning. These strong supplier–carmaker relationships were widely recognised as an important factor in the cost advantage that Toyota and Honda built up over Ford and GM.

When Japanese carmakers came to set up factories in Europe and the USA in the 1970s, they found that their supplier philosophy did not work as well as it had in Japan. They found resistance among component manufacturers in these countries, who were unused to Japanese ideas of quality and collaboration. However, they were slowly able to win some suppliers over to their way of working.

More recently, in Europe, General Motors and Volkswagen have succeeded in bringing their costs down to levels that make them competitive. However, these cost reductions have been won through a far more adversarial and price-driven relationship than is used by Japanese firms.

◄ *Mission, vision and values are defined in Chapter 2.*

The kinds of structure and systems that are found in organisations with a strong mission are reviewed in Chapter 10. ►

suppliers, distributors and so on – is bound up with the organisation's values. If people feel that an organisation stands for something that they can subscribe to, they are more likely to trust it, and will be happier with the idea of a long-term relationship. Frequently, an organisation's values are manifested through its mission and vision.

Many writers believe that mission, vision and values are of great importance. According to Peter Drucker (1973): 'That business purpose and business mission are so rarely given adequate thought is perhaps the most important single cause of business frustration and business failure.' Peters and Waterman (1982) found that strong values were one of the characteristics of excellent companies. Collins and Porras (1991, 1995, 1996) conducted a study of matched pairs of firms in a number of industries. They found that the firms which enjoyed enduring success (measured by stock market performance) over a number of decades had a clear mission and core values.

Mission statements

Organisations may issue formalised statements of their core values or purpose, such as mission and vision statements (Real-Life Application 8.8). They can also give out strong messages about what they stand for in intangible ways, such as:

- their perceived ethical stance (demonstrated by, for example, the company's expressed refusal to behave in unethical ways itself, or to own the shares of unethical companies);
- their creativity (demonstrated for example by bright and original colour schemes in its offices or on its company literature).

The target audience for these messages consists of both external stakeholders such as customers and suppliers and internal ones such as employees. Such communi-

REAL-LIFE APPLICATION 8.8

Examples of mission statements

These are often displayed prominently on the entrance foyer of the organisation's HQ, or printed in public communications such as a firm's annual report and accounts. They can be very long, or quite succinct.

'To be the undisputed leader in world travel.'

Source: British Airways

Purpose of incorporation

(a) To establish an ideal factory that stresses a spirit of freedom and open-mindedness, and where engineers with sincere motivation can exercise their technological skills to the highest level;

(b) To reconstruct Japan and to elevate the nation's culture through dynamic technological and manufacturing activities;

(c) To promptly apply highly advanced technologies which were developed in various sectors during the war to common households;

(d) To rapidly commercialize superior technological findings in universities and research institutions that are worthy of application in common households;

(e) To bring radio communications and similar devices into common households and to promote the use of home electric appliances;

(f) To actively participate in the reconstruction of war-damaged communications network by providing needed technology;

(g) To produce high-quality radios and to provide radio services that are appropriate for the coming new era;

(h) To promote the education of science among the general public.

Source: Taken from the 1946 Founding Prospectus of the Tokyo Telecommunications Engineering Corporation – later to become the Sony Corporation, quoted in Nathan (1999).

Example of vision and strategic intent

McDonald's vision is to be the world's best quick-service restaurant experience. Being the best means consistently satisfying customers better than anyone else through outstanding quality, service, cleanliness and value. Supporting this vision are five global strategies:

- Develop our people at every level of the organisation, beginning in our restaurants

- Foster innovation in menu, facilities, marketing, operations and technology

- Expand our global mindset by sharing best practices and leveraging our best people resources around the world

- Continue the successful implementation of changes underway in McDonald's USA

- Long term, reinvent the category in which we compete and develop other business and growth opportunities.

Source: McDonald's Annual Report, 1999.

---

cation of the organisation's identity is also an important way of attracting the 'right' sort of staff and discouraging people who might not fit in.

Ingredients of mission and vision

Effective missions and visions contain a number of elements (Campbell and Yueng, 1991; Collins and Porras, 1991, 1996):

- **A clear ideology, or set of values** – these may relate to the company's policies towards its employees and customers, to the quality of its products or to its beliefs about what constitutes good business practice. Sony's ideology was summarised in 1986 by Akio Morita in the Sony Pioneer Spirit: 'Sony is a pioneer and never intends to follow others. Through progress, Sony wants to serve the whole world. It shall always be a seeker of the unknown ... Sony has a principle of respecting and encouraging one's ability ... and always tries to bring out the best in a person. This is the vital force of Sony' (Nathan, 1999).

- **A core purpose** – the organisation's reason for being. Many theorists advocate that a firm's purpose should be more than just a broad statement of what it does ('We make computers for knowledge workers'). Rather, it should embrace a wider set of ideals that can inspire employees and enlist their loyalty. Sony's core purpose is 'to experience the joy of advancing and applying technology for the benefit of the public'. The purpose of the Walt Disney Company is 'to make people happy'.

- **An envisioned future** – an idea of what the company hopes to become in the future, and what it will be like to work there. The idea of the future may be expressed through:
  - *targets* – 'Achieve sales of €1 billion in four years' time' or 'Become the world leader in our industry by 2005'
  - *focus on a common enemy* – Pepsico's mission at one point was 'Beat Coke!' Komatsu, a Japanese manufacturer of earthmoving equipment, adopted the slogan 'Maru-C' ('encircle Caterpillar' – a US company that was the long-standing industry leader, with a high reputation for product quality)
  - *a role model* – to be 'the Microsoft' or 'the Mercedes' of a particular industry
  - *internal targets* – ABB, the Swedish Swiss heavy engineering group, coined the slogan, 'Think global, act local' to encapsulate the transnational strategy and architecture towards which it was striving.

Some theorists advocate that the envisioned future should be very ambitious – perhaps even unrealistically so. Such highly ambitious aims, referred to variously as *stretch targets* (Hamel and Prahalad, 1993) or as *BHAGs* ('big, hairy, audacious goals'; Collins and Porras, 1996) have one main benefit. They force people in the organisation to think beyond the constraints of its current resources and environment, and look more broadly and creatively at what might be possible.

There is no reason in theory why an organisation's mission, vision and values should not focus on financial performance and shareholder value, if it aims to create a mercenary culture, and to attract staff who are motivated by wealth and its creation. However, most writers in this area believe that mission, vision and values should have an uplifting and ethical content, along the lines of the Sony examples given above.

An organisation's mission is not the same as its strategy. A strategy is the organisation's response to its environment, and will change as the environment changes. Mission, vision and values, on the other hand, are meant to represent timeless certainties that the organisation can cling to as the world around it alters. They alter infrequently – Collins and Porras (1996) contend that they should endure for one hundred years. However, if a mission is to be meaningful, then the organisation's strategy, and the way that its members behave in practice, should be compatible with it (Campbell and Yeung, 1991).

Benefits and risks of mission and vision

There are three main theoretical advantages of a clear mission, vision and values. Firstly, they can speed up decision-making in organisations, by providing clear guidelines for behaviour and decisions that are instilled into people's everyday routines. People at all levels can thus take quick, intuitive decisions without needing to waste time consulting a manager at a higher level. Secondly, they can reduce agency costs, since if everyone in the organisation believes in the mission and values, they are less likely to try to cheat the organisation and require less supervision. Thirdly, they can enhance an organisation's reputation, particularly if the values are close to those that are espoused by important customers or other stakeholders.

Despite these potential benefits, not all organisations have explicit missions, visions or values – Benetton, for example, prefers to extol the 'Benetton system', a straightforward exposition of its strategy. There is no clear empirical evidence that the firms that have them perform better than those that do not (Bark and Baetz, 1998). Although many firms have developed mission statements, this is not necessarily evidence that they have a clear mission or vision. Commentators agree that most corporate mission statements are bland and say much the same things, so that it can be difficult to tell one firm's statement from another's. An organisation may have a clear purpose and set of values without needing a written mission statement. On the other hand, it may produce a mission statement that is far removed from the reality of how the firm thinks and acts, and give a false impression of unity and shared purpose. In such cases, a mission statement may do more harm than good (Campbell and Nash, 1992) since it gives the impression that senior management is out of touch, and makes staff feel cynical, rather than committed.

8.5.7 Hierarchical structures and control systems

We return to structures and control systems in detail in Chapter 10. ▶

Two very important elements of an organisation's architecture are its hierarchical structure (typically portrayed on its organisation chart) and the systems it uses to control and reward people's behaviour. There are also manifestations of the organisation's culture. A mechanistic culture tends to give rise to tall structures with many layers of managers and supervisors, and to detailed and pervasive control systems, while an organic structure will have fewer layers of supervision and fewer formal systems.

Structure and systems both have a strong influence on people's motivation and on the nature of their relational contract with the organisation. For example, rigid control systems imply a relational contract in which people are discouraged from taking risks and from taking actions that are not in accordance with the organisation's formal policies.

8.5.8 Information infrastructure

Information systems constitute the final element of an organisation's architecture. They can be thought of as the 'hard wiring' that underpins linkages between activities in the value chain (Section 8.1.6). They first became recognised as an important element in an organisation's success or failure in the early 1980s. This was when firms like Benetton achieved competitive advantage through early adoption of technologies such as electronic point of sale (EPOS) tills to gather information on a daily basis, analyse which items were selling well or badly and revise manufacturing schedules to reflect these sales patterns. Another influential early case was American Airlines (AA), whose load management system enabled it to analyse patterns in aircraft usage and work out how many seats on each flight should be offered at a discount, and how many held back for passengers paying full fare. AA was also able to be more flexible than its competitors in offering last-minute discounts to fill aircraft that would otherwise have flown half-empty.

Benetton's and AA's pioneering computer systems have now been widely imitated. However, information systems can be crucial in determining whether linkages between different elements in the value chain actually work in practice. Although most systems are widely available from a variety of suppliers, some firms seem better able to implement them than others, so that they are a potential source of competitive advantage, at least in the short term. Examples of important IT applications include:

- EDI and corporate extranets to link firms with their suppliers;
- ECR (effective customer response) systems to link manufacturers with retailers, and help them to understand sales patterns and plan their manufacturing;
- EPOS and bar-coding to help the manufacturing, distribution and sales activities share information;
- CAD/CAM (computer-aided design/computer-aided manufacturing) systems to enable product designers to share information quickly and cheaply with the manufacturing activity;
- sophisticated management information systems (MIS) to enable managers across the organisation to share information, compare their performance with that of other functions or divisions and 'drill down' for more detailed information to establish precisely where they are doing well or badly.

Another recent phenomenon is the use of data-mining software to find patterns in companies' data. This software can detect whether, typically, a customer that buys a pair of trousers also buys a shirt or a sweater a few days later. If a customer fails to appear for the follow-up purchase, the firm can send a voucher to tempt them back to the store. This type of *relationship marketing* information is as yet not fully exploited (few firms have enough computer capacity to process it).

Although increasing emphasis is being placed on computer-driven information infrastructure, there can be cases where less resource intensive methods work as well or better. Getting designers and salespeople to have a drink together every few weeks may be as effective in getting them to share information and ideas as networking their computers. Similarly, getting research engineers, factory supervisors or even the CEO to call on customers with the salesforce, or to man the help desk periodically, can be an effective way of passing market information around the organisation.

8.6 Configuration and competitive advantage

8.6.1 Coherence

Miles and Snow (1978) showed, in a research project covering more than 80 US firms in three different industries, that those that were successful over a sustained period of time were those that had managed to link three decisions in a coherent way:

- the marketing decision about which products to sell in which markets – what we, in Chapter 6, have called 'competitive stance';

- the manufacturing decision – broadly equivalent to the choice of value chain;

- the administrative decision – broadly equivalent to what we have called architecture.

In a similar vein, the well-known 'McKinsey 7S' framework (Waterman et al., 1980) points up the linkages between **strategy** (competitive stance in our terminology), **staff** (human resources), **skills** (competences and capabilities) and **structure**, **systems**, **shared values** and management **style** (all elements of culture and architecture).

Both these pieces of research point to the importance of coherence[16] between the different elements of strategy if an organisation is to have a sustainable position. The value chain needs to be able to develop and to supply the target customer group with the products and services they require, meeting their requirements on quality and timing, at a low enough cost for the organisation to make a financial return that satisfies its key stakeholders. This means that the competitive stance – the choice of products and target customers – must be realistic, given any limitations in the firm's value chain, just as the value chain must develop to keep pace with changes in competitive stance.

So, British Airways aims to deliver a high quality of airline service to business customers. It deploys distinctive assets within its value chain, like sleeper seats on long-distance flights, to add value to these customers. It has tried, through extensive training, to instil a culture and architecture that motivates people to deliver a high level of personal service to its customers. In 1997 it tried to change its cabin crew's pay and conditions to cut costs. This broke the relational contract between staff and airline that had sustained its levels of customer service. Service quality declined – and so did customer satisfaction and BA's profits.[17]

It may be helpful to visualise the different elements using the metaphor por-

Figure 8.7　Value chain, culture architecture and competitive stance

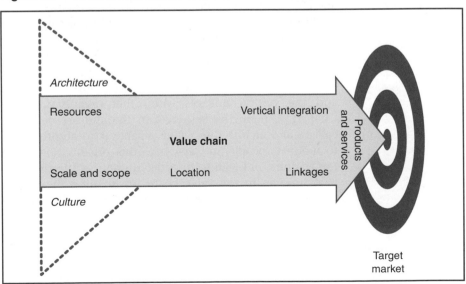

trayed in Figure 8.7. The organisation is trying to 'hit' its target market with its products and services – the head of the arrow. The value chain forms the body of the arrow that conveys the arrowhead. The architecture and culture are the flights of the arrow – they give it direction, colour and distinctiveness.

8.6.2 Distinctiveness

In order to have a sustainable position, an organisation must make itself distinctive in ways that customers find valuable or that offer some cost advantage. Distinctiveness does not normally come from the way a value chain is configured. Almost anyone who knows anything about the fashion business could replicate many elements of Benetton's value chain. They could hire some designers and a decent advertising agency to build a brand, locate two or three reliable low-cost clothing manufacturers (there are many in India and South-East Asia), link up with some retail partners and install EPOS tills and off-the-shelf software to analyse the sales results.

A firm can still make its value chain distinctive, through deploying resources that are rare and difficult to obtain, copy or substitute. These might be physical resources, though in Benetton's case the shops, tills, computers and machinery that it employs are not really difficult for competitors to acquire. More likely it will be through capabilities and competences. A firm might copy Benetton's information systems, but its managers would need time to work out how to use the mass of sales data with which they are confronted each day. They would also need experience before they could tell a temporary drop in sales of a line of clothing from a permanent fall in demand that should trigger a revision to the firm's production schedules. A competitor would also require time before it could build a brand and a reputation to match Benetton's.

There are other possible sources of distinctiveness in Benetton's value chain. It would be quite difficult for a newcomer to replicate its location decisions, since its historic and cultural ties give it first pick of all the reasonable suppliers in northern Italy. A newcomer would have to hope that it could find similarly committed and effective suppliers elsewhere. However, the parts of Benetton's value chain that are most difficult to copy are the vertical linkages with suppliers and retailers, and the strong bonds of trust that underpin them.

This is an illustration of a more general point, that the most distinctive elements of a value chain are: the capabilities, competences and other intangible resources that make it effective; the horizontal linkages between activities; and the vertical linkages with other organisations. As we pointed out in Chapter 7, intangible resources in the end are derived from an organisation's culture and architecture, which enable it to absorb and process information or to motivate people, in ways that other organisations cannot. The same two factors, culture and architecture, determine the effectiveness of horizontal and vertical linkages in the value chain, by shaping the relational contracts between the participants and the means by which they acquire and share information and knowledge.

8.6.3 First-mover advantage

There is, however, a stage at which the whole value chain may be distinctive and represent a source of competitive advantage. This is when an organisation introduces an innovative value chain that is radically different from the way that existing competitors are configured. This is the kind of advantage that Benetton had in the early 1980s, with its low costs and low levels of vertical integration. Other examples are the value chains of Southwest Airlines and of on-line retailer Amazon.com (see Chapter 3, Real-Life Application 3.5).

When an existing competitor is confronted with this kind of value chain innovation, it faces a dilemma.

- It can ignore the innovation in the hope that it will fail, or will appeal to only a small customer segment. This reaction – 'it'll never work' or 'it's just a fad' – can be quite common. Managers are quite likely to be psychologically predisposed to believe that their existing way of operating is the best, or only viable, one.

- It can abandon its existing value chain and imitate the new one. This will be a difficult decision for any firm to make. It is likely to have sunk a considerable amount of time, effort and money into building the existing value chain, and in refining the competences and capabilities that make it effective. It may have funds tied up in buildings and machinery, and emotional capital tied up in relationships with its existing people and partner organisations. Writing off these sunk costs in favour of a new and untried solution would be very risky.

- It can try to 'straddle', by using its existing value chain to serve the customers that are being targeted by the new competitors. If this works, it may give the firm competitive advantage over the new entrant, through superior economies of scale and scope. This is what US bookseller Barnes and Noble and UK retailer WH Smith are trying to achieve by combining on-line retailing with their existing bookshops. They hope to use their reputations and their capabilities in purchasing and distribution to succeed in both types of bookselling. However, when straddling goes wrong – as it did when Continental Airlines tried to launch a low-cost airline using its existing fleet and distribution channels – it can be very costly, and hurt both new and old value chains (see Real-Life Application 3.5).

The most likely reaction, therefore, is for the existing competitor to wait and see if the new value chain succeeds. If it does, then it can start to build a parallel business using the new value chain, as British Airways has done with its low-cost subsidiary, Go. Or it can take the traumatic decision to jettison old ways of working and change to the new.

In the meantime, however, the new competitor has a breathing space in which it can accumulate financial resources and build a reputation and distinctive capabilities in operating its innovative value chain. That means that, even if the value chain is eventually copied, its inventor may still possess the ingredients of competitive advantage. This is a form of what is known as **first-mover advantage**, where the first firm to launch a new product or process gains an enduring advantage over the followers.

First-mover advantage is believed to be particularly important for electronic commerce, where the early indications seem to be that the first firms to build a well-known brand will become the dominant suppliers of a particular product or service on the World Wide Web. This is the explicit reason why Amazon.com is happy to accrue losses now in order to build up a competitive position for the future in a broad variety of products.

8.7 Summary

In this chapter we have looked at how organisations configure themselves to achieve cost and differentiation advantage:

- Value chain analysis lets us pinpoint the *particular* capabilities and assets that are important to an organisation and show *precisely* where and how they are being applied to add value.

- The value chain consists of a number of primary and support activities. Each activity can contribute to cost and/or differentiation advantage by virtue of:
  - the resources deployed in the activity
  - the extent to which it is vertically integrated or outsourced
  - its scale and scope
  - its location
  - its linkages with other activities.

- Different types of generic value chain can be used for the analysis of an organisation, depending on whether it is a manufacturing-style organisation, a professional services organisation or a network.

- Value chain analysis is most valuable if used to identify the distinctive elements that give an organisation cost and differentiation advantage, rather than as a framework for cataloguing every aspect of every activity.

- Business processes can be used as an alternative to the value chain in analysing how and where an organisation adds value.

- An organisation's culture and architecture can explain how it is able to absorb and process information and motivate people so as to develop competences, capabilities and knowledge assets, and create linkages between value chain activities.

- For an organisation to have a sustainable competitive position, there must be coherence between its competitive stance, its value chain and its culture and architecture. Its value chain must also contain some elements that make it distinctive.

Typical questions

We conclude this chapter with a look at some of the questions that you may be asked that relate to organisational configuration, and how you can use the theory in this chapter to answer them.

1. *Why was the organisation's strategy not a success?*
   As always, answers to questions like this must be set in the context of the environment. It is helpful to start with an analysis of the organisation's competitive stance, using the material in Chapter 6. An analysis of the environment, using the techniques highlighted in Chapter 5, can then be used to show why the firm's choices of product and target market were right or wrong. At the

end of this part of the exercise, it should be clear what the customer requirements were, and what were the success and survival factors for a competitor in the industry.

The organisation's value chain can then be drawn (see 'Practical dos and don'ts' on p. 285). This will bring out the distinctive factors that enabled the firm to serve the target market more efficiently or effectively than its competitors. It may also highlight elements of first-mover advantage (Section 8.6.3). Or, it may make it plain that there was *nothing* distinctive about the value chain, which is a likely explanation for a firm's lack of success. If the firm was successful despite this, then the implication is that it was able to take advantage of a favourable environment.

In trying to explain failure, the value chain can be used as a framework to analyse the success and survival factors for the industry, and to explain in detail why the firm did not meet them. You may also want to look for any lack of coherence (Section 8.6.1) between competitive stance and configuration.

2. *How did the firm's culture and architecture contribute to its success?*

Start, again, with an analysis of the industry using the material in Chapter 5. Then use the theory in Section 8.5.3 and Theoretical Perspective 8.1 to demonstrate how the firm's culture – networked, mercenary, fragmented or communal – was appropriate, given the nature of the success factors in the industry at the time.

Then, move on to an analysis of the organisation's resources (Chapter 7) to pick out any competences, capabilities and learning that were important to its competitive advantage. Use value chain analysis (this chapter) to identify any important horizontal and vertical linkages. Relate those back to the culture and architecture using the material in Section 8.5.

Appendix 8.1: How value is created in the different activities

This appendix is intended as a reference resource for you to use when you try to develop a value chain analysis for an organisation. It details how each activity may use resources, vertical integration, scope, scale, location and linkages to generate cost and differentiation advantage. It also gives examples of the way in which architecture and culture underlie organisations' valuable capabilities. These detailed lists are long and a little repetitive, so you may wish to skip them on a first reading of this chapter, and return to them when you try to develop a value chain in earnest.

Not all organisations will possess all the attributes that we describe in these lists, but the following sections will give you some clues about where to look for sources of competitive advantage when mapping a value chain. The appendix is divided into four main parts, dealing with the primary activities of manufacturing-style organisations, secondary activities, professional services organisations and with network organisations.

Manufacturing-style organisations – primary activities

In this part of the Appendix (Sections A–F) we discuss the primary activities for a manufacturing-style firm. The support activities, which are broadly similar for all three types of value chain, are reviewed in Sections G–J.

A. Product design and development

Resources

◀ *We give an example of how Merck, the US pharmaceuticals company, uses risk management in innovation in Section 7.3.1.*

Innovation capabilities may lead to products with superior functionality or reliability, and capabilities in customer responsiveness may help the firm be consistently quicker to the market with new generations of product. In both cases the product design and development activity generates differentiation advantage (Real-Life Application 8.9). A capability in risk management may give cost advantage, by delivering fewer products that fail in the market place, and wasting less attention and money on unpromising products that fail to deliver. The activity may also derive advantage from superior physical resources – state-of-the-art laboratories or computing facilities – or human resources, such as designers.

Vertical integration

We look at how strategic alliances help companies to extend the range of their activities in Section 15.3. ▶

The design and development of core products is an example of an activity that many people[18] believe is too important to be outsourced completely, although selective outsourcing of part of the process is not uncommon. Automobile manufacturers will often commission specialist design houses like the Italian firm

---

REAL-LIFE APPLICATION 8.9

Digital product design and development at Sony

Following the appointment of Nobuyuki Idei as president in 1995, Sony reoriented its product range away from analogue devices, such as traditional TVs and the Walkman, towards personal computers and other products using digital technology. This move was spearheaded by its Computer Science Laboratory (CSL), which developed the Navicam digital camera that helped differentiate the Vaio laptop, the 'memory stick', a device the size of a piece of chewing gum that can be used to transfer data between digital cameras, printers and other devices, and the Aperios operating system that Sony hoped to establish as a standard for devices like the set-top boxes for cable television, which have to deal with high volumes of video and audio data.

The CSL's prime source of excellence was its human resources – some of the brightest and most creative engineers in Japan. Selected for their originality and for possessing the strength of will to challenge established thinking, they were attracted by the laboratory's culture, which offered them a great deal of personal and intellectual freedom. Inside the laboratory, dress was casual and there were no obvious signs of seniority and

power. Researchers were on short-term contracts and on high salaries related to performance. Although organic, meritocratic cultures and architectures are common in the best American research establishments, they are unusual for Japan.

The CSL's scale was small, with only 32 researchers. The personal computer development centre was separate from CSL, in San Jose, California, while CSL itself had a small offshoot in Paris specialising in human cognition. CSL was strategically located in Tokyo, out of sight of Sony's main offices there, to symbolise its detachment from the mainstream Sony culture, but close to Mr Idei's office.

CSL's head, Mario Tokoro, reported directly to Mr Idei. It also had strong linkages with operating units, to which it passed its projects for development into consumer products, and with Sony's other research laboratories, several of which were headed by CSL 'graduates'. It had developed vertical linkages with other firms, such as NTT, the main Japanese telephone company, and with Japan's Keio University, where Mr Tokoro was formerly a professor.

Pininfarina to enhance the looks of their cars. Hewlett-Packard was able to launch a new miniature disk-drive product very quickly (in under 10 months) by combining its own capabilities with expertise in micro-electronics, drive head engineering and manufacturing from three different partner firms.[19] In some industries, like microprocessors and aircraft, the cost and expertise needed to develop new generations of products are so vast that even rich firms like IBM and Boeing are unable to manage them by themselves, and seek joint ventures.

Small firms may need to outsource their product development to specialist firms with a larger skill base. However, there are risks in doing so, since they will find it difficult to prevent the knowledge from being passed on to their competitors.

Scale and scope

There are some benefits of scale in product design and development. These have less to do with cost reduction or maximising resource utilisation than with the fact that creative people tend to be more effective when working in communities where they can bounce ideas around. There may also be benefits from scope, if a firm is able to harness ideas from one product to develop another. This is why small firms may benefit from outsourcing product development to specialist firms, who are better able to afford to build and equip a community of researchers and designers who are exposed to a richer range of creative problems.

Location

The location of design facilities can be important. It may be helpful for researchers and designers to be located near their key customers, or to be able to network informally with their counterparts in other firms. A fashion or cosmetics firm may put part of its product design capacity in Milan or Paris. Also certain countries have competences in particular fields. The UK and the USA have reputations for original thinking and expertise in pure science, Germany for good engineering and Italy and Sweden for designing good-looking products. This is why firms like Honda or Ford may choose to maintain design centres in those countries, even if their main product development effort is elsewhere.

Linkages

Product design and development has important linkages with other activities. By designing products or services that are cheaper to manufacture, transport or service, it can help the operations, distribution or after-sales service activities to generate cost advantage. There may also be vertical linkages to customers, either directly or via the after-sales service activity, and to suppliers, who are also increasingly involved in the design of major components.[20] Companies are increasingly using the Internet to build customer feedback into their product design decisions, and customers are increasingly starting to expect to be involved in the process (Prahalad and Ramaswamy, 2000).

B.   Supply

The supply activity[21] is particularly important in retailing and some manufacturing organisations.

Resources

Where supply is important, it is common for considerable investment to be made in information technology resources to link firms with their suppliers. EDI (electronic data interchange) systems enable firms to place orders with suppliers without the expenditure of time and money involved in manual, paper-based procedures. Some firms, like UK food retailer Tesco, are upgrading their EDI systems into corporate extranets that they can use to communicate their requirements to suppliers. Suppliers can access extranets using a normal modem and web browser, and do not have to invest in the specialised hardware and software needed for EDI. These IT assets contribute to organisational capabilities in reliability and customer responsiveness. The firm gets differentiation advantage by ensuring that customers have the right products consistently available at the right time. However, since the IT systems can be bought commercially, and suppliers that have learned to operate with one firm can pass the benefit of their experience on to others, these capabilities do not always offer sustainable advantage.

Vertical integration

It is uncommon for organisations to keep control of the entire supply activity. If anything the trend in this area is for firms to outsource by making their suppliers responsible for delivering inputs promptly and cheaply. This passes much of the cost of holding and managing inventories upstream to the supplier.

Scale and scope

Scale and scope are not sources of cost or differentiation advantage within the supply activity itself, but do play a role in an important linkage between supply and purchasing. The purchasing activity, which handles the actual negotiations of terms and conditions with suppliers, needs to have sufficient power to insist that they adopt the firm's supply systems and procedures. This power is greater for firms that order large volumes of particular inputs.

Location

A firm's location relative to its suppliers can be important in ensuring continuity and timeliness of supply. Automobile firms like General Motors and Fiat build their newest assembly plants on large sites and insist that their suppliers build their own factories on the same complex.

Linkage

We have already mentioned (under 'Scale and scope') the supply activity's linkage with the purchasing activity. Its other important linkage is with the operations activity. Manufacturing systems like MRP (materials requirements planning) and MRPII (manufacturing requirements planning) have become increasingly common. Their purpose is to reduce inventory levels by allowing a firm to track precisely how much of each input is needed to fulfil its sales schedule, and when. The firm then orders only the precise amount of components needed, with no buffer stocks. For raw materials and bought-in components, the supply activity has to ensure a smooth flow of inputs from suppliers. An even more exacting discipline comes from JIT (just-in-time) manufacturing systems, which call upon suppliers to deliver their inputs only a few days or hours before they are needed. MRP and JIT both make strong demands on the supply activity, to make sure the correct inputs arrive at the right time and that they meet quality specifications.

Co-operation with suppliers is vital if a supply chain is to run effectively, so that vertical linkages are important in the supply activity.

C.   Operations

The operations activity sits at the heart of most organisations' competitive advantage.

Resources

Because they are so central to an organisation's competitiveness, operational activities may attract a lot of investment as firms seek to reduce unit production costs, reduce wastage, maximise the utilisation of key assets and improve output quality. Firms sometimes derive advantage from proprietary physical assets, such as machine tools and robots made to their specific design. However, as we discussed in Chapter 7, advantage is more likely to come from building superior capabilities and competences. For example, although the concepts of MRP and JIT (discussed above under 'Supply: Linkages') have been around for some twenty years and are now quite widespread, firms like Toyota are much better than their competitors at actually *operating* them. Systems like these may contribute to capabilities in innovation, reliability, responsiveness to customer requirements or speed of response, all important in the operations area.

Within a virtual value chain (see Section 8.1.2), a firm's architecture, in particular the bonds of trust it may build with its suppliers, and the resulting competences in motivating partner firms and controlling their performance, appear to be crucial. IT competences may also be important in ensuring that these vertical linkages work well. Real-Life Application 8.10 illustrates this, and a number of other facets of Benetton's operations activity.

Vertical integration

As we discussed in 8.1.2, vertical integration 'make or buy' decisions are very important to the operations activity. Increasingly, decisions about which core activities to retain in-house and which suppliers to seek for the remaining ones are seen as central to an organisation's competitive advantage, and among the main factors that distinguish one firm's value chain from another.

Scale and scope

The operations activity is an area where economies of scale (Section 8.1.3) are likely to come into play – if they exist. The availability of production economies of scale will be a major factor in determining whether an organisation pushes into global markets. The size of a factory or a restaurant has an important effect on unit costs: if it is too small, then overheads are likely to push them up, while if it is too large, management and communication problems may impede efficiency. One of McDonald's sources of advantage over its competitors has been that its restaurants, by virtue of their size and location, have the highest average sales per unit in the industry.

Economies of scope may also come into play. If there is enough similarity between the products or services that an organisation offers, then it may be able to share overheads between them and reduce unit costs. However, the opposite may happen if the demands of one type of product interfere with the production of another. Economies of scope can be easier to obtain if the organisation invests in physical resources, such as flexible manufacturing systems (FMS) and computerised scheduling systems, that are designed to maximise flexibility and give low costs even on short production runs.

Location

Location of operations can be a major influence on an organisation's cost position, and its ability to meet customer needs promptly. For example, low wage levels coupled with high education standards give some Asian countries costs advantages over Western Europe or the USA. A number of other examples are given in Section 8.1.5.

Linkages

There are invariably important linkages between operations and human resource management. Well-trained and motivated staff are important in making sure that the operations activities, which may be difficult and repetitive, are carried out pre-

---

REAL-LIFE APPLICATION 8.10

Operations at Benetton

Benetton's operations are based around its manufacturing and distribution complex at Castrette, in the Veneto region of northern Italy, near the town where the Benetton family was born and the company was founded. The company claims this complex, containing three production units linked by a fibre-optic data network, is the most modern and advanced in the world. The advanced physical assets enable the company to economise on the use of human resources – the two most modern plants between them employed only 640 people to produce 80 million garments per annum. The operation of this physical resource is facilitated by the company's long-standing technological core competences in dyeing and information technology.

The Castrette complex represents a move away from the company's historical policy of outsourcing much of its manufacturing to subcontractors, many of them owned by the company's managers and financed by Benetton. The policy is now to bring in-house those parts of the production process susceptible to automation: design, cutting, dyeing, packing and dispatching. In so doing, the company hopes to profit from economies of scale and scope. The clothes are still sewn together by subcontractors in the Veneto, with the company organising and co-ordinating their efforts, and undertaking what it calls 'the critical task of quality control'.

The company decided to retain its historical location in the Veneto even though, at the time when it conceived and built the Castrette complex in the early 1990s, it could have reduced its labour costs by 20% by moving production to Spain, and more had it relocated to South-East Asia. The location decision was based on historical loyalties, on the firm's knowledge of how to manage and motivate people in its historical heartland and on a deliberate trade-off. The Benettons judged that a stable base, with low production costs based upon technology that they controlled and understood, would offer a basis for long-term advantage. They believed that it was superior to their competitors' strategy of constantly moving manufacturing to where labour costs were lowest.

The IT in the Castrette complex enables a strong linkage between operations and the distribution activity, which is housed on the same site (see Real-Life Application 8.11). IT links to the marketing and sales activity enable the firm to alter production schedules according to demand. There are also strong linkages with the process development activity – the IT systems were largely purpose-designed and the firm's project management skills enabled the complex to be built very quickly – in only two years. There are also important vertical linkages with the remaining subcontractors, based upon strong relational contracts.

cisely. This is even more important in service businesses, where operational staff are in direct contact with customers and help to shape their view of the organisation. Where organisations are seeking to be innovative in their operations activity, then linkages with the process development activity are likely to be important. If the organisation is seeking to differentiate on the basis of being responsive to customer needs, then linkages with the marketing and sales activity are likely to be important, since the operations activity will need quick and reliable information on what the customer requires. One reason why many leading manufacturers have invested heavily in Enterprise Resource Planning (ERP) systems is to make these linkages reliable and instantaneous.

D. Distribution

In restaurants and many other service manufacturers, where production and delivery are more or less the same thing, distribution[22] does not really have a distinct identity – it can be regarded as part of operations.

In other manufacturers an efficient distribution system can give differentiation advantage by making sure that customers find the products they need when they need them. It may also give cost advantage, by enabling a firm to keep lower levels of stocks within its supply chain, and by reducing waste.

Resources

Because it bears so directly on customer satisfaction, distribution can have an important effect on competitive advantage, and so tends to attract a lot of investment in resources. It is very noticeable as a competitive weapon in retailing, where leading players invest massively in specialised physical assets, such as trucks, loading and unloading facilities and computerised monitoring systems, to make sure that products reach stores in good time, in perfect condition and with minimal wastage. Distribution may make use of capabilities in the areas of reliability, responsiveness to customer requirements and speed of response.

Vertical integration

Because of its potential importance to customer satisfaction, some producers and retailers prefer to keep the distribution activity in-house, although there are a number of specialist logistics firms to whom it may be outsourced. Some organisations, such as UK toiletries firm The Body Shop, establish a close relationship with their preferred distribution supplier, which sets up a depot within their factory.

Firms also need to decide whether to maintain their own chain of depots, or to distribute through wholesalers and/or retailers. These decisions depend partly on the availability of reliable intermediaries, and partly on the business's own scale and scope: larger businesses are more likely to find it worthwhile to handle their own distribution.

Scale and scope

Economies of scale may be available for the distribution activity. It may cost little more to deliver a full lorry load than a half-empty one, and the administrative overhead cost of running large depots and an extensive distribution network may not be much greater than for medium-sized ones. There may also be economies of

---

REAL-LIFE APPLICATION 8.11

Benetton's distribution and logistics system

Benetton's distribution activity, like its manufacturing, is located centrally at the Castrette complex, is on a large scale, and deploys advanced technological assets. The facility, known as 'Big Charley', is said to be unique in the industrialised world. Its Robostore 2000 system is capable of dividing consignments for transportation to each individual client and working out the most efficient way to group consignments for shipment. The company claims that these centralised, automated systems maximise efficiency and keep delivery lead times to a minimum and reduce transportation costs by some €5 million per annum.

The distribution activity is closely linked to production via IT links and a tunnel through which garments can be moved swiftly from factory to warehouse. There are also strong vertical linkages with the firm's marketing and sales activity, since the retailers rely upon the activity for timely delivery of the correct stock.

---

scope, provided that the organisation's different products can use the same distribution systems and resources.

Location

An organisation typically faces trade-offs in its location decisions for the distribution activity. Having a large number of small distribution points may be best if it is seeking to differentiate by offering a prompt response to customer orders, particularly if, as sometimes happens, the distribution depots are also the locations for the after-sales service activity. On the other hand, if there are economies of scale in distribution, a firm may prefer to opt for a small number of large, strategically placed depots to serve a country, or even a whole continent. This will normally only be a viable strategy in developed countries with an extensive, well-maintained transport infrastructure.

Linkages

An effective distribution activity is an important complement to the operations activity if the organisation is trying to differentiate by being responsive to customers (see Real-Life Application 8.11). It also has strong linkages with the sales activity, since if distributors and retailers are constantly being let down on deliveries, they will be less motivated to carry and promote a firm's products.

Vertical linkages to customers, distributors and wholesalers need also to be maintained in order to ensure that their requirements are known and met. Seemingly routine matters, such as the times when customers are open to receive deliveries and what kinds of lorries, packaging and pallets they can handle at their depots, can turn out to be important. Failure to take account of them can damage a firm's reputation and result in deliveries being turned away and payment being refused.

E. Marketing and sales

Resources

Marketing and sales has prime responsibility for utilising an organisation's brands and reputational assets to generate sales in the present, and with building these for the future. A distinctive capability in communication may be important in helping it to do so. The activity may have physical assets at its disposal, such as sales offices, but these are unlikely to be a source of competitive advantage unless they give the company a significantly broader coverage of the market than is open to competitors. However, a firm can gain marketing advantage by having superior knowledge assets such as customer databases and software to analyse buyer behaviour. Benetton derived much advantage in the 1980s from its competences in setting up and running IT networks to link sales outlets to the centre. The marketing activity is also an important potential source of knowledge about customers behaviour and preferences, which can make an important contribution to organisational capabilities in responsiveness to customer needs.

Vertical integration

As we have mentioned in Section 8.1.2, vertical integration decisions are very important in marketing and sales. An in-house telesales operation or salesforce will be dedicated to selling the firm's products and can be instructed precisely which customer groups to target in pursuit of a broader strategy. It can also capture valuable customer information, which might be lost if entrusted to other firms, and

---

REAL-LIFE APPLICATION 8.12

Vertical integration decisions in the marketing and sales activity

Benetton, McDonald's and Sony have long made extensive use of independently owned sales outlets that sell only their own products. Since the owner puts in most of the capital needed to set up a new outlet, such outlets represent a way of expanding quickly while keeping investment low. The firms manage the relationships with their retailers carefully, to ensure that they feel a strong association with the firm, and then rely upon their partners' entrepreneurial qualities to generate high sales at low cost. Since many competing firms follow a similar strategy, all three firms must rely for competitive advantage upon their ability to select the right store owners and then to keep them motivated.

Sony does not rely exclusively upon its own outlets. It will also sell through department stores and other outlets that it regards as compatible with its market positioning. British Airways, similarly, will sell through approved travel agents. In the UK, at least, these agents often prominently display a sign showing them to be 'BA approved'. This is a badge of respectability that helps BA's outlets differentiate themselves in an industry where there are few entry barriers to stop dishonest operators from setting up in competition. Both firms use their own reputation to complement that of their retailers.

BA and McDonald's both own and run a number of their sales outlets, typically in the most prominent city-centre locations. This gives them direct control over service quality in locations that are most likely to be sensitive to it, and enable them to capture all the profits for themselves in areas where customer traffic is likely to be high. For British Airways, these prominent outlets in prestigious locations also represent a form of advertising.

British Airways is also making increasing use of the World Wide Web as a sales channel, for both its low-cost Go! offshoot and the main airline. Highly successful firms such as Dell, the world's second-largest supplier of personal computers, and Cisco Systems, the leading supplier of Internet hardware, also make extensive use of this channel. In 2000, Cisco claimed to be transacting 84% of its business over the Internet. Although the capital costs of setting up an effective website can be high, it reduces the need for investment in outlets and to pay commission to agents and distributors. Most importantly, it enables the firm to capture the customer order information very easily, so that it can then pass the data on to its production activity and to its suppliers.

In the case of Dell and Cisco, this leads to a very lean manufacturing operation, with fast lead times and low inventories. It is also an excellent demonstration of the companies' own technology in operation. Dell is using its own proven competences in operating electronic commerce as a marketing resource. It runs seminars to show other organisations how they should adapt their own business to the web, in the expectation that they will order Dell servers to run their e-commerce operations.

feed it back to the operations and product development activities. However, an in-house sales operation represents a substantial fixed overhead expense.

Third-party agents and distributors may be more difficult to motivate and discipline, since they will often be selling other products as well. On the other hand, their independence and desire for profit may motivate them to seek out sales and cost reduction opportunities that the firm itself may not spot. They may offer the customer a more attractive range of complementary products than a firm can by itself. Also, because they focus on a particular locality and may also offer after-sales service, they may be able to build deeper knowledge of local conditions and better relationships with the community than a firm's own salesforce could. Real-Life Application 8.12 looks at a number of vertical integration decisions and the logic behind them.

Scale and scope

Marketing and sales offers the potential for economies of scope. Provided that the organisation's products complement one another well and appeal to the same target markets, then they can benefit from shared branding, advertising and reputation, and be sold through the same channels. Economies of scale are also available in marketing activities. The design of a good advertising and promotional campaign costs the same, regardless of the size of the firm, and a large campaign will benefit from discounts in the purchasing of advertising space.

Economies of scale are less frequent in the sales activity, since often an organisation finds it needs to increase the size of its salesforce or distributor network as sales increase. However, in industries such as fast-food or stationery, where customers are not particularly brand-loyal, scale may bring other benefits. A company like McDonald's may gain an advantage from having a large number of outlets, simply by being the first reputable firm that a purchaser is likely to stumble upon when hungry!

Location

Because they invariably need to show a degree of sensitivity to local requirements, firms will almost always have a sales representative located near to the customer, however far away the other value chain activities may be. For some products, it may also be beneficial to have outlets 'clustered' near others selling competitors' products. Restaurants and theatres tend to open up close to one another in entertainment districts.

Linkages

Marketing and sales has potentially vital linkages with many of the other activities, since it is an important channel through which information flows into and out of the organisation. Salespeople and distributors are in direct contact with the customers and should be better placed than many other people in the organisation to know what buyers want and whether they are satisfied. Marketing can, and almost always should, feed information on customer requirements, demand levels and customer order details to the product development, operations, distribution and finance and planning activities. Vertical linkages and distributors and retailers may also be important in gathering this information.

There may also be important linkages from other activities to help marketing and sales perform effectively. The purchasing activity will play a crucial role in helping the marketing activity obtain any available economies of scale in advertising and promotion – this is one reason why many large advertising agencies also have subsidiaries that specialise in the purchase of air-time on radio and TV. The process development activity may be important in helping set up the IT systems and processes to enable databases of customer information to be used productively – for product development, or targeted direct-mail campaigns, for example.

F. After-sales service

Because it is highly visible to the customer, good after-sales service can be an important element in an organisation's differentiation strategy. It can be particularly important for new entrants in a market where there are strong incumbent firms. By offering extended warranties, a firm may be able to reassure customers that their products are reliable, and offset some of the advantages that established firms get from their reputation.[23]

Resources

The most important resources that are deployed in after-sales service tend to be human. Some firms also invest in specialised assets such as computer diagnostics or structural testing equipment, to help diagnose and repair faults, hoping to lower their unit cost of repairs.

Vertical integration

Vertical integration decisions can be as important for after-sales service as they are for marketing and sales. This activity can generate vital information about what customers like and dislike about products and about product defects. The firm needs to capture this information and ensure that there are effective linkages with the product design, operations and marketing activities. Design and manufacturing flaws can then be put right and marketing campaigns can emphasise the features that users are known to value. It may be easier to capture this information if the after-sales service activity is kept in-house.

However, for small firms, these advantages may be offset by the potential for benefiting from third-party suppliers' scale and scope. Another reason for outsourcing sales and service is that, with marketing and sales, a local distributor may provide a more context-sensitive service than a centralised one.

Another alternative to keeping this activity in-house is to train customers to perform their own after-sales service. This is common practice for companies selling

---

REAL-LIFE APPLICATION 8.13

BA, GE and jet engine maintenance

Historically, firms that sell jet engines have left the maintenance activity to the airline operators. British Airways carried out its own jet engine maintenance until 1991, when one of its aero-engine suppliers, General Electric (GE), took over BA's engine maintenance plant in Nantgarw, South Wales. Not only does GE earn a fee from BA for the maintenance, but it also captures important product data. It has also been able to grow the business from an annual turnover of $250 million to 1999 sales of $900 million, of which less than 50% are to BA. GE is thus profiting from economies of scale in the maintenance function in a way that BA itself would have had difficulty in doing.

industrial equipment, although in some industries the trend is in the opposite direction (see Real-Life Application 8.13).

Scale and scope

Considerations of scale and scope are also important for after-sales service. Scale in this activity is important for differentiation as well as cost advantage – customers for a wide range of products, such as cars, stereos, industrial machinery and office equipment, will be attracted to a firm that can offer convenient service through a local outlet. There may also be economies of scope from having a single help-line or network of engineers handle a range of related products. For firms that are not large enough to benefit from these factors by themselves, the use of third-party service operations is an attractive option.

Location

As with marketing and sales, the need for local responsiveness in after-sales service means that firms will usually have some local representation. For small firms, or those manufacturing exceptionally large or specialised equipment, it may be that only a few people have the necessary expertise to service the products. In such a case, the after-sales service activity has to be centralised. New call-centre technology is also allowing firms to centralise some of their complaints and customer service activities for highly standardised products like computers and software.

Linkages

After-sales service has important linkages with the human resource management activity, which must ensure that people are properly recruited, trained and motivated to service products and handle complaints. It may also have a linkage to marketing and sales, since a well-equipped and modern service facility can be a powerful marketing tool in industries like automobiles, where it is visible to the customer.

Manufacturing-style organisations – support activities

Unlike the primary activities, which correspond reasonably closely to the traditional functions found in many companies, the support activities that we examine in sections G–J are often spread through a firm in ways that vary from company to company. Major decisions and programmes may be initiated and managed centrally, while small purchasing, hiring and training decisions may be taken by individual managers. When we assess a value chain, we look at the centralised and decentralised activities together, to see how they contribute to the effectiveness of the primary activities, and to the organisation's cost and differentiation advantage.

Because they are so diffused within the organisation and so integral to the organisation's smooth functioning, these activities have not often been outsourced in the past, although, as we said in Section 8.1.2, this is slowly starting to change. In the following sections, we shall only discuss vertical integration in the rare instances where it is an issue.

G. Purchasing

◄ Buyer power was discussed in Section 5.4.

Because the raw materials, components and services that an organisation buys in may represent over 50% of the value of the finished product, the purchasing activity is of major strategic importance.

Resources

The purchasing activity may have specialised knowledge assets, like supplier databases. It may use capabilities in negotiation, to get the best terms, and risk management, to offset the effects of fluctuating prices and the possibility that a key supplier may fail to deliver.

Scale and scope

Purchasing can benefit from economies of both scale and scope. Large, diverse firms are likely to attract better discounts from suppliers than small ones, and purchasing represents a fixed overhead cost that may usefully be spread across many products and services.

Location

Some large global firms centralise their purchasing decisions in order to get the maximum benefit from economies of scale and scope. However, others allow local managers to negotiate their own deals with local suppliers. They are prepared to trade off the increased responsiveness to local needs against any extra discount they may win from a centralised contract.

Linkages

Purchasing covers not only operational inputs, like raw materials, energy and advertising time, but also fixed inputs like land, buildings and equipment. Thus, it has

Table 8.7 Examples of linkages between purchasing and primary activities

Activity	Operational purchases	Fixed asset purchases
Product design and development		Laboratories, testing equipment, CAD equipment and software
Supply		Materials handling and testing equipment
Operations	Fuel, raw materials, components and subassemblies, goods for resale, third-party services: maintenance, laundry, etc.	Plant, machinery, land in prime locations, buildings, office equipment, bar-code scanners
Distribution	Fuel, third-party services	Depots in key locations, materials handling equipment, vehicles
Marketing and sales	Fuel, vehicle and office maintenance, advertising space, brochures and catalogues, hotel rooms	Offices and equipment, computer hardware and software, customer databases, market research
After-sales service	Fuel, parts, telephone services	Offices, vehicles, call-centres

important linkages with all the primary activities. These are summarised in Table 8.7. There is a particularly interesting linkage between purchasing and product design. Some firms look to gain cost advantage by standardising designs to allow key inputs to be purchased in volume and to common specifications. This strategy is seen in the automobile industry, where carmakers are seeking to build their model range around a few shared 'platforms'. It is also a feature of the fast-food and hotels industries, where firms like McDonalds and Novotel build all their outlets to a common specification, with similar décor, furnishings and, for hotels, room sizes.

H. Process development

Resources

Large firms with their superior base of human and financial resources tend to have more consistent success than small ones in implementing process improvements.[24] However, it is occasionally possible for human ingenuity to compensate for lack of other resources. Indeed, sometimes necessity, in the form of resource constraints, is the mother of invention. Toyota's lean manufacturing systems were developed in part because the firm did not have enough capital to finance large amounts of inventory. The Benetton family was able to afford to start manufacturing its own clothes because only they were able to convert cheap second-hand machines, designed for knitting stockings, to knit sweaters.

Vertical integration

Process development in some manufacturing firms is almost always vertically integrated and carried out by in-house teams of experts. Organisational processes are so specialised and integral to the specific practices of these firms that external agents cannot hope to get to grips with the intricacies of the system. However, less sophisticated processes can be outsourced, and in recent years it has been common for some organisations to pass responsibility for all the firm's processes on to suppliers of integrated systems, such as the German software company SAP. In other organisations, specialist management consultancies have been employed to re-engineer the firm's processes in order to weed out inefficiencies and areas of ineffectiveness. Consultants are also frequently employed for IT system development, which accounts for a large proportion of the fee income of major consultancies such as Arthur Andersen.

Scale and scope

Large firms can be expected to develop a wider variety of capabilities and competences than small ones, to cope with the different technologies and markets to which they are exposed. If they have a culture and architecture that encourages the transfer of learning from one product or market to another, then they may be able to gain economies of scale and scope in process development. Unilever, the Anglo-Dutch foods and detergents conglomerate, holds regular meetings to enable managers from similar countries and similar product groups to share experiences. This might enable a manager selling, say, soap powder in Nigeria to learn both from colleagues selling detergents in Asia and Europe and from those selling food products in Nigeria and other African markets.

Location

Process development often takes place where the process is carried out. However, there are exceptions. Some global manufacturers employ small teams of head-office-based experts whose role is to improve the manufacturing process world wide. The role of central management is thus to transfer best practice within the organisation, as well as to foster a culture and architecture that encourages process development locally where possible.

Linkages

Process development has linkages to most of the other activities. It may include the improvement of:

- project management and product testing methods in product design and development;
- scheduling, inspection and unloading procedures, and materials handling facilities in the supply activity;
- procedures, equipment and information technology in operations;
- vehicle and depot design and materials handling procedures in distribution;
- advertising and promotional materials, sales and market research techniques and customer information analysis in marketing and sales;
- 'scripts' for call-centre staff and fault diagnosis routines for service engineers in after-sales service.

The process development activity may also benefit from vertical linkages to suppliers of technology and advice, and also, through professional associations, to people developing and using similar processes in other organisations. Customers may also be sources of process development – Japanese manufacturers such as Toyota have a policy of helping train their suppliers to enhance their manufacturing techniques and quality standards.

I. Human resource management

Human resource (HR) management ensures that an organisation has available the skills it needs to compete effectively. It may also be a source of expertise on how to structure an organisation and nurture its culture.

Resources

Adequate human resource management is vital if an organisation is to survive. However, it appears unlikely that HR **systems** and **procedures** can offer competitive advantage. Most systems for managing and rewarding people are available to any firm, and easy to copy, although some organisations have built proprietary training programmes. The human resources themselves – the managers and staff – belong to the other activities. The difference between good and mediocre HR management tends to lie within a firm's culture and architecture, which shape the personal interactions between managers and staff.

There are some exceptions, however. Pettigrew and Whipp (1991: 242) cite firms whose communication structures are so good that competitive advantage comes from the fast and efficient exchanges between different elements of the organisation. Some companies have invested heavily in computerised communication systems, so that, for example, Microsoft's internal e-mail system allows everyone within the firm to learn about new developments and therefore think about potential applications. Other firms have invested heavily in staff training. Training was one of the reasons cited as being behind the success of British Airways' culture-change programme in the early 1980s, leading to customer responsiveness levels for which it subsequently became famous (Tushman and O'Reilly, 1996).

Scale and scope

The human resource management function is fairly neutral in respect of scale and scope. The costs of payroll systems, training programmes, and reward systems are tied fairly closely to the numbers of staff employed, and although there may be some economies of scale in, for example, training programmes, these are not usually major items of expense. There may be some advantages for large organis-ations in the range of expertise of the staff that they employ, and therefore the range of products that they may make. However, such advantages can be out-weighed by the tendency for large firms to group people in specialist functions that prevent them from working on different things. Industrial relations may also dete-riorate in a large organisation if top management becomes too remote.

Location

Human resource activities are of necessity spread throughout the organisation. Most firms employ specialist HR personnel in central and divisional human resources or personnel departments, but they are invariably outnumbered by supervisors and managers who carry out HR management activities every working day. This makes it difficult to centralise human resource management without diminishing the ability of these local managers to take effective operational decisions, or reducing their status in the eyes of their colleagues.

Linkages

Because of its all-pervasive nature, the HR management activity has potential link-ages with every other element of the organisation. The most important of these have already been highlighted in our review of the other activities.

J. Finance and planning

Resources

The main physical assets used in finance and planning are IT systems which a firm may develop itself or buy from third-party suppliers. The IT systems themselves

---

REAL-LIFE APPLICATION 8.14

Financial systems and competitive advantage at Cisco Systems

Internet hardware manufacturer Cisco Systems has configured its internal financial systems so that within 24 hours it can do a 'virtual close' – get a complete pic-ture of its profit and loss situation and balance sheet. This ability, unique among large corporations (Cisco is the world's second-largest company ranked by market capitalisation) and extremely rare among small ones, does more than simply reduce the costly disruption that accompanies the end of the financial year in most companies. Because it knows its costs so precisely, Cisco can take far better-informed pricing decisions than its competitors and has a lower risk of taking on unprofitable business.

will rarely give competitive advantage unless the organisation has competences in control and learning, which comes from the organisation's culture and architecture (Real-Life Application 8.14 gives an exception to this). Superior financial systems may contribute to an overall capability in customer responsiveness and speed of response.

Some theorists (e.g. Hart and Banbury, 1994) believe that superior planning systems can also be a source of advantage, although empirical researchers disagree as to whether strategic planning correlates with superior performance. The most recent studies suggest that there is a positive link between the existence of formal planning procedures and firm performance (Brews and Hunt, 1999) although this relationship is less clear for small and medium-sized firms (McKiernan and Morris, 1994).

Scale and scope

The challenge in most firms is to keep the fixed overhead cost of their financing and planning activities low enough to be affordable by the organisation regardless of its scale. There have been attempts in the past to build elaborate financial control and planning systems that can enable managers to run a large and diverse organisation at little more cost than a small one. However, if these are too pervasive they will interfere with the effective operation of the organisation.

The problems that arise from over-elaborate control systems are discussed in Chapter 10. ▶

Location

An important part of these activities is typically carried out centrally at corporate or divisional headquarters, so as to minimise leakages of important information and to make sure that that information is readily available to senior decision-makers. Liaison with tax authorities and other government bodies may need to be conducted centrally. Firms may also find it convenient to locate their finance functions close to financial centres or to place their headquarters in a country with a favourable tax regime. However, these decisions are easy to copy and are unlikely to be a source of competitive advantage.

These activities are rarely completely centralised. Planning has been found to be more effective if line managers at lower levels in the organisation participate[25] and most local managers will retain some control over their own budgets and financial information.

Linkages

Finance and planning have linkages to nearly all other activities, helping the organisation to absorb and transmit information and make superior decisions. Sometimes there may be significant linkages between the finance and marketing activities. Occasionally, an organisation may, through having a superior grasp of its costs, be able to set its prices more keenly than its competitors, and so gain a marketing advantage. On the other hand, if the invoicing activity is *inefficient*, then this can give an organisation a marketing *disadvantage*, since few things appear to annoy a customer more than being charged the wrong amount.

The finance activity may have useful vertical linkages to banks, venture capitalists and other institutions which can be important sources of funds and sometimes also of advice. Linkages to governments may also be important – British Airways' links with successive UK transport ministers have been important in helping the firm preserve its strategically vital dominance of take-off and landing slots at Heathrow.

Professional services

Because there are few bought-in inputs and the professionals need to be involved in every activity in the value chain, many professional service firms are highly vertically integrated. Often, they will choose to outsource only certain marketing activities and peripheral activities like catering and cleaning, and to employ outside professionals occasionally to supply specialist advice on particular problems.

Some firms, however, prefer to act as the 'server' at the centre of a network of high-class specialists (see Section 8.1.2). A construction firm may have a pool of skilled freelance bricklayers and plasterers that it trusts, and uses regularly. An advertising agency may outsource its graphic design and its media buying. Such firms will retain only certain key activities in-house – typically these will be the parts of the problem acquisition and diagnosis activity that give it control of client liaison and the overall programming of a project. Such firms will sell themselves on the size of their network, the quality of the people within it and their competences in project management. Their ability to manage interactions between these various outsiders is an important skill.

There are some benefits from scale and scope in professional services. Having a large practice enables professionals to specialise further and deepen their expertise. For example, a large accountancy firm may be able to have specialists in the taxation regulations of each country where it does business. A smaller firm might have fewer people who know less about the legislation in a given country, or may just have a few generalists who undertake both taxation and audit work. Large firms can also afford teams of administrators and researchers. By and large, very small practices with just two or three professionals can only compete with large firms because their overheads are low or because they are highly specialised. However, medium-sized firms that are big enough to need a substantial administration function can have problems in competing. Large firms' administrative overhead may not need to be much bigger, but can be spread across more, and larger, projects.

The scope of a professional firm may need to be very broad or very narrow. A small, focused firm may be able to compete with a larger one in its particular area of expertise. A large firm may benefit from being able to offer a 'one-stop shop', a single source of advice for clients on a variety of topics. The largest accountancy practices have long offered management consultancy, and are now starting to offer legal advice as well.

Some professional service firms such as medical practices or drain cleaners typically need to be located near to their clients, since problem-solving usually requires personal contact or a visit to the site of the problem. In some professions like law and software development, personal contact is less vital and firms can locate where they wish. Very prestigious professionals, such as top architects and doctors, may also be able to locate where they wish and visit clients as necessary, or even make the client come to them.

The discussion of professional services' primary activities that follows will now focus, with a few exceptions, on the various resources that they employ, and on their linkages to other activities. Real-Life Application 8.16, at the end of this section, shows how the different activities are deployed in the management consultancy industry.

K.   Problem acquisition and diagnosis

Resources

Because it can be very difficult for potential clients to tell a good professional from a convincing liar, they will place a great deal of value on a firm's reputation, which is probably the most important asset involved in problem acquisition.

Capabilities in communication, negotiation and the management of expectations may also be important. A doctor will want the patient to understand how long a treatment will take and how complete a cure will result. An architect's client must understand how much a project is likely to cost, and what compromises on appearance and fittings must be made to bring the cost down. A failure to agree on the expected outcomes may result in disappointed clients, who may insist on extra work to bring the output up to the level they were expecting, refuse to pay the full fee or take legal action. For a small firm, the cost, in terms of administration, legal fees and interest charges on the money spent to carry out the unpaid work, may be ruinous.

Linkages

There is a strong linkage between this activity and the following one, since if the initial problem diagnosis is inaccurate, extra effort will be needed at the problem-solving stage to put it right. This in turn means that the firm needs to learn effectively from the monitoring of previous projects, so that it can build that knowledge into the diagnosis of new problems.

Linkages to external networks, such as professional associations and client industry associations, and to other professionals that deal with the same customer groups, may be important in gaining new assignments. An important source of new work is where a client is referred on from one trusted professional to another. A person or firm may use a management consultant recommended by their accountant, a construction firm recommended by their architect or a specialist recommended by their local doctor.

L.   Finding possible solutions

Resources

The organisation's knowledge may be a source of cost advantage at this stage, by enabling it to come up quickly with a number of workable alternatives, and avoid wasting effort on ones that have failed in the past. Some organisations have information systems that let them access that knowledge quicker than their competitors.

Organisations may also use capabilities in innovation to develop novel or creative solutions, a source of differentiation advantage. Alternatively, they may buy in creative advice from other specialists.

Linkages

There are important linkages between solution-finding and implementation. If the solutions do not take sufficient account of potential practical problems, it may build in extra costs at the implementation stage. For example, a proposed course of medical treatment must take account of a patient's age, and any other illnesses he or she might suffer from. Architects must look at the roads around a site to make sure that it is possible to deliver the materials they are proposing to use, and to cart away the waste products.

M. Choice between solutions

Resources

This activity often requires a number of different professionals to work together – a surgeon and an anaesthetist, an architect and a structural engineer, a marketing consultant and a change management expert – to come up with the solution that meets all their professional standards and requirements. Organisations may gain competitive advantage through a superior ability to manage these professional interactions and to resolve any conflicts that result.

Linkages

This activity is likely to be important in terms of shaping the effectiveness of the implementation activity. It may also entail vertical linkages, since it sometimes involves professionals from more than one firm.

N. Implementing chosen solutions

Resources

Organisations can gain competitive advantage in this area by having competences in project management. A construction firm that consistently finishes its projects ahead of schedule may gain cost advantage, by saving on wage payments, and earn a good reputation with clients, who make valuable gains if they can start to generate income from a building more quickly than they planned. Negotiation and communication capabilities may also come into play – clients are less likely to complain if their staff are kept informed of progress and of the reasons for any variations to the agreed schedule. Some construction firms have started to use the World Wide Web for this purpose, by opening a website for each project, which all firms involved can use to consult up-to-date plans. Suppliers can also check when deliveries of building materials are due and the quantities needed.

Vertical integration

In some professions, such as management consultancy, advantage can be obtained by involving the customer in the implementation activity. As well as reducing costs, this helps the client to understand and accept (or 'buy into' or 'own') the proposed solution. This tends to make the project more effective from the point of view of the client organisation, which will not want to be reliant upon the consultant to help it run any new management systems that it implements.

Linkages

There is potentially an important linkage with the control and evaluation activity, to ensure that the organisation learns from its successes and failures. There may also be important linkages with the client organisation and its staff.

> ### REAL-LIFE APPLICATION 8.15
>
> ### Control, evaluation and learning at Boeing
>
> In many major manufacturers the research and development unit has the characteristics of a professional services organisation. It exists to find creative and effective solutions to difficult, one-off problems. This example relates to product development at Boeing, the aircraft manufacturer.
>
> Although both 737 and 747 aircraft went on to be commercial successes, both experience severe problems at the time of their launch. Their manufacturer, the Boeing Corporation, was anxious not to repeat these mishaps. It set up a team, under the name 'Project Homework', to compare the development processes of
>
> these two planes with those of earlier products, the 707 and 727. The team worked for three years and produced a document containing several hundred recommendations for good practice in aircraft development. The team members then went on to play important roles in guiding the launch of the next generation of Boeing jets, the 757 and 767. These had the most successful, error-free launches in the company's history.
>
> *Source*: Garvin (1993: 85)

O. *Control and evaluation*

Resources

Many professional organisations, like hospitals and engineers, have well-established systems for monitoring problems while they are in progress. In the case of medical establishments, this may involve substantial investment in physical assets.

It is rarer for organisations to invest heavily in evaluation of completed projects, although this is potentially important in fostering organisational learning (see Real-Life Application 8.15). Professional staff, who are typically keen to move onward to the next challenging problem, are often tempted to neglect this activity, which involves looking backward at problems they feel they have already solved.

Linkages

Control activities have a strong link to the problem acquisition activity, since an assessment of progress may well lead on to the identification and acquisition of new problems. Control and evaluation may also be linked to the activities of finding and choosing possible solutions, since it generates information that is of use in working out how to address similar problems in the future.

For example, the first time that a hospital has to treat a child that has been born HIV-positive, it has to take a guess as to which of a number of drugs and other treatments, such as diet, it should try. It will have data provided by the pharmaceuticals companies, but may have nothing that relates specifically to a child of a particular age or weight born to a mother from a specific income group with particular dietary habits. Once a hospital has worked with a number of such children, and has had a chance to monitor their progress, it gets an idea of which combinations of drugs and other treatments may be effective with children from different backgrounds.

◀ *Knowledge management was discussed in Section 7.4.5.*

Control and evaluation may also link with the process development activity. Once the organisation has discovered that a particular type of solution fits well to a specific set of problems, it can start to develop more formal procedures or

327

REAL-LIFE APPLICATION 8.16

Value chains in the management consultancy industry

The management consultancy industry includes firms of a wide variety of sizes, ranging from one-person firms to international practices employing several thousand fee-earning professionals.

Problem acquisition is the key to competitive advantage, since this holds the key to building expertise and reputation in a particular kind of consultancy, and for winning further work with the same client. Firms strive to build reputations for work in a particular field – for example, Arthur Andersen in IT systems implementation, and McKinsey and Boston Consulting Group in strategy consulting. Firms may also have a reputation for advising particular industry segments. Vertical linkages can be important for this – large, accounting-based firms such as PriceWaterhouseCoopers and KPMG will hope to have work referred on to them by other satisfied clients and by their colleagues in the audit practice. Linkages to journals are also helpful in building reputation – McKinsey is very successful in getting its consultants' work published in the *Harvard Business Review*, and offers sabbaticals to leading staff who wish to write books. They also employ specialist researchers who publish studies of particular business trends and industry sectors. Rival strategy firm Booz Allen Hamilton has attempted to counter this by launching its own strategy journal, featuring articles by its own consultants and leading business academics and journalists.

Firms also work hard to develop processes for winning work. Most have developed formats for structuring client proposals, and presentations to clients are intensively rehearsed. However, since all the firms involved have focused so much effort in this area, these routines are the basis of threshold competences rather than core competences. Perhaps more important is the ability to cost work realistically and to manage clients' expectations so that they do not insist on more work being done than was allowed for in the proposal.

The ability to field consultants with appropriate industry experience is important both for winning work, for finding possible solutions and for choosing between solutions. Firms also look for ways to allow consultants to take advantage of knowledge accumulated on similar projects in the past. As mentioned in Chapter 7, different firms have different approaches, ranging from the Lotus Notes database of past projects maintained by PriceWaterhouseCoopers to the more personal style of interaction between consultants favoured at McKinsey. Being expensive to set up and difficult to run, these knowledge management systems are potentially sources of competitive advantage.

Not all firms choose to get involved in the detailed implementation of their proposals – some, indeed, argue that they would be usurping the client's role if they did. Where they do become involved, for example in the implementation of new information and control systems, project management competences are vital, as are competences in managing change.

Among the support activities, human resource management is the most important – firms compete to recruit the best-qualified staff. Several firms, including Arthur Andersen, have their own academies where they teach new entrants consultancy techniques and imbue them with the firm's ethos.

A number of firms, such as Alexander Proudfoot, a cost reduction specialist, attempt to gain competitive advantage through process development. These firms develop highly formalised methodologies that they believe can be used to analyse certain types of problem and develop solutions. The aim of these methodologies is to standardise the projects, making them easier to manage, while reassuring the client that the process that it is undergoing has been tried and tested. These methodologies are relatively easy to copy and it is unclear if they can be the basis of a sustainable differentiation advantage.

methodologies for addressing them. This form of knowledge management can be a possible source of competitive advantage.

P. Support activities

Although support activities are generally the same as for manufacturing organisations, the emphasis is slightly different for professional services:

- The purchasing activity usually has a minor role because there are so few bought-in inputs. The most important purchasing activities are for buildings and equipment, IT and telecommunications. There are exceptions to this: hospitals, which purchase items like drugs and dressings, and schools, where stationery is a major item of expenditure.

- Process development can be an important activity. In this context, it involves taking the knowledge gained for successful projects and building it into an explicit methodology that can be used on similar projects later. Sometimes these methodologies are written up as books or articles, and used to build the organisation's reputation. For most professional services organisations, this also constitutes product development.

- Although staff are of vital importance in professional services and take up a large proportion of overall costs, the human resource management function may not attract a lot of resources. Professionals are expected to be self-motivated and their training is validated by external professional bodies, such as the councils or associations that govern medical practitioners, architects or accountants in most countries. Some firms, however, seek to gain advantage by making sure that their staff keep their professional knowledge up to date and through training in proprietary methodologies. Others pay over the odds in salaries or bonuses in order to attract and retain the highest calibre employees.

Networks

◄ *The concept of increasing returns to scale was discussed in Section 5.5.3.*

In a network value chain there are strong benefits from scale and scope – indeed, these kinds of organisation may show increasing returns to scale. Most activities have a large fixed cost element which ideally should be spread over as large a customer base as possible. No less importantly, it is usually the largest networks that are most attractive to customers (see Section 8.2).

Most of the activities can be, and frequently are, located far away from the customers. Although banks have in the past needed a network of branch offices, many of their 'back office' activities like cheque clearing are carried out centrally. Newspapers like the *Wall Street Journal* or the *Financial Times* may be written and typeset on one continent, to be printed and distributed on another.

The nature of the linkage between the different activities will be discussed in the following sections, along with the resources employed and the extent to which vertical integration influences the way in which they add value. Real-Life Application 8.17 at the end of this section, gives an example of this form of value chain for an Internet business.

Q. Network promotion and contract management

Resources

Brand and reputation are important resources in promoting a network organisation, and they are likely to be linked to the size of the network and the extent to which it has been shown to be reliable over time.

Capabilities in communication are also likely to be important to establish and advertise the organisation's brand values. Capabilities in negotiation may be important in striking deals with providers. A firm may gain cost advantage through capabilities in risk management, by minimising the number of users taken on who are unable to pay for the service, or who want to take advantage of any free introductory membership offers without eventually signing up.

Vertical integration

There may be a high level of bought-in inputs for this activity. Advertising, promotion mailings and credit-checking are all services that are freely available from outside suppliers.

Linkages

The service provisioning and infrastructure provision activities have a strong link with network promotion, since their reliability shapes the firm's reputation. Vertical linkages with customers can be important in some industries, such as financial services, where some firms seek to build bonds of trust with their clients in order to establish long-term business relationships and to sell a variety of services to each client. Vertical linkages to content providers can be important to Internet Service Providers. One reason for AOL's success is that it is able to provide proprietary content that its subscribers use in preference to that available elsewhere on the World Wide Web. This enables it to charge a subscription fee when other providers are offering basic Internet connections for free.

R. Service provisioning

Resources

From the examples in Section 8.2.3, it will be clear that physical resources play a large role in the service provisioning activity, and that organisations can gain at least a temporary advantage by having faster or more powerful machinery or computers than their competitors. Effective procedures are no less important. Organisations can gain differentiation advantage by being first with the news, by having short waiting times to log-on to the network, or by never overcharging a customer or failing to process a transaction. They can certainly attract a lot of bad publicity if they fail in these areas. Capabilities in reliability, in sensitivity to customer needs and in speed of response can therefore be important sources of competitive advantage in this activity.

Vertical integration

There are some sensitive vertical integration decisions to be taken in the activity of service provision where, as in the network promotion activity, there may be no shortage of third-party suppliers. A newspaper can use freelances or press agencies in place of its own correspondents. A bank or an on-line service provider can manage their own computer networks or subcontract it. Competitive advantage may come from taking better decisions about which activities are too sensitive to be contracted out, or from assessing where a firm genuinely has better capabilities than a third-party provider can muster.

Linkages

Service provisioning exchanges information with the network promotion activity. This activity needs up-to-date information on who the customers are and the terms of their contracts – few things upset a customer more than a mistake in their billing. The network promotion activity needs information on customer activity, to help it to decide if the customer still qualifies for membership. Some banks may exclude customers that fail to keep a minimum balance in their account, or who do not pay their salary into their bank account.

Operationally, the service provisioning activity is very dependent on the infrastructure operation activity to ensure that any physical assets are kept up to date and in good working order, and that capacity is adequate. If any sensitive parts of the service are outsourced, then vertical linkages with suppliers will also become important. Banks, for example, need to manage carefully the links with any outside bodies they use to process cheques and other transactions.

S. Infrastructure operation

There are no fixed rules to determine which particular functions belong to the infrastructure operation. For a bank, whose basic service is the provision of financial transactions, IT and telecommunications networks are the responsibility of infrastructure operation. However, for a telecommunications firm or on-line service provider, these networks essentially are the service that is being offered by the firm, and so come under the service provisioning activity. For a bank or insurer, the treasury function, which invests cash balances, is part of infrastructure operation, since a financial service firm must have a certain amount of cash available to meet the day-to-day demands of its clients, and the judicious investment of funds is a major source of profit. For most other organisations, good cash management is obviously desirable, but it is unlikely to be a major source of profit or of customer satisfaction. In most cases, therefore, it is a support activity, part of finance and planning.

Resources

Like the service provisioning activity, this activity may contribute to organisational capabilities in reliability, sensitivity to customer needs and speed of reaction. It is likely to offer technological competences in areas like IT, building maintenance or finance.

Vertical integration

These competences within infrastructure operation may also be available from third-party suppliers so that, as in the service provisioning activity, the firm may have some difficult and sensitive decisions to take about which functions are too important to outsource.

Linkages

The linkages of this activity with network promotion and service provisioning have already been covered in the discussion of those two activities.

REAL-LIFE APPLICATION 8.17

Amazon.com's value chain

Amazon.com is one of the longest-established Internet retailers, having been set up in July 1995. It pioneered the idea of selling books on the World Wide Web, and has since diversified into selling CDs, videos, games and software and many other goods, and into running Internet auctions. Apart from its main site in the US, it operates special sites for the UK and Germany.

Network promotion and contract management

Amazon originally promoted its network to potential users by word-of-mouth. It quickly built a reputation for reliability and for the unusually wide range of book titles that it offered. It also generated interest among its users by providing a medium whereby they could communicate with one another, and post reviews of the books they had read and liked (or loathed). It later began to advertise (in the UK, it used radio and posters on the London underground rail system) and it developed a system, now commonplace on the net, where other sites that referred business to it would get a small percentage of any resulting revenues. Its reputation makes it a preferred partner for many other web providers – for example, when someone uses the major search engines, such as Yahoo, it is invariably Amazon that is featured as a source of books on the topic being searched for.

Although Amazon charges no subscription fee, and uses credit card providers to process payments, it still has competences in contract management. It has patented a system whereby people who have previously registered on its site can order through a single click.

Service provisioning

Amazon invests large sums in web servers and other technology needed to keep access to its site quick and easy. Originally, the other crucial activities of inventory handling and order fulfilment were outsourced to America's largest book wholesaler. Amazon's decision to locate in Seattle was strongly influenced by the need to build strong linkages with this key supplier. It has now begun to invest in its own, state-of-the-art warehousing and logistic facilities, reasoning that, once developed, competences in these areas would be rarer and possibly more valuable than its existing Internet skills.

Infrastructure operation

One of Amazon's distinctive features has always been the ease-of-use of its software, which is developed by its own engineers. The decision to retain this capability in-house is based on a judgement that it is key to Amazon's competitive edge, although it is expensive to maintain.

Cautionary note

Although Amazon's business model has been widely praised and emulated it is, at the time of writing, unclear whether the firm actually possesses a competitive advantage over more traditional retailers. Although it boasts 130 million users in 160 countries, the company has never earned any profits, and is not forecast to do so for some time, so that there is no clear evidence that any of its resources are actually valuable.

T. Support activities

As with professional services the support activities for networks have a slightly different emphasis to those for manufacturing organisations:

- The purchasing activity is as important for networks as it is for manufacturing organisations, given the number of bought-in services and the size of the infrastructure purchases. Choosing the right suppliers may require intricate knowledge of the technologies used by the organisation, and can make a major contribution to its effectiveness.

- The process development activity is also very important strategically, since as in professional service organisations, it covers product development as well. It may involve the development of new types of contract, of new services – a new type of bank account, a colour supplement, a new type of on-line messaging service – or of enhancements to the infrastructure.

Questions for discussion

1. Are the following types of organisation manufacturing-style, professional services or network organisations?
   - A firm of painters and decorators.
   - An insurance company.
   - An insurance broker.
   - The rubbish collection department of a local authority.
   - An up-market clothing firm, such as Versace or Ralph Lauren.

2. Draw value chains for:
   - Bank of Granite (closing case, Chapter 3)
   - Daewoo's Okpo shipyard (closing case, Chapter 7)
   - the university or college where you are studying
   - another organisation where you have worked, or with which you are familiar.

   How great is the coherence between competitive stance, value chain, culture and architecture in each case?

3. Caterpillar, the US manufacturer of earthmoving equipment, has recently extended its 'CAT' brand into a line of jeans and hard-wearing leisure clothing. Why is it not afraid that Levi-Strauss will retaliate by entering Caterpillar's core business? (Try using the value chain to structure your answer.)

CASE STUDY

Navico

For James Flynn OBE, the sharply dressed founder of Navico, it was the moment of truth. Over six years, the Margate-based maker of marine communications and instrumentation equipment had grown from nothing to a respected position in the British market.

Then it suddenly ran out of steam. 'Navico had reached a plateau, and there were two ways the company could go,' says Flynn, Navico's managing director. 'Without fundamental changes, we would stagnate and slowly fade away into obscurity. Alternatively, we could transform ourselves from a small, mediocre company on the Kent coast into a big one offering quality on a global scale.'

For a 'small, mediocre company', Navico had attained levels of success of which many businesses would be proud. Founded in 1984 to design and manufacture auto-pilots, instruments and other electrical products for yachts, it had made a splash at the London Boat Show a few months later by launching a range of 11 products.

In a fragmented market with scores of specialist suppliers, Navico's all-embracing product strategy had quickly captured the attention of sailors. So too had its early adoption of new technologies for marine VHF radio telephones, which in turn brought benefits in reducing production costs.

Having started modestly with five staff in rented rooms overlooking Ramsgate harbour, Navico grew steadily to a full-time payroll of 80 by the beginning of the 1990s. But then the growth came to a halt. With the leisure marine industry drying up in a depressed economy, Navico was in danger of getting stuck on the mud flats. 'We were going nowhere. It wasn't just a change of course we needed,' says Flynn, 49. 'It was a wholehearted cultural revolution.' Adoption strategies that have since been endorsed by Winning, the (UK) Department of Trade and Industry's study of successful companies, Navico embarked on a series of changes in product development and production, together with the development of a much keener understanding of customer needs. One of the first steps by Flynn and his team was to invite sales agents from all over the world to a three-day conference to consider a range of new technical opportunities and product ideas. Small discussion groups evaluated the relevance and value of all the many concepts allowing Navico's design team to focus on the products that would have the greatest market value.

'We sell in more than 50 markets from Finland to Gran Canaria,' says Flynn. 'Our sales agents are the eyes and ears of the market. In addition to the conferences, which are now held every two years, we also have quarterly meetings with sales agents in key markets to keep track of changing customer needs.'

Agents explained to Navico, for example, how weekend sailors do not want to waste precious leisure time installing increasingly sophisticated navigation and communications systems in their boats.

Navico listened and responded by investing in training programmes for several hundred service agents around the world to provide installation and maintenance services as well as product sales.

Learning of boat-owners' preference for equipment with a consistent look and feel, Navico sought to ensure its products were complementary in appearance. It therefore began to redirect its sales effort towards boat builders.

By ensuring that Navico equipment is fitted as original equipment, it can thus encourage a steady flow of maintenance business for sales agents plus valuable follow-on after-market sales.

Feedback from sales agents, combined with market research, showed a vital need to refresh what had become an ageing product line. The four-strong team of research-and-development engineers was overstretched and the products unimpressive in appearance.

'We needed fresh eyes to assist with product presentation,' admits Navico's co-founder and technical director, Alan Wrigley, 'so we employed an outside firm of design consultants.'

The relationship with PDD, a highly successful London industrial design consultancy, is acknowledged by Flynn as a critical element in the cultural revolution and continues to this day. Navico designers work in PDD's Chelsea studios for days at a time, while staff from the consultancy are often 'in residence' at the factory to ensure that new products are designed with production factors at the fore.

'If you don't invest in new products, you quickly become an also-ran,' says Wrigley. 'But simply pouring money into research and development is not enough in itself. The marketing team gets a steady stream of conceptual ideas from customers and agents. R&D refines those into a tangible form. It's an interactive process that can involve people from all parts of the company.'

Though the in-house team handling engineering and R&D has grown to 15, the continuous flow of ideas could overwhelm the company's resources without careful control, Wrigley suggests. Weekly reviews are held to ensure the practicality and relevance of all projects. Production engineering is an integral part of the process from the outset.

Rather than plotting a solitary course as it had done since its foundation, Navico formed strategic alliances with companies active in key engineering disciplines such as radar cartography and global positioning systems (GPS) technology. This supplemented existing expertise in marine VHF, autopilots and yacht instrumentation to provide a more complete product range.

To develop a range of radar products would have obliged Navico to become proficient in yet another engineering discipline. It would also have combined a high risk and a long lead time to market without any guarantee of success. Over a period of three years, Flynn frequently visited Japan and eventually struck up a relationship with Koden Electronics, one of the three leading Japanese companies in the sector.

A joint-venture company called Konav now operates from a recently converted purpose-built factory on a greenfield site next to the main Navico factory. Konav produces a range of radars using combined Japanese and British tooling and these are then shipped to Japan and many other countries.

Despite sterling's recent sharp appreciation against the yen, the joint venture can still produce a quality product at a competitive price. Flynn warns, however, that any further strengthening of the pound will torpedo the competitive advantage of companies such as Navico and Konav competing in the global arena.

Single-cable Canbus technology developed by Bosch for the motor industry also allowed Navico quickly to satisfy customer demands for less complex wiring systems aboard craft of up to 20 metres in length. 'After the revolution we moved the design area immediately next door to production to minimise any departmental barriers. There is no point in designing it if you can't produce it, is there?' says Wrigley.

Market research among customers often has drawbacks, Wrigley warns, in merely telling you what product they want today, which is almost invariably the best product currently on the market. 'You are well behind the game if you simply copy,' he says. 'You need to be ahead of the game.'

Yet bold innovation carries risk, he says. Having worked with design consultants to create the radical Corus instrumentation system using a single screen to display six sets of information as required, Navico was shocked by the low levels of demand.

'Corus puzzled people,' says Wrigley. 'It was too far ahead of the market and took 18 months before it really started to sell. Initially we were worried. We thought we'd done something wrong, but now Corus is accepted by customers and copied by rivals.

'Product innovation attracts public attention and has great brand-building benefits. You don't want to be different for the sake of it. But if you can differentiate through customer benefits at a comparable price you're onto a winner.'

The redoubled commitment to product development has meant that the entire product line has been replaced since 1993, playing a key role in boosting turnover by 150% over the past four years.

No less important to profits has been a revolutionary approach to the production process. Once again it was recognised that a change required

CASE STUDY *continued*

input from fresh eyes, so Mike Bowerman was brought on board from Thurlby-Thandar Electronics in Cambridge as production director.

Manufacture of each of the product groups was reorganised into cells. The leader of each cell team remains constant, but investment in training enables multi-skilled staff to move between cells in response to widely variable levels of consumer demand.

Moving to a more efficient culture of operational flexibility was a painful process, Flynn recalls. 'We had to be ruthless in identifying those with key competences and those with greatest commitment to the company,' he says. 'More than 20 of the 80 staff who didn't score well on either measure had to go, though we made the transition as gently as possible with maximum support.'

The remainder settled into a simple process whereby customer orders gathered each month by the sales manager are discussed in a group meeting with the assembly manager and six team leaders. 'Talking face to face sometimes gets emotional,' Bowerman says, 'but it's a million times better than exchanging memos. If a cell team leader is going to need more staff to fulfil the week's order, then the assembly manager will re-allocate staff accordingly.'

While staff numbers have since grown to more than 110, the culture of flexibility has remained deeply ingrained. Flynn and other directors work on the shopfloor when extra hands are required.

'Not only does it give you a feel of what it's like, but it also demonstrates to everyone how much you care about customer satisfaction,' he says. 'Our management structure at Navico is already very flat. If you are prepared to roll up your sleeves and get stuck in the lines of communication are shortened even further.'

The priorities and completion dates for all orders are public knowledge for everyone in the factory. Cell members take responsibility for setting their own schedules, revising the prominent wall-mounted order board each time an item is completed and taken to dispatch.

In some cells the boards even keep a running score of the value of sales orders fulfilled. A similar strategy of openness is clear from 'Friday Hot News'

Full steam ahead with new Mayday regime

Being able to know your precise position, average speed, water depth and compass heading are all important to the yachtsman. But there is nothing more important to the serious sailor or sea-going professional than an ability to communicate.

Hand-held VHF radio telephones for use at sea have been part of Navico's product range from the outset. Their commercial importance was clear. So, too, were the implications of impending global standards for Mayday and other distress signals, together with data about the vessel's identity and location.

Vessels and shore stations throughout the world will be required to use the new equipment. It will not be necessary for commercial vessels and coastguards to monitor the emergency-only radio frequency previously used, so many old radio telephones are becoming outdated.

Commercial users have known about these changes and have been choosing new-style radio telephones for the past few years. Leisure users are now paying attention as well. Navico recognised the impact, and during its three-year cultural revolution invested almost 15% of its sales in research and development and tooling for the new product.

'Any new product is a gamble,' says James Flynn, but in this case the bet was to yield handsome returns. Though only one of more than a dozen product lines, for several years the Axis VHF radio telephone has accounted for more than a third of Navico's sales.

reports, showing the financial and sales performance of the company. This weekly update is provided to 30 key staff and posted in common areas where they can be viewed by other staff members. Part of the pay of all workers is profit-related.

The cells are also self-regulating in managing supply of components for the production process. 'We're not big enough to rely on suppliers for just-in-time deliveries,' says Bowerman. 'They will always prioritise bigger firms.' Navico therefore holds two to four weeks' stock at all times, with daily checks on empty supply boxes prompting orders sent directly from the production cells responsible.

'The change we made to our company logo was symbolic of the changes throughout the company during 1990–92,' says Flynn. 'Investing in innovative, quality products that can be produced efficiently and giving people responsibility for making them to a high standard has revolutionised Navico. Over the five years since we have seen a real-terms doubling of turnover, big increases in market share and a big jump in profitability.

Case study questions

1. What key resources can you identify at Navico, and how durable do you think they are?

2. What important decisions has Navico taken about its value chain?

3. What aspects of Navico's culture and architecture have contributed to its success?

4. How well has Navico adapted to changes in its environment?

5. If you had the opportunity (and the money) to buy shares in Navico, would you?

NOTES

1. We are following conventional practice here in using the term 'value chain', although it is rather misleading. A chain implies a nice linear sequence of links and, as you will see later in this chapter, value chains in practice are far less tidy. A more accurate term would be 'value web' or 'value network'.

2. See, for example, Huber (1993) and Lacity and Hirschheim (1993).

3. For more detail see Chapters 9 and 10 of *Gaining and Sustaining Competitive Advantage* by Jay Barney, Addison-Wesley, 1997.

4. It also happens in the job market, when applicants 'embroider' their CV to make themselves more attractive to potential employers . . . not that any of our esteemed readers would even *think* of resorting to anything so underhand . . .

5. Particularly in service industries, empirical research does not always support the idea that transaction costs *alone* can explain firms' vertical integration decisions. See Poppo and Zenger (1998) and Murray and Kotabe (1999).

6. See, for example, Donaldson (1995: ch. 6) and Chiles and McMackin (1996).

7. See, for example, Bettis et al. (1992), Chesborough and Teece (1996) and Mazur (1999).

8. See, for example, Kiely (1997) and Quinn (1999).

9. Of course, the sharing does not have to be even. Depending on the relative power of firms and their suppliers and customers, one side may be able to keep all the cost savings for itself.

10. Much of the analysis in this section comes from Stabell and Fjeldstad (1998). We have altered their terminology a little to make it easier to understand.

11. For some newspapers, this works the other way around as well – the more small advertisers there are, the more readers are likely to buy the paper.

12. The value chain presented here combines elements of Michael Porter's value chain (Porter, 1985, p. 37), The McKinsey Business System (Grant, 1998, p. 121) and the version proposed by Hill and Jones (1998).

13. Porter calls this 'technology development' and uses it to encompass both product and process development. We prefer to separate out product development from process development. It is actually quite difficult to find a logical place to analyse a firm's basic research activities within Porter's framework.

14. Porter calls this activity 'Firm Infrastructure' and includes quality control within it.

15. Notoriously, of the thirty large American firms that Peters and Waterman identified as 'excellent' and used as the basis for their 1982 book, fewer than ten were still performing strongly five years later. Peters and Waterman have also been criticised for failing to look at non-US firms and for not including a control sample of poorly performing firms, to check on whether they were following any of the same policies. This does not mean that their results were wrong, although Tom Peters has since said that in future small firms are most likely to be the source of innovation. Although their results lacked the rigour of the best academic research, they definitely struck a chord with practitioners.

16. Rumelt (1988) and Pettigrew and Whipp (1991) both draw similar conclusions about the importance of coherence.

17. 'Ayling's failings', *The Economist*, 16 January 1999, p. 76; Lennane, Alexandra; 'Still the world's favourite airline?', *Airfinance Journal*, June 1999, Issue 218, pp. 30–34.

18. For example, Hamel and Prahalad (1994), Kay (1993), Inkpen (1996).

19. Described in Cooper (1998), 'Britain's best factories 2003', *Management Today*, Supplement, 5: 3–5.

20. For a description of how Toyota involves suppliers in its design processes, and also for a very detailed description of the competences and architecture that enable Toyota to be one of the motor industry's leaders in product development lead times while using fewer engineers than its American counterparts, see Sobek et al. (1998, 1999).

21. Porter, in his original framework, called this 'Inbound Logistics'.

22. Porter refers to this as 'Outbound Logistics', which is accurate in a manufacturing context but does not properly describe the way the activity is used by retailers.

23. The economic theory behind this tactic is explained in Kay (1993: 91–92).

24. See, for example, Krasner (1982), Quinn (1985), Bolwijn and Kumpe (1990), Tushman and O'Reilly (1996), and Voss (1994).

25. See, for example, Thomas Marx (1991). Robert Grant (1998) makes a similar point.

Corporate-level strategy

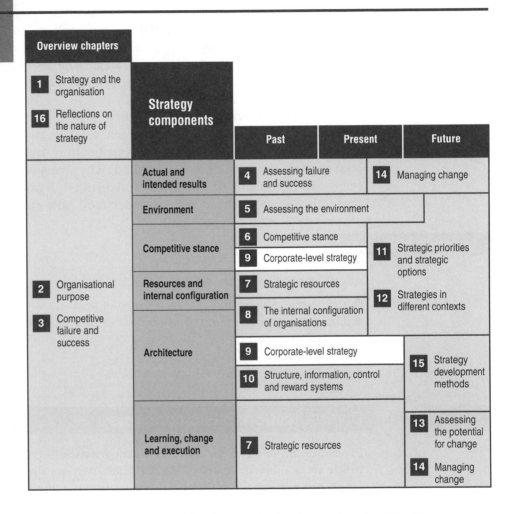

Overview chapters				
1 Strategy and the organisation				
16 Reflections on the nature of strategy				

	Strategy components	**Past**	**Present**	**Future**
2 Organisational purpose	**Actual and intended results**	**4** Assessing failure and success		**14** Managing change
	Environment	**5** Assessing the environment		
3 Competitive failure and success	**Competitive stance**	**6** Competitive stance		**11** Strategic priorities and strategic options
		9 Corporate-level strategy		
	Resources and internal configuration	**7** Strategic resources		**12** Strategies in different contexts
		8 The internal configuration of organisations		
	Architecture	**9** Corporate-level strategy		**15** Strategy development methods
		10 Structure, information, control and reward systems		
	Learning, change and execution	**7** Strategic resources		**13** Assessing the potential for change
				14 Managing change

Portfolio
A portfolio is a group of businesses or products managed within a single overarching organisational structure

In this chapter we consider the particular issues involved in the management of multi-business companies – corporations. This chapter looks at some of the issues to do with managing a **portfolio** of what may be very different types of business within a single overall structure.

It is not altogether obvious at first sight why this topic warrants a chapter to itself. According to one school of thought, there are few differences between the management of a portfolio of products and a portfolio of businesses. We agree that there are considerable parallels, and that similar techniques of analysis are used, but believe that the business portfolio poses more complex management problems. You might think that the

Hierarchical and network structures are discussed in Chapter 10. ▶

notion of a parent company managing a group of wholly owned subsidiaries through a rigid hierarchy is an out-dated and unrepresentative view of corporations today. It is true that the structures of some of the most successful major corporations look more like networks than classical hierarchies. However, large companies that own and manage a group of disparate businesses are still numerous enough for us to give special consideration to their particular needs and problems.

Let us clarify one small point first. In this book we use the term 'corporate strategy' to refer only to this very specific part of organisational life. You will find many other books on strategic management which use 'corporate strategy', in a much broader sense than we do, to refer to the overall management of large corporations.

This chapter has three parts. In the first, we look at the different types of diversification: horizontal and vertical, related and unrelated. In the second, we look at the practice of diversification: how common it is as a strategy and the reasons, good and bad, why firms employ it. Finally, we review the problems of managing a diversified organisation and look at theoretical frameworks to help us understand how effectively the organisation is tackling those problems.

Learning objectives

After reading this chapter, you should understand:

- the issues involved in managing a portfolio of businesses;
- how parent corporations can add or lose value in diversifying across a range of business areas;
- the components of synergy;
- whether, and if so how, resources can be shared across businesses.

9.1 Diversification: basic concepts

Diversification refers to the move of organisations into products and/or markets which are not directly linked to the businesses they are already in. Diversification can be more or less *related*. Related diversification is a move into products or businesses that have some similarities with the existing ones. Unrelated diversification is a move into business areas that have few or no links with what the firm already does. Diversification usually (though not always) means the **addition** of businesses, rather than the **substitution** of new ones for old.

This may be part of a deliberate strategy in which the characteristics of the industry into which a firm is diversifying are carefully matched to the organisation's resources. Sometimes, it is an emergent strategy where the organisation finds itself in new business because its customers ask it to supply a product or service they cannot find elsewhere, or because entrepreneurial employees seize opportunities in new areas. Whatever the means, the result of diversification is what is known as a 'diversified portfolio', in which a company owns a range of products or businesses in different industries or market.

A constituent part of a portfolio is commonly referred to as a 'strategic business unit' (SBU). This may be an independent subsidiary company, an operating division, or part of a division.

Organisations' portfolios can differ in two basic ways:

- They can be more or less 'related'. One of the most important debates in the theory of diversification concerns the extent to which related diversification delivers better results than unrelated.

- They can be more or less 'balanced' – with a mix of fast- and slow-growing businesses, or of large and small ones.

In the following sections, we look at what is meant by relatedness, at one particular concept of relatedness, **synergy**, and at the notion of **balance**. We also look at the possible cost of diversification, and the challenges confronting the management of a diversified corporation.

9.1.1 Relatedness

Research interest in the last few years has concentrated on what is actually meant by relatedness. Relatedness has traditionally (e.g. Rumelt, 1974) been conceived in terms of similarities between the technologies, markets, or customers used in different businesses. This kind of relatedness is assessed using standard classifications such as Standard Industrial Classification (SIC) codes, on the assumption that if two businesses share the same SIC code, they must have similar production techniques and technologies.

As strategic management theory has come to understand the importance of resources to competitive advantage, researchers have begun to realise the limitations of this view. Businesses may be superficially unrelated, but actually similar in ways which are not immediately apparent (Real-Life Application 9.1). Markides and Williamson (1996) suggest that profitable diversification is dependent on pinpointing opportunities for sharing strategic assets between two businesses – that is, *strategic relatedness*. This helps to explain why a company like Citizen sees watches and computer printers (which are not classified under the same SIC code) as related businesses even though superficially they look very different. There are enough

---

REAL-LIFE APPLICATION 9.1

Related or unrelated businesses?

A senior executive at British Steel recently expressed the view that even though his company only makes steel, it is not a single-business firm. His position was that the several types of steel that the company manufactures have such different buying characteristics and requirements and each in turn requires such different sales and production approaches, that his company could be viewed as competing in a series of unrelated markets.

By contrast, the Citizen Watch Company claims that its diversified products, which include watches, printers

for personal computers, floppy disk drives, small portable PCs, liquid crystal colour TVs, quartz oscillators, and precision machine tools and robots, share a common set of advanced, precision technologies that the company developed in the course of manufacturing watches. Citizen's president recalls how the company learned from its failures after venturing into what it now considers unrelated, non-precision businesses during the diversification boom.

Source: Markides and Williamson (1996).

similarities in the processes by which each product group is manufactured and distributed.

Markides and Williamson (1996) have identified five types of assets and resources that might be sources of strategic relatedness:

- **Customer assets** – such as brand recognition and customer loyalty. If a company spends a lot of money developing brands in one market and then diversifies into another where building brands is equally important, the company can transfer its brand-building competences into the second market.

- **Channel assets** – such as established channel access and distributor loyalty. Competences in, for example, dealer recruitment and overcoming shelf-space restrictions will be valuable across businesses that share similar levels of dependence on dealers, distributors or retailers.

- **Input assets** – such as supplier loyalty or knowledge of where to find inputs at the right price or quality, if these are in short supply.

- **Process assets** – such as proprietary technology, product or market-specific experience, and organisational systems. Two businesses that share the need to develop an effective base of skilled employees with experience in working together will have quite a high degree of strategic relatedness, even if they provide different services in different markets. A pair of businesses, one of which requires highly skilled staff and the other a base of cost-effective, low-skill workers, may in fact be less related, even though the first business' products may be 'just' up-market versions of the second's.

- **Market knowledge assets** – such as accumulated information on the goals and behaviour of competitors or customers or the typical price elasticity of demand for products.

9.1.2 Synergy

Related diversification in theory enables firms to exploit economies of scale or scope.[1] Resource sharing allows a diversified firm to reduce costs and/or to differentiate its products through, for example, providing customer-responsive distribution channels or innovative technologies. The ways in which resources can be combined or shared to achieve a whole which is greater than the units could individually is called **synergy** (see Advanced Topic 9.1.3).

9.1.3 ADVANCED TOPIC
Synergy

Synergy is a concept that we discussed briefly in Chapter 3. Restated, it is the ability to achieve something by combining elements, and which would not be achievable by these elements acting independently. This 'thing' is greater than the sum of its parts.

How possible it is to achieve synergy between SBUs has been the matter of some debate. There have been some important writers who claim that it is easy to overestimate the potential for synergy between different parts of a business, and diversified conglomerates such as Hanson Industries were famous in their heyday in the

1980s for deliberately refusing to attempt to achieve synergies between the firms in their portfolio – they thought there were more potential risks than benefits. Similar sentiments have been expressed more recently by Jerry Flint (1999: 168).

'When Alfred Sloan invented the GM management system in the 1920s, he didn't integrate operations. Quite the opposite, he created five distinct and autonomous car operating divisions, each headed by a strong leader. Did it work? Well enough to make General Motors the largest auto-maker in the world, and eventually earn it 50% of the U.S. market. GM doesn't have that system anymore. It is integrated, more integrated every day. There are no strong leaders in charge of divisions. In fact there aren't really any divisions. Decisions take forever to make, and it's hard to find anyone responsible for anything. And you know how well GM is doing. What about all the savings through integration? They are exaggerated, greatly exaggerated.'

However, although it may be that synergy is somewhat hard to obtain, there **are** occasions when it may be both possible to achieve and beneficial. In business terms synergy may refer to a number of different elements:

- *The sharing of expertise.* This may relate to management skills or technical knowledge such as in manufacturing processes or relationship marketing.
- *The sharing of information.* This may mean an exchange of information on customers – their details and preferences for cross-selling of products, for example.
- *The combining of access to financial resources.* 'Buying-power' in terms of negotiating loans or attracting investors tends to be greater in a larger organisation.
- *The sharing of sales and distribution channels.*
- *The sharing of resources.* Buildings and manufacturing facilities are common examples.
- *Achieving economies of scale in some elements of the value chain.* For example, increased buying power in purchasing raw materials.
- *Achieving economies of scope.* For example, applying FMCG skills across a range of products.
- *The sharing of systems.* For example, payroll or personnel management procedures, or computer networks.

There are many opportunities for firms to combine certain activities so that economies of scope or scale can be achieved. Raw materials supplies are cheaper if bought in bulk, and having single administrative or manufacturing facilities fully utilised across a range of products makes more economic sense than having them specialised but half-used. Hence many firms have diversified **horizontally** into products which can use some elements of a common value chain (see Real-Life Application 9.2). Other firms have diversified **vertically** into their supply chains or distribution channels. Examples include Kuwait Oil Co. which also owns a petrol retailer – Q8. By this means it hopes to reduce costs through selling a range of its products through the same sales and distribution facilities.

◀ *Vertical integration is defined in Section 1.2 and discussed in greater detail in Chapter 8.*

9.1.4 Balance

Many strategy writers, particular in the 1970s, felt that it was important for a portfolio to be 'balanced'.[2] Balance might be achieved across a number of dimensions:

REAL-LIFE APPLICATION 9.2

Diversification at Sony

Sony in 1999 comprised the following mix of businesses:

Business segment	Proportion of revenues	Proportion of profits
Electronics	63%	37%
Games	11%	39%
Music	10%	11%
Pictures	7%	11%
Insurance	5%	5%
Other	4%	−3%

The relationships between many of these businesses were clear. The games business (PlayStation hardware and software) had many technologies in common with the electronics business, whose products included TVs, audio and video equipment and computers. The two business segments could also share distribution channels and benefit from a common brand. Sony's recorded music and pictures could be played on its audio and video hardware, and by owning these businesses the company could be sure that any of its new hardware standards, such as mini-discs, would have software to run on them. Successful films could be translated into best-selling video games.

Sometimes the links were subtler. The insurance business, which sold life insurance in Japan, shared few common features with other parts of Sony, but undoubtedly benefited from the group's strong reputation. Within the other business segment were operations, such as leasing and credit cards, that had grown up to support sales in other areas.

Like every large, diversified corporation, Sony needed to make sure that, in following new opportunities, it did not spread management attention too thinly. Businesses that targeted corporate clients, like leasing and the components and professional audio equipment operations (part of the electronics business segment) already had different success factors from those that sold mainly to consumers. The financial service businesses deployed different capabilities and competences from those in electronics or video games. It takes very able managers to understand this level of diversity.

- Size – a mix of small and large businesses.
- The age or the life-cycle stage of the industry – a mix of young, fast-growing businesses and more mature ones.
- The extent to which the businesses are net producers or consumers of cash.
- The businesses' products and market characteristics.
- Geographical location.

One theoretical benefit of a balanced portfolio is a reduction of risk, since it would minimise the likelihood of all the businesses facing severe problems at the same time. A second potential benefit is that resources can be redistributed from the businesses that have them to those that need them – for example, a mature business can become a source of cash and of marketing and production expertise for a younger one. However, these benefits have not always been easy to realise in practice.

9.1.5 The costs of diversification

Although there are a number of benefits to diversification (they are discussed in Section 9.2), there are also very real costs.

The most obvious of these costs is the corporate head office – which after all has no direct customers from whom costs can be recouped, and so represents a potential 'dead weight' on the businesses. The owner or parent company will have administrative staff and a management team who are responsible for controlling the interactions between the business units and overseeing their individual contacts with the parent company. There are also hidden transaction costs, such as the cost to the business units of responding to head office requests for information. Referring decisions to corporate headquarters for approval can introduce delays that can, in some cases, lead to a loss of business to more agile competitors.

◄ Parenting skills were defined in Chapter 3.

Therefore the existence of a parent company can only be justified if it is able to cover these costs and add more value than the subsidiaries would be able to achieve themselves as independent units. The ways in which parents seek to do this are discussed in the next section.

9.1.6 Management challenges in large corporations

Large parent firms or corporations face four major decisions:

- How many and which businesses to own. The crucial question they have to answer was set out by Michael Porter (1987) as the 'better off test': will a particular business be better off – that is, better able to compete – under the ownership of the corporation than it would be if it stayed independent? If the answer to this question is 'no', then the business should not be diversified into – and if the organisation already owns it, it should be divested. This view of corporate strategy – that it is the parent's job to add value to the subsidiary – has largely replaced earlier theories that emphasised the value that the businesses would add to the parent. If the parent cannot manage an SBU successfully, then it will not be in a position to profit from its brands, distribution channels or other resources.

- How to manage the relationships, if any, between the SBUs. Each business may be a separate legal entity pursuing its own independent strategies. However, there may also be occasions when there are benefits in establishing links between the different businesses in a portfolio, in which case competences and resources need to be shared and co-ordinated across the units.

We look at organisation structures and systems in more detail in Chapter 10. ►

- The types of structures and control systems appropriate for the corporation.
- How to allocate resources between the businesses.

In the following sections, we look at each of these decisions in turn.

9.2 The practice of diversification

Like many other elements of strategic management, diversification is subject to the vagaries of fashion. Until the 1980s it was seen as such a natural and important part of the strategic management of large corporations that many important books referred to little else. The writings of Alfred Chandler (1962), Igor Ansoff (1965) and Richard Rumelt (1974) suggested that the decentralised, multi-divisional, corporation was the ideal. The success of conglomerates like Textron (with interests in activities as diverse as military helicopters, gold bracelets, chain saws, writing paper, and fine china) or Pearson (with interests in china, leisure facilities, oil, and publishing) seemed to epitomise this (Leavy, 1998; Bettis and Hall, 1983). The Boston Consulting Group's growth-share matrix (which we look at in detail in Section 9.5.1) was in common use to help companies decide what type of product or business to be in, and how to allocate resources among them. The recommended task for corporate management was to balance their portfolio of businesses and set in place appropriate control and capital appraisal systems.

In the 1980s the tide seemed to turn against diversification. Popular writers such as Peters and Waterman (1982) urged their readers to 'stick to the knitting' – to focus on areas of existing strength. Michael Porter (1987) pointed out that the 33 largest US corporations had retained fewer than 50% of the operations they had diversified into between 1950 and 1986, and that for unrelated diversification the figure was only 26%. He characterised this performance as 'dismal'. Managers began to appreciate the problems of managing diversified structures and the risk that, in the attempt to manage too many different types of things, they might lose out to competitors able to develop high degrees of specialised knowledge in a narrow area of business.

Overall, the extent of diversification by US and UK companies appears to have declined substantially during the 1980s and 1990s.[3] ITT, a prototypical American conglomerate of the 1970s and 1980s, split into three companies in 1994, based around its hotel, insurance and automotive businesses. Hanson Industries, one of the most successful conglomerates of the 1980s, decided in 1996 to split into four separate companies – energy, tobacco, chemicals and building materials. Partly, this can be attributed to the death or retirement of the people that built those conglomerates: Harold Geneen in the case of ITT, Gordon White and Lord Hanson in the case of Hanson. It proved difficult to find replacements with the necessary portfolio management abilities, a demonstration of how rare good parenting skills can be.

Another explanation in Hanson's case was that the company was aware of the changing, and less favourable, view of conglomerates in the press and financial markets. In many industries vertical integration strategies have been replaced by outsourcing, with an increasing preference for partnership relationships with suppliers and distributors such as that employed by Toyota and Marks & Spencer. Over recent times the number of industries in which firms operated decline by 14%, the number of single industry firms increased by 54% and previously diversified firms reduced the numbers of segments that they served.[4]

The management of mergers and acquisitions is reviewed in Chapter 15. ▶

It is possible to overstate the case against diversification. Part of the problem in the past has been that in the US and UK much diversification (70% of the cases in Porter's sample) has been through acquisition, which itself is a very difficult process to manage. In eastern Asia, where firms tend to favour organic growth as a means of expansion, there is much less evidence for this trend. Large corporations like Sony, Samsung, Hyundai, and Daewoo have shown little desire to cut back to 'core' businesses, or had any apparent need to. Some Western companies are still highly diversified and becoming more so: Disney, Philips, Bertelsmann, and Virgin (see Real-Life Application 9.3) are just some of the best known. America's most successful corporation, measured by total returns to shareholders, and its most admired, is General Electric, whose interests span fields as diverse as light bulbs, jet engines, power stations and credit cards. We now consider some of the possible advantages of diversification as well as looking at some of the downsides.

REAL-LIFE APPLICATION 9.3

Virgin's move into mobile phones

The Virgin Group is a UK conglomerate whose charismatic CEO, Richard Branson, is one of Britain's best-known business figures. From its 1971 beginnings in music retailing, it diversified into music production, recording and publishing, a business it has now divested. In the 1980s it made the rather startling leap into the airline business, which is now its highest profile operation. Fields into which it has since diversified include contraceptives, soft drinks, financial services, Internet service provision, rail transport, house-building and cosmetics.

On 11 November 1999, Virgin Group announced it was diversifying into mobile phones. According to Branson, this was 'perfect Virgin territory' – coming in with a simple proposition to a potentially highly profitable market that has got over-complicated and uncompetitive.

Virgin was targeting the two-thirds of the UK population that did not yet own a mobile phone. They antici-

pated that, in the future, many people would use their mobile phone to buy records, train tickets or financial services – all Virgin products.

Virgin mobile phones will miss out established UK retailers such as The Carphone Warehouse, and use its own music retailing outlets – Virgin megastores or Ourprice stores – and may also use its own direct-selling network.

When asked whether the reputation of Virgin Trains, which had not been given a good press recently, would have a deleterious effect on their move into another new business area, Branson admitted that the move into trains had been a 'massive risk' for Virgin, with a five-year goal to turn the business around. The implication was that the phones business was not such a risk.

Based on interview with Richard Branson on BBC1 TV business news, 11 November 1999.

9.2.1 Why firms diversify

Theorists have suggested a number of reasons why organisations might want to diversify:

- To seek growth and capture value added
- To spread risk
- To prevent a competitor from gaining ground
- To achieve synergy
- To control the supply or distribution chain
- To fulfil the personal ambition of the senior managers.

Diversification for growth

One of the most common reasons for diversifying is because firms perceive opportunities for growth that are not available in their core businesses or markets. It may be that the firm's managers believe that they have strategic resources that may give them an advantage in another, attractive industry. Sometimes, firms see that their suppliers or distributors are making super-normal profits, and want to capture some of that value added for themselves. For example, The Walt Disney Company now owns and operates all the hotels on its theme parks, having seen how profitable the independent hotels were that sprang up around the first Disneyland in California. Another example is the entry of large corporations – Virgin, Bertelsmann, Tesco – into Internet provision, which allows them to enter into what is likely to be an extremely important business area in the future.

A special case of this arises with successful companies that are producing such

347

large profits that there is a real problem in what to do with those profits. It may be that the structure of their existing industry prevents companies from expanding within it. They may be blocked from achieving a monopoly position, or have competitors who are too large or too strong to take on – and yet they may be extremely successful. In this case, given the market pressures for ever-increasing returns, there is little choice but to move into a new business area. However, as Grant (1998: 372) points out, history is 'littered with companies that overpaid in order to gain a position in a seemingly attractive industry', and attractive industries may not necessarily yield the desired growth.

At the opposite end of the spectrum are organisations that have become aware of the likely decline of their existing products. Perhaps they have come to the end of their life-cycles, or are threatened by substitute or competing products. There are times when it is easier to move into a new business area rather than waste resources in attempting to defend or regain a competitive position. However, it may still be worth the firm's while to remain in its old business – perhaps it is still profitable, or there may be large exit costs. The personal interests of powerful stakeholders in the organisation and managers' sentimental attachment to old products are other factors that may lead firms to retain old core businesses after it has moved into new areas.

Spreading risk

Although shareholders generally require increasing returns on their investments, many of the largest shareholders such as pension funds investments trusts, or banks also require relatively stable returns. One way for them to achieve this is to diversify their investment in stocks and shares, but another way is for the firms that they are investing in to diversify their own investments. This is so that if one SBU is in a high-risk business area, perhaps because it is new or in an unstable environment, another in a different area will balance the risk of it failing.

However, it is now generally agreed that spreading risk is a poor reason for a corporation to diversify. Investors can achieve their desired spread of investment risks by diversifying their own shareholdings, at less cost than the corporation incurs in entering and leaving businesses. This is one of the main reasons why corporations now have to justify their diversified portfolios in other ways. There are a few exceptions to this in the case of corporations which are involved in businesses or geographical locations (the former Soviet Union, or China, for example) which have less well-developed capital or stock markets, and where diversified investment strategies are simply not possible.

Preventing a competitor from gaining ground

◀ *First-mover advantage is discussed in Chapter 8. Experience effects are discussed in Chapter 7.*

Some moves into different products and markets are defensive and carried out in order to prevent a competitor or potential competitor from gaining a foothold. In this respect, the firm has to establish a position and performance so that they gain first mover advantage and build experience before the competitor has time to do so. Large conglomerates are also likely to have considerable reserves of capital and management strength, and may be able to squeeze out a smaller specialist competitor with fewer resources, for example through engaging in long-term price wars.

So size matters. There is also some recent research within a game theory framework which suggests that large conglomerates involved in multiple market places, where some of their products may even be substitutes for each other, benefit from a co-ordinated approach to product pricing across the divisions. Margins across all their divisions are likely to increase – something known as the *efficiency effect*. This is a strength that smaller, more specialist competitors lack, and which may go some way to counteracting some of the advantages which specialists appear to have. As in all of these things, there are pros and cons on both sides. Interestingly, there is also some other research which suggests that companies involved in multiple markets are less likely to start price wars or compete in other hostile ways with other similar firms because of the fear of reprisals in the remaining markets – another apparent contradiction.[5]

Achieving synergistic economies of scale and scope

Synergy is one of the reasons for diversification that is most commonly cited by managers themselves. The most obvious sources of it are the sharing of value chain activities such as purchasing, production facilities, distribution networks or finance functions. Businesses can combine their purchasing to negotiate better discounts, use their combined market power to obtain more shelf space in retailers, and share head office and IT facilities.

Synergy is not simply about combining channels or buying power, however. It may be obtained in cross-selling the products from other divisions, offering discounts to customers from other parts of the company, for example. It also relates to intangibles such a brands. The way that Virgin's brand name and corporate identity is used is a form of synergy, in that it is a brand which is distinctive and recognisable to a specific group of its potential target customers, and applicable across a wide variety of products.

Another form of synergy, identified by Hamel and Prahalad (1990, 1994) in a number of mostly Japanese corporations, comes from the use of knowledge about particular technologies or markets. These firms discovered that this knowledge could profitably be applied to businesses or products that, to an outsider, often appeared completely unrelated to the firm's original sphere of operations. Nonetheless, the genuine similarities in terms of market needs, technological characteristics, or manufacturing processes justified a move into them. We discuss these firms again in Section 9.3.1.

However, synergy is notoriously much harder to achieve in practice than in theory. There are numerous examples of companies that have moved into new areas and found them much harder to manage than they first thought. Examples in this category are Sony's much-criticised move into Hollywood (although Sony may yet have the last say on this as it is starting to look as if their acquisition of Columbia may have long-term benefits in digitisation and cross-selling of products) and Daimler-Benz in white goods (see Real-Life Application 9.4).

Furthermore, the existence of synergies does not imply an automatic need for a firm to diversify into other businesses in order to use its unique resources effectively. Licensing deals or partnerships may be much more effective methods of maximising value from proprietary technologies or brands than attempting to manage their exploitation within a corporate umbrella. Sony, for example, does not always attempt to promote or develop its music products itself, but enters into

---

REAL-LIFE APPLICATION 9.4

Daimler-Benz and DaimlerChrysler's search for synergy[6]

In the early 1990s Daimler-Benz, the German conglomerate, was involved in four major business areas

1 Mercedes-Benz   Cars and lorries
2 AEG   Electrical and electronic goods
3 DASA   Aerospace and defence goods
4 Debis   Financial services

This range of businesses had been built up through acquisitions during the 1980s, the intention being to achieve an 'integrated technology group' whose innovative technologies would benefit the car division, but part of the motivation was to compensate for stagnating vehicle sales with high-technology businesses. However, critics claimed that these objectives could have been obtained through other means, and that the company's attempt to achieve synergies between the different business units was very hard to achieve.

The company faced other difficulties. AEG in its own right was highly diversified and had problems of coordinating its business units. Eventually its appliances division was sold to Electrolux. DASA similarly contained a number of different, and in some cases duplicated, business units. And at around the time when management attention was needed to consolidate the mergers, Mercedes-Benz, the corporation's primary source of profit, experienced major problems with Japanese competitors in the crucially important American luxury car market.

In 1995 Daimler-Benz posted a loss. Some commentators suggested that the company had got so bogged down with its problems in AEG and DASA that it had failed to spot major opportunities in the vehicle division. After that Daimler-Benz restructured around seven divisions, all of whom were expected both to support the core business of transportation and achieve an annual 12% ROE target.

Since then, Daimler-Benz has merged with the US car-maker Chrysler, to form DaimlerChrysler, a merger which was, according to the company, 'carefully planned and executed'. In September 1999 DaimlerChrysler's shares had fallen by a third since their peak in April 1999 just after the merger.

---

partnerships with companies who can provide expertise on local geographical or market characteristics and have knowledge about specialised musical tastes. Disney does not manufacture the toys that bear its product characters; instead it licenses others to manufacture them, and receives handsome royalty payments in exchange. It recognises that others can do some things better than it can.

To achieve control

Another reason for diversification is the desire to achieve greater control over the firm's operating environment. Thus companies who take over their forwards and backwards supply and distribution channels might hope to achieve better control over the regularity and quality of supplies of raw materials, or the prices they pay, and in the case of distribution channels how their products are displayed or promoted. They might also hope to achieve economies of scale or scope in, for example, the numbers or range of products that can be shared within the same distribution channels.

This kind of diversification can also be a defensive move, to ensure that a firm is not squeezed out of its distribution channels by competitors. Disney Corporation bought ABC to ensure that it could still have an outlet for its TV productions, other TV networks having been acquired by its competitors.

This move into related parts of the value system is nevertheless considered to be diversification because the businesses are likely to be quite different, in terms of management, systems or structures, from the original one. This can sometimes lead such moves to fail, because the competences needed in the upstream and down-stream businesses are so different from those needed in a firm's original business. An excellent manufacturer is not always even a competent retailer. ABC is widely believed to have suffered greatly under Disney's management.

Personal ambition

◄ The achievement of personal goals through the growth of the firm is one aspect of the principal/agent problem that we discussed in Chapter 1.

Finally, one of the most likely – and common (although we know of no research that has proved this) – motives for diversifying is to achieve personal status and wealth. In the past, managers were often rewarded for the size of their empires, with less emphasis given to financial performance. Growth was the goal, and at what cost this was to be achieved was less important. This emphasis has changed in recent years, and profitability and shareholder value have become much more important.

Although not necessarily a particularly good reason for diversifying, personal ambition does not always lead to poor business decisions. The late Robert Maxwell built a publishing firm into an empire that spanned newspapers, books and the ownership of several football clubs. Although Maxwell was notoriously egotistical and, until his death, the very personification of the principal/agent problem (he raided his firms' pension funds to pay off his corporation's debts), some of his diversification decisions now look quite perceptive. In his time British newspapers and football clubs were seen as chronically unprofitable businesses that were bought only by rich people seeking to nourish their egos. Now, successful and hard-headed firms such as News Corporation are actively seeking to acquire both types of company as sources of profit.

9.2.2 Relatedness as a success factor in diversification

There has been a considerable stream of research that has found that a diversified portfolio does not always lead to good performance. Although early research suggested that diversification into *related* areas leads to improved performance whereas *unrelated* diversification does not, several exceptions to this rule have been identified, and opinion as to whether or not diversification leads to improved performance is now equivocal.[7] There are plenty of examples of hugely successful corporations that have apparently unrelated businesses in their portfolios. The performance of Virgin, Hanson in the 1980s, and Bertelsmann nowadays (but see Real-Life Application 9.8 for a note of caution) suggest that lack of relatedness *per se* is not a barrier to high performance.

Equally, examples of unsuccessful corporations full of apparently related businesses (British Steel in the 1980s) suggest that superficial relatedness is no guarantee of successful diversification.[8] One of the reasons for this is the availability of resources in an open market. A corporation may have a portfolio of businesses based on, for example, product similarities and thus their use of common raw materials. However, combining these businesses will only add value if, together, they can access this resource better or more cheaply than they could independently, without any offsetting disadvantages. At corporate level, as at business level, resources only add value if they are rare and difficult to obtain or copy.

However, if the different businesses are related through common *strategic* resources that are valuable to all of them, then diversification may still add value.

Such resources are not traded, and so the corporation is doing something that the market cannot. We look at this style of diversification, based on the sharing between the businesses or resources such as core competences, in Section 9.3.1.

REAL-LIFE APPLICATION 9.5

Quinenco

Founded in 1957, the Chilean conglomerate Quinenco owns stakes in half a dozen leading Chilean companies in a range of industries – beverages, copper and aluminium products, financial services, and hotels and resorts. In June 1997 the Luksic brothers bundled all their assets, save mining, into a holding company called Quinenco and took it public, selling 18% for $270 million. The family's 82% is now worth nearly $630 million. For the first nine months of 1998, the conglomerate reported net profits of $31.2 million, compared to $52.4 million for the comparable period in 1997.

These stakes were acquired mainly through turn-arounds, buying badly managed, money-losing firms that were ripe for rescue. For example a 30% stake in the beer manufacturer Cia. Cervecerias Unidas (CCU) was bought in 1986 for $7 million. It was a mess. It owed $350 million to 64 banks around the world, and Chile was still in economic turmoil. Today it has a market capitalisation of more than $1 billion.

In recent years the Luksics have diversified beyond Chile – a tiny country with relatively mature markets. 'The only way to have the critical mass you need in a global economy is to go into other markets, so we did that,' according to Guillermo. Between 1991 and 1995 the Luksics bought a bank, beverage companies, machine-tool manufacturers and processed-food plants in Argentina for more than $300 million. In 1997 something like 35% of the company's revenues came from Argentina, Brazil, Peru and other neighbouring nations, up from less than 10% in 1995. Its businesses include:

- Madeco, in which Quinenco has held a controlling 56% interest since 1970, is its oldest and largest subsidiary. It dominates the Chilean market for copper cables and pipes and aluminium tubes. Turnover was $795 million in 1997.

- CCU, a beverage company is about one third owned by Quinenco. CCU controls more than 90% of the $290 million Chilean beer market and is second only to Embotelladora Andina in the country's $600 million soft-drink market. For the first three quarters of last year, CCU earned $16 million on revenues of $415 million, compared with $14 million on revenues of $406 million for the comparable period in 1997. Since entering the market in 1995 CCU has become the second-largest beer seller in Argentina, where there are almost three times as many consumers as in Chile.

- Quinenco owns 71% of Lucchetti, one of the largest food companies in Chile which has leading market-share positions in pasta, edible oils and soups. In 1998, Lucchetti lost $4.3 million on revenues of $126 million, compared with a profit of $3.5 million on $113.5 million in revenues for the same period in 1997.

- Hoteles Carrera, a luxury-hotel operator 88% owned by Quinenco is expected to barely break even in 1998 compared with $645,000 in net earnings in 1997.

- OHCH is a 50–50 joint venture between Quinenco and Banco Central Hispano. OHCH's most important asset: Banco Santiago is Chile's leading bank, in which it has a 43% share and has a market capitalisation of more than $2 billion.

Some commentators have suggested that what makes the Luksics different from other family conglomerates is that they are not sentimentally attached to any of their companies, and would sell any of them if the price was right. Decisions to sell, however, have not always been applauded. One of Quinenco's prize holdings, for instance, has been VTR Telecomunicaciones, a diversified telecommunications firm that the Luksics purchased in 1987 for $7 million. In December 1997 and October 1998, the family sold off the two most lucrative pieces of VTR: its cellular phone business, for $200 million, and its long-distance service, for $227 million. They decided that VTR could never successfully compete against Cia. Telefonos de Chile, a subsidiary of Spain's Telefonica de España, which dominates both the cellular and long-distance markets in Chile. Analysts believe that the Luksics got a handsome price. But some critics say that VTR was one of Quinenco's most promising assets and the Luksics were short-sighted to sell.

Most of Quinenco's holdings are publicly traded, and investors now prefer to buy stock directly in them rather than shares in the conglomerate itself.

Based on information from Dolan (1998) and Kandell (1999).

9.2.3 Parenting

If the individual businesses are one potential source of value in a corporation; the corporate headquarters or parent is another. Recent research suggests that the success of a portfolio may be dependent, not on whether the businesses are related, but on whether the management style of the parent is appropriate for them.[9] According to these theories, some of the problems of unsuccessful diversification are due to corporations moving into businesses that are not responsive to their parenting approach and skills.

Corporations have to add something beyond and above what they could achieve by simply holding a diversified portfolio of shares, or by remaining in a tightly focused area. A head office that simply provides finance has little justification for its existence where efficient capital markets exist (Real-Life Application 9.5).

Thus for high performance it is necessary for a diversified corporation to have competences in managing a diversified organisational structure that is better able to achieve results from the business units in their portfolio than alternative methods, such as open markets. This can happen in a number of ways:

- Through the possession at corporate level of valuable knowledge, competences or capabilities. Benetton understands fashion and retailing, Sony understands the process of innovation. This knowledge enables the corporate staff to provide advice that helps SBU managers perform more effectively than they would on their own.

- Through the provision of an architecture that stimulate a greater awareness of the need for high performance than business units would have if they were subject to the discipline of less ruthless and efficient open markets, with less appropriate or up-to-date information. In the 1980s both Hanson and GEC (a UK conglomerate focused on engineering and technology, now renamed Marconi) were famous for the fierceness of the review process to which SBUs' annual plans were subjected. This was intended to make sure that those plans were watertight, and to discourage wasteful spending. Other corporations, such as General Electric and Sweden's ABB, use management information systems to let SBU managers know how their performance compares with that of other units. They also foster a culture that encourages informal competition between businesses to be 'top of the league' (Ghoshal and Bartlett, 1998).

- Through the possession of corporate level competences that let them carry out certain activities more effectively or efficiently than the businesses could themselves. Typically, these would be activities such as pre-merger planning and post-merger integration that businesses would not expect to carry out very frequently for themselves. Hanson was respected (and feared) for the way it sized up potential acquisitions, for its acumen in deciding when to strike and for its well-honed routines for installing its own procedures and managers after a new business had been acquired.

- Through identifying areas where resources may be shared and synergy achieved. One example would be where manufacturing together the raw materials for two different business units is cheaper than manufacturing them separately.

- Through a culture and architecture that encourage exchanges of competences and learning that would not be possible in an open market. This is often achieved by staff rotation, joint management initiatives, or through cross-business teams. Unilever's networked culture encourages managers from different parts of the corporation to share information freely. Managers from the same region or the same business area are encouraged to meet regularly to trade experiences and ideas. A formal HR system monitors the careers of the top 2,000 executives and moves them around the corporation to distribute their knowledge and ensure that, when they reach top positions, they have a broad understanding of Unilever's businesses.

However, there are a number of possible barriers to the effective use of parenting skills. Firstly, diversification sometimes happens in emergent fashion, decided upon for operational reasons or, where it is deliberate, may be based upon a theoretical spreading of risk in order to achieve balance. It may be some time before the head office realises what its parenting skills are, and the portfolio it accumulates in the meantime may not be related to them. It may then have problems in rationalising the portfolio.

Secondly, the managers of the SBUs may be less than open in the amount or accuracy of the information they give to the parent. In any case there is always likely to be a degree of information 'loss' in communication between two, often geographically separate, units. Knowledge may be 'locked' inside one business unit because there is no structure or mechanism for moving knowledge between the SBUs.

The research which might identify the best ways for parents to add value is at a relatively early stage. Although Michael Goold and Andrew Campbell of the Ashridge Management Centre have written considerably on the subject, it is still not well known how and why some parent companies appear better able to add value than others. Parent companies are almost by definition less expert in the businesses they oversee than the local managers, so that there is always a danger that the parent may use its power to force local managers into poor decisions.

We consider two approaches to the problem of how a corporate parent might add value in the following section.

9.3   Managing relationships between businesses

In this section we consider some of the ways in which the management of a corporation of diversified businesses have been conceptualised. As we hinted in the previous section, there are broadly two main approaches to this. The first regards linkages between the businesses as the reason for the corporation's existence, and sees the business units as needing to be managed as a synergistic whole. The second downplays the role of synergy, seeing it as either unachievable or unnecessary, and sees the corporate headquarters' parenting skills as the glue that holds the organisation together. Each business unit is regarded as an independent entity and the corporation's managers provide controls, incentives and sometimes advice to make sure that each SBU is contributing its share of profits and that the portfolio is not 'unbalanced'.

9.3.1 The corporation as a portfolio of competences and resources

In this first approach each SBU is seen as a reservoir of competences, skills and people, each of which can be transferred between different businesses as needed, to share the knowledge gained. The parenting skills deployed are those that foster such synergies. This philosophy assumes that achieving synergistic links **is** both possible and desirable. Prahalad and Hamel (1990) suggest that the most successful companies will be those that look for opportunities to exploit key skills and competences across a range of business situations. They claim that the distinguishing feature of those companies with long track records of successful diversification, like Honda and Canon (Real-Life Application 9.6), is their conceptualisation of their companies as portfolios of competencies and not just businesses.

Some of the most successful corporations of recent years, such as Sony, 3M or Procter & Gamble have made considerable efforts to spread competences across a range of their businesses, such as fast-moving consumer goods (FMCG) and marketing knowledge in the case of Procter & Gamble, coatings technologies in the case of 3M, and digitising technologies in the case of Sony (see Real-Life Application 9.7).

Robins and Wiersema (1995), who examined technology flows between businesses in diversified firms, similarly found that performance improved as 'dynamic relatedness' (where a competence accumulated by one division is used to build new strategic assets elsewhere in the firm) increased. Some other recent research (Gambardella and Torrisi, 1998) has shown that high corporate performance comes from having a small portfolio of products and a larger and diversified portfolio of competences and technologies.

We look at some of the risks involved in the management of strategic alliances in Chapter 15. ▶

The sharing of such resources can be potentially a source of advantage. Management skills, such as capabilities in innovation, or tacit knowledge, are almost impossible to pass on in the external market. It would be quite hard for Sony, for example, to share its capabilities in new product development outside its own structure except by entering into costly and potentially risky alliances with

---

REAL-LIFE APPLICATION 9.6

Core competences at Canon

The Canon Corporation is cited by Prahalad and Hamel (1990) as an example of a diversified company managed as a collection of competences. Its first business was as a manufacturer of cameras, where it developed core competences in precision engineering and optics. It then diversified into calculators, an opportunistic move that was not related to the camera business. However, the new operation was successful for many years, and gave Canon competences in electronics. For its next major move, into photocopiers, Canon used all three of its core competences and, according to Hamel and Prahalad, each other major product area that Canon had diversified into – facsimile machines, laser printer engines, inkjet printers and medical imaging equipment – has used at least two of them.

Not everyone agrees with Prahalad and Hamel's explanation of Canon's success. The core competences that they have identified are extremely broad, and it is by no means obvious that the ability to make calculators gives Canon an automatic head start in any business involving electronics. Moreover, it has never been conclusively shown that Canon's management was aware of the firm's core competences when they took their diversification decisions. It is possible that the three core competences were invented retrospectively as a way of giving a coherent explanation of the way that the company had developed.

REAL-LIFE APPLICATION 9.7

The co-ordinated approach to R&D in Sony

Sony has recently (1999) decided to alter its reporting relationships and organisational structure (see also the case study at the end of Chapter 10). This has been done for a number of reasons, some of which were to do with its recent relatively poor financial performance. However, others have more to do with an attempt to transfer learning and achieve synergies across its multiple divisions in an era where technologies are converging (probably!), and where competences in the use of digital technologies is likely to be an increasingly important critical success factor for companies in the media, software, and electronics industries.

Thus Sony has decided to retain what is probably its most important R&D functions – to do with digital technology and networks – under the direct control of the head office. Product- or division-specific R&D is still to be carried out in its divisions. The implication of this is that the divisions will focus on incremental improvements to existing product ranges, whereas critical or blue-sky projects will be managed directly by the company's most senior managers, who will then decide where any developments may best be used across the group as a whole.

---

partners. Some limited exchanges do occur, through the movement of personnel from company to company, but this is generally unpredictable and unmanageable. But the transfer of personnel *within* a corporation is relatively predictable and manageable, and may be very effective given the access to 'insider' information that a corporation has. Such exchanges, through long-term secondment of managers, or shorter-term cross unit exchanges and project work, allow learning and knowledge to be shared.

However, moving personnel or skills is not always as easy in practice as it might be in theory. Deliberate exchanges of staff across organisational boundaries can only be achieved when there is management will and commitment – SBU managers may, understandably, be reluctant to let their most able staff be transferred. Knowledge and experience tends to be product- or business-specific, and in some cases the movement of people to situations where they are not experts is an uneconomic and wasteful use of their time. So there is little point in doing this unless the businesses in the portfolio are sufficiently related to benefit from such an exchange of knowledge.

Because of the difficulties of obtaining synergy in practice, some organisations prefer the alternative approach – to maintain a portfolio of businesses as independent entities.

9.3.2 The corporation as a portfolio of independent businesses

In the second approach, corporate managers regard each of the businesses in their portfolio as independent units that may be controlled using different systems according to the businesses' needs. Each SBU 'owns' its own resources, and there is little attempt to achieve synergies between them, although it is quite common to use the smaller businesses as nurseries of management talent for the larger ones. The role of the headquarters in this case is to allocate capital to each of the SBUs, to buy and sell the business units as necessary in order to achieve a balanced portfolio, and to add value by providing certain types of parenting skills: management expertise, control and incentives.

A special case of this approach views businesses as assets to be acquired, improved, and then often sold off. Porter (1987) termed this a *restructuring* mode. Corporations under this model are simply holding companies set in place to buy up under-performing companies, improve their management, and then sell them for a greater total price than was originally paid for them. Some parts of the business, together with unwanted assets such as corporate jets and headquarters buildings, might be sold off shortly after acquisition, an activity sometimes known as 'asset-stripping'.

The best-known practitioner of this philosophy, the UK conglomerate Hanson, became very rich in its heyday in the 1980s by spotting and then turning around weak companies, to sell them later often at a considerable profit. It did this by selling off parts of the acquired companies that did not fit, replacing managers and installing its own nominees who brought in new strategies, providing investment if necessary, instigating stringent financial targets and implementing new and much more rigorous control systems.

Hanson was frequently criticised as a 'corporate raider' – an asset stripper with little regard for the well-being of the people in the companies it bought. In fact, it frequently promoted managers in the businesses it acquired to run those businesses after Hanson's own integration team had done its work. It also retained many of the acquired companies, but only those which Hanson felt it could add management value to in other ways.

One of the companies targeted by Hanson – ICI and the subsequent resulting demerger of Zeneca – is discussed in Real-Life Application 15.8. ▶

In the end, Hanson did not survive as this type of corporation long after the death and retirement of its founders (see Section 9.2). It was also a victim of its own success. Once it became known that Hanson had targeted a particular company, that company set about making any necessary improvements itself. Its share price increased, making the acquisition less good value, if affordable at all, and the pool of suitable target companies dried up.

Many of the writings which recommend that corporations should be portfolios of independent or quasi-independent business suffer from a number of weaknesses. Few take any account of how the corporate managers should deal with the issue of complexity, such as the difficulties in managing a range of different types of businesses or products within a single management structure. These problems are particularly acute for service companies. They also do not take account of the numbers of businesses that may be manageable, or how the corporate head office might add value to businesses that are virtually independent. This is a particular issue given the openness and efficiency of capital markets. For these reasons such critics have recommended that corporations manage their businesses with an eye to how they may benefit from being linked and synergies obtained.

REAL-LIFE APPLICATION 9.8

The need for synergy in Bertelsmann

Bertelsmann is one of the world's biggest media companies. It owns publishing and music businesses across 50 countries, with 60,000 employees. However, many of Bertelsmann's divisions are in mature or declining markets, and Thomas Middelhoff, who took over as Bertelsmann's new CEO in October 1998, needs to find ways of getting its businesses to work together.

This may prove challenging as Bertelsmann is famously devolved. Decentralisation has been at the core of its paradigm dating back to Reinhard Mohn, the man who rebuilt the German company after the 1939–45 war. Mohn was a fan of American management, and implemented an entrepreneurial, profit-focused, decentralised style. Bertelsmann's divisions have therefore been encouraged to operate as independent fiefdoms, concentrating on their own profitability, not the performance of the company as a whole. Middelhoff was appointed, at least in part, because of his ability to manage a geographically dispersed, devolved company populated by strong-willed managers who are not over-amenable to being told what to do.

However, although this strategy has clearly been effective in the past, many commentators now think that the divisions have to work better together. In a global digital era, it makes more sense if Bertelsmann's businesses can tap into a world-wide distribution and promotion network where the Internet, or other digital media, can be used to cross-sell the company's products. The reluctance of Bertelsmann's divisions to work together has also meant missed opportunities. Bertelsmann was probably two years late in coming to online book retailing, allowing Amazon.com to reach a dominant position, something which undermined Bertelsmann's book-club business. *Stern*, Bertelsmann's biggest magazine, provided readers with a free CD-ROM offering access to T-Online (a German ISP), even though Bertelsmann part-owns T-Online's principal competitor, AOL. Grüner & Jahr, the magazine division, when asked if they would co-operate with the music division to promote a young artist through their magazines, replied that they would do it *if* it was interesting to their readers.

9.4 Structures and systems

Organisation structure is discussed in detail in Chapter 10. ▶

The third major set of decisions to be taken by corporate headquarters relates to the corporate architecture, in particular the design of corporate reporting structures and systems. Here we look at three patterns, or 'styles', that have been observed in the extent to which the corporate head office influences the strategies and performance of the business units in their portfolio and how corporate managers exercise budgetary or financial control on them (Goold and Campbell, 1987; Goold et al., 1993).[10] (See Figure 9.1.)

Under the first style, **strategic planning**, corporate headquarters takes a very close and active interest in the setting of strategy by its SBUs. It regards them as part of a co-ordinated whole. Typically, headquarters is staffed by experienced ex-SBU managers who are qualified to offer specific advice, and who provide detailed strategic plans for each of their businesses. The targets set tend to be long term and strategic in nature, looking for penetration of particular market segments, for example. The SBU's financial performance is reviewed within the context of long-term strategic objectives for the group as a whole.

Diametrically opposed to this is the **financial control** style, where headquarters takes little interest in the strategy, but seeks to fix the performance outcomes very firmly. A subsidiary's managers commit, often after strenuous negotiations with headquarters, to short-term financial targets, knowing that if they exceed them

Figure 9.1 Strategic styles (adapted from Goold and Campbell, 1987)

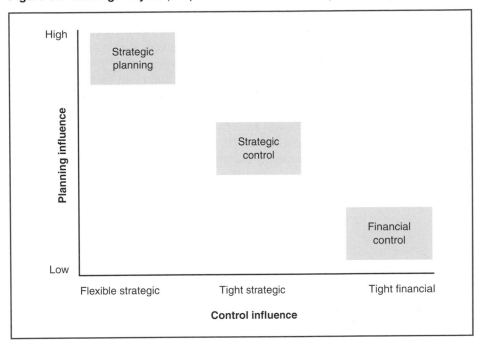

We look at de-mergers in Chapter 15. ▶

they are likely to win a handsome bonus and that if they fail to meet them they face dismissal. It is the job of the SBU managers to find ways of achieving their targets as they see fit.

This style can work well in improving the performance of autonomous SBUs. However, there are questions about whether, and if so how, the centre adds value. If the centre's management have skills in setting financial targets then they may be successful; if not, then it might be better for the business units to be sold off and managed independently. There is also the danger that the portfolio can become out of control and with little clear direction for the acquisition or disposal of companies in it.

The third style, **strategic control**, represents a compromise between the other two. Corporate staff seek to improve the strategy through advice and comment, but do not dictate it. A mixture of financial and strategic targets are set. During the 1980s, firms using this style appeared to under-perform relative to those using strategic planning or financial control. Some were acquired and broken up by restructurers like Hanson and BTR. However, in the 1990s, firms like ABB have adopted a variant of the strategic control style, where advice is not forced upon SBU managers but instead corporate headquarters acts as a forum, bringing managers from the businesses together to exchange experiences, and as a source of very high-quality advice that SBU managers are expected to call upon to help solve serious problems.

Each of these styles represents a way of allocating a scarce resource, top management attention, across a range of businesses. Each has implications for the number and type of businesses that can be in the portfolio for the style to work:

● The strategic planning style requires a lot of management attention to be given to each business, and so works best in firms whose portfolio consists of a few, quite closely related businesses, such as Cadbury-Schweppes (confectionery and soft drinks). Firms like these often look actively for synergies between their businesses (see Section 9.3.1).

- The financial control style focuses management attention on one or two simple financial statistics, which means that it can cope with quite a large number of unrelated businesses. However, these businesses cannot be too strategically complex – ideally, they should be in mature industries and not involve head-quarters staff in tricky investment decisions. As each of the SBUs is a stand-alone unit there is no attempt to manage any relationships between them or to manage any centralised plan which co-ordinates the activities of the portfolio as a whole. This style was often associated with the restructuring approach to corporate management (see Section 9.3.2).

- The strategic control style can cope with more businesses than the strategic planning style, and with more strategic complexity than financial planning. It therefore represents the natural choice for firms that seek to add value to a wide portfolio of high-technology or other fast-growing businesses. It appears to work by focusing the attention of corporate top management on the most urgent and important issues, and trusting SBU management to resolve the less pressing problems.

9.5 Portfolio balance and resource allocation

The question of the balance of a portfolio now receives less attention from theorists than it did in the 1970s. It is no longer regarded as axiomatic that an organisation's portfolio needs to be balanced – a corporation's parenting skills may direct it towards businesses that are all mature, or in a single industry sector or region.

However, an assessment of the balance of the portfolio is still useful in determining how and where headquarters should allocate cash, expertise and other scarce resources. This requires some view on which businesses are the most attractive and so should have first call on resources to fund investment and growth.

Two of the most common models used to assess this are the Boston Consulting Group Matrix – the 'Boston Box' – and the General Electric (GE) Business Attractiveness Screen, sometimes known as the Directional Policy Matrix. The GE Screen is a later model and has some more sophisticated features than the Boston Matrix, but both use graphics to represent a notional vision of the idealised diversified corporation in which industry, market characteristics and the nature of the company's range of products/businesses are balanced.

These matrices are relatively unsophisticated tools that you can use to help you to understand some aspects of a corporation's performance and strengths. Their simplicity brings both advantages and drawbacks. They give the analyst a useful overview of the shape of a corporation's portfolio, so that mapping a company's different businesses on to the Boston or GE grid is a helpful way to *start* an analysis of its corporate strategy. However, they give few indicators of whether there is any strategic relatedness between the SBUs, which is why some theorists believe them to be outdated. In order to assess relatedness, or to come to any firm conclusions about what should be done with the different businesses, you will have to carry out a deeper and more sophisticated analysis. They also have some other weaknesses which we will return to below.

9.5.1 The Boston Consulting Group (BCG) Matrix

Relative market share
The firm's market share divided by that of the market leader. Or, if the firm *is* the market leader, its market share divided by that of the no. 2 firm.

The first matrix, the Boston box, is shown in Figure 9.2. This matrix has two axes; the first is the **relative growth rate** of the markets in which the company's businesses compete; the second axis is the **relative market share** of the company's product(s) or businesses, assuming that these operate in single market places.[11] There are a number of alternative labels which we should just note – the first being that question marks are sometimes called problem children, and the second is that dogs are sometimes called cash dogs if they are still profitable.

The BCG matrix is used to assess a number of important issues to do with the balance and management of a portfolio of products or businesses. These include:

- *The risk profiles of the products/businesses.* Question marks are generally new, small and as yet untested, and are likely to be more risky than products that are older, have greater market share, and about which more is known. A company which consists only of question marks may be very successful in time, but it is rather putting all its eggs in a relatively unpredictable basket.

- *The cash demands of the products/businesses.* Question marks, being new and with small market shares, tend to require large investments of cash in order to develop them into large, successful and cash-generative businesses. Stars similarly often require cash to fund growth. Dogs, although they require little investment, because they are in declining markets, also produce relatively little income. Cash cows on the other hand are larger, have greater market shares, and because they tend to be older, bring in greater and more predictable profits. A corporation could in theory survive very nicely with only cash cows. **However**, theory on product and industry life-cycles suggests that cash cows

Figure 9.2   The Boston Consulting Group (BCG) Matrix

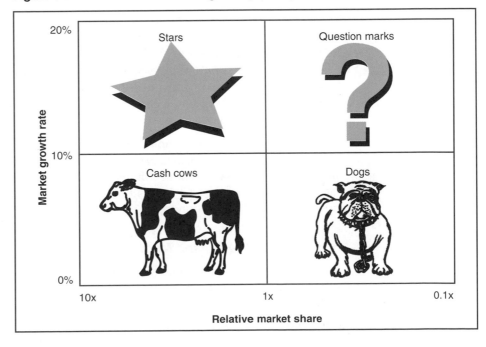

361

Figure 9.3   BCG Matrix showing product/business sizes

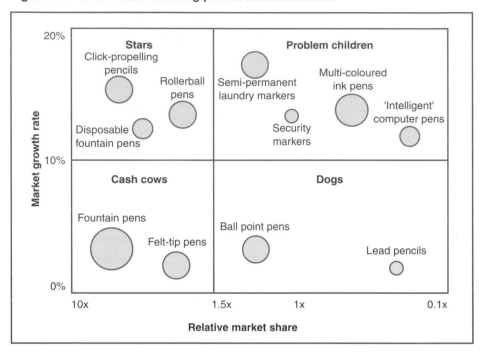

will eventually be supplanted by newer products. The company which only has cash cows is likely eventually to experience performance problems unless it has itself addressed the issue of developing replacement products – question marks. Hence it is important also to consider the developmental stage of the products/businesses in the portfolio.

- *The development cycles of products.* Product and industry life-cycles suggest that corporations needs to have a constant stream of new products coming on stream to replace older ones.

- *Resource allocation and divestment decisions.* There is an implicit assumption that relatively little should be invested in cash cows, that the cash they generate should, for the sake of future growth, be invested in stars and question marks and that dogs should be starved of investment and preferably divested.

A more sophisticated application of the Boston Matrix is shown in Figure 9.3. This shows the range of products in an imaginary pen and pencil manufacturer's portfolio, but also brings in another dimension. The size of the circles indicates the relative size of the products/SBUs within the overall corporation, and thus helps to map costs and risks in relation to the relative size of the products/businesses.

Problems with the Boston Matrix

It is asking a great deal of a simple 2-by-2 grid to encompass the complexities of corporate-level strategy, and a number of problems have been found with the BCG Matrix:

- It is difficult to define what the relevant market is, and therefore what levels of market share a product/business has. Does a company have 0.001% of the global pharmaceuticals market (dog) or 25% of the (faster-growing) German market for herbal remedies (star)? When using the matrix to assess a portfolio of business units, it is quite likely that each will be operating in a range of markets, and thus judging relative 'market' share is likely to be difficult, if not impossible!

- Underlying the model is the questionable assumption that high market share implies good profits and low growth implies a market where investment needs are, and will remain, low. These assumptions are not always true. Although research[12] suggests that there are correlations, high market share is not always a path to high profits.

- There is no hard and fast rule for drawing the lines between large/small share, and high/low growth. Indeed, the level of viability may vary considerably between the various markets – an important factor, given that this model is used to map a diverse range of products/businesses.

- Low growth markets can rebound. In fact, not all products or businesses follow a predictable life-cycle path of increase and decline. Some 'dogs' can remain profitable and viable for many, many years, and so are not automatic candidates for divestment. Some cash cows, on the other hand, may require periodic injections of investment to sustain their competitiveness.

- The simple mapping of products/businesses according to two simple dimensions ignores any potential relationships between products, and ignores synergy between, for example, dogs and stars, which may make dogs viable. There is also little consideration of the potential for learning to be transferred from dogs, which are recommended for divestment, but which may actually be repositories of considerable learning and knowledge accrued over many years of operations.

- The implication that a question mark has a low *market share* is unlikely to be accurate when the product is in a new market – where total sales are likely to be small, and the company's small number of individual sales may in fact represent a large percentage of this small market.

- The range of different types of business in a portfolio may require very different management styles, not all of which the corporate parent may be able to supply. The management of highly innovative question marks is likely to require very different skills and control systems from those needed for dogs, which should be managed in the most cost-effective way.

- There is little consideration given to the issues of motivating managers in, for example, cash cow businesses, who may be less than enchanted with seeing their hard-earned profits siphoned off to fund investment in high-risk, and as yet unsuccessful, problem children.

9.5.2 The General Electric Screen

Our second example of a portfolio-mapping matrix is the General Electric Screen (Figure 9.4). This model was developed by the large American corporation of the same name. It is a different and slightly more sophisticated model, but basically does the same job.

Figure 9.4 The GE Business Attractiveness Screen (from Robinson, Hitchens and Wade, 1978)

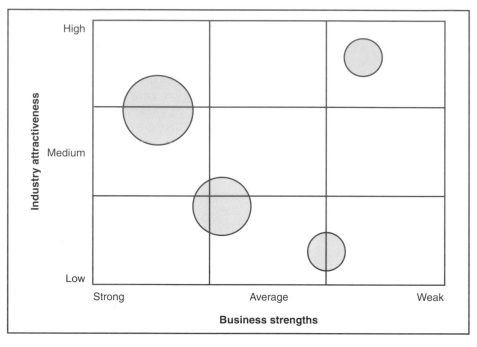

As with the Boston Matrix, it is possible to show the relative sizes of the businesses in a company's portfolio through drawing different-sized circles, and, as in the example above, it is also possible to represent different market shares. It brings together a number of key internal factors, relating to the strength of the business and external ones relating to the attractiveness of the industry in which the firm's products or businesses compete.

There are a number of measures of what influences the attractiveness of an industry. Equally there are a number of possible measures of what constitutes business strength (Table 9.1). In both business strength and industry attractiveness, the measures used would vary across different industry types, and each could be weighted according to an assessment of industry critical success factors.

Table 9.1 Measures of attractiveness and business strength

Industry attractiveness	Business strength
Market size	Relative market share
Market growth and profitability	Price competitiveness
Profit margins	Product quality
Competitive intensity and barriers to entry	Brand or business image or reputation
Cyclicality or market life-cycle	R&D capability
Scale economies	Knowledge of customers and markets
Regulation and other PEST factors	Sales effectiveness
	Geographical location
	Financial resources

Figure 9.5   Using the GE Screen to assess a portfolio's strategic priorities

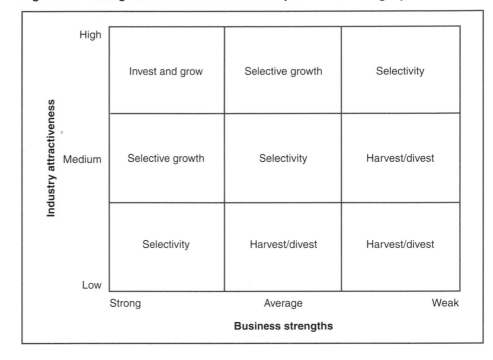

As with the Boston Matrix, the GE Screen is used to assess what strategies might be suitable for the products or businesses within the portfolio (Figure 9.5).

A product or business that is strong and in an attractive industry is clearly one that the corporation is likely to want to develop and build upon. Equally, a weak product or business in an unattractive industry is not likely to be worth investing in. In between, there are rather more selective judgements to be made. Some averagely strong businesses in middle-of-the-road industries may be invested in or withdrawn from, and what is decided will depend on other factors. In considering these wider factors, the GE Screen is more flexible than the Boston Matrix. However, there are also some provisos in the use of the GE Screen.

● The choice of appropriate measures and their weightings is a highly subjective procedure and so the screen is not a precisely objective tool.

● This matrix is dependent on enough information being available about the performance and strengths of competitors and other PEST factors.

9.6   Summary

In this chapter we have described how some companies have attempted to obtain competitive advantage by diversifying away from their original and core business. In many cases these companies still retain their original businesses, and move into additional business areas to achieve a diversified portfolio. Thus, in this chapter you have learned that:

- Companies diversify for a number of different reasons.

- Diversification does not always lead to superior performance, although companies may have competences in managing a diversified portfolio.

- Research evidence on diversification is equivocal.

- There is some historical evidence that unrelated diversification is less successful than related.

- However, what is meant by related has changed over the years and there is now a better understanding that related does not only mean superficial similarities of products or markets.

- Corporations must add value in some way in order to justify the costs imposed on the subsidiaries by the corporate headquarters. They do so by giving the businesses in their portfolio something that cannot be purchased in the market. This may take the form of:
  - strategic resources that the businesses are able to share with one another
  - corporate-level competences ('parenting skills') provided by the parent.

- There are two main approaches to understanding the management of a diversified corporation's portfolio:
  - as a group of stand-alone businesses
  - as a portfolio of competences and resources to be shared.

Typical questions

We conclude this chapter by providing some questions you may be asked about diversification and the diversified corporation, and how you can use the theory in this chapter to answer them.

1. *What are the main arguments for a firm to diversify into a new business area?*

As in most cases, this analysis needs to be set in a context of the environment the firm is operating in, as well as based on an understanding of its current range of businesses and markets. You will need to consider whether the firm is in a single, highly risky, market place, or already involved in a range of markets and business areas. You might want to carry out an analysis of the environment using the techniques highlighted in Chapter 5. Risk factors, using measures of industry stability and profitability, should be assessed for each of the businesses the firm is currently in. You might wish to use some of the portfolio models described in Section 9.5 to help to assess likely income/expenditure levels and timings as part of this analysis.

The next stage is to consider whether the firm has any competences in managing the type of business it is moving into, or in managing a diversified portfolio. If it hasn't (perhaps because it is a new, small, firm), does it have the potential to acquire them (Sections 7.1 and 7.2 in Chapter 7)? If it does have competences, are they appropriate for the particular style of the new business unit, particularly important if the new SBU is acquired as a going concern? You might also wish to ask what motivates the firm's managers to move into this area (Section 9.2.1), and question whether this is an appropriate motive or not.

2. *Critically evaluate a firm's portfolio of business units*

In order to answer this type of question you would first of all have to describe and assess the firm's portfolio of business units – it is not enough to simply list these, however. You will need to make an assessment of their relative strengths, market positions, growth rates, financial performance, etc. You might like to use one of the models we have described in Section 9.5, but there are others discussed in other chapters which you could use as well, or you might even like to develop your own matrix to take account of recent thinking on organisational learning and the transfer of competences we outlined in Sections 9.2.2 and 9.2.3.

However, even this is not enough. You will need to assess whether the portfolio is balanced (with reasons for why you judge this to be so), manageable (in terms of its transaction costs, size, and complexity, which we described in Chapter 1, Chapter 2 (Section 2.3.2) and Chapter 7), whether the head office adds value, and if so how (Section 9.2.2), and whether the size of the business gives additional sources of competitive advantage that would not be available if the business units remained independent. For this you would have to consider such issues as synergy in, for example, increased buying power of raw materials, better control over distribution channels, and transfer of learning across the business units.

3. *What strategic style should the organisation use to manage its portfolio of business units?*

This question is asking for an assessment of which of Goold and Campbell's strategic styles (Section 9.4) is most appropriate. You might start by describing some of the advantages and disadvantages of the three styles developed by Goold and Campbell. You would need to think about what types of business (and culture) are contained within the corporation, and, given the importance of synergy being achieved between the businesses, how they communicate with one another (you might like to look ahead at this stage to Chapter 10 in which we discuss the various types of organisation structure).

Then, you would need to make an assessment of when and how one style is more effective than others. Ideally, you would identify the relative performance of companies which use one approach to managing their portfolios and compare it with others who have a different approach.

Questions for discussion

1. Draw a BCG or GE matrix of:
- Quinenco (Real-Life Application 9.5);
- Sony (case study at the end of Chapter 10) or Benetton (end of Chapter 6);
- the university or college where you are studying;
- another organisation where you have worked, or with which you are familiar.

2. Has McDonald's diversified away from its core business? Is its strategy effective – if so, why?

3. What are the weaknesses of portfolio analyses?

General Electric

This case study is based on publicly available data, including material from the General Electric website.

General Electric is the ninth-largest and second most profitable company in the world. For many years it has been the epitome of the strategy-as-planning approach and the source of a number of key strategy models, for example the PIMS programme which mapped the relationship between market share and return. It was also one of the first companies to delegate strategy-making to relatively low-level 'strategic business units'. As a result, it was also one of the first organisations to use matrices for portfolio planning, for allotting cash flow and growth goals to business units. However, the emphasis since Jack Welch took over as CEO in 1981 has shifted in a very pronounced way towards a 'bubble-up and learning' approach to strategy generation, designed to release and harness the energies of people throughout the organisation.

In the period from 1981 to 1997 GE's sales have risen from $27.2 billion to $100.5 billion, and profits grown from $1.6 billion to $9.2 billion. During the same period the company cut 120,000 jobs, reducing the workforce from 288,000 to 123,000. In 1998, GE was named *Fortune* magazine's 'Most Admired Company in America' and 'The World's Most Respected Company' by a worldwide business audience in the *Financial Times*. Although Bill Gates is richer, he has not created as much shareholder value as Mr Welch has at GE.

In 1999 General Electric was involved in ten business areas:

1. Aircraft Engines
2. Appliances
3. Capital Services (this division itself contains 28 business units)
4. Industrial Systems
5. Lighting
6. Medical Systems
7. NBC
8. Plastics
9. Power Systems
10. Transportation Systems

GE is a genuine conglomerate, or multi-business, as Jack Welch prefers to call it. However, the company's array of business units is not entirely random. GE concentrates on businesses where size matters (it spent $1 million a day for four-and-a-half years to design the GE 90 aero-engine). It insists on occupying one of an industry's top two slots or getting out. In most of its businesses GE is Number 1, and is not just gaining market share, but expanding the scope of the market. But most of its business units superficially have little in common and in an era where conglomerates are being broken up General Electric Corporation of America continues to maintain a diversified portfolio with considerable evidence of success. It is currently outperforming both a number of specialised rivals and the stock-market. As Welch claims: 'These companies have nothing in common except leadership and best practices.'

However, Jack Welch is explicit that bigger is only better if the company understands and is committed to using the unique advantages of size. He intends that GE should be a big, global, multi-business company, with access to an enormous amount of information. This allows GE, by means of what he considers to be the company's learning culture, the ability to acquire, share and act rapidly on this information to their marketplace advantage. It also allows them to 'bat more frequently, to take more swings, to experiment more, and, unlike a small company, miss on occasion and swing again'.

Since 1990, GE had paid nearly $30 billion for 133 European acquisitions where some 90,000 people are now employed. GE grew fourfold in Europe, from a relatively small investment in 1990 to $24 billion in revenues in 1998, of which 11% came from exports from America. Japan is another major business area. In Japan GE acquired the business infrastructure and salesforce of Toho Mutual Life and the consumer loan business of Japan's Lake Corporation. These acquisitions, along with its other ventures there, should allow GE to double its 1998 figures of $300 million in Japanese earnings within three years. Soon, half of GE's sales and most of its workforce will be outside America.

Every new operation goes through 'GE-ification'. An acquired firm must follow hard rules, such as supplying financial information ('joining GE is like taking a drink from a fire hose' is one complaint). On the other hand, firms usually keep their names, marketing strategies and, if he or she co-operates, chief executive. In Cartagena, Spain, GE has just opened a new $600 million plastics factory. But the story, says the plant manager, has been 'less about building a site than building a culture'.

GE's good performance, according to the management team, is in part the result of a programme of management, which uses a 'tool-kit' developed in-house in 1995, named 'Six Sigma'. The 'Six Sigma' programme has been used to develop a number of new products and has helped to improve quality indicators significantly. The new products designed under the Six Sigma format involve customers closely in the process.

The Six Sigma programme trains the company's managers and staff, who are accorded titles such as 'Master Black Belts' and 'Black Belts'. Virtually every professional in the company is a 'Green Belt', extensively trained in the Six Sigma methodology. Six Sigma is a central plank of GE's ability to operate as a united global organisation. It has been described as the company's common language, more so than English. Its shared 'grammar' makes it easier to exchange ideas throughout GE. Previously two plant managers, even making the same product, had different performance measures. Piet van Abeelen, vice president for Six Sigma, suggested that: 'Without Six Sigma, if you run a plant and I run a plant, it's tough to understand your numbers. Then you can say, "Your ideas won't work, because I'm different. The commonalities are what matter. If you make the metrics the same, we can talk."' The banner inside General Electric's aero-engine servicing department in South Wales is 'In Nod: Bodlonrwydd Llwyr i Gwsmeriaid'; 'Our Goal: Total Customer Satisfaction'. Everywhere Welsh voices talk GE-speak – about 'delighting customers' or of the plant's 300 Six Sigma Green Belts and 18 Black Belts.

According to Jack Welch, his way is about taking intellectual capital and moving it around the company quickly. He does this in a number of different ways in addition to the Six Sigma system. GE has numerous councils. In Europe these include a Corporate Executive Council, a Marketing Council, Technical Council, Sourcing Council, Finance Council, Human Resources Council, Sales Council, Manufacturing Council, and a Quality Council. Each business operates similar cross-business or cross-functional networks, which meet for a day or two every few months. Almost every professional in the company sits on one of these councils. At these meetings, everybody is expected to bring ideas for how to improve profitability, or information on process improvements. Another methodology, Work-Outs, which started in 1989, are meetings that can be called by anybody to address any problem with no boss in the room. When the participants have a plan, the boss is called in and must say 'yes' or 'no' immediately.

Knowledge transfer happens in other ways too. It is a company joke that within minutes of Jack Welch's leaving a site, the phone starts ringing as other businesses ask, 'What's this thing you told Jack about?' In May 1998, in Florence, Welch heard how a Six Sigma team making turbine packages had cut the total cost by 30%. He then spent an hour grilling the team so he could tell everybody else in GE to call Nuovo Pignone. A system for managing salesforces, developed in Barcelona, is spreading world wide. A London manager in GE Capital recently told Mr Welch how his unit was using young people to teach their bosses about the Internet. Within days, the order went out that every senior manager at GE, from Mr Welch down, should spend a couple of hours a week being bossed around by an 'Internet mentor', usually a generation younger. This process is aided by what the company calls its 'insatiable' learning culture, learning from each other, across businesses, across cultures, and from other companies. Six Sigma quality, one of the threefold growth initiatives, is a product of learning. After observing the transformational effects this initiative had had on the few companies that pursued it, they invested more than

CASE STUDY *continued*

a billion dollars in a company-wide expansion of the programme.

Courses also exist in every functional discipline from finance to information management. The training unleashes a number of forces, of which content is least important. It creates networks that unify the company and leverage its diversity world wide.

At GE the culture of sharing ideas appears to be ingrained. Pay and promotion, for instance, are tied to 'boundaryless behaviour', particularly for the 3,000 managers. The company aims to globalise every activity, sourcing products and components world wide. If you live in Texas and get a strange voice asking why your credit-card payment is late, it may be because the call is coming from India; the operators assume Western names and attempt to imitate the accent of the region they cover. GE also appears to have the ability to hire people who sustain its culture. In 1999 they increased their efforts to recruit from the world-wide pool of talent that is available in the countries in which they do business; software designers in India; and product engineers in Mexico, Eastern Europe and China. According to Welch, this 'is not to arbitrage labour costs, but because these are the best people you can find'. It then moves its management talent around the world.

Case study questions

1. How does GE transfer learning across its global divisions?

2. What potential synergies do you see as being achievable between GE's ten major divisions?

NOTES

1. See Porter (1987), Hill (1988), Hill and Hoskisson (1987).

2. Balance in this context means a mixture of different characteristics.

3. See, for example, Peters (1992), Carroll (1994), Verity (1992), Leavy (1994, 1998). Grant (1998) cites a study by Davis, Diekman and Tinsley which found that the diversification index for Fortune 500 companies in the USA fell from 1.00 to 0.67 between 1980 and 1990. Research evidence from other parts of the world is less straightforward. Some recent research carried out by Hall and Lee (1999) in Korea suggests that diversification there actually produces better returns than single business firms. One theory on why this should be so is to do with the preference for Eastern firms to diversify organically, whereas Western firms tend to do so through acquisition and therefore have the problems of integration to contend with simultaneously.

4. These examples are quoted in Grant (1998).

5. See, for example, Besanko et al. (1996) and Bernheim and Whinston (1990).

6. Based on Smith (1999), Washington (1999), Flint (1999) and 'Crunch time', *The Economist*, 25 Sept 1999, Volume 352, Issue 8138, pp. 73–74.

7. See, for example, Bettis and Mahajan (1985), Palepu (1985), Geringer et al. (1989), Hitt et al. (1995).

8. See Montgomery (1982).

9. See, for example, Varadarajan and Ramanujam (1987) and Goold et al. (1994).

10. You might also like to read Goold et al. (1994) *Corporate Level Strategy*, published by John Wiley.

11. The Boston Matrix is used equally for assessing a company's portfolio of businesses in a multi-business corporation, and the portfolio of products in a single business or division.

12. The American consultancy which developed the PIMS framework, the Strategic Planning Institute, has found this relationship across many industries and time periods. However, opinions are divided about whether high market share *causes* high ROI, or whether other factors make firms profitable and also induce people to buy their products, giving them high market share.

CHAPTER 10

Structure, information, control and reward systems

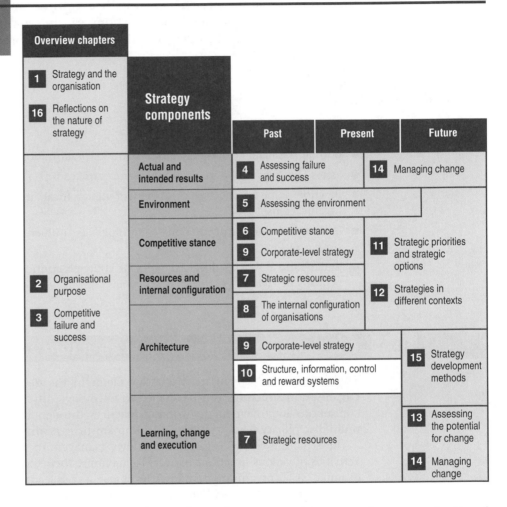

In each of the previous three chapters, we have seen how organisations' resources, value chains and parenting capabilities are affected by the way they configure their architecture: their internal communications, decision-making and control systems. In this chapter, we look more closely at these features within an organisation, all of which have a major influence on the way that a strategy operates in practice.

Organisations, unsurprisingly, are collections of people *organised* into formal relationships and different areas of responsibility who, because of this, have to communicate with each other and co-ordinate their activities in order to achieve common tasks – the organisation's strategies.

These people have different roles, and they may have different degrees of formalised power and responsibility according to, for example, whether they are 'managers' or 'employees'. Larger organisations tend to split into specialist functions, whose relative importance and location reflects the organisation's strategies. All these are elements of the organisation's *structure*, *design*, or *infrastructure* (these terms generally mean the same thing). How this is set up determines who has control over whom, who is intended to do what, who talks to whom and in what format, and how people are encouraged to carry out the tasks needed for the organisation's strategy to be achieved.

Learning objectives

By the end of this chapter you will be able to:

● outline the main structural characteristics of organisations;

● assess the impact of organisational features or contingencies on structure;

● describe some of the key principles of hierarchical, matrix, and network organisations;

● understand how information technology is influencing organisational configurations;

● understand how the different types of strategic control systems influence people's behaviour.

10.1 The basics of organisational structure

The design of an organisation is a key factor in the development of strategy. Organisation structures can be shaped to encourage innovation, new ideas and continuous improvement in working practices through the implementation of multi-disciplinary team-working and a humanistic personnel policy.

The structure of the organisation allows managers to try to co-ordinate the activities of various functions in order to maximise their skills and capabilities. For example, if an organisation chooses to pursue a cost leadership strategy, it must design a structure that facilitates close co-ordination between the activities of product design, supply, operations and distribution, so that products can be produced both reliably and cost-effectively. To achieve linkages between different activities in the value chain, the organisation must be structured so that the different functions or divisions can communicate and share their skills and knowledge. An organisation pursuing a global or multi-domestic strategy must create a structure that allows a flow of resources and capabilities between operations in different geographic locations.

Some common elements feature in most organisation's structures. Most have a single figurehead – the CEO, chief executive, chairman, president or managing director – at the top, with a **hierarchy** of managers and employees below. Even organisations that are partnerships between equals, or co-operatives in which all

Hierarchy
Hierarchy is the shape or format of reporting and decision-making relationships in an organisation. Hierarchies may be *tall* with many layers of management, or *flat*, with few.

members have an equal say, tend to appoint a managing partner, or someone else who acts as spokesperson and ultimate arbiter of decisions taken by the group. Most commercial firms or public sector organisations have a figurehead because key stakeholders want a single person who can be held accountable for the performance and spending of the organisation.

It is underneath that level that there is some variety, and there have been some interesting developments in recent years. These include:

Span of control

A manager's or supervisor's *span of control* is the number of people over whom they have direct control. These people are sometimes called their '*direct reports*'. The flatter an organisation's hierarchy, the broader that each manager's span of control tends to be.

- The fashion for 'de-layering' – removing layers of management from corporate hierarchies – in the 1980s and 1990s. This has tended to lead to an increase in the **span of control** of each remaining manager. This is linked to developments in information technology that we shall return to later.

- An increase in cross-functional team-working, in which personnel from different functions come together under a project manager, who may not be their normal line manager, to work on specific activities.

◀ *Outsourcing is covered in Section 8.1.2.*

- The outsourcing of non-core elements, so that the organisation itself has become much smaller and more focused. This has required managers to learn to manage networked organisations over which they have no direct control.

We now look at some of these issues and their implications in more detail, and try to understand what it is that shapes the structures that organisations have.

10.1.1 Achieving balance

Two of the main concerns of organisation design are to achieve an appropriate balance between two pairs of factors: **uniformity and diversity**, and **centralisation and decentralisation**.

- *Uniformity* implies standardisation, common procedures and rules defined at some common point, normally the organisation's head office.

- *Diversity* implies the modification of standards or rules in order to fit to specific cases, such as local product or service requirements, to develop new and innovative products, or to incorporate different manufacturing technologies.

- A highly *centralised* organisation is one in which control is maintained by the centre – the head office. Decisions are taken there and communicated to other parts of the organisation. Information flows are standardised – up to the top and down again.

- In contrast, organisations that are highly *decentralised* or *devolved* are ones in which control and decision-making authority is passed to local individuals, who are **empowered** to take decisions about their own areas of work without having recourse to a central authority.

Contingency

A contingency is a feature of an organisation or its environment that influences something else. For example, an organisation's structure is influenced by contingencies such as its size and the nature of its environment.

The appropriate point of balance between these different factors will vary according to different **contingencies**, such as the organisation's size, products, and industry characteristics.

Now we look at some of these issues in more detail.

Uniformity and diversity

Pressures for uniformity will be greatest when an organisation's products are stan-

373

◄ The arguments for and against standardised global production are discussed in Section 8.1.5.

Concept	Contingency theory

Contingency theory

Contingency theory is a school of organisational theory that believes that organisations' structure and behaviour are determined in predictable ways by their circumstances.[1] There has been considerable research on, for example, the relationships between: organisational strategy and structure; the work experience of senior managers and the strategies they adopt; and organisational power structures and environmental conditions. However, contingency theorists are sometimes criticised[2] for failing to take sufficient account of the power of managers' free choice and individual actions.

dardised and its customers are similar. At one extreme, a global product may require the standardisation of inputs, procedures, and systems across the world. Uniformity helps organisations to avoid wasting time and money in developing systems that overlap, or even conflict, and gives people in different parts of the organisation a common language. This makes it easier to identify best practice in one place and implement it in another. Because people will have fewer unfamiliar routines to learn, it is also easier to transfer people across production or sales locations, and get different business units to communicate and co-operate. On the other hand, organisations may face external pressures to be more diverse, so as to provide products and levels of service that are tailored to the preferences of customers in different countries and industries. These may range from legal requirements – accounting conventions and reporting requirements for tax purposes – to variations in the degree of formality that people expect in a business relationship.

Organisations thus need to strike a balance between enough uniformity to promote internal efficiency, and enough diversity to serve their customers effectively. The 'right' balance for a company will depend upon its particular circumstances (Real-Life Application 10.1).

Centralisation and decentralisation

Centralisation is the degree to which the decisions made in an organisation are

REAL-LIFE APPLICATION 10.1

Structure and uniformity

McDonald's is an international company with branches of its restaurants as far apart as China and South America. Despite the diverse environments in which it operates and the fact that many of its restaurants are managed by franchisees, until 1997 most outlets were operated using the same reward systems, the same hierarchical management structure, and the same routines for serving food. McDonald's centralised the design of its service concept, restaurant layout, the selection of franchisees and other personnel, and the design and content of training of restaurant managers and staff. The output was a predictable meal which had little variation across the world.

Company representatives established a reliable core of local suppliers two-to-three years before the first restaurant opened in a country – in some cases, introducing new farming practices, right down to importing the standard seeds. Where suitable local suppliers could not be found or developed, the restaurants imported the necessary products.

In 1997, McDonald's restructured itself into five geographical divisions each of which was to be managed independently. Since then there appears to have been increasing signs of variation in the products offered, which pander to local tastes.

taken by the central core or top management, usually located in a single head office. Policies and procedures in a centralised organisation tend to be highly formalised. Highly centralised structures are found most often, and work best, in firms with standardised products, predictable demand and, a stable and relatively simple environment.[3]

Decentralised structures, on the other hand, are more likely to be informal. They tend to be effective in market places that are fast-changing and complex, where innovation or quick customer responsiveness are critical success factors. Circumstances like these require fast action to be taken by local managers in which there is little time for decisions to be passed up to the top and back down again.

Recently there has been an increase in the numbers of network or matrix organisations where power is devolved, suggesting that the environments in which firms operate nowadays are becoming increasingly complex and dynamic. In dynamic environments, strategies cannot be systematically planned and business units need freedom to experiment, for which flexible structures are required. Devolved structures also allow corporate overheads to be reduced, although this does not always reduce costs as much as might be expected because some of those overheads must then be duplicated at local levels. Devolved functions can also suffer because they are too small and do not achieve a critical mass, and expertise can be diluted if split across too many separate sites. Theoretical Perspective 10.1 gives an idea of some of the known links between organisational contingencies and structural characteristics.

The challenge for most organisations is therefore to find the appropriate balance between control and anarchy. They will want to be decentralised enough to enable them to innovate and cope with an increasingly dynamic and turbulent environment. Ideally, decisions should be taken by managers who are close to the cus-

---

THEORETICAL PERSPECTIVE 10.1

Twelve contingencies influencing centralisation

1. The size of the organisation. Small companies can be nothing but centralised. Very large companies find it difficult to be centralised.

2. The costs involved in making any changes to products or systems.

3. The diversity of geographical locations, together with the homogeneity or heterogeneity of products and services; the technologies involved; and the interdependencies between the different operating units.

4. The relative importance and stability of the environment.

5. The requirement to make decisions fast.

6. The nature and relative importance of functional decisions. Is it important that customers get answers immediately and directly?

7. The relative workload on decision-makers.

8. The tendency for power to move to those who already hold it. This tends to mean that organisation centres tend over time to get bigger and more influential unless senior managers are careful to guard against it.

9. The willingness of senior managers to devolve decisions and the willingness and ability of others to accept responsibility.

10. Issues of motivation. Staff tend to be more motivated the more power and control they have, and so in situations where individuals need to be highly motivated, power needs to be devolved.

11. The location of competence and expertise in the organisation. Are the managerial strengths in the divisions or at headquarters?

12. The nature of the firm's planning, control and information systems. You have already seen a discussion of corporate-level strategies, and Goold and Campbell's theory on the control of multi-business organisations.

tomers and understand their needs. At the same time organisations need to achieve some degree of organisational coherence and control. Senior managers, and particularly owner/managers, like to know what is going on in their organisation. They will want to set tight definitions on, for example, financial performance or how much discount a salesman is allowed to give away to win an order. This is not necessarily what the local manager wants, or what the local market needs. The manager of a regional subsidiary may think that her particular needs are different from those in another part of the firm, because the environment is more competitive or her product is more innovative and therefore less predictable. She may also want to be in charge of her own destiny.

10.1.2. The concept of hierarchy

One of the principal ways in which organisations achieve both control and uniformity is by the setting in place of decision-making structures in which certain individuals – managers – are formally given the right to take certain decisions – a *hierarchy* of control or authority.

Organisations have two dimensions: up and down and side to side. Up and down represents the hierarchy within the organisation. Side to side represents employees at the same level, who may nevertheless be divided into specialist functions – a concept we return to in the next section. They are likely to be paid on the same scale, have similar types of responsibility, and manage similar numbers of people. Until a few years ago, most organisations were 'tall' with many levels from top to

Figure 10.1   A simple hierarchy for a large firm

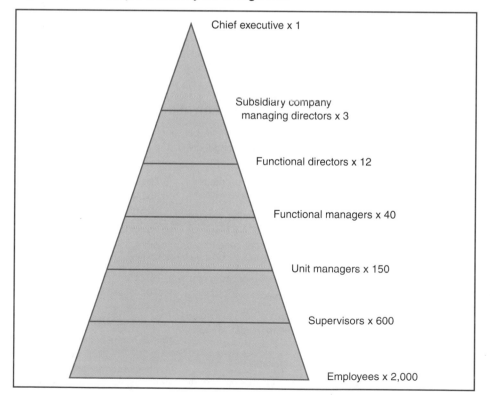

Chief executive x 1

Subsidiary company managing directors x 3

Functional directors x 12

Functional managers x 40

Unit managers x 150

Supervisors x 600

Employees x 2,000

bottom, and had a comparatively small span of control for each manager. Even in a single functional department such as marketing, there might have been as many as nine levels, from the marketing director at the top to marketing assistants at the bottom (see Real-Life Application 10.2).

The main advantage of a tall hierarchy is that the chain of command is clear. Managerial responsibilities are delimited and it is usually easy to see who has the power to make decisions on a specific issue. However, decision-making on important issues raised by lower-level staff may be slow, since every question must be passed up the organisation and the answer sent back down. During this process information can get distorted, or even lost, by middle managers who misunderstand the problem, underestimate its importance or add in concerns of their own. In a tall structure senior managers are remote from those individuals who have most contact with customers.

Employees may also feel they have little responsibility, opportunity for achievement and recognition of their worth because of insufficient delegation. There is also a lot of pressure on the time and attention of the few people who are able to take important decisions. On the other hand, there have been cases where a tall structure has increased motivation, because it offered staff a promise of regular increases in salary and status.

Thus, tall hierarchies can sometimes be quite effective, but are best suited to a stable environment where senior managers do not need to keep up to date with changing environment, and where it does not matter if decisions are taken relatively slowly.

More recently, this type of rigid hierarchy has started to break down, as you can see in Real-Life Application 10.2. Several developments have driven organisations towards flatter organisations, where there may only be three levels of management in any one department. These developments include more intense competition, information technology innovations, a more complex business environment and new theoretical thinking on the competitive importance of speed of response.[4]

Jobs in flat organisations tend to be more varied in character and type of responsibility. So, in a marketing department there may now be the marketing

---

REAL-LIFE APPLICATION 10.2

The decline of the hierarchy

In the late 1980s, a subsidiary of a major telecommunications company, boasted ten layers in its marketing department's hierarchy: marketing assistants, sales and advertising representatives and senior representatives, advertising managers, assistant brand managers, brand managers, product managers, marketing manager, market research managers, and marketing director. Nowadays the same company has a marketing director and marketing assistants still. However, the people in-between hold a number of different roles and titles, and none of them reports in such a linear fashion to the more senior managers.

In another company that we know, a hierarchy of chairman, managing director, regional director, area manager, depot manager, sales, product, technical and engineering managers, supervisors and field staff was replaced by chief executive, operations director, depot manager and field staff. Interestingly enough, staff in this firm were uncomfortable with this lack of hierarchy. Many considered that the span of control had become too large and unmanageable. About 18 months after it was abolished, a layer of area managers was added back into the structure.

director, a number of marketing or communications managers for, perhaps, different product groups or geographical areas, and a number of product or brand managers beneath them. These individuals may no longer report to a single manager, but operate in a type of matrix structure (see Section 10.3.4).

Such flat structures allow for faster decision-making, as there are fewer levels of permission to be sought. This means that individuals at lower levels are increasingly 'empowered' to take decisions that were once the prerogative of senior managers. Lower level employees need to be much more knowledgeable and competent as a result. A corresponding development is the creation of new systems for rewarding people, on the basis of their output rather than their status. As a result of the lack of managerial positions there are fewer opportunities for advancement, therefore motivation has to come from other sources. We return to the issue of control and reward systems in Section 10.4.

Charles Handy, in his book *Beyond Certainty* (1995), has suggested that 'we are leaving the age of centralised and rigid organised structures and moving into an era where self-organisation will become a key competence'. Theoretical Perspective 10.2, an extract from Handy's book, describes how the political idea of federalism is starting to be applied to organisations as they try to capture necessary flexibility and speed of response to a fast-changing competitive environment.

THEORETICAL PERSPECTIVE 10.2

Balancing corporate power

Everywhere companies are restructuring, creating integrated organisations, global networks, and 'leaner, meaner' corporate centres. In so doing, whether they recognise it or not, they are on a path to federalism as the way to govern their increasingly complex organisations. The concept of federalism is particularly appropriate since it offers a well-recognised way to deal with paradoxes of power and control: the need to make things big by keeping them small; to encourage autonomy but within bounds; to combine variety and shared purpose, individuality and partnership, local and global, tribal region and nation state, or nation state and regional bloc. It is therefore no accident that Percy Barnevik, the CEO of Asea Brown Boveri, has described his sprawling 'multi-domestic' enterprise of 1,100 separate companies and 210,000 employees as a federation. Nor is it accidental that John Akers has called IBM's restructuring a move to federalism. Basel-based Ciba-Geigy recently moved from a management pyramid with a matrix designed around businesses, functions, and regions to an organisation with 14 separate businesses controlling 94% of all the company's spending – a federal organisation.

Other examples include General Electric, Johnson & Johnson, and Coca-Cola in the United States; Grand Metropolitan and British Petroleum in Great Britain; Accor in France; and Honda in Japan. Older global companies, such as Royal Dutch Shell and Unilever, went federal decades ago, pulled that way by the demand for autonomy from their overseas subsidiaries.

The thinking behind it, the belief, for instance, that autonomy releases energy; that people have the right to do things in their own way as long as it is in the common interest; that people need to be well-informed, well-intentioned, and well-educated to interpret that common interest; that individuals prefer being led to being managed: these principles reach into the guts of the organisation or, more correctly, into its soul – the way it goes about its business day by day. Federalism properly understood is not so much a political structure or system as it is a way of life.

A federal organisation can be particularly exhausting to govern since it relies as much on influence, trust, and empathy as on formal power and explicit controls.

The first paradox is that organisations need to be both big and small at the same time. On the one hand, the economies of scale apply. At the same time, people want to identify with something closer to them and of human scale. Small may not always be beautiful but it is more comfortable. It is also more flexible and more likely to be innovative.

Federalism is not simple decentralisation with the centre acting as a banker to the separate businesses like the conglomerates of old. That loses the advantages of scale, of being able to develop lead technologies across a range of separate businesses, of combining to purchase or bid for a major contract that might involve the skills of several businesses. But neither is federalism a simple divisionalisation, the grouping of businesses under sets of umbrellas. That leaves too much power in the hands of those holding the umbrellas and pays too little attention to local needs or to the knowledge and contacts of those out in the market-place. Nor is it a matter of simply empowering those on the front line or in the separate countries. That ignores the expertise of people farther back or in other groupings. Federalism responds to all these pressures, balancing power among those in the centre of the organisation, those in the centres of expertise, and those in the centre of the action, the operating businesses. It is worth noting that Barnevik talks about centralised reporting, not centralised control, because most of his key people are not located at the centre of ABB's matrix of global business strands and national companies.

The true centres of federal organisations are dispersed throughout the operations. They meet frequently and they talk often, but they do not live together. Doing so would be a mistake because it would concentrate too much power in one group and in one place, whereas federalism gets its strength and energy from spreading responsibility across many decision points. Federalist centres are always small to the point of minimalist. They exist to co-ordinate, not to control.

In many businesses the break-up value of the operations exceeds the market value of the total enterprise. The centre has a negative added value, or, to put it another way, the transaction costs of central planning and control exceed the contribution that they undoubtedly make.

'Think global, act local' may be the fashionable slogan for dealing with this paradox, but it will not work very well as long as all real power resides in what is usually still called the Head Office or sometimes, suggestively, the Kremlin. On the other hand, a hollow corporation can soon lack direction, standards, or any sort of cohesion. This structure can work well in times of growth, but in recession, there may be no one left to take control.

It is cheaper and safer to expand one's scope by a series of alliances and ventures. When Pepsi-Cola and Whitbread jointly formed Pizza Hut UK, Pepsi needed Whitbread's knowledge of British leisure and property markets, while Whitbread needed Pepsi's pizza know-how. One without the other could not have done it. Alliances, however, are notori-ously difficult to manage. Alliances do not take kindly to orders from a head office in another country. In these cir-cumstances, power perforce has to be shared, autonomy granted, and the marriage held together by trust and common goals, two of federalism's chief ingredients.

Subsidiarity is the most important of federalism's princi-ples. It means that power belongs to the lowest possible point in the organisation. British Petroleum, which in effect went federal in 1990, devolving authority and responsibility to its separate businesses, had to decide which powers the centre would retain. The centre came up with a list of 22 'reserve powers' but, after discussions with the separate businesses, these were pruned down to the 10 most essential to the future direction of the company. In a fed-eral system, the centre governs only with the consent of the governed. Subsidiarity, therefore, is the reverse of empowerment. It is not the centre giving away or delegat-ing power. Instead, power is assumed to lie at the lowest point in the organisation and it can be taken away only by agreement. Robert Galvin tells Motorola's sales force that they have all the authority of the chairman when they are with customers.

To be effective, subsidiarity has to be formalised. Organisations need to have negotiated contracts that set the boundaries of each group's powers and responsibilities.

Finally, subsidiarity requires intelligence and information, real-time data that is broad enough to give a total picture but detailed enough to pinpoint decision points. Before the days of electronic data interchange, true holism in busi-ness was a sham. Now, the centre should be small and can be small because of the possibilities of information technology.

Federalism is about pluralism – many centres of power and expertise – and interdependence, achieved partly through holding reserve power at the centre, partly by locat-ing services or facilities needed by all in the territory of one or two. Research and development, for instance, can be located in Germany, the United States and Japan, but serve the world.

The new 'dispersed centre' of federalism is a centre that is more a network than a place. The result is a matrix of sorts, one in which every operating unit is accountable both to its respective global business sector and to its local region and that also draws on communal resources and services, wherever they may be located.

Interdependence is unlikely, if not impossible, without agreement on the basic rules of conduct, a common way of communicating, and a common unit of meas-urement.

Federalised corporate letterheads fly two flags. Some put 'a member of the X group of companies' in small let-ters in the corner. Others, such as Shell, give the federal logo pride of place. The layout will say a lot about the distribution of power, but both flags will always be pres-ent.

Authority must be earned from those over whom it is exercised

This is the practical implication of subsidiarity. In today's organisations dominated by knowledge-rich professionals, ▶

Theoretical Perspective continued

you cannot tell people what to do unless they respect you, agree with you, or both. Professionals require management by consent if they are to give their best; consent that is theirs to give or to withhold. Two major and unsuspected implications follow from it. Units have to be small so that people can get to know one another well enough to earn their colleagues' respect through their records of achievement. And people have to be around long enough to build up those records. Reputation can and does precede one into a new role but then it has to be justified. We are talking, therefore of units of less than 100 people, perhaps and of three- to five-year tenures in jobs. Organisations that think of their people as role occupants, replaceable and moveable as long as the role is properly defined, are not thinking federally. One implication is that organisations will start to require long probationary periods before they give these lifetime work guarantees. Either that or they will move to more fixed-term contracts.

Twin hierarchies (expertise and formal status position) will become more common as skills become more specialised and as task groups realise that they are temporary alliances of expertise that need to make the best use one another to get the work done – interdependence in practice. It requires notable self-confidence from those senior in the status hierarchy if they are, on occasion, to work under the direction of their juniors. Distinguishing between status and task hierarchies allows organisations to become much flatter without losing efficiency. Businesses are beginning to find that four layers of status is enough, as more of their work is organised in teams, each with its appropriate task hierarchy.

Federalism is in tune with the times – times that want to value and respect diversity and difference, times in which people want to do their own thing and yet be part of something bigger, times in which they look for structure but not imposed authority.

Adapted from Handy (1995), *Beyond Certainty.*

10.1.3 Achieving co-operation

One of the other major problems which organisations have to reconcile, is the need to co-ordinate and achieve co-operation. Organisations are, if large enough, divided into different *functional departments*, each with a different task to perform. On the smallest scale, a department may be represented by one individual; on much larger scales, a department could be a whole business, even with its own separate legal status. An example might be a unit which is responsible for developing new retail outlets, which in itself may be further subdivided into contracts specialists, architects, interior designers, and psychologists.

Traditionally, these departments have been divided into *line functions*, such as marketing, production, and R&D, which directly produce revenue, and *staff functions*, such as purchasing, legal services, finance, and personnel which are concerned with supporting the line functions. Once again, the rigid boundaries between these roles have started to break down recently.

The advantage of dividing work up into specialists is to allow people to develop much greater levels of expertise in a relatively narrow, and therefore more manageable, sphere. In an increasingly complex world, internationalisation, information technology, and speed of change have all appeared to make specialisation increasingly important, and in some ways increasingly narrow.

However, specialisation has its problems. If everyone only knows how to do one job, then someone somehow has to blend these different areas of expertise to achieve a co-ordinated outcome. Different specialists also have different ways of thinking and behaving, which makes communication difficult sometimes. Even if they speak the same national language (and this is of course not always going to be the case in an international firm) then they may not speak the same 'language'. If you are not a computer boffin, then trying to understand what a 'teccie' is saying to you may be beyond your ability. It is sometimes beyond ours anyway!

REAL-LIFE APPLICATION 10.3

The potential for functional conflict

A sales goal was set for the marketing department of an international company. The marketing campaign was so successful that the production department could not keep pace with demand. A decision was made to install a second production line, but the sales level was not sufficient to fully utilise this second line. The production manager, whose goals were based on the efficiency of his plant, was way below target and not happy. Additional production manpower needed to be urgently recruited. The personnel people did not have time to train new employees, so trained, but expensive, staff were 'poached' from competitors. The personnel department had goals based on average salaries and they were way above target. With demand buoyant and production in full swing, inventories were built up to safeguard against stock-outs. The working capital tied up in stock meant that the finance department did not meet their objectives.

The interests of departments may also be in conflict with each other, and co-operation between different areas has to be worked at quite hard to overcome this – see Real-Life Application 10.3.

We look in more detail at how companies control strategy implementation through goal and target setting in Section 10.4 later in this chapter. ▶

This example demonstrates several issues. Firstly, that developing a coherent and co-ordinated strategy throughout an organisation is a difficult task given the specialisation and divisionalisation of many organisations. Secondly, that what seems logical and desirable as a goal or objective for one department may conflict directly with the goals or objectives of another. As the departments operate both relatively independently and are interdependent of each other, the potential for conflict is high. So organisations have to develop ways of overcoming these types of problems.

Awareness of this is leading to changes in the design of organisations, where more interdepartmental interaction and more cross-functional project teams have been set up. This encourages better communication and sharing of ideas, and helps the different departments to understand each other better. It also enables the use of multiple disciplines or multi-skills to be brought together for specific projects, and allows employees to gain a better perspective of the organisation as a whole. Strategically, it addresses the need for innovation, flexibility and fast response times, such as when designing and bringing a new product to market. We look at these sorts of issues in more detail later in this chapter when we look at strategic control and reward mechanisms.

10.1.4. The impact of information systems and technology on structure and information flows

Generally speaking, until recently the more routine and repetitive the tasks, the greater the number of staff that managers in a hierarchy could cope with. Thus a regional manager of, say, a national chain of clothes shops would have been able to cope adequately with twenty shop managers, provided they all reported standardised information and they all offered the same products. In contrast, a plant manager of a multi-product electronics factory might only have been able to handle four or five subordinates, because the complexity of interactions would not allow for decision-making to be very systematised or predictable.

Information technology has changed this. Computer-integrated manufacturing systems have enabled organisations to flatten their organisational hierarchies, broaden the span of control, and decentralise decision-making despite complex manufacturing processes because some of the decision-making components originally held in someone's head, are now located within a computer program. IT-based communication systems now allow a manager to 'see' and monitor his team's work over huge distances; he or she no longer needs to be physically there. The potential span of control of a manager has therefore increased substantially, although information overload is replacing lack of relevant information as an organisational design problem.

Managers can 'talk' to far more people much faster through the medium of e-mail or video-conferencing than they could previously. This has implications for the location of specialist functions, which no longer need to be located physically near to anywhere else. As we have seen, India is subcontracting computer programming and systems design work on a real-time basis for European and American companies. Information technology is increasing the speed at which organisations fragment and become networked – in its broadest sense – relying on information transfer to do the job that once was achieved through physical proximity and contact.

10.2 Contingent links between strategy and structure

◀ There is a definition of contingency in Section 10.1.

Although some common patterns can be discerned, there appears to be no ideal organisation structure that is universally effective. Certain environments however appear to 'demand' certain structural features. In environments that are dynamic and complex, organisations seem to develop structures that are flatter, less centralised, and less formal. Large organisations tend to split up into specialist departments, and even larger organisations into divisions that are themselves divided into specialist functions.

In Henry Mintzberg's (1979) book on structures, he was explicit in linking the types of control systems, strategies, and structures he described to form a picture of an organisational *type*. To give just two of his examples he identified an *innovative* organisation, or *adhocracy* (a term originally coined by Alvin Toffler in his influential 1971 book *Futureshock*), one in which its structure is flexible and devolved, using project teams to fuse expertise from different specialists. Its control systems are similarly flexible relying for coordination on mutual adjustment among the organisation's highly trained experts, encouraged by integrating managers, standing committees, and task forces. With power based on expertise, the normal hierarchical management/staff distinction evaporates, and performance is assessed on a project-by-project basis. What he defined as the *professional* organisation relies on the standardisation of skills rather than of work processes or outputs for its coordination. So the structure emerges as highly decentralised horizontally; power over many decisions is held by the professionals. Mintzberg quite rightly cautions that each of his configurations is idealised, and admits that no real organisation is ever exactly like any one of them.

These contingent links between structure and environment and structure and strategy have been found in many empirical studies over a number of years, in many different industries and cultures. Arguably, they are among the very few known 'facts' in the whole of organisation and strategy theory. However, there has been a considerable debate about what these facts mean:

- Is there some kind of hidden force that leads structures to adapt as organisations' circumstances change? Or is it a matter of managerial choice, with managers in similar circumstances often, but not inevitably, choosing similar structures?

- Does structure follow strategy – do organisations select their structures to fit their chosen direction? Or does strategy follow structure – do organisations' structures, and the cultures and architectures that go with them, dictate the strategies that they will pursue in the future?

Whatever the cause, there do appear to be consistent patterns in the way that certain types of organisational forms are found together with certain types of products, strategies and environmental characteristics of the company. Nevertheless some organisations are able to 'buck the trend'. For example, Canon, the Japanese electronics corporation, has a very simple functional structure of the kind that would normally be found in a much smaller firm (Ghoshal and Bartlett, 1998). However, on average, organisations that conform to the prevailing patterns perform better than those that do not.[5]

Although we do not fully understand how these patterns come about, they are useful guides to the kinds of structure to recommend in different circumstances (Section 10.4).

10.2.1 ADVANCED TOPIC
Contingency theory

The ideas of determinism and free will are discussed in greater depth in Chapter 16. ▶

Whether structure 'leads' to strategy or strategy 'demands' a particular structure has been a matter of considerable debate over the years. The words 'demand' and 'lead' are in quotes above because they imply that an organisation's structure is 'shaped' by factors that are *deterministic* – that is outside the control and choice of its managers. However, as you have seen in Chapters 1 and 2, many theorists also now believe that strategy is an emergent phenomenon which comes about as a result of the organisation's communication systems, culture, and power echelons, all of which are enshrined in the structure. These in turn can be said to come about because of historical strategic choices by its managers. We look at some of the explanations for these apparent contradictions below.

The relationship between strategy, environment and certain organisational structures was first noticed by Alfred Chandler (1962). He suggested that the strategy adopted by an organisation at various stages of its development led to particular structural forms. Table 10.1 shows the development paths he identified. However, his original contingency approach can be criticised for a number of assumptions which are no longer considered correct, for example that strategy-setting is the prerogative only of senior managers and that strategic choice is a wholly rational process.

Chandler's ground-breaking work was extended considerably by writers such as Danny Miller, Lawrence and Lorsch, Burns and Stalker, Derek Pugh and John Child

Table 10.1   Strategy/structure development path for firms

Strategy	Logical structural form
Vertical integration	More sophisticated, centralised functional organisation
Internal growth and related diversification	Divisional
Unrelated diversification	Holding company

who noted links between particular organisational configurations, such as functional specialisation, and different environmental factors, such as uncertainty. Some also made links between these factors and the organisation's performance. This body of research later developed into other writings within a contingency theory framework such as that of Miles and Snow,[6] and research into organisational power. Lawrence and Lorsch, for example, described how different industries provided different sources of critical uncertainties – so that particular subunits become dominant in certain contexts.

Although contingency theory implies that there may be some sort of cause and effect mechanism in operation, there are actually a huge number of potential influences on an organisation's structure – including the deliberate choice of its managers and their beliefs about particular outcomes. Other theoretical perspectives provide potential explanations for how these variations in structural forms come about:

◀ *See Section 2.2. for a discussion of the ecological view of strategy, and Sections 2.1, 2.3, and 7.4.3 for more on organisational learning.*

- Writers such as Hannan and Freeman (1989) talk about organisational survival as an ecological mechanism: firms that are unsuited to their environment go out of business, leaving those with a suitable strategy/structure mix to thrive.

- Organisational learning processes allow for the testing of particular configurations, leaving the most successful ones to survive.

- Institutional theorists such as DiMaggio and Powell (1983) demonstrate that 'fashions' in organisational structure can be spread by outside influences, such as stock analysts and management theorists. A firm's downsizing, for example, may have nothing to do with managers experimenting themselves with removing layers of management and seeing how they work in their particular context. Rather, it may be implemented because the managers have read about other organisations' downsizing programmes, or been influenced by management consultants, and so expect that what has worked elsewhere will also be effective for them.

10.2.2   Changing contingencies during an organisation's life-cycle

Theoretical Perspective 10.3 is an extract from a widely-cited article by Larry Greiner which looks at management structures in different stages of an organisation's life-cycle. It shows how structure can affect strategy and strategy in turn can influence structure.

THEORETICAL PERSPECTIVE 10.3

Contingent links between structure, strategy and management systems

In the following extract, Larry Greiner discusses how, as an organisation develops and grows, an evolutionary period (i.e. a prolonged period of growth with no major upheaval in working practices) gives rise to its own revolution (a period of substantial turmoil). He identifies five phases of organisational development, each containing both an evolution and a revolution.

Key forces in development

Alfred D. Chandler Jr, in his book, *Strategy and Structure*, [...] proposes that outside market opportunities determine a company's strategy, which in turn determines the company's organization structure. This thesis has a valid ring for the four companies examined by Chandler, largely because they developed in a time of explosive markets and technological advances. But more recent evidence suggests that organizational structure may be less malleable than Chandler assumed; in fact, structure can play a critical role in influencing corporate strategy. It is this reverse emphasis on how organization structure affects future growth that is highlighted in the model presented in this article. ·

Five key dimensions emerge as essential for building a model of organization development:

1. age of the organization
2. size of the organization
3. stages of evolution
4. stages of revolution
5. growth rate of the industry

Each dimension influences the other over time; when all five elements begin to interact, a more complete and dynamic picture of organizational growth emerges.

Age of the organization

The most obvious and essential dimension for any model of development is the life span of an organization. The same organization practices are not maintained throughout a long time span [...] management problems and principles are rooted in time.

The passage of time also contributes to the institutionalization of managerial attitudes. As a result, employee behavior becomes not only more predictable but also more difficult to change when attitudes are outdated.

Size of the organization

A company's problems and solutions tend to change markedly as the number of employees and sales volume increase. Thus, time is not the only determinant of structure; in fact, organizations that do not grow in size can retain many of the same management issues and practices over lengthy periods. In addition to increased size, however, problems of co-ordination and communication magnify; new functions emerge, levels in the management hierarchy multiply, and jobs become more interrelated.

Stages of evolution

As both age and size increase, another phenomenon becomes evident: the prolonged growth of the evolutionary period. Most growing organizations do not expand for two years and then retreat for one year; rather, those 'that survive a crisis usually enjoy four to eight years of continuous growth without a major economic setback or severe internal disruption. The term 'evolution' seems appropriate for describing these quieter periods because only modest adjustments appear necessary for maintaining growth under the same overall pattern of management.

Stages of revolution

Smooth evolution is not inevitable; it cannot be assumed that organization growth is linear. Thus, we find evidence from numerous case histories which reveals periods of substantial turbulence spaced between smoother periods of evolution.

During such periods of crisis, a number of companies fail – those unable to abandon past practices and effect major organizational changes are likely either to fold or to level off in their growth rates.

Growth rate of the industry

The speed at which an organization experiences phases of evolution and revolution is closely related to the market environment of its industry. For example, a company in a rapidly expanding market will have to add employees rapidly; hence, the need for new organizational structures to accommodate large staff increases is accelerated. While evolutionary periods tend to be relatively short in fast-growing industries, much longer evolutionary periods occur in mature or slowly growing industries. Evolution can also be

▶

Theoretical Perspective continued

Figure 10.2   The five phases of growth

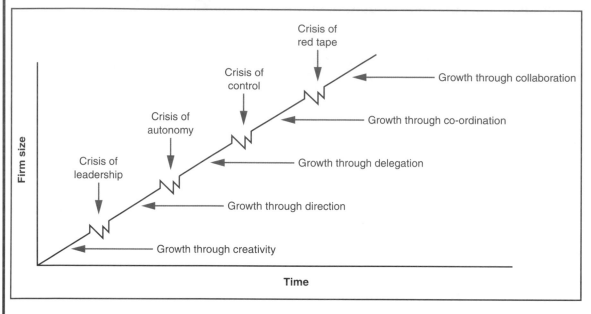

prolonged, and revolutions delayed, when profits come easily.

Phases of growth (Figure 10.2)

Each evolutionary period is characterized by the dominant *management style* used to achieve growth, while each revolutionary period is characterized by the dominant *management problem* that must be solved before growth can continue.

It is important to note that *each phase is both an effect of the previous phase and a cause for the next phase.* For example, the evolutionary management style in Phase 3 of Figure 10.2 is 'delegation', which grows out of, and becomes the solution to, demands for greater 'autonomy' in the preceding Phase 2 revolution. The style of delegation used in Phase 3, however, eventually provokes a major revolutionary crisis that is characterized by attempts to regain control over the diversity created through increased delegation.

Phase 1: Creativity ...

In the birth stage of an organization, the emphasis is on creating both a product and a market.

● The company's founders are usually technical or entrepreneurially oriented, and they disdain management activities; their physical and mental energies are absorbed entirely in making and selling a new product.

● Communication among employees is frequent and informal.

● Long hours of work are rewarded by modest salaries and the promise of ownership benefits.

● Control of activities comes from immediate marketplace feedback; the management acts as the customers react.

... and the leadership crisis. All of the foregoing individualistic and creative activities are essential for the company to get off the ground. But therein lies the problem. As the company grows, larger production runs require knowledge about the efficiencies of manufacturing. Increased numbers of employees cannot be managed exclusively through informal communication; new employees are not motivated by an intense dedication to the product or organization. Additional capital must be secured, and new accounting procedures are needed for financial control.

At this point a crisis of leadership occurs, which is the onset of the first revolution. Quite obviously, a strong manager is needed who has the necessary knowledge and skill to introduce new business techniques. But this is easier said than done. The founders often hate to step aside even though they are probably temperamentally unsuited to be managers. So here is the first critical developmental choice – to locate and install a strong business manager who is acceptable to the founders and who can pull the organization together.

386

Phase 2: Direction ...

Those companies that survive the first phase by installing a capable business manager usually embark on a period of sustained growth under able and directive leadership. Here are the characteristics of this evolutionary period:

- A functional organizational structure is introduced to separate manufacturing from marketing activities, and job assignments become more specialized.

- Accounting systems for inventory and purchasing are introduced.

- Incentives, budgets and work standards are adopted.

- Communication becomes more formal and impersonal as a hierarchy of titles and positions builds.

- The new manager and his key supervisors take most of the responsibility for instituting direction, while lower-level supervisors are treated more as functional specialists than as autonomous decision-making managers.

... and the autonomy crisis. Although the new directive techniques channel employee energy more efficiently into growth, they eventually become inappropriate for controlling a larger, more diverse and complex organization. Lower-level employees find themselves restricted by a cumbersome and centralized hierarchy. They have come to possess more direct knowledge about markets and machinery than do the leaders at the top; consequently, they feel torn between following procedures and taking initiative on their own.

Thus the second revolution is imminent as a crisis develops from demands for greater autonomy on the part of lower-level managers. The solution adopted by most companies is to move toward greater delegation. Yet it is difficult for top managers who were previously successful at being directive to give up responsibility. Moreover, lower-level managers are not accustomed to making decisions for themselves. As a result, numerous companies flounder during this revolutionary period, adhering to centralized methods while lower-level employees grow more disenchanted and leave the organization.

Phase 3: Delegation ...

The next era of growth evolves from the successful application of a decentralized organizational structure. It exhibits these characteristics:

- Much greater responsibility is given to the managers of plants and market territories.

- Profit centres and bonuses are used to stimulate motivation.

- The top executives at headquarters restrain themselves to managing by exception, based on periodic reports from the field.

- Management often concentrates on making new acquisitions that can be lined up beside other decentralized units.

- Communication from the top is infrequent, usually by correspondence, telephone, or brief visits to field locations.

The delegation stage proves useful for gaining expansion through heightened motivation at lower levels. Decentralized managers with greater authority and incentive are able to penetrate larger markets, respond faster to customers, and develop new products.

... and the control crisis. A serious problem eventually evolves, however, as top executives sense that they are losing control over a highly diversified field operation. Autonomous field managers prefer to run their own shows without co-ordinating plans, money, technology, and manpower with the rest of the organization. Freedom breeds a parochial attitude.

Hence, the Phase 3 revolution is under way when top management seeks to regain control over the total company. Some top managements attempt a return to centralized management, which usually fails because of the vast scope of operations. Those companies that move ahead find a new solution in the use of special co-ordination techniques.

Phase 4: Co-ordination ...

During this phase, the evolutionary period is characterized by the use of formal systems for achieving greater co-ordination and by top executives taking responsibility for the initiation and administration of these new systems. For example:

- Decentralized units are merged into product groups.

- Formal planning procedures are established and intensively reviewed.

- Numerous staff personnel are hired and located at headquarters to initiate company-wide programs of control and review for line managers.

- Each product group is treated as an investment center where return on invested capital is an important criterion used in allocating funds.

- Certain technical functions, such as data processing, are centralized at headquarters, while daily operating decisions remain decentralized.

- Stock options and company-wide profit sharing are used to encourage identity with the firm as a whole.

All of these new co-ordination systems prove useful for ▶

387

Theoretical Perspective continued

achieving growth through more efficient allocation of a company's limited resources. They prompt field managers to look beyond the needs of their local units. While these managers still have much decision-making responsibility, they learn to justify their actions more carefully to a 'watchdog' audience at headquarters.

... and the red-tape crisis. But a lack of confidence gradually builds between line, and staff, and between headquarters and the field. The proliferation of systems and programs begins to exceed its utility; a red-tape crisis is created. Line managers, for example, increasingly resent heavy staff direction from those who are not familiar with local conditions. Staff people, on the other hand, complain about unco-operative and uninformed line managers. Together both groups criticise the bureaucratic paper system that has evolved. Procedures take precedence over problem solving, and innovation is dampened. In short, the organization has become too large and complex to be managed through formal programs and rigid systems.

Phase 5: Collaboration ...

The last observable phase in previous studies emphasizes strong interpersonal collaboration in an attempt to overcome the red-tape crisis. Where Phase 4 was managed more through formal systems and procedures, Phase 5 emphasizes greater spontaneity in management action through teams and the skilful confrontation of interpersonal differences. Social control and self-discipline take over from formal control. This transition is especially difficult for those experts who created the old systems as well as for those line managers who relied on formal methods for answers. The

phase 5 evolution then, builds around a more flexible and behavioral approach to management.

● The focus is on solving problems quickly through team action.

● Teams are combined across functions for task-group activity.

● Headquarters staff experts are reduced in number, reassigned, and combined in interdisciplinary teams to consult with, not to direct, field units.

● A matrix-type structure is frequently used to assemble the right teams for the appropriate problems.

● Previous formal systems are simplified and combined into single multipurpose systems.

● Conferences of key managers are held frequently to focus on major problem issues.

● Educational programs are utilized to train managers in behavioral skills for achieving better teamwork and conflict resolution.

● Real-time information systems are integrated into daily decision making.

● Economic rewards are geared more to team performance than to individual achievement.

● Experiments in new practices are encouraged throughout the organization.

... and the ? crisis. Greiner in the original 1972 article hypothesised that the stresses of intensive team interactions and the constant hunger for innovation would result in 'psychological saturation' – employees would burn out. He

Table 10.2   Organisation practices during evolution in the five phases of growth

Category	Phase 1	Phase 2	Phase 3	Phase 4	Phase 5
Management focus	Make and sell	Efficiency of operations	Expansion of market	Consolidation of organization	Problem solving and innovation
Organization structure	Informal	Centralized and functional	Decentralized and geographical	Line-staff and product groups	Matrix of teams
Top management style	Individualistic and entrepreneurial	Directive	Delegative	Watchdog	Participative
Control system	Market results	Standards and cost centers	Reports and profit centers	Plans and investment centers	Mutual goal setting
Management reward emphasis	Ownership	Salary and merit increases	Individual bonus	Profit sharing and stock options	Team bonus

thought that organisations would need to resolve this crisis by developing new ways of working, even parallel structures, which gave people scope for rest and reflection. However, in a 1998 commentary, he suggests that this view is wrong.

Instead he thinks that the crisis comes about when firms run out of ways of generating growth internally, and feel compelled to seek external partners. He identifies a sixth growth phase in which organisations develop the characteristics of networks or holding companies.

10.3 Organisational designs

We now move on to look at some of the different organisational forms that have been observed, and consider some of their potential advantages and disadvantages. Decisions to design an organisation that is centralised or decentralised, tall or flat, flexible or more rigid, with more or less formal policies and procedures, are essentially umbrella decisions about how an organisation's strategy is to be achieved.

10.3.1 The simple structure

A simple structure is common in small firms (Figure 10.3), particularly where the owner is in charge. You might like to think of a small printing firm, or a design consultancy, or a small engineering firm where there are only a few staff and maybe only one or two managers or partners. Organisations with this structure are often young, as Greiner points out in Theoretical Perspective 10.3 above. A single McDonald's restaurant has this form too, even though it sits within a more complex international corporate structure.

Figure 10.3   A simple structure

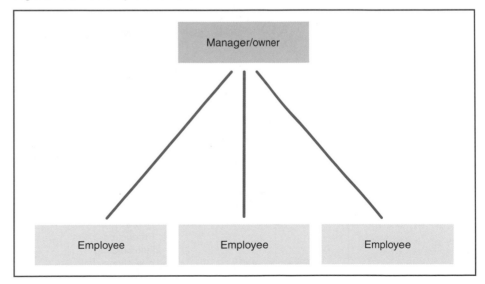

In this type of structure, which Henry Mintzberg in his influential 1979 book on organisational design called the *entrepreneurial organisation*, there is little differentiation of roles, few formal rules and procedures, and decision-making is centralised. It is therefore flexible. The manager is in charge, and the organisation small enough for him or her to be able to have considerable knowledge of what is going on and considerable input into the decisions that are taken. An organisation may deliberately be kept small for this reason.

A firm following a differentiation focus strategy, where it aims to provide a high-quality service to a limited range of customers, would benefit from a simple structure. It would allow decisions to be made quickly in response to customer requirements, and quality assured through the overall control of the principal or managing director.

However, the virtue of the simple structure – that the top people are close to everything – is also its limitation. It can only be sustained for as long as the range of activities is small enough to be accommodated within the attention span of one or two people. The simplicity of this type of design is hard to maintain:

- in larger organisations, where co-ordination between people is necessary and the management and motivation of people becomes a major concern in its own right;
- where a wide variety of tasks is being performed, some of them complex and needing the input of a variety of specialists;
- where the range of customers being served has expanded to the point where a single person cannot make sure that they are all satisfied.

10.3.2 The functional structure

The functional structure (Figure 10.4) is one of the most common in commercial

Figure 10.4   A functional structure

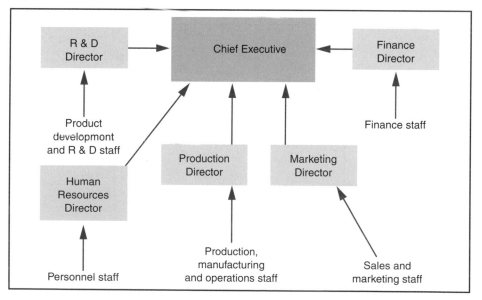

organisations. It makes one manager clearly responsible for each of the main areas of the business such as product development, operations, marketing, human resources, IT and finance. It is thus a natural second stage for a firm that has outgrown the simple structure.

Elements of this approach are also found in many public sector settings. A hospital may have a chief executive, finance, human resources, administration, medical and nursing directors, as well as management teams within these functions which are responsible for the day-to-day operations of the hospital. This structure often runs parallel to a 'professional' hierarchy of medical staff headed by a professor or consultant physician or surgeon.

A functional structure makes sense in mid-sized (say 100–500 employees) organisations, because it allows specialists to develop and practice their skills without being distracted by tasks for which they have no aptitude. It also allows different control and reward systems to be used within the different functions. A firm will probably perform better if the finance function is rewarded for maximising returns on the firm's investments and if the personnel function is rewarded for achieving high levels of staff skills, and not vice versa.

For an organisation that has a relatively narrow range of products or services and is not aiming to diversify beyond a limited set of markets, the functional structure is appropriate. It will allow the firm to develop specialised skills and be highly efficient within its limited range of activities.

On the other hand, functional structures tend to have a number of drawbacks. A functional structure asks people to specialise and to focus on a limited range of issues. This focus can lead to rigidity, as people become used to doing a certain set of tasks in a particular way, and invest time and effort in learning to do them better. The different functions thus develop their own routines, objectives and ways of viewing the world. They may become resistant to suggestions that they change to accommodate the routines and requirements of other functions. They may be reluctant to share important information or may express it in a specialised technical language that colleagues in other departments cannot understand.

This means that every functional structure contains the seeds of inter-functional misunderstandings and conflict. These conflicts are not inevitable – we have encountered firms where the marketing manager has talked knowledgeably and sympathetically about the problems of the production function, and the factory manager has shown a similar degree of knowledge of marketing issues. And not all conflict is harmful – a certain amount of 'creative tension' can help organisations to learn effectively.

However, resolving these tensions and co-ordinating the activities of the different functions requires time, effort, and management skills from the top management team. The greater the number of products, markets and technologies with which an organisation is involved, the greater the strain that is placed upon the established routines in the different departments and the greater the potential for conflict, confusion and resistance to change. This means that, rather like a simple structure, a functional structure can only cope with a limited degree of complexity in its environment before the attention of senior managers becomes spread across too many problems.

Managers can respond to this problem in different ways. They may split the organisation into smaller pieces, adopting a multi-divisional structure (Section 10.3.3). Alternatively, they may use cross-functional teams as a way of getting different functions to share information and understand each other's problems, or introduce elements of a matrix (Section 10.3.4) within the overall functional hierarchy.

10.3.3 The multi-divisional structure

The divisional or multi-divisional structure (Figures 10.5 and 10.6) is extremely common in commercial organisations. It also occurs in the public sector – a local government authority will have different divisions dealing with, say, housing, education, and waste disposal. A diversified firm that is pursuing a strategy of differentiation over a range of products and services, will benefit from a divisionalised structure. Each division can be responsive to the particular needs of its customers. A multi-divisional organisation is not so much a single integrated organisation as a set of rather independent entitles coupled together by a co-ordinating administrative system.

◀ See Section 9.2.3 for a discussion on parenting.

Each division can be measured and controlled separately using different criteria according to its market or product characteristics. A division which is responsible for the development of new products, for example, should not be expected to produce the same levels of return on investment as a division which is responsible for managing a commodity-type product which is mature and whose demand is much more predictable. For this reason, divisions are often set up as completely different companies, and even may be in partial public ownership themselves.

Multi-divisional firms tend to be older, bigger, and hence more diversified than functional organisations. Firms above a certain size (there is no fixed rule about this, but between 400 and 800 employees seems to be a natural boundary) appear to benefit from being broken up into separate units. Each unit concentrates on a particular dimension of the business – a product, a geographical area, a customer segment or any other grouping that makes commercial or operational sense.

Figure 10.5   A simple multi-divisional structure

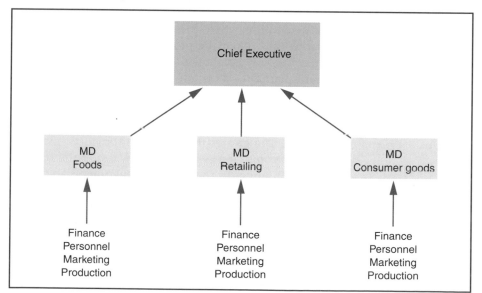

Figure 10.6   Skandia's multi-divisional structure

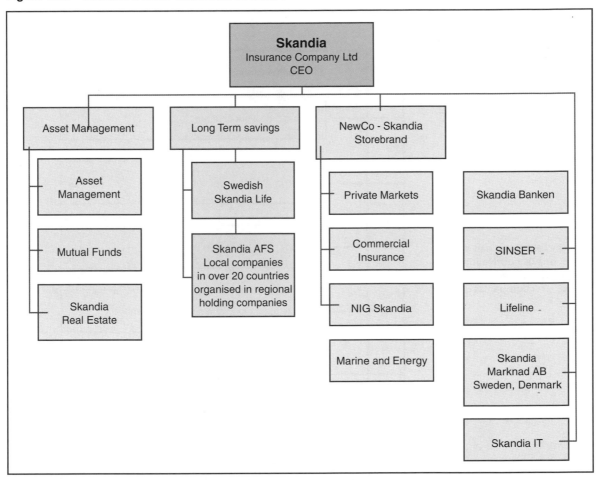

As you can see from Figure 10.6, the multi-divisional structure often contains a number of substructures, which can be of any configuration. This might include a multi-divisional division if the firm is large enough. As the figure shows, an international organisation may be particularly complex, and can contain a large variety of forms within the overall corporation. A modified example of this type of structure is sometimes known as the *holding company* structure, where a small head office simply acts as the overall owner of a range of separate companies, each of whom may have its own very different products, customers and structure and be controlled through very different types of performance targets. As you have seen in Chapter 9, the concern of the holding company in this situation is how to manage the mix of businesses within its portfolio.

There are a number of issues that need to be resolved in designing a divisional structure. Firstly, managers have to decide which dimensions of the business need to be emphasised the most. If the firm's strategy emphasises product technology or production economies of scale, perhaps it should have separate divisions for each product or type of product. If it has a global strategy emphasising the needs of particular customer segments, then there should be separate divisions for each major

Figure 10.7   Sony's multi-divisional structure in 1999

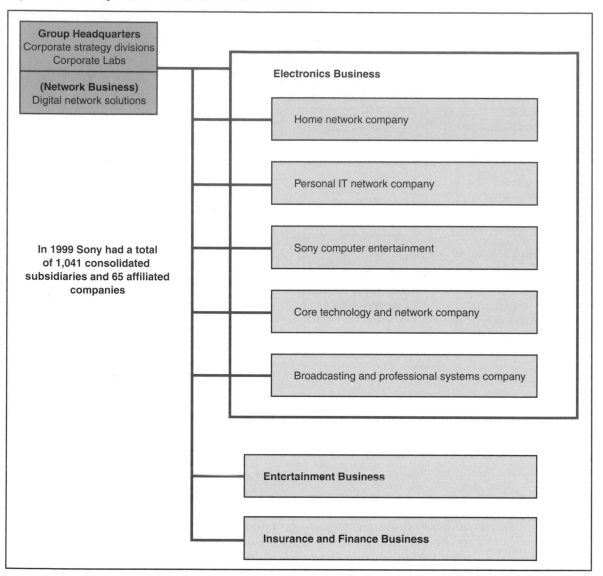

group of customers, as in Figure 10.7. If it is following a locally responsive strategy, perhaps the divisions should represent separate geographical areas.

It can sometimes be difficult to establish which dimension of a firm's activities should take priority. Sometimes, for example, production economies and customer focus are equally important. Traditionally, the answer to this dilemma has been the matrix structure (Section 10.3.4). More recent developments include the hybrid organisations discussed in Section 10.3.5.

A second issue to resolve in organisation design is how far to devolve responsibility. The tension between centralisation and decentralisation (Section 10.1.1) is felt most acutely in a large divisionalised firm. Organisations can sometimes go through several cycles of centralisation and decentralisation before finding the right balance between the two. Divisionalised structures call for some functions to

REAL-LIFE APPLICATION 10.4

The double shuffle

Long, long ago in a corporation far, far away, the following events took place. They illustrate the lengths to which people will sometimes go in order to get around corporate policy.

The corporation in question exercised a strong central control over the prices of its products. This was partly because of cultural conflict between the centre and the operating divisions. The headquarters staff, predominantly from an accounting background, distrusted the divisional managers, many of whom had risen up through the salesforce, and were trying to assert control over them. However, there were other reasons why price controls were thought to be necessary. The corporation had a very high share of its markets, and there was a genuine danger that the authorities in the USA and Europe might take action if the firm was seen to be abusing its monopoly position. It could not afford to appear to discourage competition by setting its prices to low. Also, some large customers were becoming increasingly unhappy if they found they were being charged different prices in different markets, or that other firms were being offered lower prices than they were.

In one subsidiary, located a long way from headquarters, the management grew frustrated by this. They felt that, because staff at headquarters were preventing them from offering discounts on the list price of their equipment, they were unable to compete effectively in their local markets. Almost the only time they were allowed to offer a substantial discount was as a loyalty bonus to customers who, after renting the equipment for a while, decided to buy it. So the subsidiary's management hatched the following scheme, known as 'the double shuffle'.

Every time a rental contract came to an end, the customer was offered the option of buying the equipment. If they chose not to take up that option, then the equipment, instead of being returned to the company's warehouse, was stored in a salesperson's home or garage until a buyer was found for it. The new buyer would be offered the machine at a discount that was equivalent to the loyalty bonus to which the previous renter was entitled. Once the deal was concluded, it would be entered in the accounts as if the machine had been sold to the earlier rental customer.

Eventually, the arrangement was uncovered during a routine audit by headquarters staff. There was no suggestion that people were attempting to defraud the company, or indeed do anything more serious than raise its market share. However, every senior manager who knew about the double shuffle was fired. Headquarters staff believed this action was justified because of the potential consequences if regulators or major customers had found out about the illicit discounts. They also wanted to send out a warning to other subsidiary managers who might be tempted to excesses of entrepreneurship.

---

be duplicated. Managers must decide whether the extra costs are outweighed by the benefits from allowing each division's control systems and processes to become specialised.

Devolution also brings with it the potential for 'empire building' – divisional directors building up the size of their unit in order to increase their self-esteem, their salary or their power within the organisation. Within limits, of course, such behaviour benefits the organisation as well as the director concerned. However, there is always the danger that these directors may start to dictate, ignore or even subvert corporate policy (Real-Life Application 10.4).

Just as there is potential for conflict between functions, there is also potential for conflict to develop between divisions – especially if they are interdependent and remote from central control. Products which are sold between the divisions may have to have special rates negotiated, and the rate at which transfer prices are set is unlikely to please everyone.

In the end, the divisional structure is a compromise. It is very difficult for a firm to deal with complicated problems using a simple or functional structure. There seems to be a need for an organisation's structure to become more complex in order to reflect the complexity of its environment – this is sometimes known as 'the law of requisite variety'. A divisional structure is simpler to conceive, manage and work in than a matrix structure, which is the main alternative for a large firm.

10.3.4 The matrix structure

In a matrix structure (Figure 10.8) there is no linear up-and-down hierarchy of control or decision-making. An employee might report to one manager for a particular job on a particular product, and a manager from a different department for another job. Neither of these has to be the employee's line manager, although they may be. In this way the employee's skills can be applied to the most appropriate product at the best time, rather than being tied to a particular department's own projects exclusively. It is an attempt to decentralise decision-making while still achieving some degree of co-ordination. It also allows for the flexible use of expertise.

This structure is common in professional service firms such as management consultants. PriceWaterhouseCoopers (PWC), has specialists in IT, financial systems, marketing, organisational change management and many other specialist disciplines. Each of these disciplines has a partner in charge of it who ensures that PWC keeps its consultants up to date with the latest professional developments and has a competitive range of services to offer. At the same time, there are other partners whose job it is to target particular groups of customers, such as retailers, or financial services firms, or public sector organisations. They try to ensure that PWC offers the kind of services that these customers require, and has the right marketing information to target them effectively.

A project team will be brought together to write and present a proposal to a potential client, and another, larger team will be assembled to carry out the work once the contract has been won. Each team will combine senior and junior consultants from a number of disciplines. Some of them may also have specialised in working for that particular type of customer – for example, in managing organis-

Figure 10.8   The matrix structure

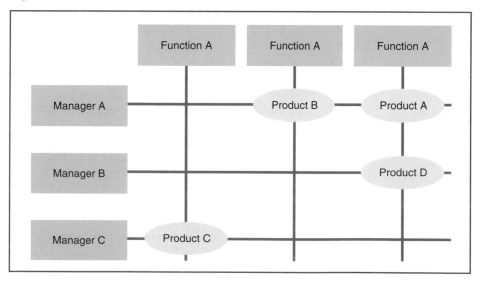

ational change specifically in retailing companies. Others may be brought in purely because of their expertise in IT or marketing and may well be more experienced and more highly paid than the consultant that is managing the project. They will defer to her when it comes to deciding at what stage they start and stop working with the client and what they include in their final report. Client liaison is the project manager's responsibility.

A consultant's line manager will be a partner who may have nothing to do with the execution of most of the projects in which he or she is involved. The partner, however, will be trying to make sure that the consultant is spending as much time as possible on fee-earning projects, attends training courses regularly and fills in his or her time sheet every month.

Problems can arise with matrix structures because accountability and responsibility – whom to blame, whom to praise; who takes action when things go wrong or right – are often confused. If PWC's project is a success, does credit go to the project manager, to the partner who is her line manager, to the partner in charge of the market segment or to the partners who supervised the various consultants involved? This can be an issue not only from the management point of view of finding who is responsible, but also from the staff point of view, that is, 'who is managing my appraisal, my pay and my development?' However, a matrix structure is particularly appropriate for organisations pursuing innovative strategies and operating within turbulent environments where constant experimentation and change is essential, and where there is considerable need for interdependence between experts such as in, for example, many software and aerospace companies.

10.3.5 Hybrid structures

Different types of structure can usefully co-exist within a single organisation. An organisation may have some divisions that operate in stable, predictable conditions, like the retail part of a high street bank. These divisions can operate perfectly well using a functional structure. Other divisions, like a bank's corporate finance division, may need to be faster moving, more innovative and combine different types of expertise in a single team. That division might be better off with a matrix structure.

Figure 10.9   IBM's customer–product structure (adapted from Galbraith, 1998)

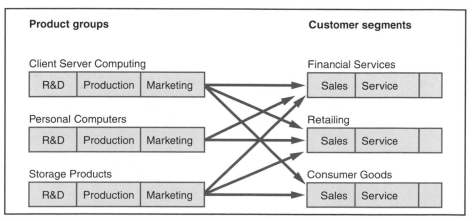

A subtler variation on this theme is where the whole organisation adopts what looks like a functional or simple divisional structure to run its day to day operations, but some parts of the business set up project teams to work on critical problems or important innovations. This kind of hybrid between a functional and a matrix structure has been called a 'hypertext organisation' (Nonaka and Takeuchi, 1995).

Another type of hybrid is the 'front–back' structure, shown in Figure 10.9. It is partially focused on customer segments and partially on products and services. In this structure there are several profit centres, each of which sells products from all over the organisation. They are not tied to one set of products from their own unit's factories, as they would be under a 'normal' divisional structure. This hybrid structure therefore combines elements of a multi-business and a single-business structure.

10.3.6 The network structure

Finally, we move on to considering what appears to be an increasingly common type of organisational structure, a network (Figure 10.10). This type of configuration is also sometimes known as a virtual organisation or a *shamrock*, a term coined by Charles Handy (1989) in his book *The Age of Unreason*.

There are several different types of network. Perhaps the most common has a single, large organisation at its centre. Other independent organisations supply it

Figure 10.10   The network structure

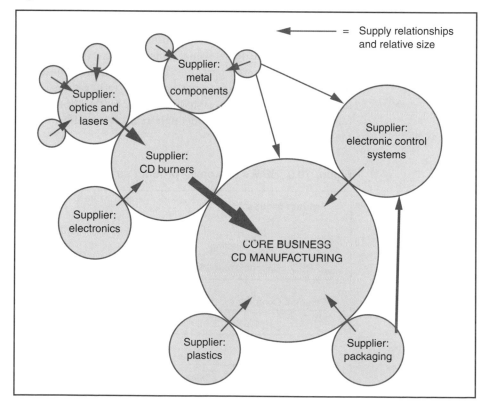

REAL-LIFE APPLICATION 10.5

Luxottica

Luxottica, a northern Italian firm, is one of the world leaders in the production of spectacle frames. It was founded by Leonardo Delvecchio, a toolmaker, who to begin with used nearby firms to produce the frames – there are some 250 firms in that part of Italy with relevant expertise. Luxottica then started a number of small (200-person) manufacturing subsidiaries of its own. It extended the network through marketing links with companies in Spain, the USA and Japan, and through an alliance with the fashion house, Giorgio Armani, to produce eyewear carrying the Armani designer label. The overseas links and the alliance with Armani were all cemented through equity investments or exchanges.

Source: Hinterhuber and Levin (1994).

---

with inputs that may be essential to its work, but that nevertheless are not considered to be the core of its activities. Other firms may act as distributors or marketing outlets, perhaps under a franchising arrangement.

◄ *The advantages and disadvantages of firms' outsourcing peripheral activities are discussed in Chapter 8.*

The last decade has seen an increasing tendency for both public sector organisations and companies to divest non-core parts of their operations. Business areas that once were part of a large firm are sold off, often to their managers, and are no longer wholly owned. In many cases strong supply relationships still exist between these organisations, although they may no longer be as exclusive as they once were. The buyer can choose to go elsewhere, and the supplier can also supply other organisations. This allows both to concentrate on what they do best, and gives them an incentive to earn greater profits by doing it well. However, not all networks are spun off from large firms – some, like that of Luxottica (Real-Life Application 10.5) are built from scratch.

A slightly different type of network operates as a confederation or strategic alliance between a number of more or less equal partners. Each partner may specialise in a certain part of the value chain (product development, marketing), have a particular expertise (website maintenance, computer network installation) or specialise in particular market segments (retailers or local governments).

Networks like this enable small firms to appear to clients as if they are large corporations, with access to a wide range of resources. If one firm in the network receives an enquiry for some business that it cannot handle itself, it calls in one of its partner organisations, or passes the enquiry on to them. Sometimes a single firm acts as the 'server' at the centre of the network, taking in the work and allocating it to the other partners.

◄ *See Chapter 7 for an analysis of core competences. See also Section 5.5.2 for a discussion of co-opetition. Strategic alliances are discussed in Chapter 15.* ►

It is not just small firms that feel the need to build such networks. In the case of hugely complex or technologically sophisticated products, it is now thought that no one firm can contain all the necessary expertise in-house. Figure 10.11 shows some of the network of which Merck, the largest pharmaceutical company in the world, is a part. It is part of this huge system because the development and distribution of drugs requires a wide range of knowledge and competences, not all of which Merck has or wishes to have itself.

However, the management of network relationships is sometimes quite difficult to do. Merck, Luxottica and Benetton all appear to be companies that have developed competences in managing these relationships. Such relationships are dependent on a number of critical factors for success. Trust has to be maintained between the organisations, difficult to do sometimes when some are potentially in competition with the others for scarce resources and even may be selling products which

Figure 10.11   Strategic alliances within the pharmaceutical industry: Merck & Co.

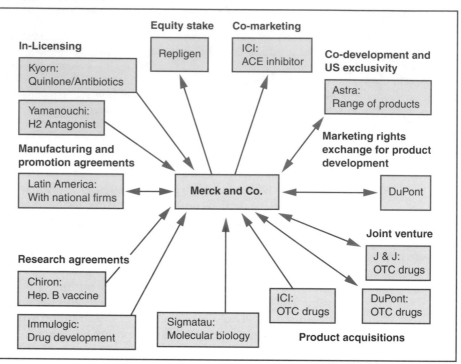

Source: Reproduced by permission of The Economist Intelligence Unit Ltd.

◄ Hold-up and other types of transaction costs are discussed in Chapter 8.

◄ The problems of managing the supply activity and the use of information technology are discussed in Chapter 8.

are substitutes for their collaborators. There is also the risk of 'hold-up': that one partner may hold the others to ransom if it feels that it has control of critical resources. For this reason, sometimes the two or more firms in a network relationship elect to exchange shares, cross-shareholdings, or set up some other type of formal or legal partnership agreement between them.

There may be logistical problems to be overcome too. If physical inputs are being supplied, then partners have to be close enough to each other for essential supplies to be delivered to the right place at the right time, and quality has to be consistently high for the buyer to be able to use the suppliers without constantly checking for faults. Communication between the two firms has to be very good. This may be through personal contact, or more often through the use of good IT systems.

Nonetheless, some theorists are starting to conceive the 'organisation of the future' as becoming more like a network than a traditional hierarchy. Two writers who have conceptualised this process are Sumantra Ghoshal and Christopher Bartlett (1998) in their book *The Individualized Corporation* (Figure 10.12). Their ideas are based on what they have observed in a number of major multinational corporations, including two widely admired engineering groups, General Electric of the USA and Asea Brown Boveri of Sweden. According to Ghoshal and Bartlett, the traditional thinking of the division as the building block of the corporation is outdated – divisions need to be replaced by much smaller and more cohesive units, and resources and responsibilities radically decentralised. The organisation becomes a

Figure 10.12   The individualised corporation (adapted from Ghoshal and Bartlett, 1998)

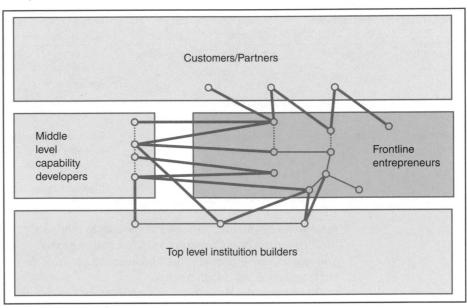

fragmented affiliation of loose alliances, coming together for specific aims, and breaking up to reform with other alliances as required. The challenge for managers is then to make individual employees feel that they belong and can contribute.

One question that needs to be answered here, however, is how such loose confederations are stopped from degenerating into disorganised anarchy. According to Ghoshal and Bartlett, their model of individualised corporations use cultural control and self-control (see Section 10.4.6). They instil a sense of discipline and direction in employees, as a substitute for the tight control through plans, budgets, reports and memos that characterises some traditional organisations. The role of their top-level managers is to put in place a set of norms and values that support co-operation, trust and self-discipline. Middle managers act as a form of glue that holds the organisation together, and spread knowledge, skills and best practices from one unit to another. Frontline managers look after the day-to-day operations and liaise with customers. They develop competences and capabilities, and manage the linkages between their units and other businesses in the corporation.

10.4   Strategic control and reward systems

The discussion of the individualised corporation shows how questions of structure lead naturally on to consideration of strategic control systems. How **do** managers get their staff and colleagues to do what they want them to do in order to achieve their idea of what the company should be doing?

A number of different kinds of control systems have been identified. These are summarised in Table 10.3. Some are imposed by outside stakeholders, others are chosen by the managers of a firm. Most organisations will make some use of all these types of control system, but have one or two that are clearly the most important. A sales-led organisation like a stockbroker is likely to use output controls to

Table 10.3 Types of control system

External control systems		Internal control systems				
External control	Market control	The system of authority	Output control	Bureaucratic control	Cultural control	Reward systems
Government	Share price	Hierarchy	Goal setting	Management information systems	Recruitment	Salary
Legislation and regulation	ROI	Appraisals	Measuring and evaluating		Socialisation	Bonuses and share options
Customers	Competitors	Rewards and punishments		Rules and procedures	Norms	
					Shared values	PRP
				Standardisation		Perks

measure performance, and reward systems to motivate people to perform better. A local government organisation may have strong external controls, from politicians and central government, and bureaucratic controls to ensure that people meet these stakeholders' requirements.

These examples show how an organisation's preference for one sort of control system is likely to vary according to its strategy, culture, structure, and environment.

We will look at each of these in some detail below, but first, Real-Life Application 10.6 introduces some of the strategic control systems in operation in McDonald's.

REAL-LIFE APPLICATION 10.6

Strategic control systems in McDonald's

In a service business like McDonald's, maintaining product consistency and quality is a considerable problem because each meal is prepared and served by different people in different locations. If a customer gets a bad meal or poor service, then the company's reputation could easily be lost.

Ray Kroc, the man who was responsible for McDonald's growth, faced the problem of maintaining standards when he expanded the company through franchising. Thousands of branches of McDonald's now exist across the world. Kroc's answer was to develop a sophisticated control system, which specified every detail of how each McDonald's outlet was to be set up and managed. In doing this, Kroc hoped that customers would always find the same level of quality in food and service wherever they went.

First, Kroc developed a comprehensive system of rules and procedures to be followed in each restaurant. The ways in which tasks such as greeting customers, cooking burgers, making fries, or cleaning tables were to be carried out were written down and then taught to each McDonald's employee in an induction process. Kroc even pioneered the notion of a company university where managers and franchisees went to learn all aspects of the company's operations. They were in turn supposed to train their employees, who were all expected to understand the restaurants' operating procedures.

Kroc's use of franchisees also helped the company to control its structure and achieve high financial performance as it grew. Kroc thought that a franchisee, who is a part owner of the business and receives a share of the profits, was more likely to be motivated to maintain high standards than a manager paid on a straight salary. This worked because Kroc was very selective in choosing his franchisees; they had to be good managers, and a franchise could be revoked if they did not maintain sufficient levels of service quality and financial performance. Each franchisee was required to provide information on a regular basis to the company's senior managers on how many meals were sold, on operating costs, etc.

10.4.1 External control; stakeholders, government and regulation

◀ We look at the kinds of demands that governments and regulatory bodies can have on an organisation in Sections 2.3.4 and 5.2.1.

Although this section is mostly about how individuals who work within an organisation can use various control systems to help implement a particular strategy, we need to briefly mention external stakeholders who can also be very powerful in forcing companies to do one thing rather than another. In fact, governments and customers can provide one of the most important controls on the strategy an organisation adopts.

◀ Buyer power is examined in Chapter 5.

Customers can demand particular products, particular features on established products or particular levels of quality or punctuality. These demands will be especially important in industries where buyer power is strong, or for firms locked into strong networks of supplier relationships (see Section 10.5.6 above). Regulatory bodies such as governments also can have strong influence on the type of strategy an organisation adopts, and the way it implements it.

In most western countries, there exists a pretty rigorous system of corporate governance. Although there are still considerable differences between countries, best practice now appears to be increasingly shared across nations. The long-standing German system of a two-tier board, comprising banks and employees in addition to managers, is starting to spread elsewhere. The underlying philosophy of this system, the broadening of participation in key decision-making, has resulted in changes to board composition in the UK, so that key decisions are not simply taken by those who are likely to benefit from them, and also resulted in the separation of the role of chairman and managing director. The USA's practice of ousting poorly-performing directors is starting to spread elsewhere, although employment legislation such as for example Japan or Germany's, provides a huge block to this occurring in some countries. Interestingly these two countries have traditionally valued long-term employment and development over short term returns – practices which were once regarded as an important source of their superior economic performance.

◀ We also look at corporate governance in Chapter 2.

Another type of external control is to use the power of externally generated and regulated mechanisms to shape employees' behaviour. The setting up of systems such as share option schemes, in which employees receive shares in the company as part of their remuneration package, is a way of attempting to overcome agency problems and align the interests of managers and employees of a company with those of the owners, the shareholders. Of course this system only works in publicly owned firms or ones where the shares are tradable. In family-controlled ones, other measures have to be taken to ensure that employees act in the owners' interest, such as strong cultural control or close personal involvement from the owners.

10.4.2 Market control

Share option schemes are dependent on open external markets, and markets are another way in which the behaviour of employees is influenced. Market control in the capitalist world has two main elements – the activities of competitors, and the regulatory effects of stock markets.

◀ Competitors' influence on strategy is dealt with in Chapter 5.

Competitors control a firm's strategy by limiting its options and activities. They may take potential customers, charge lower prices, be located in particularly favourable places or appropriate scarce resources to themselves. All these factors will act to shape or determine what the organisation itself is able to do and how it does it.

Market control is intimately bound up with the activities of competitors, because it relates to the firm's financial performance. Almost all companies nowadays are dependent on external sources of finance, whether this is from the stock market through share offerings, through venture capitalists or through banks. All these agencies will assess the potential future earnings of the firm, and will influence the direction they take according to whether they believe its future strategy is likely to be viable and effective. For companies in public ownership their performance is assessed and this assessment is made visible through indicators like the company's share price, and if this is not good, the firm's strategy is likely to be changing soon!

Economic theory assigns a lot of importance to market controls. Markets are believed to give organisations the best signals about how to make the most effective use of their resources. When one part of an organisation procures an input from another unit in the same firm, it gets an assured source of supply, and can use the organisation's hierarchy to try to make sure that its requirements are met. However, if it gets the inputs at lower than the market price, it may be tempted to buy more of them than it really needs. This diverts resources in the supplier unit that might be more profitably employed serving other units, or external customers. The supplier department, for its part, may deliver poor levels of service, because it has a captive user.

If, on the other hand, the inputs are priced above the market price, then the purchasing unit may have to raise its own prices, leading the organisation to lose market share. Furthermore, the supplier unit will appear to be more profitable than it really is. The firm's management may decide to invest more money in it, when in fact they might do better to use an outside supplier.

Many of these problems can be avoided if different parts of the same organisation trade with one another using an 'arm's length relationship' – that is, they buy and sell from one another at market prices. Relationships like this are quite normal for commonplace services like photocopying and computer maintenance. The service department charges prices close to (or perhaps just slightly lower than) those charged by commercial print shops or computer service firms. It may also draw up a 'service level agreement', which sets out what it will provide in return for the money it has paid. If it fails to meet the terms of that agreement, then it may have to repay part of the money, or its customer departments may gain the right to buy from an outside supplier. And if, at the end of the year, it turns out to have operated at a loss, then the firm's managers have a pretty clear signal that they would be better off outsourcing the service in question.

Very large organisations may set up *internal markets*, where different units bid against one another for the right to supply particular goods and services. The UK health service, for example, has a system where different hospitals compete for the right to provide hip replacement operations or orthopaedic services in their locality.

These pseudo-market arrangements are not always feasible or desirable. Sometimes there is no real market for the kind of resource that is being supplied, because it is so rare. Sometimes a firm sets up an internal supplier precisely because its managers believe that the market price is unrealistically high or that outside suppliers have too much power. And sometimes putting internal relationships on an arms length basis may destroy co-operation between different units, or even lead them to try to cheat one another.

10.4.3 The system of authority

We now move on to looking at control systems that are internal to the firm, and therefore easier for its managers to shape. Almost all organisation structures formally give some individuals – managers – the right to take decisions which affect others. And this *formal authority* is the next type of control system that we shall discuss.

It is interesting to consider why any individual would willingly join an organisation which has the ability instantly to withdraw their livelihood, or in extreme circumstances (such as the army during times of war), their life. And yet we do. Most human beings appear instinctively to accept others' rights to control our lives, perhaps because we recognise the advantages of working as a group. In organisations this is formalised into a chain of command – the hierarchy.

Managers at senior levels of this hierarchy normally have a broader range of powers than those lower down. They can take decisions with larger financial implications, and which affect more of the organisation. Their decisions are more likely to be strategic, while lower level employees' decisions will probably be operational or functional in scope. A chief executive, for example, will have the right to close down a whole factory, or relocate an office from one country to another. A design manager might only have the right to spend a certain budget and take decisions that relate to a specific product-development project.

▶ *We return to looking at how poor performance can lead to the perception of change being needed in Chapter 14. We also discussed how strategies could go wrong in Section 3.5.* ◀

The system of authority is widespread in most companies in most countries, and is accepted almost automatically by most people who work in organisations. However, there are times when it fails. There are well-documented examples of situations where senior managers have been forced out of their jobs by people whose formal rank in the organisation is lower. These acts of rebellion can come about because the senior manager fails to recognise that performance is poor, or to admit their responsibility for it. Authority can sometimes breed complacency and arrogance (Real-Life Application 10.7).

The effectiveness of the system of authority ultimately depends on external con-

---

REAL-LIFE APPLICATION 10.7

Power to the people!

The managing director of a company we know made a large number of what many of the management team regarded as hugely problematic decisions to do with the branding and marketing of the company. These problems were compounded because he 'hid' behind a small number of senior colleagues that he had worked with previously and with whom he spent most of his time. He was accused of having failed to take account of the expertise elsewhere in the firm, something which was held to have contributed to the problematic decisions he had taken.

The situation got so bad and resentment became so intense that many of the other managers started to withhold co-operation from their senior colleagues. At the same time the firm's performance declined substantially. A concerted political campaign was waged by lower level managers to remove the managing director. The weight of opinion against him, which gathered strength over time and was shared by almost everyone, eventually found its way to the main board, and this resulted in the dismissal of both the managing director and his allies.

trols wielded by stock markets or boards of directors, to force out underperforming managers. However, these bodies are not always as efficient in exercising control as they might be. Boards of directors can be formed from friends of the managers, and stock market valuations are necessarily based on imperfect knowledge and can be manipulated by skilful managers with something to hide.[7]

10.4.4 Output control

The system of authority is often expressed in terms of *targets* or *outputs*, which a manager sets for his or her employees. These can be qualitative or quantitative. Such targets can be set for all levels of the organisation – for divisions, functions or individual personnel. Actual performance is then monitored against these targets, and rewards such as bonuses given accordingly. Corrective action can be taken if performance does not appear to be matching expectations. Output controls are thus important in motivating people.

Most organisations that have got beyond the simple structure make some use of output measures. As we said in Chapter 4, 'What gets measured, gets done'. In a large organisation where people have many demands upon their attention, they will naturally tend to give priority to things that management are seen to be measuring. From the managers' point of view, setting a target is a powerful way of signalling the strategic priorities.

In the 1960s, many firms adopted the fashion for 'management by objectives', using quantitative output targets as the main way of motivating staff. They discovered, however, that output controls when used alone gave rise to agency problems, which limited their effectiveness in practice. As we shall see, output controls invariably need to be coupled with other kinds of control, but they remain a very important element in strategy implementation. When thinking about the use of output controls, there are four questions that need to be answered:

1. What output measures are being (or should be) used?
2. Are there effective procedures in place to monitor progress towards the targets?
3. Are targets at the right *level* to give people the right degree of *incentive* to achieve them – and to carry on working hard after they have been met?
4. Does the organisation have the right *combination* of targets, so that when people achieve their personal and departmental targets, they also help the organisation to achieve its strategic aims? This alignment between individual and corporate objectives is known as *goal congruence*.

A similar set of questions applies when formulating control systems to support a change in strategy. We look at each of these four topics in more detail.

Choosing what to measure

An organisation will typically set itself a number of overall goals, and then translate them into a set of more detailed targets for divisions, functions and individual employees:

● Organisational goals are likely to relate to financial measures like overall turnover, return on assets, and profitability. They may also be market control measures such as the share price (see Section 10.4.2).

◀ We looked at measures of strategic performance in Chapter 4.

- Divisional output goals might include targets as to overall levels of sales, productivity, growth or market share.

- Functional goals can include sales costs ratios; quality standards, judged perhaps by the number of returns; customer survey responses; time needed to serve customers; repeat business and so on.

- Individual goals are usually a subset of functional output goals, but where people work in teams, team-based targets are sometimes used instead. In some situations, such as in an R&D department, it is difficult to measure individual output, and then incentive systems may be tied to more general measures of performance, such as ROI or number of successful innovations developed, as 3M famously does (Real-Life Application 10.8).

REAL-LIFE APPLICATION 10.8

Innovative reward systems at 3M

3M aims to have at least 30% of its turnover generated by products introduced in the last five years. Its managers are expected to devote a high proportion (up to one seventh) of their working time to develop innovative 'bootleg' projects of their choosing, and they are paid substantial bonuses according to how many successful new products they achieve.

According to Ghoshal and Bartlett (1998), by the early 1990s 3M had over 100 core technologies, 60,000 products, 3900 profit centres and 47 product divisions.

Output targets are best if they are linked to the organisation's overall goals, such as delivering a quality product or service, being responsive to customers' needs or being efficient. An organisation pursuing a low-cost strategy might set a target for reducing costs by a given percentage each year. For each division, this might be translated into a specific target for costs as a percentage of sales. The production department of each division might be given a target for the overall costs of a specific production run, which would include the costs of any capacity underutilisation, the costs of down-times, and the costs of wastage due to poor quality levels. Targets for an individual within this department might relate to, for example, the numbers of sub-standard products that are passed incorrectly through an inspection process to be distributed to customers. There is thus a hierarchy of targets (Figure 10.13).

Measuring and monitoring

Target-setting is pointless unless the organisation also lays down procedures for assessing whether the targets are being achieved. In part this is a data-collection problem. McDonald's may set the target of serving every customer within a given period. The procedure for measuring this might be through observation from time to time, or by checking time stamps on till receipts. IT systems, such as bar code readers, can help to measure output in a factory or a supermarket.

Difficulties arise, however, in measuring more intangible activities, such as how well a research or design department is doing – where satisfactory payback or measurable success may be years down the line. Even for more common targets, such as customer satisfaction or market share, the collection of the necessary data can be

Figure 10.13 Hierarchy of targets

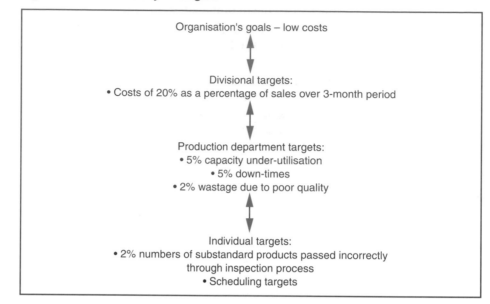

laborious and expensive. The organisation then has to decide whether the gains from knowing how well it is doing outweigh the cost of acquiring that knowledge.

Even once the data have been collected, however, there need to be procedures for using them effectively. Managers need to be able to see easily whether their targets are being met or surpassed. This means that well-designed management information systems are an important part of strategy implementation. Good managers will often supplement the formal systems with informal conversations and regular walks around their office or factory, to see how things are going. People will soon realise that something is important to their firm if it features in large print on the front page of the report that the chief executive writes every month, or if it is the first item on the agenda of every board meeting, or if it is the first thing that the managing director asks them about if they meet in the corridor.

Managers also need to be prepared to take action if a target is not being met. Depending upon the cultural norms in an organisation, this may take the form of a quiet word of encouragement, an offer of help, a formal memo expressing concern or a threat of dismissal. If a target is being surpassed, the appropriate action may be a front-page article in the company newsletter. On the other hand, people will soon realise if no one is really taking any notice of whether they achieve their targets or not, and may stop trying.

Setting the levels of targets

When working out how high or low targets should be set, the norm is to set targets that are 'stretching' – in other words, just beyond what a manager feels comfortable in achieving. For example, the marketing manager in a business unit may feel that he can increase the unit sales by 5% in the next year. His divisional director may propose that he raise his sights and aim for a 15% increase. After a process of negotiation, they may settle on a target that is 10% higher than the previous year's sales.

◀ Single- and double-
loop learning were
introduced in Chapter 7.

Although this kind of target-setting is very common, it has two main drawbacks. One is to do with the kinds of incentives it offers. Small, incremental increases in targets from year to year may move the organisation forward, but only through single-loop learning. They do not motivate people in the organisation to look beyond their existing routines. The senior management team may, however, believe that there is scope for a fundamental change in the way people work, or that the firm has fallen badly behind its competitors. They may be better off signalling this through targets that seem impossibly high – a 100% increase in sales, or a 50% reduction in costs. This kind of target, even if not met in full, can push the organisation towards the kind of radical process innovation that can give competitive advantage.

There can also be situations where it is advantageous to set people easy targets rather than challenging ones. Typically, these situations arise in bureaucratic organisations with a risk-averse culture, in industries like banking and in the public sector. In such organisations, managers may be unused to making entrepreneurial decisions, and feel paralysed, rather than stimulated, by a stretching target. It may therefore be best to give them easy goals at the beginning, and make the targets gradually more challenging as managers become used to making decisions and succeeding.

The second main drawback with setting 'stretching' targets is that managers may be motivated to manipulate the system to avoid being stretched too far. For example, our marketing manager, knowing from past experience that he will be given a target that is 5% higher than his original offer, will simply start the process by offering to match last year's sales. This may be 5% less than he knows he is capable of achieving. More subtly, if he is already close to his current year's target, he may instruct his salesforce to avoid closing orders towards the end of the year. If his target for the following year is to be based upon the current year's performance, he has an incentive not to over-achieve in the current year. That way, his new target will be easier, and he can start the new year by booking the orders that his salesforce had already concluded.

There are ways of combating this kind of behaviour – for example, by offering the salesforce extra commission on orders completed in the final month. However, this kind of agency problem can only be overcome through the kinds of cultural controls we discuss in Section 10.4.6.

Establishing the right combination of targets

Early systems of management by objectives tended to focus upon one or two key performance measures in order to give managers a clear, unambiguous aim. However, agency problems then started to appear, as clever managers found ways of achieving their targets without working too hard in pursuit of the organisation's strategic aims (see Real-Life Application 10.9).

There has therefore been a move away from using single performance measures as managerial targets. Instead, firms have begun using sets of targets that together are intended to make sure that the organisation continues to invest for the long term while sustaining profits in the short term. One technique, the 'balanced score card' (Kaplan and Norton, 1992, 1996) has been developed to help organisations to focus systematically on four sets of factors that are important to their strategic performance:

How to subvert your organisation's strategy and still get promoted

You are the up-and-coming manager of a small subsidiary of a major corporation. Unfortunately, things are not going to plan. You are meeting your sales objectives, but your unit's ROI, on which 50% of your annual bonus depends, is well down on target.

ROI, you will recall, is profit/capital invested in the unit. When the corporation set you an ROI target, it of course intended you to increase your profits – by increasing your sales and cutting out unproductive costs – and to reduce unnecessary investment, like superfluous inventory. But it's too late for all that. The end of the financial year is only three months away and, more important still, you have an interview at the end of this month for the post of general manager of a much larger subsidiary. However, unless you can show that you are on target for the year, your chances of landing that highly paid job are zero.

Happily, there is more than one way of meeting a target. First, you cancel the order for the new computer for the production control department. Of course, it would improve their efficiency hugely, but the capital cost would add to the capital invested in your department, and the depreciation charge would increase your costs, so it would bring your ROI still lower. You contemplate cancelling the order for your financial controller's new company car – but you are going to need his support to get away with this, so you let it through. However, there are plenty of other things that you can trim. The training course for the salesforce, the end of year advertising campaign and the scheduled maintenance on the factory equipment can all be cancelled or postponed. Of course, in six months' time, when sales have dried up and the factory has broken down, the unit will be in turmoil. But, by then, you'll have a new job, and it will be someone else's problem.

- *efficiency* – whose performance can be measured for example through an assessment of production costs and asset utilisation ratios;

- *quality* – which can be assessed through measuring the number of product rejects, and customer assessments of product reliability;

- *innovation* – which can be measured by counting the numbers and sales of new products introduced, and the time and costs of new product development;

- *customer responsiveness* – which can be assessed by means of customer satisfaction surveys, numbers of repeat purchases, market share, and customer service quality.

The balanced score card (Figure 10.14) emphasises the importance of considering a range of factors *simultaneously*. The complexity of modern organisations means that simple, or uni-dimensional, analyses are not enough. However, it is important to focus on those issues which are of central importance to a particular strategic goal and measure the range of factors necessary to achieve this goal.

The drawbacks of output controls

◄ We looked at different types of strategy processes in Chapter 1, and return to these issues again in Chapter 16. ►

The balanced scorecard was set up partly in response to a concern about whether output controls can be linked to an organisation's strategy. Some people also perceived a need to move away from internal performance measures such as return on investment – which tend to be based on incremental improvements on past performance rather than what should happen in the future. In order for organisations to set up a truly strategic set of output controls, they must be able to make their strategy explicit and identify clear measures that will help employees to achieve it. Goold and Quinn (1990) questioned whether many firms are ever able to do this, and of course this is also dependent on a view of strategy as planned and rational

Figure 10.14   An example of a balanced scorecard model

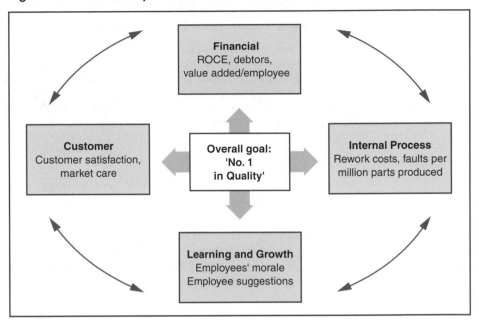

rather than emergent or political. Most managers like to focus on short-term measures of performance, which are easier to achieve and lead to bonuses for the managers concerned. In contrast, strategic performance measures need to be 'softer' and more subjective. They must assess competitive strength and market positioning and look at unit performance over the long term in the light of changing circumstances. As Goold and Quinn suggested, strategic controls need to take account of uncertainty in the business environment and the need for flexibility and creativity when developing strategy. They also need to be able to integrate the different functional level goals to achieve a co-ordinated outcome – hard to do when one function's targets may directly contradict another's.

Furthermore, output controls will always encounter sharp-witted managers who may feel, almost as a matter of honour, that they have to find a way around them. Making the controls more sophisticated may simply increase the time that is spent in trying to outwit them. This is why Ghoshal and Bartlett's (1998) individualised corporations (see Section 10.3.6 above), for example, have strong cultural controls alongside their performance targets and their state-of-the-art management information systems. It is the cultural control that prevents managers wasting their time and energy in trying to subvert the system.

10.4.5 Bureaucratic control

In addition to targets which many employees are set, organisations are full of procedures which specify, either formally and in writing or informally and through word of mouth, what an individual employee should do if and when a particular type of situation is encountered (Real-Life Application 10.10). The notion of an organisation as a collection of bureaucratic procedures is due to the work of Max Weber (e.g. Weber, 1947, 1958), who was an extremely influential German writer of the post-war years.

REAL-LIFE APPLICATION 10.10

Bureaucratic control systems in Asea Brown Boveri

Asea Brown Boveri (ABB) is one of Scandinavia's biggest and most successful companies. It operates across the world and has over 1,300 subsidiaries or related companies. Its former chief executive, Percy Barnevik, believed that the more clearly the company communicates expectations, the more free employees can be. The company as a 'policy bible' which presents clearly and precisely what practices are expected from its employees, and what the company's official policies are. It also details the company's values, thereby combining some elements of a cultural control system (see below) with a bureaucratic one.

One example of bureaucratic control systems might be a typed note issued by the personnel director to all staff detailing the appraisal process to be carried out within the organisation – specifying by whom it is to be done, on whom, when, and containing what activities. Another might be an employee's job specification – saying where their place of work is, now and potentially in the future, their salary and elements of the job they are expected to do. Yet another example is the specification of activities to be carried out in order to manufacture a particular product.

Some routines may be established by custom and practice – so that although procedures are not formally laid down in writing, all employees and their managers know what is being done, and tacitly accept, and even perhaps encourage it. As bureaucratic control which is too tight and formalised can act to stifle employee involvement and motivation, this is often a way of getting around the 'red-tape' that can develop.

Almost all organisations have some degree of bureaucratic control. The greater the stability of the organisation's operating environment and the predictability of its products' sales and development, the more formal and detailed its bureaucratic procedures are likely to be. Bureaucratic procedures are particularly appropriate for products which require standardisation and cost minimisation. When highly innovative products are being developed, in contrast, formally laid down procedures are less appropriate. The development of such products is unpredictable, their sales are erratic, and the problems met along the way are likely to be both numerous and not encountered before. In this situation, other types of control become more important. One of the most important is our next category, cultural control.

10.4.6 Cultural control: socialisation and indoctrination

A major part of cultural control is peer group pressure. A lot of our behaviour is not what we would do if we were on our own, but is shaped by how we think that others expect us to behave. We know this is what they expect, because they tell us directly, or because we see them behaving in this way themselves or expressing opinions to other people. In the same way as we tend to accept the authority of others, we are prepared to modify our behaviour to accommodate the wishes of others. We sacrifice our independence to gain acceptance into a group. And an organisation is a group.

However, we do not accept this control from just anybody. Most of us are quite selective about who we will oblige. If organisations were full of only disobliging people, then anarchy would reign and very little would be achieved. So firms spend a lot of time and money trying to recruit like-minded people, who will get on with one another. People tend to be particularly like-minded when they share similar values and when they work in the same types of jobs and share similar experiences – people who work in the same functions in other words. As we have already suggested in Section 10.1.3 above, this can lead to conflict in multi-functional organisations, simply because the cultural norms and expectations in each group are so different. The types of peer group pressure exercised in each function are likely to be quite different from one another, so to use our favourite example, accountants are likely to exert pressure to be systematic, tidy, formal in appearance and behaviour. Designers, on the other hand, may be pressured to look slightly less conventional, and to be more eccentric in behaviour and speech – to show their creative credentials.

Organisations as a whole have to make these different groups co-operate, and so, although each function is likely to retain its own cultural norms, these will sit within an overall organisational culture which will also govern an individual's behaviour. This is achieved not only by recruiting suitable people, who are attracted to the organisation because of what they perceive it stands for, but also through training and socalisation. By these means, expectations of what the organisation is 'about' can be communicated to newcomers, who will hear 'stories' which often illustrate desirable activities, observe the behaviours of their more established colleagues, and listen to their views of what is expected. Newcomers who find that they do not fit in, leave. Those that remain can then extrapolate from historical examples and make assumptions about what they should do in other situations they come upon, even if these are not precisely identical to the ones they have already encountered. As a result, cultural control is particularly effective in environments which are uncertain, fast-changing or unstable.

Family-run businesses, or those which have a family-like ethos, have particularly strong cultural control systems. Ouchi (1978, 1981) call them 'clan' firms and Mintzberg (1979) 'missionary' organisations. These types of organisation develop over time and are shaped by long-term employment, lengthy and comprehensive selection and employee evaluation processes, and strong socalisation practices such as training programmes and family-centred social events. They provide as a result an extremely strong shaper of behaviour, often dominated by the owner/founder even after they themselves have left, and are hugely resistant to change or deviant views. However, given the right environmental circumstances they can be very effective because of the bonds and strength of understanding between members. Problems might arise, however, if this environment changes.

Self-control and self-motivation

A subset of cultural control is self-control. If an organisation recruits the 'right' sort of people, it may expect that they will undertake their work willingly, without direction or supervision, and without requiring very much from the owners or directors except fair play and a reasonable salary. As a result of the need to find such individuals, because of the high knowledge content of their work perhaps, some firms spend huge amounts of resources on recruitment and selection, and then on tying people to the firm with incentives such as 'golden handcuffs'.

Many people are intrinsically motivated by the work itself, and can be 'empow-

413

ered' or relied on to take decisions which will benefit themselves and their employing organisation as a whole. Academics working in universities are often driven, not by status or high levels of pay, but by the intrinsic enjoyment of the work. People who work in a matrix organisation may have to be self-motivated, because of the lack of clarity of authority and because decisions are made without recourse to higher powers. However both these situations require employees to have a pretty strong notion of what it is the organisation is about – and what, therefore, it is that they should be doing.

10.4.7 Reward systems and sanctions

Finally we look at what perhaps many of you thought before you read this section was the only way that people were controlled – being paid, and being sacked if they did not do what they were supposed to. Both of these activities – the carrot and the stick if you like – are still very important, and probably almost universal, aspects of an organisation's control systems. The stick – the threat of dismissal – is still the ultimate deterrent, and is an extremely effective shaper of behaviour. The carrot can be tailored to encourage particular behaviours – behaviours that will, managers hope, ultimately result in the chosen strategy being implemented.

However, there have been some interesting developments in these over recent years, particularly in reward systems. Not that long ago, many employees had to 'clock-in' when they arrived at work in the morning and 'clock-out' when they left in the evening (or whatever time of day it was). No-one thought to ask what they were doing during their time at work. They were paid simply for being there, and if they needed to be there for longer, they were paid more – overtime. More recently managers have started to think that perhaps what an employee *produces* during the working day is more important, and reward systems started to address actual performance. Schemes such as performance-related pay (PRP) relate wages to actual output – measured through performance targets as suggested above. Such rewards can be tailored according to what output is desired. A firm pursuing an entrepreneurial strategy and dependent on a stream of innovative products would reward people for the number and quality of new ideas they produce, as 3M does. A firm pursuing a low price strategy will want to reward people for behaving in ways which reduce costs.

Clearly there are benefits to a strategic performance-related reward system, but there are problems too. Not that long ago sales staff were paid large bonuses, according to how many products they sold. This incentivised them, and probably made sure that turnover went up. However, sales staff can only sell the products if they are of good quality, provided in the right location, and supported by all the necessary back-up which functions such as personnel provide. But the people providing these other, equally essential, contributions were not receiving the same level of bonuses.

So there has been a move to group-based bonuses, which reward everyone for what is usually a team effort. These bonuses can be at an organisation-wide level or more localised. They can take different forms, such as a percentage of salary or share options, which are more often given to people at managerial level and which attempt to align what they do with the needs of shareholders. However, even bonuses have problems if they are team-based. If you are like our students, you will have been assessed as part of a group on occasion. This can be the source of con-

THEORETICAL PERSPECTIVE 10.4

Strategic reward systems

Source: Adapted from Lawler (1998).

Strategic reward systems have to aid the implementation of an organisation's strategy and fit with its structure and processes. To be effective these must be congruent or coherent. The reward system drives the behaviours that will achieve the organisation's strategy.

The pay schemes that are on offer influence who comes to work for an organisation. Predictably those that give the most rewards tend to get and retain the best people – and some degree of comparison with other companies is necessary to establish relative benchmarks. The type of reward also influences recruitment. High levels of risk compensation attract different types of people than those that emphasise security. The reward systems therefore need to be contingent on the desired strategic outcomes. Organisations can target the types of employees they want.

Firms can also strategically target the types of behaviour and learning they want from their staff, and targeted to achieve the development of key capabilities. High pay rates can create the sense that the organisation is elite, thus creating a self-fulfilling prophecy. Rewards can be offered differentially even within the same firm – although this has the potential to create conflict, divisiveness, and accusations of unfairness.

Traditional pay systems are geared to the job – the job is assessed and individuals paid if they fulfil the job. More recently some firms have experimented with skills-based pay. The employees are rewarded according to their abilities. In this case, people are rewarded for developing and increasing their competences, rather than moving up the hierarchy. This practice can result in a highly skilled workforce as well as create a climate of self-development and improvement. Typically this type of system has resulted in a flexible multi-tasking workforce and higher levels of employee commitment and involvement, and high levels of customer satisfaction. Skill-based pay tends to produce higher pay costs, but this is offset by greater flexibility (but paradoxically leading to reduced personnel costs as a result of lower staffing levels and reduced absenteeism and staff turnover rates).

Decisions can be taken as to whether reward systems are decentralised (left to the discretion of local managers) or centralised (set by the corporate head office). Decentralised schemes allow for local circumstances to be responded to. In a multi-business corporation, different pay schemes are appropriate because of the different business segments, products and ages of the companies within the portfolio.

Decisions can also relate to whether pay is hierarchical or egalitarian and meritocratic. Hierarchical systems are appropriate in situations where there is top-down authority, and a strong motivation for people to move up the organisational ladder. Meritocratic systems are supportive of teamwork and lateral integration. These systems are more appropriate in situations with a participative management style, and where technical expertise is a critical success factor such as knowledge-based and high-tech industries.

Objective measures of performance tend to be better motivators – because they are seen to be achievable and are transparently fair. More subjective assessments are more problematic – *because* they are subjective. However, these are sometimes the most important strategically, and therefore group based rewards are often the most helpful, because they are more able to be tied to overall business performance. However, individual performance is often hard to assess and behaviours still need to be specified and encouraged.

siderable resentment if you are in a group which is 'carrying' someone who is not pulling his or her weight. The same is true in organisations.

Theoretical Perspective 10.4 gives a concise view of some of the issues to do with reward systems and strategy.

Finally, we will just mention one type of reward – perks – which are often part of the formal system of payment within an organisation, but which also have important symbolic and cultural implications. They can be an important means of making someone feel valued, and thereby encourage extraordinary performance. These include high-status cars, trips abroad, or company expense accounts.

10.5 Trade-offs and paradoxes in organisational structures, control and reward systems

From the discussion above it should be clear that there is no one structure or set of control systems that is likely to be appropriate for all situations or strategies. In most cases managers have to strike a balance between a wide variety of conflicting demands, and reconcile many apparently irreconcilable problems. The increasing complexity and internationalisation of today's business world have just increased the number of factors competing for managers' attention. There are arguments for centralisation but also arguments for local autonomy of decision-making. Organisations have to make trade-offs between the desire to control and the need for individual flair. There are also arguments in favour of products and internal processes being uniform, and opposing arguments for their being diverse and locally customised.

If a company has a structure that allows it to minimise costs through experience effects and scale economies, it simultaneously loses the ability to customise products for customers' local needs. If the same organisation allows its staff complete autonomy of decision-making, then it risks losing any sense of organisational identity and product coherence. A devolved network structure allows the organisations at the periphery to concentrate on becoming specialists at what they do best, but this can act to prevent the necessary competences transferring to other parts of the wider organisation. If a firm satisfies one group of customers for a nominal amount of resources it is not likely to be able to satisfy another group at the same time without using additional resources. These all involve the making of choices, and trade-offs.

Similarly, trade-offs need to be made in the design of control systems. If a firm puts in place elaborate systems of output controls or bureaucratic controls, it achieves clarity. However it sacrifices flexibility – control systems like this take time to redesign, and the people who are used to them may be slow to adjust to changes. Elaborate systems will slow down a firm's responsiveness, if they require managers to seek authorisation from higher up the organisation rather than making a decision themselves. And the information needed by output control systems takes time for managers to gather and input, and time for other managers to read and interpret. Staff must have enough information to do their jobs effectively, but should not be distracted by or overloaded with unnecessary information.

By using cultural controls, organisations can improve their responsiveness and reduce their agency costs. Strongly motivated people who believe in the organisation's mission do not require expensive hierarchies of supervisors, and are less likely to indulge in behaviour that harms the firm. On the other hand, if they do make an error, or fall out of love with their employer, then the lack of supervision will increase the amount of damage that they can do. The 'rogue traders' whose illicit dealings cost Barings bank and Sumitomo Corporation hundreds of millions of dollars were highly motivated individuals. Organisations that rely on cultural controls are thus placing a lot of trust in their ability to recruit the right people.

This provides you with some choices to make when carrying out your analyses of organisations. Your task is to weigh up the pros and cons for a particular structure or control system, put this analysis into a context of what the organisation already does, what its competitors do, and what the environment is like and will be in the future. On the basis of this analysis you can make a *reasoned* assessment of the advantages of one structure and control system over another.

10.6 Summary

This chapter has looked at how organisations are organised, and what structural factors and control systems are important in particular strategic or environmental contexts.

We looked first at some of the key problems in the structuring of organisations, such as:

- uniformity and diversity
- centralisation and decentralisiation
- the height of the hierarchy, and in relation to this
- the influence of technology on a manager's span of control.

We also looked at how organisations achieve a co-ordinated outcome and co-operation, given that they are often divided into different specialist functions.

We then described some common types of organisational configurations and discussed the types of strategies and contexts in which they might be effective. These structures include:

- functional
- multi-divisional
- matrix and
- networks.

We then looked at some of the ways in which strategy is controlled within firms, both by the activities of personnel inside the organisation and by factors external to it. These include hierarchical, cultural, bureaucratic, and output types of control, in addition to the use of different types of reward systems.

Typical questions

We conclude this chapter with a sample of some of the questions you may be asked about organisational structure and strategic control systems, and show how you can use the theory described in this chapter to answer them.

1. *What might influence an organisation's choice of structure?*

   This question relates to almost all of Section 10.1. In particular you would need to consider internal factors such as the size of the organisation, its purpose or legal status, its strategy – for example whether it is focused on a small number of products and customers, or on a wider range of diverse activities, who owns or controls it, and also how much it is dependent on specialist expertise. If it is, then you would need to consider how the different types of specialist are going to be brought together in order to achieve a common outcome.

   You would also need to consider external factors, such as the dynamism or complexity of its operating environment, and also perhaps think about broadening your discussion to include the industry's life-cycle stage which we talked about in Chapter 5 – the number and strength of competitors might influence the location and available configurations of the firm itself.

2. *Suggest how an organisation can be configured to implement a multi-domestic strategy.*

In your answer to this question it would be nice to see a diagram! This might map the range of countries the firm is in, an assessment of the environment and strategy adopted in each – they may not be the same – and the types of organisational structure which might be appropriate at this local level. You may need to revisit Chapter 6 to think about the different types of international product-market strategies and their characteristics.

A multi-domestic strategy almost by definition implies a multi-divisional structure, but there may be some elements of the overall organisation, head office functions, for example, which might be located at some central point. You would therefore need to consider the ways in which communication and decision-making would flow between the head office and the various geographical locations, and even whether there would be any communication between the local divisions.

3. *You are the managing director of an entrepreneurial firm in the computer software industry. What types of strategic control system would you implement?*

This question requires an evaluation of the issues we discussed in Section 10.7. You need to identify the characteristics of the computer industry – it is dynamic and also complex. Critical success factors within this industry are innovativeness, and high levels of technical sophistication. Both factors require highly specialised skills and creative, competent and self-motivated staff.

You might wish to evaluate the different types of internal control systems (the external ones are outside your control, and so less relevant for this particular question), and prioritise the ones which you **have** to get right and those which are less important. Cultural control is likely to be particularly important, as are remuneration systems which reward creativity and technical expertise. You might also like to speculate as to how marketable such individuals are, and talk about strategies for tying them in to your particular company – like paying them large bonuses and setting up incentives for long service.

Questions for discussion

1. Why is it likely that a successful firm will have a structure similar to other successful firms in the same industry?

2. What might be some disadvantages of relying principally on cultural control to implement strategy?

3. 'The matrix structure is the only feasible way of organising for innovation in today's fragmented and turbulent world.' Discuss.

4. Describe and evaluate the relative benefits of 'carrot' versus 'stick' types of control systems.

5. How might some of the differences of opinion which develop between functions in an organisation be minimised, or made useful?

The restructuring of Sony in April 1999

Based on Sony's 1999 annual report, found at http://www.world.sony.com/, the company's own press releases, and numerous press articles.

The background to the restructuring

Sony is a Japanese-based international conglomerate which is engaged in the 'development, design, manufacture, and sale of various kinds of electronic equipment, instruments, and devices for consumer and industrial markets'. Sony's principal manufacturing facilities for these goods are located in Japan, the USA, Europe and Asia, and its products are marketed by subsidiaries and local distributors throughout the world. Sony also makes game consoles and software, recorded music, in a variety of genres and in a number of different formats, and image-based software, such as film, video and television. It has interests in satellite distribution, and some Internet-related businesses. It also has an insurance subsidiary, a leasing and credit card business, and a few other divisions such as a subsidiary which develops entertainment complexes. In 1999 it embarked on a major restructuring.

One of the major factors driving the restructuring appears to have been changes in Sony's technological environment. Of a number of relevant issues, one of the most important was digitisation. This had two related effects. Digitisation meant changes to the nature of many of Sony's electronic products, but it also changed their networking capability and therefore the potential distribution channels through which these products could be sold.

Many of Sony's divisions were increasingly involved in digital processes of one sort or another; digital camcorders increased to 60% of sales (compared to approximately 56% in the previous year); Sony's Pictures Entertainment division had digital production capabilities, and was moving towards producing films in DVD format; and some television models featured Sony's own new proprietary digital technology which created higher quality images from standard TV signals. In the future it was intended that much more would be made of the potential cross-linkages between the various digitised products and their technologies.

Products such as digital camcorders, MiniDisc systems, PCs, and Wega colour TVs had already incorporated network technologies from different parts of the organisation. For example, Sony's digital camcorder used the Memory Stick recording medium, and had facilities which allowed still images to be transferred to a PC. One MiniDisc model could be used to download music from a new satellite-delivered digital music distribution service in Japan. Some of Sony's notebook PCs had built-in miniature CCD video cameras which allowed users to capture moving or still images and store them in a computer.

However, despite these developments Sony had a difficult year in 1999. It anticipated that these economic difficulties would continue, particularly in certain locations, for example Russia, Eastern Europe and Latin America. Competition was also intensifying because a number of new competitors with new technologies entered their markets. It anticipated that its 1999 earnings would decline substantially as a result of these factors but also as a result of its investments in digitisation, networking, and the expansion of its alliance strategy to acquire new technology. Despite this, Sony planned to increase research and development expenses and had entered into a number of new strategic alliances. Partners included Fujitsu, Toshiba, Philips Electronics, Sharp Corporation Candescent Technologies, and Toyoda Automatic Loom Works.

In order to achieve growth given these circumstances, senior managers believed that they had to accelerate the pace of change within Sony and on 9 March 1999 Sony announced the changes in its group structure which would allow it to build 'new business models' appropriate for what it described as a network-centric era. Sony contrasted what they termed their new 'unified dispersed' model with their previous hierarchical or centralised business model.

CASE STUDY *continued*

The reorganisation had a number of explicit objectives:

- to maximise shareholder value;
- to enhance the company's research and development activities;
- to achieve quicker decision-making and execution in a 'rapidly changing environment' where the life-cycle of products is becoming shorter;
- to streamline its manufacturing systems.

Sony also delegated increased authority to its newly reformed business units comprising Electronics, Home Network, Digital Network Solutions, and Music Games and Pictures divisions. At the same time it 'strengthened' its group management governance structure. This separated the functions of the Board, which was to make decisions and supervise, and the Management Committee, which was to carry out day-to-day management. Sony claimed that the reorganisation clarified the Board's role as a supervisor and would improve its monitoring ability.

The new structure

From April 1999 Sony Corporation's new head office was to be divided into two functions: the group HQ, whose size was to be kept 'to a minimum', and business unit support services such as accounting, human resources and general affairs. This would allow them to compete autonomously in the open market, with a view that Sony Corporation may become a holding company in the future. For example, personnel from the corporate Human Resources division were to transfer to a newly established subsidiary company, Sony Human Capital, Inc. Some of the previously centralised support functions were to be transferred to the business units. Part of the intended function of the new head office structure was that it should be able to reorganise business units and reallocate management resources 'speedily and dynamically'.

The top managers of each business unit were to become members of the headquarters' Management Committee, 'in order to promote closer mutual ties among business units'. At the same time Sony Music Entertainment (Japan) Inc., Sony Chemicals Corporation, and Sony Precision Technology Inc. were to be brought in as 100% owned subsidiaries. The companies were previously about 70% owned and were independently listed on the Tokyo stock market. Sony planned to acquire these companies through the issue of approximately 33 million new shares.

The group's goal of creating shareholder value, and desire to achieve what it termed Value Creation Management, led Sony to introduce a new system for evaluating performance. This was to be based on the cost of capital and calculated by deducting the cost of equity and debt from after-tax operating income. Shareholder value goals for all business units were to be set by the group headquarters, but the intention was to allow each unit to design and implement their own strategies. Compensation was to be linked to these goals. The head office's role was to allocate resources speedily, and take on the role of 'active investor'.

The restructuring was also attempting to develop new marketing methods in order to deal with the increase of digital-based distribution channels. For example, in the USA, Sony sold many of its computer hardware products through its Internet web sites, some of which allow customers to configure their order – specifying their choice of CPU, memory, and hard disk drive capacity.

Digital networks were also changing the production and supply systems of Sony's manufacturing capabilities. As a result Sony reorganised its operations in Mexico, in Eastern Europe, Malaysia, and Indonesia and planned to consolidate its 70 manufacturing facilities into approximately 55 by the end of March 2003. It also planned to reduce the company's headcount by about 10%, and retrain many employees in digital technologies by the same period.

At the same time the restructuring allowed Sony to review its processes, from product development, design, procurement, and production through to logistics and sales. The objectives of this re-engineering were to reduce inventory and the times taken to move products from manufacturing to sale, as well as to improve the speed of decision-making.

The business areas

The electronics business

The restructuring mainly affected the company's major business area – the Electronics Business. Prior to April 1999 the Electronics Business comprised a number of divisions:

- **Audio** – MiniDisc systems, CD players, personal stereos, tape recorders, radios, headphones, car audio, professional-use audio equipment, and audio-tapes.

- **Video** – VCRs, DVD video players, digital still cameras, broadcast and professional-use video equipment, and videotapes.

- **Televisions** – TVs, flat display panels, personal LCD monitors, and professional-use monitors/ projectors.

- **Information and communications** – personal computers, computer peripherals, satellite broadcasting systems, cell phones, telephones, and car navigation systems.

- **Electronic components and other** – semiconductors, LCDs, electronic components, optical pickups, and batteries.

From April 1999, the Electronics Business was consolidated into three main SBUs, although it was regarded as a 'single business segment' by Sony's senior managers: the Home Network Company, the Personal IT Network Company, and the Core Technology & Network Company. Research and development laboratories and support functions were transferred from the group headquarters to the three divisions. This reorganisation aimed to delegate increased authority to these SBUs, in order to increase the speed of decision making, while at the same time 'adding more value to products and enhancing the efficiency of the production system'. Each Network Company was expected to focus on fostering growth in new business areas, as well as reallocating resources to existing businesses with the highest value-adding potential. As appropriate, the Network Companies were to be allowed to operate independently or jointly create new ventures. It was believed that these actions would enable Sony to deepen co-operation among its businesses, maximise the merits of working together, and implement group-wide strategies more quickly.

The **Home Network** division's remit was 'to establish a business model centred on digital televisions for the network-centric era' based around television, video, and audio products and high-capacity optical disk recorders, as well as focusing on the creation of home networks using digital television technology.

The **Personal IT Network** division makes phones, personal computers, and digital imaging products. Its remit was to 'create new businesses by converging telecommunications products, IT and personal AV technologies'. Its focus was on strengthening existing products such as digital camcorders and VAIO home-use PCs, as well as creating 'totally new forms of enjoyment in the network-centric era' by merging audio-visual technologies with computers and with telecommunications and network technologies.

The **Core Technology & Network** division comprises semiconductors, storage media, circuit boards and similar products. This division supplies Sony's other businesses as well as external customers with the key components for digital audio-visual products. Its objectives were to 'enhance shareholder value as an independent business unit handling recording media and devices, and by collaborating with other business units'.

The music, games and pictures businesses

In addition to the electronics business, Sony has large games, recorded music and film divisions. These divisions were left relatively untouched in the restructuring, although all are equally subject to digital technologies in the way that they make and deliver their products. The computer games division, Sony Computer Entertainment, Inc., however, was to be positioned in future as the fourth 'pillar' of the electronics business alongside the three network companies.

The challenges Sony faced in these divisions were: intensifying competition world wide; the emergence of digital distribution channels such as the Internet; the increasing convergence of media (films, TV, videos and music); the corresponding

CASE STUDY *continued*

increase in mega global media companies such as Time Warner and Bertelsmann, and the consolidation of the recorded music industry (see also end of book case studies, The European Recorded Music Industry and Bertelsmann AG).

Sony's president Nobuyuki Idei was upbeat about Sony's unique strengths in both electronics and entertainment and the Company's ability to capitalise on changes in its environment. Similarly the head of Sony's international music division highlighted the opportunities presented by the digital era:

> The advent of internet technologies presents us with new ways to extend the impact of our artists, while digital distribution will provide us with enhanced means of reaching consumers. As new lifestyles, businesses, and forms of entertainment emerge, SMEI's global resources, infrastructure, and talent position us to take advantage of these opportunities and play a key role in redefining the future of our business.

The Digital Network Solutions division and Group R&D

From 1999 Sony also created a separate division, Digital Network Solutions, which was to be managed directly by the group headquarters. Its focus was to build new network-related business platforms that directly link Sony with its customers, to create value-added services and nurture new businesses. The division's brief was not only to develop network services for the distribution of digital content, such as music and movies, but also insurance and financial services. The division includes Sony Communication Network Corporation which operates So-net, which has grown into one of Japan's largest Internet service providers since starting operations in January 1996.

Strategic R&D relating to the entire Sony Group and the development of key new technologies was to be carried out in six corporate laboratories which were to report directly to headquarters:

1. The Research Center, which researches electronic materials technologies and basic devices from a medium- to long-term view.
2. The Product Development Laboratory, which focuses on next-generation business systems and products.
3. The Architecture Laboratory, which develops software and hardware architectures for information and networkable products.
4. The Media Processing Laboratory, where system LSI (large-scale integration) and signal-processing technologies are developed for an array of hardware.
5. The Systems Solutions Laboratory, which works on basic technologies related to the Internet and Sony's computer business.
6. The D21 Laboratory, which pursues long-term R&D themes based on visions of the twenty-first century.

In the new structure research projects that need to be commercialised quickly are to be transferred to the business unit level. Research areas that involve long-term products or business domains 'best supervised by the group headquarters' would remain at the corporate level.

Financial data

All figures are million yen unless otherwise stated (¥1205US$1 as at 31 March 1999)

Group	1995	1996	1997	1998	1999
Sales/operating revenue	3,990,583	4,592,565	5,663,134	6,755,490	6,794,619
Operating income (loss)	(166,640)	235,324	370,330	520,210	338,649
Net income (loss)	(293,356)	54,252	139,460	222,068	179,004
Capital expenditures (additions to fixed assets)	250,678	251,197	298,078	387,955	353,730
R&D expenses	239,164	257,326	282,569	318,044	375,314

At year end

Net working capital	537,733	816,361	843,500	1,151,152	1,126,848
Stockholders' equity	1,007,802	1,169,147	1,459,332	1,815,555	1,823,665
Stockholders' equity per share	2,695.31	3,125.53	3,798.62	4,461.39	4,448.69
Total assets	4,223,914	5,045,699	5,680,246	6,403,043	6,299,053

Sales by business segment	1995	1996	1997	1998	1999
Electronics	3,027,434	3,283,234	3,930,292	4,377,346	4,355,001
	75.9%	71.5%	69.4%	64.8%	64.1%
Game	35,449	200,894	408,335	699,574	760,071
	0.9%	4.4%	7.2%	10.4%	11.2%
Music	481,021	506,455	570,119	660,407	718,878
	12.0%	11.0%	10.1%	9.8%	10.6%
Pictures	281,677	317,382	438,551	642,714	540,109
				(13 months)	
	7.1%	6.9%	7.7%	9.5%	7.9%
Insurance	112,831	206,802	227,920	291,061	339,368
	2.8%	4.5%	4.0%	4.3%	5.0%
Other	52,171	77,798	87,917	84,388	81,192
	1.3%	1.7%	1.6%	1.2%	1.2%
Consolidated total	3,990,583	4,592,565	5,663,134	6,755,490	6,794,619

Electronics business' sales by product category

Audio	900,180	900,400	1,029,961	1,127,788	1,072,621
	29.7%	27.4%	26.2%	25.8%	24.6%
Video	685,802	731,097	816,582	870,854	969,129
	22.6%	22.3%	20.8%	19.9%	22.3%
Televisions	544,255	554,023	704,075	709,043	702,620
	18.0%	16.9%	17.9%	16.2%	16.1%
Information and communications	413,445	540,719	764,512	894,810	914,140
	13.7%	16.5%	19.4%	20.4%	21.0%
Electronic components and other	483,752	556,995	615,162	774,851	696,491
	16.0%	16.9%	15.7%	17.7%	16.0%
Total	3,027,434	3,283,234	3,930,292	4,377,346	4,355,001

Electronics business' sales by geographic segment

Japan	1,105,152	1,379,804	1,590,820	1,843,149	1,908,600
	27.7%	30.0%	28.1%	27.3%	28.1%
USA	1,152,081	1,259,926	1,639,334	2,101,907	2,157,061
	28.9%	27.4%	29.0%	31.1%	31.8%
Europe	905,416	1,054,010	1,304,491	1,567,121	1,666,714
	22.7%	23.0%	23.0%	23.2%	24.5%
Other Areas	827,934	898,825	1,128,489	1,243,313	1,062,244
	20.7%	19.6%	19.9%	18.4%	15.6%
Consolidated total	3,990,583	4,592,565	5,663,134	6,755,490	6,794,619

CASE STUDY *continued*

Case study questions

1. Why has Sony restructured?

2. What behaviour is Sony trying to encourage through its new performance evaluation system?

3. Are the new structures and systems going to achieve Sony's objectives for them? What problems might Sony encounter?

4. Draw a map of Sony's new structure with likely channels of communication between the different divisions.

NOTES

1. Writers who have worked in a contingencies tradition include: Greenwood and Hinings (1988), Saunders (1990), Guthrie and Olian (1991), Miles and Snow (1978), Zahra and Pearce (1990), Gupta (1984), Ranson et al. (1980), Hickson et al. (1971).

2. For example, by Child (1972) and Clegg and Dunkerley (1980).

3. See, for example, Mintzberg (1979) and also the writers from the influential Aston Group who wrote about the relationship between context and structure in the 1960s and 1970s, for example Pugh and Hickson (1976), Pugh et al. (1969).

4. See, for example, Stalk (1988).

5. See the Aston studies as above.

6. See Lawrence and Lorsch (1967), Pugh et al. (1963, 1968, 1969), Child (1973, 1997), Miles and Snow (1978) and Miller (1987). See also the special issue of the *Academy of Management Journal*, 36 (6), 1994.

7. For a view of how US managers routinely manipulate their profit figures, and enhance their share prices, see *The Economist*, 11 September 1999.

PART 3

From strategic analysis to strategy formulation

Up to this point, we have been focusing upon the techniques of strategic analysis. We have seen how to analyse developments in the organisation's environment. We have learned ways of analysing the organisation's strategies in response to its environment, and the outcomes of those strategies – the resources, culture and architecture it has developed over time. All of these have given us answers to different aspects of two main questions:

- *Why has the organisation succeeded or failed in the past?* (Chapter 4 showed how to measure the extent of that success or failure.)

- *To what extent is the organisation's competitive position sustainable for the future?*

These are interesting questions (at least, we think so) but they are rather abstract and theoretical. A practising manager – you, in your next job – needs to be able to move beyond them to answer a third question:

- *Given what we know about what the organisation has accomplished up to now, and about the way the environment is likely to develop – what should the organisation do?*

In this part of the book, we start to develop our analysis of the organisation's environment, competitive stance, value chain, culture and architecture into practical proposals for its strategy in the future.

In Parts 1 and 2 we have placed great emphasis on the need for logic and rigour in strategic analysis. These are still important for the last two parts of the book, where we shall be placing a lot of emphasis on matching future strategies to the *particular* challenges that a company is facing, and of assessing which of those challenges has the highest priority. For Parts 3 and 4, another intellectual attribute becomes important – creativity. Good strategies are rarely obvious – if they were, then everyone would implement them, and they have no value, for competitive advantage is all about being distinctive.

You therefore need to be on your guard against jumping to conclusions – what is sometimes called *convergent thinking*. It is easy to fall into the trap of fixing on the first plausible strategy that comes to mind, without pausing to consider its drawbacks, or to see if there are any better, less obvious alternatives. Good strategic thinking is *divergent*, and involves looking carefully, and creatively, at *alternative* ways of responding to particular strategic challenges.

After reading this part of the book, you should be able to:

- identify the strategic issues that are confronting an organisation, and assess which of them has the highest priority;
- develop a number of alternative strategies to tackle those issues, taking account of:
  - the organisation's present competitive position
  - the context in which the organisation is operating – its sector (private, public or not-for-profit) and the stage of the industry in its lifecycle;
- assess which of those alternative strategies is the most appropriate.

Strategic priorities and strategic options

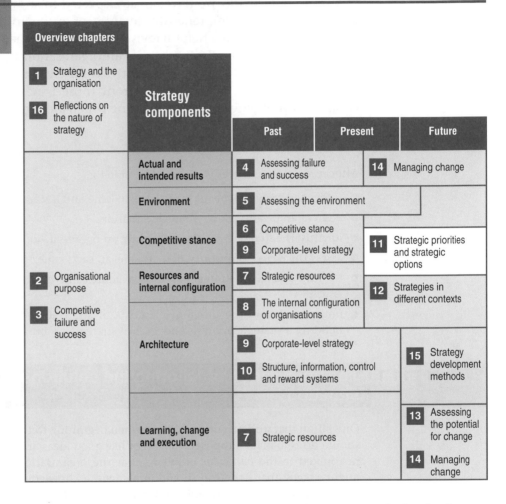

In this chapter, we take the first steps in converting analysis of what an organisation has been doing right or wrong into practical proposals for the future. In our experience, students can find this step quite a challenge, so this chapter contains a large number of practical examples to illustrate the real life strategic issues and dilemmas that confront the managers of both successful and unsuccessful organisations. We make extensive reference to firms like Sony, McDonald's, British Airways and Benetton, whose strategies have been looked at in some depth in earlier chapters.

The examples are intended to illustrate the depth and level of detail you might be expected to provide in your own analysis and proposals. We aim to show you how, by looking at companies from a number of angles and using detailed analysis of quantitative and qualitative data, you can build a coherent set of strategic proposals.

When it comes to identifying what are the issues – problems, challenges, opportunities, threats – we make extensive use of the material covered in Parts 1 and 2. In the first sections of this chapter, we use the theory and analytical frameworks we have already covered to show how they can fit together to give a comprehensive analysis of an organisation's situation. They may also serve as a helpful revision exercise. We then move on to look at how to use that analysis to assess an organisation's priorities – which issues it needs to address most urgently. We then suggest how to develop alternative strategic options to confront those issues, and conclude the chapter with a framework for evaluating which are the best options.

Learning objectives

After reading the chapter you should be able to:

- understand what is meant by a strategic issue and a strategic option;
- analyse an organisation's strategic situation;
- identify the strategic issues confronting an organisation;
- assess the degree of priority that attaches to each issue;
- identify a range of strategic options to address the most important strategic issues;
- understand how the different elements of strategic theory fit together in building a strategic analysis and a set of strategic proposals.

11.1 The importance of tailoring the solutions to the situation

One pitfall that students often fall into when beginning to think about what a firm should do is to make proposals that seem like good ideas at first sight, but that are not linked to the *particular* problems that the organisation is confronting. You might suggest that Benetton should implement a knowledge management system (to take a currently fashionable example), or embark on a series of acquisitions.[1] The problem with such suggestions is not necessarily that they are 'wrong', in the sense that they would do the organisation more harm than good. However, a good strategic analysis would need to point out *precisely* why a knowledge management programme was a *better* solution to the *specific* challenges that the company was facing that the possible *alternatives*.

This is because Benetton, like almost all other organisations, faces resource constraints. Although it is not a poor company, it does not have enough cash to pursue every available market opportunity and, at the same time, solve all its current operational problems, and fund research into every bright idea that staff or consultants bring forward. Management attention is also in limited supply, even though Benetton has many able managers, and the money and prestige to attract more.

The firm cannot give proper attention to every single problem and possibility; it can only hope to pursue a limited number of strategies with any success, so it needs to *prioritise*.

Anyone carrying out this type of analysis needs a clear idea of which of the many issues that the company is facing are the most important. Only then can possible solutions be identified. For example, at the time of writing, Benetton faces intensifying competition and declining sales in its important American markets. Clearly, these must be sorted out as a matter of urgency. If these problems result from Benetton managing their knowledge less effectively than other firms, then a knowledge management system may be an appropriate solution. However, it may also be that an acquisition of a competitor would give Benetton market knowledge, and an extra brand name, which would help it address both problems. The point here is that until we know *precisely* what the problems are in the American market, we cannot suggest which of these two alternative solutions is the more appropriate. Unlikely as it may seem, it is even possible that Benetton would be best advised to wind its American business down.

It may be that a knowledge management system is a desirable investment for the future, regardless of its relevance to the American problem. It is also possible that it could prove to be a costly and disruptive mistake that distracts management attention away from other business problems. Before we recommend it as a way forward for Benetton, we would want to know more about the firm and its industry. We would want to know how valuable knowledge was in designing and

---

Concept | **Strategic issues**

A strategic issue is something that an organisation either needs to do something about, or would benefit strongly from doing something about. Issues may be internal or external in nature, and may have a positive or negative impact on the organisation. It is helpful to conceive of a strategic issue as an important question to which the organisation must find an answer, for example:

- How should it react to the emergence of new technologies?
- What should it do about emerging or disappearing markets?
- How should it respond to changing customer requirements?
- How should it deal with newly emerging competitors?
- How should it respond to changes in strategy by existing competitors?
- How should it change its value chain or positioning in businesses where it is being out-competed in terms of differentiation or cost?
- How can it utilise its strategic resources to consolidate its lead over its existing competitors, or for expansion?
- What should it do with business units that do not fit well with its parenting skills?
- What should it do about synergies that have been identified by managers but that are not working out in practice or potential synergies between businesses that have not yet been exploited?

In managerial jargon, doing something about an issue is referred to as **addressing** it, **responding to** it or **resolving** it.

▶

Concept continued

Strategic options

If a strategic issue is a question, then a strategic option is one of several *alternative* answers to that question – things that the organisation might *do* about the issue. For example, in response to the issue 'How should it react to the emergence of new technologies?' the organisation has a number of alternatives, for example:

● It can invest heavily to become a leader in the use and application of the new technology

● It can decide to ignore the new technology because it believes that established technologies are likely to be cheaper or more reliable

● It can make a small investment now with a view to keeping its future options open.

Each of these alternatives constitutes a strategic option.

Strategic priorities

Priority is a measure of two things: the importance of an issue to the organisation's survival or success, and the urgency with which it must be addressed. The highest priority belongs to issues that, if not resolved immediately, will lead to the disappearance of the organisation – for example, a severe shortage of cash or the departure of staff with key skills.

At the other end of the scale are the strategic issues faced by a successful firm in deciding what to do with the reserves of cash that it has accumulated. Unless its shareholders are pressing for the cash to be distributed to them, the organisation can afford to take its time in responding to this issue.

In all three of these concepts – issues, options and priorities – the adjective 'strategic' is important. In this analysis, we are not concerned with minor, short-term issues or options, but with problems that will have a substantial impact on the organisation over the medium to long term.

marketing fashion goods. We would want to make sure that the company did not already have systems that did the same job. We should want to be sure that, by formalising the process of knowledge management, we did not change the firm's architecture in a way that killed designers' creativity. In short, we would want to beware of taking a fashionable, 'off-the-shelf' solution, like knowledge management, total quality management or business process re-engineering, and applying it blindly to an organisation like Benetton.

This chapter, therefore, is about making sure that we identify all the important issues that confront an organisation, and understand which of them has highest priority. It is also about making sure that we do not jump to conclusions, and that alternative options are considered – not just those that are obvious or fashionable. Finally, it is about deciding which of the alternative options is the best, and how to combine them into a coherent strategy.

Figure 11.1 maps this process, and the order in which we deal with it in this chapter.

Figure 11.1   From strategic analysis to strategic proposals

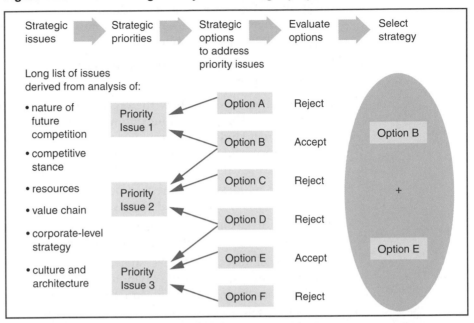

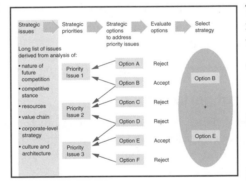

11.2   Strategic issues

There are two levels at which you will need to look at an organisation's strategic issues:

● The corporate level: Is the organisation as a whole performing adequately?

● The business level: Does a particular business have a sustainable position in its chosen industries and markets?

Depending upon the nature of your assignment as a manager or a student, you will emphasise either the corporate or the business level in your analysis. However, you will need to do both pieces of analysis in order to get a complete picture, since there are strong linkages between them:

● If you have been asked to judge the prospects of a particular business unit, you will need to know whether it is the only SBU in the firm, or whether it can look to other parts of the same corporation for cash, knowledge or other resources. You will also need to know if it is seen within the corporation as an underperforming business that needs to improve, a promising business that is expected to expand or a strong performer that is expected to sustain high levels of profitability and cash generation.

● If you have been asked to assess the prospects of the corporation as a whole, you will need to evaluate the competitive situation of the main businesses. This will tell you whether the corporation's parenting skills are adequate in managing all of the businesses in its portfolio. You will also want to look at whether the different businesses have any resources in common, to see if there are potential synergies between them.

We recommend that you undertake the analysis of the organisation's situation in the following stages:

- An initial overview of how the organisation is performing in financial and other terms. This gives a context in which to set the rest of the analysis – there are different kinds of option to be considered for a failing business than for a highly successful one. It also provides valuable clues about where to look for strategic issues at corporate and business levels.

- A review, business by business, of how the environment is changing and the implications for the competitiveness of the different business units.

- A review of the sources of each business' competitive advantage – its competitive stance, resources and value chain, and areas in which it is being out-competed.

- A review of the corporate-level strategy: the type of parenting skills being used within the organisation, the extent to which the different businesses are benefiting from them, and the potential for extending them to other businesses. This comes down to an evaluation of the organisation's portfolio of businesses, and where it might be reduced or expanded.

- A review of internal issues to determine whether the culture and architecture are appropriate and whether there are any signs of internal tensions or lack of coherence between the different elements.

- A final assessment of the major issues affecting the organisation, and the priority that needs to be attached to them.

We look at each of these steps in turn in the following sections.

11.2.1 Initial overview of performance

An analysis of performance does not show precisely the main issues facing an organisation, but it does assist us in working out where to look for them, and in determining how critical they are. With this initial overview, we are trying to answer a number of basic questions:

- Are we dealing with a successful organisation/business or an unsuccessful one?

- Are there any particular parts of the organisation or business that are significantly more or less successful than the others?

- Are there any specific functions or value chain activities that are performing particularly well or badly?

The tools used to answer these questions are the techniques of quantitative and qualitative analysis reviewed in Chapter 4.

Overall corporate performance

If the firm being analysed is a corporation with several business units, or one part of such a firm, then it is useful, if the data are available, to review the performance of the entire firm. The first step is to identify trends in the corporation's overall financial

REAL-LIFE APPLICATION 11.1

Initial overview of Sony's corporate performance

Table 11.1(a) was computed from data in Sony's 1999 annual report (available from www.world.sony.com).

Table 11.1(a) Sony Corporation (Yen billions)

Year ended 31 March	1995	1996	1997	1998	1999
Sales	3,991	4,593	5,663	6,755	6,795
Operating income (loss)	(167)	235	370	520	339
Net income (loss)	(293)	54	139	222	179
R&D expenses	239	257	283	318	375
% growth					
Sales		15%	23%	19%	1%
Operating income (loss)		N/A	57%	41%	−35%
Net income (loss)		N/A	157%	60%	−19%
R&D expenses		8%	10%	12%	18%
Operating profit margin	−4.2%	5.1%	6.5%	7.7%	5.0%
Return on total assets	−3.9%	4.7%	6.5%	8.1%	5.4%
Return on equity	−29.1%	4.6%	9.6%	12.2%	9.8%
R&D as % of sales	6.0%	5.6%	5.0%	4.7%	5.5%

It is clear that Sony has had a fairly bumpy ride over the past five years. The company recovered from the losses suffered in 1995, but profitability, on all measures, fell substantially in 1999 from the 1998 peak. This simple observation provokes questions – which businesses are responsible for the downturn, and is it a one-off phenomenon or the start of a deeper set of problems?

In the case of Sony, we pick out the corporate R&D expense for attention because of the emphasis that the corporation's mission places upon innovation. Do its actions match its slogans? We can see that R&D expense is rising steadily and is usually over 5% of sales, although fluctuations in sales turnover make it difficult to see a pattern in that statistic.

We can place these results in context by comparing them with those of Matsushita, another Japanese electronics giant (owner of the National and Panasonic brands) with a similar spread of businesses (Table 11.1(b)). It is clear that on almost all measures, Sony is outperforming its rival. Its sales are growing faster – from around half Matsushita's sales in 1995 to near-parity in 1999 – and its profits, in absolute terms and as returns on assets and on equity, are noticeably higher. If there are environmental problems at the root of Sony's 1999 difficulties, the firm still seems to be coping better than its closest rival.

Table 11.1(b) Matsushita Corporation (Yen billions)

	1995	1996	1997	1998	1999
Sales	6,948	6,795	7,676	7,891	7,640
Operating profit	260	264	374	338	194
Net income (loss)	90	(57)	138	94	14
R&D expenditures	378	400	435	481	500
% growth					
Sales		−2.2%	13.0%	2.8%	−3.2%
Operating profit		1.5%	41.7%	−9.6%	−42.6%
Net income (loss)		N/A	N/A	−31.9%	−85.1%
R&D expenditures		5.8%	8.7%	10.6%	4.0%
Operating profit margin	3.7%	3.9%	4.9%	4.3%	2.5%
Return on total assets	3.2%	3.3%	4.3%	3.9%	2.4%
Return on equity	2.8%	−1.7%	3.7%	2.5%	0.4%
R&D % of sales	5.4%	5.9%	5.7%	6.1%	6.5%

Real-Life Application continued

Data from the Fortune Global 500 (*Fortune*, 2 August 1999 and www.fortune.com) also support the idea that Sony is performing well. Its ratio of net profits to assets for the year ended 31 March 1999 is higher (at 3%, according to *Fortune*) than those of almost all other diversified electronics and electrical firms, including America's General Electric, Germany's Siemens, South Korea's Samsung and LG Electronics and Japan's Toshiba, NEC, Sanyo and Sharp. However, the Dutch group Philips boasts profit margins of 17% and its net profits are 20% of assets, and there may be other less diversified firms with even better margins.

performance – measured, for example, through return on capital employed. If the data are available, it is helpful to use results from other corporations of similar size and operating in similar industries as a basis for comparison. Other performance measures, such as growth rates and share prices that may be important to major stakeholders, are also important here. This shows whether the organisation as a whole can be said to be successful and whether any stakeholders are likely to be demanding urgent action. A sample analysis for Sony is given in Real-Life Application 11.1.

Business segment performance

It is also useful to compare the results of different divisions and business units, in terms of profitability and rate of growth (see Real-Life Application 11.2). This helps set standards by which you can judge the performance of each individual unit, which can be particularly valuable if you have no other competitive data. It may also indicate a number of other things:

REAL-LIFE APPLICATION 11.2

Sony's performance analysed by business segment and geographic market

Sony's annual report also gives a breakdown by business area of revenues, profits and assets employed for the last three years. This can be used to produce the data in Table 11.1(c).

Table 11.1(c)   Sony segmental data

Sales as proportion of total	1997	1998	1999
Electronics	68%	64%	63%
Game	7%	10%	11%
Music	10%	10%	10%
Pictures	7%	9%	7%
Insurance	4%	4%	5%
Other	4%	3%	4%
Total	100%	100%	100%

Profits as proportion of total	1997	1998	1999
Electronics	62%	59%	37%
Game	15%	22%	39%
Music	12%	10%	11%
Pictures	7%	7%	11%
Insurance	5%	4%	5%
Other	0%	−2%	−3%
Total	100%	100%	100%

Segment ROS	1997	1998	1999
Electronics	5.8%	6.7%	2.8%
Game	13.6%	16.2%	17.4%
Music	7.6%	7.8%	5.0%
Pictures	6.6%	5.5%	6.9%
Insurance	8.4%	7.0%	5.3%
Other	−0.6%	−4.1%	−3.1%
Total	6.5%	7.7%	5.0%
Segment ROA	**1997**	**1998**	**1999**
Electronics	7.9%	9.7%	4.2%
Game	44.5%	59.2%	72.3%
Music	6.3%	6.5%	5.0%
Pictures	3.6%	3.9%	4.5%
Insurance	2.7%	2.3%	1.6%
Other	−0.5%	−3.3%	−2.3%
Total	6.9%	8.3%	5.5%

From Table 11.1(c) it is clear how important the games business is becoming to Sony. Not only is it the fastest-growth business in the company's portfolio, it also offers by far the highest return on assets and by 1999 has become the largest single contributor to profits. However, revenues and margins in the electronics businesses that are the company's traditional heartland appear to be declining, so that in our subsequent analysis, we need to look for the issues underlying this decline. The return on assets in the Insurance segment is also noticeably lower than that of the other businesses, for all three years, raising questions about its place in Sony's portfolio.

We can also obtain a breakdown of Sony's businesses by geographical market (Table 11.1(d)). This points up the declining profit margins in Japan and the relatively slim margins that Sony obtains from its businesses in the USA, its fastest-growing market. This raises some further questions. Might it be possible to raise USA margins to levels found elsewhere in the group? Or is the opposite likely to happen – are profit levels in Japan and Europe, where Sony's return on assets is highest, likely to fall to US levels? Since developments in American markets often foreshadow what happens elsewhere, Sony may be looking at a sustained period of declining profit margins as the price for sustaining its global growth.

Table 11.1(d)   Sony geographic analysis

Sales as proportion of total	1997	1998	1999
Japan	44%	43%	44%
USA	23%	25%	25%
Europe	15%	15%	16%
Other	18%	17%	15%
	100%	100%	100%
Profits as proportion of total	**1997**	**1998**	**1999**
Japan	60%	61%	50%
USA	7%	13%	19%
Europe	16%	13%	20%
Other	16%	12%	12%
	100%	100%	100%
Regional ROS	**1997**	**1998**	**1999**
Japan	14.4%	15.1%	8.7%
USA	1.7%	3.3%	3.3%
Europe	6.2%	5.3%	5.3%
Other	4.8%	4.3%	3.2%
Consolidated total	6.5%	7.7%	5.0%

Real-Life Application continued

Regional ROA	1997	1998	1999
Japan	35.5%	41.3%	22.8%
USA	3.8%	9.0%	11.2%
Europe	40.5%	38.4%	44.7%
Other	35.9%	33.1%	33.3%
Consolidated total	19.3%	24.9%	17.5%

At the end of this stage of the analysis, we have established that Sony overall is a successful company, although it has experienced one or two recent setbacks. The games business has performed spectacularly well, which raises questions about how likely it is to be able to sustain its present high levels of growth and profitability. There are question-marks over the performance of the electronics and insurance businesses, and a lurking doubt as to whether margins may be likely to fall to US levels. We shall want to give all these points special attention in our subsequent analysis.

- If there are large disparities between the performance of different units, it *may* be an indication that the organisation's parenting skills are more appropriate to some businesses than to others. It may, on the other hand, be due to differences in the competitive conditions that the different divisions are facing – it will not be clear which is the real cause until you have looked at the individual units in detail.

- If a disproportionate share of profit comes from one or two units, it may indicate that the other units are superfluous and ripe for disposal – or it may show that these are 'problem children' which the corporation intends to build into major businesses.

- If the growth rates or profitability of the largest units are faltering, the organisation as a whole is quite likely to experience problems. For managers in the smaller units in the portfolio, it may be a sign that they will be expected to generate profits and cash in the short term to compensate for the lack of performance by the largest businesses.

Competitive performance of individual businesses

Once we have an idea of how well the organisation as a whole is performing, it is time to focus more closely upon individual businesses (for a single-business company, the analysis essentially starts at this point). Naturally, we are interested in overall measures of performance – growth and profitability – for each individual business. These dictate how the owners or corporate parents will perceive the business, and how likely they are to invest in it. However, at the business level, there is a strong emphasis on performance relative to competitors. We will want to look for evidence of success or failure in the market place, comparing growth and profitability with that of competitors, and looking at market share and at the results of independent quality assessments to see how customers perceive the business unit or firm.

◀ *Measures of operational performance are discussed in detail in Sections 4.5 and 4.6.*

This stage of the analysis is also where we start to get an insight into possible operational problems. It is important, if the data are available, to look at operational performance measures such as unit production costs and inventory turnover. The attitudes of employee stakeholders, as expressed through absenteeism and staff turnover statistics, may also be revealing.

REAL-LIFE APPLICATION 11.3

Operational performance at McDonald's

Although it made two small acquisitions at the end of 1999, McDonald's is essentially a single-business firm. Table 11.1(e) summarises some key aspects of its results.

Table 11.1(e) McDonald's corporate performance data

$ million (except for restaurant nos.)	1993	1994	1995	1996	1997	1998
System-wide sales	23,587	25,987	29,914	31,812	33,638	35,979
Total revenues	7,408	8,321	9,795	10,687	11,409	12,421
Operating income	1,984	2,241	2,601	2,633	2,808	3,084
Net income	1,083	1,224	1,427	1,573	1,642	1,769
No of restaurants (year end)	14,163	15,950	18,380	21,022	23,132	24,800
Growth rates	1993	1994	1995	1996	1997	1998
System-wide sales	7.8%	10.2%	15.1%	6.3%	5.7%	7.0%
Total revenues	3.9%	12.3%	17.7%	9.1%	6.8%	8.9%
Operating income	6.6%	13.0%	16.1%	1.2%	6.6%	9.8%
No. of restaurants	8.2%	12.6%	15.2%	14.4%	10.0%	7.2%
	1993	1994	1995	1996	1997	1998
Operating profit margin	27%	27%	27%	25%	25%	25%
Return on total assets	16%	16%	17%	15%	15%	16%
Return on equity	17%	18%	18%	18%	19%	19%
Debt/equity	59%	63%	62%	63%	73%	74%

Although McDonald's has been growing continuously over the past six years, it has not translated this into increases in profitability. Its return on total assets has been static, although by increasing its indebtedness, it has improved its return on equity slightly between 1993 and 1996, an example of the power of leverage. However its overall financial performance compares reasonably favourably with that of two of its major competitors: Tricon Corporation (owner of the KFC, Pizza Hut and Taco Bell fast-food brands) and Burger King (Table 11.1(f)).

Table 11.1(f) Performance data for McDonald's major competitors

Tricon Global Corporation	1993	1994	1995	1996	1997	1998
Operating profit margin	N/A	6.1%	2.5%	3.6%	2.5%	12.1%
Return on total assets	N/A	7.9%	3.6%	5.7%	4.7%	22.7%
Growth in system sales			4.8%	1.5%	0.7%	3.7%
Burger King				1996/97	1997/98	1998/99
Operating profit margin				18%	21%	21%
Return on assets				14%	16%	15%
Growth in system sales					7%	5%

Only in one year, 1998, has Tricon managed a return on assets superior to McDonald's. McDonald's growth rate also compares favourably with that of its main competitors. However, the failure to turn growth into increased returns on assets raises questions about the kinds of returns McDonald's can expect from further investment in its existing business. Looking carefully at the figures in Table 11.1(e), we can see that, throughout the period, growth in its system-wide sales (food and drink sales in McDonald's branded restaurants) has been less than the growth in restaurant numbers. This may mean that sales in existing restaurants are declining, and that all growth is coming from new outlets, which may even be taking sales from existing outlets. Or it may mean that average sales in new restaurants are lower than in existing ones, because all the most attractive locations already have a McDonald's, an example of diminishing returns to scale.

Real-Life Application continued

Having raised a question about sales/restaurant, we can try to probe further to see if we can establish precisely where the problem is. One clue comes from a 1998 poll by the American magazine *Restaurants and Institutions* in which consumers ranked McDonald's food 87th out of 91 chains. The McDonald's website helpfully provides the data in Table 11.1(g).

Table 11.1(g) Average annual sales for McDonald's restaurants

Restaurants in operation at least 13 consecutive months ($'000)	1996	1997	1998
USA			
Traditional	1,530	1,523	1,584
Satellite	425	445	459
Outside the USA			
Traditional	2,262	1,996	1,801
Satellite	488	457	450
New Restaurants in operation at least 13 months but not more than 25 months ($'000)	1996	1997	1998
USA			
Traditional	1,206	1,237	1,332
Outside the USA			
Traditional	1,710	1,431	1,357
Satellite	517	453	446

Both inside and outside the USA, new restaurants have a lower average turnover than longer-established ones, but the difference is greater outside the USA. Table 11.1(g) also shows that average sales per restaurant are increasing for all categories of restaurant in the USA, but decreasing for all categories elsewhere. The problem, if there is one, appears to be in international markets.

McDonald's website also details the numbers of restaurants in different categories, and the total sales in each of those categories. This, together with data from competitors' annual reports, enables us to calculate the data in Table 11.1(h).

Table 11.1(h) Restaurant performance analysis – McDonald's and competitors

McDonald's	1993	1994	1995	1996	1997	1998
% of sales from restaurants						
Operated by franchisees	67%	66%	64%	63%	62%	62%
Operated by the company	22%	22%	23%	24%	24%	25%
Operated by affiliates	11%	12%	13%	13%	14%	13%
Sales/restaurant ($'000)	1,665	1,629	1,628	1,513	1,454	1,451
Operated by franchisees	1,586	1,564	1,565	1,487	1,463	1,461
Operated by the company	1,878	1,789	1,798	1,738	1,627	1,614
Operated by affiliates	1,802	1,745	1,674	1,320	1,200	1,186
Growth in sales/restaurant	0.4%	−2.2%	−0.1%	−7.0%	−3.9%	−0.2%
Operated by franchisees	1.2%	−1.4%	0.1%	−5.0%	−1.7%	−0.1%
Operated by the company	−6.1%	−4.7%	0.5%	−3.4%	−6.4%	−0.8%
Operated by affiliates	1.9%	−3.2%	−4.1%	−21.1%	−9.1%	−1.1%
Tricon Global Corporation	1993	1994	1995	1996	1997	1998
% of restaurants						
Franchised		50%	52%	56%	58%	68%
Company owned		50%	48%	44%	42%	32%
Sales/restaurant ($'000)		694	706	698	767	692
Burger King					1997/8	1998/9
Sales/restaurant ($'000)					1,047	1,036

This shows that the proportion of company-operated restaurants has been steadily rising over time while the proportion operated by franchisees has fallen. Sales in company-operated restaurants have remained, on average, higher than those in franchised outlets, perhaps because McDonald's keeps the highest-volume sites for itself. However, in most years during the period, franchisee-operated restaurants have shown lower falls or higher growth in average sales than company-operated outlets. In theory, this might be because the company is taking over sites from poorly-performing franchisees, although in fact the number of restaurants in all categories is growing (we have not given these figures in Table 11.1(h)) so this explanation is unlikely. It may be that franchisees are better at responding to market conditions than company employees. In that case, there are questions about why McDonald's appears to be decreasing the proportion of franchises and increasing the proportion of restaurants operated by the company – or by affiliates, who are clearly the worst performers on this measure. Tricon has moved radically away from company-owned restaurants towards franchised outlets, and this has coincided with the sharp rise in profitability we saw in Table 11.1(f).

There are other dimensions of McDonald's performance to look at. It is a good idea in a global business to look at performance by country or region, as we earlier did with Sony. For the sake of brevity, we omit that analysis again here. One important fact to note is that McDonald's is gaining market share – its share of the US burger market rose from 42.2 to 42.7% in 1998. Its main rivals, Burger King and Wendy, also increased market share at the expense of smaller rivals.[2]

As we mentioned in Chapter 4, debtor turnover and stock turnover ratios are useful all-round measures of the way a business is managed. McDonald's inventories in 1998 amounted to 9.4 days supply of food and paper (its key purchases), just fractionally worse than the 1997 figure. This seems reasonable for a business that uses a high proportion of fresh ingredients, and indicates that operations are under control. Tricon's inventories over the past three years have also been between 9 and 10 days' supply. However, McDonalds' debtors rose from 15.5 days' sales in 1997 to 17.9 days in 1998. Since almost all sales in its company-owned restaurants will be paid for in cash, the main debtors are likely to be franchisees. The lengthening payment period may mean either that they have cashflow problems or that they are in some way unhappy with the company.

At the end of this review, we can see that McDonald's competitive performance is adequate. There are question-marks as to whether its financial returns are sufficiently high to satisfy its shareholders over the longer term, and there are questions to be asked regarding the quality of the food, the productivity of its overseas restaurants and its use of and relations with its franchisees.

11.2.2 Review of the environment

This part of the analysis draws upon the methods described in Chapter 5 – PEST, life-cycle and industry analysis. It aims to establish how a business' environment is *changing*, so the emphasis is on an assessment of *future trends* and how survival and success factors in the future are likely to differ from those in the past and the present. The kinds of issue that are likely to emerge from this analysis are:

- *How should the business respond to new potential target markets?* These might result, for example, from economic developments in regions such as Indo-China or Eastern Europe, or from socio-economic trends that increase the spending power of groups like older people and pre-teen children.

- *How should the business cope with the decline of existing markets?* The industries in which customer firms operate may be maturing or declining. Previously growing markets may, like many Asian countries in 1998 and 1999, suffer from economic decline or political unrest. Sometimes the firm's fortunes can be linked to those of a single major customer (Real-Life Application 11.4).

Practical dos and don'ts	Initial overview

We repeat here a few of the key messages from Chapter 4:

- Do not skip the quantitative analysis, however tedious you may find it. It provides essential facts to back up (or refute) conclusions that you have come to by other means. It also helps show you where to focus your qualitative analysis.

- Use data from other firms operating in similar industries for comparison wherever possible. Try not to rely upon internal data from a single firm.

- Remember – improvement is not the same as strength. A firm's results may be getting better, but it may still be performing far worse than its close competitors.

- Do not rely upon the opinions of the organisations' managers and staff in judging how successful the firm is. Some firms (Sony is quite a good example) offer a balanced perspective, talking about both their successes and their problems. Quite frequently, however, managers prefer to put a favourable gloss on the firm's performance and prospects. Let the results speak.

- Do not rely upon what casewriters say or imply about a company's success or failure, either. Devious creatures that we are, we may be trying to throw you off the scent.

REAL-LIFE APPLICATION 11.4

The UK clothing industry

In October 1999, UK clothing manufacturer William Baird confronted serious strategic problems when its contract to supply clothes to Marks & Spencer (M&S) was terminated after a relationship stretching back 30 years. This issue had been brewing for at least twelve months when it became clear that M&S was suffering an unprecedented loss of market share. M&S, which accounted for 38% of Baird's turnover, had long been the UK's leading clothing retailer, but consumers were finding its clothes insufficiently stylish and overly expensive. M&S had earlier signalled its intention to move away from its traditional reliance upon UK suppliers and take advantage of lower labour costs in regions such as the Indian subcontinent, South-East Asia and Eastern Europe. It had publicly warned its suppliers to move more of their production to these areas. It now hoped, after reducing the number of major suppliers from four to three, that those which remained would benefit from increased economies of scale, and so would be able to cut their prices and thus M&S' costs.

The issue that Baird confronted was how to respond to M&S' move. Most commentators believed that Baird would be forced to follow the obvious path of closing down the plants dedicated to serving M&S. However, Baird might also have been tempted to stay and fight – to retain the factories and try to improve their efficiency, with a view either to winning back M&S's custom or to becoming a supplier to that firm's competitors.

- *How should the business respond to changes in the competitive environment?* New competitors may have entered the market, existing ones may have altered their strategy with apparent success, while other, formerly powerful, competitors may be experiencing management problems (see, for example, Real-Life Application 11.5). Barriers to entry may have become higher or lower as the

REAL-LIFE APPLICATION 11.5

Some issues arising from changes in McDonald's competitive environment

In this real-life application, we look at three of the many issues that would be highlighted by an analysis of McDonald's present and future environment. These will be built upon later when we analyse McDonald's competitive stance, resources and value chain.

How should McDonald's respond to the increasing intensity of competition?

McDonald's is used to being unquestioned industry leader in fast food. However, a major competitor, Tricon, has been spun off from under the corporate umbrella of PepsiCo. The management team has made some radical moves to improve profitability, and are likely to be keener competitors in the future.

Its main rival in the hamburger segment, Burger King, has been strengthened by the strong financial resources and brand management capabilities of its parent firm, the drinks and food combine Diageo. Burger King has been matching, and sometimes pre-empting, McDonald's special offers and promotions tied to characters from blockbuster movies. At the same time, Burger King is claiming to have taken the lead on innovation in the segment, with the 1997 launch of three new products: the Big King, a direct competitor to McDonald's Big Mac but with a higher beef content, King Fries, a new style of french fry, that stays hotter and crisper for longer, and the Cini-Mini, a sweet breakfast roll developed by Pillsbury, one of Burger King's sister companies. McDonald's itself has not launched a major successful new product since 1983, and the 1996 launch of the Arch Deluxe was a humiliating failure. Wendy's, the third-ranking chain, has also signalled its intention to expand more aggressively, particularly outside the USA.

How can McDonald's exploit the increased brand-consciousness among consumers?

Burger King and McDonald's are both gaining share in the USA from smaller rivals, including Hardees, the fourth-ranking brand. Other, marginal, competitors such as Boston Chicken, a US fried chicken chain, and Planet Hollywood, an up-market burger chain, filed for bankruptcy (Planet Hollywood has been able to restructure its finances and continue trading). This may be a sign that American fast-food consumers are becoming more brand- and value-conscious, which will assist McDonald's by raising barriers to entry into the segment. Data from the UK also point to the importance of a major brand. A 1998 Mintel survey found that fewer than 5% of adults had visited a burger restaurant that did not belong to one of the three leading chains, or a chicken restaurant not run by KFC. 45% of adults had visited a McDonald's in the previous 12 months.

How should McDonald's react to potential shortages of a vital operating resource – people?

In 1999, owners and managers of McDonald's restaurants were finding it increasingly difficult to find and retain staff because the US economy was close to full employment. Some franchisees were printing job application forms on the paper bags in which they wrapped takeaway sandwiches.

result of social, legal or technological changes. Customer industries may be maturing and consolidating, meaning that the business has fewer, more powerful and more price-sensitive customers.

- *How should the business respond to technological changes?* New materials, innovations in production technology or new distribution channels may open up new possibilities for a business, or threaten the viability of past investments.

- *What should the business do about changing customer tastes?*

Each of these eventualities presents a business with an issue – a challenge, or a potential opportunity – to which it must consider its response. These issues must be considered in conjunction with an analysis of the relative strength of the business' competitive stance, value chain and strategic resources. This enables us to determine whether changes in industry success and survival factors are potentially favourable or unfavourable for the organisation.

11.2.3 Review of competitive stance

The review of the business' competitive stance aims to establish whether the firm is addressing the right target markets, and whether its positioning in each of those markets is appropriate. It uses the concepts and frameworks discussed in Chapter 6, and raises the following sorts of issue:

● *How should the business react in growing or declining market segments?* These may be markets that the review of the environment has highlighted as being likely to expand or contract in the future. Or they may be markets where sales are currently growing (or declining) sharply, or where the firm is able to make particularly high (or low) profits, because it has found (or failed to find) the right product mix and market positioning to attract customers. The firm may need to consider investing in the segment, or diverting resources to it.

● *What should the firm do about cases where its positioning is particularly strong or weak?* (See Real-Life Application 11.6.) If the positioning is strong, as evidenced by strong sales, good margins and positive customer feedback, then the firm may be building reputational assets that can be 'leveraged' – used for other products, in other markets or even in other businesses. Alternatively, the firm's positioning may be inappropriate for the desired target market. It may have set its prices too high or too low, or be offering services or products that have too few features, or features that customers do not want. A third possibility is that

---

REAL-LIFE APPLICATION 11.6

Competitive stance issues for Skandia Life and Sony Electronics

Skandia Life

Skandia Life offers one particular investment product in the UK which is clearly differentiated from its competitors. This is a unit trust that allows investors to select their own portfolio from a wide selection of funds. This gives the investor a high degree of flexibility – they can move their investment from fund to fund at low cost. Skandia is able to make a higher charge for administering this fund than is usual for other, simpler, investments.

In theory there is nothing to stop competitors offering a similar product, but thus far few have done so. Research has indicated that first movers in this particular investment category seem to obtain an advantage. The issue for Skandia is how to build on the lead that this product has given them. It can consider using its UK experience to market similar products in other markets, and build on its reputation in the UK for offering flexible, premium investment products.

Sony Electronics

In 1999, Sony faced several issues regarding its competitive stance in electronics, its traditional core business, for example:

● *What should it do about the Walkman?* According to Sony's 1999 Annual Report, 'Sales of compact cassette headphone stereos decreased worldwide, particularly in Asia. Also, intensified price competition in the U.S. and Western Europe hurt sales.' Although the Walkman is one of the company's most successful products, and the brand is valuable, does Sony still want to compete in a product line with declining volumes and margins?

● *How should it respond to the commoditisation of televisions?* Sony's revenues from television sales declined 3% in 1999. Lower-cost competitors from Korea are taking the market for standard televisions. Sony is trying to differentiate through a greater emphasis on larger televisions with a greater range of features. It is unclear whether it can sustain its advantage in this way. Similar problems are also afflicting its computer-display product range.

● *What should it do with the MiniDisc?* The MiniDisc format for recorded and recordable music was developed by Sony at considerable expense. It is popular in Japan but has not yet found a mass market in other countries.

the firm may have targeted the wrong segments. The customers may be too few, too poor or too price sensitive for the organisation to be able to make an adequate financial return from serving them.

- *How should the firm make life more difficult for competitors?* Sometimes a firm should consider entering, or altering its positioning in, a particular market simply to stop a competitor building a dominant market share, to make it divert cash and management attention to the competitive battle, or to hurt its cash flow. For example, it is doubtful whether General Motors makes a good return on capital on its Saturn small cars. However, it requires a presence in the US small car segment simply to prevent Japanese competitors from building relationships with large number of young automobile buyers. These buyers would then be less likely to buy GM cars as they grow older and richer, and trade up to larger models where profit margins are higher. In a global industry, it can be very useful for a firm to have a presence in all major geographic markets, including the home markets of its major competitors. This helps it stay in touch with customer requirements and gives it first-hand access to industry gossip and early exposure to announcements of new products. It also enables it to make life awkward for other firms, for example, by cutting prices in a competitor's home market. This hits the competitor's profits and cash flow, either by eroding its sales volume or by forcing it to retaliate by reducing its own prices.

- *How should the firm alter its competitive stance to react to changes in the extent of industry globalisation or in the industry's position in its life-cycle?* It may be that a firm needs to consider changing the scale or scope of its marketing effort in order to improve its competitiveness.

The issues raised in the review of competitive stance may be modified when looking at the organisation's resources and value chain. For example, if an organisation has problems in serving a particular market segment, it will often not be clear whether the decision to enter the segment was mistaken. It may be that the firm has not yet worked out how to fine-tune its value chain so as to serve the segment profitably.

11.2.4 Review of resources and value chain

The review of a business unit's resources and value chain looks at whether an organisation can continue to compete in its chosen market segments. This uses the concepts and analytical frameworks discussed in Chapters 7 and 8 – especially the value chain. In general, the analysis focuses upon whether the firm has the basis of a sustainable competitive advantage in a business, through its resources or other elements of its configuration that are difficult for other firms to imitate. It also looks for *absent* resources – for success and survival factors, highlighted during the analysis of the environment, that the firm does *not* possess. Finally, it highlights resources that can be developed in some way, for example through expansion into a new business.

For a successful business – profitable, with an effective value chain and a number of strategic resources – we first check to make sure that the success is sustainable. We then look for features – strategic resources, or other value chain attributes such as scale or location – that will form the basis of future expansion in both new and

Table 11.2   Checklist for assessment of resources and value chain

	Implication for successful business	Implication for unsuccessful business
Resources and attributes required for *survival* in future, but not possessed	Danger of catastrophic decline: high priority issues	Reason to doubt viability of business
Strategic resources and attributes whose value will *increase* as environment changes	Possible basis for aggressive expansion	Possible basis for turnaround
Strategic resources and attributes that will *retain* their value as the environment changes	Likely basis for sustained competitive advantage	Possible basis for survival or turnaround if organisation can make improvements elsewhere
Strategic resources and attributes whose value will be *diminished* by changes in the environment	Reason to doubt sustainability of competitive advantage, though organisation may still be able to survive. Possible reason for divestment.	Reason to anticipate further decline in performance. Possible reason for divestment.
Non-strategic resources and attributes that will become strategic as environment changes	Likely basis for sustained or increasing competitive advantage. Possible basis for expansion	Possible basis for survival or turnaround
Non-strategic resources and attributes that can be developed into strategic ones	Possible basis for sustained or improved competitive position, perhaps also for expansion	Possible basis for survival or turnaround
Spare resources that have no evident obvious role in current strategy	Possible basis for unrelated or speculative diversification	Possible source of funds to finance other strategic moves
Proven capacity to learn and innovate	Possible basis for sustained or improved competitive position	Possible basis for survival or turnaround if no *immediate* threat to survival

existing markets. For an unsuccessful business, the emphasis is somewhat different. We check first to make sure that the business has some features that give it a chance of surviving, and then look for resources or value chain attributes that may, if properly developed, become the basis of a sustainable position in either existing or new markets. The issues to look for are summarised in Table 11.2 and discussed in more detail below.

Issues relating to survival factors

The review of the environment should have picked out where the survival factors in an industry are likely to change in the future. Signs that this is about to happen include:

- an industry moving from growth to the mature phase of the life-cycle;
- rapid consolidation in an industry;
- firms in an industry adopting a technology that in the past has only been mastered by a few, so that a former success factor becomes a survival factor – for example, at the end of the 1990s many observers agreed that, for a retailer, an internet presence had ceased to be an optional extra and was becoming an essential part of a complete strategy.[3]

REAL-LIFE APPLICATION 11.7

Missing survival factors at British Airways?

Since 1997, the global airline industry has consolidated rapidly around a set of four global alliances. Industry observers believe that in order to remain a viable major player, an airline must have a well-defined role in an effective alliance as either:

● an efficient provider of airline services to one of the alliances, with low costs of flying and maintaining aircraft; or

● a network manager, setting the timetables and directing the strategy.

Alternatively, an airline can try to be a niche player, focused upon a particular geographic market or customer group.

In 1999, British Airways did not appear to be fulfilling any of these roles particularly well. It had previously enjoyed a strong niche position with business travellers, who paid premium fares. However, in the mid-1990s it had allowed its service quality to deteriorate in pursuit of lower costs. Although it was now attempting to upgrade the service and facilities on its planes, its differentiation features were frequently matched or anticipated by rival airlines, particularly Virgin Atlantic.

BA's cost-cutting efforts had also not had the desired effect. Despite the fact that it had reduced annual costs by £1 billion since 1997, it was still believed to be over-staffed. Although in the 1980s it had been one of the lowest cost airlines, many rivals, such as Air France and Lufthansa, had since been privatised and had raised their productivity levels.

BA did not occupy the lead role in Oneworld, its alliance with American Airlines (AA), Cathay Pacific, Iberia, Finnair and three other airlines. The senior position was occupied by American Airlines, and BA's plan for a closer partnership with AA had been turned down by the European Commission. In any case the Star alliance, involving United Airlines, Lufthansa, SAS and five other partners, seemed to be more effective in linking its partners' marketing and operations than Oneworld. Star now seemed set to incorporate British Midland, BA's domestic rival, and so gain access to some 25% of take-off and landing slots at Heathrow Airport. This gave the alliance the capacity to mount a serious challenge to BA in its core markets, although the international treaty between the USA and the UK would prevent Star from using those slots to compete with BA on the vital transatlantic route.

In late 1999, as BA announced sharply reduced interim profits, some observers were questioning whether the company actually met the criteria for survival in the industry. Its net losses for the financial year ending March 2000 were £21 million, BA's worst result in eighteen years.

Sources: Barton, Bradshaw, Brunschwiler and Bull-Larsen, 'Is there a future for Europe's Airlines', *McKinsey Quarterly*, No. 4, 1194.

Having established the criteria that need to be met by a viable competitor, we can then assess whether an organisation or business unit fulfils them (e.g. Real-Life Application 11.7). If not, then the following issues will arise:

● *How can the organisation cope with threats to its survival from missing survival factors?* Even organisations that have been very successful may confront this issue if survival factors have changed radically. For an already unsuccessful business, the implications of missing survival factors are that radical change or turnaround is likely to be needed for survival, and that shutting down the business may need to be given serious consideration.

Issues relating to strategic resources and value chain attributes

Having established whether an organisation has the wherewithal to survive, the next step is to assess how existing sources of competitive advantage will be affected by likely changes in the environment.

Sometimes strategic resources and value chain attributes can **increase their value** as a result of changes in the environment. A firm that already has a global presence and enjoys economies of scale will find these advantages enhanced if its industry matures and globalises. The strategic issues for an already successful organisation, such as McDonald's, would be *how to hammer home its advantage over weaker competitors* and *how to use these resources and value chain attributes in other businesses or markets.* The issue for an unsuccessful organisation, on the other hand, would be *how to change its strategy so that it could use these resources to improve its competitiveness.*

In order to make proposals about an organisation's future competitive strategy, we also need to identify any existing strategic resources or value chain attributes that will **retain their value** in the future environment. Typical examples would be reputational assets, a distinctive capability in innovation, a competence in a particular technology or a broadly based distribution network. An unsuccessful enterprise would confront the issue of *how to leverage these resources or value chain attributes to compensate for weaknesses elsewhere.* A successful firm would similarly be looking at *how to use these resources and attributes to increase its current advantage* (see Real-Life Application 11.8).

For both successful and unsuccessful firms it is worth considering *whether any of these existing resources might be valuable in other businesses.* For example, several UK

REAL-LIFE APPLICATION 11.8

Leveraging resources at McDonald's, British Airways and Benetton

McDonald's brand, which is already one of the best known in the world, seems set to increase further in value as fast-food consumers become increasingly brand-conscious (Real-Life Application 11.5 above). This gives McDonald's two strategic issues to address:

● *How can it use its brand to increase its advantage in the US fast-food market?* Strategic options it might consider include:

- an aggressive programme of new store openings and advertising, to take share away from weaker competitors

- introducing premium-priced products to profit from the brand values.

● *How might it use the brand in other industries and markets?* For example, McDonald's is very popular with children, and is greatly involved in the design and distribution of toys, whose promotion is tied in to the release of popular films. It might consider, as a strategic option, the launch of a line of toys under the McDonald's or Ronald McDonald brand.

British Airways, on the other hand, is less successful and faces a number of pressing problems (see Real-Life Application 11.7). However, it still has a strategic asset – its reputation. According to *Fortune* magazine (11 October 1999) it is number 3 in the list of the world's most-admired airlines, and the fourth most-admired company in the UK. The issue it faces is *how to use its reputation to offset the problems it faces elsewhere.* For example, it might consider links with medium-sized firms anxious to build business links in markets where BA has a strong presence: BA might contribute marketing expertise and give the smaller company some form of recommendation as a BA-approved partner. BA would gain the firm's travel business and enhance its standing in the broader business community.

For Benetton, an interesting strategic issue is *how to leverage its investment in production and logistics capabilities.* Many tens of millions of euros were invested in the manufacturing and distribution complex at Castrette, northern Italy, in the period 1996–99. These production facilities might be extended to different lines of clothing. The state-of-the-art distribution facilities might be used for a wider range of products. The firm also has the option to leverage its expertise in this area, either by setting up its own consultancy or by licensing its know-how in a specialist consultancy firm.

retailers, including Tesco, Sainsbury and Marks & Spencer, have used their strong reputations with customers as the basis of diversification into financial services. An unsuccessful firm is likely, in the end, to need to give priority to restoring the competitiveness of its existing business, but occasionally salvation can come from diversification.

Finally, it is important to identify any strategic resources or value chain activities that are likely to **lose their value** as the environment changes. Competitors may be close to developing resources that match the ones that have given the firm advantage up to now, as is happening to BA where competitors are eroding its domination of slots at London's Heathrow Airport. New technologies may make a firm's resources less difficult to copy or substitute. The industry may be maturing, so that existing value chain activities geared towards giving the firm a differentiation advantage may need to be replaced with ones that give cost advantage. For a successful organisation, the threat is that its advantage will be eroded and it will lose its leadership position in certain markets. An unsuccessful organisation faces the prospect of losing its remaining customers as its sources of differentiation disappear, or of deteriorating financial performance as it loses its sources of cost advantage. In both cases, the issue is: *How can the firm replace resources and activities that are losing their value?* In some organisations, there will be other resources that can be used as replacements (see Real-Life Application 11.9). Others may have a track record in learning and change that gives us confidence that they will be able to adapt their resources, or develop new ones. For an unsuccessful organisation, the question will arise as to whether it has time to develop new resources before deteriorating financial results persuade its owners to close it down or sell it off.

REAL-LIFE APPLICATION 11.9

Adversity and opportunity at Centrica

British Gas has for decades been the monopoly supplier of methane gas for cooking, heating and industrial use in the UK. It was privatised in 1986 but faced no competition until the late 1990s. It was then forced to demerge its gas distribution system, which operated the network of underground pipes, from its commercial arm, which marketed gas and gas appliances to households and firms. The distribution arm, Transco, was then forced to allow gas suppliers the same access to its network that it gave Centrica, the commercial arm.

Centrica now faces direct competition from a number of new entrants, including electricity distribution companies. In its core business, therefore, some of its most important strategic resources, such as a monopoly position in its distribution network, are under threat.

Centrica has surprised many observers with the range and effectiveness of its adaptation. It is in the process of reinventing itself as a broadly based consumer services organisation, using its reputation with consumers, its customer database and its financial assets to launch itself into new industries where these assets have strategic value. It woos customers to its credit card, Goldfish, and its home insurance arm, by offering them discounts on the gas bills. It has just acquired the Automobile Association, the UK's largest provider of motor breakdown assistance and an important insurance broker. This gives it access to another trusted brand name and to a large customer database.

It has started to use its billing systems and reputation to compete in the electricity supply industry. These resources may not be strategic – other competitors also possess them – but they give Centrica the ability to survive in the industry. It is strategically important that Centrica is able to retaliate in the electricity market against firms that threaten its cash flow by undercutting its gas prices.

Resources that are not – yet – strategic

The most likely source of replacement for strategic resources and value chain attributes that are losing their value is from resources that are in the process of being developed. Most case studies, annual reports or other sources of data for a strategic review will throw up instances of research programmes in which money has been invested, new technologies that the company is trying to turn into workable products or new approaches to delivering better quality and/or lowering costs. These resources and activities may not yet have proved their uniqueness or their value in generating cost or differentiation advantage. This may be because they are too new, or because several competitors are doing similar things and it is unclear which organisation, if any, will discover a source of enduring advantage (see Real-Life Application 11.10).

REAL-LIFE APPLICATION 11.10

Emerging resources at McDonald's and in the automobile industry

McDonald's and 'Made for You'

US consumers are becoming more affluent, and have less free time. This has increased demand for fast food, but customers are more demanding and less willing to accept standard formulations, like a Big Mac, without question. Some customers have been defecting to Burger King and Wendy's, which have long offered them more flexibility in specifying their own sandwich.

In 1998, McDonald's implemented a fundamental change to the production system in almost all its US restaurants, at a cost of $500 million. Known as 'Made for You', the new system allowed McDonald's restaurants to match Burger King and Wendy's in offering products tailored to a customer's specification – e.g. with extra cheese instead of a gherkin. It also replaced warming bins, which tended to harm the taste of the food, with an assembly line that delivered cold lettuce and hot burgers and worked from computer-generated projections of customer traffic.

'Made for You' is not in itself a source of competitive advantage – it just gives McDonald's parity with its main competitors. However, the new system has had an unexpected spin-off: it has made it far easier for McDonald's to try out new products, for example a steak, egg and cheese breakfast bagel, in small quantities in selected restaurants. Restaurants in Wisconsin and Michigan have had success with a sandwich containing a respected local brand of bratwurst sausage. McDonald's used 'Made for You' as the trigger for the development of new capabilities in product innovation and in responding to local customer preferences.

Internet purchasing systems at Ford and General Motors

On 2 November 1999, both Ford and General Motors announced that they would be transferring their purchasing systems to the Internet. Ford's system, AutoXchange, is a joint venture with Oracle, the world leader in database software. It will not only link Ford, its 30,000 direct suppliers and the second- and third-tier firms that supply inputs to them, but will also be open to other carmakers. It is intended to be a stand-alone profit-making operation and may eventually be floated separately on the stock market. GM, on the other hand, intends to retain control of its system, MarketSite, and to open it only to firms within GM's supply network. Participating small firms will be able to benefit from GM's own purchasing power if they order parts and raw materials that the carmaker uses itself.

Both approaches have the potential to save the two firms large amounts of time and money and to form the basis of important new capabilities. No strategic analysis could ignore a move of this magnitude. However, in 1999, it was impossible to predict if either system would deliver what it promised, which would generate the greater benefits or if, in the end, the two moves would simply cancel one another out, leaving the balance of competitive advantage unchanged.

Source: The Economist, 6 November 1999.

There are two categories of not-yet-strategic resources that are of interest in a strategic review. The first contains proven resources or value chain attributes that are becoming strategic because the environment is changing. Reuters, a British firm, started as a network of correspondents that furnished news stories to newspapers world wide, with a sideline in the provision of financial information. With the liberalisation of financial markets and the development of IT systems which enabled traders to react very quickly to new information, this financial information service became far more valuable than the original core business.

The second category consists of unproven resources that the organisation may be able to develop over time, such as the ones mentioned in Real-Life Application 11.10.

The resources and attributes in the first of the two categories are marginally more valuable – there is less uncertainty regarding their operational effectiveness, which has already been demonstrated in practice. But both categories offer potential sources of new advantage to a successful business, and of salvation to an unsuccessful one, and the issue is: *How can the organisation develop its marginal resources and attributes into strategic ones?*

Issues relating to spare resources

Sometimes an organisation finds itself with resources that have no application in its present strategy (see Real-Life Application 11.11). These may be manufacturing facilities that have been made superfluous by changes in the environment, people that the firm does not wish to make redundant or is legally prevented from firing, or financial assets that have been built up by a business that generates far more cash than can be reinvested. The firm will face the issue of *what to do with its spare resources*. In particular, it needs to take the decision about whether the resources

---

REAL-LIFE APPLICATION 11.11

British–American Tobacco and spare resources

British–American Tobacco (BAT) is one of the world's leading producers of cigarettes. In the 1960s and 1970s it faced the issue of how it should use the cash from its tobacco business, since most of the markets in which it was not present were closed to it because of state tobacco monopolies.

Rather than return the money to its shareholders, BAT followed a strategy, fashionable at the time, of unrelated diversification. It acquired a number of well-known firms operating in industries as diverse as paper and pulp, cosmetics and retailing, none of which generated acceptable financial returns under its management. Finally, it decided upon financial services as a business where its cash resources could be of genuine use. It acquired to major British insurers, Eagle Star in 1984 and Allied Dunbar in 1985, and in 1989 added

Farmers, one of the largest insurance companies in the USA. In 1989 it began to sell off all its interests outside the tobacco and financial services sectors.

BAT took some years to acquire the parenting skills it needed to run an insurer, but was able to build Eagle Star into a profitable operation. However, new market opportunities arose in tobacco with the fall of communism and the privatisation of state tobacco monopolies in countries like Italy. The resources tied up in Eagle Star were no longer 'spare' – they were needed for the core business. BAT took the decision to spin off Eagle Star as a separate operation, and it was acquired by Zurich Group, a Swiss insurer, in 1997.

Source: www.bat.com, accessed on 25 April 2000.

can be deployed usefully, to generate competitive advantage in some industry. Otherwise, it may need to divest them, spin them off in a separate operation or, in the case of financial resources, return them to shareholders.

Issues relating to innovation, learning and change

Even when there are no resources that are obvious candidates for 'promotion' to strategic resources, a business may still have a viable future. This will depend, however, on the organisation's capacity for developing new capabilities or other resources before competitors have the chance to do the same. Twice in recent years, at the beginning of the 1980s and the 1990s, Sony has appeared to be in trouble, with profits falling and competition increasing. Both times, a combination of product innovation and changes to its architecture and value chain have enabled it to rebound. Firms with that kind of dynamic capability confront the strategic issue of *how to utilise their capacity for innovation and learning to improve their competitive position*. After reviewing the firm's environment and competitive stance, it may be clear that product innovation is desirable in certain areas. Similarly, the analysis described earlier in this section will show if the business can benefit from enhancing a particular activity in its value chain. Sony, for example, might benefit from product development in its audio and television businesses, or from reducing its production costs in those same businesses to levels closer to those of its Korean competitors.

A strong dynamic capability can be a reason to expect a successful firm to enhance its advantage further. The ability to innovate and learn can also help an unsuccessful firm towards recovery, unless its financial or competitive situation is very poor, when there may not be enough time or funds for any necessary changes to be implemented.

11.2.5 Review of corporate-level strategy

This part of the situation analysis looks at how well an organisation is using its parenting skills, at whether all the existing businesses belong in its portfolio, and at whether the portfolio should be expanded to include new businesses.

The review of corporate-level strategy requires information relating to:

- the performance of the different businesses – from the initial overview (Section 11.2.1);
- the competitive situation of the different businesses: whether they are in attractive or unattractive industries and markets, and how quickly they are likely to grow;
- the most important resources that each business possesses, with an emphasis on strategic resources, or those that are likely to become strategic;
- the organisation's parenting skills and parenting style, using the theory introduced in Chapter 9.

The following types of issue emerge from this section of the strategic review:

- *What should the organisation do with businesses that do not appear to fit within its portfolio?* A unit may not share any important resources with the other businesses in the portfolio, and the parent may not have any skills that help it develop (see Real-Life Application 11.12). The corporation may be better off

REAL-LIFE APPLICATION 11.12

What should Sony do with its insurance business?

Sony's 1999 Annual Report wrote in extremely positive terms about its business selling life insurance to Japanese customers. It emphasised the fact that the business has been expanding while competitors have been contracting. However our analysis of Sony's results (Real-Life Application 11.2) has shown that this unit's return on assets was clearly and consistently the lowest of all the businesses in Sony's portfolio.

The match between the resources employed in this business and those required in the other businesses is unclear. It does not profit from the corporation's R&D resources and reputation for innovativeness, as the games division and various electronics businesses do. It does not furnish software for the electronics businesses' hardware, in the way that the music and pictures divisions do. It does provide a fairly safe way for the firm to invest its spare financial resources although, as we have seen, the returns are uninspiring. The Japanese insurance industry is consolidating rapidly, and globally the industry is plagued with overcapacity, so margins are unlikely to improve in the near future.

There are arguments in the other direction. The insurance business can certainly profit from the corporation's reputation for reliability. The US conglomerate, General Electric, has built a very successful $4 billion business in financial services, but this was built on a genuine synergy – GE's industrial customers wanted the firm to offer them financing facilities. Only after it had built expertise did it diversify into insurance and consumer finance. It may be that Sony was more swayed by the example of other major Japanese corporations, almost all of which have an associated bank and insurance company within their keiretsu grouping.

Sony has confounded its doubters before. Many Western commentators believed that its ventures into music and movies were mistaken, based on supposed synergies with the electronics business that did not truly exist. Matsushita, which diversified in the same way at the same time, eventually sold its film and music businesses, but Sony, after a shaky start, has been able to acquire the parenting skills needed to run them.

However, in 1999 Sony had been involved in the insurance business for twenty years. If it had not yet found a way to obtain adequate returns on its investment in insurance, then perhaps it needed to consider whether it had a future there.

selling such a unit, even if it is profitable at present, to an owner that can extract more value from it, and investing the sale proceeds in businesses it understands better. Alternatively, it may need to enhance its parenting skills in order to be able to manage the business effectively. There may also be businesses that are candidates for disposal because they are in unattractive industries, although some corporations have competences in extracting good profits from mature, declining or low-margin industries.

- *How might the corporation's strategic resources and parenting skills be leveraged into new businesses?* Contemporary theory suggests that the best way for successful businesses to develop is by using their core competences, distinctive capabilities, parenting skills and other strategic resources in businesses where they can be a source of competitive advantage (see Real-Life Application 11.13).

- *How, if at all, should the organisation attempt to profit from synergies between its businesses?* As we have already discussed in Chapter 9, synergies between businesses may be difficult to obtain in practice. Corporate managers need to decide to what extent they wish to intervene in the management of individual businesses to compel their managers, or give them incentives, to co-operate. In the case of Benetton (Real-Life Application 11.13), the decision was taken to transfer the sporting goods businesses from the Benetton family holding company, Edizione Holdings, to the Benetton clothing company, so that the different units would come under the same management.

REAL-LIFE APPLICATION 11.13

Leveraging strategic resources

McDonald's

'I think that, over time, we owe it to our shareholders, our owner operators, our employees and our suppliers to see how we can take advantage of our skills and competencies ... We know how to run a multi-unit restaurant at a high quality standard. We know how to train people, how to buy real estate and construct buildings, and how to market products. And together with our suppliers, we have a unique global supply infrastructure. If we can find a way to leverage this for the long run, then we must try.' (Jack Greenberg, CEO of McDonald's, interviewed for the company's 1999 Annual Report, p. 11).

McDonald's is seeking to use its strategic resources through investing in Chipotle, a chain of Mexican-style restaurants, and by buying the Donato's pizza business in Ohio and Aroma, a UK chain of coffee bars.

Benetton

Benetton is seeking to use its capabilities in design and distribution to become a major player in the sporting goods and sports clothing sector. It has bought a number of sporting goods brands, including Rollerblade inline skates, Prince tennis rackets and Nordica ski boots.

'"You take Benetton's power, its extremely efficient sourcing and distribution, and its knowledge of world markets, and you apply that to brands like Nordica, and you can develop a sports clothing brand as well as a sports brand," says Keith Wills, retail analyst at Goldman, Sachs & Co. in London. The Benettons are already experimenting with merchandising ski boots and clothes together. At the flagship Manhattan store, apparel is on the main floor and sports equipment upstairs. In Europe, the group is planning to launch Playlife stores to sell sports equipment and sports clothing.' ('A Cozy Deal at Benetton?', *Business Week*, 28 July 1997)

◀ *Portfolio models were discussed in Chapter 9.*

- *How should the corporation's management allocate resources between the different businesses?* As we mentioned in the introduction to this chapter, corporations, even large ones, rarely have enough cash or enough management attention to distribute between their different projects. Portfolio models such as the Boston Consulting Group matrix were originally developed to help managers prioritise the conflicting demands of different businesses.

11.2.6 Review of architecture and culture

As we saw in Chapters 7 and 8, an appropriate culture and architecture are needed to give an organisation an effective value chain and dynamic capabilities. The situation analysis needs to pick up any problems in this area. We must be alert for signs that people are not motivated in a way that helps a business give good service, or that competitiveness is in danger of being undermined by, for example, internal conflict or creeping bureaucracy.

Various kinds of evidence can indicate that all is not well with an organisation's culture or architecture. Attitudes to the company among managers or staff may be deteriorating: they may be leaving the firm to join competitors or to set up their own business, absenteeism levels are high, or staff are going on strike more frequently. Customers may be complaining about staff attitudes and defecting to other providers. Or we may be able to see, by comparing the company's culture and structure against the theoretical models set out in Chapters 8 and 10, that they do not fit the organisation's strategy and competitive circumstances.

The main kinds of issue that emerge from this part of the review are as follows:

◀ Chapter 10 discusses how structures, control and reward systems change as organisations grow. Sociability and solidarity were reviewed in Section 8.5.1

- *In what ways should the organisation consider altering its structure, systems and culture so that they are more consistent with its life-cycle stage and its future strategy?* Systems and structures need to alter to keep pace with the organisation's development. A divisional structure may be needed as the organisation expands into new services and markets. The focus of that divisional structure may need to move from, say, geographic regions to customer industries, as the organisation chooses to emphasise global synergies over local responsiveness. Control and reward systems may need to change to reflect changes in the organisation's strategic priorities – for example, to a new emphasis on reducing waste and pollution. It may be desirable for the organisation's culture to exhibit more sociability or solidarity, as the nature of competitive advantage in its industry changes over time.

- *How should the organisation respond to problems in motivating its own employees, and those of other firms in its supply and distribution network?* The formal or informal relational contracts between the firm and other stakeholders may have been broken (see Real-Life Application 11.14) or may be motivating people inappropriately. Investment houses reward successful traders with large bonuses (an element of the formal contract) and high prestige (part of the relational contract). They must be careful that traders do not feel pressured into illegal behaviour (market-rigging or the use of inside information) making large, risky investments that will earn them high rewards if successful, but will seriously damage the firm if they are not.

REAL-LIFE APPLICATION 11.14

Changing architecture at McDonald's

McDonald's has made a number of changes to its architecture since the promotion of Jack Greenberg from Chief Financial Officer to Chief Executive Officer in August 1998, in order to address several issues. Firstly, there was too great an emphasis on long service as a basis for rewards, rather than innovation. Managers who had spent ten years at the firm were still regarded as new. Secondly, these long-serving headquarters staff were taking many operating decisions, for example on pricing, without reference to franchisees or to consumer research data. Thirdly, relations with McDonald's franchisees were deteriorating, a problem that was affecting the company's sales (see Real-Life Application 11.3). The firm had broken its informal relational contract with its franchisees by opening new restaurants that were perceived as taking away customers from established franchises, and by imposing a controversial franchisee evaluation scheme.

Greenberg made a number of changes to the corporation's architecture. He fired 23% of McDonald's headquarters staff, the first such sackings in the history of the company, while bringing in new blood from firms like Tricon and General Electric. Decisions about pricing and product introduction, previously taken within the tall headquarters hierarchy, are now delegated to franchisees and local managers. Marketing information is more widely used to shape these decisions. The franchisee evaluation scheme has been abandoned.

At the same time, the firm has made decisions on its competitive stance and corporate-level strategy that are designed, in part, to repair relational contracts with franchisees. In the USA, the firm has reduced the rate at which it is opening new burger outlets and its acquisition of Donato's, a medium-sized pizza chain, is partly intended to provide new expansion opportunities for existing McDonald's franchise owners.

11.3 Establishing priorities

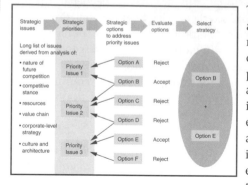

Together, the previous steps in the situation analysis are likely to highlight many issues, particularly for a large and diversified organisation. Although in practice each of these is likely to get attention from managers at some level in the organisation, only a few will be earmarked for senior management attention. These are also normally the issues to which students would be expected to give greatest prominence in their assignments.

Issues can be grouped under the following six categories (we use only three in the figure for space reasons), in descending order of priority:

1. *Survival factors and threshold resources that the organisation will no longer possess.* These issues are clearly the most urgent of all, in that they may threaten the entire survival of the organisation. In our analysis, they emerge from the reviews of the environment (Section 11.2.2) and of resources and the value chain (Section 11.2.4). Examples are BA's lack of a clear or leading role in its alliance network and equivocal brand positioning, and McDonald's relationship with its franchisees, problems in finding and retaining staff, and poor ratings for the taste of its food.

2. *Strategic advantages that are missing, being eroded by environmental change, imitated/substituted by competitors or dissipated through internal problems.* A high priority also attaches to issues that suggest that the organisation may have lost or be losing its basis of competitive advantage. Its positioning may not be distinctive (Section 11.2.3). Its existing sources of advantage within the value chain may be being eroded and it may lack evident replacements (Section 11.2.4). Inappropriate parenting skills may be eroding the competitiveness of one or more businesses (Section 11.2.5). The firm's culture and architecture may be out of line with the demands of the competitive situation (Section 11.2.6). Examples are the erosion of Sony's differentiation position in televisions and cassette tape players as the product becomes a commodity, and BA's diminishing grip on take-off and landing slots at Heathrow. The less successful the business is and the more important it is as a source of profit, the higher the priority that will need to be given to replacing its remaining sources of competitive advantage. An organisation's capacity for learning and change may need to be directed towards addressing these problems.

3. *Time-constrained issues.* These are issues that, because of external pressures, need to be resolved within a limited time frame. Governments may set deadlines for the expression of interest in a certain opportunity, or for meeting particular pollution standards. Management will not always want to place these issues high on their internal agenda, but may be forced to make a commitment. For example, it is quite likely that Sony's managers would prefer to keep growing their insurance business organically. However, they needed to make a decision

in 1999 about whether to merge the insurance arm with another company, or to commit much more capital to it, to enable it to compete with the much larger firms that were emerging as the Japanese insurance industry consolidated.

4. *Proven resources, value chain attributes and parenting skills that can be made strategic and/or leveraged into other markets.* For a successful business with few issues to consider in categories 1 and 2, these issue will have a high priority, since they represent the bases for future expansion. For an unsuccessful firm these expansion opportunities normally take lower priority than repairing the competitiveness of the core business. These emerge from the review of each business' resources and value chain (Section 11.2.4). The highest priority in this category belongs to issues whose resolution seems likeliest to lead to sustainable advantage in the future.

5. *Speculative opportunities: new markets and products with long-term potential, undeveloped or unproved resources.* These are a less certain source of potential advantage than the better proven opportunities in category 4. They are therefore likely to be given a lower priority, unless they represent a much larger source of potential profit, in which case the rewards may outweigh the greater risk. A firm may be able to generate a number of these opportunities if it is strong in learning and innovation. Again, the highest priority belongs to opportunities with the greatest potential to generate sustainable advantage.

6. *Spare resources.* As long as they do not represent a drain on the organisation's finances or management, there may be no pressing strategic need to use spare resources. However, shareholders or owners will want to see their invested capital being put to efficient use, or press for spare resources to be turned into cash that they can reinvest in another firm.

Within each category, the highest priority will clearly go to the issues with the greatest implications in terms of future profits (or losses).

11.4 Strategic options

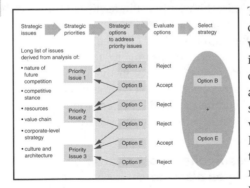

The next stage in the analysis is to develop a range of strategic options which can address the highest priority issues. For each issue, it is good mental discipline to try to seek out between two and four *different* alternatives. This is to stimulate the creative reasoning that is a vital part of top-level strategic thinking. It also helps avoid automatically gravitating towards 'obvious' strategies that may give no advantage, because competitors are following identical paths.

One option that is always available, in theory, is for the organisation to carry on with its present strategy. (This is sometimes referred to, misleadingly, as the 'do nothing option' – a better term would be 'carry on as we are'.) A continuation of the present strategy may be quite a reasonable way forward where there is no obvious way of resolving an issue, or where the present strategy is obviously successful.

◄ *Competency traps are discussed in Chapter 7. We looked at some of the factors which block managers' ability to perceive new things in Chapter 2, and return to this issue when we look at organisational change in Chapter 14.* ►

However, even highly successful organisations need to change their strategy to cope with potential new developments in the environment. Sticking too rigidly to the same strategy for too long may lead the organisation into competency traps.

Alternative strategic options may differ from one another along two dimensions. They can try to do *different things*: one option may be to match competitors' products and service, while another may be to try to raise levels of service well beyond what customers receive at present. And they can try to achieve things in *different ways*: when copying a competitor's product, a firm can opt to use its existing value chain, or to change its product development processes and distribution systems so that they too are more like those deployed by the competition. We can look at these two dimensions in greater detail.

11.4.1 Doing different things

In confronting a strategic issue, an organisation has a number of alternatives to consider, each of which involves differing degrees of internal change, and change to the competitive dynamic within the industry. It can attempt to:

- catch up with or match competitors' offerings;
- use advantages in one area to compensate for disadvantages elsewhere;
- neutralise competition;
- go beyond competitors' offerings;
- withdraw from, or outsource, the relevant business or activity;
- make a minimum investment so as to 'reserve the right to play' later;
- seek new competitive arenas.

We examine each of these alternatives in turn and give examples of how they might be applied to a selection of real strategic issues.

Catching up with or matching competitors' offerings

This 'copycat' strategy may involve introducing products that compete directly with a competitor's, in the way that Burger King launched its 'Big King' to match McDonald's 'Big Mac'. It can also involve emulating their processes, as McDonald's did when it launched 'Made for You' (see Real-Life Application 11.10). This kind of strategy is basically defensive, aiming to fix a weakness rather than build on strength, and contains a tacit admission by a firm that, in this area of its operations, it cannot do any better than its competitors. However, it might be right for an organisation to conduct a 'holding operation' to build survival factors in one part of its business, while it tries to build advantages elsewhere.

Using advantages in one resource area or part of value chain to offset disadvantages elsewhere

Strategy is about trade-offs, and businesses frequently take judgements about where they can use strategic resources to offset areas where they may possess only the bare minimum requirements for survival. A common example is where an established firm uses its cash reserves to fund price reductions in order to combat a new entrant with a superior product.

In its TV business, Sony is trying to use its reputation and its strength in innovation to sell television sets with advanced features, and offset the superior competences of Samsung in low-cost production of generic products. McDonald's uses its reputation, its capabilities in delivering consistent quality and the strength of its distribution activity to offset American consumers' low perceptions of the taste of its food.

A strategic option like this may involve changing a product's positioning – its price or advertising – to emphasise the organisation's particular areas of advantage. It may also require the organisation to enhance those particular resources and value chain activities, to make sure that they form the basis of a genuine differentiation or cost advantage.

Neutralise competition

A special case of the use of resources to offset weakness is when the organisation takes steps to eliminate or neutralise competitors, rather than to out-compete them. This typically involves the use of financial assets and sometimes capabilities in negotiation. Strategic options that come under this heading include:

- **Acquisition of bothersome competitors**. Microsoft, feeling threatened by Quicken, the market leader in PC software for managing personal finances, tried to acquire it. Unfortunately for Microsoft it was prevented from so doing by the US anti-trust authorities.

- **Industry consolidation/rationalisation**. This is another acquisition-based strategy, typically used in a declining industry plagued by overcapacity. Stronger firms will buy up weaker competitors and then take them out of commission. This brings supply in line with demand and allows the remaining assets to make an adequate financial return. Skandia, for example, is leading the consolidation of the Scandinavian insurance industry, through an agreed acquisition of controlling stakes in Storebrand of Norway and Finland's Pohjola. A variation on this theme is where producers swap assets to give each firm control of a particular product or market niche.

- **Litigation and lobbying to erect or penetrate barriers to entry**. A firm may use, or threaten, a lawsuit alleging patent infringement to discourage firms from launching competing products. It is also possible for new entrants to use legal proceedings alleging anti-competitive behaviour as a lever to prevent incumbents from retaliation. EasyJet, a low-priced UK airline, went to the courts to try to prevent British Airways from launching Go, a subsidiary that competed directly with easyJet. Although BA won the legal battle, easyJet won a great deal of favourable publicity during the proceedings. Firms may also lodge anti-dumping suits and lobby parliaments and governments to win protection for foreign competitors – the US steel industry has used this tactic consistently over several decades.

Going beyond competitors' offerings

Some of the most thrilling stories in strategic management are of 'breakthrough' strategies: product or service innovations that transform the nature of competition in an industry. Another word for this is **outpacing**. In the 1970s and 1980s, Toyota was able, through its manufacturing systems, to cut the delivery lead time on its cars to levels unimaginable by its competitors. Freeserve, a British Internet service provider (ISP), transformed the UK industry by introducing a service that required users to pay no monthly subscription, and pay only the cost of their telephone calls. Although this business model was quickly copied, Freeserve was able to build and hold a position as the UK's leading ISP, ahead of established firms like AOL.

There are more mundane 'leapfrog' strategies that also come into this category, where firms try to outdo one another with successive product offerings. In appealing to long-haul business class passengers, BA announced a refit of its planes with more luxurious sleeper seats. Virgin Atlantic promptly countered with the introduction of double beds on some of its flights. Similarly, Sega and Sony are attempting to gain advantage over one another with successive generations of computer games consoles.

A breakthrough strategy often consists of more than a product innovation. Often, as in the Toyota example, there are innovations in the value chain as well: product development and production processes may be re-engineered, and new distribution channels pioneered. Typically, changes to the architecture and culture will be needed to make all this possible.

Withdrawal or outsourcing

The different ways of withdrawing from a business are reviewed in Chapter 15. ▶

The opposite extreme from the breakthrough strategy is to withdraw from a business, market segment or value chain activity. Withdrawal from a business, segment or activity may not mean closing it down. Often an activity will be spun off as an independent unit or sold to a third party, or the people and assets will be redeployed in other areas.

◀ *The advantages and disadvantages of outsourcing are discussed in Chapter 8.*

A corporation may decide to withdraw from a business because it does not believe that it has appropriate parenting skills, or because it believes that there are more attractive opportunities elsewhere. Similarly, a business may decide to withdraw from a particular market segment because it doubts its ability to compete effectively, or because it would make a better return by using its resources to serve different customers. Skandia has expressed its intention to become a global leader in unit-linked investment products (investments tied to the performance of stock-market investments). It has been steadily withdrawing from other businesses, such as property and casualty insurance (in Italy and the UK) and reinsurance.

A business may also decide to withdraw from particular activities in the value chain, such as distribution or maintenance, by outsourcing them. It is becoming increasingly difficult for firms to sustain their position if they have weaknesses at any point in the value chain. A firm may therefore do best to focus its own resources in the activities where the firm has a sustainable advantage, and buy other activities in from specialists who will bring it at least a threshold capability.

Finally, where an organisation has spare or under-utilised resources, it may decide simply to cut them back rather than seek an alternative use for them. Superfluous cash reserves can be returned to shareholders as a special dividend or through a repurchase of some of the firm's shares.

Reserving the right to play

Sometimes a firm does not want to be drawn into the kind of commitment needed to match or surpass competitors, but does not want to withdraw completely from a business, market or activity. In that case, it can try to 'reserve the right to play'[4] – make the minimum investment needed for it to acquire the necessary threshold resources. This investment can be in people and research facilities or take the form of a stake in, or a joint venture with, another firm. If the business or activity starts to show greater promise, then the investment can be increased. If not, then the firm will not have wasted too much money, and may have gained knowledge that it can use elsewhere.

This is a common strategy in emerging industries or markets, where it is not yet clear which technologies will prevail, or indeed whether there is any profit potential at all. Benetton tried to reserve the right to play in Internet retailing by taking a stake in a start-up, Boo.com. If it became clear that Internet retailing was vital to its future, then it hoped to draw upon Boo.com's e-commerce experience for its core business. Even though Boo.com experienced severe financial difficulties and at one stage was forced to cease operations, Benetton had limited its losses to an affordable sum.

Firms also adopt this kind of option for new technologies, which they judge will be profitable in the future but which are a long way from generating profitable products. Japanese firms such as Sharp followed this strategy with liquid-crystal diodes (LCDs). They started by allocating a few scientists to the technology, and gradually developed core competences. When laptop PCs came to the market, Sharp and Toshiba were able to gain a lucrative, dominant, position in the supply of flat-panel displays for them.

One attraction of this strategy is that it enables firms to learn from the mistakes made by those of their competitors who have decided to make a greater early commitment. The drawback is that, if these other firms make a successful breakthrough, they may gain early-mover advantages in market position, reputation and distinctive capabilities that will be difficult for their followers to match.

Seek new competitive arenas

◀ *Diversification is discussed in Chapter 9.*

Good products, strategic resources and value chain activities may give an organisation the basis for diversifying into new business, markets or product areas. A move of this kind may need to be accompanied by a withdrawal from another section in order to free up necessary resources.

We begin the process of considering strategic options for McDonald's and Sony in Real-Life Application 11.15.

REAL-LIFE APPLICATION 11.15

Real strategic issues and options

In this real-life application, we take two of the strategic issues that we picked out earlier in our analysis of McDonald's and Sony, and look at alternative options to address them. Please note that what we say here and in subsequent real-life applications in this chapter are our opinions and suggestions, set out purely for the purposes of illustration and discussion.

How should McDonald's react to the shortage of unskilled labour

In 1999, McDonald's, like all its competitors, was threatened by a labour shortage in the USA. A long-lived economic expansion saw unemployment fall to unprecedentedly low levels. The labour shortage meant that many of the people who might once have been ready to consider working in a hamburger restau-

▶

rant could now find better-paid or more prestigious employment elsewhere. The danger for McDonald's was that the term 'fast-food' might become a misnomer if there were not enough staff to service peak-hour lunch queues.

This is one issue where 'carry on as we are' represents a valid option. There are no historical precedents for a prolonged period with such low unemployment, so McDonald's might decide simply to live with labour shortages for a few months. However, if the present situation endures, as some economic commentators think it might, McDonald's might be caught out if competitors are better prepared.

Matching competitors, none of whom had yet solved this problem, would carry little risk. One option might be for McDonald's to lead its competitors in launching a joint industry scheme designed to train older people, or to make it easier for people like single mothers with young children to join the workforce. This would also reinforce the firm's reputation in the community, but might be costly to run.

For this issue, there are no obvious options using advantage from other areas to compensate for the threatened poor service or to neutralise competition. However, long term, McDonald's might consider a radical redesign of its restaurant systems to use less labour. This option has risks attached, since it might involve considerable investment in developing and installing new food preparation systems or in automating order-taking and serving, which would be wasted if the labour market loosened. On the other hand, an extreme version of this option, which would see a McDonald's restaurant transformed into some kind of technological wonderland where people come to see their food prepared as much as to eat it, would increase differentiation advantage. (Yes, it's far-fetched, but it is important to try to be creative – a parallel phenomenon is visible in the trendy Sushi restaurants in London, New York, as well as Tokyo, where a conveyor belt and robots are used to deliver freshly and visibly-prepared sushi to customers.) A small-scale research effort along these lines, perhaps in collaboration with a catering equipment manufacturer or a university food science department, might qualify as reserving the right to play.

Withdrawal from the US fast food business or from any area of the value chain affected by labour shortage is not a realistic option – the business is too important to the corporation. McDonald's might consider new competitive arenas. However, it is difficult to think of any US businesses into which McDonald's might real-istically think of diversifying that are not subject to the same labour shortages as fast food. Diversification is not an option that addresses this issue, though it might be considered in relation to some of their other problems (see Real-Life Application 11.8). However, McDonald's might seek to increase its penetration of overseas markets, where unemployment is higher, to provide a profit stream to offset any decline in US income.

How should Sony react to commoditisation in the TV business?

Sales in Sony's television business have declined in the face of price competition, from other producers such as Samsung, which is unlikely to ease. This business is probably too important for 'carry on as we are' to be an option – rather, Sony needs to think of ways of ensuring acceptable levels of profitability in future, or to get out altogether.

Under the heading of 'matching competition', Sony might seek ways of keeping its own production costs at competitive levels. One option would be to relocate some manufacturing activity to countries with lower labour costs. Another option would be to re-engineer the production process to take out further costs. However, since Sony would need to commit a lot of time and money to this option, it would make more sense to conceive of it as a way of going beyond competition, bringing production costs, say, 30% below competitors' likely future levels, rather than merely matching them.

Sony is presently trying to use advantages in technology and reputation to combat price competition, by shifting its product range towards TVs with wide-screens and other advanced features. Samsung and its fellow Korean corporations have, however, already shown themselves to have decent reputations and have introduced TVs with features that come close to matching Sony's. Digital and wide-screen TVs are themselves likely to become commodity products quite soon. To the outside observer (Sony's management may know better) it is difficult to think of anything that Sony can do with a television that Samsung cannot quickly match. There are thus no obvious options that would use Sony's advantages in other areas to compensate for any future cost disadvantage.

There are, however, a number of options that involve neutralising competition. Sony might seek to acquire a Korean competitor, some of which have overextended themselves financially, or establish joint ventures with either Samsung itself or with one of its weaker fellow-countrymen. Sony might also seek to collaborate with its Japanese rival, Matsushita, or with Philips.

Withdrawing from the television business would warrant serious consideration, if it became an area where Sony could no longer compete effectively, though this would involve writing off considerable investments throughout the world. It would also relieve the competitive pressure on firms like Philips and Samsung, which might then feel emboldened to threaten some of Sony's other businesses.

Sony might wish to reserve the right to play in the TV business, to obstruct competitors and retain an interest in the technology. There are possible synergies with the games and computer businesses, and also with commercial video. An option along these lines might involve reducing the TV business to a smaller operation producing high-end TVs that are a test-bed for advanced technologies which may later be incorporated into other products. The reduced TV business might be expected to break even financially, but not to make a high return on capital.

11.4.2 Doing things in different ways

You will by now be familiar with the variables that an organisation's managers can manipulate when trying to vary its strategy: the corporate strategy that determines the businesses in which an organisation competes and, for each of those businesses, the competitive stance, value chain, resources, culture and architecture. Different strategic options will involve different degrees of change to these variables, individually or together.

◄ *Changes to competitive stance are often analysed using the Ansoff matrix (Chapter 6).*

The changes that can be targeted and implemented most precisely are changes to corporate-level strategy and to competitive stance. These involve:

● entering or withdrawing from industries or markets;

● moving resources from one business area to another;

● developing or withdrawing products and services;

● moving a product's positioning up- or down-market.

Burger King's launch of the 'Big King', and Skandia's withdrawal from Italian commercial insurance, are examples of these relatively straightforward strategic moves, which did not require significant changes to their value chains or architecture.

However, not all strategic options involve changes to corporate-level or marketing strategy. An organisation may attempt to alter its value chain to improve the cost-effectiveness or reliability of different processes. These kinds of change are somewhat more difficult to implement, because they involve disruption to established routines, and the development of new ones. However, they are a vital part of an organisation's strategic repertoire.

An organisation's culture and architecture can also be the basis of strategic options aimed at improving ways in which information is gathered and communicated, and the motivation of people in and around the organisation. Changes in this area may be aimed at improving levels of innovativeness or customer service.

New capabilities and competences may also be required in order for the organisation to cope with a changing environment. This may mean recruiting new human resources to bring in additional skills, or implementing training programmes for existing staff. It may also require changes to the culture and architecture to help people to develop new routines.

However, it would be wrong to restrict strategic thinking to any single part of the strategic mix – strategic moves frequently combine several different elements in a holistic package. Moving a product to a more up-market positioning, for example, is not normally just a simple matter of changing the pricing and advertising. The value chain may need to be changed to deliver higher levels of service and support. The physical assets used to manufacture the product may need to be upgraded so that new features can be incorporated and the proportion of defective products reduced. The culture and architecture will also need to be addressed: the structure and control systems may need to change to empower staff to respond more directly to customer needs, reward systems will need to reflect the emphasis on quality, and the management information systems will need to gather and monitor customer

---

REAL-LIFE APPLICATION 11.16

Holistic strategic change at McDonald's

In its 1999 Annual Report, McDonald's declared its intention of transforming itself into 'a destination, rather than just a convenient place to stop'. On one level, this is simply a strategic repositioning of the McDonald's brand, product and service. However, it implies far-reaching change affecting many elements of the company's strategy.

● The product range will need to be extended to include more interesting signature dishes, and these will have to change more frequently to sustain customer interest.

● This means that the product development activity in McDonald's value chain will need to be completely re-engineered to deliver more elaborate menus and to raise the pace of product innovation. This may imply a significant cultural change in that part of the organisation, including an increased willingness to encourage suggestions from franchisees and restaurant staff.

● The restaurants may need to be re-designed to encourage people to stay longer. The colour scheme may need to be more subdued and the seating replaced (seats in McDonald's restaurants

are designed specifically for customers who are expected to stay for a short time).

● Service processes may need to change so that staff, instead of staying behind the counters to take orders, venture out to encourage customers to order desserts, or refill their drinks. This implies a major retraining programme for restaurant owners and managers as well as their staff.

● The strategy will only be successful if the average value of a customer order in a McDonald's outlet increases. Monitoring, control and maybe even reward systems will need to change in order to give this value more prominence.

McDonald's will not need to change everything. Its distribution activity is already capable of delivering a wide variety of fresh ingredients, and is unlikely to need much upgrading. Its brand remains a strategic asset under its new strategy. It is already a destination for children's parties, and may have capabilities there that can be built upon. Its new acquisitions may also have relevant skills.

Practical dos and don'ts	**Strategic option development**

- Do not restrict yourself to options that have been mentioned by the firm's management or by outside observers such as journalists or case-writers. There is no guarantee that they have correctly identified all the issues, or all the possible ways of addressing them. Try to do better!

- Remember that there is almost always more than one way of addressing a particular issue.

- Try to look at each issue from a number of the different angles set out in Section 11.4.1. What would the strategy be if we tried just to copy the most successful competitor? What would it be if we tried for a ground-breaking innovation? If we withdrew from the business or market affected by the issue, could the resources be put to good use elsewhere?

- It may also be fruitful to try to think of different ways of achieving a given outcome. If an organisation has a weakness in after-sales service, should it fix the problem by improving the organisation of its own service department, or by outsourcing the activity? Or should it decide to ignore that problem and compensate through superior product innovation, or by repositioning its product further down-market and trying for extra sales volume?

- Do not focus exclusively on product/market changes and diversification. Enhancements to the value chain, culture and architecture can be equally important strategically.

- Try to be creative. There is no harm, at this stage in the process, in putting forward ideas that at first sight are slightly impractical – they may trigger other, more sensible ideas. Brainstorming the issues in groups can be helpful. Any truly mad suggestions can be eliminated at the evaluation stage (Section 11.5).

- A strategic option may address more than one issue – for example, McDonald's purchase of the Donato's Pizza chain worked on several levels. It addressed a market opportunity, it represented a way of leveraging McDonald's competences and capabilities in restaurant management, it brought new ideas and competences into the McDonald's organisation, and it helped to provide new profit opportunities for frustrated franchisees. Moves like this, which advance an organisation in several directions at once, are helpful because they lower the risk that management attention will be diffused over a wide range of initiatives.

satisfaction data. Real-Life Application 11.16 discusses some of the challenges posed by McDonald's strategy in 1999.

11.5 Evaluating strategic options and establishing the proposed strategy – the RACES framework

Once the organisation's strategic options have been determined, they have to be narrowed down into a coherent future strategy. This means that we have to seek out a set of options that, taken together:

- address all the high priority issues;

- are consistent with one another, and with the elements of the existing strategy that are going to remain;
- give the organisation the factors required for survival in its chosen industries, and one or more attributes that will make it unique.

This is the stage in our analysis at which creativity must be tempered by practical realities. There is no point in recommending a strategy, however imaginative, that the organisation cannot put into practice for lack of money or skills, or that will be rejected by powerful stakeholders. In order to form part of the organisation's future strategy, a strategic option **must** meet the following criteria:

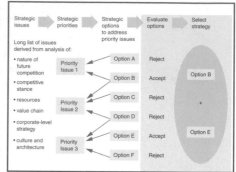

- **Resources** needed to implement the option must be available, or the organisation must be able to obtain them quickly.
- It must be **Acceptable** to powerful internal and external stakeholders, for example the firm's owners, regulatory bodies and key managers and staff.
- It must be **Consistent** with other proposals and existing strategies.
- It must be **Effective** in resolving the issues that it is intended to address.

A strategic option should also contribute to the

- **Sustainability** of the organisation's competitive advantage, by contributing some element of uniqueness to its future strategy.

You may find the various acronyms to be made from Resources, Acceptability, Consistency, Effectiveness, Sustainability (RACES, SCARE, CARES) helpful in remembering these five criteria, each of which we discuss in more detail below. We also look at what happens when there is conflict between different criteria – for example, when the most effective option is the least acceptable.

11.5.1 Resources

The first consideration in determining whether an option should be accepted or rejected is the practical one of whether the organisation has, or can obtain quickly enough, the resources needed to put it into effect.

Physical assets

It can be helpful if the organisation already possesses the land, buildings, equipment and software needed to implement a strategic option. Frequently, however, these things can be purchased if the organisation needs them, so it is often more important to ensure that it has the financial resources to buy them and the competences to use them.

There are cases, however, when the lack of physical resources may be a reason to reject an option. This happens when the resources concerned are difficult to buy on the open market, perhaps because supply is controlled by a competitor. For example, there is an increasing shortage in the UK of prime sites for large retail outlets.

Financial assets

Most strategic moves cost money. There will be up-front costs of market research and R&D. Cash may be needed for additions or improvements to production facilities or sales outlets, for recruiting new staff and making existing people redundant, for training and advertising. If sales volumes increase, then the firm is likely to need extra working capital to finance inventories and debtors. **If the funds for all this are not available then the option will need to be rejected in favour of something more affordable.**

It is therefore important to prepare an estimate, however crude, of the likely cost of an option, and to analyse an organisation's cash flows and balance sheet to look for possible sources of cash from:

● *Cash generated by existing operations*. Remember that cash is not the same as profit. If the firm is already investing heavily in its existing operations, then it may have no funds available from this source, even if it is profitable.

● *Loans*. An organisation's borrowing capacity is normally determined by its gearing and interest cover. If gearing is already high and/or interest cover low, a firm is likely to have difficulty in obtaining new loans, unless they can be secured against existing assets.

● *Share or bond issues*. If the firm's prospects are good, or its managers have built a following among investors, then it may be able to raise new funds in the capital markets or from private shareholders. If it can make a sufficiently strong case, it may be able to ask the market to fund a specific strategic option, such as an acquisition, expansion into a major new market or the development of a completely new range of products. Young firms in fast-growing industries may find that venture capital is available, at a price, even if they have no track record in their current firm.

● *Asset disposals*. By selling plant, buildings or parts of the business, firms may raise cash to reinvest elsewhere.

● *Improved use of working capital*. By reorganising its operations to cut the amount of inventory or reduce the level of debtors, a company can release capital for investment.

Sometimes an option may be self-financing. Investments in new systems to cut costs or lower inventory may save a firm enough money in the short term to pay for themselves.

Competences and intellectual assets

We have already shown in Chapter 7 how difficult it may be for an organisation to build competences and intellectual resources. Therefore, two important judgements need to be made:

● *Does the organisation already have the skills needed to put the option into practice?*

- *If not, can the organisation acquire the intellectual resources it needs quickly enough?* If the organisation has a good track record in learning, then the answer to this question may be 'yes'. Otherwise, the organisation will need to buy in or borrow these resources, if they are available. They may, however, be obtainable from consultants or from other businesses that belong to the same corporation or strategic network.

The skills of the change agent are reviewed in Chapter 14, and the challenges of post-merger integration in Chapter 15.▶

The competences and knowledge that are needed may go beyond product and process technology. A strategic option may imply substantial changes in structure, systems or culture, and the management of these changes requires specialist skills. The management of a merger or acquisition, if this forms part of the proposed strategy, also calls for particular competences.

Human resources

Even if the organisation does not need to acquire new knowledge or competences, a strategic option may require it to increase the number of people with a particular skill, such as software engineers or salespeople. It may also need to strengthen its management with people with experience in, for example, electronic commerce, running sales operations in Thailand or managing the implementation of large-scale IT systems. In determining whether to accept or reject an option, we need to decide:

- Whether the organisation's existing staff can implement the option, with relevant training if necessary. This requires a judgement about whether those people have the right level of education, and the right attitude and motivation, to take on board any new skills.
- Whether new employees can be recruited to supplement the existing staff. This involves questioning whether there is an adequate supply of people with the relevant education and training who will come for the pay offered. It also requires a judgement on how easy the organisation will find it to attract people with the right degree of motivation. Organisations with a poor reputation or with a strong and unusual culture may find it difficult to recruit enough of these people.

Reputational assets

The importance of reputational assets will depend on the nature of the strategic option and the industry at which it is aimed. For options aimed at improving internal processes, they will be largely irrelevant. In emerging industries, or in new segments of established industries, the lack of an established brand need or reputation may not be a problem. In the airline industry, firms like Virgin Atlantic, easyJet and Air One have been able to establish themselves in competition with established airlines with strong reputations. Options aimed at entering or expanding in a brand-sensitive market, on the other hand, will be hard to achieve if the firm does not have a strong brand.

A firm does not necessarily need reputational assets in the precise segment that the strategic option is targeting. Reputation can be transferred from one business to another, as Richard Branson did when he used a brand built in the music industry to start an airline. Reputational assets can be bought by acquiring another company or can sometimes be built quickly through advertising and sales promotion.

Time

Finally, it is important to assess whether the organisation has sufficient time at its disposal to make a success of the option in question.

As we noted in Section 11.3, some opportunities have a very obvious time constraint attached to them, but for any strategic option it is worth asking if the organisation can implement it before competitors do something that destroys its benefits. If competitors are going to be clearly first to market with a new product, or will have made further advances before a catch-up strategy has time to take effect, then maybe the option should be discarded.

For an unsuccessful organisation, the owners or controlling stakeholders will be another source of time constraints. Any proposed changes in the strategy will need to take effect before stakeholders lose patience and shut the organisation down.

11.5.2 Acceptability

Organisations, as we have seen, contain various groups of stakeholders who typically differ in what they want from the organisation, and in the power they have to achieve their own desires and/or frustrate those of other people. If a strategic option falls foul of a powerful stakeholder group, then it may not be possible to implement it. The organisation may lose time, money and customers if it tries to do so.

◀ *The concept of stakeholders was introduced in Chapter 1. The analysis of stakeholder power is discussed in Chapters 13 and 14.* ▶

In order for an option to meet the criterion of acceptability,[5] it must first meet the objectives of the *controlling* stakeholders. It should help the organisation to achieve the financial returns and growth that those stakeholders are seeking. It should not involve more (or less) risk than they are prepared to accept, and be compatible with any requirements they have regarding ethics, social responsibility and so on.

The sources of obstacles to change, and the management of the change process are reviewed in Chapter 14. ▶

The second requirement, if an option is to be judged acceptable, is that any objections from powerful stakeholders can be overcome. Most significant shifts in strategy will upset some people, who fear that they will lose power or status, or that they will end up doing more work for the same, or less, reward. If those people have the power, and the desire to use it, then they can block an option through political manoeuvring, strike action or simple refusal to do as they are asked. The resulting conflict may alienate customers, or take management attention away from everyday operations, so that the organisation becomes less effective.

For an option to be acceptable therefore, it must clearly be possible to manage the change process in such a way as to limit the damage from such conflict, or to avoid alienating powerful stakeholders.

◀ *The concept of relational contracts is introduced in Section 8.5.4.*

The assessment of acceptability will draw upon an analysis of the organisation's culture and architecture. In particular, it will be important to understand the nature of the relational contracts between the organisation and its different internal and external stakeholders. It is by upsetting these relational contracts that an organisation can trigger damaging resistance to change.

There is rarely a simple 'yes' or 'no' answer to the question 'Is this option acceptable?' Most proposals, however radical, can become acceptable if the management

Unacceptable strategic change at British Airways

In the 1980s, British Airways followed a differentiation strategy based on customer service. Customer service in the air is largely delivered by cabin crew, whose attitudes were thus crucial to the success of BA's strategy. The relational contract between cabin crew and the airline involved a high degree of recognition for their efforts, as well as a profit-sharing package.

In the mid-1990s, when British Airways' strategic emphasis moved towards cost leadership, and it tried to change cabin crew working conditions, its management tried to push these changes through in a way that showed little respect for the cabin crew. The informal relational contract between the airline and these stakeholders was broken and in 1997 the cabin crew mounted a strike.

BA had underestimated the strength of the resistance and the power that this group of stakeholders exerted through its close relationship with passengers. Many customers who had in the past benefited from the cabin crew's hard work were sympathetic to their cause. The dispute cost BA millions of pounds in lost revenue and eroded its reputation for customer service and as a good employer.

is prepared to spend enough effort and money on winning over the key stakeholders, or if the organisation is so obviously on the brink of disaster that radical solutions need to be tried. However, acceptability can be used as a criterion on which to *rank* proposals, and a decision can then be made as to whether the most acceptable proposal is also the best overall. We return to this point in Section 11.5.6 below.

11.5.3 Consistency

We have already mentioned the need for a strategy to be coherent – for value chain, culture and architecture all to be configured to deliver the chosen combination of cost and differentiation advantage in the chosen markets, and to sustain advantage for the future.

We look at new venture divisions as one way of managing incongruent or inconsistent strategies in Section 15.2.2. ▶

Once our chosen strategic options have been accepted, the new strategy of which they will form part should also be coherent. That means that the strategic options that are selected must be consistent or congruent with one another, and with any parts of the existing strategy that are being maintained. Particular points to look out for include:

- *Brand values and reputation.* A strategic option should not undermine the organisation's reputational assets. For example, it would be difficult for Sony to launch a line of cheap, disposable products without confusing consumers who are used to its products being long-lived, reliable and priced at a premium. If it wanted to extent its products in this direction, it might need to launch a new brand, as BA did with its cut-price Go airline.

- *Culture and architecture.* A new option should not undermine the values and relational contracts that are important for sustaining motivation and innovativeness elsewhere in the organisation.

- *Value chain.* An organisation should beware of overloading its value chain or stretching it in too many potentially conflicting ways. Careful judgements are required as to whether a new product or new form of positioning will force people to do mutually contradictory things – for example, produce custom-designed and mass-produced items at the same time, using the same equipment.

Inconsistency is not always a barrier to adopting an option. In a poorly performing organisation, or one that is threatened by a changing environment, a clean break with past strategy may be needed. However, the fact that this may be difficult to manage needs to be acknowledged.

11.5.4 Effectiveness

An effective option is one that resolves the strategic issue that it is intended to address. The entire process of option development that we have mapped out in Sections 11.2–11.4 is designed to produce effective options, and we shall not go into further detail here. Certain options may however creep into your proposals that will fail the effectiveness test – for example, generic 'good ideas' (or management fads) like empowerment, total quality, business process re-engineering and knowledge management, **if** they do not address a particular strategic issue.

Some options, however, may be *more* effective than others. For example, a wholesale replacement of a firm's product line may be more effective in meeting future customer needs than a more gradual, piecemeal adaptation. However, the more gradual approach may be more compatible with the organisation's skill base. It may be less risky and involve fewer redundancies among long-serving employees, and so be more acceptable to owners, senior managers and staff. Effectiveness, like acceptability, is a criterion on which alternative options can be ranked.

We look at strategies at different stages of the life-cycle in Chapter 12. We also look there at strategies in other contexts, such as the public sector. ▶

Certain types of strategy are likely to be more or less effective according to the context in which they will be used. For example, effective strategies in mature industries are those which address the key issues of a declining growth in sales and an increasingly large and powerful competitor group, and respond to the needs of a sophisticated, and potentially bored, customer base. In newer industries, an effective strategy is one that makes the most of rising market demand and builds a strong competitive position for the future.

11.5.5 Sustainability

◀ *Strategic resources, including dynamic capabilities, are examined in Chapter 7. The issue of sustainability is discussed in more detail in Chapter 8.*

Within the options that are accepted for incorporation into the proposed strategy, there will need to be some that give the organisation a reasonable expectation of sustainable advantage. Remember that our definition of a strategic option is that it is large scale and long term. That means that at least some of the options should be aiming to develop products and build strategic resources and unique value chain attributes that will give the organisation some form of cost and/or differentiation advantage over the longer term. In fast-changing environments, this is likely to involve the development of dynamic capabilities. Other strategies may be needed in order to produce short-term success in order to allow the development of other longer-term benefits, but long-term options cannot be ignored altogether.

A major focus for long-term sustained success is therefore the development of strategic resources – those which are rare, and difficult to imitate or substitute.

11.5.6 Combining the RACES factors to reach a decision

At the end of your RACES analysis you will end up with set of options, each of which should be given a ranking on how well it meets each of the five criteria. It may be helpful to summarise the analysis in a matrix (see Real-Life Application 11.18). The final task is to decide which options to accept and which to reject.

Sometimes an option will rank low on several of the criteria, and can obviously be rejected. Sometimes there will be a clear winning option that ranks highest on most of the criteria and scores acceptably on all of them. More frequently, however, you will be confronted with one of the following two situations:

- Several options perform adequately on all the criteria, but there is no clear winner. The option that scores highest on effectiveness, for example, is not the one that scores highest on acceptability. You are forced to judge which criterion is the most important.

- Every one of the available options fails on at least one criterion, and you are forced to judge which of them is, on balance, the least bad.

These are precisely the kinds of compromises and trade-offs that confront practising managers, and there is no easy formula for judging them. It may be comforting to realise that once you have got this far in the analysis, and eliminated the truly ridiculous options, there are no right or wrong answers. It is, however, important to phrase your argument carefully, so it is clear that you understand the trade-offs you are making, and the precise reasons why, in the end, you favour one option over another. The following guidelines may help:

- Options for which the resources clearly are not available or obtainable should normally be rejected. However, if the option represents a very valuable opportunity, and other criteria are met, it may be worth looking again to see if there are creative ways of finding the resources needed. If the organisation is in deep trouble, then it may seriously be worth considering the gamble of taking resources from a failing operation to fund a speculative opportunity.

- Low effectiveness will also normally be a reason for rejecting an option, although the entire analytical process we have mapped out here, tying options to specific issues, is designed to minimise the number of ineffective options that are analysed.

- A trade-off will frequently be necessary between acceptability and effectiveness. The options that enable the organisation to make radical advances in the market place, or in reducing costs, can often imply substantial changes to people's working practices and involve giving power to people who understand new markets or new technologies. People who are wedded to established practices, or who hold power under the existing structure, can be expected to resist these changes. In the end, effectiveness must win out over acceptability, since an organisation that is not effective in meeting the needs of customers will not be able to afford to keep its other stakeholders happy for very long. However, this does not mean that an option that risks internal conflict by forcing through fast and radical change is better than one involving more gradual change, which staff may find more acceptable. Each case will need to be judged on its separate merits.

- Not every option will need to meet the sustainability criterion, but those that do may merit preference over those that do not.

Evaluating options for McDonald's and Sony

In this real-life application, we illustrate the use of the option evaluation framework by applying it to the options described in Real-Life Application 11.15. These evaluations represent our views only, and we do not necessarily expect you (or the two firms' management) to share them. The important thing is for you to see how our argument takes shape.

Rating of McDonald's options for addressing its potential shortage of unskilled labour against RACES criteria – we use high, medium, or low. An alternative is to use marks out of ten

Option	Resources	Acceptability	Consistency	Effectiveness	Sustainability	Overall evaluation
Carry on as we are	High: resources obviously available	High: problems unlikely with internal stakeholders, and no evidence of shareholders demanding action	High: this *is* the existing strategy	Medium: will be effective if economy reverts to trend but not if labour market remains tight	Low: no additional contribution to sustainable advantage	Essentially this is a bet on economic conditions reverting to 'normal' patterns
Launch joint industry training scheme with competitors	Medium/high: would require expansion of existing training facilities, but risk is shared with competitors	High: would accord with firm's existing social policies, and no threat to any existing employee	High: will enable most existing strategies and policies to be maintained	Questionable: are there many employable people out there who could be brought into the workforce?	Low: advantage would be shared with competitors	Reject on grounds of limited effectiveness
Automation of order-taking and serving	Medium-low: would require substantial investment in new equipment, capabilities and competences, but firm has $300m in cash and generates $3bn in operating cash flow	Medium: existing serving staff might fear for their positions, but little tradition of their organising to resist management; franchisees might need to be convinced of need and effectiveness; other stakeholders unlikely to be perturbed	Low: would diminish likely appeal of McDonald's as destination restaurant	Medium: effective if technology works and if unemployment remains high; otherwise danger of wasted effort	High: might give competitive advantage if economic conditions remain unchanged	Reject: not effective enough to offset problems with resources, acceptability and consistency

Real-Life Application continued

Option	Resources	Acceptability	Consistency	Effectiveness	Sustainability	Overall evaluation
Automation plus: McDonald's as technological wonderland	Low: even greater advances required than for automation option, although probably financially affordable	Medium: similar to automation option	High: would assist in transformation of McDonald's as destination restaurant	High: *If* works; would work as differentiation factor even if labour market conditions changed	High: *If* technology functions and in absence of similar moves by competitors	High risk option with high potential rewards
Small-scale automation research by third party	High: lower commitment, more affordable version of previous option	High: any threat to jobs would be beyond career horizon of typical McDonald's employee	High: as previous option	Moderate: would leave main implementation problems unsolved, if labour market tightened further in short term	Moderate: risk that any knowledge might 'leak' to competitors	Slower but lower risk version of previous option
Increase penetration overseas	High: no new competences needed, and adequate funds available	High: only conceivable problems are with existing non-US franchisees, but overseas markets far less saturated than US markets	High: consistent with current strategy	Moderate–low: it would take a great deal of overseas expansion to compensate for a major downturn in the USA, which in 1999 accounted for 50% of sales and 44% of operating income	Medium: all major fast-food operators have international presence, but McDonald's widely believed to be better than most at adapting global formula to local conditions	Perhaps worth diverting some investment from US markets to other markets, but not a complete solution

The final judgement on which option to adopt would depend on the analyst's views on likely developments in the US labour market, and on their attitude to risk. The adventurous option is the 'technological wonderland'. The more conservative option would be a combination of overseas expansion and small-scale investment in automation. 'Carry on as we are' makes sense if the analyst is convinced the problem will simply go away of its own accord.

Rating of Sony's options for reacting to commoditisation in the TV business against RACES criteria

Option	Resources	Acceptability	Consistency	Effectiveness	Sustainability	Overall evaluation
Relocate production to low labour-cost countries	High: Sony already operates plant in many countries, and finance will be available. Although highly indebted by Western standards (1999 debt/equity ratio was around 140%), interest is well covered by profits (interest cover ~7) and company generated $5.5 bn in cash from operations in 1999	Moderate: move would excite opposition from employees/unions in Japan and elsewhere (e.g. Wales); certainly in Japan this opposition might be powerful	Medium: neither supports nor conflicts with other major strategies	Medium: unclear whether problem lies in cost of labour, in production methods or in cost of components	Low: a move that is easy to copy	Possible component of broader package; does not rate high on any important criterion
Re-engineer production process	Low: if Sony had the competences to do this, they would probably already have exercised them; might possibly acquire from consultant or Japanese manufacturing specialist	High: using ingenuity to deal with a threat is compatible with the Sony culture, even if it is more oriented to product than process innovation; workforce could be sold on this as alternative to job losses	Medium: pursuit of cost advantage not central to Sony strategy, but might generate competences that could find use elsewhere in corporation	High: if it works; otherwise would waste time that might be used to pursue alternative	High: new routines could form basis of enduring advantage in TV and other manufacturing businesses	If resource problem can be overcome then this is a good option; but that is a big if, and beating the Koreans at their own game will not be easy

Real-life Application continued

Option	Resources	Acceptability	Consistency	Effectiveness	Sustainability	Overall evaluation
Acquisition of Korean competitor	Moderate–low: Sony has the capital, but its track record with acquisitions is not good	Very low: Korea and Japan have long-standing animosity	Neutral: neither supports nor subverts existing strategy	Moderate–low: would the Korean firms that are doing poorly enough to be available for purchase have the competences and capabilities that Sony seeks?	Moderate–low: same doubts as for effectiveness	Reject – too many minus points
Joint venture with Korean competitor	Medium: Sony has experience of a number of joint ventures	Low: the Korean–Japanese antagonism is still an obstacle; if the proposed partner were a successful firm, then it would probably want control; Sony's management might find this unacceptable	Neutral	Similar comments apply as for previous option	Similar comments apply as for previous option	Dubious: a successful partner would want an unacceptable degree of control, an unsuccessful one would not deliver the necessary competences
Joint venture with Matsushita or Philips	Medium: as with previous option	Low for Matsushita: ancient rivalries would die hard; but Sony and Philips have collaborated successfully before, e.g. on development of compact disc	Medium: may have wider benefits in forging links with global rival	Depends on whether any economies of scale from joint operation could outweigh Samsung's sources of lower costs	Moderate: economies of scale might keep new competitors at bay for some time	Worth considering if economies of scale are genuine
Withdraw from TV business	High: no new competences needed, and cash available to fund re-training, business may be saleable as going concern	Moderate–low: Sony's management might perceive withdrawal as unacceptable humiliation; workforce might also resist	Low: would lose synergy benefits and would give Samsung a source of cash to invest in competing with Sony elsewhere	High: the problem would certainly be resolved, albeit at some short-term cost	Low: offers no benefits unless it frees up cash to be invested in sustainable advantage in another business	Consistency considerations probably rule this option out

Option	Resources	Acceptability	Consistency	Effectiveness	Sustainability	Overall evaluation
Reduce presence in TV industry but retain up-market foothold	High: no new competences needed	Moderate: can be presented as a return to core values of innovation; redundancies could be limited to less powerful workforce outside Japan	High: retains synergy benefits and nuisance value to competition	Medium: will probably work in the short term, but unclear how long the up-market niche can be defended	Medium: TV business may yet be source of important innovations	Broadly viable, if imperfect solution

None of these options is perfect, and the choice between them will depend on wider strategic considerations. If Sony wishes to develop core competences in low-cost manufacturing, then the TV business is a good place to start, and the re-engineering option should be chosen. If Sony is considering a pruning of its portfolio then televisions might be considered for disposal. If the synergy benefits are paramount, then the option of reducing presence to an up-market foothold might be best, perhaps as part of a joint venture with Philips.

Practical dos and don'ts   ## Option evaluation

- Try to resist the temptation to jump straight to what seems to be the 'obvious' right answer, and use the RACES criteria, for that option only, to show that it works. Your arguments and your proposals will be improved if you can look at a range of alternatives, evaluate each of them, and demonstrate why your proposal is the best and why you have rejected the others.

- Make sure that your proposals, taken together, add up to a complete and coherent whole. Together, they must address all the high priority issues that you have identified. In addition, it should be clear from your proposals:
  - why anyone should want to buy the organisation's products or services in future
  - how the organisation will earn an acceptable return while serving its users
  - how it will *sustain* its position in a changing world.

  If you do not have answers to these three points, then your proposals do not constitute a complete or viable strategy.

- Do not forget the financial analysis. Putting forward sets of proposals without checking whether the organisation has enough money to implement them is not a sensible idea.

- Do not underestimate the problems that employees may have in accepting ideas that may (you think) be for the good of the organisation as a whole. Try to imagine yourself in the situation of each set of stakeholders – senior management, junior management, operational staff, suppliers and so on – and thinking 'Would I really like it if this were happening to me?'

- Competitors are also stakeholders. When considering acceptability, do not neglect the possibility that they may retaliate, or call in regulators or lawyers to block, or at least delay, a proposal.

- When assessing the effectiveness of an option, remember to think of the downside – the things that may go wrong, and their cost.

11.6 Summary

In this chapter we have set out a framework for developing strategic proposals that are tailored to the particular challenges and opportunities confronting an organisation. This framework has five stages:

1. The identification of the strategic issues confronting the organisation – the challenges, problems and opportunities. The strategic issues are phrased as questions: 'What should the organisation do about X?' 'How should it respond to Y?' Strategic issues are identified from a thorough analysis of the organisation's performance, its future environment, its competitive stance, its resources, its value chain, its culture and its architecture.

2. The determination of the organisation's strategic priorities. At this stage, the list of issues is reduced to a more manageable size. Issues relating to threats to an organisation's survival take the highest priority, followed by issues relating to how an organisation can obtain or protect sources of sustainable advantage. If these issues do not consume all available resources, then the organisation can turn its attention to how to use them in new ways, how to develop new resources and what to do with spare ones. Some issues require a quick decision, and they take priority over those that do not.

3. The identification of strategic options, the possible alternative answers to the questions posed by a strategic issue. Different options will vary in the extent to which they call on the firm to match, outdo or neutralise competition, to expand into new competitive arenas and withdraw from old ones. They will also make use of different combinations of changes to the organisation's corporate-level strategy, competitive stance, resources, value chain, culture and architecture.

4. The evaluation of each of the options to determine which to accept and which to reject. For this, we suggest the use of the RACES criteria: resources, acceptability, consistency, effectiveness and sustainability.

5. The combining of the options that have been accepted into a coherent strategy that addresses all the high priority issues.

Typical questions

We conclude the chapter with a review of the kinds of question that you may encounter using this material, and the way in which the material in this chapter might be used to answer them.

1. *What are/were the main challenges or problems facing the organisation (at a given point in time)?*

   This is simply a different way of asking you to analyse the organisation's situation and identify the strategic issues confronting it. You then need to show which issues have (or had) the highest priority.

2. *Why did the organisation's managers decide on a particular course of action?*

   Again, it is advisable to analyse the organisation's situation and establish strategic issues and strategic priorities. You then need to show how the course of action taken was a reasonable way of responding to one or more of the high-priority issues. You may also want to look at some of the main alternative options, and demonstrate why the managers might have thought their course of action was the best available.

3. *Was the organisation correct to follow the course of action that it did?*

This is a development of the previous question. You should look at the alternative options available to the organisation and use the RACES framework to assess whether the strategy that the organisation adopted was superior to the main alternatives. You may also be able to introduce evidence on the organisation's performance after the decision, to see how it worked out in practice.

4. *How well does/did the organisation stand (at a given point in time)?*

This type of question calls upon you to exercise your powers of judgement, based upon the strategic issues you have identified. You may find it helpful to classify the issues according to the categories in Section 11.3. There will be a number of issues in the first two categories, indicating potential threats to the organisation's survival and to its sources of competitive advantage. You will want to assess whether the organisation has viable options available to help it to meet those threats. You will then want to assess whether the organisation has viable ways of addressing the issues in categories 4 and 5, which would enable it to profit from its existing resources and develop new ones. You then need to arrive at a balanced assessment of how realistic it is to expect the organisation to profit from its opportunities while fending off the threats.

5. *What course of action would you recommend for the organisation?*

This involves use of all five stages of the framework laid out in this chapter: issue identification, establishing priorities, identifying options, evaluating the options and combining the selected options into a recommended strategy.

Questions for discussion

1. What is the difference between a strategic issue and a strategic option?

2. What alternatives did McDonald's have to implementing 'Made for You'? Do you agree with its decision to become a chain of 'destination' restaurants?

3. When might you expect an organisation to give serious consideration to strategic options that:
   (a) require resources that will be very difficult to obtain?
   (b) will be unacceptable to significant parts of the management or workforce?
   (c) will be inconsistent with large parts of the existing strategy?
   (d) have a high risk of being ineffective – of failing to achieve their aim?
   (e) do not give sustainable advantage, even if effectively implemented?

CASE STUDY

Gillette loses face

From 'Gillette blames Asia – and a few organizational lapses – for its stock's slide. But the biggest problems are right under its nose', by Jeremy Kahn. *Fortune*, 8 November 1999, pp. 105–110.

Nicked. Cut. Creamed. Over the past two years, headline writers have left no pun unturned in describing Gillette's performance. And if things keep going like this, the images are only going to get bloodier.

Anyone who watches the market knows the general contours of the story: A stalwart American stock – a company that since 1990 had pulled off not one but two of the greatest product launches ever, the Sensor and Mach 3 razors – suddenly finds itself tanking on an epic scale. By mid-1997, as the Asian economic crisis swept west, Gillette's earnings started to plunge (some 62% of its sales and 60% of its profits come from outside the US). Compounding the shortfall was the company's recent $1 billion development and rollout of the triple-blade Mach 3, the most expensive launch in its history. By the end of the year, earnings growth had ceased completely; by the end of 1998, Gillette lagged its peer group – including Procter & Gamble and Unilever – in five-year total return to shareholders. And on 28 September of this year, Gillette announced it would miss its quarterly sales targets – the fourth time in five quarters that it has fallen short of revenue or profit estimates, or both. The next day the company's stock dropped another 9% to $33; that's 48% below its high for the year. In fact, the stock hasn't been this low since October 1996, when the Dow was at 6000.

True, Gillette, which is based in Boston, still owns the $7 billion worldwide razor and blade industry. The Mach 3 is its most successful new product ever, hitting $1 billion in sales in just 18 months, something it took Sensor six years to do. Gillette is also the world leader in ten other product categories including alkaline batteries (Duracell), epilators (Braun), pens (Papermate), and toothbrushes (Oral B). And the company still has at least one well-placed friend in Warren Buffett who for now hasn't moved to sell any of Berkshire Hathaway's 96 million shares.[6] Obviously, the issue for Buffett – and

for Gillette – is whether this is just a (big) dip or the beginning of a long slide.

Until two years ago, Gillette was a fat, happy company; cushioned by years of double digit growth, it was able to ignore a nasty snarl of problems just below the surface. The Asian crisis may have been painful in the immediate sense, but as Constance Maneaty, an analyst at Bear Stearns, points out: 'There are companies with greater exposures [to international markets] that have been making the estimates, like Colgate.'

The real damage Asia inflicted on Gillette was to expose the company's underlying weaknesses: a culture plagued by inertia, inefficiency, and nostalgia; mismanaged inventories and receivables; a Goldbergian corporate structure cobbled together over years of acquisitions; and, more important, three decades-old divisions that have consistently and badly underperformed.

Some of the company's logistical glitches have already been addressed. At the mundane level, for example, Gillette has been criticized for not moving inventory or collecting on credit sales as quickly as other makers of consumer goods – tying up capital that could be put to better use elsewhere. (Last year it overestimated demand for its razor-blades and got stuck with hundreds of thousands in warehouses in December.) Now the company is finally installing software to help avoid the routine invoicing and delivery problems that have prevented it from collecting money on time.

Gillette has also begun rehabbing its structure. A new $535 million reorganization will shutter 14 factories and 12 distribution centers world-wide, consolidate 30 offices, cut 4,700 jobs (11% of Gillette's workforce), and save $200 million a year. It will also try to streamline what has been a complex sales process. Until early this year, each of its product divisions operated autonomously: A given retailer was subjected to a seemingly endless stream of Gillette salespeople – one representing Braun, another peddling toothbrushes, a third pushing razors – none of whom knew much about what the others were doing. And this scene would be repeated in every market around the world. The new scheme should allow the sales staff to present 'one face' to each customer.

All of that helps. In the end, though, those fixes skirt Gillette's real problem: it has been years since this company was more than just half great. Of Gillette's six businesses, three – razors and blades, Duracell batteries, and Oral B toothbrushes – are superstars. But Braun's profits fell 4% last year, dropping below 1996 levels. Gillette's toiletries, such as shaving cream and Right Guard deodorant, are down (earnings are 40% below their 1988 level, and profit margins are just 4%, compared with almost 40% for blades). And its stationery products group, which includes Papermate, Parker and Waterman brand pens, has also flagged (profits fell 31% last year). Back when Gillette's overall earnings were leaping forward 15% to 20% a year, it was easy, convenient even, to ignore that these divisions were sucking wind. Now it's impossible. (Certainly, Henry Kravis isn't ignoring it. He recently filed to sell KKR's 51 million Gillette shares, which the firm received when it sold Duracell to Gillette in 1996, but hasn't done so because of their falling price.)

To analysts the solution is simple: Amputate. Gillette's three weak businesses account for 40% of its $10.1 billion in annual sales but less than 20% of profits, and that figure is dropping every quarter. There's no doubt that investors would like to see the company leaner. 'Wall Street is wondering if the new CEO is going to roll up his sleeves and decide that some of the poor divisions are not as strategic as they were seen to be three to five years ago,' says Mark Godfrey, an analyst at Invesco, which owns about 33,000 shares.

That new CEO is Michael Hawley, who took over in February. Hawley has worked practically his entire career – 38 years for Gillette, all but 14 of them away from company headquarters, mostly on international assignments in Hong Kong, Britain, Colombia, and Australia. Compared with his predecessor, Alfred Zeien, an extroverted salesman who relished proselytising for Gillette on Wall Street, Hawley is affable but reserved. Still, he shares Zeien's vision of Gillette as a company driven by technological innovation and superior products –

exactly the sort of R&D-intensive strategy that produced Sensor in 1990. At that time, Gillette's razor business was threatened by disposables, which commanded more than 50% of the market and were moving it quickly toward commoditization. Gillette countered with a lavish campaign aimed at re-establishing brand loyalty (its 'Best a man can get' ads). Then it backed up those ads with a demonstrably superior product – one that segmented the market and commanded a hefty premium from consumers. The result was that Sensor actually reversed the ascent of the disposable razor.

That formula – the use of superior technology and savvy advertising to segment markets and prevent commoditization – came to be known informally as 'the Gillette way'. And it's a model the company has returned to again and again, from Duracell's Ultra batteries to Oral B's $5 CrossAction toothbrush. But Gillette's efforts to apply this formula to its weaker divisions have been unconvincing.

While analysts urge Gillette to offload those divisions, Hawley plans to rescue them. But what if they're not worth saving? Gillette brass bristles at this kind of talk. It tends to engender long, quixotic speeches about Braun's leading market share in hand blenders. Almost to a man, these guys are company lifers. They've done tours of duty in every part of Gillette and feel a nostalgic affection for those hand blenders and after-shaves and Parker pens. They like to talk about 'permanence'. During the 1980s, Gillette fought off two hostile takeover attempts by corporate raiders that wanted to split it up; that they might have saved the company only to break it apart themselves a decade later is anathema to them.

This rather sentimental (or if you prefer, paternalistic) mindset means Gillette risks throwing good money after bad. Take Braun: Gillette bought the company in 1968, at a time when it feared electric shavers would doom the company's blade and razor business. That hasn't happened, in part because of the success of Gillette's own wet razors. But now Gillette is left with a business that doesn't fit so well with the rest of the company. Braun isn't even the clear leader in electric shavers, a market that has been in decline for the past four years. And

CASE STUDY *continued*

while Braun is about to unveil a self-cleaning electric shaver in Japan that Gillette thinks will eventually be a hit world wide, it isn't clear that this will be a Sensor-type breakthrough that can revolutionize the industry.

Moreover, holding onto Braun as is means that Gillette is also stuck manufacturing coffeemakers, kettles, and depilatory devices. And even if those products have great market share, they have lousy profit margins. Archie Livis, the executive vice-president in charge of Gillette's diversified group (Braun, Oral B, and stationery) notes that those small appliances represent only 33% of Braun's sales, but 'what happens is the Street equates Braun with small appliances'. That's why Braun is cutting back spending on this part of its business. But why not sell it altogether? The best answer Livis can supply is, 'At this point in time we wouldn't want to toss the baby out with the bathwater.'

The only part of Braun worth keeping at the moment is its $550 million electric toothbrush business. Already run as a joint venture between Braun and Oral B, it is the fastest-growth category in the entire Gillette product line, with a 65% market share, profit margins that exceed the company average, and a $200 million to $300 million refill business. This part of Braun could easily be merged with Oral B completely, creating a $1.2 billion tooth-care unit. 'If they would carve out the electric toothbrushes, they could sell the rest of Braun', says Bear Stearns' Maneaty.

Gillette's toiletries are also a drag on the overall operation, with the lowest profit margins at the company. And although Gillette leads the market in shaving cream, that's not the case with deodorant or shampoo. Last year, Gillette finally decided to bite the bullet and pare back some of its holdings. It sold Jafra cosmetics, and it's now looking to offload the White Rain hair-care line.

But if toiletries is a loser, you'd never know it from listening to Gillette executives. Peter Hoffman, Gillette's senior vice-president in charge of grooming and batteries, insists that Gillette's shave-preparation business dovetails well with its razor business. Fair enough. As for deodorants: 'All our experience has taught us it is the next logical step in the grooming process,' he says. 'So when men and women get ready for the day, those functional toiletries they use, that have some cosmetic overtone, you would define as the shaving process and the deodorant process.'

But this logic could be extended infinitely. Why doesn't Gillette make clothing? Or shoes? After all, once people shave and deodorize, most of them engage in what we would define as the dressing process. Edward DeGraan, Hoffman's boss, has a slightly better explanation. 'Gillette does best in products that can demonstrate functional improvements,' he says. 'In products that move away from that kind of core premise, we do less well.' But while the company has tried to apply the Gillette way to its toiletries, the basic problem remains: there's not much difference between Gillette's stuff and everybody else's, except that Gillette's costs more. That means toiletries become a kind of loss leader for Gillette's shaving business. But would retailers refuse to stock Gillette's blades – the best-selling blades in the world – just because they aren't getting Right Guard too?

Of Gillette's three weaker divisions, stationery may best lend itself to improvement through the Gillette way. Parker sold the same damn pens for 20, in one case 40, years. John Darman, the mastermind behind the Mach 3 launch and now senior vice-president in charge of the stationery group, is looking to change that. He has introduced new advertising, which has already reversed Papermate's sliding market share during the all-important back-to-school season; a redesigned model line is set to launch early next year; and an R&D crew is working on a breakthrough – new inks, redesigned grips – that will do for writing what Sensor did for shaving. 'We are not going to be a problem for this company starting next year,' Darman says.

Darman is persuasive, but his plan will work only so long as Gillette doesn't have to spend too heavily to implement it. Even Hawley is cautious. 'The danger is to make a big capital investment on something that doesn't have the type of margin and volume that a Mach 3 does,' he says.

It has to be hard for Gillette, after so many years as a stock market stud, to find itself down and out.

Indeed, simple denial may explain why, rather than facing the facts and sharply lowering earnings estimates for the year, the company has continued to set aggressive targets – and miss them. That in turn has created a credibility problem with Wall Street. 'I think the stock reflects all this frustration that investors have felt for the past two years and skepticism about the timing of a recovery,' says Wendy Nicholson, an analyst at Salomon Smith Barney, who recently lowered her fourth-quarter estimates for Gillette. 'At its current price, any credible good news ought to be good for shareholders.'

With Asia on the rebound and Hawley's restructuring well under way, good news isn't impossible. But without a few sharp cuts, Gillette may never be the growth stock it used to be.

Case study questions

1. What were the most important strategic issues confronting Gillette in November 1999?

2. What options had Gillette selected to address these issues? What were the main alternatives?

3. Do you agree with Gillette's proposed strategy? Why (or why not)?

NOTES

1. A knowledge management system is an off-the-shelf programme developed by management consultants to put in place some of the strategies for managing knowledge that we discussed in Section 7.4.5.

2. *Financial Times*, 17 April 1999.

3. See, for example, 'The e-volution of Big Business', *Fortune*, 8 November 1999, pp. 60–91.

4. The term 'reserving the right to play' comes from Courtney et al. (1997).

5. The term 'acceptability' comes from Johnson and Scholes (1998).

6. Berkshire Hathaway is an American investment firm with a policy of making large, long-term investments in a few selected corporations. Warren Buffett, its president, has achieved near-legendary status among US investors for his ability to select firms whose share-value will rise.

Strategies in different contexts

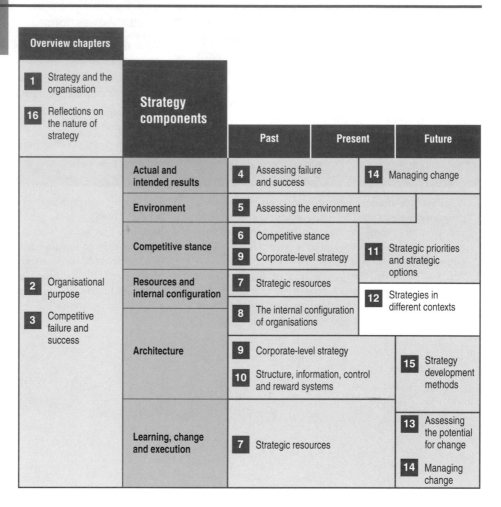

Most of this book has been to do with relatively large companies; organisations which are in the business of making money for their shareholders and which compete with other firms in order to make profits. Not all organisations are like this, however. For some, financial considerations, although still important, may be subordinate to other objectives. For others they do not have the size to implement the sorts of strategies we discuss elsewhere. So here we look at strategies for organisations other than large commercial firms.

Public sector organisations have particular strategic choices to make. In many state-owned concerns, competition and value for money have become increasingly important, and many of the principles outlined elsewhere within this book will be equally appropriate there. But public sector organisations have constraints and opportunities all of their own and we will consider some of these. We also consider strategies for organisations in the not-for-profit sector, charities, who also have to operate in an environment that is increasingly competitive, but where all income has to go to the charity's beneficiaries. In these circumstances there are issues of ethics, stakeholders and reinvestment which particularly need to be considered.

In this chapter we also look at strategies which might be suitable for firms other than the big companies that we have discussed in much of this book. An enormous number of people across the globe are employed in organisations that will never have more than perhaps two or three employees. These are the family-owned businesses that are there principally to provide employment for their owners.

However, even large firms have started small at some stage, and have had to go through the pains of growing. So, we look at strategies that are appropriate at different stages in the company/industry life-cycle. In addition to discussing the general features of the different stages, we touch upon the turnaround strategies that might be considered by firms in crisis. We also look at strategies in industries characterised by hypercompetition and increasing returns. We conclude with a review of strategies for electronic commerce.

Learning objectives

By the end of this chapter you should be able to:

- describe the environmental characteristics of the public and not-for-profit sectors;
- understand which strategies are appropriate for public and not-for-profit organisations;
- describe a variety of strategies which are likely to be appropriate for small and/or new firms;
- understand how strategies are likely to vary at different stages of an industry's life-cycle;
- assess what strategies are suitable for industries which are characterised by hypercompetition and increasing returns, for electronic commerce and for firms confronting a turnaround.

12.1 Strategic management in the public sector

First we consider some of the issues to do with the strategic management of the public sector. This is something of a problem, because the public sector is not a single entity. It comprises, for example:

- Government departments of a number of different types; national, local, and international. Examples include the European Commission, the UK's Civil Service and Ministries, the USA's Senate, and more local agencies such as the UK's county and district councils, Départements and Mairies in France, and Länder in Germany.

- Agencies which are directly controlled by governments at either a national or local level. These include air traffic control services, the armed forces, social welfare agencies, police and courts, and tax offices.

- Government agencies which are quasi independent in terms of their management and funding, and which are controlled principally by regulation. These include schools, universities, hospitals and utilities.

In fact, there are huge national differences in the set-up, structure, and control of these different agencies, which are beyond the scope of this book to discuss. However, all public sector organisations are ultimately dependent on the state for their funds.

12.1.1 The public sector environment

In many countries, although not all, the state means an elected government which can change at any time, but which typically 'reigns' for between four and seven years. Given that governments are frequently changed because the electorate wants a change of policy, this means that the immediate environment in which public sector organisations operate changes more frequently, and more radically, than that of commercial organisations.

Another typical characteristic of public sector organisations is that they are in existence to provide a service – sometimes directly to the government which funds them, as in the case of the Civil Service in the UK or the federal agencies and bureaux in Australia and the USA – but in many cases to beneficiaries who do not pay for them (or at least not directly).

In some cases, public sector organisations have two or even more customers or user groups, the consumers of the service *and* other government or private agencies who will refer individuals (see Real-Life Application 12.1).

Andersen et al. (1994) in a discussion of the American public sector, point out how big, complex and varied are the public programmes that a government typically manages. The architecture of public sector agencies is thus often extremely complex, both internally and externally. Many public programmes are administered by multiple agencies, which are independent entities but interdependent in the services that they provide. Most programmes cross traditional organisational and administrative boundaries.

For example, schools are often the responsibility of both economic and social development departments of the government. They are a provider of community services such as day care, as well as the site of traditional instruction and education. They are also the place where health issues (usually the responsibility of another department) such as drug abuse, teen pregnancies, and AIDS are tackled. Students who attend schools are also likely to be involved to a greater or lesser extent with other organisations which also deal with education and welfare issues. No single agency has overall responsibility for education services in their totality. The public sector is summarised in Figure 12.1.

Figure 12.1 **The public sector environment** (from Poister and Streib, 1999)

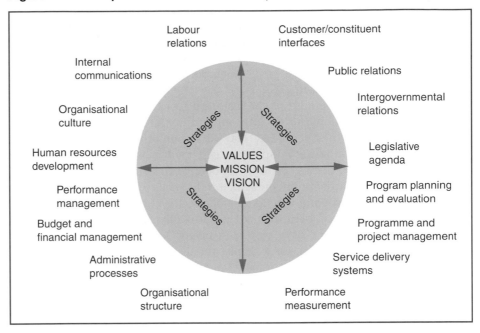

Who is the customer? The case of the Probation Service

The Probation Service in the UK is a government agency which supervises offenders. Its role includes providing welfare advice to the offender and his or her family, but also involves monitoring compliance with court orders and rehabilitating prisoners after their release. Probation Officers also provide advice on sentencing to the criminal courts. The Probation Service is funded by the government, partly by local and partly by central government, although this is about to change to a single central government source. It is managed by full-time managers, who have to report to both a management committee appointed by the courts and government inspectors, although this itself is also about to change to a government-appointed committee.

Given this background, the Probation Service has to please a number of different masters. It has to satisfy the central government that it is doing what it is set up to do – ultimately to reduce or minimise offending. It has to satisfy local governments that it is providing adequate *local* services to its residents, it has to satisfy the management committee *and* central government inspectors that it is being managed effectively, and giving value for the money which the government is providing from taxes and for which it is itself accountable to the public. On a day-to-day basis it has to provide the judges and magistrates in the courts with the information and service that they require (despite the fact that they do not pay directly for it), and last but not least, it has to be concerned that offenders are receiving the high-quality services that *they* need.

The culture and architecture of public sector organisations

The public sector environment thus has many diverse interest groups, inside and outside an agency's own structure. Because of this and the fact that there is often no direct benefit from working with colleagues towards a common goal, such as the profitability of the organisation, public sector organisations can be extremely political. This is compounded by the fact that all public agencies or departments compete with one another for a share of a finite budget; there is no opportunity to increase income through increasing sales. As Johnston (1998) says, public sector organisations are often characterised by small fiefdoms which make the process of gaining support and commitment to an overall goal difficult.

This has certain cultural implications. It tends to reduce risk-taking and creativity because of the potential for political conflict to develop when individuals step out of line.

Because of the historical focus on cost management rather than profit generation, there is little opportunity for highly creative or entrepreneurial performance to be rewarded. Reward systems therefore tend to be based on salary and the movement up structured grades, with few bonus or performance-related pay schemes. Because of some of these issues, the public sector can find it hard to attract entrepreneurial individuals, or those who would introduce new and better working practices. Public sector cultures have tended to notice poor rather than good performance. Paradoxically, however, few traditional public sector organisations have cultures whereby low standards are either measured or dealt with through, for example, the dismissal of the staff member concerned. Sackings are rare and are usually only carried out for the most serious offences – such as criminal activities. Having said that, there is a wide spread of different cultures in the public sector, and treating all departments as if they are the same is problematic given the heterogeneity of the sector.

Trends in the public sector environment

Recent times have seen a considerable move in the UK and the USA (although there are considerable regional differences elsewhere in the world) away from directly controlled and funded structures and towards regulatory and market mechanisms of control in the public sector.[1] Departments have been devolved into commercial quasi-businesses, or profit centres, that are less subject to direct government control. In some cases these have been encouraged to seek funding from non-government sources (Real-Life Application 12.2).

The move towards the commercialisation of the public sector partly reflects a world-wide trend away from centralist approaches, but is also the result of the recession of the 1980s and early 1990s which left many governments short of the tax income which could be used on services. Andersen et al. (1994) tell how New York State, in 1991, posted the USA's then largest budget deficit, $6 billion. This record was superseded in 1992 by California, which registered a deficit of $11 billion. This political and economic climate has led some government agencies to look for alternative sources of funding, such as lotteries, or to enter into partnerships with other agencies, both public and private. In the UK this has become formalised by the present government into what it has termed its public/private partnership initiative. At the same time there has been a considerable move towards the contracting out of non-essential services, a move that parallels similar cutting back to core businesses in the private sector.

The move from government departments to profit-generating entities has provided something of a challenge for public sector agencies who have had to cope with what, in many cases, is a radical shift in culture and operating expectations. The management of change has therefore been a fact of life for many senior managers in former public sector organisations. Even when not completely commer-

REAL-LIFE APPLICATION 12.2

The commercialisation of the public sector

In the UK, of the 100 firms in the FTSE index, 20 are privatised former public sector agencies such as British Telecom (BT) and BG Group (gas) and a number of electricity and water companies. Many are now owned by foreign companies (see also Real-Life Application 12.3 below). The old utilities now face competition for once-captive customers.

A similar pattern of events has happened elsewhere. In Italy Benetton has been able to shop for what it regards as 'bargain basement' companies – formerly public utilities.[2] It bought large stakes in the GS supermarkets business and Autogrill, Italy's main motorway service business, when they were sold off by IRI, Italy's state-owned industrial conglomerate. Benetton is now eyeing the operating contract for Italy's fourth mobile phone network, for which it has teamed up with BT, among others. It is also hoping to win the management contract for the two Rome airports, where it is competing against BAA. The privatisation of Italy's motorway network is due to happen in the year 2000, and Benetton intends to take a stake in a consortium that will bid for it.

Gilberto Benetton sees some possible synergies between the mobile phone business and GS supermarkets, through which it could arrange distribution, but otherwise the point about taking over privatised businesses is that the Benettons believe that they can offer management expertise and quickly raise profitability. 'These are great companies where there is massive potential for improvement,' he says.

The Italian government is also privatising all its opera houses, including La Scala Milan, an option which the British government also considered for the Royal Opera House Covent Garden (see also Real-Life Application 12.5). Although the ROH is not strictly a public sector organisation, it receives its charter and large subsidies from the government, and the govern-ment recently considered its privatisation and flotation on the stock exchange. As the government said, there would be 'many benefits in the financial disciplines of privatisation' although, given its recent track record financially, it is debatable whether the City would have backed a stock market flotation.[3]

In Sweden the paper manufacturer AssiDoman, a firm created in 1994 from the royal Swedish forests and two existing pulp and paper companies, was able to become more commercial as a result of partial privatisation in 1994. Whereas in the old days a call from the trade union to a local politician had been enough to prevent job losses, the new AssiDoman has been free to cut staff and rationalise production across its various sites.[4]

In Dublin the ministry of public enterprise has approved a preliminary plan put forward by the national carrier, Aer Lingus, to establish an alliance with a strategic industrial partner, the first stage in the government's plan to privatise the state airline, and follows the authority's announcement that it would privatise Telecom Eireann. The formation of the industrial link will be followed by the public flotation of shares. This will involve the sale of stock to Aer Lingus' employees intended to help secure their approval on the inevitable restructuring of the labour force. Should the alliance prove successful, the relationship may be expanded to include some kind of cross equity involvement or the purchase of Aer Lingus' equity by the outside party. The Irish government has adopted a more conciliatory approach to employees in nationalised industries which are to be privatised. During the sale of stock in Telecom Eireann, some 14.9% of the company's equity capital is to be sold to workers in exchange for agreed job cuts and changes in working practices. The government is likely to seek a Dublin and a London listing for Aer Lingus stock.[5]

cialised, most departments have had to become very much more business-like and accountable in recent years.

Governments who have to impose a competitive framework on what were once monopolistic situations have also faced some problems. Privatised government departments can retain many of the advantages of a monopoly for some time following deregulation. The former state-owned airlines, in what is now a deregulated environment, still retain considerable control of key slots at major airports throughout the world, which predictably they are very reluctant to give up. For this reason, many former government-run agencies are heavily regulated in the period following privatisation, being bound by rules as to how much money they

REAL-LIFE APPLICATION 12.3

Consolidation in the UK's electricity industry

In 1996 the British government was considering allowing mergers between some of the recently privatised electricity companies. The Monopolies and Mergers Commission (MMC), Britain's anti-trust authority, acknowledged that the mergers could have been against the public interest yet went on to recommend that both the bid by PowerGen (an electricity generator) for Midlands Electricity (a distributor) and the bid by National Power for Southern Electric (also a generator/distributor) should be allowed. In 1995 the government had already permitted a similar merger between Scottish Power and ManWeb. The MMC suggested that the mergers would help British electricity firms compete abroad through their increased size and because they would possess a wider range of skills and experience.

However, there was considerable criticism of the decision to allow the industry to consolidate like this, especially as PowerGen and National Power already controlled 90% of Britain's electricity generation between them. Allowing the mergers between generators and distributors would reduce competition in a market which already had monopolistic tendencies and make the government regulator's task harder. As a result, commentators worried that new entrants would be blocked from entering the market and prices would rise. The firms were already highly profitable and the price of electricity was high. These prices were eventually reduced by the regulator, although not by as much as some thought should have happened.

On the other hand, allowing the firms to merge would have allowed them potentially to achieve synergies and reduce costs. These costs could have been passed on to the consumer, although it was suggested that these benefits had in fact gone to shareholders instead.

There were some who already thought that the government's privatisation and industrial policy was in a mess and that regulation of the utilities was something you could 'drive a power station through'. Other countries with private utilities, such as America or Japan, had set up combined generators and distributors which acted as regional monopolies, and were heavily controlled by a very large number of regulators. Instead, the UK government had chosen to split the generation, transmission and distribution of electricity into separate businesses. This was supposed to encourage competition by letting regional electricity firms shop for the best price from a range of generators. It was also meant to provide the regulator and his small number of staff with enough easily-obtainable information to set prices accurately by comparing the performance of the different firms. Allowing the mergers would reduce the amount of information available to him and he was said to have strongly opposed them. In fact, he was subsequently granted increasing monitoring and enforcing powers. Allowing the generators and distributors to consolidate into a vertically integrated duopoly in effect reversed the government's original policy.

can make, what functions and services they will provide, and how they will be managed. In the UK most of the privatised organisations are overseen by government-appointed regulators (Real-Life Application 12.3).

12.1.2 Strategic options for public sector organisations

This move to impose the economic and commercial disciplines of the private sector on to some public sector departments has been paralleled by recommendations that public sector organisations adopt the strategies, management practices, and systems of private firms. The public sector traditionally has been concerned to maximise inputs. Management and operational structures were designed to implement government policy through planning, budgeting, and evaluation and review processes. This environment has now been replaced with a greater concentration on outputs in terms of the efficient uses of resources and the effectiveness of outcomes.

Many public sector departments have begun to bring in private sector practices such as strategic planning procedures which have encouraged managers to consider longer-term objectives and any systematic change initiatives which might be necessary. This forces consideration of any long-term resource implications, such as the level of IT infrastructure which might help the co-ordination of effort across the organisation and the multiple agencies involved in providing services. It also starts the process of moving the organisation away from the ad hoc management which has tended to characterise the public sector in the past; and provides information which can be used to influence the political agenda for the future.

However, there has been quite a lot of discussion in the literature as to whether these business-based procedures are appropriate. They do not really address the unpredictable political dimensions of the public sector environment, and even though many public sector organisations are less dependent on government funding than they used to be, taking a long-term view is still more difficult than in commercial firms. Berry and Wechsler (1995) found that 85% of public sector agencies worked to less than five-year time-frames, and many worked to one-year periods. The relatively short-term appointments of governments and ministers, whose political priorities filter down eventually to most, if not all, public sector agencies, mean that environmental or regulatory change is regular and for the most part unpredictable.

These sorts of issue constrain the strategic choices that public sector executives can take. Senior management decision-making in the public sector may be driven more by short-term expediency than a longer-term view of what will benefit the organisation and its users. Except in quasi-business units operating in competitive environments, for which the theory discussed throughout the rest of this book is largely applicable, concepts such as competitive advantage and competitive stance also assume a different meaning in this sector. Many free-market thinkers in the UK and the USA take the attitude that the public sector should only perform duties that the private sector is unable and unwilling to assume. From their point of view, a 'weakness' in a public sector organisation is not necessarily a bad thing – it may represent a welcome opportunity to return that activity to the private sector.

According to Poister and Streib (1999), 'strategic management in the public sector is concerned with strengthening the long-term health and effectiveness of governmental units and leading them through positive change to ensure a continuing productive "fit" with changing environments'. This means ensuring that the architecture, value chain, systems and resources (such as competent staff, finances and infrastructure) are in place which allow for the planning, implementation and evaluation of service delivery, and the management of specific projects on time and within budget.

It also includes setting in place performance management systems and human resource development policies that allow the organisation to adapt to changing circumstances, and the setting up of budgeting and administrative systems to monitor specific programmes and outputs. These systems and structures have to allow for the efficient implementation of policies within a politically complex setting involving national and local party politics, as well as possible conflicts within an organisation and between rival agencies. Perhaps even more importantly, they have to be transparent and effective enough to satisfy powerful external stakeholders such as government ministers, who have an ethical and public accountability brief. The effectiveness of public sector managers is often judged purely on whether their budgets are met.

Summarised, this type of environment means that the strategic focus for many traditional public sector managers is:

- Setting in place a value chain, systems and structures that will allow the agency's users to be served effectively and efficiently. This focuses attention on communication and linkages between different parts of the agency itself, minimising disruptive internal and inter-agency political activity, and minimising the duplication and thus costs of particular elements. The value chain for a government agency will typically be of the 'professional services' type (see Section 8.1.2).

- Developing co-operative relationships between agencies for implementing and evaluating policies. This is an extension of the internal architectural issues mentioned in the previous paragraph. Once again it requires the setting in place of structures and culture which facilitate inter-agency communication, as well as providing clear lines of responsibility and accountability.

- Providing transparent accountability to both the public and politicians. This requires the development of clear financial systems which may need to be made available to public scrutiny in a number of different formats. It also requires the creation of departments which have responsibility for both monitoring public concern, and reporting on the work of the agency. The requirement for public accountability means that a core competence for many public sector departments is the management of the interface with the various 'customer' groups.

- Promoting the organisation's values, mission, vision, and strategies. This is not only important in order to make the agency's services known to those that may benefit from them, but is also important in 'selling' the agency to those responsible for funding and controlling it. This counts as a 'problem acquisition' activity in the professional services' value chain.

- Soliciting and achieving sufficient resources to implement a politically-set agenda. This is linked to the activities discussed in the previous paragraph, and is important because of the limited amount of funding available to competing agencies. The most successful in attracting funds may be those that are best able to 'sell' their work to those ultimately responsible for financing them, so that capabilities in communication and in managing customer expectations are important.

- Developing knowledge assets and capabilities. The staff of the best-run public sector organisations invariably have a comprehensive understanding of the issues affecting the groups that use their services, and a knowledge of where to locate the resources to help them.

- Influencing a future legislative agenda – another aspect of the problem acquisition-activity in a public sector organisation. This is a tricky issue, because it can be argued that state agencies should be simply undertaking the work that the public requires them to do without question. However, they are obviously in the best place to understand some of the key issues facing their particular clientele, and it is arguable that they would be failing in their duty if they were not to bring these issues to the notice of the wider public.

- Putting in place an effective control and evaluation activity, including mechanisms for soliciting and assessing feedback from external stakeholders, such as end-users or customers and constituents as well as the wider media and general public. This has a similar function, and requires similar systems, to the market research function in commercial organisations.

- Monitoring trends and changes in the agency's environment that might affect its policies or the ability to serve its mission. Given the radical and often unpredictable changes in the public sector's environment, accurate predictions may be impossible to achieve, but managers in the public sector would be less than effective if they did not attempt to assess what might happen, and what they should do given different circumstances.

12.2 Strategic management in the not-for-profit sector

Organisations in the charity, not-for-profit or voluntary sector (we shall use the term NFP as an all-embracing short-cut) generally provide a service to people who would otherwise not receive it.[6] As such they are sometimes used by governments instead of statutory agencies. They are given grants or tax relief in exchange for providing a specialised service to certain groups of constituents. In other cases they are created to provide something which the NFP's founders believe is lacking – whether this is financial aid, advice, or practical help to a particular group of people.

The NFP sector is as varied as the public sector or commercial firms, and is a large group. There are well over 200,000 registered charities in Britain alone, a country of about 57 million people. In 1997 the NFP sector had an annual turnover of £13 billion, employed 466,700 people with a wage bill of £6 billion, and contributed £3.6 billion to the economy.[7]

NFP organisations are involved across the range of educational, research, welfare, economic, social and spiritual activities. They include youth clubs, parent–teacher associations, research or grant-making foundations, religious bodies (such as churches or mosques), hospices, schools, universities, hostels for homeless people, international aid agencies, and organisations with a quasi-political function such as Greenpeace or Amnesty International.

Some of these are charities – regulated by governments in terms of what they can and cannot do, and with tax benefits as a result – and some are independent organisations funded from public donations. NFP organisations can range from very small concerns, with perhaps one or two workers, to very big organisations such as Oxfam, or Médecins sans Frontières, which not only employ many hundreds of both paid and voluntary staff, but are international in their operations and therefore complex. Managing such organisations is no less challenging than managing a large international corporation. In some ways the NFP environment – internally and externally – is considerably more complex than that of either the public or private sector.

12.2.1 The NFP environment

One of the most important distinguishing features of NFP organisations, and one of the most challenging to manage, is their employment culture, which can be informal and driven by a high commitment to the values of the organisation. Many of the people who work for NFPs are volunteers. In addition, there may be a relatively small group of paid employees who undertake the management and

REAL-LIFE APPLICATION 12.4

Salt Lake City's YWCA

The Young Women's Christian Association (YWCA) of Salt Lake City is a NFP membership organisation, housing ten human service programmes that serve the greater Salt Lake City area. Approximately seventy individuals staff the programmes and fill administrative positions. A volunteer board of directors is responsible for ensuring that the agency receives adequate funding and that the programmes are providing appropriate services.

The YWCA's programmes are funded mainly through charitable sources such as government grants, funding agencies, foundations, and individual donors. The YWCA receives over half its $1.2 million in revenue from government grants of various sorts.

Over much of its 100 year existence, the YWCA experienced a period of informal, emergent, growth and an external environment characterised by a fragmented structure of funding. In the 1970s and 1980s, competitive forces intensified as a result of the entry of commercial businesses into the recreation industry. The YWCA's 'gym and swim' strategy gave way to a new strategic direction – human services.

As fundraising and grant-giving became big business in the 1970s, forces within the NFP sector changed. The number of NFP agencies increased, precipitating greater competition for funding and clients. A programme director remarked, 'Competition is foreign to the YWCA, because we're a NFP, and NFPs aren't supposed to compete with each other.'

The effects of this competitive intensity led to funding sources becoming more powerful and demanding of the programmes they funded, requiring them to operate more like businesses, with greater accountability. The YWCA responded to this environmental challenge by increasing its level of formalisation with the appointment of a professional director and the implementation of a formal strategic planning system in 1993.

According to a member of the strategic planning committee: 'Our strategy process is to first clearly and realistically assess our current state. Once we do an assessment, our next step in that strategy is to define the goals, the problems, the obstacles to begin to do problem solving – resourcing, networking, developing a plan, and moving forward.' However, in some quarters individual efforts were considered more important than strategic plans, because only the actions of individuals had a first-hand effect on the agency's clients. The strategic planning process required discipline to which the informal organisation was not accustomed.

Conflict developed. The formal majority argued for more patience with the formal strategic planning process. This perspective contended that the answer to the YWCA's solvency problem was to systematically raise more revenue. The informal minority maintained that the YWCA needed to focus on programme quality. A board member commented that one of the 'unhealthy' ways that the YWCA solved philosophical differences was for people to 'drop out': 'Instead of standing in there and fighting toe to toe about differences, some board members have resigned.'

Based on Maranville (1999).

administration of the organisation. Volunteers, and also the staff who work in a NFP organisation often for relatively low levels of pay, tend to be hugely committed to the cause which the NFP organisation promotes, and are rewarded principally by the intrinsic nature of the work. However although committed to the organisation and its mission, they can also have a tendency towards what Charles Handy (1988) has called 'strategic delinquency'. They may put their own ethos and values in front of the organisation's goals, and be reluctant to recognise any priorities other than their own interpretation of the main aims of the organisation. This can sometimes result in the internal management of the organisation itself being neglected – to the ultimate detriment of the client group it is supposed to help.

Farmer and Fedor (1999) point out that volunteers are often even more difficult to control than 'normal' employees, since the sanctions which are used in commercial organisations, such as threats to livelihood, are not available. They will not work unless they want to. They have less to lose if they leave, and have to be interested and involved in the work. Volunteers tend therefore to either be highly active or become disenchanted and leave (Real-Life Application 12.4). The 'reliability' of volunteers in terms of their psychological or actual withdrawal from the organisation is a major problem in the NFP sector, and is one of its most distinguishing features. NFP managers therefore have to pay considerable attention to their volunteers. They need to be cherished and valued and notice taken of what they think is important. Symbolic management is therefore an important method of control and motivation in NFP organisations.

Corporate governance in NFP organisations

On top of this complicated mix of employment status is a management committee or board of trustees which has fiduciary responsibilities. Charities are more explicitly and directly accountable to their income providers than a commercial organisation. Key donors often have roles on the management committee of the charity, and are very keen to see value for their money (Real-Life Application 12.5).

These management committees often comprise volunteers, and in some cases representatives from the client group which the NFP serves, as well as donors. Board members have substantial power in setting the NFP's policies and strategic direction, much more so than shareholders do in the private sector. The management team may thus find itself overruled by well-meaning but unqualified trustees who may be following their own political or moral agenda. Many NFP organisations therefore have to deal with a difficult micro-political environment, and with board members who are powerful because of their control of funds.

Many NFPs are heavily dependent on a single source of income, frequently government funding. According to Coble (1999) charities in the USA receive about 31% of their revenues from government sources; 18% from private contributors; 39% from dues, fees, and charges; and about 11% from other sources. Governments often dictate the direction the NFP takes through the types of project that it will fund, and the performance criteria it sets for renewing this funding. NFP organisations have therefore to manage the relationships with their key external stakeholders very carefully. In this way they are similar to many public sector organisations.

The importance of fundraising

◄ *The value chain of a network organisation is discussed in Section 8.1.3.*

Many NFPs are network organisations – they exist to link donors and volunteers with the users who will ultimately benefit from their activities. A vital part of the network promotion activity is the raising of the funds needed to enable the organisation to operate. In general NFP managers spend considerable time in developing and maintaining sources of income. In the case of charities with a diverse donor body, they are competing for what seems to be a declining pool of available money. Drucker (1995) suggests that NFP managers deal with this environmental feature by targeting specific stakeholders to build what he calls donor constituencies, long-term relationships with key suppliers of funds.

Finding sources of funding therefore dictates much of the work of NFPs. They submit grant applications for a certain amount of money and often get less than they request, something which requires a rethinking and restructuring of their original plans. Many charities have become extremely sophisticated in the marketing techniques they use to target potential donors, and database management and relationship marketing have become hugely important tools in NFP management. However Sargeant and Kahler (1999) suggest that the general public is becoming fatigued with the deluge of increasingly sophisticated solicitations from charities, making it difficult for an individual charity to make its voice heard. This has not been helped by the occasional case reported in newspapers where donations have been entirely swallowed up by administration costs leaving nothing for the intended recipients of donors' money, which have tended to make the public wary of donating, particularly to unknown NFPs.

REAL-LIFE APPLICATION 12.5

Power, politics and funding of the Royal Opera House, Covent Garden

The Royal Opera House, in London's Covent Garden, is arguably the UK's premier opera and ballet company. It is legally a charity which receives government funding managed by a government agency, the Arts Council. The Royal Opera House receives an annual grant of £15 million and has received £98.5 million of taxpayers' money in the past five years. In order to receive this it is obliged to sign a contract which covers its financial responsibilities, among other things. However, it is also supported by large-scale private donations, and in recent years has also received a substantial grant from the government-set-up National Lottery.

It needs this money; the Royal Opera House has the best-paid staff of any UK charity, with an average salary of over £40,000, twice the national average wage.[8] Sir Jeremy Isaacs, its director until the end of 1997, was on a salary of £120,790. It funds some of the most expensive operatic 'superstars' who typically are paid several thousands pounds per performance.

It has also undergone a major redevelopment recently, reopening at the beginning of 2000 (albeit with some hiccups). The ROH was awarded £78.5 million of National Lottery money towards the £214 million costs of rebuilding and loss of income from its temporary closure. It was left needing to raise £100 million from private sources. At the end of 1999 £82 million had been raised, with another £6 million pledged.

Much of this was due to the efforts of Vivien Duffield, who had been vice-chairman of the Royal Opera House for two years and a board member for many years. A wealthy individual, she is an important donor to the ROH, and is a powerful source of additional donations through her contacts. Her power and management style has caused resentment in some quarters: 'who does she think she is, telling us how to run the place, just because she has bunged in a few million?'[9] Her influence has shaped some of the policies which the ROH has adopted. She opposed the plan to perform in a tent beside Tower Bridge during the closure and

encouraged the company to put on Ligeti's *Le Grand Macabre*. However, she has denied influencing some other policy decisions with which she had been accused of tampering.

The Royal Opera House nearly went bankrupt in 1997. It was only an eleventh-hour intervention by private trusts with a £2m facility which enabled the ROH to go on trading. These donors made it clear that they would not bail the charity out again. This crisis was only one of many to have beset the ROH in recent years. A 1997 government committee's report into the management of the Royal Opera House was said to be 'the most damning report ever written', claiming that 'The Royal Opera House is now at the lowest point in its long and distinguished history.' After detailing the financial crises, personnel changes and political ineptitude that characterised the previous few years, the Arts Council, the Department of Culture, even the Charity Commissioners, all came in for heavy criticism. But the report's harshest censure was reserved for the opera house's managers and board. They were judged to be guilty of incompetence and disastrous financial planning and misjudgements. The committee's report said: 'We would prefer to see the Royal Opera House run by a philistine with the requisite financial acumen than by the succession of opera and ballet-lovers who have brought a great and valuable institution to its knees.'[10] The committee recommended that the opera house's chief executive, chairman and board should leave immediately.

Interference from Mrs Duffield and other powerful and/or rich members of the board was cited by Mary Allen, the departed chief executive, in her book on her times at the Royal Opera House as a reason for the difficulties she experienced. In this she described how she never felt able to take decisions without constantly having to refer to the numerous powerful individuals who comprised the board, or who made large donations. Each of whom had their own ideas as to how the Opera House should be run.

Many have responded by changing their fundraising focus to become more commercial. There is some evidence (e.g. Parker, 1998) that the NFP sector is relying less on direct donations and is increasingly providing some services for fees. Many NFP organisations have started to separate into cost and profit centres. The cost centres deliver the services for which clients are not expected to pay. The profit centres are set up to raise funds through commercial activities, marketing, and managing investments – anything which will make money, which can then be used to fund the NFP's services. Because of this ability to generate potentially unlimited income, such NFP organisations are more like commercial firms than traditional charities or public sector organisations. However, the reporting regime is generally less demanding than that of private firms, with no obligation to disclose directors' remuneration, and no powerful shareholders to mount a hostile takeover bid.

Nevertheless, they have some important differences, the most important of these being the question over what NFP organisations do with their funds. By definition, they are there to provide a service; therefore any income should be directed towards providing that service and not towards paying high salaries or perks to employees, or indeed reinvesting in the organisation's infrastructure. There is of course a balance, in that reinvesting in the organisation may provide benefits in the longer-term and well-paid staff may be more effective in achieving the NFP's aims.

Judging effectiveness

The goals which NFP organisations aspire to and against which their effectiveness can be judged are quite different from public sector or commercial firms. Although NFPs must live within their financial means, 'profits' are not relevant except as a means to an end. Providing education, emergency aid, or welfare services, or whatever else the NFP's mission is, are instead more important goals. It is therefore quite difficult to judge an NFP's effectiveness by any normal measures. Is an NFP organisation with a growing balance sheet and money in the bank more effective than one that is running into debt because it is providing a high level of service that the community wants? Is the NFP with low costs more effective than one with high expenses but correspondingly higher levels of income?

In fact each of an NFP's stakeholders might have different ways of judging effectiveness. Donors might consider the achievement of value for their money the main criterion for judging success (however judged, and each donor may have very different ways of doing this). Governments, for example, will want to ensure that the money they put into a charity which is providing hostels and services for homeless people is actually and demonstrably taking people off the streets. The homeless people who use this charity will want the accommodation to be clean and provided in a safe environment, and the staff and volunteers who man the hostels will want to feel that they are doing a good job, and are appreciated by managers and users alike. There will also be a judgement of effectiveness from other agencies such as the police, who may put pressure for the charity to be closed if they are receiving too many calls for help; neighbours of the hostels will judge it effective if they are not hassled as they walk to their homes; and local hospitals and doctors may judge effectiveness by whether their workload of problem cases is increased or not. Some of these objectives are likely to be in conflict with others. For example, providing high numbers of places for high-risk homeless people is

REAL-LIFE APPLICATION 12.6

Stakeholder objectives in universities

Stakeholders are currently arguing about strategies for the university sector in the UK. Teachers argue for maintaining the quality of education, measured in terms of things like low ratios of students to staff, and high spending on library facilities; within shrinking budgets, managers focus on cost-saving measures and rational-isation of programmes; and politicians are attempting to encourage wider access to higher education at the same time as they try to contain spending on universities and obtain what they see as better value for money.

almost inevitably going to lead to complaints from neighbours as their quality of life goes down. Another example of conflicting objectives is given in Real-Life Application 12.6.

Understanding what effectiveness means and balancing conflicting objectives can lead to problems in defining the level of service required or to be provided. It is often also quite difficult to assess whether an NFP's mission, however defined, is being achieved. In the example above, it is a relatively easy task to assess whether the charity is providing accommodation; all it needs to do is count up bed occupancy. But if its mission is also to reduce long-term homelessness, how can it judge whether it has done this? Reducing homelessness is a much more complex task, which involves political and economic decisions, and co-ordination between a wide variety of different agencies, both statutory and voluntary.

This is not to say that NFPs should not attempt such broad missions. Some of the biggest, best-known, and powerful NFP organisations have extremely widespread political aims as their *raison d'être*. Greenpeace and Friends of the Earth (see end of chapter case study), both international organisations with a brief to crusade on ethical and 'green' issues, are campaigning bodies with large research and public relations arms. Arguably both have been extremely effective in achieving publicity for their causes. *Proving* that they have been responsible for achieving any changes to corporate or government practice is a much harder task, however.

12.2.2 Strategic options for NFP organisations

The same caution is needed when applying the concepts of strategic management to not-for-profit organisations as was highlighted in the case of public sector organisations. Although NFPs compete with one another for resources (funds and volunteers), a very aggressive competitive stance is likely to antagonise stakeholders and to harm the organisation. Another unusual attribute of NFPs is that their objective may, in theory, be to work themselves out of existence – by eliminating cancer, or poverty in Africa. Strategic management in NFPs needs to be concerned with three principal strands:

1. *Putting in place the value chain, architecture, structure and systems that allow the NFP's mission to be implemented.*

   In this respect the task is identical to that of commercial or public sector organisations. The difference is in the types of control and management systems that need to be selected (bureaucratic and cultural for the most part), and in coping with the singular and highly political nature of the staff, trustees, management committee and funding structure. The competing demands of the different stakeholder groups, each of which is likely to have its own (and often different) objectives, cultures, and sources of power, means that a survival factor for an NFP is the reconciliation and bridging of these different perspectives.

2. *Developing the fundraising infrastructure that allows income to be generated, in quantity, and in as regular, predictable and reliable a form as possible.*

   In order to do this an assessment needs to be made of the potential sources of funds, and whether the NFP is what Parker (1998) terms a 'has-been', 'celebrity' or 'star' category:

◄ The Boston Consulting Group matrix was introduced in Chapter 9.

   ● *Has-beens* (the NFP equivalent of 'dogs' in the Boston Consulting Group matrix), because they are perceived to be old-fashioned or out-dated, even though they may be well known, are at risk of losing both sponsors and clients. In order to achieve sufficient income such organisations need to raise their public profile and be seen to be rejuvenating their operations and mission.

   ● A *celebrity* organisation (analogous to a 'star' business unit in the BCG classification) is usually well known, but has not yet built up sufficient resources to meet demand. This type of organisation should be able to attract new donors relatively easily, and this needs to be the area of most attention.

   ● A *star* organisation (confusingly, the NFP answer to a BCG 'cash cow') already has a good public profile and high levels of financial support, and only needs to be worried about the threat of new competition for funds coming into their particular field.

   The increased competition from other NFPs and an increasingly charity-sated public mean that considerable management attention has to be paid to wooing, and keeping, donors, and in positioning the organisation so that it can attract a sufficiently wealthy and committed group of supporters. This may involve similar marketing and segmentation competences to those used in commercial firms to target customers.

3. *Providing* visible *evidence that the management of the NFP is being carried out in a professional and competent manner.*

   This is an important task given the dependence of many NFPs on the goodwill of the general public and/or their donors. There is some evidence that adopting various professional management practices borrowed from commercial organisations, such as strategic planning, customer satisfaction surveys, cutting costs and change management procedures are likely to enhance people's impressions of effectiveness. NFPs which are judged effective also tend to have management committees or boards of trustees with higher social standing; therefore NFPs which need to raise their esteem in the eyes of the public and key stakeholders might do well to upgrade the standard and status of their board's membership.

12.3 Strategic management for new and/or small firms

Although grouped together in this section, we need to clear up a small point first: small firms are not always new, although almost all new firms are small. Most small firms have no intention of becoming any larger. By far the majority of small firms are what have come to be known as 'mom and pop' concerns – organisations which provide employment for the owner and his or her family and possibly a few other employees.

◀ We discussed the principal-agent issue in Section 1.3.2.

In these types of organisation the strategy is what the owner wants it to be. There is no principal/agent problem, or much in the way of emergent strategies – or even 'strategies' at all as we have used them in much of this book. The owner's strategy might be to provide long-term income free from the interference of colleagues or bosses, to provide an enjoyable way of spending the day, as a social service, or to maintain a business so that it can one day be passed on to the children. Farms and stately homes are often in this latter category. In fact, many small firms pursue strategic objectives that actually run counter to the conventional definitions of busi-

Figure 12.2 The five stages of company growth (adapted from Churchill and Lewis, 1983)

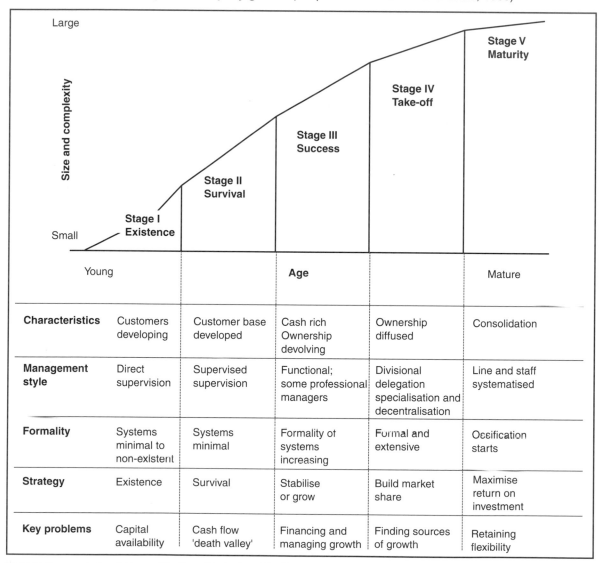

	Young		Age		Mature
Characteristics	Customers developing	Customer base developed	Cash rich Ownership devolving	Ownership diffused	Consolidation
Management style	Direct supervision	Supervised supervision	Functional; some professional managers	Divisional delegation specialisation and decentralisation	Line and staff systematised
Formality	Systems minimal to non-existent	Systems minimal	Formality of systems increasing	Formal and extensive	Ossification starts
Strategy	Existence	Survival	Stabilise or grow	Build market share	Maximise return on investment
Key problems	Capital availability	Cash flow 'death valley'	Financing and managing growth	Finding sources of growth	Retaining flexibility

ness success that we have used in this book, such as return on capital, growth in turnover, and profits (see Jennings and Beaver, 1997).

A different animal is the firm that is small only because it is new. These organisations are owned and managed by *entrepreneurs* – people whose objective is the growth and development of their firms into large money-making concerns. Whether they are able to do this depends to a great extent on the skills and abilities of the owner to *lead* and *delegate responsibility* to what may become in time a large and increasingly complex organisation with many employees.

12.3.1 The strategic environment for small firms

◄ *We looked at Greiner's model of organisational growth over time in Section 10.2. We also look at organisational configurations in Chapters 8 and 10.*

Along with Larry Greiner, a number of other writers have discussed the issues of managing company growth, for example Churchill and Lewis (1983). Figure 12.2 summarises some of the key issues identified by these writers.

These stages can be summarised as a gradual move from informal to formal, paralleling the move from small to large as the firm matures. As we suggested above, of course not all firms will move through these stages, and a lot of management writing in recent times has focused on how to enable old, large firms to retain the informality of a young, entrepreneurial business.

Much of the research on small firms has concentrated on the personalities of successful entrepreneurs, but another major area of interest has been the other factors which influence the success or otherwise of growing firms.[11] This research suggests that flourishing high growth companies are more focused in their objectives, with a strong emphasis on forecasting and the management of financial data. On the other side of this equation, inadequate accounting systems, lack of capital budgeting abilities, poor stock control, poor record-keeping and over-controlled and demotivated employees are known factors in small business failures. Predictably, small firms that start (and remain) undercapitalised are inclined to be unsuccessful.

Unlike large firms, which have at least some chance of shaping and controlling the environment in which they operate, the small firm lacks resources. It has little option but to take whatever the environment throws at it, and adapt as best it may – minimising the harmful consequences of any changes which might occur. Small firms are in industries which are either new (see Section 12.4.1 below) and probably quite chaotic, or more mature and dominated by larger and more powerful firms. In both cases the environment is likely to be relatively uncontrollable and hostile.

◄ *Chapter 5 looks at some of the factors in the environment that are important to firms' success.*

A number of studies have suggested that industry structure or context may have a greater impact on new venture performance than either strategy or the founder's entrepreneurial characteristics.[12] The environment is particularly important for retailers, one of the most common types of small business, whose location is critical. Firms in urban areas tend to have lower survival rates compared with those in rural areas, and those located near large magnet or 'attractor' stores or complementary outlets are more likely to be successful.

There are some other important success factors. Some studies have suggested that firms in sectors with high barriers to entry have a lower tendency to fail. When large amounts of money are concerned, the founders are likely to make a more thorough assessment of the business' prospects. However, other studies have also suggested that the manufacturing sector has the highest annual bankruptcy rates (three times the average) compared with service and retail firms (approximately half the average rate for all businesses). There are some variations between different subsectors in these areas too. Professional services have lower failure rates compared with other services, probably because they have to overcome hurdles before they are founded, such as industry accreditation.

12.3.2 Success and survival factors for small firms

Many of the strategies which small firms may adopt are not strictly strategic by our normal criteria as applied to large firms. For most small firms the short term is a more important consideration than thinking five years ahead, and dealing with practical considerations is equally important to the survival of the firm. For a large organisation these issues would form a relatively minor and localised functional concern.

Although generic skills in managing finances and personnel are useful, the management of a small business is very different from that of a large corporation. Flexibility, multi-tasking and dealing with a multiplicity of roles are the competences needed by small business owner/managers. The management of strategy is primarily a process of responding to changes in the environment, and using scarce resources (both financial and managerial) to maximise the gains for the owner, however he or she defines these.

Having a strong and balanced management team is often a critical factor in the success of a small firm, especially if it is one whose owner wants it to grow. It is one of the reasons why venture capitalists (VCs) will often assess the strengths of the management team as a whole, rather than the owner alone. VCs will often appoint one of their own staff to work as part of the team and provide specialist expertise that may not be available elsewhere. However, obtaining suitable 'professional' and specialised managers, who have the skills which the original owner does not themselves possess, can be a real problem for small firms. They cannot provide the same level of salaries and benefits that managers could expect from larger organisations. The way that many small firms overcome this is by promising a share of the ownership of what is hoped will become a large and successful firm in the future.

For a firm to be successful over a sustained period there must also be a capability to adapt to changing circumstances and very different internal and external conditions. An entrepreneur needs to be able to initiate and implement change and develop new products and systems. There appears to be an inverse relationship between the age of a business and its likelihood of failure, perhaps because, by definition, older firms have already demonstrated a successful capacity to adapt and develop, and have built competences and capabilities which allow this process to continue. Strategies which are likely to be successful are also contingent on the industry or sector in which they are applied. For example a successful strategy for a retailer is likely to be based on the ability to choose and negotiate a good site close to an attractor store and then to manage cash flow and stock control effectively.

According to Gadenne (1998), success in retailing is also linked with a focus on: (i) pricing products lower than those of competitors; (ii) emphasising high sales turnover; (iii) emphasising cost reduction; (iv) checking quality of products; (v) using outside borrowed funds; and (vi) searching for cheap sources of finance. The value-for-money factor in the retail industry suggests that small retail firms may only be able to compete successfully when both low price and good quality are achieved.

For firms in service industries, important strategic issues relate to the welfare and motivation of employees – involving them in decision-making, assessing performance and rewarding accordingly, and emphasising staff training. In addition a number of financial management factors are important: (i) not using outside borrowed funds; (ii) not searching for cheap sources of finance; (iii) maintaining large cash balances; (iv) emphasising high sales turnover; and (v) not keeping high levels of inventory.

For manufacturing firms, success factors are: (i) having a specialised understanding of products/customers and competing on the basis of price/cost; (ii) acquiring knowledge of competitors' activities in order to establish a market niche which will not attract retaliation from larger and more powerful competitors; (iii) employing consultants or professionals, e.g. accountants; and (iv) finding cheap sources of finance.

12.4 Strategic management at the different stages in an industry's life-cycle

There are close links between strategies which are prevalent at the early stages of an industry's life-cycle[13] and strategies which are likely to be chosen by a small firm at its own early stage of development – after all, it is often the small firm which creates a new product and thus a new industry. The industry grows with the firm and its eventual competitors. But the correlation is not exact – a large, older, firm *can*

Figure 12.3   The industry life-cycle

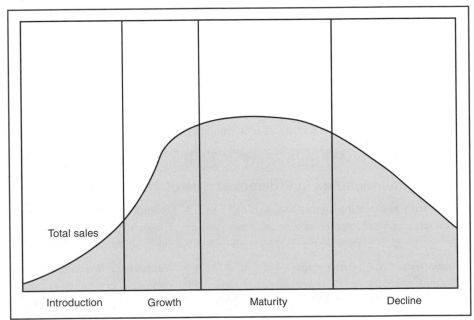

◀ We looked at different types of environmental conditions in Chapter 5. We also looked at the industry life-cycle in the same chapter, Section 5.3.

◀ We looked at the relationship between portfolio models and the industry life-cycle in Chapter 9.

innovate and create an industry, and small firms can enter into an established industry – given certain conditions.

As a reminder we repeat a picture of an industry life-cycle in Figure 12.3 (see Real-Life Application 12.7 for some examples of firms at the different stages). Remember that this is a rather simplistic model of an industry over an indeterminate period of time, in which the stages can vary in length enormously. Each industry will also vary in overall size, complexity and stability. Don't forget, too, that it is not easy to define an industry.

When we are looking at strategies that are likely to be effective at different stages of an industry life-cycle, factors such as the characteristics of the industry need to be taken into account. For example, industries in a high growth phase tend to be complex and dynamic, although these correlations are not perfect. Mature industries tend to be more stable and in many ways simpler. But there are some exceptions to this general rule. Industries such as software remain fast changing, even when mature. We return to look at some of these special types of industry environment in Section 12.4.5 below when we consider strategies under conditions of hypercompetition.

As we discussed in Chapter 5, there are four important determinants of strategic behaviour in an industry: the power of customers, the power of suppliers, the likelihood of new firms entering the industry, and the threat of substitute products. The strength of each of the four forces changes with the maturity of the industry.[14]

The strategies which firms adopt are also influenced by the industry's structure – how many firms there are, how large they are – which also changes with the industry's life-cycle, along with the size, structure, and strength of the competing firm itself (Table 12.1). Because of all these factors, when an industry matures, the strategies adopted by firms within it tend to change.

12.4.1 Strategies for the introductory phase of an industry

The strategic environment for introductory-stage organisations

We look at the development of innovation by mature companies in new venture divisions in Section 15.2. ▶

At the beginning of the introductory phase, a single firm has created and sold a single new product – the start of a new industry. The firm in question, and its competitors when they start up, will quite often be small, like Internet start-ups in the US and Europe, and will offer only a single product or service. Where a large company is involved, it may well be through an independent division, such as the e-commerce divisions of large firms like Procter & Gamble, with many of the characteristics of a small firm.

REAL-LIFE APPLICATION 12.7

European industries in different stages of the life-cycle

Industries at the introductory stage

Examples include: Internet service providers; website designers; on-line banks; digital camera manufacturers.

Industries at the growth stage

Examples include: mobile phone service providers; PC manufacturers; cook and chill food manufacturers.

Industries at the mature stage

Examples include: sugar refiners; food supermarkets; retail banking; china tableware makers.

Industries at the decline stage

Examples include: SLR camera manufacturers; coal mining; high street butchers.

Table 12.1 Life-cycle stage characteristics

	Introduction	*Growth*	*Maturity*	*Decline*
Growth rate of sales	Rising slowly	Accelerating	Level	Declining
Competitors	Few but increasing	Increasing consolidation Exit of weakest firms Fight for share beginning	Stable oligopoly Firms interdependent – market signalling Cartels may develop	Declining Exit of firms
Customers	Few and rich	Widening Increasingly discerning	Mass market Repeat purchasers	Moving away
Entry barriers	Technology	Start-up costs Competence and learning curve effects	Competitors	Over-capacity
Products	Little choice Poor quality	Growing availability Increasingly differentiated	Differentiated High quality	Shrinking choice
Typical pricing	High. Cost-plus	Penetration	Price wars to take share	Cut
Profits	Negative	Increasing	High	Declining
Unit costs	High	Declining	Low cost/ efficiency focus	Low
Typical advertising	Information and education	Mass-market awareness Persuasion and differentiation	Brand maintenance	Reduced

At this stage products and their technologies are undeveloped, and the customers who buy them are what marketing theorists term *innovators* or *early adopters* who are prepared to put up with unreliable technology and service for the sake of being at the forefront of new things.

Strategic options for introductory-stage organisations

The main strategic challenges faced by the innovator and its competitors in the introductory phase of an industry are:

● To build reputational assets, not just for themselves, but also for the industry as a whole. Once the industry becomes 'respectable', people will be readier to invest in it and to consider buying its products.

- To develop the product or service, and the associated supply and distribution chain, to the point where they are robust enough to serve a mass market. The industry will then be ready to move into its growth phase.
- To avoid cash flow problems as start-up costs mount while customers remain few. The firm will need to reinvest any income in building market positions and in developing the product; this means that, although prices charged for the new product are high, profits are likely to be low and cash flow negative.

The size of the firms will often limit the size of the competitive arena in which they will compete. Firms that are seeking to build a mass market may focus on their home market, where they can rely upon the goodwill of local customers and are in a position to respond quickly to problems with the product or its service. Nokia, in the early days of the mobile telephone industry, built a secure base in Scandinavia before it expanded into the rest of Europe. This is a traditional route for many manufacturers. However, the Internet has made it possible for firms selling some products like software or fine foods, which do not require a service network, to bypass this local phase before they internationalise. The availability of reliable commercial distributors and postal delivery services has made an integrated distribution network unnecessary for such firms. Such sales and distribution media may help firms build to a viable scale more quickly than if they were restricted to their home country.

Within the chosen markets the natural positioning strategy is one of differentiation on functionality and, to a lesser extent, reliability. Early adopters are rarely price sensitive, and are more interested in advanced features and the availability of after-sales service (Real-Life Application 12.8). Product and production technology are unstable, so that, even if the funds are available, it is very risky to build lots of capacity and sophisticated systems in an attempt to obtain strong cost advantages.

For a small company at this stage, it will be natural to restrict the scope of operations to a few products and to outsource many value chain activities. It may, for example, hire manufacturing capacity from other firms, use agents and distributors

REAL-LIFE APPLICATION 12.8

AOL

America Online (AOL) is the largest internet service provider in the world. Almost three-quarters of AOL members' time, and nearly 40% of the time that all Americans spend on the web, is spent within AOL's web space. It started off life as an on-line video-games firm called Control Video Corporation in the early 1980s. At the time AOL was not involved in its subsequent major competitive arena, the Internet. Since then it has transformed itself into, first a proprietary on-line service and then into an Internet service provider. With more than 18 million subscribers and $5 billion revenue in 1999, its sales outstrip those of the next 20 Internet companies combined.

Throughout its life, it has been criticised by commentators for moving into business areas that it did not understand, and for providing poor levels of service – notoriously when it began to offer an unlimited time/fixed fee deal. It has always confounded its critics, and has argued that its customers are far more interested in its technical capabilities than its reliability. Having said that, its recent deals with Sun Microsystems, developers of Java software, and Netscape, signal that it is now moving into a more sophisticated and demanding customer arena. Predictably commentators are suggesting that it does not have the capability to deal with this.

for sales and service, and work out of serviced office accommodation. Amazon.com, in its early days in the book trade, relied upon a nearby book whole-saler to manage its inventory.

However, if the product and the associated technology are very new, then a firm may find itself forced to integrate vertically, simply because it cannot find suppliers, distributors or service agents with the necessary expertise. In the 1960s, an early UK entrant into the super-conducting magnets industry, Oxford Instruments, found that it could not obtain sufficient supplies of liquid helium. Although it had little expertise in gas production, it had to form its own subsidiary to supply this vital ingredient, needed to maintain the magnets at the near-absolute-zero temperatures at which they operate.

Elsewhere in the value chain, strategic priorities are likely to be:

- **R&D:** developing genuine capabilities in innovation, to stay at the leading edge of product development. Incremental innovations to the new product may allow the leading firm to build on its original creation, but at this stage of the life-cycle firms often aim for breakthroughs that will set their product or service apart from competitors.

- **Production:** building capabilities in producing to a reliable standard of quality, increasing scale, lowering costs, and improving the management of the process.

- **Marketing:** although a firm will want to build its own brand and reputation, it will often be as concerned with building the reputation of the industry. A firm may help to found an industry association, to establish guidelines for product safety or for good practice. It may also practise some odd-seeming competitive behaviours, such as publicly praising competitors that have behaved in a 'responsible' fashion. When the financial derivatives industry found itself with a poor public profile, after several firms had taken heavy losses on futures and options in the early 1990s, one major player, J P Morgan, acted to try to reassure customers. It made its proprietary risk management methodology, developed at great expense, freely available, so that customers and regulators could see that, with the right tools, financial derivatives were a respectable arm of an investment portfolio.

The culture and architecture of the firm will also be developed at this time. A communal culture and informal structure are typical at this stage in a firm's development, as people work long hours together to solve challenging problems. Management time needs to be invested in educating, and building relationships with banks and venture capitalists or other sources of financial capital. Once these people have understood the nature of the industry, they can be of great assistance in helping the firm and the industry to develop to maturity. The expertise and network of contacts that the Californian venture capital firm, Kleiner Perkins, has developed, after advising early Internet firms such as AOL, Amazon.com and Netscape, makes it a valuable and sought-after partner for newer start-ups.[15]

12.4.2 Strategies for the growth phase of an industry

The strategic environment for growth-stage organisations

Once the growth phase starts, a product or service is becoming established in the minds of consumers. The original firm and its early competitors are beginning to learn how to make improvements to the product and the processes used to produce and sell it, so that quality is generally higher. Consumers are becoming increasingly sophisticated and able to make choices about the levels of service or product differentiation that they require. There are likely to be an increasing number of competing firms, who see money to be made in copying the original product, or in creating new 'me-too' ones that are slightly different.

At this stage, there is considerable consumer-led demand for products. This means that some firms can survive for a considerable period even though they are inherently weak and unlikely to endure more competitive conditions. In order to survive, they may need to do no more than provide a usable product, and basic levels of service. In fact such firms may choose to deliberately differentiate themselves on relatively low quality and low price – a position which they may continue through to more mature phases if they possess the other success factors for this strategy of managing their costs.

The growth phase resembles the introductory phase in some important regards. The R&D and marketing strategies used in the earlier phase may still be valid. Technology may not yet have stabilised, so that it will still be risky to invest in physical assets with the sole aim of acquiring cost advantage. Some firms may find that they have achieved cost advantages through routines that they have developed incrementally over time. However, the enhancement of these advantages is likely to take second place to the challenge of meeting demand.

Strategic options for growth-stage organisations

At this stage, where demand is increasing at the highest pace, the main challenge for firms lies in keeping up with it, and in establishing a viable position in the market place (Real-Life Application 12.9). This implies keeping abreast of technological developments and ensuring that products are compatible with any emerging standards. New uses may be appearing for the product or service, and so firms may be directing themselves towards new customer groups. Those with sufficient production and management capacity may also be looking to expand geographically.

More ambitious firms will seek to differentiate themselves from competitors, typically on the basis of reliability. During the growth phase of the PC industry in the UK, firms would advertise the number of hours that their products had been tested at the factory. This was intended to show that they were not prone to the frequent hardware crashes that had bedevilled earlier generations. Other areas of differentiation might be better levels of customer service, additional features (such as recording capability or Dolby noise reduction in the case of the Sony Walkman), higher levels of product quality, or different product designs. If a firm can demonstrate that it is consistently at the cutting edge of innovation, and associate its name with product standards in the industry, this can also be valuable in building reputation.

For manufacturers, production capacity has to be increased rapidly, and this has implications for the recruitment and training of personnel and the location of suitable manufacturing plants as well as the logistics of moving the product from where it is made to where it is sold. Controlling the quality of the product is still an issue – especially for service manufacturing firms like McDonald's where the product is simultaneously manufactured and consumed in locations which are

◄ *Service manufacturing was defined in Section 8.2.*

506

REAL-LIFE APPLICATION 12.9

Managing growth at Intel

Microprocessor chips are a fundamental component of personal computers. Intel have been estimated to have supplied up to 80% of the chips built into PCs in the last few years, and for twenty years or so until 1999 posted average earnings growth of 30% p.a. However, the company did not start off in this business. Intel was founded in 1968 to offer replacement parts for mainframe computer memories. But in 1970, Intel introduced the world's first DRAM (dynamic random access memory) computer chip, and by 1972 this was the world's largest selling semiconductor, accounting for over 90% of Intel's sales revenues. DRAMs remained Intel's core business throughout the 1970s and early 1980s.

Intel had a new process technology, the first to give viable 'yields' (the yield is the number of functioning DRAMs that are etched on each wafer of silicon). There were three major types of technological competencies involved in making such semiconductor products: (1) circuit design, (2) process technology development (TD), and (3) manufacturing engineering. TD was a silicon-based competence: it involved the sequence of physical steps necessary to put multiple layers of masks on a chip. Circuit design was not a silicon-based competence: it referred to the ability to define patterns on each layer of mask. DRAMs required a very tight relationship between circuit design and TD. Intel viewed TD as its distinctive competence because TD had made the difference in its initial success.

In the early stage of the DRAM industry, when production volumes and minimum acceptable yield levels were relatively low, the difference between the activities and concerns of TD and manufacturing engineering was not particularly important. Intel had also developed a distinctive competence in integrating TD and manufacturing. This resulted in the ability to make rapid incremental process changes and to stay ahead of competition. Intel emphasised being first to market with premium-priced products and first to move into new markets as existing ones matured. As the largest volume product, DRAMs were viewed as the 'technology driver' on which Intel's learning curve depended, and the company routinely allocated resources to its successful and fast-growing DRAM business.

Texas Instruments and Mostek were early entrants into this market. Also, large, vertically integrated Japanese firms targeted the semiconductor memory industry as strategic. Their determination to dominate led to aggressive capacity expansion and price competition. The difference between competitors' product offerings quickly disappeared and new DRAM generations followed each other in highly predictable two- to three-year cycles.

As the DRAM industry matured, customers demanded tens of thousands of units of a single product and demanded high quantities of DRAMs with guaranteed performance, reliability, and price. This, in turn, shifted the basis of competition in the industry towards the large-scale, precision manufacturing competence necessary to achieve very high yields for each new DRAM generation immediately. And this shift favoured the tightly managed manufacturing-oriented firms, such as Texas Instruments and the Japanese, over the more innovative but less disciplined TD-oriented Intel. In time, DRAMs became a commodity product. The new key factor determining profitability in the DRAM market was manufacturing capacity. To be a viable competitor, a company needed to be willing to commit increasingly large capital investments to DRAM capacity and to develop the necessary discipline in manufacturing to obtain high initial yields and continuous yield improvements quickly for each DRAM generation.

The changing basis of competition in the memory business strained the relationships between Intel's TD and manufacturing groups. TD scientists continued to see their task in terms of process innovation, revolutionary change, and technical elegance. Manufacturing engineers, in contrast, now saw their task in terms of stability, incremental change, and technical simplicity in order to reach higher yields. Increasing the emphasis on large-scale manufacturing engineering competence was difficult for Intel. The early technical heroes at Intel had been TD scientists who understood a fundamental physical phenomenon and converted it into a working product prototype. As process technology began to evolve more quickly, each generation of product not only required a new process but an entirely new set of capital equipment. Thus it became very disruptive to current production to carry out process technology development on the line. As Andy Grove, Intel's chief executive, suggested, Intel encouraged 'constructive confrontation' between competing technologies and their internal champions as it learns its way into the future in a high-risk, hyper-competitive environment (Burgelman and Grove, 1996).

Struggling to maintain a competitive advantage, Intel continued to rely on innovative TD efforts through several successive DRAM generations. But some of these remained niche products, and Intel fell behind in manufacturing yields and market share relative to top Japanese producers such as Fujitsu and Hitachi. By 1980, Intel's market share had dwindled to less than 3% (ninth in the industry). By 1984, DRAM production was restricted to one out of Intel's eight manufacturing plants and the company had moved to focus on a different product group – microprocessors.

Principally adapted from 'Fading memories: A process theory of strategic business exit in dynamic environments' by Robert Burgelman, *Administrative Science Quarterly*, March 1994.

spread across a wide geographical area. Even for tangible product manufacturers, however, quality control is an issue – not because the knowledge of how to maintain quality is not there, but simply because corners are sometimes cut in an attempt to maximise output.

There are no patterns for culture and architecture for firms at this stage of the life-cycle. Some firms, like Compaq in the PC industry, may find it advantageous to formalise their structures and systems to cope with the management problems of increasing size, and to move towards a mercenary culture as a way of driving growth within the firm. Other competitors may find it preferable and effective to stay with the informal structures developed earlier, since the formalisation of systems will take management attention away from the main priority, meeting demand.

Towards the latter part of this stage (and don't forget there are no neat cut-off points between the different phases, or even an automatic progression from one stage to another), there will be an increasing consolidation of the industry, in which the stronger firms start to take over or squeeze out some of the smaller or weaker firms. For the larger and stronger firms this is a way of buying in innovative knowledge that they have not had the time or competence to develop themselves, in the form of personnel from smaller, more creative, firms. It is also a way of increasing market share, and acquiring additional distribution channels. Smaller or weaker firms, therefore, can contemplate withdrawal through sale to one of their stronger competitors, the negotiation of a suitable price being a major consideration. This strategy should not always be considered an admission of failure. Quite the opposite; it is often a recognition that not all owners of small firms can, or should want to, develop their companies into major concerns. They may be better employed in creating something new, then moving on to develop something else – being serial entrepreneurs in other words.

12.4.3 Strategies for the mature phase of an industry

The strategic environment for mature-stage organisations

In the mature phase of an industry, sales growth slows but is not yet in decline. This stage can last for many years, with small increases and decreases in sales growth rates as economies pass through cycles of boom and recession, fashions come and go, or new marketing campaigns are carried out by the major firms to rekindle the sales of their mature products (Real-Life Application 12.10).

Sometimes by this stage the industry has consolidated into an oligopoly. This is most likely to happen in industries where there are appreciable economies of scale

REAL-LIFE APPLICATION 12.10

Classical music recording life-cycles

There are a number of record (or more accurately now-adays, CD) companies which specialise almost exclusively in recording and producing classical music. They include Deutsche Grammophon, Deutsche Harmonia Mundi, Teldec Classics, or Classics for Pleasure. Almost all are subsidiaries of the large global music and entertainment companies such as Sony or EMI. All are having to face an increasingly competitive business environment provoked in part by the improved reliability and technology of the soundcarrier – the CD. In the past, record companies had a reliable source of repeat sales in music fans who had managed to break or scratch their records. This problem no longer exists – and once a customer has a copy of Beethoven's ninth symphony, only the most obsessive or dedicated of fans will want to buy multiple copies of the same work. The same problem does not apply to pop or rock genres which benefit from a diet of new compositions and constantly changing fads.

The classical industry has fought back, although sales overall are still pretty stagnant. There is increasing differentiation of the companies. Deutsche Grammophon has positioned itself as the high-quality, high-price producer. It rarely if ever sells CDs at budget prices, and equally rarely uses anything but the most

reputable and thus expensive artistes (which is not necessarily the same as the most famous). Other companies have focused on selling low-cost CDs of the most popular works. New labels such as Chandos, Hyperion, and particularly Naxos have attempted to broaden the customer base (and incidentally stimulated competition) by providing cheap but high-quality recordings. They have done this partly by sourcing some of the recordings from the former Soviet Union, countries which have a long and highly reputable classical music tradition but where the costs of soloists and orchestras are much less than in the West. Other firms such as Classic FM have specialised in promoting famous artistes (often those who are visually attractive, or who have some other interesting or memorable attributes) who perform popular or undemanding pieces, often repackaged into relatively short extracts from various works on the same CD. Other labels such as Harmonia Mundi have focused on unusual or specialised pieces, such as early music or modern compositions – contemporary classical, a segment which has surprised many commentators by its success. Sales of works by living composers such as Pärt, Gorecki, or John Taverner have in some cases rivalled those of more conventional 'pop' artistes.

or scope. In such cases all the major firms know one other, watch each other's actions carefully and respond to any competitive moves.

Sometimes, however, the industry will remain fragmented. This is most likely to happen when there are many possible sources of advantage, none of which gives a competitor a position of overwhelming strength. This allows firms that are out-competed in some areas to retain a viable position because of their strengths in others. Fragmentation is also likely in industries like restaurants and fashion, where sheer inspiration and ingenuity may allow a small firm to compete with a large one, at least for a time.

Typically, by the time an industry matures, product and process technologies have stabilised, so that it becomes more difficult to differentiate the product or service on functionality. This is the problem that British Airways faces with economy class air travel, or Sony with its Walkman cassette tape player. Customers, many of them repeat buyers, have become familiar with the product or service and have developed a clear idea of what constitutes value for money. This makes it more difficult for firms to sustain positions based on premium prices, since few buyers will pay over the odds for something which is little different from what is offered by competitors.

Strategic options for mature-stage organisations

The nature of the challenge confronting firms in the mature industry often changes from achieving differentiation advantage to achieving and sustaining cost advantage. At the same time, firms must avoid triggering a damaging price war, particularly in oligopolistic industries where price moves will quickly be noted and copied. There are a number of reasons why such a war might develop. Extra capacity, ordered when the industry was still growing in the expectation that growth would continue, may come on stream when the industry has matured. There will be a temptation for firms to cut their prices to try to utilise the extra capacity, and get some return on the sunk investment. At the same time, salespeople who may have grown used to large bonuses when the market was growing may press for price reductions to help them make their targets. However, since most of the firms in the industry will be in a similar situation, a round of price cuts will simply lead to a reduction in profits for all competitors. Damaging price wars of this kind occur periodically in industries such as automobiles, air travel and insurance.

◄ We looked at some of the special issues to do with managing an international strategy in Section 6.5.

Firms can respond to these challenges by seeking new competitive arenas. Though they will have an established presence in some markets, there may still be opportunities for them to find new target customer groups and expand into new geographical areas, in order to escape from existing competitive pressures and gain economies of scale. The larger firms in a mature industry are likely to be building a broad, and most likely global, product market scope.

Methods of international expansion are explored in Chapter 15. ►

Within established markets, brand names and corporate reputation will by this stage be well developed, and customers will have learned which firms and which products are suited to their needs. Those firms that can, will seek to differentiate on the basis of reputation and image, to reap the kinds of price premiums that BMW and Mercedes, for example, obtain in the automobile industry. Firms with a well-developed innovation capability may look to product innovation as a path to differentiation advantage, like Sony in consumer electronics and Virgin Atlantic in air travel. However, these are likely to be small, incremental innovations, designed to create demand for repeat purchase and respond to customer requirements for product enhancements, with major breakthroughs being few and far between.

The main thrust of R&D effort at this stage of the life-cycle typically shifts from product innovation to process innovation. This is part of a general emphasis within the value chain of improved efficiency, cost advantage and exploitation of strategic resources. Peripheral activities in which the firm has no distinctive capability may be outsourced, including those into which the firm integrated vertically at an earlier stage in the industry life-cycle.

Where economies of scale are available, firms may seek to profit from them through investment in large production and distribution facilities. In fragmented industries, firms may look to compete, as Benetton and McDonald's do, by building chains of franchised or semi-autonomous operations, that are agile enough to compete with small firms, but benefit from the parent company's brands, reputation, and administrative systems.

Marketing activities are devoted to maintaining continued awareness of the brand and building customer loyalty, so that customers do not defect to competitors. Radical price reductions are typically avoided unless a firm believes that it has achieved a significant cost advantage, or to try to 'kill off' a competitor that has cash flow problems. However, cut-throat competition of this kind is rarely appro-

◀ We introduced the concept of industry rules of the game in Chapter 5.

priate in a mature industry, since it can incite strong competitors to retaliate in kind. It is better to try to retain a stable base of competitors that understand the industry 'rules of the game'.

Building customer loyalty is also an important consideration for the firm's architecture. Links to customers through staff secondments and regular visits can be important in building loyalty through personal friendships, and in furnishing information that enables firms to update their product and service to meet customer needs.

As the processes and technologies stabilise, the firm's culture and architecture are likely to change to reflect the new circumstances. People's roles within the firm typically become more closely defined and specialised at this stage in the life-cycle. This tends to lead firms to adopt sophisticated control systems and formalised structures, although whether the choice is a functional, divisional, matrix, or hybrid structure will depend upon the size and scope of the organisation, and upon the nature of the industry. A networked or mercenary culture may be appropriate, depending on the competitive situation.

We look at the various alternative strategic methods, such as mergers, acquisitions and alliances, in Chapter 15. ▶

◀ We looked at portfolio theory and corporate level strategy in Chapter 9.

Firms in a mature industry also have to start to think about what they do if and when sales start to decline – and when this will be is, of course, dependent on the nature of the industry. Therefore they need to consider moving into different areas – diversifying – either through acquiring other firms in different areas of business, or through the in-house development of new products themselves. The choices of these new products or business areas will be dependent on the dominant strategic logic,[16] and whether they are considered to fit into the firm's portfolio of products and businesses (Prahalad and Bettis, 1986). Part of this process may be a consideration of whether the firm has any non-essential functions or business areas which could be devolved, sold or closed down.

We should note here that not all theorists agree with the view, described above, that firms involved in a mature industry should downplay product innovation and abide by established industry rules of the game. Charles Baden-Fuller and John Stopford (1992) believe that the concept of a mature industry is misleading. They cite a number of case studies of firms that have successfully introduced radical product and marketing innovations in industries, such as steel cutlery, that were widely seen as mature and unexciting. Such innovations were typically accompanied by a far-reaching transformation of the organisation's culture and architecture.

We look at strategies for organisational transformation in Chapter 14. ▶

12.4.4 Strategies for the decline stage of an industry

The strategic environment for decline-stage organisations

By the final phase of an industry's life-cycle, sales have begun to decline and substitute products have taken over (Real-Life Application 12.11). However, it is still possible for declining industries such as cigars and fountain pens to be extremely profitable.[17] As long as there are not too many companies competing for a shrinking customer base, profits can be obtained in the decline phase, sometimes for many years. These are the 'cash dog' products, whose costs are minimal and which need little investment, since demand is predictable, the remaining customer base is likely to be loyal, and the product and process technologies are stable.

◀ A 'cash dog' is a category in the Boston Matrix which we describe in Chapter 9.

REAL-LIFE APPLICATION 12.11

Declining industries in Germany

In Germany, according to the industry classification of the German Federal Statistics Office, six manufacturing industries representing more than 10% of German production reported a shrinking index for at least ten years since 1986. These industries were (1) mining, (2) textile production and clothing, (3) leather manufacturing and processing, (4) iron production, (5) the foundry industry, and (6) aerospace, ship, and rail manufacturing.

Using foundries as an example, the overall market declined by an average negative growth rate of −2.5% per annum between 1987 and 1997. The number of foundries in Germany declined between 1992 and 1997 by an average of 5.8% per annum, and the average annual production volume of a sample of firms in this industry declined by 7% per annum over the five years between 1988 and 1992.

Source: Schefczyk and Gerpott (1998).

Strategic options for decline-stage organisations

The challenges for a firm at this stage of an industry are to maximise the profits to be obtained from the industry, to minimise the investment needed and to avoid a destructive price war between firms with high exit costs that are determined to stay in the industry.

At this stage in the life-cycle, withdrawal can be a very attractive option for a firm which does not believe that it has the reputation or other resources that are needed to profit from the decline, or that has more attractive opportunities elsewhere. If the firm is wise, it will itself have created the substitute products that have taken away the sales from the old industry, or will have diversified into other products with greater prospects for growth.

For many firms, therefore, decisions at this stage relate to winding up the business, selling it or its assets for as much as possible, or simply moving its employees and facilities to be used in other areas. Withdrawal will be viable if exit costs are not too high, or if there is another company that is willing to purchase the assets and take on the staff. However, in some areas and industries there may be political issues which make withdrawal difficult or expensive, and others where the costs of closure may be greater than those of staying in business.

Firms that cannot or do not want to quit the industry immediately may pursue a 'harvesting' strategy. They produce and sell what they can, with minimal investment in marketing and fixed assets, until demand dries up, and then they withdraw from the industry. This is an effective strategy if competition in the industry remains benign, so that the company can enjoy the fruits of its past investment without worrying about aggression from its competitors.

However, firms which believe that they have some form of sustainable advantage may prefer a more proactive strategy. One option is to focus on a profitable niche market where the organisation may have built good relationships in the past, or where its resources are particularly valuable. In the steel industry, some players have focused on the development and production of unusual alloy steels for specific applications. Others have focused on providing undifferentiated steel products, such as the reinforcing rods used in concrete, in a particular geographic area. They employ a low-cost technology, the mini-mill, that takes steel scrap as its raw material and is economic at lower output volumes than the integrated steelworks used by the major global competitors.

If a firm believes that it has the basis for competitive advantage over a broad competitive arena, then it may make sense to attempt to lead the industry into an orderly decline, with a view to dominating it for the rest of its life. A leadership strategy involves a measure of upfront investment intended to frighten competitors out of the industry, and at the same time to make it easy for them to withdraw. For example a firm might invest aggressively in new, low-cost production facilities and in marketing, to build market share. This would demonstrate that the 'leader' was committed to the industry for the long term. At the same time it might make public pronouncements about its belief that the industry's decline was permanent. These would be aimed at competitors whose owners or managers were sentimentally attached to the industry, and who might be tempted to hold on in expectation of a future upturn. Finally, it might ease competitors' path out of the industry by assuming some of their exit costs. It might buy their plant, hire their people and assume their commitments to fill orders and maintain service and the supply of spare parts for existing users. Sometimes, governments or supra-national bodies such as the European Commission can be persuaded to assist in restructuring an industry.

Once the threat of a price war in a declining industry has been averted, the strategies that the remaining firms should pursue are straightforward. It makes sense to profit from the stability and predictability of the environment by simplifying everything. Product features can be minimised, production schedules optimised by making a limited range of products and aiming for long production runs. Competences can be refined and systems and structure can be simplified and made extremely efficient.

It may be possible to enhance profitability further by differentiating the product. Brand names in the industry will be very well known and may have grown quite prestigious with age. The dwindling band of users may take pride in their association with an old-fashioned product or service, and be open to marketing campaigns based upon special editions or collectors' items. Dunhill, an English manufacturer of tobacco pipes, has founded a club for pipe smokers, the Fellowship of the White Spot. Members receive a regular newsletter in which they are informed of gatherings of pipe aficionados and are offered limited edition pipes made in special shapes and decorated in silver.

It is not unknown for industries in apparently terminal decline to be rejuvenated. The Yo-yo is a toy which we remember from our childhoods (too many years ago!), but which had not been seen (in the UK at least) for many years. Suddenly at the end of the 1990s it has reappeared – in an improved format admittedly, but still recognisably a Yo-yo.

Turnaround strategies

As industries mature and go into decline, it becomes more likely that certain firms will themselves decline to the point of crisis. Although research (Slatter, 1984) has shown that poor management and poor financial controls are the most common causes of corporate crisis, falls in demand, increased competition, and other environmental problems, such as increases in input prices or interest rates, were a factor in 30–40% of corporate crises. One-off errors, such as a failed large project or acquisition, can also reduce a firm to a critical state. No strategic option can be guaranteed to be effective in such circumstances. Sometimes the only option is ignominious withdrawal. In the 1980s, following an unsuccessful acquisition, the UK defence electronics firm Ferranti was bought by its long-time rival GEC – for £1!

Where a recovery strategy, or turnaround, is possible, it tends to contain a number of elements:

- A financial restructuring, often including asset sales. Sometimes, the assets that have to be sold are those that the firm would rather keep. When the UK leisure group Stakis was being revived in the late 1980s, it found itself forced to retain casinos it wanted to sell, for want of a buyer, and to sell instead the nursing homes that it wanted to keep and expand.

- A change of competitive arena. This may imply moving products and brands up- or down-market, the identification of new customer groups or the development of new brands to replace those with a tarnished image.

We look at the management of organisational transformations and strategic change in more detail in Chapter 14. ▶

- A transformation of the culture and architecture – possibly the most demanding of all management tasks. Frequently it will require a change of leadership, or at least the injection of new skills and ideas into the management team. Business process re-engineering (see also Section 14.5.2) is a technique that may be appropriate in these extreme circumstances.

Sometimes, where an organisation has the funds available, a judicious acquisition may be a vital stage in a turnaround. America's venerable long-distance telephone operator AT&T has tried to revitalise itself through its acquisitions of cable television firms. These have given it access to people's homes, and therefore the ability to compete with the new entrants with more modern technology that were threatening its business (though some commentators doubt this strategy will work).[18]

12.4.5 Strategies in hypercompetitive industries

◀ *Hypercompetition and increasing returns were introduced in Chapter 5.*

Another situation that warrants a special mention is that of hypercompetitive industries.[19] These typically (although not always) arise when there are increasing returns to scale. In industries like PC processor chips, computer games consoles and PC operating systems the competitor that is best at getting its technology adopted as the industry standard is able to gain an unusual degree of control. This poses particular strategic problems. Companies that dominate their industry, such as Intel and Microsoft, face the challenge of staying ahead, while those that are contesting their dominance have to try to establish a credible alternative standard. In such industries the race to become dominant can be fierce.

The management of innovation is discussed in Chapter 15. ▶

Both leader and challenger firms will follow outpacing strategies based upon strong product development activity. Their aim is to come up with a significant technological advance that will establish the next generation of their product as the industry standard. This makes it important that their culture and architecture foster capabilities in innovation. They will also need to develop capabilities in communication, to help them to persuade an overwhelming mass of customers to adopt their standard. Strong marketing capabilities helped Sony to achieve, and then sustain, leadership in computer games consoles with its 'power of Playstation' advertising campaign. Intel has gone further – its 'Intel inside' branding exercise appeals directly to PC end-users, over the heads of its own direct customers.

No less important for a firm seeking a dominant position in a hypercompetitive industry, is establishing a strong network of complementary firms (Real-Life

REAL-LIFE APPLICATION 12.12

Strategic networks in hypercompetitive industries

One of the crucial factors that helped JVC to establish VHS as the industry standard in video recorders, in competition with Sony's Betamax, was its alliance with other manufacturers, such as Thomson of France, to ensure worldwide availability. This made it worthwhile for film companies to make their software available in VHS format.

In the Internet retailing industry, the early movers such as Amazon.com have tried to cultivate networks of complementary sites that will cross-refer business to one another. For example, users of the Alta-Vista search engine always find, along with their search results, a link to Amazon.com. If they follow the link,

they are offered a selection of books relating to the search topic. The aim is to make Amazon the standard place to look for a wide variety of items.

In the emerging industry for Internet-enabled mobile phones, early leadership has been seized by the Symbian alliance that includes Psion, a British manufacturer of handheld computers, together with the three dominant producers of mobile phones, Nokia, Motorola and Ericsson. Microsoft, which wants to make its Windows CE the standard operating system in these devices, has formed an alliance with British Telecom, a substantial operator of mobile phones.

Application 12.2). For example, producers of video games hardware or computer operating systems will need to forge relationships with software firms that will write compatible games and other applications. The operating system firm will benefit from a good relationship with the designer of the microprocessor on which their product will run, so that the two can optimise their respective products to take advantage of one another's features. Both will want some form of relationship with the leading producers and users of computer hardware that, they hope, will use their products. They may also try to involve end-users in helping to specify the next generation of product.

◄ The problems of diversification are explored in Chapter 9. Problems with mergers and acquisitions are discussed in Chapter 15. ►

As an alternative to networks, firms sometimes use vertical integration, typically by acquisition, to assure themselves of supplies and distribution outlets. Sony and Matsushita both bought record labels and Hollywood studios in the 1980s, to ensure artist and character availability for the next generation of audio and visual hardware and software. Sony bought Psygnosis, a leading computer games manufacturer, to ensure that games were available for its consoles. This has the same drawbacks as any diversification strategy. Neither Sony nor Matsushita found it easy to manage their media subsidiaries and both lost a great deal of money in learning.

Competing firms will try to get users, software suppliers and other important complementary firms locked into their standards as early as possible. They will do this by *signalling* their intentions for the next generation of technology several years in advance. Intel did this with successive generations of its 8086 and Pentium processors, and Sony adopted the same tactic when it announced its Playstation II games console two years ahead of launch. Microsoft is similarly famous (or infamous!) for announcing new versions of its software well in advance of the eventual release date.

Once a product is established, attention will turn to expanding and entrenching its leadership position. Tactics that are employed include:

- Frequent upgrades to keep competitors aiming at a moving target. Intel, for example, launches new versions of its Pentium processor every 3–6 months
- Aggressive pricing. New products will have a high price at launch, to profit

from the early adopters of new technology, who tend to be price insensitive. Prices will be decreased a few months after launch, to encourage high-volume adoption of the standard, and may be dropped substantially to counter the launch of a competing product, as Sony did with its Playstation console just before the launch of Sega's Dreamcast.

- Moves into new products and markets. Intel moved successfully into the manufacture of computer motherboards, and made it known that it had the capacity to manufacture computers. Over a sixteen-month period, Amazon.com diversified from being a pure bookseller into the sale of music, electronics, toys, videos, video games, software, home improvement goods and gifts, as well as competing in the on-line auctions industry. Not all these moves will be successful – Intel never manufactured computers under its own label, and withdrew from the manufacture of graphics cards. Many observers doubt that Amazon can compete successfully with specialist on-line firms such as eToys (toys) and eBay (auctions). However, these moves serve to keep competitors guessing and force them to spread their resources thinner if they want to compete on all fronts.

For a firm that is seeking to compete with an established leader, there are two main possibilities. One is to launch a new product or technology that dramatically

REAL-LIFE APPLICATION 12.13

Competing with an 800 pound gorilla – AMD and Cyrix versus Intel

Intel has had a dominant position in the supply of processors for personal computers that dates back to IBM's adoption of its 8088 processor for the first IBM PC. Its 1999 share of the market was approximately 90%. Demand for PCs forced it to license other chip-makers to produce processors on its behalf, and this gave them an entrée into the market. Starting with the 80386 processor in the late 1980s, Cyrix and Advanced Micro Devices (AMD) were able to use these licences to produce clones of Intel's chips. Although they were able to make some improvements of their own to Intel's design, which enabled their chips to work faster than the market leader's, they competed largely on price.

Intel fought back, using legal action to try to curtail the two firms' activities. Finally, it launched the Pentium processor, which gave it a proprietary brand, the courts having ruled that it could not register a number, such as 80386, as a trade name. The product also had certain features that its competitors were unable to emulate satisfactorily. AMD and Cyrix differentiated their products on price, and stayed in business because PC manufacturers wanted an alternative supplier to limit Intel's power. However, they were not very profitable.

When Intel launched its Pentium II processor, it adopted a new, proprietary standard for the connection between the processor and the motherboard. This was intended to entrench Intel's advantage, but it left open to AMD and Cyrix a market for users who wanted a faster processor to fit their old-style motherboards. They were able to build on this to establish an alternative standard for motherboards, which they used for a range of processors with expanded capabilities. Meanwhile, Intel retaliated with its Celeron range of inexpensive processors, designed to compete with Cyrix and AMD for price-sensitive customers.

AMD then acquired a small firm which had developed a technology for rendering the three-dimensional images used in computer games that was superior to Intel's. With this 3D-Now technology, AMD had genuine hopes of challenging Intel's dominance, and its Athlon processor was enthusiastically reviewed in the computer press. However, its profitability was still poor, and in the third quarter of 1999 it shipped 4.5 million units compared with Intel's 27 million and recorded a loss of $105 million. It was expecting to break even in the fourth quarter. At a 1998 conference, AMD's Chairman and CEO, W.J. Sanders III, had compared its struggle with Intel to that of a monkey competing with an 800 pound gorilla.

Source: www.vnunewswire.com and www.amd.com accessed on 27 November 1999.

outperforms the existing one, and establishes itself as the new standard, as has happened with successive generations of video games consoles. The second is to fasten on to a market or segment that the leader has opened up and then abandoned (Real Life Application 12.13).

However, strong competitors may not remain invincible for ever. Microsoft has recently come under attack from software developers who have created a rival operating system, Linux, which is distributed free via the Internet. This has been developed as a deliberate attack on the dominance of Microsoft, although it is not as yet a credible alternative system for most users. Microsoft's dominance has also been under attack from the other 'side' – the regulatory and legislative bodies of the USA, who have recommended the breaking up of the company as a way of dealing with its otherwise (apparently) unassailable power.

12.5 Strategies for electronic commerce

Our final context is, at the time of writing, still new and has been little explored in the strategy literature. It relates to **e-commerce**: the use of the Internet and, more specifically, the World Wide Web as media for offering goods and services. The web is having a profound impact on certain industries, such as bookselling, and is widely predicted to change the nature of competition in others. Forrester Research, an American consultancy, forecast in 1999 that business-to-business e-commerce would grow from $43 billion in 1998 to $1300 billion in 2003, and business-to-consumer e-commerce from $8 billion to $108 billion over the same period. Electronic commerce in Europe, where the usage of the Internet by consumers and businesses is lower than in the USA, is forecast to grow at similar rates after 2001.

Stock markets, particularly those in the USA, have shown an appetite for Internet-related shares and have given them valuations many times higher than would be accorded to traditional businesses with similar revenue streams. At the beginning of 2000, the stock market value of Amazon.com, the leading on-line book retailer, exceeded that of all America's traditional booksellers and publishers combined although in common with other e-commerce stocks its shares underwent a radical correction in value in April. In February 2000 Reuters, an established UK provider of financial information and news, was able to increase its market value by over 40% by announcing a strategy for offering information over the web.

The Internet has many applications within organisations' value chains. Ford Motor Company uses it to give every employee up-to-date product design, quality, and delivery information. Sun Microsystems, a leading manufacturer of computer workstations and web servers, uses advertisements on its own website and on sites frequented by technicians to attract and recruit high quality staff (Brown, 1999). The Internet has made the operation of virtual value chains considerably cheaper and easier. However, in this section, we focus on **e-businesses** – organisations that use the web as the principal way of reaching customers, or as the basis of services that could not be offered by other means.

◀ We discuss virtual value chains in Section 8.1.2.

12.5.1 Competitive stance

The most important decisions to be taken in e-commerce relate to **competitive stance**. A firm must decide which goods or services to offer and how to differentiate its offerings from those of on-line competitors and traditional, off-line, providers.

One basic service that firms can offer is that of access to the Internet itself. Internet service providers (ISPs) provide an access point, such as a telephone number, through which subscribers can log on to the Internet. Different ISPs compete on the basis of the speed with which their users can access the net, and availability – the extent to which users can be sure of logging on at the first time of dialling, without getting an engaged tone. It is difficult for one ISP to obtain an enduring advantage on either of these factors, since its competitors can catch up simply by installing more modems and servers. Thus, the ISP industry in most countries is a commodity business where competition is largely on price. In the UK and some other European countries, ISPs often give access to their services for free, but take a percentage of the connection charges that its users pay their telephone company. In the USA, where local telephone charges are usually not metered, most ISPs charge subscribers a flat monthly charge. Vendors of access via cable, satellite or ADSL, a form of high-speed telephone link, are at present able to charge a premium, since they offer access speeds some 40 times faster than conventional telephone modems.

ISPs can attempt to add value by offering some form of exclusive content that is independent of the World Wide Web. These on-line service providers – the best known are America Online (AOL), AOL's subsidiary CompuServe and the Microsoft Network (MSN) – have become **channels** connecting content providers with their audience. They have to differentiate their output from one another, and from ISPs, through the quality of the content that they offer. In January 2000, AOL took steps to ensure the availability of high-quality content through its merger with Time-Warner, a major publisher and a leading producer of films and television programmes.

Another form of web service is the **portal**. Typically based around a search engine, portals aim to be the first port of call for a user seeking information or entertainment via the net. Some sites have set themselves up as portals for specialised communities such as the computer or advertising industries. The largest portals, such as Yahoo (the most successful), Excite and Netscape, cater to a broader audience, but also have sections dedicated to serving specialised communities.

◀ *The role of brands and reputation in customer choice is discussed in Section 7.2.5.*

Apart from acting as channels and/or portals, electronic businesses may compete more directly with traditional ones. According to Philip Evans and Thomas Wurster (1999), they do so by acting as **navigators** or **infomediaries**, giving their users access to abundant, detailed product information, and the tools to process it quickly. In this way, they reduce their users' dependence on reputations, brands and supplier relationships when making choices between products and services. Typically, virtual businesses offer far more information, a broader selection of goods and services and lower prices than traditional navigator firms such as insurance brokers, travel agents and booksellers. Don Tapscott (1995) has coined the term **disintermediation** for the process by which traditional brokers and intermediaries see their role reduced and taken over by virtual businesses.

Forrester Research has identified three types of navigator whose activities are particularly suited to electronic commerce:[20]

- **Aggregators** are firms that give users access to comprehensive, up-to-date price and service information from a number of providers in a fragmented market, and usually also a means of ordering the product they require. Examples are Chemdex, a service for selling laboratory chemicals to researchers and companies in the fields of bioscience and pharmaceuticals (see Real-Life Application 12.14). CitySearch, a site that offers information on places to visit and where to eat in major American cities, and Amazon.com.

- **Auctioneers** offer ways for people to dispose of surplus or perishable items, and for buyers to find bargains. They also channel payment from buyer to seller, so that both can strike a deal with a person or firm they have never met or heard of, with little risk of fraud. Examples are eBay and QXL, well-known auction sites for second-hand items and collectibles, lastminute.com, where customers can find last-minute deals on airline seats and hotel rooms, and Adauction, which sells off unused advertising space on big websites such as Yahoo.

- **Exchanges** match buyers and sellers in markets where they would otherwise have difficulty in communicating, set prices and handle the details of contracts and payment. One example is NTE (Real-Life Application 12.14).

E-businesses may fulfil more than one of the various roles of channel, portal, navigator, aggregator, auctioneer and exchange. Amazon.com operates as both an aggregator and an auctioneer. Whichever roles they seek to fill, they must generate revenue from subscription charges, from commissions or mark-up on goods and services purchased through their site, and by charging for advertising space on it. Users will not renew their subscriptions or stay on a site to complete transactions unless they find the content interesting and relevant.

A site's capacity to attract and retain users for long periods of time is called **stickiness** and appears to be one of the main success factors in electronic commerce.

REAL-LIFE APPLICATION 12.14

Chemdex and NTE

Chemdex was created to meet a need from biological researchers, who use specialised chemicals in their work. Previously, the only way to find these was to look laboriously through suppliers' catalogues, which were bulky and often out of date, and phoning to see if the item was in stock. All this was taking up valuable research time. Chemdex persuaded the suppliers to put their catalogues on to its web site – which suited them, since the catalogues were expensive to produce and distribute. It then added a search engine and information on the properties of each chemical so that researchers could find what they wanted quickly and easily. It also developed software which helped the firms that employed the researchers aggregate their orders to each supplier, so that they could get bulk discounts and reduce the number of invoices to be processed. It earns its commission on each order by saving time and money for both buyers and sellers.

National Transport Exchange (NTE) makes a market in lorry (truck) space in the USA. It gets information from several hundred lorry fleet managers about where their vehicles are headed and how much space is available. A fleet manager who has sent a load from (say) Denver to Pittsburgh may find that his truck has nothing to carry on its journey back to base, and will offer that space through NTE. Based on its knowledge of available capacity, NTE sets a price for shipping a container-load of goods from Pittsburgh to Denver. A shipper can, through NTE's site, book that space at a price well below what it would normally pay to charter an empty lorry, obtain a contract with the transport firm and make payment. By using the web, NTE can make its service available to anyone that can afford a PC and modem, including small businesses that want cheap space and individual truckers who might want to offer it.

Source: 'Business and the Internet', supplement to *The Economist*, 26 June 1999, pp. 17–20.

Advertisers can see which sites are 'stickiest' and will pay the highest rates to the firms that run them. The two most profitable e-businesses, AOL and Yahoo, are both able to retain users for longer than average: 10 hours per month for AOL, 1 hour per month for Yahoo. (According to Brown (1999), the corresponding figures for Excite and Netscape are a little over 30 minutes per month.)

Evans and Wurster (1999) identify three other dimensions that may differentiate an e-business from its competitors:

- **Reach** – the size of a firm's network, i.e. number of customers it connects with, and the variety of products and services that it offers them.
- **Richness** – the depth and detail of information that a firm delivers to its customers and collects about them.
- **Affiliation** – the extent to which a firm acts on the side of the consumer, rather than the producer.

For a conventional business, there is a trade-off between richness and reach – it is difficult and expensive to offer in-depth advice and information about a wide range of subjects to a large number of clients. On a well-designed website, this trade-off no longer exists – vast amounts of information can be made available for little extra cost. This is one of the main reasons that e-businesses have been able to win customers from traditional ones.

Richness is one of the ways in which different Internet brands compete with one another, and is one of the ingredients of 'stickiness'. Alongside its comprehensive catalogue, Amazon.com offers richness in the form of interviews with authors, articles about best-selling books and readers' own opinions on books they have read. Some e-businesses also use the other aspect of richness, customer information, to a limited degree, by e-mailing their customers a birthday greeting, for example, as Yahoo does.

Affiliation is an untested aspect of electronic commerce. Conventional discount retailers, such as the US retail chain Wal-Mart and its UK subsidiary, Asda, have always tried to differentiate themselves by casting themselves as being on the side of the consumer against the producer. They claim to pass on to the consumer the economies that they get from purchasing in bulk. Although Amazon.com has won customers through its low prices and by claiming to offer impartial advice, it has not risked alienating publishers by claiming to take the customer's side.

As conventional producers start to offer products over the web, the trade-off between richness and affiliation is likely to become increasingly important. A company like Sony can offer richer information about its recording artists, in the form of detailed biographies and recording histories, than Amazon and CD-Now, because they control that information. On the other hand, consumers that hit Sony's website will find information only about Sony's products, and will know that there is a danger that, because of the website's clear affiliation, the information they find will not be objective or complete.

At the time of writing (in Spring, 2000) it is not clear whether customers will desert established names like Sony in favour of newer sources that may be cheaper, more comprehensive and more objective. Some firms that sell directly to end-users over the Internet are developing ways of getting round this trade-off. Computer manufacturer Dell, for example, offers comprehensive and ostensibly dispassionate information about printers and other peripherals (which it does not manufacture) alongside the information it gives about its own computers. In some industries, including hotels, airlines and housebuilding, competing firms have combined to set up joint websites, in an attempt to shut new e-businesses out of the market.

12.5.2 Resources

Most observers agree that reputation is a crucial resource for an e-business. The first firm to establish a reputation as the premier site for a particular purpose or community will become the first place to which most users will point their browsers. If they find what they want there, then they will not bother to look elsewhere. This will then be the site through which providers will want to offer their goods or services, and where advertisers will want to post their banners. A reputation for reach, ease of use and reliable service will often be important in establishing a site as number one in its field – news and gossip about good and bad service travels easily over the net, through a process which we might call 'word of mouse'!

It is quite rare for a newer entrant to knock out an established player, although there are some famous examples. Yahoo was not the first search engine on the web, but established itself as the leader because of superior ease of use and its ability to develop stickiness. CD-Now, one of the very first on-line retailers, was overtaken by Amazon.com as market leader selling recorded music over the Internet. Amazon was able to transfer its reputation and its competences in site design and administration very effectively from books to music. As a rule, however, there appear to be very strong first-mover advantages in electronic commerce.

Some authors believe that consumers are more comfortable shopping on-line with retailers who also have an established presence and reputation in the physical world. This gives buyers some reassurance about the firm they are dealing with and so reduces their fear of credit-card fraud. It also means that they have somewhere to return faulty goods or to seek after-sales service. This mixing of on-line and off-line retailing is referred to as a 'clicks and mortar' strategy. However, there are few, if any, instances of successful traditional retailers that also dominate their segment in e-commerce.

While a *firm's* reputation may be a source of advantage in electronic commerce, Evans and Wurster (1999) believe that the value of some *product* brands may suffer. Customers who have plenty of objective product information will no longer need the reassurance of brands like Sony's, which are badges of quality and reliability. On the other hand, brands like Coca-Cola, Nike or Armani, which convey a particular image or lifestyle, may do well. Their owners can use their websites to offer games or multimedia experiences that reinforce the brand values.

Evans and Wurster also point out the potential value of an unused resource – customer information. Excite, a portal, is said to collect 40 gigabytes of customer data each day. As data mining software becomes more sophisticated and powerful, the potential to use it to target customer needs more precisely with, for example, customised newsletters, home pages and special offers, will become greater. Tapscott (1995) coined the term **molecularisation** for this process, the opposite of mass marketing, where each customer becomes, in effect, a market segment in his or her own right. Products are designed and targeted precisely for that individual.

Value chain

◀ *The value chain of network organisations is reviewed in Section 8.2.3.*

Most 'pure' e-businesses are network organisations – they exist to link buyers and providers. Within the value chain of these networks, the service provisioning activity appears to have a key role, with two aspects of it being particularly important. These same two elements of the value chain are also crucial for firms that are not 'pure' electronic businesses, but are nonetheless using the web as a distribution channel.

The first of these value chain elements is the provision of a secure, user-friendly website. A survey carried out for IBM and quoted in the guide to CeBIT2000, a major computer industry trade fair, indicated that 65% of on-line purchases were never completed – having selected their purchases, customers dropped out at the point when they were required to pay.[21] At the time of writing, a website that is easy to navigate and a simple ordering process that instils confidence in the customer appear to be strategic resources, and the process development activity has a crucial role in developing them. Market leaders such as Amazon.com have invested considerable resources in building a lead in these areas. However, as the technology of electronic commerce matures, these are likely to become threshold resources rather than strategic ones – a change that may well have occurred by the time you read this book.

The second crucial aspect of service provisioning relates to the **fulfilment** of electronic transactions – packaging and delivery of the goods to the customer. Here again, the IBM survey indicates that many firms have failed to master this activity. Only half of the customers who did make an on-line purchase received a confirmation or delivery date from the vendor, and 'a significant proportion' of goods ordered failed to arrive. This was not because the sellers were dishonest – no payment was taken for the transactions – but because they were ineffective. The major US Internet retailers suffered adverse reactions from customers and an average 31% fall in their share price because they were unable to fulfil orders for Christmas gifts in time for 25 December 1999.[22]

The importance of fulfilment explains why Amazon.com has spent some $300 million to build a distinctive competence in this area. In 1999 and early 2000, it announced the opening (or major expansion) of six distribution centres in the USA, and it is expanding its centre in the UK.

12.5.3 Architecture and culture

There have been no rigorous studies conducted of the architectures and cultures of successful e-businesses. However, stories in the press convey a fairly uniform impression that these firms have flat hierarchies and youthful, organic cultures where hard work, long hours and high personal achievement are expected. Most employees receive share options, which give them the prospect of considerable wealth if the firm succeeds. However, they are also motivated by the prospect of changing the world[23] (see Real-Life Application 12.15).

The most successful electronic ventures appear to have distinctive **external** linkages, which are important in developing stickiness. These are of three kinds:

- **Relationships with customer communities.** These can be developed through the kinds of interactive communities that Yahoo and Amazon.com have both managed to foster. These give the firm's managers information – in the form of

REAL-LIFE APPLICATION 12.15

Amazon.com's culture and architecture

Work hard, have fun, make history

It would be impossible to produce results in an environment as dynamic as the Internet without extraordinary people. Working to create a little bit of history isn't supposed to be easy, and, well, we're finding that things are as they're supposed to be! We now have a team of 2,100 smart, hard-working, passionate folks who put customers first. Setting the bar high in our approach to hiring has been, and will continue to be, the single most important element of Amazon.com's success.

During our hiring meetings, we ask people to consider three questions before making a decision:

● Will you admire this person? If you think about the people you've admired in your life, they are probably people you've been able to learn from or take an example from. For myself, I've always tried hard to work only with people I admire, and I encourage folks here to be just as demanding. Life is definitely too short to do otherwise.

● Will this person raise the average level of effectiveness of the group they're entering? We want to fight entropy. The bar has to continuously go up. I ask people to visualise the company 5 years from now. At that point, each of us should look around and say, 'The standards are so high now – boy, I'm glad I got in when I did!'

● Along what dimension might this person be a superstar? Many people have unique skills, interests, and perspectives that enrich the work environment for all of us. It's often something that's not even related to their jobs.

Source: Jeff Bezos, CEO of Amazon.com, in his firm's 1998 Annual Report, http://www.amazon.com/exec/obidos/subst/misc/investor-relations/1998annual_report.html accessed on 16 February 2000.

e-mail feedback and ordering data – from which they can see what their customers' interests and concerns are. This can be fed back into product innovation and process design. Sometimes, these relationships come from membership of the community in question. One of Chemdex's founders, David Perry, had an earlier career as a biotechnology researcher, which gave him an intuitive grasp of the kinds of problem confronting his target users.

● **Relationships with providers.** Because content is important in persuading users to spend time on a site, relationships with the best content providers can be a source of competitive advantage, particularly if this gives a site something exclusive to offer. AOL has long cultivated these relationships, co-operating with media firms such as Time-Warner, MTV and Nickelodeon to adapt their TV and journalistic content to the web. It also established an incubator, the 'Greenhouse', which offered aspiring content providers finance, management advice, and an outlet on AOL's network. In return, AOL gained the right to buy an equity stake in the provider if it chose to. The best-known product of the Greenhouse is the Motley Fool, a finance and investment advice site that was originally available only to AOL subscribers, though it is now accessible through any ISP.

● **Relationships with other e-businesses.** Most virtual firms encourage other sites to display links to them by offering them a percentage of the revenue from any sales that result. Pioneered by Amazon.com, this system is now standard across the web, but is expensive – Amazon gives its associates 15% of the value of any sales that they generate.

12.5.4 Other Internet-related business opportunities

Electronic commerce offers opportunities to a variety of organisations that supply related goods and services. The most profitable Internet-related firms are those like IBM, which supply hardware and software. These may not themselves be e-businesses, although three of the largest, Cisco Systems, Sun Microsystems and Dell, make extensive use of electronic commerce in their own purchasing and selling, and have intranets that play a major role in their internal administration. However, their products play a crucial role in enabling firms to operate websites that can handle large numbers of transactions without crashing.

Other suppliers that may profit from e-commerce are those which can take on part or all of the task of fulfilment. Firms with established capabilities, such as those that run mail-order catalogues or logistics providers, may have an opportunity to sell their services to e-businesses who wish to outsource this activity. In Japan, the main chains of convenience stores are offering their services as points to which suppliers may deliver goods and customers collect them, pay for them and return them if faulty. This facility may prove popular with Japanese consumers, who prefer to pay cash and make little use of credit cards, the standard medium for e-commerce transactions.

Another type of supplier specialises in management skills and advice. These 'Internet incubators', such as Idealab! and CMGI, offer Internet start-ups accounting skills, legal advice and some managers and staff, in return for an equity stake. Typically, they nurture a new firm through the first six months of its existence.[24]

12.6 Summary

This chapter has discussed some of the strategic issues facing organisations in environments other than those we have spent most of the rest of the book discussing. We have looked at some of the strategic issues and some of the strategic options available to organisations who operate in the public and not-for-profit sectors, and firms which are small. We have also looked at some of the strategic considerations for firms at the various stages in their industry's life-cycle, including the special case of hypercompetition, and considered some of the strategic issues facing companies in the field of electronic commerce.

- *Public sector* organisations are those whose ultimate source of funding is the state, although there are many different types of public sector organisations. Some of the major strategic issues facing public sector agencies are:
  - coping with the uncertainty of political environment, such as externally controlled funding and priority setting
  - the regularity of changes in the external environment, in the form of government elections
  - how best to provide the service for which they are in existence
  - balancing a complicated mix of political agendas, agencies with shared responsibilities for the same clientele, and different 'customers' with potentially conflicting requirements.

- *Not-for-profit* organisations are those which provide a service to people who would probably otherwise not receive it. They are funded through donations and grants, although many receive funding from the government in recognition of the services they provide. Like the public sector, NFP organisations are a heterogeneous group ranging across the spheres of education, research, welfare, economic, social and spiritual activities.

- The NFP environment is also complex and requires organisations to balance varied personal and political agendas, as well as manage a staff group which often comprises a high proportion of volunteers.
- Raising funds is a major strategic problem for NFP managers.
- NFPs have to be visibly circumspect with their funds, and maintain effective relationships with the public and their donors.
- A key issue is how to put in place the architecture and structure which allows their mission to be accomplished – but defining this is sometimes problematic.

● We also looked at strategies for firms at the early stage in their life-cycle.

- Small and or/new firms are relatively heavily controlled by factors in the environment.
- Firms which are currently small but are intended to be high growth are run by entrepreneurs. Whether such firms become large concerns in time is dependent on the ability of the owner to delegate and set in place management systems and structures which will help him or her to control an increasingly complex organisation.

● We looked at the strategic issues facing firms at different stages of their industry contexts – introduction, growth, maturity, and decline stages – and also at some special types of mature industries. Industries tend to become larger, consolidated, and more stable as they mature, although there are some exceptions to this general rule.

- Strategies at the early stage of the industry life-cycle are mainly to do with getting the company better known, and developing the infrastructure which allows sales to be achieved.
- Strategies at the growth stage are to do with milking the demand, and improving quality. Differentiation of products and firms is likely to occur at this stage.
- Strategies in the mature phase are about maximising income and increasing market share. Price wars are possible, and the industry may be quite oligopolistic. Economies of scale are important.
- Strategies in the decline stage are about exiting from the industry – developing substitute products, minimising exit barriers, or milking the product for whatever profits still remain.
- Strategies in hypercompetitive industries require the establishment of a dominant position, and its subsequent maintenance through ongoing innovation. It may also require a strong understanding of the strategic synergies and networks between different product groups, technologies, and firms.

Finally, we looked at some of the issues to do with managing in an Internet environment. As we write, this is too new an area to have been subject to much research and there are few theoretical models which apply particularly to e-commerce. However, we considered some of the bases of competitive advantage for companies who are principally involved in these types of commercial activities.

Typical questions

We conclude this chapter with a look at some of the questions that you may be asked that relate to strategies in different contexts, and how you can use the theory in this chapter to answer them.

1. *What are the main challenges facing a public sector organisation (at a given point in time)?*

This has many similarities with the analysis you would carry out for a private sector organisation – in that you would need to think about what is happening in the organisation's environment, particularly whether it is likely to encounter any significant changes in its funding or brief. You would then need to assess whether its internal architecture is likely to be able to deal with it and implement any brief it may be given.

2. *How well is an NFP achieving its objectives?*

You may find it helpful to classify the issues according to the categories in Section 12.2. Apart from anything else you should discuss what the organisation's objectives are, and how these have been arrived at. This may not be a particularly straightforward issue, given the wide variety of stakeholders in NFPs. You will then want to assess whether the organisation is carrying out its work effectively. Given that two of the principal problems for most NFPs are the management of volunteers, and obtaining funding, you might like to think about what other organisations are likely to be competing for the limited 'pot' of funds and whether the culture and management systems are likely to allow the organisation to attract and retain its volunteer workforce.

3. *What course of action would you recommend for a small firm in the growth stage of an industry?*

This is quite a complicated question which will require you to bring together a number of different concepts and issues. It involves use of not just the material in this chapter on industry life-cycles which we discussed in Section 12.4, but also consideration of the issues to do with company life-cycle stages we discussed in Chapter 10, Section 10.2, and organisational configurations in Chapter 8. Internal features such as its size and structure affect the organisation's capabilities and whether it is likely to be able to capitalise on the types of opportunities that are available in a growing market – whose characteristics you would also need to describe.

Similarly complicated analyses would be needed to answer similar questions about strategies for a large or a small firm in the introductory, mature, or decline phase of an industry.

Questions for discussion

1. What are the strategic issues facing firms selling exclusive gifts over the Internet?

2. Why might a chief executive of a public sector agency wish for his or her department to be privatised?

3. What problems might an NFP organisation encounter if its chief executive attempted to bring in a more 'professional' or bureaucratic style of management and control systems?

4. What would the owner of a small but fast-growing manufacturing firm need to do to minimise the risk that the firm fails?

A campaigning NFP: Greenpeace

Based on Greenpeace and Friends of the Earth websites © Friends of the Earth 2000; Scott, A. 'Friends of the Earth launches toxic release web site'. *Chemical Week* 161 (6): 20, 1999: Smith, G. 'Are we talking to ourselves?' *NonProfit World* 16 (5): 14–15, 1998.

Greenpeace's *raison d'être*

According to its 1998 annual report, Greenpeace is a 'global environmental campaigning organisation' which organises public campaigns 'for the protection of oceans and ancient forests, for the phasing-out of fossil fuels and the promotion of renewable energies in order to stop climate change, for the elimination of toxic chemicals, against the release of genetically modified organisms into nature and for nuclear disarmament and an end to nuclear contamination'. It is independent of any political party or faction. It also explicitly rejects violence against either persons or property.

Recent campaigns have been fought against:

- The oil company Shell dumping its disused Brent Spar oil platform in the ocean.
- Nuclear power, and the discharge and reprocessing of toxic or nuclear waste. In 1985 French nuclear testing in the South Pacific became the subject of considerable discussion when Greenpeace's ship *Rainbow Warrior* was sunk by the French Secret Service.
- Harmful chemicals, including PVC, a material that releases dioxins when it is produced and burned, and chlorine-free paper manufacture.
- Genetically engineered produce, and for any such produce to be identified by labelling. Greenpeace has been extremely visible recently, in its activities to destroy fields of experimental GM crops in Europe.
- Drift-net fishing, over-fishing, and factory trawlers. Greenpeace recently campaigned to have the albatross protected, as thousands were caught on the lines used to catch blue-fin tuna.
- Whaling and killing of seals.

Campaigns in recent months have started to harness the power of new technology. The Organisation for Economic Co-operation and Development's intended Multilateral Agreement on Investment was blocked by 'a network of citizens groups' mostly oganised through the Internet.

These campaigns have some similarities with those of another campaigning NFP – Friends of the Earth.

Friends of the Earth

Friends of the Earth (FoE) is the largest international environmental network organisation, with groups in 60 countries. In the UK it comprises a network of campaigning local groups, which work in 220 locations throughout the British Isles. Over 90% of its income comes from individual donations, the rest from special fundraising events, grants and trading.

FoE claims that it carries out programmes to 'conserve natural resources and to protect the planet from environmental disasters'. It has recently campaigned:

- on proposed international trade agreements and for an environmentally sound US trade policy;
- on ensuring corporate accountability on the part of major companies and politicians;
- on environmentally sound alternatives to economically-driven business practices;
- against road building, road pollution and the use of fossil fuels;
- against tax exemptions for pesticides and fertilisers in the USA;
- against the building of a pipeline through the Amazon forest.

Over the years FoE claims that it has won many battles with government and industry – achieving bans on ozone-destroying CFCs, reduced trade in rainforest timber, and increased support for cleaner energy technologies. Its tactics include 'empowering citizens around the country to address environmental problems affecting them' which it does through direct action as well as through providing information, analysing business, government and state spending, and through promoting legal test cases. Friends of the Earth is non-political and believes that it can achieve its aims best by working with people with very different party political perspectives.

An example of their tactics is their recently launched chemical-release data website, which charts emissions at UK chemical plants and utilities. In its first two days of operation, about 3,000 people logged on to the site. FoE's senior pollution campaigner Mike Childs explained that 'by putting this information on the Internet it's accessible to company shareholders and investors'. It will also put pressure on the industry from communities near the plants and the financial community. The site appears to have worked; it has provoked a discussion in the press, and stimulated the companies 'named and shamed' to defend their activities. However, as with Greenpeace, their actions have led to a heated debate as to the scientific basis for their claims.

Structure

Greenpeace is an international organisation whose central office is funded by its affiliated national offices. Greenpeace International was established in 1979, when Greenpeace offices in Europe, the Pacific, and North America joined in an alliance that would later become the *Stichting Greenpeace Council*. It has been based in Amsterdam since 1989.

All Greenpeace national offices are represented at an annual Council Meeting. This makes recommendations on overall direction and policy, sets the annual budget ceiling, and elects the international Board. The board is accountable to the council. In turn, the board elects a chair, and appoints an Executive Director (ED) who is responsible for the day-to-day management of Greenpeace International. The ED is assisted by a team of programme directors and is accountable to the board. The board is responsible for approving the organisation's financial statements, audits and accounts, for ensuring that council decisions are implemented, and for approving the long-term political and campaign direction of the organisation.

The 33 national offices contribute 18% of their income to the international organisation. The voting status of the national offices is determined by their financial and campaign performance. National offices are funded entirely by individual donations and, to a lesser extent, from the sale of merchandise. The majority of funding is raised in a handful of countries. However Greenpeace's activities are global, and the countries which contribute the most income do not by any means always receive the most aid.

Greenpeace campaigns are supported by an infrastructure of professional employees, and they suggest that funding and managing this infrastructure is a priority in order to provide effective support for their environmental activities.

The international office oversees Greenpeace's international campaigns, co-ordinates its fleet of campaign vessels, and ensures the internationally consistent development of policy and campaign focus of the offices world wide. The International Executive Director leads the organisation, in wide consultation with the management of the national offices who meet twice yearly.

When considering the type of management structure it needed, Greenpeace thought about imitating the United Nations, which makes decisions by unanimous agreement of the security council. It briefly tried this model but found it too slow and compromising for an activist organisation. On the other hand, they rejected a highly centralised decision-making structure which would have undermined many of the strengths of the national offices and would have made it difficult 'for the voices of our new colleagues in the developing world to help shape our work'. They arrived at a model that balances a number of conflicting pressures – Greenpeace International (Stichting Greenpeace Council) which performs central co-ordinating functions, and the national offices which are licensed by the international organisation to use the name 'Greenpeace'. As they say 'the International executive director makes decisions built on wide consensus when possible, but places a higher value on fast, clear decisions than exhaustively negotiated compromise'.

CASE STUDY *continued*

Greenpeace believed they needed:

- fast, uncompromising decisions based on participation and consultation;

- rigid centralisation of some functions (like assigning ships' schedules and co-ordinating international campaign and media work) and widely distributed responsibility for others (pressuring national representatives to international treaties, challenging local contributions to global problems);

- transparency to their supporters and the public about how resources are allocated and how decisions get made. Towards this end, they publish an annual report which includes financial statements for Greenpeace International and consolidated information for Greenpeace world wide (see below).

Funding

Greenpeace receives its support, both financial and otherwise, primarily from the more than 4 million individuals who support it in more than 150 countries world wide. It explicitly states that it does not solicit or accept money from any business interest, political group, or government anywhere in world – independence which they believe is crucial. As they say their '*sole political stance is the protection of the environment*'.

By the end of 1998, Greenpeace had 2.4 million financial supporters (1997, 2.5 million), the result of their efforts to strengthen the number of regular supporters as opposed to one-time donors. They suggest that this strategy improved their financial situation.

In the UK a recent funding campaign was a scheme called 'Frontline'. This was set up in response to a 'jaded' donating public, and a more cynical population. They asked a proportion of their supporters to give £20 per month on standing order. The donor rewards were comparatively slender: the occasional video, a briefing or two from Head Office, and invitations to public meetings. Nevertheless this became 'one of the great success stories of British fundraising'. 'Frontline' now has over 4,000 members, and income from the scheme represents over 10% of the UK organisation's entire annual income.

In 1998 Greenpeace launched an affinity credit card that featured a new, biodegradable plastic. Greenpeace suggests that this is less harmful to the environment because it is not made from PVC.[25] Like other affinity cards, a percentage of every purchase is paid to Greenpeace to support its environmental activism.

Financial information

Greenpeace International (US $000s)

Selected income and expenditure	1998	1997	1996	1995	1994
Income					
Total income	31,926	32,146	30,616	36,482	30,415
Expenditure					
Programmes					
Toxics	1,680	2,379	2,059	4,354	4,640
Climate	2,103	3,972	1,688	1,496	3,837
Nuclear and disarmament	1,535	2,035	3,316	6,593	3,509
Biodiversity		2,617	3,714	3,377	5,653
Oceans	1,287	860			
Forests	1,904	1,551			
Genetically modified organisms	787	448			
Programme Support					
Media and communications	1,820	1,224	2,745	3,817	1,654
Marine operations and other support	5,878	6,001	5,636	3,541	5,040
Fundraising	1,548	1,315	1,948	1,846	1,880
Administration	4,816	5,952	5,624	5,788	2,566
Total expenditure	**28,822**	**30,315**	**33,332**	**37,739**	**33,572**

Balance sheet	1998	1997	1996	1995	1994
Fixed assets	10,560	13,894	16,237	16,025	13,294
Total assets	31,859	27,047	29,507	47,067	49,876

Greenpeace 'World Wide' (US $000s)

Selected income and expenditure	1998	1997	1996	1995	1994
Income					
Total income	125,297	125,648	139,895	152,805	137,358
Expenditure					
Programmes					
Oceans	7,885	6,611			
Forests	5,532	3,304			
Genetically modified organisms	3,349	1,007			
Biodiversity		10,680	11,302	8,335	13,014
Toxics	8,938	13,602	10,263	12,508	12,422
Climate	7,473	13,394	9,348	8,164	12,464
Nuclear and disarmament	9,957	8,461	9,877	13,543	10,109
Programme Support					
Media and Communications	9,957	10,898	16,438	11,305	7,842
Other Support	10,164	10,282	10,777	13,631	18,511
Public Information and Outreach	10,832	15,732	14,548		
Fundraising	24,303	23,857	39,011	59,453	45,992
Administration	18,199	21,118	23,736	26,855	18,978
Total expenditure	**117,951**	**128,024**	**145,300**	**153,794**	**139,332**
Balance sheet	1998	1997	1996	1995	1994
Fixed assets	20,745	24,429	27,605	26,425	23,088
Total assets	117,760	103,554	121,463	133,550	123,581

Case study questions

1. What are the major strategic issues facing Greenpeace?

2. Is Greenpeace's structure effective? Explain your answer.

3. What does Greenpeace need to do to ensure its success over the next five years?

NOTES

1. Johnston (1998), Berry (1994), Poister and Streib (1999), Berry and Wechsler (1995), Nutt and Backoff (1992), Bryson (1995), Andersen et al. (1994).

2. Sarah Cunningham (1999) 'Benettons have designs on expanding family firm'. *The Times*, 24 May 1999, p. 50.

3. John Harlow (1997) Privatisation plan for Royal Opera, *The Sunday Times*, 9 November 1997, p. 9.

4. Edward Carr 'Survey of Business in Europe (3): Wake up or die – New ways to manage old companies'. *The Economist*, 23 November 1996.

5. 'Aer Lingus seeks partner before IPO', *Euroweek*, 11 September 1998.

6. For more information on not-for-profit organisations see Armstrong (1992), Coble (1999), Farmer and Fedor (1999), Handy (1988), Herman and Renz (1998), Horton Smith (1999), Maranville (1999), Parker (1998), Sargeant and Kahler (1999), Shoichet (1998).

7. Ian Murray, *The Times*, 25 April 1997, p. 6.
8. 'City Comment: Sweet charity for top bosses', *The Daily Telegraph*, 26 June 1998: p. 33.
9. 'The Royal Opera House: The House that Vivien built'. *The Daily Telegraph*, 23 November 1999.
10. 'ROH crisis: Damned, blamed, accused, scorned', *The Guardian*, 4 December, p. 8.
11. See, for example, Gadenne (1998), Watson and Everett (1999), Chapman (1999), Jennings and Beaver (1997), Fenwick and Strombom (1998), Sandberg and Hofer (1987), Shane and Kolvereid (1995), Chandler and Hanks (1994).
12. See, for example, Sandberg and Hofer (1987), Chandler and Hanks (1994), Shane and Kolvereid (1995).
13. The analysis in Sections 12.4.1–12.4.3 draws heavily on the pioneering work of Michael Porter (1980).
14. See Michael Porter, who discusses strategic options at the various stages of the industry life-cycle in his 1980 book *Competitive Strategy*.
15. Warner, M., 'Kleiner Perkins: Inside the Silicon Valley Money Machine', *Fortune*, 26 October 1998, pp. 110–118.
16. 'Andy Grove: How Intel makes spending pay off', *Fortune*, 22 February 1993, p. 58. Prahalad and Bettis (1986).
17. This insight came from Porter's collaborator Kathryn Rudie Harrigan. See Porter (1980).
18. 'Ma Bell restored', *The Economist*, 11 December 1999, pp. 85–86.
19. The strategic options discussed in this section are adapted from those put forward by Richard D'Aveni in Chapter 6 of *Hypercompetitive Rivalries*, Simon & Schuster (1995).
20. 'Business and the Internet', *The Economist*, supplement to issue of 26 June 1999, p. 20.
21. Glover, Tony, 'IBM Report Reveals Integration Nightmare', *CeBITVIEWS*, 24 February–1 March 2000, pp. 60–64.
22. The Fright after Christmas. *The Economist*, 5 February 2000, pp. 85–88.
23. 'How to be a Great e-CEO', *Fortune*, 24 May 1999, pp. 40–46.
24. 'Brands Hatch', *The Economist*, 23 December 1999, pp. 26–27.
25. 'Greenpeace introduces environmentally friendly credit card', *Bank Marketing*, Washington, May 1998, 30 (5) 13.

Strategy implementation

The first three parts of this book have mainly been focused on assessing an organisation as it has been and as it is now, and understanding how that influences its strategic positioning and the choices which its managers make. Part 4 now moves on to looking at some of the practicalities of strategic *management* – the *implementation* of the strategies which we have been discussing in other parts of this book. For much of the time this means managing change – changing parts of the organisation and/or its strategies – to a greater or lesser extent. This challenge can only really be avoided in the rare cases when the organisation can afford a 'carry on as you are' strategy. Even then, managers need to manage the incremental change that occurs as new ideas and initiatives emerge within the organisation. They also need to be on guard to make sure that the organisation's values and operational effectiveness are not slipping, and to avoid strategic drift.

First, therefore, in Chapter 13, we consider some of the factors that might act to prevent particular strategies being achieved. This can relate to employees' ability to cope with novelty, particularly problematic if large-scale changes are proposed. Less dramatic change is easier for the people in an organisation to cope with, and therefore strategies that are incremental or relatively small in scale are generally easier to implement. It can also relate to the way in which organisations have built up routines, competences, or architectures which are dedicated to one way of seeing the world and one type of strategy, and which may also act to block strategies which are different from the norm.

In fact, for most organisations, most of the time, change requires only incremental alterations to the organisation's existing strategic positioning, architecture or value chain, and these changes are relatively easily managed through the use of effective leadership, and some practical skills, which we describe in Chapter 14. In extreme cases, however, the survival of the organisation requires radical surgery – a turnaround – and this is one of the special cases of organisational change that we discuss. In Chapter 14 we also examine some specialised, and often commercially 'packaged', models of organisational change – total quality management (TQM) and business process re-engineering (BPR).

In Chapter 15, we look at some of the different methods by which strategies may be implemented, through acquiring or merging with other firms, through entering into alliances with firms who can bring complementary skills, knowledge, or resources, or through in-house development of new products and markets. We also briefly consider some of the issues to do with cutting back an organisation to a smaller core, such as divestment and management buy outs (MBOs).

After reading Part 4, you should understand:

- the individual and organisational factors which make change hard to bring about or, alternatively, more likely to happen;
- the skills required to bring about strategic change;
- specialist models of organisational change – turnarounds, BPR and TQM;
- some of the issues involved in the management of innovation;
- when mergers, acquisitions and strategic alliances may be suitable strategic methods.

CHAPTER 13

Assessing the potential for change

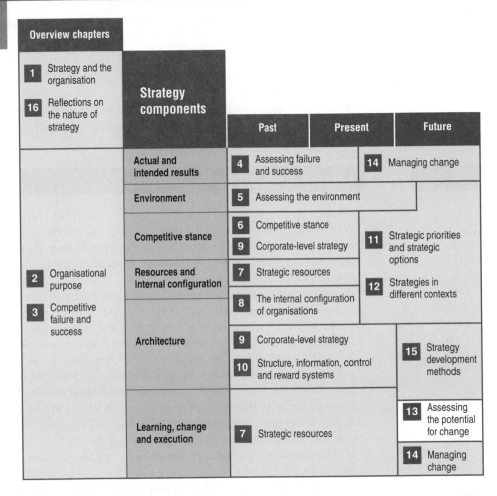

Previous chapters have helped you to analyse strategic situations (discussed in Part 2) and design possible strategies (discussed in Part 3), and this chapter will consider ways of making them happen. This, for the manager in the real world, is often the most difficult part of the strategy process. In the following sections we look at some of the factors which might influence anyone who tries to move an organisation to a new strategic position. This involves going deeper into the concept of acceptability that we introduced in Chapter 11.

In this chapter you will learn to:

- identify the problems involved in changing organisations;

- understand the different types of change which an organisation may implement, and the risks involved;

- identify forces for and against change, and assess the likelihood of successful change;

- analyse an organisation's culture so as to identify the elements which will need to alter to support a change in strategy, and assess whether this has been done effectively;

- assess an organisation's change programme in the light of what theory tells us about effective and ineffective change management.

13.1 Levels and types of change

Change is all around us. Look at the towns near where you live – would you recognise them if you went back 50 years in time? We are changing too. Every day some of our cells replace themselves as they age, and other parts of our body react to their environment – think of a skin tan. Organisations are the same. Every day they are slightly different from the day before – they have found a new customer, an employee has left, a new product has been developed or an old one improved.

For many organisations the speed at which they change has increased substantially recently. Competition is fiercer, employees are more mobile, and technological developments have meant that change is easier to achieve than it used to be. Product life-cycles are considerably shorter than even a few years ago – think of televisions, mobile telephones or cars. Look at the example of changes in products providing recorded music (Figure 13.1). In the early days major new developments came along at perhaps forty- or fifty-year intervals at the most. Nowadays, they appear every few years and the time between significant changes appears to be getting less all the time. So change is no longer unusual.

What is relatively unusual is significant or radical organisational change. Most of us do not have major heart surgery every week; most organisations do not have a major restructuring or strategy change regularly. Most new products are incremental improvements on existing ones, or breakthroughs developed by breakaway firms. The types of changes which organisations encounter regularly *tend* to be relatively small scale or localised.

Table 13.1 shows the different levels and types of change in an organisation, and the needs to which they are a response. This chapter relates mostly to the top half of the table. Functional changes in, say, marketing or HR strategy usually involve relatively little disruption, are localised and are relatively cheap to implement. However, a note of caution needs to be sounded at this point. Small changes in one part of an organisation often involve change in another. An organisation launching a new product may also need to invest in new skills (people), a new plant (technology), and a new structure (administrative changes). Changes in organisation

Figure 13.1   The life-cycles of recorded music products

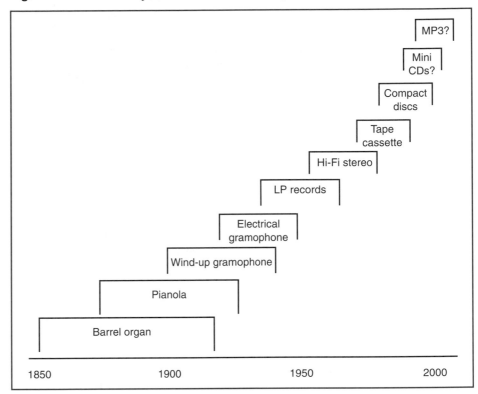

structure may imply new systems, new job descriptions, new reward schemes, and new production processes. It is important to consider the whole picture, even when recommending change in only one part of the organisation.

◄ 'Carrying on as we are' as an option was discussed in Section 11.4.

Most strategic decisions, by definition, imply major changes – a change in direction, a change in activities, changes in organisation structure and systems. The strategy of 'carrying on as we are' requires little alteration to existing structures, systems or processes. It implies a wish to do these better, but this is likely to involve only a minor degree of change. Emergent or incremental patterns of strategy development also imply relatively little change, building as they do on existing paradigms and ways of thinking about the world.

One well-known model of strategy development is called 'logical incrementalism'. This is discussed in more detail in Chapter 16. ►

These types of strategy are common, with good reason. Significant change is difficult, costly, and demanding of staff time and energy; it is heavy on organisational resources; and it is also relatively risky because of the uncertainty involved (although as you have already seen in Chapter 5, doing nothing can be risky too). The bigger each of these elements is, the more problems involved. So there can be a number of difficulties in achieving strategic change, and, as you might imagine, it is likely that organisations would rather avoid facing them.

◄ We looked at some of the environmental factors that require organisational turnarounds in Section 12.5.4.

However, there are times when organisations simply have to embark on major change programmes, or even turnarounds. In Section 13.6 we review the main reasons why this should be so. First, however, we consider some of the problems (and also benefits of course) which might result from attempted change. An aware-

Table 13.1 Levels and types of organisational change

Frequency of occurrence	Need	Principal level of change	Types of change
Very rare	Turnaround, normally in response to major changes to the organisation's operating environment	Organisation-wide	Values, paradigm, culture, styles of management, organisation structure; organisational competences
Rare	New mission, goals and strategy often in response to major decline in organisational performance	Senior management; management team and often organisation-wide	New objectives; corporate strategy; management structure; organisational competences
Quite common	Improved organisational competitiveness	Management and functional level	Organisation structure; functional strategies; systems and management roles; empowerment; management by objectives; performance management; job descriptions; policies
Common	Major product or market initiative	Management team, functions	New marketing operations; HR policies; division's structure
Very common	Improved efficiencies	Team, or functional	Functional strategies; organisation of tasks; job enrichment; training; computerisation of systems

ness of these issues is important in allowing both students and practising managers to:

● assess the acceptability of a proposed change;

● design change programmes that have a chance of overcoming the most predictable obstacles.

These obstacles to change may arise at both the individual and the organisational level, and, first, in Section 13.2 we look at personal reasons why people may object to change. In Section 13.3 we examine two models that have been proposed of the way in which people adapt to change – identifying the stage that people have reached in these models is helpful for assessing the likely strength of resistance and for deciding what needs to be done next. Then in Section 13.4 we move on to some organisational barriers to change.

13.2 | Barriers to change: individual

Not everyone thinks that change is a good thing. There have always been those who regret any new developments, and who long for the 'good old days'. Others, for example Alvin Toffler (1970) in his book *Future Shock*, while not necessarily being against change *per se*, argue that the rate of change is now out of control; we have reached the point where people simply cannot cope any more. He might be even more shocked at how much faster the rate of change is nowadays, thirty years on.

On an individual level people often find it difficult to cope with considerable change. It appears to be inherently stressful, as individuals have only a limited ability to take on and cope with new things. This of course varies with the individual; what may make *me* collapse in a heap may be an interesting and stimulating challenge for *you*! The fact is we are all different, and experience different levels of stress or strain according to our individual constitutions and experiences. We are all different, too, in our ability to manage and deal with the stress we feel. Nevertheless, at some point most people will begin to feel uncomfortable if change is excessive (see Real-Life Application 13.1). For many years now it has been accepted that there are links between stress and subsequent ill health – in the form of cancer, heart attacks and even less serious problems such as colds or eczema.

If change is self-inflicted, then coping with it is somehow easier, although it can still be stressful. When change is imposed, particularly if it is something you do not agree with (and don't forget, what benefits the organisation as a whole might not mean improvement for every person in it), then emotions like fear, anxiety and resentment are likely to be very strong. In these circumstances resistance and conflict can result, which is why major change strategic programmes, which after all are usually set in motion by one or two senior managers, are often accompanied by high levels of hostility, increased politicking, increased absenteeism, and high staff turnover rates.[1]

REAL-LIFE APPLICATION 13.1

The effects of changes in the Queensland Hospital system

In recent years, governments have actively pursued reforms of the Australian public sector. A main objective of health sector reform has been to reduce hospital waiting lists and increase the overall level of efficiency of the public hospital system. This is in a context of high demand for hospital services, an ageing population, new medical technologies and treatments, and a growing community expectation for the provision of the most advanced care available. In one Queensland hospital, over a year there was a 16% increase in the number of theatre cases and admissions; the average daily number of inpatients increased by 6%, the occupancy rate increased from 86 to 92% and the average length of stay fell by 14%.

Yet, the government allocated only limited funds to achieve this. These changes had to be achieved without increases in staffing levels or salaries, and inevitably this burden fell on individual members of staff. One of the major effects of these increases in work intensity was a decline in staffing well-being and morale. Increases in demand for counselling for stress-related issues, high staff turnover and absenteeism levels were seen. Periodically the strain also showed in the form of industrial disputes, although the underlying professionalism of health workers restrained the kinds and extent of industrial action pursued; striking was still perceived as unprofessional and unethical.

From Cameron, A. (1998) 'The elasticity of endurance: Work intensification and workplace flexibility in the Queensland hospital system', *New Zealand Journal of Industrial Relations*, 23(3): 133–151.

Figure 13.2 shows some of the forces that may be influential in encouraging an individual to consider or welcome change. This is an example of a *force field* analysis originally proposed by Kurt Lewin (1952). He was highly influential in theorising about the factors which encourage people, or indeed organisations and nations, to change – he was interested in the reconstruction of post-war Germany, for example. His view was that unless there are good reasons why people believe they should change, they will not. Hence the forces encouraging change will need to be stronger than the forces supporting the status quo if change is to be achieved – the 'force field'. On the right hand side you will see some of the factors which might act to block change. On the left hand side you can see some of the elements which might act against these to force change. They 'meet' in the middle and, depending on the relative strength of the two sides, change will be more or less likely.

We will now look in more detail at some possible reasons why change is resisted by individuals. Many of these are emotional responses, although some are also quite rational.

13.2.1 Fear of the new

First of all, when things around us are changing there is uncertainty about the new situation. It appears that people generally need at least some degree of stability and certainty in their lives, and it is the uncertainty of change which provides much of our anxiety and stress.[2] Certainty is needed in order to plan for the future of children, or to take on an expensive commitment – a mortgage for example. If we anticipate that the future will be different, however, then we may worry about whether we will like it. We might also recognise that, in the short term at least,

Figure 13.2   Force field of factors influencing individual change

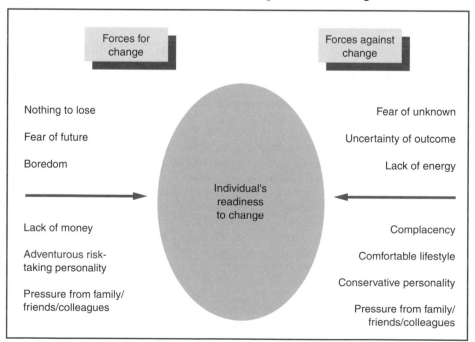

there will be a period of considerable disruption and hard work as wrinkles are ironed out, and we and others around us learn to cope with the new ways. Change that is imposed by others also reduces our sense of autonomy or control of our own destinies – and the sense of not being in control is a well-known factor in stress-related illnesses.

13.2.2 Fear of incompetence

A similar fear is whether we will be able to cope with what the future holds. We know that we can do what we have done previously. In the future, if this is different from what we do now, then there is always a degree of anxiety about whether we have the skills to cope with it. This is why experienced and capable staff may resist the introduction of computers into their work, particularly if more junior people around them are likely to find it easier to cope. Self-esteem is an important element in well-being.

13.2.3 Change fatigue

Individuals seem only able to cope with a limited amount of stimulation, before they become disoriented or dysfunctional. This appears to be due to a function of the brain's ability to process information; if there is too much, then a psychological mechanism kicks in which acts to block off new stimuli and prevents the individual from taking on board further novelty. Weick (1995: 89) suggests that under demanding situations conservative decisions will result as people retreat into familiar, and thus psychologically comfortable, territory. This may be one reason why absenteeism increases during periods of organisational change, and why negative or dysfunctional activities such as 'stalling', pretending to work but not doing so, or stretching tasks much longer than necessary, become more prevalent (Ashforth and Mael, 1996: Ashforth and Lee, 1990).

13.2.4 Emotional and rational resistance

Fear and fatigue may be the most powerful reasons for resistance to change, but people can also resist change on other grounds. They may feel aggrieved that they were not consulted about the proposals, or asked to be involved in the implementation. They may genuinely believe that the proposals are mistaken, and would make the organisation's position worse. Or they may simply not care enough about the organisation to make the effort needed to change their existing routines. This may be because they are not committed to its values or, in a fragmented culture, they may feel more committed to their personal or professional goals than to the organisation's. Doctors, for example, may feel more deeply about curing people, or advancing the frontiers of medical science, than about keeping their hospital's budget in balance, even if financial considerations are important to the hospital's strategy.

13.3 The coping cycle

However much individuals may welcome or resist change, there appears to be a relatively standard pattern of acceptance and 'internalisation' of change. A number of models of this process have been devised, most based on a classic piece of theorising in the 1950s by Kurt Lewin. He identified a pattern of freezing, 'change', and 're-freezing' to explain the developments over time of an individual's acceptance of changing circumstances.

The first stage, *freezing*, implies a relatively steady state in which there is comparative stability, unchanging routines and a psychological state of relative contentment.

The next stage, *moving* or *change*, is characterised by uncertainty, a movement away from what has gone before, but little idea as yet of what future path will be taken. It is a period of instability and experimentation.

The final stage, *re-freezing*, is back to a period of stability – but stability with different characteristics from the previous period of 'freezing'. The experimentation and stability of the previous period have been resolved, to result in a new direction, new approaches and a period of psychological contentment again.

Obviously this type of model is only an approximation of what happens in reality, both on an individual and an organisational level. It also assumes a relatively stable environment – but if the world outside is constantly changing, then re-freezing may not be either possible or desirable. However, it is useful in helping us to understand some of the behavioural or mental differences at each stage of the change process.

Another model by Colin Carnall of individual psychological adaptation to change in organisations, which is based on similar principles to Lewin's, is shown in Figure 13.3.

The first stage, *denial*, is when individuals pretend to themselves that externally

Figure 13.3   The coping cycle (from Carnall, 1995)

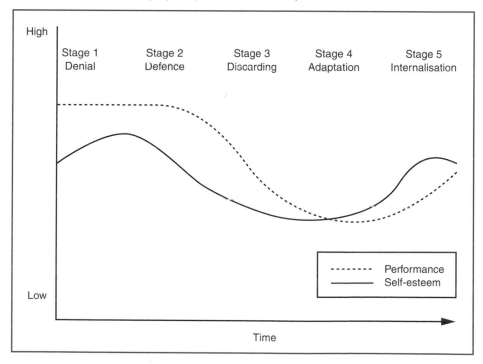

imposed change is not happening. It is characterised by attachment to traditional ways of approaching things even if they are clearly problematic. Behaviour remains unaltered, even though it may be becoming increasingly inappropriate. There is a refusal to recognise either that change may be occurring at all, or that it could be beneficial.

At the second stage, *defence*, externally imposed change has been recognised, but by no means accepted. There is a clinging to and defence of old ways, and a refusal to consider that new approaches could be beneficial. Paradoxically, self-esteem may actually rise at this stage. There can be a sense of bonding with colleagues as they fight a 'common enemy' – the managers who have introduced change. However, depression can also start to bite and behaviours sometimes become defensive and negative. This results in resistance to, or even sabotage of, the efforts of those imposing the change. Ashforth and Lee (1990) have written an interesting paper which catalogues these types of defensive behaviours in organisations. We will return to these issues in the next chapter in the section on power and politics.

Defensive responses are common during periods of uncertainty. Most of these responses arise because people perceive that change is threatening. Even when it is self-imposed or broadly welcomed, the uncertainty which is its result requires time for people to adapt and get used to the idea that things will be done differently from now on. A period of what is almost grieving for the old ways, and a gradual acceptance of the new has to take place.

During the third stage, *discarding*, the individual starts to realise that change is going to happen and even may have some benefits. A process of 'disengaging' with the old ways starts to take place. There is an acknowledgement that perhaps they were not all they were cracked up to be, and maybe the new ways aren't quite as bad as was first thought.

This process continues with the next stage, *adaptation*, where behaviour changes and there is an acceptance that change has become a reality and has to be made to work. There is further disengagement with the old ways of approaching things, and at this stage the individual perhaps even starts to 'sell' some of the benefits of the new approaches to others who are further behind in the adaptation process.

The final stage, *internalisation*, is where the individual had adapted totally to his or her new environment. It has become increasingly difficult to imagine any other way of approaching things; the old ways are but a distant memory – and it may seem incredible that they were clung to for so long.

It is impossible to say how long this cycle takes, or indeed if everyone will go through it. Some people never get beyond the denial stage, and change programmes in organisations are characterised by high levels of staff turnover for just this sort of reason. Many different factors will influence the process of adaptation; individual adaptability and readiness to accept change; the amount of chance already experienced and whether change fatigue has set in; the types and scales of changes; and the perception, or not, that change will bring benefits.

◄ *The concepts of power and stakeholder were introduced in Sections 1.2.1 and 1.2.2. We also look at the power enshrined in organisational structures in Section 10.4.*

By understanding the stage that important individuals and stakeholder groups have reached in the coping cycle, you can get clues about how likely they are to resist further change, and what form that resistance might take.

In addition to individual inertia or resistance to change, there are considerable organisational barriers to change. We will now consider some of these.

13.4 | Barriers to change: organisational

◀ We have looked at the effects of the organisation's history on where it is now in Chapters 1, 2, and 3.

As we have discussed elsewhere in this book, organisations are the result of a range of historical processes. They have been shaped by political activities of negotiation and bargaining, and by a long period of *reification*. This happens through a gradual process of experimentation and adaptation: if something works it is continued with; if it doesn't, it is discarded. The results are the physical manifestations of the organisation: products and services, buildings and their contents, control systems. Organisations are therefore the result of their historical successes. This has considerable implications for anyone attempting to move an organisation in a significantly different direction (Real-Life Application 13.2).

For much of the time this gradual and iterative adaptation works well. However, if something radical happens to make an organisation mis-aligned or badly adapted to its environment, significant organisational change may be required. There is likely to be strong resistance to this from within the organisation. As you have already seen, change is disruptive. Job security may be threatened, and behaviour patterns and values questioned. People are required to take more risks, undertake new challenges, be more flexible – in other words they may have to adapt personally to change; this takes time and can be stressful. But there are other, organisational reasons why change may be resisted. We will now look at some of these in more detail.

13.4.1 Dominant logic and the paradigm

As we saw in Chapters 1 and 2, most organisations have a set of principles that guide the behaviour of those who work in them. These may not be articulated, or even consciously recognised by those who work there, but they will be there, even though there may also be a number of subcultures with different values within the overall organisation.

REAL-LIFE APPLICATION 13.2

Sony's physical manifestations

Sony began in 1946 in post-war Japan as a company which made magnetic tape. It was founded by two individuals who remained in charge of the company for many years, until both died fairly recently at a grand old age. Most of the company's senior managers have been with the firm for many years.

Its products developed from the company's early learning about audio technology and it was one of the first companies to produce a transistor radio based on miniaturisation technologies. Since then it has produced headphones, radios, cassette players, tape recorders, personal stereos, televisions, video recorders, hi-fi components, digital audio tape recorders/players, car audio systems, professional audio equipment, audio tapes, CD players, video cam-eras, digital cameras, digital satellite systems, on-line audio, computer games, and DVDs. Although many of these products are superficially very different from each other (televisions and CDs for example), the vast majority are the outcome of Sony's learning and development over time – almost all products can trace their roots back to the founders' own preferences.

The firm's architecture, despite a recent restructuring (see the case study at the end of Chapter 10) is still heavily based around the needs of innovation and building on core technologies of sound production and miniaturisation.

Imagine what Sony would do if the demand for music or audio products dried up completely – unlikely, we know!

These values tend to become more homogeneous, over time. The influence of the founder of the firm is always strong, and persists sometimes for decades after he or she has departed (Schein, 1983; see also Real-Life Application 13.2 above). This happens because founders recruit people to support or succeed them that they think will help their own values to persist. This process is then replicated throughout the organisation as it grows and recruits more staff. In time, organisations develop identities and convey something of themselves and their values to the outside world, so that those who think they share these values apply to work there. Once they arrive, those that find they have made a mistake leave; those that find they are suited, stay.

This mutual attraction of like-minded individuals and organisations is reinforced over time by socialisation processes. There is an adjustment of ideas and values as part of the social bonding processes that occur between groups of people. Training, the passing on of traditional ways of doing things, and the telling of stories about successes and failures, also ensure that over time people in organisations develop similar world views and approach things in a similar way. This becomes the *dominant logic* against which all new activities are measured, and which indeed determines whether new things are considered at all. Another term for this is the *paradigm*, the cultural norms and assumptions that, consciously or unconsciously, govern most organisational activities.

The dominant logic affects the type of information from outside the organisation which is gathered and given attention. There are many examples of firms that commission market research, and then reject its findings because it does not give the answer that they wanted or expected – showing, for example, that the firm's products were not as well regarded by the customers as the firm thought. Information can be selectively gathered internally too. Even successful and well-regarded firms can fall prey to this.

Managers' ability to *perceive* the need for change is clearly a potential block to change taking place. The organisation's dominant logic, value systems, data-gathering and market intelligence processes are all geared to what has worked well in the past (see Real-Life Application 13.3). If changes in external circumstances erode the organisation's competitiveness, then clearly things need to be different. Poor performance is often an indicator of this, and can help to overcome the persistence of the dominant logic and bring about an awareness of the need for change.

◄ *Dominant logic as and the paradigm are defined in Section 1.2.5.*

◄ *The selectivity of information gathering is discussed in relation to contingency theory in Section 10.1 and Theoretical Perspective 10.1.*

13.4.2 Culture, structures, and systems

Even if senior managers are persuaded that change would be beneficial, there are still a lot of hurdles to overcome before it can be brought about. Many of these are linked with what we have just been talking about – the information-gathering systems and decision-making processes that together form an organisation's structure and operations. In fact, most of these actions are intimately bound up with one another. They can be modelled as a network or web, with each element relating to each of the others in a reciprocal way (Figure 13.4).

At the centre of the web is the **paradigm**, the values and beliefs or dominant logic which, as you have already seen, is the 'glue' which guides behaviour and shapes organisational decision-making. It is different from the organisation's mission, which is the conscious message the organisation broadcasts to its stake-

The dominant logic at 3M and IBM

3M

The US corporation, 3M, has been one of the world's most consistently innovative companies. Starting from the invention of wet-and-dry sandpaper in 1910 and masking tape shortly afterwards, it developed a broad range of products, based around expertise in coatings and powder technology, but ranging from office equipment through reflective road signs to Scotch-Brite scourers for cleaning dishes.

It is famous for setting targets for innovation: 15% of its people's time is to be allocated to projects of their own, to foster creativity; 25% of turnover is to be derived from products developed during the previous three years. Staff get promotion and the membership of prestigious internal societies through successful innovation. As an example of a 'corporate value statement', 3M's is 'never kill a product idea'.

But 3M is less good at measuring the profitability of its products, and as the product line has proliferated, profitability has dropped. Given a succession of leaders with backgrounds in chemical engineering and steeped in the values which produced innovations like the Post-It note, 3M has found it difficult to cut back marginal products and to limit research to areas where it has product or marketing strength.

IBM

Despite a dominant global market share and high-qual-ity products, between 1991 and 1993 IBM suffered a combined loss of nearly $16 billion, making it one of the biggest corporate failures in history. During the period of the company's greatest success and growth, the 1970s and 1980s, IBM had taken advantage of the world's growing demand for calculating machines and the increasing size of businesses. The speed and reliability of IBM's mainframe computers made the heavy initial investment worthwhile for large organisations.

Then small, and convenient, portable computers began to be developed, which showed that flexibility and convenience could be matched with computing power. For some time, IBM chose to ignore the spectacular growth of PCs, claiming that they were unlikely to be able to solve the types of problems that IBM's mainframes handled. By the early 1990s IBM's market share had declined significantly.

Most of the company's senior management team had come from a work background in the mainframe division. Very few had worked elsewhere within the company, and almost none had worked outside the company for any significant period. In addition, reports indicated that IBM had become arrogant and complacent; one of the world's largest and most profitable companies, many employees appeared to think that 'Big Blue' could not be toppled – it was too big, too successful, and too good to be challenged by the 'upstart' PC.

holders. The paradigm consists of unconscious behaviours and decision rules, built up over time. It is rare for an organisation to be able to articulate what its paradigm is; it can only be observed and inferred from the other elements of the web. This makes it nearly impossible to change directly – it has to be 'worked on' through changes to the other elements.

Stories are the tales told by organisational members to each other and to outsiders about what has gone on in the organisation. They form an important part of organisational 'sense-making' in which individuals learn how and what to think by finding out what others think. They are also an important element in the socialisation or acculturation processes of new members. As stories form part of the history of the organisation they are impossible to change. Anyone wishing to minimise the influence of particular stories on how individuals within the organisation think, in order to bring about cultural change, has to hope that new stories will take their place. As you can imagine, this process is hard to control or direct artificially.

Company reports and accounts, biographical books, and press articles are a good source of officially sponsored stories – the ones the senior managers want to promote (Real-Life Application 13.4).

Figure 13.4   The cultural web (from Johnson, 1992)

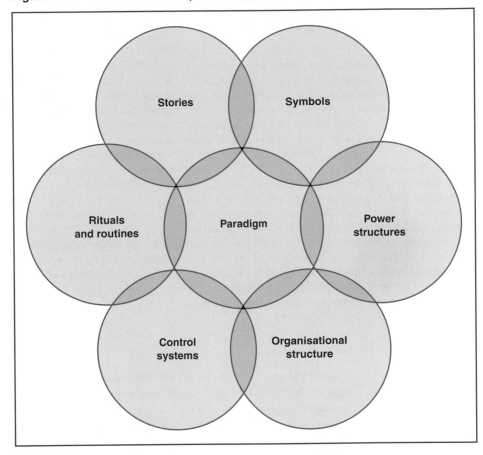

Corporate stories in McDonald's and Benetton

McDonald's

The opportunities at McDonald's extend right to the top. Senior Chairman Fred Turner started his career with McDonald's working in a restaurant, and Chairman and CEO Mike Quinlan began in the mailroom.[3] And, of the more than 13,000 McDonald's restaurant managers in the USA, 70% of them started as crew.

Crew members are not only trained in specific skills in operating a restaurant and serving customers, but they also learn valuable lessons in teamwork, discipline, and responsibility that will contribute to their success later in life, no matter what career they ultimately choose to pursue.

People from all walks of life – from Olympic medallists and broadcast journalists to movie stars and politicians – credit a first job at McDonald's with having equipped them with the ingredients for success.

Source: McDonald's 1998 Annual Report.

Benetton

Alessandro Benetton, 32, Luciano's son:

'Nobody in the family likes to buy yachts – we like to grow.'

'In everything we do, we keep the basic values of our family.'

'We need entrepreneurs. I'm not sure every one will work out, but even when you fail, you learn a lot.'

Source: Levine, J. (1996) 'Even when you fail you learn a lot', *Forbes*, 11 March: 58–60.

REAL-LIFE APPLICATION 13.5

Symbols in McDonald's and Sony

McDonald's

McDonald's employees at all levels make abundant use of the abbreviation QSCV – standing for Quality, Service, Cleanliness and Value. These are the four principles laid down by Ray Kroc to define what the company stands for, and what it offers its customers. This is a quite rare example of an organisational value that is deeply held (and so part of the paradigm) but is also actually articulated.

Another symbolic aspect of McDonald's paradigm is the belief that its success comes from taking under-achieving or poorly qualified people and transforming them – as you can see from the stories we mentioned in Real-Life Application 13.4. The training rituals that are part of the everyday experience of arriving and working also show how deeply ingrained this belief is. The great symbols of this part of the paradigm are the company's famous 'Hamburger Universities', the bases for its corporate training programmes.

Source: McDonald's 1999 Annual Report.

Sony

In the Founding Prospectus written in 1946, Ibuka, one of Sony's two founders, set out his vision of the future company as being designed by and for engineers 'establishing a stable workplace where engineers could work to their hearts' content . . . creating an ideal workplace, free, dynamic and joyous where dedicated engineers will be able to realise their craft and skills at the highest possible level'. For a while this document was only available to be seen by special request, although it apparently could be recited verbatim by many employees. It is now on the company's website.

You would be correct in thinking that this example could also be considered to be a 'story' – as with many strategy concepts, it is not always easy to put things into one neatly defined box.

Source: Nathan (1999).

Symbols are the ways in which the organisation is represented – both to itself and to the outside world. Sometimes these symbols are tangible objects such as headquarters buildings or company cars which indicate the importance of particular people or roles. Sometimes they are intangible – particular types of language or behaviour (Real-Life Application 13.5).

Symbols are an important way in which organisations' members learn to make sense of the world around them, and are also key indicators of what behaviour is expected. Some symbols *are* open to being altered by those attempting strategic change (Real-Life Application 13.6). A move in emphasis from salaries paid for simple attendance at work to bonuses paid for particular skills, the rewarding of new product development, as in 3M for example, are symbols of senior managers' values and expectations.

Other symbols are less open to manipulation because their importance is not consciously recognised or they are too deeply buried in the ethos of the organis-

REAL-LIFE APPLICATION 13.6

Changing language as a symbol of changing values

Most UK rail and bus companies have stopped talking about 'passengers' and insist on the use of the word 'customers'. A passenger is a piece of human cargo that is carried from A to B. A customer is a person that has a right to expect politeness and good service in exchange for the money he or she has paid.

By itself the change of terminology means nothing. As part of a broader package of change measures, it has some significance.

ation to be changed without destroying what it is about. Think of a university's graduation ceremony or 3M's rewards for successful innovators as shown in Real-Life Application 13.3 above. Any move to abolish these would encounter such resistance that it would simply not be worth attempting – unless it was vital to a strong message about a fundamental change in what the organisation stands for.

Power structures are the dominant groups that reflect historical successes and the achievement of power by key individuals. In 3M they were the engineers, in IBM the mainframe designers and salespeople, in Benetton the founding family. Each of these cases furnishes clear evidence about what each company unconsciously believes about itself. 3M believes that success comes from engineering excellence, IBM that it comes from selling large computers to handle a firm's total data requirements, and Benetton that it comes from close-knit family-style relationships. Power structures are likely to be enshrined in the formal **organisational structure** or configuration. This is the organisation's formalised decision-making processes. There are, however, occasions when dominant individuals or groups are not reflected in the formal structure – a problem that makes achieving change particularly difficult. In some organisations, for example, power may reside with union representatives. In the case of British Airways, as we discussed in Chapter 11, a degree of power resides with the cabin staff, who are the people who have to deliver the service that makes BA competitive.

Control systems are the ways in which certain behaviours are rewarded and encouraged, or vice versa. As we have mentioned in Chapter 4, the things a company measures are powerful indicators of what it really thinks is important. The amount that it invests in measuring them, and the frequency with which controls take place, are also useful clues (Real-Life Application 13.7).

Sometimes the *absence* of control systems can be an indication that the organisation believes deeply that certain things are *unimportant*. For example, if an organisation has no effective systems for measuring quality or customer satisfaction, this is powerful evidence that it does not care deeply about either of those things, however loudly it may claim otherwise.

◄ Routines were introduced in Chapter 1 and discussed further in Chapter 3.

You should by now be familiar with the concept of **routines**. As these are, for the most part, unconscious, they are sticky. Because of this they are quite difficult to assess and therefore change. A firm's **rituals** are similar to its routines, but concerned with expressed behaviours that indicate the importance of particular things. An induction ceremony, like the training course which new employees undergo at McDonald's Hamburger University, is one example. These are perhaps some of the simplest things to alter.

13.4.3 Diagnosing the degree of change needed

You can use the cultural web to identify a change gap. Draw a cultural web of the

Figure 13..5   Cultural web prior to the intended change

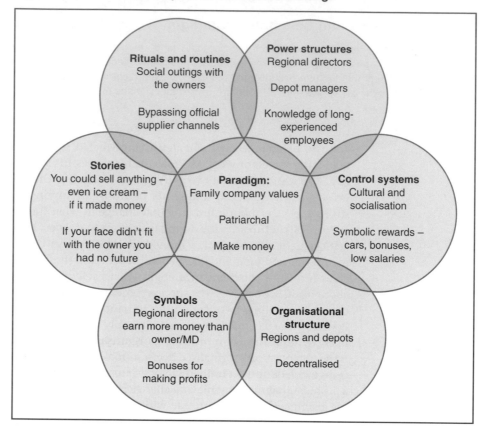

organisation as it is now. Then draw one of the organisation in the future once all the changes you think are necessary are implemented. This is likely to highlight quite graphically many of the steps that will be needed in order to get to that point. An example is given in Figures 13.5 and 13.6 for Morgan Williams, the case study you will find at the end of Chapter 14.

13.4.4 Evaluating the consistency of change initiatives

One could expand the cultural web to incorporate other elements to make a more comprehensive organisational web (Figure 13.7). Usually, change in one of these areas will imply the need for change in others. An organisation launching a new product may also need to invest in new skills (new staff or training existing employees), new plant (information technology, or manufacturing machinery), and a new structure (location of decision-making). Changes in an organisation's structure may imply new systems, new job descriptions, new reward schemes, and new staff locations.

◀ The importance of coherence in a strategy was discussed in Section 8.5.1, the related idea of consistency as a criterion for evaluating strategic options is introduced in Section 11.5.

You will see from this figure how difficult organisation-wide change might be. All the elements are interlinked; all are the result of the organisation's history and experience; and disturbance of only one element, for example the formal structure, will achieve little unless other elements are simultaneously altered. As we have already mentioned, successful strategy is *coherent*, each of these elements

Figure 13.6 Cultural web after the intended change

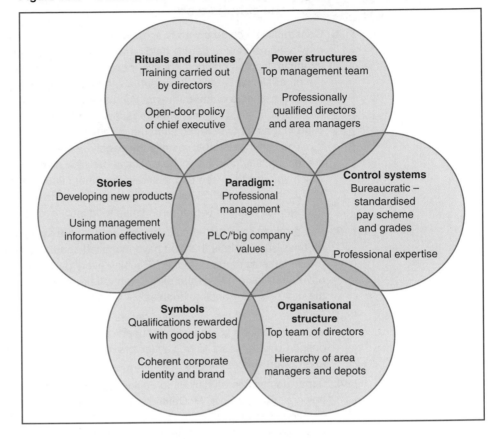

supporting one another in allowing the organisation to deliver value to its customers and users. Thus, there has to be a sense of consistency and cohesion about the message of change if it is to be effective.[5] There is no use in changing reward systems if functional responsibilities are not tackled at the same time – mixed messages would result, and management's commitment and their ability to implement the change would be questioned. Similarly, a stated intention to move towards, for example, a more proactive product development strategy would not be accepted if management did not simultaneously provide reward systems which supported this move.

If an organisation's paradigm is to be changed, it must be tackled in all of its manifestations. It is no use simply changing the organisation's structures and control systems, which tend to be the most obvious levers for managers to pull when they are trying to do something – or to be seen by their superiors to be doing something. Tackling power structures, by hiring and promoting some types of people, and firing or demoting others, may be important, but will not necessarily give the right messages to the people that remain if other actions (or lack of action) contradict this.

Think back to the organisations where you have worked, however briefly. It is the stories, symbols, rituals and routines that you will remember most vividly, because they shape the reality of most people's working lives. Thus, these need to

Practical dos and don'ts   **The cultural web**

1. Constructing a cultural web is an iterative process. It is best to start with one or two elements of it, deeply held paradigmatical beliefs or values for example, that are obvious from your observations or case study. Then identify the other elements of the web – rituals, control systems, etc. – that belong with the elements of the paradigm you have written down. As you are doing this, other rituals, routines, structures, systems and so on will come to your mind that are not yet reflected in the paradigm you have conceptualised so far. You can then start to identify the deeply-held beliefs that are expressed in these structures and behaviours. These are new elements of the paradigm, which you can then see expressed in the other cultural elements – which should make you rethink what the paradigm comprises. You may need to go through this process two or three times to identify everything.

2. In a properly constructed cultural web, each of the structures, systems, rituals, routines and symbols that you have identified should correspond with one or more elements of the paradigm. Equally, every part of the paradigm that you have identified at the centre of the web will be manifested in at least one of the other six surrounding 'bubbles'.

3. Fill in as much of the *descriptive details* of the elements of the cultural web as you can, don't be content with a superficial list. Having said that, concentrate only on what appears to be key factors, or you will end up with an enormous and unworkable catalogue of issues.

4. It may sometimes be difficult to decide where in the web a particular factor belongs. For example, McDonald's Hamburger University has been mentioned as both a symbol and a ritual. The trick here (as with a PEST analysis) is not to agonise too much about niceties of classification – after all, many of the 'bubbles' overlap. Just write the factor down under a sensible heading, to make sure it is included in the analysis.

5. Many of the most important elements of culture are intangible, and may not be easily discernible from a written case study, or even from a visit to a company if you were to do some primary research. The cultural web often requires a more intuitive style of analysis than, say, the value chain. You may need to 'read between the lines' of a case study or other evidence, to guess at what is running through the minds of the people involved.

6. You may find that you are not able to draw a complete web, because you have no information on things like stories, or rituals and routines. It is still worth using the evidence that you have to construct as complete a picture of the web as possible. You may also find it helpful to interpret other kinds of evidence, such as artefacts. For example, the kinds of easy-to-use keyboards that McDonald's has designed for its tills is evidence that making effective use of people with low educational standards is part of its paradigm. Tangible artefacts are not included in Johnson's cultural web but, as with most models, you should feel able to extend and adapt it if you have good grounds for doing so.[4]

Figure 13.7   An organisation's web

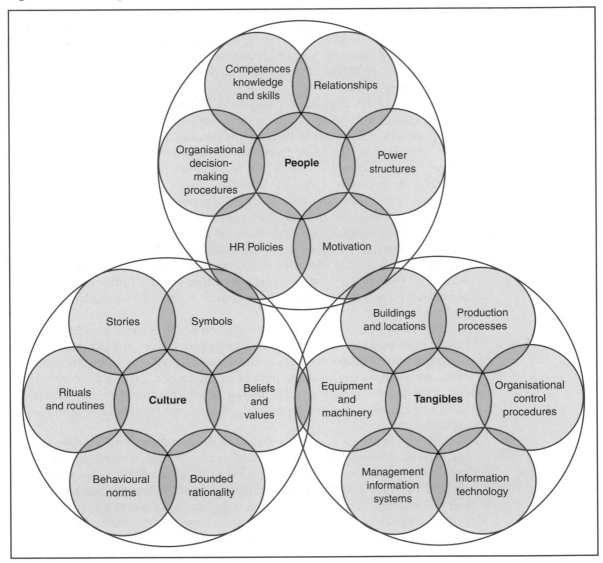

be worked on, alongside the organisation's structures and systems, if a change programme is to succeed. Unfortunately, these elements of the web, commonly referred to as 'soft factors', are the trickiest to influence in a way that leads to predictable results. Partly because of this, they are also the ones that many traditional, 'rational', 'hard-headed' managers find it most difficult to justify spending time and money on. We return to this issue in Chapter 14.

13.4.5 Power structures

One of the major elements that may need to be tackled in a strategic change programme, and indeed usually is tackled, is an organisation's power echelons. These

◀ We looked at ways of identifying powerful groups and the sources of their power in Section 1.2.2.

◀ Resource-dependency theory, and information control theories of power are covered in Chapter 10.

are the dominant individuals and groups who set the organisation's direction, and who in general are tied most strongly into the dominant logic – which they have had the greatest part in setting. They are also likely to have the greatest access to information and resources. They are the senior managers and functional staff who attend the organisation's most important meetings, and who make the most significant decisions. While *all* employees hold power to some extent, this group holds relatively more.

An organisation's dominant power echelons develop over time. They will start to emerge around the founder of the organisation, as he or she recruits like-minded people to act as their agents. During the increasing formalisation of an organisation, the most favoured individuals will be placed in positions where they can control resources and information, and where they can therefore take the decisions which the founder, or their successor, thinks appropriate. Over time they are also likely to become increasingly numerous in number, and influential through their connections to external stakeholders and to important individuals in other parts of the organisation. This means that when the strategic position of the organisation has to change they are likely to prove a considerable obstacle – because of their shared beliefs about how to do things, their ability to derive strength in these beliefs from each other, their considerable control over resources, and because of their formalised authority positions.

A number of writers, for example Miles and Snow (1978) have identified the contingent links between the strategies an organisation follows and the characteristics of its dominant managerial echelons. Organisations following cost leadership strategies, for example, are likely to have large production or finance departments. Organisations following entrepreneurial or innovative strategies, in contrast, are likely to have larger and more powerful research and development or marketing departments.

Although possible, it is unlikely that all of the members of a dominant echelon will perceive the need for change at the same time. In fact, the inability to do so is one reason why new managers may need to be appointed – as we shall see in Chapter 14. This means that if the organisation needs to adopt a radically different and new strategy, there will be a considerable number of 'losers' – many of whom, as you can imagine, are likely to be less than happy to lose their power and control over events. One common way of attempting to deal with this is to replace the managers in charge of important departments, reduce their budgets and the size of their departments, or marginalise them to less powerful roles. We shall return to this issue in the next chapter; these policies do not always work out as well as the change instigator would like!

13.4.6 External stakeholders

As you have learned, some of an organisation's powerholders are more powerful than others. Some are found within the organisation – key employees and managers – but others are found outside it – the organisation's wider stakeholders. All of these may have some interests in maintaining the organisation's status quo. However, there may also be other external stakeholders whose interests can influence the change process. In the case of particular industries, like banking or defence for example, external stakeholders can be extremely powerful.

External stakeholders who might influence change include:

- *Customers* who may lose their preferred supplier if that organisation changes strategic direction significantly. If that buyer–supplier relationship is a long-standing and critically important one, then there is likely to be concern at the possibility of change.

- *Suppliers* are similarly likely to be extremely worried if an important customer decides to move into a different business area.

- *Governments* or government agencies may also have significant concerns if an organisation decides to change. Their concerns, however, are likely to be restricted to their own suppliers, quasi-governmental organisations, or perhaps to companies whose size or positioning in particularly critical products – arms or aerospace, for example – would provide a significant threat to national security if they were to change.

- *Competitors* may be considerably affected by proposed changes. These might make the organisation a more effective competitor, or alternatively may take it away from its established products or markets. They themselves may have to change in the attempt to take up the customer base that has been freed up. They may have to increase capacity beyond the point at which they can cope, thereby losing the goodwill of existing customers. Or they can ignore everything, and see other competitors gain from the situation and steal market share.

- *Residents and neighbours.* An organisation's move away from its traditional products may offer grounds for concern for those living in the area. Traffic may increase, pollution may begin to be more of a concern, or employment prospects in the area may decline.

The way in which such stakeholders make their feelings known, and whether they are effective in modifying the change the organisation intends to bring in, depends on their relative power, as it does with internal stakeholders. Some can influence change through access to, or control over, legislation or political policies. Environmental pressure groups which have no formal political role, can sometimes be very effective in mobilising public pressure (see Real-Life Application 13.8).

REAL-LIFE APPLICATION 13.8

Shell's clash with Greenpeace

Royal Dutch Shell decided to dispose of redundant North Sea oil rigs by cutting them up on site. Greenpeace, the environmental group, mounted a strong publicity campaign to raise public concern about the effects of this decision on the wildlife around the rigs. After people started to boycott Shell petrol stations in protest, it was forced to reconsider its policy. Eventually, the company decided to bring the oil rigs ashore and dispose of them there, even though some scientists believed that this would be even more harmful to the environment.

This illustrates the importance of careful stakeholder analysis in strategic decision-making. Greenpeace had no formal role in the decision process, but it did have a track record in issues of this kind. Royal Dutch Shell simply failed to anticipate its interest in the situation, or the strength of the public feeling it could stir up.

13.4.7 Organisations' resources, capabilities and competences

Achieving organisational change is likely to be extremely demanding on all sorts of resources – time, human, as well as financial. This means that during the period of change, resources may get diverted from existing products or markets, resulting in their own decline and a relatively rocky period for the company as it adjusts to its new situation and resettles to some degree of strategic stability. When they change, organisations seem to re-acquire some of the vulnerability they had when they were new (Amburgey et al., 1993).

Paradoxically, the organisations most likely to be in a position to attempt radical change are those that are strong enough not to need it! One of the reasons why there are so few long-lived corporations may be that, by the time the need for change is accepted, the organisation is weakened to the point that it may be threatened by the change process itself. Organisations that identify the need for radical change early, and embark upon it before they are in crisis, are rare. One example is the Xerox Corporation, which embarked upon a massive change in culture and manufacturing systems while it still dominated the world photocopier market, with a 40% share.

13.5 Ways in which change may be resisted or promoted

In assessing the extent to which a particular stakeholder group may pose an obstacle to change (or a force in favour of it), we need to take a realistic view on what precisely they can do about it – and whether it will matter. People and stakeholder groups can block change in several ways:

- They can lobby powerful outside stakeholders – governments, pressure groups, customers, suppliers – and power echelons within the company to take account of their objections.

- They can attempt to sabotage the change through strikes or overt refusal to do what they are told.

- They can simply ignore the proposals and quietly carry on with their established routines. The people concerned may not see this as actual resistance – it may be a natural human reaction to change fatigue, or to proposals that have not been effectively planned or communicated.

As a counterbalance, there will in most organisations be some people who are enthusiasts for innovation, and are happy to try out new ways of working. Depending upon the size and influence of this 'early adopter' group, it can be a powerful force in favour of change.

13.6 Forces for strategic change

You might think that given the potential difficulties, significant change would never be contemplated. Nevertheless, radical change programmes that attempt to change culture, strategy, or the organisation as a whole, are not unknown. There are a number of potential reasons for this.

The first factor is that the world has become a much smaller place. For commer-

Figure 13.8   Forces which influence an organisation's readiness to change

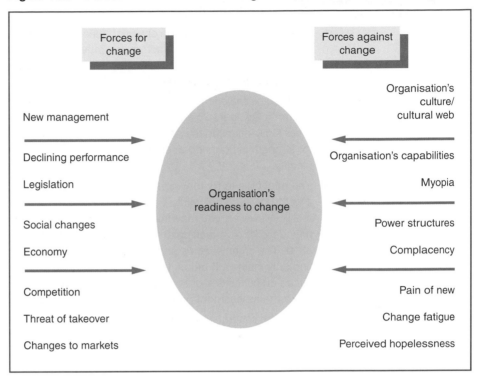

cial organisations competition has increased hugely. Nowadays threats are not only posed by local firms, but also from companies based thousands of miles away. Traditional political and physical barriers between countries have broken down, leading to the development of international trading regions such as the EU or ASEAN. Transport and communication costs have reduced, again increasing the potential for global competitors to enter what used to be relatively protected domestic markets. The fashion for protectionism or state ownership appears to be breaking down, leading to once protected organisations becoming open to competition and the financial disciplines of the global market place. However, not only have markets become more open and international, but consumers the world over have generally become more sophisticated. They are far more knowledgeable about the contents of products, or 'green' issues and this, and other profound changes in consumer awareness, has meant that companies have had to make, in some cases, radical changes to their products and operations.

A force field similar to the one shown for individuals in Figure 13.2, can be drawn for the organisation's readiness to change (Figure 13.8). This force field has implications for the management of change. Even when there may be very strong forces encouraging change in an organisation, success is not automatic, and entrenched interests may make the process of adaptation long and fraught. However, those implementing change can use the force fields to identify potential troublespots as well as to emphasise and illustrate the more positive aspects of change.

We shall now look in more detail at some of the factors that can act to unblock potential areas of resistance to change.

Practical dos and don'ts	Force fields

1. Force fields are organisation specific. Although we have given examples of some of the most common factors you may encounter, there will be other factors that may be found in various settings, and you are perfectly at liberty to bring in any that seem relevant.

2. List precise evidence for the force field factors you identify. Show financial performance figures over time – to identify trends, or comparative figures with other similar firms in the same industry. Describe the evidence that you have for strength of bounded decision making or for the power structures you identify.

3. You might like to try to weight the various factors, as long as you realise that it would be extremely difficult if not impossible to measure them precisely in reality. However, you may think that in a particular organisation its culture and bounded decision making are *so* strong that it deserves a weighting of 9 out of 10. The organisation's performance may be less important in this instance and only merits a 5 out of 10 weighting. Carry out the same exercise for the forces on both sides of the model. Although very subjective, this can help to make the assessment process at least slightly more objective.

4. Do not be content with simply making a list. Understand why, and how, each of the factors you identify might influence the change process in the organisation you are looking at.

13.6.1 Poor or declining performance

Poor or disappointing financial results create a strong reason for changing. This is often the symptom that accompanies many of the other forces for change. It can lead to the threat of takeover because a firm's share price declines, perceptions of weakness can lead to a threat of debt recall by lenders, and aggressive initiatives from competitors who perceive an opportunity.

◀ *Strategic drift is covered in Section 3.5.1.*

Poor performance can come about because of a number of different factors. Many have to do with the quality of management. Managers may have become complacent, which frequently leads to strategic drift. As you have seen with IBM they can fail to notice a competitor who steals sales. They may have failed to keep up to date with the skills needed in a changing competitive environment, for example in information technology, or they may simply have become lazy and greedy. These may be harsh words, but the Anglo-American firm Hanson Industries used to specialise in finding companies with just these characteristics, taking them over, removing layers of 'fat' (such as unnecessary directors' perks, layers of management, or over-high costs), and significantly improving the financial performance of their targets (and their own wealth!).

Companies whose performance is poor often find that it provides the spur to taking the necessary, but difficult, decisions. Such evidence can provide a crisis of confidence in the leadership, who may be replaced to bring in new managers with different and perhaps more appropriate skills, or forced to implement the sorts of changes which are necessary. Poor financial performance is an important indicator

REAL-LIFE APPLICATION 13.9

Performance-induced changes at McDonald's

McDonald's said in June 1998 it would cut 525 jobs, or 23% of the 2,300 workforce at its headquarters – the US fast-food group's first corporate job losses. The cuts were designed to reduce bureaucracy, streamline decision-making, reduce costs and improve focus. 'While eliminating jobs is a painful process – both personally and culturally – it is necessary to make these changes to refocus and realign with our restaurants and, where appropriate, bring home office resources closer to them,' Jack Greenberg, the new president and chief executive, said.

The company had been plagued by unrelenting US competition and menu flops. The world's biggest fast-food chain had lost its way. In the US profits had barely changed in the preceding three years. This meant that big changes were looming, apart from the job losses. Eight new products were being test marketed in the USA. 'If they don't make the national menu, that's not a failure,' Mr Greenberg says. 'The failure would be not to test them, or to test them for five years before you decide, which is what we have traditionally been guilty of. We have been taking much too long to develop an idea and get it to the market, then too long to decide whether we want to do it or not.'

For many years, McDonald's scarcely seemed to need new products. But by 1996 things had started to go wrong. In the USA, which accounted for 40–45% of operating profits, sales growth slowed and sales per store fell, hitting profits. It also found itself losing market share to Burger King and Wendy's, its two biggest rivals.

Taken from *Financial Times*, 18 June 1998, 'McDonald's announces first corporate job losses'; and *Financial Times*, 3 September 1998, 'A mission to buff up the golden arches: Interview with Jack Greenberg'.

of underlying problems, of whatever description, which focuses attention on potential causes (Real-Life Application 13.9).

13.6.2 New management

One of the most common reasons for change is the appointment of a new chief executive or management team. This is a bit of a chicken and egg situation however. As you have seen above, a new manager is often instated as a result of poor performance prior to his or her appointment, with the specific brief to bring about change (Real-Life Application 13.10).

However, new managers also make considerable changes even when this is not an underlying motive behind their appointments, and the greater the difference between their previous experience and the new situation, the greater the number of changes they will make – not always successfully.[6]

13.6.3 Political, legal, economic, and social events

Issues such as concern for the environment, public pressure to avoid trading with certain countries, for example Iraq and Cuba, government laws, state economic pressures, such as the encouragement of lead-free petrol, and the creation of new trading blocs such as the European market, all imply change for organisations within them, and trading with them.

There are many examples where legislation has brought about huge changes in the strategies and profiles of organisations affected by it. Deregulation is a major stimulus for organisations to become more market-driven and competitive. As you have already seen, firms in the airline industry changed considerably, but think

REAL-LIFE APPLICATION 13.10

Management-induced changes at McDonald's

Michael Quinlan, chief executive of McDonald's, in May 1998 announced that he was to hand over to Jack Greenberg – only the fourth CE in its 43-year history. Mr Quinlan will continue as chairman.

McDonald's grew dramatically during Mr Quinlan's 10-year reign to operate in 109 countries, but suffered loss of market share and weak profits in its main market, the USA, after new products failed to live up to expectations and in the face of intense competition from rivals such as Burger King.

Mr Greenberg's appointment – which took effect in August 1998 – followed a series of moves by McDonald's to recover its poise. In July 1997, the company announced a big management shake-up that propelled Mr Greenberg to the job of turning around the US business as chief executive of the US operations. In May 1998, McDonald's US figures met analysts' expectations for the first time in three quarters, reporting net profits up 5% in the first quarter to $362.2 million on sales of $8.2 billion.

In some ways, Mr Greenberg, 55, was an unlikely choice for the job. An ex-accountant, he had joined McDonald's as chief financial officer 16 years previously, and until becoming head of the US business in 1996, had little operational experience. In his short time with the US operation, he had already made big changes. He decentralised the business, splitting it into five regional divisions with a degree of autonomy; brought in new managers from outside; announced a plan to change the kitchen equipment in all the US restaurants; and started testing new menu items.

Source: Financial Times, 1 May 1998, 'McDonald's chief names successor: Fast food appointment follows attempts to recover market share'; *Financial Times*, 18 June 1998, 'McDonald's announces first corporate job losses'; and *Financial Times*, 3 September 1998, 'A mission to buff up the golden arches: Interview with Jack Greenberg'.

also of the changes which companies and public sector organisations in the former Soviet Bloc are having to face now.

13.6.4 Competition

Increasing competition can also often stimulate change. British Airways is a very good example of a company which brought in a major organisational and cultural change programme when it recognised the threat from a shift away from its protected position and a previously narrow group of national competitors, to what was about to become world-wide competition.

REAL-LIFE APPLICATION 13.11

Competition-induced change at Apple Computer

Apple Computer in the early 1990s is a good example of a firm needing to change in response to three forces: the increase in size, complexity and specialisation of competitors; technological innovation; and the increasing tendency for firms in the industry to operate globally. Innovations that had been developed by Apple were being copied and used in cheaper rival products. Apple lacked the scope and scale of operations that were needed to build and maintain market share while offering high-quality products at premium prices. It also lacked certain development skills and the financial resources needed to fund research and development.

Apple introduced a range of cheaper, lower-performance Macintosh machines, it implemented a cost-reduction programme, more sophisticated operations management processes designed to deliver innovation on schedule, and a divisionalised structure that focused on the functional aspects of the business. At the same time, it tried to introduce more discipline into the culture, while retaining its positive elements of empowerment, flexibility and freedom.

13.7 Summary

In this chapter we have looked at some of the organisational and individual factors which might influence the change process. We first of all looked at the different types of change programmes that can be found in organisations. These cover a range of complexity:

- organisational-wide cultural or structural change, which is relatively rare, and quite difficult to tackle;
- strategy and management structure, less problematic and more common;
- functional strategies, structure, and systems, quite common and relatively easy to implement.

Then we looked at some of the factors that might influence the success of these change programmes. Specifically we have looked at how individuals can react to the possibility of change according to individual attributes and differences in their situations. Many of the individual factors that act to block the acceptance of change are to do with the uncertainty of the future, and fear of not being able to cope.

We then looked at how individuals adapt to change, by going through a process known as the coping cycle, in which change is internalised and accepted over time.

Next we looked at organisational factors which influence the change process. We examined some of the issues to do with the organisation's culture, dominant logic, structure and stakeholder power which might act to block change. We saw how to map these factors in a cultural web.

Balanced against the factors which might mitigate against change are those which might lead to change being accepted more readily. Many of these are to do with factors external to the organisation such as developments in its technological or economic environment and increased competition. Often these 'drivers' of change become known through a decline in the firm's financial performance, and result in the appointment of a new manager who stimulates the change process.

At both individual and organisational levels it is possible to draw a map of a force field, which graphically represents the forces which encourage and, on the opposite side, act to block change.

Typical questions

We conclude this chapter by reviewing some of the questions you are likely to be asked about strategic change, and how you can use the theory in this chapter to answer them.

1. *What factors are likely to block the success of a planned change programme?*

This is a wide-ranging question about both individual and organisational issues, and you will need to revisit many of the preceding chapters in this book to answer this question. For example, we have often said that an organisation is the product of its history and experimentation over time, and it is particularly important when contemplating any type of change programme to understand where the organisation 'has been'. Only then can you assess how easy it might be to break its traditional or expected direction.

First of all you should think about what the organisation's stakeholders – employees, managers, and external ones – are like in general (Chapter 1, Section 1.2.1). You should also want to look at the culture of the organisation or functions (Chapters 1 and 8), decision-making processes and bounded rationality (Chapter 1, Section 1.2.3), and the power of important stakeholders (Chapter 1, Section 1.2.2). Understanding where important powerholders have come from, what they think, and how they are likely to respond are important features of any change programme you might recommend.

You might also want to use the tools in this chapter, such as a force field analysis (Sections 13.2 and 13.4), or cultural web (Section 13.4.2), to assess the depth of attachment to previous ways of working held by the organisation as a whole – so that you consider the implications of how changes to one part of the organisation may have a knock-on effect on others.

2. *What environmental factors might lead to an organisation-wide strategic or cultural change programme being contemplated?*

This is a relatively straightforward question, in which you would use the factors identified on the right-hand side of the force field (Section 13.5) as a guide to the type of environmental features which might lead to change being considered. You can add categories of your own to this list as appropriate – it is not exhaustive.

The first thing to identify here is any evidence that change is necessary; organisations are very unlikely to want to take the risk of trying something completely new unless there are pressing reasons for doing so. Why change a winning formula after all? This means making an assessment of the organisation's performance and looking for evidence that its resources, value chain and architecture (Chapters 6 and 7) are not delivering sustainable competitive advantage. You may also be looking for evidence of strategic slip and particularly performance relative to the firm's competitors. Understanding the firm's relative standing can help you to make a judgment about whether the organisation is performing at its best and therefore whether change is necessary or not.

You would also want to take a closer look at what changes there have been in the environment – the wider one, as well as the organisation's more local competitive environment. You will always want to be aware of factors that will alter the nature of the competitive game. Tools like PEST (Chapter 5, Section 5.2) or industry analysis (Chapter 5, Section 5.4) are useful here.

Questions for discussion

1. What conclusions about the organisation's paradigm might you draw from the following:
- Benetton's controversial 'United Colours of Benetton' advertising campaigns of the 1990s, featuring Aids victims, wounded soldiers and people of different races embracing.
- 3M's policy of encouraging every employee to spend 15% of their time on their personal projects, whose results are not monitored by the firm.

2. Some firms embrace change as a continuous and ongoing part of their culture. Do you think any of the issues and problems described in this chapter apply to these types of organisations? Defend your answer.

3. Force fields can be criticised for being impossible to measure. The relative weighting of each of the forces is thus impossible to assess. Do you agree with this criticism? How can this problem be overcome?

4. Use the cultural web to assess the change 'gap' in an organisation of your choice.

5. 'Change which is imposed on an individual by his or her manager is always going to be resisted.' Discuss.

Oticon

Based on the Oticon case study in Burnes (1996: 203–208)

Oticon, a Danish company founded in 1904, was by 1979 the world's top manufacturer of hearing aids. However, in the 1980s its fortunes plummeted and it lost money and market share. In 1987, the company's performance was so poor that it lost half its equity.

Oticon had been a very traditional, departmentalised and slow-moving company. It had a distinguished past but now it was a small company operating in an increasingly competitive global market-place. Though it had 15 sites around the world and 95 distributorships, it was competing in an environment which had come to be dominated by Siemens, Philips, Sony, 3M and Panasonic. Although the company was strong in the state-subsidised markets of Scandinavia and northern Europe, it was weak in the more open markets of America and the Far East. More importantly, it had the wrong products. Oticon manufactured the standard 'behind the ear' hearing aids but customers increasingly preferred the 'in the ear' variety. Also, Oticon was strong in analogue technology, while its customers were moving towards a preference for digital technology.

Oticon began to change with the appointment of Lars Kolind as President of the company in 1988. He was only the third person to hold this post in the company's history. In his view the company had been sleeping for ten years and, in the next two years, he worked hard to turn the situation round. Cost-cutting measures were implemented. He pared the company down, cut staff and increased efficiency, and reduced the price of the company's hearing aids. By 1990 Oticon made a profit margin of 4% and was growing at 2% per year. However, the market was growing at 6%.

Kolind did not think the company had a future. He had been searching for sources of sustainable competitive advantage: 'I looked at technology, audiology. I looked at distribution strength. I looked at everything, but there was nothing we could do better than the competition.'

Nevertheless, he did not give up. Instead, Kolind resolved to 'think the unthinkable'. On New Year's Day 1990, the solution came to him, to design a new way of running a business that could be significantly more creative, faster, and more cost-effective than the big players, and that could compensate for Oticon's lack of technological excellence, capital, and general lack of resources.

Kolind realised that the industry was totally technology-focused, and that the main thrust was to make hearing aids smaller. He, on the other hand, thought this exclusive focus on technology was short-sighted. He believed Oticon was not in the hearing-aid business *per se*; they were in the business of 'making people smile; restoring the enjoyment of life that hearing impairment can destroy'. To this end, the company adopted a new mission statement:

To help people with hearing difficulties to live life as they wish, with the hearing they have.

To achieve this required knowledge of people's lifestyle and how hearing impairment affects this, and an understanding of the social stigma associated with hearing impairment and the use of hearing aids. He saw that Oticon could compete and thrive by providing a new holistic approach to customer care – by understanding customer lifestyle needs.

Kolind had the vision for Oticon's role in meeting customers' needs, but he still had to find a way of implementing it. He believed the key lay in the mix of expertise necessary to produce a hearing aid: micro-mechanics, microchip design, audiology, psychology, marketing, manufacturing, logistics, and all-round service capability. If Oticon were to move away from merely making hearing aids and instead provide a total package of support for people with hearing difficulties, it would have to develop a whole new concept in hearing-aid service. It would need to combine this expertise in a new way and add new areas of expertise to the organisation. In short, they would have to move from a technological orientation to a knowledge orientation. They had to build a learning organisation where experts would put aside their expertise and work as a team.

Kolind began by redefining his role as CEO. Instead of seeing himself as the captain that steers the ship, he saw himself as the architect who designs it rather than controls every action. Beginning with the head office, which comprised the finance, management, marketing and product development functions, the company decided to abandon the concept of a formal organisation. The reason for starting with the head office was simple – it was the source of the organisation's core competence. If it could be made to work effectively, the rest of the organisation might follow.

Formal structures, job descriptions and policies were seen as creating barriers to co-operation, innovation, and teamwork rather than facilitating it. Therefore, Oticon got rid of departments, departmental heads and other managerial and supervisory positions and even budgets. Job descriptions, titles and everything else which created barriers between members of staff were also eliminated. This took place in a region, Scandinavia, which has a long history of industrial and social democracy. Denmark in particular has led the way with the creation of a strong co-operative movement.

The concept of creating chaos out of organisation and expecting anything other than a disaster seems fraught with danger, and managers realised the potential problems of the direction Oticon was embarking on. Oticon's management was convinced that without a clear direction which everyone understood and believed in, the company would fragment and collapse into a disorientated mass of individuals, each pursuing their own course of action. To avoid this, the management and staff openly and at length debated the new strategy for the company, and the implications for how Oticon would be structured and would operate. Kolind commented that: 'the entire staff discussed not only where we were going but why we were doing so, ... and we also got as far as having everybody think that this fundamentally made a lot of sense . .. so there was consensus on the strategy'.

Oticon's values also meant that staff were treated as responsible adults, who would not overspend or misspend budgets, and who did not need to have their behaviour controlled by managers.

Oticon now operates on a project basis. Anyone can start a project, provided that person has the permission of one of five senior managers. Some projects are also initiated by management. The main criterion for acceptance is that a project is customer-focused. Anyone can join a project, provided that person has the agreement of the project leader. The basis idea, going back to the concept that Oticon treats everyone as an adult, is that it is the individual's responsibility to fill his or her day usefully. If people do not have anything to do, it is their job to find something useful to do – either by starting a project or by joining one.

Communication is at the centre of this new approach to work. Partly this is facilitated by computer. Each desk has a computer; these list all the projects on offer and the team leader's name along with the tasks involved. Usually the team leader will try to recruit the skills he or she needs, but individuals are also expected to seek out opportunities. There are no demarcation lines; if an R&D specialist or a secretary wants to work with a marketing group, then all they have to do is have a chat with the project leader in order to sign on.

The physical embodiment of this new 'structureless' structure is the workplace. Gone are individual offices, gone are corridors; all the walls were taken out and everyone works in the same open-plan office. Staff gather where they wish to work. Instead of individual offices, everyone has a little filing cabinet on wheels. Staff come in each morning, pick up their mobile office and trundle it to where they are working that day. Oticon is also a genuinely paperless office. All incoming mail is scanned into the computer and then shredded. Oticon wants staff to move around from project group to project group as work requires. It does not want this process hindered by staff having to transport masses of paper, as happens in most offices.

This requires everyone to have access to, and be able to use, a computer. However, the emphasis at Oticon is on face-to-face, informal communication

CASE STUDY *continued*

(e-mail is used but not extensively). This is why the office is littered with stand-up coffee bars to encourage small, informal (but short) meetings. Three or four people will meet to discuss an issue or exchange ideas and information and then return to where they are working that day and follow up ideas and suggestions. These are usually fed straight into the computer and are available to everybody else. There is also an expectation not only that all information is open to staff in this manner, but that staff actually want to know the information. Therefore, rather than putting up barriers or operating on a need-to-know basis, Oticon tries to be transparent about all aspects of its business, whether it be new products, staff salaries or finance in general. The view is that the more a person knows, the more valuable he or she is to the company.

Staff did not take to this radically new way of working overnight. They had not originally been recruited for their teamworking and project management skills, and some found it hard to come to terms with these new arrangements. Nor did they welcome the loss of routine and clear authority relationships, or find the resultant uncertainty easy to adjust to. This was especially the case with managers for whom the loss of their power base, information monopoly, and status symbols was difficult to accept. In addition, under the new arrangement, managers were reclassified as project leaders and had to compete for the best staff, rather than having their own dedicated subordinates.

Kolind anticipated resistance and sought to overcome this by involving staff in planning the transformation of the company. Small groups of staff

were selected to handle such projects as designing the new electronic infrastructure, locating a site for the new head office and selecting an architect. Also, all staff were given IT skills training. Indeed, they were all given a home PC and encouraged to identify their own training needs. Despite this, prior to the move to the new building, Kolind found it necessary to issue an ultimatum to staff: accept the new arrangements or leave.

However, the biggest boost to the new arrangements came when staff could see that they actually worked better than the old ones. Improvements were clear. Fifteen new products had been launched (twice as many as the company had had previously); new product lead time had been halved; the company's sales were growing at 20% per year, after a period of ten years without real growth; Oticon's market share increased from 8% in 1990 to 12% in 1993; and in 1995 Oticon launched the world's first digital hearing aid, the DigiFocus – in effect a four gram computer which fits in the ear but has the processing power of a desktop machine. Not only was this a technological breakthrough for which Oticon won a number of major innovation awards, but it also allowed Oticon to regain its position as one of the world's top three hearing aid producers.

Case study questions

1. What organisational and individual barriers might have blocked the acceptance of Kolind's new vision?

2. Why did Kolind believe that the organisation needed to change?

3. Draw a cultural web of Oticon before Kolind's arrival, and one three years later.

NOTES

1. See, for example, Gabarro (1987), Pfeffer (1992) and Rieple (1998).
2. Writers who have examined emotions and change include Weick (1995), Armenakis et al. (1995, 1996), Armenakis and Fredenberger (1995), Vince and Broussine (1996), Fineman (1993). A lot of the writing on the after-effects of mergers is also interesting in terms of looking at the emotions of uncer-

tainty; see, for example, Chatterjee et al. (1992), Nahavandi and Malekzadeh (1988) and David and Singh (1993).

3. The report fails to mention that this was while he was enrolled at Chicago's Loyola University.
4. For an example of an augmented version of Johnson's web, which also demonstrates the use of the cultural web to diagnose the extent of

change needed, see Heracleous and Langham (1996).

5. Pettigrew and Whipp (1991) discuss these issues comprehensively.

6. John Gabarro (1987) *The Dynamics of Taking Charge*, Harvard Business School Press, Boston, Mass., provides an interesting summary of some of these issues.

CHAPTER

14

Managing change

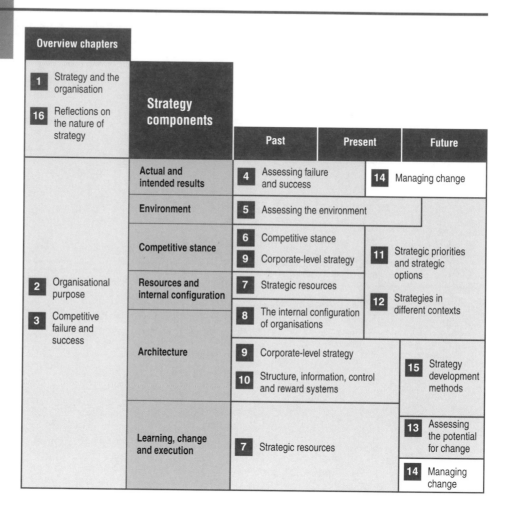

This chapter continues on from Chapter 13 to consider some of the practical activities that managers can carry out in order to bring about change – and we are talking about significant organisational change for the most part.

Given the need for change, one question is: Can it be managed? The answer is 'yes', but a qualified 'yes'. Change can be unpredictable – the outcome of a change programme may not be the one which the senior manager implementing it expects or wants. After all, as you have seen in Chapter 13, organisations are collections of thinking individuals, all of whom have some degree of power and wilfulness, and who may not agree with what a colleague is attempting to do.

Change can also be an expensive and difficult process – and the bigger the change programme, the more expensive and difficult it will be. Fewer problems will be experienced in less drastic change programmes, but even then, it is not something to be contemplated without care. If you wish to recommend change, then the ramifications and potential downsides must always be considered – as well as the potential upside of course.

The fact that it is such a problematic process is one of the reasons why a large consultancy business has grown up specifically to help managers contemplating organisational turnarounds, or trying to improve competitiveness. Some of these have been developed into specific methodologies, such as Business Process Re-engineering (BPR) or Total Quality (TQ) programmes. We look at these later in this chapter.

Learning objectives

By the end of this chapter you will understand:

- some of the factors which might make the intentional management of change more or less successful, including:
  - the role of leadership
  - the importance of power and politics
  - the role of particular activities, including changing people, restructuring, and managing symbols;
- the special nature of organisational turnarounds;
- where total quality and business process re-engineering might be appropriate strategies, and their dangers.

14.1 The role of leadership

◀ *The organisational ecology viewpoint of strategy development was discussed in Section 5.4.2.*

There are many influential writers on organisations who suggest that change cannot be managed deliberately. This includes classic research by for example Lieberson and O'Connor (1972) and writers adopting a Darwinian or ecological view on organisational survival and development, such as Hannan and Freeman (1977). These writers suggest that organisations are large and unwieldy bodies whose direction cannot be deliberately manipulated by a single person. However, their writings have since been subject to considerable discussion and criticism. Many other theorists, although acknowledging their views, believe that leaders can and do make a difference, even though the results of their actions may take time to appear and be hugely shaped by other factors such as the environment.

Writers who believe in the importance of the leadership role suggest that the activities of the person acting as the *change agent* is critical. The instigator of significant change is usually the chief executive or managing director. However, sometimes other individuals have successfully acted as change agents. Such 'champions' of change are known to share many of the characteristics of 'transformational' leaders (see Howell and Higgins, 1990).

Change agents need to be special people: both practical and visionary; detailed and broad; considerate and ruthless; team players and individualistic; empathetic and detached, as well as politically astute and resistant to stress. Buchanan and Boddy list fifteen competences which particularly characterise effective change agents (see Theoretical Perspective 14.1). These refer to change agents at all levels in an organisation, not just the chief executive. In all cases the change agent is likely to need a mixture of these different attributes, whose relative importance will vary according to the situation. Pettigrew and Whipp (1991: 145) suggest that leading change needs 'the use of varying leadership approaches over time; a combination of practices to address shifting competitive circumstances', although whether these multiple approaches can be carried out by the same person is debatable.

Although many of the change agent characteristics are likely to be relevant across a number of different organisational environments, some attributes are more important in some situations than others. The more senior the manager, the more important is the ability to address the structural, political or power elements of the change role. Lower level managers simply do not have to pay attention to this combination of elements to the same extent, even though they also need to use political skills to effect change.

What someone leading change does, and how successful he or she is, depends on

---

THEORETICAL PERSPECTIVE 14.1

The fifteen competences of change agents

Adapted from Buchanan and Boddy (1992)

Goals cluster

1. Sensitivity to changes in personnel, top management perceptions and market conditions, and how these impact the goals of the project in hand

2. Clarity in specifying goals and defining the achievable

3. Flexibility in responding to changes outside the control of the project manager

Roles cluster

4. Team building abilities to bring together stakeholders and develop effective groups and allocate responsibilities

5. Networking skills in establishing and maintaining contacts within and outside the organisation

6. Tolerance of ambiguity to be able to function comfortably and effectively in an uncertain environment

Communication cluster

7. Communication skills to be able to transmit effectively to colleagues and subordinates the need for change and challenges to individual tasks and responsibilities

8. Interpersonal skills, including selection, listening, collecting appropriate information, identifying the concerns of others and managing meetings

9. Personal enthusiasm in expressing plans and ideas

10. Stimulating motivation and commitment in others

Negotiation cluster

11. Selling plans and ideas to others; creating a desirable vision of the future

12. Negotiating with key players for resources or changes in procedures, or to resolve conflict

Managing up cluster

13. Political awareness in identifying coalitions, and in balancing goals and perceptions

14. Influencing skills to gain commitment to projects from potential sceptics or resisters

15. Helicopter view, to take broader view of priorities

three things: (1) their own attributes – personality, skills and experiences; (2) the cultural and strategic positioning of the organisation; and (3) the contingent relationship between these two groups of factors. Buchanan and Boddy (1992), along with Kotter (1995) and Pettigrew and Whipp (1991), indicate how important it is for change agents to understand the situation they are in. They need to have the necessary expertise to make correct decisions, to know when people are trying to pull the wool over their eyes, and to understand the art of what is possible.

In organisations which have cultures in which individuals make their own decisions, adhocracies for example, a change agent who attempts to manage the process by telling people what to do is likely to encounter considerable resistance. In this type of environment, the change agent perhaps needs to have a more laid-back style, paying attention to altering important symbols such as reward systems, or persuading his or her colleagues about the benefits of change. In contrast, in an organisation where control is bureaucratic and where decision making is centralised, a more dictatorial style might be effective – and even expected.

Bourgeois and Brodwin (1984) identified five distinct leadership approaches in the implementation of change. The first two imply top-down change, the latter three describe processes that increasingly involve people lower down the organisation. Whichever is appropriate depends on the nature of the situation:

◀ Cultural and strategic typologies were discussed in Sections 14.4, 10.5 and 13.5.

◀ The role of control and reward systems in implementing strategy were discussed in Chapter 10.

1. The strategic leader defines changes of strategy and then hands over to senior managers for implementation. Here, the strategic leader is primarily a thinker, not a doer, and may enlist the help of specialist change management consultants. The style of implementation tends to be coercive. It also requires the leader to be in possession of complete information, which is interpreted correctly.

2. The strategic leader decides major changes of strategy and also defines the specific changes to structure, personnel, systems, etc, that need to be made for the change to be implemented.

3. The strategic leader together with senior managers formulate proposed strategic changes. The aim is to reach a consensus on change strategies, which are then implemented by the managers. The style of implementation is collaborative, however this has its downside in that managers jockey for power in the absence of a clear political direction.

4. The strategic leader focuses on establishing a clear mission and purpose for the organisation and exerts influence towards the development of an appropriate culture. Decisions about change at the business and functional levels are decided and implemented by senior managers. This approach, however, requires making explicit what may be hidden and deeply buried cultural elements, and, as we discussed in Chapter 13, some elements of culture are notoriously difficult to manipulate.

5. Managers throughout the organisation are encouraged to participate in ideas for change. The strategic leader establishes a framework for evaluating these proposals, the implementation of which is undertaken by senior managers. There are obvious implications in this model for the direction the change process will take – its outcome is unpredictable.

In fact, the issue of who should instigate change is an interesting one. Beer et al. (1990) found that company-wide change programmes which were directed by top management were quite likely to fail. The ones that succeeded did not employ formal training or communication programmes, but instead started at the bottom of the organisation and were driven by individuals or task groups who championed specific facets of change. This research points up an interesting paradox of how, or indeed if, senior managers can direct non-directive change process. Beer et al.'s conclusion is that top management's role is to support but not interfere, to create a climate for change, specify the general direction of change but not specific solutions, and then to communicate the lessons of success and failure. To summarise, their recommendations are that top management should:

● Mobilise commitment to change through joint diagnosis and team efforts.

● Develop a shared vision for change – emanating from task teams.

● Foster consensus for the new vision – management giving support and encouragement.

● Replace managers who cannot work under the new system.

● Spread revitalisation to all departments, without pushing from the top – even allowing some reinventing of wheels.

● Institutionalise change through systems.

● Monitor and adjust strategies in response to problems.

14.2 The role of power and politics in strategic change

◄ We first looked at organisational power and politics in Section 1.2.2.

Having suitable leadership attributes and choosing appropriate behaviours are important elements in achieving change, but change agents will achieve very little unless they are powerful – in other words that they can get other people to do their bidding (Hardy, 1995). Of course this is a bit tautological – after all, power often comes from being an effective leader. But before we move on to consider in more detail in Section 14.3 some of the specific actions someone attempting to bring about change might take, we will briefly look at some of the things which may increase their power and influence, in what is usually a fairly difficult period for all concerned.

Change is easier to achieve from a senior management position – after all power resides in hierarchy. However, hierarchical position on its own is not usually enough; it has to be sanctioned by those lower down the hierarchy. People in fact *choose* to allow power to be ceded to others – something which Jean-Jacques Rousseau and David Ricardo in the eighteenth century called the 'consent of the governed'.[1] There have been many examples of lower level individuals refusing to accept the authority of nominally higher level managers – by industrial action, sabotage or working to rule. In some cases, resistance has been so effective that they have been able to effect the removal of the more senior manager (see Real-Life Application 14.1), and see also the Morgan Williams case study at the end of this chapter).

◄ You were first introduced to the concept of defensive behaviours in Section 13.4.

Although there is little research in this area, we suspect that change investigators are more likely to be ousted than managers operating in a period of relative stability. Anyone attempting significant change is likely to experience considerable hostility, fear, resistance and resentment, even within an organisation that on one level knows it *has* to change. This can manifest itself in defensive behaviours which

REAL-LIFE APPLICATION 14.1

Politics and conflict in Merck & Co

Merck is one of the largest pharmaceutical companies in the world. It is based in New Jersey. Over the years, the company's innovative research and development has created many blockbuster drugs, which have earned it millions of dollars in profits. Merck had sales of $24 billion in 1997 but knowledge capital estimated at $48 billion. Like all the other major pharmaceutical companies, however, Merck had been experiencing increased competitive pressures in the mid 1990s. R&D costs were increasing, and consumers had become more powerful in reducing the price of drugs. This reduced the profits of the large pharmaceutical companies.

For many years Merck was headed by Dr P. Roy Vagelos, a famous researcher who pioneered the development of many of its new drugs, and the company had dramatic success under his leadership. Vagelos, who planned to retire when he reached 65 in November 1994, decided to appoint Richard J. Markham as his successor as CEO over four other top managers who were senior to Markham, and just prior to this Markham was named president of Merck. Vagelos believed that Markham, a brilliant marketing expert, not a R&D scientist, was best suited to tailor the company's strategy to its new competitive environment. Describing him as an 'agent of change', Vagelos believed that he could alter the company's focus and give it a new way to compete in the 1990s and beyond. However, in July 1993 Merck announced that Markham had resigned.

It appears that Markham's new strategy, with its emphasis on marketing rather than research, had caused a high level of conflict in Merck's top management team. Merck's success had been built on its R&D

skills, and its scientists had hitherto been the acknowledged heroes of the corporation. In contrast, Markham's new strategy took both resources and prestige away from the scientists.

Markham had also come into conflict with Merck's top managers over his proposed $5 billion purchase of Medco, a company that specialised in supplying cheap generic drugs through mail order. In purchasing Medco, Merck would control a significant part of the distribution of generic drugs and have avenues for selling generic drugs of its own, a significant change in direction away from its focus on the premium drugs segment.

However, such a radical change in strategy was apparently too much for Merck's top management team, and even for his mentor, Vagelos, to take. It called for a new position for the company, one that would require leadership from cost-conscious marketing- and production-oriented managers, who would directly threaten the power and status of Merck's R&D-oriented top management team. These top managers had already lost out when Vagelos had made Markham his successor, and they resented Markham's quick rise to power in the company.

Top managers began to lobby against his new strategy and for a change in leadership. They formed a coalition to convince Vagelos that Merck would only suffer from the changes Markham was proposing and that the company should retain its R&D focus. With dissent in its top management team and facing criticism from the board of directors, the company decided to end its experiment. Markham resigned.

Adapted from: *Strategic Management: An Integrated Approach*, Charles Hill and Gareth Jones (1998: 470–1).

can minimise the chance of the change initiatives thriving (see Theoretical Perspective 14.2).

Managing politically and developing a power base is therefore a prerequisite for a change agent, where there is considerable doubt over the future strategy of the organisation and a number of potential routes for it to go. Political activity and jockeying for position increases; newly powerful people emerge, and the period is characterised by *un*certainty. Change can be a time of high risks and high rewards.

Perhaps the easiest way of getting change accepted is to clearly demonstrate that it works, through improvements in financial performance for example. This is a nice chicken and egg situation, however. Change can be resisted to such a point that any potential benefits cannot occur – such that the success which would have

THEORETICAL PERSPECTIVE 14.2

Defensive behaviour in organisations

Ashforth and Lee (1990) identify many defensive behaviours that can be put under the general heading of 'negative power' – political behaviours which block or inhibit the ability of others to achieve things. Many appear to be an attempt to minimise the personal risk of losing one's position or job during periods of uncertainty. They include:

● over-conforming – never bending rules or challenging senior managers

● buffing – rigorously documenting or fabricating documents

● passing the buck – attempting to reduce the chance of being blamed for a mistake

● playing dumb – pretending not to know something

● stalling – pretending to do something when not doing so

● playing safe – not taking risks

● justifying – providing excuses for behaviours

● scapegoating – blaming others

● misrepresenting – failing to tell the whole truth

● protecting 'turf' – defending one's position or staff, even when unjustified

● escalating commitment to losing courses of action – continuing to defend a mistake after it has become clear it is a mistake

Source: Ashforth and Lee (1990)

◀ *We introduced some of the factors which help to develop a power base in Section 1.2.2.*

allowed the change to be accepted does not happen. A nicely paradoxical self-fulfilling prophecy! So, given that this is a potential problem, other political skills become particularly important.

Many of these are the leadership characteristics and behaviours of change agents identified in Section 14.1. But power also comes from charisma, or what French and Raven (1959) termed referent power. Charisma is difficult to define or explain, but basically refers to the ability to inspire devotion – from both genders. Charisma inspires loyalty and following, and many of our most well-known business leaders have it. So do many politicians, Nelson Mandela being one well-known example. The use of charismatic behaviours, such as making people feel important and cherished, is arguably far more important during periods of uncertainty when people are generally feeling quite distressed.

Power can also be increased through specifically political activity. This is increasingly important the higher up the organisation you go. There are very few chief executives who are not skilled in the politics of management. By this, we mean the deliberate manipulation of factors in order to achieve an improved and more powerful position for themselves. A corollary to this is often a weakening of the position of others.

Power as you saw in Section 1.2.2 is derived from control over, or access to, information, knowledge, and resources, as well as the presenting of information on these sorts of issues in the best possible light through:

● The manipulation of facts and figures. This is not the same as lying, but instead relates to the presentation of data in such a way that they are shown positively.

● The manipulation of the image. This can relate to organisational data but also can be done by the individual, in respect of his or her appearance and in what they say and how they say it.

● The deliberate alteration of channels of communication, so that only chosen

THEORETICAL PERSPECTIVE 14.3

Managerial political actions for change

Activity areas	Mechanisms				Key problems
	Resources	Elites	Sub-systems	Symbolic	
Building the power base	Control of resources	Sponsorship by an elite	Alliance building	Building on legitimisation	Time required for building
	Acquisition of/ identification with expertise	Association with an elite	Team building		Perceived duality of ideas
	Acquisition of additional resources				Perceived as threat by existing elites
Overcoming resistance	Withdrawal of resources	Breakdown of division of elites	Foster momentum for change	Attack or remove legitimisation	Striking from too low a power base
	Use of counter intelligence information	Association with change agent	Sponsorship/ reward of change agents	Foster confusion conflict and questioning	Potentially destructive; need for rapid rebuilding
		Association with respected outsider			
Achieving compliance	Giving resources	Removal of resistant elites	Partial implementation and participation	Applause/reward Reassurance	Converting the body of the organisation
		Need for visible 'change hero'	Implementation of 'disciples'	Symbolic confirmation	Slipping back
			Support for 'young Turks'		

Adapted from Buchanan and Boddy (1992)

individuals get to hear about important pieces of information, or at least hear of them in time to do anything about them.

Buchanan and Boddy (1992) neatly summarise the political mechanisms of change in Theoretical Perspective 14.3. Many of these activities we discuss further in Section 14.3 below.

Figure 14.1 A change kaleidoscope

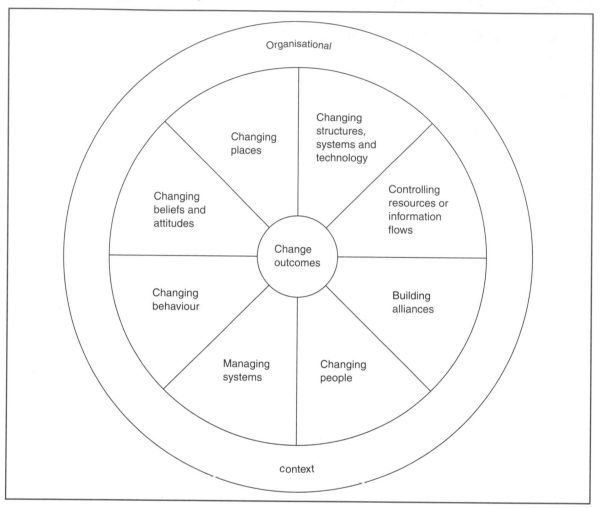

	14.3	**The practicalities of managing change**

We are now going to consider in more detail some of the policies and actions a senior manager may adopt to achieve change. These are summarised in a change kaleidoscope in Figure 14.1 (Balogun and Hope-Hailey, 1999).

14.3.1 Changing people

One of the most common ways of achieving change is by changing people. Personnel change at all levels of an organisation brings with it new ideas and visions of the future, new values and new energy. A company that is looking to change from a technical to a market-led culture may recruit more marketing people. Some companies have steadily increased the number of graduate trainees who have language skills as part of the process of becoming more international. The recruitment of top management from publicly quoted companies, to head up what were formerly government agencies in the old Soviet Union and elsewhere, has been an effort to instil a commercial culture into the public sector. Some research carried out in France (Courpasson, 1990) suggests that there seems to be a period of about two years during which the benefits of newcomers remain potent and they are still able to perceive things from a new angle. After this time they tend to go 'native' – a process which you will recognise has links with the coping cycle described in Section 13.3.

The appointment of a new chief executive, as we have already seen, is often the result of the perceived need by shareholders of companies to introduce change, perhaps because of poor performance by the newcomer's predecessor. And on their arrival, new chief executives are well known for replacing existing management with their own chosen employees.[2] This appears to be based on a number of different motives and has several potential benefits. Firstly, new managers bring similarly novel ways of perceiving things; they can bring with them new skills and experiences. However, appointing newcomers also has more overtly political aspects. Replacing existing managers at one stroke removes potential troublemakers who may resist the change efforts with people who are likely to be supporters of the new chief executive, and who can act as his or her agents – doing their bidding and acting as their eyes and ears. Existing managers can be marginalised from decision making and removed from the control of resources.

Group members can derive strength from each other. Whereas it is relatively easy to marginalise or remove a single unco-operative individual, it is much harder to deal with a group of unco-operative individuals. Because of this, change programmes are often accompanied by a radical shake-up in both organisational structures and personnel. The disbanding of existing relationship networks is one effective way to break up hostile group responses to change, in other words to 'divide and rule'. However, this policy does have some problems in that it also breaks up the communication channels which are necessary for organisations to be effective – and for change to be seen as successful.

Although these types of actions are common, and have a very long pedigree (they were recommended by Machiavelli in the fifteenth century), they have to be used with some care. Employees see colleagues and friends forced to leave, not always with a positive future to look forward to, although they may understand and even secretly support the reasons for their departure, a programme of redundancies or dismissals often adds considerably to the sense of uncertainty and stress which accompanies change. As a result, what sometimes happens during major change programmes, and it is also a well-known problem in mergers, is that many of the best people – those who are more marketable – depart as a result of the anxiety and discomfort that tends to be prevalent. This leaves the organisation with a skills shortage and an increasingly reduced ability to implement the change which has been introduced or achieve any improvements in performance. This process appears to underpin some of the 'vicious circle' or 'downward spiral' models of organisational decline.[3]

14.3.2 Building alliances

The above section for the most part is about controlling. Another option is enabling. An alternative, or in fact usually a concurrent, policy may be to promote or push forward in other ways selected staff from within the existing organisation – people who may have been held back in the previous regime. They can provide a particularly important symbol of the future, undertaking the change management tasks, and acting as a bridge between the old and the new, and between staff and senior management.

Allies can be an important source of personal support, as well as acting as agents of change in their own right. This type of political action probably needs to be targeted at important powerholders within the organisation – assuming that these can be identified, although allies in the outside world can also be very helpful if they can bring in resources or useful information. One problem encountered by newcomer chief executives attempting change is that they cannot know all the hidden bits of the organisation they have inherited – the relationships, the favours owed, the jealousies and dislikes. Most importantly of all, they do not know the hidden holders of power, who perhaps lack formal authority, but who have particular knowledge or understanding of how the informal organisation operates. These types of hidden structures can mean the difference between successful change and failure.

Finding good people to be on your side is therefore critical, and the new executive needs to quickly build a network of supporters around them. This can be done by picking out key people and cherishing them – through the use of charismatic behaviours, but also through rewarding them tangibly by, for example enhanced salaries, and also by promoting them to key posts, where they can control resources or important information.

14.3.3 Controlling resources or information flows

Rewarding key allies acts at the same time to remove unwanted individuals from key decision-making roles, and remove resources from their control. Both are important factors in achieving change, both symbolically and practically; it is very difficult to influence the direction of a firm if you no longer have decision-making powers within it or do not know what is going on. As suggested in 14.3.1, this can be achieved explicitly through demoting or dismissing people, but also more subtly by removing people from decision-making committees. Sidelining people – or giving them a 'sideways push' – is one well-established way of moving people away from key roles while at the same time allowing them to retain their job and dignity.

Controlling resources and information is an important element in successfully implementing change as these are key elements identified in theories of organisational power.[4] You may also wish to read Machiavelli's *The Prince*; he has some interesting points to make on these issues.

14.3.4 Changing structures, systems and technology

◀ We discussed the strategy/structure debate first in Section 10.3

An extension of the activities described in the previous section is the changing of the organisation's structure. Strategy and structure appear to become congruent over time, probably through an iterative process. But if a more radical and deliberate move is needed, then the structure has to be congruent with the new strategic direction. This often means a radical alteration to the organisation's locations, its reporting relationships, and its channels of communication and decision-making.

A restructuring is very likely to change the culture of an organisation. It modifies work and functional groupings by altering the way in which people communicate with each other. But reward, appraisal, monitoring, budgeting and control systems are also capable of changing people's beliefs and attitudes towards behaving in particular ways.

14.3.5 Changing places

A similar type of challenge to the status quo, which therefore results in a change in culture, can occur by deliberately moving people around the organisation. Subcultures develop in organisations around differences in function, role and level. Culture can, therefore, be changed by moving people from one function or role to another, thereby bringing people in contact with entirely different ways of seeing things. Japanese companies such as Sony are well known for shuffling people frequently from one function to another, partly to transfer learning, but also to develop innovative new products which require the challenging of established assumptions. Many of the American and European companies described in this book are doing the same.

14.3.6 Changing beliefs and attitudes

Beliefs form through observation, interaction, participation and communication. Applying these concepts in practice can change the beliefs and attitudes of members of an organisation. Implementing, for example, quality circles achieves the purpose of improving the quality of products or services, but also of changing people's beliefs and attitudes towards quality. Formal communication can help to implant and reinforce new attitudes to the organisation and its activities; management education is another way that initiatives towards improved quality and customer service, for example, can be implemented. Training programmes aimed at socialisation into new values and beliefs can also be helpful – but tend to be a long-term solution.

British Airways spent a small fortune on training its staff in customer care, marketing, and human resource management policies which emphasised empowerment and local autonomy of decision-making. Their training programme was a fundamental element in their cultural change programme, and continued over many years. British Airways is often held up as an example of one of the few companies to have successfully achieved a major cultural change, but it took a very long time, and considerable expense and top management support and encouragement (Real-Life Application 14.2).

14.3.7 Changing behaviour

Although culture change is not easily achieved through introducing new techniques or methods, some behavioural change can lead to changes in beliefs and attitudes. Training in new skills, for example, is likely to change people's beliefs

REAL-LIFE APPLICATION 14.2

Cultural change in British Airways

In 1981, British Airways lost almost £500,000. Passengers had horror stories of their experiences with the airline. When the announcement was made by the British government that the firm was to be privatised, *The Financial Times* newspaper commented that only masochists would buy the stock.

Five years later, however, BA's profits were the highest in the industry, 94% of its employees bought stock in 1987 when the firm went public, and passengers were commenting on how improved the service was. With essentially the same workforce, flying largely the same routes, and using the same technology, British Airways has become one of the world's leading airlines. This came about because of what has been described as the 'cultural revolution' engineered by the airline's chairman and chief executive, Lord King, and Sir Colin Marshall.

After deciding that they were in the service business rather than the transportation business, virtually the entire 37,000 person workforce was put through a two-day culture change training programme entitled 'Putting People First'. Almost all of the 1,400 managers went through a five-day version entitled 'Managing People First'. What separated this programme from most normal management training sessions was its magnitude, the consistency with which it was applied throughout the organisation, and the support of top management.

The programme's emphasis was on instilling a new culture, but this ran alongside some other changes. An appraisal scheme was instigated that measured not only what managers did but how they did it, and a new compensation programme was brought in which paid bonuses of up to 20% of salary based on how managers behaved.

One of the key areas for emphasis was to ensure that staff understood that they were in a highly competitive situation, in which their success was based on the quality of service they offered customers. A fundamental part of this was expecting staff to use their initiative, and not be bound by an inflexible rule-book.

Source: Based on Tushman and O'Reilly (1996).

about their own capabilities. Making them carry out another person's job for a short time may make them more aware of the wider implications of what they do, and what the organisation as a whole is capable of.

14.3.8 Managing symbols

One common and relatively easy way of indicating that change is on the cards is to change some of the most important organisational symbols (see Real-Life Application 14.3). Changes to a firm's reward system, so that employees are rewarded for the amounts of profits they make rather than just for turning up at work, is an important symbol that making money is important. Promoting a previously lowly marketing manager to a key committee is a symbol that customer awareness and product differentiation strategies are becoming more important. A corollary is likely to be a symbolic loss of power for others – accountants for example. I think you can imagine how they might react!

One term that you will often see for a major strategic, cultural and organisational change programme is a **turnaround**, used when a company's performance is turned from declining or poor to improving and successful.

REAL-LIFE APPLICATION 14.3

Symbolic changes at Siemens

In the mid-1990s, Siemens, the 150-year-old German conglomerate, faced increased competition and needed to improve its speed of response and innovation. Heinrich von Pierer, Siemens' CEO, responded by challenging some of the firm's deeply-held beliefs. He started talking of 'tearing down barriers within the company', creating a 'climate for honest open dialogue' and 'optimising entire process chains', which was a contrast to the firm's normal language. He also introduced a company-wide process improvement programme called TOP ('time-optimised processes') which aimed to improve growth, profitability and innovation. But whereas in the old days everything would have been organised centrally, each business unit was now responsible for bringing about its own change.

Von Pierer also sought a clearer market orientation for the company's R&D, to bring together technology push and market pull approaches. Previously Siemens had not particularly looked elsewhere for guidance, but it now started to benchmark itself against its competi-

tors, and studied retailers and financial services to improve its own logistics and customer service. Von Pierer put more emphasis on profitability, creating some 250 independent and entrepreneurial business units. Employees were to be paid by results rather than by seniority, and staff were expected to assess their superiors as well as being assessed by them. Siemens also planned to introduce a stock-options scheme for its directors – a relative novelty in Germany. Senior management positions are now only open to those with international experience.

There are signs that the company's performance has improved. Over the past few years Siemens has seen productivity gains of up to 10% – DM 30 billion and increased profits. Its market shares have improved in most areas of its business. Inventions are up 50%, and 70% of its products are less than five years old, compared with 50% before the programme started.

14.4 Organisational turnarounds

◄ We looked at some of the factors which give rise to the need for organisational turnarounds in Section 12.4.4.

◄ We first discussed bounded decision-making, and enacted environments in Chapter 1. We also looked at culture, resources and competences – all factors which can influence an organisation's ability to change – in Chapters 7 and 8.

The management of corporate turnarounds[5] has spawned an entire industry of consultants and books recommending ways in which they should be carried out.[6] The question therefore is: are they any different from other types of change programme? The answer is probably yes – mainly because of the scale of changes and disruption likely to be caused. Corporate turnarounds are needed when an industry comes to the end of its life-cycle, and/or when a company's previous management have failed to spot changes in the firm's competitive environment so that its performance declines substantially in relation to its competitors. This is not as uncommon as one might hope – after all, if you were managing a large firm, you would think that maybe its performance is one of the major things that you might be concerned about. However, for all the reasons we have discussed previously, an organisation's managers are sometimes unable to make the changes themselves.

Some writers[7] on declining firms think that they begin their slide into problems up to ten years before they finally fail – through bankruptcy, or take-over. Causes range from small management teams, which leads to impoverished decision-making, autocratic management, and lack of consultation, all of which are often exacerbated by stress and the departure of the most competent managers. As with the factors which cause strategic slip, organisations in crisis appear to have a number of common elements (Table 14.1).

By the time the organisation reaches crisis point, a newcomer – a new chief executive, or perhaps a specialist corporate 'doctor' – a consultant specialising in turnarounds, may need to be brought in. This can happen several times over an organisation's life (Real-Life Application 14.4).

Table 14.1   Cases of organisational crises

Causes	Effects
Management blinded by previous success	Entrapment and self-deception
Loss of vision	Lack of clear goals
Small teams Stress	Impoverished decision-making
Autocratic management 'Tucked-away' manager	Lack of consultation of sources of expertise within the organisation, lack of empowerment and commitment
'Cronyism'	Decisions based on politics rather than 'rational' competitive factors
Departure of most able staff	Loss of key skills
Hierarchy orientation	Outdated structures and poor communication Excess bureaucracy and administrative procedures
Concern for consensus and fear of conflict	Desire for acceptance leads to group think and impoverished decision-making Lack of creativity
Tolerance of incompetence[8]	Excess personnel

REAL-LIFE APPLICATION 14.4

Turnaround management at Apple

Over the course of Apple's history it has experienced a number of competitive cycles. IBM PCs emerged, Microsoft's Windows operating system imitated Apple's previously unique functionality, and the basis of competition shifted to cost, quality and efficiency. Apple Computers' board of directors replaced the founder, Steve Jobs and subsequently his successor, John Sculley as CEO. Sculley was replaced by Michael Spindler, who was seen as having the operational skills needed to run the company in a mature market. Spindler's task was to emphasise efficiencies and lower margins and reshape Apple to compete in its new market environment. However, Apple's performance stagnated and its board chose a turnaround expert, Gil Amelio, to finish what even Spindler could not do. Eventually, Jobs returned as CEO to refocus Apple's product line and launch the successful iMac line.

Source: Tushman and O'Reilly (1996).

This implies that there are particular turnaround management competences which are transferable across firms and industries, and this may be true – to some extent. However, specialist turnaround agents usually concentrate on a small number of industries. Hanson Industries in its heyday in the 1980s was a corporate turnaround specialist, who concentrated on a small number of low-tech industries in which they could apply some generic skills.

Some of the major components of the management of a turnaround are summarised in Table 14.2.

Table 14.2   Turnaround management

Leadership characteristics	Organisational outcomes
Envisioning	New strategic direction
Accessing finance; financial management skills/tight control	Competitive repositioning Space for survival, restructuring debt Productivity improvements
Bias for action/decisiveness	Energised organisation
Ruthlessness	Organisational restructuring Retrenchment – focusing on cost control and personnel reduction
Communicating, visibility and contact Symbolic action (such as eliminating perks, public recognition, promoting individuals and departments, and using the metaphor of a sick patient)	Values and culture change, increased motivation

You will see that many of these activities are similar to those for less-radical change programmes. However, perhaps one of the most important of the tasks required in a turnaround is to obtain financing – or the promise of it. The crisis

---

REAL-LIFE APPLICATION 14.5

The even newer IBM

The business press has trumpeted that the saving of a national icon is the biggest achievement of Louis V. Gerstner Jr., but it is likely that business historians will record the leadership skill he demonstrated in resurrecting the company as a mere preamble to the way he harnessed the technology power of IBM to help propel world commerce to a new economy – e-business. That should prove to be the broader achievement that goes beyond his stated intent in joining the firm. 'When I came to IBM [as chairman and CEO] in 1993, frankly my fondest wish was for the company to return to its former position of leadership'.

Under Gerstner, IBM already has made its mark with the e-business strategy that evolved from its network-computing push of 1995. From a standing start, IBM turned itself into a multibillion-dollar e-business, transforming core business processes, such as the way it sells and the way it buys. Nearly $20 billion of the company's revenue – about 25% of the total – is related to the Internet. In December 1998 alone, IBM bought more than $600 million in goods and services over the Internet. By streamlining procurement processes and taking them to the Web, IBM says it will save $240 mil-

lion in 1999. In 1998 more than 14 million customer questions and problems were resolved via online support systems, avoiding more than £300 million in call-centre and field-specialist support costs.

In seeking a position of leadership for IBM, Gerstner is not talking about the kind of leadership IBM enjoyed in the past – 'not leadership based on proprietary technology that kind of locked customers in'. Yet six years ago when Gerstner, then CEO at RJR Nabisco Inc., was tapped to succeed John Akers at IBM, some analysts were not only surprised but also critical of the selection. They anticipated a technologist, but this was a professional manager who began his life's work in 1965 at McKinsey's management consultants, and who served in senior management at American Express for 11 years.

Gerstner proceeded to prove he was exactly what was needed to transform the stumbling computer company into a technology and services firm. His first step was to reverse a strategy of dismantling that his predecessor John F. Akers had begun to implement. Instead of buying into the argument that creating 'Baby Blues' (Akers had proposed more than 10) was the only route to profitability, efficiency, and shareholder value, Gerstner recognized the greater value in keeping it whole. This was a wellfounded wager. It was backed up by the whole experience of having been an IBM customer trying to implement an aggressive information technology strategy during his time at American Express. 'I joined IBM with the mindset of a customer' is one of Gerstner's favorite expressions.

With a focus on keeping IBM whole, Gerstner began the process of doing something about the culture he inherited, which some observers described as a troubling replay of a Soviet-style bureaucracy. The basic issue was a culture that had been inbred for 40 years and sustained by success, says Jones. 'If you have a practice of hiring [candidates] out of school, with no work experience, over time the result becomes a workforce with a very unique set of business practices'. Gerstner implemented a practice of tough love and setting policies in place to encourage desired behaviour. One is an increased investment in performance-based pay programmes. For example, since 1994 IBM has increased its variable pay pool (a pool of cash distributed to employees based on the performance of the company, each business unit, and each individual employee) by more than 60% to $1.6 billion in 1998. Stock options are also being emphasized. IBM nearly doubled the number of employees who were granted

stock options in 1996, doubled that number again in 1997, and then tripled it in 1998.

Line management is forced to involve itself with what it once considered a lot of remote, arcane technical issues. In a networked world, issues of business strategy – things like speed, competitiveness, cycle time, or globalization are so interconnected with technical issues that it really doesn't make sense to discuss them separately. However, despite many encouraging signs, Gerstner believes two serious challenges remain. The first is that IBM's transformation is nowhere near complete. 'We've sustained it for more than six years now, and that's good. But in any turnaround there's the very natural tendency to look around one day, take a deep breath, and tell yourself you're out of the wood. That's a very dangerous time.' The second challenge Gerstner sees is in executing IBM's Internet strategy. 'We stuck our necks out and said that the Net would be used for transactions of all kinds – commerce, of course, but also education, government services, supply-chain management, health-care delivery. Now everything is an 'e-' this and an 'e-' that. Our challenge now is to capitalize on this mind-share and convert it into hardware and software sales and services engagements.'

Adapted from Teresko (1999)

requires fast and radical changes without the resources available in times of growth. Obtaining finance requires some considerable selling skills, and credibility with bankers and investors. Another difficult task is to manage the balance between the old business, which needs to be maintained and milked as far as possible, and the move into new business areas. This is not easy, but it can be done (Real-Life Application 14.5).

Now we move on to look at a couple of particular types of change programmes which address the need to alter specific elements of the organisation's value chain or architecture. These change programmes have been associated with specialised methodologies, and are often implemented by outsiders – management consultants.

14.5   Value chain enhancement options

Total Quality (TQ) and Business Process Re-engineering (BPR) are ways of enhancing an organisation's value chain, and enabling it to deliver better levels of service and output quality at lower cost. They are probably most appropriate to mature businesses with established routines, but can in theory be applied in any context. Both have been used in the public as well as the private sector.

There are considerable similarities between TQ and BPR. Both are ways of getting an organisation to review its processes, examine how well they are enabling it to add value and reformulate or even eliminate them. Total Quality is more concerned with improving the way that existing tasks operate, so as to make the organisation's current value chain work better. Business Process Re-engineering is intended to initiate more sweeping and fundamental changes to the value chain, probably involving the elimination of some tasks. Both may involve major changes to an organisation's routines and culture, substantial commitments of management time and often large investments in external consultants to aid the process.

Total Quality in the 1980s and BPR in the 1990s were 'hyped' as cures for all organisational ills. This persuaded some managers to adopt them, with high expectations, but without taking sufficient account of the specific issues of effectiveness and acceptability in their particular organisations. In practice, both types of programme have a high failure rate – of the order of 50–70%. This has led to a backlash of criticism of the two techniques as being better at generating fee income for consultants than they are at generating improvement for their clients.

The truth is probably somewhere between the two extremes. Neither TQ nor BPR is appropriate for every organisation. Both have led to major improvements in some organisations that have benefited from top management commitment, planned the implementation carefully and let the programmes run long enough to overcome initial setbacks and attain their full effect. Like all major programmes involving structural and cultural change, TQ and BPR will not succeed without this commitment or patience, and may fail anyway if they run foul of an entrenched culture, or if they upset powerful stakeholders.

14.5.1 Total quality

Sometimes known as Total Quality Management (TQM), Total Quality Planning (TQP) or Total Quality Control (TQC), Total Quality is commonly associated with Japanese organisations. In fact, it was 'invented' by American theorists W. Edwards Deming and J. Juran, who failed to interest companies in their own country in the technique but found a readier audience in Japan as it sought a way of rebuilding itself after the Second World War. Japanese firms adopted and refined the ideas during the 1960s. TQ was then re-exported to the USA and Europe after Japanese imports started to penetrate there during the 1970s. Deming and Juran, along with influential TQ proponents, Philip Crosby and Avi Feigenbaum,[9] became sought-after consultants.

Total Quality, as it is commonly understood, combines concepts derived from all these authors. At its heart is a particular conception of what constitutes 'quality'. For the purposes of a Total Quality programme, a product or service is of good quality if it meets a customer's requirements in terms of size, weight, functionality, reliability, lead time for delivery, price and any other attributes that the customer may think are important. For a customer looking for a car that will be driven mainly on short trips in crowded city centres, any small car is a 'good quality' car as long as it is weatherproof, reliable, manoeuvrable and cheap to run. A large luxury saloon car, although it is more comfortable and contains more sophisticated electronics, is not really of higher quality for this group of customers – it will be too large and it will cost too much to purchase and to run. Features in excess of the customer's requirements – such as the luxurious 'extras' in the large car in our example, or delivery times that are faster than a customer actually wants – are not needed and so the resources needed to design and produce them can be diverted to other uses.

Quality is measured from the point of view of the customer, and most processes in a firm have several customers, some external (the people who order and use the product) and some internal – the people that use the physical and information outputs of the process. For example, for most firms that sell to other businesses, the sales department has at least two sets of external customers: (i) the end-users, who want good, reliable products and services, and (ii) the purchasing staff, who want keen prices and reliable ordering and delivery procedures. Its internal customers may include: the production staff, who need reliable information on what they must produce and how to package it; the financial staff, who need to know what prices and payment terms have been agreed; and distribution staff, who need to know whether their usual lorry will fit into the customer's depot. Quality is achieved, at each stage of the value chain, by satisfying each of these customers. Internal customers must be satisfied so that they are able to satisfy their external customers in their turn.

Most Total Quality theorists believe that an organisation should strive to meet customer requirements 100% of the time – that it should aim for zero defects. They believe that the cost of failing to achieve zero defects – rather confusingly termed 'the cost of quality' – is invariably greater than the cost of the systems needed to sustain that level of performance. The cost of quality includes wastage from low-grade output, the costs of putting errors right before or after delivery, price reductions needed to compensate dissatisfied customers and the value of business lost when dissatisfied customers turn to other suppliers and warn potential customers about their bad experiences. In a mass market, they point out, even a small proportion of defective products, say 1%, can translate into a large number of dissatisfied customers and a substantial cost of quality.

There are several weapons that organisations can use to direct themselves towards zero defects. In a manufacturing operation, statistical process control techniques[10] can be introduced, to give an early warning of when a production process is in danger of moving 'out of control' and producing output that does not meet the agreed production specification. More generally, TQ theory advocates that firms should not content themselves with fixing quality problems one by one as they arise. Instead, they should analyse the problems in depth to establish their root cause, which can then be fixed to make sure that the problem does not recur. This sometimes requires substantial changes to the organisation's processes and systems.

Two philosophies are central to this idea of Total Quality:

- 'Kaizen', a Japanese term meaning 'continuous improvement'. This is the notion that a firm should never be satisfied with its existing quality levels, but should always be seeking further improvements to bring each of its processes closer to the goal of zero defects.

- Under TQ an organisation should actively seek ideas for improvement from everywhere in the organisation. Often this happens in the framework of 'quality circles' where employees involved in a process, either as producer or consumer, meet regularly to discuss ways of improving it. For this to work, managers must be open to criticism of existing practices and to suggestions for improving them from more junior employees.

The introduction of total quality into an organisation requires a number of phases. Typically, some time will be spent estimating the cost of quality, as a way of convincing the people involved that the effort of implementing TQ is worth-while. Quality circles or similar discussion forums will be set up, which makes it necessary to train some employees in group facilitation techniques, so that they can lead the discussions. All participants in these groups need to be trained in a variety of analytical techniques that help them to analyse and prioritise quality problems. Finally, some training is often needed for the firm's managers to help them to learn how to coach their employees to produce workable suggestions and how they themselves should respond to them and champion them.

It can be difficult to achieve the major cultural change that is often required if a firm is to implement total quality effectively (Grant et al., 1994). This is particu-larly the case if the existing culture is mechanistic and the structure and architec-ture are attuned to pushing instructions from the top of the hierarchy to the bottom, rather than suggestions from the base of the hierarchy upwards.

14.5.2 Business process re-engineering

BPR has a shorter history than TQ – it dates from a 1990 *Harvard Business Review* article by Michael Hammer, entitled 'Re-engineering work – don't automate, oblit-erate!'. This started from the premise that computerising existing processes wasted the opportunity, provided by modern IT, to remodel business processes from scratch. By rethinking processes entirely, unnecessary steps and wasteful duplica-tions of effort between departments could be eliminated. This should be done in one radical swoop, rather than incrementally, as the Kaizen approach of TQ implies.

Hammer and his followers[11] suggest that organisations should organise around outcomes, not tasks. For example, one process may require the procurement of inputs and the payment of their suppliers. This may at present be organised into a number of tasks, with one department finding suppliers and negotiating terms, another issuing purchase orders, another receiving deliveries and a fourth process-ing supplier invoices. However, not all these tasks may be needed for the desired outcomes – a steady supply of goods from a (reasonably) happy group of suppliers – and even if they are all needed, they may not need to be divided between differ-ent people. During a re-engineering programme, people are invited to decide what a process is intended to *achieve*, and then to question existing assumptions about the tasks and who performs them.

Other principles of re-engineering are to avoid the same data being keyed in more than once (since this gives scope for error) and to eliminate tasks involving just the keying in and checking of data created by others. It is better to give the people who use the outputs from a process the responsibility for carrying it out and the authority to take the necessary decisions. They may use expert systems to help them take complex decisions without reference to higher authority. So, for example, the system for ordering inputs can be linked to the factory scheduling system, so that the people who use the material can be made responsible for the accuracy of the data and the effectiveness of the schedules.

A BPR change programme typically involves a re-engineering project team, drawn from throughout the organisation, which looks at a specific definable process – Hammer and Champy (1993) believe that no organisation can handle more than one of these processes at a time. The team maps the people and tasks currently involved and develops ideas for redesigning them. They are supported by a re-engineering champion or 'Czar' whose role is to help the team to sell its proposals to the managers and staff involved.

Hammer and Champy claim that a number of benefits emerge from a successful re-engineering programme. Work that was formerly divided between different functions is brought back together to be carried out by 'process teams' who are able to take a more holistic view of tasks and their consequences. The people who work in those teams benefit from performing more interesting, multi-dimensional work rather than repetitive specialist tasks, and from being empowered to take decisions. These changes, Hammer and Champy argue, necessitate other changes in the way people are trained and managed. Training needs to be replaced by more broadly based education, so that people can handle the wider variety of tasks and challenges. Structures become flatter. These empowered and better-qualified employees need, and will tolerate, less supervision. For their managers, coaching and leadership skills become more important than financial and administrative ones. For all concerned, the management of processes leads to a greater orientation on the customer.

Business Process Re-engineering has been reported as giving spectacularly good results in certain cases, and it still boasts many ardent proponents.[12] However, these days, they are outnumbered by its critics, and even BPR's greatest enthusiasts admit that a substantial number of re-engineering projects fail.[13] Hammer himself has gone on record as admitting that he underestimated the human problems involved in implementing BPR which, like TQ, implies a substantial change in culture if it is to succeed. The degree of change, and the danger of damage is exceptionally high with BPR, which one commentator has compared to 'chemotherapy – a radical treatment that destroys a lot along the way'.[14] Apart from the normal problems entailed by radical organisational change, BPR has suffered because many managers have viewed it as a way of eliminating jobs and people, rather than improving work processes.[15] This understandably can lead people involved in re-engineering teams to be defensive, and to avoid proposals that might threaten their own jobs.

Even when changes are identified and implemented as a result of a BPR programme, there may be unforeseen problems. Some firms have reduced their head-count greatly, only to be caught out by an unexpected upsurge in demand (Bernstein, 1998). One study has found that, although some staff indeed find that their re-engineered jobs are more rewarding, they also find them more stressful and intensive, and that managers, rather than acting as coaches, maintain pressure for improvements in productivity and financial performance (Knights and McCabe, 1998).

14.6 | Summary

This chapter has introduced you to some of the issues to do with the implementation of strategic and organisational change. Following on from Chapter 13 which outlines some of the organisational and individual responses to change, we have examined some of the ways in which change might be managed, or managed more effectively. This might be through:

- the use of leadership skills. We looked at some of the personality characteristics and attributes which agents of change may need to have, given different organisational and environmental contingencies.

- developing an adequate power base. Leadership skills are clearly important here too, as is charisma in dealing with hostile or defensive responses from individuals who feel threatened by the change. But we also looked at some of the other important power sources during periods of change, such as having allies in place to do one's bidding, removing those individuals who are likely to be unsupportive, and controlling information and resources.

We then looked at some of the practicalities of managing change through:

- changing people – promoting some, and removing or marginalising others;
- building alliances with powerful people who are supportive of the new direction, and who can bring resources and expertise;
- controlling information flows and resource allocation. This is often achieved by changing the organisation's structure and formal channels of decision-making and communication;
- changing systems, processes and technology. This forces people to face up to doing things in a different way, and can change behaviour and culture as a result;
- training and socialisation processes. This can be achieved through training programmes which are designed to make people aware of different approaches to work and through improving skills and competences in new areas. Change can also be achieved by the movement of staff around the organisation so that they encounter different ways of approaching things, and learn more about the concerns of people in different functional areas.
- managing symbolically, for example by:
  - changing the ways in which people are rewarded
  - a senior manager behaving visibly differently
  - selectively promoting or enhancing certain roles.

We also discussed the special case of organisational turnarounds, and looked at where total quality and business process re-engineering might be appropriate strategies, and their dangers.

Typical Questions

We conclude this chapter by reviewing some of the questions you are likely to be asked about strategic change, and how you can use the theory in this chapter to answer them.

1. *How well was the change programme managed?*

You will want to use the cultural web (Section 13.4.2) to identify the main features of the culture and see whether the change programme tried to focus on just one or two, such as structure and control systems, and neglected the rest, or whether it attempted to alter a whole range of organisational factors. You will also want to assess whether the change agent had the right characteristics (Theoretical Perspective 14.1), and whether he or she did the right things (given the context) and used the appropriate range of behaviours at their disposal (Sections 14.1, 14.3). You may want to conclude by reviewing how successful the programme turned out to be (see below).

2. *How successful was the change programme?*

You may want to use the cultural web (13.4.2) as a framework to review which elements of the culture have genuinely changed. You may also want to look back to the motives for change to determine how well the programme has addressed the issues that originally provoked it. You can review how well the obstacles to change have been overcome. But don't forget that a question like this is about *performance* (Chapter 4). Have sales and profits started to rise, or at least stopped falling? Have customers commented favourably on the organisation since the change?

Questions for discussion

1. There are a number of consultants who promise that they can turn around a failing company. Evaluate the pros and cons of bringing in such a person.

2. What might be the effects if an organisation's chief executive decides to promote its design director to main board level from his or her previous position within the marketing department?

3. How would you approach the management of change in an international retailer whose performance has declined significantly thanks to competition from Internet-based firms?

4. 'The organisation's paradigm cannot be changed deliberately.' Discuss.

Morgan Williams Ltd

Adapted from Morgan Williams plc, case study written by Alison Rieple and published by European Case Clearing House, Cranfield.

Organisation background

Morgan Williams Ltd is a British company whose sales are largely European based. Its principal products are the sale and installation of specialist electrical and ground-breaking equipment, mainly to the manufacturing and construction industries. The company in its present form is the result of a merger of two privately owned British companies. The logic behind the merger was that the joint organisation would benefit from synergy to be obtained by the companies combining their sales networks, and smoothing out of their dependence on cyclical market or environmental circumstances (both companies' sales were heavily dependent on different elements of the weather). It was also anticipated that customers would benefit from the convenience of depots which could provide the complete range of both companies' products.

Williams Ltd had been in existence for over 100 years. Very few new products had been developed in recent times. The company's products were industry standards, and had very strong brand images within their particular market place. The company was heavily unionised and bureaucratic, and staff were comparatively well paid. The company may not have been profitable for several years prior to the merger.

Morgan Ltd, in contrast, was formed in the 1970s. The entrepreneur who had founded the company had built it up from very small beginnings to a substantial size until he sold the company and retired. It had been highly profitable for many years and at the forefront of developments of innovative products or product applications. However, in recent years competitors had entered their market place providing similar products at reduced prices, which had started to erode margins, and innovation had declined. The culture of the company was said to be highly entrepreneurial and unbureaucratic, albeit paternalistic. One perception of the company was that the owner allowed his staff to sell anything as long as it was profitable. Large cars and grandiose job titles substituted for large salaries. In general, the company was said to be like a large family, with a strong sense of loyalty and commitment to the owner.

Almost immediately following the owner's sale of Morgan, the company was merged with Williams. Despite the hopes for synergistic benefits, the post-merger period proved exceptionally problematic. Over 800 different staff grades were identified in the combined company. Managers from the two companies who were doing broadly comparable jobs would find themselves receiving wildly different salaries and benefits. As a result there was considerable dissatisfaction over the unfairness of these practices.

The intended synergies had also been hard to achieve. Contrary to expectations the companies' product and market characteristics had turned out to be very different, and the staff from each side in practice had little involvement with the other's products. Each company's employees found it hard to understand the other's point of view or way of working. In some areas there was literally no communication, let alone co-operation, between the two camps and the company of the time was described as a hot-bed of political activity and ill-will.

The change programme

As a result of these evident problems a new chief executive, Paul Wilson, was appointed. His previous work experience was as managing director of a highly successful subsidiary of a large British PLC. He had also had experience of company restructurings and acquisitions. Paul Wilson regarded his brief as to 'normalise' the company – 'It needed someone to impose some sense on to it, to give it a national identity, and to stamp out the factions which were going off all over the place.' He was welcomed with open arms as someone who could sort out the mess, and who had a strong vision of what the company could become in the future.

591

CASE STUDY *continued*

In order to help him to achieve this he appointed a new senior team: a marketing director, a new recruit but someone with whom he had worked closely in his previous company; an operations director, who had previously been a sales director in Williams, where he had worked for 25 years; another operations director who had been a regional director in Morgan, again having spent nearly all his career there; a human resources director who was a new appointment brought in from a major PLC; and a finance director, who had worked in Morgan Williams since the merger, having been involved in setting it up. He was a major shareholder in the company.

Paul Wilson also instituted a sweeping programme of changes to the staff, systems and structure of the organisation. Staff salaries and benefits were rationalised, and performance-related pay and share options schemes were introduced. The existing structure was dismantled. Two regions under the direction of two operations directors were set up to replace the six which had existed previously in both companies. After a short time, this structure was also disbanded, and the ex-Williams' operations director was dismissed. Ten area managers were appointed to oversee the 30 depots, all of whom reported to the remaining operations director.

Depots were relocated or extended to allow them to provide the complete range of products, and to improve facilities. Large sums were spent on training staff to deal with the combined product ranges and to encourage commitment to the new company. New product development was encouraged and new markets opened up in Eastern Europe. Paul Wilson believed that products which were obsolete in the UK still had some potential there.

Employees who were unwilling or unable to accept the new terms, or who appeared unlikely to help the company to move forward, were made redundant or dismissed – Paul Wilson generally regarded personnel standards as very low. Many of the company's managers were replaced by new appointments, some of whom came from the chief executive's previous company. At one point this group comprised 30% of senior managers. Although he had not known all of them personally, he knew *of* them. They were thus a 'known quantity', with successful previous track records and generally higher academic qualifications than the Morgan Williams' managers. Some of the most important managers in Morgan Williams, such as the marketing director and the head of one of the product development divisions, came from this source.

Paul Wilson believed that these changes were essential. The quality of existing staff and the political factions which existed in the company on his arrival meant that he felt he needed to remove those who were backward looking or whose values were out of line with those he thought necessary for competitive success in the future.

However, although this basis for selection was accepted by many to be a necessary policy given the situation, many of the new appointments were also considered less competent than those they had replaced, and they became a source of considerable friction. Although it was said that the problems within the company had not begun to be addressed until Paul Wilson's arrival, the sheer number of changes he had instituted appeared to have caused a considerable degree of anxiety. Some believed that this had prevented employees from concentrating on what they should have been thinking about – how to win more business.

One problem concerned the apparently privileged relationship which his former colleagues were believed to have with the chief executive. This group therefore became a particular focus for resentment and were blamed for much of the company's woes – its financial performance was in steady decline at this time although there were many potential explanations for this, not least of which were an unlucky run of weather and an increasingly hostile economic environment.

The performance of the marketing director was a matter for particular concern. He was in a critical role, given Paul Wilson's stated objectives of product and market development, but was widely regarded as not up to the job. Despite this, he was said to have been effective in his previous company. He was accused of having failed to get to grips with marketing in general and the issue of branding specifically. Many believed his decisions had been made on the basis of inappropriate assumptions about the company's product and market characteristics – assumptions which were shared by Paul Wilson, and which were thought to originate in their common work background. Many of the chief executive's other key decisions on, for example, the structure and operating policies of the company, were also criticised on the same basis. His apparent unwillingness to relinquish these views, preferring instead to concur with the marketing director, had led to many 'heated' discussions between Paul Wilson and the operations and finance directors.

Given that many of the staff within Morgan Williams were believed to be less competent than required for the future success of the company, the chief executive's removal of poor staff had been an important component of the change process. However, although he had been responsible for the dismissal or redundancy of a considerable number of employees, he failed to dismiss the marketing director, or indeed the other problematic new managers, despite the fact that most thought their performance was poor. His former colleagues were thus seen to be getting away with things and not dealt with in the same ruthless way that others had been. Paul Wilson was accused of inequity, and also of allowing incompetent staff to remain in key roles – having a potential, if unquantifiable, effect on the organisation's performance. Despite the alternative explanations for the company's poor performance, almost all managers within Morgan Williams felt that its financial position was worse than it could or should have been. These opinions appear to be held by outside analysts too. The company's share price fell from a high of £2.32p to 38p over the three years following Paul Wilson's appointment.

This perceived failure to take action brought to a head problems between the chief executive and the finance director, resulting eventually in their not talking to each other. In fact, disagreements between the two individuals had emerged previously over the company's strategic position, and the wisdom of expansion into Eastern Europe when there were so many problems in the UK to be tackled. Partly as a result of these disagreements, there appeared to be considerable lack of clarity elsewhere in the company about its strategic position. Similar disagreements, although not apparently so violent, had emerged between the operations director and the chief executive.

Paul Wilson's credibility within the organisation was in crisis. Eventually he agreed to dismiss the marketing director, at about the same time as some of the other most problematic of his former colleagues were also dismissed. The removal of these managers appeared to symbolise a significant decline in the chief executive's power within the organisation. In May 1995, following publication of the first major loss for the company, an emergency board meeting was convened, at which Paul Wilson resigned.

Case study questions

1. What were the most critical issues facing the company on Paul Wilson's arrival?

2. Evaluate the advantages and disadvantages of appointing a new coalition of managers from the chief executive's former company.

3. How could the problems which arose as a result have been overcome?

4. Why did Paul Wilson leave?

NOTES

1. Power issues like this have also been discussed more recently by writers such as Jeffrey Pfeffer (1992), an American academic, and the French philosopher Michel Foucault (1980).

2. See Gabarro (1987), Gouldner (1954), Rieple (1997), Pfeffer and Salancik (1978).

3. If you are interested in learning more about this, then articles by Hambrick and D'Aveni in the October 1992 edition of *Management Science* and the March 1988 issue of the *Administrative Science Quarterly* make interesting reading.

4. See, for example Pettigrew's writing on information centrality (Pettigrew, 1973), Pfeffer and Salancik's work on resource dependency (1978), Hickson et al. (1971) and Ranson et al. (1980).

5. For further reading on the subject of turnarounds, see Barker and Duhaime (1997), and 'Ma Bell restored', *The Economist*, London, 11 December 1999: 53–54; Barker and Mone (1994), Pearce and Robbins (1994); Armenakis et al. (1995, 1996); Pant (1991); Robbins and Pearce (1992), O'Reilly (1999).

6. There is even an organisation which represents turnaround consultants – The Turnaround Management Association.

7. See, for example, Hambrick and D'Aveni (1992). Lorange and Nelson (1987) in their work on corporate crises, and John Gabarro (1987, 1988), in his work on new managers who fail to take charge, also make some pertinent points on factors that lead to organisational failure.

8. Alison Rieple's research on managerial ruthlessness (1996) found similarly.

9. See, for example, Crosby (1979); Deming (1986, 1993); Feigenbaum (1983) and Juran (1988).

10. See, for example, Deming (1943) and Shewhart (1939).

11. See, for example, Hammer (1990), Hammer and Champy (1993); and Talwar (1993).

12. Apart from Hammer and Champy's own books and articles, success stories are reported by Stewart (1993) 'Reengineering; The hot new managing tool', *Fortune*, 23 April 1993, p. 40 – although *Fortune's* editorial team has now joined the ranks of the doubters. More recently, *Management Today* has highlighted two examples of good practice: 'Krone (UK) technique', *Management Today*, Vol. 5 (1998) supplement, 'Britain's Best Factories', pp. 31–36; 'Highly commended: Eli Lilly, Basingstoke', *Management Today*, November 1998, p. 94. There are also websites devoted to BPR at www.prosci.com, www.brint.com/BPR.htm and www.bprc.warwick.ac.uk.

13. A 1994 report 'The State of Re-engineering' by James Champy's own consulting firm, CSC Index, found that fewer than 50% of firms aiming for increases in market share obtained them. ('Reengineering reviewed', *The Economist*, 2 July 1994, p. 66.)

14. The quotation is taken from page 86 of 'The Big Ideas', *Fortune*, 22 November 1999, pp. 84–86. See also Blair et al. (1998).

15. 'Why he hates re-engineering', *Fortune*, 31 October 1994; Hammer, Michael, 'Hammer Defends Reengineering', *The Economist*, 5 November 1994, p. 70.

CHAPTER 15

Strategy development methods

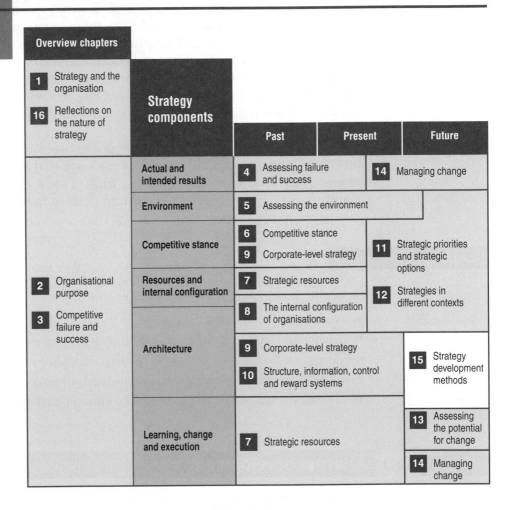

This chapter looks at some of the different ways in which companies can implement their chosen strategies. Previously we have looked at the various strategic options available to firms such as entering or withdrawing from industries and markets, developing new products and services, catching up with or outpacing competitors in existing markets, developing new competences; and enhancing the organisation's value chain and architecture.

Once these decisions are taken, the next step is for the organisation's managers to decide which methods are going to be used to achieve the chosen strategy. Methods divide broadly into development *internally*, within the firm's own functions or divisions, such as innovation or incremental growth in existing markets; or *externally*, such as the development of strategic relationships with other companies, mergers or acquisitions.

We shall not spend much time in this chapter on internal development, doing what the organisation already does, perhaps slightly better or in slightly different markets. This is probably the most common strategic method but is also the least complicated. Instead, we shall concentrate on the methods that take the organisation further away from what it does now. We look particularly at the management of innovation, which has its own peculiar problems and so warrants a section of its own. We also look at diversification or expansion into new markets or business areas, particularly abroad. This can be achieved through licensing, or the use of agents and franchises; relationships such as strategic alliances and joint ventures; or through mergers and acquisitions.

All of these methods of development are likely to require significant investment, and so we look at some of the ways that finance can be raised to undertake such activities. Finally we look at some of the ways in which a business can cut back through divesting parts of the business or through management buy-outs.

Learning objectives

So by the end of this chapter you should be able to:

- identify some of the major issues to do with the management of innovation;
- describe the ways in which organisations can raise finance for expansion;
- outline the benefits and drawbacks of mergers, acquisitions and alliances;
- assess the relative benefits of the main methods of expansion;
- describe the features of management buy-outs and divestments.

15.1 Internal development

Internal development, which is sometimes called organic growth, is a common strategic method. Strategies follow incrementally from what has gone on before. This is not to say that the organisation does nothing new, simply that it uses for the most part the same product manufacturing systems, structures, channels and markets that it already has. Internal development is comparatively controllable and avoids the risks and unpredictability which can be associated with acquisitions or mergers. On the other hand, internal development usually takes longer than buying into a ready-made strategic position already developed by another company – and delay can provide risk in its own right.

◀ *We looked at generic and product/market strategies in Section 6.4.*

Internal development is most closely associated with product development or market building strategies, but can also be used as a means of implementing diversification strategies. If a manufacturing organisation wishes to forward integrate, for example, into retailing, it may choose to set up its own shop network, but this is likely to take time, during which competitors may be able to improve their own competitive position. In addition, new skills and capabilities are needed for retailing, and the development of these both take time and may also take management away from activities that currently generate revenues. It therefore may be easier and quicker for the firm to buy a retail chain or set up an alliance with an established retailer who has the specialist knowledge that this requires.

Internal development forces a firm to bear all the financial risk of product development or new market entry, but also enables it to appropriate all the resulting profits for itself, rather than sharing them with a partner.

15.2 Innovation

The management of product innovation is a form of internal development which many writers claim is a competence in its own right, and also essential for economic success in certain industries.[1] However, whether innovation is necessary for all firms and how it should best be managed has been the subject of considerable debate. There are many potential benefits for successful innovators. As we discussed in Chapter 8, Section 8.5.3, first-mover firms can take time to build up defensible positions by the time competitors have become aware of the need to copy them, if indeed they can. On the other hand, as we will see later in Sections 15.2.3 and 15.2.4, innovation can be a high-risk strategy. It can be expensive, time consuming, and sometimes take much longer to show benefits than firms hope for at the outset. It is also something that not all firms can do well (Figure 15.1).

◀ *Innovation as a rare and distinct competence is discussed in Chapters 3 and 7.*

Another area where there has been considerable debate is where innovation should be developed within a company. This debate is polarised into those who recommend the adoption of separate units or *new venture divisions* to manage innovation, and those who think that innovation should be integrated throughout an organisation. There are powerful arguments both for and against.

Innovation means that *new* products are developed, and new equals risk. It also equals expense, which some firms may be willing to take because of the potentially large rewards that may result. However, this is not a strategy that all firms would be able, or indeed would wish, to follow. As you discovered in Chapters 6 and 11, there are many different types of strategy which firms can choose, and not all of these involve the creation of new products.

Figure 15.1   First-mover winners and losers

	Technology leaders	Technology followers
Competitive winners	Pilkington (float glass)	Matsushita (VHS) Compaq (PC)
Competitive losers	EMI (medical scanner) Xerox (PC)	Kodak (instant photos)

However, there are many firms that *do* wish to innovate. For them, a few problems have to be overcome. The development of innovation tends to require structures and cultures which are very different from those which are focused on controlling costs or making standardised products. An innovation is about creating something other than what the company already makes. It is therefore likely to originate in people who are rebels or rule breakers, who may be relatively 'unmanageable' and independent-minded, with a tendency to dress and behave informally (although this behaviour is not the same as a complete lack of discipline; Michael Eisner, the boss of Disney, is claimed to have said that the only people he allowed to roll on the floor and have tantrums were his three-year-old children!). Any managerial attempt to impose strict control on these individuals is likely to meet with hostility and quite possibly the departure of the staff concerned. For innovation, the organisation's cultural environment, its reward systems and behavioural norms need to be directed towards encouraging new ideas. Thus bonuses would be paid for the numbers of new products developed rather than a reduction in the numbers of faulty products produced.

◀ *We looked at the different types of product/culture control systems in Chapter 10.*

Organisations that are adopting more stable strategies and attempting to minimise costs are likely to be more bureaucratic. Rules will be laid down and, in general, followed. Behaviour and clothing are likely to be more formal, and unconventional behaviour frowned on. Reward systems are more likely to be based on regular payments for simply turning up to work, or for minimising the number of defects. In this context individuals who take risks are likely to be pretty unpopular.

Because of these very different types of needs, the attempt to integrate innovation into organisations that are focused primarily on other types of strategies is likely to be fraught with conflict. As a result, a number of writers have put forward recommendations that innovation should be developed in separate divisions, whose culture and systems are geared up entirely to developing new products. Existing products can then be managed separately in the main part of the organisation. However, this model is not without its own disadvantages, as we will discuss in Section 15.2.2 below.

15.2.1 The development of innovative products: two examples

So what does the development of a new product look like? We will use as our example the Post-It Note from 3M, a company which is commonly cited as the model innovative firm, and the Sony Walkman, from a company which is similarly commonly identified as a classic example of the Japanese approach to innovation management. It is important to remember, however, that these are only two examples; other new products in other firms may have been developed in different ways. First some background.

The first thing to say about innovation is that it is *not* creativity, although this is part of it. Most people and most organisations have more new ideas than they can ever do anything with. Innovation is more than this. Obviously a new idea is the basis for a new product, but this has to be married with the ability to make it and then sell it. It is clear then that innovation requires the input of many people, not just the originator of the idea. There are a number of names for the people involved:

◀ *We looked at 3M's reward and control systems in Section 10.4.4.*

- The *champion* is the person who pushes the idea forward; he or she is sometimes called an *intrapreneur* (an entrepreneur who works *in* a company) or a 'hero'.

- The *sponsor* – the person who takes the idea to other parts of the company, sells its potential benefits to other people in other departments – and acts to protect the product champion from interference from other people.

- The *mentor* or *coach* is the individual who can encourage, train, and push someone into following through a new idea, and bring in necessary expertise.

- The *godfather* (or mother!) is the senior manager who provides the financial support and gives permission for the product to be developed.

There are also a number of other words you might hear in connection with innovation development. *Boot-legging* refers to the working on new product ideas in little unofficial or semi-official pockets (*skunk-works*) within a company, often using time and resources intended for another purpose. Skunk-works are now almost officially sanctioned in 3M and Sony.[2]

3M's Post-It Note was developed by a single determined individual, Art Fry. He had noticed that the slips of paper he used to mark hymns in church fell out. Elsewhere in 3M another engineer, Spence Silver, had developed a peelable adhesive some four years previously, for which a commercial application had not yet been found. Fry pinched some of this adhesive and made some rough prototypes of a non-sticky, sticky paper for his hymn book. He also used the products and equipment of other divisions to improve his idea. Eventually he was given official permission to develop it. However, when he was told that the machine that would produce the sticky papers would take months and be far too expensive to make, he developed a crude version in his own house and brought it into work. The marketing people then surveyed customers and found that they didn't see a need for a weakly sticky note. Determined not to be put off, and convinced that his product idea had a future, he distributed some samples to people around the company, including the secretaries of influential senior managers. Their potential was spotted, and mainstream production of Post-It Notes began.

The Sony Walkman, in contrast, originated because of an awareness of market needs and by bringing together different parts of the corporation to work on the technological aspects. Sony's engineers were at the time attempting to develop a small cassette recorder that could be used by reporters to record interviews – the machines that they were forced to use at the time were large and very cumbersome. In order to master the miniaturisation issues, they worked first on a machine that only played back – it did not record. However, they discovered that this prototype had such good sound quality that it was a potential new product in its own right. Meanwhile, in another part of Sony, another group of engineers were working on lightweight headphones as part of an ongoing project focusing on all sorts of miniaturisation. Both projects were driven by Sony's design objectives of the time to achieve better sound quality and greater portability for all its products. The connection between the two projects was made by Masura Ibuka, Sony's chairman, who had visited both departments and saw the potential links. Although Sony's marketing department was not initially enthusiastic about the product, it was championed by Ibuka and Akio Morita, who both felt it had great potential.

Thirty thousand of the early prototype models were made and sold within three months in Japan. By this stage each of its technical components had been fully developed independently and simply needed to be brought together. The Walkman soon went into full production, selling 1.5 million units within two years, and its successors still bring in huge sales world wide. Sony even now has over 50% of the market in both Japan and the USA.

15.2.2 Structures and cultures for innovation

◀ *We describe the role of corporate headquarters in the management of multi-business corporations in Chapters 3 and 9.*

Sony and 3M encourage innovation in very different ways; both very successfully. We now consider whether there is a single best way that innovations can be developed. In the early days of thinking about these issues, those writing about it could be divided into two broad camps – those who recommended innovativeness being integrated throughout an organisation and those who advocated the setting up of separate units. The writer who has been a particular proponent of the 'separatist' new venture division (NVD) approach is Robert Burgelman, an American academic who wrote about these issues mainly in the early 1980s, but the approach has been advocated and described by others since.[3] The main feature of an NVD is that it is set up as a separate operating company which attempts to mimic the free and easy atmosphere of entrepreneurial small firms. In this model the role of the corporate headquarters is to provide overall direction and finance, but otherwise to be relatively hands-off. The NVD is likely to be considerably smaller than the main part of the company.

The main advantages of a separate NVD are that all its systems, structures and culture can be geared towards the development of high-risk, high-cost and often 'messy' and unpredictable new products. Staff can be specialists in innovation, and can be allowed to behave in ways which might be problematic in the main part of the organisation. Close contact can be achieved between a relatively small number

---

REAL-LIFE APPLICATION 15.1

Raytheon's New Product Center

Raytheon is a major US defence and electronics corporation that manufactures Beech aircraft, power stations, as well as domestic electrical appliances across the world. Its New Product Center was responsible for the development of the company's product innovations and blue-sky activities. Normal R&D activity was carried out within the operating divisions.

The 50 or so NPC staff worked on as many as 60 new product ideas at any one time. Each member worked on perhaps four or five projects, rotating them at will. A mild renegade spirit existed within the NPC, something which did not fit precisely with the wider Raytheon system. Little of their work was charged directly to the operating divisions (it was self-supporting initially and eventually paid for by the company's headquarters and also received income from licensing), although the majority of work was commissioned by the divisions. When products appeared to be ready for mainstream production, they were taken over by one of Raytheon's eight business divisions. This process was one of the hardest – and was considered to be the 'make or break' issue. Key staff within the NPC spent a considerable amount of time establishing relationships with people in other parts of the company in order to understand their businesses, and NPC staff were commercially aware as well as knowledgeable about manufacturing and technological issues.

The NPC managers needed to persuade the divisions to 'adopt' another 'child' and get the marketing and manufacturing managers on board. This process was smoothed by the close relationships between the NPC managers and those elsewhere in the firm, but was also dependent on their understanding the divisions' business needs before the development started. Ideas generated solely within the NPC were less likely to succeed than those with a product champion in the client division.

Source: Kanter et al. (1991).

of people, and cross-functional boundaries between, for example, technologists, designers and financial specialists are less likely to be problematic.

The main disadvantages are that there are few opportunities for the transfer of innovative capabilities or learning to the main part of the organisation, which might be able to benefit from it. There is also a problem in what to do with an innovation if it becomes successful and needs to be developed into a mature product. In Raytheon's New Product Center, their name for a new venture division (see Real-Life Application 15.1), this is achieved through considerable support from the corporation's head office, and a concerted effort to discuss the many potential new products developed by the unit with other divisions within the company.

Because of these problems, a number of writers have recommended that innovation be integrated throughout an organisation.[4] Such authors are concerned for firms to develop not a single innovation, but a *stream* of innovations. Some of these innovations may extend the features of existing products, some will be radically different, but all will be built on the knowledge and competences which are to be found throughout the organisation as a whole and on which its existing core products are based. The integrated model also allows the learning accrued during the process to be transferred elsewhere.

◀ *We described 3M's culture and dominant logic in Chapter 14.*

There are, however, some provisos with this model. It has to be done with top management support. They have to be willing to tolerate risk-taking and some level of inefficiencies, and they also have to set in place structures which bring together different people and therefore potentially engender conflict. 3M and Sony (Section 15.2.1) are both commonly cited as examples of companies where innovativeness is enshrined in their whole ethos. However, it is worth noting that both firms have innovative cultures – and have had since their inception. They do not attempt to manage a different type of strategy, such as price-leadership, within the same environment – and as a result, they are sometimes outcompeted on cost. They have also not had to attempt to manage the change process of moving a bureaucratic organisation to a more entrepreneurial one.

In fact, such polarised models of innovation development are rarely found in practice and most firms use a more complex hybrid-structure approach to new product development. As Drazin et al. (1999) suggest 'large, complex initiatives, characterised by long time horizons and a project management structure composed of multifunctional, interdependent teams, are increasingly more common venues for creative action'. Examples they give include the development of new aircraft and motor cars, defence contracting and space projects. In all of these cases, although the initial spark of a creative idea was important, the process was not that of an isolated individual or a small group unit, but instead a large-scale, long-term project which brought together at some time a large number of experts from different parts of the companies concerned.

◀ *You might like to revisit Sony's statement of strategic intent in Section 8.5.6 for a view of their explicit intentions towards innovation.*

Looking at Sony in Real-Life Application 15.2 and also at the end of Chapter 10 Case Study, it is clear that their corporate strategy mixes regular reinvention of their main business foci (recent developments are based around digitisation and networking technologies, for example), incremental improvements to existing products within the local divisions, and completely new product development. Some of this is under the control of the head office, and some controlled locally. Research and development is carried out through the corporation, and their businesses are focused around a small number of core technologies, which fuel product development in each of the relevant areas. However, it is interesting to

REAL-LIFE APPLICATION 15.2

Innovation at Sony

Since its founding in May 1946, Sony has developed many innovative products and claims that it maintains a 'leading position in the development of new technologies'. Recently this has been focused on networking. In 1999 Sony created the Digital Network Solutions division, based in the group headquarters. The focus of this department is the distribution of digital content, such as music and movies, but also insurance and financial services. Sony's reports explicitly identify the firm's desire to create unique, fun products, by drawing on the 'many audio-visual technologies' that they have developed over the years. It states a commitment to R&D in electronics, and in integrating audio-visual and information technologies.

Examples of recent Sony product innovations:

- New Walkman models offering recording facilities, extended playing time and improved sound quality.

- Mini-Disc (MD) Walkmans, MD decks, MD Hi-fi systems, and car MD players. MD decks that can be connected to a PC to allow editing and that can digitally down-load music from the SKY PerfecTV! digital satellite broadcasting service.

- PCs with audio-visual capabilities such as the ability to create video CDs and edit music from MD decks.

- Notebook PC models with built-in miniature CCD video cameras.

- A distributed audio-visual network server system that incorporates Sony's new operating system.

- DVD optical pickups. Sony claim to have introduced the industry's first sensor-free model, an innovation which will help reduce the size of CD-ROM drives in notebook computers.

- The industry's first low-temperature Poly-Si TFT LCD screen.

- A 21-inch computer display with a flat-surface CRT.

- A high-capacity 200MB floppy-disk system.

- The Memory Stick integrated circuit recording medium.

- The 'next generation' PlayStation game console which allows for, among other things, delicate facial expressions and the fluttering of clothes on a real-time basis. The PlayStation is based on innovations in two semiconductors – a parallel rendering engine and a 128-bit CPU.

(Based on Sony's 1996, 1997, 1998 and 1999 annual reports).

---

note that key technology and knowledge development – 'blue sky' projects, for example – are carried out in the six laboratories sited in the company's headquarters and controlled directly by the top team.

Other structures which appear to be becoming increasingly common in industries where creativity is a critical factor, are networks involving a major company and a smaller more creative firm. This type of collaboration is common in, for example, the recorded music and software industries, where expertise and knowledge are located in separate specialist units. Similarly, other forms of network structure are becoming more common, which bring together expertise from many different organisations, sometimes across international boundaries. More often these networks are based within a narrow geographical area, which facilitates both formal and informal exchanges of ideas and knowledge (Real-Life Application 15.3). We return to looking at strategic alliances in Section 15.3.

◀ *The different structural forms including networks are described in Chapter 10.*

15.2.3 Risks of innovation

Even the companies who specialise in innovation do not always get it right, and just to illustrate how expensive it can be when this happens, Real-Life Application 15.4 reports on the case of the digital video disc.

A further problem in predicting innovation success concerns the local nature of

An innovation-supportive infrastructure

A third of all the venture capital raised around the world goes on nurturing innovations in one place – Silicon Valley, the industrial strip between San Francisco and San Jose in northern California. Most of the $5 billion a year in venture capital invested there is also raised there. Most of the entrepreneurs starting up new businesses there have moved there. And most of the wealth they generate stays there. The factories there have added 250,000 new jobs since the Californian economy emerged out of recession in 1992, and around 3,500 new companies are created there annually.

Silicon Valley's godfather was Fred Terman, an engineering professor at Stanford University in Palo Alto. In the late 1930s, Terman persuaded two of his students, William Hewlett and David Packard, to form a company in a lock-up garage nearby instead of back east where most talented graduates headed at the time. To keep more of his entrepreneurial graduates in the region, Terman later persuaded Stanford to turn a tract of its peach groves into a campus-like industrial park, and to offer part-time business and engineering degrees to technicians at local firms. The Stanford Industrial Park is home to Hewlett-Packard (California's biggest manufacturer) as well as Xerox's famed Palo Alto Research Centre (PARC).

To this day, Stanford remains the engine room of Silicon Valley's growth, churning out almost as many new start-ups each year as it does engineering and business graduates. And like the region's founding firms, later ones spawned in Stanford's classrooms – including Sun Microsystems, Silicon Graphics, Cisco Systems and Yahoo! – have set up shop in the neighbourhood, too. This is because nowhere else in the world can they get access to such a concentration of professional skills needed to bring an innovation to the market place. It is this web of local services – from chip designers and specialist software writers to patent lawyers, high-tech marketeers, headhunters and PR experts, not to mention super-smart venture capitalists – that make innovation in Silicon Valley so easy.

Source: The Economist, 20 February 1999: 'Silicon envy'.

◀ *We looked at the complexities of managing in an international environment in Section 6.4.*

markets. Products which are developed in one country do not necessarily transfer elsewhere. Sony's MiniDisc, which was brought out in 1992, has sold five million players in Japan, but fewer than 20% of this outside Asia. The same goes for digital audio tape and the Advanced Photo System, even when this involved an international consortium (it was jointly developed by several Japanese firms and Kodak).[5]

An organisation may invest considerable time and resources in developing a breakthrough technology, only to have an imitator reap the benefits. Sometimes, this is because the product is launched prematurely. Apple Computer launched a handheld computer, the Newton, with several innovative features, including the ability to recognise handwriting. Unfortunately, the handwriting recognition software was unreliable, and the Newton was an expensive flop. Another firm, Palm, learnt from Apple's mistakes, realising that most users wanted a simpler machine that could exchange information with a PC. They gained market leadership in handhelds with a well-designed device that carried out this key function simply and reliably.

Another reason why an innovator may fail to gain any reward from a technological breakthrough is for lack of *complementary assets* (Teece, 1987) such as sales and distribution channels. EMI, a British firm now better known for its music business, pioneered the magnetic resonance image scanner, now in common use in hospitals, in the 1970s. However, it lost out in the crucial USA market to General Electric, which had superior manufacturing and marketing facilities. EMI lost so much money through its failed US venture that it was forced to merge with Thorn, a UK rival.

REAL-LIFE APPLICATION 15.4

The perils of innovation

There was no treat beneath the Christmas tree for Japan's consumer-electronics firms. The ¥2.2 trillion-a-year ($17 billion) industry was hoping that the new Digital Video Disc (DVD) would give it the same lift that the VCR provided spectacularly in the early 1980s. Yet sales of DVD players – proclaimed as the greatest gadget to come out of consumer-electronics laboratories in decades – remained stubbornly earthbound – fewer than 750,000 units in 1997. Intoxicated with the technology, Japanese electronics firms believed they would have no trouble selling 1m DVD players across the world during 1997, with sales hitting 20 million a year by 2000. If so, the DVD market would be worth ¥3 trillion a year – more than the entire sales of the Japanese consumer-electronics industry today.

When DVD was launched in November 1996, nobody expected it to take off immediately. Only a couple of dozen DVD titles were on the shelves and the handful of players on the market at the time cost more than ¥100,000. But 1997 was supposed to be different. All the big manufacturers, including Toshiba, Matsushita, Pioneer and Sony, now make cheaper, better – even portable – DVD machines. Some 300 DVD titles are available in Japan and more than 250 in America. Yet telly addicts on both sides of the Pacific have stayed loyal to their dull, old video machines.

The biggest drawback seems to be that DVD cannot record – a version that can is at least a year away and the subject of a battle over standards. August 20, 1997, was the deadline for Sony and Philips to abandon their proprietary version of the recordable DVD and to throw their weight behind a common standard. They did not, which meant another tussle similar to the debilitating war between Sony's Betamax and the Matsushita camp's VHS in the 1980s. It was largely because of memories of this war that, in 1995, Sony and Philips reluctantly agreed to pool their ideas for the new DVD with eight other consumer-electronics giants in a group known as 'the DVD forum'. This compromise at least allowed the pre-recorded version of the DVD to emerge.

The irony is that both rival designs are now obsolete. Improvements in solid-state laser technology means that high-density DVDs can record up to six hours of television programmes against the one or two hours offered by the traditional designs. Both Sony and Matsushita have high-density DVD designs waiting in the wings.

The DVD manufacturers also now have to worry about substitute products. A new type of digital-television satellite is looming over the Japanese horizon, which will offer 300 digital video channels with a quality every bit as good as that of DVD. Japanese viewers will then have a selection of films broadcast almost continuously thrown in with their monthly satellite-TV subscription.

Source: *The Economist*, 3 January 1998: 'Slipped disc: Consumer electronics: Digital Video Disc disappoints' and 23 August 1997: 'Shan't play: The war over digital video discs'.

15.2.4 Time scales for innovation success

From the previous section it is clear that innovation can be unpredictable and expensive. How expensive is very difficult to establish and there has been very little published research on the matter, but a large-scale study of new ventures carried out in the late 1970s (Biggadike, 1979) found that it took an average of 8 years for

Table 15.1 Performance of diversification into existing markets
(Biggadike, 1979)

Years	ROI	Cash flow/sales	PBT
1–2	−40%	−90%	−39%
3–4	−14%	−29%	−10%
5–6	−8%	−13%	−5%
7–8	7%	−4%	−4%
<18	17%	3%	9%

Note: These figures relate to performance in the year in question, not cumulative performance over time.

The benefits of innovation at Intel

Intel is the market leader in computer microprocessor chips – a position based almost entirely on its innovative capabilities. Intel's chips are installed in more than 80% of all the personal computers sold world wide. Between 1992 and 1997 Intel's sales nearly quadrupled to $21 billion, and net profits quintupled to $5 billion. During this period the firm's 486DX microprocessor sold for over $300, but cost about $20 to make, a fact which helped to make it the tenth most profitable big public company in the world. Since then its Pentium chip has maintained the firm's dominance in the market.

Its main rivals are tiny in comparison. Advanced Micro Devices (AMD) and Cyrix, have a combined market share of less than 6%. Both firms had to play catch-up and were forced to develop cloned versions of Intel's chips through using reverse engineering or by licensing the technology.

a company's diversifications to reach profitability, and 8–10 years before ROI equalled that of mainstream activities (see Table 15.1). Another study has suggested that 46% of the resources devoted to product development go to unsuccessful projects and 35% of new products fail commercially (Crawford, 1979). For many companies therefore, innovation is not an option; they do not have the finance, or the ability to take such risks or such a long-term view.

On the other hand, for companies that do succeed in developing innovations, the rewards can be significant (Real-Life Application 15.5).

15.3 Strategic alliances

Strategic alliances
Strategic alliances are the formal relationships that are set up between different organisations.

We suggested in Section 15.2.2 that an alliance is a common structure in industries where innovation and product development are critical success factors. They allow firms to become specialists. Their products or services are bought in as necessary and married with expertise from within the firm or with groups of firms to develop a specific new product or technology. In fact *strategic alliances* of all descriptions have become an increasingly common method of strategy development in other types of industry in recent years.[6]

15.3.1 Reasons for strategic alliances

Alliances may have any number of different purposes, not only the development of innovative new products, and can take a number of different forms (see Section 15.3.2 below). They can offer a firm certain benefits:

- The firm can learn from other organisations with complementary competences; this is sometimes called co-specialisation. Alliances which allow the partners to bring together complementary skills are common between companies from the same country, as well as between firms in different countries. Some of the most important of these alliances are between firms in different industries, which allow each to develop new products which neither firm could have achieved on its own. An example of this is Siemens and Toshiba who used their alliance to improve their competitive position in DRAM and semiconductor technologies. Siemens brought the product development skills which Toshiba lacked whereas Toshiba brought process management competences and considerable experience in managing technology alliances (Doz and Hamel, 1997).

- The firm can bypass protected markets. China in recent years, and Japan after the Second World War, would not allow full ownership of local companies by overseas firms. The only way in which foreign companies could gain access to these markets or the specialist knowledge found there was by the creation of joint ventures with locally-owned firms. Many countries, developed and developing, still restrict access to part or all of their economy – for example, giving their national airline control over key routes. The oneworld alliance between, for instance, BA and American Airlines and their other partners (see end of chapter case study) allows each firm access to some, if not all, of the partners' protected positions, thereby squeezing out their joint competitors. Of course the firm in such protected markets also benefits from bringing in knowledge and contacts from elsewhere, if not immediately, then perhaps at some point in the future.

- The firm can expand into newly opened markets about which there is little external knowledge. The countries of the former Soviet Union, for example, are now open to foreigners, but conditions there are still very different from those that potential inward investors know and understand. In these situations it is helpful to have a local partner who knows the accepted ways of doing business, has the necessary contacts, or understands the particular requirements of local customers (see, for example, Real-Life Application 15.6). Alliances in these situations are often about establishing an early foothold in a market – which may in time expand hugely.

- The firm can spread risk. In the inward investment situation described in the previous paragraph, the benefits to the outsider firm are obvious, but the local firm also benefits from, say, the greater business expertise of the foreign part-

REAL-LIFE APPLICATION 15.6

Bank alliances in South Africa

In 1998 two local banks forged alliances with foreign partners around custodial services. The Standard and Corporate Merchant Bank and the Bank of New York (BNY) entered into a strategic alliance to offer South African investors an integrated global custody solution with all its value added services and a single point of contact. Nedbank and State Street Bank and Trust Company signed a memorandum of understanding in which they will work as primary partners in a long-term alliance to provide services to institutional investors in South Africa. So instead of working through two institutions, SA investors can work through a single channel to manage its global custody needs.

With SA opening up to international markets, Mark Kerns, MD in charge of BNY's product development, suggested that 'we saw an opportunity around South Africa's increasing globalisation. BNY offers a joint assessment of technological and operational requirements by product specialists against the background of future investment strategies. We bring capability, education and other assistance.' Derick Nel, of Nedcor, explained that the alliance 'is particularly significant in SA within the context of the phasing out of exchange controls and a rapid move in the financial markets towards electronic settlement.' For State Street, CEO and chairman Marshall Carter explains that the alliance 'will enable State Street to provide comprehensive custodial services to the growing institutional markets in SA and represents a significant opportunity for us to expand upon our existing position in the global marketplace.'

Based on article in *Finance Week*, 3 Sept 1998: 76/35, pp. 49–50.

ner, thus reducing the risk on both sides. Similarly, developing a new product with a partner allows some of the associated risks and costs to be shared, although of course it means that any rewards will be shared too.

● The firm can move into a new business area quickly. Alliances can short-cut the time taken to develop a significant market position, and this is a potentially important factor in industries which are highly competitive or unstable. BP was able to establish a strong market presence in mainland Europe through its alliance with Mobil – a process which was estimated would have taken 8 years if they had followed an internal development route. As also suggested above, many companies invested heavily in alliances in Eastern Europe in the 1990s, anticipating the eventual dynamism of the markets there. Daewoo, for example, invested over $2 billion in equity-sharing joint ventures across the former Soviet Union between 1994 and 1997.[7]

● The firm can reduce competition. If you remember, in Chapter 5, Section 5.5.2, we discussed the idea of co-opetition, or as Doz and Hamel (1998) spell it, co-option, which is common in rapidly evolving industries. Some alliances are prime examples of collaboration between firms aimed at also reducing competition from each other. Although we do not know of any empirical research to confirm this, we would imagine that, once in an alliance, firms are much less likely to want to put their partners out of business!

15.3.2 Forms of strategic alliance

Alliances can take a number of different legal and cultural forms:

Joint ventures

These are separate legal companies jointly owned by one or more partners. They are usually set up with a specific purpose in mind, for example the joint development of a product or the introduction of a product into a new international market. Sony came into the record business in 1968 when it entered into a joint venture with CBS Records, a relationship that was cemented in 1988 when it purchased CBS for $2 billion. It is also weaving a network of 13 global joint ventures with cable operators in Asia, Latin America and India. There are also many

---

REAL-LIFE APPLICATION 15.7

Airbus Industrie

Airbus is at present a 'Groupement d'Intérêt Economique', an EU legal structure which makes no profits or losses in its own right. These accrue to its owners: Aerospatiale Matra of France (37%), DaimlerChrysler Aerospace (Dasa) of Germany, British Aerospace, and Casa of Spain. The four partners manufacture the components of Airbus planes in their own factories. Final assembly is carried out either by Aerospatiale Matra in Toulouse or by Dasa in Hamburg. All four partners now agree it would be better to merge the 30-year-old alliance's activities into a single limited company, which could cut costs by closing factories or combining activities if necessary. However, discussions among the four Airbus partners about changing its structure have not yet resulted in the exchange of details about the value of their Airbus assets, which would be a crucial step towards creating an independent company. Each member has been concerned with the needs of its own nation's airlines, and these vary widely.

examples of this type of alliance in manufacturing. Turnipseed et al. (1999) suggest that 'Boeing, nor any other aircraft manufacturer, will likely ever launch a major aircraft project alone again.' Boeing's major competitor, Airbus Industrie, is itself a joint venture, although one of an unusual nature (see Real-Life Application 15.7).

Equity exchange

This involves the taking of a share stake in one company by another, and often by two companies in each other. The proportion of equity exchange can vary from a few percentage points up to 100% (although strictly speaking, once one party acquires a majority stake in another, it becomes an acquisition rather than an alliance and one firm becomes a subsidiary of the other. As with may strategy issues, the distinction is not that clear-cut). Obviously the larger the proportion of shares cross-owned, the bigger the involvement and commitment. Sony Music Japan, along with two other Japanese record companies Nippon Crown and Toshiba-EMI (itself a joint venture), bought 5.5% stakes in a leading Japanese independent music label Avex DD in order to develop the Japanese music market. Some of the airlines in the world-wide alliances (see the end of chapter case) took equity stakes in their future partners. BA took a 49.9% stake in the French airline, TAT European Airways, which it eventually acquired in full. It also took a 24.6% stake in USAir, which it then sold prior to its linking up with USAir's rival, American Airlines, in the oneworld alliance.

Informal agreements

◀ We looked at networks and various other forms of organisational structure in Chapter 10.

Although not in a formal sense an alliance, one common arrangement is for two managing directors to, say, reach a friendly agreement as to which of them will set up retail outlets in a particular geographical area. Larger firms may agree to work towards a common set of standards as in the case of the DVD (Section 15.2.3 above). Such informal arrangements are common in areas where there are long-standing friendships and relationships between firms, such as in the Italian clothes manufacturing industry (see for example, the Benetton case study at the end of Chapter 6) or the Japanese system of Keiretsu.

Contractual arrangements

These are where a legal contract is set up which defines specifically the areas of co-operation. This category may be subdivided into:

● **Licensing**. Licensing is the allocation of specific rights by one firm (the *home firm* or *parent firm*) to a partner firm. The partner may be given local manufacturing rights for a patented product, or licensed to market locally produced items under the home firm's brand name. In exchange, the home firm receives a royalty payment for each item made or sold. This arrangement is common in media-based industries, where licences are issued for the manufacture of toys based on the characters in a TV programme. In the music industry it is common for the owner of a music copyright to license another firm to broadcast or perform it, or incorporate it on a compilation CD. Licensing allows brands and product ranges to be extended, and also means that the parent firm does not have to bear the development costs involved in setting up in a foreign market. However, the home firm takes certain risks when it devolves production to a licensee. The partner may turn out not to have the same levels of competence or the same interest in maintaining standards or protecting a brand name. By licensing proprietary knowledge a firm also loses control over it. Although many specific products may be protected by patents, the knowledge which is contained in their production is not, and may be used by the licensee to develop their own competing product. Paradoxically, however, a successful licensing agreement may also have the opposite effect, and reduce the partner's incentive to develop its own, potentially superior, products.

- **Franchises.** This involves the sharing of profits and ownership between the senior partner and a franchisee, who agrees to sell the company's products in a defined format. Typically, such shops are owned independently of the parent group, but their owners agree a certain layout and colour scheme for the store, and undertake to sell only goods and services specified by the franchisor. Franchising is particularly common in service industries, including fast-food restaurants (McDonald's, Pizza Hut), hotels (Hilton, Holiday Inn), print-shops (KallKwik) and household repairs (PlumbCenter for plumbing, DynoRod for drain clearance). Franchisees may be small businesses, but it is also quite common for them to be large companies that manage several outlets within the same franchise. Pizza Hut's UK franchisee, for example, is Whitbread, a major diversified brewer and restaurateur in its own right.

- **Distribution rights.** This arrangement allows a separate firm the right to distribute another company's products. This type of arrangement is common in international businesses, where a firm with local geographical knowledge will agree to sell another firm's products without getting involved in their manufacture. These use local *agents* who sell the firm's products for a percentage of the sales price. Agents, unlike franchisees, are rarely bound by an exclusivity deal and often sell other firms' products at the same time. Once a product is established, firms may choose to take greater control over distribution by setting up directly-owned subsidiary companies.

- **Manufacturing agreements.** These are contracts stipulating that a particular element of a completed product will be provided by a specific partner organisation. Often these types of contract will specify time-scales for delivery, and expected standards of cost and quality. Close strategic relationships between manufacturers have allowed Japanese electronics firms to reap the cost benefits in just-in-time deliveries, but manufacturing contracts are also common in many other industries.

15.3.3 Success and failure factors in alliances

Although there can be many benefits in alliances, how they are going to be set up and managed needs to be carefully considered.

In the first place, alliances can be short-lived. In some studies it has been estimated that a quarter of joint ventures last less than three years and the median life span for alliances is only about seven years – not that this should be taken as an indicator of failure; the alliance's objectives may well have been achieved by this point.[8] However, it is quite common for an alliance to be cut short, perhaps due to cultural incompatibility, mistrust, or a sense that the other partners are getting more out of it than they deserve. There is some evidence that alliances between a strong and a weak firm rarely work. This is because the *perceptions* of the partners need to be that there is an equality of exchange. The scale of commitment and risk-taking is an issue here, as is the perception that one partner may be getting more than its fair deal of valuable knowledge. So a consideration needs to be whether an alliance's firms have similar strengths, and whether an alliance is likely to bring equal benefits to both sides. There is also considerable evidence that fit – operational and strategic needs as well as culture – is an important factor in alliance success. We return to cultural compatibility when we look at mergers in Section 15.4.

So, for most alliances the partners need to consider any potential down-sides, and so do you if you are recommending a firm goes down this route; these include the costs of exit, or potential damage to a competitive position as a result of a breakdown in a previously successful relationship, or the loss of important knowledge. It is for these reasons that many companies prefer to keep their most important competences in-house, and not risk a partner inadvertently gaining access to them.

In fact, what will happen at the end of an alliance is an important issue. Many are set up with specific time frames and goals in mind, although others are not. Toshiba attempts to minimise the risk of any problems by setting up what are in effect prenuptial agreements which detail what each partner would do in the case of the alliance not working out. Bleeke and Ernst (1991, 1995) found that more than 75% of alliances ultimately end in the acquisition of one of the partners by

Figure 15.2   Strategic alliance options (from Faulkner and Bowman, 1995)

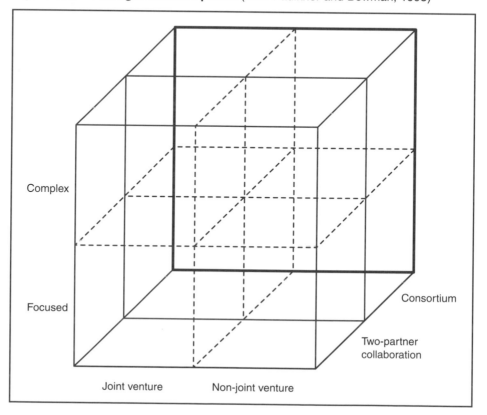

the other. This should not be taken as an indication of failure, as acquisitions sometimes are (see Section 15.4). It may indicate that the alliance worked very well.[9]

Another factor that needs to be considered is the structure of the alliance. David Faulkner has categorised these according to a variety of characteristics (Figure 15.2). Each of these categories tends to have its own needs and suitable management styles. The management of a complex consortium, which brings together multiple partners to work on multi-stranded problems in order to develop a complicated new product, for example, is likely to be more difficult to manage than a simple collaboration between two partners with a specific focus, such as a distribution agreement.

Negotiating skills in setting up the alliance in the first place can be extremely important, not only in setting up the right structure, but in creating a framework of trust and co-operation. Making sure that all eventualities are thought of, with explicit instructions for what each partner should do if things go wrong, is important even before the alliance gets started. Another issue concerns financing. The level of investment, the timing of calls for further injections of capital, and the financial implications of early termination are all issues that need to be considered.

In addition, you should think about how an alliance is going to be managed once it comes into existence. Who will work there – expatriates or locals in the case of an international joint venture? Who will resolve any conflicts that develop? Resolving crises and integrating diverse cultures are particularly vital competences in the management of strategic relationships. And how the alliance partners will communicate with one another is particularly problematic if they come from different countries and are located thousands of miles apart.[10]

15.4 Mergers and acquisitions

15.4.1 Why firms make acquisitions

An acquisition can be a relatively cheap and quick route into a new market or new product area. The parent acquires existing knowledge about customers and market characteristics, particularly important if the parent is expanding abroad and adopting a locally responsive strategy (see Real-Life Application 15.8).

It also buys a ready-made infrastructure through which additional products might be put, and which may be located closer to some of the parent's other target markets. The parent may also acquire a product, which may complement their existing products, or which would bring in new technologies or knowledge.

Other motives that have been commonly cited as being behind acquisitions include:

- *The potential to achieve operational synergies.* These may relate to the sharing of distribution channels, the maximisation of manufacturing plant utilisation, or the shared use of systems, buildings and infrastructure.

- *Increases in power*, such as relative power over buyers or suppliers, or relative to competitors.

- *Increased market share.* This may accrue from the purchase of a competitor, or

Concept	**Mergers and acquisitions**

A **merger** is the creation of a new legal firm by the bringing together of two or more previously independent companies. It often, although not always, implies a consensual element to the deal, where both firms agree to combine. It also often, although not always, implies a relative equality in the size and strength of the combining firms.

An **acquisition** is the buying of one company (the 'target') by another. Another word for an acquisition is a takeover. Unlike a merger it often implies a degree of unwillingness from the acquired company to be bought, in which case it is often described as a hostile takeover. It usually refers to the purchase of a smaller firm by a larger one. Sometimes, however, a smaller firm will acquire management control of a larger or longer established company and keep its name (and often its stock market quotation) for the combined entity. This is known as a **reverse takeover**.

Both acquisitions and mergers can be financed by capital from the purchasing company (a 'cash bid'), by offering shareholders in the target shares ('paper') in the acquiring firm or in the merged entity, or by a combination of the two. Paper bids are more common in firms which are in public ownership and in mergers. Acquisitions are often purchases of small, privately owned firms, whose price can be met from existing financial resources.

Accountants and lawyers place great store on the formal difference between an acquisition and a merger. For strategists, the distinction is less clear-cut and not really important, so that the two words are often used interchangeably. In some cases it is impossible to say whether a deal is a merger or an acquisition and both in any case require similar management of the integration process. This has led some to suggest that any differences between the two are simply semantic. Managers use the term 'merger' when they want to emphasise the equality of the arrangement, and 'acquisition' if they want to show that one party is firmly in charge.[11]

from greater financial strength which gives a better chance of increasing sales (Real-Life Application 15.9).

- *Cost reductions*. These may result from increased buying power, or improved efficiencies in resource utilisation and operating synergies.

- *Financial credibility* to increase sales, profits, and thereby increase the chances of obtaining capital from external sources.

- *Managing an underperforming firm better than its existing management*. This often happens when the share price falls below an acceptable P/E ratio, indicating complacent or incompetent management.

- *Reducing competition or overcapacity in an industry*. A firm may decide to take a bothersome smaller competitor out of the market place, while strengthening its management team and capabilities with those of the acquired unit. Or it may look to end a period of extreme price competition by merging with a competitor and retiring some of its manufacturing capacity. This second strategy may be particularly appropriate in a mature or declining industry.

REAL-LIFE APPLICATION 15.8

Mövenpick moves into southern Africa

Switzerland-based Mövenpick Hotels & Resorts is expanding into southern Africa with the acquisition of 55% of South African-based Karos Hotels. The deal pre-empts a $24 million investment into the rebranding and refurbishment of eight of Karos's 15 southern African properties over the next 12 to 18 months. The remaining underperforming properties will be disposed of by the year-end.

Positioned in the upper end of the mid-market, Mövenpick operates 37 hotels throughout Europe and the Middle East. Mövenpick CEO Windfuhr said that with an operating sales volume in excess of $762 million, the firm has the financial liquidity to grow faster than it has previously and plans are to sign management contracts with about 20 more hotels south of the equator within five years. He said he is confident that, because Mövenpick has chosen to enter the tough South African market with instant, countrywide representation in key destinations, it will succeed where other key international players – most of whom have built expensive 'one-off' establishments – are finding the going tough. Mövenpick's low entry costs (approximately one-tenth that of originating costs) means it will be able to offer highly competitive room rates of between $32 and $47 a night – almost half that of its competitors. The group also enjoys a high awareness among consumers with South Africa's leading inbound tourism markets. Windfuhr said Mövenpick's image transfer is already generating valuable business with European travel agents who are packaging South Africa tours exclusively using the Mövenpick product.

Based on an article by Elizabeth Sheridan in *Hotel and Motel Management*, 15 October 1998, 213 (17): 6.

● *Reducing the threat to management of having their own firm taken over.* Some mergers are clearly defensive in nature. Managers opt to merge with another organisation that they feel comfortable working with. The merged firms become too large for another firm to be able to afford and its managers hope in this way to avert the threat of being taken over by a firm that might impose uncomfortable changes in their ways of working – or simply sack them. This tactic can, however, backfire, since the proposed merger can act as a signal to competitors, and to the financial markets, that the two firms are 'in play' – potential candidates for takeover. Other firms may then step in with hostile bids for one or both candidates, thus bringing about precisely the outcome the managers hoped to avoid. We saw this with Banque Nationale de Paris' takeover bid (Real-Life Applications 1.2 and 1.3) for its main rivals, Banque Paribas and Société Générale. Both these banks had announced that

REAL-LIFE APPLICATION 15.9

Intended merger synergies

The proposed merger between Irish Life and Irish Permanent promises to create a major competitor in Ireland's financial-services market. Some commentators suggested that a merged organisation would be a formidable rival for Ireland's other major banks. Irish Life is capitalised at about 1.6 billion Irish pounds (approx. €1 billion). Irish Permanent is capitalised at about I£800 million.

Both offer strong brands. Irish Life leads the Irish market in life and pensions, while Irish Permanent is strong in several retail lines, particularly residential mortgages. Of particular value to Irish Life would be Irish Permanent's extensive national branch network. Irish Permanent has a small life and pensions business, while Irish Life has a small mortgage operation. Their combination could appeal to a big segment of the Irish population, and could result in revenue synergies rather than cost-cutting synergies.

Source: 'Merger would create Irish financial giant' in *Best's Review*, December 1998, 99(8): 16.

they had agreed to merge earlier in the month, anticipating that they might be less prone to a takeover if they combined.

- *Personal ambition*. Many mergers appear to be driven by some managers' drive for power and status, and the need to be bigger and better than their competitors. Needless to say this is often not acknowledged as a reason! However, merchant banks, management consultants and other professionals, who may stand to earn large fees from deals in which they act as advisers, have been known to play upon their clients' egos. Quite a number of deals are rumoured to have been initiated by these advisers, typically over a large meal accompanied by lots of alcohol and flattery!

- *Lack of imagination*. Some large mergers are seriously believed by many commentators to occur because the two management teams simply could not think of anything else to do to drive their businesses forward. One example where this was suggested is the recent merger between GrandMet and Guinness to form Diageo, the world's leading drinks conglomerate, although this has since revealed the potential for genuine cost savings.

Fundamentally, the aim of an acquisition is to produce improvements for both companies compared with their situation if they had continued independently. However, managing acquisitions, especially international ones, requires considerable skills in its own right, and many have been anything but successful.

15.4.2 Possible problems with mergers and acquisitions

Much research has been conducted into the performance impact of acquisitions using criteria such as return on total assets or net worth, and share price.[12] Most studies have found that at least 50% of acquisitions are unsuccessful. By no means all acquisitions result in increased profitability in either the long or the short term, and for most the result is at best neutral.[13] Although acquisitions can increase market power, these do not appear to result in improved profits. Researchers who have analysed share price movements during and after a merger concluded that, five years after acquisition, only 50% of acquiring organisations had outperformed the stock market. A study by McKinsey and Co. suggested that most organisations would have received a better rate of return if they had put their money in the bank rather than purchased another company.[14] There is even some evidence that merged firms invest less in innovation and produce fewer R&D outputs such as patents after the combination than other firms in the same industry.

There appear to be several reasons for the failure of an acquisition. These are discussed below.

Operational weaknesses or the real value of the acquired company are not apparent until after acquisition

Acquisitions of less profitable firms tend not to be as successful as those of profitable ones. This implies there are few bargains in acquisitions, which is especially true given the relatively open nature of capital markets. But managers also appear able to overestimate their ability to turn a poorly-performing firm around, although Electrolux is one exception to this general rule. In its core business of household appliances, it has turned around a number of firms who were experiencing difficulties, including Electro Helios in Sweden, Arthur Martin in France, Zanussi in Italy, and White Consolidated in the USA. However, on the few occasions that the company ventured outside the major home appliance business it did not do so well, and some sent Electrolux's profits into a three-year slump (Haspeslagh and Jemison, 1986).

This means that companies need good information about the strengths and weaknesses of the firms that they acquire. However, this is not always easy to come by. Exxon Corporation bought Reliance Electric for $1.2 billion in 1979 with the understanding that Reliance could inexpensively commercialise an innovation from Exxon's research laboratories. After the acquisition, Exxon discovered that Reliance was not able to manufacture at any cost advantage. Exxon paid a $500 million premium on its purchase of Reliance for a capability that did not exist. (Haspeslagh and Jemison, 1986).

Firms ought to be able to discover the true situation of the organisations that they acquire during the *due diligence* process that occurs before the legal contracts are signed. The acquiring firm's advisers go through the target organisation's accounts and other records, to ensure that all is in order. However, differences in accounting and legal standards between countries can sometimes make it quite difficult to arrive at a clear picture of the target firm's circumstances. Sometimes, the target firm's owners and management may deliberately falsify the records in order to inflate the amount they receive for the business. And even where all is in order, the due diligence process is normally undertaken by legal and accounting specialists, who are not qualified to judge the target firm's operational capabilities. Some of the best-known acquirers do not rely upon due diligence, but 'stalk' their acquisition candidates over several years, building up a picture of their strong and weak points from published sources and industry rumours.

An expensive bid may have over-extended the acquiring company

The amount of investment that an acquisition involves means that shareholders will expect high levels of returns, which are hard to achieve in the short term and which may encourage managers to make mistakes. The pressures from investors 'to turn a company round' quickly is very high. In particular, if the acquisition involves a diversification, it may place great demands upon the attention of the parent firm's top management, and distract them from important issues in the core business. Many organisations also have to borrow heavily to make an acquisition, thereby substantially increasing their gearing ratios and thus their own vulnerability.

As noted in the previous section, practised acquirers tend to accumulate information about their targets over a long period. They use these data to assess precisely how much the company is worth to them. This means that they are able to strike quickly if, because of a temporary operational problem or a fall in the stock market, the target's share price dips. The acquirer can then move quickly to pick up the target firm cheaply. They are also in a position to judge whether to walk away from the deal if, as sometimes happens, a bidding war starts to push up the price of the acquisition.

Hoped-for synergies do not materialise

Despite synergies being identified in advance, there are many reasons why they

REAL-LIFE APPLICATION 15.10

Failed merger synergies at Daimler/Chrysler

Daimler, the parent company of Mercedes-Benz cars, merged in November 1998 with the American car firm Chrysler. This was hailed in some quarters as an 'inspiration', because of the neat fit of the firms' products and markets. The company intended to maximise the scope for cross-fertilisation of ideas. 'If you can meld Chrysler's effervescence in design, good supplier relations and its paperless design with Mercedes-Benz's quality, the potential is really limitless'. A new Chrysler Cirrus could use the chassis of the Mercedes-Benz C Class, the Dodge Durango and Mercedes-Benz M Class sport/utilities could share parts, and Mercedes-Benz engines could be used in Chrysler's cars. Chrysler hoped to learn German self-discipline and there were also hopes that Daimler could imbue itself with Chrysler's flexibility and cost control abilities. The merger should have also enabled global purchasing and technology sharing. However, the merger resulted in two purchasing agents, one from Chrysler, one from Daimler, overseeing departments that buy seats, steering wheels and other interior components for Mercedes-Benz and Chrysler respectively. Only one person would be needed.

There have been other tensions in the integration too, and more than one commentator has suggested that they de-merge. Not everyone at Chrysler is dedicated to the merged company, which many have

suggested is actually a takeover by the Daimler side. Some complain of the wear and tear of commuting between Michigan and Stuttgart. There are problems in salaries, as the Americans generally earn much more than their German counterparts, which can be problematic when a German boss makes less than his American subordinate.

In May 1998 prior to the merger there was talk of keeping two head offices – one in Auburn Hills, outside Detroit, and the other in Stuttgart, home of Mercedes. By 1999 it was intended that there would be one headquarters – in Stuttgart. Auburn Hills is likely to manage the Chrysler brand and be home to some specialist departments, such as IT and legal affairs. However, at their headquarters there has been no attempt to merge the companies' identities. The Chrysler pentastar logo is an integral part of the building design at DC headquarters in Auburn Hills, MI. And the famous Mercedes logo sits atop DaimlerChrysler headquarters in Stuttgart, Germany. Chrysler's marketing and sales operations will function with little interference from Daimler, however, because the merged company is adamant about marketing its brands separately. Mercedes' product plans were outlined at the Frankfurt show on a stand far removed from Chrysler's, which was in another exhibition hall.

◄ The problems of generating synergy were explored in Chapter 9.

may not be realised (Real-Life Application 15.10). Synergies in distribution may be scuppered by different product characteristics that require different modes of transportation, or different groups of customers may in fact require different types of marketing or distribution approaches from those expected.

In fact, the growing trend towards the mergers of firms in related areas of business has paradoxically meant that acquisition success rates may have declined. The full integration of two or more organisations is rather problematic. They are dependent on the wide-scale integration of people, as well as the imposition of common financial control and accounting systems. In the past acquiring organisations may have been more content to adopt a hands-off approach.

The acquisition integration process is managed badly

◄ We looked at the management of change in Chapter 14.

During the post-merger period, managers are often called upon to manage significant organisational change. Both organisations will bring distinctive, political, cultural and technological structures. In order to capture synergies, the combined firm must *change* these in at least one, and probably both, firms. As you have already seen, change brings about considerable distress and uncertainty, and organisations during this type of situation are highly unstable.

Who should manage the change is an interesting question. A common solution is to appoint an executive from the parent company, but these managers may have been so hyped up by the chase that the implementation is seen as an anticlimax for which they have no enthusiasm or energy. This person must also bring general management expertise to the job and general management skills are not as general as many would suggest.[15] And they may not be accepted or trusted in the acquired firm. Whether they are depends not only on the manager's personal skills, but also on the role they played in the pre-acquisition period and whose 'side' they are perceived to be on.

How fast changes should be implemented is also an important, but as yet unresolved, issue. There are advantages and disadvantages both to making changes immediately after an acquisition and to making them only after a suitable waiting period. Many authorities advocate making changes immediately, which minimises the uncertainty and stress for employees and shows that the new management has a clear direction for the merged business. On the other hand waiting a bit allows learning and understanding on the part of both firms, for new managers often do not understand the true realities of their new partners. As Haspeslagh and Jemison (1986) say, they have heard some managers suggest, 'The key is to move as fast as possible', but they also heard, 'Move carefully'. Those who advocated 'Put in your own people' were counterpointed by those who said 'Leave them alone; they are the ones who know their business'.

There are insuperable difficulties in achieving operational or cultural fit

In many acquisitions there are very many more differences between the firms than managers had expected, even if the due diligence process has been carried out thoroughly beforehand. Strategic and cultural fit (for example, the degree to which a target firm augments or complements its partner's market position, structure, technological competences, administrative practices, behavioural norms, reward systems) appears to be an important determinant of acquisition success but is hard to achieve in practice. Successful takeover specialists such as Electrolux acknowledge that they examine very carefully whether prospective acquisitions will be able to adapt to the parent's way of doing business, and pay as much attention to this as to the financial aspects of the acquisition (von Krogh et al., 1991). However, Cartwright and Cooper (1996) point out that well-used expressions like 'cultural fit' and 'cultural compatibility' are ill-defined, and question whether being compatible necessarily means being alike. They draw a parallel with marriages that work even though the two partners seem incompatible.

What an acquirer can get to know about a prospective partner is also limited to what is known as its 'front-stage' or 'front room' culture – things that can be made explicit and communicated. Its 'back stage' culture – less tangible things like its paradigm, beliefs, and other unconscious guides to behaviour which may be hidden even to the firm's employees themselves, let alone an outsider – is much harder, if not impossible, to ascertain before the companies are brought together. The organisation's cultural artefacts may be visible and give some idea of its historical priorities and values, but still may not give an adequate picture of the

◄ We discussed the concept of paradigm and values in Chapter 8, and the cultural web in Chapter 14.

617

company's cultural web as a whole. This means that companies may perceive similarities where there are few, and anticipate fewer problems than in fact they encounter.

Even being in similar business areas does not guarantee a similar culture, a common language or a proper understanding of the other organisation. A company's assets may be configured and used in very different ways, and managers often underestimate the degree to which systems are idiosyncratic. Haspeslagh and Jemison (1986) have an example. After the merger that created Japan's Kangyo Bank, the managers had to publish a dictionary of more than 200 words to ensure the correct interpretations of key terms. Even apparently straightforward words had completely different interpretations in the two banks.

Although there will always be cultural differences between merging firms, this process is sometimes (although not inevitably) made worse in international acquisitions because of national cultural differences. The Dutch prefer egalitarian relationships. Dutch acquirers of German firms that attempted to set up power-sharing relationships in merged firms have fared worse than acquirers who set up rule-governed and clearly hierarchical relationships between units (von Krogh et al., 1991).

For this reason a number of writers have suggested that full integration is not always the ideal model for successful acquisitions. Whether this is necessary depends on the type of strategic benefits intended. Some acquisitions need interdependence of decision-making, and cannot allow the organisations to remain

REAL-LIFE APPLICATION 15.11

Electrolux Components Group

Few acquirers have built up more experience at absorbing companies than Electrolux, which developed a proven corporate routine for doing so. It excelled at each of four key tasks: preparing a blueprint for consolidation, managing the rationalisation process, moving to best practice, and harnessing complementarity.

After buying a number of competitors, each with full product lines, the firm faced a difficult problem. The component manufacturing and salesforces could be largely integrated. But moving away from developing and manufacturing a fairly full line of appliances in each company would fundamentally change the character of each organisation. Yet the group was well aware that carrying many different product lines would entail internal duplication and competition and it turned its attention to world-wide coordination issues.

It set up a task force to examine opportunities for global synergies between the companies. At the component level it was decided that there was some scope for standardisation and rationalisation, given similarity in their needs. As a result, the Electrolux Component group was formed in early 1987 with responsibility for

all strategic component production world wide. It was decided that half of the sales should go outside the group, and at least 20% of internal needs should continue to be sourced elsewhere. Because more than 50% of the group's component production came from one of the acquisitions, Zanussi, Zanussi's managing director was appointed to head this group in addition to remaining as MD of Zanussi. During its purchase of Zanussi, Electrolux had made efforts to portray the acquisition not as a takeover, but rather as a partnership. As a senior Zanussi manager commented: 'We have had a lot of exchanges, and learned a lot from them, but we have not had a single Swedish manager imposed on us.'

In Europe a new organisation was created to co-ordinate product development, marketing strategies and brand positioning of all the company's appliance brands. The group reported directly to Leif Johansson, head of Electrolux's household appliance division. The group established four broad design families: Alpha, Beta, Gamma, and Delta. Alpha was to be the 'prestige' range and its development was to be the responsibility of Electrolux. Beta, assigned a 'warm and friendly' appeal, was to be developed and marketed under the Husqvama umbrella. Gamma, was to be 'young and aggressive,' and the responsibility of Electro Helios. Finally, Delta with an 'innovative' image was under the overall charge of Zanussi.

The allocation of four broad product-based families, responsibilities and brand positioning recognised the differentiation of the group's products in what marketing managers would call the brand space – thereby increasing the combined market share potential. More important, it also corresponded to a conscious exploitation of existing differences. Market research clearly showed, for example, that the average Zanussi customer was younger and was an earlier adopter than the Electrolux customer. At the same time, the approach helped to revive and stimulate Zanussi's innovative culture and drive, which had languished somewhat during the difficulties that preceded the takeover. That the company did this consciously is reflected in the following comment from Johansson of Electrolux, who suggests that:

'When we acquire, we go in with a clear plan. We have a list of actions ready for twice as much impact as we need. And we have a strong sense of what we want to achieve in three months, in six months and in nine months. The fact that you have a plan does not mean that you cannot change it. But to go into an acquisition without a plan usually becomes a disaster. We usually say that we have a window of around a year to make the major changes that are needed. We set up task forces involving management at different levels, and give them two weeks to work and then report to us and to the acquired company (at that stage we are still two parties). Then, we keep doing this at a very quick pace:

study, report back, get new direction, go back, study, etc. That gives us a continuing process . . . The key is first to concentrate on real issues. We generally don't hold big discussions about principles or what organisational structure will be needed in the future. Rather we concentrate on what creates the real improvement in results, and those are generally tough decisions, like whether to make investments, or to get one service organisation out of two, etc. The way we get acceptance is to talk about it, argue, explain in a clear voice, never be political and be extremely clear. Secondly, to see to it that the acquired company managers actually grow, that they get more, that they are also winners in this change.

What we tried to do was to build on the know-how and the strengths that existed in the Zanussi group, as it related to brands, as it related to innovative capacity, etc. I think what we have done is to build on the old strengths of Zanussi and get more emphasis on that, rather than change too much. The skills necessary were there, but what was lacking was both financial resources and a strategy as it relates to the European market.'

The Zanussi acquisition was to become a major source of group-wide branding knowledge and by 1988, Electrolux could clearly be satisfied with its acquisition. After going from a massive loss of $120 million to a profit of $60 million, the firm was well integrated into Electrolux's ongoing operations, upon which it had had a major impact. Electrolux had become much more balanced in product range and market presence, and it had built a vertical strength in components.

Adapted from Haspeslagh and Jemison (1986).

autonomous. These require a full consolidation of the operations, structure, and culture of both organisations as in the case of Electrolux, the Swedish appliance manufacturer which bought its Italian competitor Zanussi, and then had to streamline the operations of what had been two direct competitors (Real-Life Application 15.11). However, this may take considerable time, resources, and effort.

Other acquisition types have a low need for strategic inter-dependence and a high need for autonomy – for example, British Petroleum, which diversified into foodstuffs and bought Hendrix, a Dutch animal feed business. The acquired operations are managed at arm's length, except in a few specific areas in which collaboration is needed. Yet other types of acquisitions have high needs for interdependence *and* a high need for the merged firms to remain autonomous, as in the case of ICI, the British chemical company, which, having acquired Beatrice Chemicals, had to find a way to preserve the entrepreneurial character of the acquired company while leveraging ICI research into them. This presents the most complex managerial challenges. These acquisitions require capabilities both to be transferred and simultaneously preserved in a context that is different from the acquirer's.

Such variations in the degree of integration may vary across different elements of the value chain. Some units may remain independent. Other units may need to collaborate. Yet others may be fully combined, all within the same overall acquisition.

The full absorption model appears to be the most common, even if this is not always required or indeed achievable. This illustrates a paradox that occurs in acquisitions. Because of the costs of integration and the effects of disruption, the acquired firm's performance may be a function of the autonomy it is allowed to have. But granting too much autonomy limits the parent's learning about the nature of the acquired company's business or technologies, for which it presumably paid a large premium.

◀ We looked at capabilities, competences and strategic resources in Chapter 7.

So managers have to manage the process of capability-transfer quite carefully. Paradoxically again, the more strategic the capabilities to be transferred, the more difficult this transfer will be. A strategic capability is one that is not easily imitated. They are embedded in the tacit skills and routines of a group. The more difficult a capability is to imitate, the longer it will take to learn and transfer. Alliances may be one way of dealing with this problem, especially if an acquisition is thought of as a potential outcome. Learning and transfer of knowledge can take place in a relatively risk-free environment, which has a get-out option, unlike a full merger.

Another way of attempting to overcome these problems is to use a cross-organisational team to jointly devise a new way of working. During the SmithKline Beecham merger, employees from all levels and functions across both firms were involved in over 300 teams, each of which had a clear set of goals, and produced recommendations and implementation plans, complete with timetables. The process also helped to reduce conflict and create a new firm with a common culture (von Krogh et al., 1991).

In fact conflict and resistance to new and unfamiliar views is common in mergers. This has a number of different causes, not simply a 'normal' resistance to change. Acquisitions, particularly full absorptions, can provide a threat to established roles and economic security, as well as being beset with considerable uncertainty about the future. Even if high-level managers get on well, there may be mini-culture clashes throughout the combined firm, so that a merger of 'equals' may actually be perceived as a takeover at local levels.

It is well known that people respond to a threat from outsiders by banding together against the 'enemy'. In mergers there are plenty of opportunities for almost anyone to feel that they have come off worse than others, or that their situation now is worse than it used to be – this is known as *relative deprivation*. These sources of stress can have the effect of making people resistant to new ideas, and make people cling to their old established habits more strongly than they might otherwise do.

Key managers in the acquired company leave

Partly as a result of the high levels of uncertainty and discomfort which typically accompany mergers and acquisitions, they are characterised by high levels of staff turnover. This can mean that employees leave for other jobs, or simply do not come to work with the same degree of commitment as previously. Absenteeism levels rise, and productivity can decline. This is a particular problem in companies where critical resources are lodged in the knowledge and skills of key members of staff. In industries with a high knowledge content, such as advertising and financial services, personnel are the firm's assets and, if they leave, the price which the acquirer has paid for the company can appear very poor value.

The reaction of competitors may be misjudged

The intentions of American Airlines and British Airways to merge at least some of their operations and routes (see end of chapter case study) produced a reaction that they appear not to have anticipated. Their competitors went hot-foot to complain to the competition authorities on both sides of the Atlantic about the likely monopolistic position of the two firms on some routes. Perhaps a more predictable response came from BA's old enemy, Virgin Atlantic's Richard Branson, who painted the banner 'No way BA/AA' on many of his planes' tail-fins and who has complained publicly about what he thinks is their attempt to stamp out competition. BA and AA also appear not to have been aware of the reaction from the European Commission's competition regulators who objected to the number of key slots the airlines would have controlled.

15.4.3 Factors in merger failure and success

As we pointed out at the beginning of Section 15.4.2, the success rate of mergers and acquisitions is, on almost all measures, disappointing. The discussion in the previous section will have shown the importance of careful research before the merger occurs and careful planning and handling of the post-merger integration process. Certain firms, like Hanson Industries and Electrolux, develop corporate-level capabilities in planning and implementing acquisitions, which are important elements of their parenting skills.

Research has shown that certain types of takeover deal appear to have a higher probability of success than others (Healy et al., 1997). Friendly bids are more likely to generate positive financial returns (measured by cash flow) than hostile ones, partly because the *bid premium* (the amount over and above the quoted share price that a bidder has to pay to gain control of the target) is lower. These benefits are enhanced when the deal is financed through equity rather than debt. When there is a high degree of overlap between the businesses of the bidder and the target, there are higher average financial returns and a lower probability that the deal will be unprofitable.

15.5 Trade-offs between internal development, acquisitions and alliances

It is important to understand that internal development, strategic alliances and mergers and acquisitions *are not strategies* in their own right. They are means to an end: alternative ways of achieving particular strategies, such as entering a new market, developing a new product or reducing the level of competition in a declining industry. Table 15.2 summarises what we have said in earlier sections about their respective advantages and disadvantages. In choosing between them, managers are trading-off three different types of risk (see Figures 15.3(a) and 15.3(b)).

- *Financial risk* is the risk that money will be invested for insufficient return. Because of the sums involved, this is highest in the case of a major acquisition which, if it goes wrong, can bring down an entire corporation. It can be quite high with internal development, since one firm is bearing all the risks of a new venture. This risk can, however, be reduced by the policy followed by some Japanese firms (Hamel and Prahalad, 1994) of keeping initial investments in new technologies small at the beginning, and gradually committing more resources once the potential becomes clearer. However, this option is only available for ventures with a long time horizon. A well-structured alliance agreement, in which cost and risk are shared between partners, may be the best way of reducing financial risk – but then, of course, the rewards must also be shared, and there are other potential drawbacks.

- *Market-entry risk* is the risk that a new venture will fail because there is no market for its products or services, because it arrives in the market too late or because it lacks the knowledge and skills to penetrate the market effectively. This risk is highest for internal development, where a firm may be venturing into markets and technologies where it has no experience. It is lowest for an acquisition, where a firm typically buys a package of products and resources that have proved their value in the market place. Alliances again represent an intermediate position – the overall package is unproven, but the partners in the alliance should be able, between them, to provide all the necessary resources.

- *Cultural risk* is the risk that the venture will fail because it cannot develop a viable working culture. This risk is lowest for internal development, since the new venture will have a homogeneous culture of its own. On the other hand, this risk is very high for alliances, mergers and acquisitions, particularly those that involve firms from several different nations. In an alliance, there is the problem of establishing mutual understanding and consistent objectives between the different partners. The cultural problems associated with mergers and acquisitions were discussed in Section 15.4.2. However, there appear to be benefits from experience in managing alliances and acquisitions, and firms can

Table 15.2   Relative merits and drawbacks of internal development, acquisitions and alliances

	Advantages	Disadvantages
Internal development	Keep control Retain all benefits	Limited to own resources Take all risks
Mergers and acquisitions	Ready-made products, markets, know-how, organisation	Acquisitions are: ● difficult to value ● difficult to integrate
Alliances	Pool resources and know-how Spread risk, capital commitment	Partners' goals may conflict Organisational confusion Lose control of know-how and technology

Figure 15.3(a)   Trade-offs: risk of market failure versus cultural risk

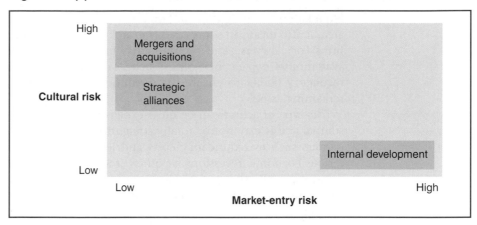

Figure 15.3(b)   Trade-offs: financial versus cultural risk

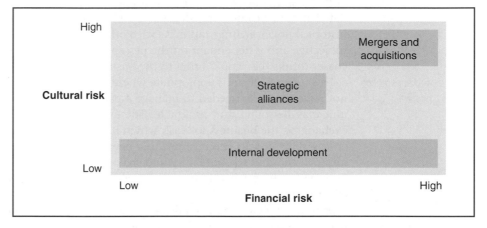

develop capabilities in areas like post-merger integration that can reduce cultural risk.

There is no one method, out of internal development, strategic alliances, mergers and acquisitions, that is clearly best in all circumstances. A firm's management (and you!) will have to judge which approach is best suited to the industry in which they are operating and the particular capabilities of their organisation.

15.6   Divestment

Up to this point we have been looking mainly at methods for expanding a business. We now turn our attention to a different possibility: the selling off or closing of parts of a business in order to concentrate on core business areas, or even in order to raise necessary funds. Methods for achieving divestment are explained below.

Liquidation

Liquidation is a straightforward (in theory) shutting down of a business or business area. It also means in some cases the bankruptcy and enforced closure of a firm by firms of lawyers and accountants known as *liquidators* such as Price-WaterhouseCoopers or Deloitte Touche. These firms are appointed by the courts or regulatory bodies to ensure that creditors get the maximum benefits from any remaining assets.

◀ *We looked at exit barriers in Chapter 5.*

This type of action can be quite expensive, since liquidators' fees may be substantial and it may not be totally straightforward. There may be considerable exit barriers such as redundancy costs and legal challenges. It is more common in serious economic recessions; at other times liquidation is relatively rare, as most firms, especially those in public ownership, will have been bought by stronger competitors a long time before they become bankrupt.

Sale to an external buyer

This is a straightforward option. Just like selling a house or a car, a price is negotiated and the business transferred. Key issues are the price which is often based on historical price/earnings ratios. As with other sales, however, this process is hugely subjective and is dependent on the perceptions of strategic synergies that the purchaser thinks they could bring to the business.

◀ *We looked at parenting skills in Chapter 9.*

This type of action is appropriate where the existing parent believes that it does not have the skills needed to manage a particular business unit, even though the unit may be sound and profitable. The existing parent believes it can benefit by exchanging the business for cash which it can reinvest in an area that fits its parenting skills. It sells the business to a new owner who believes it has the skills to improve the unit's profitability and make it worth more than was paid for it. If both parties have a good understanding of their relative skills, then both will benefit from the transaction.

In other cases a complete business will be sold by its owners. This is a common path for 'serial entrepreneurs' – people who have no interest in managing mature, stable businesses, but instead enjoy the challenge of creating new firms again and again.

Asset swaps

In this type of arrangement, a company exchanges a part of its business with another firm. The motivation behind this is usually for each firm to maximise synergies between business areas and concentrate on core areas. In the 1980s these swaps were common in low-margin businesses like bulk chemicals, where different firms tried to specialise in one or two products to maximise economies of scale and retire excess capacity. The valuation of the swap is clearly a key issue.

Float-offs

Float-offs, which are sometimes known as spin-offs, or de-mergers, involve part of an organisation being set up as an independent company. This usually happens in big publicly-owned corporations which have got too large and unwieldy, and

REAL-LIFE APPLICATION 15.12

The float-off of Zeneca

In the early 1990s, ICI, a large British multinational conglomerate which was involved in a wide range of chemicals and agricultural businesses, decided that it was under-valued by the stock market. It was thus at risk from predators such as Hanson Industries, which had taken a 4% stake and were rumoured to be interested in buying the company and splitting it up to release greater value. In the summer of 1993 ICI's managers decided that one way of combating this was to do the breaking up themselves, and so floated off part of the company as Zeneca and retained the name ICI for their more traditional chemicals businesses. Zeneca concentrated on pharmaceutical and agrichemical business areas. This restructuring involved over 500 companies in more than 180 locations.

Zeneca's demerger was one of the first to test whether splitting a company in half creates two stronger businesses or simply two smaller companies. There is some evidence that it worked. In 1996 they made pre-tax profits of £878 million, double 1993's figures. Both companies' shares are traded on the stock market, and the value of both following the break up was higher than that of the combined firm. Zeneca in 1996 had a market capitalisation of £12.8 billion and ICI of £6.8 billion, implying that the combined business would have been valued at more than £19 billion compared with a value of £9.9 billion for the combined firm before the demerger. Zeneca's share price rose from just over 600p at the time of the demerger to above 1300p in 1996. ICI's went up from around £6 to above £9.

Since then, other firms have followed suit. Ciba has sold off its chemicals divisions, and Dow Chemical has sold its Marion Merrell arm to Hoechst, which in turn has announced plans to demerge its drugs unit from its main chemicals business.

Zeneca's chief executive, David Barnes, believes that the demerger was a liberating force, albeit an unquantifiable one, unleashing a sense of renewal into the company that would not have happened if they had stayed with ICI. One of the key decisions was opting for an entirely new name, calling the new business Zeneca rather than, e.g. ICI Biosciences, although this also meant that they lost an extremely well-known brand name. But this symbolised that this was a new company, with a new set of values, and a new organisational structure. At the same time as changing the name, managers took the opportunity to revamp the structure of the company, throwing out the layers of bureaucracy that had built up at ICI. The old organisation's matrix structure, with chains of command for territories, for products and for functions, was all swept out with the demerger. What remained was said to be leaner and much quicker to respond to the market.

There have been other consequences of the demerger, however. One result is that the two companies are now much smaller than they would otherwise have been and thus more vulnerable to takeover. In 1996 two of Zeneca's giant Swiss rivals, Sandoz and Ciba-Geigy, announced plans to combine. With a total market value of more than £40 billion, the new company, Novartis, was the largest merger ever. It means that Zeneca was highlighted as the potential next player in the consolidation of the drugs industry, most probably as prey for Roche of Switzerland, Glaxo Merck or SmithKline Beecham. The market remains convinced that a bid for Zeneca is just a question of when, not if. However David Barnes is determined to maintain Zeneca's independence: 'I object to the idea that "everyone's merging and therefore you have to",' says Barnes. 'In most mergers, one of the parties has embedded difficulties, and merging is really not the cure,' he says. However he does not rule out making an acquisition himself. With no debts and a market value of over £12 billion, Zeneca is not in the top 10 in the pharmaceuticals industry, but it is still a sizeable company, and one that could finance a deal if it chose to.

Based on Owen and Harrison (1995) and Lynn (1996).

where the break-up value of the company appears to be greater than the value placed on it by stock markets as a single entity. A business unit is formed into a separate public company with its own equity issue, which is offered to shareholders on the open market (Real-Life Application 15.12). The parent often, but not always, retains a large stake in the floated company. These happen more often when the floated unit is profitable, and also increases when there is a fashion for them, as tends to happen when stock markets are buoyant.

Management buy-outs

Another way for a firm to divest a part of its business that it no longer wants is by selling it to its managers – a management buy-out or MBO. A variation on this theme is a management buy-in (MBI), in which a group of managers or entrepreneurs is brought in to manage a unit, financed in the same ways as if the existing management team were doing it. However, there is some evidence that MBIs have a much higher failure rate than MBOs, particularly during the recession of the early 1990s.[16] Another variation which has grown in importance recently is the institutional buy-out. Here financiers set up the deal and own the majority of the company, offering managers a generally small stake (10% rather than 30%) and involving them in negotiations at a relatively late stage.

In an MBO, managers acquire full financial control of the business unit that they are already running. Often this involves them in taking a substantial equity stake while investing only a small proportion of the total funding involved; the rest comes from venture capitalists, an issue of shares, a bank loan or some combination of these. The vendors divest businesses which may be performing poorly or failing to create synergies with their other activities. Financiers are attracted to these because MBOs offer the potential to earn higher financial returns than by investing in larger companies or in traditional start-up businesses.

In 1997 there were 430 MBOs in the UK with a total value of £4.4 billion, plus 230 management buy-ins valued at £6 billion – a combined increase of 33% on 1996.[17] Management buy-outs can involve large sums. The managers of the British Levington horticulture business had to raise £25 million to buy the unit from Fisons. In Switzerland the June/July 1996 MBO of Saia-Burgess Electronics cost $109 million, and that in Schaffner Electronik $130 million (see Higgins, 1996). Table 15.3 shows some of the benefits of a management buy-out.

There are, however, some problems with MBOs:

● The vendor has to obtain the best price for its own shareholders. The managers

Table 15.3 Management buy-out issues

Advantages to the vendor	● It allows the firm to concentrate on its core businesses
	● The vendor can reduce debt levels, and perhaps allow it to get rid of a loss-making activity
	● Relationships between the parent's and MBO's managers are likely to be good, allowing any desired interdependencies of activities to continue.
Advantages to the managers	● The management team is likely to be highly committed to the future success of the unit because of their personal financial involvement and likely financial gain
	● The unit is bought by a management team who know the business. This is likely to help the corporate image of both the newly floated firm and the parent, and should help the firm to retain customers and enable them to obtain future finance
	● There is a continuity of both employment for staff and trading relationships with suppliers and customers.

REAL-LIFE APPLICATION 15.13

A cynic's view of an MBO

Once upon a time there was a divisional manager, an average type of bloke who put in just enough effort to keep out of trouble, and whose division performed accordingly, not disastrously, but not too brilliantly either. This division was a bit of a backwater anyway, not strictly related to the corporation's mainstream business, which is why one day top management decided to dispose of it. Rumours of this impending change gradually seeped into the consciousness of our manager, who felt somewhat unnerved by the thought of new and presumably more demanding bosses. Musing gloomily with his colleagues on this unpleasant prospect, he had a sudden brainwave. 'Why don't we buy out the business ourselves?' he cried, signalling to the barman for another round of drinks. 'We'd get top managers off our backs, and in a few years' time, when we floated, we'd make a fortune.' Seized with unwonted energy, he and his colleagues swooped into action, convincing top management, appointing advisers, securing finance, mortgaging houses, and then working

like billyo in their new company for two years so as to improve performance and thus ratchet up their share of the equity still further.

Some of the executives left behind in the original corporation remarked scathingly on the sudden progress of the former division, but our manager was undeterred, pointing (quite accurately) to the sting of envy in their comments. Came the flotation, and the company was valued at twice the buy-out price. Our manager and his team, who owned substantial equity stakes, were multi-millionaires. 'We're rich! We're rich!' he crowed. Then he woke up.

It is likely that these types of MBO conditions, which were alleged to be common in the 1970s, no longer exist. MBO financiers are much more sophisticated these days, the deals are more transparent, and valuations more accurate.

Source: van de Vliet, Anita, 'The management miss-out', *Management Today*, London, November 1996, pp. 62–64.

may not be the only bidders and because of their knowledge of the business may offer a lower price than competing bids (although if this becomes public knowledge, that could depress the offers from elsewhere).

- If the unit is loss-making, is the current management team the best people to carry on with the job?

- Valuing the unit is hard to do accurately. Does the unit's recent financial performance give a true indication of its future performance and thus value (see Real-Life Application 15.13)?

- The vendor is unlikely to be particularly happy at seeing the unit's performance improve post-sale, thereby exposing its own management failings.

- The motivation of the unit's managers is likely to decline if the MBO fails and the company is sold to another buyer. Many of the managers might leave, taking their knowledge of the business with them.

- MBOs are often funded with high levels of gearing, making profits harder to achieve and involving high levels of personal financial risk to the managers concerned.

Appendix 15.1: Raising finance

Many of the expansion methods described in this chapter require considerable financial resources. Some of this may be available from retained profits, but even big conglomerates sometimes need to obtain large sums which they cannot immediately find from their own pockets. In these cases firms need to obtain money from elsewhere.

There are many potential sources of these funds. In capitalist societies it is almost certain that the economy would collapse if these services were not available. They include:

Banks

The types of funds available from banks are usually *loans* of one sort or another. These often have a specified date by which time the loan has to be repaid and require regular payments of *interest* – an amount of money (typically between 5 and 30% per year) which is roughly equivalent to the opportunity cost of the money – in other words, its unavailability to the bank to be invested elsewhere. In some countries at different times (according to government tax policies), loans are a cheaper way of obtaining funds than the issuing of shares, although firms rarely want to over-extend their borrowings because of the risk that they could default on interest payments.

Loans may be **secured** or **unsecured**:

- A *secured* loan is given on condition that if the loan is not repaid the bank gains an asset such as a building or plant, which would probably be sold in order to recover the costs of the loan. This is like a private individual taking out a mortgage on a house purchase.

- An *unsecured* loan is given without any hold over tangible assets. Unsecured loans are quite rare, and would normally only be issued if the bank had considerable faith in the company's long-term viability. Interest rates on this type of loan would almost certainly be higher than for a secured loan. There are a number of companies which carry out assessments of other firms' risk profiles, giving information about numbers and types of creditors, previous debts unpaid, and trading record as an aid to financiers making appropriate loans.

Loans can also be long term (usually more than ten years) or short term.

Equity markets (also known as stock markets)

Equity markets are organisations set up to trade in publicly-owned stocks and shares. They are almost always heavily regulated by the governments of the countries in which they exist, which delimit their activities and the types of financial instruments that they can administer.

The types of funds available for stock markets include **shares**, **preference shares** and **debentures**. Most companies will use a range of these types of source of finance in order to spread risk and also vary the types of repayments that they have to make.

Shares

Shares, sometimes known as *ordinary shares*, are legal documents allocated by firms to individuals or other firms who become shareholders. They are the partial owners of the firm and can make decisions about the firm's operations and personnel. Shares normally, although not always, attract annual payments known as dividends, and if the company is publicly owned, these shares can be traded on the open market. Shares form part of a firm's equity capital. Issuing new shares is subject to a number of rules about size and financial performance, and dilutes the company's balance sheet equity. Firms issue shares when their balance sheet is very strong, and when they have special projects that require large injections of capital. However, increasing the number of shares issued dilutes the percentage of the firm that other shareholders own, which they may not wish to give up, and has risks in the need for dividends to be paid in the future.

Preference shares

Preference shares are a variety of share in which dividend payments are usually of a fixed amount. This can be quite risky if a company's performance is unstable. Preference shareholders have to be paid first, before ordinary shareholders. A company chooses preference shares if the costs are less than those of raising other types of finance such as debentures.

Debentures, gilt-edged stocks or bonds

These are financial instruments which confer no ownership benefits on the holder. They cannot vote on company issues. Debenture holders obtain defined amounts of interest each year, which has to be paid even if the firm makes no profits. These types of instrument have a defined period of existence, at the end of which they must be redeemed (paid back).

Venture capitalists

Venture capitalists are individuals or organisations which specialise in providing finance to high-risk businesses who are relatively young and for whom more traditional forms of finance are not available or are too expensive. They also invest in management buy-outs and buy-ins, and other types of company flotations. Venture capitalists usually fund their investments through a mixture of loans and the issuing of equity capital, some of which is normally bought by the managers of the new venture. Venture capitalists usually vet the management teams of the ventures very carefully, and often place one or more of their own staff on the management team until it has shown that it can manage the business properly

Whenever finance has to be obtained, a number of critical issues will need to be considered:

- What amount of money can be obtained? Financiers will consider a number of key issues in order to decide whether to make funds available. These will include an assessment of the viability of the project under consideration, and this may include a judgement on the calibre of the management team concerned. Part of this assessment will also include the team's historical performance, relative to competitors', and price/earnings ratios. This will also be used to assess whether interest payments on the funds would be covered.

- Can the firm repay a loan or debenture when it becomes due? For most companies in a healthy financial state this is not a problem; they can take out a new loan, or issue new debentures, but circumstances can change and high levels of borrowing can push a company into not being able to afford to service the debt.

- Can interest payments or dividends be met? (The amounts called for will vary from country to country, and will also depend on the current cost of capital, which is partly dependent on inflation rates.) This will relate not only to the date that the finance is obtained, but at all times in the future until the debt is repaid, or shares withdrawn.

- The timing of payments, and when financing will be required. Venture capitalists talk of the 'death-valley curve', when income goes way below the break-even line. This happens when a firm is expanding so much that its costs are astronomical, and because of the, often large, lag in income, it may not be able to pay creditors or interest payments.

15.7 Summary

In this chapter we have looked at some of the main ways in which organisations can achieve their chosen strategies. We have not looked at perhaps the most common path, continuing what the organisation already does, as this is relatively straightforward. Instead we have looked at the strategic methods which take the organisation further away from its current activities by developing new products in-house – innovation, or by moving into new business areas and markets.

We discussed a number of alternative places where innovative new products can be developed:

- new venture divisions, in which the systems, structures, and cultures foster creativity and new product development without disrupting work in the main part of the firm;

- integrated throughout a firm, which allows the firm's staff and existing products to benefit from the learning which happens when a new product is developed.

Both of these have their advantages and disadvantages, and we also looked at some hybrid models of innovation development which attempt to combine the best of both these worlds. We also briefly discussed some of the risks and time-scales involved in new product development.

We then considered the different ways that an organisation can move into new markets or business areas:

- Building alliances with other organisations, through:
  - joint ventures
  - equity exchange
  - informal arrangements
  - contractual arrangements
  - licensing
  - franchising
  - distribution and manufacturing rights
- Buying or merging with other organisations.

We considered some of the advantages and disadvantages of mergers and acquisitions as methods of entering new markets, and also of gaining access to new knowledge which may be used to develop new products. The advantages are:

- a strong market position can be obtained relatively quickly;
- a competitor can be disabled;
- a firm can acquire complementary knowledge and operating synergies.

However, there are also some disadvantages:

- the value of an acquisition may be less than hoped for – based on the price paid and also on the value expected to derive from intended synergies – which may or may not be realised;
- there may be considerable difficulties in integrating two organisations which are likely to have very different cultures and systems;
- key personnel may leave.

Finally we looked at some of the ways in which organisations can restructure or become smaller, by selling off part of the company to its managers, or by floating off part of the company.

Typical questions

We conclude this chapter with a look at some of the questions that you may be asked that relate to strategic methods, and how you can use the theory in this chapter to answer them.

1. *Has an organisation's acquisition of another company been a success?*

This question is quite difficult to answer! The first problem is in deciding what time period you are going to use to measure success. It may be anything from one year to ten years. Acquisitions are often unprofitable in their first years, as all the rationalisation and integration of systems and structures costs a lot of money, but taking a ten-year period means that it is impossible to ascribe success or not to the acquisition alone. In any case, profits are not the only way of measuring success – and this is the second problem that you will have to think about: How are you going to define success? It may be profits, or return on assets, or resource utilisation or any other financial ratio that you choose to use (Section 15.4 and Chapter 4). It may be increased turnover, or improved market share – both allow the firm extra bargaining power *vis à vis* their suppliers (see Section 15.4 but also Porter's five forces model in Section 5.4) and the ability to set market prices – especially if they have taken over one of their major competitors. However, the acquisition might not produce any financial benefits in the short term, but sets the firm on the route to a sustainable position in the longer term through allowing it access to a new market. It might also allow it to gain additional proprietary knowledge which can then be used to develop new products.

2. *Why should a firm choose innovation as a strategic method?*

As is always the case with questions like this, your answer must be grounded in an analysis of the organisation's culture and architecture (Chapter 8) and structure (Chapter 10), and its current strategic position and resources. It is helpful to understand the organisation's current strategies and whether it has any competences in new product development (Chapter 7). An analysis of the environment (Chapter 5) will give an idea of whether innovation is a critical factor in organisational success. At the end of this analysis, it should be clear whether innovation is a desirable strategic method for the organisation, given its own internal position and the needs of the external environment.

You should also give an indication of some of the likely benefits – in increased sales (Section 15.2) or creating a dominant market position, for example, but also some of the potential down-sides and risks of innovation (Section 15.2.3).

3. *A firm is considering a strategic alliance with a foreign partner. What should they do to improve its chances of success?*

One of the first issues to consider is what is the alliance for. Is it to swap knowledge in order to jointly develop new products? If so, then consideration has to be given to whether the partner's skills are complementary and compatible. A second issue here is one of trust and how the exchange is to be controlled (Section 15.3). You would need to consider the history and location of both firms: Do they have a track record of alliances, and are they located in a country where alliances are accepted ways of doing business? Both will make the alliance more likely to be successful. One of the issues is the type of structure to be set up; a joint venture may be the more successful route in situations where the partners do not know each other and where a new product or market is being developed. Franchises are more appropriate where a product already exists and where the partner wants to retain more control over its sales. You should also think about what might happen if things go wrong (Section 15.4.2).

Questions for discussion

1. Alliances may be a way of overcoming a firm's internal weaknesses. Do you agree that this is a good use for them?

2. What are the disadvantages of innovation as a strategic method?

3. Describe five potential problems in acquisitions, and how they might be overcome.

4. You are a venture capitalist thinking of investing in an MBO. What are the key factors you should be considering?

The merger of Glaxo and SmithKline Beecham

The merger of Glaxo Wellcome and SmithKline Beecham to form GlaxoSmithKline (GSK) was approved by the European Commission in May 2000 and by the US Federal Trade Commission (FTC) in December 2000. Because of delays by the regulators Glaxo and SmithKline had to delay the merger from its original announcement in January. It was hoped to have completed the deal by August 2000. In order to secure FTC approval, GlaxoSmithKline had to divest a number of businesses to competitors such as Roche and Novartis. It was also prevented from retaining some of its key sales and marketing staff in these businesses, who had built up considerable expertise in the drugs they represented.

GSK is now arguably the world's largest (by sales and market share) pharmaceutical company. It has sales of approximately £17 billion, market share of 7.3% and a market capitalisation of £130bn. Pfizer's acquisition of Warner-Lambert in July 2000 formed the world's second largest pharmaceutical firm with 6.7% of the market and fractionally lower revenues (although its total revenues from all its products including non-drugs are larger and some regard it as the market leader; it also has a bigger market capitalisation at current exchange rates of nearly $300bn) The remaining largest pharmaceutical firms, Merck, Novartis and AstraZeneca, each have between 4% and 5%.[i]

The pharmaceuticals industry is a fragmented one with small major players, a large number of smaller biotechnology firms which act as specialised partners to the larger corporations, and a new sector – speciality or emerging pharmaceuticals.[ii] They market niche drugs rejected by the majors, but unlike the biotechnology firms, do not invest in speculative, long-term research that may never bear fruit and are likely to benefit from new technologies, such as the Internet, which provide cheaper marketing and distribution channels.

However, conventional wisdom suggests that bigger is better, hence the current rash of mergers in the pharmaceutical industry (AstraZeneca and Pharmacia/Monsanto are other recent ones). Some of the reasons for this are to achieve the largest marketing reach, the lowest costs and the resources to develop any new drugs or exploit new research techniques in an increasingly sensitive regulatory environment, and last but not least, to satisfy the constant demand from investors for large profit increases. Yet, historically, big, merged pharmaceutical companies have lost market share and created less value than independent firms such as Merck, ScheringPlough and Pfizer. These have preferred to find growth from streams of 'blockbuster' medicines.[iii]

Commentators have suggested that there are a number of reasons for the relatively poor performance of the merged firms. First, the newly merged entity is complex and large, and problems can arise from attempting to impose controls onto a previously informal and flexible structure. Thus the added costs of co-ordination can end up eclipsing any potential economies of scale. Second, simply getting bigger does not necessarily improve the risk profile of a company's R&D portfolio[iv]. But perhaps another problem is that the disruption of the merger and the stereotypical risk-averse culture of a larger organisation can depress the scientific creativity that is a critical factor for success in the industry, so much so that key researchers leave.

GSK are positive about their reasons for merging, and their desire to create an industry leader.[v] In addition to broadening its product portfolio, GlaxoSmithKline has strengthened its sales and marketing position throughout the world. The merged company is now either number one or two in terms of market share in many of its key business areas.[vi] In the first half of 2000, GlaxoSmithKline posted an 11% increase in sales to £8.62 billion, including pharmaceutical sales of £7.37 billion.

In time, it hopes to achieve cost savings of £1.6 billion as the result of procurement initiatives, operational efficiencies and network rationalizations, although not all commentators agree that this is achievable, given the little overlap between the two companies' portfolios. However, its 15,000 scientists will now have £2.5bn a year to spend on the search for new drugs. This includes a move into developing drugs systematically through an understanding of the genetic causes of disease, a once-in-a-lifetime opportunity with the recent sequencing of the human genome. This is likely to turn into a race to own the intellectual property. Doing this costs a lot of money and with an enlarged R&D budget, GSK thinks it will be in a good position to win this particular race.[vii] Some commentators have suggested that this particular stream of research may end up bankrupting many of the weaker firms, if not the whole industry.[viii]

In order to overcome the problems of size and bureaucracy and combine the advantages of scale with the flexibility of smaller units, GSK intends to restructure. Research will be divided among profit centres that will compete for resources from GSK's HQ and, eventually, from external sources. Particularly promising lines of inquiry will be passed on to a centrally-managed drug development unit which can benefit from economies of scale. This is similar to a structure developed by the recently merged Pfizer-Warner-Lambert. The new set-up has been interpreted by some as an imposition of SmithKline's financial rigour and performance-related culture on Glaxo's more traditional model, but may also reflect the merged company's increasing leanings towards the USA.[ix]

Although GSK's corporate headquarters will be in the UK, it has large US operations and the head of research will be based in Philadelphia, where the new group's operational headquarters will be located. Approximately 45% of revenues will come from the United States and 33% from Europe.[x] The company's new Chief Executive, Jean-Pierre Garnier, is already based in the States and will stay there. Many of the company's senior executives will also relocate to the USA, although most of the research and production facilities will remain in the UK.

i   Business: The new alchemy *The Economist*; London; 22 Jan 2000 vol. 354 no. 8154 pp 61–62; *Financial Times* 27 Dec 2000: Long-awaited union comes into being; *Financial Times* 18 Dec 2000 £130bn GlaxoSmithKline merger clears crucial US antitrust hurdle; Richard Evans (2000) Wedded bliss? Don't bet on it *Barron's*; 24 Jan, vol. 80 no. 4 p. 20.
ii FT 07 Nov 2000 Ugly ducklings swan into the middle ground.
iii FT 21 Aug 2000 LEX COLUMN: Pharmaceuticals; The new alchemy *The Economist*; London; 22 Jan 2000 vol. 354 no. 8154 pp. 61–62
iv FT 21 Aug 2000 LEX COLUMN: Pharmaceuticals.
v   27 Dec 2000; Financial Times Long-awaited union comes into being.
vi 11.6 percent share of the central nervous system drug market, 6.1 percent of the gastrointestinal and metabolic drug market, 16.7 percent of the anti-infective market, 17.7 percent of the respiratory market, and 26 percent of the vaccines market according to *The Economist* The new alchemy, 22 Jan 2000 Volume 354 No. 8154.
vii FT 20 Nov 2000 Pfizer gives new shape to research & development.
viii Independent on Sunday 11/2/01.
ix FT 11 Nov 2000: Drugs giant plans radical research move: GlaxoSmithKline to separate R&D into eight competing centres to encourage innovation.
x   Kevin Gopal; GlaxoSmithKline: Merger mania, part I *Pharmaceutical Executive* Feb 2000; vol. 20: 2 pp. 34–36

Alliances in the global airline industry

There are now over 500 alliance deals across the world between airlines. These inter-airline agreements range from simple code-sharing on one route (where airlines sell seats on each other's flights) to co-operation on schedules, shared ticketing, gate facilities and baggage handling, mutual frequent-flyer programmes, block space, give back or free sale arrangements, joint marketing and promotion and the fixing of fares and franchise agreements. However, the nature of these deals has changed significantly in recent times. No longer are alliances merely informal arrangements between a couple of carriers to share flight codes and cross-sell tickets. Now they are becoming virtual mergers, bypassing national rules against foreign ownership, and are coalescing into five large groups:

- *Qualiflyer Alliance* (ten airlines including Swissair, Sabena, Balair, Air Europe, AOM, LOT Polish Airlines, Volare and LTU International Airways)
- *SkyTeam* (Delta Air Lines, Air France and Aeromexico, and now Korean Air)
- *Wings* (KLM/Northwest/Continental)
- *Star Alliance* (Lufthansa, United Airlines, Air Canada, Varig, SIA, ANZ, Ansett, SAS and Thai Airways International, plus numerous small regional airlines which act as feeders)
- *oneworld* (American, Austrian Airlines, British Airways, Cathay Pacific, Canadian Airlines and Qantas) (Table 15.4).

The two major groups, Star and oneworld, are roughly equal in size. Star members have a total fleet of 1,446 aircraft, and oneworld partners have 1,524. Star carriers serve 654 destinations in 108 countries; oneworld serves 632 in 138 countries. Star has 184 million passengers per year versus 174 million for oneworld. Combined total passenger traffic of the two groups represents roughly a quarter of the world's overall annual scheduled passenger traffic.

Star has been operating since 1996 but the creation of oneworld in September 1998 spurred Star to attempt to sign up many of the potential new partners it had been courting previously, including Singapore Airlines, All Nippon Airways, Air New Zealand and Ansett.

Oneworld similarly has expanded well beyond its founding members. Cathay's decision to join oneworld was influenced by the fact that Thai Airways had already joined Star, and Singapore Airlines intended to do the same. For Qantas, the oneworld alliance is critical to remedy weaknesses and low profitability in its network to European destinations. The airline will now combine with former arch-rival Cathay Pacific to offer one-stop services to a host of European cities. Finnair became a fully-fledged member of the oneworld coalition in August 1999, strengthening the alliance's northern European market and providing competition for SAS of Star. Iberia has made a statement of intent to join, and talks are under way with Dragonair, Swissair, Emirates and Japan Airlines. Dragonair is a Hong Kong-based airline that is majority-owned by the Chinese government but in which Cathay Pacific has a stake, and holds the key to maximising the alliance's access to mainland China. Recently LanChile confirmed its plans to become a member and Aerolineas Argentinas, in which both Iberia and American have an equity share, is also a likely entrant. This would give oneworld a Latin American link to counter Star's Varig of Brazil. Lot Airlines of Poland already has links with BA and American Airlines and would act as oneworld's entree to Central Europe.

Many of these airlines already had marketing or operating agreements with one or more of the alliance partners. However, few of the participating airlines have taken equity in each other's companies, although some of oneworld's partners have cross-shareholdings. BA owns 25% of Qantas, while American Airlines' parent company is a major shareholder in Canadian Airlines.

There have also been some changes in partners. Before it joined oneworld, Finnair had close ties with Lufthansa and the Star alliance as a whole, Swissair and Sabena (which participate in the Qualiflyer Group) and with Delta Air Lines, Air France's strategic partner. Austrian Airlines has recently left the Qualiflyer group. Swissair, which has recently signed a code-share agreement with Qantas, is reported to be interested in the oneworld option even though it

Table 15.4   The major oneworld alliance airlines

Airline	Passengers (millions)	Cargo operating per year (metric tonnes)	Revenues per year (billions)	Aircraft
American Airlines	93	679,663	16.9	856
British Airways	41	816,000	14.5	330
Canadian Airlines	11	114,168	2.0	131
Cathay Pacific	10	635,000	3.9	62
Qantas Airways	19	359,000	4.8	145

Source: Morrocco et al. (1998).

CASE STUDY *continued*

is a member of the Atlantic Excellence/Qualiflyer Group. Despite the proliferation of alliances there are still a number of airlines out on their own. Garuda Indonesia, Philippine Airlines and Malaysia Airlines are all showing relatively poor performance, and because they are state-support carriers who can fly whether they make a profit or not, have found it hard to join alliances where commercial concerns are uppermost. However, joining an alliance at a late stage is still possible for airlines that *do* improve their performance. Korean Air, having gone through a period of losses and poor safety, has now become profitable and joined the SkyTeam alliance. For other outsiders such as Virgin Atlantic, the lack of allies is a problem and Richard Branson, Chairman of Virgin has admitted that despite his dislike of them, he may be forced into joining one or setting up his own group.[18] Others are not interested in joining up. Emirates maintains that it prefers bilateral deals, as did Japan Airlines, which had bilateral agreements with American, Canadian and Qantas, although it has now succumbed and joined oneworld.

Opponents of these alliances, such as Richard Branson, see them as stifling competition, and suggest that fares inevitably go up as a result. In fact business-class fares have risen since the alliances came into existence. A number of other commentators have suggested that the main benefits of alliances accrue to airlines, not customers, although industry managers predictably do not agree. Nevertheless these alliances have increased at a time when there was a major crisis in Asian economies, and in an industry where profits are fairly low at the best of times. Cathay Pacific, which until recently was sceptical of airline alliances, made a loss for the first time in 1998 and has now joined the largest group. Many other loss-making airlines in Asia have similarly speeded up their attempt to join an alliance.

For passengers, there are, nonetheless, some benefits. The airlines' alliances generally mean: improved flight connections since schedules are co-ordinated more closely and passengers can complete a journey on several airlines using one ticket (although there have apparently been some concerns from passengers who are left wondering who will be the operating carrier on their flight); transferable frequent-flyer benefits between member airlines; improved freight and mail services; shared premium lounges; and corporate sales deals.

For airlines the improved benefits to passengers can be used as marketing tools and help to increase revenues. Synergies can be found in a number of areas, thus reducing costs, for example, in cross-selling tickets and sharing sales networks and in combining buying power for new aircraft or equipment. Similarly, they can increase their route networks without the capital outlay that would otherwise be involved. Sharing routes allows excess capacity to be reduced. The potential savings from having two or more airlines sharing an under-used and very unprofitable long-haul route are huge. If they can use two fewer wide-bodied aircraft on that route by filling seats in other planes, alliance partners can save about $100 million a year in operating costs, while maintaining the same revenues.[19]

Most international airports are so congested that an airline's profitability on a given route depends on whether it has slots in peak periods. Many of these slots are allocated to state-owned airlines (or those that were state-owned prior to deregulation but still hold these assets). Alliances are a way of overcoming these monopolistic positions, and also of getting round legislation that prevents foreign ownership of national airlines: the maximum stake foreign investors may hold is 25% in the USA and 49% in the EU. Such rules block takeovers or mergers, inhibiting the establishment of pan-national groups. Such structural barriers have probably delayed the consolidation of the airline industry; in other similar industries this occurred between 20 and 50 years ago.[20] Also, because of its structure, consolidation may not lead to the same benefits as in other industries such as car manufacturing, where the strongest and fittest companies survive and the weakest go under. Instead, it means that the airlines can collude in price-fixing cartels, weak airlines are protected from closure, and barriers to entry are high, as newcomers cannot hope to match the allies' global network of routes.

In fact, American and BA's oneworld alliance has been considered a second best option by some writers, who suggest that a better choice would have been a bilateral agreement. Both airlines control internationally important routes, and do not really need other partners. However, they have been prevented from joining together. Their intended relationship produced predictable reactions from competing airlines who complained that AA and BA together already controlled about 60% of the passenger slots in their market and would enjoy 100% control over some routes. The European Commission, as upholders of fair competition, judged that such a link was anti-competitive and proposed that BA should give up slots at Heathrow in compensation, a price BA was unwilling to pay. The two-way alliance was thus blocked,

and oneworld was formed. In the face of the onslaught the duo's reaction was to do everything they could to make sure that the three other alliances were also subjected to scrutiny by Brussels.

Case study questions

1. Are GSK's reasons for merging sound?
2. Where is GSK's growth going to come from in the future?
3. What do you think the future of the pharmaceutical industry is likely to be?
4. Evaluate the benefits of being in the oneworld alliance for American Airlines.
5. Should Virgin Atlantic join an alliance? Justify your answer.

NOTES

1. Two of the most powerful early proponents of the importance of innovation were Peters and Waterman (1982). There have been many since then, however, including Burgelman (1983, 1984), Kanter (1989), Peters (1988), Nonaka and Takeuchi (in their various guises, e.g. 1988, 1990, 1995), and Tushman and O'Reilly (1996).
2. See Drazin et al. (1999); also Drazin and Schoonhoven (1996).
3. See, for example, Kanter et al. (1991), Burgelman and Sayles (1986), Burgelman (1983, 1984), Kanter (1985, 1989), Shrader and Simon (1997); Garud and Van de Ven (1992); Chesbrough and Socolof (2000); Simon et al. (1999). A more recent term for the NVD is internal corporate venturing.
4. See, for example, Quinn (1985), Nonaka and Takeuchi (1995), Nonaka (1988, 1990, 1991), Peters and Waterman (1982), Leonard-Barton (1992), and Inkpen (1996).
5. 'Will it play in Penang?', The Economist, 2 May 1998.
6. See, for example, Spekman et al. (1996), Bleeke and Ernst (1995), Stiles (1994), Faulkner and Bowman (1995), Doz and Hamel (1998).
7. Examples taken from Mockler (1999: 7).
8. See, for example, Cartwright and Cooper (1996) and Bleeke and Ernst (1991, 1995).
9. Research currently under way by the authors suggests that this proportion can go down to as low as 35% in the recorded music industry.
10. See, for example, Mjoen and Tallman (1997).
11. See, for example, David and Singh (1993).
12. See, for example, Chatterjee et al. (1992), Buono and Bowditch (1989), Buono et al. (1985), Cartwright and Cooper (1993, 1996), Haspeslagh (1989), Nahavandi and Malekzadeh (1988), Ingham et al. (1992), David and Singh (1993).
13. However, a cautionary note here concerns the firms' historically different accounting procedures and practices which can distort performance comparisons. Similarly, the massaging of financial results, both pre- and post-acquisition, can lead to misleading interpretations. Prior to the acquisition, managers may revalue properties or goodwill, or move costs from one year to another. In the year after the acquisition, profit levels may represent one-off savings as a result of rationalisation, pension-fund raids, or asset stripping. As one of our Dutch colleagues commented, managers can 'pick apples from the lower branches'.
14. Quoted in Cartwright and Cooper (1996).
15. Kotter (1982) and Gabarro (1987) have useful things to say on this point.
16. Study carried out by Nottingham University's Centre for Management Buyout Research quoted in Sarah Perrin, 'The buy-out is back', Management Today, May 1998, pp. 78–82.
17. Figures compiled by the Centre for Management Buy-out Research quoted in Perrin (1998: 78–82).
18. See Airfinance Journal, October 1998, Issue 210, page 21: BA and AA to expand their alliance with global partners.
19. This estimate comes from Bickers (1998).
20. See Jebb (1998).

Reflections

Part 5 is quite short – a single chapter. At the beginning of this book you were introduced to a number of basic ways in which strategy has been described and conceptualised. Through the book you have been introduced to many of the most important aspects of strategic management. Part 5 is therefore an extended theoretical commentary which pulls together the views of some of the most influential strategy theorists. This is an opportunity for you to think in a bit more depth about some of the issues we have raised, and to reflect on what strategy is really all about.

CHAPTER 16

Reflections on the nature of strategy

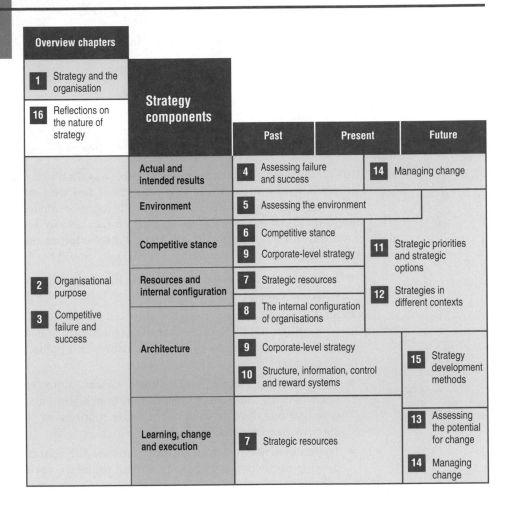

W e have now reached the end of our exploration of the nature of organisations, strategy and competitive advantage. In this chapter we give you the opportunity to reflect on what we have tried to show, and to investigate some alternative points of view. This chapter is more abstractly theoretical in its approach than any other in the book. It contains few real-life applications and only a very short end-of-chapter case study, but it covers a number of topics that you may find quite intellectually demanding.

After reading this chapter you should:

● have a basic appreciation of the way in which the theory of strategic management has developed over time;

● understand the main schools of strategic management thought and the nature of the differences between them;

● be able to critique the intellectual stance that we have adopted in writing this book.

16.1 Our own view of strategy

Part of our motivation for writing this book was that, like many authors, we have strong views about the world that we did not feel were adequately presented by other writers. Although we have tried, in the name of intellectual balance and good teaching, to put our views across in an even-handed way, we would not be human if we did not let our biases show. Here is a selection of the basic preconceptions that underlie our view of what strategy is, and should be:

● Managers are imperfect, idiosyncratic human beings, who are at best boundedly rational.

● Strategic decisions are strongly influenced by managers' own histories and pre-conceptions, by the culture that the organisation and its industry have developed over time, and by power relationships and political processes within the organisation.

● These human, cultural and political factors, along with differences in the environment, cause every organisation to evolve along a unique path. No two organisations develop exactly the same routines, or 'feel' the same to their employees, customers or suppliers.

● These differences between organisations are the reason why some are able to develop distinctive resources. It is these resources, above all, that explain the existence of competitive advantage, the phenomenon that enables some organisations to succeed while others fail.

● However strong the macro-political influences on an organisation or within a nation may be, sooner or later the laws of economics will reassert themselves. Organisations that do not have some distinctive resources will decline and possibly die.

● Organisations, through their members, are capable of learning and changing. Competitive advantage will be sustained longer in organisations that have developed routines for doing this.

● Effective motivation of an organisation's people is a crucial factor in enabling the organisation to develop effective routines, to learn and to change – in other words, to develop sustainable competitive advantage.

- What managers do makes a difference. Although they may be only boundedly rational, managers can improve the effectiveness of their strategic decisions by:
  - finding ways to obtain and process more information
  - thinking logically about what they should do
  - thinking about what they would need to do to implement their decisions and persuade other people to help them.

If you review the content of the previous fifteen chapters, you will see that these assumptions about human nature and organisations permeate every one of them. We believe that there are strong theoretical arguments and, for the most part, empirical evidence to support every one of these propositions. They also coincide with what we have observed in the various organisations that we have worked for, consulted in, or researched.

However, there are many eminent researchers and scholars who have contrived, through their own idiosyncratic and boundedly rational thought processes, to arrive at different conclusions. In the following sections, we move on to consider some of the major schools of strategic management theory which have emerged over the last thirty years or so.

16.2 Schools of strategic thought

When it started to be thought of as a distinct domain (probably in the 1960s), strategic management was often called business policy, particularly in America where its teaching started to become commonplace. The original omission of the word 'management' is interesting, and reflects the apparent lack of awareness or understanding at the time of how strategy actually happens – how it is brought about, who creates it, where it takes place, how it is *made*. More recently there has been a much greater focus on understanding the social processes that give rise to particular outcomes, and some have even questioned whether organisations have or even need a grand, overarching strategy at all. So it is possible to trace developments in the theorising which has taken place about the strategy process over the years.

Those who have developed the field of strategic management theory can be gathered into distinct groups. The categorisation we use in this chapter is:

- **visionary** – strategy as the results of the activities and vision of a single leader;
- **planning** – strategy as a process of analysis, target-setting and monitoring;
- **decision-preference** – strategy as the outcome of individual thought processes influenced by the backgrounds of the people involved;
- **process** – strategy as the outcome of sociological processes within the organisation that are strongly shaped by its history;
- **political** – strategy as the outcome of a set of negotiations where the relative power of the participants may be as important as the merits of their proposals;
- **ecological** – strategy as a process of experimentation and adaptation to the environment, where it is inevitable that some organisations will fail;
- **organisational anarchy** – an absence of strategy, organisations succeeding without any coherent pattern of strategic decisions being discernible.

Other authors have also categorised writing on strategy. A commonly cited frame-

THEORETICAL PERSPECTIVE 16.1

Schools of strategic thought

Richard Whittington, writing in 1993, identified four main schools of strategic theorising. He called them the Classical; the Processual; the Evolutionary; and the Systemic according to their position on a process/outcome axis, as shown in Figure 16.1.

Figure 16.1   Schools of strategic theorising

```
                    OUTCOMES
                 Profit-maximising

        CLASSICAL    |    EVOLUTIONARY

PROCESSES           |
Deliberate  ————————+———————— Emergent

        SYSTEMIC     |    PROCESSUAL

                    |
                 Pluralistic
```

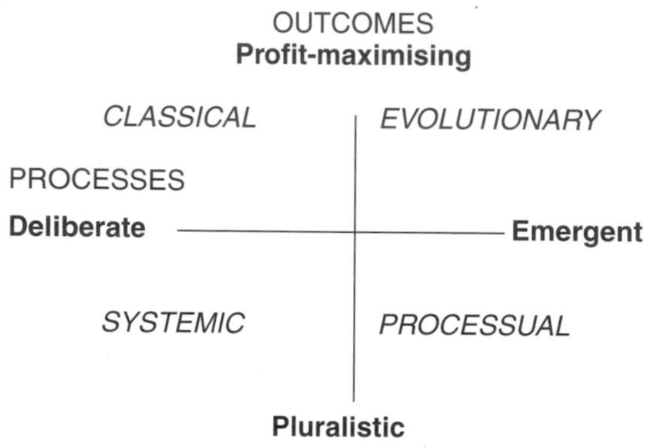

The classical model is perhaps the traditional approach to strategic management or business policy, in which profit maximising is considered the principal and probably the only objective for a firm; strategies are decided and planned in a rational fashion by the chief executive or the 'organisation', with little account taken of any unpredictable responses which might come from other competing firms or individuals with different objectives. Whittington puts writers such as Chandler (1962), Ansoff (1965, 1991) and Porter (1980, 1985) into this group.

Processualists emphasise the messiness of organisational life. They understand that strategic processes are often irrational, not planned, and subject to the whims and vagaries of markets and other people even within the same firm. For them, bodging, compromise, bargaining or just getting by is the way that strategy happens – they think that the way people operate in organisations is too haphazard to

follow a rigid pre-set plan. However, they are optimistic about organisations surviving in these circumstances; they accept that markets are not perfect, profit maximising is an unrealistic goal and satisficing is a perfectly valid way of making strategic decisions. Writers in this group include Cyert and March (1963), Mintzberg (1987) and Pettigrew (1990).

Systemic theorists, as with classical theorists, accept that strategy can be planned and deliberate, and that individuals can and do carry out intentional actions, but also understand it as taking place within a framework of systems, in which both strategic ends and means are inextricably linked to the cultures and power structures of the local social systems in which they take place. They are often far away from the singular profit-maximisation view of organisations. These writers accept that managers may have other reasons for working, professional pride or social conscience, for example. Writers in this group include Granovetter (1985) and Marris (1964).

Finally, Whittington identifies the evolutionaries, who rather dismiss the ability of individuals to create and implement strategies at all; instead, because of the unpredictability of the environment, strategies emerge as the result of an iterative and selective process, in which those which are suitable survive and thrive, while those that do not, die – a principle which also applies to the organisations in which they occur. Writers in this group include Hannan and Freeman (1977, 1988) and Williamson (1991b).

Whittington described how each of these models had come from their writers making very different interpretations of the firm's situation and different assumptions about the strategy processes that go with them.

Other strategy typologies

New classifications of types of strategy continue to be developed: if you want to help to develop the field of strategic management, you might wish to develop your own! Examples are those of McKiernan (1996) and Mintzberg et al. (1998) – see Table 16.1.

Table 16.1 Categories of strategy

McKiernan's (1996) categories	Mintzberg et al.'s (1998) ten schools
1. Planning and process	1. Design
2. Positioning	2. Planning
3. Resource	3. Positioning
4. Learning – subdivided into six groups:	4. Entrepreneurial
5. Natural selection	5. Cognitive
6. Incremental	6. Learning
7. Cultural	7. Power
8. Political	8. Cultural
9. Visionary	9. Environmental
10. Patterns of strategy development.	10. Configurational.

work, by Richard Whittington (1993) is summarised in Theoretical Perspective 16.1. He identified four major groups of strategic theorising: processual, systemic, evolutionary, and classical.

Essentially, the ideas presented in these groups fall within a continuum of more deliberate ⇔ more emergent strategic processes. On a cautionary note, almost all of the writings in these categories apply principally to commercial companies, and particularly to large firms. Specific theories relating to strategies in small firms and in the public and non-profit sectors tend not to fit easily into these groups. Strategies in these sectors have been discussed separately in Chapter 12.

Where each of us stands in terms of accepting these views will influence how we analyse situations. For example, if you are someone who believes in a planned, rational, approach to assessing problems, when faced with a strategic problem you are likely to begin calculating potential returns from investments, and ignore the political implications of what you propose, or how these investments would be managed. If you are someone who prefers to look at the behavioural aspects of employees, you are likely to ignore the financial implications of the human resource policies that you recommend. It is a rare student – or academic – who deals with all of these issues equally.

Determinism versus free will

An important part of the debate between the different schools of strategy described relates to the extent to which organisations can be considered to be in control of what happens to them. Many schools of strategic thought start from the notion that what an organisation can achieve is largely shaped by factors that managers cannot control directly: its environment, or complex political and cultural processes. Other theorists assume a degree of free will – that managers can have some significant influence over their organisations, and even create or invent their environment. These theorists differ, however, in their assessment of the extent to which managers can shape those events by careful planning in advance.

This is in part a reflection of a highly topical and sometimes heated debate in the psychological and sociological literature about how much of what we do is the result of our own *free* will. Many thinkers believe in a degree of *determinism* – that factors other than our own free choices *determine* what we do – in other words shape, constrain, encourage, or otherwise make one thing more likely than another. Do you 'decide' to do a degree because you have thought through all the implications, because you are expected to go to college by your family who believe that it will improve your career prospects, or because you are genetically 'programmed' in that direction?

Sociologists such as Anthony Giddens (1974, 1979, 1984) and Roy Bhaskar, (1978, 1989) suggest that it is actually the *interplay* between deterministic and free-will factors that result in human choices.

In the following sections, we look in turn at each of our seven categories of strategic thought, and review the direction that strategic management theory appears to be taking.

16.2.1 The visionary approach to strategy

The visionary (or leadership) approach is perhaps the original view of strategy, based as the word is on the tactics of warrior leaders. It is linked with early theorising on entrepreneurship, and the notion of powerful wealth creators. In this group strategy is held to be the result of the activities and vision of a single individual, who sets and controls the organisation's agenda. Writers who have identified this model say that organisational strategy decision-making is dominated by the views and wishes of this individual – possibly with a small group of close allies or advisers – who is unlikely to be willing to tolerate views which deviate from his or her own to any significant extent. Most new firms are likely to have been created by such an individual. However, this model can also apply to larger or more established firms, even those which are in public ownership.

Such a style of strategy-making is likely to be found in an architecture which is centralised around the leader, or what Handy (1985) terms a spider's web culture, where systems, procedures and the organisation's structure bring decision-making back to the centre. One good example of this in practice was Robert Maxwell, the British media mogul, who was known to insist that anything costing over £500 was approved and signed off by him personally. This was in a company whose annual turnover was several million pounds.

Criticisms of this approach to understanding strategy tend to focus around the fact that, in a large organisation, a single individual simply cannot be all powerful. This is particularly true in a public company, where banks or shareholders are extremely influential in shaping what the organisation does. Individuals are dependent on getting others to carry out their wishes, and therefore how they 'sell' their vision to organisational stakeholders, how they persuade others to support them, and how they control the strategies that they have chosen are important considerations which tend to be ignored by the visionary writers. The environment is also discounted. Indeed, some critics of the visionary approach claim that what the leader does counts for nothing in influencing the firm's performance when compared with the effects of the environment (see the ecological school below).

Writers in this group include Schumpeter (1950), Drucker (1970), Pinchot (1985) and Mintzberg (1973).

16.2.2 The planning approach to strategy

The second of our categories, the planning approach, has been perhaps the most influential way of theorising about strategy over the years. It assumes that organisations (sometimes, although not always, personified in the chief executive) undertake a process of analysis, establish goals as a result, and then achieve these through setting targets and measuring outcomes. Analytical tools, such as PEST or value chain analysis are used to identify suitable opportunities which are then assessed against criteria to lead to a final selection of strategy.

Many strategy books and courses adopt this approach, even when their authors and teachers acknowledge that this is not how life is in reality. Most teach a very rational way of thinking about things – the skills of analysis, measurement and evaluation. Much academic writing on strategy can also be put into this tradition.

Some of it, such as the work of Igor Ansoff and Michael Porter, has been extra-ordinarily influential in shaping the field.

Four main criticisms have been levelled at the planning approach. Firstly, many of the writers in this school paid insufficient attention as to whose goals were being adopted. Many works assumed that the *organisation* made the decision, whereas in fact organisations have no ability to do this. *Individuals* decide, so who actually makes the decision and sets the plan in place is an important consideration which is often ignored. Secondly, as with the visionary approach, authors writing in this tradition are said to give insufficient weight to the problems of implementing strategies.

In a large organisation, a strategic plan involves a potentially enormous number of other people, not all of whom will agree with the chief executive's intentions. They may do their best (often with great effect) to sabotage his or her perfectly rational plans. The planning approach is also said to ignore the unpredictability and dynamism of the environment. What is assumed in a plan at one point in time, may not be the reality at the time that the plan is put into action. Finally, human beings may be only boundedly rational, unable to consider all necessary eventualities, and yet the incompleteness of information gathering and processing is rarely considered by the planning school.

Writers in this category include Selznick (1957), Chandler (1962), Ansoff (1965), Andrews (1971), Porter (1980, 1985), Quinn (1980), Baden-Fuller and Stopford (1992) and Rumelt (1997).

16.2.3 The decision-preference approach to strategy

Our third category marks a move away from understanding strategy as a rational, thoughtful, profit-maximising process to giving more weight to evidence that people's decision-making is not as rational or free-thinking as it could be. Writers in this school pay particular attention to the psychological processes of bounded decision-making that predispose managers towards particular strategic paths whatever the environmental opportunities.

Such preferences become strongly embedded within firms. Individuals are attracted to organisations that appear to share the same values as they do. Schein (1992) and Hambrick and Brandon (1988), for example, identified the tendency of firms to become increasingly homogeneous as they age. This happens through parallel processes of the recruitment and socialisation of newcomers and the departure of unsuitable new recruits. Over time these processes become self-reinforcing, as the organisation develops a manifest identify which attracts some potential employees, and repels others. Organisations can therefore become increasingly filled with people who have a tendency to make the same types of decisions.

◀ *Bounded decision-making and culture were discussed in Chapters 2 and 14.*

Writers in the decision-preference group suggest that the most influential people in the company, those who have the power to shape the organisation's strategy, are likely to share similar ways of viewing the world, and so make similar decisions (a phenomenon sometimes known as *groupthink*, especially when it leads to mistaken decisions). This homogeneity can lead to swift, effective decision-making. Having similar views to others reduces the potential for conflict, and if the organisation is suited to its environment, there is no need to collect information on competitors or potential customers in markets which are not

◀ Models of organisational failure were reviewed in Chapter 3.

close to where the organisation already operates. When there are changes to the organisation's environment, however, then problems can occur. If managers only pay attention to a narrow set of issues and information, and expect that the future will resemble the past, then external changes can be overlooked, so that the organisation's performance slips.

Theorists of this school can be criticised, however, because of their focus on the individual at the expense of external factors. For the most part they ignore the influence of the wider environment, and the responses which organisations have to make to competitors' actions. As with the planning school, writers in the decision-preferences school appear to assume that an organisation's managers have a free choice in the strategies they adopt. This school also fails to address the issue of who and why decision-preferences become discarded. Although decision preferences are persistent, organisations also *can* and *do* change their strategies, even when the same staff are in place. It can also be argued that people are not constrained as much as some would suggest. For example, although research has identified links between demographic profiles and strategic preferences, these correlations are by no means perfect, allowing scope for individual choice.

Writers in this category include Reger and Huff (1993), Huff (1990), Weick (1990), Simon (1947, 1957), March and Simon (1958) and Myers (1962), all hugely influential people who have written about decision-making processes within organisations.

16.2.4 The processual approach to strategy

The processual approach sees strategy as emerging from the organisation's systems and processes, which develop over time and reflect the organisation's historical strategies. Like the decision-preference approach, it attributes a lot of importance to the systems and structures that strategic decision-makers set in place for gathering and processing information on customers or competitors. It assumes that these systems emphasise the kind of information that decision-makers already think is important, and give less prominence to data that might challenge their worldview. Unlike the previous category, however, it emphasises the way *systemic* aspects of an organisation – how people communicate with each other, how it pays its staff, how it processes information, what its staff **do** on a daily basis – shape strategic choices. These activities become embedded in routines, systems and structures as well as tangible things like buildings and equipment in a process called *reification* (from the Latin words for 'to make into a thing').

Writers in this group have identified how the organisation's information-gathering and attention systems are focused on particular aspects of the environment. Existing competitors are likely to be monitored, and particular aspects of their strategic performance such as their pricing policies and profit ratios, measured carefully. Other potential opportunities in the environment are likely to be missed altogether, or rejected as being too far away from what the organisation 'does'. Internally, too, there will be strong systematic shapers of future strategy. The types of financial or management information which are monitored within the organisation will tend to relate to assessing the performance of existing strategies, and how it could be improved, rather than what *might* be achieved with *different* strategies.

Some writers in this category place great importance on the competences and abilities of an organisation's staff, so that strategies are adopted because they make the most of what the organisation already does well. Moving into new business areas, on the other hand, requires considerable investment in learning.

In fact, all these systems and structures represent a considerable investment of finances, time and learning, so that there are costs involved in dismantling them in order to do something different. These costs, combined with managers' inherent decision-preferences as described in the previous section, are seen as making radical change unlikely. Writers in this group have suggested that organisations have a strong tendency to do in the future what they have done in the past, and that any change to strategy will be incremental – based on slight changes to what the organisation already does.

However, writers in this school can be criticised for their failure to take account of the fact that organisations can and do change significantly sometimes. They also tend to ignore how it is that systemic elements are selected; writers in other categories would suggest they are the result of political bargaining or environmental selection. Processualists also do not explain particularly well how it is that individuals within organisations respond to unknown situations, where the organisation's systemic elements cannot provide solutions based on history.

Key writers who have written about processual influences on strategy include Cyert and March (1963), Argyris and Schön (1978), Burgelman (1988, 1996), Prahalad and Hamel (1990), Stacey (1992), Senge (1990), Nonaka and Takeuchi (1995) and Quinn (1980). Others have focused more specifically on cultural influences on strategy, for example Grinyer and Spender (1979), Pettigrew (1985), Johnson (1987, 1992), Feldman (1986) and Peters and Waterman (1982).

Penrose (1959), Teece (1980), Wernerfelt (1984), Barney (1991) and Grant (1991) are all authors who have written about the resource-based view of the firm, which emphasises the importance of capabilities and learning.

16.2.5 The political approach to strategy

Another gradual development over the years of strategy theorising has been to question whether organisations do have single goals, or a single organisational 'mind'. Early strategy texts, if they ever considered the matter, often seemed to assume that the *organisation* made decisions, with little consideration of who within the organisation *actually* made the decisions. For writers in this group, in contrast, strategy-making is a political process, not only the preserve of the chief executive, but the result of the bargaining and negotiation taking place between the many individuals and groups in an organisation. Strategy, in this conceptualisation, is therefore the pooled *outcome* of a number of individual objectives, the pattern in which can only be identified retrospectively.

◀ *Organisational power is covered again in relation to structures and the management of change in Chapters 10 and 14.*

Clearly power has a part to play in this; some individuals are more powerful than others. Because of their authority position, their control over critical resources, or their expertise, in important areas, they are in a better position to achieve their particular objectives. Even if the most powerful person in an organisation is normally the chief executive, some degree of compromise or accommodation of other people's objectives can act to modify his or her original intentions.

More than most of the other groups, the political school focuses upon the internal workings of the organisation. It is thus open to the criticism that, by focusing on the process leading to the decisions, it ignores the content of those decisions – whether they are good or bad, and how one can tell which is which. Writers in this group, at least in the early days, paid little attention to how or why certain individuals became more powerful than others.

This group is relatively under-represented in the mainstream strategy literature, although recent research on, for example, strategic alliances have started to examine the political dimensions of such relationships. Key writers in this area are Burns and Stalker (1961), Burns (1977), Hickson et al. (1971), Ranson et al. (1980), Child (1972), Pettigrew (1973, 1977, 1992) and Pfeffer and Salancik (1978).

16.2.6 The ecological approach to strategy

Our next group looks at strategy as an experimental process, in which different things are attempted and only those that succeed are pursued. Those strategic activities which do not appear promising are allowed to die off or are ignored. Tom Peters, in some of his recent writings on innovation, has suggested that organisations should deliberately attempt to develop large numbers of novel activities in order to improve the chance that any one would be promising, a view which Peter Drucker also advocated in 1985.

This approach to strategy-making allows the organisation, through carrying out small-scale experiments, to adapt to changes in its environment, and is said to be particularly appropriate in fast-changing and dynamic industries. However, it is expensive, because of the waste of effort in trying different things, and a company in a simple, stable environment may not get much benefit from the constant experimentation. It may also lead to conflict, as people's pet ideas are rejected.

In this school of writing, the environment is regarded as especially important in shaping the destiny of the firm – another form of determinism. Some writers, such as Lieberson and O'Connor (1972), have focused entirely on such deterministic elements at the level of the whole firm, and suggested that whatever a company's leaders do, it has absolutely no impact on their organisation's performance compared with the effects of the environment. Although their research was later replicated by Weiner and Mahoney (1981) and their results questioned, even this second study found that the leader accounted for a relatively small proportion of their firm's performance. Hannan and Freeman (1977, 1984) similarly examined firms' adaptation and survival. They developed what they called a 'population ecology perspective', which mirrors the natural selection theories of the biological sciences. They discovered that there were regularities in the forms of organisations that survived within particular environment niches. Based on their view that organisations are slow-moving systems, constrained by investments in fixed assets, power structures and resource allocation mechanisms, they suggest that companies are rarely able to respond to changes in their environment fast enough. Only those firms which are already appropriately adapted thrive and therefore survive; those that are not, do not, and what leaders do plays little role in this success or otherwise.

◀ *Hannan and Freeman's population ecology theory was discussed in more detail in Chapter 5.*

Other writers in this category include Pugh et al. (1963, 1968), Miller et al. (1988), Burgelman (1991, 1994, 1996) and Van de Ven (1986, 1992).

16.2.7 Organisational anarchy

Most strategic management theorists assume that in every organisation, however chaotic, a pattern of actions will emerge, which an observer can recognise as its strategy. Our final, very small group of writers question this and ask whether all organisations have, or *need* to have, a strategy at all.

The term 'organisational anarchy' comes from a much-cited (1972) article by Michael Cohen, James March and Johan Olsen. They compare decision-making in certain types of organisation[1] to a garbage can in which problems and potential solutions rattle around, fired by the energy of participants, with a certain number of decisions emerging as problems and solutions collide.

In 1995, Andrew Inkpen and Nandan Choudhury wrote an article suggesting that strategy writers were conditioned to think that strategy *had* to exist even when there is evidence that in some cases it does not. Inkpen and Choudhury argued that not having a strategy at all may be quite helpful for organisations which operate in fast-changing environments, where there is little certainty over which of any intended strategies might be most effective. Similarly, there is so little stability in the environment that no micro-level organisational decisions have the opportunity to be collated into anything resembling a pattern. In these circumstances, attempting to impose a strong strategic framework on to the organisation could result in opportunities being missed, and the organisation being left behind.

Other theorists, such as Gerry Johnson (1987) and Romanelli and Tushman (1994) have implicitly accepted that there will be times that organisations do not have any clearly definable strategies. They suggest that this is simply an undesirable, short-term and unintentional phase, which Johnson terms 'flux', in between periods when the organisation does have a strategy. In contrast, Inkpen and Choudhury suggest that it can be a normal, and indeed desirable, situation for a firm. Such a view has also found some support in, for example, Pascale's (1996) view on the Japanese way of doing business. He suggests that they are somewhat distrustful of a single 'strategy' because this focuses attention away from what is going on at the peripheries of the organisation, where changes in customers, technology or competitors are noticed.

Inkpen and Choudhury's work is an interesting, unorthodox view on strategy processes, which we think is likely to spawn further writings. It has as yet been subject to very little empirical research. However, a truly anarchic organisation will be inefficient because no learning or repeated behaviour takes place, and so is likely to be outcompeted if other firms can develop more economic ways of operating. This is likely to happen unless the environment is exceptionally unstable.

16.2.8 The future of strategy theorising

The seven schools we have outlined above differ in several ways. They differ in the extent to which they see strategy as a rational response to a set of challenges. They differ also in the extent to which they see strategy development as the outcome of individual as against group processes. These variations are often more differences of emphasis than differences of fact. We doubt whether any of the theorists from the decision-preferences school would deny the existence of political processes within organisations, but in the interests of readability and manageability they simply prefer to focus on one relatively straightforward aspect of organisational life rather than another.

As we suggested at the beginning of Section 16.2, the traditional way of thinking about strategy has tended to be dominated by writers who seemed to assume that organisations had a 'mind', and a singular and rational one at that. These assumptions have been challenged by many modern scholars who believe that strategy needs to be understood as something more complicated. Some of them see it as a mistake to think of strategic decisions as being taken by 'organisations' or even by chief executives or top management teams. They have tried to show, by observing real organisations and their managers, that strategy processes can be set in train and influenced by managers and staff at many levels, and by external stakeholders. Others have tried to demonstrate, again through observing real decision-making processes, that the development and implementation of a strategy is not always rational. They believe that, like many other types of decision-making, strategic decisions can be subject to a messy, political process of resistance, compromise, bargaining, and negotiation as well as the influence of emotions.

Particularly in Europe, it is fair to say that the critics of the idea of strategy as rational processes of analysis and planning have become increasingly influential. However, the rational view still has some very powerful adherents. Some of them believe that strategy implementation can be made into a rational process if strategists understand their organisations well, and plan carefully enough. Others believe that strategic management is simply about setting the right direction for the organisation, and that the processes of strategy development and implementation, while interesting, are part of a different field of study.

REAL-LIFE APPLICATION 16.1

Honda – the facts and their interpretation

In 1975, the Boston Consulting Group (BCG), an influential management consultancy specialising in strategy, wrote a report for the UK government setting out alternatives for the British motorcycle industry. Within that report they analysed Honda's success in the US market. They painted a picture of how Honda had cleverly planned its penetration into the USA with small motorcycles sold to ordinary households, at a time when US producers focused on selling large machines to motorcycle enthusiasts. Honda than used this initial breakthrough to build volume in the USA, and gain reputation and economies of scale, which enabled them to gradually move up-market and to expand internationally.

In 1980 Richard Pascale, a US academic, decided on a whim to interview the Japanese executives who had managed Honda's US operations at the time. The picture they painted was very different from the calculated strategy described by BCG. They suggested that Honda's US success was the result of a set of happy accidents. The managers had started by trying to sell Honda's larger bikes, which however were not robust enough for American road conditions. The move to smaller motorcycles happened partly because there was nothing else for them to sell, partly because US

retailers had expressed interest after the Japanese managers had been spotted using the bikes to travel around. Henry Mintzberg, a very influential Canadian academic and author, was most taken with Pascale's account, and used it extensively to support his ideas about emergent strategy. According to him, Honda's success came about because, rather than planning everything in advance, they adapted to market conditions as they encountered them.

Andrew Mair, a British academic who has made a long study of Honda, does not dispute the details of Pascale's account. However, he has found documents that suggest that it was always Honda's intention to market their smaller motorcycles in the US, and that the manufacturing capacity to support those sales was planned well in advance. He suggests that the real basis of Honda's success, in the US and elsewhere, was not its use of avoidance of planning, but in its ability to handle ambiguity.

Source: Boston Consulting Group, 'Strategy Alternatives for the British Motorcycle Industry', HMSO, London, 30 July 1975; Pascale, Richard, *Managing on the Edge*, Simon and Schuster, New York, 1990; Mair (1999).

A related debate has taken place over the extent to which strategy can be seen as an *intentional* action. Some theorists say that, for something to qualify as a strategy, it must be a carefully formulated military-style plan of campaign – which is what the term *strategos* originally meant in Greek. At the other extreme are scholars holding the view that strategy is an *outcome* – a pattern that emerges from a stream of decisions or events. For people who hold this view, a strategy cannot be specified in advance, but only be seen or assessed retrospectively, and when we pick out patterns in an organisation's actions and call them its 'strategy', we may be doing nothing more than making a set of events *look* logical, when they actually happened by chance.

In fact the debate over how strategy *really* happens is still raging. A recent edition of the *California Management Review*[2] was devoted to discussing the interpretation of a single strategic case study, Honda's entry into the USA with its motorbikes (Real-Life Application 16.1). Some of today's most eminent strategy theoreticians wrote short articles critiquing each other's perspectives using this case as an exemplar. Some of these writers preferred an emergent view, some a competences view and some a planned view of the process. Indeed, if you want to understand the critiquing process a bit better, reading these articles would be a good start.

It is unlikely that we have yet discovered all the potential ways of thinking about strategy. For example, theorists have yet really to get to grips with what strategy means in virtual businesses, where the main links are electronic rather than interpersonal, and where organisational membership can be fluid. Nor has strategic management theory fully absorbed the implications of e-business, where business models are invented and implemented rapidly, and then changed before anyone has had time to assess their effectiveness.

Mintzberg et al. (1998) have summarised developments in the strategy field in a graph which shows the numbers of writers in each of their groups over time (Figure 16.2). It neatly illustrates the gradual move away from an emphasis on the rational towards those that identify the more processual aspects of the strategy process.

Perhaps future theorists may move away from emphasising one view of strategy over the others, and start to see the different schools as aspects of a single phenomenon. Research may examine how these strategy processes vary over time within the same organisation, or how they interrelate with each other. Hart and Banbury (1994) have found that firms that are able to use a range of strategy-making processes, from visionary through planning to processual, are more successful, on a variety of measures, than those with just one mode of developing strategy. They believe that this range of routines makes the organisation more adaptable as its environment changes. Research by Bailey and Johnson (1996, 2000) has found that a range of different types of strategy processes operate simultaneously within the same company – although usually one or two tend to dominate. Which styles are prevalent vary according to the organisation's size, maturity and industry sector.

To summarise, we have identified a large number of historical models of strategy processes. These are not intended to be prescriptive – you do not need to decide which one of these boxes you fit into, although thinking about these issues might help you to understand where your own preferences and biases lie. We have described them to help you to understand that thinking about strategy is not a simple matter, or one that is immutable. When analysing organisations it is helpful to decide which of the 'lenses' we have identified are most appropriate, perhaps taking an eclectic approach. As Michael Goold (1996) says:

Figure 16.2   Evolution of the ten schools (from Mintzberg et al., 1998)

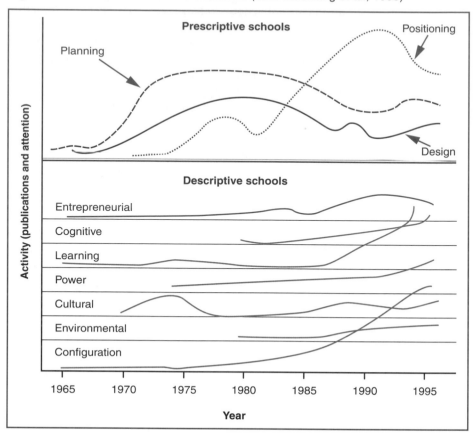

I remain, therefore, an unrepentant synthesiser. No strategic approaches or theories are likely to contain all the truth and all the answers. At best, they will offer partial insights and partial assistance. This may lead the academics to fight fierce rhetorical battles with the emphasis on undermining the weak points in their opponents' theories and approaches. Wise practitioners, however, in deed of all the help they can get, will continue to make use of what is valuable in each approach, even though they recognise its limitations. So, even after extra time, the contest between the planning and learning approaches to strategy remains undecided. Rather than moving to a penalty shootout to resolve the debate, perhaps we should instead all agree to plan to learn – or else to learn to plan.

16.3   Summary

In this chapter we have introduced you to a large number of writers, each of whom has addressed the complexity that is strategic management in a different way. From the discussion of their various approaches, we hope that you can see that strategy is not a concept which any single approach can capture in its entirety.

We have described seven different approaches to strategic management: the visionary, planning, decision-preference, processual, political, ecological and organisational anarchy. We also introduced other well-known conceptualisations of strategy theorising, notably the writings of Whittington (1993), McKiernan (1996) and Mintzberg et al. (1998).

Since ideas presented in this chapter are intended for reflection rather than practical application, we do not include our usual review of the questions you are likely to be asked about them.

Questions for discussion

1. 'The cataloguing of different schools of strategic thought is a pointless activity pursued by academics with nothing better to do.' Discuss.

2. Look at the description of our own preconceptions about strategy in Section 16.1. From which school of strategic thought is each of them drawn? What are the main arguments for and against them?

3. How would you expand future concepts of strategy to take account of virtual organisations and e-commerce?

4. Look again at the Honda case (Real-Life Application 16.1). Which of the three points of view do you think is correct?

CASE STUDY

Strategy decision-making in IBM

Adapted from Case Studies 'The Rise of IBM' and 'The Fall of IBM' in *Strategic Management*, C.W.L. Hill and G.R. Jones (1995), Houghton Mifflin, pp. C167–C202.

IBM was at one time one of the most successful computer companies in the world. In 1971 it held 75% of the world mainframe computer market. Although IBM's domination of the mainframe market produced record increases in revenues and profits every year, its performance masked some major problems that were developing during the 1970s and 1980s. The first major problem was that the mainframe computer market was starting to mature. Low-cost global competitors began offering IBM's customers mainframe systems at a lower cost than the expensive IBM systems. In turn, minicomputers and PCs were developed by companies such as DEC and Apple, both of which were to provide severe competition for IBM as the technological capabilities and low costs of the new computers superseded that of mainframes.

To respond to the threat of low-cost competition in the mainframe market IBM spent $10 billion to produce low-cost computers over a six-year period. However, IBM's push to reduce manufacturing costs did not fit well with its strategy of offering high-quality customer service using its salesforce to sell and service its machines. Other problems were emerging. The life span of a mainframe computer was shortening and IBM was forced to replace its leased computers every two or three years, making it difficult to recoup the high levels of development costs. Its strategic response was to continue to produce high-quality machines, protect its mainframe market from competitors and to hang on to its customers at all costs by supporting its very expensive, but successful, salesforce.

In 1986 DEC introduced its new VAX 9000 minicomputer which shocked IBM's mainframe managers because it had the same speed and capacity as IBM's largest 370 mainframe, but cost only 25% as much. For the first time, mainframe managers were forced to accept that minicomputers might be a substitute for mainframes.

Almost all of IBM's top managers had risen up the ranks of IBM from the mainframe division. A core belief was that computing power was everything; big machines meant big revenues. For example, IBM's mainframe managers saw the potential earning power of the minicomputer as insignificant when compared to the huge revenues generated by its mainframes. IBM's top managers also did not want competition from a new computer division inside the company. Even its renowned salespeople were oriented to selling and servicing the mainframe; they were not oriented towards satisfying customer needs, which might be more appropriate for a minicomputer or a workstation sale.

In the end, the minicomputers that the company brought to market were too big and too expensive to compete with DEC's machine and too small to compete with IBM's own mainframes. The company's attempt to introduce a two-division structure (one making minicomputers and the other making mainframes) to try to solve these problems created huge divisional rivalry between mainframe and minicomputer managers as they saw themselves in direct competition for resources. Managers in both units failed to co-operate or to share technological resources to develop new ranges of machines.

Similar problems faced IBM's introduction of the PC, which had been made in response to the development of the personal computer by Apple. Although initially successful, IBM's PCs were quickly cloned by competitors at a much lower cost. However, IBM continued to charge premium prices and did not reduce its own costs. IBM's north American PC market share dropped from 37% in 1985 to 12% in 1992.

IBM had developed a highly bureaucratic organisational structure, which meant that managers of the personal computer division had to get approval from the corporate management committee to cut prices – a process that sometimes took months. Its top management committee, staffed primarily by managers from its mainframe division, found it difficult to respond quickly to the rapidly changing computer environment. A potential project for a new product would be approved after six committee members rated two competing processes, which could take months or years; then the committee would meet to finalise the product plan. During this process if any committee member disagreed with the project, it would be sent back for further review or scrapped.

In 1991 revenues fell 5% from 1990, the first decline since 1946. The company's 1991 loss of $2.8 billion was the first loss in IBM's history. In 1992 IBM's losses increased to $5 billion on $65 billion in revenues.

Case study question

1. How would theorists from each of the seven schools (visionary, planning, decision-preference, processual, political, ecological and organisational anarchy) explain the decline of IBM? Which explanation do you find most compelling?

NOTES

1. Cohen et al. said that this type of behaviour was particularly common in public, educational, and illegitimate organisations. They took a university as their main example – we cannot imagine why!
2. See articles by Mintzberg, Rumelt, Pascale, and Goold in *California Management Review*, Volume: 38 Issue: 4 1996. For an illuminating view of how these, and other, authors have selected some parts of Honda's story and ignored others to find data that supports their arguments, see Mair (1999).

PART

6

Case Studies

The UK food retailing industry in 1998

Introduction and early history

Introduction

This case charts the rich history of the UK's *food retailing* (also known as the *grocery*)[1] industry to 1998 when the 'big five' multiple grocers, Tesco, Sainsbury, Asda, Somerfield and Safeway, together commanded 78% of the market.[2] It looks briefly at the origins of the industry, reviews the reactions of UK food retailers to the changes in their environment since the introduction of self-service in 1950, describes the industry structure in the 1990s, and concludes with a review of the strategies of the principal players.

The early history of the UK grocery industry

In pre-industrial Britain most people lived directly off the land, with farmers' surplus being sold in the market. Industrialisation, however, brought people into cities in search of work, so that large amounts of food had to be amassed in one place and redistributed. Shops supplanted street traders because of the need to store large quantities of produce and offer more variety. The nineteenth century saw an increase in Britain's population and their per capita incomes,[3] and two important developments in food technology, the can and the refrigerator, which enabled shoppers to forgo their daily visit to the market and buy food in greater quantities at less frequent intervals.

Of today's significant players, Sainsbury, Somerfield and the Co-operative movement can all trace their history back to this era. Twenty-eight men from Rochdale, known as Rochdale Equitable Pioneers Society formed the Co-operative movement in 1844. Their aim was to make food available to working people at a reasonable price. A share of any profit or surplus was returned to members in proportion to their purchase – in the form of a 'dividend' (the 'Divi').

This case study was written by Adrian Haberberg, based on a first draft prepared under his supervision by Driton Tali, MBA student at the University of Westminster. It is intended for classroom discussion rather than to illustrate good or bad handling of an administrative situation. (© Adrian Haberberg, 1998.)

Tinned food evolved in direct response to the need of the Navy: by the mid-1870s, most grocers stocked tins, mainly of cheap Australian meat, and by the early 1920s cheap tinned vegetables, fruits, and jam were available to almost everybody. At the same time, refrigeration technology was being improved. By the 1870s, ice-making had been perfected, and in 1880 the first successful consignment of frozen meat arrived in the UK from Australia. Commercial refrigerators appeared soon after, though domestic models took longer to develop.

By 1900, 'multiple' grocers (those with a chain of outlets in different towns and cities) had become prevalent,[4] though the service they provided was quite traditional:

> ... the customer was discouraged from touching any goods until they had been requested from an assistant, approved of and, of course, paid for. Marble counters separated the customer from the assistant, in a white apron, who would expertly cut the cheese and shape the butter, wrap up the provisions in a flash and, as a finale, tot up the bill ... in an instant. There was a chair for anyone whose feet were killing them, and would madam care for the goods to be sent to her home?[5]

Two world wars left British shopping habits largely unaltered, although food was rationed and women's roles and attitudes were changing, war having exposed them for the first time to large-scale employment in industry.

Changes in the food retailing industry 1950–80

The consumer

The needs and lifestyles of UK consumers underwent a major transformation between 1950 and 1980 (Exhibit 1.1). The post-war austerity of the 1950s was transmuted into the free-wheeling consumption of the 1960s and, to a lesser extent, the 1970s. An increased proportion of women in employment increased the demand for 'one stop' shopping. Increasing car ownership made it possible for people to travel further to shop and to carry larger quantities of goods home with them. Foreign travel increased demand for products such as exotic fruit and vegetables.[6] Once inside the stores, consumers responded to marketeers' increasingly sophisticated use of packaging and brands, frequently promoted on television.

During the 1970s the UK economy experienced considerable problems, with

Exhibit 1.1 Social and structural changes in UK society 1960–80

	1960	1970	1980
1. Population (1960 = 100)	100	106	107
2. Real personal disposable income (1960 = 100)	100	130	172
3. Females in employment (1960 = 100)	100	108	120
4. Percentage of homes owning:			
(a) Refrigerators	22%	66%	93%
(b) Freezers	–	< 3%	50%
(c) Cars	30%	50%	58%
(d) Televisions	75%	91%	96%
5. Number of people taking holidays abroad	4m	6m	10m

Source: The food industry – economics and politics (CAB, 1983, p. 129)

occasional short booms brought to an end by high inflation and currency crises. The slumps that followed each boom, combined with an underlying decline in the competitiveness of many UK producers on quality and price, led to ever-increasing levels of unemployment. Price became an important consideration for consumers.

The triumph of the supermarket

Self-service retailing became established in the USA during the Great Depression of the 1930s,[7] as a way of containing costs (and hence prices), using fewer staff to offer a wider range and quantity of merchandise. Sainsbury's is widely credited with opening the UK's first self-service store in Croydon, south-east London, in July 1950 (although Tesco claims its first self-service outlet opened in 1948). The Croydon store was soon Sainsbury's busiest outlet[8] and by 1960 *supermarkets*, low-price, high-volume, self-service stores carrying a wide variety of food, were common. Their spread was facilitated by a relaxation in building controls in the mid-1950s.

It became apparent that many of the supermarket's advantages were augmented as the stores themselves became larger. A store with a wide range of goods saves customers the time that, with traditional shopping, they might spend moving between and choosing between specialist shops. Large stores also offered advantages to the retailer.[9] Small shops may need one or two staff who, for large parts of the day, may be under-utilised. Larger shops, however, can vary the number of staff employed to meet fluctuations in demand (e.g. at Christmas), and can redeploy staff between tasks – from checkouts to checking stock, filling shelves and carrying out maintenance – to maximise productivity. Improvements in food technology, which prolonged the shelf-life of many products, made it possible to serve these larger stores with less frequent bulk deliveries.

Tesco opened its first *superstore* in 1967, and ten years later there were 150 UK superstores.[10] Superstores typically occupy 2,000–4,000 square metres and today sell everything from baked beans to fine wines. Some may also sell clothing, offer services such as dry cleaning, pharmacies, post-office and film developing and have a petrol forecourt. Most are located outside town centres with a free car park. *Hypermarkets*, which occupy about 10,000 square metres of space, and typically offer an extended range of clothing, hardware and electrical goods as well as food, began to open in the UK in the 1970s, a few years after their appearance in France. In 1960 the average size of a new store opened by Sainsbury's was 5,800 sq. ft, by 1980 it increased to 14,800 sq. ft, and the average store opened by the late 1980s had an area of 32,300 sq. ft.[11]

This increase in average outlet size resulted in a decline in the number of outlets needed to serve the community. The 1951 Census of Distribution counted 284,000 food shops, compared with the 121,000 shown by 1979 government statistics.[12] In order to survive, the small stores adapted themselves into *convenience stores* carrying a limited range of goods such as essential groceries, toiletries, cigarettes and newspapers and keeping longer hours than larger outlets. They were often run by, and catered for the specialist needs of, people belonging to immigrant minorities, such as those from the Indian subcontinent or the Caribbean. In order to compete with the branding and purchasing power of larger chains, they would sometimes join *affinity groups* such as Spar and Londis.

The rise of the multiple grocer

It has been estimated that at the turn of the century independent retailers accounted for 80% of the grocery market.[13] However, along with the benefits that came from having larger outlets, the bigger grocery firms began to find other advantages over their smaller rivals in the years following the Second World War. Alongside the obvious cost savings from volume discounts and faster stock turnover, there were more subtle benefits that developed over time. They could experiment with store layouts and pass from store to store the results – for example, that low-value staples like milk should be put at the rear so that, en route to these products, shoppers would see the rest of the merchandise. They acquired the ability to conduct and interpret sophisticated market research giving a better match of price and product characteristics to consumers' needs. Specialised procurement expertise, allied to heightened purchasing power, allowed large firms to specify a mix of products precisely adapted to meet those needs. Smaller grocery firms, on the other hand, had relatively limited procurement expertise, stocked narrower ranges, and needed to rely on manufacturers to adapt existing product lines.

This led to some changes in the industry structure (Exhibit 1.2). In the decade between 1961 and 1971, the total number of shops declined by approximately 13% and in the 1970s, while the number of shops fell by almost a third, the number of firms which had only one outlet fell by 40%.[14]

The multiple firms adopted a variety of strategies to promote their growth. There were mergers and acquisitions, with Tesco in particular acquiring six other multiples with a total of 878 shops in the period 1955–68 and closing the smallest and most uneconomic of their shops.[15] In order to serve their customers better and keep costs low, most of the retailers introduced computers during the 1960s.[16] Some also sought to build market share by passing cost savings on to their customers[17]; retailers increased their advertising expenditure by 533% in money terms between 1970 and 1979.[18]

Until 1964, manufacturers had enjoyed 'retail price maintenance': the right to set the prices at which retailers could sell their products. The owners of strong brands also were able to obtain favourable terms for the amount of space dedicated to their products and for retailers' participation in their promotional campaigns. Grocers, unable to offer discount on manufacturers' brands, resorted instead to offering rebates based on consumers' total purchase (the co-operative movement's 'dividend') or 'trading stamps'.[19] However, after pressure from leading retailers, retail price maintenance was abolished in 1964 and retailers were able to compete directly on price.

A number of discount grocers were born in this period, including Victor Value,

Exhibit 1.2   Grocery sales by type of retail outlet (%)

	1950	1957	1961	1966	1971	1975	1978	1980
Co-operatives	23	23	20	16	14	14	15	14
Independents	57	55	53	48	43	37	27	25
Multiples (10+ branches)	20	22	27	36	43	49	58	61

Source: A.C. Nielsen, *Annual Review of Grocery Trading*, Oxford, 1981.

Shopper's Paradise and Kwik Save Discount. Price competition also began to feature in the major grocers' strategies. In 1978 Tesco, by then clearly second in terms of market share, withdrew amid much publicity from the use of trading stamps and launched a series of price reductions under the heading of 'Operation Checkout'. Sainsbury, the established market leader, responded in kind with 'Discount 78'.

With the abandonment of resale price maintenance, manufacturers and suppliers lost most of their influence over the way their products were sold in the major UK supermarkets. They were in any case a fragmented, inefficient, largely domestically based industry,[20] and were now faced with declining numbers of individual customers or buying points for their products. For example, whereas in 1960, 500 multiple grocer buying points accounted for 28% of food trade, by 1970, 202 buying points accounted for 42%. In 1971, 27% of grocery turnover was accounted for by ten retailers.[21]

The 1980s – the 'golden age' of British grocery retailing

Economic and social progress

The Conservative government of Margaret Thatcher came to power in 1979 with a mandate to end the stagflation of the 1960s and 1970s. Its policies gave rise initially to a sharp rise in inflation and a vicious recession in the early 1980s. However, they also led to a resurgence in the competitiveness of UK industry and commerce which delivered rising standards of living to much of the country's population for most of the decade (Exhibit 1.3). Even though by the end of the decade economic growth had faltered, car ownership in the UK increased by almost 70% between 1971 and 1990, so that the proportion of households with regular access to a car rose from 52% to 68%.[22]

Among the tenets of the Conservatives was an emphasis on 'free market' principles and the encouragement of an 'enterprise culture' through the removal of disincentives to business growth. *Laissez-faire* policies were evident in a number of areas: mergers and acquisitions were rarely challenged by the state and the local government administrations who controlled land development were instructed not to refuse permission without a compelling reason, such as major traffic problems or the erosion of the countryside.[23]

Meanwhile, the growing to adulthood of people born during the post-war 'baby-boom' greatly increased spending on new types of food as tastes and lifestyles underwent further change. National advertising eroded regional and local differences in patterns of consumption. Increasing environmental and health awareness stimulated demand for low fat foods and organically produced vegetables and whole-

Exhibit 1.3   UK economic indicators

	1980	1985	1987	1988	1989	1990
(a) Population (millions)	56.4*	56.6	56.9	57.1	57.2	57.4
(b) Real GDP (% change year on year)	−1.7	3.5	4.8	4.3	2.3	0.8
(c) Industrial production (1985 = 100)	92.5	100.0	105.7	109.5	109.9	109.3
(d) Average earnings (1985 = 100)	58.2	100.0	116.3	126.6	133.1	151.6

* = 1981 data

Sources: 'Discount Grocery Retailing', IGD 1993; (a) p. 6, (b) and (c) p. 7, and (d) p. 8.

foods. While the numbers of women in employment increased, the average size of the family fell gradually, and the proportion of single person households rose. The amount of time that the average person had available for shopping therefore changed; while non-working women spent on average 4.56 hours per week shopping for groceries, working women spent only 2.93 hours.[24] Thus demand increased for 'one stop shopping' and convenience products like ready-prepared meals.

Competitive strategies

All of the four largest grocery combines increased their market share in the 1980s (Exhibit 1.4). Some, such as Sainsbury, grew organically, while others, such as Argyll (owner of the Safeway stores), grew by acquisition. Within the UK food-retailing sector there were 69 mergers and acquisitions from 1982 to 1986.[25] The trend towards larger store sizes also continued, with the number of hypermarkets and superstores increasing from 239 in 1980 to 580 in 1989.[26]

If 1970s competition was on price, in the 1980s it was based on adding value. Typical 1980s grocery stores offered mediocre service with unattractive interiors, narrow aisles, harsh lighting and too few checkouts, where sometimes only cash was accepted. They were replaced by accessible, attractive, architecturally distinctive stores with in-store bakeries, florists, pharmacies, delicatessens, coffee bars, heel bars and customer service desks. The products became more distinctive with organic vegetables, exotic (for British tastes) fruits such as yams and mangoes and reduced fat foods such as the Healthy Eating Range Tesco introduced in the second half of the 1980s.[27] Many of the discount formats born in the 1960s and 1970s – Victor Value, Shopper's Paradise and Pricerite, for example – disappeared, while others, such as Kwik Save, attempted to follow their larger competitors up-market.

Apart from the general trading of the major stores, four other elements of strategy came to prominence in the 1980s: retailers' own brands, information technology, changing relationships with suppliers and internationalisation.

Own brands in food retailing

The French hypermarket retailer Carrefour initiated its own brand 'Produits Libres' in 1976. Own brands were first introduced in the UK in 1977.[28] The first 'generation' of own-brand products were staple products such as bacon or baked beans. This type of product is still sold by most leading retailers at prices typically 25–45% below those of leading manufacturers' brands.[29] Their packaging is simple, in tune with the low price positioning.

Exhibit 1.4 Top five British grocers' shares of total grocery sales

Company	% share			
	1982	*1984*	*1988*	*1990*
J Sainsbury plc	9.5	11.6	14.5	16.3
Tesco plc	8.7	11.9	14.8	15.7
Argyll Group plc	3.8	5.1	9.7	11.2
Asda plc	4.6	7.2	7.9	10.4
Dee Corporation/Gateway plc	n.a.	7.3	11.4	7.8

Source: R.D. Bromley and C.J. Thomas, *Retail Change*, UCL Press, 1993, p. 44.

Exhibit 1.5   Retailers own-brand shares in food retailing 1981–90

Country	(% of total food sales)		
	1981	1985	1990
Belgium	16	16	18
France	19	19	20
West Germany	5	10	16
Italy	5	7	8
Netherlands	13	21	27
UK	17	25	36

Source: Euromonitor.

From the mid-1980s onwards, retailers began to sell more up-market own-label products. Initially these products were still basic staples, although packaged to compete more directly with the brand leaders' products. These today are the most common own-brand variant in most countries.

Own brands developed strongly in the UK (Exhibit 1.5), accounting for 100% of Marks & Spencer's sales, 65% of Sainsbury's and 50% of Tesco's.[30] The majority of UK own-branded goods were, and still are, imitations of manufacturers' products, but a few retailers began to offer products that were differentiated from both manufacturers' and other retailers' offerings. Marks & Spencer (M&S)[31] led the way with a range of cook-chilled and fresh foods, but were imitated by Tesco, Sainsbury, Asda and Safeway.

Chill-cooking technology appeared in the 1980s. It safeguarded the flavour of complex dishes and sauces better than canning or freezing, so allowing the production of more appetising and exotic recipes than was previously possible. Cook-chilled dishes were also convenient for the customer, who needed simply to heat them in a conventional or microwave oven.

Information technology and logistics

The development of successful own-label products was greatly helped by information generated by efficient centralised stock control and distribution systems put in place during the 1970s and early 1980s. The major UK retailers' sustained profitability had enabled them to invest heavily in these systems.[32]

The core of these systems was data gathered at the checkout using electronic point of sale (EPOS) systems. This could be fed to systems monitoring inventories in stores, at central warehouses and within the distribution network, to trigger reordering. Links to accounting systems made administrative procedures simpler and faster. EPOS also offered managers ways to monitor internal efficiency measures, such as the average time it takes for a checkout operator to handle an item and deal with a customer, takings per hour and numbers of mis-scans.[33]

EDI (electronic data interchange) links to suppliers' computer systems allowed automatic reordering and computerised tracking of where orders were in the distribution chain, so that action could be taken in the event of a delay. By the end of the decade the large UK food retailers could supply stores smoothly and predictably within 12 hours of an order being transmitted, as compared to 24 hours in the early 1980s and 48 hours in the late 1970s.[34]

In order for this system to work effectively without complex and wasteful duplication of deliveries, it was necessary to invest in composite warehouses and trucks. These could simultaneously handle storage and delivery of frozen foods, fresh meat and fish and dry groceries, each of which needed to be kept at different temperatures. The first composite warehouse was opened by Tesco in 1988.

The result was a significant and progressive reduction in retailers' inventories and the amount of capital tied up in them. In some firms, being at the cutting edge of IT development may have stimulated innovation elsewhere in the organisation.

Supplier retailer relationships

In part, retailers' reductions in inventory were achieved by passing back some of the cost and risk to the manufacturer/supplier.[35] Pressure was placed on suppliers to develop just-in-time production and distribution systems to match the retailers'.

The large grocers were able to exploit the availability of their own brands and their ability to control the allocation of selling space to squeeze out nationally advertised brands. This allowed them to demand ever-larger discounts, including back-dated discounts, from manufacturers and suppliers and to impose ever more stringent conditions of supply,[36] though the amount of credit that was demanded from suppliers was still well below what was common elsewhere in Europe. During the 1980s, food manufacturers' profits increased at only half the rate achieved by the major food retailers.[37]

Internationalisation

By the late 1980s, amidst fears that the UK grocery market was approaching saturation,[38] retailers became interested in other markets. In June 1987, Sainsbury acquired Shaw's – a supermarket group operating on the East coast of the USA – for

Exhibit 1.6 Profitability of food retailers 1989–90

	Net profits as % of	
Company	Assets	Sales
United Kingdom		
Kwik Save	14.6	3.8
Tesco	12.1	5.1
Marks & Spencer	11.7	7.2
Argyll	10.5	4.6
J Sainsbury	10.5	4.8
Asda	5.8	3.9
Continental Europe		
Ahold (Holland)	5.7	1.4
Comptoirs Modernes (France)	4.9	1.7
Delhaize- Le Lion (Belgium)	4.9	1.5
Carrefour (France)	4.6	1.2
Promodes (France)	4.2	1.7
Au Printemps (France)	3.9	1.3
Asco (Germany)	2.4	1.5
Casino (France)	2.0	0.9

Source: © The Economist Newspaper Limited, London, 23 February 1991.

$261 million.[39] Ian MacLaurin, Chairman of Tescos, declared 'Tesco is anxious to expand abroad should the right opportunity come along. Group executives have been looking at the US market with acquisition in mind for some time.'[40]

US net profit margins tended to be lower than in the UK, mostly below 1% in the mid-1980s.[41] Various legal restrictions, including those on hours of opening, meant that European retailers' net profits were also low by UK standards (Exhibit 1.6). However, margins did not always translate into returns on assets – Kwik Save, the most profitable chain of all, was a discounter with a long history of undercutting rivals on price.

Strict anti-trust legislation had prevented US retailers from expanding nationally[42] until enforcement of anti-merger policy was relaxed in the 1980s.[43] US food retailers had therefore only been able to build brand identities at the regional level. National retail chains like Sears, K-Mart and Wal*Mart were best known for their clothing and hardware.

US food retailers' own brands were thus weaker than those in the UK, making it easier for food manufacturers to refuse to supply them with own-label products.[44] Their strategies tended to emphasise price: either 'hi–lo' pricing with periodic promotions and discounts or EDLP (every day low prices) featuring more consistent low prices.

UK food retailing in the 1990s

Industry structure

The four major multiples continued to increase their grocery market share in the 1990s (Exhibit 1.7) at the expense of co-operatives and the independent sector. In March 1998,[45] Somerfield agreed to merge with Kwik Save to become the fifth major player.

Exhibit 1.7   Grocery market shares 1992–97 (% share)

Company	1992	1993	1994	1995	1996	1997
Tesco	18.2	18.7	19.3	21.8	22.5	23.6
J Sainsbury	22.5	21.6	22.0	21.1	20.7	19.6
Asda	10.4	10.5	10.9	11.7	12.8	13.5
Safeway	8.6	9.1	9.2	9.6	10.3	10.8
Kwik Save	6.7	7.2	6.9	6.6	6.5	5.8
Somerfield/Gateway	5.6	4.6	4.8	4.5	4.5	4.5
Wm. Morrison	2.8	3.3	3.6	4.0	4.2	4.0
Iceland	3.1	3.3	3.4	3.2	2.9	3.0
Waitrose	1.6	1.5	1.4	1.6	1.6	1.6
Aldi	0.2	0.2	0.3	0.8	0.9	0.8
Netto	–	0.4	0.6	0.7	0.8	0.9
Lidl	–	–	–	0.3	0.5	0.6
Other multiples	3.0	5.4	4.9	2.9	2.0	2.7
Co-operative	8.5	7.3	6.6	6.3	5.5	5.0
Symbol	1.8	1.6	1.3	1.1	1.0	0.8
Other independents	7.0	5.3	4.8	3.8	3.3	2.0

Source: Mintel.

Exhibit 1.8 Grocery shop numbers in Great Britain, 1993–97

Change %	1993	1994	1995	1996	1997	
Multiples	5,325	5,593	5,667	5,826	6,349	19.2
Co-ops	2,395	2,324	2,362	2,316	2,263	−5.5
Independent	32,662	31,601	31,382	28,400	28,319	−15.3
Total	40,832	39,519	39,411	36,982	36,931	−8.5

Source: Mintel.

The UK retail grocery industry in 1990 had 42,446[46] retail outlets, but by 1997 this total had fallen to 39,631. The government's attempt to curb supermarket growth had little impact – between 1993 and 1997 there was an increase of 19% in the number of retail outlets owned by multiples (Exhibit 1.8).

Competitive developments

The high profit margins in the UK and the returns earned by Kwik Save attracted entrants from abroad. European discounters Aldi and Netto opened their first UK shops in 1990, followed by Ed (Erteco) in 1993, and Lidl in 1994. US retailer Costco opened the UK's first warehouse club in 1993.[47]

Their entry, at a time when the UK economy was in recession, triggered a round of highly publicised price cuts. Tesco reduced prices on 500 own-label items in August 1991, Sainsbury responded with a promotion called 'Why Pay More' and Asda announced its own price reductions for the pre-Christmas period when retailers have traditionally made much of their profits. In December 1992, Sainsbury reduced the prices of 50 selected products by up to 50% and Tesco and Safeway responded with price cuts on 1,000 items. In the following three years, the price of a typical basket of eleven basic items fell by 29% in Sainsbury, 23% in Kwik Save, 16% in Tesco and 14% in Aldi.[48]

However, price was by no means the only competitive weapon that the leading food retailers had at their disposal in the early 1990s. They built upon their 1980s' investments in product development, supply chain management and distribution – by 1994, all supermarkets with an area of over 25,000 sq ft and 89% of smaller supermarkets deployed EPOS systems.[49] Most major chains introduced schemes to improve staff motivation to generate cost-saving suggestions and improvements in customer service, while at the same time cutting back on headquarters staff – Tesco announced 800 headquarters redundancies in February 1994, and Sainsbury announced 650 job losses the following month.[50] They also turned their attention to expansion, both in the UK and abroad.

Sainsbury earmarked £800 million a year for new stores.[51] Tesco acquired the French supermarket Catteau (which, however, it sold again in 1997),[52] Global T.H. in Hungary and Slavia in Poland, and opened Tesco outlets in the Czech Republic and Slovakia. Marks & Spencer, who had for many years traded in Canada without great success, now opened branches in France and Spain. In defiance of all stereotypes of English and French cuisine, M&S found a ready market in Paris for their cook-chilled meals.

However, competition laws were seen as limiting the scope for further domestic or international mergers. Some European retail chains have signed pacts with one another with a view to reducing costs by bolstering their bargaining power with

Exhibit 1.9 Consumer expenditure on chilled ready meals

	£ million	Index
1992	238	100
1993	267	112
1994	288	121
1995	310	130
1996	338	142
1997	364	153

Source: IGD.

suppliers and jointly developing new store concepts and distribution networks. While some sceptics reckon that retailers will in practice be reluctant to share know-how with allies who may one day become competitors, there are now around 15 such pacts. The European Retail Alliance was formed in 1989 by Britain's Argyll, France's Casino and Holland's Ahold.[53] Other alliances where UK grocery retailers are involved are Intercop (which includes Britain's CWS), Deuro-Buying (Asda (UK), Carrefour (F), Makro (NL) and Metro (D)), and Intergroup Trading (which includes the affinity group Spar).[54]

In their home market, the grocers extended the range of products and facilities on offer in their stores to embrace clothing, newspapers, books, videos, CDs, pharmacies, financial services and baby-changing facilities. They identified the potential for selling takeaway food both to consumers going to the store specifically for that purpose and to grocery shoppers.

Tesco, Sainsbury, Asda and Safeway extended their own-brand ranges, offering similar products to Marks & Spencer but at lower prices. By the end of the decade, all five companies were putting a strong emphasis on developing ready meals, with a new frozen or chilled ready meal being launched practically every month and apparently finding a ready market (Exhibit 1.9). In 1998, Mintel was predicting the launch of new premium ranges from leading supermarket chains, aimed at consumers wanting to replicate a restaurant-quality meal.

Supermarket chains also attempted to enhance the service offered by extending their opening hours, and offering home delivery and loyalty cards.

Shopping hours

Shopping hours had long been tightly regulated by the government in the UK, with some restrictions on opening hours dating back to the nineteenth century.[55] In the early 1990s, the enforcement of these laws was relaxed, and the main food retailers, apart from Waitrose and M&S who refused on principle to break the law, began to open on Sundays.[56]

The inevitable change in the law came in November 1995, and many of the main supermarket chains then progressively extended the opening hours of selected branches until 8.00 p.m., 10 p.m. or in some cases 24 hours (excluding Sundays, when food shops are allowed to open for only six hours). For example, Sainsbury's store in Islington, in North London, stayed open 24 hours on Friday, with 10.30 p.m. to 1.30 a.m. the busiest period. The move was popular with many types of customer from families to shift workers and taxi-drivers.[57] Because most large stores were staffed all night to receive deliveries, the marginal cost of extending opening hours was quite small.

Home delivery/home shopping

Iceland, a specialist frozen food retailer targeting lower income customers, was the first multiple to launch a national home delivery service, available from 770 stores. Other home delivery services included Tesco Direct (in 21 stores mainly in London), Sainsbury's Order & Collect (in 32 stores, extended nationwide in April 1998) and Somerfield (34 stores). Safeway, Waitrose and M&S also tested services. The primary customers for these services were people without access to a car and busy working professionals.[58]

Loyalty cards

Further developments in firms' IT capability led to the introduction of loyalty cards. These, when presented at the checkout, gave the shopper 'points', typically one point per pound of expenditure. After accumulating a certain number of points, typically 250, the customer was sent or could collect vouchers that could be used to purchase goods in the issuer's stores. In some cases the points could be donated to charity or translated into 'air miles', which in sufficient quality entitled the holder to free air travel.

While retailers hoped that loyalty cards would build customer loyalty to a particular supermarket brand, they also valued the potential for capturing information about buying patterns and so developing closer relationships with customers. Information systems registered which products customers bought, how often, in which combination and how they reacted to price changes, advertising, etc. Customers could then be targeted with special promotions relevant to their needs, or sent reminders with money-off vouchers if they had not visited the store recently.

Following Tesco's launch of its Clubcard in February 1995, most other grocery chains, apart from Asda and Wm. Morrison, launched their own loyalty cards. Some food retailers started to offer combined loyalty and credit cards, whose use in the retailer's own stores earned the customer extra loyalty points.

Social responsibility and the environment

As people became more conscious of environmental and ethical issues, social responsibility began to play a more prominent part in grocery retailers' strategies.[59] Sainsbury's in 1997–98 donated a total £3.4 million to charitable organisations and community projects.[60] Sainsbury and Tesco periodically (and often simultaneously) run promotions where shoppers who spend a minimum amount can earn vouchers that enable the school of their choice to purchase computing hardware and software. Tesco claimed that by the end of 1997 it had given 31,000 computers to schools, together with an extensive range of software and training.[61] Food retailers have also begun to adopt environmentally friendly policies, such as the use of solar power for refrigerated lorries, recycling, and the purchase of wood and paper products from sources certified as managed for environmental sustainability.

Customer requirements

Expenditure on food outside the home continued to grow, through restaurants, fast food outlets and takeaway food shops. In the 1990s, the proportion of women

Exhibit 1.10   Factors influencing choice of store for main grocery shopping

	(% of respondents citing)	
	1995	1998
Quality of products	50	59
Location / easy to get to	53	55
Attractive prices	52	54
Wide range of products	45	43
Measures to ease queues at checkout	37	42
Fresh food service counter (e.g. deli, fish)	25	34
Longer opening hours	38	33
Good own label range	26	29
Cash point facilities	16	27
Express checkouts	22	26
Customer loyalty cards	6	22
Cash back facility	n/a	22
Financial services	n/a	2

Source: Mintel

that worked, and so had less time to spend on food preparation, had increased. An increasing proportion of the population lived in single- and two-person households, and found it more economic to use single portion prepared foods.

They and other consumers were becoming more selective but also more eclectic in their buying preferences. Mintel research showed that British consumers were increasingly interested in quality (Exhibit 1.10) whereas shoppers in continental Europe placed greater emphasis on price. Consumer spending on vegetarian ready meals grew by 70% in the period 1993–98.[62] Ethnic variants were the fastest growing sector, accounting for over half of sales, with Indian, Chinese, Italian and Thai the most popular recipe dishes.[63]

Unresolved problems

Despite the enduring success of the industry, a number of problems remained at the end of the 1990s. Firstly, government policy on out-of-town developments had wavered. In 1994 Safeway and Asda were each refused planning permission for out-of-town superstores.[64] Secondly, public concerns had been expressed as to how it was that the leading UK food retailers were so much more profitable than their counterparts abroad.

In August 1998, the UK government's Office of Fair Trading announced that it was investigating the dominance of the leading supermarkets, following complaints from farmers that falling market prices for farm produce were not being passed on to consumers. *The Sunday Times*, an influential weekly newspaper, had at intervals throughout the 1990s published comparisons between retail prices in the UK, the USA and continental Europe. In their leading story on 23 August 1998 they claimed that British shoppers were charged the highest prices in the Western world, supporting this claim with detailed comparative data for the cost of a basket of everyday items in various capital cities.

On 23 November 1998 the BBC broadcast a documentary in its 'Panorama' programme which echoed the concerns of the OFT and *The Sunday Times*, and also showed interviews with suppliers detailing what were claimed to be unfair practices on the part of the supermarket chains. Among those claims were: that supermarket buyers would, without prior negotiation or notice, reduce the agreed prices for meat and produce; that they would require suppliers to purchase their packaging from a particular source when similar materials were available more cheaply elsewhere (the implication being that the supermarket had some preferential agreement with the packaging supplier); that they would demand charitable donations from their suppliers which would then be passed on to the charity disguised as contributions from the supermarkets themselves.

Some operational problems had also proved intractable. Despite the industry's heavy investment in EPOS, many customers still experienced long queues at checkouts. Express checkouts and self-scanning facilities seemed not to be having the desired impact, perhaps because of customers' technophobia.[65] A study by management consulting firm McKinsey found that labour productivity in UK food retailing was only 75% of that in France, although the same study pointed out that in total factor productivity (labour and capital combined), 'the United Kingdom sets the global standard jointly with France' and that the UK 'defined global best practices in logistics and space management'.[66]

Meanwhile, in the USA, Wal*Mart, the world's largest retailer and America's sixth largest company by market capitalisation, had entered the grocery market, opening 150 Supercentres (200,000 sq ft grocery stores) per year.[67] This had triggered among US supermarket chains a wave of defensive mergers and an eagerness to learn the efficient retailing practices at which Wal*Mart excelled, and where European food retailers were reckoned to be well ahead of their US counterparts. In December 1997, Wal*Mart had acquired Germany's Wertkauf hypermarket group, and had announced an interest in acquisitions in other countries, including the UK.[68]

Industry players in 1998

Independent grocers

Independent food retailers' power and influence have declined dramatically from the 1970s, when there were some 62,000 independent shops with a combined market share of over 40%. In 1993 they controlled only 13% of the grocery market. Until the early 1990s, their main competitive advantage was their legal right to open for longer hours than the major retailers and to trade on Sunday. Once food superstores were able to match them in this area, they found themselves under increasing pressure. In 1992 Nisa, the largest association of independent retailers, formed a buying consortium with another 28 independent organisations.[69] This aimed to combine the purchasing power of its members, but co-ordination and communication problems meant that the hoped-for benefits failed to materialise. Independent retailers lost further market share and their numbers continued to fall.

However, the traditional open market, with its low overheads and fresh fruit, vegetables and fish, has remained a feature of most sizeable UK towns. Vending machines and other electronic sales outlets had also shown growth in the 1990s.

Co-operative food retailers

Co-operative societies hold an important place in the UK's social history. However, this has not enabled them to retain the dominant position they once had in UK food retailing. Nevertheless, the UK's 50 independent co-operative societies still command a total of 2,263 food outlets, and a grocery market share of 5%. Some of the societies have only a few stores, but two of the major elements of the movement are the Co-operative Wholesale Society (CWS) and the Co-operative Retail Society (CRS) (Exhibit 1.11).

The CWS was founded in 1863 as a wholesale supplier of a wide range of food and other products to the growing retail co-operatives. Over the years it acquired a number of troubled co-operatives and so became a retailer in its own right. CWS supplies some 4,500 Co-op own-brand food and non-food products to other retail societies. It is a major player in the UK funeral, travel agent and optician industries and is Britain's biggest farmer, working 50,000 acres of land, most of which it owns. It also has a substantial share in the Co-operative Bank.[70]

The CRS was created in 1934 to take Co-op trading to areas without local societies, and has since absorbed nearly 200 formerly independent societies.[71] It has 480 food stores of which 197 are supermarkets of over 8,000 sq. ft and 291 are small stores under 8,000 sq. ft. There have been periodic discussions with a view to merging CRS with CWS, most recently in February 1997, but without result. There was also a move by a private firm to buy CWS in 1997, but this came to nothing amid accusations that top CWS managers had supplied confidential information to the prospective purchaser.

All co-operative societies are governed by representatives elected by the society's members. This makes them immune from hostile takeover, but has been said to slow down decision-making. Nonetheless, the two major societies have followed, and in some cases led, the main trends in retailing over the years. CWS has some of the UK's oldest ranges of own-label products, and the CRS launched its own range in 1997. CRS launched a new logo, incorporating the rainbow emblem of the international Co-operative movement in 1997 and completed its EPOS installation programme in June 1998.

The 'Divi', having at one stage been converted to a form of trading stamp, now has a new incarnation as the CWS's loyalty card. This was rolled out in 1997 after a two-year trial in Northern Ireland and Scotland, which the society reported was very successful, and gives customers a 5% discount on own-label products and a 2% discount on other items. The CWS is hoping this card, which gives 50% more than other loyalty cards, will win back lapsed customers and retain existing ones.

Exhibit 1.11 Co-operative food sales and trading profit (£ million)

	Year ending January			
	1995	*1996*	*1997*	*1998*
CWS				
Sales (excl. VAT)	1036	1013	1043	n/a
Pre-tax profits	43.4	37	32.2	n/a
CRS				
Food sales (excl. VAT)	1,074	1,263	1,235	1,210
Total sales (excl. VAT)	1,348	1,556	1,542	1,538
Trading surplus	38	27	11	(23)
Trading margins (%)	2.8	1.7	0.7	(1.4)

Source: Mintel.

Discounters

A small group of retailers have remained faithful to the discounting strategies that were popular in the 1970s. By keeping their cost structures lean and their stock turnover high, they are able to offer top brands, together with a few secondary or exclusive labels, at prices 5–10% below those of comparable products from the leading retailers. Their target market is the 56% of the UK population that falls into the lower income groups (C2, D and E).[72]

The most prominent of these firms is Kwik Save, but it was joined in the 1990s by Northern European rivals Aldi, Netto and Lidl. All four firms paid special attention to the north of the country, with its relatively dense population, high level of unemployment and low average household incomes.[73] The 1990s also saw the first appearance in the UK of American-style 'warehouse clubs'.

Kwik Save Group plc

Kwik Save was founded as Value Foods in Wales in 1958 by Albert Gubay. Gubay gained notoriety through his persistent infringements of local laws on shop opening (he stayed open until 9 p.m. on Fridays) and his undercutting on price, which led some manufacturers to refuse to supply him, as they were then legally entitled to do. A 1964 visit to the USA introduced him to a strategy of selling a selected range of products at low prices while keeping overheads to a bare minimum. A trial store deploying this strategy was soon doing more business than Gubay's three larger supermarkets, and the formula was quickly rolled out. The firm was floated on the stock exchange in 1970 as Kwik Save Discount, when it had 24 stores, and had expanded to over 200 outlets by 1980, despite Gubay's resignation from the group in 1973.[74]

The original Kwik Save stores minimised warehousing and administration costs by offering only 800 lines, as against the 4,000 normal for competitors. The product range was gradually expanded so that in the 1990s a Kwik Save store might have 1,500–3,000 lines, predominantly leading brands. Outlets were located in busy high street locations in densely populated areas.

Despite its competitive prices, low margins and low-cost image, Kwik Save's profits grew by 19% per annum through the second half of the 1980s, generating the highest return on capital employed in the UK food retailing sector.[75] Growth continued in the early 1990s, aided by Kwik Save's first national press and poster campaign, which centred around the slogan 'All the best labels – no designer prices'. However, competition from the major multiples, in particular Asda with its

Exhibit 1.12   Kwik Save Group plc, turnover and profitability, 1993–97

	Year ending August				
	1993	1994	1995	1996	1997
Turnover (excl. VAT)	2,651	2,800	2,992	3,254	3,010
Operating profit (£m)	126	135	125	90	74
Pre-tax profit (£m)	126	136	125	3	74
Operating margins (%)	4.8	4.8	4.2	2.8	2.6
Sales per sq. ft per week (£)	10.4	10.2	9.1	9.1	8.9

Source: Mintel.

strong price positioning, and from the continental discounters such as Aldi and Netto, put profits under pressure (Exhibit 1.12).

Kwik Save responded in a number of ways. In 1996 it began a restructuring programme with capital investment of £50–60 million projected for 1997–98. The costs of store closures, consultancy fees, new systems and store refurbishment hit profits further, with each store refurbishment costing around £70,000. Store closures in 1996–97 reduced turnover by 3%, although like-for-like sales in the remaining stores also declined.

In July 1997, the company launched a programme of weekly promotions, designed to highlight Kwik Save's value, with 200 lines being heavily promoted each month. It backed this up with the 'Call Cut Costs' campaign, which encouraged customers to telephone a 24-hour free phone number if they found lower prices in competitors' stores. The promotion led to a number of price reductions in the first few months of operation.[76]

In July 1998, however, Kwik Save merged with Somerfield, resulting in the loss of Kwik Save's own brand and almost 700 jobs at its Welsh head office.[77]

Netto, Aldi and Lidl

Three firms, Netto, Aldi and Lidl, all recent entrants, follow similar strategies. They are not publicly quoted, and none of the three releases much financial information.

Netto Foodstore Limited is owned and operated by Dansk Supermarket, a Danish company that operates retail chains in Denmark, Germany, Poland as well as the UK. It was formed in 1977, primarily as a response to Aldi's entering the Danish food-retailing market.[78] In the eight years after opening its first UK supermarket in 1990 in Leeds[79] it built a chain of 117 stores, mostly in the north. A few shops in London and South-East England were acquired from the French discounter Erteco when it exited the UK market. The stores are located on high streets, and carry a range of approximately 650 lines, with only one product choice being available per product category. Stringent cost control is said to keep Netto's prices 15–20% below those of leading retailers. Netto and Aldi turnover and profit for 1992–96 can be seen in Exhibit 1.13.

Albrecht Discount ('Aldi') holds over 5,200 stores in Germany, Austria, Denmark,

Exhibit 1.13   Netto and Aldi, turnover and profit 1992–96

	1992	1993	1994	1995	1996
Netto Foodstore Ltd					
(year ending August)					
Turnover (excl. VAT) (£m)	82	148	206	276	293
Pre-tax profit/loss	(1.4)	(0.6)	1.7	2.0	(1.9)
Aldi Ltd					
Year ending December					
Turnover (excl. VAT) (£m)	179	267	380	545	632
Pre-tax profit (£m)	6	11	12	13	15

Source: Mintel.

France, Luxembourg, the Netherlands, the USA and the UK. Its 1993 turnover of $20.9 billion gave it 12th place among the world's largest retailers.[80] Its first UK store opened in Birmingham in 1990.[81] By March 1998 Aldi had 195 stores in the UK with 30 more expected to open before the end of that year, most in the south of England to reduce the firm's northern bias.

Lidl Ltd was the UK subsidiary of Germany's Lidl & Schwartz. Its first 40 UK stores started trading in November 1994, a further 40 had opened within a year and by 1998 there were 130 stores all over the country. Lidl operates 'neighbour-hood stores' of 3,000–9,000 sq. ft, offering around 600 product lines, the vast majority of which are food. IGD estimates its UK turnover at over £350 million.

A 1994 estimate gave discounters 16% of the market for packaged groceries, double what it had been in 1991, but pointed out that such goods generated less than 25% of major grocers' sales.[82]

Warehouse clubs

In November 1993 Costco, the third largest US chain of warehouse clubs, opened the first such UK outlet in Thurrock, 30 km to the east of London.[83] The second, Cargo Club, was opened in London in March 1994 by Nurdin & Peacock, a British wholesaler.[84]

Warehouse clubs typically have a sales area of 100,000 sq. ft and offer a range of 3,500–4,500 food and non-food lines at prices 25% or more below those in major supermarkets. Customers, mostly individuals or small businesses, must pay an annual membership fee to be able to purchase goods, which are sold in bulk with a restricted range of pack sizes. Warehouse clubs were the fastest-growing forms of retailing in the USA, but some critics doubted that UK consumers were as ready as their US counterparts to drive long distances to shop or to buy in bulk.[85] Indeed, 1994 estimates that there would be 50 such outlets in the UK by the year 2000 seemed, in 1998, to be rather wide of the mark.

Regional food retailers

Bradford-based[86] Wm. Morrison Supermarkets plc (Exhibit 1.14) is the largest of the regional grocery retailers with 86 stores averaging 36,000 sq. ft. The group, of which 30% is owned by the Morrison family, accounts in 1998 for 4% of UK food

Exhibit 1.14   Wm. Morrison Supermarkets plc. Financial performance (£000s)

	Year ending February				
	1993	1994	1995	1996	1997
Turnover	1,316.7	1,538.4	1,779.4	2,099.4	2,176.0
Operating profit	79.9	96.0	114.4	126.2	133.8
Net profit	54.5	63.3	73.0	79.2	82.8
Total assets	619.1	706.1	829.3	1,105.8	1,037.8
Sales per sq. ft per year per (£)	792.2	764.8	790.7	807.2	816.2
EPS (p)	7.41	8.61	9.91	10.67	11.01
Shareholders' funds	361.0	415.2	477.9	545.6	614.5
Gearing	15.3	7.0	5.5	28.6	14.9

Source: Wm. Morrison Supermarkets plc Published Accounts.

expenditure, although in its northern heartland its market share is much larger: 16% in Yorkshire and 12% in north-east England.[87] The company had plans to expand in southern England by the end of 1998.

Morrisons is widely regarded as the most successful and efficient of the small regional grocery multiples, with tight control over its costs.[88] Own-label products account for around 50% of sales. It does not have a loyalty card, preferring to feature a thousand products on special offer each week. It had pioneered a 'Market Street' concept for its shops, aiming to provide 'traditional values in a modern format'. This concept involved a number of fresh food shops within Morrisons stores, including a butcher, fishmonger and bakery.

In 1997, Morrisons announced a strategic link up with the Midland Bank (the UK brand of BSBC) to develop in-store banking and financial services. The in-store bank offers a comprehensive range of personal banking services, including co-branded accounts. The 'Midland Brand at Morrisons Bonus Saving Account' launched in January 1998 paid interest of 6%.

Waitrose, by contrast, is focused on the affluent south of England. It was founded in 1906 by Wallace Waite, Arthur Rose and David Taylor. In 1937 it was acquired by John Lewis Partnership plc,[89] a diversified British retailer which also operates a chain of department stores that are differentiated, among other things, through their low-price promise, 'Never Knowingly Undersold'. The group was famous for its monthly sales reports, widely followed as a barometer of UK consumer confidence, and for being owned by its employees, or 'associates'. Waitrose's 117 stores accounted for 48% of the group's turnover.

Waitrose did not follow its parent's low-price strategy; in fact, it is the most up-market of all the grocery multiples. Waitrose's product offer is centred on quality and its stores are said to feel radically different to other food retailers, bearing a closer resemblance to a large delicatessen. The company has been able to improve its profitability (Exhibit 1.15) and is pursuing a strategy of building stores in affluent residential areas in London and south-eastern England.

Tesco plc

Tesco in 1998 was the UK's largest supermarket and superstore group with 568 stores. It traces its roots back to market stalls run by its founder, Jack Cohen, in London's impoverished East End just after the First World War. Its first store was opened in 1929, the firm was floated on the London Stock Exchange in 1947 and it opened its first supermarket in 1956.

Tesco's shops were historically located on high streets and were large by the standards of the time – a 1961 supermarket entered the record books as Europe's largest.

Exhibit 1.15 Waitrose Ltd. Financial performance (£ millions)

	Year ending January		
	1996	1997	1998
Turnover (excl. VAT)	1,380	1,461	1,585
Operating income	46.0	35.7	32.3
Total assets	534	572	614

Source: FAME.

Its original positioning was summed up in the title of Cohen's autobiography: *Pile it High and Sell it Cheap*. However, the firm's rather down-market reputation did nothing to inhibit its expansion from its roots in London and southern England, aided by a series of acquisitions:

1955	Burnards	19	London stores
1957	Williamsons	70	branches
1959	Harrow stores	20	branches
1960	John Irwins	212	branches in North West England
1964	Charles Phillips	97	self-service stores
1968	Victor Value chains	280	stores
1987	Hillards	40	stores in Yorkshire
1994	William Low	57	stores in Scotland and North England
1997	Irish Food Retailing Businesses of Associated British Foods		

Sources: Various trade publications

Sir Jack Cohen (as he had become) stepped down as chairman in 1979, and under his successors, Sir Leslie Porter and Sir Ian (later Lord) MacLaurin, Tesco attempted the difficult transition towards a more up-market, value-added positioning. This move is widely agreed to have been a remarkable success.

Tesco opened its (and the UK's) first out-of-town superstore in 1967 and in the 1980s such units became a cornerstone of the company's strategy because of their inherent economic advantages and the impression created on customers by their more attractive shopping environments. Smaller stores were closed, and the total number of units fell from around 600 in the 1970s to about 400 in the early 1990s. By 1992, however, the group appeared to be contemplating a partial reversal of that strategy. In that year it opened its first branches of Tesco Metro, a relatively small city centre outlet 'meeting the needs of workers, high street shoppers and the local community'[90] and Tesco Express, a combination of a local petrol station and convenience store.

Along with most other UK retailers, Tesco installed its first computers in the 1960s.[91] In the 1980s it was arguably the first UK retailer to grasp the full potential of IT in retailing and to build Electronic Data Interchange links with its suppliers. By 1998, these had been developed into an Extranet (using Internet technology) designed to aid two-way communication between Tesco and its suppliers and forming part of the Efficient Consumer Response (ECR) initiative launched in January 1996.[92] This was claimed to have saved the company £60 million in its first two years, well ahead of its initial £100 million five-year target.

More public initiatives included a 'Green Policy' of reducing energy consumption, recycling waste paper, switching from using CFC gases (which are believed to damage the ozone layer) in refrigerators etc. In a series of industry 'firsts', it began offering 'cash-back' facilities at checkouts in 200 stores in November 1989, introduced its 'one in front' scheme aimed at reducing queues in 1994,[93] was the first grocery retailer to introduce a loyalty card in 1995, launched its takeaway food concept, 'Tesco To Go and Tesco To Stay' in June 1997,[94] and in 1998 became the first grocery retailer to sell domestic gas.

Profits leapt from £100 million in 1986 to top £500 million in 1992, and Tesco became established as one of the most powerful and sophisticated food retailers.[95] In 1995 it ousted arch-rival J Sainsbury as Britain's biggest grocer.

Tesco expanded into continental Europe in 1992 with the acquisition of French

Exhibit 1.16   Tesco plc. Financial performance (£ millions)

	Year ending February				
	1993	1994	1995	1996	1997
Turnover (excl. VAT)	7,581	8,600	10,101	12,094	13,887
Operating profit	496	521	617	724	774
Net profit	362	299	381	466	520
Total assets	4,465	4,972	5,908	6,216	6,622
EPS (p)	18.6	15.2	18.9	22.2	24.1
Shareholders' funds	2,694	2,759	3,104	3,588	3,890
Gearing	47.5	29.3	24.6	14.7	13.9
UK performance					
Turnover (excl. VAT) (£m)		8,347	9,655	11,560	14,621
Operating profit (£m)		513	600	713	760
Operating margins (%)		6.1	6.2	6.2	5.8
Sales per sq. ft per year (£)		758.1	763.8	862.9	944.6

Source: Tesco's published accounts.

supermarket Catteau, but struggled to reproduce its UK success there. In five years like-for-like sales in France increased only 1.1%, and in 1997 Tesco sold Catteau to the French group Promodes. Overseas expansion in Eastern Europe saw greater success, and helped to fuel continued profit growth after 1993 (Exhibit 1.16). More recently Tesco ventured into the Far East with the purchase of a stake in Lotus in Thailand.[96]

Much of the firm's strategy for the 1990s was encapsulated in the advertising slogan 'Every Little Helps – give the customer what they want under one roof' adopted in 1993. Baby-changing facilities were made available in every store, and all products bought in Tesco carried two promises: a 'No Quibble' money-back or product replacement guarantee (emulating a policy most widely associated with Marks & Spencer) and 'Unbeatable Value'; if the same product could be bought cheaper from a competitor within a three-mile (5-km) radius, Tesco would refund twice the difference and drop its price. In the words of Ian MacLaurin, 'Tesco always listens to the customers and we work hard to develop close relationships with our customers in order to serve them well'.[97]

The 1995 introduction of the Clubcard loyalty card was a valuable coup; for many people, it was the event that confirmed Tesco's position as leader of the UK food-retailing industry. In 1998 there were approximately 5 million Clubcard members. Clubcard has become central to Tesco's marketing strategy and certain of the firm's alliances: points could be earned in B&Q, the leading UK DIY retailer, and on gas purchased from Energi, the supplier whose services were marketed in Tesco stores. Its cousin, Clubcard Plus, was also the basis of Tesco's entry into the financial services industry. In 1998 the firm offered or planned to offer a savings account with an attractive rate of interest, a Visa credit card, a budget account, foreign currency facilities, home insurance and personal loans.

Another initiative that attracted media attention was Tesco Direct, its home shopping service. After trials in West London, starting in 1996, the service was extended to 231 stores. The main users were working professionals, who tended to have access to the Internet,[98] which was the means by which 59% of orders were taken – the remainder were received via the telephone or by fax. Tesco publicly forecast that home shopping was eventually likely to account for between 5% and 30% of its turnover.

Attention was also given to internal improvements. A staff empowerment scheme was rolled out to the 250 stores during 1997,[99] with a view to involving staff more in decisions relating to areas such as complaints, customer loyalty, sales growth, cost control and stock management. This was followed in March 1998 by the announcement of an agreement with the retailing worker's union, USDAW, to set up staff forums in order to improve channels of communication between staff and management.

J Sainsbury plc

In 1869, John James and Mary Ann Sainsbury opened a shop at 173 Drury Lane, in what is now London's West End theatre district. A second shop and depot followed four years later, and the firm gradually extended its operations throughout England, mainly through organic growth, although a 1936 acquisition was important in establishing the firm in England's Midlands. Sainsbury's first Scottish supermarket was opened in Glasgow in 1992. By 1998, nine million customers each week were being served in 391 Sainsbury's supermarkets, of which 9 were in Scotland, 8 in Wales and 4 in Northern Ireland.

Although the firm has been a public company since 1973, it had always been managed by the Sainsbury family. In 1998 the firm's website carried pictures of four generations of male Sainsburys, every one of whom had spent all or part of their career in the company, almost all in senior management positions.[100]

It was under the leadership of John James' grandson, Alan (chairman from 1956 to 1967), and his son John D Sainsbury (chairman from 1969 to 1992) that the company truly could be said to have seized the initiative in UK food retailing. Alan had been responsible for the 1950 introduction of self-service supermarkets to the UK. The firm believed that good quality, by attracting customers, would generate benefits of scale that could then be passed on to customers through low prices. The slogan 'Good Food Costs Less at Sainsbury's' was coined in 1959, and through the 1960s, 1970s and 1980s the company built a strong following among consumers, in particular the middle classes. The confidence that Sainsbury inspired in its customers helped the firm to persuade them to eat avocado pears and drink wine – both novelties for most UK consumers in the 1970s. Its own brand was highly regarded, and in 1998 accounted for 40% of lines and 66% of sales.[101]

By the late 1970s, the firm had a secure leadership position within UK food retailing, and looked for avenues for expansion. In 1977 it opened its first Savacentre hypermarket, the fruit of a 50–50 joint venture with British Home Stores, a retailer of clothing and home furnishings. Sainsbury bought out its partner in 1989, and by 1998 Savacentre operated 13 hypermarkets generating operating profits of £31 million on turnover of £864 million.

In 1981 Sainsbury entered the UK market for DIY ('do-it-yourself') products for home and garden improvements, with the opening of its first Homebase store. Homebase was a joint venture with Belgian retail group GIB of which Sainsbury held 75%. The DIY sector grew strongly in the 1980s as more British people bought their own homes and disposable incomes rose, but the recession at the end of the decade, which was accompanied by a sharp fall in property prices, led to fierce price competition. However, Homebase remained profitable; by 1994 it held fourth place in the sector and posted operating profits of £24 million on sales of £328 million. In 1995 it was one of the most profitable operators in the industry, although its turnover was less than one-quarter of that of market-leading B&Q.[102] In March 1995 Sainsbury acquired Texas Homecare, then the second largest DIY chain with sales double those of Homebase, though its 1994 profit was only £8 million. Some 40 of Texas' stores were sold and the remainder converted to the Homebase format. At the time one observer called this 'a miscalculation of momentous proportions which they will regret for years', but in 1998 Homebase contributed operating profits of £56 million on sales of £1,235 million from 298 stores.

Sainsbury's overseas turnover was the highest of any UK grocery retailer, although its European expansion was limited to a branch opened in Calais to sell alcoholic drinks to British day-trippers attracted by the lower levels of tax and duty on alcohol charged in France.[103] A more serious strategic move had been the purchase of Shaw's, a US supermarket chain. This commenced with the purchase of a 21% stake in 1983, and the remaining shares were acquired four years later. Shaw's positioning, 'high quality at value-for-money prices', was similar to Sainsbury's own, and the Shaw own brand was also unusually well regarded by American standards, accounting for 40% of 1998 sales of $2.8 billion. Shaw's contributed $62 million to the group's 1998 operating profit.

In October 1994, Sainsbury had acquired a 16% stake in another US chain, Giant Food, which was based, like Shaw's, on the USA's east coast, but south of Shaw's New England stronghold. This move was well received by observers and was widely expected to lead to a full bid,[104] but in May 1998 Giant Food, including Sainsbury's stake, was acquired by the Dutch grocer Ahold. Plans to expand closer to home through the acquisition of Scottish chain William Low had been frustrated by Tesco, which bought Low's itself.

Throughout the 1980s and early 1990s Sainsbury's market share in the UK and profits continued to rise. In 1992, a 21% increase in pre-tax profits saw a triumphant Sainsbury overtake Marks & Spencer as the UK's most profitable UK retailer.[105] However, a turning point came three years later. Although the

Exhibit 1.17   J Sainsbury plc. Financial performance (£ million)

	Year ending March				
	1994	*1995*	*1996*	*1997*	*1998*
Turnover (incl. VAT)	11,224	12,065	13,499	14,312	15,496
Operating profit	796	899	854	745	854
Net profit	142	539	478	403	487
Total assets	5,491	5,732	6,754	7,285	9,124
Sales per sq. ft per year (£)	736.4	699.4	527.9	540.2	567.6
EPS (p)	28.0	29.8	26.8	22.0	26.1
Shareholders' funds	3,040	3,289	3,543	3,671	4,150
Gearing (%)	18.0	18.3	16.5	17.9	18.9
Sainsbury's Supermarkets					
Turnover (excl. VAT)	8,339	9,014	10,214	10,852	10,836
Operating profit	695	784	779	661	735
Operating margins (%)	8.3	8.7	7.6	6.4	6.8
Sales per sq. ft per year (£)	944	965	1046	1045	997

Source: J Sainsbury's published accounts.

Homebase division already had an established loyalty card, the supermarket group was surprised by the launch of Tesco's Clubcard. Afraid of the impact of loyalty schemes upon its operating margins, Sainsbury delayed its response for several months, until customer defections made it clear that it needed a competing scheme. By the end of 1995, Tesco had become the market leader and Sainsbury's sales per sq ft and operating profits were in sharp decline (Exhibit 1.17).

A number of reasons were advanced for the company's decline. In the company's own words, it was 'a family retail business with international links, which retains strong personal links with its past, rather than ... an international retail operation'.[106] David Sainsbury, who had taken over from his cousin John as chairman in 1992, also came under criticism as being too laid back and indecisive by comparison with his predecessor, and spending too much time on interests outside the company.[107] Some critics were forthright about the company: 'It is hierarchical and old fashioned and there is too much deference. Decision-making is extremely convoluted. There are hundreds of meetings but they rarely come to a conclusion'.[108]

The group responded in a number of ways. In a rare outside recruitment move, Kevin McCarten was brought in from Procter & Gamble as marketing director in October 1996. In March 1997, Dino Adriano moved over from Homebase to become chief executive of Sainsbury's supermarket division. Consultants were brought in for a complete review of the company's brand identity. With new marketing slogans such as 'Better Quality ... Same Price' launched in March 1997, 'Fresh Foods, Fresh Ideas' launched in September 1997 and 'Taste the Difference', the firm hoped to persuade customers that freshness was the most important point of difference at Sainsbury's.

In May 1997, the Group was split into four component businesses, each with its own board and strategy. More operational power was delegated down the line, and staff councils were set up to improve communication within the business. Sales and marketing departments were reorganised and a system of category management was established to promote closer relationships with suppliers.[109]

Although Tesco's Clubcard was widely expected to be a prelude to its entering the banking sector, it was actually Sainsbury that in February 1997 became the first UK supermarket company to launch a bank. Sainsbury's Bank, a 55–45 joint venture with the Bank of Scotland, claimed to have attracted 600,000 customers and deposits of over £1.4 billion by October 1997,[110] and 700,000 customers and £1.5 billion of deposits by December 1998.[111] The products on offer in 1998 included an instant access savings account, a Christmas Saver Account,[112] Classic and Gold Visa credit cards, personal loans, mortgages and home insurance. Further products such as pet insurance were planned.

In July 1997, Sainsbury became the first British supermarket to introduce the radio-linked scanner. This enabled customers to scan their own purchases and was available in 32 stores in 1998, and the company plans to have them available in all new stores.

Home shopping is available in 20 stores and home delivery is being rolled out to 32 of the larger stores. Sainsbury opened its first takeaway shop in West London in summer 1998. Friday night 24-hour shopping was extended to 51 stores.

Asda plc

Yorkshire butchers Peter and Fred Asquith founded UK's third largest food retailer in 1965. In 1998 Asda (an abbreviation of Associated Dairies) had 216 stores serving over 6.2 million customers per week. It was successful during the 1970s and 1980s with a strategy of building superstores where prices were some 5% below those at Sainsbury and Tesco. However, a number of strategic errors were reported to have been committed at the end of the 1980s.

In its core business, Asda attempted to match the facilities at the stores that Tesco and Sainsbury were building in the company's northern England heartland. The firm raised prices to recoup costs, but found its customers deserting it for lower priced competitors. Prices then were pushed up further to recoup lost revenue, further alienating customers, 75% of whom came from areas where the average income was at or below the national mean. This was compounded by a programme of ill-judged mergers and acquisitions. In April 1985 Asda merged with furniture retailer MFI, and later also with carpets and furniture group Allied Maple in what was intended largely as a move to defend all three firms against possible predators.[113] Synergies between the three constituent parts of Asda–MFI were minimal, and none of the three managements truly understood the others' businesses. This, Britain's biggest ever retail merger, was unwound in November 1987 but left Asda deep in debt, a situation compounded by the £700 million acquisition of the Gateway group's 61 largest supermarkets in 1989. This too was debt financed, and left the group unable to finance capital expenditure, while the Gateway stores turned out to have been significantly over-valued.[114] When chairman and chief executive John Hardman was ousted in June 1991, the group was in dire financial straits with debts of over £1 billion.

After several months without a CEO, Asda recruited Archie Norman as chief executive at the end of 1991. Norman was an ex-partner with management consultant McKinsey who had previously played a major part in the transformation of the ailing Woolworth chain of general stores into the successful Kingfisher retailing group.

What followed was a classic corporate turnaround. Disposals of peripheral businesses, property and some stores, together with a rights issue, reduced debt to manageable levels. The chain implemented a strategy of pursuing sales volumes by setting prices 5–7% below those of major competitors while reducing costs through improved productivity and purchasing terms.[115] The chain also moved to differentiate itself in a number of ways: through holding 'Singles Nights' to bring lonely customers together in its stores, through 24-hour trading (then a novelty) in the pre-Christmas period and by notices in the stores encouraging customers to ask for assistance.

The company launched George, a clothing range designed by George Davis, founder of the Next chain, with a view to establishing Asda as the UK's second clothing retailer after M&S. In 1998 it was estimated to have achieved a 2% share of the clothing market, greater than that of many specialist fashion retailers. Asda also became Britain's fourth largest music retailer, with 6% of the CD market.

Recruitment and staff motivation proved vital in implementing these strategies. Staff were offered share options on the same basis as directors – by 1995, 36,000 of the 68,000 employees had accepted. A suggestion scheme, 'Tell Archie', set up in July 1993, attracted 14,000 suggestions in the first 18 months and a total of 30,000 by the middle of 1998. Rewards for successful suggestions ranged from small gifts such as pens, through theatre trips to weekends abroad.

There were moves to establish clear profit responsibilities for product and cat-

Exhibit 1.18   Asda plc, financial performance (£ millions)

	Year ending April				
	1993	1994	1995	1996	1997
Turnover (excl. VAT)	4,614	4,822	5,285	6,042	6,952
Operating profit	190	197	251	316	372
Net profit	157	(126)	179	228	308
Total assets	2,870	2,645	2,842	3,278	3,751
Sales per sq. ft per year	596.6	591.4	643.7	716.2	790.4
EPS (p)	3.97	4.36	5.9	7.71	9.09
Shareholders' funds	1,568	1,376	1,493	1,658	2,061
Gearing (%)	4.9	6.0	0	16.3	12.3
Asda Retail financial performance					
Turnover (excl. VAT) (3m)	4,396	4,794	5,257	6,010	6,883
Operating profit (£m)	196	208	247	313	365
Operating margins (%)	4.5	4.3	4.7	5.2	5.3
Sales per sq. ft per year (£)	542.8	589.4	640.3	712.4	728.6

Source: Asda's published accounts.

egory management at firm and store level. An egalitarian management style was developed, with open-plan offices even for senior directors and no reserved parking spaces. Board meetings were held in stores and followed by meals in the staff canteen, after which directors talked with customers and 'colleagues', as all Asda employees were termed.[116]

From its low point in 1992 when operating profits fell to £182 million, Asda has shown consistent improvement (Exhibit 1.18) although like-for-like sales were reported to have slowed in 1998.[117]

Asda in 1998 was in the fourth year of its Breakout programme, designed to differentiate it from its competitors in terms of value by offering a wide range of fresh food, larger stores, friendly service, 'service with personality' and more non-food products. One recent innovation was the 'Store of Takeaway', where Asda's chefs prepared and served meals to eat in store or at home. The range included the Curry Pot, China Town, Hot Wok, Chicken Rotisserie, Salad Bar, custom-made Pizzas and fish and chips. The company claimed that prices were up to 50% below those in specialist takeaways.

Asda does not have a loyalty card, preferring to compete on the basis of everyday low prices. The company claims to monitor the prices of 12,000 lines each week, to check that it is offering the best value. In September 1997 it launched a card offering discount telephone services[118] and started a trial of in-store financial services, in conjunction with the British bank TSB, which, if successful, was to be extended to at least 100 stores.

Safeway plc

Originally the UK subsidiary of the US chain of the same name, Safeway opened its first UK store in 1963. In 1987 Safeway's British operations were acquired by the Argyll Group, which had previously operated supermarkets under a variety of banners. Most of its stores were re-branded as Safeway, and by 1992, 85% of Argyll's profit came from Safeway business. In 1998 the company had 471 stores in the UK.

Exhibit 1.19   Safeway plc, financial performance (£ millions)

	Year ending March				
	1994	*1995*	*1996*	*1997*	*1998*
Turnover	5,608	5,815	6,069	6,590	6,979
Operating profit	365	383	418	462	410
Net profit	253	93	301	294	241
Net assets	3,204	3,258	3,530	3,764	4,095
Sales per sq. ft per year (£)	659	669	733	771	779
EPS (p)	22.6	8.3	26.4	26.8	22.1
Shareholders' funds	1,776	2,018	1,939	1,887	2,007
Gearing (%)	14.8	17.9	12.8	33.3	38.3
Safeway's					
Turnover (excl. VAT)	5,608	5,815	6,069	6,590	6,979
Operating profit	365	383	417	462	410
Operating margin (%)	6.5	6.6	6.9	7.0	5.9
Sales per sq. ft per year (£)	568	624	655	684	700

Source: Companies' published accounts.

In the 1980s Safeway concentrated on cost control and profitability, perhaps at the expense of giving adequate attention to customer requirements. Despite a number of programmes to improve service, such as Queue Busters, a successful initiative to reduce queues, and Shop & Go, a self-scanning system available in 149 stores, critics believed that the company had neglected non-family customers. They also pointed to some urgent operational issues, such as the need to develop Safeway's non-food business and address problems in its supply chain. A 1997 re-branding exercise, Safeway 2000, was not a success and merger discussions were reportedly held with Asda early in 1998, but curtailed after a premature leak to the press.

More recently, however, the company has refocused its marketing on the family, with some apparent success (Exhibit 1.19). Baby-changing and crèche facilities have been introduced at a number of stores.

Safeway's ABC loyalty card, launched in autumn 1995, had attracted some nine million cardholders by 1998. A 1997 relaunch made ABC's terms the most generous of the major grocers' cards, with customers spending more than £160 in any month getting double points and those spending more than £240 being rewarded with triple points. A savings account offering an attractive interest rate was launched in conjunction with Abbey National, a UK retail bank, in January 1998.

Although critics believe that existing stores are in need of renewal, Safeway continues to expand. In a joint venture inaugurated in August 1997, Safeway took management control of 15 Wellworth stores in Northern Ireland to which three stores were to be added in 1998. Fifteen new stores were planned for the British mainland in 1998 and a successful start claimed for a joint venture with BP, a major oil company and petrol retailer, to develop a new convenience store/petrol station format.

Somerfield plc

Somerfield has the most tangled history of all the major UK supermarket groups. It traced its origins to a small Bristol grocery store opened by J.H. Mills in 1875. It expanded slowly until 1950, when a Bristol financier took a major interest and renamed the firm Gateway. Gateway was bought by Linfood Holdings in 1977 and 100 stores brought under the Gateway banner. Linfood already owned the Frank Dee supermarket business (founded from a wholesaler spun off from J.H. Mills some years earlier) and in 1983 the Frank Dee Supermarkets were re-branded as Gateways, while Linfood renamed itself The Dee Corporation. The logical change of group name to The Gateway Corporation came five years later, following the acquisition of several other supermarket chains including the UK hypermarkets business of the French company Carrefour.

The group experienced profit problems until, in 1989, it was acquired for £2.1 billion by Isosceles in a highly geared takeover of the kind that was then fashionable. In the early 1990s, the Isosceles Group, under different management teams, implemented a number of strategies in its attempts to improve business, selling the largest Gateway stores to Asda and a number of smaller ones to Kwik Save and launching the Food Giant discount chain. Success eluded the firm until a new management team, recruited in 1993, found a successful retail format under the Somerfield name. The group was renamed Somerfield Stores in 1994 and floated on the Stock Exchange as Somerfield plc in 1996.

Most of the profit improvement since 1994 (Exhibit 1.20) came from improved control of costs. The Price Check programme of price reductions and promotions, dating from 1994, was also a significant factor in the firm's revival. However, more recent investment has focused on customer service, improved stock availability, own-brand development and staff training. Somerfield's loyalty card offered Premier Points, a scheme also used by a number of petrol retailers, where customers accumulated points redeemable for consumer goods at Argos, a chain of catalogue retailers. By 1998 Somerfield had issued 15 million cards and the company was reporting a 5% increase in customer loyalty.

Somerfield in 1998 had 564 stores, many located on large housing estates and suburban high streets. Stores were smaller than the typical Sainsbury or Tesco: new stores had an average sales area of 13,000 sq. ft. They boasted a high frequency of store visits, although a lower average customer spend than its rivals' superstores. Most of its customers are in the C1/C2 social groups. Home delivery is available in 30 stores nationwide and home shopping, launched in autumn 1997, was to be extended to at least five stores in 1998.

In March 1998, Somerfield merged with Kwik Save, with all Kwik Save super-

Exhibit 1.20   Somerfield, financial performance (£ millions)

	Year ending April			
	1994	1995	1996	1997
Turnover (excl. VAT)	3,110	3,156.3	3,161	3,200.6
Operating profit/loss	43.4	(27.4)	101	115
Operating margins (%)	1.4	0.8	3.2	3.6
Total assets	1,703	1,631	1,498	959
Sales per sq. ft per year (£)	495.9	511.8	526.8	539.1
EPS (p)	6.4	(13.4)	21.8	26.6
Shareholders' funds	1,216	1,142	722	288.4
Gearing (%)	7.1	4.5	4.3	38.8

Source: Companies' published accounts.

markets to be converted to the Somerfield format within four years.[119] The company claimed that the two firms had much in common in terms of store sizes and price positioning, and that the merger offered £50 million in potential cost savings. In August 1998, Somerfield announced its interest in acquiring Booker, a troubled £660 million cash-and-carry wholesaling group. The acquisition of Booker would make Somerfield Britain's largest food-buying concern behind Tesco and Sainsbury. The combined company is predicted to have sales of £11 billion and profits of £295 million.[120]

NOTES

1. As in most other countries, grocers in the UK also sell a wide variety of non-food household products such as detergents and small kitchen utensils, but food is the most important element of their turnover.

2. Mintel, *Food Retailing*, June 1998. Other estimates, calculated on different definitions of the total national food market, place this figure at around 50%.

3. In 1851, 25 million people lived in the UK, 50 years later there were 37 million, an increase of 48% (*Annual Abstract of Statistics*, Spring 1990).

4. One of the most successful chains belonged to the Scottish entrepreneur Thomas Lipton, whose empire grew between 1871 and 1900 from a single shop in Glasgow to more than 450 throughout the UK. His name survives on an internationally available brand of tea. J. Sainsbury and Somerfield also trace their history back to this era.

5. *The Economist*, 'Obituary for Lord Sainsbury', 7 November 1998, p. 154.

6. *Sainsbury's Annual Report*, 1995.

7. P. Kotler and G. Armstrong, *Principles of Marketing*, Prentice-Hall, 1991, p. 388.

8. *Sainsbury's Annual Report*, 1990.

9. G.J. Bliss, 'A Theory of Retail Pricing', *Journal of Industrial Economics*, June 1988, pp. 337–40.

10. M. Josef, 'Superstore Trading Profile', *Grocery Market Bulletin*, July 1990, pp. 1–7.

11. *Sainsbury's 125 Years*, p. 11. A square foot is an imperial measure of area: 1 square metre is about 11 sq. ft.

12. J. Burns, J. McInerney and A. Swinbank (eds) *The Food Industry: economics and policies* edited by Heinemann in association with the Commonwealth Agricultural Bureaux, 1983, p. 128.

13. J.B. Jeffreys, *Retail Trading in Britain 1850–1950*, CUP, 1954.

14. 'Trouble in Store', *TEST*, p. 30.

15. *Tesco Student Pack*, 1987, p. 3.

16. R. Newman, 'The use of computers in supermarket groups', *Retail and Distribution Management*, December 1975, pp. 12–16.

17. N. Wrigley, 'Antitrust regulation and the restructuring of grocery retailing in Britain and the US', *Environment and Planning*, A24, 1992, p. 729.

18. Saatchi & Saatchi, *1980 Annual Report*.

19. Customers earned a certain number of stamps for each pound that they spent; these were accumulated in books which could then be exchanged for consumer durables or other items selected from the stamp-issuer's catalogue. Grocery and petrol outlets competed on the number of stamps offered per pound of expenditure. These stamps survived the end of retail price maintenance, and were indeed the basis of periodic consumer 'crazes', but fell rapidly out of fashion once Tesco stopped offering them in 1978.

20. *The Times*, 9 February 1990, p. 21.

21. S.W. Howe, *Bilateral Oligopoly and Competition in the UK Food Trade*, Vol. V, 1973, p. 81.

22. Department of Transport, *Transport Statistics*, 1994 edition.

23. 'Trouble in the Store', *Retail Locational Policy in Britain and Germany* (TEST), 2–07, p. 21.

24. 'Study by the Henley Centre', *The Independent*, 24 March 1995, p. 4.

25. J. Fernie, *Retail Distribution Management*, 1990, Kogan Page, p. 42.

26. Retail Trade Association, *Euromonitor*.

27. *Tesco Student Pack*, 1987.

28. *Own Brand in Food Retailing across Europe*, OXIRM, 1994.

29. According to a study undertaken in 1982 by Niesen.

30. D. Parker and N. Tree, 'The Business Year 1993–4', *Business Studies Magazine*, 1994, p. 4.

31. M&S were the long-standing market leader in UK clothing retailing with a strong up-market niche position in food retailing.

32. E.J. Lynch (1990) 'The impact of EPOS on market-

ing strategy and retailer–supplier relationship', *Journal of Marketing Management*, 6, pp. 157–68.

33. D. Knights and H. Wilmott, *New Technologies and the Labour Process*. Macmillan, 1988, p. 150.

34. *Euromonitor*.

35. W.S. Howe, 'UK retailer vertical power, market concentration and consumer welfare', *Journal of Retail Distribution Management*, 18 February 1990, p. 19.

36. K. Davies, C. Gillinghan and C. Sutton, 'Development of own-label product strategies grocery and DIY in the UK', *International Journal of Retailing*, 1, 1986, pp. 6–19.

37. N. Wrigley and M. Lowe, *Retailing, Consumption and Capital*, Longman, 1996, p. 35.

38. *Retail Saturation: Examining the Evidence*, OXIRM, 1989.

39. *Sainsbury's Annual Report*, 1988, p. 3.

40. *The Times*, 1 October, 1987, p. 23.

41. D. Litwak, 'The nations top grocery corporation', *Supermarket Business*, 1987, 42, p. 95.

42. N. Wrigley, 'Antitrust regulation and the restructuring of grocery retailing in Britain and the USA', *Environment and Planning*, 1992, A24, p. 152.

43. NatWest Securities, *US food retailing: The European connection*, 1993, London.

44. N. Wrigley and M. Lowe, *Retailing, Consumption and Capital*, Longman, 1996, p. 103.

45. *The Independent*, 10 July 1988, p. 18.

46. IGD.

47. Warehouse clubs are stores of hypermarket size which admit only customers who have paid a membership fee. They sell food and non-food items in bulk packages at heavily discounted prices.

48. *Sunday Times*, 6 August 1995.

49. IGD, 1994.

50. *The Economist*, 19 March 1994.

51. *Sainsbury's Annual Report*, 1993, p. 4.

52. *Tesco Annual Report*, 1997.

53. M. Giles, 'Retailers are cousin havoc in high street', *The Economist*, 4 December 1993.

54. IGD.

55. Shop Hours Regulating Act of 1886 and the 1911 Shop Act.

56. A. Baldwin, *Financial Times*, 28 November, 1991, p. 22.

57. *Verdict*, March 1998.

58. Mintel.

59. P. Wilkinson, *Corporate Community Involvement*, 11 May 1998.

60. *Sainsbury's, Facts and Figures*, 1998.

61. IGD.

62. *Blue Book*, 1998.

63. IGD.

64. *Financial Times*, 5 November 1994.

65. Mintel.

66. *Driving Productivity and Growth in the UK Economy*, McKinsey Global Institute, 1998.

67. *The Economist*, 31 October 1998.

68. *Financial Times*, 23 December 1997, p. 21.

69. G.D. Jonquieres, *Financial Times*, 26 November 1992.

70. *An Outline of the Co-operative Movement*, 1998.

71. *Co-operation*, 150, p. 4.

72. CSO – Verdict.

73. IGD.

74. D. Channon (1992) *Kwik Save Group plc*, Imperial College London/ECCH case study 392–065–1.

75. IGD.

76. Mintel.

77. *The Independent*, 10 July 1998, p. 18.

78. IGD.

79. Leeds is a large English city in Yorkshire, approximately 300 km north of London.

80. *The Economist*, 4 March 1995.

81. Birmingham is England's second largest city and is situated in the Midlands, 200 km north of London.

82. *The Economist*, 19 March 1994.

83. *Financial Times*, 2 December 1993.

84. *The Economist*, 19 March 1994.

85. *Financial Times*, p. 5, 30 October 1993.

86. Bradford is located just to the west of Leeds, in Yorkshire.

87. IGD.

88. *Financial Times*, 7 September 1997, p. 23.

89. *John Lewis Partnership plc*, 1998, John Lewis.

90. http://www.tesco.co.uk/information/fact_file/Company_History.asp, 13 December 1998.

91. Newman, R., 'The Use of Computers in Supermarket Groups', *Retail and Distribution Management*, December 1975, pp. 12–16; *Tesco Student Pack*, 1997, p. 5.

92. ECR is an interactive electronic data exchange linked to leading suppliers, which traces every item purchased in the store. It enables suppliers almost real-time access to sales data, which can speed restocking and cut back on forward ordering if necessary, reducing wastage.

93. If there are customers queuing at a checkout, another checkout will be opened until all checkouts are open. If a customer has to wait longer than 5–10 minutes, then he or she gets a 50p voucher.

94. *Tesco Annual Report*, 1998.

95. *Financial Times*, 10 April 1993, p. 11.

96. *Financial Times*, 19 May 1998, p. 32.

97. Sir Ian McLaurin, Tesco's CEO, *The Times*, 13 February 1995, p. 23.

98. Mintel.

99. *Tesco Annual Report*, 1998.
100. http://www.j-sainsbury.co.uk/company/history/ FamilyTree.html.
101. *Sainsbury's 125 Years*.
102. *The Sunday Times*, Business Section, 22 January 1995, p. 6.
103. Duties on wine, beer and spirits were far lower in France than in the UK, and increasing numbers of British people were finding it worthwhile to make special trips to purchase their drinks there.
104. *Sunday Times*, Business Section, 4 October 1994.
105. *The Times*, 14 May 1992, p. 22.
106. *Sainsbury's Annual Report*, 1998.
107. David Sainsbury had long been interested in politics, using some of his family's considerable wealth to back centrist politicians and parties.
108. *The Guardian* (2), 4 January 1996, p. 2.
109. *Sainsbury's Annual Report*, 1998.
110. Verdict.
111. http://www.j-sainsbury.co.uk/finres/1998_final, 13 December 1998.
112. Customers paid £10 or more a month by direct debit and received 3.23% interest plus a further 3% if no withdrawals were made until November.
113. G. Davis, *Cases in Retail Management*, Pitman Publishing, 1994, p. 46.
114. N. Wrigley and M. Lowe, *Retailing, Consumption and Capital*, Longman, 1996, p. 122.
115. 'Asda's Open Plan', *Management Today*, December 1995, pp. 50–54.
116. 'Asda's Open Plan', *Management Today*, December 1995, pp. 50–54.
117. Verdict, April 1998. The slow-down was attributed to customers taking advantage of more aggressive price promotions from rival supermarkets, during a period when Asda had not been running any major new promotions.
118. *Financial Times*, 18 September 1997, p. 30.
119. *The Times*, 10 July 1998, p. 23.
120. *The Sunday Times*, Business, 23 August 1998, p. 4.

The world-wide recorded music industry

Overview of the origins and growth of the music industry

Birth

In 1877 Thomas Edison's recording of 'Mary had a little lamb' introduced into the world a technology that would grow into a 40 billion-dollar industry.[1] Ten years later Emile Berliner took Edison's sound-producing machine based on a rotating cylinder (later improved by Alexander Graham Bell) and flattened it to produce a disk – the first recognisable record. Berliner's invention which allowed copies to be stamped from one original (something that was not possible with a cylinder) turned what had been conceived of as a dictating machine for business into a source of home entertainment.

Further technological improvements to the gramophone and the record were made and commercial birth followed in the early 1900s when the first sound recordings were released for sale to the general public.

From cylinder to CD and beyond

The development of sound recording and reproduction was not achieved via large technological leaps, but rather through a stream of improvements, each building on the last.

During the early 1990s the disk format gradually replaced the cylinder and progress was made on improving the quality and number of copies that could be made of a recording, in the 1890s for example, the limit had been around 250. The First World War unexpectedly produced a boost to record sales. Soldiers, using increasingly portable machines, played records to remind them of home, and record companies recorded marching songs, patriotic ballads and sentimental love songs and sent them to the front.

This case study was written by Jon Gander and Alison Rieple, University of Westminster. It is intended for classroom discussion rather than to illustrate good or bad handling of an administrative situation. © Copyright 2000 Jon Gander and Alison Rieple.

Following the war Jazz music became popular, with Paul Whiteman's 'Whispering' achieving sales of over a million in 1920.[2] With the promise of the industry now demonstrated by increasing record sales, attention was turned to trying to improve the quality of sound recording and reproduction which was plagued by scratching and hissing. This poor sound quality was in direct contrast to the superior quality of the sound produced by another medium rapidly growing in popularity, the wireless. Improvements were not restricted to industry efforts, and a number of enterprising amateurs attempted to find a solution. One, a Professor McKendrick, designed a gramophone that employed a length of tubing filled with peas. Unfortunately although the peas did indeed absorb most of the scratchy sound, most of the required sound was also absorbed!

The solution was the replacement of acoustic with electronic recording techniques. Acoustic recording involved the musicians performing in front of a large horn which conveyed the sound to the stylus, the vibrations of which 'cut' the tracks in the record, whereas electrical recording employed a number of microphones which, strategically placed, allowed the sound from the different instruments to be more easily picked up. Sound reproduction improved dramatically with electrical recording, and by 1927 had been adopted as the industry standard. As well as improving the quality of the recorded sound, electrical recording also allowed greater freedom in the type of music performed as the sensitive needle of an acoustic recording required clear, steady singing if it was to cut the track and not jump.

During the late 1940s and early 1950s a number of different record sizes and speeds were introduced. By reducing the speed of the turntable and cutting more grooves in the record (from 85 to around 300) the LP (long-playing record) was able to 'hold' more music. Columbia Records demonstrated the benefit of their new product by comparing a pile of 78's that stood eight feet high with the equivalent music on LP format that measured only fifteen inches. Another major music company of the era, RCA resisted the adoption of the LP and countered Columbia's move by introducing a new format of their own, the 45 rpm on a seven-inch disc. For two years the formats competed for the market's attention. RCA eventually accepted the LP with Columbia in turn adopting the 45 for single songs, and the 78-rpm record was gradually phased out.

Referred to as the 'battle of the speeds', this episode in the music industry characterised what is now a familiar dynamic, the development and introduction of new technologies and products that challenged and attempted to dislodge the incumbent and become the new industry standard. There was, however, room for more than one format, as was proved by the music cassette introduced in the early 1960s by Philips. By nature of its portability, the cassette took up a complementary position rather than a replacement one.

Examples of successfully adopted technologies include stereo, the Dolby recording system, high-fidelity (hi-fi) reproduction and compact discs (CDs), introduced in the early 1980s. A notable failure in this increasingly relentless drive for improved sound recording and reproduction was the introduction of quadraphonic sound (a system involving four speakers) in the late 1960s/early 1970s.

A number of other new formats have since been introduced with varying degrees of success. Sony's MiniDisc has a following mainly restricted to Japan, where some 8% of households own a MiniDisc player.[3] A relaunch in 1996 failed to boost sales in the USA. The Digital Audio Tape (DAT) was not adopted by the general public and is now primarily used by professionals in recording studios. Recordable CDs or

CD-Rs have yet to make any significant penetration in the market, though the recent fall in price is helping to encourage interest.

In the second half of the 1990s products have been launched that bundle various existing media and technologies. Enhanced CDs combine the audio of the traditional CD with multimedia options. Designed to be played on a PC, the package includes video clips, band information, lyrics, etc. A new variation of this theme has been to link the CD to information on the Internet rather than on the CD itself. Sony who calls its enhanced CD, 'CD-Extra', has perhaps been the most active with the release of 40 albums (mainly in the USA) on the format.

DVD (Digital Versatile Disc) video was launched in 1997, heightening expectations that DVD audio will soon follow. DVD's promise is based on its ability to store on the same sized disc as a CD, the complete repertoire of an artist, video footage, interviews, as well as a wide range of relevant data. As of 1999 the official launch of the format with the accompanying hardware has yet to be announced. This is principally due to industry wrangles over developing an industry-wide specification, licensing, and accord on patent ownership. The original DVD consortium of Philips, Sony, Pioneer, Thomson, Matsushita, Mitsubishi, Victor, Toshiba and Time Warner was split by a breakaway group comprising Sony, Pioneer and Philips. Sony and Philips are reported to be working on a DVD audio format aimed as a direct replacement for the CD. Compatible with CDs, it will have the same playing time and will offer surround sound, based on an improved sound quality system called Direct Stream Digital (DSD).

Internet-based sound technology is based on software which digitally compresses music into files (the most common format being MP3) that can be transmitted via a telephone wire or satellite. There are two main ways by which the music can be played. Using technology dubbed 'streaming', music can be played online in real time, or the file can be downloaded and stored to be played back at a later date. The downloaded files can either be stored on a PC and transferred onto recordable CD, or the software needed to play the MP3 file on a PC can also be downloaded.

The development of musical styles

Though classical music formed the majority of recorded repertoire at the beginning of the twentieth century, new musical styles with more widespread appeal soon began to appear. Dance music was introduced around 1910 and was soon followed by Jazz music around 1915. The music industry during this period was controlled by music publishers and composers, who wrote the songs and arrangements which were then sold to record labels for use by their contracted artists.

From 1917 to around 1940 one particular group of New York publishing firms dominated the industry to such an extent that the music was named after the area where most of their offices were located, Tin Pan Alley (near Broadway). Bing Crosby's 'White Christmas' (by Irving Berlin) was a classic example of the sentimental, optimistic style that epitomised the output of Tin Pan Alley writers.

The first signs of a new paradigm – that of performer writers – came in the late 1930s, when a number of bands under the direction of people such as Count Basie and Glenn Miller wrote and performed their own musical arrangements. The 1940s saw the emergence of Rhythm and Blues (R&B) and Country music, the further development of which led, in the mid-1950s, to the musical style that was to revolutionise the music industry, Rock 'n' Roll. With its appeal to a younger audience,

Exhibit 2.1   Record sales 1945–60 in millions (USA)

1945	109	1953	219
1946	218	1954	213
1947	224	1955	277
1948	189	1956	377
1949	173	1957	460
1950	189	1958	511
1951	199	1959	603
1952	214	1960	600

Source: Billboard.

Rock 'n' Roll injected both increased revenue through rising record sales (Exhibit 2.1) and encouraged a new generation of writer performers to contribute to the music industry's development and structure.

Music's progress

Since the 1960s there has been an explosion and also fragmentation in musical styles. Exhibit 2.2 illustrates this.

Exhibit 2.2   Indicative development of musical styles

1960s	The Nashville sound (Country and Western) The Motown sound (Soul) (Sam Cooke) The further development of Rock 'n' Roll into 'Rock' with its heavier and more complex beat (The Beatles) Psychedelic rock (Cream)
1970s	Heavy Metal (Motorhead) Reggae music (Bob Marley and the Wailers) Funk (Kool and the Gang) Disco (Donna Summer) Glam rock (T-Rex) Punk rock (Sex Pistols)
1980s	New wave (Spandau Ballet) Alternative music (The Smiths) Jazz funk (Level 42) Mainstream rock of solo singers (Springsteen/Madonna) Rap music (Snoop Doggy Dogg) House music (Masters at Work)
1990s	Grunge (Nirvana) Hip hop (A Tribe called Quest) Trip hop (Portishead) Brit pop (Oasis) Lo-fi (Stereolab) Lounge (Air) Acid jazz (James Taylor Quartet) Drum and bass (Goldie) Techno music (Chemical Brothers) Speed garage Death metal/Thrash (Napalm Death) Hard core (fast Techno) (Carl Cox)

Exhibit 2.3 **Soundcarrier sales of selected genres**

	1990	1991	1992	1993	1994
Rock	36.1	34.8	31.6	30.2	35.1
Country	9.6	12.8	17.4	18.7	16.3
Pop	13.7	12.1	11.5	11.9	10.3
Urban Contemporary	11.6	9.9	9.8	10.5	9.6
Rap	8.5	10	8.6	9.2	7.9
Classical	3.12	3.2	3.7	3.3	3.7
Jazz	4.8	4	3.8	3.1	3
Gospel	2.5	3.8	2.8	3.2	3.3
Soundtracks	0.8	0.7	0.7	0.7	1
Children's	0.5	0.3	0.5	0.4	0.4
Other	7.5	6.5	7.4	6.6	9.2

Source: Recording Industry Association of America (RIAA).[4]

As the above represent cultural movements their appearance and subsequent development are difficult to date. There is often a delay between the originators of a kind of music and its adoption and subsequent classification by the industry and in addition to this, trends are often re-invigorated by later bands interpreting the work of earlier artists.

In an attempt to maintain a roster of acts that is in tune with the musical style of the day, record companies can get left behind. For example, the massive popularity of disco music in the 1970s and its subsequent free-fall from popularity caught the record companies by surprise, leaving them with unsold stock and tied to expensive contracts with their new unpopular artists. A more recent example was the rush to sign 'Brit Pop' bands similar to Oasis and Blur. In the UK the 'Brit Pop' phenomenon stalled, leaving the record companies and their associated labels with contracts with unwanted bands.

The increasing profusion of musical styles makes the tracking of each genre's popularity difficult. Exhibit 2.3 gives the percentage of sales (dollar volume) of all soundcarrier formats in the USA.

The industry

The business of music involves a long chain of activities connected to the creation, production, distribution and reproduction of a piece of music. Viewed in its widest sense the industry can be described as a process involving three main components: the artist[5] and their music (software); the means of transmitting or distributing the music to the customer; and the method by which it is played (hardware). Such a definition embraces the consumer electronics industry, software manufacturing and development companies, broadcasting and multimedia groups and retail outlets.

Exhibit 2.4 traces the development of a record with the attendant activities necessary to bring it to market. Though the activities have been separated, this is not meant to suggest that each activity is carried out by a different firm. The degree to which the activities are handled in-house is dependent on the size of the firm and the nature of the contract with the artist.

Exhibit 2.4   Music industry activities from songwriter to consumer (from Fink, 1996)

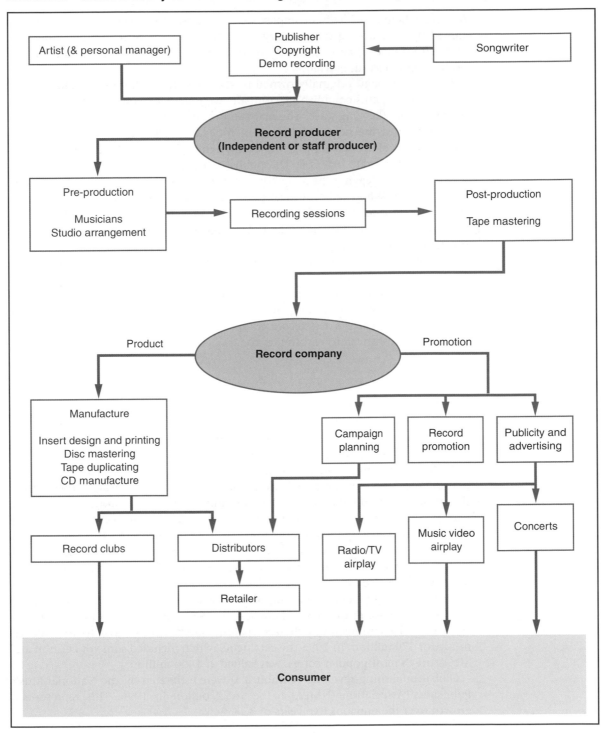

Copyright

An understanding of such a complex web of relationships and transactions is best gained by approaching the industry from its starting point, copyright. There are two main sources of copyright: copyright on the song and its lyrics, and copyright on the sound recording itself.

The song, though originally owned by the creator(s) of the music and lyrics, is transferred to a music publishing company to protect, exploit and collect revenue deriving from the song's use. The main source of royalties comes from the sale of records, termed 'mechanicals'. In the UK, for example, a record company must, by law, pay 8.5% of the dealer price to the copyright holder. Elsewhere in Europe there exists a uniform rate of 9.3%. The publisher then usually takes a 30–50% commission on this, leaving the songwriter with the remainder. To collect fees for use of the song (TV and radio) a local performing rights organisation is contracted, such as the Broadcast Music Inc. (BMI) in the USA or the Performing Rights Society (PRS) in the UK, which then divides the income equally between the publisher and the songwriter.

The sound recording of the music made by the artist also has copyright, which is owned by the record company. The 1988 UK Copyright Act defined the owner of the copyright to the sound recording as the 'person by whom the arrangements necessary to make the recording are undertaken'.[6] Depending on the nature of the contract with the artists, the record company then pays a royalty on records sold. This can vary, with 'stars' earning up to 25%.

Publishing

The distinction between publisher and record company is historical and reflects the original importance of printed music and the separation of the person who wrote from the person who recorded the song. There are currently very few independent publishing firms; most are now part of a record company.

Publishing revenues can be subdivided into four categories: broadcast, public performance, mechanicals and print. Broadcast involves the royalties owing from the music played on the radio, television and in films (synchronisation). Public performance covers music being used in concerts that are not broadcast. The 'mechanicals' category includes the royalties from the recording and reproduction (in records, CDs and other music formats) of copyright music. Printed music sales include songbooks and musical scores as well as income from the rental and public lending of CDs and videos.

An indication of the growing importance of music publishing is demonstrated by the rise in value of back catalogues. In 1984 Michael Jackson's publishing company ATV famously bought the majority of the copyrights to the Beatles' music for $70 million. In 1995 the catalogue, which included some of Lennon and McCartney's most popular songs, was valued at $400 million.

Global publishing revenues (Exhibit 2.5) were estimated by the National Music Publishers' Association (NMPA) to be $6.22 billion in 1996. This represents a growth over the previous five years of 32%.[7]

Exhibit 2.5   Global publishing revenues 1996 (US$ millions)

Broadcast	1,496
Public performance	1,105
Mechanicals	2,654
Print	613

Source: IFPI, NMPA published in *M&C* 29 July 1998, p. 13. *Note*: Information is not current

Recorded music

The industry terms recorded music the soundcarrier market. A 'soundcarrier' refers to the type of format on which the music is recorded, CDs, vinyl, music cassettes (MCs), etc. To reach the finished product a deal needs to be signed with the artist, the music is produced (recorded) and the master copy is then reproduced at a manufacturing plant. The resulting record is then marketed and distributed to various retail outlets.

The costs involved in the above sequence are high and, when considered alongside the risk of an artist or album flopping, provide for a significant source of risk. Costs derive from a number of sources, such as signing an artist, producing a record, manufacturing, distribution and marketing. Cost structures are of a highly variable nature due to the variety of contracts between the label and its artists,

Exhibit 2.6   Approximate CD cost structure in the UK

	£
Selling price to consumer	13.99
Selling price net of VAT	11.91
Retailer's buy-in price	7.24
Retailer's gross margin[i]	4.67
Distribution costs[ii]	(0.72)
Physical manufacturing costs[iii]	(0.65)
Artist royalty[iv]	(1.61)
Mechanical royalty[v]	(0.68)
Other artist and repertoire costs[vi]	(1.61)
Other overheads[vii]	(1.32)
Profit before interest and tax (PBIT)[viii]	0.65

Notes:
i.   A Monopolies & Mergers Commission (MMC) report of 1994 based on data collected from the five major retailers in the UK concluded that average gross profit margin was 33.1% with a PBIT of less than 1%.
ii. The cost reported in Exhibit 2.5 is based on 10% of dealer price. This figure is clearly an estimated average as costs associated with a soundcarrier will vary according to a number of factors, such as volume and area covered.
iii. This includes design and printing of the CD booklet as well as the manufacture of the CD itself. As with distribution, manufacturing costs can vary.
iv. Royalty rates vary according to the perceived worth of an artist. The royalty of 20% of dealer rate has been assumed for this table. Industry observer Cliff Dane: 'In the early 1960s bands like the Kinks and The Who earned a 2–3% margin ... by the 1980s that had risen to 10–15% and now it is over 20% for superstars.'[8] Until the mid-1980s artist royalties were based on 90% of sales. This was to account for the time when brittle records broke in transit, a tendency that was solved by the 1950s. There is also a delay between when the record is sold and when the record company sends the royalty payment. Penny Nagle of V2 Records (independent) states that the majors (large companies such as Sony, Warner and EMI) can take up to 18 months, while her label accounts to the artist within 6.[9]
v.   Mechanical royalty is used here as an all-embracing term to describe royalties payable to the publisher and songwriter for use of the song and lyrics (includes TV/radio/adverts).
vi. This entry includes costs associated with the artists and includes un-recouped advances, and recording costs.
vii. This refers to administration and marketing.
viii. This estimate is derived from the published accounts of the major UK record companies.
Source: C. Dane Media Research Publishing – 1996.

varying retail discount structures and general fixed and variable costs. Exhibit 2.6 presents a typical breakdown of costs.

Promotion and marketing

A significant marketing effort is required to ensure that the artist gets sufficient exposure, in what is a very crowded market place, to create both awareness and interest in the new album or single.[10] Estimates of typical marketing expenditure vary according to the label's distribution objectives.

Extreme examples include those of major artists such as Michael Jackson. Of the reputed $40 million spent on Jackson's CD HIStory, 75% was allocated to marketing spend. A typical budget is, however, in the region of £500,000.

Marketing and promotional activities involve a series of timed appearances on TV and radio stations, poster campaigns, interviews for youth magazines and representations to disc jockeys to convince them to play the song. The title given to people who promote the new single or album to the radio stations is 'plugger' and they, if successful, can have a powerful effect on the initial sales of a newly released single or album. For example, the Oasis hit single 'D'You Know' was played 18 times in one afternoon by the UK radio station Radio 1.[11]

The first week's sales after a record's release are seen as crucial, as the exposure received by a Number 1 single can further increase sales. In October 1998 the top five singles in the UK charts were new releases. A music magazine editor commented, 'I can remember when it was a big occasion for a single to go straight in at No. 1. Now it's so common that every No. 1 this year (1998–1999), apart from one, has been a new entry.'[12] An example of the power of radio and the vital role of a carefully planned and leveraged promotional campaign can be seen in Robbie William's first record after leaving the successful boy band 'Take That'. His first solo album did not impress the record label and was given weak marketing support – it sold 40,000 copies. However, one song from the album was picked up by radio stations and played frequently. The song became a hit and album sales shifted to another gear. The subsequent album was given a greater promotional effort and initial sales reached 40,000 copies a week.

The advantages of securing a high charting new release has led the UK to the practice of discounting. New singles can cost less than half the standard £4 for the first week of release, after which the price is raised.

Another source of promotion comes in the form of soundtrack albums. Films such as 'Robin Hood Prince of Thieves', 'The Bodyguard' and 'Trainspotting' linked the music and the film together, and by combining promotional efforts, bolstered the sales of each.

Concerts and tours are usually timed to coincide with the launch of a new album and thus provide extra marketing support. Tours are also a major source of revenue for the artists as they can receive between 60 and 90% of the gross profit from the event.[13] While a record company might provide marketing support, tours and concerts are organised and funded by specialised companies.

Profit

'This is a very lucrative business when you have a hit, but only one in five makes money and one in ten is a hit.'[14]

An often expressed view among industry commentators and executives is that most albums now need to sell 1 million copies to make a reasonable profit.[15] Yet, of the hundreds of releases by a major music company, few reach this level. In 1996 PolyGram, for example, managed to achieve this with only 34 of its albums. A Boston Consulting Group report estimated that 95% of debut albums fail, and that, largely as a consequence of this, the industry as a whole writes off around $5 billion in unrecoverable investment annually.[16] However, successful records enjoy healthy returns on volume. An example reported in the *Financial Times* in 1997 stated that with 3 million copies sold, PolyGram would achieve profits of $2 per album, rising to $3 for sales of 5 million and $5 if sales topped 10 million. When examples such as Madonna (180 million soundcarrier sales to 1995) and Alanis Morissette (28 million copies of her debut album – 'Jagged Little Pill') are considered, the importance of hit songs and major acts is clear. A further example of this imbalance was evidence when an 18.5% fall (one quarter) in Sony's record sales was explained by a 'drop in demand for Celine Dion albums'.[17]

Artists

The relationship between artists and their record company is often stereotyped as antagonistic. There are numerous high profile cases of artist vs company wrangles. Among the most notable include the artist formerly known as Prince who wrote the word 'Slave' on his cheek for one of his last videos for Warner, and George Michael who had headphones with the legend 'Phoney' in place of the Sony logo.

Much of the tension can be traced to the way contracts are structured. Although signing-on fees are used (though usually restricted to major stars), most of the deal is based around the number of records sold. A record contract will involve a promise to record a certain number of albums for which the artists will receive an advance per album. This advance is then used to pay for the recording costs of the album, which is then deducted from the artist's royalties. So, although the artist will have money after the record has been made (the advance is greater than the anticipated recording and production costs), by how much depends on his or her perceived or demonstrable record selling potential. Large sums of money will only accrue to the artist after a certain number of records have been sold. Robert Fripp (Tangerine Dream) offers the following analogy: 'Signing a record deal is like getting a mortgage, except when you've paid it off the building society still owns your house.'

From the record label's perspective, however, such caution reflects the hit-and-miss affair of the music industry. The eventual ruling in *Georgios Panayiotou (George Michael) and Others vs Sony Music Entertainment UK Ltd*, 1994 supported this view and agreed with Sony that signing an artist exclusively over a long period was a justifiable way of protecting their investment.[18]

Distribution

A number of factors can make distribution a difficult and costly activity. The product has a relatively low unit price, retail outlets are large in number and the markets are geographically dispersed. Record companies either use their own distribution networks or sign agreements with other firms (either specialist independent distributors or distribution systems of the major record companies) to place the product in areas they cannot reach. Being able to reach a range of international markets allows record companies to take advantage of differences in taste. For example, the British band Shampoo are almost unknown in Europe but enjoy strong sales in Japan.

As well as an opportunity for increasing revenue, artists promoted and distributed across a range of international markets can protect themselves from the volatile fashions and fads operating in their home market. A notable example are the Irish group, U2, who have had their longevity put down to an international fan base.

The function of distribution and logistics operates in quite a hostile environment as demand can be sudden and erratic with some records moving extremely quickly while others move not at all. The challenge is compounded by the fact that record sales are subject to large seasonal variations. In the UK, for example, 40% of sales occur in the run up to Christmas.

Artists and repertoire

Artists and repertoire (A&R) perform functions akin to the role of the research and development department of other industries. Often ex-musicians, they are close in attitude and age to the artists and are thus more able to recognise new talent, and assess their likely sales potential, than older and arguably more remote senior managers. In 1998, the average age of a music industry director was 46. Even with A&R staff of similar age and attitude, liaising with artists remains a difficult exercise.

Exhibit 2.7 World sales 1969–98 (retail value, US$ millions)

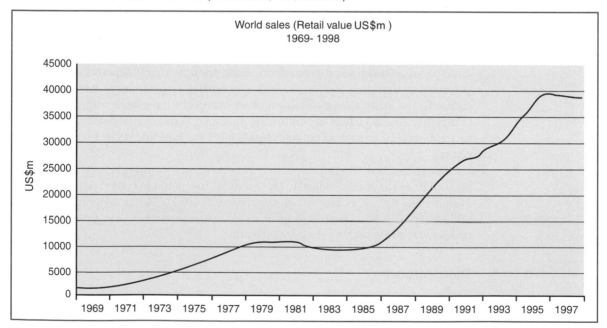

Source: The International Federation of Phonographic Industries (IFPI) World Record Sales 1969–1990; The Recording Industry in Numbers 1998.
Note: Information is not current

Exhibit 2.8   World sales by region (retail value, US$ millions)

Year	Europe	Asia	Middle East	Africa	Australasia	Latin America	North America
1991	10,708	5,307.5	278.6	244.8	610.7	1,172.4	8,448.8
1992	10,811	6,416	218.5	205.5	601.7	1,235.1	9,617.1
1993	10,525	7,058.9	279.9	204	612.6	1,520.1	10,623.8
1994	11,598	8,417.2	312.7	205.3	684.4	1,766.6	12,732.7
1995	13,358	9,737.9	345.9	263.7	790.8	1,746.3	13,056.5
1996	13,357	9,052.7	438.4	251	936.8	2,216.3	13,209.3
1997	12,673	8,351.6	453.8	233.4	853.5	2,575.9	12,883.5
1998	13,003	7,847	349	243.2	707	2,353.2	14,162.7

Source: IFPI; The Recording Industry in Numbers 1998 and 1999. *Note*: Information is not current

Exhibit 2.9   World soundcarrier unit sales 1981–98 (millions)

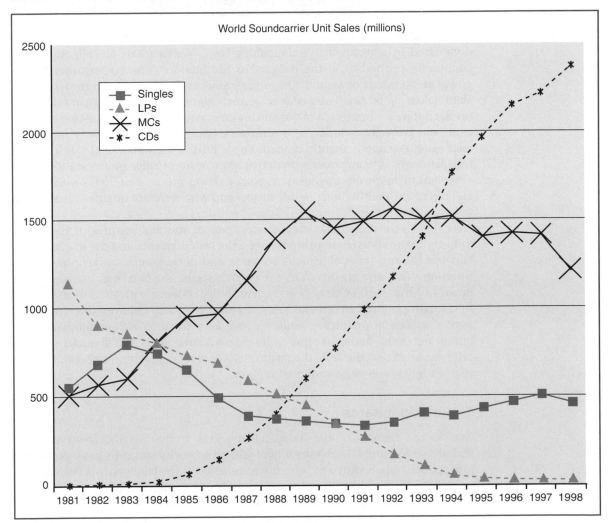

In 1998 CD sales saw continued growth with an increase of 6% on 1997. Sales of other formats declined; MCs (cassette tapes) by 10%, Singles by 11% and LPs by 12%. The 'singles' soundcarrier category is the total number of singles sold in all formats (vinyl, CD and cassette).

Source: IFPI; The Recording Industry in Numbers 1991–1998. Pre 1991 figures are taken from BPI year books. *Note*: Information is not current

One A&R man from a major label was told that the US group Rancid would only talk to him if he dyed his hair green. However, the newly green-haired A&R man still did not get the band as they signed up to a smaller independent label. A&R also play a role in the production of the records, providing advice on the development of the artist's music, though this can depend on whether a personal relationship has formed between them and the artist.

World sales

Exhibits 2.7, 2.8 and 2.9 show world sales by geographic area and soundcarrier type.

The players

The recorded music industry and its related business area, music publishing, are dominated by a group of five companies, Sony, Warner, BMGE, EMI, and UMG, commonly referred to in the industry as the 'majors'. These companies have a global market share of around 80% of the soundcarrier market, with the remaining share taken up by the 'independent' sector. Quantitative definitions do not exist on the difference between a major and an independent. The dividing line is drawn using market share estimates and turnover data, but as no commonly agreed criteria exist, the line is slightly blurred. Music Business International (MBI) defines independents as 'companies who derive most or all of their profits via the direct exploitation of music copyrights ... whose shares are at least 50% owned separately from the multinational music majors and who were not originally bankrolled by any of the majors.'[19]

As the above definition demonstrates, one of the key features of the music industry is the close relationship between the independents and the majors. Deals between the two types of firm are common and range from joint ventures to distribution deals, and are driven by the need to secure the two basic ingredients for music industry success: finance and talent. Independents, with their stronger links to changing cultural trends and less risk-averse company cultures, often make for a more successful A&R team, while the majors, with their well-established distribution networks, manufacturing facilities, marketing skills and financial strength offer the artist and the label the chance to compete in a larger number of markets with a higher level of promotional support.

The independents

One of the features of the independent sector is that an independent rarely remains so for long. The majors often build up minority stakes in small promising independent labels with a view to full acquisition if the labels' artists become successful. As Clive Calder, founder and co-owner of Zomba (an independent label), said '... the pattern so often now in the past five to ten years has been for small independent labels to grow off the back of the major companies and their systems (via giving away ownership stakes in return for investment)'.[20]

Investment and access to a major's distribution and marketing network is not the only reason for the surrender of ownership stakes. With a small roster of artists, the independents are vulnerable if an act's sales suddenly drop. Factory, the Manchester based independent label that enjoyed success during the 1980s with acts such as New Order and the Happy Mondays, sought an alliance with a major label due to financial pressures.[21]

Working together can bring out differing cultural attitudes between the major and independent that can put a strain on the deal. However, says Osman Eralp, an industry executive with experience in both an independent and a major: 'It's not a question of good guys versus bad guys. It's more about the way large companies tend to work with smaller entrepreneurial companies, because they have to report to shareholders who demand changes when things get uncomfortable.'[22]

As well as cultural differences, the attitudes of some artists can mean that the maintenance of an arm's length, part ownership, relationship is necessary. Sony had a five-year agreement to invest in Creation records (49%) with rights to buy the remaining share. By the time this had fallen due (1997), Sony had acquired Oasis who had signed to Creation records in 1993. Not wanting to imperil the relationship with the lucrative but temperamental Oasis, they paid the label's co-founders Alan McGee (who had also threatened to leave if Sony took the option to buy) and Dick Green £12 million cash to extend the 49% agreement for a further five years. Such issues have led some commentators such as Peter Kriesky (Mercer Management) to warn that, 'This is not a business where unfriendly takeovers make any sense.'[23]

Recently, independents have been exploring alternative sources of funding. These include floating a minority stake in themselves on the stock market,[24] establishing alliances with other media players such as between Telstar and Capital Radio (UK), or more imaginatively between K-Tel and Playboy Online.

The majors

Until Universal's merger with PolyGram, the majors were the six largest (by size of roster and soundcarrier market share) record companies in the world. The group currently consists of EMI, Universal Music Group (including the recently acquired PolyGram), Sony Music Entertainment (SME), Warner Music Group and Bertelsmann Music Group Entertainment (BMGE). All the companies except EMI (subject to a successful completion of their merger with Time Warner – see below) are owned by a larger parent company.

EMI (Electric Music Industries)

In 1898 operating under a licensing agreement granted by Emile Berliner, the London branch of the Gramophone Company was established. In 1899 the company bought a painting called 'His Master's Voice' (HMV) and adopted it as their trademark. The company expanded rapidly, establishing offices and manufacturing facilities in Europe, India, Africa and Australia. By 1906, 60% of the company's profits were from operations outside the UK.[25] With the opening of the first HMV shop in 1921 the company had interests in the manufacture of gramophones, the production and manufacture of recorded music and the sale of the finished product to the customer. A merger with Columbia Gramophone company followed in the early 1930s and the newly named EMI was born.

In the late 1940s and early 1950s, a period of American music dominance, EMI's strong European presence won licensing agreements with the Hollywood film and record studio MGM (Metro Goldwyn Meyer) and Paramount Record Corporation to distribute their products in Europe.

A succession of successful acts in the 1960s and 1970s, such as the Beach Boys, The Beatles, Pink Floyd and Queen, helped the company to further expand its retail division and, by acquiring publishing companies, establish in 1973 its publishing arm, EMI publishing.

EMI's publishing division currently holds a back catalogue that includes David Bowie, Sting and a 50% stake in Jobete Music, controllers of the valuable Motown catalogue.[26] EMI's 1998 Annual Report claimed that EMI had over 1 million copyrights. Industry analysts believe that EMI is the leader in music publishing, with Music Business International,[27] suggesting that 'It would not be unreasonable for EMI Music to have 20–25% of the world publishing market.'[28]

EMI's interests in electronics and hardware manufacture appeared to end when, in 1954, it sold its radio and electronics division to Thorn, a major UK electronics company with interests in TV manufacture and rental, domestic appliances and lighting. However this decision was reversed when Thorn bought EMI in 1980 and brought recorded music and the means by which to listen to it together again. The reunion proved a temporary one with Thorn/EMI selling off more than 60 businesses between 1985 and 1993.[29] The rationalisation programme was to enable a greater concentration on two markets: the rentals division (at the time it was the world's leading company) and the music operation.[30] This newly focused approach was accompanied by a string of acquisitions of independent record companies including the $500 million purchase of the world's largest independent, Virgin Records. However, in 1996 Thorn and EMI de-merged. Since then EMI has been subject to almost constant industry speculation over its acquisition. The list of possible suitors has included Bertelsmann, Seagram (parent company of Universal), Walt Disney, Viacom, Microsoft and News Corporation.

Until recently, EMI was the only major with a significant involvement in retailing through its ownership of the HMV retail chain.[31] In 1997 EMI spun-off HMV to form a joint venture with Advent International under the name HMV Media Group (in which it has a 45.2% stake).[32] The company therefore remains primarily focused on producing and publishing music.

After a year searching for a new CEO, Eric Nicoli, previously CEO of United Biscuits and a non-executive EMI director for six years, was appointed in March 1999. Responding to a 2% fall in EMI's share price when news of his appointment was announced, Mr Nicoli said: 'I think my lack of industry knowledge will be an advantage not a disadvantage. It will mean I won't have any preconceived notions of what is the right thing to do and what is the wrong thing to be doing.'[33]

At the end of January 2000, Warner Music Group and EMI announced their intention to merge. The new operation will be headquartered in New York with overall management control in Time Warner's hands. Eric Nicoli will become co-chairman along with a Time Warner executive. Concern over the merged

Exhibit 2.10   EMI (£ millions)

	1993/94	1994/95	1995/96	1996/97	1997/98	1998/99
Revenues	1,760.50	2,189.00	2,705.10	2,491.10	2,352.70	2,375.5
Operating income	246.1	249.9	365.2	374.9	341.8	227.1

Source: Company accounts for year end 31 March 1999.

companies' combined market share has led to some speculation that the deal could be subject to an investigation by European competition authorities. If the deal goes through, costs savings of around £300 million are thought to be available.

Universal Music Group (UMG)

Formed in 1924 as Music Corporation of America (MCA), MCA's original focus was as a talent agency. In the late 1960s, by buying the record company American Decca and merging with Universal International Pictures, MCA's operations expanded considerably. The resulting entertainment conglomerate was forced by the US Justice Department to give up its talent agency business and to agree not to acquire any major film/TV or record company for seven years, moves prompted by fears that the company would exploit its range of business activities and damage competition.

After the requisite pause the music division (operating under the name MCA) continued to build up its repertoire through acquisition. These included ABC's record division (1979), part ownership of the Motown label and Geffen records, a major US independent label.

In 1990 Matsushita, a Japanese Electronics conglomerate, bought MCA in what at the time was the largest ever Japanese acquisition of a US company[34]: $6 billion bought the new owners the whole MCA group, which includes its film and TV interests, its music division and theme parks. Performance during the first few years under new management was described by the *Financial Times* as erratic and by 1994 American executives disgruntled with the level of investment made by Matsushita[35] were publicly asking for independence.

In April 1995 Matsushita sold 80% of its interest in MCA to Seagram the Canadian drinks company for $5.7 billion.[36] Under new CEO Edgar Bronfman, a large number of management replacements were made including chairman Lew Wassermann who had been with the company since 1946, president Sid Shienberg, and CEO of MCA Music Al Teller.[37] Successors were found from within the music industry, with Bronfman's use of ex-Warner executives leading to the changes in personnel being labelled one of 'Warnerisation'. In December 1996 the group changed its name to Universal Music.

Bronfman demonstrated a greater willingness to invest in the record division. While strong in the USA, MCA relied on distribution and licensing deals with BMGE to market its product elsewhere. Universal Music International was established to redress this balance, and an aggressive expansion programme was undertaken. This is reflected in the number of overseas offices increasing from 4 in 1993 to 28 in 1997. These branches allowed Universal to reduce their reliance on BMGE for overseas distribution and brought about a great number of joint venture deals with local labels in order to gain access to new talent. An example of this is Aqua the Danish group, who have had success in Scandinavia as well as the UK, Japan, and the USA. Despite these efforts Universal was still overly focused on US artists, who it then marketed overseas. Its largest purchase during this period was a 50% stake in US label Interscope. Interscope had become available after Warner had dropped the label following the controversy generated by the violent content of some of its rap songs. With a turnover far lower than the other majors, a weaker roster of local artists (non-US), and continued, though reducing, reliance on

Exhibit 2.11   Universal ($ millions)

	1994	1994/5	1995/6	1996/7	1997/8
Revenues	1,293	1,257	1,205	1,500	1,580
Operating income	192	123	24	72	90

1994 and 1995 year ending 31 January; 1995/6 restated to cover year ending 30 June; 1996/7 onwards year end 30 June
Source: Company accounts and M&C 13/1/99.

BMGE's greater international presence, Universal remained the smallest of the major music companies, and was accordingly often referred to as a mini-major.

In late 1998 the $10.4 billion take over of PolyGram by Universal's parent company Seagram swiftly brought Universal up the ranks of the major music companies. The music operations of the two companies were brought together under the name Universal Music Group (UMG). The newly formed group lifted the combined music company's soundcarrier market share almost 10% higher than Sony, its nearest competitor.

Press releases from the combined group (Universal and PolyGram) for fiscal year 1998/99 state that revenues totalled $6.3 billion.

PolyGram

PolyGram's origins lie in a joint venture between two major electrical companies, Siemens (German) and Philips (Dutch). Siemens had entered the music business through the acquisition in 1941 of Deutsche Grammophon, originally established in 1898 by the British Gramophone Company. Philips' activities began in 1950 (Philips Phonographic Industries) under the label Phonogram. The 1962 joint venture was consolidated in 1972 when they adopted the unifying name PolyGram.[38] Philips later went on to buy out Siemens' 50% share, completing the buyout in 1985.

Philips has a long history of electronics innovation, notably the music cassette, and as joint developer (with Sony) of the Compact Disc. Jan Timmers (ex-president) commenting on the link between music and the consumer electronics industry described the relationship as symbiotic 'which, according to my (Jan Timmers') dictionary means: The intimate living together of two dissimilar organisms in a mutually beneficial relationship'.[39]

PolyGram's music operations were strengthened by the purchase of labels including the US label Mercury (1970) and the UK label Decca in 1980. However, PolyGram's share of the important US soundcarrier market was low and a merger with Warner Music was proposed in 1984. The deal was seen by the two companies as mutually beneficial as Warner was weak outside the USA. However, the merger was blocked by regulatory bodies in Germany and the USA, over concerns that the resulting group would be too powerful. With growth via a major merger frustrated as a strategy, PolyGram embarked on a series of smaller scale acquisitions and joint ventures that included A&M records, Motown, UK Label Island Records and Def Jam. When Go! Discs – a leading independent record label in which PolyGram had taken a 49% stake in 1987 – was acquired, Andy MacDonald, its founder, resigned declaring it as 'an oppressive acquisition'.[40]

From the early 1990s, PolyGram's diversification into film and TV production and distribution began to turn the company from a music company into an entertain-

Exhibit 2.12 PolyGram (NLG millions)

	1993	1994	1995	1996	1997
Revenue	6,733	7,605	7,563	7,947	9,304
Operating income	N/A	1,111	1,152	1,113	1,307

Source: Company accounts, year end 31 December 1997.

ment company. In 1992 it established PolyGram Filmed Entertainment (PFE) to co-ordinate and manage its interests in this area. Acquisitions included TV companies such as Propaganda Films, Island Pictures, MFP/Meteor, a leading independent Benelux film production and distribution company, and Vision Video Ltd, a large UK video production company. Joint ventures were established with MTV networks to launch MTV Mandarin and MTV Asia, with Warner Bros to co-finance and distribute Castle Rock Pictures, and with the Sundance cable and satellite channel owned by Robert Redford.

PolyGram's music operations experienced growth in the mid-1990s. By 1995–96 it had become the world's largest record company by market share (see Exhibit 2.12). The company was the leader in the classical soundcarrier market with a global share of around 40%,[41] and had CD manufacturing facilities in Germany, France, USA and the UK. Its publishing division had a catalogue of 385,000 titles and was believed to be the fifth largest publisher with sales of $180 million.[42]

Warner Music Group (WMG)

Warner Bros Records was established in 1958. In 1969 The Kinney Corporation (owners of US record companies Elektra and Atlantic) bought Warner Bros Records and folded it into its existing group to form WEA (Warner Elektra Atlantic). In 1989 Warner merged[43] with Time Life to form what was then the world's largest media conglomerate[44] and renamed its music division Warner Music Group (WMG).

Despite carrying a debt of around $15 billion in 1996, Time Warner's media interests were further strengthened by the merger with Turner Broadcasting Systems (which included the 24-hour news channel CNN). Despite concern that the newly merged group would command too strong a position in the USA media industry, the Federal Trade Commission approved the deal and 'the most powerful broadcasting organisation the US has ever seen'[45] came into being.[46] It has interests in film, TV (Warner Bros), cable networks (e.g. CNN), pay TV stations including HBO (largest in the USA) and publishing interests through its subsidiary Time Inc. It also owns 50% of Columbia House, the largest music and video club in the USA.[47]

Initially, WMG retained a separate status within the group, protected by former Warner CEO Steve Ross, who became chairman of the newly formed Time Warner. Time Warner's core business was defined as the creation and exploitation of intellectual copyrights. In the early 1990s Warner expanded operations in South East Asia,[48] establishing joint ventures with local companies, and purchased independent labels in Europe and Latin America.

After Steve Ross's death in 1992, Gerald Levin, the new CEO, gradually restructured WMG, bringing the three major labels (Atlantic, Elektra and Warner Bros) under the control of a new body, Warner US. Warner Music International (WMI) was created to manage the group's overseas interests.

Exhibit 2.13   Warner Music ($ millions)

	1994	1995	1996	1997	1998
Revenues	3,986	4,196	3,949	3,691	4,025
Operating income	720	690	744	467	493

Source: Company accounts, year end 31 December and M&C 19 January 2000.

Levin's arrival brought about a paradigm shift in stressing that the systems by which copyrights were delivered were as important as the copyrights themselves.[49] Structural changes followed. A-vision, a former subsidiary of Atlantic distribution, was made into a separate division and renamed Warner Video. Interests in multimedia were similarly collated and formed into a new division, Warner Active, which made acquisitions in software development companies (Hyperbole and Accolade). WMG has also established ADA (Alternative Distribution Alliance) designed to improve the company's links with the independent sector.

WMG includes the music publishing division, Warner Chappell.[50] Warner Chappell was ranked Number 2 in the world by revenue in 1997 with revenues of $475 million[51] and boasts a catalogue of 1 million copyrights.[52]

In mid-January 2000, the US internet company America Online (AOL) announced a $183 billion bid for Time Warner. The two companies will merge to create AOL/Time Warner. As there is little overlap in industry sectors there is little likelihood of regulatory opposition. Only six years ago, Warner's New Media division had rejected a plan to acquire AOL.[53]

Sony Music

Sony Corporation's business divisions maintain a very strong presence in both hardware and software activities and are organised in five major divisions: Electronics (video, television, audio); Game (computer games and consoles); Music (Sony Music Entertainment – SME); Picture (film and television); and Insurance. By far its most important division is Electronics, contributing just over two-thirds of group revenues, with most of the remainder split evenly beween its Game, Music, Pictures and Insurance divisions.[54]

The Sony Corporation's history is marked by a series of electronic inventions. In 1954 it launched its first transistor radio, in 1979 the Walkman personal stereo, in 1982, in partnership with Philips the Compact Disc. Sony has also played a key role in the consortia that have developed enhanced CDs and DVD technology. Sony became the market leader in home-use game machines within three years of the launch of its console. Sony is also the market leader in digital camcorders. In recent years Sony has entered the portable PC market with its Vaio 505 Superslim Notebook, and has announced deals with software companies such as Sun Microsystems and Microsoft.

Sony entered the record business in 1968 when it began a joint venture with CBS Records, which it was to take over in 1988 for $2 billion.[55] Sony's purchase of CBS Records and the Hollywood studio Columbia Pictures in 1989 was a move into the ownership of entertainment content, not just the hardware it is played on. The move can in part be explained by the need to supply entertainment content (music, video, etc.) for its hardware. The commercial failure of its technically

Exhibit 2.14   Sony Music (¥ millions)

	1993/4	1994/5	1995/6	1996/7	1997/8	1998/9
Revenues	461,752	481,021	506,455	570,660	660,407	718,878
Operating income	N/A	N/A	40,129	45,216	54,084	38,147

Source: Company accounts, year end 31 March.

superior video recorder (Betamax) was in part due to Sony's inability to supply the market with the necessary content to play on their machines.[56]

In 1992–93 SME with 18.7% world market share was the largest of the majors, largely due to strong positions in the world's top two markets, the USA and Japan.[57] However, the contractual dispute with George Michael led to industry accusations that Sony did not understand how to manage artists. Sony's inability or unwillingness to sign successful Rap acts, then (1996) the best selling genre in the USA,[58] appeared to back this up. Perhaps as a reaction to this perception and as a way of increasing market share in Europe, SME created a separate division in 1995, Sony Music Independent Network Europe (SINE). With an espoused artist-friendly mission, their role is to establish and support the company's relationships with independent labels and their artists; deals have been struck with labels in the UK, Benelux countries and Germany. These deals are flexible and vary from buying a minority stake in the smaller label to offering advice and marketing co-ordination. SINE therefore gains access to emerging and often volatile new talent, without the danger of losing the artists by attempting to fully control them.

Sony/ATV Music Publishing will, following the acquisition of PolyGram by Universal, become the smallest of the publishing groups among the majors.

Bertelsmann Music Group Entertainment (BMGE)

Bertelsmann AG, BMGE's parent company, began as a book publisher in early nineteenth century Germany. Significant growth took place in the 1950s driven by the success of its book clubs. The company now has interests in multimedia, TV/film production, book and newspaper publishing and recorded music and music publishing. It is currently Europe's largest media conglomerate by revenue.[59]

Bertelsmann's interest in the music industry dates from 1958 when it established its music division to manage its German record label, Ariola. Although Bertelsmann added Arista, a US record company, in 1979, the company's music business was relatively small. The $300 million acquisition of the record business of RCA (Radio Corporation of America), a major label with a long history in the music business, enabled Bertelsmann to get out of the middle and become a fully fledged major. The resulting company, Bertelsmann Music Group (BMG) was formed in 1987 and divided into two divisions, BMG International and BMG North America.

BMG's history is characterised by internal growth and a selective rather than an aggressive approach to acquisitions. Their cautious approach to investment, and an unwillingness to fund acquisitions through debt have prevented BMGE from acquiring a number of the artists and market share available. Some of the larger record companies available for sale (A&M, Island Records, Chrysalis Records and Virgin Music) were not acquired. While the larger deals were passed over by BMG, smaller more regional record companies have been acquired such as Riccordi

Exhibit 2.15   BMGE (DM millions)

	1993/94	1994/95	1995/96	1996/97	1997/98	1998/9
Revenues	5,736	6,777	7,338	7,329	7,911	8,100

Bertelsmann does not release profits by division.
From 1996/97 revenues from its multimedia division were quoted separately.
Source: Company accounts.

(Italian) in 1994 for $300 million, or Fun House (Japanese) for $90 million. More characteristic however are joint ventures with local record companies, which allow Bertelsmann to establish a presence in a large number of markets around the world and build up a more regional repertoire. John Preston (ex-chairman of BMGE UK) stressed this policy when stating the belief that '. . . if you don't have a strong local repertoire in each market you don't have a sustainable economic position.'[60] As of 1998 the company had interests in over 200 record labels.[61] BMGE's world-wide coverage plus interests in CD manufacturing plants (its 1997 Annual Report claimed it was number 2 in the world for CD production) enabled it to sign distribution and manufacturing agreements with other record companies, notably MCA.

Over its 12-year history BMG doubled its revenues and increased the scope of its activities considerably. In recognition of its growing portfolio, notably with its interests in multimedia (stakes in 100 software companies) and TV and film broadcast/production, BMG was renamed BMG Entertainment (BMGE) in 1994. In 1998 this was taken one stage further by the division of BMGE into two autonomous units, BMG Entertainment (music companies) and CLT-UFA (TV/film/radio).

Bertelsmann's interests in online media include genre-specific web sites, the first major to do so, and minority or 50% interests in new media firms, such as a joint venture with America Online. These internet investments, allied to the fact that it is the world's largest record club,[62] point to BMGE being well placed to respond to the possibilities of e-commerce.

Soundcarrier market shares

The calculation of soundcarrier sales across a global market and large volumes was immeasurably improved with the advent of point of sale data capture programmes. Using bar codes, information on the sale can be collected and relayed to a database. Pioneers of this approach were the US company, Soundscan (1991). After compiling the data, they are sold to the record companies. However, even Soundscan does not claim to capture the whole US market and estimation is required to produce a final figure. This recency in accurate data collection methods and equipment has limited the amount of historical market share data available.

Nevertheless, companies' own analysis of their market share often differs from those of industry observers such as Music and Copyright (M&C), the music industry newsletter produced by the *Financial Times* or Music Business International's (MBI) Annual Report of the Music Industry. In 1993 the chairman of PolyGram suggested that companies outline how they compute their market share. This has not been taken up.[63]

One procedure commonly used by the majors is to take the trade value of their sales to calculate, in conjunction with estimates of the total value of the market that year, their percentage. However many of the majors do not reveal in detail the revenues from various activities commonly grouped within the music division such as publishing, record clubs, video and film and TV production. For example, none of the majors publishes separate figures for revenues from music publishing, as opposed to those of soundcarrier sales. Indeed, such is the commercial sensitivity surrounding such information that the consultants handling the Universal/PolyGram deal had difficulty in establishing the companies' relative contributions. With the majors involved in numerous deals with independents, companies sometime claim revenue from independently owned copyrights, a phenomena referred to as 'doublecounting'.[64] The result is that industry observers (such as MBI) calculate market share from a combination of information sources, such as unit sales, company revenues and chart shares.

Market shares of the majors in selected countries

Music and Copyright estimates of market shares are arrived at through M&C research, information from National IFPI groups, and data from national music sales tracking companies such as CIN (UK) and Soundscan (US). Although the quality of information has improved over the years, some countries continue to be difficult to track reliably and are therefore excluded. These are China, Russia, India, South Africa and Turkey. The retail values for some countries in 1995 and 1996 are shown in Exhibits 2.16 and 2.17. For the years 1997 and 1998 the market shares are based on wholesale value as differing taxes and retailer margins make retail values unreliable (Exhibits 2.18 and 2.19).

Exhibit 2.16   Retail value 1995

Country	Value ($m)	BMGE (%)	EMI (%)	PolyGram (%)	Sony (%)	Warner (%)
Australia	680.5	6.4	18.2	13.1	26.5	18.3
Austria	409.4	14.8	20.2	21.3	11.7	13.5
Brazil	1,053.1	14.5	15	20.9	18.5	15.5
Canada	1,113.1	8	10	19.9	12.9	23.5
France	2,391.8	11	18.5	31.5	24.5	13
Germany	3,269.6	14.5	21.5	22.5	12	12.5
Italy	582.7	23.9	15.4	19.3	15.5	17.2
Japan	7,552.1	7.6	13.7	13	17.6	7.2
Mexico	299.0	15.7	12.5	10.4	19.6	12.8
Netherlands	716.5	13.2	15	22.9	14.2	8.2
Portugal	140.2	10	20.9	15.7	16.6	12.4
South Korea	505.3	5.4	4.8	9.9	5.1	3.5
Switzerland	449.2	13.3	17.4	21.9	14.4	15
Taiwan	336.4	5	6	17	5	14
UK	2,571.6	9.2	21.5	21.6	13.4	11.2
US	12,102.0	12.4	9.8	13.5	13.9	21.6

Source: Music and Copyright, 8 May 1996, p. 7.

Exhibit 2.17   Retail value 1996

Country	Value ($m)	BMGE (%)	EMI (%)	PolyGram (%)	Sony (%)	Universal (%)	Warner (%)
Austria*‡	396.7	13.4	26	17.7	13.6	2.5	18.4
Brazil	1,394.5	14.5	15.8	19.8	16.6	1	14.8
Canada*†	911.6	8	10.3	17	18.5	14.1	23.9
Czech Republic	98.4	11	26	16	6	N/A	12
France	2,318.0	11	16	33	22.5	2.8	13
Germany*‡	3,179.3	17.3	26.1	19.6	14.2	2.3	16.4
Italy*	637.5	20	17.5	18.8	18.7	3.4	21.6
Japan*	6,762.3	7	14	13.5	17.5	2.8	6
Mexico	399.3	15.9	12.7	13.9	17.8	1.5	11.5
Portugal	157.9	12.47	21.64	16.71	14.4	2.9	9.22
South Korea	516.6	5.9	5.9	10	6.4	1.9	4.9
Spain	584.9	12.5	22.5	16	16.5	4.2	14
Sweden	340.0	13.3	24.52	14.95	15.71	4.53	15.32
Switzerland*‡	401.3	16	17.3	19.2	16.5	2	22.1
UK‡	2,709.8	8.3	22.5	20.4	12.4	3.1	9.6
US	12,298.0	13.48	7.93	13.46	14.32	10.35	10

Source: Music and Copyright, 16 July 1997, p. 7.
Notes: *Based on chart shares; †nine months only; ‡album shares only.

Exhibit 2.18   Market shares of the majors 1997 (by wholesale value)

Country	Value ($m)	BMGE (%)	EMI (%)	Sony (%)	UMG (%)	WMG (%)
Argentina	173.4	17	14	21.5	25.5	12.5
Australia	443.5	8.5	19	23	22	14.5
Austria	193.3	15.5	18	11.5	19.5	9.5
Belgium	195.3	15.5	18	11.5	19.5	9.5
Brazil	799.4	17	13	16	24	14
Canada	690	10.5	15	15	25	16
Columbia	125.9	14.5	7.5	28.5	9.5	5
Denmark	168.1	10	27.5	15	21	10
France	1,302.20	5	21	19	35	7.5
Germany	1,797.90	18.5	18.5	13	25.5	9.5
Hong Kong	158.9	11	11.5	8.5	29	12.5
Indonesia	119.8	11	8	13	21.5	13.5
Italy	409.2	18	20	18	28.5	15
Japan	4,647.20	7.5	10.5	16	13.5	6.5
Mexico	333.6	16.5	12	18	19	9.5
Netherlands	341.2	14.5	16.5	17	28.5	6
Norway	137.4	9	18	14	25.5	10
Poland	93.7	13	20.5	10	18	9
Portugal	107.7	12	21.5	16.5	23.5	6
South Korea	198.5	6.5	12.5	10	16.5	7
Spain	397.5	10.5	23.5	14	18.5	22
Sweden	212.4	10	19.5	15	19.5	13
Switzerland	214.9	11.5	14.5	11.5	23	12
Taiwan	367	12	11	10	25	6
Thailand	134	1.5	4	3.5	4	2
UK	1,736.60	8	24.5	12	25	7.5
US	7,037.90	12	12.5	15	26.5	19

Source: Music and Copyright, 14 July 1999, p. 13.

Exhibit 2.19   Market shares of the majors 1998 (by wholesale value)

Country	Value ($m)	BMGE (%)	EMI (%)	Sony (%)	UMG (%)	WMG (%)
Argentina	189.1	15.5	14.5	23.5	25.5	12
Australia	367.3	7.5	17.5	25	22	15
Austria	184	14	14	12.5	20.5	13
Belgium	205.8	12.5	19.5	16.5	26	6.5
Brazil	703.8	16	11	18	25	10
Canada	671	10.5	14	16.5	23	17.5
Columbia	83.9	10	5	33.5	13.5	5
Denmark	163.1	9	31	15	17	14
France	1,334.1	6	17	26	38	10
Germany	1,744.3	17.5	14	14.5	23.5	13
Hong Kong	97.8	11	10.5	16	24	9.5
Indonesia	47.9	10	6.5	11.5	18	10
Italy	412.2	12	19	20.5	25.5	21
Japan	4,480.7	5.5	10.5	18.5	11.5	6
Mexico	353.1	15	11	18.5	17.5	10
Netherlands	314.7	12.5	13.5	18	27.5	8.5
Norway	145.4	8.5	15	18	23.5	11
Poland	102.1	11	15	12.5	15.5	10
Portugal	122.9	9	17	17.5	31	8.5
South Korea	92.7	7.5	8.5	12.5	13.5	10
Spain	444	12.5	17.5	16.5	17	19
Sweden	224.7	9	17	18	19	15
Switzerland	256.6	10	12.5	13.5	22	10
Taiwan	290.7	8.5	9.5	14	26.5	4.5
Thailand	90.1	1	2	5.5	4.5	2
UK	1,852.1	7.5	19	14	23.5	11
US	7,851.4	12	13	18	24.5	19

Source: Music and Copyright, 14 July 1999, p. 13.

Challenges facing the industry

Convergence of media

DVD (Digital Versatile Disc) technology presents the music industry with a new challenge. Advances in the compression of data not only allow for more music to be placed on the disc, but a variety (as the name suggests) of multimedia content, such as film and text. The resulting convergence of format with the different media threatens the traditional view of the 'record' as solely a music carrier.

Piracy

Unauthorised copying of copyright music has been a subject of industry concern ever since music cassettes allowed consumers to copy recordings. The industry responded by issuing skull and crossbones stickers with the legend 'Home taping is killing music'. The CD format and the widespread availability of the required copying technology has led to an increase in the number of pirate organisations manufacturing illegal CDs. The industry, through its representative body the IFPI,

Exhibit 2.20   Estimated piracy rates

Area	Percentage of total unit sales
Latin America	Around 50%
Eastern Europe	70%
Western Europe	Less than 10%
Middle East/Turkey	Around 30%
Africa	40%
Asia (excluding Japan)	30%
Japan	Less than 10%
North America	Less than 10%

Source: IFPI; The Recording Industry in Numbers 1998.

monitors piracy levels (based on raided stores, and the uncovering of illegal CD manufacturing plants) closely. It is estimated that one in every three soundcarriers on the global market infringe copyright, with the emerging markets of Asia, Latin America and Eastern Europe returning the highest piracy levels. The IFPI estimates that in 1996 world-wide pirate sales reached $5 billion in retail value[65] (see Exhibit 2.20).

The Internet

The Internet as one 'gigantic photocopying machine'[66]

The ability to record a song digitally, to transfer the music as an MP3 file across the Internet, and to play it in its digital form prompted the CEO of the IFPI to warn of the 'death'[67] of the industry. Robert Kohn, chairman of Goodnoise, an independent music company, has an equally strong opinion: 'MP3 is unstoppable. Any initiative now is like launching Betamax two years after VHS has become the standard. The real solution to piracy is to make music cheaper to buy than it is to steal.'[68] Alain Levy of PolyGram interviewed in 1995 was more cautious: 'Buying music is a social experience, and the packaging of a product is very important.'[69] Demonstration of the music industry's determination to protect copyright can be seen in the Recording Industry Association of America's (RIAA) $6.75 billion lawsuit against the most popular music site MP3.com. RIAA is a lobby group for the record industry. MP3.com has responded by counter-suing for damages because of the RIAA carrying out 'unfair business practices'. The case is scheduled to go to court in April 2000.

The necessity of responding to the new technology increased in urgency when, after much resistance by the major music companies,[70] Diamond Multimedia Systems, a US company, succeeded in introducing a portable MP3 player in late 1998. The machine, called the Rio, allows music to be digitally stored and played back through headphones.

The challenge embodied by the Internet is not restricted to piracy; by offering an alternative to the physical form of soundcarriers and their distribution, it has far-reaching implications on the current structure and nature of the music industry. Encouraged by a low cost-per-sale ratio that will continue to decline, some independent record labels are beginning to use the Internet to distribute their product digitally. Artists, including established stars such as the Beastie Boys,[71] Duran Duran[72] and David Bowie, have also flirted with the medium by releasing songs on the Internet. Such moves can, however, bring about conflict. When Creation records announced its intention of starting on-line retailing, Sony, which owns 49% of the label, blocked the move by warning Creation that it would be breaching contract if it distributed outside the UK. In another example, Warner Bros forced Tom Petty to withdraw from the Internet a song he had made available for free downloading.

On-line digital distribution

With the introduction of a portable MP3 player, and an estimated 17 million MP3 files being downloaded every day,[73] the majors' attitude had recently turned from hostile to a more active and involved approach. In December 1998 a joint development programme involving all the majors and technology companies such as Microsoft, IBM and AT&T was announced.[74] The project, called the Secure Digital Distribution Music Initiative (SDMI), is aimed at developing an industry standard security encryption system to prevent unauthorised copying. SDMI also set up the Portable Device Working Group (PDGW) made up of over 50 electronics companies and software developers to develop an industry standard machine. However, Stan Goman, CEO of Tower records, a major music retailer, is not optimistic about the majors' ability to develop a tamper-proof encryption system. 'They're fooling themselves. ... These kids can break into the Pentagon on their computers, so they're going to figure out a way to crack the system. There's no way out of it. If the record companies thought home-taping was a drag on their sales, wait until MP3 gets going.'[75]

In early 1999 IBM and the majors announced their intention to pilot an on-line distribution system in order to evaluate the effectiveness of the developed encryption technology and customer reaction to this particular buying process. Christened the Madison project,[76] it was scheduled to run for six months. The programme was to be limited to a thousand participants who could choose from a catalogue, and download the music to their PC in 3–6 minutes. The obtained recording could then be 'burned' onto a recordable CD with the customer offered the facility of printing a copy of the cover of the CD. Though the body was initially scheduled to have come up with an industry standard by Christmas 1999, no firm agreement has yet been reached.

In advance of such an announcement most downloadable music is presently restricted to 30–45 second samples of songs. A number of other alliances between the majors and technology companies point to a more wholehearted embracing of digital distribution, and a preparation for a digital future. In May 1999 Sony and Microsoft announced that they would form a non-exclusive alliance to provide streaming and downloading facilities, bringing together Sony's content with Microsoft's new software package MS Audio 4. A similar alliance between UMG and the technology company Intertrust, has also been announced. While all the new software packages for digital music files claim that they will satisfy the SDMI requirements for secure download architecture, it is not clear which system will become the accepted standard for digital music compression.

Tension exists between first entry advantages and the loss of revenue through piracy and insufficient encryption technology. The debate is exemplified by the current disagreements beween Sony's electronics division and its music operation, over the release of a Sony Internet music player.

717

On-line retailing

On-line retailing (using the Internet to place an order for a soundcarrier to be delivered) as opposed to on-line digital distribution (ordering and receiving music through the Internet) was initially blocked by the majors who controlled the copyrights to the recordings. The first commercial attempt made by video rental chain Blockbuster and IBM in 1993 stalled after the majors refused to licence their repertoire. Concerned about the possible problems created by channel conflict, they restricted music sold via the Internet to collections unavailable through traditional channels. This policy, however, was gradually eroded, with the majors gradually granting third party distribution licences for selected repertoire. Sony, soon followed by the rest of the majors, also began to operate websites from which visitors can order CDs and read artist-specific information. The websites come in a number of different varieties; music genre, the record label, or the individual artists themselves.

Most on-line sales are restricted to the USA, although European sales, particularly in Germany and the UK, are beginning to increase. Sales in the USA have grown considerably from a retail value of $49 million in 1997 to $250 million in 1998.[77] The introduction of a new channel enabled new on-line companies to enter the music retailing market. Though initially these companies such as Cdnow and N2K generated sales of $16.2 million and $5.9 million respectively and together held 45% of on-line music sales in 1997, their future, given the entrance of the music majors into on-line distribution, is uncertain.

Predictions on the future size of the on-line market vary. One research company, Forrester, predicts on-line sales to reach $4 billion by 2002, while Jupiter Communications settles on a more conservative $1.4 billion.[78] Variations aside, that the market is attractive is demonstrated by Amazon's successful entrance into CD retailing in 1998. In their first quarter of trading they captured the largest share of the market with sales of $14.4 million.[79]

Innovation, either technological or musical, has ensured that the music industry has always operated in a dynamic environment. In the 1930s the rise of the radio was blamed for record sales that plummeted from $104 million in the USA to $6 million in 1932. It took until 1941 for US sales to return to their 1927 figure.[80] The advent of Music Television in the 1980s seemed initially to offer the same threat. Today it is the growth of the Internet as an entertainment and communication medium, in conjunction with the development of related software to distribute and play music in digital form, that represents a significant threat to the current structure of the music industry.

The union of Time Warner, AOL and EMI is seen by analysts as a response to the new technology, and has prompted rumours of further industry consolidation.[81] David Endhoven, the manager of one of EMI's most successful artists, Robbie Williams, is pessimistic: 'Power will be concentrated into fewer hands and it will make it much harder for new artists to succeed. Decisions will be made by a very small committee of accountants and lawyers looking for instant hits. It will serve the needs of face-less one-hit wonders rather than helping talented artists develop.'[82] Alan McGee, however, is unconcerned: 'Smaller bands are not going to need record companies anyway – they'll just sell their stuff directly over the Internet. They have nothing to worry about.'[83]

Soon after the establishment of the World Wide Web, the Director General of the

IFPI spoke of the threat it represented: 'We know, at some time in the future, recorded music will be widely available on-line, interactively, and as a major part of multimedia products; but at present we rely almost exclusively on retailers for the revenue which drives our industry. Our challenge in terms of developing rights for producers, is how to get from here to there, with an industry intact.'[84]

NOTES

1. Music publishing and recorded music sales.
2. Gammond, P. and Horricks, R. (1980) *The Music goes Round and Round*. Quartet Books: London.
3. MBI, 1998, 'World Report'.
4. Fink, M. (1996) *Inside the Music Industry*, Second Edition (p. 24), Simon & Schuster, Macmillan: New York.
5. 'Artist' will be used to refer to a group or individual.
6. Monopolies and Mergers Commission, *The Supply of Recorded Music*, HMSO, 1994 (p. 51).
7. M&C, 29 July 1998; 'Global publishing'.
8. Dane, C., quoted in *The Economist*, 23 December 1995, 'Musical chairs'.
9. Barker, Adam, 'When royalties are held to ransom', *The Times*, 17.2.98.
10. *The Guardian*, 10 June 1998: Music week estimated that for the first 5½ months of 1998, 6,663 albums and 3,658 singles had been released in the UK.
11. *The Times*, 26 October 1998.
12. *The Guardian*, 26 October 1998, 'Younger generation misses out'.
13. Fink, M. op. cit., p. 102.
14. *The Economist*, 23 December 1995, 'Val Azzoli President of Warner Atlantic'.
15. *Financial Times*, 2 June 1997, 'Bankable pop stars'.
16. *The Guardian*, 15 February, 'Sounding out the band'.
17. *The Observer*, 'Rock is on the Block', 17 May 1998.
18. The judge in George Michael's case reportedly lost his sympathy for the singer on discovering that as part of a renegotiated deal with Sony prior to the case George Michael had been given £11 million.
19. MBI, December 1998.
20. MBI, December 1998.
21. *The Guardian*, 12 January 2000, 'Back to the Factory'.
22. Former MD of A&M Records UK who had previously worked for an independent (*MBI*, December 1998).
23. *Financial Times*, 25 January 2000, 'Rivals face up to exile on main street'.
24. Edel, a German independent with 1997 turnover of $119.5m, raised around $50m from a 23% flotation.
25. Annual Report 1997.
26. Acquired in 1997 for around $382m (*Financial Times*, 2 July 1997).
27. MBI, February 1999, page ix.
28. United States National Music Publishers association estimated global sales to be worth $6.22bn in 1996.
29. Including the television manufacturer Ferguson, Kenwood, the kitchen appliance manufacturer, its lighting division (Thorn's oldest business established in 1928) and a 59% stake in Thames Television.
30. The *Financial Times* traces this decision to the losses made in technology development R&D programmes (9 June 1993).
31. The MBI world report stated that there were three international retailers of music – HMV, Tower and Virgin.
32. The sale generated $165m.
33. *Sunday Times*, 14 March 1999, 'Yorkie man takes on his toughest role'.
34. $6.5bn for the MCA group which included Geffen records, Universal Studios and theme parks.
35. *The Independent*, 19 November 1994. They had recommended buying CBS and Virgin.
36. M&C, 5 June 1996.
37. Who had been with the company since 1973.
38. DG had been trading outside Germany under the name Polydor. PolyGram is thus the union of Polydor and Phonogram.
39. Burnett, R. (1996) *The Global Jukebox* (p. 56).
40. After issuing a press release that termed the deal an 'oppressive acquisition' (*Financial Times*, 24 August 1996).
41. M&C, 25 March 1998.
42. M&C, 25 March 1998.
43. Five years later the company was still servicing a debt of $15bn.
44. Above Walt Disney.
45. MBI, 1997 (p. 17), 'World report'.
46. The deal added an extra 2bn to the existing debt.
47. Annual Report 1997/98.
48. Following a relaxation in inward investment restrictions.
49. M&C, 11 March 1995.
50. Chappell was bought from PolyGram.
51. M&C research, 11 February 1998.
52. Annual Report 1997/98.
53. *The Washington Post*, 16 January 2000, 'Like Bambi going up against Godzilla, it was not a fair fight'.

54. Annual Report 1997/98.
55. M&C, 4 August 1993.
56. Nathan, J. (1999) *Sony: The Private Life*, Harper-Collins: London.
57. M&C, 1 September 1993.
58. M&C, 4 December 1996.
59. *The Guardian*, 21 April 1999, 'Fragmented industry'.
60. 'Local repertoire stems internationalism', December 1996, *MBI*.
61. M&C labelled BMG's strategy as a 'joint venture strategy to link up with small labels and production companies' (16 March 1994).
62. Reuters – Business Wire, 12 March 1998.
63. M&C, 1 September 1993.
64. MBI, February 1999.
65. International Federation of Phonographic Industries (IFPI) Network, February 1998, 'Going for the jugular'.
66. Nimmer, D., a Los Angeles copyright lawyer quoted in *The Economist*, 27 July 1996.
67. Channel 4 News, 9 February 1999.
68. *New York Times*, December 1998, 'Recording industry aims to sell music via the internet'.
69. *The Economist*, 23 December 1995, 'Musical chairs'.
70. *New York Times*, 27 October 1998, 'A once proud industry fends off extinction'.
71. Against the wishes of their label EMI (*M&C*, 27 January 1998).
72. Credited as the first major label single to be commercially distributed over the internet (*MBI*, October 1998).
73. *The Observer*, 25 July 1999. 'Online music puts record labels in a spin'.
74. Headed up by Leonardo Chiariglione, largely responsible for the creation of MP3. *The Times*, 26 March 1999.
75. *New York Times*, 10 December 1998, 'Two big firms converging to change the sale of music'.
76. *Financial Times*, 8 February 1999.
77. M&C, 27 January 1998, '1997 figures from Jupiter Communications'.
78. MBI, October 1998, 'Turning direct delivery into profit still a distant prospect'.
79. M&C, 4 November 1998.
80. Gammond, P. and Horricks, R. (1980) *The Music Goes Round and Round*, Quartet Books: London.
81. *The Guardian*, 24 January 2000, 'EMI and Time Warner form giant music group'.
82. *Financial Times*, 25 January 2000, 'End of the industry formerly known as "record"'.
83. Ibid.
84. Burnett, R. (1996) *Global Jukebox*, Routledge: New York.

Bertelsmann Music Group Entertainment (BMGE) and Bertelsmann AG

BMGE

BMGE is the music and entertainment division of Bertelsmann AG, a large multinational publishing and media conglomerate ranked by revenue among the top 500 companies in the world. Bertelsmann's history can be traced back to 1835 when Carl Bertelsmann established Bertelsmann House, a printing business in the small north western Germany town of Gütersloh. Early publications concentrated on religious texts, and the company's operations remained relatively modest (400 employees) for the following 100 years. Reinhard Mohn, whose grandfather had married Carl's daughter, took over from his father Heinrich Mohn in 1947, and began to transform the small family firm. The younger Mohn's first strategic move was to start a 'Lesering', Germany's first book club, an idea reputedly[1] derived from watching US soldiers distribute books to prisoners of war during Mohn's period of internment in a Kansas camp. The book club and the increase in volume sales that it generated were to drive the company's early growth during the 1950s.[2] In the 1960s Mohn took the first step in creating a media company by buying a controlling interest in UFA (a German TV/Film production company). The 1970s saw further evidence of Mohn's media ambitions with the acquisition of Gruner & Jahr, a German magazine and newspaper company. In 1977 Mohn took the company's interests outside Germany with the purchase of 51% of an American company, Bantam Books (the remaining stake being bought in 1981), and in 1979, the acquisition of Arista, a US record company.

In 1981 Mohn stepped down as CEO, leaving Mark Wössner to complete the transformation of the family concern into one of the world's biggest media and publishing conglomerates. Mohn's legacy continues to influence the company. The current chief executive, Thomas Middelhoff, describes Mohn as perhaps 'the most important entrepreneur Germany has ever had'.[3] Before retiring Mohn ensured that the company would remain private by transferring around 70% of his shares

This case study was written by Jon Gander and Alison Rieple, University of Westminster. It is intended for classroom discussion rather than to illustrate good or bad handling of an administrative situation. © Copyright 2000 Jon Gander and Alison Rieple.

in the company to the specially created Bertelsmann Foundation, a non-profit organisation which continues to hold the majority of shares and is currently chaired by ex-CEO Mark Wössner.

The creation of BMG

In the mid-1980s the company's fledgling music division based on the Ariola (founded in 1958 by Bertelsmann) and Arista (acquired in 1979) labels was struggling. Michael Dornemann, later to head the division, described the situation: 'The music company was in some trouble because that was a time when medium sized companies were in a trap between neither being a (stand-alone) label, developing artists and licensing to the majors, nor being a major.'[4]

Bertelsmann's response was the $330 million acquisition of the US label RCA. The resulting company, Bertelsmann Music Group, was formed in 1987 and divided into two main divisions, BMG International and BMG North America.

A new approach . . .

As well as being CEO of BMG, Dornemann also headed up the North American operation, while ex-PolyGram executive Rudi Gassner was brought in to run the International division. Though RCA's distribution network and valuable back catalogue (Elvis Presley) were useful additions to a music business intent on becoming a major player, BMG also inherited a weak roster of acts and a loss-making US operation. Culture and operating systems also presented the new owner with challenges. Both Dornemann and Gassner felt that under its previous owner, General Electric, RCA had been run as an appendage of a hardware company and not as an entertainment company. One of the resulting features of this approach was bureaucracy. Gassner described the culture he found in RCA's international offices as centralised and internally focused, characterising the attitude as 'If I have a memo from New York, and something goes wrong, then I am covered'.[5]

This centralised culture stood in direct contrast to the new owner's commitment to decentralisation – a principle that had been laid at the centre of Bertelsmann's written constitution, first developed in the 1970s and later reinforced in 1988. Stemming from Reinhard Mohn's belief in the advantages of a company made up of independent entrepreneurs, the company's core values are described in the document as 'decentralised, pluralistic and participatory'. The result of translating these values into operating principles was a flat and decentralised organisational structure that conferred a wide degree of autonomy onto divisional managers, who were encouraged to behave like 'the owner of any mid-sized company'.[6]

Alongside cultural issues there was the wider concern of assessing the inherited businesses, and creating a co-ordinated whole with BMG's existing businesses. Gassner described the situation he found to be one of 'a patchwork of companies around the world. It had no mission, no goals and in total it didn't make any money.'[7]

Goals, or rather financial objectives are, along with decentralisation, one of the defining characteristics of Bertelsmann. All divisions are subject to *Betriebsergebnis*. 'Betriebsergebnis' is a German accounting term roughly meaning return on assets and is the only German word used in BMGE, a company that has English as its official language.[8] Set at around 15%, all divisions are required to frame their investment decisions in order to meet the required return. Financial targets are then cascaded down through to local operations. As well as providing a standard against which to evaluate business decisions, the system also provides the basis for bonuses that Gassner described as enabling senior management to make up half their salary again.

Selected developments and events in BMG's development

(1) 1988–1993

A rationalisation programme followed Bertelsmann's takeover of RCA, and companies were set up to bring together and manage the newly strengthened music publishing and distribution functions. RCA's record club, for example, was reorganised to become BMG Direct. This reorganisation of existing assets and companies was accompanied by an investment plan to add to the company's asset and skills portfolio. A number of newly established companies were also set up during this period. BMG video, initially part of the international division before expanding into the US division, was created to produce, develop, promote, and distribute videos. Beginning with music videos it went on to broaden its range by moving into children's sports, and feature film videos.

Between 1998 and 1992, BMG expanded into numerous international markets establishing a local branch office in each country to help to build BMG's market share in the region, distribute licensed and own repertoire from other regions, and develop and promote new emerging talent in the area. Branches were established in Eastern and Central Europe, South America, Scandinavia, Europe and seven in South East Asia. In contrast to the arguably traditional music company approach of attempting to find the next big star (usually North American or English) to promote and sell their records globally, BMG developed a strategy based on the identification and promotion of regional talent, with a more local appeal. This involved purchasing or forming strategic alliances with small labels such as the French labels Vogue and Avrep, the Scandinavian labels Stageway and Norsk,[9] and the Italian label DDD.

BMG also began to move into multimedia by establishing joint ventures with American software and computer game companies. In 1992 New Technologies was established to manage and seek out more potential partners. In 1993 BMG purchased 50% of US software company, Crystal Dynamics. BMG's interest in home entertainment was further underlined by BMG's alliance with TCI (Telecommunications Inc.), a US cable television company, to operate a music themed channel.

Either through contracts, or in exchange for investment in the company, BMG's alliances brought increased revenue and improvements in both production and distribution efficiencies to BMG's operations. Key among these agreements was the 1988 deal with MCA/Geffen. The contract gave BMG the right to produce and distribute the label's music product, such as Nirvana and Guns 'n Roses, outside the USA. The contribution of this arrangement to BMG's revenue was acknowledged by BMG itself and MBI, for the year 1992/93. The *Financial Times* estimated the value of the arrangement to have been $400 million. This partnership strategy is further demonstrated by the fact that two-thirds of BMG's UK sales for the period

(1992/93) had come from labels with which BMG held distribution contracts. Other examples for the period include the agreement with 20th Century Fox to market and distribute its film music soundtracks.

However after five years, the RCA label, whose market share had improved slightly, remained the sleeping giant it was when Bertelsmann took it over. For the year 1992/93 Dornemann stated that RCA would 'barely break even'.[10] Attempts to improve RCA's fortunes led Dornemann to make a number of personnel changes. Three different presidents over the period failed to revive the label, and Dornemann's efforts drew some criticism. One executive fired after three months complained that he 'had (had) responsibility over certain areas but little authority to do anything'.[1]

Fortunes of Arista, another of BMG's US labels, were, however, a direct contrast. The style of the president and original founder of the label, Clive Davis, was very different from the ex-Boston Consulting Group strategist Dornemann. Though criticised by senior executives at Bertelsmann for not adhering to Betriebsergebnis, Davis' skill at discovering and handling big stars such as Janis Joplin, Bruce Springsteen, and Barry Manilow was delivering dividends in the shape of Whitney Houston. After a dip in sales following her earlier success, her soundtrack album for the film 'The Bodyguard' sold 27 million copies and generated revenue of around $200 million.[11]

In the early 1990s with BMGE's European market shares lagging behind those of the other European music companies, PolyGram and EMI, the possibility of purchasing Virgin records (then the world's largest independent), with its strong roster of talent, seemed to offer a way of breaking out of what the *Financial Times* called the 'second division'. However, after protracted negotiations, talks broke up and the company was bought by EMI in 1992. The later success of Virgin acts such as Janet Jackson and the Smashing Pumpkins appeared to vindicate EMI's acquisition. By 1994, Virgin was the UK's largest selling label, helping EMI to overtake PolyGram to become the UK's leading distributor.

Responding to questioning as to why BMG had failed to buy Virgin, Dornemann, after describing how he assessed Virgin's value to be $700 million ($300 million less than EMI's successful offer), commented that, 'You shouldn't go too far from return on investment even for strategic reasons'.[4] Return on investment targets frame Bertelsmann's approach to acquisitions, which (as company policy) have to be depreciated over 10 years, and cannot be funded by debt that exceeds 1.5 times cash flow. An ex-BMG executive described this approach to valuation: 'BMG undervalues a lot of properties because they look at everything in isolation. They calculate current performance and then run the numbers out a few years, never taking into account any operating synergies or business combinations.'[1]

Their approach to acquisitions runs counter to the behaviour of the other major media and music companies. In the early 1990s, when Time Warner, Sony and Matsushita were all carrying billions of dollars of debt as a result of their purchases (Warner Brothers Records, CBS Records and MCA respectively) in the entertainment industry, Bertelsmann's burden was a relatively light $240 million.[12] BMG's attitude to acquisition is rooted in the beliefs of Reinhard Mohn, who, described as 'a financial conservative'[1] was reluctant to fund growth through debt. 'We don't like to go to the banks',[3] as Middlehoff was later to comment.

However, after five years of effort BMG was comfortably inside the groups of companies known as the majors (see Exhibits 3.1–3.3).

Exhibit 3.1   Soundcarrier market shares (%) of the majors in Europe

	Europe 1994
Warner	12.4
Sony	13.1
BMG*	16.8
EMI	22.4
PolyGram	18.6

* BMG's market share includes MCA products which it was licensed to distribute outside the USA.
Source: Music and Copyright estimates 18 January 1995, IFPI, Music and media.

Exhibit 3.2   Soundcarrier market shares (%) of the majors in Japan and the USA

	Japan		USA	
	1993	1994	1993	1994
Warner	6.9	7.6	22	21
Sony	16.9	17.3	17	15
BMG	5.4	6.6	12	12.9
EMI	14.4	11.7	12	11
PolyGram	9.6	10.8	12	13
MCA	7.9	8.7	10	11

Source: Music and Copyright estimates 22 August 1995 and 30 March 1995, IFPI, music and media.

Exhibit 3.3   World soundcarrier market shares, October 1992–September 1993

	Company	Market share (%)
1	PolyGram	15.6
2	Sony	15
3	Warner	14.4
4	EMI	13.9
5	BMG	10
6	MCA	6.1

Note: Sales of MCA product outside the USA have been allocated to MCA not BMG (its licensee and distributor outside the USA).
Source: Music and Copyright estimates 18 January 1995.

(2) 1994–1999

In 1994 Bertelsmann restructured the company's activities which had previously been divided into BMG, magazines, printing, international book and record clubs, books, international publishing and electronic media. In May 1994 the group's activities were brought under the supervision of four divisions, Books (publishing and clubs), Gruner & Jahr (Magazine and Newspaper publishing), Industry (printing, paper manufacture and other industry services) and BMG Entertainment (BMGE). The renaming of BMG to include Entertainment reflected BMG's development of its multimedia, broadcasting and video/film interests.

BMGE was now Bertelsmann's fastest growing division, a trend that Dornemann felt would continue, by predicting that BMGE's contribution to group revenues would rise to 40% in the next five to eight years.[13] Increases in revenue had come at a price, however, and the 1993/94 annual report stated that BMGE 'was burdened by the cost of launching numerous new projects'.[14] How far the burden had bitten into profitability was uncertain – given the reluctance of Bertelsmann to publish profits per division. Music and Copyright however estimated that BMGE was Bertelsmann's least profitable division for this period with a contribution of less than 10% of net profit. The fact that growth was achieved at the expense of profitability seemed to be reinforced by Dornemann himself when he stated in an interview that as the aim was to grow the company: 'profitability is by definition not so good'.[15]

BMGE continued to build local repertoire through a combination of acquisition, joint venture and minority purchases in promising smaller labels. From 1994 to 1996 Music and Copyright estimated that BMGE had made 15 major acquisitions at a cost of around $500 million. Detailed accounts of the amounts involved in acquisitions or minority purchases are not released by the company; in their absence estimates and comments by senior executives at BMGE are the best substitutes available. For example, John Preston, chairman of BMG International UK & Ireland, voiced the belief that 'If you don't have a strong local repertoire base you don't have a really sustainable economic position. . . . We have invested enormously and developed on a regional basis.'[16] Investments for the period include the purchase of US label Windham Hill (annual sales around $40 million) and Italy's largest independent record company, Riccordi. Shares were acquired in US labels such as CMC, Loud and a 25% stake in Zomba, a large UK-based independent label with annual sales estimated at around $500 million. One noticeable concentration of investment was in South East Asia. For an estimated $90 million,[17] BMGE bought the Japanese independent Fun House, then the largest deal in the Japanese record industry. The company had previously bought a 50% stake in Elite Record (Taiwan) and a majority share in Hong Kong-based Music Impact.

BMGE continued to exploit its widespread distribution network. In 1995 BMGE became the first major to be granted a license by a state-owned company to distribute Chinese music and in 1997 agreements were signed with Richard Branson's new record label V2 (covering North America) and Australian label Mushroom records (North America, UK and New Zealand). One relationship was however being cut back: 1994 saw MCA and Geffen begin to establish branches in Europe signalling their desire to be less dependent on BMGE. Music and Copyright estimated that the reduced reliance on BMGE, who had acted as their agent, would produce a fall in BMGE's European revenues of around $100 million per annum.[13]

BMGE's multimedia interests also increased with investments in software and development companies with US firms such as Novell Inc. and Philips Electronics. A new company, Bertelsmann Ventures, was established to aid the search for suitable investment partners, one such being a Canadian company developing a digital jukebox. BMG Interactive Entertainment invests in software development and production alliances with US companies. It also entered into joint ventures with Sage Technology to develop a compact disk replication system (NeuRom), the aim being to increase the replication time by 50%, and with Anya, a Spanish company producing Sports CD-ROMs.

Bertelsmann's television and radio production and broadcast operation, UFA's, merger in 1996 with CLT, another media group headquartered in Luxembourg, brought to an end a period of mixed fortunes for the division. A long-running dispute with another privately owned German media company, Kirsch, over decoder compatibility, and regulatory blocks from the German authorities over Bertelsmann's attempts to become sole owners of the six TV companies it had interests in, stymied the division's growth. It reported losses of $500 million, also resulting from failed attempts to establish alliances in the European pay-TV market.[18] However, the merger created Europe's largest commercial broadcaster with radio and TV stations in Germany, France, the Benelux countries, UK, Sweden and the Czech Republic. Companies include RTL Radio (formerly Radio Luxembourg) and a 37.5% stake in Premier, a pay-TV station.

Citing the need to give two different business areas the requisite autonomy after the merger, Bertelsmann's entertainment interests were divided into BMGE (music companies) and CLT–UFA (film, radio, television) with Dornemann having a place on the CLT–UFA board.

The restructuring extended to BMGE's music operations. After a period in which *The New York Times* commented that 'executives have passed through at a startling rate',[19] the underperforming European division was divided into two operations – GSA (Germany, Switzerland, Austria) and Eastern Europe/the UK/Central Europe. Strauss Zelnick's (head of BMGE North America) responsibilities were extended to include some of the companies of BMGE International which now were managed from the New York base.

In April 1999 UMG and BMGE established an Internet-based joint venture, getmusic.com. The site combines the product from both companies and allows visitors to obtain information about their favourite music and order CDs on-line. The new alliance, by offering a greater choice of artists, is designed to combat the problem of Internet commerce, namely attracting traffic. BMGE had previously been the first of the majors to set up genre-based music websites in 1996. Music product from UMG will be introduced onto these sites. BMG Online, the company established in 1998 to co-ordinate and develop BMGE's on-line activities, has established partnerships with new media companies such as AOL (America Online) and Liquid Audio to develop and test new technologies such as on-line distribution and listening to music over the Internet.

As a result of Universal's $10.4 billion acquisition of PolyGram in 1999, BMGE became the smallest of the major international music companies by market share. Industry observers estimate the consequent loss of their distribution deal with Universal to represent $50 million in revenues, and doubts continue to surround the profitability of BMGE. Without full disclosure of divisional profits the true situation is unobtainable; however, the presence of rumours surrounding the possibility of BMGE being floated as a private company point to an industry-held belief that 'exposure to shareholder discipline' is needed.[18] The company line on flotation, however, is consistent, with Strauss Zelnick, CEO of BMGE, being the latest executive (February 1999) to deny the existence of any such plans. Asked about BMG, Middelhoff responded: 'We have only one objective ... we have to improve its profitability.'[3]

Exhibit 3.4   Global market shares (%)

	BMG	EMI	Sony	UMG	WMG
1995	11	14	15.5	22	15
1996	12	14	15.5	26.5	15
1997	11	15	15	23	12
1998	10.5	14	18	22	13

Source: Music and Copyright, 14 July 1999.

Market shares

The figures in Exhibit 3.4 include the combined market shares (historic) of Universal and PolyGram who merged in late 1998. Universal was previously MCA, having changed its name after being bought by Seagram in 1995.

The 1995 and 1996 figures have used the retail value of sales. For the years 1997 and 1998 the market shares are based on wholesale value as differing taxes and retailer margins make retail values unreliable.

The market share of the majors between 1995 and 1998 can be seen in Exhibit 3.5. Note that, in Exhibit 3.5, the retail values are given for 1995 and 1996, but for 1997 and 1998 the market shares are based on the wholesale value as differing taxes and retailer margins make the retail values unreliable.

Exhibit 3.5   Market shares of the majors, 1995–1998

Retail value 1995

Country	Value ($m)	BMGE (%)	EMI (%)	PolyGram (%)	Sony (%)	MCA (%)	Warner (%)
Australia	680.5	6.4	18.2	13.1	26.5	2.4	18.3
Austria	409.4	14.8	20.2	21.3	11.7	2	13.5
Brazil	1,053.1	14.5	15	20.9	18.5	–	15.5
Canada	1,113.1	8	10	19.9	12.9	15.6	23.5
France	2,391.8	11	18.5	31.5	24.5	–	13
Germany	3,269.6	14.5	21.5	22.5	12	2	12.5
Italy	582.7	23.9	15.4	19.3	15.5	–	17.2
Japan	7,552.1	7.6	13.7	13	17.6	6.2	7.2
Mexico	299.0	15.7	12.5	10.4	19.6	–	12.8
Netherlands	716.5	13.2	15	22.9	14.2	3	8.2
Portugal	140.2	10	20.9	15.7	16.6	0.7	12.4
South Korea	505.3	5.4	4.8	9.9	5.1	0.6	3.5
Switzerland	449.2	13.3	17.4	21.9	14.4	–	15
Taiwan	336.4	5	6	17	5	1.5	14
UK	2,571.6	9.2	21.5	21.6	13.4	2.7	11.2
USA	12,102.0	12.4	9.8	13.5	13.9	9.7	21.6

Note: MCA's market share in the countries above for which no figure has been given is guestimated by M&C to be around 2.5%.
Source: Music & Copyright 8 May 1996, p. 7.

Retail value 1996

Country	Value ($m)	BMGE (%)	EMI (%)	PolyGram (%)	Sony (%)	Universal (%)	Warner (%)
Austria*‡	396.7	13.4	26	17.7	13.6	2.5	18.4
Brazil	1,394.5	14.5	15.8	19.8	16.6	1	14.8
Canada*†	911.6	8	10.3	17	18.5	14.1	23.9
Czech republic	98.4	11	26	16	6	–	12
France	2,318.0	11	16	33	22.5	2.8	13
Germany*‡	3,179.3	17.3	26.1	19.6	14.2	2.3	16.4
Italy*	637.5	20	17.5	18.8	18.7	3.4	21.6
Japan*	6,762.3	7	14	13.5	17.5	2.8	6
Mexico	399.3	15.9	12.7	13.9	17.8	1.5	11.5
Portugal	157.9	12.47	21.64	16.71	14.4	2.9	9.22

▶

Exhibit 3.5 continued

Country	Value ($m)	BMGE (%)	EMI (%)	PolyGram (%)	Sony (%)	Universal (%)	Warner (%)
South Korea	516.6	5.9	5.9	10	6.4	1.9	4.9
Spain	584.9	12.5	22.5	16	16.5	4.2	14
Sweden	340.0	13.3	24.52	14.95	15.71	4.53	15.32
Switzerland*‡	401.3	16	17.3	19.2	16.5	2	22.1
UK‡	2,709.8	8.3	22.5	20.4	12.4	3.1	9.6
USA	12,298.0	13.48	7.93	13.46	14.32	10.35	10

Notes: MCA changed its name to Universal in December 1996.
• Based on chart shares   † Nine months only   ‡ Album shares only.
Source: Music and Copyright 16 July.

By wholesale value 1997

Country	Value ($m)	BMGE (%)	EMI (%)	Sony (%)	UMG (%)	WMG (%)
Argentina	173.4	17	14	21.5	25.5	12.5
Australia	443.5	8.5	19	23	22	14.5
Austria	193.3	15.5	18	11.5	19.5	9.5
Belgium	195.3	15.5	18	11.5	19.5	9.5
Brazil	799.4	17	13	16	24	14
Canada	690	10.5	15	15	25	16
Columbia	125.9	14.5	7.5	28.5	9.5	5
Denmark	168.1	10	27.5	15	21	10
France	1,302.20	5	21	19	35	7.5
Germany	1,797.90	18.5	18.5	13	25.5	9.5
Hong Kong	158.9	11	11.5	8.5	29	12.5
Indonesia	119.8	11	8	13	21.5	13.5
Italy	409.2	18	20	18	28.5	15
Japan	4,647.20	7.5	10.5	16	13.5	6.5
Mexico	333.6	16.5	12	18	19	9.5
Netherlands	341.2	14.5	16.5	17	28.5	6
Norway	137.4	9	18	14	25.5	10
Poland	93.7	13	20.5	10	18	9
Portugal	107.7	12	21.5	16.5	23.5	6
South Korea	198.5	6.5	12.5	10	16.5	7
Spain	397.5	10.5	23.5	14	18.5	22
Sweden	212.4	10	19.5	15	19.5	13
Switzerland	214.9	11.5	14.5	11.5	23	12
Taiwan	367	12	11	10	25	6
Thailand	134	1.5	4	3.5	4	2
UK	1,736.60	8	24.5	12	25	7.5
USA	7,037.90	12	12.5	15	26.5	19

Source: Music and Copyright 14 July 1999, p. 130.

Exhibit 3.5 continued

By wholesale value 1998

Country	Value ($m)	BMGE (%)	EMI (%)	Sony (%)	UMG (%)	WMG (%)
Argentina	189.1	15.5	14.5	23.5	25.5	12
Australia	367.3	7.5	17.5	25	22	15
Austria	184	14	14	12.5	20.5	13
Belgium	205.8	12.5	19.5	16.5	26	6.5
Brazil	703.8	16	11	18	25	10
Canada	671	10.5	14	16.5	23	17.5
Columbia	83.9	10	5	33.5	13.5	5
Denmark	163.1	9	31	15	17	14
France	1,334.10	6	17	26	38	10
Germany	1,744.30	17.5	14	14.5	23.5	13
Hong Kong	97.8	11	10.5	16	24	9.5
Indonesia	47.9	10	6.5	11.5	18	10
Italy	412.2	12	19	20.5	25.5	21
Japan	4,480.70	5.5	10.5	18.5	11.5	6
Mexico	353.1	15	11	18.5	17.5	10
Netherlands	314.7	12.5	13.5	18	27.5	8.5
Norway	145.4	8.5	15	18	23.5	11
Poland	102.1	11	15	12.5	15.5	10
Portugal	122.9	9	17	17.5	31	8.5
South Korea	92.7	7.5	8.5	12.5	13.5	10
Spain	444	12.5	17.5	16.5	17	19
Sweden	224.7	9	17	18	19	15
Switzerland	256.6	10	12.5	13.5	22	10
Taiwan	290.7	8.5	9.5	14	26.5	4.5
Thailand	90.1	1	2	5.5	4.5	2
UK	1,852.10	7.5	19	14	23.5	11
USA	7,851.40	12	13	18	24.5	19

Source: Music and Copyright 14 July 1999, p. 13.

Exhibit 3.6   BMGE's operational divisions

BMGE North America

BMGE North America's portfolio of companies includes:

- the four main music labels *Arista*, *RCA, Ariola* and *Windham Hill*. These provide the majority of musical content for BMGE's music operations and are managed as separate companies.

- *BMG Canada* looks after the company's activities north of the border.

- *BMG Direct* is the music club division, made up of five clubs catering for general as well as specialised music sectors such as BMG Jazz, and Sound and Spirit, a large Christian music club. It is described as the world's largest record club.[20] In 1998 bmgmusicservice.com was established, enabling customers to order on-line.

- *BMG Distribution* provides marketing sales and payment support for BMG's labels in North America. It also handles the supply of CD-ROM and Video products to retailers in the USA.

- *BMG Special Products* produces customised music for companies such as Shell Oil, Avon, Starbucks, and Burger King. In December 1998, a retail music label Buddha records was formed to create customised compilations for businesses using BMG's back catalogue.

- *BMG Video US* distributes sports, fitness special interest and feature film videos.

- *BMG Publishing* was formed in 1987. Revenue is roughly divided into royalties (50%), performance (30%), synchronisation (15%) and printed music sales (5%). BMGE controls the copyright to more than 700,000 songs from its record labels RCA, Arista, Ariola, Windham Hill and the 130 plus catalogues it has acquired (artists including B.B. King, Barry Manilow and the Beach Boys).

BMG Entertainment International

Based in New York it manages BMGE's music interests outside North America. It is divided into four regions:

- Asia Pacific

- UK – Central Europe

- GSA (Germany, Switzerland, Austria) – Eastern Europe

- Spain – Latin America

- *BMG Video International* distributes videos to more than 40 countries. Originally distributing the music from BMG-owned labels plus product from other music companies such as MCA or Geffen, it has diversified into film, special interest and children's videos.[21]

- *BMG Classics* is based in New York; it owns classical labels such as Catalyst and distributes products from Melodiya (Russian) and Conifer Classics.

Storage Media Division

This is made up of three companies *Sonopress*, *Topac* and *The Technology Group*. Sonopress is a CD and cassette manufacturer with around 11 CD and music cassette (MC) factories based in countries such as Brazil, Ireland, and the USA. It operates licences from other companies such as Microsoft, Apple and IBM as well as music companies such as MCA. An estimated 40% of Sonopress's turnover is derived from non-BMGE companies. Established in 1994, Bertelsmann claims it is the world Number 2 in the production of CDs and Number 1 in the world for CD-ROMs. Topac is involved in the package design of the CD, printing of jacket sleeves and booklets and other inlays. It is developing digital printing capabilities and hologram technology. The Technology Group is a division designed to keep track of latest technological developments and cultural trends. It is charged with forming research and investment alliances with technology companies.

Bertelsmann AG

Bertelsmann AG, BMGE's parent company, is a holding company deriving its income from the profit contributions of its 600 individual companies, operating in around 50 countries (see Exhibit 3.10 for consolidated statements of income). Despite the multinational source of income, Bertelsmann's headquarters are still in the small town of its birthplace, Gütersloh, although BMGE is based in New York. A media conglomerate run from a town with a population of 94,000 is unusual, as Mark Wössner commented 'In some ways it would be an advantage if we could run our business from New York' but, 'we have been here 163 years'.[22]

Bertelsmann employees for 1997/98 are shown in Exhibit 3.7. The head office and central services employ 634 personnel, 600 of whom are in Germany. Personnel costs for the period were DM 5.383 billion.

Bertelsmann's numerous companies are grouped into five divisions, as well as BMGE, there is a book division, a newspaper and magazine division, an industrial services division and its newly formed multimedia division. In line with Mohn's principle of decentralisation, business units and divisions are run separately. While they are encouraged to collaborate on specific projects, such co-operation is only entered into if both partners feel that the arrangement suits their individual business needs. Intra-company negotiations are conducted in the same manner as with outside companies. For example, Sonopress, Bertelsmann's CD manufacturing operation, has to bid for contracts with BMGE's record companies in the same way as other manufacturers, the result being that 35% of BMGE CDs are produced by competitors. Gerd Schulte-Hillen, the head of the newspaper and magazine division, described the individualism and independence resulting from such an approach as being 'the motor of innovation'.[23] When asked if he would work with BMGE to promote an artist, he replied in the negative, adding, 'We do it only if it's interesting for our readers.'[24] The flip-side to such an approach is the reduction in possible cross-divisional synergies. Dornemann, however, is dismissive of synergy, describing it as 'a contradiction to focus'.[1] Focus, however, can come at a price. In one instance the magazine division distributed free software for one of the multimedia division's competitors.

Perhaps as an acknowledgement of the costs of such a trade-off, an in-company survey (1997/98) among managers from all divisions and levels revealed a desire to establish closer links. The result of this finding was to establish in 1999 a 'Corporate University'. The initiative aims to encourage discussion and cross-company learning through 'virtual classrooms' in order to create 'closer co-operation across national borders and product lines'.[6] This project complements other cross-company communication and co-operation initiatives such as BMG Distribution's intranet/extranet service BMG Central (established in 1998) and the

Exhibit 3.7   Bertelsmann employees 1997/98

	Germany	International
Book	5,564	12,841
Magazines	6,456	5,587
Music	1,869	9,871
Industry	8,564	5,568

Source: Annual report 1997/98.

Exhibit 3.8   Bertelsmann's operational divisions (other than BMGE)

Book

The purchase in 1998 of America's largest publisher, Random House, for around US$1.2 billion – turned Bertelsmann into the world's leading publishing company. It was the company's largest ever acquisition, and was quickly followed by the acquisition of 50% of barnesandnoble.com, the on-line retail division of Barnes and Noble, for $200 million. In early 1999 Bertelsmann launched BOL (Bertelsmann Online) to begin on-line retailing under its own name. Initially set up in Germany, France, the UK and the Netherlands there are plans to extend the operation to include Spain and Asia.

Bertelsmann is the biggest book club in the world with over 25 million subscribers worldwide and 10% of the market in North America.[25] Book clubs in France, Spain and Germany supply 700,000 books daily.[2] In 1998 BCA, the UK's leading book club, was added to the list. Bertelsmann has recently expanded its special interest book division with the purchase of Springer and Doyma, European scientific publishers. This growth is in contrast to other media firms with publishing interests. For example, Rupert Murdoch (Harper-Collins) and Viacom (Simon & Schuster) were both reported as trying to sell their publishing divisions. Book publishing is described 'as getting away with lower profits than would be tolerated in other industries'. Publishers' margins[26] have been reduced, a result of being squeezed by the growing margins of retailers and the ever-increasing demands of authors.

Industry

Claimed by Bertelsmann to be Europe's largest media service company,[27] it includes 18 printing, services and technical support companies. The companies provide services such as direct marketing support, electronic marketing information systems incorporating electronic point of sales systems, communication and logistical system set-up and support, accounting systems and call centre set-up.

Grüner & Jahr (magazine division)

One of Europe's largest printing and publishing houses with a portfolio of 80 magazines and 9 newspapers world wide. Publications include: *Flora*, Europe's second largest gardening magazine, *Stern* (Germany), *Parents* (US), *Family Circle* (UK), *Computer & Co.*, Europe's biggest selling computer magazine and *Rtv* the biggest selling television programme magazine in Europe.

Multimedia

The multimedia division has grown out of BMGE and currently operates as a separate division within Bertelsmann. The division has formed partnerships with US-based software developers bringing it into the area of computer games (Sega), CD-ROM technology, and interactive digital music transmission. The operation currently has stakes in over 100 multimedia companies such as NuvoMedia, a company involved in developing an electronic book and Pixelpark, a leading German Internet design and management company. In 1995 Bertelsmann formed a joint venture with America Online (AOL) to provide Internet services to Europe. The company has continued to build up its interests in the new media sector forging alliances with companies such as the Internet search engine Lycos in 1998. A special division, Bertelsmann Ventures has been established in the USA to continue to seek out suitable partners. As the end of year results stated in Exhibit 3.2 do not include the revenues from Bertelsmann's many joint ventures and operations in which it has minority shares, financial performance in this area is undervalued. Bertelsmann estimate that total divisional revenues, if these unconsolidated revenues were to be added, would come to DM 923 million.

Executive Network which links around 1,400 managers through interactive communication technologies.

The growing convergence[24] within the entertainment industry presents Bertelsmann's autonomous culture with a challenge. How to balance the entrepreneurial spirit, arguably an advantage in fast growing markets such as multimedia and software, with the need to integrate its media products in line with consumer needs. As Thomas Middelhoff stated on becoming CEO of Bertelsmann: 'On the one hand we will keep a decentralised structure. On the other there is a strategic need to co-operate more than in the past.'[23] An example of Middelhoff's 'strategic need' is evidenced by Bertelsmann allowing a small start-up company, Amazon.com, to grab a leading share in the on-line book sales sector.

In the keynote speech at the German Multimedia Congress in April 1999, Middelhoff again highlighted the balancing act required. He defended the presence of internal competition that is generated from maintaining a decentralised structure, yet demanded more 'imagination in the mutual marketing of our products'.[28] Middelhoff also signalled Bertelsmann's intention to become a multimedia company involved in interactive media communications at both the content provision and distribution levels, by predicting that, by the turn of the millennium, 50% of their turnover would come from the electronic media industry.

Performance

As a private company the detail contained in Bertelsmann's financial reports is limited (Exhibit 3.9). Profit, for example, is not broken down by division. Revenues from 50% owned multimedia businesses are not included in the exhibit. Prior to 1992/93, BMG revenues were: 1988/89 $1.77 bn (representing 23% of Bertelsmann's sales); 1989/90, $2.09 bn (25%); 1990/91, $2.09 bn (23%); 1991/92, $2.4 bn (25%) (Music and Copyright 29 September 1993, p. 13.)

Exhibit 3.9   Revenues by division (DM million)

Division	1992/93	1993/94	1994/95	1995/96	1996/97	1997/98	1998/99
Book	5,837	6,074	6,815	6,890	7,108	7,249	8,300
Grüner & Jahr	3,623	3,713	4,384	4,579	4,813	5,192	5,400
BMGE	4,947	5,736	6,777	7,338	7,329	7,911	8,100
Industry	2,882	2,994	3,408	3,549	3,571	3,369	3,800
Multimedia					196	313	480

Exchange rates for the deutschmark (DM) against the US$ have been averaged over the calendar year. US$1 = DM:

1990	1991	1992	1993	1994	1995	1996	1997	1998
1.62	1.66	1.57	1.68	1.62	1.43	1.5	1.73	1.76

Sources: 1992/93 and 1993/94 figures obtained from M&C, 15 March 1995; 1994 to 1999 from company's accounts.

Exhibit 3.10 Bertelsmann AG Financials

Consolidated statements of income (DM million)	1999	1998	1997	1996	1995
Total operating revenue*	25,978	22,985	22,475	21,551	20,616
Other operating revenue	1,704	1,338	945	959	716
Cost of materials (and services purchased)	27,758	26,826	26,758	27,132	26,548
Royalty and licence expenses	23,239	22,540	22,606	22,429	22,354
Personnel costs	26,261	25,383	25,095	24,950	24,655
Depreciation and amortisation	21,115	2,839	2,884	2,765	2,712
Other operating expenses	28,144	26,955	26,328	25,759	25,700
Income from investments	869	11	254	233	11
Interest income (expense)	2,279	2,149	2,154	2,135	2,111
Results from ordinary business activities	1,755	1,642	1,537	1,307	1,263
Income taxes	2,845	2,520	2,515	2,402	2,446
Net income	**910**	**1,122**	**1,022**	**905**	**817**
Allocation of Profits					
Income applicable to minority shareholders	293	317	237	222	249
Losses applicable to minority shareholders	35	56	14	19	10
Change in retained earnings	371	596	540	463	371
Dividends of Bertelsmann AG	281	265	259	239	207
Thereof to holders of profit participation certificates	148	145	141	1,327	132
Thereof to shareholders	133	120	118	102	75

• Approximately two-thirds of Bertelsmann's revenues are derived from operations outside Germany.

Consolidated balance sheet	1999	1998	1997	1996	1995
Assets					
Non-current assets					
Intangible assets	4,281	1,878	2,063	2,306	1,996
Property, plant and equipment	3,351	2,677	2,801	2,702	2,431
Investments	3,214	2,000	1,920	863	486
Current assets					
Inventories	1,569	1,278	1,322	1,230	1,269
Receivables and other assets	6,692	5,363	4,931	4,708	4,041
Marketable securities	22	12	11	21	15
Cash	369	415	360	388	415
Prepaid expenses	198	148	148	139	107
Total assets	**19,696**	**13,771**	**13,556**	**12,357**	**10,760**
Stockholders equity and liabilities					
Capital stock	938	938	938	610	610
Profit participation certificates	1,343	1,305	1,253	1,209	1,155
Retained earnings	1,890	1,365	1,014	895	492
Dividends of Bertelsmann AG	281	265	259	239	207
Minority interests	895	727	726	569	577
Provisions					
Provisions for pensions and similar commitments	2,572	2,185	1,998	1,886	1,646
Other provisions	4,460	3,584	3,481	3,442	3,153
Debt	**3,700**	**684**	**1,092**	**665**	**489**
Other liabilities	3,100	2,317	2,421	2,491	2,101
Deferred income	517	401	374	351	330
Total stockholders equity and liabilities	**19,696**	**13,771**	**13,556**	**12,357**	**10,760**

Source: Annual reports.

NOTES

1. 'The Betriebsergebnis factor', *Forbes*, 23 May 1994: pp. 118–124.
2. 'Making a mark', *The Economist*, 10 October, 1998.
3. 'Bertelsmann's new media man', *Fortune*, 23 November 1998.
4. 'Dornemann embracing danger, avoiding risk', *Music Business International*, June 1994: pp. 11–13.
5. 'BMG's five year man', *Music Business International*, April 1996: 18.
6. Bertelsmann AG 1997/98 Annual Report.
7. 'A new major order', *Music Business International*, 1992: 2 (12).
8. 'Rudi Gassner and the International Committee of BMG International', Harvard Business School, 20 October 1995: European Case Clearing House, Cranfield University.
9. 'BMG looks for new talent in the East', *Music Business International*, October 1993.
10. 'An overnight success – after six years', *Business Week*, 19 April 1993.
11. 'BMG finds profit in Asia and cautiously moves into multi-media', *Music and Copyright*, 29 September 1993.
12. 'Bertelsmann coming to America – the sequel', *The Economist*, 16 November 1991.
13. *Music and Copyright*, 3 August 1994.
14. 'BMG Entertainment is the fastest growing Bertelsmann division', *M&C*, 15 March 1995, p. 13.
15. *Music Business International*, June 1994.
16. 'Local repertoire stems internationalism', *Music Business International*, December 1996, p. 58.
17. *Music and Copyright*, 27 March 1996.
18. *Music and Copyright*, Corporate Report, 15 January 1997.
19. 'A once proud industry fights off extinction', *New York Times*, 8 December 1996.
20. Reuters – Business Wire, 12 March 1998.
21. Annual report states that the company owns video rights to 300 feature films, e.g. Pulp Fiction.
22. Mark Wössner, *The Economist*, 7 November 1998.
23. 'Bertelsmann's Bismarck', *The Economist*, 7 November 1998: pp. 103–104.
24. The ability to transmit, store and enjoy film, text or music via a PC and the Internet.
25. 'Random thoughts', *The Economist*, 28 March 1998.
26. *The Economist* described them as 'skinny', 28 March 1998.
27. Bertelsmann AG Annual Report 1996/97.
28. Bertelsmann – a strategy for the 21st century. Extract from keynote speech, 7th German Multimedia Congress, Stuttgart 26 April 1999: www.bertelsmann.com.

Ryanair

Background

As the year 2000 began, Ryanair's chief executive, Michael Leary, could afford to be satisfied with the airline's performance. Recently released six monthly figures had revealed a 23% increase in profitability, in spite of several new routes being launched, and had forecast that Ryanair would carry 6 million passengers during the year. Load factors[1] were in excess of 70%, two of its competitors had gone out of business and the economic outlook in Ireland and the UK, its two major markets, remained bright. His company had been one of the pioneers in Europe of the 'no-frills' style of airline – lower levels of legroom and in-flight service than on a traditional carrier, but at much lower prices. He was aware, though, that yet another low-cost airline was about to start operations at its Stansted airport hub and that the Ryanair formula, itself copied from the USA, could be developed by others.

This case study starts by outlining the economic and regulatory background to Ryanair's development. It then looks at the development of low-cost, 'no-frills' airlines in Europe. Finally, it reviews Ryanair's history, its strategy and the competitive challenges that the company faced in 2000.

Ireland's economic growth

The airline industry has traditionally been sensitive to economic growth cycles. As an Irish airline, Ryanair has been able to take advantage of being based in Europe's fastest growing economy. Exhibit 4.1 shows GDP per head in constant 1995 prices and also the total number of international passengers using Ireland's airports as well as limited data on the total number of trips undertaken by residents of Ireland.

This case study was prepared from published sources by Adam Simmons, University of Westminster. It is intended for classroom discussion, rather than to illustrate good or bad handling of an administrative situation. (© Adam Simmons, 2000.)

Exhibit 4.1   Irish GDP and international passenger growth 1993–98

Year	GDP/head (1995 IR£)	Trips abroad by Irish residents (millions)	Passengers (millions)
1993	9913	2.056	7.1
1994	10449		8.3
1995	11396		9.6
1996	12190		10.9
1997	13365	3.053	12.1
1998	14386		13.6

Source: Central Statistical Office, Ireland, *Travel and Tourism Intelligence* (No. 1, 1999).

Exchange rates

The airline industry is characterised by a higher use of foreign exchange than almost any other. All aircraft purchases and leases and fuel are paid for in US$, wherever in the world the transactions take place, foreign personnel are paid in their own currency rather than that of the airline's home base and much, if not most, of its revenue will be in foreign currency (in the case of Ryanair, over 75% of revenue is not in Irish Punt – see Exhibit 4.7b for more details).

Exhibit 4.2 shows the movement in exchange rates between Ryanair's reporting currency (IR£) and the other two currencies in which it trades most, namely the British pound and the US dollar.

Exhibit 4.2   Exchange rate movements 1994–99

	IR£ per £	IR£ per US$
1994	1.0233	0.6676
1995	0.9843	0.6236
1996	0.9754	0.6246
1997	1.0810	0.6599
1998	1.1632	0.7018
Q1 1999	1.1619	0.7116
Q2 1999	1.1978	0.7456
Q3 1999	1.2026	0.7507
19 Jan. 2000	1.2788	0.7781

Source: Economic Trends and Financial Statistics, Central Statistical Office (UK).

Regulatory and financial issues affecting the European airline industry

Liberalisation

Ryanair was established at a time not only of a period of prolonged growth in its home market but also when discontent with high fares and limited or non-existent competition was increasing. The industry structure within Europe had barely changed since the end of the Second World War.

Until the mid-1980s, the airline industry was heavily regulated. Under guidelines laid down under the Chicago Convention, which took place in 1944, commercial airline services were regulated by bilateral (i.e. government to government) agreements which stipulated:

- which airlines were designated to fly a particular route (usually one or two from each country);
- what fares could be charged;
- how many seats could be sold; and
- which airports could be used.

With the exception of the bilateral agreements between the UK and both Ireland and Holland which were liberalised in the mid-1980s, commercial air services in Europe were not fully deregulated until 1993.

The first package of liberalisation measures took effect in 1987; this package allowed any number of airlines to compete on routes within the European Community, as long as neither of the governments at each end of a proposed new route objected to the fares charged. Prior to this package, many routes were carved up between the flag carriers of the two nations served, with each providing 50% of the total capacity.

The second package, which came into force with the single European market at the start of 1993, gave airlines access to almost all international routes within the EU. This package, however, had little impact; big carriers have not to date taken significant advantage of the changes. According to the Association of European Airlines, by the end of 1995 not one of its 26 members – which include most of the continent's leading carriers – had availed themselves of the new freedom. Developments resulting from the package continued to be patchy, it said. 'This is obviously an indication of the difficulties in identifying new opportunities and successfully penetrating unfamiliar markets.'

But smaller airlines have been less inhibited by national boundaries. Ryanair's main international base is in the UK and not Ireland, while Debonair, although based at Luton, operated several routes completely outside the UK. (Debonair ceased operations in October 1999.)

One of the main reasons why small airlines, rather than large established carriers, are benefiting from the third package is a continuing scarcity of slots at Europe's busiest airports. Flag carriers remain reluctant to split their operations (the Go operation being an exception – see below) between two or more airports in the same metropolitan area. The low-cost newcomers concentrate on point-to-point traffic rather than interlining and do not necessarily need to use the most congested hubs. Indeed, Ryanair does nothing to encourage hub through-traffic between Dublin and its European destinations via Stansted, and tells passengers that baggage carried in the aircraft is taken at the passenger's own risk!

A Europe-wide regulation on the allocation of slots took effect in February 1993. This confirmed the long-standing principle of grandfather rights, under which a carrier which holds a slot for a season has first claim on it for the equivalent period of the following year. It allowed airlines to exchange slots but permitted governments to protect them for certain domestic services. And it made two gestures in the direction of new market entrants – the first by creating a pool of new, unused or returned slots, of which half would be available to newcomers, the second by warning that airlines would lose slots if they failed to use them for 80% of the time allotted.

Regulation

Although economic regulation of airline operations is now non-existent, European governments and their agencies continue to exert control on the industry. For instance, Eurocontrol, based in Brussels, allocates scarce airspace to airlines and effectively acts as a constraint on the number of 'paths' available in the skies. While the USA with a landmass similar in size to Europe, has only one air traffic control system, Europe has one for each sovereign state. As these systems were all developed independently, the capacity of air traffic control in Europe is therefore somewhat less than for the USA.

A second means through which governments have been able to exert control is by permitting the national flag carrier (Alitalia in Italy, for example) to retain a monopoly on ground handling at major airports. The retention of such monopolies, however, is due to be phased out under European Union law.

As well as airline services being regulated, airports all over the world, including the USA, have traditionally been owned by national or local governments. In the UK, however, almost all airports have been privatised or are run by private sector firms on behalf of public sector owners.

Low-cost, 'no-frills' airlines

Traditions

Before deregulation, airlines were unable to compete on price, so the only way for an airline to differentiate itself was through service. Traditionally, air travel was for the wealthy and therefore a high quality of service was expected in terms of aircraft meals, free drinks in first class, higher seat pitch[2] and so on. By contrast, rail travel became much more rapidly a commonplace means of transport and so dispensed with service 'frills' relatively early on in its evolution.

Low-cost airlines have been able to develop a new business model more akin to travelling in standard class rail. It is important to note that most passengers will spend no more than two hours in a low-cost airline's plane (including boarding time), somewhat shorter than the rail journey from London to Manchester which took around 2½ hours in early 2000.

However, the airline industry has rarely been entirely free of price competition. It is notorious for its volatility and sensitivity to changes in economic cycles. It is also characterised by high levels of fixed costs and so, when demand turns down, airlines have always had little choice in the short term but to reduce prices to try to alleviate the inevitable excess capacity. Prior to deregulation, this was done through offering 'special' discounted prices with strict conditions attached, or by offloading excess seats unofficially through special outlets ('bucket shops') that were not allowed to advertise the name of the airlines whose tickets they were selling cheaply.

Exhibit 4.3   Selected responses to survey on no-frills airlines

	All (%)	Experienced no-frill travel (%)	Intend to travel on no-frill (%)
Not bothered about the lack of in-flight catering	34	55	66
Would not fly long haul on a no-frills carrier	29	37	40
Good that no travel agent is required	19	35	46
No ticket to worry about	16	22	29
If a no-frills airline flew to my destination, I would consider it first	21	34	49

Source: No Frills/low cost airlines, Mintel (February 1999).

Passengers' attitudes to no-frills airlines

Before the advent of no-frills airlines such as Ryanair, many people believed that such services could not be viable in Europe and advanced the argument that passengers would be unwilling to dispense with the traditional levels of airline service.

In February 1999, Mintel published a report on passengers' attitudes to no-frills airlines, undertaken in November 1998 with 1983 adults. A selection of the responses is shown in Exhibit 4.3.

It is interesting to note that, even on longer flights, many passengers would not be concerned about the lack of catering. At present, the longest sector flown in Europe on a 'no-frills' basis is by easyJet, between Luton and Athens. This flight takes 3½ to 4 hours.

The issue of in-flight catering, particularly on short haul flights, was highlighted in a second Mintel report on consumers' attitudes to in-flight meals (*Onboard Catering*, June 1999). Of 340 respondents, the statement with which most people agreed (59%) was that the main benefit of meals served on board was that they helped to pass the time. Twenty-five per cent of respondents felt that the portions of these meals were too small.

Passenger volumes on low-cost airlines

Although air travel continued to grow strongly in Europe and world wide in the latter half of the 1990s, budget air travel grew even faster. Exhibit 4.4 shows the rate of growth in air travel between 1988 and 1998 of airline passengers between the UK and the rest of the world.

According to Andrew Light, aviation analyst at Salomon Smith Barney, low-fare travel was the fastest growing segment of the European aviation market during 1999. In the USA, 24% of air travellers use low-fare airlines. In Europe, the figure is just 2.8%.

Mr Light forecast that European low-cost travel would reach only half the US level, because Europe's airports are more congested than American. European airlines also face greater competition from rail than do US carriers, especially that in France, Germany and Spain, all of which have dedicated high-speed rail networks that are being expanded.

But the European low-fare market is still growing strongly. Mr Light calculated

Exhibit 4.4   Growth rates of international air passengers to and from UK

Millions of passengers	Ireland	Other W. Europe (including Turkey)	Other	Total
1988	3.52	46.67	21.08	71.27
1993	4.36	53.53	30.25	88.14
1998	8.53	73.70	43.21	125.44
% change p.a. 1988–1998	9.2	4.7	7.4	5.8
% change p.a. 1993–1998	14.3	6.6	7.4	7.3

Source: CAA (UK).

that the budget market grew by 40% during 1998 to 10.9 million passengers and predicted that final figures for 1999 would show growth of 60% during the year.

UK–Ireland traffic has exhibited the strongest growth in the last five years (Exhibit 4.4). While traffic has grown throughout Western Europe, the range of growth levels between 1993 and 1998 is large. Ireland's is the largest, but other countries are not far behind (Holland 11.9%, Finland 12.3%, Denmark 13.3%), while France has barely grown (0.9% per annum) and Greece has actually fallen (20.5%). The fall in French traffic may be attributed to the Channel Tunnel, with London–Paris journeys down by some 20% since it opened in 1996. However air passenger volumes between the UK and Belgium have increased by almost 13% per annum between 1996 and 1998, despite competition from high-speed cross channel rail services.

Ryanair's history

Success for a new entrant is more likely at times of high demand and Ryanair was established during a period of strong growth in the aviation sector.

The Ryan family were no strangers to the airline business when Ryanair was launched; they had significant stakes in Guinness Peat Aviation which, during the 1980s, became the world's largest aircraft leasing company and Boeing's biggest ever customer. GPA hit financial difficulties in the early 1990s and has since been absorbed into GE Capital, a division of General Electric Company (USA).

The history of Ryanair may conveniently be divided into two parts: from its founding in 1986 to 1991, and from 1991 onwards, when it effectively relaunched as Europe's first no-frills airline.

1986–91

Ryanair started operations in July 1985 between Waterford and London, Gatwick, using an 18-seat Bandeirante propeller aircraft, against a background of stagnant traffic levels between Ireland and the UK; from 1974 to 1985, passenger volumes varied little from 1.5 million, having peaked in 1979 at 2 million before falling back to the historical average.

In November 1985, the liberalisation package was signed between UK and Ireland, thanks in part to lobbying by the Irish tourist industry. As a result of this new Air Services Agreement, Ryanair was able to commence Dublin–London flights in May 1986, using a 44-seat turboprop (Hawker Siddeley HS748). It offered an unrestricted return fare of IR£95, which was 20% cheaper than any other on the market and 55% cheaper than other airlines' restricted fares. In the previous year, 1985, passenger numbers on the London–Dublin route totalled 993,000. On average, there were 16 daily flights to Heathrow (6 by BA, 10 by Aer Lingus (EI)) and 2 to Gatwick (one Danair, one EI).

By 1989, Ryanair had introduced jets into its fleet (starting in 1986). Although its fleet and customer base had grown, so had its losses: in 1988, the airline had recorded an operating loss of IR£3 million and a net loss of IR£7 million. These losses were no doubt influenced by higher competition on the routes it served. For example, prior to liberalisation in 1987, there were on average 14 flights per day between Dublin and Manchester, whereas just one year later there were 50.

Ryanair's route structure in 1989 was focused principally on linking Ireland and the UK. Its network was as follows:

- between **Dublin** and: Paris, Munich, Liverpool, Luton and Cardiff
- between **Luton** and: Shannon, Kerry, Cork, Waterford and Galloway
- between **Knock** and: Leeds, Manchester, Luton, Coventry

Routes which had been axed by 1989 included Dublin to Glasgow, Manchester and Birmingham; Knock to Birmingham; and Luton to Brussels.

Knock airport was built in the early 1980s (principally as a result of lobbying by a priest who urged the Irish government to enable holy sites in the area to be made more accessible) and was generally regarded as a white elephant. While Aer Lingus insisted on a subsidy for flying to Knock, Ryanair saw an opportunity to serve the expatriate market in the UK and developed a route structure to serve this market.

Ryanair Holdings had developed a divisional structure by 1989.[3] Its five divisions were:

- **Ryanair** (responsible for UK/Ireland flights);
- **Ryanair Europe** (development of London–Europe network);
- **Ryanair Engineering** (aircraft maintenance);
- **Ryanair Fleet Management** (acquisition, by purchase or lease, of aircraft for the two airline divisions); and
- **Ryanair Tourism**, whose main objective was to invest in hotels and other tourist infrastructure.

The budget allocation process between these divisions was based on who could present the best case to the holding company board, rather than the board designating which divisions should be targeted for fast growth. It should be pointed out that separation of Ryanair's flight operations between two divisions was necessary to overcome regulatory obstacles: Ryanair Europe was UK registered and was therefore eligible to be designated as a UK carrier on routes to and from other European countries.

By 1991, Ryanair was carrying 650,000 passengers annually on 23 routes. It was using three different types of aircraft, had two classes of seating and had been through five chief executives in four years. Furthermore, the airline had also accumulated losses of IR£19 million (IR£9 million in 1990 alone). It was at this point that four key decisions were made which transformed Ryanair:

- cut the number of routes served from 23 to 4 (Dublin to Liverpool and London, London to Cork and Knock).

Exhibit 4.5 Southwest Airlines: a global inspiration

The model for Ryanair's operation was Southwest Airlines of the USA. Southwest started operations in 1971 as a local carrier within Texas, but, once deregulation occurred in the USA in 1978, the airline gradually spread to the rest of the USA; by October 1999, Southwest was flying to 56 airports in 29 states and was the fourth largest American airline, consistently profitable (no losses recorded since 1972). It operated 308 Boeing 737s (making it the world's largest operator of the world's most popular aircraft) and no other aircraft.

Each aircraft had an average flight length of 1 hour 25 minutes and operated for around 12 hours per day. By contrast, a full service airline operating a 737 into a mainstream airport would expect around 8 hours daily flying time from its short haul aircraft.

The Southwest model has been adopted not just by Ryanair but also by easyJet.

In 1998, Southwest Airlines had an operating margin of 16.4% (13.7% in 1997). This margin, however, is somewhat lower than Ryanair's, which has been around 26% since 1997.

- replace turboprops with jets (BAC 1–11s);
- make Stansted, rather than Luton, its main London hub; and, above all
- develop a no-frills strategy.

In addition, employee numbers were reduced by some 15% to 500 personnel.

1992 onwards

From 1992, Ryanair wholeheartedly adopted and extended the Southwest model (Exhibit 4.5). For example, Ryanair did not offer its passengers peanuts (which form a part of Southwest's branding) or any other food, as food waste would increase the time required to clean the aircraft and hence turnaround times. In 1994, it replaced its fleet of 100-seater BAC 1–11s with Boeing 737s, each with 130 seats. By 2000, Ryanair owned 21 of these older 737–200s, which have an average age of 18 years and are depreciated over 20 years. In typical 'full service' airlines, there would be around 95 seats with a two-class configuration.

Ryanair posted its first pre-tax profit of IR£300,000 in 1992. In July 1997, Ryanair

Exhibit 4.6(a) Ryanair profit and loss accounts 1995–99

Year ending March	1st half 99/00	1999	1998	1997	1996	1995
Revenue	153,181	232,929	182,606	134,940	110,058	86,179
Staff expenses		31,372	24,135	25,353	21,195	17,252
Directors' emoluments		550	498	10,211	9,419	5,213
Depreciation		28,517	19,799	8,546	5,257	3,460
Operating income	41,534	53,455	44,325	21,426	19,201	14,263
Interest (net inflow)		5,019	2,441	(1,086)	1,682	413
Pre-tax profit		59,705	48,383	21,511	20,566	15,657
Tax		14,443	12,529	7,162	7,205	3,652
Retained income	33,396	45,262	35,854	14,349	13,361	12,005

Source: EXTEL; figures in IR£000.

became a public company, listing on both the Irish and New York stock exchanges and, in July 1998, a listing was acquired on the London exchange. Key accounting information is shown in Exhibits 4.6(a)–4.6(d).

With a profit margin of over 25% in 1999, Ryanair became Europe's most profitable airline.

Exhibit 4.6(b)   Turnover by region 1996–99

Year ending March	1999	1998	1997	1996
UK	128.5	111.4	79.2	58.3
Ireland	56.0	54.5	52.9	49.5
Other Europe	48.4	16.7	2.8	2.2
Total	232.9	182.6	134.9	110.0

Source: EXTEL; figures in IR£m.

For any scheduled airline to be successful, it needs to attract traffic at both ends of each route. Ryanair's key source of revenue growth since 1996 has been in attracting passengers from France, Italy and Scandinavia on to its flights.

Exhibit 4.6(c)   Ryanair turnover analysis 1998–99

Year ending March	1999	1998
Scheduled ticket revenue	203.9	160.5
In-flight sales	15.9	10.7
Car hire	3.6	2.8
Other	9.5	8.6
Total	232.9	182.6

Source: EXTEL; figures in IR£m.

While most of Ryanair's revenue comes from the sale of tickets on its scheduled flights, there are other sources. Ryanair used to sell duty free goods on its flights but, in July 1999, duty free sales for flights within the EU were abolished. Such sales were a significant source of revenue for flight attendants, who received a commission on each sale. In addition, Ryanair has a marketing agreement with Hertz car rentals which pays Ryanair a sum for each rental secured from Ryanair passengers. In August 1999, in-flight sales were reported to be running at 6% of total revenue, which is not significantly lower than for the year to March 1999.

Exhibit 4.6(d)   Ryanair balance sheets 1996–99

On 31 March	1999	1998	1997	1996
Fixed assets	160.3	103.3	50.2	34.6
Cash	124.9	51.0	23.9	44.3
Total assets	314.9	172.8	87.8	89.4
Short-term liabilities	90.1	56.2	38.4	41.5
Total net assets (including provisions)	215.9	106.1	36.8	36.4
Funded by:				
Long-term debt	18.3	1.1	33.7	4.8
Share capital	6.6	6.3	5.0	14.0
Share premium	102.9	55.9	0.0	0.0
Retained earnings	88.1	42.8	(1.9)	17.7

Source: EXTEL; figures in IR£m.

The company's gearing has varied significantly over the last four years. By going public in 1997 and 1998, it received major inflows of equity capital which enabled it to reduce debt levels to a tenth of shareholders' funds by 1999.

Ryanair has not traditionally paid dividends: all profits are reinvested in the business.

Current network

Ryanair's funds have been used to develop its route network. In any business, expansion involves costs and the airline industry is no exception. Developing new routes requires more aircraft, hiring personnel at the new points on the network, and promotional costs.

The network has evolved since its inception. As Exhibit 4.7(a) demonstrates, the first phase of network development was concerned primarily with links between Ireland and the UK. Most of Ryanair's recent expansion, however, has been through the development of a hub at Stansted airport serving destinations in Europe.

Ryanair's average load factor for 1998–99 was 73%. Exhibit 4.7(b) shows that, in spite of new routes developed in summer 1999, this load factor has not changed significantly.

Exhibit 4.7(a) Ryanair network development (showing routes operating in January 2000)

	Started	Average no. of weekday flights*		Started	Average no. of weekday flights*
Between Dublin and			**Between Stansted and**		
Birmingham	1993	4	Cork	1987	3
London Stansted	1991	11	Kerry	1997	1
London Luton	1986	2	Derry	1996	2
London Gatwick	1994	4	Knock	1987	2
Bristol	1997	3	Stockholm (Skavsta)	1997	3
Cardiff	1996	1	Rimini	1998	1
Bournemouth	1996	1	Venice	1998	2
Glasgow Prestwick	1994	3	Pisa	1998	2
Leeds	1996	3	Toulouse (Carcassonne)	1998	1
Liverpool	1988	3	Lyon (St Etienne)	1998	1
Manchester	1994	4	Malmo (Kristianstad)	1998	1
Teesside	1997	1			
Brussels (Charleroi)	1994	3	Oslo (Torp)	1997	2
Paris (Beauvais)	1994	4	Frankfurt (Hahn)	1999	3
			Genoa	1999	2
Between Prestwick and			Turin	1999	2
Paris (Beauvais)	1998	2	Ancona	1999	1
London Stansted	1995	7	Aarhus	1999	2
			Biarritz	1999	1

* In winter timetable, 1999–2000.
Sources: http://www.ryanair.ie; *Financial Times* (various).

Exhibit 4.7(b)   Load factors on selected routes, October 1999

Between Stansted and	Seats during month	Passengers	Load factor (%)
Ancona	8,060	6,301	78.2
Biarritz	8,583	5,182	60.4
Carcassonne	13,817	9,561	69.2
Cork	29,937	25,388	84.8
Frankfurt	14,969	11,312	75.6
Genoa	18,104	11,482	63.4
Kerry	11,718	8,137	69.4
Knock	19,778	15,494	78.3
Kristianstad	11,718	8,524	72.7
Oslo	14,969	11,012	73.6
Pisa	22,913	18,604	81.2
Rimini	8,060	6,274	77.8
St Etienne	8,060	5,135	63.7
Stockholm	36,731	22,152	60.3
Treviso	16,120	13,062	81.0
Average	243,536	177,620	72.9

Source: CAA Statistics, OAG Airline Guide.

As a result of having two different aircraft sizes (the 200 series has 130 seats and the 800 series has 189 seats), Ryanair is able to alter capacities without altering frequencies and therefore has a more flexible fleet. Loads on the Frankfurt route were below average, and so the larger aircraft which were being used on the route have been transferred to city pairs where demand justifies the extra capacity.

Relationships with airport operators

To develop new routes, airlines require access to airports. This in turn means that capacity has to be available in the air (European air space is discussed earlier) and also at airports.

Although airports and airlines in Europe have both traditionally been in the public sector, the ownership structure has been separated. In the UK, for instance, BAA was the government agency owning London's airports and British Airways operated flights. In practice, however, governments have sought to restrict access to principal airports in their countries to protect their flag carriers from competition, and so access to airports was very often not driven by market-based principles. For instance, in 1994, the French government tried to shield Air France from competition at Orly airport in Paris by saying that no slots were available for foreign airlines. The government only relented when British Airways and British Midland took their case to the European Commission.

Ryanair has at times had fractious relationships with the airports it serves; for instance, in August 1999, Ryanair's chief executive accused Manchester and Kerry airports of introducing 'unjustifiable passenger taxes' and warned that the airline would reduce its traffic to airports which operate 'anti-customer' pricing practices. In December 1999, Ryanair was threatening to withdraw services between London and Knock as a result of new passenger charges being imposed by Knock's airport authorities. Disputes between Ryanair and Dublin airport in particular over lower charges to encourage new route development have hindered Ryanair's growth at its home base and so just about all its European growth has taken place at Stansted, owned and operated by the now privatised firm BAA plc.

Ryanair has often been the first operator to fly international routes into the airports it serves. As a result of putting these airports, such as Charleroi and Hahn 'on the map', Ryanair has been able to secure significant cost advantages, not only by flying into secondary, less attractive airports but by persuading these airport operators in some cases, to subsidise Ryanair's operations (at Torp airport, near Oslo, the airport authorities were reported to be paying for the costs of Ryanair's call centre there). Clearly, further airlines which elect to fly to these airports will not be able to get such favourable terms.

According to a study undertaken by the University of Westminster's Transport Study Group,[4] airport charges per passenger were around £10 less for a low-cost carrier than for a full service carrier (British Midland Airways) serving European routes based at Heathrow.

Dublin Airport

Aer Rianta, an Irish parastatal organisation, owns and manages Dublin, Shannon and Cork airports, the three largest in Ireland.

Dublin airport in particular mirrors the strong growth in the Irish economy. Between 1979 and 1986, total passenger numbers at Dublin declined from 2.8 million and then increased to around 2.9 million by 1986. Following liberalisation of the UK–Ireland market at this time, Dublin's passenger numbers increased to 5.1 million by 1989.

By 1997, the airport was handling in excess of 10 million passengers. This increased in 1998 to 11.6 million and the projection for 1999 is 12.4 million. For the last five years, Dublin has been the tenth fastest growing airport in the world, averaging 8.6% growth per annum.

The importance of the UK market to Dublin airport is shown in Exhibit 4.8. Although a similar breakdown is not available for other Irish airports, the volume of transit and transatlantic traffic is smaller at Shannon and non-existent at Cork, and therefore the proportion of traffic from these other airports to and from the UK will be even higher than at Dublin.

As an Irish airline, it is notable that most of its European network is based in the UK and not in Ireland (details of Ryanair's network are given below). One of the major sources of contention between Aer Rianta and Ryanair has been the former's intention to raise passenger charges as a result of the loss of duty free sales for passengers flying within Europe. Consequently, Ryanair has not expanded its Dublin

Exhibit 4.8 Analysis of passenger volumes at Dublin airport 1997–98 ('000s)

	1998	*1997*
UK	6,919	6,361
Mainland Europe	3,385	2,850
Transatlantic	674	535
Other (domestic and transit)	663	587
Total	11,641	10,333

Source: http://www.aer-rianta.ie/htmlonly/dublin/htm/index/data/con048.htm

network while the airport charges incurred by Ryanair are deemed to be too high: Ryanair was set to inaugurate five routes from Dublin to continental Europe in summer 1999, but withdrew the plans when the airport authorities would not commit themselves to lowering its charges.

Stansted airport

History and growth rates

Stansted airport, situated some 50 km to the north-east of London, is a legacy of the Second World War. It was built as an American military airfield in 1944 and, because of the requirement for heavy payloads, was built with a runway of sufficient length for all modern-day jet aircraft.

Stansted had traditionally been cast in the role of 'poor relation' to the other BAA airports in the south-east, Heathrow and Gatwick. In 1991, when its new terminal opened at a cost of £400 million, Stansted's passenger throughput was only 1 million. The capacity of the terminal was 8 million, however. In effect, Stansted was 'a regional airport serving the local community in terms of services ... provided but international in terms of infrastructure', according to Stansted's managing director, John Stent.

Two airlines have been responsible for growth at Stansted. In early 1990s, Air UK (now KLM uk) developed a network there (see the section on 'Buzz' (p. 760) for more details). However, since 1995, Ryanair has been the lead airline at Stansted with its Irish and European routes based there.

Within the space of 14 months, Stansted increased its 30 scheduled routes in May 1998, to 62 routes by June 1999, thanks to a large extent to Ryanair's expansion of its continental network and the introduction of Go, BA's low-cost subsidiary in May 1998. The arrival of Buzz increased the number of routes further, with the introduction of five new destinations between January and March 2000 alone.

For the year ending March 1999, Stansted processed 7.3 million passengers, up from only 3.3 million in 1995. The breakdown of passenger numbers at Stansted for this year was:

Ryanair	2.3 million
KLM uk	1.6 million
Go	0.6 million
others	2.8 million

(*Note*: Go only started operations in May 1998).

These figures demonstrate that growth at Stansted has been driven principally by the low-cost carriers (the growth of Luton, a smaller airport the same distance from London as Stansted, is similarly attributable to the development of easyJet and Debonair). For the period January to December 1999, Stansted processed 9.4 million passengers, a 38% increase on the previous year, with traffic on scheduled flights to Europe doubling from 2.4 million in 1998 to 4.8 million. In September 1999, Ryanair operated 49 daily flights on average (12 of which were to Dublin), Go 33 and KLM uk 40 (of which 17 were on 'Buzz' routes). Total daily flights from Stansted during this month were 193, of which 176 were on scheduled services.

Stansted has grown for negative as well as positive reasons. It is extremely difficult for airlines to acquire new slots at Heathrow and Gatwick, due to congestion. Gatwick, for example, processed 29 million passengers during 1998, but with the same runway capacity as Stansted. Some airlines have therefore moved part of their operations to Stansted as no alternative was available (El Al Israel Airlines, for instance) while SAS and Alitalia at least have the consolation of being able to compete directly with Ryanair and other low-cost carriers by setting up Stansted routes.

Passenger numbers through Stansted by early 2000 were such that the terminal was having capacity problems. £200 million is being spent on its expansion, however, with a view to doubling capacity by 2006. In the short term, however, another year of high growth in 2001, as in the previous three years, could cause capacity problems. The problem with growth at airports is that, once the passenger volumes reach a particular level, the airport becomes more attractive to airlines and so demand for slots increases.

Surface access

As well as being given a new terminal building, Stansted also was added to the railway network by building spurs to both the north and south from the London Liverpool Street–Cambridge line. Until Spring 1999, the service comprised two trains per hour from London, taking 41 minutes. As the airport has grown, services have been added from Cambridge and the London service has four trains per hour for much of the day. Further railway infrastructure work is required to increase these frequencies, as the spur lines and platforms at Stansted are approaching capacity.

Stansted is further from central London than either Heathrow or Gatwick and therefore is more expensive to reach by rail. However, both Ryanair and Go offer special deals so that passengers can obtain discounts on rail fares at railway stations on production of evidence that the traveller will be flying or has flown with the airlines. Ryanair sells these 'special offer' tickets on board its aircraft as a means of alleviating the loss of income from in-flight duty free sales.

Stansted is located close to the M11 motorway. As a result of a new dual carriageway road from London to Redbridge, in north-east London, the attractiveness of Stansted to passengers arriving by car has also increased.

Ryanair's marketing strategy

Markets

Traditionally, airlines have segmented passengers into two broad categories, business and leisure.

- **Leisure.** This segment is highly price sensitive, with frequency of flights and their timings of little importance. Customers in this segment have traditionally been willing to book in advance to procure a cheap fare.
- **Business.** The principal requirements for the business segment have been the ability to book late and to have a choice of frequencies at convenient departure times.

This segmentation is now seen as too crude, however; one of the unexpected outcomes of the introduction of low-cost flights has been the high proportion (between one-third and a half) of budget airline passengers travelling on business. These passengers are either chief executives of small businesses or self-employed; in other words, the fare is being paid out of the passenger's own pocket rather than a corporate travel budget.

Leisure passengers have also been segmented further to the advantage of low-cost carriers. While most leisure traffic uses inclusive tour holidays (and therefore are not a target for Ryanair, easyJet and Go), there is a growing segment of independent holiday travellers who prefer to make their own plans and therefore book flights independently of hotels and car hire.

A leisure category of particular importance to Ryanair is the 'visiting friends and relatives' (VFR) market, which forms a significant proportion of traffic between the UK and Ireland.

The 'Product'

Ryanair is quite explicit in its advertising that passengers will receive a no-frills service on board its flights: no food, no pre-assigned seats, and so on. Ryanair has been criticised, however, for being less than forthcoming about the airports that it serves in continental Europe. Exhibit 4.9 summarises an investigation by Watchdog, a popular English TV programme specialising in consumer affairs, following complaints sent in by viewers about these airports.

With the exception of Dublin airport, Ryanair uses no primary airports; invariably, the airfields into which Ryanair flies are further from the town which they serve than primary airports. In the case of Frankfurt-Hahn, the airport is more than 100 km from the city centre, as are Torp (Oslo) and Skavsta (Stockholm). A consequence of using these secondary fields is that, to compensate for lack of access to a high-speed rail link into the centre of a city, Ryanair lays on buses for its passengers.

From Ryanair's point of view, these airports are undoubtedly preferable; their lack of congestion, both on approach and on the ground, enables a 20-minute turnaround (Ryanair ceased taking cargo in 1997 to improve the turnaround time on the ground from 30 minutes). Although passengers have a longer trip to and from their destination, the lower fares paid by Ryanair's passengers compensate for the extra journey time.

Frequencies

The only high-frequency international route operated by Ryanair is between Dublin and London, with over 20 flights per day each way. Otherwise, each route is operated with between one and four daily flights during the week. For example, during winter 1999/2000, Lufthansa operated 14 daily flights and BA 8 flights between London's airports and Frankfurt, compared to Ryanair's three flights to Hahn.

Southwest Airlines considers three flights a day to be the minimum requirement, particularly for business travellers, as these customers need to change flights if meetings overrun or are cancelled.

Exhibit 4.9   Ryanair under scrutiny

Ryanair is a budget airline who advertise flights to Oslo. The prices are considerably lower than other airlines at around £80 but Ryanair don't always tell you that its flights don't actually go to Oslo. They go to a tiny place called Torp which is 110 kilometres away from the Norwegian capital, the equivalent of flying to Oxford for London. There is a 55 miles per hour speed limit in Norway and a bus or car journey along the country roads takes an average of 90 minutes. The return bus trip costs around £12 and a taxi £120.

Oslo's main city airport is Fornebu, a ten minute car ride from the centre. British Midland, SAS and Braathans, the Norwegian airline, all fly to Fornebu. They and all other international flights will be transferring to the new Oslo airport, Gardemoen, when it opens in October. Gardemoen is 47 kilometres from Oslo and there will be a high-speed train link to the city centre taking 33 minutes. Ryanair however will continue to fly to Torp.

Eight out of ten Ryanair operators did not tell Watchdog researchers that Torp is a 90-minute journey from Oslo and two didn't even mention the name Torp at all.

Tim Jeans, director of sales and marketing at Ryanair, told Watchdog: 'Torp is designated as an Oslo airport by the International Air Transport Association. Ryanair do, he says, tell passengers at the point of booking that the flights go to Torp and would always volunteer the information as to the airport's location when asked by a passenger.'

Source: Watchdog, BBC1, 24 September 1998.

Reliability

One of the key indicators of performance for an airline is reliability. This indicator can be manipulated, but at a price: an airline's performance in this area can be improved if more time is scheduled at airports for turning aircraft around. Longer turnaround times, however, have a negative impact on the utilisation of the aircraft fleet. Exhibit 4.10 shows punctuality data for Ryanair and its competitors on the routes shown. Where available, punctuality information for 1997 is also given.

As Europe's airways get increasingly crowded, delays to all destinations have increased, and future figures are expected to be worse. However, Ryanair's average delays exceeded those of its competitors both in 1997 and 1998.

Price

The characteristics of airline pricing are similar to those of many services: most of the costs are fixed and the marginal cost of servicing a customer is very small. In order to extract as much consumer surplus as possible, airlines have traditionally had a fare without restrictions, which is very high, and have then sold off other seats cheaply but subject to restrictions. For example, one means commonly used to prevent business passengers travelling at a cheap fare is to insist that the passenger must incur a Saturday night away. While this is not a problem for leisure passengers, this restriction has generally meant that business travellers pay a significantly higher price than leisure traffic.

To give an indication of price differentials between Ryanair and full service airlines, two Ryanair routes were examined. In each case, the fare quotation was requested for 11 days in advance with a midweek departure and a return flight one day later. The results of the queries are shown in Exhibit 4.11.

The average fare paid per passenger between April 1998 and March 1999 was IR£42, or just over £36, excluding tax.

Exhibit 4.10 Average delays from Stansted for Ryanair and its competitors, 1997 and 1998

		Number of flights 1998	Average delay (mins)	
			1998	1997
Between Stansted and	Airline			
Carcassonne	Ryanair	417	19	
St Etienne	Ryanair	631	13	
Knock	Ryanair	1,423	25	14
Cork	Ryanair	2,577	23	16
Dublin	Aer Lingus	3,927	7	6
Dublin	Ryanair	7,774	16	14
Kerry	Ryanair	855	26	14
Pisa	Alitalia	111	38	
Pisa	Ryanair	826	25	
Rimini	Ryanair	416	33	
Rome (Ciampino)	Go	1,003	10	
Rome (Fiumicino)	KLM uk	119	31	
Venice (Treviso)	Ryanair	896	29	
Venice	Go	46	9	
Kristianstad	Ryanair	692	26	
Stockholm (Arlanda)	SAS	1,010	14	
Stockholm (Skavsta)	Ryanair	2,023	22	17

Source: CAA (UK) Punctuality Statistics.

Exhibit 4.11   Fares comparison on two Ryanair routes

In £, excluding taxes	Ryanair	Full service airlines
London–Dublin	125–196	218–291
Dublin–Paris/Beauvais	154–233	399–477

Source: Ryanair online booking, MSN Expedia £1 = IR£1.2646 (2/1/2000).

Distribution

As late as 1997, some 75% of all Ryanair's tickets were sold through travel agents. Also at the time, Ryanair's flights appeared on two major computer reservations systems. By contrast, when easyJet started operations in 1995, no intermediaries were used; the only means of purchasing a ticket was directly from easyJet.

In 1997, Ryanair unilaterally reduced the commission paid to travel agents from 9% to 7.5% of the ticket's value. In spite of a threatened boycott by some Irish travel agents, the reduction was pushed through. Since this time, Ryanair's proportion of direct sales has increased to around 40%.

The company remains committed to the use of intermediaries; however, it believes that, when expanding into Europe, a small-scale, low-cost airline without offices in the cities it serves has inadequate resources to market all its tickets directly and so expects to continue using travel agents for the foreseeable future. By contrast, easyJet has no intention of using travel agents in any city that it serves.

Customers' opinions of Ryanair

Exhibit 4.12 summarises customers' views on Ryanair, while Exhibit 4.13 gives a selection of more detailed comments on Ryanair's services, all posted between January 1999 and January 2000. It should be noted that these comments were not part of an organised survey; rather, the information was posted onto the Internet by individuals.

Exhibit 4.12   Customers' opinions on Ryanair flights

Flight	1	2	3	4	5	6	7	8
Route	SOT–DUB	STN–KRI	STN–SKA	BHX–DUB	LTN–DUB	STN–DUB	DUB–STN	STN–DUB
Frequent flyer?	Yes	No	Yes	Yes	Yes	Yes	–	–
Would you fly Ryanair again?	Yes	Don't know	Yes	Yes	Yes	Yes	Yes	No
Service (/10)	7	–	5	9	9	6	10	1
Delay (/10)	7	–	5	9	9	6	10	1
Comfort (/10)	5	–	5	6	6	9	9	0
Value (/10)	10	–	9	10	10	10	10	0

Notes: SOT – Southampton, DUB – Dublin, STN – Stansted, KRI – Kristianstad, BHX – Birmingham, LTN – Luton, SKA – Skavsta

Exhibit 4.13   Comments on passengers' experience in flying Ryanair

Flight 1: Very hard to find out how to book with Ryanair and the phone number is constantly busy on account of frequent deals offered in UK's tabloids. However rates are low and flights frequent enough to allow last minute booking options. Love their adverts which quote the price to a destination and then 'including stupid government tax of 30 pounds' . . .!

Flight 2: It is stupid wearing high-heeled shoes when working as an airhostess. Lightweight women in such shoes bounce the weak floor in an airplane harder than a male airhost, you will notice this when you are awakened in your sleep as they run through the cabin. Furthermore, high-heeled shoes are considered not convenient in emergency situations.

Flight 3: Cheap and relatively cheerful service. Have to pay for all drinks except water but the fares can be quite low, on this occasion less than half the cost of SAS, so who cares about being charged for a Coke? Return flight left about 15 minutes late but made up time en-route. Skavsta is an 80-minute bus ride from central Stockholm; a bus meets all flights and costs SwKr120 return.

Flight 4: Bargain basement price makes Ryanair very attractive. Return flight delayed due to shortage of co-pilot. Captain kept the passengers amused with a witty commentary as to the whereabouts of the missing pilot. Cabin crew were very friendly (and pretty too!). Seats are a little on the cramped side but as it's such a short flight it's not difficult to live with. Have to pay for your own drinks, but who cares!

Flight 5: Flight delayed both ways due to dense fog at Luton. Delays were in the order of 30 minutes outbound, 1 hour inbound. Usual friendly crew, with particularly amusing comments from the flight deck.

Flight 6: A great airline. Best way to book is over the net. Fares are unbelievably low – US$10 from Dublin to Paris exclusive of taxes at certain times. You get what you pay for – just the seat – everything else is charged for but most flights are less than 45 minutes so what exactly do you need? Not great for families and hence few/no crying children on board. No pre-allocation of seats so everyone turns up early and flights leave and arrive on time.

Flight 7: We left Dublin 10 minutes early, and flying the brand new Boeing 737–800 it was like a dream. The seats were very comfy and a bit of leg room. Cabin crew were very nice and great crack, I would fly them any day. And their fares are rock bottom, with as little as £6 one way they beat Aer Lingus anyday!

Flight 8: While all the airlines suffered problems due to the Stansted air crash just before Christmas, Ryanair's lack of staff and any semblance of organisation made the whole experience much worse for Ryanair's passengers. The other airlines had cleared their backlog by mid-afternoon on 23 December. I finally arrived in Dublin on the 23rd at 10.00 pm (arrived Stansted 10 am that morning). By the way, Ryanair also lost my luggage.

Source: http://www.carsurvey.org/air/

Competitive analysis

Who are Ryanair's competitors?

By 2000, Ryanair could be said to be facing competition on three fronts: from other low-cost operators, low-cost divisions of large international airlines and surface transport. There is evidence, however, that when a low-cost carrier enters a new market, it generates new passenger volumes rather than just taking market share from incumbents.

Competition from other airlines

As 2000 commenced, Ryanair faced competition on several fronts from flag carriers, low-cost subsidiaries of large European airlines and other no-frills carriers. Just four years earlier, Ryanair's only major competition had been with Aer Lingus out of Ireland and with British Midland on the London–Dublin route; now, there were three new competitors, two owned by much larger airlines with access to far higher levels of funds than Ryanair. Furthermore, ferry companies had acquired high-speed vessels which cut some 2 hours off the sailing time between the UK and Ireland.

Aer Lingus

Aer Lingus's history is that of a classic flag-carrying airline: owned by the public sector, short on capital and having interests outside of aviation (Aer Lingus until recently owned the Copthorne Hotel chain). It has been heavily restructured and received state aid from the Irish government.

Aer Lingus is a full service airline which, apart from four gateways in the USA, is focused on Europe. During the winter 1999/2000 timetable, it operated an average of 64 daily flights between Ireland and Europe, including the UK. During 1998, the latest year for which figures were available, it flew 5 million passengers on its European network, 2 million of whom were carried between Ireland and London. Thus, Ryanair and Aer Lingus (excluding its American network) were equal in size in terms of passengers carried.

Aer Lingus had some 5,000 employees compared to Ryanair's 1,200. It was, however, cutting down on staff numbers; in December 1999, aircraft maintenance was contracted out to a subsidiary of Lufthansa, Germany's national airline.

In spite of the improved profitability (Exhibit 4.14), Aer Lingus remained under-capitalised; for the years ending 1998, it had negative working capital of IR£70 million, up from IR£50 million in 1997. Funding requirements, estimated by Salomon Smith Barney, an American investment bank, are at least IR£150 million. These funds are required to fund the growth opportunities afforded by an alliance (see below), strengthen its overall capital base and cushion against any potential industry downturn. The company has also stated its intention to own at least half its fleet. Currently, more than half is leased, whereas Ryanair owns all the aircraft it operates.

By November 1999, Aer Lingus was the only 'flag carrier' in the EU, with the exception of Greece's Olympic Airways, which was not part of one of the major airline groups or alliances. However, Aer Lingus signed agreements to join the oneworld alliance (comprising British Airways, American Airlines, LAN Chile, Iberia and Cathay Pacific) and will be participating fully in 2001. Joining such an alliance was considered the only viable option by Aer Lingus and their advisers.[5]

By far the most important arena of competition between Aer Lingus and Ryanair is on the Dublin route.

Exhibit 4.14   Aer Lingus financial summary, 1996–98 (IR£ million)

Year	Turnover	Profit before exceptional items	Capital employed
1996	766	36	190
1997	802	41	153
1998	901	52	209

Source: http://www.aerlingus.ie/company/accounts/gfhilite.html

Exhibit 4.15   Passenger volumes between London and selected destinations 1997–98

	1998	1997
Dublin	4,078,489	3,717,134
Paris	2,838,253	2,819,847
Frankfurt	1,905,526	1,772,531
New York	3,885,582	3,515,956

Source: CAA statistics.

Exhibit 4.16   Flights between Dublin and London (all airports)

Year	Aer Lingus	Ryanair	British Midland	CityJet	BA
1985	11	0	0	0	6
1989	23	6	6	0	6
1993	12	10	8	0	0
1997	18	21	8	7	4*
1999 (Sept.)	19	21	8	4	7*

* Operated by CityFlyer Express
Source: Nigel Dennis, 'Low cost carriers and scheduled airline operations', CAA Statistics.

Dublin–London

Dublin–London is now Europe's busiest air route; prior to 1997, Paris–London was busier. Exhibit 4.15 shows total passenger numbers travelling between selected destinations and the five London airports (Heathrow, Luton, Gatwick, City and Stansted). Exhibit 4.16 shows that, in 1997, Ryanair was the largest carrier on the Dublin–London route, accounting for 37% of passengers. However, in the first half of 1999, Aer Lingus had captured 37% of this market – a 16% increase in passenger numbers – while Ryanair's passenger volume had declined by 1%, giving it a 32% share.[6]

Of the 5 million passengers carried in 1998 by Ryanair, some 25% used the London–Dublin route (in 1986, Ryanair carried just 50,000 passengers between Dublin and London; by 1990, 290,000 were carried, and by 1994 this figure had risen to 820,000). The resources devoted to this route by Ryanair clearly exceed all others: in January 2000, 17 out of 89 of Ryanair's average weekday flights were on this route. Given the historical and commercial ties between the UK and Ireland as well as the proximity of the two markets, it is not surprising that Aer Lingus also devotes a large element of its resources to the route (in January 2000, 22 out of 71 European flights, excluding Irish domestic services).

Before Ryanair started on the route in 1985, there were just under 1 million passengers; by 1988, traffic had doubled to 1.97 million and, by 1996, the volume recorded was 3.34 million. Competition on the route became so intense that British Airways withdrew in 1991; at present, the only BA presence on the London–Dublin route is via one of its franchise operators (CityFlyer Express).

Other routes

Exhibit 4.17 gives an indication of the load factors on routes where Ryanair faces direct competition from Aer Lingus. While Aer Lingus overall has higher load factors, it should be remembered that it needs a higher load factor than Ryanair to break even, due to its higher cost base.

Exhibit 4.17   Load factors on routes from Dublin where Ryanair and Aer Lingus compete (%)

	Ryanair	Ryanair	Aer Lingus	Aer Lingus
	1999 (January–May or June)	1998	1999 (January–May or June)	1998
Birmingham	Low 60s	Low 60s	Low 70s	High 60s
Glasgow/Prestwick	77	61	79	68
Manchester	Low 70s	High 60s	Low 70s	Low 80s
Paris/Beauvais	Low 70s	67	Low 70s	76
Brussels/Charleroi	Low 60s	61	68	High 60s

Source: http://www.sbpost.ie/archives/01–08–99/biz-finance/personal-f/high.html.

easyJet

easyJet is a privately run airline which started operations in November 1995. Its main base is at London Luton airport, with smaller hubs at Liverpool and Geneva. Its full network from Luton is:

UK:	Edinburgh, *Glasgow*, Inverness, Aberdeen, Belfast and Liverpool
Spain:	Madrid, Barcelona, Malaga, Palma
Other:	Nice, Zurich, Geneva, Amsterdam, Athens

(*Italicised* destinations are in competition with Ryanair)

There are similarities between Ryanair and easyJet: use of secondary home airports, exclusivity of Boeing 737s, no seat allocation and no in-flight catering (although easyJet offers snacks for sale on board). There are, however, two key differences between the two carriers:

- easyJet has never used travel agents as a distribution channel. The two methods of purchasing an easyJet 'ticket' (as with Ryanair, no paper tickets are issued) are by telephone or on the Internet. The telephone access numbers have been publicised from the beginning, as each aircraft carries the number in large characters on the side of the aircraft. On average, over 50% of easyJet's purchases were being made on-line.

- easyJet uses primary airports at its destinations. For example, easyJet flies to Barcelona airport and not Girona, which is 100 km by motorway from Barcelona, less intensively used and presumably cheaper.

Since its inauguration, easyJet and its chairman, Stelios Haji-Ioannou, have developed a public relations image similar to that of Richard Branson: taking on the 'Big Guys', bringing cheap air fares to the people, and so on. Publicity has been generated for easyJet by its legal actions against the start-up of British Airways' Go subsidiary and by the 'Airline' series shown on ITV during 1999.

In 1998, a national opinion poll indicated a 72% brand recognition for easyJet in the UK.[7] Thanks to the diversifications discussed below, this figure has probably increased.

easyJet has become a member of the easy Group. The easy brand, with its distinctive orange colouring and logo, has been developed across other businesses. In 1998, a set of Internet cafés was established, initially in London, Edinburgh and Amsterdam. These cafés are typically much larger than previously established Internet cafés (the one at London Victoria, for example, has 400 machines, compared to a typical 10 to 20 for most cafés) and offer access at around £2 per hour, half the rate found elsewhere. There are posters around the cafés inviting customers to book easyJet flights on-line. The cafés are aimed more at people who have experience in using PCs and the Internet, as the availability of assistance is small compared to traditional Internet cafés.

In January 2000, the easy group launched easyRentacar, with daily hire rates starting at £10. Again, this is less than half the rate of established car rental companies. The ability to charge lower prices is due to each vehicle being a mobile advertisement for the group, being painted in the easy orange and having the easyJet name and contact details painted on each car. Initial locations are likely to be at Luton, easyJet's home base, and in Scotland, which forms a large part of easyJet's current network.

easy group's latest venture is to set up easyBank, an Internet only bank, established in June 2000. At the time of writing, no further details were available.

Irish Sea Ferry Operators

In 1984, 70% of Great Britain–Ireland passengers travelled by sea; by 1990, the airlines' share had increased to 53% of the total, and, by 1998, air travel accounted for 56% of the volume of traffic between the UK and Ireland. Exhibit 4.18 illustrates air transport's share of the market for the selected European states.

While the airlines actually caused a reduction in sea crossings prior to 1990, the introduction of high-speed ferries between Holyhead/Liverpool and Dun Laoghaire/Dublin has enabled the ferry operators to grow at a similar pace to their airline rivals. In 1993, weekly capacity during peak period was for around 27,700 cars, while the equivalent figure for 1998 was 68,500.[8]

In 1993, some 640,000 cars were carried on ferries between the UK and Ireland, but this had risen to 915,000 by 1999. The growth in the number of passengers without cars was somewhat slower however, averaging 4% annual growth over this period. Figures for the first nine months of 1999[9] suggest that growth has ceased.

Exhibit 4.18   Summary of model split between UK and NW European states

Country	Year	Air	Total	% air
Belgium	1996	647	2,975	22
	1997	716	2,764	26
	1998	691	2,882	24
France	1996	2,557	13,524	19
	1997	2,642	14,735	18
	1998	2,753	14,792	19
Germany	1996	2,798	4,861	58
	1997	2,919	4,934	59
	1998	2,884	4,892	59
Ireland	1996	2,858	5,247	54
	1997	3,261	5,845	56
	1998	3,503	6,247	56
Netherlands	1996	1,618	3,070	53
	1997	1,872	3,409	55
	1998	1,958	3,670	53

Source: Overseas Travel and Tourism (series MQ6), Office of National Statistics.

Reaction from the major carriers

Go

Go is a subsidiary of British Airways operating from Stansted. The airline was launched in March 1998, flying initially to just three destinations: Rome (Ciampino, its secondary airport), Milan and Copenhagen. By December 1999, however, Go was flying to 17 destinations, with an 18th (Glasgow) due to start in March 2000. The full list of destinations is:

UK: Edinburgh, *Glasgow* (from March 2000)
Portugal: Lisbon, Faro

Spain: Malaga, Alicante, Madrid, Bilbao, Barcelona
Italy: Milan, *Venice*, Bologna, Rome
Other Europe: *Lyon*, Zurich, Prague, Munich, Copenhagen
(*Note: Italicised* destinations are in competition with Ryanair.)

Although direct competition with Ryanair is limited, Go flies to the primary airports of the city it serves (except Rome): Ryanair flies to St Etienne and Treviso rather than Lyon and Venice airports. Go will also be flying to Glasgow airport, which is closer to the town centre rather than Prestwick, which is where Ryanair flies.

In the first 18 months of operation, Go posted losses of some £21 million on a turnover of £33 million. Clearly, much of the losses were due to start-up costs and, thanks to the resources of its parent, British Airways, these losses have not been an obstacle to further expansion. For example, the leases on Go's aircraft are guaranteed by British Airways.

Buzz

Unlike Go, which was created from scratch, Buzz was created out of an existing airline, namely KLM uk, a 100% owned subsidiary of KLM, the Dutch airline.

Unlike other low-cost carriers, however, Buzz did not have to acquire new aircraft; rather, a proportion of KLM uk's fleet has been rebranded and dedicated to the Buzz operation. KLM therefore has two distinct brands operating from Stansted.

Buzz started operations in the first week of January 2000, flying between Stansted and Berlin, Dusseldorf, Frankfurt, Lyon, Milan, Paris and Vienna. Most of these routes were previously flown by KLM uk.

KLM uk's previous strategy was twofold: it flew routes from over 20 UK airports into Amsterdam to link into the parent's network and it also had a set of routes from, principally, Stansted to a number of destinations in both the UK and mainland Europe. During September 1999, KLM uk operated some 35 daily flights from the UK to Amsterdam, 20 domestic flights and 20 flights from Stansted to international destinations other than Amsterdam.

For its expansion to Hamburg, Helsinki, Bordeaux and Marseilles in March 2000, Buzz acquired 737s and thus became the only low-cost carrier still in business to have more than one aircraft type in its fleet.

While the seat pitch of 32 inches, unchanged from when the aircraft were operated by KLM uk, is generous by budget airline standards, there is no free food on offer. Meals are available either in advance or on the aircraft at £5.50 for breakfast or £7.00 for lunch or dinner. Like Go and easyJet, Buzz is a ticketless airline.

To what extent do new entrants on to a route grow the market?

One of the key arguments which have been put forward by low-cost operators to expand service in the face of reluctant airport authorities and governments is that when low-cost operators enter a route, they expand traffic rather than take share from existing operators.

Exhibit 4.19 shows two routes, London to Frankfurt and to Stockholm, which Ryanair entered in September 1998 and April 1999 respectively. In the case of

Exhibit 4.19   The impact of new, lost-cost entrants on routes

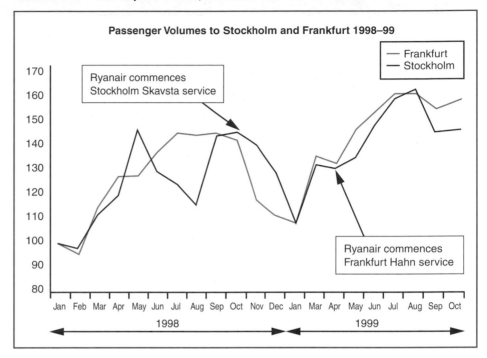

London–Frankfurt, Ryanair has been competing directly with KLM uk (now Buzz) on this route from Stansted. Since Ryanair's entry, there has been no evidence of decline in KLM uk's market share, around 9.5% of the total.

The exhibit also includes the average growth exhibited by members of the Association of European Airlines, whose members generally include the national flag carriers. Between January 1998 and October 1999, growth was around 13.6%.[10]

Further evidence of market growth comes from an examination of the London–Nice market (see Exhibit 4.20). Although the British airlines serving the route have gained passengers, albeit with a loss of market share after easyJet's entry, the increased competition caused Air France to withdraw from the route.

Exhibit 4.20   Passenger volumes on London–Nice, 1996–99

	1996	1997	1998	1999
Total	606,249	661,182	866,842	983,492
BA	56%	55%	52%	51%
British Midland	18%	18%	13%	12%
easyJet	9%	25%	28%	31%
Other	18%	1%	7%	6%

Source: http://www.easyJet.com/uk/news/2000120_01.html.

Competitors in mainland Europe

At present, there are no serious low-cost competitors in mainland Europe. Reasons given for this lack of competition include:

- airport authorities unwilling to reduce charges for new entrants;
- more rigorous labour laws, making personnel costs expensive (this is the principal reason for Virgin Express having a subsidiary registered in Ireland);
- high-speed railway services; and
- greater competition from cars, as journeys within mainland Europe do not need to use the channel tunnel or ferry services – for example, a trip by car from Paris to Brussels will be significantly cheaper per kilometre than to London.

This is not to say, however, that there are no airlines with the potential to enter the market. In Italy, for example, Air One competes with Alitalia, but exclusively on domestic routes. In the winter 1999–2000 timetable, Air One operated 68 weekday flights, principally between Rome, Milan, Naples and Turin, using an all economy layout. Previously, Air One had operated between Stansted and Milan using a two-class configuration, but this service was not operating in early 2000. Another potential entrant into European-wide no-frills service is Spain's Air Europa which has 46 Boeing aircraft and operates principally within Spain. In December 1999, it was reported however, that the carrier was in talks to join the KLM–Northwest–Alitalia alliance. Iberia, the principal Spanish airline, is a member of oneworld.

Low-cost airlines: the early casualties

In the USA, very few of the new airlines which set up in business following deregulation of the airline industry in 1978 are still operating. Although the process of liberalisation in Europe is much more recent, there have already been two UK-based airlines which have gone bankrupt, both in the latter half of 1999.

Debonair

Debonair commenced operations in June 1996, some seven months after easyJet, with three routes from Luton: to Barcelona, Munich and Münchengladbach (near Dusseldorf). While both airlines were headquartered at Luton, Debonair differed from easyJet in several ways:

- Debonair established hubs at Munich and Barcelona, in addition to Luton.
- A breakeven load factor of 57%, compared to a little over 50% for easyJet. The higher load factor was due to a higher seat pitch of 33 inches.
- A more explicit focus on business travel (a budget airline with frills and a less 'populist' promotional campaign).

By the end of 1998, Debonair had eight BAe 146 jet aircraft and one turboprop flying on nine routes. In a move to increase its share of business travel, Debonair started paying travel agents 20% commission which, at the time, was more than double the industry average of 9%.

In 1999, Debonair acted as a franchisee for Air France, Swissair and Lufthansa, operating routes on behalf of these airlines from Paris, Zurich and Munich respectively.

At the beginning of October 1999, Debonair ceased trading and its aircraft were grounded. The Debonair collapse prompted a war of words between some rivals. easyJet said on its web site that neither Debonair nor AB Airlines (see below) was able to compete with British Airways' attempt to eliminate competition. It said Go, BA's low-cost subsidiary, 'pays no attention to whether it makes a profit or a loss, but has the sole intention of reinstating a BA monopoly and then raising fares'.

Debonair's average utilisation for its fleet in July 1999 was 7.2 hours; by contrast, easyJet's 737s average 10.4 hours. Furthermore, during 1998, Debonair's average load factor was 58.3%; by comparison, easyJet's and Ryanair's were 70% or higher.

AB airlines

AB airlines started out in 1993 as Air Bristol – a carrier established specifically to fly between Bristol and Toulouse, the sites of two Airbus manufacturing plants.

At the end of 1995, AB started operations between London Gatwick and Shannon and added in 1997 Lisbon (May) and Berlin (December). In July 1998, AB expanded operations further by codesharing[11] with Debonair (see above) on a route between Gatwick and Nice and also commenced services to Barcelona.

Whether AB airlines could be regarded as a 'low-cost' airline in the Southwest, easyJet or Ryanair mould is debatable: during 1997, its average load factor was 57% and its three aircraft (two different types) were being utilised on average for 5.5 hours per day.

In August 1999, AB airlines went bankrupt and, as no buyers were found, ceased trading. In its last year of reporting (year ending November 1998), AB reported pre-tax losses of £10.6 million on revenues of £17.2 million and indeed had shown no pre-tax profits whatsoever since 1995.

The future

As more of the major carriers developed their own low-cost operations, with access to their parents' funds and resources such as primary airports and greater purchasing power, Michael Leary needed to consider Ryanair's future expansion strategy: to what extent could Ryanair continue to follow its unique strategy in Europe and resist the lure of primary airports?

Early in 2000, both Air France and Lufthansa were considering whether to set up low cost subsidiaries alongside KLM and British Airways. Furthermore, within a few years, high-speed rail travel would be available between London and Marseille, Nice, Bordeaux, Toulouse, Amsterdam and major cities in Western Germany as well as Brussels and Paris. Indeed, the infrastructure is already in place to serve many of these city pairs: all that is missing are the services!

Ryanair has ordered 25 new Boeing 737–800s, each seating 189 passengers, at a reported total cost of $1.2 billion, with five aircraft being delivered annually, the first in March 1999. Unlike other no-frills carriers, Ryanair will own all these aircraft. Would Ryanair find the passengers to fill this increase in capacity?

NOTES

1. The load factor is the proportion of the seats available on a particular flight that have been sold.
2. The seat pitch is the distance from the front of one row to the front of another. A lower seat pitch gives a passenger less space than a higher one.
3. AVMARK *Aviation Economist*, August 1989.
4. 'Low cost carriers and scheduled airline operations' (Nigel Dennis, 1999).
5. 'Advice and assistance in relation to a strategic alliance for Aer Lingus' (Salomon Smith Barney, July 1999).
6. *Sunday Business Post*, Ireland (1 August 1999).
7. easyJet Annual Report, 1997/98.
8. *Ireland Outbound, Travel and Tourism Intelligence* (No. 1, 1999).
9. Stena Group, Third Quarter Report, 1999.
10. *Airline Business*, various issues.
11. Codesharing occurs when one airline flies a route on behalf of two or more. Revenues and costs are usually split equally between the partners.

Has Siemens lost its way?

Introduction

Siemens AG is today a giant in the electronics industry and one of Germany's leading concerns. It is a company with a long family tradition and has left its imprint upon many of the most important events of the nineteenth and twentieth centuries. Siemens has, however, recently faced less successful times. This case study sets out to explore the issue as to whether or not the company, which was 150 years old in 1997, has lost its way in the modern economic world.

The early period: 1847–1914

The beginning of what was to become Siemens AG can be traced back to the establishment of 'Telegraphenbauanstalt Siemens und Halske' in 1847. Werner Siemens was the driving force behind the company and remained so for the rest of his life.[1] Within twelve years of its foundation the company had subsidiaries in Russia (1853) and Britain (1857). By 1865 the company's English operations had become substantial and the English subsidiary changed its name to Siemens Brothers. Major company projects during 1848–72 are set out in Exhibit 5.1.[2]

By 1892, the company's products were at the forefront of technological progress in the fields of communication and energy production and it was already a respected competitor in world markets. In the same year, the company built a power station at Erding in Bavaria and opened a subsidiary in the United States (this subsequently closed in 1904). Siemens and Halske obtained the first patent for an X-ray tube in 1897, just two years after Roentgen's invention of the process.

Continued prosperity led in 1890 to the company becoming a limited partnership, and in order to cope with even further expansion the decision was taken in 1897 for the company to go public. Since the family could not provide all of the capital, the Deutsche Bank acquired an important shareholding.

This case was written by Tony Fowler of Sheffield Hallam University to facilitate classroom discussion. It is not intended to illustrate good or poor handling of an administrative situation. (© Tony Fowler, 1997.)

Exhibit 5.1   Major Siemens' projects during 1848–1872

Year	Project
1848	A telegraph link between Berlin and Frankfurt
1853	An extensive telegraph system in Russia
1867	An extensive telegraph system in Russia
1871	The London–Tehran telegraph link
1872	The Ireland–United States cable link

A second new company named Siemens–Schuckert GmbH (which was to become a public company in 1927) was established in Berlin in 1903, to deal with the electric power engineering side of the business. The large Siemensstadt factory was opened in 1913 as the company's new headquarters in north Berlin.

Two World Wars: 1914–45

At the outbreak of the First World War, Siemens had a turnover of 403 million marks and employed 63,000 workers. Not surprisingly, orders for civilian electrical equipment slowed considerably and the company began production of communications devices for the military as well as explosives, gun locks for rifles, and later in the war, aircraft engines.

The company was able to operate with comparatively low wage costs due mainly to its success in withstanding a series of strikes. The company was also able to benefit from the successful operation of a co-operative 'Werkverein' (Work Association) to which, rather than trade unions, most workers belonged. The company was able to establish this 'Werkverein' in exchange for some modest social concessions to the workforce.[3]

Although the First World War initially led to massive military orders to equip the German navy and to supply field telegraph systems and munitions, the eventual defeat of Germany hurt Siemens and Halske badly. The early post-war period saw the expropriation of the Siemens subsidiaries in Russia and Britain. The British subsidiary was not returned to the Siemens family after the armistice although it retained its name for business purposes. The company as a whole, however, survived the war and the German revolution of 1918 in a comparatively intact state.

The 1920s witnessed renewed expansion of the German economy and the company benefited from this. In 1923, it started producing radio receivers for the consumer market and set up a Japanese subsidiary (Fusi Denk, later known as Fuji Electric).[4] Co-operation with AEG led to the foundation of a joint light-bulb company named Osram. Contracts for large quantities of telephone equipment were successfully negotiated with the German Post Office. The company also obtained a contract to supply the German Railways with signalling equipment. The real superiority of the company's products was, however, shown in orders for electric locomotives, cable networks and power stations in countries as far afield as Japan, the USSR and Ireland. Productivity per man doubled between 1923 and 1928 and a 14% dividend was paid from 1928 to 1930.[5] By the end of the decade, the company was accounting for one-third of the German electrical manufacturing industry's production and nearly the same proportion of its employees.

The economic crisis of the early 1930s led throughout the world economy to dramatic losses of production, the creation of mass unemployment and the imposition of significant cuts in money wages, events that, in Germany, contributed to the rise to power of Hitler and the Nazi regime.[6] Siemens and Halske was forced to cut dividends and lay off workers but remained on a relatively sound financial footing until the Nazi government's rearmament helped to produce orders in 1935. During the rest of the decade, the company manufactured a wide range of equipment for the war effort. Siemens Apparate und Maschinen GmbH was founded in 1933 in order to take advantage of the demands provided by German rearmament.

It is, however, difficult to evaluate the company's activities at this time. Certainly Siemens, along with many German companies, came to regard the National Socialists as a bulwark against Communism and a guarantee that trade unions would be abolished. Although there is some evidence that Carl Friedrich von Siemens was repelled by the Nazi anti-semitism, the company did little or nothing to hinder Nazi militarism.

There is also no doubt that the company, in common with other large German businesses during the Nazi period, employed slave labourers during the war, many of whom died from illness, malnutrition and exhaustion. It is also alleged by death camp survivors – but denied by the company – that Siemens supplied gas chamber equipment to the concentration camps.

From 1940 onwards, the company was devoting virtually all of its manufacturing capacity to military orders. In 1944 it helped develop and manufacture the V2 rocket.

The Allied victory created major problems for Siemens. The destruction of much of the Berlin plant, the dismantling of factories in Poland and the Russian occupied zone and the confiscation of patents and capital abroad taken together accounted for losses of about 2.5 billion marks or 80% of the company's capital. It would require years of rebuilding for the company to recover its pre-war potential.[7]

Recovery and expansion: 1945–79

Siemens was able to adapt rapidly to the new political and economic realities of post-war Germany. The Berlin plant was rebuilt at a cost of DM 4.7 billion but the headquarters of Siemens and Halske was transferred to Munich and that of Siemens–Schuckert to Erlangen. Both of these locations were in the American Occupation Zone, which was considered to be less risky than West Berlin. Although the plants in Munich and Erlangen had also suffered war damage, they were soon rebuilt and transferred to peacetime production. By the early 1950s, Siemens and Halske was once again producing railroad, medical, telephone and power-generating equipment as well as consumer electronics products. The company developed the capacity which enabled it to profit from the boom in pent-up consumer demand which first appeared during the 1950s and continued during the 1960s.[8]

The recovery of the company can be seen from the figures in Exhibit 5.2.[9] Turnover grew by a multiple of 40 during the period 1950 to 1979 with the most rapid growth coming in the 1950s. The workforce grew by a multiple of over five during the same period, although there was a significant slowdown in this rate of growth during the 1970s. This slowdown reflected a watershed in the post-1945 economic development of most of the Western world, especially West Germany.

Exhibit 5.2   Siemens' workforce and turnover 1946–79

Year	Workforce (in thousands)	Turnover (in millions)
1946	60	227*
1950	81	700†
1960	209	4,063
1970	301	11,763
1979	334	28,022

* In RM
† In DM following the 1948 currency reform

> For West Germany, the time after 1973 was a particularly bitter period of awakening until the early 1970s, the country had been spared any major economic crisis. . . . All this changed dramatically in 1973 and West Germany turned into a laggard in the international growth race, with the lowest real GDP growth of the six largest industrialised countries.[10]

Siemens' post-war recovery, like its rise to prominence a hundred years before, owed much to its research and development programme. In the early 1950s, the production of high-quality chips and semiconductors was patented and the first international direct dialling system followed in 1953. In the same year, Siemens entered the field of data processing, an area that was to become increasingly important for the company. It introduced its first mainframe computer in 1955. In 1954, it established Siemens Inc., an American subsidiary based in New York, and sold an electron microscope on the US market.

Siemens has also become increasingly involved with the production of nuclear power stations both for the domestic and overseas markets. Its first nuclear reactor went into service in 1959 at Munich Garching. This area of activity has brought the company into conflict with the active environmentalist lobby in Germany. All of this expansion has taken place in conjunction with increasing wages and benefits to staff and rising levels of profits.[11]

Siemens' products were used on the Mariner IV probe to Mars, and in 1965 its high-speed passenger train went into service with the German Railways. In 1968, it began to construct nuclear power stations in Latin America.

By 1966, the rapid expansion of Siemens and the company's increased involvement in the international arena necessitated a structural reorganisation. Siemens and Halske and Siemens–Schuckert were merged to form Siemens AG and the larger company was organised on the basis of six divisions and five central functional areas.

The 1970s were prosperous years for Siemens.[12] The slowdown in the world economy did force the company to recruit fewer additional workers,[13] but sales grew to DM 21 billion and profits to DM 606 million in 1976. In 1977, Siemens entered a joint venture with Allis-Chalmers in the USA in the turbine generation field. Siemens' status as an electrical manufacturer rose to the point where they were seen as replacing Westinghouse as the main threat to General Electric in everything from motors and switchgear to generators and nuclear reactors. At this time it had also increased its share of the West German mainframe computer market to 21% and was beginning to be perceived as a threat by the market leader IBM.

Siemens did, however, encounter some major problems when attempting to enter the micro-circuit technology market in the late 1970s. In spite of its huge budget it did not have the required flexibility to compete with the market leaders. It did eventually manage to enter a joint venture with Philips to develop advanced micro-circuits.

Mixed fortunes in the 1980s

In 1981, Peter von Siemens retired and was succeeded by Bernhard Plettner. This meant that for the first time since the company was founded in 1847, direct control of the company moved out of the hands of the Siemens family.

The early years of the decade seemed at the time to indicate a continuation of the growth and expansion of the period 1950–70. In spite of a brief downturn in 1983, the figures for turnover followed an upward trend. The workforce fell between 1980 and 1983, but had surpassed its 1980 level by the end of 1985. These developments can be seen from the figures in Exhibit 5.3.[14]

This upward trend in company fortunes is confirmed by the figures for profits after tax, which rose from DM 802 million in 1983 to DM 1,528 million in 1985.

The company's lack of success in the area of micro-circuits continued into the 1980s and its components division lost money until 1987. In the event, Siemens was forced to buy chips from Toshiba to meet its commitments until its own chips became available in 1988.

Exhibit 5.3   Siemens' workforce, turnover and net profits 1980–85

Year	Workforce (in thousands)	Turnover (DM million)	Net Profit (DM million)
1980	344	31,960	633
1981	338	34,561	509
1982	324	40,000	738
1983	313	39,471	802
1984	328	45,819	1,066
1985	348	56,616	1,528

Siemens owed part of this success in the early years of the decade to the financial difficulties encountered by AEG, its major competitor in the electrical industry. It seemed at the time that it was also due to Siemens' decision to diversify into other fields like electronics and the production of nuclear power stations rather than to concentrate upon its near monopoly as a supplier of the German Post and Telecommunications systems. This recipe for success seemed likely to continue throughout the decade, but it was not to be; the fortunes of the concern took a turn for the worse in 1986.[15] The magnitude of the difficulties is revealed by the figures set out in Exhibit 5.4.[16]

Exhibit 5.4   Siemens' turnover and net profits 1984–89

Year	Turnover (DM billion)	Net Profits (DM million)
1984	45.8	1,066
1985	54.6	1,528
1986	47.0	1,474
1987	51.4	1,275
1988	59.4	1,391
1989	61.1	1,577

There was a 14% drop in turnover between 1985 and 1986 which was only partially corrected during the following year. This was a dramatic deterioration and it resulted in a reduction of dividend per share from DM 12 to DM 11. The company gave some reasons for these difficulties, and these are set out below. The figures also showed a 14% fall in profits between 1985 and 1986 to DM 1,275 million and the indications were that most of these profits had been earned from interest payments on the firm's financial investments rather than by making and selling goods.[17]

The company's poor results led to the resignation of the 73-year-old chairman of the Supervisory Board, Bernhard Plettner, in 1988. He was replaced by the former finance director, Heribald Närger, a man who had nine years' experience in his former role and was equally committed to the company's traditions.

The company chairman, Karlheinz Kaske, retained his position and endeavoured to explain away the results as *minor difficulties caused by an unfavourable business environment*. His analysis was as follows: a decline in economic activity had led to a reduction in demand in important markets both at home and overseas. The fall in the value of the dollar in terms of the DM had led to tougher competition both at home and overseas and to a reduction in the DM value of profits transferred from the Siemens subsidiary in the USA. In the light of these difficulties (Kaske carefully avoided the word crisis), many of the stakeholder groups (especially shareholders and workers) involved with the company would need to make sacrifices. In addition to the cut in dividends, there would have to be a rigorous cost-cutting exercise involving reductions in staffing and investment. These cuts were not, however, allowed to prevent an increase in expenditure on research and development since this was regarded as crucial to the company's policy of concentration on the growth sectors in the European and US markets.[18]

Bernhard Plettner and the new company chairman, Karlheinz Kaske, were responsible for the ambitious programme of acquisitions and research and development embarked on by the company during this period. Siemens launched a programme to develop its own microchips, acquired the Rolm subsidiary of IBM for $844 million in 1988 and spent $24 billion on research and development during 1983 and 1988. All of these actions were aimed at yielding long-term benefits, but had an inevitable impact on short-term earnings. The firm cut its dividend in 1988.

It would be wrong to overstate the difficulties faced by Siemens. The company was still very powerful and had access to liquid assets of DM 23 billion. Nevertheless the decline in profits and dividends drew the attention of leading commentators. *Der Spiegel*[19] interpreted the results as an indication that the company was in danger of failing to match world standards in fields important for the future of electronics. *Manager Magazin*[20] wrote about a 'revolutionary restructuring of the system of management' being planned by Kaske and Närger.

The main features of Kaske's strategy for the future of Siemens were announced as long ago as 1981, and were as follows:

● to seek to become the world leader in the rapidly expanding markets for:
  – office automation
  – factory automation
  – telecommunications;
● to concentrate on certain key geographical markets, for example the US market, which accounted for 30% of Siemens' turnover in the electro-technical industry, and the Far East;

- to set the standards for the world in semiconductor technology by catching up with the leading American and Japanese concerns.

In the event, the company's hopes for a breakthrough in particular product ranges and in the US and Far Eastern markets during the 1980s were not realised.

Kaske's restructuring of the company

The structure of the company as it existed during the period 1966–87 is set out in Exhibit 5.5. This operated as a form of *matrix structure* with the *Central Divisions* on one side of the matrix and the *Business Groups* on the other.

One of the biggest problems faced by Siemens during this period was a lack of speed and flexibility in decision-making. Kaske set out to design a structure that would enable the company to get nearer to the market and the customer. He wished to simplify the decision-making processes in a way that would help the company to discover, develop and support entrepreneurial talent.

In principle, in the old structure, the Board of Management should have played an important role, but in practice, it was very large, containing 31 members, and total reliance on this body would have made strategic decision-making an even longer process. This problem necessitated the delegation of important decisions, such as whether or not to continue to produce in South Africa, to the still unwieldy *Central Committee*, with 14 members with an average age of nearly 60, and the seven strong and similarly ageing *Investment Committee*.[21]

This delegation gave Närger a considerable amount of power, since he was present when all important decisions were taken. The rest of the Supervisory Board, however, played a much less significant role. As a former banker, Närger did not fit in well with the image of the 'typical Siemens manager'. It was certainly true that a large percentage of such managers had worked for the company all of their lives, and were therefore likely to accept the chief tenets of the traditional Siemens culture: e.g. the search for large-scale solutions and complete systems.

This culture was also reflected in the habit of referring to the company not as a 'Konzern' or 'Firma' but simply as *'das Haus Siemens'*. There was also a predominance of conservative older men on the Board. Although this may have been inevitable at that stage in the historical development of such a large company, it did carry with it a serious disadvantage. There was a suspicion that the younger,

Exhibit 5.5 Siemens' organisational structure (1966–87)

SUPERVISORY BOARD						
BOARD OF MANAGEMENT						
CENTRAL DIVISIONS						
Finance	Research and Technology		Personnel	Sales and Marketing		Business Administration
BUSINESS GROUPS						
Components	Energy & Automation	Medical Engineering	Communications & Information Systems	Electrical Installations & Automotive Systems	KWU	Telecommunication Networks & Security Systems
REGIONAL OFFICES			SUBSIDIARIES		ASSOCIATED COMPANIES	

more energetic managers, who were more attuned to the technological and business needs of such a rapidly changing electronics market, may have seen their career prospects blocked by the 'old guard'. The slow reaction time of the company was well known, and *Manager Magazin*[22] has commented on the absence of an efficient decision-making process. It was claimed that in many divisions an issue had to pass through up to seven hierarchical levels before a final decision was reached.

In Kaske's view, the old structure had become impossible to manage. In his opinion, the nature of the matrix structure had created a number of problems. In particular, there were conflicts between heads of the groups and the five central (functional) departments. It was also difficult to co-ordinate sales and personnel policy for the company as a whole. The process was made even more difficult by the fact that investment decisions had to be made by the Central Investment Committee rather than being handled primarily by the group concerned. It was argued that this resulted in delays, intrigues and a general failure to adapt quickly to market needs.

In an attempt to solve these organisational problems, a small managerial committee was established consisting of Kaske himself, Plettner, Närger and the chief administrator, Max Günther. The latter, a respected conciliator of conflicting interest groups, had been selected to devise the new structure and also to persuade existing managers to accept it. Günther's sudden death in January 1988 made this task much more difficult. There was understandably a fear among a number of managers that a reorganisation would cost them their jobs or damage their power positions within the existing hierarchy.[23]

In the new structure (Exhibit 5.6), the Board of Management was to behave like a holding company, giving up control of day-to-day activities in order to concentrate upon the strategic development of the company as a whole. The seven (partly overlapping) broad business groups were dissolved and replaced by over twice as many but more market-oriented business units. Two additional features of the new structure were redefined: Central Functional Departments and the Regional Units.

Exhibit 5.6 Siemens' organisational structure (1989)

SUPERVISORY BOARD					
BOARD OF MANAGEMENT					
CENTRAL DIVISIONS			**CO-ORDINATING COMMITTEES**		
Business Planning & Development	Finance & Control	Personnel	Telecommunications and Security Systems	Energy & Automation	KWU
Research & Development	Production & Logistics	Regional Offices			
15 BUSINESS UNITS					
Semi conductors	Passive Components & Electron Tubes	Factory Automation Systems	Automotive Systems	Medical Engineering	System Sales
Indirect Sales	Private Communication Systems	Security Systems	Telecommunication Networks		Environmental Technology
Plant Power (KWA)	Power Transmission & Distribution		Transportation Technology	Power Generation & Distribution	
REGIONAL UNITS	**SUBSIDIARIES**		**ASSOCIATED COMPANIES**		

One of the changes concerned the organisation of 'Sales'. In the old structure each group had its own sales department dealing with important customers such as the railway and the postal services. These sales departments did not, however, sell directly to the customer but to the company's own Sales/Distribution Department which completed the sale. This department had 147,000 staff, of whom one-third were based in Germany. It was argued that this situation frustrated the group sales staff and meant that the central sales department could not possibly develop the specialist knowledge required for individual products ranging from electronic control equipment for steelworks, to laser printers and tomographs. This system was another factor contributing to the slowness with which Siemens could respond to changing market conditions.

This weakness in the sales area was recognised by Kaske and plans were developed to break down the centralised structure and give greater influence to the new product-based business units. Reforms were also made in the key central division Research and Development. It is argued by some observers that too many of the 40,000 employees of this division are engaged in areas of research seen as far too remote from the market. Kaske stressed that priority should be given to meeting the needs of customers. In this respect, he listed the following as priority areas:

- Medical diagnostics
- Automobile technology
- Office and Production Automation
- Communication technology
- Materials analysis
- Micro-electronics.

There was no guarantee that the reforms in production, marketing and organisational structure would prove to be successful. Entrenched special interests and the conservatism of many existing senior managers were factors likely to inhibit progress.

Some commentators argued that Kaske's record was one of good intentions which he was unable to carry into effect and there was also some doubt as to whether or not Närger had the dynamism required by such a task. But the future of Siemens, of the West German electronics industry and even, some might argue, of the national economy, depended on whether the reforms – which one might almost describe as 'corporate perestroika' – could be carried through.

The prospects of success were set out in *Der Spiegel* in 1988 as follows:

> Kaske had five years in which to accomplish these tasks. Five years in which it would be decided whether or not Siemens could retain its position as an important international company or not.

Kaske maintained that economic growth and the welfare of the economy as a whole was coming to depend more and more on the performance of the electronics industry. One expected this industry to set the pace of technical advance for the economy as a whole. Kaske was confident in the ability of his team to deliver a top-class performance in the future.

There was no shortage of money with which to accomplish the changes; what was missing was a willingness to do so. In this respect the falling dividends were aimed as much at those within the firm as those outside. It was a signal as to the position of the firm and the urgency for change.

A review of company performance at the end of the 1980s

Siemens as a 'flagship' of German industry

Paradoxically, the very size, wealth and prestige of the company may have contributed to its difficulties at the end of the 1980s. A concern with 359,000 employees in 123 countries throughout the world automatically came under the microscope of politicians and the media and could not afford to be found wanting. The performance of Siemens was seen as symbolic of the German economy as a whole and the news of the reduced dividend inflicted further strains on the financial markets only a month after the 1987 Stock Exchange Crash.

The complete product portfolio

Siemens prided itself on 'being able to do everything' while its competitors followed a more pragmatic strategy of mutual co-operation which allowed companies to concentrate upon areas where they are strong and avoid areas of relative weakness. This strategy also had the advantage of satisfying the wish of some customers not to become too reliant upon one supplier.

The relationship with the state

The company was accused of being over-reliant on the state for orders and subsidies and in need of the stimulus of international competition in domestic markets. It was certainly true that the attitude of Siemens' management was influenced strongly by the traditional 'special relationship' between the company and the German postal service. For years, the Federal Post Office entrusted the fixing of technical standards to Siemens staff and this led almost inevitably to a situation where the product which met these standards came from Siemens. The Siemens Director for Communications was even allowed to sit on the Administrative Board of the Federal Post Office.

It was therefore no surprise that the order for glass fibre optic television cables was issued just after Siemens had opened the most modern fibre optics factory in the world at Neustadt. This cosy arrangement did have advantages for Siemens, but immunity from competitive forces is no incentive to produce systems capable of standing up to international competition. This was demonstrated by the technical faults which hindered the launch of the Siemens car phone system.

The special relationship with the Federal Post Office is coming to an end in the near future. The Federal Post Office is being split up into three independent enterprises and competitors such as SEL and AEG, who are willing to pool their technological expertise with European and American partners, will soon present a serious threat to Siemens' market position. The introduction of the Single European Market in 1992 has changed matters further since it requires that national postal services are eventually compelled to accept open tendering from foreign as well as domestic suppliers. While this opens up other European markets to Siemens, it also requires it to defend its position in the German market.

There is no doubt that, taken together, these three factors go a long way to explaining why Siemens had failed to attain the objectives set out by Kaske in 1981.

New leadership in the 1990s

In spite of the reorganisation in 1989, in comparison with its major competitors, Siemens remained the electronics company with the lowest productivity and the highest unit costs. It would seem that Kaske had failed to deal with the real problems of the company. As we have seen, the company was only able to sustain its heavy and sometimes wasteful research and development budget because of its protected position in key markets. Market deregulation will put an end to that.

Karlheinz Kaske (64) was succeeded on 1 October 1992 by Heinrich von Pierer (51). It is worth noting that these two men are very different individuals, not just in terms of their ages. Indeed, von Pierer is a complete contrast to all of his predecessors at the helm of Siemens. Educated in law and economics, he is only the second non-engineer to lead the company. He also has a relaxed and open attitude to his job. His overriding aim is to improve the profitability of the company. It was hoped that he would bring a new perspective to bear and would be able successfully to address the company's problems.

Plan A: The TOP programme

After the rapid and costly expansionist policies of Kaske, the first task of von Pierer was to consolidate. With this in mind, he tightened further Kaske's existing rationalisation policy. In this respect, the whole of the company's value chain was examined for economies. The proportion of in-house production was to be reduced and the company was to turn to out-sourcing when possible. Joint ventures were to be broken off or sold if they were thought to be unprofitable.

A new programme called *Time Optimised Process* (TOP) was initiated in 1994 to reduce the company's costs as soon as possible. The aim was to save DM 30 billion. The innovations cycle was to be reduced by half and productivity was to rise by 30%. The rate of return on turnover was to increase from 2% to 5%.

Kaske had already tried to initiate a company-wide productivity drive in 1990, but progress was held up at the time partly by the conservative forces at senior levels within the company. Effective change had to wait for von Pierer. He was fortunate in that the passing of time had removed many of the older and more conservative elements from the Board.

It was realised that this would involve a radical change in the attitudes of key members of the Siemens team. Rather than behaving like civil servants, they would need to learn to be entrepreneurs. In the case of individual products the barriers that existed between the various business functions would need to be removed and an overview taken of the development of the product from the research laboratory to the delivery to the customer. Only when this has been done and a team responsible for the whole of the value chain has been established, can the team be expected to understand, monitor and control the process.

The TOP programme included some spectacular rescue actions like the cost-reduction programmes in semiconductors, energy production and Siemens–Nixdorf, but was not formulated into a comprehensive company-wide scheme. For example, there was no clear indication of the strategic areas on which Siemens should concentrate. It is simply a recovery programme and no clear Siemens strategy for the future is yet visible.

The majority of Siemens' employees have not been impressed by the programme. Most of them regard it as simply a programme for reducing jobs and as offering nothing in terms of working conditions and leadership. In 1994 awareness of the scheme was not high, and a campaign to address this problem was not commenced until 1995 – some time after the official start of the scheme.

One of the major problems was that the workforce tended to associate the scheme with the major restructuring programmes mentioned earlier that were mostly concerned with cost cutting and job shedding. This has led many to redefine the programme as *Total ohne Personnel* (totally without personnel) or *Total ohne Perspective* (totally without perspective or prospects): in many respects these sentiments are not totally unfounded.

Kaske's legacy for the company has been unfortunate in a number of respects. During the 1980s, when Siemens had numerous customers and protected markets, the chance to instigate productivity programmes was let slip. This now had to be attempted in much more difficult circumstances. At the same time, there is no strategy for internal growth that will enable jobs lost in one area to be recouped by growth in new areas. For many years, the company grew mainly by means of acquisitions. The failure to identify key areas in which the company could foster internal growth was a major problem in this respect.

Von Pierer has been accused of meddling too much in the day-to-day activities of the organisation without providing enough clear guidance on future strategies. He has, however, given the chiefs of his 17 business units[24] more responsibility. Whereas previously nearly all projects had to be approved by the Board, von Pierer now allows decisions on projects up to DM 10 million to be made at the business unit level. This involved about 80% of the company's investment decisions and frees up the Board to consider strategic issues.

He has attempted via the TOP programme to change the culture of the company, '... to make every worker feel responsible for the success of the company', but, as we have seen, the results of this are subject to some dispute at this stage.

As Exhibit 5.7 demonstrates, there has been an increase in turnover and profits in every year since 1992, but apart from 1995 and 1996 the growth in profits has been very modest. The effects on the size of the workforce have, however, been more marked with the total falling by nearly 10% during the period 1992–95 before recovering a little in 1996.

The company's performance in comparison with its great rival General Electric has been poor, and even von Pierer admits to the company lagging behind its American competitor. He feels that the position in Germany was not helped during the early 1990s by the boom in business following Re-unification. At the time when, in the USA, a recession was focusing minds on necessary reforms, Siemens was able to avoid the necessity to make the required changes.

It is even possible to argue that much (about a third) of the recent increase in profits is due to the financial activities of the company rather than genuine production and sales of electrical products. Siemens is in many respects still a bank that also has an electrical business. Von Pierer has still not managed to increase the rate of return on turnover above a meagre 2.6%. The target rate of 5% still eludes him.

Exhibit 5.7   Siemens' workforce, turnover and net profits, 1990–96

Year	Workforce (in thousands)	Turnover (DM billion)	Net profits (DM million)	%*
1990	373	63.2	1,668	2.6
1991	402	73.0	1,792	2.5
1992	413	78.5	1,955	2.5
1993	391	81.6	1,982	2.4
1994	376	84.6	1,993	1.9
1995	373	88.7	2,084	2.3
1996	379	94.2	2,419	2.6

*Net profits as a percentage of turnover.

Der Spiegel has accused von Pierer of not being discriminating enough in his evaluation of the contribution of each division to group profits. There does not seem to be a minimum acceptable rate of return target similar to that operated by Daimler-Benz. In his defence, von Pierer has argued that it is not that easy for Siemens, since the company operates in so many different areas, he regards it as impossible to apply the same minimum target rate of return to all divisions. *He is also reluctant to play employees and shareholders off against each other in this way. He argues that both groups are stakeholders in the company, and Siemens does not want to make good profits at the expense of the workforce.* This statement does not, however, sit too easily with the recent cut-backs in the size of the workforce and the perceived impact of the TOP programme.

Siemens is still accused of being slower than its competitors in the innovatory process, but while there is still room for improvement the company is second only in its record on innovations to Asea Brown Boverie.

It has been suggested in the *Financial Times* that the company should be divided into separate low-tech and high-tech branches, since different strategies are appropriate in each area. Von Pierer rejects this suggestion, however, since he believes that in reality it is impossible and unwise to make such a distinction when technological advances are being made in all areas. He argues that the company has achieved through its reorganisation the de-centralisation necessary to give it the required flexibility in today's business environment. *He argues that the company can now best be thought of as a fleet of boats travelling together but often at different speeds.* The company now possesses over 250 business entities and each of these can react to market forces in the same way as a medium-sized company.

Von Pierer insists that business strategy must at any one time contain a mixture of conservative and progressive elements. Siemens is, for example, ahead of the field in its activities in emerging markets.

One of the positive factors is that the electronics market is expected to grow over the next few years at a rate of between 6 and 7% per annum. If the company can maintain its position in the face of this growth, it should be able to remain one of the giants of the industry. It does remain true, however, that many of the basic criticisms of the company made at the end of the 1980s remain true today.

Plan B: A change of course?

The company's profits during 1996 were up by 16% on the previous year and yet the investors remained unimpressed. Because of an apparently gloomy outlook for the fortunes of the company, the shareholders have recently sold Siemens' shares in large numbers. *At the time of its 150th anniversary the company found itself with about 380,000 workers and in a difficult economic situation.*

Some critics argue that the main problem has been that so far von Pierer has not decided on a clear course of action. Recent events may be forcing him to do so and in this respect can be regarded as a change of course. Will he conclude that a further tightening of the rationalisation programme is called for, since the TOP programme has not produced the results he hoped for, or will he – as Siemens has done for decades – aim to keep as many jobs in Germany as possible on social grounds?

Der Spiegel is clear on the matter:

> If von Pierer does not want his company to descend into international mediocrity, it will be necessary to raise both productivity and profits dramatically. This does not seem likely to be possible without the sale of many parts of the business and the loss of thousands of jobs.[25]

Peter von Siemens, the great-grandson of the company's founder, has recently criticised the company's rate of return of 2.6% as unacceptable. 'For this kind of return the milkman on the corner would no longer be willing to open his shop.'[26]

Motivated by increasing pressure on all sides, von Pierer may now be willing to drive forward the reorganisation of the company. It is clear that if he wishes to retain his job in the new millennium, he will need to have achieved his objectives and no one expects him to give up his position without a fight.

Von Pierer believes that of the *eight business segments* (Exhibit 5.8) in which the company currently operates, *none* can in its current form remain competitive in the long term. The company can only earn lasting returns from the segments in which Siemens is in first or second position in the world.

All of the Siemens' companies will be carefully examined in order to establish whether or not they have a leading competitive position and, if not, what are the chances of their attaining one.

The proposals have been set out in *Der Spiegel*:

> In those areas where it looks unlikely that Siemens can attain a leading position, other companies may be acquired or joint ventures with competitors established. Even in the central area of energy production and distribution it is questionable as to whether or not Siemens is strong enough in the longer term to withstand alone the pressures of international competition.

Siemens' subsidiaries that do not achieve their targets will be detached and sold. There will be no long-term cross-subsidisation in the name of long-term strategy. The company will undertake a clearing up operation of unwanted activities.[27]

Exhibit 5.8 Market segments, 1996

Segment	Workforce (thousands)	Turnover (DM million)	Profits (DM million)
Industry	98.3	24.7	524
Communication	66.1	22.0	920
Energy	39.5	13.8	452
Information	34.1	13.6	52
Transport	28.6	8.3	130
Components	35.1	8.0	876
Medicine	22.4	7.1	30
Lighting	26.2	5.7	369

Previously von Pierer was reluctant to join in the debate concerning the importance for the company of shareholder value. As we have seen, he has in the past argued that Siemens were not a company interested in short-term profit maximisation. Now he is increasing the tempo himself and speaks of a great need for action to 'plug-up' the holes through which the company is losing money as quickly as possible.

Unfortunately there are problems for the company in many of the market segments in which it is active. These problems have been set out in *Der Spiegel*:[28]

> There is great concern for the area of *Medical Technology*. This branch has suffered for years as a consequence of the cost-curbing legislation in the health industry. This year the needy subsidiary will make modest profits but nothing will come of this. In the previous, the American authorities shut down the production of the American subsidiary of Siemens because of alleged poor quality production. Von Pierer believes that in this segment Siemens must lose about 2000 jobs world-wide. Even then, he doubts whether the company can continue alone in all areas of this segment.
>
> The prospects in the *industrial area* are even more gloomy. Because of the weak state of the economy, many firms are deferring their large orders. As a consequence, Siemens cannot find enough paying customers.
>
> In the previous year the effervescent profits in the *Silicon Chip* business were able to balance out the losses in other areas. The good times are, however, over. The prices for memory chips are under pressure throughout the world and, as a consequence, the Siemens order book has suffered.
>
> Even in the area of *Public Communication*, up until now a virtual gold mine, there are signs of danger. This year Telekom is completing the digitalisation of the network that has earned Siemens a turnover in the billions in the previous two years.
>
> The *Siemens–Nixdorf (SNI) subsidiary* is also in trouble and only remains in 'the black' because of transfers of millions of DM from the parent company. Analysts are agreed that Siemens cannot any longer drag along weak subsidiaries like SNI.

With these problems in mind, Siemens has already announced a number of measures that would tend to indicate that von Pierer is at last ready to embark upon a radical reorganisation of the company. He has stated that the full consequences of the globalisation of its markets have yet to be faced by the company and these may be the first real steps in this direction. The main *measures* are as follows:

- The ailing medical branch will in future, for the first time, offer cheap mass-produced articles. The heart pacemaker section has been sold and in the next few months other fringe areas will be sold.

- There will also be further rationalisation in the area of transport technology.

- Von Pierer will install a man he trusts in the industrial area, the former McKinsey manager, Edward Krubasik. His job will be to decide whether or not Siemens should stay in such fringe areas as the production of paper or sugar-making machinery.

- Von Pierer is hoping to achieve an optimal regional mix of production and this is likely in the longer term to mean the relocation of production outside Germany. The German share of production is scheduled to fall from 40% today to under 30% within the next ten years. Production in Asia will double and will also grow strongly in North and South America.

Conclusions

Siemens has grown enormously over the past 150 years. During the period *1847–1914* Siemens became a public company and began to establish itself in the international arena. Although the company suffered considerable disruption during the two world wars which spanned the period 1914–1945, it survived in spite of the problems caused by reparations and the partition of Germany.

Although it took many years of rebuilding for the company to regain its pre-war potential, the years between 1945 and 1979 are rightly regarded as a period of recovery and expansion. When the immediate aftermath of the war had subsided, the company was able to benefit from the *Wirtschaftswunder* and continued to prosper even into the 1970s. It was at this time that the company first encountered the problems created by its size and inflexible decision-making machinery.

The 1980s were, as we have seen, a mixed period, and in the middle of the decade the fortunes of the company deteriorated. This was partly due to the instability in the international business environment that was affecting all companies, but was also due to the particular problems of Siemens and the German economy. Almost for the first time it was necessary for the leaders of the company to reconsider the way in which the company was organised and the direction in which it was moving. First *Karlheinz Kaske* and then *Heinrich von Pierer* embarked on radical reorganisations and rationalisation programmes designed to re-establish the company in the international market place. It is clear that Kaske's attempts failed to produce the change of direction and culture required, but judgement on the policies of von Pierer cannot at this stage be finally made.

There have been some positive signs, but the overall picture is not yet promising. For example, during 1996/97 Siemens managed to achieve an increase in productivity of 8% but this was not enough to improve company fortunes and its image with investors. Firstly, its competitors also performed well and, secondly, these gains had to be balanced by the effects of the falling price levels faced by the company in many of its international markets and by significant currency losses. At the same time, wage costs were rising in Germany and this was damaging the competitiveness of the company's German operations. The total effect of all of this was negative for Seimens.

An investment analyst interviewed in *Der Spiegel* argues that Siemens has followed a policy of selling profitable areas (e.g. high-performance printers) and has used the cash to try to strengthen weaker areas. He views this as a mistaken policy that must stop if Siemens is to regain the confidence of investors. The company must pull out of unprofitable activities.

> Siemens is not a social concern and is not invincible. Profitable areas can be offset against loss-making areas but the only way to create secure long-term jobs is by investing in the technologies of the future.[29]

There needs to be more evidence of a radical reorganisation of the company along these lines before we can conclude that the company is being rescued by von Pierer and can no longer be charged with *having lost its way*.

NOTES

1. Siemens' company history – internal company documents.
2. Paula Kepos (ed.) (1995) *International Directory of Company Histories* (Vol 2), Gale Hardcover.
3. Tony Fowler and Ian King (1988) *Siemens* (An unpublished bilingual case study).
4. Kepos *op cit.*
5. Fowler and King *op cit.*
6. Henning, F.W. (1997) *Das Industrialisierte Deutschland.* Uni-TB.
7. Fowler and King *op cit.*
8. ibid.
9. Giersch, H., Paque, K.H. and Schmiedling, H. (1994) *The Fading Miracle*, Cambridge University Press, Cambridge.
10. Siemens *op cit.*
11. Fowler and King *op cit.*
12. Kepos *op cit.*
13. Giersch et al. *op cit.*
14. Siemens *op cit.*
15. Fowler and King *op cit.*
16. Siemens *op cit.* Siemens' Annual Reports.
17. *Der Spiegel*, 12/88.
18. Fowler and King *op cit.*
19. *Der Spiegel op cit.*
20. *Manager Magazin*, 4/88.
21. These were standing committees of the company.
22. *Manager Magazin op cit.*
23. Fowler and King *op cit.*
24. This has been expanded from the 15 designated by Kaske.
25. *Der Spiegel*, 7/97.
26. ibid.
27. *Der Spiegel op cit.*
28. ibid.
29. Peter Thilo Hasler in *Der Spiegel*, 7/97.

The British Broadcasting Corporation

The British Broadcasting Corporation (BBC) is one of the oldest broadcasting organisations in the world, and a British institution. Known to many insiders and longer term employees simply as 'the Corporation', it was founded and began broadcasting in 1922 in Britain not long after the invention and early development of radio around the beginning of the century. The BBC was also arguably the first organisation in the world to begin broadcasting high definition (by 1930s standards) television pictures on a regular basis from its transmitter at Alexandra Palace in the suburbs of north London in 1936. At the beginning of the year 2000, however, the BBC faced a very different world to that of the 1920s and 1930s. One of the main questions is how its role as a British 'public service' broadcaster can fit into the rapidly changing and increasingly competitive and globalised communications industry of the twenty-first century.

The following extract is the opening statement from the BBC Report and Accounts for 1998–99:

> We aim to be the world's most trusted broadcaster and programme maker, seeking to satisfy all our audience in the UK with services that inform, educate and entertain and that enrich their lives in ways that the market alone will not. We aim to be guided by our public purposes; to encourage the UK's most innovative talents; to act independently of all interests; to aspire to the highest ethical standards; to offer the best value for money; to be accountable to our licence payers; to endeavour to be the world's leading international broadcaster; and to be the best – or learn from the best – in everything we do.

The Governors have endorsed the following key objectives for the BBC in 1998/99.

1. Secure the BBC's role as a standard setter of programme quality, in new as well as existing services, continuously innovating, developing and refreshing output across all genres.

This case has been written by Clive Helm, University of Westminster, for the purposes of classroom discussion. It is not intended to illustrate good or poor handling of an administrative situation. © Copyright Clive Helm 2000.

2. Serve the whole audience effectively, responding to the needs of the different groups of licence payers and communicating the value of the BBC's services to them.

3. In the light of the BBC's strong commitment to education, embrace the opportunities presented by new initiatives and new broadcasting technologies and ensure that educational purposes underpin programming on a broad front.

4. Strengthen popular drama, entertainment and situation comedy on television.

5. Demonstrate increased value for money throughout the BBC.

6. Maximise the potential for creativity and efficiency of digital production.

7. Agree and implement plans for responding to new political institutions in Scotland, Wales, Northern Ireland and London.

8. Secure the position of the World Service within the context of a global strategy for the BBC in television, radio and online.

9. Continue to improve the effectiveness of the BBC's two main commercial businesses – BBC Worldwide and BBC Resources – while trading fairly.

10. Build on the improvement in two-way communication between staff and management and ensure that all who work for the BBC play their part in delivering BBC goals and strategies.

The BBC is principally funded by means of a compulsory 'licence fee' payable by anyone using their services. The licence fee income for the period 1996–97 to 1998–99 is shown in Exhibit 6.1 and the expenditure for 1998–99 is shown in Exhibit 6.2.

Exhibit 6.1   BBC licence fee income 1996–97 to 1998–99

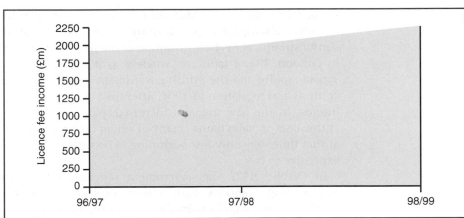

Source: BBC Report and Accounts 1998–99.

Exhibit 6.2   **BBC licence fee expenditure 1998–99**

Expenditure	£m
BBC1	752
BBC2	406
National and regional television	185
National, regional and local radio	149
BBC Radio 1	37
BBC Radio 2	42
BBC Radio 3	62
BBC Radio 4	89
BBC Radio 5 live	55
BBC1 & 2 Widescreen	30
BBC Choice	34
BBC News24	50
BBC Parliament	2
Digital radio	6
BBC Online	23
Digital development costs	9
Restructuring	31
Corporate Centre	60
Licence fee collection costs	133
Total Expenditure	£2155

Source: BBC Report and Accounts 1998–99.

Outline history of the BBC and the British Broadcasting Industry: origins and early history

In June 1896 Guglielmo Marconi filed the first patent at the British Patent Office for 'wireless telegraphy apparatus' and in the following month gave the first public demonstration of his new invention at the headquarters of the General Post Office in London. Use of radio, or 'wireless' as it was commonly called in those days, spread rapidly, and the British government responded by introducing a system of controls and regulation in 1904. After the First World War ended in 1918, popular interest in the new medium increased, particularly with a growing number of enthusiasts or 'radio hams', many of whom built their own equipment as radio sets at that time were only just beginning to become commercially available, and were expensive to buy.

In October 1922 the government sanctioned the formation of the British Broadcasting Company with a share capital of £100,000 owned jointly by a number of major radio manufacturers of the time, notably the Marconi, Western Electric and General Electric companies. It began regular daily broadcasts in November, and in the following year was granted an exclusive licence to broadcast in the UK by the Postmaster General of Great Britain.

In December 1922 John (later Lord) Reith was appointed as the first General Manager. Born in 1896 with a strong Presbyterian Scottish background and upbringing, Reith had very definite views on the role that the new medium of broadcasting should play. His vision of the BBC was of a broadcaster with a strong mission and social purpose to 'educate, inform and entertain', while being imbued with a firmly moral ethic, and making, as he put it, 'no concessions to the vulgar'. He also felt strongly that broadcasting in Britain should be kept as a monopoly with what he described as a 'unity of control'. Funding for the BBC was to be principally by means of a compulsory 'licence fee' payable by anyone using a radio in Britain and collected by the Post Office, together with a levy of 10% on the sales of all new radio sets sold.

In the months following these early beginnings the BBC's output began to grow to several hours a day to include news bulletins, talks, religious addresses, plays, orchestral concerts, children's programmes and variety shows. In 1923, a government committee – the first of many over the years to come – met to discuss the future of broadcasting in Britain. In line with Reith's wishes, the committee rejected the idea of allowing the financing of the new medium of radio by advertising as had happened in the USA, and decided on the continuation of the licence fee. They also concluded that, 'the control of such a potential power over public opinion and the life of the nation ought to remain with the state'. In the same year, the first edition of the *Radio Times*, a magazine published by the BBC listing its programmes, went on sale.

As the cost of radio receivers fell rapidly, sales boomed. The number of licences issued priced at 10 shillings (50 pence), rose rapidly from just over 35,000 in 1922 to around 600,000 in 1923 and continued to grow. Despite the high-minded ideals espoused by Reith however, from the outset the BBC was not immune to criticism. While it may have sought to inform, educate and entertain, there were those who felt that some of its output was rather highbrow and intellectual for popular tastes. As an organisation, some viewed the BBC as elitist and paternalistic, a criticism that was to echo down the years to the present day. A visitor to the offices near the Savoy Hotel in London, described them as, '... next to the House of Commons, quite the most pleasant club in London – there were coal fires and visitors were welcomed by a most distinguished gentleman who would conduct them to a private room and offer whisky and soda'. In the early days, radio announcers were reputedly expected to wear evening dress while on air and to speak according to a set of conventions and with a style of pronunciation that came to be known as 'BBC English'. One contemporary observer noted that at that time, 'most employees had very little experience of broadcasting ... mainly they were a mixture of enthusiasts who believed in the possibilities of radio'.

On 1 January 1927 the BBC became a public body, the British Broadcasting Corporation, constituted under a Charter which was to be reviewed by the government periodically after a number of years. The Charter's purpose was to set out the role and standards for the BBC while at the same time giving it a separation from direct state influence, a system of public obligation and government regulation that came to be known as the 'public service' model of broadcasting. A Board of Governors was appointed whose role was to see that the BBC was properly managed and accountable both to the government and licence fee payers. John Reith was appointed as the first Director General.

During the 1930s radio ownership continued to grow rapidly so that by the end of the decade almost all the population of Britain could receive programmes. In 1932 the BBC moved into Broadcasting House, a large, imposing, purpose-designed building located in a prominent position in central London which housed all its

Exhibit 6.3   BBC top organisational structure 1935

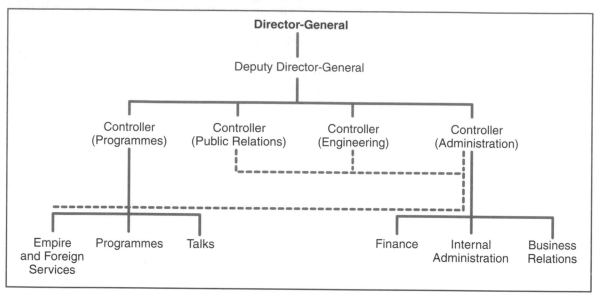

facilities and offices and from where the King, George V, gave the first Christmas message on radio to the nation. In the same year, the 'Empire Service' began short wave broadcasts to Australia, India, parts of Africa and Canada. This was followed by the introduction of foreign language broadcasts to other parts of the world. These networks, which came to be called External Services, were financed by a grant directly from the government and not from the licence fee.

The top organisational structure of the BBC in 1935 can be seen in Exhibit 6.3.

The birth of television

During the early 1930s, the BBC had been collaborating closely with Electrical and Musical Industries (EMI), a company with interests in music publishing and recording as well as radio manufacturing and electronics, to develop a workable technology for television. In November 1936, after several years of experimenting with different systems, the first regular television broadcasts began from the BBC's transmitter at Alexandra Palace in the suburbs of north London. Initially, television was only available in the London area and, as with the beginnings of radio, very few people owned television sets due to their low availability and high cost. Like radio, the new television service was also funded by a licence fee. John Reith, however, was uncertain about the new medium and apparently showed little enthusiasm for it. In his diary he wrote, '... to Alexandra Palace for the television opening. I declined to be televised or take part.' In 1938, having set the tone of British broadcasting for years to come, he left the BBC to become the first government appointed chairman of the new British state airline, Imperial Airways.

Television broadcasting was stopped by the Second World War in 1939 when a Mickey Mouse cartoon that was showing was abruptly blacked out. Radio continued however, encouraged by the government, both as a means of entertainment and morale raising, as well as a source of news and government information.

English and foreign language services were expanded and continued to broadcast news and information throughout war-torn Europe and many other parts of the world in over 45 different languages. These wartime broadcasts, together with the BBC's perceived freedom from direct state control, helped to create and foster an international reputation for the quality and impartiality of its news reporting.

After war ended in 1946, television in Britain resumed – with the same Mickey Mouse cartoon that had been interrupted in 1939 – and gradually spread to most of the country as ownership of sets increased, although progress in building a transmitter network was slowed by post-war materials shortages. By the end of the 1940s, as well as its single television channel, the BBC was operating three radio networks; the 'Home Service' carrying primarily news and speech, the 'Light Programme' delivering popular music and light entertainment and the 'Third Programme', which was almost exclusively dedicated to classical music.

The 1950s and the launch of commercial television

The first competition in British broadcasting came in 1954 with the government's passing of an Act of Parliament allowing commercial television – television paid for by carrying advertising – to begin operating in the UK. The system of 'Independent Television' (ITV) was to be regulated by an Independent Television Authority (ITA) which would own the transmitters, select and appoint which television companies would be allowed to operate, set standards for programmes and regulate the standards and amount of advertising on the new networks.

The ITV system was set up on a regional basis with a different television contracting company covering each of fourteen different areas of Britain, as well as Independent Television News (ITN) which was jointly owned by all the regional companies and provided a news service to the whole network. The franchisees who bid for the contracts to run the new ITV regions were in the main consortia of companies who already had interests in businesses such as newspaper publishing, film production and distribution, ownership of theatres and cinemas, and other areas of the entertainment industry. In order to try to avoid complete regional monopolies, the franchise for the Greater London area, which was seen as being the most financially attractive, was split between two contractors, Associated-Rediffusion Television which operated on weekdays, and Associated Television which operated at weekends. These two companies, together with the two others which gained the contracts for the other most heavily populated and therefore most lucrative franchise areas, became the main 'network companies' which produced and provided most of the programming to the rest of the ITV system. The smaller regional companies acted mainly as distributors of this material but had a contractual obligation to produce a certain amount of locally oriented news and programming. The first ITV broadcast took place on the evening of 22 September 1955 and the first television commercial seen by the British public was for 'tingling fresh' Gibbs SR toothpaste.

For a commercial broadcaster whose income comes from advertising revenue, the price that advertisers can be charged for airtime is usually directly related to the size of the audience watching – audience ratings are therefore all important. The ITV system, however, was quite strictly regulated by the ITA in terms of programme quality and content and the amount and type of advertising that could be carried. Direct sponsorship of television shows by advertisers, as happened in the USA, was not allowed. Initially programmes could only be broadcast after 7 p.m. However this was soon changed so that the TV companies could transmit between 9 a.m. and 11 p.m., but only to a maximum of 35 hours a week. There was also a short-lived restriction on broadcasting between 6 p.m. and 7 p.m., which was known as 'toddler's time' and which was intended to allow parents time to put small children to bed.

Many advertisers jumped at the new opportunity offered to promote their products directly to an audience of British consumers sitting in the comfort of their living rooms through the powerful medium of television. Following some initial losses after start-up, several of the ITV franchisees quickly became very profitable; one of the smaller companies' shares, for example, multiplied in value 28-fold after two years, and owning a commercial television station at this time was famously described by one investor as 'a licence to print money'.

The advent of commercial television was seen by some of the senior management at the BBC as a major threat not only to the Corporation but also to the standard of British broadcasting as a whole. One executive at the time dismissively criticised ITV's output as being 'a collection of wiggle dances, giveaways, panel games and light entertainment'. From the beginning, although the commercial system was highly regulated, its programming was determinedly more populist and innovative than the BBC's, some of which now seemed staid by comparison. There was a greater emphasis on light entertainment and comedy and on formats copied from American television, such as quiz and talent shows. By this time there was also a growing international trade in television programming and ITV, as well as producing its own shows, also tended to import more of its output from the USA – American police series such as 'Seventy Seven Sunset Strip' and westerns such as 'Bonanza' proved to be particularly successful with British and other European audiences.

The popular success of ITV posed BBC executives at that time with a dilemma: should they try to fight back and get into an audience ratings battle with the commercial network or try to stay truer to Reith's founding ideals of public service broadcasting? Eventually it was decided that the BBC would not try to compete with the commercial network head on, but would instead be prepared to let its average share of audience ratings fall to one third of the total. To the surprise of many, however, this did not happen – after an initial swing to ITV, the audience settled down to a roughly even split. Eventually the BBC responded to the commercial channels' challenge to a degree by introducing its own versions of some of the kinds of shows that ITV had made popular and by buying in more American programming of its own.

The beginning of commercial television also revived the public, political and media debate that had been going on for many years, indeed since the BBC began, about the role of public service broadcasting. The BBC still viewed itself, and was seen by many, to be an integral part of the fabric of British national culture. It tended to be the natural channel to broadcast occasions of national importance such as addresses by the Queen or Prime Minister, the opening of Parliament, or major sporting and cultural events. Critics, however, questioned whether it was necessary to have a public service broadcaster financed by a compulsory fee at all when a commercial system could now provide television for free. The ITV companies in particular argued fiercely that the licence fee gave the BBC an unfair advantage. There were those who thought that it amounted to a compulsory tax on the viewing public, some of whom, with the beginning of choice in broadcasting, might not actually want to watch the BBC's programmes at all. There was also a body of opinion that the BBC could be funded in other ways, perhaps by subscription or advertising, or a combination of both. This debate was to carry on and intensify over the decades to come.

Broadcasting in other parts of the world

In contrast to the public service, monopoly type of model that characterised the birth of broadcasting in Britain, the development of radio and television in the USA had followed a very different pattern. Radio station KDKA, which started transmitting in November 1920 from a shack on the roof of the Westinghouse company's plant in East Pittsburgh, is generally claimed to be the first commercial station to begin regular broadcasts in America. By 1922, 600 commercial stations were operating either independently or in chains and licensed by the US Federal Communications Commission. In 1926 the National Broadcasting Company (NBC) was founded as a subsidiary of the Radio Corporation of America. It rapidly acquired existing chains of stations as well as setting up more of its own. The Columbia Broadcasting System (CBS), which also operated a string of stations, was founded in the following year.

The first television broadcast in America was made by NBC from the World's Fair in 1939. Large-scale introduction of television was delayed by the Second World War, but by 1954 there were around 400 stations operating across the USA. By the beginning of the 1980s this number had grown to around 10,000 radio and 1,200 commercial television stations, a large majority of which were either directly owned by or affiliated to the three major networks, NBC, CBS and their newer and smaller rival, the American Broadcasting Company (ABC).

Television in the USA was therefore almost wholly commercial, unlike in Britain. Advertisers in the USA were also allowed to directly produce and sponsor radio and television shows which often prominently featured their products, a practice which was not allowed in the UK. Criticisms of American television tended to be that it was overly commercial and that its programming sometimes aimed at the lowest common denominator in terms of quality and content. In 1967 the Public Broadcasting System (PBS) was created as the first alternative network, financed by a mixture of public and private funding, and carrying a range of programmes that attempted to be less commercial and in some cases were educational. British programming from both the BBC and ITV networks formed a significant part of PBS's output.

In most Western European countries, broadcasting generally developed along lines broadly similar to those in Britain – a public service or state broadcaster funded by a licence fee alongside a fairly tightly regulated single, or number of, commercial channels, although in some countries the public service broadcaster also carried advertising. In Russia and Eastern Europe all the official broadcasting organisations were very much more directly under the control of the state.

Radio and television in Australia, Canada, New Zealand and South Africa, all countries with a historic and cultural link to the UK, also tended to follow the same duopolistic form of public service network, sometimes financed directly from the government, alongside a number of regulated commercial channels. In Australia and New Zealand in particular, the Australian Broadcasting Corporation and the Broadcasting Corporation of New Zealand were to some extent modelled directly on the BBC whose personnel had been drafted in to help to set them up with technology and expertise in their early days.

The 1960s and 1970s

By the middle of the 1960s the BBC had learned to live with the challenge posed by ITV in Britain as both channels vied for the attentions of the British television audience. They both produced a range of popular, generalist programming that tried to appeal to most sections of the public at some time, including news and current affairs, light entertainment and comedy, sport, drama and feature films. Both channels also had an obligation to produce a certain amount of educational programmes for schools. In 1964 the BBC was given permission by the government to begin a second channel, BBC2, which aimed at a more upmarket audience and had more of a bias towards factual and arts programming than the existing channel, which now became BBC1.

The international market place

Although some programming on both the BBC and ITV networks was imported, particularly from the USA, much of it was produced directly by the BBC and the ITV companies themselves for the British home audience. It therefore tended to have a distinctive British quality and cultural slant. Both the BBC and ITV exported programmes to a large number of foreign markets, most notably to Western Europe, Australia, Canada, New Zealand and also to the USA.

Among broadcasters around the world, the BBC had developed a reputation for producing high-quality programming, particularly in areas like historical and classic drama, and factual programming in subjects such as natural history and popular science. Some of these programmes were co-productions which tended to be large, prestige projects which would be expensive for one network to undertake alone and which were therefore financed, produced, and possibly distributed, jointly by the BBC and one or more other broadcasters in other countries. In the USA, the world's largest television market, some of the BBC's output tended to be seen as being more educational in nature rather than as entertainment. Although some programme material was sold to the major networks, a significant proportion of the BBC's American sales was therefore either to the PBS system or one of the other US public networks which had appeared to provide less purely commercially driven programming. On the whole, British comedy and light entertainment, although selling well in some countries like Australia and New Zealand, did not transfer well to the US mainstream market, probably due to cultural differences. Some British comedy shows, however, did sell successfully to smaller American stations and networks where they tended to find a specialist audience, sometimes achieving a cult status.

The job of selling programmes abroad was handled by the wholly owned commercial arm of the Corporation, BBC Enterprises, which had been formed in 1962.

As well as exporting programmes, BBC Enterprises' other main activities included the exploitation of copyrights held by the BBC through sales of records and cassette tapes, film library material and character merchandising. Selling programming in foreign markets was not always a very profitable activity, especially in some smaller countries where sales did not always cover costs. Revenues from BBC Enterprises were £3.7 million in 1973 against total income from the licence fee of £128 million.

The BBC in the 1960s and 1970s

By this time, the BBC had grown to become a large organisation employing around 24,000 people full time, which had come to see itself not just as a broadcaster but in some ways as a national institution. With a management structure organised largely along the lines of a hierarchical bureaucracy, it was now based not only in Broadcasting House and various other buildings around the centre of London, but also in a new, large, specially built complex spread over several acres of west London known as Television Centre, which is still the main headquarters of its television operations. Television Centre had been designed to house all the administrative offices, studios, technical resources and many other kinds of facilities needed for television production – the scenery department alone reportedly covered more than one acre. There were also similar but smaller specially built facilities centres in several other British cities.

At this time, the BBC was also maintaining 12 orchestras, a full-time choral society and choir and a training academy for musicians. Although some creative people involved in programme production such as performers, directors and technicians worked on a freelance or contract basis, the majority of staff were employed permanently and paid on a system of fixed, graded salary scales. A significant proportion of employees, especially in managerial grades, tended to be graduates from leading universities, particularly Oxford and Cambridge. Recruitment and promotion for many posts tended to be carried out following appraisal processes and procedures that were similar to those in the British civil service. It was (and still is) customary for the Director General to be knighted by the Queen and given the title 'Sir' in the New Year Honours list.

During the 1960s television became the dominant broadcasting medium as radio listening went into decline. In 1964 the BBC's radio division had also faced a further threat from a new breed of broadcaster, a number of offshore, unlicensed 'pirate' radio stations that had begun to transmit continuous pop music to a growing and increasingly affluent young audience. The BBC at this time had no pop music station. Pirate stations were illegal under British regulations but avoided legal action by operating from ships moored just outside UK territorial waters. After strong lobbying of the British government by the BBC, offshore broadcasting was outlawed under an Act of Parliament in 1966. In the same year, three years after the first pirate station went on the air, the BBC started its own pop station, Radio 1, and the other three radio networks were renamed Radios 2, 3 and 4. Shortly afterwards the first of a chain of around 20 BBC local radio stations around Britain was launched. This was both to fulfil a public service obligation to local community broadcasting and also in response to what was seen as a need for more locally rather than nationally based programming based on differing needs throughout the country. Legitimate independent commercial radio began in Britain in 1973.

The 1980s

The 1980s saw many further rapid changes in British broadcasting including further deregulation and the growth of new technologies such as satellite and cable television and the Internet, all resulting in ever-increasing competition for the BBC.

New rivals

Channel 4, a second terrestrial ITV channel, began broadcasting in November 1982 and in early 1983 the BBC's new breakfast time television show, the first in Britain, was closely followed by its new commercial rival, TV-am, a channel devoted solely to breakfast TV. In January 1984, Sky Television, the majority of which was owned by Rupert Murdoch's News International, a multinational media corporation, was launched as the first pay satellite television service in Britain. Sky offered several channels for a monthly fee to subscribers who also needed to buy a satellite dish and decoder box in order to receive its programmes.

In 1985 the government's Cable Authority began granting local franchises to operators to begin installing networks in British towns and cities and connecting up subscribers to cable. Until this time, cable television in Britain had been limited to about 14% of households, but over the next few years it spread rapidly throughout the country. This followed the example of the USA where, by 1984, 44% of all homes had been cabled. In the same year, Cable News Network (CNN), an American based, round the clock news channel, became available in Britain for the first time.

Over the next few years, many more satellite and cable channels were launched in the UK, as shown in Exhibit 6.4, many of them carrying specialist types of programming such as feature films, music or sport. As had happened earlier in the USA, there was much industry talk about the fragmentation of audiences and speculation that perhaps this was the end of broadcasting and the beginning of the era of 'narrowcasting'.

There were also changes in the ITV network that had now become known as Channel 3. Over the years, several of the original franchisees had changed and while the regional structure remained intact, a relaxation in the regulation on takeovers within the industry had led to a number of mergers between some of the ITV companies, a process of consolidation that seemed likely to continue.

Government policy

In 1985, yet another government committee was formed under Professor Sir Alan Peacock as chairman to once again consider the future of broadcasting in Britain, and, in particular, alternative ways of financing the BBC. A series of opinion polls had shown that around two-thirds of the British public were actually in favour of funding the BBC through advertising rather than by paying the compulsory licence fee. The Peacock committee concluded that the BBC should not have to

Exhibit 6.4   Selected UK satellite and cable channels 1984–93

Start	Channel	Delivery	Programming
1984	Sky Channel (Sky One)	C/S	General entertainment
1984	Screensport	C/S	Sports
1984	The Children's Channel	C/S	Children's programmes
1984	Premiere*	C	Feature films
1985	Bravo	C/S	Feature films
1985	Home Video Channel	C	Feature films
1985	The Arts Channel	C	Ballet, drama, opera
1985	Lifestyle	C/S	Women's programming
1986	Indra Dhnush (AsiaVision)	C	Asian entertainment
1986	Vision	C	Religious programmes
1987	Super Channel	C/S	General entertainment
1987	MTV Europe	C/S	Music
1987	CNN International	C/S	News programmes
1987	Cable Jukebox	C	Pop music
1988	The Landscape Channel	C	Nature and music
1989	Japansat	C/S	Japanese language
1989	The Discovery Channel	C/S	Documentaries
1989	Eurosport	C/S	Sports
1989	Sky Movies	C/S	Feature films
1989	Sky News	C/S	News programmes
1990	The Movie Channel	C/S	Feature films
1990	Sky Sports	C/S	Sports
1991	Sportscast	C/S	Sports
1991	The Comedy Channel*	C/S	Comedy programmes
1992	The Adult Channel	C/S	Adult programmes
1992	The Parliamentary Channel	C/S	UK Parliament
1992	The Learning Channel	C/S	Educational service
1992	The European Family Christian Network	C/S	Religious programmes
1992	UK Gold	C/S	Repeat programmes
1992	TV Asia	C/S	Asian programmes
1993	UK Living	C/S	Women's programming
1993	The Family Channel	C/S	Family entertainment
1993	QVC – The Shopping Channel	C/S	Home shopping

* No longer operating.
Delivery: C (Cable only); C/S (Satellite-delivered to cable or direct to home).

carry advertising in the immediate future, but that there should be further moves to deregulate the broadcasting industry and that government broadcasting policy should seek to 'enlarge both the consumers' choice and programme makers' opportunities'.

Part of this policy was a requirement that, by 1990, the BBC and ITV companies should aim to commission around 25% of their original programming from outside contractors rather than produce it in-house. Although a small proportion of programme production had always been made by external, independent producers, this move hastened the growth of an independent television production industry in the UK making programming primarily for the BBC and commercial networks. Channel 4, the newest commercial channel, in fact had few production facilities of its own: instead it commissioned most of its original output from independent production companies or bought in programmes from the international market place, making it a model of what came to be called in the industry a 'publisher broadcaster'. Many of the newer cable and satellite channels, some of which had very low programming budgets compared to the traditional terrestrial broadcasters, also relied primarily on low-cost, bought-in material.

The BBC in the 1980s

By the late 1980s, there was a growing awareness among senior managers that the BBC would have to respond to the rapid changes that were happening in their industry. As if deregulation and the rapidly increasing competition from satellite and cable were not enough, there were also two other major threats that faced the Corporation towards the end of the 1980s. Firstly, for many decades it had enjoyed a steadily increasing revenue from licence fees as the number of households with television grew and also as viewers switched from black and white television to the higher priced licence for colour: by the end of the 1980s this growth had come to an end. Secondly, the BBC's Charter, which was periodically reviewed by the government, was due for renewal in 1996. With the explosion of television channels that had occurred, once again there was growing public and media debate about whether a publicly funded broadcaster was really necessary, throwing the future renewal of the Charter into doubt.

The BBC's Governors and top management realised that they would have to respond quickly to these challenges to justify the continuation of the licence fee to both the government and the public, and also to convince them that it was money well spent. In 1988, in conjunction with proposals put forward by consultants, a wide-ranging, five-year plan for restructuring and reorganising large parts of the BBC was formulated. Broadly its objectives were:

- to cut costs through reductions in overheads, staffing and disposal of unnecessary premises; and
- to reduce in-house production capacity and make greater use of outside services and suppliers.

In addition, another set of goals was developed as the basis on which it was hoped the Corporation could move into the 1990s and beyond. These were:

- to seek to maximise income from sources other than the licence fee;
- to investigate opportunities for commercial partnerships;
- to seek to compete in global markets.

Into the 1990s

In 1992 John Birt became Director General of the BBC, having been deputy since 1986. Birt had had a long career in British television, both in programme making and in management, and had formerly been Director of Programmes at London Weekend Television, the ITV weekend contractor for the London area.

A period of change: the introduction of 'Producer Choice'

Faced with the goals set out in the plan, Birt set about attempting the major task of restructuring large parts of the BBC, particularly the areas concerned with pro-gramme production. Over the next few years, working with external consultants, Birt and a team of senior managers began to spearhead moves to increase efficiency under a wide-ranging set of new initiatives that were branded under the label 'Producer Choice'.

The main thrust of Producer Choice was to create an internal market in pro-gramme making resources by separating the purchasing and supply of these resources within the BBC. This meant that the internal purchasing of in-house facilities used to make programmes such as studios, lighting, editing suites and so on, as well as personnel, would be now financially distinct from the cost of pro-viding them from within the organisation. A price would now be put on these facilities so that in-house users and purchasers, in this case BBC producers (who are responsible for the overall production and delivery of finished programmes), would have greater flexibility and a more accurate and accountable way of budg-eting and monitoring the production costs of their programmes. Previously, the costs of providing and using BBC internal production facilities had never been fully assessed or quantified: costing and pricing these facilities would now enable shows to be costed and budgeted more accurately. Producers could now also shop around. They could compare the price of the in-house facilities offered by 'BBC Resources', as the newly created division was to be called, with those offered by outside suppliers which they now had the discretion to use if they felt that these offered better value.

At the same time, BBC Resources were encouraged to market and sell their pro-gramme-making facilities to outside customers as well as internally within the BBC. Alongside this system of 'market testing', a wide range of other internal overhead and support services were set stringent efficiency targets that were based on com-parisons with the outside private sector.

The greater accountability offered by Producer Choice also enabled a 'slim-down' of other production and administrative areas where there appeared to be over-capacity. By 1996 the number of permanent jobs in BBC Resources was reduced from around 11,000 to around 6,800, with a reduction of several hundred other jobs in other general administrative and support functions. At the end of the same year, BBC Resources as a unit reported a trading surplus of £15 million while sup-plying 78% of the BBC's facilities requirement, and in the British production facili-ties market as a whole it was reportedly the biggest provider of television and radio facilities in the UK, having gained a 22% share of the total market.

Some radio and television production departments where there was thought to be overlap and duplication were also merged. This was particularly the case in one of the BBC's largest and most prestigious departments, news, which was respon-sible for producing the BBC's output of newscasts for all its television and radio channels. This was now merged with another department called Current Affairs which was more concerned with the production of lengthier feature programmes devoted to news analysis and issues of current interest. Television and radio news operations were also combined. Journalists, who had previously worked exclus-ively either in radio or television, were now expected to work in both media as required by production schedules. Technical staff were also required to work more flexibly and in some cases adopt a wider range of roles and skills, a process known as 'multi-skilling'. The trend to multi-skilling was to some extent facilitated by developments in technology, which meant that some of the hardware and equipment used in television and radio production was becoming easier and required less specialised training to use.

The productivity and efficiency gains achieved by these changes, as well as the sale and disposal of over 1 million square feet of surplus buildings and floorspace over the same period, were estimated at over £100 million with annual savings of more than £50 million expected in years to follow. At the same time, both the BBC and ITV were given permission by the government to sell off their transmitter networks, and in 1997 the BBC's transmission system was sold to Castle Transmission Services for £244 million, resulting in the transfer to Castle of about 500 BBC staff.

Not unnaturally, the wide-ranging changes and restructuring brought about by Producer Choice attracted criticism and reaction from some of the employees affected, as well as the in-house union that represented them within the BBC. However, although there were some relatively minor instances of resistance such as short strikes and 'go slows' in some areas, on the whole there was no large-scale industrial action.

There was a general move within BBC Resources towards employing production staff more on fixed term contracts or a freelance basis as needed by programme-making schedules, and away from full-time, permanent, salaried employment. Some full-time staff were offered, and chose to take, redundancy payments that were calculated on the basis of the number of years that they had been in employment. Many of these people were then re-employed by the BBC in similar roles on flexible, short-term contracts or as self-employed freelances, who could also work elsewhere in the industry.

Some of these employees however, particularly those who had been with the BBC for a large part of their working lives, disliked the change from a culture characterised by a stable employment and clearly defined roles to one where they might have to undertake varying tasks and where employment was less certain. They resented what they saw as the lessening of career security and the uncertainties presented by the new, more flexible structure, ways of working and employment practices. Many felt that the BBC was no longer the organisation it once was. There were reports that morale among some staff had fallen to an all-time low in the Corporation's history. In this new, more commercial climate, producers also claimed to be increasingly unsure about what their goals now were in making programmes: Were they supposed to be going all out to chase audiences and ratings, or were they to make shows that aimed for something higher, more in the public service BBC tradition?

The decision to merge the news and current affairs departments and combine radio and television news was also generally unpopular with many of the journalists employed there. There was widespread dissatisfaction and claims that these moves would undermine the quality of news output, supposedly one of the BBC's main strengths. Several journalists, some of whose names were familiar to British audiences, took the opportunity to express their views by publishing articles in other newspapers, and one well-known television newscaster, Martyn Lewis, left the BBC after many years there.

John Birt also came in for criticism of his management style. To most BBC staff, the Director General was traditionally a remote and lofty figure. Birt, however, reportedly exacerbated this by communicating to employees through circulars and reports in a style loaded with management jargon that was derisively dubbed 'Birtspeak'. Other critics, including producers and programme makers who felt that they had borne the brunt of the cost savings and efficiencies imposed by Producer Choice, also pointed to his apparent increasing fondness for using management and design consultancies and advertising agencies, as well as the growing cost and amount of executives' time being reportedly taken up with exercises such as ongoing strategy reviews and management 'awaydays'. The cost of management consultants to the BBC had now risen to around £8 million a year – money that could, they claimed, have been better spent on creating programming. It was pointed out that even after all the restructuring of the last few years, the BBC still employed around 23,000, although not all full time, and while there were now many less people involved in programme making, there had been a rapid growth in the number of managers in some areas, notably a department of around 300 corporate policy-makers. Even a former BBC chairman, Marmaduke (now Lord) Hussey, took the opportunity to make a speech in the House of Lords, the upper chamber of the British parliament, lambasting the present BBC for 'too much bureaucracy, over bloated policy units and too much time spent on expansion in management'.

There were also problems with the implementation of some Producer Choice initiatives which did not always go smoothly or achieve the intended result. Apart from employees' reluctance to change working practices and the difficulties in designing and putting into practice new processes and procedures, it was found that anomalies sometimes occurred in trying to make the internal market actually work. Transactions and trading between various BBC departments, for example, could become inordinately time consuming, complex and bureaucratic, causing frustration and increased costs. There was also the issue of whether it was really appropriate to compare and benchmark efficiency and performance measures derived from an examination of private sector industry firms with the internal departments of a large organisation like the BBC.

The BBC's Charter was renewed in 1996 for a further ten years, but as well as seeking cost savings and efficiencies, Birt's new strategy also encompassed plans to try to ensure the longer term future of the Corporation. Among these was the formation in 1994 of a new commercial and international division, BBC Worldwide, to replace BBC Enterprises. Worldwide's prime, stated purpose was not only to ensure that licence payers benefited fully from the BBC's assets, but also to engage in commercial activities generating sustainable, increasing cash flow which could be passed back to the BBC. An important consideration was that Worldwide was to be financed and managed quite separately from licence fee-funded activities in order not to breach the terms of the BBC's public service Charter.

The top organisational structure of the BBC in 1994 can be seen in Exhibit 6.5.

The dawn of digital

The 1990s also saw the beginnings of the digital revolution in television. As well as holding out the promise of better quality pictures and sound, digital technology meant that many more TV channels – potentially up to several hundred – could now be sent either by terrestrial signals or by cable or satellite to those who had digitally equipped sets.

In the BBC's 1997 Annual Report, John Birt wrote:

> The entire broadcasting industry is experiencing massive changes and so far we have seen only the tip of the iceberg. Digital technology will allow choice and encourage

Exhibit 6.5   BBC top organisational structure 1994

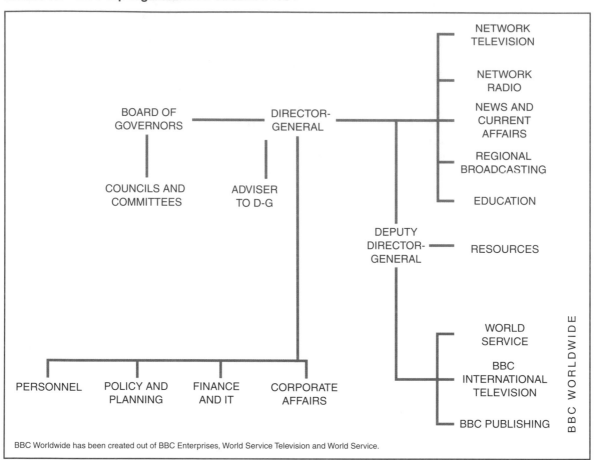

BBC Worldwide has been created out of BBC Enterprises, World Service Television and World Service.

competition on an unprecedented scale. Broadcasting will become more disparate and more global, and certainly more commercial. The BBC cannot live in isolation from those changes. We have repeatedly said that we must adapt or die. We intend to take a leading role in exploiting the new technology, pioneering new services in the future as we have done in the past.

As well as an explosion of new channels, digital and cable also offered the possibility of delivering a whole host of other telecommunication, information and interactive services into the home. Another major trend was the convergence of digital, Internet and telecom technologies which offered a multitude of new 'infotainment' possibilities. Not so long before, the Internet had been seen by some broadcasters as a threat – an alternative source of home information and entertainment, particularly with the young and computer literate. The potential outcomes of these technologies coming together, such as the development of Internet television, brought about the possibility of partnerships with other operators in these rapidly evolving industries.

Between 1992 and 1998, the BBC's annual audience share in the UK dropped from 32% to 29.5%, the first time it had fallen below what was considered to be the psychologically significant figure of 30% (see Exhibit 6.6). Over the same

Exhibit 6.6   Independent Television commission survey 1998: channel viewing

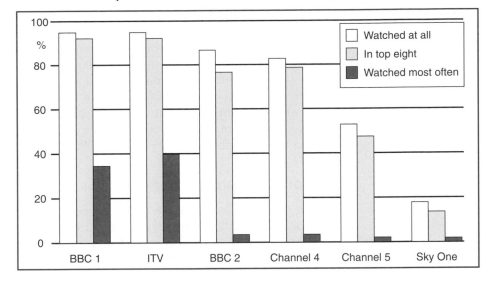

period ITV's share fell from 42% to 32%. This followed the pattern in the USA where the major terrestrial networks now had less than 50% of the audience following the growth of satellite and cable.

New products and services

In the late 1990s, the BBC launched a plethora of new services. As well as the existing BBC1 and 2 channels, several new licence fee-funded channels were launched on digital terrestrial, cable and satellite platforms free to licence payers: 'News 24', a round-the-clock, rolling news channel; 'BBC Choice', a selection of the best shows from the two existing networks; and 'BBC Inform', an information and data service. At the same time, BBC Worldwide launched several new commercial pay channels and entered into various partnerships and international distribution deals. Among these were:

- 'BBC World', a wholly owned round-the-clock news and information channel;
- 'BBC Prime', a wholly owned channel featuring the 'best of the BBC';
- a joint venture with Flextech plc, a British-based pay TV operator, to begin three new subscription channels in Britain – 'UK Horizons' (factual programming), Arena (arts) and 'UK Style' (living and leisure);
- a partnership with the Discovery Channel in the USA, which specialises in nature and wildlife programming, to co-produce and distribute programmes and also start three new pay channels in America – BBC America, Animal Planet and People and Arts – on satellite and cable;
- BBC Online, the BBC's website and on-line news service, including 140,000 pages of information and over 50,000 news stories;
- the publication of a growing number of new magazines and CD-ROM titles based on BBC shows, as well as 120 book titles, 151 video titles and 126 audio titles;

- a 20% stake in UK TV Australia, a pay TV channel joint venture with Pearson plc, a British media group, and Fox Television of the USA.

By 1998, the BBC World channel was available on cable or satellite in 187 countries and claimed 52 million subscribers worldwide, while BBC Online claimed to be the UK's most visited site on the Internet. Other new channels and on-line services were also planned for the future. In 1998 BBC Worldwide's total sales had grown to £409 million with profits before tax of £12 million.

Details of BBC Worldwide's joint ventures, sales history, cash flow to the BBC, and financial statements for 1998–99 can be seen in Exhibits 6.7 to 6.12. The profiles of the Worldwide board members in 1998–99 are given in Exhibit 6.14.

BBC Worldwide and its brands

At the beginning of 1999, the new chief executive of BBC Worldwide, Rupert Gavin, who had recently been recruited from the Internet and multimedia division of British Telecom, announced his aggressive new commercial strategy for BBC Worldwide. The strategy was to be that Worldwide would be first and foremost driven by the creation of programme brands for the global TV market, which could then be exploited and fed through a 'brand pipeline' to channels and other media formats around the world. This development and international commercialisation

Exhibit 6.7 BBC Worldwide joint ventures 1998–99

Name of entity	Nature of entity	Partner	Date entered
UK Channel Management Limited	Joint Venture	Flextech	April 1997
UK Gold Holdings Limited	Joint Venture	Flextech	April 1997
Animal Planet (Latin America) LLC	Associate	Discovery	March 1998
People and Arts (Latin America) LLC	Associate	Discovery	March 1998
Animal Planet LLC	Associate	Discovery	March 1998
JV Programmes LLC	Joint Venture	Discovery	March 1998
JV Network LLC	Associate	Discovery	March 1998

	UK Channel Management Ltd (£m)	UK Gold Holdings Ltd (£m)	Animal Planet (Latin America) LLC (£m)	People and Arts (Latin America) LLC (£m)	Animal Planet LLC (£m)
Turnover	3.9	21.4	0.4	2.5	5.8
Loss before tax	(16.2)	(0.3)	(3.6)	(4.1)	(6.6)
Taxation	–	0.1	(0.1)	(0.4)	–
Loss after tax*	(16.2)	(0.2)	(3.7)	(4.5)	(6.6)
Fixed assets	–	–	1.0	4.4	26.0
Current assets	5.4	15.5	1.2	1.1	5.1
Non-current assets	1.1	1.4	–	–	–
Liabilities less than one year*	(8.0)	(10.5)	(0.3)	(0.2)	(4.5)
Liabilities more than one year*	(10.6)	(67.0)	(7.0)	(11.6)	(40.0)

* BBC Worldwide has no obligation to fund losses or liabilities of these entities and has not consolidated its share of losses or liabilities into the annual financial statements.
Source: BBC Worldwide Report and Accounts 1998–99.

Exhibit 6.8 BBC Worldwide sales history, excluding joint ventures 1993–94 to 1998–99

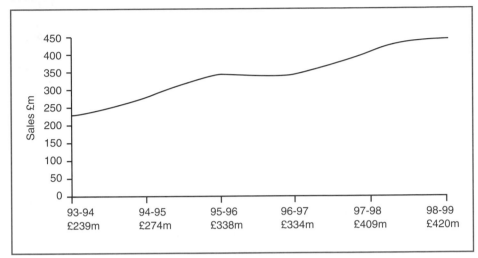

Source: BBC Worldwide Report and Accounts 1998–99.

Exhibit 6.9   BBC Worldwide cash flow to the BBC

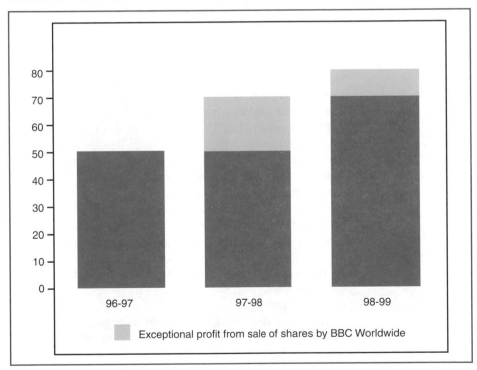

Source: BBC Report and Accounts 1998–99.

Exhibit 6.10   BBC Worldwide consolidated profit and loss account 1998–99

For the year ended 31 March	1999 £m	1998 £m
Turnover (including share of joint ventures)	446.3	422.0
Less: Share of joint ventures	(26.0)	(13.1)
Group turnover	420.3	408.9
Cost of sales	(264.6)	(274.8)
Gross profit	155.7	134.1
Distribution costs	(109.4)	(106.3)
Administrative expenses	(34.9)	(35.6)
Group operating profit/loss	11.4	(7.8)
Share of operating profit in joint ventures	–	–
Share of operating profit in associates	0.6	0.6
Total operating profit/loss	12.0	(7.2)
Profit on sale of investments	8.4	20.7
Profit before interest and taxation	20.4	13.5
Interest receivable	0.8	0.5
Interest payable	(1.3)	(2.2)
Profit on ordinary activities before taxation	19.9	11.8
Tax on profit on ordinary activities	(7.8)	(8.5)
Profit on ordinary activities after taxation	12.1	3.3
Equity minority interests	(0.1)	(0.1)
Retained profit for the financial year	12.0	3.2

The above results are derived from continuing operations.
Source: BBC Worldwide Report and Accounts 1998–99.

of branded entertainment products followed an approach long followed by major Hollywood studios such as Disney. At this time, one of the BBC's most successful programmes was Teletubbies, a morning show for pre-school children, featuring four lovable, cuddly toy characters, which had been a great hit in the UK. Another BBC success story was TV cook Delia Smith who was enormously popular and had a very large following in Britain. Both Teletubbies and Delia Smith had generated very large sales of spin-offs such as books and other licensed merchandise. Gavin described Worldwide's 'battle plan' as 'to take all the brands, whether it is Delia, Teletubbies . . . or new brands in the pipeline, and apply the same process: build the brand, get it on TV, exploit it internationally and make it happen over a wide range of formats'. Both Delia Smith's show and Teletubbies were made by independent production companies – Teletubbies was the creation of independent producers Ragdoll Productions who had an interest in the ultimate copyright and licensing rights to the Teletubby characters. The Teletubbies had also been a hit in the USA where revenue from merchandising in the first year alone reportedly amounted to over $800 million.

In the rapidly changing and internationalising television and media industry (see Exhibit 6.13), John Birt was of the opinion that one of the BBC's main assets was the BBC brand itself, which was considered to be well known and highly regarded throughout the world. He had been quoted as saying:

> The best values of the BBC lie in a dedication to programme quality. . . . The BBC will concentrate on the kind of broadcasting most at risk in a commercial market place –

Exhibit 6.11   BBC Worldwide consolidated balance sheet 1998–99

As at 31 March	1999 £m	1998 £m
Fixed assets:		
Tangible fixed assets	9.6	8.4
Investment in programmes for future sale	95.2	85.3
Investments		
Investments in joint ventures	27.8	215
Share of gross assets	(96.3)	(77.1)
Share of gross liabilities	68.5	55.6
Adjustment to reflect effective obligation	0.0	0.0
Interests in associated undertakings	0.2	0.1
	105.0	93.8
Current assets:		
Stocks	13.7	13.2
Debtors	116.1	119.6
Cash at bank and in hand	21.1	13.0
	150.9	145.8
Creditors: amounts falling due within one year	(167.9)	(166.5)
Net current liabilities	(17.0)	(20.7)
Total assets less current liabilities	88.0	73.1
Creditors: amounts falling due after more than one year	(16.9)	(16.9)
Provisions for liabilities and charges	(1.5)	—
Net assets	69.6	56.2
Capital and reserves:		
Called up share capital	0.2	0.2
Profit and loss account	69.1	55.8
Equity shareholders' funds	69.3	56.0
Equity minority interests	0.3	0.2
	69.6	56.2

Source: BBC Worldwide Report and Accounts 1998–99

Exhibit 6.12   BBC Worldwide: Turnover and profit analysed by type of business 1998–99

Turnover analysed by type of business

	1999 (£m)	1998 (£m)
Programme distribution	134.5	126.0
Channels	31.2	26.3
Group turnover	420.3	408.9
Share of joint ventures	26.0	13.1
Turnover	446.3	422.0

Profit before interest and taxation analysed by type of business

	Operating result 1999 (£m)	Sale of investments 1999 (£m)	Total 1999 (£m)
Publishing and new media	15.2		15.2
Programme distribution	13.2	8.4	21.6
Channels	(16.4)		(16.4)
Profit	12.0	8.4	20.4

Source: BBC Worldwide Report and Accounts 1998–99.

Exhibit 6.13 ITV Network companies ownership, March 1999

Owner	Company	Area of UK covered
Granada Group	Granada TV	North West England
	Yorkshire TV	Yorkshire
	Tyne Tees TV	North East England
	GMTV (share)	UK Breakfast time
Carlton Communications	Carlton TV	London (weekdays)
	Central TV	East and West Midlands
	West Country TV	South West England
	GMTV (share)	UK Breakfast time
United News and Media	Anglia TV	East of England
	Meridian TV	Southern England
	HTV	Wales and West of England
Scottish Media Group	Scottish TV	Central Scotland
	Grampian TV	Northern Scotland
	GMTV (share)	UK Breakfast time
Ulster	Ulster TV	Northern Ireland
Border and Cumbrian Newspaper Group	Border TV	Scottish Borders

Exhibit 6.14 BBC Worldwide board member profiles 1998

Peter Teague, BBC Worldwide's Director of Finance and Information Technology, is Acting Chief Executive of BBC Worldwide until Rupert Gavin takes up the post of Chief Executive on 1 July 1998. At that point Peter becomes Managing Director of the UK Region and Deputy Chief Executive. Peter, a qualified chartered accountant, joined BBC Worldwide in January 1997 from AT&T Unisource Communications Services. He began his career in 1976 at Peat Marwick Mitchell as an Audit Senior. After spending the majority of his post-qualification career in venture capital and corporate finance advisory roles, he joined ISTEL in 1987 as Director, Finance.

Mike Phillips is Director of the Rights Agency, which provides a link between BBC Worldwide and BBC programme makers in the exploitation of commercial rights and handles all BBC co-productions. Mike joined BBC Worldwide Television as Deputy Managing Director in June 1996 from his post as Managing Director of Thames Television. He was also a director of the Thames parent company, Pearson Television.

Peter Phippen is BBC Worldwide's Managing Director, UK Region, with responsibility for magazine, book, video and spoken word publishing, and BBC Worldwide's television joint venture with Flextech. He joined IPC Magazines in 1982 as a graduate trainee, leaving five years later to join BBC Magazines as Marketing Director. From 1 July Peter became President and Chief Executive Officer of BBC Worldwide Americas Inc., to drive forward our business throughout the Americas.

Mark Young is the Managing Director for BBC Worldwide's activities in Europe, the Middle East, Africa and India. He was appointed Finance and Commercial Director in June 1994 and was Managing Director of BBC World until November 19967. Mark joined the BBC in 1993 as Chief Assistant to the Deputy Director-General. Prior to that, he was Head of Business Affairs at Independent Television News. He previously spent five years with the publishers, William Coffins.

Sam Younger took up his post as Managing Director, BBC World Service, in November 1994. He is responsible for BBC World Service's international radio broadcasts in 44 languages, listened to by 140 million people each week. Sam was Assistant Editor of Middle East International before joining BBC External Services, as a talks writer in 1979. His career with BBC World Service has included time as Director of Broadcasting, Controller Overseas Services, Head of the Arabic Service and Head of Current Affairs, World Service in English. Sam has been a director of BBC Worldwide since December 1995.

Carolyn Fairbairn is BBC Worldwide's Director of Strategy, devising strategies to maximise BBC Worldwide's commercial opportunities both in the UK market and in key territories around the world. Previously, Carolyn was a member of the Downing Street Policy Unit, with responsibility for policy development in health and social services. Prior to this she spent seven years working as a management consultant with McKinsey and Company, with a particular focus on the information technology and broadcasting sectors.

Jeff Taylor is BBC Worldwide's Director of Global Brand Development, the division which develops and markets properties with multiple media global potential. Jeff joined BBC Worldwide in February 1996 as Director of Consumer Publishing. He joined from Sony where he was European Marketing Manager for Consumer Video, responsible for Western and Eastern Europe.

Jeremy Mayhew is BBC Worldwide's Director of New Media. Jeremy joined BBC Worldwide in 1995 as Director of Strategy and New Media Development. Jeremy joined from the BBC where he was Head of Strategy Development, Corporate Strategy, advising the Director-General and Board of Management on major policy and managerial issues. Previously, he was Special Adviser at the Departments of Trade and Industry and Social Security and was a consultant in the communications practice of Booz Allen & Hamilton. Jeremy has also worked as a producer on current affairs and documentary television programmes.

Source: BBC Worldwide Report and Accounts 1998–99.

original entertainment, intelligent news and current affairs, a comprehensive service of education and the full reflection of our national culture. These are the BBC's historic broadcasting strengths, by which our audiences judge us, and where we believe we lead the field.

Conclusion

There were those who were not so sure about the Corporation's future. Both media commentators and politicians once again raised the issue of the conflict that seemed to be growing between public accountability to licence payers and commercialism, while the BBC pursued what seemed to be an increasingly aggressive commercial strategy through its Worldwide arm. Critics rounded on the fact that the new digital 'News 24' channel, which had cost £30 million of licence fee payer's money to set up, was as yet only available to the very few who had digital TV, and at the end of 1998 was attracting a small audience of only 120,000. As for the digital revolution, while some analysts were predicting that by the year 2003 around 45% of British households would be equipped for digital TV, the signs were that its mainstream launch in early 1999 had been met with what seemed to be a general apathy by the British public. Writing in *The Guardian* in February 1999 under the headline, 'Dawning of the Digital Age is One Big Yawn to the British Viewer', one journalist reported the findings of a market survey which suggested that many consumers were confused by all the new media choices on offer and, although generally open to the idea of pay television, thought that digital TV had in fact little new to offer.

There were also accusations that, in a more competitive television environment, there had been some 'dumbing down' of programmes and in particular that the BBC1 channel had gone down-market in an attempt to chase ratings. There were also those who feared that in becoming more commercial and international, the BBC was in danger of losing its public service ethic and purpose. Former prominent British film producer David (now Lord) Puttnam, who was also chairman of the National Endowment for Science, Technology and the Arts, had been quoted as saying,

> ... No public service broadcaster can hope to be involved in every single aspect of the digital economy. (The BBC) must play to its strengths, its specific and very well honed strengths. In an increasingly expensive and fragmented broadcasting environment, the BBC, well led and well motivated, has to re-establish the argument for the universal licence fee as one of the most equitable and truly sustainable forms of social justice of the modern era.
>
> Its core role, its mission, needs to be defined as tightly as possible. To use a metaphor I've become increasingly fond of, the BBC needs to be more of a 'keep' than a 'castle', a possibly smaller organisation, but one with higher walls, guarding a unique national treasure house of innovative talent, critical standards and most important of all, truth.
>
> ... Creativity drives everything that's good about the BBC. At its best, it's the lifeblood of the Corporation. ... In my experience, creativity becomes stifled as soon as you attempt to over-manage it, if you constrain it too tightly within structures against which it will constantly, and for the most part unproductively, chafe.
>
> ... Public service broadcasting was born out of passion, and a commitment to an ideal of 'quality' in the first half of this century – I believe that only similar passion will sustain it in the increasingly hostile environment of the next century.

On the other hand, there were others who questioned why it should be assumed that the BBC was the sole bastion of quality broadcasting in Britain and who argued that, as in other forms of media, there was no reason why quality could not just as well be delivered by the commercial sector as by a public service broadcaster whose compulsory licence fee was now an anachronism. Writing in the national press, politician Gerald Kaufman, chairman of the government's Culture, Media and Sports Select Committee, expressed his view that:

> ... As a smaller and smaller proportion of households watch BBC television, the outcry against the licence fee will grow angrier ... an organisation whose existence depends upon a regressive 'poll tax' is in the long run, unviable. ... The Chancellor should do the decent thing. He should privatise the BBC, use the income from its sale to finance tax cuts to the present licence payers (a double vote winner) and force this increasingly weird anomaly to enter the real world of competitive broadcasting.

Even among some of the most ardent supporters of public service broadcasting, there were doubts as to whether the BBC, positioning itself as a 'quality' broadcaster with a distinctive British heritage, could compete globally in an increasingly competitive environment against some of the world's biggest diversified media companies such as Time Warner, Disney and Viacom, all of whom were aggressively pursuing the new opportunities presented by the changing world of digital communications and entertainment. In a rapidly shifting and evolving industry, developments in early 1999 had included the purchase by Microsoft for $500 million of a 5% stake in NTL, the British cable operator and owner of the former ITV transmitter network, and the acquisition of Flextech by TCI, a $50 billion international cable giant headed by John Malone who had been described by US Vice President Al Gore as, 'the Darth Vader of the information age'.

Further denting the BBC's credibility at the end of the 1990s was its loss of the rights to broadcast two major British sporting events. It was outbid by Sky for the UK football Premier League, and by Channel 4 for the English Test Match cricket series which had traditionally been shown by the BBC for many years. Sky was also eagerly pursuing other major sports events and had made a bid to buy Manchester United, one of the UK's leading football clubs. It seemed increasingly likely that, in future, major sporting occasions would be appearing on pay channels like Sky, which were also beginning to charge viewers extra to watch these events on a 'pay per view' basis.

John Birt's tenure as Director General ended in the year 2000. With growing uncertainties hanging over the next renewal of the BBC's Charter by the government in 2006, it was announced in June 1999 that his successor would be Greg Dyke, an executive with a long career in British commercial television and with a reputedly strong commercial and populist instinct. Dyke was quoted as saying that he wished to maintain and develop the ethos of public service broadcasting by 're-igniting the great traditions of the BBC', while at the same time aggressively developing the profit-making potential of the Worldwide division by giving it greater autonomy and freedom to operate separately from licence fee-funded activities.

In the conclusion of his statement in the BBC's 1998 annual report John Birt wrote the following:

> The nature of broadcasting is changing rapidly. If the BBC is to continue to offer distinctive but genuinely popular service it must adapt. It is already doing so, but the challenges are immense, in terms of funding, technology and competition. . . .
>
> In the digital world of multi-channel choice, the need for the BBC will be greater, not less. Real choice means genuine programme diversity that guarantees something for everyone. That is what the BBC exists to deliver. We will sustain the services that audiences know and trust, but we will also launch new ones and so continue to extend choice. . . .
>
> In striving to bring the benefits of the new technologies to every home in the land, the BBC will remain true to its long-standing public service values and principles. The BBC in 1998 is a confident and dynamic institution. We are serving our audiences better than ever. We are alert to the world around us. We are ready to face the formidable challenges to come. We are, and intend to remain, one of the great cultural institutions in the world.

SOURCES

This case study has been compiled from the following sources:

BBC Report and Accounts: 1973–74, 1993–94, 1994–95, 1995–96, 1996–97, 1997–98 and 1998–99.
BBC Worldwide Report and Accounts: 1998–99.
Briggs, A. (1985) *The BBC: the First Fifty Years*. Oxford University Press.
Financial Times, London: 11 February 1999 and 21 April 1999.

Head, S. (1986) *World Broadcasting Systems – A Comparative Analysis*.
Macdonald, B. (1994) *Broadcasting in the UK*. Mansell.
Rosen, P. (ed.) (1988) *International Handbook of Broadcasting Systems*. Greenwood.
The Sunday Times, London: 13 June 1999.
The Guardian, London: 26 January 1999, 17 February 1999, 19 February 1999, 4 March 1999, 24 March 1999 and 25 June 1999.

References

Albert, M. (1993) *Capitalism against Capitalism.* Whurr, London.

Amburgey, T.L., Kelly, D. and Barnett, W.P. (1993) Resetting the clock: the dynamics of organisational change and failure. *Administrative Science Quarterly,* 38: 58–73.

Amit, R. and Schoemaker, P.J.H. (1993) Strategic assets and organizational rent. *Strategic Management Journal,* 14: 33–46.

Andersen, D.F., Belardo, S. and Dawes, S.S. (1994) Strategic information management: Conceptual frameworks for the public sector. *Public Productivity and Management Review,* 17 (4): 335–353.

Andrews, K.R. (1971) *The Concept of Corporate Strategy.* Dow Jones Irwin, Homewood, IL.

Ansoff, H.I. (1965) *Corporate Strategy.* McGraw-Hill, New York.

Ansoff, H.I. (1991) Critique of Henry Mintzberg's 'The Design School'. *Strategic Management Journal,* 12: 449–461.

Argyris, C. and Schön, D.A. (1978) *Organizational Learning: A Theory of Action Perspective.* Addison Wesley, Reading, MA.

Argyris, C. and Schön, D.A. (1996) *Organizational Learning II: Theory, Method and Practice.* Addison Wesley, Reading, MA.

Armenakis, A. and Fredenberger, W. (1995) Process strategies for turnaround change agents: Crisis and non-crisis situations. *Journal of Strategic Change,* 4 (1): 19–31.

Armenakis, A., Fredenberger, W., Cherones, L. and Feild, H. (1995) Symbolic actions used by business turnaround change agents. *Academy of Management Journal,* Special Edition (Best Papers Proceedings, p. 229).

Armenakis, A., Fredenberger, W., Giles, W. and Cherones, L. (1996) Symbolism use by business turnaround change agents. *International Journal of Organizational Analysis,* 4 (2): 123–134.

Armstrong, M. (1992) A charitable approach to personnel. *Personnel Management,* 24 (12): 28ff.

Arthur, W.B. (1996) Increasing returns and the new world of business. *Harvard Business Review,* July–August: 101–109.

Ashforth, B. (1994) Petty tyranny in organizations. *Human Relations,* 47 (7): 755–778.

Ashforth, B.A. and Lee, R.T. (1990) Defensive behaviour in organisations: A preliminary model. *Human Relations,* 43 (7): 621–648.

Ashforth, B.E. and Mael, F. (1996) Organizational identity and strategy as a context for the individual. In J. Baum and J. Dutton (eds) *Advances in Strategic Management,* vol. 13 (pp. 17–72). JAI Press, Greenwich, CT.

Baden-Fuller, C. (1989) Exit from declining industries and the case of steel castings. *Economic Journal,* 99: 949–961.

Baden-Fuller, C. and Stopford, J.M. (1992) *Rejuvenating the Mature Business: The Competitive Challenge.* Harvard Business School Press, Cambridge, Mass.

Bailey, A. and Johnson, G. (1995) *The processes of strategy development* Cranfield University School of Management Working Paper.

Bailey, A. and Johnson, G. (1996) *Logical or processual: defining incrementalism.* Paper presented to Academy of Management Conference, Cincinnati, August.

Bailey, A. and Johnson, G. (2000) A framework for a managerial understanding of strategy development. In Elfring, T. and Volberda, N.W. *New Directions in Strategy: Beyond Fragmentation.* Sage Publications (forthcoming).

Bailey, A., Johnson, G. and Daniels, K. (2000) Validation of a multi-dimensional measure of strategy development processes. *British Journal of Management* (forthcoming).

Balogun, J. and Hope-Hailey, V. (1999) *Exploring Strategic Change*. Prentice-Hall Europe, Hemel Hempstead.

Bark, C. and Baetz, M. (1998) The relationship between mission statements and firm performance: An exploratory study. *Journal of Management Studies*, 35 (6): 823–853.

Barker, V.L. and Duhaime, I.M. (1997) Strategic change in the turnaround process: Theory and empirical evidence. *Strategic Management Journal*, 18: 13–38.

Barker, V.L. and Mone, M.A. (1994) Retrenchment: Cause of turnaround or consequence of decline? *Strategic Management Journal*, 15 (5): 395–406.

Barney, J. (1986a) Strategic factor markets: Expectations, luck and business strategy. *Management Science*, 32 (10): 1231–4121.

Barney, J. (1986b) Organizational culture: Can it be a source of sustained competitive advantage? *Academy of Management Review*, 11 (3): 656–665.

Barney, J. (1991) Firm resources and sustained competitive advantage. *Journal of Management*, 17 (1): 99–120.

Barney, J. (1999) How a firm's capabilities affect boundary decisions. *Sloan Management Review*, Spring: 137–145.

Beauchamp, T.L. and Browe, N.E. (eds) (1983) *Ethical Theory and Business* (2nd edition). Prentice Hall, New Jersey.

Beer, M., Eisenstat, R.A. and Spector, B. (1990) Why change programs don't produce change. *Harvard Business Review*, November–December: 158–166.

Benjamin, R. and Wigand, R. (1995) Electronic markets and virtual value chains on the information superhighway. *Sloan Management Review*, Winter: 62–72.

Bernheim, B.D. and Whinston, M.D. (1990) Multi-market contact and collusive behaviour. *Rand Journal of Economics*, 1–26.

Bernstein, A. (1998) Oops, that's too much downsizing. *Business Week*, 8 June: 38.

Berry, F.S. (1994) Innovation in public management: The adoption of strategic planning. *Public Administration Review*, 54 (4): 322–330.

Berry, F.S. and Wechsler, B. (1995) State agencies' experience with strategic planning: Findings from a national survey. *Public Administration Review*, 55 (2): 159–168.

Berthon, P., Hulbert, J. and Pitt, L. (1999) Brand management prognostications. *Sloan Management Review*, Winter: 53–65.

Besanko, D., Dranove, D. and Shanley, M. (1996) *The Economics of Strategy*. Wiley, New York.

Bettis, R.A. and Hall, W.K. (1983) The business portfolio approach – where it falls down in practice. *Long Range Planning*, April: 95–104.

Bettis, R.A. and Mahajan, V. (1985) Risk/return performance of diversified firms. *Management Science*, 31: 785–799.

Bettis, R.A., Bradley, S.P. and Hamel, G. (1992) Outsourcing and industrial decline. *Academy of Management Executive*, 6 (1): 7–22.

Bhaskar, R. (1978) *A Realist Theory of Science*. Harvester Press, Brighton.

Bhaskar, R. (1989) *Reclaiming Reality*. Verso, London.

Bickers, C. (1998) Sharing the pain. *Far Eastern Economic Review*, 161 (40; October): 79–80.

Biggadike, R. (1979) The risky business of diversification. *Harvard Business Review*, May/June: 103–111.

Blair, H., Taylor, S.G. and Randle, K. (1998) A pernicious panacea: A critical evaluation of business re-engineering. *New Technology, Work and Employment*, 13 (2): 116–128.

Bleeke, J. and Ernst, D. (1991) The way to win in cross border alliances. *Harvard Business Review*, November–December: 69: 127–137.

Bleeke, J. and Ernst, D. (1995) Is your strategic alliance really a sale? *Harvard Business Review*, January–February: 97–108.

Bolwijn, P.T. and Kumpe, T. (1990) Manufacturing in the 1990s: Productivity, flexibility and innovation. *Long Range Planning*, 23 (4; August): 44–57.

Bourgeois, L.J., & Brodwin, D. (1984) Strategic implementation: Five approaches to an elusive phenomenon. *Strategic Management Journal*, 5: 241–264.

Bower, J.L. (1970) *Managing the Resource Allocation Process: A Study of Planning and Investment.* Harvard University Press, Cambridge, Mass.

Bower, J.L. and Doz, Y. (1979) Strategy formulation: A social and political process. In D.E. Schendel and C.W. Hofer (eds) *Strategic Management.* Little, Brown, Boston, Mass.

Boyd, B., Norburn, D. and Fox, M. (1997) Who wins in governance reform? Conventional Wisdom 1, Shareholders 0. In H. Thomas and D. O'Neal (eds) *Strategic Discovery: Competing in New Arenas.* Wiley, Chichester, pp. 237–259.

Brandenburger, A.M. and Nalebuff, B.J. (1995) The right game: Use game theory to shape strategy. *Harvard Business Review,* 28 (4): 353–374.

Brandenburger, A.M. and Nalebuff, B.J. (1997) *Co-opetition.* Harper–Collins, London.

Brews, P.J. and Hunt, M.R. (1999) Learning to plan and planning to learn: Resolving the planning school/learning school debate. *Strategic Management Journal,* 20 (10): 889–913.

Brown, E. (1999) 9 ways to win on the web. *Fortune,* 24 May: 48-61.

Brown, J.S. and Duguid, P. (1991) Organizational learning and communities of practice: Toward a unified view of working, learning and innovation. *Organization Science,* 2 (1): 40–57.

Brown, S. (1994) Retail location at the micro-scale: Inventory and prospects. *The Service Industries Journal,* 14 (4): 542–576.

Brown, S.L. and Eisenhardt, K.M. (1997) The art of continuous change: Linking complexity theory and time-paced evolution in relentlessly shifting organizations. *Administrative Science Quarterly,* 42 (1; March): 1–34.

Bryson, J.M. (ed.) (1995) *Strategic Planning for Public and Non-profit Organizations.* Jossey-Bass, San Francisco.

Buchanan, D.A. and Boddy, D. (1992) *The Expertise of the Change Agent: Public Performance and Backstage Activity.* Prentice Hall, Hemel Hempstead.

Buono, A.F. and Bowditch, J.L. (1989) *The Human Side of Mergers and Acquisitions: Managing Collisions between People, Cultures, and Organizations.* Jossey-Bass, San Francisco.

Buono, A.F., Bowditch, J.L. and Lewis, J.W. III (1985) When cultures collide: The anatomy of a merger. *Human Relations,* 38 (5): 477–500.

Burgelman, R.A. (1983) A process model of internal corporate venturing in the diversified major firm. *Administrative Science Quarterly,* 28 (2): 223–244.

Burgelman, R.A. (1984) Managing the internal corporate venturing process. *Sloan Management Review,* 25 (2; Winter): 33–48.

Burgelman, R.A. (1988) Strategy making as a social learning process. The case of internal corporate venturing. *Interfaces,* 18 (3): 74–85.

Burgelman, R.A. (1991) Intraorganizational ecology of strategy making and organizational adaptation: Theory and field research. *Organization Science,* 2: 239–262.

Burgelman, R.A. (1994) Fading memories: A process theory of strategic business exit in dynamic environments. *Administrative Science Quarterly,* 39 (1; March): 24–56.

Burgelman, R.A. (1996) A process model of strategic business exit: Implications for an evolutionary perspective on strategy. *Strategic Management Journal,* 17: 193–214.

Burgelman, R.A. and Grove, A.S. (1996) Strategic dissonance. *California Management Review,* 38 (2): 8–28.

Burgelman, R.A. and Sayles, L.R. (1986) *Inside Corporate Innovation: Strategy, Structure and Managerial Skills.* Free Press, New York.

Burnes, B. (1996) *Managing Change: A Strategic Approach to Organisational Dynamics.* Pitman, London.

Burnett, R. (1996) *Global Jukebox.* Routledge: New York.

Burns, J.M. (1978) *Leadership.* Harper & Row, New York.

Burns, T. (1977) *The BBC: Public Institution and Private World.* Macmillan, London.

Burns, T. and Stalker, G.M. (1961) *The Management of Innovation.* Tavistock, London.

Burton, J. (1995) Composite strategy: The combination of collaboration and competition. *Journal of General Management,* 21 (1): 1–23.

Calori, R., Lubatkin, M. and Very, P. (1994) Control mechanisms in cross-border acquisitions: An international comparison. *Organization Studies,* 15 (3): 361–379.

Camerer, C.F. (1991) Does strategy research need game theory? *Strategic Management Journal,* 12: 137–152.

Cameron, A. (1998) The elasticity of endurance: Work intensification and workplace flexibility in the Queensland public hospital system. *New Zealand Journal of Industrial Relations,* 23 (3): 133–151.

Campbell, A. and Nash, L. (1992) *A Sense of Mission.* Addison-Wesley, Reading, Mass.

Campbell, A. and Yueng, 5. (1991) Building a sense of mission. *Long Range Planning,* 24 (4): 10–20.

Cannella, A.A. Jr and Hambrick, D. (1993) Effects of executive departures on the performance of acquired firms. *Strategic Management Journal,* 14: 137–152.

Carnall, C. (1995) *Managing Change in Organisations.* Prentice Hall, Hemel Hempstead.

Carroll, G.R. (1994) Organizations: The smaller they get. *California Management Review,* 37 (1): 28–41.

Cartwright, S. and Cooper, C.L. (1993) The role of culture compatibility in successful organizational marriage. *Academy of Management Executive,* 7 (2): 57–70.

Cartwright, S. and Cooper, C.L. (1996) *Managing Mergers, Acquisitions and Strategic Alliances* (2nd edition), Butterworth Heinemann, Oxford.

Chaganti, R. and Sambharya, R. (1987) Strategic Orientation and Characteristics of Upper Management. *Strategic Management Journal,* 8 (4): 393–401

Chakravarthy, B. and Lorange, P. (1991) *Managing the Strategy Process: A Framework for a Multibusiness Firm.* Prentice Hall, New York

Champy, J. (1994) Reengineering reviewed. *Economist,* 2 July: 66.

Chandler, A.D. (1962) *Strategy and Structure.* MIT Press, Cambridge, Mass (2nd edition, 1969; 3rd edition, 1990).

Chandler, G.N. (1996) Business similarity as a moderator of the relationship between pre-ownership experience and venture performance. *Entrepreneurship Theory and Practice,* 20 (3): 51–65.

Chandler, G.N. and Hanks, S.H. (1994) Founder competence, the environment, and venture performance. *Entrepreneurship Theory and Practice,* 18 (3): 77–89.

Chandler, G.N. and Jansen, E. (1992) The founder's self-assessed competence and venture performance. *Journal of Business Venturing,* 7 (3): 223–236.

Chapman, P. (1999) Managerial control strategies in small firms. *International Small Business Journal,* 17 (2): 75–82.

Charan, R. and Colvin, G. (1999) Why CEOs fail. *Fortune,* 21 June: 31–37.

Chatterjee, S. and Blocher, J.D. (1992) Measurement of firm diversification: Is it robust? *Academy of Management Journal,* 35: 874–888.

Chatterjee, S. and Wernerfelt, B. (1991) The link between resources and type of diversification. *Strategic Management Journal,* 12 (1): 33–48.

Chatteriee, S., Lubatkin, M.H., Schweiger, D.M. and Weber, Y. (1992) Cultural differences and shareholder value in related mergers: Linking equity and human capital. *Strategic Management Journal,* 13 (5): 319–334.

Chesborough, H.W. and Socolof, S.J. (2000) Creating new ventures from Bell Labs technologies. *Research Technology Management,* March–April 43 (2): 13–17.

Chesborough, H.W. and Teece, D.J. (1996) When is virtual virtuous? Organizing for innovation. *Harvard Business Review,* January–February: 65–73.

Chiesa, V., Manzini, R. and Noci, G. (1999) Towards a sustainable view of the competitive system. *Long Range Planning,* 32 (5): 519–530.

Child, J. (1972) Organization structure, environment and performance: The role of strategic choice. *Sociology,* 6: 1–22.

Child, J. (1973) Organizational structure, environment and performance: The role of strategic choice. In G. Salaman and K. Thompson (eds) *People and Organizations.* Longman, London.

811

Child, J. (1974) Managerial and organisational factors associated with company performance. *Journal of Management Studies,* 11 (3; October): 175–189.

Child, J. (1997) Strategic choice in the analysis of action, structure, organizations and environment; retrospect and prospect. *Organization Studies,* 18 (1): 43–76.

Chiles, T.H. and McMackin, J.F. (1996) Integrating variable risk preferences, trust and transaction cost economics. *Academy of Management Review,* 21 (1): 73–99.

Churchill, N.C. and Lewis, V.L. (1983) The five stages of small business growth. *Harvard Business Review,* May/June: 30–39.

Clegg, S. and Dunkerley, D. (1980) *Organization, Class and Control.* Routledge, London.

Coble, R. (1999) The non-profit sector and state governments: Public policy issues facing non-profits in North Carolina and other states. *Non-profit Management and Leadership,* 9 (3): 293–313.

Cohen, M.D., March, J.G. and Olsen, J.P. (1972) A Garbage Can Model of Organizational Choice. *Administrative Science Quarterly,* 17:1–25.

Cohen, W.M. and Levinthal, D.A. (1990) Absorptive capacity: A new perspective on learning and innovation. *Administrative Science Quarterly,* 35 (1): 128–152.

Collins, J.C. and Porras, J.I. (1991) Organizational vision and visionary organizations. *California Management Review,* Fall: 30–41.

Collins, J.C. and Porras, J.I. (1995) Building a visionary company. *California Management Review,* 37 (2; Winter): 80–101.

Collins, J.C. and Porras, J.I. (1996) Building your company's vision. *Harvard Business Review,* September–October: 65–77.

Collis, D.J. and Montgomery, C.A. (1998) Creating corporate advantage. *Harvard Business Review,* May/June: 71–83.

Courpasson, D. (1990) Les nouvelles pratiques d'acces à l'emploi bancaire. *Annales des Mines,* June: 42–48.

Courtney, H., Kirkland, J. and Viguerie, P. (1997) Strategy under uncertainty. *Harvard Business Review,* November–December: 67–79.

Crawford, C.M. (1979) New product failure rates: Facts and fallacies. *Research Management,* September: 9–13.

Cronshaw, M., Davis, E. and Kay, J. (1994) On being stuck in the middle or good food costs less at Sainsbury's. *British Journal of Management,* 5 (1): 19–32.

Crosby, P. (1979) *Quality is Free.* McGraw-Hill, London.

Cyert, R.M. and March, J.G. (1963) *A Behavioural Theory of the Firm.* Blackwell, Oxford.

D'Aveni, R. (1994), *Hypercompetitive Rivalries,* Free Press, New York.

D'Aveni, R. (1995) *Hypercompetitive Rivalries.* Simon & Schuster.

Daft, R.L. (1995) *Organizational Theory and Design.* West Publishing Company, St. Paul.

Datta, D.K. (1991) Organizational fit and acquisition performance: Effects of post-acquisition integration. *Strategic Management Journal,* 12 (4): 281–297.

Davenport, T.H., De Long, D.W. and Beers, M.C. (1998) Successful knowledge management projects. *Sloan Management Review,* Winter: 43–57.

David, K. and Singh, H. (1993) Acquisition regimes: Managing cultural risk and relative deprivation. *Corporate Acquisitions: International Review of Strategic Management,* 4: 227–276.

David, K. and Singh, H. (1994) Sources of acquisition cultural risk. In G. Von Krogh, A. Sinatra and H. Singh (eds) *The Management of Corporate Acquisitions.* International Perspectives.

Day, G. (1994) The capabilities of market-driven organizations. *Journal of Marketing,* 58 (October): 37–52.

De Chernatony, L., and McDonald, M.H.B. (1998) *Creating Powerful Brands in Consumer, Service and Industrial Markets.* Butterworth Heinemann, Oxford.

Deal, T. and Kennedy, A. (1982) *Corporate Cultures: The Rites and Rituals of Corporate Life.* Addison-Wesley.

DeMaio, A., Verganti, R. and Corso, M. (1994) A multi-project framework for new product development. *European Journal of Operational Research,* 78: 178–191.

Deming, W.E. (1943) *Statistical Adjustment of Data.* John Wiley & Sons, New York (republished in 1964 by Dover Publications, New York).

Deming, W.E. (1986) *Out of the Crisis.* Massachusetts Institute of Technology Center for Advanced Engineering Study, Cambridge, MA.

Deming, W.E. (1993) *The New Economics for Industry, Government, Education.* Massachusetts Institute of Technology Center for Advanced Engineering Study, Cambridge, MA.

Dess, G.G, Gupta, A., Hennart, J. and Hill, C.W.L (1995) Conducting and integrating strategy research at the international, corporate, and business levels: Issues and directions. *Journal of Management,* 21: 357–393.

Dierickx, l. and Cool, K. (1989) Asset stock accumulation and sustainability of competitive advantage. *Management Science,* 35 (12): 1504–1513.

DiMaggio, P.J. and Powell, W.W. (1983) The iron cage revisited: Institutional isomorphism and collective rationality in organizational fields. *American Sociological Review,* 48 (April): 147–160.

Dolan, K.A. (1998) Like father, like sons. *Forbes,* 162 (6): 136–140.

Donaldson, L. (1995) *American anti-management theories of organization.* Cambridge University Press, Cambridge

Douglas, S. and Wind, Y. (1987) The myth of globalisation. *Columbia Journal of World Business,* Winter: 19–29.

Doyle, P. (1998) *Marketing Management and Strategy* (2nd edition). Prentice-Hall Europe, London.

Doz, Y.L. and Hamel, G. (1997) The use of alliances in implementing technology strategies. In M. Tushman and P. Anderson (eds) *Managing Strategic Innovation and Change.* Oxford University Press, New York.

Doz, Y.L. and Hamel, G. (1998) *Alliance Advantage: The Art of Creating Value through Partnering.* Harvard Business School Press, Cambridge.

Drazin, R. and Schoonhoven, C.B. (1996) Community, population, and organization effects on innovation: A multilevel perspective. *Academy of Management Journal,* 39: 1065–1083.

Drazin, R., Glynn, M.A. and Kazanjian, R.K. (1999) Multilevel theorizing about creativity in organizations: A sensemaking perspective. *Academy of Management Review,* 24 (2): 286–307.

Drennan, D. (1992) *Transforming Company Culture.* McGraw-Hill, London.

Drucker, P. (1970) Entrepreneurship in business enterprise. *Journal of Business Policy,* 1 (1): 3–12.

Drucker, P. (1973) *Management: Tasks, Responsibilities and Practices.* Harper and Row, New York.

Drucker, P. (1985) *Innovation and Entrepreneurship.* Heinemann, London.

Drucker, P. (1994) The theory of the business. *Harvard Business Review,* September–October.

Drucker, P. (1995) *Managing the Non-profit Organization.* Butterworth-Heinemann, Oxford.

Edeleman, D.C. (1998) *Patterns of Deconstruction: The Orchestrator.* Boston Consulting Group Inc.

Edvinsson, L. (1997) Developing intellectual capital at Skandia. *Long Range Planning,* 30 (3): 366–373.

Edvinsson, L. and Malone, M.S. (1997) *Intellectual Capital.* HarperBusiness, New York.

Eisenhardt, K.M. (1989) Agency theory: An assessment and review. *Academy of Management Review,* 14 (1): 57–74.

Eisenhardt, K.M. and Brown, S.L. (1998) Time pacing: Competing in markets that won't stand still. *Harvard Business Review,* March–April: 59–69.

Evans, P. and Wurster, T.S. (1999) Getting real about virtual commerce. *Harvard Business Review,* November–December: 84–94.

Farkas, C.M. and Wetlaufer, S. (1996) The ways chief executive officers lead. *Harvard Business Review,* May–June: 110–122.

Farmer, S.M. and Fedor, D.B. (1999) Volunteer participation and withdrawal: A psychological contract perspective on the role of expectations and organizational support. *Non-profit Management and Leadership,* 9 (4): 349–367.

Faulkner, D. and Bowman, C. (1995) *The Essence of Competitive Strategy.* Prentice Hall, Hemel Hempstead.

Feigenbaum, A.V. (1983) *Total Quality Control* (3rd edition). McGraw-Hill, New York.

Feldman, S.P. (1986) Management in context: An essay on the relevance of culture to the understanding of organizational change. *Journal of Management Studies,* 23 (6): 587–607.

Fenwick, G.D. and Strombom, M. (1998) The determinants of franchisee performance: An empirical investigation. *International Small Business Journal,* 16 (4): 28–45.

Fineman, S. (ed.) (1993) *Emotions in Organizations.* Sage, London.

Fink, M. (1996) *Inside The Music Industry* (2nd edition). Simon & Schuster/Macmillan, New York.

Fiol, C.M. (1991) Managing culture as a competitive resource: An identity-based view of sustainable competitive advantage. *Journal of Management,* 17 (1): 191–211.

Flaviàn, C., Haberberg, A. and Polo, Y. (1999) Subtle strategic insights from strategic groups analysis. *Journal of Strategic Marketing,* June: 89–106.

Flint, J. (1999) A letter to Jurgen Schrempp. *Forbes,* 31 May: 168.

Ford, C.M. and Giola, D.A. (1995) *Creativity in Organizations: Ivory Tower Visions and Real World Voices.* Sage, Newbury Park, CA.

Foucault, M. (1980) *Power/knowledge: selected interviews and other writings 1972–1977.* Harvester Press, Brighton.

French, J.R.P. and Raven, B.H. (1959) The bases of social power. In D. Cartwright (ed.) *Studies in Social Power.* University of Michigan Press, Michigan.

Gabarro, J. (1987) *The Dynamics of Taking Charge.* Harvard Business School Press, Boston, Mass.

Gadenne, D. (1998) Critical success factors for small business: An inter-industry comparison. *International Small Business Journal,* 17 (1): 36–56.

Galbraith, J.R. (1998) Linking customers and products. In S.A. Mohrman, J.R. Galbraith, E.E. Lawler III and Associates (eds) *Tomorrow's Organization.* Jossey-Bass, San Francisco.

Gambardella, A. and Torrisi, S. (1998) Does technological convergence imply convergence in markets? Evidence from the electronics industry. *Research Policy,* 27 (5): 445–463.

Gammond, P. and Horricks, R. (1980) *The Music Goes Round and Round.* Quartet Books, London.

Garud, R. and Van de Ven, A.H. (1992) An empirical evaluation of the internal corporate venturing process. *Strategic Management Journal,* 13: 93–109.

Garvin, D.A. (1993) Building a learning organization. *Harvard Business Review,* July–August: 78–91.

Garvin, D.A. (1995) Leveraging processes for strategic advantage. *Harvard Business Review,* September–October: 77–90.

Geringer, M.J., Beamish, B.W. and daCosta, R.C. (1989) Diversification strategy and internationalization: Implications for MNE performance. *Strategic Management Journal,* 10: 109–119.

Ghemawat, P. (1991) *Commitment: the Dynamic of Strategy.* Free Press, New York.

Ghoshal, S. and Bartlett, C.A. (1987) Managing across borders: new organizational responses. *Sloan Management Review,* Fall: 43–53.

Ghoshal, S. and Bartiett, C.A. (1998) *The Individualized Corporation.* Heinemann, London.

Giddens, A. (1979) *Central Problems In Social Theory.* Macmillan, Basingstoke.

Giddens, A. (1984) *The Constitution of Society; Outline of the Theory of Structuration.* Polity Press, Cambridge.

Giddens, A. (ed.) (1974) *Positivism and Sociology.* Heinemann, London.

Giersch, H., Paque, K-H. and Schmiedling, H. (1991) *The Fading Miracle.* Cambridge University Press, Cambridge.

Glover, T. (2000) IBM report reveals integration nightmare. *CeBITVIEWS,* 24 February–1 March: 60–64.

Goleman, D. (1996) *Emotional Intelligence.* Bloomsbury, London.

Goffee, R. and Jones, G. (1996) What holds the modern company together? *Harvard Business Review,* November–December: 133–148.

Goold, M. (1996) Learning, planning, and strategy: Extra time. *California Management Review,* 38 (4; Summer): 100–103.

Goold, M. and Campbell, A. (1987) *Strategies and Styles: The Role of the Centre in Managing Diversified Corporations.* Blackwell, Oxford.

Goold, M. and Campbell, A. (1998) Desperately seeking synergy. *Harvard Business Review,* September–October: 131–143.

Goold, M. and Quinn, J.J. (1990) The paradox of strategic controls. *Strategic Management Journal,* 11: 43–57.

Goold, M., Campbell, A. and Alexander, M. (1994) *Corporate-Level Strategy: Creating Value in the Multi-Business Company.* Wiley, New York.

Goold, M., Campbell, A. and Luchs, K. (1993) Strategies and styles revisited: strategic planning and financial control. *Long Range Planning,* October: 49–60.

Gouldner, A.W. (1954) *Patterns of Industrial Bureaucracy.* Free Press, New York.

Granovetter, M. (1985) Economic action and social structure; the problem of embeddedness. *American Journal of Sociology,* 91: 481–510.

Granstrand, O., Patel, P. and Pavitt, K. (1997) Multi-technology corporations: Why they have distributed rather than core competencies. *California Management Review,* 39 (4): 8–25.

Grant, R. (1991) The resource-based theory of competitive advantage: Implications for strategy formulation. *California Management Review,* 33 (3): 114–135.

Grant, R. (1998) *Contemporary Strategy Analysis* (3rd edition). Blackwell, Oxford.

Grant, R.M., Shani, R. and Krishnan, R. (1994) TQM's challenge to management theory and practice. *Sloan Management Review,* 35 (2; Winter): 25–35.

Greenwood, R. and Hinings, C.R. (1988) Organisational design types, tracks and the dynamics of strategic change. *Organization Studies,* 9 (3): 293–316.

Grinyer, P.H. and Spender, J.-C. (1979) *Turnaround – Managerial Recipes for Strategic Success.* Associated Business Press, London.

Grunert, K.G. (1996) Automatic and strategic processes in advertising effects. *Journal of Marketing,* 60 (4): 88–101.

Gupta, A.K. (1984) Contingency linkages between strategy and general manager characteristics: A conceptual examination. *Academy of Management Review,* 9 (3): 399–412.

Gupta, A.K. (1986) Matching managers to strategies: point and counterpoint. *Human Resource Management,* 25 (2): 215–234.

Guthrie, J.P. and Olian, J.D. (1991) Does context affect staffing decisions? The case of general managers. *Personnel Psychology,* 263–292.

Guthrie, J.P., Grimm, C.M. and Smith, K.G. (1991) Environmental change and management staffing: An empirical study. *Journal of Management,* 17 (4): 735–748.

Hall, E.H. Jr and Lee, J. (1999) Broadening the view of corporate diversification: An international perspective. *International Journal of Organizational Analysis, 7* (1): 25–53.

Hall, E.H. Jr and St John, C.H. (1994) A note of diversity measurement. *Strategic Management Journal,* 15: 153–168.

Hall, R. (1992) The strategic analysis of intangible resources. *Strategic Management Journal,* 13: 135–144.

Hambrick, D.C. and Brandon, G.L. (1988) Executive values. In D.C. Hambrick (ed.) *The Executive Effect: Concepts and Methods for Studying Top Managers.* JAI Press, Connecticut.

Hambrick, D.C. and Cannella, A.A. Jr (1993) Relative standing: A framework for understanding departures of acquired executives. *Academy of Management Journal,* 36 (4): 733–762.

Hambrick D.C. and D'Aveni, R.A. (1988) Large corporate failures as downward spirals. *Administrative Science Quarterly,* 33 (1): 1–23.

Hambrick D.C. and D'Aveni, R.A. (1992) Top team deterioration as part of the downward spiral of large corporate bankruptcies. *Management Science,* 38 (10): 1445–1466.

Hambrick, D.C., and Mason, P.A. (1984) Upper Echelons: The Organization as a Reflection of Its Top Managers. *Academy of Management Review 9:* 193–206

Hamel, G. and Prahalad, C.K. (1989) Strategic intent. *Harvard Business Review,* 67 (3): 63–77.

Hamel, G. and Prahalad, C.K. (1993) Strategy as stretch and leverage. *Harvard Business Review,* 71 (2): 75–84.

Hamel, G. and Prahalad, C.K. (1994) *Competing for the Future.* Harvard Business Press, Boston, Mass.

Hammer, M. (1990) Re-engineering work – Don't automate, obliterate! *Harvard Business Review,* July–August: 104–112.

Hammer, M. (1994) Hammer defends reengineering. *The Economist,* 5 November: 70.

Hammer, M. and Champy, J. (1993) *Re-engineering the Corporation: A Manifesto for Business Revolution.* Harper–Collins.

Hammer, M. and Stanton, S. (1999) How process enterprises really work. *Harvard Business Review,* November–December: 108–118.

Hampden-Turner, C. (1990) *Charting the Corporate Mind.* Blackwell, Oxford.

Hampden-Turner, C. and Trompenaars, F. (1993) *The Seven Cultures of Capitalism.* Doubleday, New York.

Handy, C. (1985) *Understanding Organisations* (3rd edition). Penguin, Harmondsworth.

Handy, C. (1988) *Understanding Voluntary Organisations.* Penguin, Harmondsworth.

Handy, C. (1989) *The Age of Unreason.* Penguin, London.

Handy, C. (1995) *Beyond Certainty.* Hutchinson, London.

Hannan, M.T. and Carrol, G.R. (1992) *Dynamics of Organizational Populations: Density, Legitimation and Competition.* Oxford University Press, New York.

Hannan, M.T. and Freeman, J. (1977) The population ecology of organisations. *American Journal of Sociology,* 8 (2).

Hannan, M.T. and Freeman, J. (1984) Structural inertia and organizational change. *American Sociological Review,* 49: 149–164.

Hannan, M.T. and Freeman, J. (1989) *Organizational Ecology.* Harvard University Press, Cambridge, MA.

Hannan, M.T., Carroll, G.R., Dundon, E.A. and Torres, J.C. (1995) Organizational evolution in a multinational context: Entries of automobile manufacturers in Belgium, Britain, France, Germany, and Italy. *American Sociological Review,* 60: 509–528.

Hansen, M., Nohria, N. and Tierney, T. (1999) What's your strategy for managing knowledge? *Harvard Business Review,* March–April: 106–116.

Hardy, C. (1995) *Power and Politics in Organizations.* Dartmouth, Aldershot.

Hardy, C. (1996) Understanding power bringing about strategic change. *British Management Journal,* Special Issue (March): S3–S16.

Harris, L.C. and Ogbonna, E. (1999) The strategic legacy of company founders. *Long Range Planning,* 32 (3): 333–343.

Hart, S. and Banbury, C. (1994) How strategy-making processes can make a difference. *Strategic Management Journal,* 15: 251–269.

Haspeslagh P. (1989) Emphasizing value creation in strategic acquisitions. *Mergers and Acquisitions,* 24 (2): 68–71.

Haspeslagh P.C. and Jemison, D.B. (1986) *Managing Acquisitions: Creating Value Through Corporate Renewal.* Free Press, New York.

Haspeslagh, P.C. and Jemison, D.B. (1987) Acquisitions: myths and reality. *Sloan Management Review,* 28 (2): 53–58.

Hayes, R.H. and Abernathy, W.J. (1980) Managing our way to economic decline. *Harvard Business Review,* July/August: 67–77.

Hazen, M.A. (1997) Response to the revolt against cultural authority: Power/Knowledge as an assumption in organization theory. *Human Relations,* 50 (9): 1079–1084.

Healy, P.M., Palepu, K.G. and Ruback, R.S. (1997) Which takeovers are profitable? Strategic or financial. *Sloan Management Review,* 38 (4): 45–57.

Healy, P. and Ruback, R. (1997) Which takeovers are profitable? Strategic or financial? *Sloan Management Review,* Summer: 45–57.

Hedberg, B. (1981) How organisations learn and unlearn. In P.C. Nystrom and W.H. Starbuck (eds) *Handbook of Organizational Design,* Vol. 1 (pp. 3–27). Oxford University Press, Oxford.

Hedley, B. (1976) A fundamental approach to strategy development. *Long Range Planning,* 9 (60): 2–11.

Hellgren, B. and Melin, L. (1993) The role of strategists' ways-of-thinking in strategic change processes. In J. Hendry and G. Johnson (with J. Newton) (eds) *Strategic Thinking: Leadership and the Management of Change* (pp. 47–68). Wiley, Chichester.

Henderson, R.M. and Clark, K.B. (1990) Architectural innovation: The reconfiguration of existing product technologies and the failure of established firms. *Administrative Science Quarterly,* 35: 9–30.

Heracleous, L. and Langham, B. (1996) Strategic change and organisational culture at Hay Management Consultants. *Long Range Planning,* 29 (4): 485–494.

Herman, R.D. and Renz, D.O. (1998) Non-profit organizational effectiveness: Contrasts between especially effective and less effective organizations. *Non-profit Management and Leadership,* 9 (1): 23–38.

Hickson, D.J., Hinings, C.R., Lee, C.A., Schenk, R.E. and Pennings, J.M. (1971) A strategic contingencies theory of intraorganizational power. *Administrative Science Quarterly,* 16 (2): 216–229.

Higgins, K. (1996) Swiss learn the art of the buy-out. *Corporate Finance,* 141 (August): 8.

Hill, C.W.L. (1988) Internal capital market controls and financial performance in multidivisional firms. *California Management Review,* 33 (3): 114–135.

Hill, C.W.L. and Hoskisson, R.E. (1987) Strategy and structure in the multi-product firm. *Academy of Management Review,* 2: 331–341.

Hill, C.W.L and Jones. G.R. (1998) *Strategic Management – An Integrated Approach,* 4th Edition, Houghton Mifflin, Boston.

Hill, T. and Westbrook, R. (1997) SWOT analysis: It's time for a product recall. *Long Range Planning,* 30 (1): 46–52.

Hinterhuber, H. and Levin, B. (1994) Strategic networks: The organization of the future. *Long Range Planning,* 27 (3): 43–53.

Hirsch, P.M. (1975) Organisational effectiveness and the institutional environment. *Administrative Science Quarterly,* 20: 327–344.

Hirt, M.A., Ireland, R.D. and Hoskisson, R.E. (1995) *Strategic Management: Competitiveness and Globalisation.* West, St Paul.

Hoffman, W.M. and Moore, J.M. (eds) (1990) *Business Ethics: Readings and Cases in Corporate Morality.* McGraw-Hill, New York.

Hofstede, G. (1980a) Motivation, leadership, and organisations: Do American theories hold abroad? *Organisational Dynamics,* 9 (1): 42–63.

Hofstede, G. (1980b) *Culture's Consequences: International Differences in Work-Related Values.* Sage, London.

Hofstede, G. (1991) *Cultures and Organizations.* McGraw-Hill, London.

Horton Smith, D. (1999) The effective grassroots association, II: Organizational factors that produce external impact. *Non-profit Management and Leadership,* 10 (1): 103–116.

Howell, J.M. and Higgins, C.A. (1990) Champions of change: Identifying, understanding and supporting champions of technological innovations. *Organizational Dynamics,* 19 (1): 40–55.

Huber, R.L. (1993) How Continental Bank outsourced its 'crown jewels'. *Harvard Business Review,* January–February: 121–129.

Huff, A.S. (1990) *Mapping Strategic Thought.* Wiley, Chichester.

Hunt, J.W. (1987) Hidden extras: How people get overlooked in takeovers. *Personnel Management,* 19 (7): 24–26, 28.

Hunt, J.W. (1990) Changing pattern of acquisition behaviour in takeovers and the consequences for acquisition processes. *Strategic Management Journal,* 11 (1): 69–77.

Hunt, J.W., Lees, S., Grumbar, J.J. and Vivian, P.D. (1987) *Acquisitions: The Human Factor.* London Business School/Egon Zehnder International.

Hutchison, C. (1996) Integrating environmental policy and business strategy. *Long Range Planning,* 29 (1): 11–21.

Ingham, H., Kran, I. and Lovestam, A. (1992) Mergers and profitability: A managerial success story? *Journal of Management Studies,* 29 (2): 195–208.

Inkpen, A.C. (1996) Creating knowledge through collaboration. *California Management Review,* 39 (1): 123–140.

Inkpen, A.C. and Choudhury, N. (1995) Seeking a strategy where it is not: Towards a theory of strategy absence. *Strategic Management Journal,* 16: 313–323.

Jebb, F. (1998) Survival of the biggest. *Management Today,* November: 52–57.

Jemison, D.B. and Sitkin, S.B. (1986) Corporate acquisitions: A process perspective. *Academy of Management Review,* 11 (1): 145–163.

Jennings, P. and Beaver, G. (1997) The performance and competitive advantage of small firms: A management perspective. *International Small Business Journal,* 15 (2): 63–75.

Jensen, M.C. and Meckling, W.H. (1976) Theory of the firm: Managerial behaviour, agency costs and ownership structure. *Journal of Financial Economics,* 3: 305–360.

Johnson, G. (1987) *Strategic Change and the Management Process.* Blackwell, Oxford.

Johnson, G. (1992) Managing strategic change: Strategy, culture and action. *Long Range Planning,* 25 (1): 28–36.

Johnson, G. and Scholes, K. (1988) *Exploring Corporate Strategy,* 2nd edition, Prentice-Hall, Englewood Cliffs.

Johnson, G. and Scholes, K. (1999) *Exploring Corporate Strategy,* 5th edition, FT–Prentice Hall, Harlow.

Johnston, J. (1998) Strategy, planning, leadership, and the financial management improvement plan: The Australian Public Service 1983–1996. *Public Productivity and Management Review,* 21 (4): 352–368.

Juran, J.M. (1988) *Juran on Planning for Quality.* Free Press, New York.

Kandell, J. (1999) Strains in diversity. *Institutional Investor,* 33 (3): 97–102.

Kanter, R.M. (1985) Supporting innovation and venture development in established companies. *Journal of Business Venturing,* 1: 47–60

Kanter, R.M. (1989) Swimming In Newstreams: Mastering Innovation Dilemmas. *California Management Review,* 31 (4): 45–69.

Kanter, R., Richardson, L., North, J. and Zolner, J. (1991) Engines of progress: Designing and running entrepreneurial vehicles in established companies. *Journal of Business Venturing,* 6 (3): 145–163.

Kaplan, R.S. and Norton, D.P. (1992) The balanced scorecard: Measures that drive performance. *Harvard Business Review,* January–February: 71–79.

Kaplan, R.S. and Norton, D.P. (1996) Using the balanced scorecard as a strategic management system. *Harvard Business Review,* January–February: 75–85.

Kay, J. (1993) *Foundations of Corporate Success.* Oxford University Press, Oxford.

Kearns, K.P. (1994) The strategic management of accountability in non-profit organizations: An analytical framework. *Public Administration Review, Washington,* 54 (2): 185.

Kiely, T. (1997) Business processes: Consider outsourcing. *Harvard Business Review,* May–June: 11–12.

Kim, D.H. (1993) The link between individual and organisational learning. *Sloan Management Review,* Fall: 37–50.

Kinkead, G. (1999) In the future, people like me will go to jail. *Fortune,* 24 May: 190–200.

Klepper, S. and Simons, K.L. (1996) Innovation and industry shakeouts. *Business and Economic History,* 25 (1): 81–89

Kloss, L.L. (1999) The suitability and application of scenario planning for national professional associations. *Non-profit Management and Leadership,* 10 (1): 71–83.

Knights, D. and McCabe, D. (1998) What happens when the phone goes wild? Staff, stress and spaces for escape in a BPR telephone banking work regime. *Journal of Management Studies*, 35 (2): 163–194.

Kolb, D.A. (1984) *Experiential Learning: Experience as the Source of Learning and Development*. Prentice-Hall, Englewood Cliffs.

Kotter, J.P. (1982) *The General Managers*. Free Press, New York.

Kotter, J.P. (1995) Leading change: why transformation efforts fail. *Harvard Business Review*, March–April: 59–67.

Krasner, O.J. (1982) The role of entrepreneurs in innovation. In Sexton, Kent and Vesper (eds) *Encyclopaedia of Entrepreneurship*. Prentice-Hall, Englewood Cliffs.

Lacity, M.C. and Hirschheim, R. (1993) The information systems outsourcing bandwagon. *Sloan Management Review*, Fall: 73–86.

Lave, J. (1988) *Cognition in Practice: Mind, Mathematics and Culture in Everyday Life*. Cambridge University Press.

Lawler, E.E. III (1998) Strategic pay systems. In S.A. Mohrman, J.R. Galbraith, E.E. Lawler III and Associates (eds) *Tomorrow's Organization*. Jossey-Bass.

Lawrence, P.R. and Lorsch, J.W. (1967) *Organization and Environment. Managing Differentiation and Integration*. Harvard University Press, Cambridge, Mass.

Lawrence, T.B. and Phillips, N. (1998) Commentary: Separating play and critique: Postmodern and critical perspectives on TQM/BPR. *Journal of Management Inquiry*, 7 (2): 154–160.

Leavy, B. (1994) Two strategic perspectives on the buyer–supplier relationship. *Production and Inventory Management Journal*, 35 (2): 47–51.

Leavy, B. (1998) The concept of learning in the strategy field: Review and outlook. *Management Learning*, 29 (4): 447–466.

Lennane, A. (1999) Still the world's favourite airline? *Airfinance Journal*, 218 (June): 30–34.

Leonard-Barton, D. (1992) Core capabilities and core rigidities: A paradox in managing new product development. *Strategic Management Journal*, 13: 111–125.

Levering, R. and Moskowitz, M. (2000) The 100 best companies to work for. *Fortune*, 10 January: 53–63.

Levinthal, D.A. (1995) Strategic management and the exploration of diversity. In Montgomery, C.A. (ed.) *Resource-based and Evolutionary Theories of the Firm*, Kluwer, Boston, MA.

Levinthal, D.A. and March, J.G. (1993) The myopia of learning. *Strategic Management Journal*, 14: 95–112.

Levitt, B. and March, J.G. (1988) Organizational learning. *Annual Review of Sociology*, 14: 319–340.

Levitt, T. (1983) The globalization of markets. *Harvard Business Review*, May–June: 90–102.

Lewin, K. (1952) *Field Theory in Social Science*. Tavistock/Routledge & Paul, London.

Lewis, D. (1998) Non-governmental organizations, business and the management of ambiguity. *Non-profit Management and Leadership*, 9 (2): 135–151.

Lieberson, S. and O'Connor, J.F. (1972) Leadership and organizational performance: A study of large corporations. *American Sociological Review*, 37: 117–130.

Lindblom, C.E. (1959) The science of muddling through. *Public Administration Review*, 19 (2): 79–88.

Lindblom, C.E. (1968) *The Policy Making Process*. Prentice Hall, Englewood Cliffs, New Jersey.

Lissack, M.R. (1997) Of chaos and complexity: managerial insights from a new science. *Management Decision*, 35 (3): 205–218.

Lorange, P. and Nelson, R.T. (1987) How to recognize – and avoid – organizational decline. *Sloan Management Review*, 28 (3; Spring): 41–48.

Lorenz, A. (1999) Rolls Royce fuels industrial power deals. *Sunday Times*, Business Section, 1 (August): 3.3.

Lorsch, J.W. (1986) Managing culture: The invisible barrier to strategic change. *California Management Review*, 28 (2): 95–109.

Lynn, M. (1996) Fortress Zeneca. *Management Today,* May: 72–76.

Mair, A. (1999) Learning from Honda. *Journal of Management Studies,* 36 (1): 25–44.

Makadok, R. (1998) Can first mover advantages be sustained in an industry with low barriers to entry/imitation? *Strategic Management Journal,* 19: 683–696.

Maranville, S.J. (1999) Requisite variety of strategic management modes: A cultural study of strategic actions in a deterministic environment. *Non-profit Management and Leadership,* 9 (3): 277–291.

March, J.G. (1991) Exploration and exploitation in organizational learning. *Organization Science,* 2: 71–87.

March, J.G. (1999) *The Pursuit of Organizational Excellence.* Blackwell, Oxford.

March, J.G. and Simon, H.A. (1958) *Organizations.* Blackwell, Cambridge, Mass.

Markides, C.C. and Williamson, P.J. (1996) Corporate diversification and organizational structure: A resource-based view. *Academy of Management Journal,* 39 (2): 340–367.

Marris, R. (1964) *The Economic Theory of Managerial Capitalism.* Macmillan, London.

Marx, T.G. (1991) Removing the obstacles to effective strategic planning. *Long Range Planning,* 24 (4): 21–28.

Mazur, L. (1999) Why marketing is too important for outsourcing. *Marketing,* 8 July: 16.

McGahan, A.M. and Porter, M.E. (1997) How much does industry matter, really? *Strategic Management Journal,* 18 (Summer, special issue): 15–30.

McKiernan, P. (ed.) (1996) *Historical Evolution of Strategic Management,* vols I and II. Dartmouth, Aldershot.

McKiernan, P. and Morris, C. (1994) Strategic planning and financial performance in UK SMEs: Does formality matter? *British Journal of Management,* 5 (special issue): S31–S41.

Melin, L. (1985) Strategies in managing turnaround. *Long Range Planning,* 18 (1): 80–86.

Miles, R.E. and Snow, C.C. (1978) *Organisational Structure, Strategy, Process.* McGraw-Hill, New York.

Milgrom, P. and Roberts, J. (1982) Predation, reputation and entry deterrence. *Journal of Economic Theory,* 27: 280–312.

Miller, A. and Dess, G. (1993) Assessing Porter's 1980 model in terms of its generalisability, accuracy and simplicity. *Journal of Management Studies,* 30 (4): 553–585.

Miller, D. (1987) The genesis of configuration. *Academy of Management Review,* 12 (4): 686–701.

Miller, D. (1990) *The Icarus Paradox.* Harper Business, New York.

Miller, D. (1992) The Icarus paradox: How exceptional companies bring about their own downfall. *Business Horizons,* 35 (1): 24–35.

Miller, D. and Friesen, P.H. (1982) Successful and unsuccessful phases of the corporate life-cycle. *Organisation Studies,* 4 (4): 339–356.

Miller, D. and Friesen, P.H. (1984) *Organisations: A Quantum View.* Prentice Hall, Englewood Cliffs.

Miller, D., Droge, C. and Toulouse, J.-M. (1988) Strategic process and content as mediators between organizational context and structure. *Academy of Management Journal,* 31 (3): 544–569.

Mintzberg, H. (1973) Strategy making in three modes. *California Management Review* 16 (1): 44–53.

Mintzberg, H. (1975) The manager's job: folklore and fact. *Harvard Business Review,* July–August: 49–61.

Mintzberg, H. (1979) *The Structuring of Organisations: A Synthesis of the Research.* Prentice Hall, Englewood Cliffs.

Mintzberg, H. (1983) *Power In and Around Organisations.* Prentice Hall, Engelwood Cliffs.

Mintzberg, H. (1987) Crafting strategy. *Harvard Business Review,* July–August: 65–75.

Mintzberg, H. (1991) Generic strategies. In H. Mintzberg and J.B. Quinn (eds) *The Strategy Process* (2nd edition). Prentice-Hall, Englewood Cliffs.

Mintzberg, H. (1996) Reply to Michael Goold. *California Management Review,* 38 (4): 96–99.

Mintzberg, H., Ahlstrand, B. and Lampel, J. (1998) *Strategy Safari.* Prentice Hall, London.

Mintzberg, H. and Waters J.A. (1985) Of strategies, deliberate and emergent. *Strategic Management Journal,* July–September: 257–272.

Mjoen, H. and Tallman, S. (1997) Control and performance in international joint ventures. *Organization Science,* 8 (3): 257–274.

Mockler, R.J. (1999) *Multinational Strategic Alliances.* Wiley, Chichester.

Montgomery, C.A. (1982) The measurement of firm diversification: Some new empirical evidence. *Academy of Management Journal,* 25 (2): 299–307.

Morrocco, J.D., Thomas, G. and Bruce, D. (1998) 'Oneworld' alliance to expand quickly. *Aviation Week and Space Technology,* 28 (149): 13–32.

Murray, J. and Kotabe, M. (1999) Sourcing strategies of US service companies: A modified transaction-cost analysis. *Strategic Management Journal,* 20 (9): 791–809.

Myers, I.B. (1962) *Introduction to Type: A Description of the Theory and Applications of the Myers–Briggs Type Indicator.* Consulting Psychologists Press, Palo Alto.

Nadler, D. and Tushman, M. (1988) What makes for magic leadership? *Fortune,* 6 June: 115–116.

Nahavandi, A. and Malekzadeh, A.R. (1988) Acculturation in mergers and acquisitions. *Academy of Management Review,* 13 (1): 79–90.

Nathan, J. (1999) *Sony – The Private Life.* Houghton Mifflin, Boston and New York.

Nelson, R.R. and Winter, S.G. (1982) *An Evolutionary Theory of Economic Change.* Harvard University Press, Cambridge, Mass.

Nevis, E.C., DiBella, A.J. and Gould, G.M. (1995) Understanding organizations as learning systems. *Sloan Management Review,* Winter: 73–85.

Nonaka, I. (1988) Toward middle-up-down management: Accelerating information creation. *Sloan Management Review,* 9–18.

Nonaka, I. (1990) Redundant, overlapping organizations: A Japanese approach to managing the innovation process. *California Management Review,* 32 (3): 27–38.

Nonaka, I. (1991) The knowledge creating company. *Harvard Business Review,* 69 (November/December): 96–104.

Nonaka, I. and Takeuchi, H. (1995) *The Knowledge-Creating Company: How Japanese Companies Create the Dynamics of Innovation.* Oxford University Press, Oxford.

Normann, R. (1977) *Management for Growth.* Wiley, New York.

Nutt, P.C. and Backoff, R.W. (1992) *Strategic Management of Public and Third Sector Organizations.* Jossey-Bass, San Francisco.

O'Neill, H., Pouder, R. and Buchholtz, A, (1998) Patterns in the diffusion of strategies across organizations: Insights from the innovation diffusion literature. *Academy of Management Review,* 23 (1): 98–114.

Ocasio, W. (1997) Towards an attention-based view of the firm. *Strategic Management Journal,* 18 (Summer Special Issue): 187–206.

Ohmae, K. (1989) Managing in a borderless world. *Harvard Business Review,* May–June: 152–161.

Oliver, C. (1997) Sustainable competitive advantage: Combining institutional and resource-based views. *Strategic Management Journal,* 18 (9): 697–713.

O'Reilly, B. (1999) The mechanic who fixed Continental. *Fortune,* 140 (12): 176–186.

Ouchi, W.G. (1978) *Theory Z.* Addison-Wesley, Reading, MA.

Ouchi, W.G. (1981) Organisational paradigms: A commentary on Japanese management and theory of organisations. *Organisational Dynamics,* 9 (4): 36–43.

Owen, G. and Harrison, T. (1995) Why ICI chose to demerge. *Harvard Business Review,* 73 (2; March/April): 133–142.

Pablo, A.L. (1994) Determinants of acquisition integration level: A decision making perspective. *Academy of Management Journal,* 37 (4): 803–836.

Palepu, K. (1985) Diversification strategy, profit performance and the entropy measure. *Strategic Management Journal,* 6: 239–255.

Pant, L.W. (1991) An investigation of industry and firm structural characteristics in corporate turnarounds. *Journal of Management Studies;* 28 (6): 623–641.

Parker, L. (1998) Non-profit prophets: Strategy in non-commercial organisations. *Australian CPA,* 68 (6): 50–52.

Pascale, R.T. (1996) The Honda effect. *California Management Review,* 38 (4): 80–91.

Pearce, J.A. II and Robbins, D.K. (1994) Retrenchment remains the foundation of business turnaround. *Strategic Management Journal,* 15 (5): 407–417.

Penrose, E. (1959) *The Theory of the Growth of the Firm.* Oxford University Press (2nd edition, 1995).

Perrin, S. (1998) The buy-out is back. *Management Today,* May: 78–82.

Peteraf, M.A. (1993) The cornerstones of competitive advantage: A resource-based view. *Strategic Management Journal,* 14 (3): 179–191.

Peters, T. (1988) *Thriving on Chaos.* Macmillan, London.

Peters, T. (1992) Rethinking scale. *California Management Review,* Fall: 7–29.

Peters, T. and Waterman, R. (1982) *In Search of Excellence.* Harper & Row, New York.

Pettigrew A.M. (1977) Strategy formulation as a political process. *International Studies of Management and Organisation,* Summer: 78–87.

Pettigrew, A.M. (1985) *The Awakening Giant.* Blackwell, Oxford.

Pettigrew, A.M. (1990) Longitudinal field research on change: Theory and practice. *Organization Science,* 1 (3): 267–292.

Pettigrew A.M. (1992) On studying managerial elites. *Strategic Management Journal,* 13.

Pettigrew, A.M. and Whipp, R. (1991) *Managing Change for Competitive Success.* Blackwell, Oxford.

Pettigrew A.M. (1973) *The Politics of Organisational Decision Making.* Tavistock, London.

Pfeffer, J. (1992) *Managing with Power: Politics and Influence in Organizations.* Harvard Business School Press, Boston, MA.

Pfeffer, J. and Salancik, G.R. (1978) *The External Control of Organisations: A Resource Dependency Perspective.* Harper & Row, New York.

Pinchot, G. (1985) *Intrapreneuring.* Harper & Row, London.

Poister, T.H. and Streib, G.D. (1999) Strategic management in the public sector. *Public Productivity and Management Review,* 22 (3): 308–325.

Poppo, L. and Zenger, T. (1998) Testing alternative theories of the firm: Transaction cost, knowledge-based and measurement explanations for make or buy decisions in information services. *Strategic Management Journal,* 19 (9): 853–877.

Porter, M.E. (1979) How competitive forces shape strategy, *Harvard Business Review,* March–April: 137–145.

Porter, M.E. (1980) *Competitive Strategy.* Free Press, New York.

Porter, M.E. (1985) *Competitive Advantage.* Free Press, New York.

Porter, M.E. (1987) From competitive advantage to corporate strategy. *Harvard Business Review,* May–June: 43–59.

Porter, M.E. (1990) *The Competitive Advantage of Nations.* Macmillan, London.

Porter, M.E. (1996) What is strategy? *Harvard Business Review,* November–December: 61–78.

Porter, M.E. and van der Linde, C. (1995) Green and competitive: Ending the stalemate. *Harvard Business Review,* September–October: 120–133.

Prahalad, C.K. and Bettis, R.A. (1986). The Dominant Logic: A New Linkage Between Diversity and Performance. *Strategic Management Journal,* 7 (6): 485–501.

Prahalad, C.K. and Doz, Y. (1987) *The Multinational Mission: Balancing Local Demands and Global Vision.* Free Press, New York.

Prahalad, C.K. and Hamel, G. (1990) The core competence of the corporation. *Harvard Business Review,* 68 (3): 79–91.

Prahalad, C.K. and Ramaswamy, V. (2000) Co-opting customer competence. *Harvard Business Review,* January–February: 79–87.

Prokesch, S.E. (1997a) The management of intellectual capital. *Long Range Planning,* 30 (3; June; special issue).

Prokesch, S.E. (1997b) Unleashing the power of learning: An interview with British Petroleum's John Browne. *Harvard Business Review,* September–October: 147–168.

Pugh, D. and Hickson, D. (1976) *Organization Structure in its Context: The Aston Programme, I.* Gower, Farnborough.

Pugh, D.S., Hickson, D.J., MacDonald, K.M., Hinings, C.R., Turner, C. and Lupton, T. (1963) A conceptual scheme for organisational analysis. *Administrative Science Quarterly,* 8: 289–315.

Pugh, D.S., Hickson, D.J., Hinings, C.R. and Turner, C. (1968) Dimensions of organisational structure. *Administrative Science Quarterly,* 13 (June): 65–105.

Pugh, D., Hickson, D.J., Hinings, C.R. and Turner, C. (1969) The context of organization structures. *Administrative Science Quarterly,* 14 (1): 91–114.

Quinn, J.B. (1980) *Strategies for Change: Logical Incrementalism.* Irwin, Illinois.

Quinn, J.B. (1985) Managing innovation: Controlled chaos. *Harvard Business Review,* 63 (May–June): 78–84.

Quinn, J. (1989) Strategic change: 'logical incrementalism'. *Sloan Management Review,* Summer: 45–60.

Quinn, J.B. (1999) Strategic outsourcing: Leveraging knowledge capabilities. *Sloan Management Review,* Summer: 9–21.

Quintas, P., Lefrere, P. and Jones, G. (1997) 'Knowledge management: a strategic agenda', *Long Range Planning,* pp. 385–391.

Ramanujam, V. and Varadarajan, P.R. (1989) Research on corporate diversification: A synthesis. *Strategic Management Journal,* 10 (6): 523–551.

Ranson, S., Hinings, B. and Greenwood, R. (1980) The structuring of organizational structures. *Administrative Science Quarterly,* 25 (1): 470–474.

Rayport, J.F. and Sviokla, J.J. (1995) Exploiting the virtual value chain. *Harvard Business Review,* November–December: 75–85.

Reger, R.K. and Huff, A.S. (1993) Strategic groups: A cognitive perspective. *Strategic Management Journal,* 14: 103–124.

Reich, R. (1998) The new meaning of corporate social responsibility. *California Management Review,* 40 (2; Winter): 8–17.

Reid, W. and Myddelton, D. (1996) *The Meaning of Company Accounts.* Gower, Aldershot.

Rhenman, E. (1973) *Organisation Theory for Long Range Planning.* Wiley, London.

Rieple, A. (1997) The paradoxes of new managers as levers of organizational change. *Strategic Change,* 6 (4; June/July).

Rieple, A. (1998) 'An analysis of the structural factors which led to the enforced departure of a chief executive', unpublished doctoral thesis, Cranfield University, England.

Rieple, A. and Vyakarnam, S. (1996) The case for managerial ruthlessness. *British Journal of Management,* 7 (1): 17–33.

Robbins, D.K. and Pearce, J.A. (1992) Turnaround: Retrenchment and recovery. *Strategic Management Journal,* 13 (4): 287 Count: 23–309.

Robins, J. and Wiersema, M.F. (1995) A resource-based approach to the multibusiness firm: Empirical analysis of portfolio interrelationships and corporate financial performance. *Strategic Management Journal,* 16 (4): 277–299.

Romanelli, E. and Tushman, M.L. (1988) Executive leadership and organisational outcomes: an evolutionary perspective. In D.C. Hambrick (ed.) *The Executive Effect. Concepts and Methods for Studying Top Managers.* JAI Press, Connecticut.

Romanelli, E. and Tushman, M.L. (1994) Organizational transformation as punctuated equilibrium: An empirical test. *Academy of Management Journal,* 37 (5): 1141–1166.

Roos, G. and Roos, J. (1997) Measuring your company's intellectual performance. *Long Range Planning,* 30 (3): 413–426.

Rumelt, R.P. (1974) *Strategy, Structure and Economic Performance*. Harvard University Press, Boston, Mass.

Rumelt, R.P. (1982) Diversification strategy and profitability. *Strategic Management Journal*, 3: 359–369.

Rumelt, R.P. (1988) Evaluating business strategy. In H. Mintzberg and J.B. Quinn (eds.) *The Strategy Process: Concepts, Contexts and Cases*. Prentice Hall, Englewood Cliffs, NJ.

Rumelt, R.P (1995) Inertia and transformation. In C.A. Montgomery (ed.) *Resources in an Evolutionary Perspective: A Synthesis of Evolutionary and Resource-Based Approaches to Strategy*. Kluwer, Norwell, Mass.

Rumelt, R.P. (1996) The many faces of Honda. *California Management Review*, 38 (4; Summer): 103–111.

Rumelt, R.P. (1997) The evaluation of business strategy. In H. Mintzberg and J.B. Quinn (eds) *The Strategy Process: Concepts, Contexts, Cases* (3rd edition). Prentice Hall, Englewood Cliffs, NJ.

Saloner, G. (1991) Modeling, game theory and strategic management. *Strategic Management Journal*, 12: 119–136.

Sandberg, W. and Hofer, C. (1987) Improving new venture performance: The role of strategy, industry structure and the entrepreneur. *Journal of Business Venturing*, 2 (1): 5–28.

Sargeant, A. and Kahler, J. (1999) Returns on fundraising expenditures in the voluntary sector. *Non-profit Management and Leadership*, 10 (1; Fall): 5–29.

Saunders, C.S. (1990) The strategic contingencies theory of power: Multiple perspectives. *Journal of Management Studies*, 27 (1): 1–18.

Schefczyk, M. and Gerpott, T.J. (1998) Determinants of corporate efficency in a declining industry: An empirical analysis of German foundries. *Management International Review*, 38 (4): 321–344.

Schein, E.H. (1983) The role of the founder in creating organisational cultures. *Organisational Dynamics*, 12 (Summer): 13–28.

Schein, E.H. (1992) *Organisational Culture and Leadership* (2nd edition). Jossey-Bass, San Francisco.

Schein, E.H. (1993) How Can Organizations Learn Faster? The Challenge of Entering the Green Room. *Sloan Management Review*, (Winter): 85–92.

Schumpeter, J.A. (1950) *Capitalism Socialism and Democracy* (3rd edition). Harper & Row, New York.

Scudder, G.D., Schroeder, R.G., Van de Ven, A.H., Seiler, G.R. and Wiseman, R.M. (1989) Managing complex innovations: The case of defense contracting. In A.H. Van de Ven, H.L. Angle and M.S. Poole (eds) *Research on the Management of Innovation*. Harper & Row, New York.

Selznick, P. (1957) *Leadership in Administration: A Sociological Interpretation*. Row Peterson, Illinois.

Senge, P. (1990) *The Fifth Discipline: The Art and Practice of the Learning Organisation*. Doubleday, New York.

Shane, S. and Kolvereid, L. (1995) National environment, strategy, and new venture performance: A three country study. *Journal of Small Business Management*, 33 (2): 37–50.

Shanley, M.T. and Correa, M.E. (1992) Agreement between top management teams and expectations for post-acquisition performance. *Strategic Management Journal*, 13 (4): 245–266.

Sheehan, R.M. Jr (1999) Achieving growth and high quality by strategic intent. *Non-profit Management and Leadership*, 9 (4): 413–428.

Shenkar, O. and Yuchtman-Yaar, E. (1997) Reputation, image, prestige and goodwill: An interdisciplinary approach to organizational standing. *Human Relations*, 50 (11): 1361–1381.

Sherman, S. (1993) Andy Grove: How Intel makes spending pay off. *Fortune*, 22 February: 56–60.

Shewhart, WA. (1939) *Statistical Method for the Viewpoint of Quality Control.* Graduate School of the Department of Agriculture, Washington DC (republished in 1989 by Dover Publications Inc., New York).

Shoichet, R. (1998) An organization design model for nonprofits. *Non-profit Management and Leadership,* 9 (1; Fall): 71–88.

Shrader, R.C. and Simon, A. (1997) Corporate versus independent new ventures: resource, strategy and performance difference. *Journal of Business Venturing* 12 (1): 47–66.

Simon, H.A. (1947) *Administrative Behaviour.* Free Press, New York.

Simon. H.A. (1957) A behavioural model of rational choice. In H.A. Herbert (ed.) *Models of Man.* Wiley, New York.

Simon, M., Houghton, S.M. and Gurney, J. (1999) Succeeding at internal corporate venturing: Roles needed to balance autonomy and control. *Journal of Applied Managemant Studies* December 8 (2): 145–159.

Simons, R. (1995) *Levers of Control: How Managers use Innovative Control Systems to Drive Strategic Renewal.* Harvard Business School Press, Boston, Mass.

Slatter, S. (1984) *Corporate Recovery.* Penguin, London.

Slatter, S. and Lovett, D. (1999) *Corporate Turnaround: Managing Companies in Distress.* Penguin, London.

Smith, D.C. (1999) So much for synergy. *Ward's Auto World,* 35 (4): 60.

Smith, K.G., Smith, K.A., Olian, J.D., Sims, H.P., O'Bannon, D. and Scully, J.A. (1994) Top management team demography and process: The role of social integration and communication. *Administrative Science Quarterly,* 39: 412–438.

Sobek, D.K. II, Liker, J.K. and Ward, A.C. (1998) Another look at how Toyota integrates product development. *Harvard Business Review,* July–August: 36–49.

Sobek, D.K. II, Ward, A.C. and Liker, J.K. (1999) Toyota's principles of set-based concurrent engineering. *Sloan Management Review,* 40 (2; winter): 67–83.

Somers, M.J. and Bird, K. (1990) Managing the transition phase of mergers. *Journal of Managerial Psychology,* 5 (4): 38–42.

Spekman, R.E., Isabella, L.A., MacAvoy, T.C. and Forbes, T. III (1996) Creating strategic alliances which endure. *Long Range Planning,* 29 (3): 346–357.

Spender, J.-C. (1989) *Industry Recipes – The Nature and Sources of Managerial Judgement.* Blackwell, Oxford.

Stabell, C.B. and Fjeldstad, Ø.D. (1998) Configuring value for competitive advantage: On chains, shops and networks. *Strategic Management Journal,* 19: 413–437.

Stacey, R. (1992) *Managing Chaos; Dynamic Business Strategies in an Unpredictable World.* Kogan, London.

Stacey, R. (1995) The science of complexity: an alternative perspective for strategic change processes. *Strategic Management Journal,* 16: 477–495.

Stalk, G., Jr. (1988) Time: The next source of competitive advantage. *Harvard Business Review,* July/August: 41–52.

Stalk, G., Evans, P. and Shulman, E. (1992) Competing on capabilities: The new rules of corporate strategy. *Harvard Business Review,* March–April: 57–69.

Stanworth, J. (1994) Penetrating the mists surrounding franchise failure rates: Some old lessons from new business. *International Small Business Journal,* 2 (1): 59–63.

Starr, L. (1990) R&D/Technology integration across the Atlantic. *Research–Technology–Management,* 33 (2): 16–18.

Stearns, T.M., Carter, N.M., Reynolds, P.D. and Williams, M.L. (1995) New firm survival: Industry, strategy, and location. *Journal of Business Venturing,* 10 (1): 23–42.

Steiner, G.A. (1969) *Top Management Planning.* Macmillan, New York.

Stern, J.M., Stewart, G.B. and Chew, D.H. (1998) The EVA financial management system. In J.M. Stern, G.B. Stewart and D.H. Chew (eds) *The Revolution in Corporate Finance* (pp. 474–488). Blackwell, Malden, MA.

Stewart, TA. (1993) Reengineering; The hot new managing tool. *Fortune,* 23 April: 40.

Stewart, T.A. (1998) The next big idea. *Fortune,* 21 December: 81–83.

Stewart, TA. (1999) See Jack run Europe. *Fortune,* 27 September: 140 (6): 124–136.

Stiles, J. (1994) Strategic alliances: Making them work. *Long Range Planning,* 27 (4): 133–137.

Talwar, R. (1993) Business re-engineering: A strategy-driven approach. *Long Range Planning,* 26 (6): 22–40.

Tapscott, D. (1995) *The Digital Economy: Promise and Peril in the Age of Networked Intelligence.* McGraw-Hill, New York.

Teece, D.J. (1980) Economies of scope and the scope of the enterprise. *Journal of Economic Behavior and Organization,* 1 (2): 223–247.

Teece, D.J. (1987) The competitive challenge: *Strategies for Industrial Innovation and Renewal,* Mosi Balinger.

Teece, D.J., Pisano, G. and Shuen, A. (1997) Dynamic capabilities and strategic management. *Strategic Management Journal,* 18 (7): 509–533.

Teresko, J. (1999) Driving success at new blue. *Industry Week,* 6 December: 56–67.

Toffler, A. (1970) *Future Shock.* Random House, New York.

Trompenaars, F. and Hampden-Turner, C. (1997) *Riding the Waves of Culture.* Nicholas Brealy Publishing Ltd, London.

Tsai, W.M.-H., MacMillan, I.C. and Low, M.B. (1991) Effects of strategy and environment on corporate venture success in industrial markets. *Journal of Business Venturing,* 6 (1): 9–28.

Tulle, S. (1999) The EVA advantage. *Fortune,* 139 (6): 122.

Turnipseed, D., Rassuli, A., Sardessai, R. and Duns, C.P. (1999) A history and evaluation of Boeing's coalition strategy with Japan in aircraft development and production. *International Journal of Commerce & Management,* 9 (1/2): 59–83.

Tushman, M.L. and O'Reilly, C.A. (1996) *Winning Through Innovation: A Practical Guide to Leading Organizational Change and Renewal.* Harvard Business School Press, Boston.

Tushman, M.L. and O'Reilly, C.A. (1996) Ambidextrous organizations: Managing evolutionary and revolutionary change. *California Management Review,* 38 (4; Summer): 8–30.

Tushman, M.L., Newman, W.H. and Romanelli, E. (1986) Convergence and upheaval: Managing the unsteady pace of organisational evolution. *California Management Review,* 29 (1; Fall): 29–44.

Useem, J. (2000) Welcome to the New Company Town. *Fortune,* 10 January: 45–47.

Van de Ven, A. (1986) Central problems in the management of innovation. *Management Science,* 32: 590–607.

Van de Ven, A. (1992) Suggestions for studying strategy process: A research note. *Strategic Management Journal,* 13, Special Issue, Summer: 169–188.

van Witteloostuijn, A. (1998) Bridging behavioral and economic theories of economic decline: Organizational inertia, strategic competition and chronic failure. *Management Science,* 44 (4): 501–519.

Varadarajan, P.R. and Ramanujam, V. (1987) Diversification and performance: A re-examination using a new two-dimensional conceptualisation of diversity in firms. *Academy of Management Journal,* 30 (2): 380–393.

Varadarajan, P.R. and Ramanujam, V. (1990) The corporate performance conundrum: A synthesis of contemporary views and an extension. *Journal of Management Studies,* 27 (5; September): 463–483.

Vergin, R. and Qoronfleh, M. (1998) Corporate reputation and the stock market. *Business Horizons,* 41 (1): 19–26.

Verity, J. (1992) Deconstructing the computer industry. *Business Week,* 23 November: 44–52.

Vince, R. and Broussine, M. (1996) Paradox, defense, and attachment: Accessing and working with emotions and relations underlying organizational change. *Organization Studies,* 17 (1): 1–21.

Von Krogh, G., Sinatra, A. and Singh, H. (eds) (1994) *The Management of Corporate Acquisitions. International Perspectives.* Macmillan, New York.

Voss, C.A. (1994) Significant issues for the future of product innovation. *Journal of Product Innovation Management,* 11 (5): 460–63.

Ward, S., Light, L. and Goldstine, J. (1999) What high-tech managers need to know about brands. *Harvard Business Review,* July–August: 85–95.

Warner, M. (1998) Kleiner Perkins: Inside the Silicon Valley money machine. *Fortune,* 26 October: 110–118.

Washington, F.S. (1999) DaimlerChrysler: Some key people depart. Is Daimler running the show? *Ward's Auto World,* 35 (5): 47–54.

Waterman R., Peters, T. and Phillips, J. (1980) Structure is not organization. *Business Horizons* 23 (3; June): 14ff.

Watson, J. and Everett, J. (1999) Small business failure rates: Choice of definition and industry effects. *International Small Business Journal,* 17 (2): 31–47.

Weber, M. (1947) *The Theory of Social and Economic Organizations.* Free Press, New York.

Weber, M. (1958) *The Protestant Ethic and the Spirit of Capitalism.* Charles Scribners, New York.

Weick, K.E. (1990) Cartographic myths in organisations. In A.S. Huff (ed.) *Mapping Strategic Thought.* Addison-Wesley, New York.

Weick, K.E. (1993) The collapse of sensemaking in organizations: The Mann Gulch disaster. *Administrative Science Quarterly,* 38 (4): 628–652.

Weick, K.E. (1995) *Sensemaking in Organizations.* Sage, Thousand Oaks.

Weiner, N. and Mahoney, T.A. (1981) A model of corporate performance as a function of environmental, organisational, and leadership influences. *Academy of Management Journal;* 24 (3): 453–470.

Wernerfelt, B. (1984) A resource-based view of the firm. *Strategic Management Journal,* 5: 171–180.

Whitby, S., Parker, D. and Tobias, A. (1998) Nonlinear dynamics and duopolistic competition: a R&D model and simulation. Refereed paper presented at the British Academy of Management conference, Nottingham, September 1998.

Whittington, R. (1993) *What is Strategy and Does it Matter?* Routledge, London.

Wiersema, M.F. and Bantel, K.A. (1992) Top management team demography and corporate strategic change. *Academy of Management Journal,* 35 (1): 91–121.

Wiersema, M.F., and Bantel, K.A. (1993) Top management team turnover as an adaption mechanism. *Strategic Management Journal,* 14 (7): 485–504.

Wiig, K.M. (1997) Integrating intellectual capital and knowledge management. *Long Range Planning,* 30 (3): 399–405.

Williamson, O.E. (1975) *Markets and Hierarchies: Analysis and Anti-Trust Implications.* Free Press, New York.

Williamson, O.E. (1991a) Comparative economic organization: The analysis of discrete structural alternatives. *Administrative Science Quarterly,* 36 (2): 269–296.

Williamson, O.E. (1991b) Strategizing, economizing and economic organisation. *Strategic Management Journal,* 12: 75–94.

Wood, A. (1998) Zeneca stays independent: Counting on internal growth. *Chemical Week,* 160 (14): 24–26.

Yelle, L.E. (1979) The learning curve: Historical review and comprehensive survey. *Decision Science,* 10: 302–328.

Yeoh, P.L. and Roth, K. (1999) An empirical analysis of sustained advantage in the US pharmaceutical industry: Impact of firm resources and capabilities. *Strategic Management Journal,* 20 (7): 637–653.

Yip, G.S. (1992) *Total Global Strategy.* Prentice Hall, Englewood Cliffs, NJ.

Zahra, S.A. and Pearce, J.A. (1990) Research evidence on the Miles-Snow typology. *Journal of Management,* 16 (4): 751–768.

Index

Note: the text within the case studies at the end of each chapter has not been indexed.